Praise for *Family Law: Text, Cases, and Materials*

'*Family Law: Text, Cases, and Materials* is a fantastic core text offering a thorough explanation and exploration of the essential areas covered in most family law courses. It offers a perceptive analysis of controversial issues including appropriate contextual material to enable students to really engage with both law and policy.'

Dr Thérèse Callus, Associate Professor of Law, University of Reading

'Engaging and appropriately pitched for my undergraduate students. Its clear and accessible contents has something to offer students of all abilities.'

Dr Sara Fovargue, Reader in Law, University of Lancaster

'*Family Law: Text, Cases, and Materials* draws extensively on a broad range of sources from statutes and case law to academic commentary and official reports. The authors deftly and seamlessly integrate these sources alongside their own, often critical and challenging, views in such a way that encourages students to look beyond the mere black letter of the law and consider the effects that these legal provisions have on families in society.'

Philip Bremner, Lecturer, University of Sussex

'A first-rate text with analysis by experts in the field, which usefully highlights the intersection between family law and other areas of law.'

Dr Andy Hayward, Lecturer in Family Law, Durham University

'Chosen by a focus group of my students as their favourite of the family law texts available, this book provides an approachable, comprehensive review of the law. Using extracts from key materials, the authors analyse the effectiveness of the law and its underlying messages, putting the law in a critical context that is thought-provoking and accessible. I am very pleased to see a new edition.'

Polly Morgan, Lecturer in Law, University of East Anglia

'An excellent resource which allows students both to broaden their reading and consider key debates.'

Dr Sharon Thompson, Lecturer in Law, Cardiff University

FAMILY LAW

OXFORD
UNIVERSITY PRESS

Great Clarendon Street, Oxford, OX2 6DP,
United Kingdom

Oxford University Press is a department of the University of Oxford.
It furthers the University's objective of excellence in research, scholarship,
and education by publishing worldwide. Oxford is a registered trade mark of
Oxford University Press in the UK and in certain other countries

First edition 2007
Second edition 2011
Impression: 1

Published in the United States of America by Oxford University Press
198 Madison Avenue, New York, NY 10016, United States of America

British Library Cataloguing in Publication Data
Data available

Library of Congress Control Number: 2015936773

ISBN 978–0–19–966418–4

Printed in Great Britain by
Ashford Colour Press Ltd, Gosport, Hampshire

PREFACE TO THE THIRD EDITION

Much has happened in the four years since the second edition of this book was published. As usual, the courts have been busy producing a wealth of new case law, but there have also been many important statutory developments affecting all areas of family law. For many practitioners and litigants before the family courts, these are challenging times in family justice.

As in the previous editions, we have endeavoured to provide readers with a thorough understanding of the law relating to families and to do so in a way that stimulates critical reflection on the law. We ask how and why the law has developed as it has, what policies it claims to be pursuing, whether it balances the rights and interests of individuals, families, and the wider public appropriately, and how it operates in practice. As in the second edition, the material in this edition of the book is fully integrated with the Online Resource Centre.

The Online Resource Centre provides a wealth of useful information, not least of which are our regular updates on changes to the law since the manuscript of the book was completed. It also contains questions, supplementary text and materials, and suggestions for further reading. Some of these augment the topics covered in the book, while others provide information for interested readers on material which is less central to family law and not covered systematically in the book. A guide to using this book and the online materials is found on the Online Resource Centre.

One significant change since the last edition has been the arrival of a new member of the authorial team. Shortly before the revisions to the text began in earnest in early 2014, Sonia Harris-Short was appointed as a District Judge. While we are fortunate that she has remained involved in writing the book, she was not able to continue with all the chapters for which she was previously responsible, and so Rob George joined the team. Consequently, Joanna Miles continues to be responsible for the chapters relating to adults (2–7), Rob George is responsible for the private law children chapters (8–11), and Sonia Harris-Short for the public law children chapters (12–13). As previously, we co-wrote chapter 1.

We are grateful to the team at OUP, and especially to John Carroll who was patient and helpful in the development of this new edition. We are also grateful to our colleagues and students who have helped us in our thinking about family law. Particular thanks are due to Peter Dunne, for guidance on terminological usage in relation to transgender issues, and to Irene Ding for research assistance to Joanna Miles. We have endeavoured to state the law as it was on 1 December 2014.

This edition is dedicated to Phil Harris (1947–2012) and Val Harris (1947–2012).

New to this edition:

- consideration of some of the contemporary challenges facing the family justice system
- full coverage of the Marriage (Same Sex Couples) Act 2013
- discussion of the Supreme Court's decision in *Jones v Kernott* (2011) and subsequent case law, and its implications for ownership of the family home

- analysis of the Law Commission's recommendations (2014) in relation to matrimonial property agreements
- consideration of the meaning of 'welfare' following the Court of Appeal decision in *Re G* (2012)
- revised consideration of the relationship between the welfare principle and human rights following recent domestic and European court decisions
- updates on the surrogacy case law, including *Re X* (2014) on applications for parental orders and *G v G* (2012) on the court's power to revoke a parental order
- detailed updates on parental responsibility, including new discussion of the position of 'alternative families' seeking parental responsibility and applications to have parental responsibility revoked
- a fully revised chapter on private disputes over children following the Children and Families Act 2014, addressing child arrangements orders
- detailed analysis of relocation law following the Court of Appeal's reinterpretation of previous authority in *K v K* (2011) and subsequent cases
- full analysis of significant new public law children cases from the Supreme Court in *Re J* (2013) and *Re B* (2013) and from the Court of Appeal in *Re B-S* (2013)
- a fully updated discussion of adoption following recent reforms to law and practice, as well as important new case law, including the Court of Appeal's recent review of step-parent adoption in *Re P* (2014)

SHS
JM
RG

PREFACE TO THE FIRST EDITION

This book has two principal aims: to provide readers with a thorough understanding of the law relating to the family and to do so in a way that stimulates critical reflection on that law: how and why has the law developed as it has, what policies is it seeking to pursue, does it achieve the right balance between the rights and interests of individual family members and wider public interests, how does it operate in practice?

As part of the *Text, Cases, and Materials* series, alongside our own description of and commentary on the law, the book includes a large number of extracts from primary sources, both statute and case law, and from official data, academic commentaries, qualitative research findings, and policy and reform papers. Several of these extracts are edited for use in the book. Deletions are indicated by ... and textual insertions and editorial amendments made by us are contained in square brackets. We have generally removed all original footnotes and references from the extracts; where an original footnote is retained, we have indicated this in the footnote. The occasional footnotes attached to extracts are otherwise our own.

Many valuable resources for family lawyers are now available on the internet. Wherever a source to which we have referred is online, we have indicated this by use of the Online Resource Centre logo in the bibliography. Only where a source is available exclusively online have we included the full website details in the bibliography. Readers wishing to access any of that material can visit the Online Resource Centre, where they will find links to all sources marked with the Online Resource Centre logo. The Online Resource Centre also provides links to a number of websites of general use and interest to the family lawyer.

Inevitably, it has not been possible to cover all of the issues relating to families in England and Wales today that we might have wished to include. In particular, we do not discuss public funding for family proceedings, criminal offences against children and reasonable chastisement, international child abduction, inter-country adoption, the law relating to the elderly and other vulnerable adults, the law of succession, immigration law, private international law, European law relating to the family, or housing law. We have been able to give only brief attention to the laws of taxation and social security, formalities for marriage and civil partnership, wardship, and disputes regarding the child's name and relocation. We have, however, included material on some of these topics in the Online Resource Centre.

There are a number of people to whom we are immensely grateful, for reading draft chapters, advising on specific issues, or both: Stuart Bridge, John Eekelaar, Jonathan Herring, Matthew Jolley, Mavis Maclean, Judith Masson, Jo McCaffrey, Clare McGlynn, Howard Miles, Cheryl Morris, Rebecca Probert, Daniel Robinson, Nick Wikeley, and the anonymous reviewers for Oxford University Press. We have also benefited greatly from the research assistance of Gemma Nicholls, Anna Shadboldt, Phil Harris, and Andrew Brown. Any errors and omissions are, of course, our own. We also thank all the students whom we have taught family law and the wider family law community: we have learnt a lot from them all, and still have more to learn. Thanks are also due to Angela Griffin, our original commissioning editor at OUP, and to Melanie Jackson and the rest of the team who have seen us through the project and accommodated our various needs.

Sonia Harris-Short is responsible for chapters on the law relating to children: chapters 8–13. Joanna Miles is responsible for chapters covering issues relating to adults and financial and property disputes: chapters 2–7. We co-wrote chapter 1. This book has been written as a teaching and learning aid for undergraduate family law courses. The information and commentary contained in this book do not, and are not intended to, constitute legal advice to any person in relation to a specific case or matter. We have endeavoured to state the law as it was at 1 October 2006. Twice yearly updates on developments in areas of law addressed in the book will be posted on the website.

SHS
JM

ACKNOWLEDGEMENTS

We are grateful to all authors and publishers of copyright material used in this book and in particular to the following for permission to reprint from the sources indicated:

Extracts from Law Commission Reports, Legal Services Commission Reports, DFES, DHSS, Cafcass and ONS publications are Crown copyright material. Crown copyright material is reproduced with the permission of the Controller, HMSO (under the terms of the Click Use licence). Parliamentary material is reproduced with the permission of the Controller of HMSO on behalf of Parliament. This book contains public sector information licensed under the Open Government Licence v1.0 (http://www.nationalarchives.gov.uk/doc/open-government-licence/open-government-licence.htm).

American Bar Association and the author for extract from *Family Law Quarterly*: Mary Ann Glendon, 'Is there a future for separate property?', (1974) *Family Law Quarterly* 315.

Ashgate Publishing and the authors for extracts from S. Cretney, 'Divorce Reform: Humbug and Hypocrisy or a Smooth Transition?', in M. Freeman (ed), *Divorce: Where Next* (Aldershot: Dartmouth, 1996); F. Kaganas, 'Contact, Conflict and Risk', in S. Day Sclater and C. Piper (eds), *Undercurrents of Divorce* (Aldershot: Ashgate, 1999); and B. Neale and C. Smart, 'In Whose Best Interests? Theorising Family Life Following Parental Separation or Divorce', in S. Day Sclater and C. Piper (eds), *Undercurrents of Divorce* (Aldershot: Ashgate, 1999).

Susan Boyd for extracts from S. Boyd, 'From gender specificity to gender neutrality? Ideologies in Canadian child custody law', in C. Smart and S. Sevenhuijsen (eds), Child Custody and the Politics of Gender (London: Routledge, 1998).

Cambridge University Press for extract from J. Pahl, 'Individualisation in Couple Finances: Who Pays for the Children?', (2005) 4 *Social Policy and Society* 381.

Gingerbread for extract from 'Government plans for child maintenance: Gingerbread briefing (2011)', briefing paper on child support reforms at www.gingerbread.org.uk/file_download.aspx?id=7360.

Hart Publishing, an imprint of Bloomsbury Publishing Plc, for extracts from N. Wikeley, *Child Support: Law and Policy* (Oxford: Hart Publishing, 2006); M. Maclean and J. Eekelaar, *The Parental Obligation: A study of parenthood across households* (Oxford: Hart Publishing, 1997); and S. Day Sclater, A. Bainham, and M. Richards, 'Introduction', A. Bainham, 'Parentage, Parenthood and Parental Responsibility', and M. Johnson, 'A Biomedical Perspective on Parenthood' in A. Bainham, S. Day Sclater, and M. Richards (eds), *What is a Parent? A Socio-Legal Analysis* (Oxford: Hart Publishing, 1999).

The Incorporated Council of Law Reporting for extracts from Appeal Cases [AC], Family Division Law Reports [Fam], and Weekly Law Reports [WLR].

Jordan Publishing Ltd for extracts from *Child and Family Law Quarterly and Family Law Reports* [FLR]: R. Deech, 'The unmarried father and human rights', (1992) 4 *Journal of Child Law* (continued as *Child and Family Law Quarterly*) 3; L. Smith, 'Clashing symbols?

Reconciling support for fathers and fatherless families after the Human Fertilisation and Embryology Act 2008', (2010) 22 *Child and Family Law Quarterly* 46; P. Hayes, 'Giving due consideration to ethnicity in adoption placements—A principled approach', (2003) 15 *Child and Family Law Quarterly* 255; C. Smith and J. Logan, 'Adoptive parenthood as a "legal fiction"—Its consequences for direct post-adoption contact', (2002) 14 *Child and Family Law Quarterly* 281; J. Eekelaar, 'Family law: Keeping us "on message"' (1999) 11 *Child and Family Law Quarterly* 387; J. Eekelaar, 'Beyond the Welfare Principle', (2002) 14 *Child and Family Law Quarterly* 237; N. Wikeley, 'A duty but not a right: Child support after *R (Kehoe) v Secretary of State for Work and Pensions*', (2006) 18 *Child and Family Law Quarterly* 287; P. Harris and R. George, 'Parental Responsibility and Shared Residence Orders: Parliamentary Intentions and Judicial Interpretations', (2010) 22 *Child and Family Law Quarterly* 151; J. Herring and R. Taylor, 'Relocating Relocation', (2006) 18 *Child and Family Law Quarterly* 517; B. Lindley, 'Open Adoption—Is the Door Ajar?', (1997) 9 *Child and Family Law Quarterly* 115; and *Re C (HIV Test)* [1999] 2 FLR 1004 (Fam Div), 1006 -17.

Robert Mnookin for extracts from *Law & Contemporary Problems*: R. Mnookin, 'Child-custody adjudication: Judicial functions in the face of indeterminacy', (1975) 39 *Law & Contemporary Problems* 266.

Oxford University Press for extract from J. Dewar, 'Land, Law and the Family Home', in S. Bright and J. Dewar (eds), *Land Law: Themes and Perspectives* (Oxford: OUP, 1998).

Oxford University Press Journals for extracts from *International of Law, Policy and the Family and Current Legal Problems*: I. Ellman, S. McKay, J. Miles, and C. Bryson, 'Child Support Judgments: Comparing Public Policy to the Public's Policy' (2014) *International Journal of Law, Policy and the Family* 28; E. Jackson et al, 'Financial Support on Divorce: the Right Mixture of Rules and Discretion?', (1993) 7 *International Journal of Law and the Family* 230; T. Campbell, 'The Rights of the Minor: As Person, As Child, As Juvenile, As Future Adult', (1992) 6 *International Journal of Law and the Family* 1; M. Freeman, 'Taking Children's Rights More Seriously', (1992) 6 *International Journal of Law and the Family* 52; and H. Reece, 'The Paramountcy Principle: Consensus or Construct?', (1996) 49 *Current Legal Problems* 267.

Polity Press for extract from C. Smart and B. Neale, Family Fragments? (Cambridge: Polity Press, 1999).

Reed Elsevier (UK) Ltd trading as LexisNexis for extracts from All England Law Reports [All ER], and Family Court Reports [FCR].

Springer for extract from L. Flynn and A. Lawson, 'Gender, sexuality and the doctrine of detrimental reliance', (1995) 3 *Feminist Legal Studies* 105. Permission conveyed through Copyright Clearance Center, Inc.

Sweet & Maxwell Ltd for extracts from *Law Quarterly Review* and *Journal of Social Welfare and Family Law*: J. Eekelaar, 'Do parents have a duty to consult?', (1998) 114 *Law Quarterly Review* 337; and A. Morris, 'Couples and benefits claims: a comment on Relying on the State, Relying on Each Other', (2000) 7 *Journal of Social Security Law* 228. Reproduced by permission of Thomson Reuters (Professional) UK Limited.

Taylor & Francis Ltd for extracts from *Journal of Social Welfare and Family Law*: N. Harris, 'Unmarried cohabiting couples and Social Security in Great Britain', (1996) 18 *Journal of Social Welfare and Family Law* 123; L. Fox-Harding, 'The Children Act 1989 in Context: Four

Perspectives in Child Care Law and Policy (1)', (1991) 13 *Journal of Social Welfare and Family Law* 179; M. Burton, 'Third party applications for protection orders in England and Wales: service provider's views on implementing Section 60 of the Family Law Act 1996', (2003) 25 *Journal of Social Welfare and Family Law* 137; A. Kewley, 'Pragmatism before principle: the limitations of civil law remedies for the victims of domestic violence', (1996) 18 *Journal of Social Welfare and Family Law* 1; and extracts from C. Gibson, *Dissolving Wedlock* (London: Routledge, 1994); and J. Pahl, *Private Violence and Public Policy: The Needs of Battered Women and the Response of Public Services* (London: Routledge and Kegan Paul, 1985). Reproduced by permission of Taylor & Francis Books Uk.

Wiley-Blackwell for extracts from *Child and Family Social Work and Modern Law Review*: B. Luckock and A. Hart, 'Adoptive family life and adoption support: policy ambivalence and the development of effective services', (2005) 10 *Child and Family Social Work* 125; G. Douglas, 'The Intention to be a Parent and the Making of Mothers', (1994) 57 *Modern Law Review* 636; and E. Jackson, 'Conception and the Irrelevance of the Welfare Principle', (2002) 65 *Modern Law Review* 176.

Every effort has been made to trace and contact copyright holders but this has not been possible in every case. If notified, the publisher will undertake to rectify any errors or omissions at the earliest opportunity.

OUTLINE TABLE OF CONTENTS

TABLE OF CONTENTS

3   FAMILY PROPERTY AND FINANCES   123

7   PROPERTY AND FINANCES WHEN RELATIONSHIPS END   443

8 FUNDAMENTAL PRINCIPLES IN THE LAW RELATING TO CHILDREN   537

11 PRIVATE DISPUTES OVER CHILDREN   728

12 CHILD PROTECTION 820

13 ADOPTION 903

TABLE OF CASES

H

TABLE OF STATUTES

TABLE OF STATUTORY INSTRUMENTS

TABLE OF INTERNATIONAL INSTRUMENTS

ABBREVIATIONS

ASBO	anti-social behaviour order
ACA 2002	Adoption and Children Act 2002
ADR	alternative dispute resolution
AID	artificial insemination by donor
BAAF	British Association for Adoption and Fostering
BME	black and minority ethnic
BSA	British Social Attitudes
CA 1989	Children Act 1989
CA 2004	Children Act 2004
CAA 2006	Children and Adoption Act 2006
Cafcass	Children and Family Court Advisory and Support Service
CAO	child assessment order
CASC	Children Act Sub-Committee, Advisory Board on Family Law
CB	child benefit
CFA 2014	Children and Families Act 2014
CFR	Children and Family Reporter
C-MEC	Child Maintenance and Enforcement Commission
CMOPA 2008	Child Maintenance and Other Payments Act 2008
CMS	Child Maintenance Service
CPA 2004	Civil Partnership Act 2004
CPAG	Child Poverty Action Group
CPC	child protection conference
CPS	Crown Prosecution Service
CSA	Child Support Agency
CSA 1991	Child Support Act 1991
CSA 2010	Crime and Security Act 2010
CSEW	Crime Survey for England and Wales
CSMCR 2012	Child Support Maintenance Calculation Regulations 2012
CTC	child tax credit
DCA	Department for Constitutional Affairs
DCLG	Department for Communities and Local Government
DCMS	Department for Culture, Media and Sport
DCSF	Department for Children, Schools and Families
DEO	deduction from earnings order
DFE	Department for Education
DFES	Department for Education and Skills
DH/DOH	Department of Health
DHSS	Department of Health and Social Security
DPMCA 1978	Domestic Proceedings and Magistrates' Courts Act 1978
DSS	Department of Social Security
DTI	Department of Trade and Industry
DVCVA 2004	Domestic Violence, Crime and Victims Act 2004
DVPN	domestic violence protection notice
DVPO	domestic violence protection order

DWP	Department for Work and Pensions
ECHR	European Convention on Human Rights
EEA	European Economic Area
EHRC	Equality and Human Rights Commission
EPO	emergency protection order
FLA 1986	Family Law Act 1986
FLA 1996	Family Law Act 1996
FLRA 1969	Family Law Reform Act 1969
FLRA 1987	Family Law Reform Act 1987
FPC	Family Proceedings Court
FPR 2010	Family Procedure Rules 2010, SI 2010/2955
GRA 2004	Gender Recognition Act 2004
HFEA	Human Fertilisation and Embryology Authority
HFEA 1990	Human Fertilisation and Embryology Act 1990
HFEA 2008	Human Fertilisation and Embryology Act 2008
HMIC	Her Majesty's Inspectorate of Constabulary
HMRC	Her Majesty's Revenue and Customs
HO	Home Office
HRA 1998	Human Rights Act 1998
ICCPR	International Covenant on Civil and Political Rights
IFS	Institute for Fiscal Studies
IRO	independent reviewing officer
IVF	in vitro fertilization
JSA	income-based jobseeker's allowance
LASPO 2012	Legal Aid, Sentencing and Punishment of Offenders Act 2012
Law Com	Law Commission
LCD	Lord Chancellor's Department
LPA 1925	Law of Property Act 1925
LRA 2002	Land Registration Act 2002
MA 1949	Marriage Act 1949
MCA 1973	Matrimonial Causes Act 1973
MIAM	Mediation Information and Assessment Meeting
MOJ	Ministry of Justice
M(SSC)A 2013	Marriage (Same Sex Couples) Act 2013
NRP	non-resident parent
OECD	Organisation for Economic Cooperation and Development
ONS	Office for National Statistics
PHA 1997	Protection from Harassment Act 1997
PR	parental responsibility
PRO	parental responsibility order
PSO	prohibited steps order
PWC	parent with care
SAA 1985	Surrogacy Arrangements Act 1985
Scot Law Com	Scottish Law Commission
SGO	special guardianship order
SIO	specific issue order
TOLATA 1996	Trusts of Land and Appointment of Trustees Act 1996
UNCRC	United Nations Convention on the Rights of the Child 1989
WTC	working tax credit

1

INTRODUCTION TO FAMILY LAW

The purpose of this chapter is to introduce you to:

- the idea of family law
- some key themes and debates which feature in several areas of family law and are dealt with in later chapters of the book
- this book and its companion Online Resource Centre

We hope that you will find it helpful.

1.1 FAMILIES AND FAMILY LAW IN ENGLAND AND WALES TODAY

1.1.1 WHAT IS 'FAMILY'?

This apparently simple question is actually a complex one to which people might offer different answers in different contexts. To many, 'family' implies a group linked by blood relationship and by marriage, and commonly by a shared home. The world of advertising would have us believe that we all live, or at least grew up, in nuclear families: households composed of two parents and their children. However, the reality of domestic life for many people diverges from that traditional image, as figures from the 2011 Census show.[1]

In 2001, the census showed that just over half (51 per cent) of the usually resident adult population was married;[2] by 2011, the proportion had fallen to 47 per cent.[3] This is a continuation of a trend seen since the 1970s, with the popularity of marriage declining and divorce becoming much more common.[4] Increasing numbers of couples live together without getting married and 47 per cent of children are now born to parents who are not married.[5]

---

[1] ONS (2013a). We provide more detailed statistical information on several of the issues identified here in later chapters.

[2] ONS (2003).

[3] ONS (2013a).

[4] For discussion of this trend with possible reasons for it, see ONS (2012a).

[5] ONS (2014c).

Thirty per cent of households in England and Wales contain dependent children: of those, 50 per cent are headed by a married couple, 13 per cent by a cohabiting couple, and 24 per cent by a lone parent.[6] Some children are adopted, fostered, or otherwise 'parented' by people other than their biological parents. Same-sex couples are gaining social acceptance and legal recognition: they can marry, register a civil partnership (which bestows rights and responsibilities akin to those of spouses), adopt children together, or become parents using assisted reproduction. Some households, particularly in certain ethnic minority communities, comprise 'extended' families of more than two generations and/or adult siblings.[7] Many people, particularly in early and late adult life, share households with friends in platonic relationships. Increasing numbers of young people remain in their parents' homes into adulthood. Many individuals live alone, but are nevertheless members of families by virtue of blood and other ties; some couples physically live apart and yet still regard themselves as being 'together'. In one way or another, all of these groups may consider themselves 'family'.

Whether, to what extent, and how the law recognizes this diversity in family life is of central importance for family lawyers. The supportive and protective functions of 'family law' are reserved to those the law accepts as 'family'. For those whom the law rejects, denied formal recognition of their family status, solutions must be found elsewhere. For example, those who have not formalized their relationships by marriage or civil partnership cannot access the specialist financial remedies applicable on divorce to spouses and civil partners. The general law of contract, trusts, and property must be relied upon to determine financial and property disputes between such individuals on relationship breakdown. A key issue for contemporary family law is therefore to decide which social 'families' to admit to 'family law', how to regulate their relationships, and whether to confer more extensive rights and duties on some categories of family than others, for example by privileging marriage.

1.1.2 WHAT IS FAMILY LAW?

Defining 'family law' is also surprisingly complicated. In jurisdictions with codified laws, we might expect to find a code containing the Family Law of that country.[8] Identifying a corpus of family law for England and Wales is less straightforward. Much of the law that regulates family life here is specifically devised for families, but to some extent aspects of the general law are relevant too.

The shape and focus of family law has also changed substantially over the decades. As Rebecca Probert has highlighted, a family law textbook written in the 1950s would have looked very different from ours.[9] At that point in the social and legal history of the English family, marriage—then meaning only opposite-sex marriage, of course—was almost universal, cohabitation almost unheard of, and divorce rare by comparison with today's standards. It was therefore more natural to focus on law governing the ongoing relationship between the spouses (and not much else). Much has changed since then. The law relating to children has dramatically expanded, such that the parent–child relationship now takes centre stage, regarded by some commentators as the central relationship of family law. And rather than the functioning family, it is the pathology of family breakdown that has come

---

[6] Authors' calculations from ONS (2013a). The remaining 12 per cent of dependent children live in other types of household.

[7] ONS (2014b), 21.

[8] Müller-Freienfels (2003).

[9] Probert (2004a), 903–5.

to preoccupy the discipline. Divorce and its financial consequences, domestic violence, disputes over the upbringing of children, and protection of children from abuse within the home now constitute the core of family law.

In recognition of the breadth of contemporary 'family' and 'family law', this book examines the law relating to a wide range of 'families', not just those based on marriage, and addresses issues relevant to the ongoing family, as well as those arising on relationship breakdown.

1.2 THEMES AND ISSUES IN CONTEMPORARY FAMILY LAW

You will find that studying family law involves quite a lot of 'black letter' law, particularly in areas which are regulated closely by statute. However, our understanding and evaluation of the law is considerably enriched by thinking about various theoretical and policy implications of the social issues with which family law is concerned. Indeed, an important feature of contemporary family law scholarship is the identification of broad trends in the way in which law has been used to regulate the family in many western jurisdictions.[10] Throughout this book, you will encounter a number of inter-related themes, issues, and perspectives on family law. We introduce the most important of these in this section in order to set the scene for the specific debates that you will read about in the following chapters.

1.2.1 A RIGHTS-BASED APPROACH TO THE FAMILY?

Welfare versus rights

Family law has oscillated between rights-based and welfare-based approaches to the family. Should family law be based on the notion that individual family members have rights and duties that they exercise against each other and against the state? (And, if so, what rights should those be?) Or should family law, and family dispute resolution, be based on welfare-based criteria, seeking to achieve the 'best' outcome for the parties in their particular circumstances? The rights–welfare spectrum relates closely to a similar tension between law based on rules and law based on discretion, which we discuss next. A lawmaker who wishes to enforce rights and duties may naturally adopt a rule-based approach. But a lawmaker concerned to achieve the best outcome in all the circumstances of the individual case may prefer to rely on discretion, affording decision-makers flexibility to produce optimal outcomes.

As Stephen Parker has related,[11] historically, both rights-based and welfare-based approaches have been evident in legal regulation of the family. One or other predominates at particular points in time, but neither is ever completely absent. Put at its most basic, from an approach initially dominated by rights (principally those of the husband and the father), the twentieth century witnessed a clear shift towards a welfare-orientated approach (exemplified by the welfare principle and the redistribution of property and finance on divorce), and now a new rights-based model is doing battle with the welfare approach.

---

10 See, e.g., Dewar (2003).
11 Parker (1992), 321–5 on which the following draws.

In general terms, a rights-based approach reflects the view that the state should not seek to bring about certain consequences, such as maximization of social welfare, but simply protect individuals' rights to pursue their own vision of the 'good life'. Pre-twentieth century rights-based family law consisted of a fairly rigid system of rules prescribing fixed roles for each family member which were ostensibly applied without regard to the implications for the individuals concerned. A utility-based model, by contrast, involves identifying a social goal and balancing individual interests to attain it. Broad discretion is conferred on judges to conduct this interest-balancing exercise guided only by vaguely defined 'goals and standards'. However, as Parker explains, growing dissatisfaction with the broad discretionary nature of a welfare-orientated approach led to a renewed focus on a more rule-orientated, rights-based approach. Needless to say, the rights of contemporary family law are rather different in substance from those of the nineteenth century, not least in being (on their face) gender neutral. But the result has been an uneasy tension as family law tries to accommodate both welfare and rights. As Parker puts it, 'by the late 1980s...a kind of normative anarchy reigned within family law, with some measures tugging in the direction of rights and others in the direction of utility'.[12]

Contemporary rights in family law: the European Convention on Human Rights

The Human Rights Act 1998 (HRA 1998) has intensified this ideological 'struggle' between rights and utility in family law. The HRA 1998 gave effect to the European Convention on Human Rights (ECHR) in domestic law. Despite continuing opposition and scepticism, a more rights-based approach to the family is therefore unavoidable. The HRA 1998 has implications for statutory interpretation, the development of case law, and the exercise of judicial discretion. Consequently, sound knowledge of the HRA, the ECHR, and the Strasbourg jurisprudence is essential for any family lawyer. In this section, we introduce the key ECHR Articles likely to be encountered by family lawyers.

 ONLINE RESOURCE CENTRE

Readers requiring information on the operation of the HRA 1998 will find further guidance and materials on the Online Resource Centre.

Article 3

In some areas of family law—child protection and domestic violence—the most basic human rights may be at stake.

Article 3

No one shall be subjected to torture or to inhuman or degrading treatment or punishment.

---

[12] Ibid, 325.

Article 3 subjects the state to a negative obligation: it must not perpetrate abuse itself or through its agents. Like other Convention rights, Article 3 has also been held to impose positive obligations on the state, here requiring the state to take reasonable steps to protect both adults and children from abuse perpetrated by others.[13] In extreme cases, Article 2—the right to life—may also be implicated; it too imposes positive obligations on the state. The state's obligations towards children who are suffering or at risk of suffering harm are particularly far-reaching.

Article 6

Article 6—along with Article 8[14]—creates procedural rights for those involved in family law disputes, whether between the state and family members (e.g. child protection and adoption) or between private individuals (e.g. disputes between parents about arrangements for children).

Article 6(1)

In the determination of his civil rights and obligations or of any criminal charge against him, everyone is entitled to a fair and public hearing within a reasonable time by an independent and impartial tribunal established by law. Judgment shall be pronounced publicly but the press and public may be excluded from all or part of the trial in the interests of morals, public order or national security in a democratic society, where the interests of juveniles or the protection of the private life of the parties so require, or to the extent strictly necessary in the opinion of the court in special circumstances where publicity would prejudice the interests of justice....

Procedural rights are as important as substantive rights (i.e. the right to a particular outcome), bringing both instrumental and non-instrumental advantages. Conferring procedural rights on individuals likely to be affected by the outcome of a decision-making process may improve the accuracy and quality of that decision: those individuals may have unique knowledge to contribute to the process and so should be allowed to participate. But procedural rights also perform a dignity-protecting function: they acknowledge affected individuals' entitlement to participate in decisions affecting them, rather than simply subjecting them arbitrarily to the closed decision-making of a third party. Whether doing so makes any practical difference to the outcome does not matter for these purposes—what matters is that the affected individual is heard.

Ascertaining what 'fairness' requires under Article 6 involves weighing the applicant's demands against the exigencies of the particular procedure involved and the rights of other parties to those proceedings,[15] in a manner similar to the proportionality exercise conducted under Article 8 (below). Articles 6 and 8 have been found to apply both to court-based and out-of-court decision-making, and may support various rights, for example: to participate in decision-making affecting the applicant;[16] to be legally represented

---

13 *Z v United Kingdom* (App No 29392/95, ECHR) (2001).
14 *W v United Kingdom* (App No 9749/82, ECHR) (1988).
15 *Ashingdane v United Kingdom* (App No 8225/78, ECHR) (1985).
16 *Re M (Care: Challenging Decisions by Local Authority)* [2001] 2 FLR 1300.

before decision-making forums;[17] to legal aid;[18] to adequate notice of proceedings (rather than 'without notice' proceedings, conducted without notifying the respondent);[19] to be given access to key evidence;[20] and to be given access to a court or other forum to enforce legal rights.[21] Articles 6 and 8 also offer protection regarding the effect of delay on the disposal of cases,[22] and the privacy or otherwise of legal proceedings and judgments in family cases.[23]

Article 8

Article 8 is a key provision for family lawyers, carrying potential significance for almost any sort of family law dispute. Any case under Article 8 will have three stages: demonstrating that the right applies; showing that the state has interfered with the right; determining whether that interference can be justified by the state.

Article 8

1. Everyone has the right to respect for his private and family life, his home and his correspondence.

2. There shall be no interference by a public authority with the exercise of this right except such as is in accordance with the law and is necessary in a democratic society in the interests of national security, public safety or the economic well-being of the country, for the prevention of disorder or crime, for the protection of health or morals, or for the protection of the rights and freedoms of others.

To establish a case under Article 8, the applicant must first show that the complaint falls within the scope of Article 8(1). The right to respect for private life and the right to respect for family life arise most commonly in family law cases; the right to respect for the home may also be relevant, for example, in relation to rights to succeed to a tenancy or to occupy property.

The right to respect for private life has been particularly important for those who have traditionally struggled to establish 'family life' rights, such as same-sex couples and transgender people, or where no family ties currently exist. The scope of private life protection, while not unlimited,[24] is potentially extremely broad, covering 'physical and psychological integrity', 'physical and social identity', 'gender identification, name and sexual orientation and sexual life', 'personal development', 'personal autonomy', and 'the right to establish and develop

---

[17] E.g. on children's rights to participate in legal proceedings: *Sahin v Germany* (App No 30943/96, ECHR) (2001).

[18] *Airey v Ireland (No 1)* (App No 6289/73, ECHR) (1979).

[19] In the context of child protection proceedings, see 12.6.2.

[20] E.g. in relation to child protection: *TP and KM v United Kingdom* (App No 28945/95, ECHR) (2001); *Re A (Sexual Abuse: Disclosure)* [2012] UKSC 60.

[21] See, e.g., 6.4.7 on parents' rights to enforce child support.

[22] E.g. in relation to child-related disputes: *Glaser v United Kingdom* (App No 32346/96, ECHR) (2000); *Re D (Intractable Contact Dispute: Publicity)* [2004] EWHC 727; see chapter 11.

[23] In relation to disputes about children's upbringing: *B and P v United Kingdom* (App Nos 36337/97 and 35974/97, ECHR) (2001); *Re B (A Child) (Disclosure)* [2004] EWHC 411; and in relation to disputes between adults: *Clibbery v Allan* [2002] EWCA Civ 45.

[24] *M v Secretary of State for Work and Pensions* [2006] UKHL 11; cf Scherpe (2006c).

relationships with other human beings and the outside world'.[25] It has been invoked in various situations.

The right to respect for family life is the most frequently invoked provision of the Convention in domestic family law proceedings, in both private and public law cases. Establishing the existence of family life is not always straightforward. A well-established line of authority makes it clear that Article 8 affords respect only to existing family relationships: it does not safeguard the 'mere desire' to found a family or create new familial relationships.[26] Moreover, until recently the European Court of Human Rights has clearly favoured the traditional heterosexual married unit, where 'family life' between the various individuals, including children of the marriage, is established automatically by the simple fact of the marital tie.[27] Establishing family life where the adult parties are unmarried has been more difficult.[28] However, the Court has been increasingly willing to embrace de facto as well as de jure family life.[29] Importantly, this has included relationships between transgender, gay, and lesbian parents and their children.[30] Most recently, as we discuss in chapter 2, the European Court has held that both opposite-sex and same-sex cohabiting couples living in a stable de facto partnership fall within the notion of 'family life', whether or not they have children.[31]

Once the applicant has established the existence of one of the relevant interests protected by Article 8 (whether private life or family life, etc) it must then be determined whether the state has, prima facie, interfered with the right. This raises the question of what the right 'to respect' for private and family life entails. Article 8 imposes a range of specific obligations on the state. Many of those are negative: for example, prohibiting the state from removing children from their parents. Others are positive, requiring the state to act in a particular way. As noted earlier, sometimes Article 8 imposes procedural obligations: for example, requiring that parents be given the opportunity to be consulted about decisions made by the state in relation to their children.[32] We shall come across many examples of Article 8 obligations throughout the book. By way of example, here are some types of situation in which Article 8 might plausibly be invoked—we shall see later whether successfully or not:

- to achieve the legal recognition of transgender people's preferred gender;

- to protect the competing interests in cases of domestic violence: the victim's right to physical and psychological integrity, versus the alleged perpetrator's right to remain undisturbed in his own home;

- to recognize the parental status of unmarried fathers;

25 *Van Kück v Germany* (App No 35968/97, ECHR) (2003), [69].

26 *Fretté v France* (App No 36515/97, ECHR) (2003), [32]. The European Court has suggested that Art 8 may protect a potential relationship between a father and a child once the child is born even if there is no existing relationship between them (*Anayo v Germany* (App No 20578/07, ECHR) (2010)), but that can be seen as being about the recognition of a family relationship rather than the creation of one.

27 *Al Nashif v Bulgaria* (App No 50963/99, ECHR) (2003).

28 *Marckx v Belgium* (A/31, ECHR) (1979).

29 *Lebbink v Netherlands* (App No 45582/99, ECHR) (2004).

30 *X, Y and Z v United Kingdom* (App No 2180/93, ECHR) (1997); *Salgueiro De Silva Mouta v Portugal* (App No 33290/96, ECHR) (2001).

31 *Schalk & Kopf v Austria* (App No 30141/04, ECHR) (2010), [90]–[95]; *Vallianatos v Greece* (App Nos 29381/09 and 32684/09, ECHR) (2013), [73].

32 *W v United Kingdom* (App No 9749/82, ECHR) (1988).

- to protect the competing interests of parties to disputes relating to the upbringing of a child following parental separation, particularly arrangements about children's living arrangements;
- to protect the mutual family life interests of parents and children where it is proposed to take a child into state care, and to protect their ongoing relationship once a care order has been made;
- to protect parents' interests when adoption of their child is proposed.

Article 8 is a 'qualified' right, which means that even if the state is prima facie obliged to respect the right in a particular way it may be justifiable for it to do otherwise. As we can see from the examples just given, in many Article 8 cases individuals will be asserting competing rights, and some decision clearly has to be made between them. Protecting one person's rights will necessarily entail encroaching on the rights of the other; for example, protecting a non-resident parent's right to spend time with his child against the wishes of the parent with whom the child mainly lives will necessarily interfere with the latter parent's right to respect for family life.

Article 8(2) provides the framework within which we resolve these conflicts and ascertain the true extent of each party's right. Once it has been demonstrated that the applicant has a right under Article 8(1) which has been interfered with in some way by the state, the burden then shifts to the state to justify its action. Article 8(2), in common with the other qualified Convention rights, sets out three basic criteria that must be met in order for the interference to be justified: it must be (i) 'in accordance with the law'; (ii) pursue one of the legitimate aims specified in the list in Article 8(2); and (iii) be 'necessary in a democratic society'. In practice, the first two requirements of Article 8(2) are usually easily satisfied. Often, the state will have acted in accordance with domestic law to protect the rights and interests of a child, unquestionably a 'legitimate aim'.

The most difficult test to satisfy is showing that the interference with the applicant's rights was 'necessary in a democratic society'. This test comprises several requirements: the interference must correspond with a pressing social need, be based on relevant and sufficient reasons, and be proportionate to the aim being pursued. The key concept here is proportionality, the tool used to resolve conflicts between competing parties' rights, or between rights and other 'legitimate aims'. The concept of proportionality is also relevant to several other provisions, including Articles 6 and 14. The Strasbourg Court has also used criteria akin to those found in Article 8(2) when seeking to ascertain the scope of positive obligations under various Articles.[33] The proportionality test requires the decision-maker to carry out a balancing exercise, weighing the various rights and interests in order to determine whether the degree of interference with the applicant's rights is no more extensive than is required to meet the needs of the stated aim. But applying the proportionality test is not a mechanical, value-neutral exercise: it is impossible to determine the proper relationship between competing rights and interests without ascribing each of them relative weight—the question is a normative rather than factual one: 'which right ought to prevail?'; or 'how extensive ought the state's obligation to be?'.

---

[33] *Rees v United Kingdom* (App No 9532/81, ECHR) (1986), [37]; *Osman v United Kingdom* (App No 23452/94, ECHR) (2000), [99], quotation of Commission decision, para 91.

Article 12

By contrast with the breadth of Article 8, Article 12 has a very specific focus.

Article 12

Men and women of marriageable age have the right to marry and to found a family, according to the national laws governing the exercise of this right.

The rights protected under Article 12 are expressed in unqualified terms and, although subject to 'national law', at least as regards the right to marry, it is impermissible to read into Article 12 the same limitations as set down in Article 8(2).[34] The position as regards the right to found a family is more uncertain.[35] Although the European Court has generally interpreted Article 12 cautiously and conservatively, evolving social conditions and trends may prompt change. As we shall see in chapter 2, European Court decisions concerning the right of transgender persons to marry[36] and recognizing same-sex couples as having family life under Article 8[37] may signal a shift away from the traditional concept of marriage as a heterosexual, biological-sex-based relationship, to one based more broadly on gender and social function. Article 12 has also become potentially important in the field of reproduction as individuals seek to take advantage of new reproductive technologies. The controversial issue of whether Article 12 offers a legal basis for an individual right to become a parent, whether through natural intercourse, assisted reproduction, or adoption, is discussed in chapters 9 and 13.

Article 14

Article 14 is the Convention's non-discrimination clause. As we shall see in chapter 2, it has been used with notable success in the English courts since the HRA came into force to advance the legal rights of same-sex couples.

Article 14

The enjoyment of the rights and freedoms set forth in this Convention shall be secured without discrimination on any ground such as sex, race, colour, language, religion, political or other opinion, national or social origin, association with a national minority, property, birth or other status.

The principle of non-discrimination has been described by Baroness Hale as 'essential to democracy'—guaranteeing that power is not exercised arbitrarily, everyone is valued equally, and where distinctions are drawn between different groups such distinctions have a rational basis.[38]

---

[34] *R (Baiai) v Secretary of State for Home Department* [2008] UKHL 53, [15].
[35] Ibid, and see *R (Mellor) v Secretary of State for the Home Department* [2001] EWCA Civ 472, [28]–[29]. For further discussion, see pp 634–5.
[36] *Goodwin v United Kingdom* (App No 28957/95, ECHR) (2002).
[37] *Vallianatos v Greece* (App Nos 29381/09 and 32684/09, ECHR) (2013).
[38] *Ghaidan v Godin-Mendoza* [2004] UKHL 30, [131]–[132].

Article 14 is not a free-standing anti-discrimination provision: it guards against discrimination only in the exercise of other Convention rights. Any claim under Article 14 must therefore begin by demonstrating that the factual circumstances of the case fall within the scope of one of the other rights. However, this does not require the applicant to demonstrate that that other right has itself been breached. Article 14 also demands that if the state chooses to grant rights beyond those required by the Convention, it must not do so in a discriminatory way: it must grant that right equally unless the difference in treatment can be justified.[39]

A resistance to rights?

The return to a rights-based approach to the family, prompted by the HRA 1998, gives previously excluded groups such as transgender people and same-sex couples a more promising language in which to argue for change, providing them with rights that they can assert against the state in order to demand legal recognition. However, the rights-based discourse has not met with unanimous support from family lawyers. Some family lawyers, including some family judges, have shown deep-seated resistance to the (re)introduction and potential predominance of rights-based reasoning. The continuing ambivalence about the rights of individual family members has meant that the impact of the HRA 1998 on the balance between welfare and rights in family law has varied considerably depending on the nature of the dispute.

There are various reasons for this resistance.[40] For some conservative groups, the perceived alliance between strong liberal values and human rights discourse breeds concern that, by emphasizing individualism, equality, and non-discrimination, rights-based reasoning will undermine the traditional family unit and the values it protects.[41] More moderate commentators are concerned that the individualistic focus of rights-based reasoning is inappropriate when dealing with the interdependence of contemporary family life.[42] Scepticism about rights-based reasoning is particularly strong in cases relating to children, where there are concerns that focusing on rights will lead to children's interests being marginalized. Jane Fortin, for example, has warned that the 'Strasbourg jurisprudence may not always augur well for British children' and that rights-based discourse, including the discourse of children's rights, may be hijacked by the parental rights lobby, particularly fathers, to further their own claims and interests at the expense of the child.[43] Those concerns are understandable. It is only fairly recently that the notion of parents holding autonomous 'proprietary' rights over their children has given way to a welfare-based discourse which strives to put children's interests at the heart of the decision-making process.[44] For many family lawyers, the principle that children's interests should be paramount in decisions concerning their future welfare and upbringing is sacrosanct; to revert to reasoning dominated by the individual rights of parents would be a retrograde step.

Despite these concerns, family law has not escaped the pressures of a domestic legal, political, and social culture increasingly wedded to the concept of rights. Rights-based arguments

---

[39] Ibid, [135].
[40] Harris-Short (2005), on which the following draws.
[41] E.g. Hafen and Hafen (1995–96).
[42] E.g. Herring (1999a), 232–5; Diduck (2011b).
[43] Fortin (1999a), 251.
[44] Parker (1992), 321–5.

have found a natural home in family law disputes. A rights-based, more rule-orientated approach can lead to more principled, 'just' outcomes.[45] The discourse of rights demands that the individual needs and interests of all family members are identified and weighed. Clear articulation of the parties' individual needs and interests may bring predictability, transparency, and accountability in family law decision-making. It can also address concerns that welfare-based approaches allow legitimate rights and interests to be obscured by children's interests.

One of the most controversial issues in carrying out the balancing exercise demanded by Article 8(2) is the weight to be accorded to the child's interests, in particular whether they are to be the paramount consideration such that any interference with an adult's rights will automatically be deemed 'necessary in a democratic society' if undertaken with the aim of protecting a child's rights and interests. This is an important issue, not least because of its implications for the traditional welfare-orientated approach of English law, explored in depth in chapter 8. It exemplifies, more clearly than any other area of family law, the ideological struggle between welfare and rights in the post-HRA era.

1.2.2 RULES VERSUS DISCRETION

The legislature has adopted two principal modes of law-making in relation to the family: (i) the imposition of rules; and (ii) the creation of judicial (or executive) discretion (though recent cases have tended to term this an 'evaluation' or 'value judgment'[46]). Some legislation creates prescriptive, exhaustive rules to govern particular disputes; child support law is the classic example of this approach. Here, the courts' function is confined to determining the meaning of statutory language and applying it to the facts of the case, though this is not a straightforward or value-neutral task. Other legislation confers wide discretion on the family courts: the statute may set down broad principles, or just indicate relevant factors for the courts to consider, giving no close indication of the 'right' outcome for any particular case. Many areas of family law, such as decisions about future arrangements for children's living arrangements and financial provision on divorce, are heavily discretionary. Here, the courts' role is very different: interpretation of the legislation is less difficult and less important to the determination of individual cases. Instead the emphasis is on the courts' assessment of the individual circumstances of each case, and on their judgement of what will be a 'fair' outcome, or one which best promotes the welfare of particular family members, guided only rather loosely by general statutory principles.[47]

As noted earlier, this contrast between rules and discretion is associated with the contrast between rights-based and welfare-based approaches to family disputes. It is also connected with broader questions about the social function of family law: should family law endeavour to modify the behaviour of individuals within families, or should it simply offer an (apparently) morally neutral forum for decision-making?

There are various pros and cons to rules and discretion. Does discretion create inconsistency and so unfairness? Are rules equally capable of yielding unjust outcomes? Does

---

[45] Dewar (1998a), 473.

[46] *Re B (Care Order: Proportionality: Criterion for Review)* [2013] UKSC 33, [44], [57], and [199]; *Re B-S (Adoption: Application of s 47(5))* [2013] EWCA Civ 1146, [72].

[47] This has implications for the proper handling of case law in the family field, an issue discussed on the Online Resource Centre.

discretion render the system unpredictable and so impede private negotiation? Are rules preferable insofar as they can be used by the state to try to affect our behaviour? A strong reason in favour of discretion in family law is that family life is so variable that it would be impossible to lay down sufficiently nuanced rules in advance. Discretion thus maximizes 'individualized justice', achieving the fairest outcome in each individual case.[48] However, rules also have advantages. As Carl Schneider has observed, rules have 'democratic legitimacy': they are publicly accessible and readily susceptible to public debate. They also further one of the most fundamental principles of justice: that like cases should be treated alike. It is suggested that where the rules to be applied are clear and democratically sanctioned even losing parties should feel satisfied that they have been treated fairly rather than abandoned to the vagaries of individual judges' personal prejudices and preferences.[49] Yet, as Schneider also points out, this confidence in the capacity of rules to guard against a sense of injustice in family disputes may be naïve. Rather than passively accept defeat, the losing party is very likely to contend that the rules are wrong or have been unfairly applied to the circumstances of their case. Falling back on the individualized justice afforded by discretion, our disaffected litigant is likely to call for a more careful examination of the individual circumstances of his or her case in order to ensure justice is done.

A particular concern of opponents of discretion is that it hampers negotiated settlements. It is often said that parties 'bargain in the shadow of the law',[50] that they negotiate in light of what they anticipate a court would order in their case. This can sometimes be difficult, given the highly discretionary—and so rather unpredictable—nature of family law.[51] By contrast, rules would provide clear guidance about how a court is likely to resolve the dispute, helping parties to negotiate settlements out of court, but also performs the important normative function of telling disputants how society believes the dispute ought to be resolved.[52] As we shall see in various chapters, this normative function of family law has become particularly important and controversial in the context of divorce and post-divorce parenting, as the state has sought through more subtle and diffuse methods to re-inject some sense of 'family values' and 'responsibility' in the wake of the removal of 'fault' from family law. We are not faced then simply with a choice between rules and discretion, but more fundamentally with a dilemma regarding the proper purposes of family law: to modify behaviour in line with some moral code (better effected by rules), or to resolve practical problems by reference to more (apparently) value-neutral principles. Dewar has observed that there has indeed been a shift in several jurisdictions (particularly in areas such as child support, spousal support, and post-divorce parenting) away from discretion (and welfare), partly as a result of attempts to reinvigorate the moral messages conveyed by the law with a view to delivering more 'just' and principled outcomes for men, women, and children.[53] But the recent promotion of other rights—such as the right to autonomy—raises concerns that other rights-based gains (e.g. to equal treatment) may be lost.[54]

[48] Dewar (1997), 311–14.
[49] Schneider (1992), 74–7.
[50] Mnookin and Kornhauser (1979).
[51] On the other hand, it has been suggested that this very uncertainty provides the parties an incentive to settle so as to avoid the unpredictable outcomes in court: Harris (2008).
[52] Ibid.
[53] Dewar (1997), 313–16 and Dewar (1998a), 473–4.
[54] Diduck (2011b). See further below, 1.2.7.

1.2.3 WOMEN'S AND MEN'S PERSPECTIVES ON FAMILY LAW

The interests of some groups and individuals have at various times been neglected by family law. Commentators from various schools of thought and proponents of reform have sought to draw attention to these omissions. Feminism has long been the most dominant of these discourses, highlighting the historical oppression of women by the law in general and family law in particular. By contrast, the turn of the twenty-first century has witnessed a burgeoning fathers' rights movement and the growth of masculine studies which have sought to encourage equivalent examination of the position of men within the family.

Feminist perspectives

There is a wealth of literature bringing a variety of feminist perspectives to family law. Feminist scholars do not speak with one voice, various schools of thought taking very different approaches to a range of family law issues. For example, views differ sharply on whether women have legitimate claims to ongoing financial support following divorce; and on whether perceived judicial bias towards women in disputes about children's living arrangements should be supported as recognizing and valuing women's care-giving role, or resisted as further entrenching traditional stereotypes portraying women's natural and appropriate role as resting within the private realm of the family. However, despite the diversity, feminist writers share some core concerns which have an important bearing upon many areas of family law.

The 'difference' of gender

The first such concern is the issue of gender itself and whether gender does and/or should make a difference. For 'liberal feminists', gender is unproblematic: all that is required to secure true equality is the removal of legal and structural barriers to women's full participation in the public sphere.[55] For 'difference' or 'cultural feminists', however, gender is crucial: they focus on 'the perception that women and men have differing modes of reasoning and different socially-constructed roles which are explanatory of women's inferiority and exclusion from the gendered, male, world'.[56] The work of Carol Gilligan, an educational psychologist, is most closely associated with the 'difference' school of feminist thinking. Based on her research into the moral development of boys and girls, she suggests that men and women think differently and approach moral problems in different ways.[57] Although controversial, Gilligan's work has a potentially important application to many legal issues. She describes the 'ethic of care', which she identifies with feminine thinking, as an approach which sees moral problems within a web of complex relationships to be resolved through dialogue and communication. This supports a model of family justice based more firmly on negotiation, mediation, and other forms of alternative dispute resolution than the adversarial, rights-based approach of traditional adjudication. Gilligan's work on the importance of resolving disputes by situating them within the context of the realities of people's lives has also been advanced as the most appropriate model for resolving disputes about children's

---

[55] Barnett (1998), 17–18.
[56] Ibid.
[57] Graycar and Morgan (2002), 194–5.

living arrangements, in preference to the abstract, rights-based reasoning which has come to dominate recent debates.[58]

Gender also matters for the radical feminist school. Gender is here understood as the manifestation of power disparities between men and women as created and sustained by the law. As Barnett explains, 'from this perception, woman's role is determined by her socially constructed gender, which ensures her inequality and subordination in relation to law and society which is characterised by male dominance'.[59] The insights of radical feminists have made an important contribution to our understanding of men's violence against women, particularly within the domestic sphere.

The public/private divide

A second core concern of feminist writers is the world's division into 'public' and 'private' spheres, and the role of that division in securing what O'Donovan terms 'the universal oppression of women'.[60] It is argued that whereas men have been identified with the rational, economically productive world of work and politics, women have been identified with the emotionally driven world of the family where work is undertaken for love not money.[61] This has led to an economic and power imbalance between the sexes which, in turn, has secured men's dominance over women in all spheres of life. Moreover, it is argued that the exclusion of women from the public sphere of government, politics, and work, and the reluctance of public bodies to intervene in what is regarded as the quintessentially private realm of family life, have rendered women invisible to the law and allowed dominance, inequality, violence, and abuse to continue unchecked. The law's historically muted response to the problem of domestic violence provides a strong example of legislators' reluctance to intervene in the 'private affairs' of family members. It is sobering to remember that it was only in 1991 that rape within marriage was criminalized. As Barnett argues, 'that which law does not explicitly proscribe infers implicit acceptance'. In the now seminal phrase, 'the personal is political'.[62]

Women as mothers

The confinement of women within the private sphere of domestic life is closely related to feminism's third core concern: women's traditional mothering role and its implications for achieving women's equality. Whether the reproductive and maternal role of women should be a cause for celebration or concern, it has relevance to several areas of family law, from financial provision on divorce to disputes about children's living arrangements. The close association between the enduring inequalities faced by women and their child-bearing and child-rearing responsibilities has been the subject of much comment by both radical and liberal feminists.

For radical feminists, women's mothering role can be deeply problematic. Katherine O'Donovan argues that women's confinement in the private sphere as a result of their reproductive and child-rearing role has secured their subordination to the dominance of men, who, she contends, are able to maintain this dominance and authority by distancing

---

58 See, for example, Neale and Smart (1999).
59 Barnett (1998), 18.
60 O'Donovan (1985), 15.
61 Ibid, 8–9.
62 Barnett (1998), 65–6.

themselves from the domestic work of raising a family. She argues that women's continuing subordination is rooted in both biology and culture: law and society has constructed male and female roles on the basis of an interpretation of biology that dictates that 'biological differences should determine the social order'. Thus the answer for a radical feminist is to free women from mothering: 'to abolish current methods of biological reproduction through the substitution of artificial methods and the socialisation of child care'.[63]

Liberal feminists have similar concerns about how traditional assumptions about the 'natural', biologically determined role of women within the family have limited women's opportunities in the public world of work, although their solutions to this problem are less drastic. Clare McGlynn's analysis of the 'ideology of motherhood' underpinning judicial decision-making in family law within the European Union is instructive for domestic lawyers, particularly regarding disputes about children's living arrangements and the perceived bias operating against fathers in such cases. According to McGlynn, the 'ideology of motherhood' reflects a deep-rooted belief that 'all women need to be mothers, that all mothers need their children and that all children need their mothers'.[64] This belief permeates the law such that motherhood is simply accepted as the natural, appropriate, and inevitable role for all women. From here, child-care is readily understood as the primary responsibility of women, underpinned by a welfare discourse that identifies the physical and emotional needs of all young children with their mothers. To protect this core relationship, the mother–child relationship is thus privileged by the law to the detriment of women's equality in the wider public sphere. However, as McGlynn points out, this privileging of motherhood is not just damaging for women but also for men, denying fathers an active caring role within the family. The answer for McGlynn is not to negate the importance of the mothering role, but to reject the privileging of motherhood over fatherhood. It is, she argues, 'parenting' not 'mothering' which should be valued, opening up an egalitarian vision of life in which both men and women are free to participate as equal partners in the private and the public spheres.[65]

However, the world of gender neutrality to which liberal feminist scholars such as McGlynn would aspire is not a vision shared by all feminists. Indeed, in a world which remains deeply gendered, entrenching 'formal equality' within the law based on a gender-blind vision of life may be a cause of further oppression for many women. As noted above, for some feminists, gender does make a difference and the key to achieving equality is not to ignore and suppress those differences but to ensure the law attributes equal value and respect to female experiences. On family law issues bearing upon the mother–child relationship, cultural/difference feminists would thus be more receptive to approaches which sought to support and uphold the mothering work of women and the perhaps unique mother–child bond, seeing it not as a source of oppression but as a source of empowerment and strength.

Men and the family

Much less developed than feminist jurisprudence is a growing body of work focusing on men's engagement with the law. Many men are increasingly disenchanted with what they perceive as the bias towards women in family law, particularly the law relating to children.

---

[63] O'Donovan (1985), 15–16.
[64] McGlynn (2001), 326, citing Anne Oakley.
[65] Ibid, 326–30.

This disenchantment has coincided with an important 'repositioning' of fatherhood in contemporary political, legal, and cultural thought. Recent years have seen the strong emergence of what Richard Collier terms the idea of the 'new democratic family'.[66] Central to this model of the family is a vision of fatherhood which is active, engaged, and emotionally involved. Thus we see a move away from the dominant normative construction of the father as detached economic provider, towards a more 'progressive' idea of father as 'hands-on' parent. This re-visioning of fatherhood was strongly promoted by the Labour Governments of 1997–2010, which introduced a range of initiatives aimed at encouraging and supporting fathers, particularly economically and socially vulnerable men, to engage successfully in family life.[67]

However, as Collier explains, this emerging image of the 'new' 'hands-on father' is not unproblematic. The 'new father' is just one of several conflicting popular images of fatherhood in contemporary discourse.[68] There remains, for example, strong political and cultural allegiance to the concept of the father as the 'guarantor of social and familial order'. Firmly rooted in appeals to traditional notions of masculinity, the father is here perceived as strong and authoritarian, the disciplinarian within the family charged with ensuring correct behaviour. He is expected to provide a positive role-model for his children, particularly his sons, by fulfilling his primary role as economic provider. Yet, strongly contradicting these overwhelmingly positive images of fatherhood, is continuing suspicion and distrust about the role of men in family life. Thus the negative perception of at least some men as irresponsible and feckless, the 'deadbeat dad' who is superfluous to the family, remains entrenched in popular discourse. Still further away from any positive conception of the father is the legal, political, and cultural acceptance of the dangerous family man—a man who callously subjects his family to harmful violence and abuse.

Moreover, there are serious concerns about the extent to which the rhetoric surrounding the emergence of the new 'hands-on' father is rooted in the actual practices of family life. Indeed, as Richard Collier argues, there would appear to be a serious disjuncture between the rhetoric and the reality of 'new fatherhood'.[69] Rather than a revolution in the traditional gendered division of labour in the UK, the empirical evidence strongly suggests that women continue to take on the bulk of the domestic labour whilst men remain principally committed to paid employment outside the home.[70] Despite various recent initiatives, parenting and employment practices thus remain deeply gendered, the evidence suggesting that rather than embracing the opportunity for change, men, and perhaps some women, remain resistant to political pressure—or feel economically unable—to cede their traditional roles.

This debate signals some important dangers for family law. The recent focus on fatherhood and the rhetoric surrounding the 'new' 'hands-on' father has led to what Collier describes as a 'devaluing and systematic negation of the social importance of mothers and mothering'.[71] This devaluing of motherhood is particularly problematic given it appears to be occurring against a 'mythical' understanding of contemporary fatherhood. Family law decision-making based on unfounded assumptions about contemporary equality between the sexes risks betraying the investment made by women in their parenting role, and

---

[66] Collier (2003), 245.
[67] Ibid, 245–7, 249–51. See also Gillies (2009), 52.
[68] Collier (2003), 257–9 on which the following draws. See also Collier (2014).
[69] Ibid, 255–6.
[70] See data cited in chapter 3.
[71] Collier (2003), 266.

ultimately the welfare of the child. The extent to which the role of fathers has changed, and whether such changes demand a different approach by the law to parent–child relationships, will be an important question throughout the child law chapters.

1.2.4 GENDER IDENTITY

Gender is important in various parts of family law. Terminology here can be confusing: although the law talks in terms of 'opposite-sex' and 'same-sex' relationships,[72] it is clear that what actually matters most of the time legally is not 'sex' in a narrow, biologically-determined sense, but a person's legally recognized 'gender'.[73] Until recently, marriage could be contracted only by parties of the opposite legal gender. Civil partnership can still be contracted only by parties of the same gender. An individual's legal gender may also determine whether and how they can become a child's parent and/or gain parental responsibility. It is important to emphasize that the issue here is one of legal gender (i.e. whether the person is male or female), not sexual orientation (i.e. whether one is sexually attracted to members of the opposite or same gender).

Legal gender is generally uncontroversial.[74] However, matters are less straightforward for transgender (or 'trans') and inter-sex persons. There are thought to be just a few thousand trans people in the UK,[75] and up to 1 per cent of people at birth cannot be decisively labelled male or female on biological criteria (by reference to their reproductive anatomy).[76] The problems that these people encounter under a law which seeks to place everyone into one of two boxes—male or female—raise interesting questions, not least, why does the law insist on categorizing us in that way? While trans people self-identify as either male or female and so might accept this 'binary' male/female taxonomy, inter-sex individuals (in particular) may regard themselves as belonging to a 'third' gender or reject the concept of gender entirely.[77]

In medical terms, sex is determined by various factors, the first immutable, the others more or less susceptible to medical intervention: chromosomes (XY for male, XX for female); gonads and other internal sex organs; genitalia; and secondary sexual characteristics generated by hormones, such as body hair and body shape. Gender is connected to biological sex and much of the development associated with gender happens in the womb,[78] but it is also influenced by upbringing, lifestyle, and self-perception (which might have a neurological as well as psychological aspect).[79] Usually, these factors are congruent: biological sex is obvious from birth, and legal gender follows from it. However, for inter-sex and trans people, matters are more complex.

In inter-sex cases, the individual's physiology is ambiguous, featuring both male and female characteristics. A judgement is simply made about which legal gender to ascribe to the individual concerned.[80] In transgender cases, by contrast, the chromosomes, gonads, and genitalia all unambiguously denote one biological sex, yet the individuals self-identify

---

[72] E.g. Marriage (Same Sex Couples) Act 2013.
[73] E.g. Gender Recognition Act 2004.
[74] Some sources, including the European Court of Human Rights, now refer to non-trans people as 'cis-sexual' or 'cisgender'.
[75] DCA (date unknown).
[76] Chau and Herring (2004), 204.
[77] Ibid.
[78] NHS (2014).
[79] *Bellinger v Bellinger* [2003] UKHL 21, [5].
[80] E.g. *W v W (Physical Inter-Sex)* [2001] Fam 111.

as of the other gender. This phenomenon is commonly understood to be a psychiatric condition, diagnosed as 'gender dysphoria', though recent research suggests that it may have a biological cause during foetal development.[81] Following assessment at a Gender Identity Clinic, medical treatment available to deal with this condition now involves hormonal treatment to alter secondary sexual characteristics; living in society as the other gender, with psychiatric therapy and support; and ultimately, and if clinically appropriate, surgery to remove unwanted gonads and genitalia, and construct genitalia and bodily features of the other sex.[82]

English law—following the leading decision *Corbett v Corbett*[83]—for a long time declined to recognize transgender individuals in their preferred gender, even after they had undertaken extensive surgery, insisting that gender must be determined for legal purposes exclusively by reference to the chromosomal, gonadal, and genital evidence. English law came under repeated challenge before the European Court of Human Rights, applicants complaining of breaches of Articles 8 and 12. After several decisions in which the matter was essentially left to the state's margin of appreciation, finally, in *Goodwin v UK* the Court held that English law was in breach of both Articles.[84] The English courts being unable to remedy the breach through human rights compliant interpretation of the relevant statutes,[85] Parliament enacted the Gender Recognition Act 2004 (GRA 2004). The Act provides a procedure whereby individuals can obtain full legal recognition in their preferred gender, confirmed by a certificate. Notably, there is no requirement that individuals undergo gender confirmation surgery before recognition can be granted—such treatment is not clinically appropriate for all patients. But a formal diagnosis of 'gender dysphoria' must be made.[86] If an individual does not use this procedure, the *Corbett* position stands, and they remain classed in their birth-assigned gender (corresponding with their biological sex) for all legal purposes.

We explore in chapters 2 and 9 the key areas of family law where legal gender matters. However, as family law becomes increasingly gender neutral—for example, marriage is available to all couples, whether opposite-sex or same-sex, and legal parentage can be acquired by couples of the same sex by various means—the question increasingly arises whether we need to retain the concepts of sex and gender in law at all.[87]

1.2.5 SEXUAL ORIENTATION

For centuries, individuals with non-heterosexual orientation were outlaws. Anal intercourse, even if consensual, was a serious criminal offence, subject to the death penalty until 1861. The offence of gross indecency—introduced in 1885—was aimed explicitly at gay behaviour. Lesbianism, by contrast, inhabited the shadows: the suggestion in 1921 that lesbian acts be brought within the scope of the offence of 'gross indecency' was dismissed on the basis that criminalization would 'tell the whole world there is such an offence,... bring it to the notice of women who have never heard of it, never dreamed of it. I think this is a very

---

[81] NHS (2014).
[82] Ibid.
[83] [1971] P 83.
[84] (App No 28957/95, ECHR) (2002).
[85] *Bellinger v Bellinger* [2003] UKHL 21.
[86] GRA 2004, ss 2–3.
[87] For versions of this argument, see Polikoff (2008) and Herring (2014).

great mischief'.[88] Needless to say, quasi-conjugal relationships between same-sex couples received no legal recognition—and some consider that that should still be the case.

However, over the last 60 years English law's approach towards gay and lesbian individuals, their sexual relationships, their place in civil society, and their relationships has been transformed. Kees Waaldijk has suggested that most countries follow a series of standard legislative steps towards recognition of same-sex relationships: first, homosexual acts are decriminalized and any distinctions between opposite-sex and same-sex sexual relations, such as the age of consent, are removed from criminal law; secondly, the civil law prohibits any discrimination against homosexuals in employment and the provision of goods and services; thirdly, family law is extended to embrace same-sex relationships in various ways, ending finally with acceptance of same-sex marriage.[89] In the UK, as in many western countries, lesbian, gay, and bisexual people have now clearly 'arrived' in family law, prompting questions about the proper regulation of same-sex—and opposite-sex—relationships, some of which draw on lessons learned from the feminist project.

Just as feminism is not a single school of thought, nor are advocates for gay and lesbian rights a homogenous group, and some criticize the way in which the new liberalism has been achieved and the potential implications of reform. The principal motive for reform has been equality. As we noted above, Article 14 ECHR has been used successfully on several occasions in Strasbourg and domestically to further the cause of gay and lesbian law reform, even though sexual orientation is not expressly enumerated as one of the prohibited grounds of discrimination.[90] The concept of equality is not, however, straightforward. The argument that same-sex couples should be treated in the same way as opposite-sex couples is conceptually simple, carries political and legal weight, and is readily accepted by the general population. As Craig Lind argued presciently a decade ago,[91] it was inevitable in today's political climate that this version of equality would take us inexorably towards the 'full equality' symbolically enshrined in same-sex marriage.[92] However, equality is more complex than this suggests. True equality does not necessarily require that all people be treated the same. Sometimes it demands that different people be treated differently. The crucial question for family lawyers thus remains whether 'admission to marriage and other forms of heterosexual family regulation enhance the "real" equality of lesbians and gay men?'[93]

The main concern here is the potentially 'normalizing' effects of formal equality arguments and their suppression of the diversity of gay and lesbian life.[94] As Edwin Cameron asks: 'on whose terms – and on what basis – is recognition to be gained? Are our relationships to be recognised only if they are in all respects, save for the gender of our partners, indistinguishable from traditional heterosexual marriages?'[95] The dilemma is a very real one for political activists. It is through emphasizing the 'sameness' of homosexuality that the greatest legal and political mileage has been made. So, Cameron asks, is assimilation to the heterosexual norm and rejection of the rich diversity and difference of same-sex relationships to be the inevitable price of equality?

---

88 Lord Birkenhead, quoted in Playdon (2004), 136.
89 Waaldijk (2003).
90 See *da Silva Mouta v Portugal* (App No 33290/96, ECHR) (1999).
91 Lind (2004), 115–19.
92 Marriage (Same Sex Couples) Act 2013.
93 Lind (2004), 119.
94 See further Norrie (2000); Harding (2014).
95 Cameron (2001), v.

1.2.6 CULTURAL DIVERSITY

The cultural and religious diversity of the population of England and Wales raises important issues for family law. The 2011 Census revealed that 7.8 million people or 14 per cent of the usual resident population of England and Wales are from an ethnic minority community.[96] There is considerable diversity within the ethnic minority population, which includes those of Indian, Pakistani, Bangladeshi, Black Caribbean, Black African, Chinese, and mixed-race origin, as well as a growing number of European migrants. Religious identity is also an increasingly important consideration. While the majority religion within Great Britain remains Christianity, with over 33 million people (59 per cent of the total population in 2011) identifying as Christian, the next largest religious groups are Muslims (2.7 million); Hindus (817,000); Sikhs (423,000); Jews (263,000); and Buddhists (248,000).[97] Just over a quarter of people identify as having no religion.

Given this diversity, religious and cultural factors play an important role in family disputes. The family sits at the heart of most cultural and religious communities. It is through the family that cultural and religious practices and beliefs are transmitted and preserved for the next generation. Cultural and/or religious practices are therefore often particularly strongly entrenched within the protected, private realm of family life. Traditions surrounding core family practices such as marriage and child-rearing are particularly resistant to change and, within immigrant communities, are often strongly defended when felt to be under threat from the assimilating pressures of the majority population. As John Eekelaar observes: '[i]t is natural that adults should be deeply concerned about the cultural context in which their children grow up. They tend to see it as part of their own interests'.[98] Respect for cultural identity is also a key part of liberalism's respect for individual liberty and choice, respect that extends to both adults and children.

The difficult question facing multicultural societies is to what extent minority practices and beliefs, whether rooted in religion or culture, should be accommodated within the law when in conflict with the normative standards of the majority population. An overly prohibitive approach can lead to charges of cultural imperialism, even racism. An overly tolerant approach can constitute an affront to the mores of the majority population, who may then complain that their own traditions and values are being undermined and eroded. Perhaps more persuasively, the application of different principles and standards to different ethnic and religious groups generates concern that vulnerable individuals within those communities are being denied equal treatment and protection under the law. The suggestion in 2008 (at least as reported in the media) by Dr Rowan Williams, then Archbishop of Canterbury, that some form of legal pluralism was 'unavoidable' in the UK and that Islamic courts should be able to apply Sharia Law to a range of family disputes caused a popular outcry.[99] It was condemned by David Cameron, then leader of the Opposition, as 'dangerous' and 'illiberal',[100] though religious bodies already play an important role in family law, both formally and informally.[101]

---

[96] ONS (2012b).
[97] ONS (2012c).
[98] Eekelaar (2004), 178.
[99] See <http://news.bbc.co.uk/1/hi/uk/7239409.stm>.
[100] See <http://news.bbc.co.uk/1/hi/uk_politics/7264740.stm>.
[101] Douglas et al (2012). See further below, p 26.

The potential for difficulty arises in several areas of family law, and the cultural norms and practices at stake are hugely significant to the communities in question.[102] There is no clear policy in English law determining how cases involving sensitive cultural or religious issues should be dealt with. It has been said that the starting point of the law is 'a tolerant indulgence to cultural and religious diversity and an essentially agnostic view of religious beliefs'.[103] Minority practices with respect to marriage have attracted considerable attention. The first wave of immigration following the Second World War raised the difficult question of whether polyg-amous marriages and child marriages entered into abroad should be recognized by English law.[104] Inter-generational conflict between first and second wave immigrants and their children generated disputes over arranged marriages, argued by the younger generation to be forced and so invalid.[105] In the context of divorce, women from various communities have looked to English law to help address difficulties in obtaining a divorce in accordance with their personal religious law.[106] Intra-cultural and religious disputes concerning marriage and divorce require the English courts to navigate a difficult path between according appropriate respect to the cultural and religious mores of the community, whilst seeking to do justice between the parties in accordance with the norms of English law. This task is made particularly difficult when dif-fering interpretations of the cultural/religious norms and practices at the heart of the dispute are advanced by the opposing parties. Clearly, Parliament and the courts must be responsive to the potential difficulties caused, especially for women, by traditional family practices. However, there are again no simple answers. Measures intended to protect vulnerable individuals within ethnic minority communities, such as refusing to recognize polygamous or child marriages on the basis of protecting basic human rights and promoting gender equality, can have the opposite effect, leaving the most vulnerable groups unprotected and driving prohibited prac-tices, such as polygamy, underground.[107] Prakash Shah suggests that a more effective response is to afford official recognition to these diverse cultural and religious practices, bringing them within the protective scope of English law.[108]

Cultural and religious conflict can also arise in various contexts relating to children. In the private law arena, disputes between parents of different religious and/or ethnic back-grounds over the upbringing of their children are increasingly common.[109] The weight to be accorded to cultural and religious identity in the context of adoption has also been con-troversial, trans-racial adoption dividing many commentators and communities.[110] Less well recognized, but equally important, is the potential impact of different child-rearing practices within ethnic minority communities on the outcome of disputes about children's living arrangements after parental separation. In contrast to the model of the nuclear family which predominates in the West, the extended family has a much more central role in many Asian and African cultures, as is reflected in the typical household size amongst ethnic minority communities in Great Britain.[111] Care must be taken that parents, particularly

---

[102] Murphy (2000), 650–1.
[103] *Pawndeep Singh v Entry Clearance Office, New Delhi* [2004] EWCA Civ 1075, [67].
[104] See Shah (2003).
[105] Matrimonial Causes Act 1973 (MCA 1973), s 12: see 2.7.1.
[106] See 5.5.7.
[107] Shah (2003), 399.
[108] Ibid.
[109] See, for example, *Re J (Child's Religious Upbringing and Circumcision)* [2000] 1 FCR 307; *Re G (Education: Religious Upbringing)* [2012] EWCA Civ 1233: see 8.2.1.
[110] Eekelaar (2004), 182.
[111] ONS (2014b).

mothers, from these communities are not unfairly prejudiced in disputes about where children should live because they fail to comply with the patterns of child-care predominating in western nuclear families.[112] Members of the extended family should not be overlooked as full-time carers for children because of the much less significant role played by equivalent relations within western families. Similar considerations apply in the public law context. On the one hand, social workers and the courts must be alert to the dangers of cultural imperialism in misinterpreting culturally rooted child-rearing practices as harmful or abusive.[113] On the other hand, social workers and the courts must be equally alert to the danger of the 'culture' argument being manipulated by parents with the result that vulnerable children are left in dangerous situations of abuse.[114]

1.2.7 STATE INTERVENTION VERSUS PRIVATE ORDERING

One of the most fundamental debates in family law is about how far the state should intervene in family life, rather than leaving people to make their own arrangements. The extent to which the law can exert moral force in contemporary family life is closely tied to its willingness to intervene in family decision-making. The more emphasis placed upon the privacy of the family unit, the more difficult it is for the state to enforce its normative standards and interests. The problem is particularly acute in the context of family breakdown. If the state is neutral about how such disputes should be resolved, families can be left to settle their own problems. By contrast, if the state is committed to promoting, for example, a particular model for the division of family assets on divorce in order to protect particular family members, it may be expected to try to enforce its view of the 'right' or 'preferable' outcome through the law. However, state intervention in family life has always been controversial.

The privacy of the family unit is fiercely protected within liberal western thought. Intervention in this protected realm by outside agencies has typically been perceived as harmful and undesirable. However, as Andrew Bainham explains, the private realm is not 'naturally preconstituted'.[115] Its boundaries are constructed by the state to serve the state's interests. Whilst the concept of family privacy is an important constraint on state intervention, it is not an inherent good. Consequently, where the privacy accorded to the family unit serves the wider public interest the state will happily adhere to a 'hands-off' approach; but when the family fails to serve that wider public interest, the state will intervene. Bainham illustrates this point with the example of child-rearing. Child-rearing can be understood as a private matter subject to state intervention only when certain norms are breached. However, child-rearing may more accurately be understood as an inherently public matter which, whilst typically delegated to parents, remains subject to the state's overriding control and scrutiny.[116]

Whichever conceptualization is preferred, the public interest in regulating the family is such that state intervention into the private realm will sometimes be justified. This will most often be the case when the family is in crisis, for example where children are being abused within the family home. The state may also have an interest in enforcing financial obligations

---

[112] See *Re K (Residence Order: Securing Contact)* [1999] 1 FLR 583.
[113] See *Re K* [2005] EWHC 2956.
[114] Eekelaar (2004), 190.
[115] Bainham (1990), 206–7.
[116] Ibid.

between family members. The difficulty lies in deciding when the privacy of the family should be protected and when the public interest, whether social, economic, or moral in nature, is sufficiently strong to merit intervention.

Debates concerning the location of the public/private boundary, the proper role of the state, and the practical limits of governance have become particularly acute in light of criticisms of the family justice system and increasingly determined efforts by successive governments to move family disputes out of the courts. It is through the law and its effective implementation in the courts that governments have traditionally sought to regulate families, particularly at the point of breakdown. However, in recent years, government would seem to have lost faith in the family courts as an effective mode of family governance. More fundamentally, such has been the dramatic withdrawal of 'law' from family dispute resolution, that serious questions are now raised as to whether the state has abandoned its normative and regulatory aims within this sphere.

The role of the family court

More flexible and informal than other parts of the legal system, the family justice system prides itself on its conciliatory approach to family disputes. Relatively few families therefore find themselves in the family court which, as it has evolved, has itself acquired a distinctive character. Current policy initiatives are nevertheless strongly focused on diverting even those relatively few warring family members away from court and into other dispute resolution mechanisms.

One means by which this policy is being pursued is through the recent reforms to legal aid which have seen a significant re-allocation of public funding for the resolution of family disputes. Opponents of the reforms argue that the provision of public funding to those who are unable to afford the costs of private legal advice and representation is essential to secure access to justice, whether obtained via lawyer-led negotiation and settlement of a dispute or, far less commonly, by resort to contested litigation and adjudication of the issues. Matrimonial matters were within the scope of the original legal aid scheme, part of the welfare state, from its inception in the late 1940s. However, in the era of cuts following the global recession, the Coalition Government made radical proposals for the 'reform' of legal aid,[117] the most important aspect of which for our purposes was the removal of entire areas of private law family disputes from the scope of public funding for legal advice and legal representation, in particular, those concerning arrangements for children, financial relief following relationship breakdown, and financial provision for children.[118] The principal justification offered for the cuts was the need to reduce financial spending, but the relevant consultation papers suggested that an ideological motivation was also at play.[119] Family court cases were regarded as having lower priority for funding, since they 'result[ed] from a litigant's own decisions in their personal life',[120] and consequently litigation was 'unnecessary'.[121] By contrast, those who managed to settle their cases by agreement out of court were regarded as 'able and willing to take responsibility'[122] for their own affairs: by implication, litigation is 'irresponsible'.

---

117 MOJ (2010b).
118 See chapters 11, 7, and 6.
119 Eekelaar (2011); George (2012a), ch 1.
120 MOJ (2010b), para 4.19.
121 Ibid, paras 2.11, 4.209, 5.6, and 5.14.
122 Ibid, para 4.157.

Despite strong opposition and warnings by opponents about the effects the reforms would have on vulnerable adults and children,[123] the Legal Aid, Sentencing and Punishment of Offenders Act 2012 (generally known as 'LASPO') was enacted, effecting cuts to family legal aid from April 2013. LASPO removes public funding for lawyers' services for all private law disputes, other than: (i) for victims of 'domestic violence', provided that they can evidence that abuse in one of the prescribed ways;[124] (ii) where a child who is the subject of the proceedings is at risk of 'harm' from another party.[125] Funding is also (in theory) available on an 'exceptional' basis where necessary to protect the applicant's rights under Article 6 ECHR,[126] though early indications suggest that this exception is being applied very narrowly.[127] However, while funding is no longer provided for solicitors to help parties negotiate settlements out of court, it *is* available for mediation in all private family law cases, with a small fee payable to lawyers who provide advice and assistance in support of this process.

One important effect[128] of LASPO has been a significant drop in the number of family court cases starting at all, particularly private law cases.[129] This effect was predicted—indeed, desired—by the government, and was intended to support an increasingly clear policy aim of moving private family law away from court-based solutions towards 'private ordering', where direct negotiation and settlement are promoted out of court. Various forms of non-court dispute resolution now operate outside the formal court structure, some involving lawyers, some not. As more disputes move out of court, the legal process is arguably becoming increasingly marginalized, with therapeutic, social work interventions, and mediation strongly encouraged as more promising alternatives to the legal process.

Non-court dispute resolution

There are numerous alternative means of resolving family disputes, collectively known as non-court dispute resolution.[130] We consider two approaches here.

Mediation

The most high-profile non-court dispute resolution option is mediation. While mediation might include a therapeutic element designed to enable the parties to adjust to the future, for example to help them to cooperate in joint parenting after separation, it does not aim to reunite couples. Family mediation involves an impartial third party, the mediator, assisting the couple to reach an agreement about the future arrangements for their property, finances, and children. The mediator's role is purely facilitative: he or she has no power to impose a settlement on the parties. As Walker explains, 'it is seen as a more sensible way of settling

---

[123] E.g. Eekelaar (2011), Williams (2011), George (2011).
[124] LASPO, Sch 1, paras 11–12; SI 2012/3098, r 33.
[125] LASPO, Sch 1, para 13; SI 2012/3098, r 34.
[126] LASPO, s 10: see *Airey v Ireland* (App No 6289/73) (1979–80) 2 EHRR 305, Miles (2011c), (2011d).
[127] MOJ and Legal Aid Agency (2014), but see *R (Gudanaviciene) v Director of Legal Aid Casework* [2014] EWCA Civ 1622, and cf *Q v Q* [2014] EWFC 31 with *Re K and H (Children)* [2015] EWCA Civ 543.
[128] Another, discussed on the Online Resource Centre, is the increase in parties going to court without lawyers ('litigants in person'): MOJ (2014a), 21. Litigants in person often struggle to represent themselves effectively and have considerable support needs: Trinder et al (2014).
[129] MOJ (2014a), 19.
[130] Previously known as 'alternative dispute resolution' or ADR.

family disputes and as a civilised and civilising procedure, a process which returns to, or keeps control in, the couple'.[131]

Interest in mediation as an alternative to lawyer-based dispute settlement on relationship breakdown first peaked in the 1990s, when it became a key component of subsequently abandoned divorce law reforms. Mediation was envisaged for the future as 'the norm rather than the exception', to be used for all aspects of a divorce, including finances and property, as well as children's arrangements.[132] Many commentators were concerned that those debates were based on polarized (and rather distorted) depictions of what mediation and lawyers/the legal system were each supposed to offer.[133] Mediation was said to have been 'dangerously idealised'[134] as the harbinger of cheap conflict-free divorce, while law and lawyers were pilloried for fanning the flames of conflict and invariably viewed as inevitably and irrationally inducing contested litigation.

Research has never supported either stereotype,[135] yet despite the lack of clear evidence of its claimed benefits, mediation returned to the spotlight as a central feature of the Family Justice Review 2011[136] and as a privileged area for receipt of public funding following the LASPO legal aid reforms. Mediation now sits at the centre of the private law family justice system. Since 2014, applicants in private law children or finance proceedings have been required to attend a Mediation Information and Assessment Meeting (MIAM) before applying to the court.[137] That application must contain either the mediator's confirmation of attendance, or a claim by the applicant (or certification from the mediator) that the case falls within one of the prescribed exceptions: for example, the mediator is satisfied that the case is unsuitable for mediation, whether because the other party to the dispute is not willing to mediate, or for some other reason; or domestic abuse has resulted in police investigation or an application for protective civil orders in the last year.[138] Family courts are now also required to consider, at every stage, whether non-court dispute resolution is appropriate for the parties.[139]

However, the aim to achieve a significant increase in mediation clients has yet to materialize. Despite the public funding changes prioritizing mediation, the number of mediation assessments, mediation starts, and mediation agreements all dropped dramatically in the first year of the new funding scheme, reversing what had been a rising trend.[140] This drop is generally attributed to the fact many couples had previously attended mediation on the suggestion of their solicitors, reflecting family lawyers' settlement-oriented approach to dispute resolution.[141] As fewer people can now afford solicitors, this natural conduit of clients into mediation has dried up, and clients have yet to make direct approaches to

---

131 Walker (2000), 401–2.
132 LCD (1993), para 7.11.
133 E.g. Eekelaar, Maclean, and Beinart (2000), ch 1; Walker (1996); Eekelaar (1995).
134 Brown and Day Sclater (1999), 158.
135 See below.
136 Norgrove (2011), paras 4.94 et seq.
137 Children and Families Act 2014 (CFA 2014), s 10(1).
138 Family Procedure Rules 2010 (FPR 2010), r 3.8; Practice Direction 3A (2014), paras 17–21.
139 Ibid, para 3.3.
140 MOJ (2014b), 21. Meetings assessing suitability for mediation dropped by 57 per cent, the number of cases starting mediation dropped by 39 per cent, and agreements following mediation dropped by 37 per cent.
141 E.g. Davis, Cretney, and Collins (1994), Eekelaar, Maclean, and Beinart (2000), Eekelaar (1995), Maclean and Eekelaar (2009).

mediators in substantial numbers. Various measures have been put in place to try to rebuild mediation numbers.[142]

Arbitration

Another form of non-court dispute resolution, currently much less commonly used, is arbitration. In arbitration, the parties attend some form of hearing in front of an independent third party, the arbitrator, who determines the dispute, much as a judge does in court. Outside family law, arbitration is well recognized and widely used, governed by the Arbitration Act 1996. However, arbitration has had a slow start in family law disputes. As recently as 2008 it was merely being suggested that it *might* be possible to use the Arbitration Act for family disputes—and then only for financial disputes following relationship breakdown.[143]

However, the Institute of Family Law Arbitrators, a non-profit organization to accredit suitable arbitrators and provide guidelines on family arbitration, was established in 2012. In *S v S (Financial Remedies: Arbitral Award)*,[144] Sir James Munby P approved an application for a consent order in financial remedy proceedings which reflected an award made under this scheme,[145] and gave guidance as to how similar cases should be addressed. The President considered that where parties voluntarily agree to undertake arbitration, then '[i]n the absence of some very compelling countervailing factor(s), the arbitral award should be determinative of the order the court makes'.[146]

A rather different arbitration took place in *AI v MT*.[147] The parties were observant orthodox Jews who, following their separation, sought to have all their family law issues—relating both to finances and to their children—resolved by arbitration before the New York Beth Din (the rabbinical court, adjudicating over issues under Jewish law, including divorce). The parties initially proposed that this would be binding arbitration, but Baker J refused to endorse that plan since it would involve the parties agreeing to oust the court's jurisdiction, which is not permitted as a matter of public policy.[148] Non-binding arbitration then took place and, two years later, resulted in a determination which the court endorsed as a consent order. However, as Baker J noted, the court remained in overall control of the process and would not have endorsed an order which it considered outside the bounds of what was acceptable.

Is private ordering in family disputes a 'good' thing?

The reduction in the number of families going to court and consequently (one might assume) the increase in those resolving their disputes either entirely privately or through a form of non-court dispute resolution, might be viewed as a positive thing: this approach promotes autonomy and reduces the state's involvement in people's lives. However, questions arise about such claims.

At a fundamental level, the non-interventionist policy associated with private ordering sends out a strong message about the value placed on the rights and interests at stake in

---

142 MOJ (2014d).
143 Thorpe (2008).
144 [2014] EWHC 7.
145 See 7.7.1.
146 [2014] EWHC 7, [19].
147 [2013] EWHC 100.
148 *Hyman v Hyman* [1929] AC 601.

family disputes. For this reason, this approach towards the family has been subjected to cogent criticism, particularly by the feminist school, on the basis that it reinforces the status quo and legitimizes 'structural inequalities between the sexes'.[149] It is argued, for example, that the state's formerly non-interventionist policy in areas such as domestic violence allowed abuse of vulnerable family members to go unchecked. Private ordering on family breakdown runs a similar risk. If parties' agreements on matters such as finances or children are not subjected to outside scrutiny and control, power rather than principle may dictate the outcome of negotiations.[150]

Specific concerns arise concerning mediation. While some separating couples do make fair and sensible arrangements about finances and children by themselves, in other cases there is a considerable power imbalance between the parties: one party may flatly refuse to negotiate or mediate, and/or they may not understand their legal rights. How, if at all, can mediation be used where one party has abused the other, and what safeguards can help identify such cases and ensure that the funding available for lawyers' services in such cases is accessed instead?[151] Since children may not participate directly or at all in the process, can mediation ensure that their interests are given adequate attention?[152] The extent to which 'autonomy' is promoted in a dispute resolution process unable to address these basic inequalities of power is questionable. Moreover, it is not just power imbalances between the parties that are problematic. There is a danger that mediation simply replaces one set of professionals (lawyers and judges) with another (mediators), who may be unable to maintain a neutral, orchestrating role and avoid interposing their view of the 'right' outcome.[153] Does mediation thus simply become a form of informal adjudication without the safeguards of formal legal process?[154]

It might be said that, to be acceptable, a private agreement must be negotiated on a relatively level playing field by parties who understand the rules of the game they are playing. There are therefore important benefits for parties who are trying to resolve their family disputes out of court, whether via mediation or not, being able to rely on the partisan help and advice of a lawyer.[155] For example, there is nothing inherently wrong in a party to a divorce seeking to uphold his or her rights to proper financial support. A 'bad' privately mediated agreement could leave that individual in a vulnerable position (potentially at a cost to the state). As Eekelaar puts it, the government's 'diminished concept of what constitutes justice in regard to family matters' has the effect of 'depriv[ing] legal rights of all effect' in the family context.[156] These concerns are echoed by George who observes that the effect of cutting access to legal advice and family courts may be 'to withdraw justice from the family, and leave the weak at the mercy of the powerful'.[157]

The nature of the 'autonomy' being promoted in arbitration is open to rather different criticism. Ferguson has observed that there is a difference between the parties negotiating an outcome (e.g. with a pre-nuptial or separation agreement or through mediation) and

[149] Bainham (1990), 207.
[150] George (2012a), ch 1.
[151] See, e.g., Raitt (1996); Greatbatch and Dingwall (1999); Hunter (2011).
[152] See, e.g., Diduck (2003), 118–19; Pearce (2013).
[153] Dingwall (1988); Piper (1996); Davis (2000), para 18.6.
[154] Stylianou (1998).
[155] Eekelaar, Maclean, and Beinart (2000); see also Davis (2000), 20.1.
[156] Eekelaar (2011), 313.
[157] George (2012a), 21.

the parties agreeing to be bound by an outcome selected by someone else.[158] The autonomy involved in the former might be considered more deserving of the law's respect than the latter: agreeing to an outcome arguably involves greater expression of autonomy than agreeing to a process by which someone else will determine an outcome. Ferguson suggests that the autonomy argument 'operates here as a smokescreen for ideological reform in which law withdraws from intimate family life':[159] arbitration can be seen as a way for the wealthy to 'buy' a quicker tribunal (and a more controllable one, since the parties choose the arbitrator) to resolve their disputes than is available for those left to use the court system.

Consequently, while there are potential benefits to be had from encouraging at least some family disputes to be resolved out of court, there are concerns about denying people the *possibility* of going to court. If the normative and protective function of family law is to be taken seriously, there is a strong argument that legal intervention is needed in some family disputes.

1.3 CONCLUDING THOUGHTS

Family law is an intellectually stimulating and challenging subject, but it also matters beyond the lecture room. Family law affects real people and their lives on a daily basis. Family life can be full of love and happiness, a rich and rewarding experience—but it can also be a cause of great pain and sadness. Families often turn to the law for help. Getting the law right is therefore important. We hope you enjoy studying it as much as we do.

 ONLINE RESOURCE CENTRE

You will find materials supplementing the discussion in this chapter on the Online Resource Centre which we hope you will find useful. In addition to the topics addressed here, you will find sections on:

- *The Sources of Family Law*: Statute Law; Case Law; International and European Law; Non-Legal Sources.
- *The Family Justice System*: including, the family courts; resolving family disputes out of court; some current challenges facing the family justice system and changes made in response to them.

   Also available on the Online Resource Centre are:

- *A Guide to using this textbook and the Online Resource Centre*
- *Supporting materials for each chapter*: Questions, suggestions for further reading, and supplementary materials for each chapter, including updates on developments in family law since this book was published.

The Online Resource Centre is found at **www.oxfordtextbooks.co.uk/orc/familytcm3e/**.

---

[158] Ferguson (2015), (2013a).
[159] Ibid.

2

FAMILY RELATIONSHIPS
BETWEEN ADULTS

CENTRAL ISSUES

1. English family law has recently opened its doors to same-sex relationships and transgender people. Once outlaws, same-sex couples can now marry. Once in legal limbo, trans people can have their preferred gender formally acknowledged, and form relationships in that gender. Only same-sex couples can register a civil partnership.

2. Many legal consequences flow automatically from two status-based relationships: marriage and civil partnership. The law of nullity—which sets out the grounds on which a marriage or civil partnership is void or voidable—identifies who has the right to acquire each status, and tells us something about the law's conception of each status.

4. For many faiths, marriage is the basis for family life. English marriage law currently gives a privileged position to Anglican rites in the formation of (opposite-sex) marriage. Only monogamous marriages can be created in England and Wales. But English law has had to deal with questions raised by the marriage traditions of other faiths practised in this country.

5. English law increasingly recognizes relationships that have not been formalized in marriage or civil partnership, but tends still to focus on couples. Relationships between platonic companions, adult relatives who share a home, and individuals in relationships across different households receive less attention. Should law move 'beyond conjugality' and recognize the wider range of relationships that are important to people's domestic lives and identities?

2.1 INTRODUCTION

A man and a woman go through a civil marriage ceremony to give the woman the status necessary to acquire a British passport; after the ceremony, they go their separate ways.[1]

---

[1] *Vervaeke v Smith* [1983] 1 AC 145, see below p 85.

Another couple go through a Sikh marriage ceremony and live together as husband and wife for nearly 40 years.[2] A same-sex couple cohabit for over 20 years until the death of one partner, who had been nursed by the other for several years following an accident.[3] Two unmarried elderly sisters live together for their entire life, for the last 30 years in the house built by their brother on land inherited from their parents.[4] Which of these relationships is recognized in English law, on what basis, and with what consequences?

This chapter seeks to answer the first two parts of that question in relation to these and other examples. There are many situations in which legal recognition of relationships between two or more adults is relevant, several (but by no means all) of which are addressed in this book: for example, determining rights to inherit on intestacy, calculating welfare benefits entitlements, accessing remedies against domestic violence and financial remedies on relationship breakdown, protection of the shared home in the event of insolvency, enjoyment of tax exemptions, and eligibility to apply to adopt a child together.

Identifying which relationships are recognized for such legal purposes, and how, used to be relatively easy. Family law focused on (opposite-sex) marriage and the legal consequences that flow automatically from it. Little recognition was afforded to unmarried opposite-sex couples, none to same-sex couples, and blood relatives appeared only on the periphery. Transgender people were not recognized in their preferred gender and so, if heterosexual, were unable to marry their chosen partner. Those excluded from law's concept of family sought admission to it for the dignity, status, and legitimacy that flows from legal recognition, and for access to the accompanying rights and responsibilities.

Status-based family law has rapidly expanded in response to these claims. Since 2005, same-sex couples have been able to formalize their relationships by registering a civil partnership, a status which confers almost all of the legal consequences of marriage, and following implementation of the Marriage (Same Sex Couples) Act 2013 (M(SSC)A 2013) in 2014 they have been able to marry. 'Trans' people can obtain legal recognition of their preferred gender and formalize relationships with their partners, whether by marriage or civil partnership. Identifying these status-based relationships is largely straightforward: legal recognition flows from the fact of marriage or civil partnership, proved (and, in the case of civil partnership, created) by registration.

Increasing recognition has also been granted to relationships not formalized in marriage or civil partnership. Cohabitants, opposite-sex and same-sex, have acquired more legal recognition, albeit far less extensive than that of spouses and civil partners. Identifying 'non-formalized' relationships is less straightforward than ascertaining whether parties are married. The law recognizes these relationships where they *function* like a family or, more specifically, like spouses. This 'functional' approach to identifying relationships involves a close factual inquiry into the parties' everyday lives.

However, recognition of these relationships has prompted further questions. Commentators have asked whether marriage is an unnecessary legal concept.[5] They are not advocating the abolition of marriage, but asking why we attach certain legal rights and duties to some relationships, traditionally marriage, and not others. The fact that parties happen to be spouses or civil partners may not be a necessary or even sufficient reason for

---

[2] *Chief Adjudication Officer v Bath* [2000] 1 FLR 8, see below p 82.
[3] *Fitzpatrick v Sterling Housing Association Ltd* [2001] 1 AC 27, see below p 109.
[4] *Burden and Burden v United Kingdom* (App No 13378/05, ECHR) (2008), see below p 118.
[5] E.g. Clive (1980), Hoggett (1980).

particular legal consequences to arise, either at all or from that type of relationship alone. The next candidates for legal recognition tend to be couples who cohabit in a relationship akin to marriage or civil partnership. But what about individuals who share a home, who may or may not be blood relations, and do not have an intimate (sexual) relationship? Why focus on couples or pairs, and not on wider networks?

The basic question is what characteristics of relationships *should* be relevant to determining the scope of legal recognition in each context. The answer depends on what we think is the purpose or function of each law and so which relationships ought therefore to be included. But there may be other objectives at stake: should the law actively promote marriage by attaching certain privileges exclusively to it, and continue to impose special rules on entry into marriage, to preserve a particular understanding of what marriage itself entails? Or should a more neutral stance be taken on relationship-form, and attention focused instead on families' practical situations, regardless of status? We consider some of the evidence relevant to debates on these questions in the last section of the chapter. First, we examine the demographic data about families in England and Wales today.

2.2 FAMILY RELATIONSHIPS IN ENGLAND AND WALES

The transformation of family law reflects substantial change in patterns of relationship formation in recent decades. But, as Rebecca Probert has observed, it is possible amidst the undoubted change to overlook the continuity: most couples are married and stay married.[6]

2.2.1 MARRIAGE AND CIVIL PARTNERSHIP

The proportion of married couple households is high. In 2013, of the 18.2 million families in the UK ('family' here consisting of couples or lone parents, with or without dependent children), around two-thirds—12.3 million—were married couples.[7] But the number of marriages contracted each year has declined markedly since the all-time high in the 1970s,[8] a trend common across Europe.[9] In 2009, the marriage rate (i.e. the number marrying per thousand unmarried people in the population aged over 16) was at its lowest since these calculations began in 1862, and the number of marriages contracted in England and Wales was the lowest since 1895 (when, of course, the population was much smaller). The last few years have seen a recovery in both the rate and the raw number of marriages taking place. But obtaining an accurate picture of the married population is complicated by the fact that the data exclude the large number of marriages apparently contracted abroad by UK residents—so the decline in marriage may not be as 'precipitous' as the data suggest.[10] As many as 10 per cent of marriages between UK residents may now be occurring abroad, as 'wedding package holidays' become popular.[11]

---

6 Probert (2012a), 74–5.
7 ONS (2013d).
8 Wilson and Smallwood (2007).
9 OECD (2014).
10 Probert (2012a), 83.
11 Government Actuary's Department (2005), ONS (2014e), 3.

Figure 2.1 Marriages: England and Wales, 1932–2012

Source: Reproduced from the Office for National Statistics, by Crown copyright © 2014; ONS (2014e).

However, while the marriage rate and overall number of marriages have dropped, the number of *remarriages* has stayed fairly constant since the 1970s, having risen after divorce law was liberalized in 1969. Remarriages (for one or both parties) therefore now constitute a large proportion of total marriages—over a third of all marriages contracted in England and Wales in 2012.[12]

The average age at marriage has significantly increased since the 1970s, the mean age at *first* marriage for both sexes now being in the early 30s.[13] So those who do marry are now doing so later, in most cases following a period of cohabitation.[14]

Marriage practices vary between ethnic groups. For example, Census data looking at family types by reference to the country of birth of the 'family reference person' show that families based on marriage are most common (and cohabitation least common) where that person is of Middle Eastern or Asian origin.[15]

The data discussed so far concern opposite-sex marriage. At the time of writing, it is early days for same-sex marriage, the first of which were celebrated on 29 March 2014. By the end of June 2014, 1,409 marriages had been formed.[16] Many of those who may have wished to form a same-sex marriage will have been unable to do so immediately having already become civil partners—the process for converting a civil partnership to a marriage was not put in place until December 2014, so those couples had to wait. (The only alternative would have been to dissolve the civil partnership, hardly an attractive option, or to seek an annulment, for which it would be most unlikely that grounds would be available.) The figures

---

12 ONS (2014e), 9.
13 Ibid, 8.
14 Beaujouan and Ní Bhrolcháin (2011), 8–10.
15 ONS (2014e), 11–12; see also ONS (2005), 22.
16 ONS (2014f).

capturing the first civil partnership conversions will give a better sense of the demand for same-sex marriage.

In the meantime, civil partnership, first registrable in December 2005, has proved to be considerably more popular than anticipated. By the end of 2012, 60,454 partnerships had been registered in the UK.[17] There were twice as many registrations in 2006 than in subsequent years, doubtless including a large backlog of couples who had been waiting (some for decades) to formalize their relationship.[18] The total number of registrations to date is nearly triple the lower end of the original projection that by 2050 there would be between 21,000 to 42,500 civil partnerships in Great Britain.[19] It will be interesting to see how many new civil partnerships are formed now that same-sex marriage is possible.

2.2.2 COHABITATION

It is hard to measure the incidence of cohabitation and characteristics of cohabitants since such relationships are unregistered. But various surveys and the Census give a good sense of their prevalence. As marriage rates are falling, cohabitation is increasing, particularly amongst younger cohorts, and is the fastest growing family type. There were 2.9 million opposite-sex cohabiting couple families in 2013, up from just over 2 million in the 2001 Census, of which 1.2 million had dependent children.[20] There were an estimated 89,000 same-sex cohabiting couples in 2013.[21] Government projections suggest that by 2033 there will be 3.8 million (opposite-sex) cohabiting couples and that many more older people will be cohabiting, not least as current cohorts of young cohabitants age without converting their relationships into marriage and those who divorce cohabit rather than marry new partners.[22]

Amongst opposite-sex couples, cohabitation is commonly used as a prelude to marriage, which the rising age at first marriage indicates is being postponed. Increasing numbers of couples may not marry at all, despite evidence of widespread intentions to do so.[23] Older cohabitants are more likely to be divorced and perhaps to cohabit instead of marrying. Recent figures suggest that by the tenth anniversary, half of cohabiting couples have married each other, while four in ten have separated—leaving just 10 per cent cohabiting long term.[24] But the average duration of cohabiting relationships is increasing: the median duration is now three years.[25] The British Social Attitudes survey in 2006 found a mean duration of 4.6 years for past cohabitations; relationships ongoing at the date of the survey had lasted on average 6.9 years, 8.5 where the couple had children.[26] So while cohabiting relationships are on average shorter than marriages, they are not universally characterized by a lack of commitment.[27]

---

17 ONS (2013b).
18 Ross et al (2011).
19 DTI (2004), 33–6.
20 ONS (2013d).
21 Ibid, 5.
22 ONS (2010d) and ONS (2014g), fig 8 and associated text.
23 See Coast (2009), de Waal (2008), discussed at p 115 below.
24 Beaujouan and Ní Bhrolcháin (2011), cf Wilson and Stuchbury (2010), discussed by the former at n 41.
25 Beaujouan and Ní Bhrolcháin (2011), 13 and n 41.
26 Barlow et al (2008).
27 Lewis et al (1999); Smart and Stevens (2000).

Another significant demographic change is the boom in births outside marriage. Nearly half of births now occur outside marriage, and just under a third of births are registered by parents who are living together.[28] Data from the Millennium Cohort Study of children born in 2000 show that cohabitants' relationships are less stable than those of spouses. Three years after the birth, while 95 per cent of mothers who were married at the birth were still with the father, only 83 per cent of originally-cohabiting mothers were with him, nearly a third having married him by then; and after five years, more cohabiting parents had separated.[29]

We discuss some of the policy questions raised by this growth in cohabitation and its apparent instability as a family form in the last part of the chapter in light of further empirical data about the characteristics of individuals who do and do not marry.

2.2.3 OTHER RELATIONSHIPS WITHIN AND BETWEEN HOUSEHOLDS

Not everyone lives in couple-based families. Three in ten households—7.7 million in total—contain an individual living alone, and a very small proportion of households consist of two or more unrelated adults not living as a couple.[30] Other households contain more than one family, or several adult generations of the same family, elderly siblings or friends who live together for companionship, or adult children living with and caring for their elderly parents.[31] Nearly 10 per cent of British adults 'live apart together': couples who share an intimate relationship, without living in the same household.[32]

2.3 GENDER IDENTITY AND SEXUAL ORIENTATION

Historically, many 'family' relationships were not legally recognized because they failed to fit the law's family template: a married couple with children, or as Katherine O'Donovan once called it, the advertisers' 'cornflakes family'.[33] However, human rights arguments have been used to extend the legal conception of family to non-traditional family forms. We examine two issues here in order to set the scene for the current law discussed in this chapter: briefly, gender identity and the treatment of transgender people in law; and, at greater length, relationships between same-sex couples. How the law deals with these issues reveals some important features of the law's (traditional) view of what marriage, in particular, is all about.

2.3.1 DETERMINING GENDER

The recognition of adult relationships is one area in which the legally recognized gender of each person matters, though less so than formerly. As noted at 1.2.4, although the law refers

---

[28] ONS (2014c), (2013b).
[29] Calderwood (2008).
[30] ONS (2013d).
[31] Law Com (2002), para 1.7.
[32] Duncan et al (2013); Haskey and Lewis (2006).
[33] O'Donovan (1993), 30.

to 'opposite-sex' and 'same-sex' relationships,[34] the key criterion is not 'sex' in a narrow, biologically-determined sense, but a person's legally recognized 'gender'.[35] We adopt the law's terminology on that basis.

Until recently, only couples of the opposite legal gender could marry. The arrival of same-sex marriage in English law changes that, of course. But it remains the case that only couples of the same gender can become civil partners.[36] And we need to know for some legal purposes whether a marriage involves a same-sex couple or not.[37] So it remains necessary that each of us has a legally determined gender. That question is not straightforward for individuals who do not identify with the gender assigned to them at birth—transgender ('trans') people.[38]

As we noted at 1.2.4,[39] the Gender Recognition Act 2004 provides a procedure for trans people to have their preferred gender recognized for all purposes, including marriage and civil partnership law, following adverse rulings by the European Court of Human Rights regarding the UK's previous refusal to recognize preferred gender.[40] The common law position—whereby legal gender is determined on purely biological criteria—was established in *Corbett v Corbett*, and continues to apply if a gender recognition certificate is not obtained under the 2004 Act procedure. *Corbett* concerned the validity of a marriage contracted between a man and April Ashley, who was born a biological male but self-identified as female and had undergone gender confirmation surgery. At the time, a marriage would be void if not contracted between 'a man and a woman'.[41] What is most striking about Ormrod J's decision that April Ashley was legally a man is the exclusive, question-begging nature of the reasoning, a feature that we shall encounter elsewhere in this chapter: he sets up the issue in such a way that his answer is unavoidable. His view about the 'essential role of a woman in marriage' is also noteworthy:[42]

Corbett v Corbett (otherwise Ashley) [1971] P 83 (Fam Div), 105–6

ORMROD J:

...[S]ex is clearly an essential determinant of the relationship called marriage because it is and always has been recognised as the union of man and woman. It is the institution on which the family is built, and in which the capacity for natural hetero-sexual intercourse is an essential element. It has, of course, many other characteristics, of which companionship and mutual support is an important one, but the characteristics which distinguish it from all other relationships can only be met by two persons of opposite sex....

Since marriage is essentially a relationship between man and woman, the validity of the marriage...depends, in my judgment, upon whether the respondent is or is not a woman.... The question then becomes, what is meant by the word "woman" in the context of a marriage,

---

34 E.g. Marriage (Same Sex Couples) Act 2013.
35 E.g. Gender Recognition Act 2004 (GRA 2004).
36 See 2.6.1 below.
37 E.g. availability of marriage solemnized by a religious body, availability of particular grounds of nullity.
38 Cf inter-sex people—discussed at 1.2.4.
39 See the Online Resource Centre for fuller account of the history and current law.
40 *Goodwin v United Kingdom* (App No 28957/95, ECHR) (2002).
41 See Gilmore (2011).
42 Diduck and Kaganas (2006), 47–50.

> for I am not concerned to determine the "legal sex" of the respondent at large. Having regard to the essentially hetero-sexual character of the relationship which is called marriage, the criteria must, in my judgment, be biological, for even the most extreme degree of transsexualism in a male or the most severe hormonal imbalance which can exist in a person with male chromosomes, male gonads and male genitalia cannot reproduce a person who is naturally capable of performing the essential role of a woman in marriage. In other words, the law should adopt in the first place . . . the chromosomal, gonadal and genital tests, and if all three are congruent, determine the sex for the purpose of marriage accordingly, and ignore any operative intervention.

Ormrod J's words stand in stark contrast to the language used by Judge Martens in his dissenting judgment in *Cossey v United Kingdom*, one of the early—unsuccessful—challenges to English law's refusal to recognize the preferred gender of transgender persons.

Cossey v United Kingdom (App No 10843/84, ECHR) (1993)

JUDGE MARTENS (dissenting):

4.5.1 . . . [It] is arbitrary and unreasonable in this context to ignore successful gender reassignment surgery and to retain the criterion of biological sex.

4.5.2 This is all the more so because Mr Justice Ormrod's arguments are clearly unacceptable. Marriage is far more than sexual union, and the capacity for sexual intercourse is, therefore, not "essential" for marriage. Persons who are not or are no longer capable of procreating or having sexual intercourse may also want to and do marry. That is because marriage is far more than a union which legitimates sexual intercourse and aims at procreating: it is a legal institution which creates a fixed legal relationship between both the partners and third parties . . . ; it is a societal bond, in that married people (as one learned writer put it) "represent to the world that theirs is a relationship based on strong human emotions, exclusive commitment to each other and permanence"; it is, moreover, a species of togetherness in which intellectual, spiritual and emotional bonds are at least as essential as the physical one.

Given the GRA 2004 and the extension of marriage to same-sex couples, the family law problems that transgender persons experienced might largely be regarded as a thing of the past. However, we shall see at 2.6.1 below that at least one anomaly remains. In one sense, transgender people seeking recognition of their preferred gender in order to marry posed less of a 'threat' to traditional marriage than claims for same-sex marriage: the trans person living in their preferred gender in an opposite-sex couple did not challenge the opposite-sex model of marriage, merely questioned how legal gender would be determined for these purposes. By contrast, recognition of same-sex marriage would prove far more controversial. But we may note here that Judge Martens' remarks in *Cossey v United Kingdom* might apply whatever the parties' legal genders.

2.3.2 SAME-SEX RELATIONSHIPS: THE ROAD TO SAME-SEX MARRIAGE

One might assume that by 'same-sex' we mean gay or lesbian. But where the law is concerned about parties' respective legal genders, that is all that it is concerned about; the parties' sexual orientation is legally irrelevant.[43] However, in reality, of course, relationship recognition is most pressing for those in couple-relationships, which usually have a sexual aspect. For many of those couples, achieving the right to marry has been the ultimate goal. Now that English law permits marriage by couples of the same sex, we focus here on that most recent development, providing only a brief overview of the history leading up to that point.[44]

The road to recognition for same-sex couples

Judicial developments

In 1985, a Court of Appeal judge had no hesitation in saying

> I am…firmly of the view that it would be surprising in the extreme to learn that public opinion is such today that it would recognise a homosexual union as being akin to a state of living as husband and wife. The ordinary man and woman…would in my opinion not think even remotely of there being a true resemblance between those two very different states of affairs.[45]

And so, a woman was denied the right to succeed to the tenancy that had been held in the name of her deceased lesbian partner, on the basis that they could not be regarded—in the terms of the governing statute—as having lived together 'as husband and wife',[46] as opposite-sex cohabitants would be. The European Commission on Human Rights found no violation of Article 14 in conjunction with Article 8: it was legitimate for the state to protect 'the family' (including opposite-sex cohabitants)—which Ms Simpson and her partner were not.[47]

Yet fifteen years later, while the House of Lords was still not prepared to regard a same-sex couple's relationship as akin to husband and wife (a finding which would have conferred stronger legal protection), it was prepared to find that they were members of each other's 'family', thereby acquiring some protection under different tenancy succession legislation:[48]

Fitzpatrick v Sterling Housing Association Ltd [2001] 1 AC 27, 44, 51

LORD NICHOLLS:

I am in no doubt that this question should be answered affirmatively. A man and woman living together in a stable and permanent sexual relationship are capable of being members of a family for this purpose. Once this is accepted, there can be no rational or other basis on which the like conclusion can be withheld from a similarly stable and permanent sexual relationship between two men or between two women…. Where sexual partners are involved, whether heterosexual or homosexual, there is scope for the intimate mutual love and affection and long-term commitment that typically characterise the relationship of husband and wife. This love and affection and commitment can exist in same-sex relationships as in heterosexual relationships. In sexual terms a homosexual relationship is different from a heterosexual

---

[43] Green (2011).
[44] See Cretney (2006a) for a fuller history.
[45] Watkins LJ, *Harrogate BC v Simpson* (1985) 17 HLR 205, 209.
[46] Housing Act 1980, s 50(3).
[47] *Simpson v United Kingdom* (App No 11716/85, ECHR) (1986), [7].
[48] Rent Act 1977, Sch 1, paras 2(2) and 3(1); for commentary, see Sandland (2000), Diduck (2001).

relationship, but I am unable to see that the difference is material for present purposes. As already emphasised, the concept underlying membership of a family for present purposes is the sharing of lives together in a single family unit living in one house...

LORD CLYDE:

The concept of the family has undergone significant development during recent years, both in the United Kingdom and overseas. Whether that is a matter for concern or congratulation is of no relevance to the present case, but it is properly part of the judicial function to endeavour to reflect an understanding of such changes in the reality of social life.

Lord Slynn observed in *Fitzpatrick* that the exclusion of same-sex couples from the tenancy succession legislation's more beneficial, quasi-spousal category might be regarded as incompatible with the European Convention on Human Rights (ECHR) once the HRA 1998 came into force.[49] The House of Lords soon reached that conclusion in *Ghaidan v Godin-Mendoza*, shortly before the enactment of the Civil Partnership Act (CPA 2004).[50] It was successfully argued that the survivor's rights under Article 14 in conjunction with Article 8 (right to respect for the home) were violated by denying a same-sex partner the security of tenure enjoyed by an opposite-sex partner on the tenant's death. The argument before the House of Lords focused on whether the undoubted difference in treatment of a same-sex couple compared with an opposite-sex unmarried couple in this context could be justified. Baroness Hale explained eloquently why it could not:

Ghaidan v Godin-Mendoza [2004] UKHL 30

BARONESS HALE:

138. We are not here concerned with a difference in treatment between married and unmarried couples. The European Court of Human Rights accepts that the protection of the 'traditional family' is in principle a legitimate aim: see *Karner v Austria* [(App No 40016/98)]...para 40. The traditional family is constituted by marriage. The Convention itself, in article 12, singles out the married family for special protection by guaranteeing to everyone the right to marry and found a family. Had [the Rent Act, the tenancy succession legislation] stopped at protecting the surviving spouse, it might have been easier to say that a homosexual couple were not in an analogous situation. But it did not. It extended the protection to survivors of a relationship which was not marriage but was sufficiently like marriage to qualify for the same protection. It has therefore to be asked whether opposite and same-sex survivors are in an analogous situation for this purpose.

139. There are several modern statutes which extend a particular benefit or a particular burden, granted to or imposed upon the parties to a marriage, to people who are or were living together 'as husband and wife'[51]...Working out whether a particular couple are or were in such a relationship is not always easy....What matters most is the essential quality of the relationship, its marriage-like intimacy, stability, and social and financial inter-dependence.

---

[49] [2001] 1 AC 27, 34.
[50] [2004] UKHL 30.
[51] See 2.8.2 below.

Homosexual relationships can have exactly the same qualities of intimacy, stability and inter-dependence that heterosexual relationships do.

140. It has not been suggested to us that the nature of the sexual intimacies each enjoys is a relevant difference. Nor can the possibility of holding oneself out as a legally married couple be a relevant difference here...[not least given the inability of same-sex couples to marry at this stage].

141. The relevant difference which has been urged upon us is that a heterosexual couple may have children together whereas a homosexual couple cannot. But this too cannot be a relevant difference in determining whether a relationship can be considered marriage-like for the purpose of the Rent Act. First, the capacity to bear or beget children has never been a prerequisite of a valid marriage in English law.... Even the capacity to consummate the marriage only matters if one of the parties thinks it matters: if they are both content the marriage is valid.[52] A marriage, let alone a relationship analogous to marriage, can exist without either the presence or the possibility of children from that relationship. Secondly, however, the presence of children is a relevant factor in deciding whether a relationship is marriage-like but if the couple are bringing up children together, it is unlikely to matter whether or not they are the biological children of both parties. Both married and unmarried couples, both homosexual and heterosexual, may bring up children together. One or both may have children from another relationship: this is not at all uncommon in lesbian relationships and the court may grant them a shared residence order so that they may share parental responsibility. A lesbian couple may have children by donor insemination who are brought up as the children of them both: it is not uncommon for each of them to bear a child in this way.[53] A gay or lesbian couple may foster other people's children. When the relevant sections of the Adoption and Children Act 2002 are brought into force, they will be able to adopt: this means that they will indeed have a child together in the eyes of the law. Thirdly, however, there is absolutely no reason to think that the protection given by the Rent Act to the surviving partner's home was given for the sake of the couple's children.... It is the longstanding social and economic interdependence, which may or may not be the product of having brought up children together, that qualifies for the protection of the Act....

142. Homosexual couples can have exactly the same sort of interdependent couple relationship as heterosexuals can. Sexual 'orientation' defines the sort of person with whom one wishes to have sexual relations. It requires another person to express itself. Some people, whether heterosexual or homosexual, may be satisfied with casual or transient relationships. But most human beings eventually want more than that. They want love. And with love they often want not only the warmth but also the sense of belonging to one another which is the essence of being a couple. And many couples also come to want the stability and permanence which go with sharing a home and a life together, with or without the children who for many people go to make a family. In this, people of homosexual orientation are no different from people of heterosexual orientation.

143. It follows that a homosexual couple whose relationship is marriage-like in the same ways that an unmarried heterosexual couple's relationship is marriage-like are indeed in an analogous situation. Any difference in treatment is based upon their sexual orientation. It requires an objective justification if it is to comply with article 14. Whatever the scope for a 'discretionary area of judgment' in these cases may be, there has to be a legitimate aim before a difference in treatment can be justified. But what could be the legitimate aim of singling out heterosexual couples for more favourable treatment than homosexual couples? It

---

[52] See 2.7.6 below.
[53] See now the Human Fertilisation and Embryology Act 2008, discussed at 9.4.3.

cannot be the *protection* of the traditional family. The traditional family is not protected by granting it a benefit which is denied to people who cannot or will not become a traditional family. What is really meant by the 'protection' of the traditional family is the *encouragement* of people to form traditional families and the *discouragement* of people from forming others. There are many reasons why it might be legitimate to encourage people to marry and to discourage them from living together without marrying. These reasons might have justified the Act in stopping short at marriage. Once it went beyond marriage to unmarried relationships, the aim would have to be encouraging one sort of unmarried relationship and discouraging another....But,...it is difficult to see how heterosexuals will be encouraged to form and maintain such marriage-like relationships by the knowledge that the equivalent benefit is being denied to homosexuals. The distinction between heterosexual and homosexual couples might be aimed at discouraging homosexual relationships generally. But that cannot now be regarded as a legitimate aim. It is inconsistent with the right to respect for private life accorded to 'everyone', including homosexuals, by art 8 since *Dudgeon v UK* (1981) 4 EHRR 149. If it is not legitimate to discourage homosexual relationships, it cannot be legitimate to discourage stable, committed, marriage-like homosexual relationships of the sort which qualify the survivor to succeed to the home. Society wants its intimate relationships, particularly but not only if there are children involved, to be stable, responsible and secure. It is the transient, irresponsible and insecure relationships which cause us so much concern.[54]

144. I have used the term 'marriage-like' to describe the sort of relationship which meets the statutory test of living together 'as husband and wife'. Once upon a time it might have been difficult to apply those words to a same-sex relationship because both in law and in reality the roles of the husband and wife were so different and those differences were defined by their genders. That is no longer the case. The law now differentiates between husband and wife in only a very few and unimportant respects. Husbands and wives decide for themselves who will go out to work and who will do the homework and child care. Mostly each does some of each. The roles are inter-changeable. There is thus no difficulty in applying the term 'marriage-like' to same-sex relationships.

And so the House of Lords interpreted the Rent Act provision under s 3 of the HRA 1998 to include same-sex couples, ensuring compatibility with Convention rights.

The creation of civil partnership

As noted above, 2004 also marked the enactment of the CPA 2004, which for the first time permitted same-sex couples to formalize their relationships in order to acquire the vast majority of the rights and duties of marriage, without the label 'marriage'. The Act also reinforced *Ghaidan v Godin-Mendoza* by amending legislation dealing with cohabitants to ensure that it covered same-sex as well as opposite-sex couples, by requiring same-sex couples to demonstrate that they live together 'as if they were civil partners'.[55] But although the institutions of marriage and civil partnership, and their non-formal analogues, were kept semantically distinct, they were intended to operate socially and legally in the same way[56] in order to achieve equality for same-sex couples.[57]

---

[54] See also *Rodriguez v Ministry of Housing of the Government of Gibraltar* [2009] UKPC 52.

[55] See, e.g., CPA 2004, Sch 8, para 13(3), amending Rent Act 1977, Sch 1, para 2(2).

[56] There are some exceptions in the conditions for creating valid marriage and civil partnership: see 2.5 below.

[57] Women and Equality Unit (2003a), paras 1.1–1.2.

Hansard, *Official Report*—**Civil Partnership Bill Debates,** Hansard HC Deb, vol 426, col 776, 9 November 2004: Report Stage

Deputy Minister for Women and Equality (Jacqui Smith):

We introduced [the Bill] with a specific purpose, which is to provide legal recognition for unrelated same-sex couples who do not currently have the option, which is available to opposite-sex couples, to marry. We seek to create a parallel but different legal relationship that mirrors as fully as possible the rights and responsibilities enjoyed by those who can marry, and that uses civil marriage as a template for the processes, rights and responsibilities that go with civil partnership. We are doing this for reasons of equality and social justice... We had some discussion about this in Committee, and our view was that, unless there was an objective justification for a difference in the approaches taken to civil marriage and civil partnership, no difference should exist. There are very few areas in which any difference does exist. The whole point, however, is that civil partnership is not civil marriage, for a variety of reasons, such as the traditions and history—religious and otherwise—that accompany marriage. It is not marriage, but it is, in many ways—dare I say it?—akin to marriage. We make no apology for that.

The introduction of civil partnership attracted vocal opposition, notably from those who were unconvinced by the government's denials that civil partnership was essentially 'gay marriage':

Hansard, *Official Report*—**Civil Partnership Bill Debates,** Hansard HL Deb, vol 660, cols 403–5, 22 April 2004: 2nd Reading

Baroness O'Cathain:

The Government have stated many times, even in recent months when they knew that the Bill was about to be introduced, that they do not intend to legalise same-sex marriage.... [On] 11 February this year [Lord Filkin]... said: "The concept of same-sex marriage is a contradiction in terms, which is why our position is utterly clear: we are against it, and do not intend to promote it or allow it to take place"...

...The Government's consultation document on civil partnerships said: "It is a matter of public record that the Government has no plans to introduce same-sex marriage". So apparently we are all agreed. Only gay rights groups want gay marriage. The rest of us are opposed to it. There is just one problem: despite what has been said already in this debate, I firmly believe that this Bill creates gay marriage... The Government may deny this, but I am sure that the man in the street will see this as being a gay marriage... The Guardian on 30 June called civil partnership: "legal marriage in all but name". It is just wrong to create a parody of marriage for homosexual couples.

The CPA 2004 reinforced the policy position that it was not a 'gay marriage' Act by providing that those who had contracted a same-sex marriage abroad in a jurisdiction that permitted same-sex marriage would not be recognized as spouses in English law—instead, they would be treated as civil partners.[58] The attempt of Susan Wilkinson and Celia Kitzinger, who

---

[58] CPA 2004, ss 212–18, Sch 20.

had married in Canada, to obtain a declaration that that was incompatible with their rights under Articles 8, 12, and 14 ECHR failed.[59] They had argued that to offer same-sex couples the 'consolation prize' of civil partnership rather than the 'gold standard' of marriage was offensive and demeaning, breaching basic principles of equality. They rejected the government's 'separate but equal' approach on the basis that marriage is still regarded as the superior institution.[60] The President found no breach of Article 12—the right to marry under the ECHR still extends to opposite-sex couples only—and no breach of Article 14 in conjunction with Article 8, on the basis that the parties' private life was not engaged by refusal to recognize their relationship as marriage; the reasoning on that point is incompatible with later ECHR authority.[61] He did regard the complaint as falling within the ambit of Article 12, and found a clear difference of treatment compared with an analogous opposite-sex couple that needed justification under Article 14. However, he was satisfied that the government had discharged that burden: the difference of treatment pursued a legitimate aim—the protection of the traditional family based on marriage—and did so in an appropriate and proportionate manner.

The President's approach to marriage in finding that justification was characterized by the sort of exclusive reasoning seen in *Corbett v Corbett*:

Wilkinson v Kitzinger [2006] EWHC 2022

SIR MARK POTTER P:

118. It is apparent that the majority of people, or at least of governments, not only in England but Europe-wide, regard marriage as an age-old institution, valued and valuable, respectable and respected, as a means not only of encouraging monogamy but also the procreation of children and their development and nurture in a family unit (or "nuclear family") in which both maternal and paternal influences are available...

119. The belief that this form of relationship is the one which best encourages stability in a well regulated society is not a disreputable or outmoded notion based upon ideas of exclusivity, marginalisation, disapproval or discrimination against homosexuals or any other persons who by reason of their sexual orientation or for other reasons prefer to form a same-sex union.

120. If marriage...is[,] by longstanding definition and acceptance, a formal relationship between a man and a woman, primarily (though not exclusively) with the aim of producing and rearing children as I have described it, and if that is the institution contemplated and safeguarded by Article 12, then to accord a same-sex relationship the title and status of marriage would be to fly in the face of the Convention as well as to fail to recognise physical reality.

To this, one might respond with the words of one Canadian court: 'Stating that marriage is heterosexual because it has always been heterosexual is merely an explanation for the opposite-sex requirement of marriage; it is not an objective that is capable of

[59] *Wilkinson v Kitzinger* [2006] EWHC 2022; for commentary see Bamforth (2007a), Harding (2007), Auchmuty (2008), Monaghan and Harding (2010).

[60] *Wilkinson v Kitzinger* [2006] EWHC 2022, [5]–[6].

[61] *Schalk and Kopf v Austria* (App No 30141/04, ECHR) (2010).

justifying [different treatment]'.[62] The President's reasoning was criticized for adopting a 'heteronormative' approach, presupposing traditional gender roles at odds with many contemporary opposite-sex relationships.[63] It sits awkwardly alongside Baroness Hale's judgment in *Ghaidan*, particularly as she made clear that procreation is not (as a plain matter of English law) a necessary correlative of marriage—but many same-sex couples do raise children.[64] Nor is it obvious how the practice of marriage in its traditional form is promoted by excluding from its ambit same-sex couples who wish to lead a similar life.[65]

Developments under the ECHR

However much the reasoning in *Wilkinson v Kitzinger* might be open to criticism, there seemed little immediate prospect that English law's pragmatic compromise—giving same-sex couples the legal consequences of marriage without the word itself—would be challenged successfully under the ECHR. Indeed, whereas it had for years been *behind* the trend in relation to the transgender issues discussed above, English law was already substantially ahead of what the ECHR required in relation to same-sex couples.

The House of Lords recognized same-sex couples as 'family' in *Fitzpatrick* several years before the European Court held in *Schalk and Kopf v Austria*[66] that they have a 'family life' for the purposes of Article 8. The following year, legislation conferred on same-sex couples the controversial right to adopt children jointly, a few years before ECHR jurisprudence prohibiting discrimination against prospective adopters on the grounds of their sexual orientation.[67] And civil partnership itself was introduced before there was any suggestion from the European Court that same-sex couples should be given some way of formalizing their relationships in law—and there is still no requirement that they should.[68] The only requirement is that they do not treat same-sex couples differently from opposite-sex unmarried couples without having strong justification for doing so, on the basis that such treatment is *necessary* to pursue a legitimate aim.[69]

It is also clear that there is no right to same-sex marriage under the ECHR or other international human rights law. The right to marry is enshrined in various terms in several human rights instruments.[70]

European Convention on Human Rights (1953), Article 12

Men and women of marriageable age have the right to marry and to found a family, according to the national laws governing the exercise of this right.

---

[62] *Halpern et al v Attorney General of Canada et al* (2003) 169 OAR 172.
[63] Harding (2007); Auchmuty (2008).
[64] See 2.7.6 below; see also Strasser (2014), 48–9.
[65] See also *Secretary of State for Work and Pensions v M* [2006] UKHL 11, [113].
[66] (App No 30141/04, ECHR) (2010).
[67] See 13.5.2.
[68] Though see remarks about the developing European trend in *Vallianatos v Greece* (App Nos 29381/09 and 32684/09, ECHR) (2013), [91]–[92].
[69] *Karner v Austria* (App No 40016/98, ECHR) (2004), *Vallianatos v Greece*, above.
[70] Art 12 ECHR is considered more generally at 2.4.3.

International Covenant on Civil and Political Rights (1966), Article 23

1. The family is the natural and fundamental group unit of society and is entitled to protection by society and the State.

2. The right of men and women of marriageable age to marry and to found a family shall be recognized....

Charter of Fundamental Rights of the European Union (2000), Article 9

The right to marry and the right to found a family shall be guaranteed in accordance with the national laws governing the exercise of these rights.

Of these, only the EU Charter was passed following the creation of registered partnership schemes and same-sex marriage. Article 9 does not mention same-sex partnerships, but does not refer to 'men and women', accommodating the possibility of same-sex marriage.[71] Although the Lisbon Treaty makes the EU Charter legally binding on EU institutions and member states implementing EU instruments,[72] the European Court of Justice has declined to recognize registered partnerships as equivalent to marriage under EU law.[73] And the UN Human Rights Committee has held that the exclusion of same-sex couples from marriage does not breach Article 23 of the International Covenant on Civil and Political Rights (ICCPR).[74]

The position under the ECHR was considered in *Schalk and Kopf v Austria*, in which the applicants unsuccessfully challenged Austrian law's refusal to permit same-sex marriage.[75] Austrian law had created a form of registered partnership that carried less extensive legal consequences than marriage. Messrs Schalk and Kopf objected that their inability to marry violated their rights under Article 12, and Article 14 in conjunction with Article 8. They sought to rely by analogy on the developments in relation to trans people (discussed above) and on the wording of Article 9 of the EU Charter. The Court was unanimous in its decision on Article 12:

Schalk and Kopf v Austria (App No 30141/04, ECHR) (2010)

58. The Court is not persuaded by the applicants' [living instrument] argument. Although, as it noted in *Christine Goodwin*, the institution of marriage has undergone major social changes since the adoption of the Convention, the Court notes that there is no European consensus regarding same-sex marriage. At present, no more than six[76] out of forty-seven Contracting States allow same-sex marriage.

---

[71] See the Commentary to the Charter, cited by the European Court of Human Rights in *Schalk and Kopf v Austria* (App No 30141/04, ECHR) (2010).

[72] On the supposed UK opt-out from this aspect of the Treaty, see Barnard (2008).

[73] *D and Sweden v Council* (C-122/99P) [2001] ECR I-4319; Caraccioclo Di Torella and Reid (2002).

[74] Views of 17 July 2002 (*Joslin et al v New Zealand*, CCPR/C/75/D/902/1999).

[75] See Bamforth (2011).

[76] More do so now, but still a relatively small minority.

59....[T]he present case has to be distinguished from *Christine Goodwin*. In that case...the Court perceived a convergence of standards regarding marriage of transsexuals in their assigned gender. Moreover, *Christine Goodwin* is concerned with marriage of partners who are of different gender, if gender is defined not by purely biological criteria but by taking other factors including gender reassignment...into account.

60. Turning to the comparison between Article 12 of the Convention and Article 9 of the [EU Charter],...the latter has deliberately dropped the reference to men and women....The commentary to the Charter...confirms that Article 9 is meant to be broader in scope than the corresponding articles in other human rights instruments...At the same time the reference to domestic law reflects the diversity of national regulations, which range from allowing same-sex marriage to explicitly forbidding it. By referring to national law, Article 9 of the Charter leaves the decision whether or not to allow same-sex marriage to the States. In the words of the commentary: "...it may be argued that there is no obstacle to recognize same-sex relationships in the context of marriage. There is, however, no explicit requirement that domestic laws should facilitate such marriages."

61. Regard being had to Article 9 of the Charter, therefore, the Court would no longer consider that the right to marry enshrined in Article 12 must in all circumstances be limited to marriage between two persons of the opposite sex. Consequently, it cannot be said that Article 12 is inapplicable to the applicants' complaint. However, as matters stand, the question whether or not to allow same-sex marriage is left to regulation by the national law of the Contracting State.

62. In that connection the Court observes that marriage has deep-rooted social and cultural connotations which may differ largely from one society to another. The Court reiterates that it must not rush to substitute its own judgment in place of that of the national authorities, who are best placed to assess and respond to the needs of society.

A majority of the Court also found no breach of Articles 14 and 8: the lesser legal consequences attaching to Austrian registered partnership, compared with marriage, were a matter for individual states to determine within their margin of appreciation. That being so, English civil partnership law, which gives civil partners almost identical rights to those of spouses, clearly does not breach the ECHR. However, the Court has recently noted the growing European trend for same-sex couples to be given some means of formalizing their relationship. It may only be a matter of time before states are required to provide *some* sort of registration scheme for same-sex couples, albeit not yet equivalent to marriage or indeed marriage itself.[77]

The arrival of same-sex marriage in English law

Although not currently required by international human rights law, several jurisdictions around the world[78] have now recognized same-sex marriage, and England and Wales is one of the latest to join that group. With relatively little forewarning (the issue having not appeared as a manifesto commitment of either coalition party) and no human rights law requirement to do so, in 2012 the Coalition Government conducted a consultation exercise

---

[77] *Vallianatos v Greece* (App Nos 29381/09 and 32684/09 ECHR) (2013), [91]–[92]. Contrast the Grand Chamber's reversion to the traditional view of Art 12's scope in discussion of transgender people's relationships in *Hämäläinen v Finland* (App No 37359/09, ECHR) (2014), [96], noted by Dunne (2014).

[78] Including the Netherlands, Belgium, Spain, Sweden, Norway, Denmark, Portugal, Iceland, France, Finland, Scotland, Canada, most US states, Argentina, Uruguay, South Africa, and New Zealand.

on same-sex marriage—or 'equal marriage', as it called it.[79] It elicited the largest response of any consultation process in UK history, attracting over 228,000 individual responses (over half of which supported the proposal to allow same-sex couples to marry in a civil ceremony) and 19 petitions against the proposal (between them collecting half a million signatures). The government's consultation response summarized the key arguments for and against the basic proposition.

HM Government, *Equal Marriage: The Government's Response* (2012)

3.4 Within the 53% of people and organisations[80] who agreed with allowing same-sex couples to have a civil marriage some expressed views on the nature and importance of marriage. This included their belief that it is right to allow same-sex couples to express their love and happiness in the same way as opposite sex couples, and to allow them to have access to marriage which is socially and legally seen as a strong bond between the couple.

3.5 Respondents acknowledged that the introduction of civil partnerships was a significant step forward in society. A few respondents, who agreed with the proposals, nevertheless felt that there are too many differences, both practically and symbolically, between marriage and civil partnerships. For example, respondents commented that "civil partnerships can be seen as a second class form of registration" and that the difference means that "same-sex relationships are demeaned by dismissing them as 'only civil partners' and 'not really married'". Stonewall[81] commented in their response that "by insisting marriages and civil partnerships be kept separate, organisations and individuals perpetuate the notion, even if inadvertently, that relationships between same-sex couples are not as valid as those between heterosexual couples" ....

3.7 In a similar vein, most respondents who agreed with the proposals saw allowing same-sex couples to have a marriage ceremony as a matter of equality, and/or human rights. Many individuals and organisations, including the National LGBT Partnership felt that "access to civil marriage is an important step forward for [lesbian, gay, bisexual, and trans] people, and the ban on civil marriage is arguably the last major inequality in English and Welsh law for LGB&T people".

3.8 In addition to the equality benefits of the proposals, a number of those who agreed with them felt that allowing same-sex couples to marry would be good for society as a whole, and would reflect the position of society and social views regarding same-sex couples. The National Union of Students also commented that;

"these steps would also have a positive impact on wider public attitudes towards LGBT people and ultimately contribute to a more inclusive society where there is more choice and acceptance".

3.9 However, others disagreed with these views and did not believe that same-sex couples should be able to get married. Most of these responses commented that this was because it did not fit in with the current legal definition of marriage, as being between a man and a woman. Of those who indicated they were against the proposals, most said that this was because the true meaning of marriage could not include same-sex couples. The

---

[79] Government Equalities Office (2012).
[80] Excluding the petitions.
[81] The gay, lesbian, and bisexual campaign group.

Catholic Bishops Conference of England and Wales quoted the definition included in the Catechism:

"The matrimonial covenant, by which a man and a woman establish between themselves a partnership of the whole of life, is by its very nature ordered to the good of the spouses and the procreation and education of offspring"....

3.11 The same view was expressed in responses, including the response from the Church of England, who raised their concern that our proposal changed the definition of marriage, as outlined in Christian teachings and Canon Law (that marriage is "...a union permanent and lifelong for better for worse, till death them do part, of one man with one woman, to the exclusion of all others on either side..."). This belief was also echoed by the Muslim Council of Britain, who quoted the Qu'ran (53:45): "He himself created the pair, male and female"....

3.12 The Catholic Bishops Conference of England and Wales with whom others (for example the Evangelical Alliance) agreed, saw marriage as based on "the biological complementarity of male and female and on the possibility of children". They also raised concerns that changing the definition of marriage in the way proposed would conflict with their view that the distinguishing purpose of marriage is having and raising children rather than just being about love and commitment – which could for example be the love and commitment between an aged parent, or two siblings living together....

3.14 Many also felt that allowing same-sex couples to marry would be bad for society as a whole. They believed it would, for example, have wider negative consequences or send out the wrong message to children. Respondents raised concerns that the role and place of marriage in society would be taken too lightly, or that it would "bring about more instability to marriages in this country". They saw marriage between a man and a woman as of fundamental benefit to society, In contrast, some responses, including that of the Evangelical Alliance, felt that allowing same-sex couples to get married would have a negative impact on all people's marriages, and therefore society, as the institution would be "diluted".

Many of the objections put against same-sex marriage in the consultation exercise have been put elsewhere. In the following extract, Mark Strasser—writing from a US perspective—challenges the argument that recognizing same-sex marriage would threaten 'traditional marriage'. Much of what he says resonates with Baroness Hale's speech in *Ghaidan v Godin-Mendoza*, extracted above:

M. Strasser, 'Family, Same-Sex Unions and the Law', in J. Eekelaar and R. George (eds), *Routledge Handbook of Family Law and Policy* (Abingdon: Routledge, 2014), 50–3

Sometimes, the alleged harm of same-sex marriage is that it undermines the purpose of marriage, namely, 'the need to provide a biological father and mother committed to each other, hopefully for life, for the purpose of rearing healthy children'. But this is incorrect, at least in part, because there is no single purpose for marriage. Individuals who will not or cannot procreate are not (and should not be) precluded from marrying on that account, which suggests that the state recognizes that marriage serves a variety of purposes, only one of which is that it provides a setting in which children might thrive. But same-sex couples fulfill many of the purposes of marriage, including providing a place where the young can be nurtured, and this provides a strong policy reason why they should have their relationships recognized. In cases in which the relationship must be dissolved, the state has interests implicated in ensuring an orderly dissolution of the relationship, including an equitable distribution of property, the provision of support in appropriate cases, and visitation and custody awards where children are involved. But the state's interests in assuring an orderly breakdown of long-term relationships are implicated whether the couple is composed of individuals of the same sex or different sexes.

But does giving same-sex couples the right to have civil partnership not provide all the protection that is necessary to advance the state's purposes? This is where it is necessary to turn to arguments based on equality and equal respect:

When the US Supreme Court struck down Virginia's interracial marriage ban in *Loving v Virginia*, the Court reasoned that the prohibition was 'designed to maintain White Supremacy' and as such was 'invidious racial discrimination' that had no legitimate independent purpose. The Court would presumably also have rejected a 'separate but equal' status as stigmatizing and hence unconstitutional. One must wonder what legitimate, independent purpose is served by refusing to permit same-sex couples to marry. The point here is not to undermine the desirability of same-sex couples having a legal status for their relationships even if it is a civil partnership rather than a marriage, because even a separate status would afford many of the emotional, religious, and tangible benefits afforded by marriage. Those are important and are not to be taken lightly. Nevertheless, by creating a separate status, the state sends additional messages, for example, that it does not want the institution of marriage to be tainted by permitting those with a same-sex orientation to have access to it. Yet, that is presumably exactly the kind of message that the state should not be sending insofar as it wishes to promote respect for all persons. By the same token, when the state makes marriage a restricted institution only open to certain individuals even though those denied access would both benefit from and serve the purposes of the institution, the state sends additional messages, for example, that marriage itself is simply yet another pawn to be used in the culture wars. But sending such a message does more to demean the institution in the eyes of many than permitting same-sex couples and their families to enter the fold ever could.

Perhaps it would be thought that recognizing same-sex marriage somehow sends a message of disapproval to those who oppose such unions. But it is of course true that individuals who oppose same-sex unions are not being told that they cannot marry. So, too, individuals who believe that it is important for individuals to marry within their faith are not somehow being denigrated when the state permits individuals of different faiths or no faiths to marry. The recognition of same-sex marriages does not imply that different-sex marriages are not valuable, just as the recognition of interracial, interreligious or intergenerational marriages does not imply that intra-racial, intra-religious or intra-generational marriages are not valuable.

The government promoted the Marriage (Same Sex Couples) Bill[82] in simple terms, echoing the view of marriage expressed by Judge Martens in *Cossey* (extracted at 2.3.1 above) in relation to transgender individuals' right to marry:

---

[82] For analysis of the parliamentary and associated debates, see Eekelaar (2014), Harding (2014), (2015).

Hansard, *Official Report*—Marriage (Same Sex Couples) Bill Debates, Hansard
HC Deb, vol 558, col 125, 5 February 2013: 2nd Reading

The Minister for Women and Equalities (Maria Miller):

Mr Speaker, you and I know that every marriage is different – indeed, any husband or wife of
a member of this House has a distinct set of challenges to face every day – but what marriage
offers us all is a lifelong partner to share our journey, a loving stable relationship to strengthen
us and mutual support throughout our lives. I believe that that should be embraced by more
couples. The depth of feeling, love and commitment between same-sex couples is no different from that depth of feeling between opposite-sex couples. The Bill enables society to
recognise that commitment in the same way, too, through marriage. Parliament should value
people equally in the law, and enabling same-sex couples to marry removes the current differentiation and distinction.

The Bill inevitably attracted opposition in Parliament. A major focus of the debates was the
need to secure the position of religious bodies, particularly the Church of England, which
do not wish to solemnize marriages between same-sex couples, whilst providing a mechanism to enable those religious bodies that do wish to solemnize such marriages to do so. But
others fundamentally objected to the Bill, taking the position of the Coalition for Marriage,
which had gathered one of the main petitions on the proposition: 'I support the legal definition of marriage which is the voluntary union for life of one man and one woman to the
exclusion of all others. I oppose any attempt to redefine it.' One of the leading opponents in
the House of Lords took his inspiration from Lewis Carroll, but behind that literary façade
his reasoning shares much with that of Ormrod J in *Corbett* (extracted at 2.3.1 above) in
refusing to accept the possibility of an alternative view of who might marry whom. He may
perhaps be forgiven for taking the view he does, given Lord Filkin's remark on behalf of the
then Labour Government during the Civil Partnership Bill debates ten years earlier that
'same-sex marriage' was a 'contradiction in terms'.[83]

Hansard, *Official Report*—Marriage (Same Sex Couples) Bill Debates, Hansard
HL Deb, vol 745, col 942, 3 June 2013: 2nd Reading

Lord Dear:

"I don't know what you mean by 'glory', Alice said. Humpty Dumpty smiled contemptuously.
Of course you don't – till I tell you. I meant 'there's nice knock-down argument for you!' But
'glory' doesn't mean 'a nice knock-down argument', Alice objected. When I use a word,
Humpty Dumpty said, in rather a scornful tone, it means just what I choose it to mean – neither more nor less".[84]

I would suggest that if we substitute the word "marriage" for "glory" we get somewhere
very close to the essence of today's debate. As Humpty Dumpty might have said: "There's a
nice knock-down argument for you. Marriage means just what I choose it to mean – neither
more nor less".

---

83 Referred to by Baroness O'Cathain in the extract above on p 41.
84 Quoting from Lewis Carroll, *Through the Looking Glass*, ch VI.

> If we move away from Lewis Carroll's Alice and back through the looking glass, we find ourselves in a world where an ill considered Bill seeks to overturn centuries of tradition, heedless of public opinion and the views of religious leaders and blind to the laws of unintended consequences. It seeks to alter totally the concept of marriage as we have always known it, it seeks to divide a nation with an argument that hides behind the concept of equality when in reality it is about sameness, and it stands on its head all considerations of electoral mandate.

Is marriage what same-sex couples (should) want?

Same-sex marriage is highly controversial wherever it is raised, opposed not only by conservative religious organizations and other 'traditionalists', but also—for very different reasons—by some feminist and radical queer commentators.[85] For some, marriage is an icon, and as such an important prize to be won, even if civil partnership or some other institution affords identical rights and duties. But for others, marriage is a patriarchal monolith to be avoided in favour of more diverse, egalitarian ways of living, or simply an irrelevance in contemporary society.

The government's consultation exercise asked two questions to the 'consumer base' for same-sex marriage:

HM Government, *Equal Marriage: The Government's Response* (2012)

Question 7: If you identify as being lesbian, gay or bisexual and were considering making a legal commitment to your partner, would you prefer to have a civil partnership or a civil marriage?

Of the 43% of respondents who said this question was relevant to them:

6% would prefer a civil partnership
81% would prefer a civil marriage
7% no preference
6% don't know

Question 9: If you are in a civil partnership would you wish to take advantage of this policy and convert your civil partnership into a marriage?

Of the 17% of respondents who said this question was relevant to them:

87% would take advantage of this policy
6% would not take advantage of this policy
8% don't know

So there is clearly very strong support for marriage, with only a tiny minority wishing to stick with civil partnership, despite the advent of same-sex marriage. This may disappoint those more radical pro-gay rights commentators for whom same-sex marriage is viewed as a mixed blessing. Does legal recognition come only at the cost of being required to behave in a way that conforms to heterosexual models of relationship? Couples who fear that might

---

[85] For discussion of the various viewpoints, see Crompton (2004), Eskridge (2001), Norrie (2000), Finnis (1993), Bamforth (2001), (2007b), Auchmuty (2008).

prefer the distinctiveness of civil partnership, if they chose to register their relationship with the state at all: this may be the standpoint of the 6 per cent minority noted above.

A. Diduck, 'A Family by Any Other Name... or Starbucks™ Comes to England', (2001) 28 *Journal of Law and Society* 290, 292–4

Boyd and other... scholars have previously brought to our attention the deradicalizing potential of widening the net of traditional families, however, and I wish to argue that important lessons can be learned from their insights. Boyd, for example, says that each time a case to redefine spouse or family is brought forward, a challenge to heteronormativity is made, but often the way that legal arguments have to be formulated and, I would add, the way the decision is ultimately framed means that the potentially disruptive gay/lesbian subject is absorbed back into familiar roles and his or her disruptive potential is displaced. We can see evidence of this in the *Fitzpatrick* case. In arguing first for legal recognition as a spouse, and alternatively as family, Fitzpatrick was forced to submit that his relationship with Mr Thompson was 'akin to marriage', and the way the court framed its decision seems to suggest that it agreed.

Diduck finds traditional equality arguments problematic because applicants must demonstrate that they are treated differently from analogous individuals. The claim's success hangs on gay and lesbian applicants showing that their relationships are the same as heterosexual ones: this 'retains the pitfall of instantiating in law characteristics, relationships, and subjectivities already dominant'.[86] Craig Lind argues that this creates new demarcations: homosexuality per se no longer bars admission to 'family', but those whose relationships fail to make the grade in other respects—for example, because not monogamous, or because not perceived as being sufficiently committed—remain excluded:[87]

C. Lind, 'Sexuality and Same-Sex Relationships in Law', in B. Brooks-Gordon et al (eds), *Sexuality Repositioned* (Oxford: Hart Publishing, 2004), 122–4, 126

[A]lternative ways of living domestic lives are being marginalised by the... process of normalisation. People who are unsuited to these lifestyles remain outsiders in society. And the question we must ask ourselves is whether or not we have really progressed when we have managed to enlarge the group of the privileged and retain our prejudices in relation to others.

But others take a different view, either regarding normalization as unproblematic or rejecting the view that the concept of family will remain fixed. The 'conservative approach', outlined by Lind in this extract, rejects the notion that marriage is institutionally unacceptable and embraces normalization:

For some..., what distinguishes people with same-sex desire from those with different-sex desire is only their desire. In all other respects lesbians and gay men are 'normal'. Furthermore, their identity is perceived as immutable. And inequality arising out of an immutable, unchosen,

---

[86] Diduck (2001), 304.
[87] See further Eskridge (2001); Halley (2001); Norrie (2000).

characteristic, it is argued, is unjust. The argument goes on to assert that society could easily remedy that inequality by extending the privileges of the majority to the minority. Sexuality should be an irrelevant consideration in legal regulation; in the regulation of family relationships, for example, lesbians and gay men should be able to attract exactly the same legal regulation as different-sex couples. Society would, in effect, acknowledge the 'normality' of lesbians and gay men by adapting its significant institutions to provide for them. Even amongst those who acknowledge the constructed nature of sexuality there are those who take the view that a socially responsible sexuality is a constrained sexuality...Fitting same-sex desire into the normal patterns of life is an acceptable way of controlling it so that it becomes socially responsible rather than socially obnoxious. Normalisation of sexuality should occur...

Recent research amongst younger generations of same-sex couples who had formed civil partnerships, along with the responses to the equal marriage consultation noted above, suggests that most such couples do indeed just want to be normal—or 'ordinary'—rather than to be at the vanguard of a radical movement experimenting with alternative forms of relationship.[88] Notably, these couples have grown up and spent all or most of their adult lives in a time when the advances in gay rights and relationship recognition (all bar same-sex marriage) had already been made:

B. Heaphy et al, *Same-Sex Marriages: New Generations, New Relationships*
(Basingstoke: Palgrave Macmillan, 2013), 5

Indeed, notable findings from our research include the common belief among younger same-sex partners that gender and sexual inequalities in relationships have largely been overcome, and that *couple-centred* life remains the obvious and natural answer to life-political questions about how to live and relate. These beliefs partly influenced many partners' claims to have 'ordinary' marriages,[89] which in turn were grounded in a conviction that contemporary heterosexual and same-sex relationships were much the same. This is linked to a conviction that heterosexual and same-sex relationships are now equal in the eyes of the law, and are generally accepted as on a par with each other in day-to-day life. It is also linked to the strong sense that active commitments are more important than gender and sexuality in the making of 'good' relationships and marriages. Such beliefs and claims were thought to be evidenced by real changes that had taken place with respect to sexuality in law and in everyday life, which enabled younger same-sex couples to live their lives relatively free from the constraints encountered by previous generations. While previous generations of feminist and lesbian and gay liberationists linked the cultural privileging of the couple and marriage to constraining power, the tendency among our younger same-sex partners was to link their personal privileging of the couple and marriage to the historically increased quanta of power that sexual minorities have over their ordinary lives. At the same time, their beliefs that their relationships were more similar to, rather than different from, their heterosexual generational peers were grounded in a conviction that the latter tended to be less 'traditional' and more equal relationships than was the case for their parents' generation. This implied that gender was nowadays relatively insignificant in shaping heterosexual relationships and marriages. This is the imagined social world that many younger same-sex partners invoke in telling their stories of their 'ordinary' relationships.

---

[88] Cf Mitchell et al (2009).
[89] This term was being used in relation to civil partnership; see also Peel (2015).

Heaphy et al emphasize that the 'ideals of ordinariness...cannot simply be equated with the "normalisation" or "assimilation" of these relationships' of the sort that would trouble Diduck. Rather the claim to be ordinary is viewed as a claim to be part of the common 'mass of people (heterosexual and non-heterosexual) in "the middle" who must work at creating "mature" and "responsible" relationships'.[90]

However, while these couples may reject the role of radical relationship innovators, the wider recognition of same-sex couples, culminating in their right to marry, may mean that these couples unwittingly have a transformative effect on marriage, for opposite-sex as well as same-sex couples:

C. Lind, 'Sexuality and Same-Sex Relationships in Law', in B. Brooks-Gordon et al (eds), *Sexuality Repositioned* (Oxford: Hart Publishing, 2004), 126

Giving same-sex couples access to ordinary family regulation will, it is argued, go some way (if not all the way) towards addressing the concerns of feminists and others about the patriarchal nature of family regulation. Recognising same-sex relationships will force an internal transformation in the basic tenets of all relationships...Although the desire to be married is regarded as a conservative phenomenon...the desire to compel the state to recognise same-sex marriage is radical. It brings into public discourse a different way of being married. Same-sex couples will be bound to behave differently from the norm of marriage...This is particularly true in relation to gendered roles and other unquestioned behavioural patterns in different sex family lives...For this reason same-sex relationships destabilise the ideal of marriage. Same-sex couples introduce a reflective element into expectations of behaviour in relationships. As a result of this characteristic they will, it is argued, reveal different ways of being married. In particular, they will undermine gendered power in relationships. A more equitable family ethic will emerge. Same-sex families will, in effect, live the feminist ambition for a family life characterised by real equality. In doing so they will, in effect, foster its achievement beyond their own families. Ideologically suspect relationships will benefit from the disruption to the norm that normalisation of abnormal relationships will cause.

The transformative potential is not limited to 'leadership by example', however. The fact that there is a debate surrounding same-sex marriages will create (indeed, has created) a discourse around the nature of marriage, adult relationships and state regulation. It has increased the scope and variety of relationships that are socially recognised and the mechanisms that the state is prepared to use to regulate them. It has, in effect, led to a tangible increase in the diversity of recognised family forms in society. This, it is argued, is a radical departure from the married/single binary which has been the dominant feature of modern family life....

As Baroness Hale noted in *Ghaidan* in the extract above, modern marriage is already substantially changed from the institution of a few decades ago, not least in law. The anticipated popularity of same-sex marriage may take us further in de-gendering marriage, not only in law but also in how spouses organize their daily lives.

---

90 Heaphy et al (2013), 170.

2.4 STATUS-BASED RELATIONSHIPS: MARRIAGE AND CIVIL PARTNERSHIP

English law recognizes two formalized relationships: marriage and civil partnership. Both are status-based relationships recognized simply by virtue of the parties completing state-prescribed formalities; the legal existence or validity of such a relationship does not generally depend upon the parties subsequently behaving in a particular way, so, for example, they need not cohabit.[91] As we shall see, there are some differences in the law governing the formation and validity of and exit from marriage by opposite-sex couples, marriage by same-sex couples, and civil partnership (which only same-sex couples may form). But the legal effect of all marriages and civil partnerships are otherwise essentially identical,[92] and so we discuss them in parallel throughout this chapter and the rest of the book, noting and exploring differences as we encounter them. We begin by examining the essential legal nature of such relationships and the right to form them, before turning to the conditions that must be satisfied in order to create them.

2.4.1 THE NATURE OF MARRIAGE AND CIVIL PARTNERSHIP

Marriage has long been regarded as multifaceted: at once a religious institution, a contract between the parties, and a legal status from which particular rights and responsibilities flow, both between the parties themselves, and vis-à-vis the spouses and third parties, including the state.[93] As such, marriage is difficult to categorize juristically:

K. O'Donovan, *Family Law Matters* (London: Pluto Press, 1993), 43–4

As a contract, so presented in legal discourse throughout the history of the common law, it cannot stand. Its terms are not negotiated by the parties, but prescribed by law. It is not a contract freely entered into by any adult but is open only to certain persons under specified conditions according to law. Termination of marriage can occur only as denoted by law, and not by the partners. Within the legal married state, the law's prescriptions allocate roles ascriptively, according to gender, and not according to the wishes of the parties. Legal marriage requires the sacrifice of personal autonomy but not on equal terms for the parties. An ascriptive quality, gender, is incorporated in the legal institution [notably, the marital rape exemption, see 4.2.3]. This differentiation of partners produces inequality.

Where the notion of marriage as free contract is rejected, writers tend to use the word 'institution' instead, and this may be an appropriate word. When one enters an institution one does so on terms set by that body, one is bound by rules to which one consents on entry. However, the membership may collectively agree a change of rules. It is not easy to apply this analysis to marriage. It is the law, not the partners, which lays down the rules, not only of entry, but also of membership. Collective agreement on the alteration of the

---

[91] *Draper v United Kingdom* (App No 8186/78, ECHR) (1980), [60].
[92] M(SSC)A 2013, s 11(1), subject to Schs 3 and 4.
[93] *Lindo v Belisari* (1795) 1 Hag Con 216, 230; *Niboyet v Niboyet* (1878) 4 PD 1, 11; *Bellinger v Bellinger* [2001] EWCA Civ 1140, [99] and [128].

rules by the partners is not possible. We are up against something not easily analysed in institutional terms. Marriage has contractual and institutional elements, but it is also *sui generis*, a law unto itself.

As for its religious aspect, much of current marriage law has origins in ecclesiastical law. But it is questionable whether the contours of contemporary, secular marriage law should continue to be shaped by Christian doctrine in a multi-cultural, multi-faith society in which it has been possible to contract a civil marriage since 1836.[94] Indeed, several changes in marriage law over the years—of which the introduction of same-sex marriage is only the most recent—have taken the institution of marriage as recognized by law progressively further away from its ecclesiastical roots.[95]

The nature of civil partnership attracted attention during parliamentary debates. Section 1 of the CPA 2004 describes civil partnership as a 'relationship'. Some thought it ought to be described as a 'contract'. The government disagreed:[96]

Hansard, *Official Report*—Civil Partnership Bill Debates, Hansard HL Deb, vol 662, cols 1361–2, 24 June 2004: Report Stage

Minister of State for the Criminal Justice System and Law Reform (Baroness Scotland of Asthal):

The noble Lord wishes to describe civil partnership as a contract. However, civil partnership is not governed by the law of contract and there is no room for individual variation of the statutory rules governing eligibility, or governing formation or dissolution of a civil partnership, nor of those setting out its consequences.

The change of status from single person to civil partner affects a couple's relationship with each other. After the formation of their civil partnership they would have an entirely new legal relationship with each other. Forming a civil partnership also affects their status; in other words, their position as an individual in relation to everyone else. Each would now be a civil partner. This change of status is permanent in that on the ending of a civil partnership, civil partners do not revert to being single people. They will be marked by having been in a civil partnership in that they will be former civil partners or a surviving civil partner. Civil partnership is a new statutory relationship that provides same-sex couples with legal recognition of their life together as a couple.

While marriage and civil partnership combine contract and status, save for one recent change which we discuss below at 2.5.3, it is clear that civil partnership has no religious aspect in law. Adopting the rules that apply to civil marriages, no religious service may be used while the registrar is officiating at the signing of the civil partnership document (the act which creates a civil partnership).[97] The original decision to create the separate institution

---

94 Marriage Act 1836.
95 Note also the introduction and gradual liberalization of divorce (chapter 5), and the narrowing of the prohibited degrees of relationship, discussed at 2.6.1 below. Contrast the implicit view of the Church of England (2013) that introduction of same-sex marriage would uniquely have that effect, despite its opposition to the earlier developments having been cast in similar terms: Woodhead (2014).
96 See also *Bull v Hall* [2013] UKSC 73, [26] and [36].
97 CPA 2004, ss 2(5) and 6.

of civil partnership rather than simply permit same-sex marriage was influenced by the fact that many regard marriage as a religious sacrament incapable of accommodating same-sex unions. Indeed, special rules now govern whether and when a same-sex marriage may be solemnized by a religious body. But once created, however created, they all have the same effect in law.

One of the key debates today is the extent to which spouses and civil partners can devise their own terms for the relationship by agreement. Since marriage arises from the parties' mutual consent, should they be similarly free to divorce simply because both wish to do so? Should they be free to agree their property and financial arrangements on separation?[98] For the time being, the law formally continues to prescribe the grounds for divorce, to require application to court to terminate the legal status, and (despite increased weight attaching to marital agreements) retains the power to intervene in parties' financial settlements: as O'Donovan observes, having joined the club, members cannot simply change the rules as it suits them.

2.4.2 THE SIGNIFICANCE OF STATUS

Historically, marriage had a profound and unequal effect on the legal status of the individuals concerned:

W. Blackstone, _Commentaries on the Laws of England_, vol 1 (1765, Facsimile edn: Chicago: University of Chicago Press, 1979), 430

By marriage, the husband and wife are one person in law: that is, the very being or legal existence of the woman is suspended during the marriage, or at least is incorporated and consolidated into that of her husband: under whose wing, protection, and _cover_, she performs every thing ... Under this principle, of an union of person in husband and wife, depend almost all the legal rights, duties, and disabilities, that either of them acquire by the marriage.

The common law doctrine of unity fused husband and wife's legal personalities into one person, and, as Lord Denning once pithily put it, that person was the husband.[99] This fiction generated some slightly surprising consequences. For example, spouses were unable to sue each other in tort.[100] Nor (still) can they be guilty of conspiring with each other.[101] That dubious benefit aside, lack of distinctive legal personality caused wives substantial disabilities, as we shall see in chapters 3 and 4 when we examine the laws of family property and domestic violence. As John Stuart Mill put it in his essay on _The Subjection of Women_: 'If married life were all that it might be expected to be, looking to the laws alone, society would be a hell upon earth'.[102] But over the course of the late nineteenth century and throughout the twentieth century, wives' legal disabilities and husbands' rights of control were gradually

---

[98] See 5.7.2 and 7.7.

[99] _Midland Bank v Green (No 3)_ [1982] Ch 529, 538.

[100] Until the Law Reform (Husband and Wife) Act 1962.

[101] This exemption is now justified on the basis of marital sanctity and confidentiality, rather than marital unity: Criminal Law Act 1977, s 2(2)(a), _Midland Bank v Green (No 3)_ [1979] Ch 496, 521. The Law Commission has recommended its abolition: Law Com (2009), para 5.16.

[102] (1869), 465.

removed. Marriage has, at least in theory, developed from legally-condoned patriarchy to a 'partnership of equals':

Sheffield City Council v E and another [2004] EWHC 2808, [2005] Fam 326

MUNBY J:

111. . . . [I]n *Durham v Durham* (1885) . . . Sir James Hannen P described the contract of marriage in these terms:

"It is an engagement between a man and woman to live together, and love one another as husband and wife, to the exclusion of all others. This is expanded in the promises of the marriage ceremony by words having reference to the natural relations which spring from that engagement, such as protection on the part of the man, and submission on the part of the woman." . . .

116. It seems to me that . . . these observations about the husband's duty to protect and maintain and the wife's duty of submission have now to be read with very considerable caution. Indeed, I doubt that they any longer have any place in our contemporaneous understanding of marriage, . . . as a civil institution whose duties and obligations are regulated by the secular courts of an increasingly secular society. For, although we live in a multicultural society of many faiths, it must not be forgotten that as a secular judge my concern . . . is with marriage as a civil contract, not as a religious vow . . .

131. Today both spouses are the joint, co-equal heads of the family. Each has an obligation to comfort and support the other. It is not for the husband alone to provide the matrimonial home or to decide where the family is to live. Husband and wife both contribute. And where they are to live is, like other domestic matters of common concern, something to be settled by agreement, not determined unilaterally by the husband. In so far as the concept of consortium—the sharing of a common home and a common domestic life, and the right to enjoy each other's society, comfort and assistance—still has any useful role to play, the rights of husband and wife must surely now be regarded as exactly reciprocal.

The notion that spouses owe each other legal duties to comfort, support, and cohabit is problematic. None of them is specifically enforceable,[103] but divorce may be obtained on the basis of desertion, separation, or behaviour such that the petitioner cannot reasonably be expected to live with the respondent.[104]

Civil partnership has nothing like the history and ideological baggage of (opposite-sex) marriage.[105] It is a creature of modern statute largely replicating existing matrimonial legislation, the exemption from criminal liability for conspiracy included. The common law doctrines of unity and consortium presumably have no application to civil partnership[106] or to same-sex marriage. However, as Munby J observed in the *Sheffield* case, it is doubtful whether those doctrines have any modern significance for opposite-sex spouses: although never formally abolished, they have been compromised substantially by legislation.[107]

---

103 The action for restitution of conjugal rights was abolished in 1970: Law Reform (Miscellaneous Provisions) Act: see Cretney (2003a), ch 4 and Gaffney-Rhys (2006).
104 Matrimonial Causes Act 1973 (MCA 1973), s 1. See chapter 5.
105 Though see the concerns of commentators such as Diduck (2005), discussed at 2.3.2.
106 Harper et al (2005), 42.
107 Bridge (2001), 15.

We examine particular rights and duties arising from marriage and civil partnership throughout the book.[108] It will be clear that, while their status is less distinctive than it was historically, spouses and civil partners still enjoy a special position in English law, particularly compared with cohabitants whose de facto relationships—discussed at 2.8.2 below—attract rather fewer, less intensive legal consequences.

2.4.3 A RIGHT TO MARRY, OR NOT TO MARRY?

Marriage and civil partnership are vehicles for the acquisition of distinctive rights and duties, many of which cannot be created by private contract. Whether one has the right to form a marriage or civil partnership is therefore a vital question. It has been said that English law has always recognized the right to marry,[109] but the right is enshrined in Article 12 ECHR and other international conventions. The importance and universal recognition of this right was described by Baroness Hale in a case concerning procedural restrictions placed on marriages by non-EEA (European Economic Area) nationals in an effort to prevent sham marriages contracted purely for immigration purposes:

R (On the Application of Baiai and others) v Secretary of State for the Home Department and others [2008] UKHL 53

BARONESS HALE:

44....As Chief Justice Warren...said [in *Loving et ux. v Virginia* 388 US 1 (1967), landmark US Supreme Court decision quashing bans on mixed-race marriages] "Marriage is one of the 'basic civil rights of man', fundamental to our very existence and survival". Even in South Africa, where marriage is not constitutionally protected because of fears that this might entrench a particular model of marriage within a multi-cultural society, "the provision of the constitutional text would clearly prohibit any arbitrary state interference with the right to marry or to establish and raise a family. The text enshrines the values of human dignity, equality and freedom" (see *Minister for Home Affairs v Fourie*, Case 60/04 Constitutional Court of South Africa, para 47, Sachs J). Denying to members of minority groups the right to establish formal, legal relationships with the partners of their choice is one way of setting them apart from society, denying that they are "free and equal in dignity and rights".

45. Even in these days, when many in British society believe that there is little social difference between marrying and living together, marriage still has deep significance for many people, quite apart from the legal recognition, status, rights and obligations which it brings. "Marriage law...goes well beyond its earlier purpose in the common law of legitimising sexual relations and securing succession of legitimate heirs to family property. And it is much more than a piece of paper." (Sachs J, para 70). It brings legal, social and psychological benefits to the couple when they marry, while they are married and when it ends.

Article 12 expressly preserves the right of states to govern the exercise of the right. Although not required by Article 12 to do so, Parliament has now exercised that right to confer on

---

[108] For exhaustive analysis of the effects of marriage, see Lowe and Douglas (2015), ch 4.

[109] *R (On the Application of the Crown Prosecution Service) v Registrar General of Births, Deaths and Marriages* [2002] EWCA Civ 1661, [20]; *Aquilar Quila and others v Secretary of State for the Home Department* [2010] EWCA Civ 1482.

all individuals the right to marry a person of either sex in English law. But however a state defines marriage, the state's freedom then to govern the exercise of the right to marry, so defined, is not unlimited. In this extract, Lord Bingham responds to the suggestion that the right to marry in Article 12 is an absolute right:[110]

R (On the Application of Baiai and others) v Secretary of State for the Home Department and others [2008] UKHL 53

LORD BINGHAM:

13. If by "absolute" is meant that anyone within the jurisdiction is free to marry any other person irrespective of age, gender, consanguinity, affinity or any existing marriage, then plainly the right protected by article 12 is not absolute. But equally plainly...it is a strong right....In contrast with articles 8, 9, 10 and 11 of the Convention, it contains no second paragraph permitting interferences with or limitations of the right in question which are prescribed by law and necessary in a democratic society for one or other of a number of specified purposes. The right is subject only to national laws governing its exercise.

14. The Strasbourg case law reveals a restrictive approach towards national laws. Thus it has been accepted that national laws may lay down rules of substance based on generally recognised considerations of public interest, of which rules concerning capacity, consent, prohibited degrees of consanguinity and prevention of bigamy are examples....But from early days the right to marry has been described as "fundamental", it has been made clear that the scope afforded to national law is not unlimited and it has been emphasised that national laws governing the exercise of the right to marry must never injure or impair the substance of the right and must not deprive a person or category of person of full legal capacity of the right to marry or substantially interfere with their exercise of the right....

16. The Strasbourg jurisprudence requires the right to marry to be treated as a strong right which may be regulated by national law both as to procedure and substance but may not be subjected to conditions which impair the essence of the right.

In *Baiai*, it was held that it was legitimate to seek to prevent sham marriages for immigration purposes by imposing restrictions on the right to marry, but that such restrictions must be proportionate and non-discriminatory in their operation; the scheme in question failed that test.[111] Other notable cases involving the UK have involved marriage by prisoners; the adverse finding in *Draper v United Kingdom*[112] prompted reform to allow marriages in prisons. Such restrictions must also have a clear basis in law: so a general statutory discretion not to issue marriage licences to remand prisoners could not lawfully be exercised on the basis that a particular marriage would frustrate an impending trial, the defendant's intended wife then no longer being compellable as a witness.[113]

Domestic rules regarding capacity to marry and the formalities required to create a marriage must also be compatible with Article 12. For example, Article 12 was invoked, without

---

110 Art 12 is inapplicable in this sense to civil partnership; however, analogous restrictions on access to civil partnership might breach Art 8.

111 See also *O'Donaghue v United Kingdom* (App No 34848/07, ECHR) (2011).

112 (App No 8186/78, ECHR) (1980).

113 *R (On the Application of the Crown Prosecution Service) v Registrar General of Births, Deaths and Marriages* [2002] EWCA Civ 1661; *Frasik v Poland* (App No 22933/02, ECHR) (2010).

substantial analysis or adjudication, to permit the Prince of Wales to contract a civil marriage; it had previously been understood that members of the Royal Family were able to marry in England and Wales only in an Anglican ceremony.[114] But Article 12 is relevant to the wider populous too, and on examining the law of nullity we shall see how current English law fares under Article 12.

Recent cases in the English courts have also considered what is in effect the right *not* to marry, implicit in Article 12. A marriage to which one or both parties is not consenting is voidable, but the courts have developed their inherent jurisdiction to intervene where it is feared either that an impending marriage would be forced,[115] or that one party may lack the mental capacity to consent to marriage or be unable to make a fully informed, genuine choice to enter a particular marriage.[116] The marriage in the latter type of case might often be valid, since English law takes a narrow view of what must be understood and consented to for a marriage to be valid. But the 'serious emotional and psychological harm' that might nevertheless be suffered has been held to justify the grant of protective orders designed to 'ensure that any marriage really is what [the individual] wants'.[117]

2.5 CREATING A VALID MARRIAGE OR CIVIL PARTNERSHIP

The law does little to provide *positive* definitions of marriage and civil partnership. The most famous, if 'positively misleading',[118] definition of marriage comes from the nineteenth century: 'I conceive that marriage, as understood in Christendom, may...be defined as the voluntary union for life of one man and one woman to the exclusion of all others.'[119]

This statement was not accurate even when it was first made, not least because marriage can be terminated by divorce, so may not endure for the parties' joint lives. But, rightly or wrongly, it is nevertheless frequently cited as a starting point for discussion of marriage, in particular in attempts to resist same-sex marriage. We discover rather more about the law's conception of marriage and civil partnership from the *negative* law of nullity. That law performs a dual function. It sets out those characteristics or conditions that are so fundamental to the law's understanding of marriage and civil partnership that if one or more of them is absent or not satisfied, the relationship cannot or may not be regarded as valid. It also provides a mechanism whereby an apparent marriage or civil partnership which fails to satisfy any of those criteria can be unravelled.

2.5.1 THE LAW OF NULLITY: VOID, VOIDABLE, AND NON-MARRIAGES

It is important to appreciate the distinction between nullity and divorce (or, in the case of civil partnership, dissolution). Divorce entails the termination of what had been a valid

---

114 See (2005) FL 345; for comment, Probert (2005b).
115 See now statutory remedies created by the Forced Marriage (Civil Protection) Act 2007.
116 See *Re SA (Vulnerable Adult with Capacity: Marriage)* [2005] EWHC 2942.
117 Ibid, [126] per Munby J.
118 Probert (2007a), 323.
119 *Hyde v Hyde* (1866) LR 1 P&D 130, 133, per Lord Penzance.

marriage. Nullity is concerned with the validity of a purported marriage from its inception. However, the distinction is not clear-cut, as the law of nullity distinguishes between void and voidable marriages and civil partnerships:

Law Commission, *Report on Nullity of Marriage*, Law Com No 33
(London: HMSO, 1970)

3. . . . [T]he present distinction between valid, void and voidable marriages corresponds] to factual differences in the situations of the parties which call for different relief from the courts. The difference between the three types of marriage may be summarised thus:

(a) A valid marriage is one which is in no sense defective and is, therefore, binding on the parties (and on everyone else); it can only be terminated by death or by a decree of divorce, which decree acknowledges the existence of a valid marriage and then proceeds to put an end to it.

(b) A void marriage is not really a marriage at all, in that it never came into existence because of a fundamental defect; the marriage is said to be void *ab initio*; no decree of nullity is necessary to make it void and parties can take the risk of treating the marriage as void without obtaining a decree. But either of the spouses or any person having a sufficient interest in obtaining a decree of nullity may petition for a decree at any time, whether during the lifetime of the spouses or after their death. In effect, the decree is a declaration that there is not and never has been a marriage.

(c) A voidable marriage is a valid marriage unless and until it is annulled; it can be annulled only at the instance of one of the spouses during the lifetime of both, so that if no decree of nullity is pronounced during the lifetime of both spouses, the marriage becomes unimpeachable as soon as one of the spouses dies.

4. In many Civil Law countries marriages which we would regard as void are treated as voidable in the sense that a marriage once formally celebrated cannot be disregarded until it has been set aside. This seems to be based on the importance which those countries place on official records. The English view, however, is that registration of a marriage merely records the celebration of marriage and affords no guarantee of its validity. To require legal proceedings to be instituted before partes could regard themselves as free from a marriage which was palpably invalid because, for example, one party was already married to another or was under the age of 16, would, in our view, add needlessly to the expense to the parties and to the public.

Although no court proceedings are needed to 'end' a void marriage, they may still be desirable: to provide the certainty of a court order definitively stating the legal position; and to invoke the court's jurisdiction to make financial orders between the parties.[120] It may seem surprising that a void marriage should attract any legal consequences. However, to give one example, an innocent party to what is later discovered to have been a bigamous marriage might have compromised his or her position assuming the marriage to be valid to a point where his or her need for financial relief is as great as that of a party to a valid marriage.

---

120 *S-T (formerly J) v J* [1998] Fam 103.

Whether a remedy is awarded depends on the court's discretion; where the applicant is responsible for the relationship's invalidity, no remedy may be forthcoming.[121]

The last, rather curious category is the 'non-marriage'. These are purported marriages which depart so far from what constitutes a marriage under English law, usually because no attempt has been made to comply with the required formalities, that they cannot be regarded even as a void marriage and so *no* legal consequences flow from them. This is a particularly grave conclusion when one or both parties honestly believed the marriage to be valid. As we shall see below, it seems that the courts have recently been stretching the boundaries of this category in forced marriage cases in order to achieve just outcomes, but on a questionable legal basis.

2.5.2 THE PRACTICAL IMPORTANCE OF THE LAW OF NULLITY

If the significance of the law of nullity were measured by reference to the number of nullity decrees granted, we would conclude that it was relatively unimportant. In 2011, just 345 petitions were filed for nullity, compared with 129,298 divorce petitions.[122] This in part reflects the limited scope of the grounds for nullity and the breadth of the bases on which divorce may be obtained. However, much more significant is the role of the law of nullity in delineating the scope of the right to marry or form a civil partnership, and the unknown numbers of individuals who might thereby be prevented from doing so. Restricting access to these institutions to certain types of relationships tells us something about the law's view of the social function of marriage and civil partnership. The most interesting questions, then, are why have *these* entry requirements been imposed; and why are the grounds on which a marriage or civil partnership may be voidable not relegated to the law of divorce.

2.5.3 FORMAL REQUIREMENTS FOR CREATING MARRIAGE AND CIVIL PARTNERSHIP

Before we examine the grounds for nullity, we must outline the formal requirements for creating a marriage or civil partnership. Since marriage and civil partnership transform the parties' legal status, both between themselves and as against the world, it is unsurprising that public formalities must be performed. The rules are intended to ensure that the parties are free to marry and consent to do so, and to establish with complete certainty who enjoys the legal status of spouse or civil partner.[123] Requiring parties to jump through specific procedural hoops, rather than permitting them to create marriages by whatever method they privately choose, is compatible with Article 12.[124] Specifically, a state does not violate Article 8, 12, or 14 in refusing to recognize religious marriages and requiring parties who wish to have a religious ceremony additionally to complete further formalities to create a civil law marriage.[125]

---

[121] See p 498.
[122] MOJ (2012), table 2.5.
[123] Law Com (1973a), Annex, para 4.
[124] *X v Federal Republic of Germany* (App No 6167/73, ECHR) (1974).
[125] *Şerife Yiğit v Turkey* (App No 3976/05, ECHR) (2009); *Muñoz Díaz v Spain* (App No 49151/07, ECHR) (2009).

English law relating to formalities for marriage suffers from 'bewildering' complexity, entirely the product of history,[126] and the introduction of same-sex marriage—to which yet more rules apply—has further complicated matters. Separate rules govern the creation of civil partnership. The formal requirements for marriage and civil partnership can broadly be divided into three categories:

(i) the preliminary procedures—giving public notice of intention to marry or register a civil partnership in order to allow interested parties to lodge objections (e.g. on the ground that the parties do not have the capacity to marry);

(ii) rules that must be satisfied and procedures that must be completed to create the marriage or civil partnership—regarding the time and location of the ceremony, the identity of the celebrant, the presence of witnesses, and (for marriage) the exchange of particular words or (for civil partnership) the signing of the civil partnership document; and

(iii) bureaucratic registration requirements, recording and so proving the existence of the marriage or civil partnership—in the case of marriage, this is a separate stage; in the case of civil partnership, the act of registration both creates and records the legal status.

Marriage formalities

In the case of marriage, different rules govern stages (i) and (ii), depending on the location and/or religious format, if any, of the intended ceremony, and, if it is a marriage between a same-sex couple, on whether the solemnizing authority has the power to marry them at all. The registration requirement (iii) is universal.

For marriages conducted in a civil ceremony, the situation is straightforward: whether the ceremony is conducted in a register office or other premises approved for the solemnization of marriage (e.g. several stately homes, hotels, and other venues),[127] any couple—opposite- or same-sex—may be married in a civil ceremony. The option of civil marriage was created in 1836.[128] Previously, marriage could *only* be solemnized in a religious ceremony in an Anglican church, though Jews and Quakers were permitted to use their own marriage practices. Since 1992, civil ceremonies have outnumbered religious ceremonies, in 2008 accounting for two-thirds of all marriages.[129]

The Church of England still enjoys a privileged position as the one religious body which can both use its own forms of preliminary procedure and whose own buildings, ceremony, and celebrants are qualified to create and register marriages without any further state sanction.[130] However, the Church will only—and under the current state of the legislation can only—conduct marriages between couples of the opposite sex.[131] Jews and Quakers[132] may still use their own marriage practices, but must complete the preliminaries applicable to civil marriage.[133] Adherents to other Christian denominations and other religions[134] may straightforwardly marry opposite-sex couples in their own

---

126 Law Com (1973a), Annex, para 6.

127 Marriage Act 1949 (MA 1949), ss 46A–B.

128 Marriage Act 1836.

129 ONS (2010b).

130 MA 1949, Part II.

131 See M(SSC)A 2013, ss 1(3)(4), 2, 11(6).

132 MA 1949, s 47.

133 Ibid, s 26(1)(c)(d).

134 See *R (Hodkin and another) v Registrar General of Births, Deaths and Marriages* [2013] UKSC 77.

religious premises following completion of the civil preliminaries, provided further requirements regarding the registration of the building and presence of an authorized celebrant are satisfied.[135] Any faith group that wishes to conduct same-sex marriages must specifically 'opt in' to do so, a procedure which requires the written consent of the relevant governing authority.[136] This mechanism is not available to the Church of England.[137]

Same-sex couples who have a civil partnership but wish to marry have since December 2014 been able to convert their civil partnership to a marriage, either using a simple one-stage process at a register office, or a two-stage process in which the conversion is completed at another venue, enabling the couple to hold a ceremony to celebrate the occasion either at approved premises or at religious premises which have been registered for marriage of same-sex couples using the opt-in procedure.[138]

Civil partnership formalities

Until recently, civil partnership was clearly a non-religious institution: the original CPA 2004, like the rules for civil marriages, barred the use of religious premises as a venue for creating a civil partnership and required that the registration be conducted by a civil registrar, not a religious celebrant. This scheme frustrated faith groups such as Liberal Jews and Quakers who wanted to be able to host registration ceremonies. The Equality Act 2010 accordingly removed the bar on use of religious premises, leaving the matter instead to the decision of each faith group, just as the M(SSC)A 2013 leaves the matter of same-sex marriage to individual faith groups to decide.[139] However, the registration process must still be conducted by a registrar, not by the religious celebrant.

Consequences of failing to comply with formalities

Failure to comply with the prescribed form does not necessarily render the marriage or civil partnership void.[140] Some defects may result in nullity—see 2.6.2 below. Other breaches do not affect validity, though someone—usually the registrar or equivalent person—may be guilty of a criminal offence.[141] Conversely, if failure to comply with the formal requirements is sufficiently fundamental, the resulting union may be regarded as a non-marriage—see 2.6.2 below.

Reform?

Rationalization and simplification of the law in this area is long overdue, and may in time be required in order to avoid a challenge under Article 14 ECHR in conjunction

---

[135] MA 1949, ss 26(1)(a), 35, 41–4; Places of Worship Registration Act 1855.

[136] MA 1949, ss 26A, 26B.

[137] The situation of the Church in Wales is dealt with by M(SSC)A 2013, s 8.

[138] Marriage of Same Sex Couples (Conversion of Civil Partnership) Regulations 2014, SI 2014/3181.

[139] CPA 2014, ss 6–6A. Marriages and Civil Partnerships (Approved Premises) (Amendment) Regulations 2011, SI 2011/2661.

[140] See 2.6.2.

[141] MA 1949, ss 75–7; CPA 2004, ss 31–3. Parties may be guilty of perjury if they make false declarations: Perjury Act 1911, s 3, CPA 2004, s 80.

with Articles 12 and 9, barring discrimination in the exercise of the right to marry on grounds of religion. It is not obvious that the special status of the Church of England regarding opposite-sex marriage, and the relatively disadvantageous positions of other faiths and denominations, should be maintained.[142] However, following recent ECHR case law, it might be argued that the universal availability of civil marriage to members of all faiths or none means that there is no violation of Article 14 in conjunction with Article 12.[143] Reform proposals would provide uniform rules for *all* marriages (and now civil partnership), and in other respects provide a marriage law far better suited to twenty-first-century social conditions in this jurisdiction.[144] John Eekelaar has made the following proposal:

J. Eekelaar, 'Marriage: A Modest Proposal', (2013) 43 *Family Law* 83, 84

It seems that our marriage law, confused though it is, has developed by making a series of accommodations with various groups and points of view. This is not a dishonourable history. Most people see marriage as a major event in their personal lives, which for many can only be adequately expressed if it has been brought about in a manner in accordance with a deeply held belief, or in a way that holds strong meaning for them. The logical (if radical) outcome of recognising this is that it should not matter what type of ceremony accompanies the formation of the marriage if it fulfils those requirements for the parties. The attempt to impose conditions, and especially to segregate the religious from the secular, fails to do this sufficiently and can lead to ludicrous consequences. There is the further advantage that this strategy would make the secular law relating to the consequences of marriage available to all unions which the parties see as being a marriage, provided only that certain preliminary formalities are fulfilled.

A comprehensive review of the law relating to marriage ceremonies might be undertaken soon, following a government consultation on whether non-religious belief organizations, such as Humanists, should also be permitted to solemnize marriages. The government concluded that the issues raised called for a more thorough examination of the area, possibly by the Law Commission.[145]

ONLINE RESOURCE CENTRE

More detailed discussion of the formal requirements for the creation of marriage and civil partnership may be found on the Online Resource Centre.

---

142 Cf the concession made by the UK Government in *O'Donaghue v United Kingdom* (App No 34848/07, ECHR) (2011), [110] that excluding Anglican marriages from special immigration rules (considered in *R (Baiai) v Secretary of State for the Home Department* [2008] UKHL 53) violated the Convention.

143 *Muñoz Díaz v Spain* (App No 49151/07, ECHR) (2009), though the complaint in that case was one of ethnic rather than religious discrimination, so the point may still be open: [79]–[81]. Cf *Şerife Yiğit v Turkey* (App No 3976/05, ECHR) (2009), where Turkish law, which recognizes no religious marriages at all, was upheld.

144 General Register Office (2003); Probert (2002a), (2004b); Barton (2002).

145 MOJ (2014c), (2014e).

2.6 GROUNDS ON WHICH A MARRIAGE OR CIVIL PARTNERSHIP IS VOID

The grounds on which marriage and civil partnership are void, summarized in the table below, are identified in the MCA 1973, s 11 and CPA 2004, s 49. They fall into two categories: (i) the first addresses the parties' 'capacity' to marry or 'eligibility' to form a civil partnership; (ii) the last concerns the failure to observe specified formalities.

Grounds on which marriage or civil partnership void	
Marriage: MCA 1973, s 11	*Civil Partnership: CPA 2004, s 49*
[no equivalent ground]	Void if parties not of the same sex
Parties within the prohibited degrees	Parties within the prohibited degrees
Both parties not over 16	Both parties not over 16
Either party already a spouse or civil partner	Either party already a spouse or civil partner
Rules regarding polygamy breached	[no equivalent ground]
Certain formalities disregarded	Certain formalities disregarded

2.6.1 CAPACITY TO MARRY OR FORM A CIVIL PARTNERSHIP

With the exception of minimum age, the rules relating to capacity do not wholly bar individuals from becoming a spouse or civil partner. The issue is whether the given *couple* have the capacity to marry *each other*.

Gender pattern: the same-sex requirement for civil partnership

The principal distinction between marriage and civil partnership still lies in the parties' legal genders (not their sexual orientation), albeit in a new way: while spouses may be of any gender pattern, civil partners must still be of the same sex.[146]

Gender for these purposes is determined by reference to a person's legally recognized gender, as opposed to self-defined gender; a transgender person's preferred gender will therefore only be their legal gender if they have a gender recognition certificate.[147] A trans person in an originally opposite-sex marriage can now remain married (now in a same-sex marriage) after receiving legal recognition of their preferred gender under the GRA 2004, provided that their spouse consents.[148] However, because civil partnership remains a same-sex only institution, there remains an anomaly for trans individuals who have a civil partnership with their same-sex partner before obtaining gender recognition. Unless that partner is also seeking recognition of their preferred gender (in which case they will remain a same-sex

---

[146] CPA 2004, ss 3(1)(a) and 49(a).
[147] See 2.3.1 above.
[148] GRA 2004, ss 3(6A)–(6C), 4(2), 11A.

couple, now of the other legal gender, so still eligible for civil partnership),[149] the trans person must choose between keeping their civil partnership (as a same-sex couple, in the eyes of the law) and so not having the preferred gender recognized, or having the preferred gender recognized and converting their civil partnership to a marriage.[150] The European Court had previously justified English law's refusal to allow a couple to remain married if one of them obtained legal gender recognition under the GRA 2004, such that they became a same-sex couple. But that was in the context of a legal regime which maintained a clear distinction between the traditional institution of marriage (opposite-sex) and civil partnership (same-sex).[151] That clear distinction has now gone, so it is unclear how the state could justify preventing civil partners retaining that status after one of them has their preferred gender recognized.

So gender still matters—but not only for rare case of the trans person who wishes to retain a civil partnership post-recognition. Some opposite-sex couples might wish to register a civil partnership rather than marry but cannot do so. England and Wales is in an extraordinary position internationally, recently joined by Scotland, in affording same-sex couples *more* formal relationship recognition options than opposite-sex couples. Same-sex couples can marry or have a civil partnership; opposite-sex couples can only marry. All other jurisdictions that recognize same-sex marriage having earlier introduced a registered partnership option have either abolished the latter (with prospective effect—so existing partnerships remain intact but no new ones can be formed),[152] or the latter option is available to all couples.[153]

Does English law's lopsided position breach the opposite-sex couple's rights under Article 14 in conjunction with the right to respect for family and private life under Article 8? Ferguson et al, applicants in a case against the UK Government, lodged with the European Court before the 2013 Act was passed, would say so.[154] Given the date of the application, the case complained about the exclusion of both same-sex couples from marriage and opposite-sex couples from civil partnership. It was recently declared inadmissible.[155] The reasons for that decision are not in the public domain, though the advent of same-sex marriage may have made the case, as formulated, difficult to sustain. But the argument for opposite-sex civil partnership is not therefore unsustainable: it merely requires modification in the new legal environment. Particularly relevant here is the recent European Court decision that a Greek law creating civil partnerships only for *opposite*-sex couples was discriminatory.[156] The Court reiterated that any discrimination on the ground of sex or sexual orientation requires 'particularly weighty reasons' to justify it; no such reasons were found to justify the Greek policy.

Applying that test to the English context, in order to justify the different treatment of opposite-sex couples, the government must identify a 'legitimate aim' for excluding them from civil partnership, and demonstrate that that exclusion is 'necessary' in order to pursue that aim: that latter test is strict in the context of different treatment

---

149 Ibid, ss 4(2)(c), 5B, 11B.
150 Ibid, ss 4(3) and 4A(3).
151 *Parry v United Kingdom* (App No 42971/05, ECHR) (2006).
152 E.g. the Nordic countries.
153 E.g. France, the Netherlands, New Zealand.
154 Ferguson et al (2011).
155 DCMS (2014b), 20.
156 *Vallianatos v Greece* (App Nos 29381/09 and 32684/09, ECHR) (2013).

based on sexual orientation.[157] Yet it is wholly unclear what legitimate aim the current position promotes, whether to justify the general bar or the very specific impact on trans persons in civil partnerships noted above. The government sought to justify the retention of civil partnership (at all) on the basis that it is an 'established mechanism' for recognizing same-sex relationships,[158] and further sought to justify not extending it to opposite-sex couples on the basis that it had been 'unable to identify a need'[159] for it and that 'it has not been made clear what detriment opposite sex couples suffer by not having access to civil partnerships'.[160] Yet none of this amounts to a legitimate aim. It seems particularly odd to suggest that civil partnership should be kept as it is as a means of recognizing same-sex relationships when marriage—hitherto an extremely well-established mechanism for recognizing opposite-sex relationships—has just been opened up to same-sex couples. The European Court has always accepted protection of the traditional family based on (opposite-sex) marriage as a legitimate aim,[161] but it is hard to see that it is legitimate (never mind necessary) to 'protect' civil partner-ship by excluding opposite-sex couples from it. And it seems equally difficult to argue that the newly *non*-traditional concept of marriage requires protection by preventing opposite-sex couples from formalizing their relationships through civil partnership instead—is marriage, newly configured, not equally 'threatened' (if at all) by same-sex couples retaining a choice of institution?[162]

Such analysis was notably absent from the government's recent review of civil partner-ship, which was guided by the following principles:

DCMS, *Civil Partnership Review (England and Wales): A Consultation* (2014a), para 1.7

- Any changes should deliver clear benefits to individuals and society.

- We should avoid taking action that we believe would be detrimental to society or individuals' relationships.

- The fundamental nature of civil partnership as legal recognition of the relationship and public expression of commitment of a loving couple should not be altered, for example to encompass siblings or carers and those they care for.

…We should avoid acting prematurely, before the impact of same sex couples having access to marriage is known.

There is a notable omission amongst these 'principles' of any commitment to equality and non-discrimination, despite that having been the government's basic case for promoting same-sex marriage. It is striking that in its conclusions following the review it noted that, 'Almost no respondents mentioned benefits other than in terms of advancing equality if

---

[157] Ibid.

[158] Government Equalities Office (2012), 2.19.

[159] Ibid, 2.20.

[160] HM Government (2012), 7.9.

[161] E.g. *Schalk and Kopf v Austria* (App No 30141/04, ECHR) (2010); *Parry v United Kingdom* (App No 42971/05, ECHR) (2006).

[162] Compare the reasoning of Baroness Hale in the extract from *Ghaidan v Godin-Mendoza*, at 2.3.2 above.

civil partnerships were opened up to opposite sex couples',[163] as if equality were not a desirable end itself.

The government also queried whether there was a demand for opposite-sex civil partnership (whilst simultaneously expressing alarming concerns about the potential cost of permitting it—costs which would only arise if there *were* huge demand).[164] A preoccupation with the question of 'demand' (low or high) is arguably misplaced. As one MP put it: 'Equality matters. Even if only a few people are being discriminated against, we should all want to stop any such discrimination.'[165] However, the government's own consultation would suggest that there is a demand for it. Twenty per cent of unmarried heterosexual respondents who answered the relevant question said that they would rather form a civil partnership than marry.[166] Contrast that with the 6 per cent of gay, lesbian, and bisexual respondents to the same-sex marriage consultation who said that they would prefer civil partnership to marriage.[167] Neither response can be regarded as nationally representative. But on its face, it seems curious to retain civil partnership only for same-sex couples in the face of those responses. Indeed, various empirical research projects reveal an appetite for civil partnership amongst opposite-sex couples who want the legal consequences of marriage without what they regard as the negative connotations of that institution.

A. Barlow and J. Smithson, 'Legal Assumptions, Cohabitants' Talk and the Rocky Road to Reform', (2010) 22 *Child and Family Law Quarterly* **328, 336–7**

Both of our qualitative studies confirmed that Ideologues [those in long-term, committed relationships in which one or both partners have an ideological objection to marriage] who were choosing not to marry for very clear reasons are capable of adopting a legally rational approach, other than in relation to marriage itself. Participants in this group had almost all made wills, made declarations of ownership in respect of the family home and drawn up next of kin documents in each other's favour. The one legal step they were not generally prepared to take was that of getting married, however advantageous this might prove to be in terms of issues like pensions and inheritance tax. Many expressed their frustration that there was no mechanism other than marriage – often objected to for its patriarchal baggage – through which they could achieve parity with married couples. The symbolism and values associated with the language of marriage was a problem for some:

'The "marriage" word is what's value-laden with all the concepts that we dislike. That's what I object to. If they called it something like "civil contract and joint responsibilities", then fine.' (Peter, long term cohabitant, no children)

Whereas the term 'civil partnership' was much more positively viewed, as Hannah summed up –

'I think just the language of civil partnership is quite interesting. The "civil" clearly is making a statement about it being, you know, not religious; being secular. And "partnership" is clearly about . . . For me it communicates something about equality, um in terms of two equal people

---

163 DCMS (2014b), 2.30.
164 See debate at Hansard HC Deb, vol 563, cols 979–81, 996, 20 May 2013.
165 Julian Huppert MP, Hansard HC Deb, vol 563, col 1010, 20 May 2013.
166 DCMS (2014b), para 2.19.
167 See HM Government (2012), extracted above at p 50.

> making that...Progressing to that point where they want to register their partnership. Whereas marriage comes with so many things in terms of society's expectations or belief about it that, you know, it's very difficult to separate out the legal stuff and the religious stuff from the kind of, um...The way our society operates around traditional male-female relationships.' (Hannah, long term cohabitant)

Other couples whom Barlow and Smithson interviewed felt so strongly against marriage that they were prepared not to marry, despite serious concerns about the impact of inheritance tax and the risk of the surviving partner and children being left homeless. A policy that tries to encourage marriage will have no impact on this group.

> Yet the legal and psychological needs of this very committed and legally rational group would easily be met by the extension of a marriage-like civil partnership to different-sex couples along the lines of the Dutch model. The couples here were not looking for any lesser commitment than marriage – indeed a number considered themselves far more committed to each other than the average married couple – but the patriarchal and quasi-religious tenets embedded within even civil marriage was not something this group were prepared to sign up to, whatever the cost. To view this form of partnership as 'marriage-like' would be to misunderstand the nature and motivations for this style of cohabitation relationship and exposes a weakness in family policy if it fails to provide legal safeguards for what seem to be the 'strong and stable' families it stated it wants to support.

There is clearly a constituency for whom civil partnership would confer its own 'intrinsic value', distinct from marriage.

The government ultimately justified its decision not to change civil partnership '[g]iven the lack of consensus on the way forward'.[168] But that observation could have applied with equal if not greater force to its proposals for same-sex marriage. So, English law remains in a curious position. The government failed to offer any specific analysis of the case for *phasing out* civil partnership by barring new entrants, the stance taken in all other jurisdictions with the same type of regime. Unless that step is taken or civil partnership is opened up, English law may yet prove vulnerable to ECHR challenge on this issue.[169]

There remains the intriguing question of how the courts would react to an opposite-sex couple who managed to dupe a civil registrar into thinking that they were a same-sex couple and registered a civil partnership accordingly. What legal status, if any, would flow from that? If the purported civil partnership were void it would attract legal consequences—as we noted above, curiously, even a void marriage or civil partnership has some legal effects. Alternatively, the purported civil partnership might be regarded as so beyond the pale as to be a 'non-civil partnership',[170] with no legal consequences at all: it had been said that 'a marriage void for the reason that the two parties are of the same sex is not merely void but a meretricious marriage which cannot give rise to anything remotely matrimonial in character'.[171] Since any such couple would know that their actions constituted a

---

[168] Ibid, 4.

[169] The first challenge seems imminent: Bowcott (2014).

[170] We discuss the equivalent concept of 'non-marriage' below at p 77.

[171] *S-T (formerly J) v J* [1998] Fam 103, 146. Cf *Talbot v Talbot* (1967) 111 Sol Jo 213. Contrast recent cases of forced marriage contracted abroad where the courts have refused to recognize the marriage at all rather than declare it to be voidable: e.g. *B v I* [2010] 1 FLR 1721, discussed below at p 87.

direct, essentially political challenge to the law of civil partnership, depriving them of access to 'void' status and its associated remedies may not be unjust.[172] But the category of 'non-marriage' and 'non-civil partnership' is a conceptually problematic one that may be better reserved to cases involving thoroughly defective formalities, particularly given the plain language of s 49 of the CPA 2004, which suggests such cases should simply be classed as void.

Prohibited degrees of relationship and associated formalities

The law of marriage has always barred unions between certain relatives. Over the centuries, the range of prohibited relationships has gradually narrowed[173] and the degree of prohibition on one remaining category (step-relations) relaxed. The most recent relaxation, removing all restrictions on marriages between parents- and children-in-law, was prompted by a decision of the European Court of Human Rights. B and L, both divorced, were father- and daughter-in-law. They had been cohabiting for some time, along with B's grandson (L's son), and wished to marry, but were barred from doing so under the law then in force until both B's first wife (the mother of B's son whom L had married) and B's son (L's first husband) had both died (a quite unpredictable eventuality), or unless they invoked a costly and cumbersome procedure, with 'no discernable rules or precedent', to obtain a personal Act of Parliament permitting their marriage. The majority of a group appointed by the Archbishop of Canterbury had earlier concluded that this bar could not be justified.[174] The restrictions were held to breach B and L's right to marry under Article 12.

B v United Kingdom (App No 36536/02, ECHR) (2006)

36 Article 12 expressly provides for regulation of marriage by national law and given the sensitive moral choices concerned and the importance to be attached to the protection of children and the fostering of secure family environments, this Court must not rush to substitute its own judgment in place of the authorities who are best placed to assess and respond to the needs of society. . . . [A] large number of Contracting States . . . have a similar bar in their law, reflecting apparently similar concerns about allowing marriages of this degree of affinity.

37 The Court must however examine the facts of the case in the context pertaining in the United Kingdom. It observes that this bar on marriage is aimed at protecting the integrity of the family (preventing sexual rivalry between parents and children) and preventing harm to children who may be affected by the changing relationships of the adults around them. These are, without doubt, legitimate aims.

38 Nonetheless, the bar on marriage does not prevent the relationships occurring . . . There are no incest, or other criminal law, provisions to prevent extra-marital relationships between parents-in-law and children-in-law being established notwithstanding that children may

---

172 See Law Com (1970), para 32.
173 E.g. Marriage (Enabling Act) 1960; Marriage (Prohibited Degrees of Relationship) Act 1986. See Cretney (2003a), ch 2.
174 Archbishop of Canterbury's Group (1984).

> live in these homes. It cannot, therefore, be said that in the present case the ban on the applicants' marriage prevents any alleged confusion or emotional insecurity to the second applicant's son...

The Court was also unimpressed that the private Act of Parliament route had enabled some parties in the applicants' position to marry. In response to the government's argument that the bar should be retained because this procedure ensured that exceptions were made only in cases where no harm would arise, it commented:

> 40...that there is no indication of any detailed investigation into family circumstances in the Parliamentary procedure and that in any event a cumbersome and expensive vetting process of this kind would not appear to offer a practically accessible or effective mechanism for individuals to vindicate their rights. [The Court] would also view with reservation a system that would require a person of full age in possession of his or her mental faculties to submit to a potentially intrusive investigation to ascertain whether it is suitable for them to marry...

The in-law restrictions were subsequently repealed.[175]

The current law—identical in effect for marriage and civil partnership—is most clearly set out in the CPA 2004.[176] Different rules apply to: (i) consanguineous and some adoptive[177] relationships, where marriage or civil partnership is absolutely barred; and (ii) step-relationships, where it is permitted in certain cases:

Civil Partnership Act 2004, Sch 1, Part 1: Prohibited Degrees of Relationship[178]

Absolute prohibitions

1 (1) Two people are within prohibited degrees of relationship if one falls within the list below in relation to the other.
Adoptive child
Adoptive parent
Child
Former adoptive child
Former adoptive parent
Grandparent
Grandchild
Parent
Parent's sibling
Sibling
Sibling's child

(2) In the list "sibling" means a brother, sister, half-brother or half-sister.

---

[175] Marriage Act 1949 (Remedial) Order 2006, SI 2007/348.

[176] CPA 2004, s 3(1)(d), (2); MCA 1973, s 11(a)(i).

[177] Adoption and Children Act 2002 (ACA 2002), s 74: adopted persons remain members of their birth family for the purposes of these rules; within their adopted family they are barred only from parent/child unions.

[178] Following *B v United Kingdom* (App No 36536/02, ECHR) (2006), para 3 was not commenced and is due to be repealed. For marriage, see MA 1949, s 1 and Sch 1, as amended.

Qualified prohibitions

2 (1) Two people are within prohibited degrees of relationship if one of them falls within the list below in relation to the other, unless—

    (a) both of them have reached 21 at the time when they register as civil partners of each other, and

    (b) the younger has not at any time before reaching 18 been a child of the family in relation to the other.
    Child of former civil partner
    Child of former spouse
    Former civil partner of grandparent
    Former civil partner of parent
    Former spouse of grandparent
    Former spouse of parent
    Grandchild of former civil partner
    Grandchild of former spouse

  (2) "Child of the family", in relation to another person, means a person who—

    (a) has lived in the same household as that other person, and

    (b) has been treated by that other person as a child of his family.

Where parties falling within the qualified prohibitions wish to marry or become civil partners, additional formal preliminaries apply, though it seems that failure to comply would not invalidate the union.[179]

The rules prohibiting marriage between relations were based originally on biblical grounds.[180] Latterly, the prohibitions were justified by reference to the genetic health of any offspring of such unions.[181] It is curious that identical restrictions apply to civil partnerships and same-sex marriages, since same-sex couples cannot (yet[182]) procreate with the genetic material of both partners. Moreover, genetic problems can arise between unrelated persons and between cousins, who may marry in English law, and the prohibitions extend to adoptive and step-relations. So the rules are better rationalized on social grounds: the undesirability of relatives forming conjugal relationships disrupting other family relationships. The special limits imposed on marriages between step-relations reflect concerns about abuse of power by older family members; barring such marriages may deter people from pursuing these relationships at all. The criminalization of sexual activity between family members now largely corresponds with the remaining prohibited degrees.[183] One curious exception relates to adoptive relationships, where marriage between adoptive parent and child is absolutely barred, even though sexual activity between them, once both

179 MA 1949, ss 16(1A)–(2B), 27B–C; Marriage (Registrar-General's Licence) Act 1970, s 3; CPA 2004, Sch 1, Part 2.

180 Canon law has biblical origins: Leviticus chs 18 and 20; Deuteronomy 27; 1 Corinthians 5.

181 Law Com (1970), paras 51–3; Archbishop of Canterbury's Group (1984); cf Human Fertilisation and Embryology Act 1990, s 31ZB.

182 Except in the controversial case of mitochondrial donation, which it is contemplated would only be used in case of medical need, not simply as a means of permitting two women to be genetically related to the child: see 9.4.3.

183 Sexual Offences Act 2003, ss 64–5, and where one party is under 18, ss 25–9; cf *Stübing v Germany* (App No 43547/08, ECHR) (2012).

are adult, is apparently permitted.[184] However, the law fails to pursue the social rationale to its logical limit. For example, why are adopted relatives (aside from parent and child) excluded from the prohibitions?[185] Why can people marry former *cohabiting* partners of their parents without restriction? While step-grandparents and child are barred from marrying before both are 21 where the younger has at *any* time when under 18 been treated as a child of the step-grandparent's family in the same household, the criminal law seems not to ban sexual activity between them once the child is over 16 and they no longer share a household.[186] Given these inconsistencies, the prohibited degrees may yet be subject to further reform.[187]

The age of the parties and associated formalities

Until 1929, the minimum age for marriage was 12 for a girl and 14 for a boy.[188] The basic rule now is that no person under the age of 16 may enter into marriage or civil partnership.[189] In the case of marriages between step-relations, the prohibited degrees rules raise the age limit to 21. The Law Commission considered but rejected the argument that marriages of children should be merely voidable (valid unless annulled at the instance of one of the parties); or ratifiable (void unless affirmed by the parties after majority is attained).[190] Under-age marriages are therefore void, and so vulnerable to challenge by third parties, even many years after the child in question has reached majority and is happily married, and even if both parties were ignorant that either of them was under 16 at the time of marriage. The basic age rule corresponds with the criminal law of sexual offences against children[191] and child abduction,[192] so it may be surmised that it is designed to protect children from undesirable sexual activity. The age limits also reflect the seriousness of marriage and civil partnership and the obligations inherent in them, and the need for a mature consent.[193]

Mature minors, aged 16 or 17, may validly marry or become civil partners. But special formal requirements apply, depending on whether the marriage is preceded by civil or (in the case of opposite-sex marriage) Anglican preliminary procedures. Save in the rare case of widowed children, some Anglican marriages, all marriages preceded by civil preliminary procedures, and civil partnerships involving 16- and 17-year-olds ordinarily require the consent of a parent with parental responsibility and/or of another statutorily defined 'appropriate person'.[194] Where those eligible to consent are absent, inaccessible, or under a disability, the court may consent instead, or the registrar may dispense with the consent requirement. If a person whose consent is required refuses to consent, court consent may be obtained.[195] Court consent is required where the child is a ward of court. However, failure

---

[184] ACA 2002, s 74.

[185] Law Com (1970), para 50; sexual activity between adult adoptive relations is not criminal.

[186] Sexual Offences Act 2003, s 27(4).

[187] See Gaffney-Rhys (2005), 957; cf Cretney (2006b).

[188] Age of Marriage Act 1929 raised age to current level of 16; see Cretney (2003a), 57–8.

[189] MCA 1973, s 11(a)(ii), MA 1949, ss 2 and 3; CPA 2004, ss 3(1)(c) and 4.

[190] Law Com (1970), paras 16–20.

[191] Sexual Offences Act 2003, principally ss 5–13; in the case of sexual offences involving mature minors, note the marriage/civil partnership exception in ss 23 and 28.

[192] Child Abduction Act 1984, s 2.

[193] For international human rights instruments in this field and comparative examples, see Gaffney-Rhys (2009).

[194] MA 1949, s 3; CPA 2004, Sch 2, Part 1. For analysis of these rules, see Probert (2009a).

[195] MA 1949, s 3(1); CPA 2004, Sch 2, Part 2.

to *obtain* appropriate consent will not of itself invalidate a marriage or civil partnership.[196] Only where an appropriate person positively registers *dissent* and no court consent is substituted is the marriage or civil partnership void.[197] In the case of Anglican marriages preceded by the publication of banns, parental consent is not required; but if the parent or other appropriate person has publicly and openly declared his or her dissent in church when the banns are published, any later marriage under those banns will be void.[198] In the case of civil partnership, dissent renders the partnership void even if the parties were unaware of the impediment; the position in relation to marriage is arguably less clear.[199]

The age limits selected by English law may not be compatible with the marriage practices of some minority religions observed in the UK. An application to Strasbourg challenging this as incompatible with Articles 9, 12, and 14 ECHR was declared inadmissible, the age limits falling with the state's freedom to regulate marriage.[200]

The requirement of parental consent for child spouses was originally designed to prevent imprudent marriages. However, as Munby J has observed, in contemporary society where the average age at marriage is now over 30, the numbers of teenagers marrying at all is relatively small[201] and children whose parents withhold consent to marriage are simply likely to cohabit instead. The greater concern now is not to prevent unwise marriages by children, but forced ones: not to uphold parental rights to resist a child's proposed marriage, but to prevent an abuse of parental power by forcibly engineering a marriage.[202] Prior to the Forced Marriage (Civil Protection) Act 2007, the courts developed their wardship and inherent jurisdiction to protect children (and vulnerable adults) in such cases;[203] and immigration rules now place an age bar of 18 on marriage visas.[204] The duress entailed in such cases renders the marriage voidable, and we consider this issue further below in that context.

Monogamy

Under English law, marriage and civil partnership are monogamous and mutually exclusive states: one may only have one spouse or civil partner at any one time and one cannot simultaneously be a spouse and a civil partner.[205] A marriage or civil partnership contracted where either party is already a spouse or civil partner is automatically void, regardless of the parties' knowledge, and remains void even if the other spouse or civil partner subsequently dies or a divorce is obtained. Parties who knowingly give false information regarding their status in this regard for the purpose of procuring a marriage or civil partnership commit an offence.[206] However, the statutory offence of bigamy is confined to marriage.[207]

---

196 In the case of civil marriages, MA 1949, s 48(1)(b). The parties may be guilty of perjury: Perjury Act 1911, s 3(1); CPA 2004, s 80.

197 MA 1949, ss 30 and 49(b); CPA 2004, s 49(c).

198 MA 1949, ss 3(3) and 25(c); for marriages under common licence, ss 16(1)(c), (2) and 25(c).

199 The issue turns on the effect of ss 49(b) and 25(c) on the declaration of voidness made by ss 30 and 3(3) respectively.

200 *Khan v United Kingdom* (App No 11579/85, ECHR) (1986).

201 Compare the figures for 2008 with 1981, ONS (2010c), table 5.

202 *A Local Authority v N, Y and K (By her Children's Guardian)* [2005] EWHC 2956, [78]–[84].

203 Ibid; see also Probert (2009a).

204 Cf *R (Quila, Bibi) v Secretary of State for the Home Department* [2011] UKSC 45.

205 MCA 1973, s 11(b); CPA 2004, ss 3(1)(b), 49(a).

206 Perjury Act 1911, s 3; CPA 2004, s 80.

207 Offences Against the Person Act 1861, s 57.

Cases may arise where one party's original spouse or partner has been missing for some time, and is honestly and reasonably presumed to be dead. A second union will nevertheless be void if it transpires that the 'deceased' was still alive at the time of the ceremony. However, it is possible to apply for a declaration that the missing party is presumed to be dead, thereby dissolving the marriage or civil partnership.[208] The missing party is presumed dead if continuously absent for seven years and the applicant has no reason to believe that he or she has been alive during that time.[209] Once the declaration has been made, the 'survivor' may then validly form a new marriage or civil partnership, even if the 'deceased' later appears and the declaration is varied or revoked.[210]

Polygamy

Rules about polygamous unions apply only to marriage, and in practice only to opposite-sex marriage. Since no jurisdiction permits polygamous civil partnership or same-sex marriage, the issue does not arise there. Polygamy has required attention from English law as a result of migration from jurisdictions where polygamy is lawfully practised.[211] English law does not itself permit the creation of polygamous marriages, so any purportedly polygamous marriage created by a ceremony conducted in England and Wales will at best be void,[212] and may be treated as a non-marriage. To create a valid marriage through a ceremony conducted, for example, in a mosque, that ceremony must comply with the formal requirements set out in the MA 1949 for non-Anglican religious marriages, and will create a monogamous marriage.[213]

But does English law recognize polygamous marriages contracted abroad by those domiciled in England and Wales?[214] There is a distinction between actually and potentially polygamous marriages. If a man takes more than one wife, both marriages are actually polygamous. A marriage is only *potentially* polygamous when a husband takes his first wife under a law permitting him to take another. In 1972, Parliament adopted a policy of cultural assimilation: any polygamous marriage, whether actually polygamous or potentially so, contracted by someone domiciled in England and Wales would be void. As Sebastian Poulter observed:

> the provision was framed so widely that it was liable to bar, for example, Muslims from the Indian subcontinent who had acquired a domicile of choice here, from returning to their countries of origin to enter into a first marriage through an Islamic wedding. This restricted them in their choice of ceremony since an Islamic form of marriage cannot validly be contracted in England.[215]

---

[208] Presumption of Death Act 2013, ss 1 and 3(2).

[209] Ibid, s 2.

[210] Ibid, s 6(2).

[211] See 1.2.6. On associated immigration rules, see Immigration Act 1988, s 2; Immigration Rules, r 278; *Bibi v United Kingdom* (App No 19628/92, ECHR) (1992).

[212] *R v Bham* [1966] 1 QB 159.

[213] See p 2.5.3 above.

[214] Recognition of marriages contracted abroad by those domiciled abroad is an issue of private international law: see Collins (2014), ch 17; *Official Solicitor v Yemoh* [2010] EWHC 3727.

[215] Poulter (1998), 50–1.

After unsatisfactory judicial attempts to mitigate the resulting harshness the Law Commission recommended reform.[216] If a *potentially* polygamous marriage is contracted abroad by someone domiciled in England and Wales, it is now valid.[217] If a second marriage is then celebrated abroad by either party, the first marriage will not be invalidated since validity is determined at the start of marriage. But if either party to that second marriage is domiciled in England and Wales, that second—actually polygamous—marriage will be void.[218]

2.6.2 DISREGARD OF FORMAL REQUIREMENTS

Void marriages

The rules about which formal defects invalidate particular types of marriage are as labyrinthine as the laws relating to the formalities themselves. The MA 1949 is silent about the effects of failing to comply with some formalities, but in the absence of provision expressly rendering a marriage void, it will be valid despite the formal defect.[219] We have already considered the effect of breach of the requirements regarding mature minors and step-relations.

Some formal requirements are mandatory—their non-observance will render the marriage or civil partnership void, though only if (in the case of marriage) the parties are guilty of 'knowing and wilful disregard' of the fact that they are failing to comply with that requirement. It has not been decided whether the parties need know only that they have failed to comply with the relevant formality, or whether it must additionally be shown that they know that the effect is to invalidate the marriage; the CPA 2004, s 49(b) simply requires that both parties 'know' of the relevant defect. Broadly speaking, a marriage or civil partnership is void where the parties know that the ceremony or registration was conducted: without completion of the key preliminary requirements; in a place other than that specified in the original notice; after expiry of the period of time following completion of the preliminaries during which the marriage or partnership may be celebrated; or without a properly authorized celebrant or registrar being present.[220]

Other requirements are directory—their non-observance may involve a criminal offence by the registrar or other responsible person, but will not invalidate the union, even if the parties know that they have failed to comply with them. For example, breaches of the rules regarding the time of the ceremony, public access to it, the presence of witnesses, use of the prescribed words, and failure to register are not invalidating.[221]

Non-marriages

Some departures from the formal requirements are so substantial that the courts have held there to be no marriage at all.[222] *Hudson v Leigh* offers an illustration. The parties

---

216 Law Com (1985a).
217 MCA 1973, s 11(d).
218 Ibid.
219 *Campbell v Corley* (1856) 4 WR 675.
220 MA 1949, ss 25, 30, and 49; CPA 2004, s 49(b)(c).
221 Law Com (1973a), Annex, para 120; see also MA 1949, ss 24 and 48.
222 Cf Le Grice (2013), who rejects the category of non-marriage entirely.

wished to marry. The wife, a devout Christian, wanted to marry in a religious ceremony, but the husband, a wealthy 'atheist Jew', did not. They compromised. They would have a Christian ceremony (in South Africa) which would satisfy the wife that they were 'married in the eyes of God', but it was agreed by them and the celebrant that the service would not create a legal marriage. Specific passages from the normal wedding service were accordingly omitted, in particular, the question whether anyone present knows any lawful impediment to their marriage, and any reference to the parties as 'lawful' husband or wife, or to their being 'lawfully' married. The service proceeded as planned. The parties then returned to London where, it had been understood, they would get married in a civil ceremony. Unfortunately, their relationship broke down between fixtures, and the wife began divorce proceedings.

But could they divorce? Not if there were no valid marriage to begin with. And the wife would not be entitled to a decree of nullity and the right to apply for financial orders consequent upon that decree unless there was a void marriage. The wife argued that the South African ceremony had created a lawful marriage, or at least a void marriage, contending that cases suggesting the existence of a third category—the so-called 'non-marriage'—were wrongly decided. The husband argued that the ceremony amounted only to a non-marriage, and that the wife therefore had no right to apply for financial orders. The husband won. The South African ceremony was certainly defective as a result of South African marriage formalities law so at least void.[223] But the judge went further, holding there was no marriage at all:

Hudson v Leigh [2009] EWHC 1306

BODEY J:

69. I would find it unrealistic and illogical to conclude that there is no such concept as a ceremony or event which, whilst having marriage-like characteristics, fails in law to effect a marriage. Such is the ingenuity of human beings that we will always be able to come up with some sort of ritual or happening which one party claims created a marriage but which the other says fell short of doing so. Rare though this will be, the law has to be able to determine the issue without being constrained (except of course where statute so requires) to go down the nullity route.... Rebecca Probert [(2002a) suggests that] the 'marriage within a play' example (such as in Romeo and Juliet)...is a 'non-marriage'...because it in no way ever purports to be a real marriage, a feature which she suggests is linked to, but distinct from, the issue of the parties' intentions. The concept of 'non-marriage' should she argues: "...also apply to alternative, self-devised rituals, should anyone wish to argue the legal validity of, for example hand-fasting or a broomstick wedding" (these being old rites here and on the continent, thought by some in days gone by to create married status).[224]

70. It is inherently difficult to come up with examples (of a questionable ceremony, ritual or event) which do not appear fanciful; but take a nervous and eccentric couple who wished to have a full dress-rehearsal of their wedding ceremony, so as to be sure that everything would go alright on the day. Assume that the vicar was present and that he used the full wording

---

[223] The formal validity of the marriage was governed by South African law, as the law of the place where the ceremony had occurred. For fuller discussion of applicable law in case of a foreign marriage, see *Assad v Kurter* [2013] EWHC 3852.

[224] See Probert (2009b) on the falsity of these beliefs.

of the marriage service. Assume wedding-outfits, bridesmaids, flowers, music, an Order of Ceremony and the presence of many of the intended guests, but with its being known that the occasion was not the real thing. What if that the relationship were then to break down prior to the actual wedding day?

71.... [I]t was but a rehearsal and was neither arranged to, nor intended to, nor was it purporting to achieve any legal outcome at all (even though in principle the parties' underlying wish and purpose was to be married).... I distinguish the possible example of where the minister is intending to celebrate a marriage in the normal way, but where the parties are participating for a (perhaps) drunken bet, or dare: that is a very different matter and would call for quite different considerations should it arise...

Bodey J then set out key factors for determining the status of a purported marriage:

79.... [I]t is not in my view either necessary or prudent to attempt in the abstract a definition or test of the circumstances in which a given event having marital characteristics should be held not to be a marriage. Questionable ceremonies should I think be addressed on a case by case basis, taking account of the various factors and features mentioned above including particularly, but not exhaustively: (a) whether the ceremony or event set out and purported to be a lawful marriage; (b) whether it bore all or enough of the hallmarks of marriage; (c) whether the three key participants (most especially the officiating official) believed, intended and understood the ceremony as giving rise to the status of lawful marriage [under English law[225]]; and (d) the reasonable perceptions, understandings and beliefs of those in attendance [though these cannot be decisive in converting an occasion which all three participants fundamentally meant not to be effective into a marriage in law]. In most if not all reasonably foreseeable situations, a review of these and similar considerations should enable a decision to be satisfactorily reached.

He accordingly made a declaration that there never was a marriage.

It may be felt that no injustice was done to the wife in that case, who was apparently deliberately trying not to create a marriage in the South African ceremony. The same might not always be said about the apparently growing number of ceremonies conducted in England and Wales in which parties marry in accordance with their own religious rites but who (entirely innocently) fail to comply with the formal requirements necessary to create a marriage recognized in English law.[226] Many of these marriages may be solemnized on religious premises; these can be authorized as registered premises for civil marriages, but it appears that relatively few have been.[227] Some of these marriages take place on private premises. Unlike actors in a stage play or couples rehearsing, these couples may honestly believe that they are validly married in the eyes of the state as well as their god—and the women, in particular, may be left especially vulnerable by a finding of non-marriage.

For example, in *Gandhi v Patel*,[228] the parties had a lavish Hindu wedding conducted by a Brahmin priest in an Indian restaurant in London, but did not observe any formal requirements of English law; they could only have created a valid marriage by marrying 'again' in a register office or other approved or registered premises.[229] Unbeknownst to the

---

225 *El Gamal v Al Maktoum* [2011] EWHC 3763, [81].
226 See Talwar (2010), Gaffney-Rhys (2013), 58.
227 ONS (2010a), table 3.43; see 2.5.3 above.
228 [2002] 1 FLR 603.
229 Which could include a temple: MA 1949, ss 35, 41–4; Places of Worship Registration Act 1855.

wife, the husband was already married, so any marriage would in any event have been void for that reason. But would the restaurant marriage even count as a void marriage, given the informal circumstances of its creation? The issue arose when the husband died having made no financial provision for the wife in his will. She sought to apply to court under its powers to redistribute property from the deceased's estate amongst certain family members.[230] To be eligible to make that application, she had to prove at least a void marriage,[231] a claim which the beneficiaries of the husband's estate rejected. The judge decided that the ceremony created only a non-marriage, relying on dicta in another case, *A-M v A-M*, concerning the celebration of a wedding under Islamic rites in a private flat:

A-M v A-M (Divorce: Jurisdiction: Validity of Marriage) [2001] 2 FLR 6 (Fam Div)

HUGHES J:

58...A marriage which purports to be conducted under [the Marriage Acts] may nevertheless be void for want of formality...But unless a marriage purports to be of the kind contemplated by the Marriage Acts, it is not...a marriage for the purposes of s 11.... No doubt it is possible to envisage cases where the question whether a particular ceremony or other event does or does not purport to be a marriage of the kind contemplated by the Marriage Acts is a fine one. *Gereis v Yagoub* [1997] 1 FLR 854 was one such, where [the judge] concluded that but for the absence of notice to the superintendent registrar and the lack of registration of the building the ceremony would have been one valid in English law; the decision may have been a merciful one. It is clear, however, that the present ceremony did not begin to purport to be a marriage according to the Marriage Acts, with or without fatal defects. It was not conducted under the rites for the Church of England, nor was there ever any question of an application for, still less a grant of, a superintendent registrar's certificate, and it was conducted in a flat which was clearly none of the places which were authorised for marriage. The ceremony was consciously an Islamic one rather than such as is contemplated by the Marriage Acts...[N]obody purported to conduct or take part in a Marriage Act 1949 ceremony, and the fact that no one applied their mind to how English law would view what they did does not alter that conclusion...[T]he...ceremony is neither a valid marriage in English law nor one in respect of which jurisdiction exists to grant a decree of nullity.

However, the courts have struggled to provide a coherent account of which formal requirements are so essential to creating a Marriage Act-style marriage that their omission plunges couples into the legal black hole of non-marriage. Whilst at first sight appealing, the notion that the parties' intentions should be relevant is problematic. Upsetting parties' intentions and beliefs about the validity of their marriage may often appear harsh: in *Dukali v Lamrani*, the parties, following in the footsteps of many others before them, celebrated their marriage in a notarized ceremony in the Moroccan Consulate. They had given no notice of intention to marry, the notary was not an authorized person, and the Consulate was not an approved premises—it was held to be a non-marriage.[232] However, Rebecca Probert has cogently

---

[230] Inheritance (Provision for Family and Dependants) Act 1975.
[231] Ibid, ss 1(1)(a) and 25(4).
[232] [2012] EWHC 1748.

argued that parties' intentions (and those of the celebrant and others present) should neither rescue something from being a non-marriage because of its egregious lack of formalities, nor cause a non-marriage to emerge from a ceremony that is formally valid.[233] If party intentions were relevant, even determinative, why would we bother having formal requirements at all? And can we even ascertain the parties' intentions sufficiently reliably to determine such an important issue of legal status?

R. Probert, 'The Evolving Concept of Non-Marriage', (2013) 25 *Child and Family Law Quarterly* 318, 333–4

From a pragmatic point of view, the difficulties of placing weight on the intention of the parties alone are obvious. After all, it will be rare for a case to come to court where the parties are in agreement about their intentions. If they have discovered some flaw in their ceremony and wish to remedy it, it would be simpler, quicker and cheaper to go through a new ceremony of marriage rather than to litigate over the status of the first. If they have separated, then at least one of them may wish to deny that there was ever any intention to marry. And if one has died, then, despite sympathy for the survivor, claims based solely on intention should be regarded with caution.

And it is not, after all, a simple conflict between intention and form. Couples manifest their intention to enter into a legally binding marriage by going through a ceremony in a prescribed form. As Lord Brougham put it in *Warrender v Warrender*, each nation lays down its own forms and solemnities, 'compliance with which shall be deemed the only criterion of the intention to enter into the contract' . . .

Moreover, given that many of the disputed ceremonies involve religious weddings, ascertaining whether there was an intention to enter into a legally binding ceremony of marriage may be difficult. . . . [Their conduct following the ceremony, e.g. in starting to live together and to commence a sexual relationship] may, of course, simply indicate that they regarded the religious ceremony as sufficient to legitimate their subsequent relationship, regardless of its legal standing. For those with strong religious convictions, a ceremony that is valid in the eyes of their god may well be more important in this sense than one that is legally valid. In short, intention alone is an unsatisfactory criterion by which to assess the validity of a marriage.

Instead, she argues, the answer to what will yield a non-marriage can be discerned by careful reading of the MA 1949. Thus, total non-compliance with formalities (as in *Dukali*) will clearly result in a non-marriage; but, she argues, provided the parties have either given the required notice or married in an authorized location, their marriage will be valid, notwithstanding innocent[234] breaches of the other formal requirements.[235] If we are dissatisfied with that, the answer lies not in undermining formality law by allowing party intention to influence the outcome unpredictably, but instead in reforming our formality law to make it easier, in particular, for adherents to minority faiths to create valid marriages through their own religious ceremonies.[236]

---

233 Cf *Galloway v Goldstein* [2012] EWHC 60.
234 Cf 'knowing and wilful disregard', which will result in a void marriage.
235 Probert (2013a); e.g. *MA v JA* [2012] EWHC 2219.
236 See 2.5.3 above.

Rescuing a non-marriage: the presumption of marriage

The courts have sometimes been prepared to rescue individuals from a finding of non-marriage via the presumption of marriage. This presumption comes in two forms: it may be presumed that parties are married, despite the lack of positive evidence of a valid ceremony, where they have cohabited for such a period of time and in such circumstances that they are reputed to be married; alternatively, where there is evidence of a ceremony having taken place and the parties have subsequently lived together as husband and wife, it will be presumed that the ceremony complied with the formal requirements of English law.[237]

In *Chief Adjudication Officer v Bath*,[238] the parties went through a Sikh wedding ceremony which did not fulfil English law's formal requirements; there was no marriage certificate. Nevertheless, the couple lived as man and wife for nearly 40 years, during which time the man paid his tax and national insurance contributions on the basis that he was married. The woman later applied for a widow's pension, but her application was refused because there was no evidence of a valid marriage. The Court of Appeal held the marriage to be valid: the facts required to demonstrate that the marriage was void owing to defective formalities could not be proved. However, Evans LJ also considered, alternatively, that the presumption of marriage saved the marriage. His conclusion, and the other non-marriage and presumption cases, have been cogently criticized by Probert: it is one thing to presume that a valid marriage occurred when there is no evidence of any ceremony, or no evidence that the ceremony that did occur was formally valid, quite another to presume a marriage where the only known ceremony was plainly invalid and there is no evidence that a further ceremony might have occurred.[239]

By contrast, it was conceivable in *A-M v A-M (Divorce: Jurisdiction: Validity of Marriage)*[240] that the parties, domiciled abroad, might have contracted an Islamic marriage by proxy, the wife having granted power of attorney to her husband for this purpose. But Probert queries whether the English courts should presume that a marriage has been contracted in these circumstances. In that case, it was advantageous to the wife to presume a marriage, but in other circumstances the assertion of a marriage by proxy, a procedure readily open to abuse, might be undesirable as a matter of policy, not least since the UK is a signatory to the UN Convention on Consent to Marriage which requires that consent be given in person.[241] She concludes that the courts are using the presumption of marriage in an unprincipled manner in order to achieve fair outcomes for parties to non-Christian faiths who seem to be particularly susceptible to a finding of 'non-marriage' for want of proper formalities.[242] Again, the better solution lies in reform of marriage formalities.

---

[237] *Chief Adjudication Officer v Bath* [2000] 1 FLR 8, [20].

[238] Ibid.

[239] Probert (2002a), 412–13. See *Al-Saedy v Musawi* [2010] EWHC 3293, [72]; *MA v JA* [2012] EWHC 2219, [83].

[240] [2001] 2 FLR 6.

[241] Probert (2002a), 416.

[242] Cf the Coptic Orthodox Christians in *Gereis v Yagoub* [1997] 1 FLR 854.

2.7 GROUNDS ON WHICH A MARRIAGE OR CIVIL PARTNERSHIP IS VOIDABLE

Since a voidable marriage or civil partnership is valid unless and until annulled on the application of one of the parties during their joint lives, we might ask why these grounds should exist at all, rather than simply leaving dissatisfied parties to divorce. However, the concept of the voidable marriage is important for faith groups, since to annul a marriage because of some impediment present from the outset is doctrinally distinct from dissolving a valid marriage.[243] The category of voidable marriage has therefore been retained—and extended to civil partnership (notwithstanding the wholly secular nature of that institution). Annulment of voidable unions now takes effect prospectively: the existence of the marriage or civil partnership prior to the decree is unaffected.[244]

The voidable grounds for opposite-sex and same-sex marriage and for civil partnership are mostly shared, and it will be assumed in the following discussion that principles from the case law relating to marriage apply to civil partnership. However, some sex-related grounds—concerning failure to consummate and venereal disease—do not apply to civil partnership, and failure to consummate does not apply to same-sex marriage. Why this should be is intriguing in two senses: why they should apply only to (opposite-sex) marriage, and why they should apply to any marriage at all.

Grounds on which marriage and civil partnership voidable	
Marriage: MCA 1973, s 12(1)	*Civil Partnership: CPA 2004, s 50*
Lack of valid consent by either party	Lack of valid consent by either party
Either party suffering from mental disorder rendering 'unfit' for marriage	Either party suffering from mental disorder rendering 'unfit' for civil partnership
Respondent pregnant by a third party at time of marriage	Respondent pregnant by a third party at time of civil partnership
Grounds relating to gender recognition	Grounds relating to gender recognition
Respondent had venereal disease at time of marriage	[no equivalent ground]
Grounds relating to non-consummation	[no equivalent ground]
—*opposite-sex marriage only*—*no equivalent for same-sex marriage: s 12(2)*	

Nearly all of the grounds on which marriage and civil partnership may be avoided may be regarded as in some way relating to a defect in the parties' consent,[245] either in the sense that no consent was given, or that the apparent consent was vitiated by the presence or absence of some crucial factor or condition with or without which the consent could not be fully effective. Since all voidable grounds can be raised only by a party to the

---

243 Law Com (1970), Part III.
244 MCA 1973, s 16; CPA 2004, s 37(3).
245 Law Com (1970), para 24(b).

relationship, the spouses essentially have a discretion to determine whether the grounds matter to them at all.[246]

Statutory bars prevent decrees of nullity in some circumstances.[247] Several of the voidable grounds are subject to specific bars which we examine below. But a general, estoppel-type bar applies to all grounds:

Matrimonial Causes Act 1973, s 13(1)[248]

The court shall not . . . grant a decree of nullity on the ground that a marriage is voidable if the respondent satisfies the court—

(a) that the petitioner, with knowledge that it was open to him to have the marriage avoided, so conducted himself in relation to the respondent as to lead the respondent reasonably to believe that he would not seek to do so; and

(b) that it would be unjust to the respondent to grant the decree.

This provision, which replaced the old defence of approbation, was considered in *D v D (Nullity: Statutory Bar)*.[249] The court noted differences between the old defence and s 13: the matter need no longer be considered from the perspective of public policy, but simply in terms of what is required to do justice between the individual parties. The test's two-part nature may make it hard to invoke. Given the jurisdiction to make financial orders on nullity decrees, and the ready availability of divorce, the bar may rarely be imposed.

2.7.1 LACK OF VALID CONSENT

Consent lies at the heart of both marriage and civil partnership. The need for consent—and the right not to be married without it—is recognized by several international human rights instruments.[250] The issue has arisen recently in relation to forced marriage and parties with limited mental capacity, often in cases concerned to prevent such marriages going ahead at all, rather than in subsequent nullity proceedings. It may seem odd that so important an issue as lack of consent should not render a marriage void—indeed, that was the position at common law. However, such a marriage could subsequently be ratified by the non-consenting party, and the need for close factual investigation of alleged lack of consent makes it better suited to the voidable category. So the MCA 1973 made that change, on the Law Commission's recommendation.[251]

The MCA 1973 and the CPA 2004 provide that marriage or civil partnership will be voidable wherever one party did not 'validly consent' to it, enumerating situations in which that might be so: 'duress, mistake, unsoundness of mind, or otherwise'.[252] Lack of consent may be relied on by either party, not only the party whose consent it is claimed was lacking.

---

[246] *Sandwell MBC v RG and others* [2013] EWHC 2373.

[247] MCA 1973, s 13; CPA 2004, s 51.

[248] CPA 2004, s 51(1).

[249] [1979] Fam 70.

[250] Universal Declaration of Human Rights, Art 16; UN Convention on the Elimination of All Forms of Discrimination Against Women, General Recommendation No 21; UNCRC, Arts 19 and 35; UN Convention on Consent to Marriage, Minimum Age for Marriage and Registration of Marriage, Art 1.

[251] Law Com (1970), paras 11–15; cf McClean and Hayes (2011), 79–80.

[252] MCA 1973, s 12(1)(c); CPA 2004, s 50(1)(a).

Proceedings on this ground must ordinarily be initiated within three years of the marriage or civil partnership.[253]

Before examining the bases on which consent might be vitiated or absent, we must identify what it is that must be consented to. *Vervaeke v Smith* is instructive on this point and on English law's attitude towards the institution of marriage. The petitioner was a Belgian prostitute who married an Englishman in order to acquire British nationality and so avoid deportation.[254] The couple parted immediately after the ceremony, never intending to live as husband and wife and never doing so. The issue of the marriage's validity arose years later when the petitioner sought to inherit from her second 'husband'. She could only succeed (at that time) if the first marriage were void[255] for want of consent. She failed in the English courts, but subsequently obtained a decree of nullity in Belgium which she then sought to have recognized in England. In the course of considering—and refusing—that application, the House of Lords approved remarks of Ormrod J:

Vervaeke (formerly Messina) v Smith and others [1983] 1 AC 145, 151–3

"Where a man and a woman consent to marry one another in a formal ceremony, conducted in accordance with the formalities required by law, knowing that it is a marriage ceremony, it is immaterial that they do not intend to live together as man and wife.... [I]f the parties exchange consents to marry with due formality, intending to acquire the status of married persons, it is immaterial that they intend the marriage to take effect in some limited way or that one or both of them may have been mistaken about or unaware of some of the incidents of the status which they have created. To hold otherwise would impair the effect of the whole system of law regulating marriages in this country, and gravely diminish the value of the system of registration of marriages upon which so much depends in a modern community. Lord Merrivale in *Kelly (orse. Hyams) v. Kelly*...said: 'In a country like ours, where the marriage status is of very great consequence and where the enforcement of the marriage laws is a matter of great public concern, it would be intolerable if the marriage of law could be played with by people who thought fit to go to a register office and subsequently, after some change of mind, to affirm that it was not a marriage because they did not so regard it.'..."

Interestingly, Lord Hailsham went on to contrast the approaches of English and Belgian law, the latter having granted a decree of nullity where the former would not. As the Belgian court had put it in this case:

"According to section 146 Civil Law, there is no marriage when there is no consent. The consent being an essential condition and element of the marriage, the lack of consent has as consequence the absolute invalidity of that marriage. As the parties...delusively indulged in a marriage ceremony without in fact really consenting to a marriage, they behaved against public policy. The disturbance of public order, the protection of what belongs to the essence of a real marriage and of human dignity, exact that such a sham-marriage be declared invalid."

---

253 MCA 1973, s 13(2)(4)(5); CPA 2004, s 51(2)–(4). Cf *B v I* [2010] 1 FLR 1721, a decision under the inherent jurisdiction addressed below in relation to duress.

254 Cf the new rules designed to prevent such marriages considered in *R (On the Application of Baiai and others) v Secretary of State for the Home Department* [2008] UKHL 53.

255 Would the English courts' reasoning apply equally now that the marriage is merely voidable? Cf Bradney (1984) on duress cases.

While English law reaches the opposite result, it is striking that its reasons for declaring the marriage valid are at root very similar to the reasons offered by Belgian law for reaching the opposite conclusion: upholding the seriousness of the institution of marriage as a matter of public policy.[256]

Duress

The law on duress has received considerable attention in cases involving forced marriages. It is important to appreciate the difference between forced and arranged marriages:[257]

Re SK (Proposed Plaintiff) (An Adult by Way of her Litigation Friend)
[2004] EWHC 3202

SINGER J:

7. . . . [T]here is a spectrum of forced marriage from physical force or fear of injury or death in their most literal form, through to the undue imposition of emotional pressure which is at the other end of the forced marriage range, and that a grey area then separates unacceptable forced marriage from marriages arranged traditionally which are in no way to be condemned, but rather supported as a conventional concept in many societies. Social expectations can of themselves impose emotional pressure and the grey area . . . is where one may slip into the other: arranged may become forced but forced is always different from arranged.

Statutory civil remedies and criminal offences now exist to protect potential and actual victims of forced marriages. The courts have also developed the inherent jurisdiction to protect suspected victims[258] and generally to ensure that vulnerable individuals are able to give full and genuine consent to any marriage proposed for them, beyond what the law of nullity requires by way of consent for the marriage to be valid.[259] Prevention is better than cure.[260]

ONLINE RESOURCE CENTRE

We examine the civil and criminal law responses to forced marriage on the Online Resource Centre.

Our principal concern here, however, is with the diagnosis and cure: to determine when a marriage or civil partnership may be annulled owing to duress. Forced marriages are voidable under the MCA 1973; arranged marriages, to which both parties consent, are not. One difficulty in this scheme has been encountered (and simply sidestepped) in recent cases involving the recognition of forced marriages contracted abroad. The victims brought their

---

256 See also *SH v KH* 2006 SC 129 in Scots law.
257 See generally Mody (2015).
258 *Re SK (Proposed Plaintiff) (An Adult by Way of her Litigation Friend)* [2004] EWHC 3202.
259 *Re SA (Vulnerable Adult with Capacity: Marriage)* [2005] EWHC 2942.
260 *NS v MI* [2006] EWHC 1646, [7] per Munby J.

proceedings too late in terms of the MCA 1973: as noted above, nullity petitions based on lack of consent must be brought within three years of the ceremony. That period cannot be extended, say, because the victim of a forced marriage was prevented by family circumstances (which may be tantamount to false imprisonment) from seeking assistance and bringing proceedings.[261] The courts have sought to 'avoid' the time bar by granting declarations under the inherent jurisdiction that the ceremony created no marriage capable of recognition in English law—that is, treating the case as one of non-marriage.[262] Whilst the outcome may appear just, releasing victims of forced marriages without incurring the stigma (in their community's eyes) of a divorce, it must be doubted whether these cases are rightly decided under the law as it stands,[263] and the court's jurisdiction to make financial orders is not available following a finding of non-marriage, to the potential detriment of the victim 'spouse'.

That problem aside, the chief difficulty lies in navigating Singer J's 'grey area' between forced and arranged marriages. The courts have shown considerable sensitivity towards minority cultural practices.[264] It is clear that the duress may come from the other party to the marriage or from third parties. However, the law is uncertain because competing lines of authority espouse different tests, one subjective, the other objective. Since there are Court of Appeal decisions on both sides, that court and those below it remain free to apply either test until the Supreme Court resolves the issue.[265] However, the subjective test is generally preferred, some judges and commentators considering that it already represents the law.[266] When assessing cases decided before 1971 espousing an objective test, it may be important to bear in mind that lack of consent then rendered a marriage void, rather than voidable, and so a stricter test may have been considered desirable.[267] But whichever test were applied to these facts, the reported cases would arguably have been decided the same way.

The objective test

In *Buckland v Buckland*, the husband, a member of the armed forces serving in Malta, found himself in an awkward position. Falsely alleged to be the father of a young girl's child, he was told by his senior officers and lawyer that his only escape from prosecution and imprisonment for under-age sex would be to marry the girl. The judge set out a three-stage test in declaring the marriage void (as it would have been then):

---

[261] Cf s 13(4): extension in case of mental disorder only.

[262] *B v I* [2010] 1 FLR 1721; *SH v NB* [2009] EWHC 3274; *KC and NNC v City of Westminster Social and Community Services Department and anor* [2008] EWCA Civ 198; *Re P (Forced Marriage)* [2011] EWHC 3467; *XCC v A* [2012] EWHC 2483; for criticism, see Probert (2008a) and (2013a), 330–2.

[263] Cf *A Local Authority v X* [2013] EWHC 3274, where the court required that a decree of nullity be sought: the marriage being void on grounds of age as well as voidable for non-consent, there was no bar to be avoided by granting a declaration instead.

[264] *NS v MI* [2006] EWHC 1646, [37]; see also Scottish cases, e.g. *Mahmud v Mahmud* 1994 SLT 599; for criticism, see Bradney (1984), (1994); Lim (1996).

[265] *Young v Bristol Aeroplane Co Ltd* [1944] KB 718; *Ashburn Anstalt v Arnold* [1989] Ch 1, 21.

[266] *NS v MI* [2006] EWHC 1646; Masson, Bailey-Harris, and Probert (2008), 2-041.

[267] Bradney (1984), 279. Note also, however, that when void, no time bar would have applied to forced marriages, a problem that has been avoided in recent cases by invoking the inherent jurisdiction: *B v I* [2010] 1 FLR 1721.

Buckland v Buckland (orse Camilleri) [1968] P 296 (Probate Div), 301

SCARMAN J:

[I]n a case where it is alleged that the petitioner's consent to marriage has been vitiated by fear, it must be shown, first, that fear of sufficient degree to vitiate consent was present; and, secondly, that the fear was reasonably entertained....[A] third proposition may be stated to the effect that, even if the fear is reasonably entertained, it will not vitiate consent, unless it arises from some external circumstance for which the petitioner is not himself responsible.

The conclusion which I have reached, on the facts in the present case, is that the petitioner agreed to marry the girl because he was afraid, and that his fear was brought about by an unjust charge preferred against him...The fear which originated in this way was greatly strengthened by the advice given to the petitioner by his own solicitor and by his superior officer. I am satisfied that when he presented himself in the church for the marriage ceremony, he believed himself to be in an inescapable dilemma—marriage or prison: and, fearing prison, he chose marriage...

Accordingly, in my judgment, he is entitled to a declaration that the marriage ceremony was null and void.

The test was elaborated in *Szechter v Szechter*.[268] A Polish Jewish woman in very poor health married an academic at Warsaw University (who divorced his wife, with her full consent, to facilitate the plan) in order to enable the woman to escape totalitarian Poland, where she had been imprisoned for offences against the regime. She had served several months of imprisonment and lengthy interrogation before trial, during which time she faced various very serious threats; the circumstances were causing her already fragile health to fail. The court considered *Buckland* on the way to annulling the marriage.[269] As McClean and Hayes have observed, however, given *Vervaeke v Smith*, it seems odd to say that the woman did not consent to marry in this case where she did so precisely in order to acquire the status necessary to flee:[270]

Szechter v Szechter (orse Karsov) [1971] P 286 (Probate Div), 297–8

SIR JOCELYN SIMON P:

[T]he instant case seems to me to be stronger than...*Buckland v. Buckland*. It is, in my view, insufficient to invalidate an otherwise good marriage that a party has entered into it in order to escape from a disagreeable situation, such as penury or social degradation. In order for the impediment of duress to violate an otherwise valid marriage, it must, in my judgment, be proved that the will of one of the parties thereto has been overborne by genuine and reasonably held fear caused by threat of immediate danger (for which the party is not himself responsible) to life, limb or liberty, so that the constraint destroys the reality of consent to ordinary wedlock.

Two Court of Appeal cases approved this line of authority. Both involved arranged marriages which were held to be valid; indeed, it is questionable whether either case would have succeeded

---

[268] [1971] P 286.
[269] Polish law was formally determinative, but the position under English law was also considered.
[270] McClean and Hayes (2011), 88.

under the subjective test, considered below. In *Singh v Singh*,[271] a young woman married under parental pressure—not under a threat to life, limb, or liberty, but rather out of a sense of reluctant duty to her parents and religion. In *Singh v Kaur*,[272] it was the husband who gave in to family pressure. Aged 21 and having always lived at home, he was threatened that if he did not marry, he would lose his job in the family business, and have no income or transport:

Singh v Kaur (1981) 11 Fam Law 152 (CA)

ORMROD LJ:

[O]ne can see that, through our English eyes, he is in a sad position but, at the same time, he has to make up his mind, as an adult, whether to go through with the marriage or whether to withstand the pressure put upon him by his family. It is quite clear that this court cannot possibly…hold that this marriage is invalid by reason of duress unless it can be shown that there were threats to his life, limb and liberty. Quite clearly, the evidence falls far, far short of that. There was no threat of that kind and…it would be a very serious matter if this court were, even if it could in law, to water down Sir Jocelyn Simon's test…because there are many of these arranged marriages, not only in the Sikh community in this country but in other communities, and not only Asiatic communities. There are other European communities who adopt this custom, and it would be a most serious thing for this court to introduce any less rigorous burden of proof in these matters than that which the court decided was right in the case of *Singh v Singh*…

The subjective test

The alternative, subjective test requires no particular type of threat, but simply focuses on the state of mind of the party in question, which is not measured against any objective standard of steadfastness. The test originates in *Scott v Sebright*: the young bride was blackmailed by a rogue who had borrowed her fortune to pay his debts, and threatened her with bankruptcy, scandal-mongering within the drawing rooms of polite London society, and (immediately before the ceremony) death, should she not marry him. That last threat would clearly have satisfied the objective test, but the court did not express itself so narrowly:

Scott (falsely called Sebright) v Sebright (1886) LR 12 PD 21 (Probate Div), 23–4, 31

BUTT J:

The Courts of law have always refused to recognize as binding contracts to which the consent of either party has been obtained by fraud or duress, and the validity of a contract of marriage must be tested and determined in precisely the same manner as that of any other contract. True it is that in contracts of marriage there is an interest involved above and beyond that of the immediate parties. Public policy requires that marriages should not be lightly set aside, and there is in some cases the strongest temptation to the parties more immediately

---

271 [1971] P 226.
272 (1981) 11 Fam Law 152.

interested to act in collusion in obtaining a dissolution of the marriage tie. These reasons necessitate great care and circumspection on the part of the tribunal, but they in no wise alter the principle or the grounds on which this, like any other contract, may be avoided. It has sometimes been said that in order to avoid a contract entered into through fear, the fear must be such as would impel a person of ordinary courage and resolution to yield to it. I do not think that is an accurate statement of the law. Whenever from natural weakness of intellect or from fear—whether reasonably entertained or not—either party is actually in a state of mental incompetence to resist pressure improperly brought to bear, there is no more consent than in the case of a person of stronger intellect and more robust courage yielding to a more serious danger. The difficulty consists not in any uncertainty of the law on the subject, but in its application to the facts of each individual case....

Here, however, the facts clearly pointed to the conclusion that no true consent had been given.

Having received only passing reference in *Singh v Kaur*,[273] the subjective test found support from the Court of Appeal in *Hirani v Hirani*.[274] A young Hindu woman was threatened with eviction from the family home should she not submit to an arranged marriage, precipitated by her parents' abhorrence of her dating a Muslim. Ormrod LJ delivered the short judgment, curiously overlooking the previous Court of Appeal cases endorsing an objective test to which he had been a party. He adopted a limited reading of *Szechter v Szechter*, at odds with his reading of the case in *Singh v Kaur*. Like the judge in *Scott*, he drew an analogy with contract:[275]

Hirani v Hirani (1983) 4 FLR 232 (CA), 234

ORMROD LJ:

...[T]he matter can be dealt with quite shortly by referring to a recent case in the Privy Council dealing with duress and its effect on a contract. It is a case called *Pao On v Lau Yiu Long* [1980] AC 614. Lord Scarman, giving the opinion of the Privy Council and dealing with the duress question, at p. 635 said this:

'Duress, whatever form it takes, is a coercion of the will so as to vitiate consent.'

He then quoted a dictum of Kerr J in another case...:

'There must be present some factor "which could in law be regarded as a coercion of his will so as to vitiate his consent".'

The crucial question in these cases, particularly where a marriage is involved, is whether the threats, pressure, or whatever it is, is such as to destroy the reality of consent and overbears the will of the individual. It seems to me that this case, on the facts, is a classic case of a young girl, wholly dependent on her parents, being forced into a marriage with a man she has never seen and whom her parents have never seen in order to prevent her (reasonably, from her parents' point of view) continuing in an association with a Muslim which they would regard with abhorrence. But it is as clear a case as one could want of the overbearing of the will of the petitioner and thus invalidating or vitiating her consent.

---

[273] (1981) 11 Fam Law 152.
[274] (1983) 4 FLR 232.
[275] Note *Mahmood v Mahmood* 1993 SLT 589, 591.

Hirani was applied in *P v R (Forced Marriage: Annulment: Procedure)*,[276] the facts of which would readily satisfy the objective test. A British Pakistani family took their daughter to Pakistan for a relative's funeral. During the visit, the parents arranged a marriage which the daughter was forced to go through with under threat of violence in circumstances where she was unable to escape owing to illness, close supervision, and lack of funds and knowledge of the local area. Her apparent assent during the ceremony was caused by her mother standing behind her and pushing her head to create the appearance of a nod. The marriage was patently voidable for want of consent.

Mistake

Mistakes only vitiate consent and render marriage (and presumably civil partnership) voidable where they relate either to the identity (not merely the attributes) of the other party, or to the nature of the ceremony. Such mistakes may be spontaneous or induced by the fraud of the other party or a third party. Other mistakes will not render marriage or civil partnership voidable, though the courts have a protective jurisdiction to prevent marriages involving vulnerable individuals going ahead under such misapprehensions.[277]

Mistake as to identity

C v C [1942] NZLR 356 (High Court, New Zealand), 358–9

CALLAN J:

The topic was carefully considered...in...*Moss v Moss*...: "But when in English law fraud is spoken of as a ground for avoiding a marriage, this does not include such fraud as induces a consent, but is limited to such fraud as procures the appearance without the reality of consent"..."Error about the family or fortune of the individual, though produced by disingenuous representations, does not at all affect the validity of the marriage".... Now my duty is to accept that statement of law and apply it to the facts of this case, and I have a clear opinion that this is a case of real consent although induced by fraud, and not a case of no consent or absence of consent. The petitioner truly consented to marry the human being to whom she was married by the Registrar. It is true that he was married under the name of Michael Miller, the Australian boxer, whereas in truth he is Samuel Henry Coley, a New Zealander, not a boxer at all, and a person of very different fortune of the person he represented himself to be, of no fortune at all really. But I am also satisfied that Michael Miller, as a human being, meant really nothing to this lady. What she was interested in was the man before her, the man who, after this very rapid courtship, proposed marriage to her, and she accepted that human being because she believed, on his fraudulent representations, that his position as to fortune and his prospects were ample for starting her in a good way in the married state...The point was that she was willing to marry this man whom she believed to be able to support her, and the identity of Michael Miller in the matter was

---

[276] [2003] 1 FLR 661.

[277] *Re SA (Vulnerable Adult with Capacity: Marriage)* [2005] EWHC 2942: concern that a marriage arranged for a deaf and dumb young Pakistani woman should only proceed with her full and genuine consent to the specific marriage proposed.

> merely accidental. It is possible to conceive a case...where this principle can be applied successfully. Suppose A. proposes marriage to B. by correspondence, never having seen B. before, but really on what A. knows about B.'s family circumstances and so on, or perhaps A. has not seen B. for very many years, and that proposal is accepted, and then on the day of the marriage C. fraudulently impersonates B., and gets away with it, because A. does not know the present personal appearance of B. There would be, I should think, a case of no true consent. But that is not this case.

However, the line between mistakes as to identity and attributes may not be certain. In *Militante v Ogunwomoju*,[278] the court voided a marriage involving an illegal immigrant who had assumed the identity of someone living legally in the UK. *Moss v Moss* was cited, but the refined arguments of *C v C* were not considered in the very short judgment. One commentator notes that it is not known whether the petitioner 'thought she was marrying another man, or simply [as in *C v C*] that she thought the man had a different name'.[279]

Mistake as to the nature of the ceremony

In these cases, a language barrier often creates the confusion. For example, in *Valier v Valier (otherwise Davis)*,[280] the Conte Jerome Valier, an Italian resident of France who had fallen on hard times, was working in a garage and was 'not quick on the uptake' when spoken to in English. He went through a marriage ceremony with May Winifred Davis, aspiring actress, at St Giles', London register office. Not realizing that he had thus been married, he later married the Marchesa Balbi in Italy. His London marriage was annulled on the ground that he had no idea when he attended the register office and signed a document, which he never subsequently saw or read, that he was contracting a marriage. In Italy, engaged couples must sign a document at the town hall and wait three weeks before obtaining a licence to marry, the marriage then being solemnized at the town hall and thereafter in church. He mistakenly thought that he was merely performing this preliminary. The marriage was annulled.[281]

Unsoundness of mind

Ability to give valid consent to marriage or civil partnership requires mental capacity to do so. The appropriate test for determining capacity was analysed in a case concerning a woman referred to as 'E'. E had spina bifida and hydrocephalus, and was alleged to have a mental age of 13 and to be vulnerable to exploitation. She had formed a relationship with an older man, S, who had several convictions for serious sex offences. E's local authority, SCC, applied under the inherent jurisdiction for injunctive relief to prevent their planned marriage.[282] Munby J had to identify the appropriate test for capacity to marry so that the expert witnesses charged with assessing E's capacity could be properly instructed. The starting point is that adults are presumed to have capacity; it is for those who assert that an

---

278 [1993] 2 FCR 355.
279 Douglas (1994a).
280 (1925) 133 LT 830.
281 See also *Mehta v Mehta* [1945] 2 All ER 689.
282 The jurisdiction to issue such injunctions was confirmed in *M v B, A and S (By the Official Solicitor)* [2005] EWHC 1681.

individual lacks capacity to prove that. No one, including the court, can consent to marriage on behalf of someone lacking capacity to marry; and the court cannot interfere with the decision of someone who does have capacity, just because it thinks the decision unwise.[283] Capacity is assessed on an issue-by-issue basis, rather than as a general matter. The test is whether the individual understands the nature and quality of the relevant transaction. In the case of marriage, what does that involve?

Sheffield City Council v E and another [2004] EWHC 2808, [2005] Fam 326

MUNBY J:

68. . . . The law . . . can be summed up in four propositions. (i) It is not enough that someone appreciates that he or she is taking part in a marriage ceremony or understands its words. (ii) He or she must understand the nature of the marriage contract. (iii) This means that he or she must be mentally capable of understanding the duties and responsibilities that normally attach to marriage. (iv) That said, the contract of marriage is in essence a simple one, which does not require a high degree of intelligence to comprehend. The contract of marriage can readily be understood by anyone of normal intelligence.

So, what are the duties that normally attach to marriage?

132. . . . Marriage, whether civil or religious, is a contract, formally entered into. It confers on the parties the status of husband and wife, the essence of the contract being an agreement between a man and a woman to live together, and to love one another as husband and wife, to the exclusion of all others. It creates a relationship of mutual and reciprocal obligations, typically involving the sharing of a common home and a common domestic life and the right to enjoy each other's society, comfort and assistance.[284]

Importantly—given the undesirability of E's intended spouse—Munby J held that the test is also a general one: did E have the capacity to marry *generally*, not to decide to marry S, *specifically*. So the test was one of capacity to enter this type of transaction (marriage), not a test of the wisdom of the specific marriage contemplated:[285]

85. . . . [T]he *nature of the contract of marriage* is necessarily something shared in common by all marriages. It is not something that differs as between different marriages or depending upon whether A marries B or C. The implications for A of choosing to marry B rather than C may be immense. B may be a loving pauper and C a wife-beating millionaire. But this has nothing to do with the nature of the contract of marriage into which A has chosen to enter. Whether A marries B or marries C, the contract is the same, its nature is the same, and its legal consequences are the same. The emotional, social, financial and other implications for A may be very different but the nature of the contract is precisely the same in both cases.

---

283 *Sheffield City Council v E* [2004] EWHC 2808, [18]–[23], [101].
284 We considered the general validity of this statement at p 57 above.
285 Cf the theoretical scope for a court considering the marriage of a minor to withhold consent on best interest grounds: see Probert (2009a), 249.

This decision has been criticized, not least in the light of a more recent decision that whether an individual has capacity to decide to *live with* someone is to be addressed in the context of the particular context and proposed partner.[286] It has been noted that the decisions on capacity to marry on which Munby J relies predate more sophisticated case law dealing with capacity in relation to medical treatment, and that it is somewhat unreal to deal with marriage as an abstract proposition rather than to consider capacity to marriage in the context of the social reality of the particular marriage.[287] At one point Munby J opined that:

> 144. There are many people in our society who may be of limited or borderline capacity but whose lives are immensely enriched by marriage. We must be careful not to set the test of capacity to marry too high, lest it operate as an unfair, unnecessary and indeed discriminatory bar against the mentally disabled.

That remark encapsulates what some feminist scholars consider entails a failure to protect the vulnerable in this area, potentially breaching the state's positive obligations under the ECHR:[288]

J. Herring, N. Barker, and M. Fox, '*Sheffield County Council v E*', in R. Hunter et al (eds), *Feminist Judgments: From Theory to Practice* (Oxford: Hart Publishing, 2010), 355

BARKER AND FOX LLJ[289]

21.... [A]lthough there are certain (largely unarticulated) social norms and ideals associated with marriage, it is impossible to capture the range of relationships that may be encompassed within the legal framework of marriage in an abstract definition. Marriage should not be universalised. Nor should it be idealised. In contrast to commonly held romantic notions of what marriage is, we must recognise that legal marriages... "need not be loving, sexual, stable, faithful, long-lasting, or contented". All too often they are unpleasant, abusive and violent. In this context, it is appropriate that E should, at a minimum, be aware of the fact that sometimes marriage is not pleasant and have the capacity to weigh the potential benefits *and* risks inherent in a marriage to S.

22. On this basis, we reject Munby J's view that marriage is a universal and simple contract. Once it is recognised that marriage no longer has (or should have) what Professor O'Donovan referred to... as a sacred, magical status, and that there is no universal fixed essence of marriage, it can be seen that the analogy with medical treatment is appropriate. Just as there are different types of medical treatment, there are varieties of marriage. Just as the level of risk involved in medical treatment depends on the type of treatment and who administers it, the level of risk within marriage depends on the spouses and other circumstances.

---

[286] *York CC v C* [2013] EWCA Civ 478.

[287] Herring, Barker, and Fox (2010), Herring (2013).

[288] On that point see ibid (2010), 359. Cf *Sandwell MBC v RG and others* [2013] EWHC 2372 (COP) in which Holman J declined to declare that it was in the incapacitated party's best interests to initiate nullity proceedings, given the benefit he derived from being married.

[289] This extract comes from an imagined Court of Appeal decision overturning Munby J's decision.

'Or otherwise'

One other situation which might vitiate an apparent consent involves intoxication. Probably only extreme intoxication temporarily depriving the individual of *capacity* to consent will suffice; mere loss of inhibition through drink, which causes the individual to provide a consent that he or she would not have given when sober, will not:

Sullivan v Sullivan, falsely called Oldacre (1818) 2 Hag Con 238 (Consistory Court), 246, 248

SIR WILLIAM SCOTT:

Suppose three or four persons were to combine to [procure a marriage] by intoxicating another, and marrying him in that perverted state of mind, this Court would not hesitate to annul a marriage on clear proof of such a cause connected with such an effect. Not many other cases occur to me in which the co-operation of other persons to produce a marriage can be so considered, if the party was not in a state of disability, natural or artificial, which created a want of reason or volition amounting to an incapacity to consent… [But i]f he is capable of consent, and has consented, the law does not ask how the consent has been induced.

2.7.2 MENTAL DISORDER RENDERING PERSON 'UNFIT' FOR MARRIAGE OR CIVIL PARTNERSHIP

This ground[290] may be relied upon by either party, and must ordinarily be invoked within three years of the ceremony.[291] It must be distinguished from mental incapacity vitiating consent. Here, the individual is competent to consent, but the nature of his or her disorder is such that he or she is nevertheless 'unfit' for marriage or civil partnership at the time of the ceremony. This is more difficult territory than the consent ground, as it appears to require an evaluation of the individual's behaviour and an understanding of what it is for which he or she must be 'fit'. In *Bennett v Bennett*, Ormrod J posed the question as follows: 'Is this person capable of living in a married state, and of carrying out the ordinary duties and obligations of marriage?'—but did not elaborate.[292] In *Bennett*, the wife was occasionally violent and periodically hospitalized with neurosis. The court remarked that she might be a person to whom it would be difficult to be married and would need an understanding husband. But her mental illness was not so extreme as to make her unfit. Indeed, Ormrod J's experience of the divorce courts suggested to him that there were many people of normal mental state who might be thought considerably less fit for marriage than this wife.[293] It remains to be seen what qualities are necessary to render someone fit for civil partnership.

The existence of a marriage or civil partnership provides a statutory defence to some of the sexual offences involving persons with mental disorders, though not for those offences involving individuals with disorders impeding that person's choice regarding the sexual activity in question, or for those offences involving inducements, threats, or deception.[294]

---

290 MCA 1973, s 12(1)(d); CPA 2004, s 50(1)(b).
291 MCA 1973, s 13(2)(4)(5); CPA 2004, s 51(2)–(4).
292 [1969] 1 WLR 430, 434.
293 Ibid.
294 Sexual Offences Act 2003, s 43; cf ss 30–7.

2.7.3 THE RESPONDENT WAS PREGNANT BY ANOTHER AT THE TIME OF THE CEREMONY

This ground[295] may only be relied upon by the other party, must ordinarily be invoked within three years of the ceremony, and that party must have been ignorant that the respondent was pregnant by another at the time of the ceremony.[296] The ground was introduced in 1937, the courts having declined to regard such mistakes as sufficiently fundamental to vitiate husbands' consent to marriage—pregnancy is an 'attribute' only, and not an issue going to the wife's identity.[297] It has been suggested that the ground is justified on two bases: that the husband only married the wife because he believed the child to be his own; and/or that the husband believed the wife to be chaste.[298] The latter is rightly regarded as inappropriate to modern conditions. The lack of equivalent ground upon which it can be complained that a male partner is fathering children elsewhere suggests that the concern is not (male) sexual fidelity or chastity. It may be better to leave female infidelity resulting in pregnancy, in extreme cases, to the law relating to duress (as in *Buckland*) or to the divorce courts.

In the case of civil partnership and same-sex marriage, it is (currently) biologically impossible for one female to be pregnant *other than* by someone who is not her (female) civil partner. Where the parties have together embarked on a course of assisted reproduction, necessarily using donor sperm, the non-pregnant party ought not to be allowed to complain.[299] The requirement that she be ignorant of her partner's pregnancy at the time of the civil partnership registration goes some way to ensure justice, and the general, estoppel-type bar to nullity practically eliminates the possibility of annulment in such cases.

2.7.4 GROUNDS RELATING TO GENDER RECOGNITION

The continuing importance of gender to both marriage and civil partnership is emphasized by two voidable grounds relating to trans people, which continue to apply despite the advent of same-sex marriage.

If one party was unaware at the time of the ceremony that the other person has previously obtained legal recognition of their preferred gender under the GRA 2004, the marriage or civil partnership will be voidable on the application of the first party, who may not wish to continue in the relationship given this discovery, even though the marriage or civil partnership is not void.[300]

The second ground caters for trans people who are spouses or civil partners when they apply for legal gender recognition, though is now perhaps of chief significance for civil partners. As we noted at 2.6.1, where the parties are married before one of them obtains legal gender recognition, that marriage can continue as such following recognition if both parties

---

[295] MCA 1973, s 12(1)(f); CPA 2004, s 50(1)(c).
[296] Ibid, s 13(2)–(5); s 51(2)–(4), (6).
[297] *Moss v Moss* [1897] P 263.
[298] Hayes and Williams (1999), 503–4. The authors question why this particular 'attribute' mistake should have been selected; why not the belated discovery that one's spouse is a convicted rapist?
[299] See 9.4.3 on Human Fertilisation and Embryology Act 2008, s 42.
[300] See MCA 1973, ss 12(1)(h) and 13(3); CPA 2004, ss 50(1)(e) and 51(6).

consent.[301] But a pre-existing civil partnership must be annulled before the trans partner can obtain a full gender recognition certificate, because the civil partnership cannot endure once the parties are of the opposite legal gender. So the trans partner initially receives an interim certificate that renders the partnership voidable,[302] and either party has six months from the issue of the certificate in which to apply for a decree of nullity.[303] Once the full certificate is issued, if the parties wish to continue to share a legal relationship, a special procedure allows them to reconstitute their relationship as spouses, without being subject to the usual waiting periods.[304] The equivalent procedure for spouses would be used by couples who wish to continue their post-gender-recognition relationship as civil partners, despite the availability of same-sex marriage.

2.7.5 A GROUND UNIQUE TO MARRIAGE: VENEREAL DISEASE

A marriage, but not a civil partnership, may be annulled on the ground that the respondent had communicable venereal disease at the time of the marriage. Civil partners aggrieved in similar circumstances must seek dissolution instead. It is not clear what 'venereal disease' covers,[305] and in particular whether only serious infections such as HIV are included, or all sexually transmitted diseases, including minor, relatively common, and readily treatable conditions such as chlamydia. It is significant that the ground was introduced in the pre-antibiotic age. This ground may be relied on ordinarily only within the first three years of marriage, and only if the petitioner was ignorant of the problem at the date of the marriage.[306] Given the reasons offered by government for not adopting this ground for civil partnership and its abolition in some other jurisdictions, its retention for marriage must be questioned:

Hansard, *Official Report*—Civil Partnership Bill Debates, HC Standing Committee D, col 162, 26 October 2004

Mrs McGuire [Parliamentary Under-Secretary of State]:

[T]he Government's intention in drafting the Bill was that civil partners would be treated in the same way as spouses except where there was justification for a difference in treatment. This was one matter on which we felt that there was justification for difference. It is a medical fact that men and women may carry certain sexually transmitted infections for many years without knowing it, and we do not believe that it is appropriate in present-day circumstances to include that as a ground for nullifying a civil partnership. The deliberate transmission of a sexually transmitted infection might well be considered as a basis for dissolution, as a factor proving unreasonable behaviour.

---

301 GRA 2004, ss 3(6A)–(6C), 4(2), 11A. Cf the previous situation, *Parry v United Kingdom* (App No 42971/05, ECHR) (2006).
302 MCA 1973, s 12(1)(g); CPA 2004, s 50(1)(d).
303 Ibid, s 13(2A); s 51(5).
304 MA 1949, s 39A; CPA 2004, s 96 and Sch 3.
305 MCA 1973, s 12(1)(e).
306 Ibid, s 13(2)–(5).

I suggest that were we starting now to create marriage law, it would be highly questionable whether we would include such a provision in that law. It is a provision from a bygone age when, perhaps, we were less informed about sexually transmitted diseases. The Government have clearly stated in their national strategy for sexual health and HIV that we need to de-stigmatise the whole issue of sexually transmitted infections if we are to tackle the increasing infection rate...Suggesting that sexually transmitted diseases should be treated differently from any other communicable diseases in that regard is counterproductive to that aim.

2.7.6 GROUNDS UNIQUE TO OPPOSITE-SEX MARRIAGE: FAILURE TO CONSUMMATE

An opposite-sex marriage may be annulled where not consummated owing either to the wilful refusal of the respondent or to incapacity of either party.[307] The disapplication of these grounds for same-sex marriages[308] might suggest that same-sex marriage, like civil partnership, is somehow to be regarded as a sexless union. However, the difference can be explained rather more prosaically. As we shall see below, consummation is defined—very specifically—in terms of penile penetration of the vagina. Self-evidently, such a concept cannot apply to same-sex relationships. But it is questionable whether the ground should exist even for opposite-sex marriages. Indeed, close examination of the definition of consummation will cause many of our *assumptions* about what the ground might be about, and so why its retention might be justified, to fall away. The government clearly has no appetite for what is a long overdue fundamental review of marriage law, but the retention of non-consummation leaves us with interesting questions about what these grounds say about the nature of (opposite-sex) marriage, an issue that we explore below.

Neither non-consummation ground is subject to the three-year limitation period applying to most of the other voidable grounds, and so may be raised at any time until consummation occurs. Until the introduction of the special gender recognition ground, wilful refusal to consummate was the only ground clearly related to problems post-dating the marriage, rather than facts present at the time of the ceremony; it has been noted that the statute does not expressly confine incapacity to cases where the condition existed at the time of the ceremony, leaving open the possibility of a nullity decree on grounds of supervening incapacity.[309] Despite suggestions that this ground should be demoted to the law of divorce, it remains part of nullity law.[310] It is necessary to examine three issues: first, the meaning of 'consummation'; and then the two ways in which lack of consummation may give grounds for nullity: incapacity and wilful refusal to consummate.

Consummation

Both grounds rely on the concept of consummation:

---

[307] Ibid, s 12(1)(a) and (b).
[308] Ibid, s 12(2).
[309] Masson, Bailey-Harris, and Probert (2008), 2-027.
[310] Cf Morton Commission (1956), paras 88–9, 283; Law Com (1970), para 27.

D-E v A-G, falsely calling herself D-E (1845) 1 Rob Eccl 279 (Consistory Court), 298

DR LUSHINGTON:

Sexual intercourse, in the proper meaning of the term, is ordinary and complete intercourse; it does not mean partial and imperfect intercourse: yet I cannot go the length of saying that every degree of imperfection would deprive it of its essential character. There must be degrees difficult to deal with; but if so imperfect as scarcely to be natural, I should not hesitate to say that, legally speaking, it is no intercourse at all. I can never think that the true interest of society would be advanced by retaining within the marriage bonds parties driven to such disgusting practices. Certainly it would not tend to the prevention of adulterous intercourse, one of the greatest evils to be avoided…If there be a reasonable probability that the lady can be made capable of vera copula—of the natural sort of coitus, *though without power of conception*—I cannot pronounce this marriage void. If, on the contrary, she is not and cannot be made capable of more than an incipient, imperfect, and unnatural coitus, I would pronounce the marriage void.[311] [Emphasis added]

The cases have been preoccupied then, not with the question of fertility, but with what 'ordinary and complete intercourse' entails. No other form of sexual activity counts. The case law makes for extraordinary reading. Often, the issue is whether the wife has a sufficiently accommodating vaginal cavity which can be penetrated, and whether the husband is capable of sufficient penile penetration of it. The 'impervious cul-de-sac' of the wife in *D-E v A-G* was deemed insufficiently deep, at 2½ inches, to permit consummation. As medical science advanced, so too did the courts' willingness to accept artificially created, or extended, vaginas as meeting the requirements, though only when created in a biological female.[312] As for the husband's contribution, ejaculation in the vagina, at least, is not required, but an erection of some endurance is: the efforts of the husband whose erection 'collapsed' immediately upon penetration could not 'without a violation of language be described as ordinary and complete intercourse'.[313] The courts have been divided on the acceptability of *coitus interruptus* for these purposes,[314] but no less authority than the House of Lords has condoned the use of condoms, further underlining the fact that procreation need not be intended or anticipated as a possible by-product of the exercise.[315] This point is driven home by *Clarke (otherwise Talbott) v Clarke*,[316] in which *despite* the wife's conceiving a child by a rogue, persistent sperm, the marriage was nevertheless unconsummated for want of actual intercourse. Whether any sexual satisfaction is obtained is irrelevant to the legal perfection of the intercourse,[317] and intercourse need only occur once for the marriage to be consummated. The parties' sexual compatibility is therefore not the issue; that is a matter for the divorce courts. Pre-marital intercourse between the parties does not preclude a finding of non-consummation if the act is not repeated after marriage.[318] We turn now to the two grounds based on the concept of consummation.

311 Now only voidable.

312 *S v S (otherwise C)* [1954] 3 All ER 736; *SY v SY (orse W)* [1963] P 37; cf *Corbett v Corbett* [1971] P 83. Unless the courts review their approach to consummation in such cases, the marriages of trans women remain vulnerable to voidability on this ground, though the estoppel bar to nullity may apply: MCA 1973, s 13.

313 *W (orse K) v W* [1967] 1 WLR 1554.

314 *Cackett (orse Trice) v Cackett* [1950] P 253; cf *Grimes (otherwise Edwards) v Grimes* [1948] P 323.

315 *Baxter v Baxter* [1948] AC 274.

316 [1943] 2 All ER 540.

317 *SY v SY (orse W)* [1963] P 37.

318 *Dredge v Dredge (otherwise Harrison)* [1947] 1 All ER 29.

Incapacity

The incapacity to consummate may be physical. If it is curable by non-dangerous surgery, a refusal to undergo treatment might amount to wilful refusal.[319] Alternatively, the incapacity may be psychological. In *Clarke*,[320] the wife had an invincible repugnance to sexual intercourse, described in the language of 1940s psychology as 'frigidity'. Care must be taken to differentiate incapacity from wilful refusal, since while a spouse may plead his or her own incapacity, wilful refusal may only be relied on by the other party. In *Singh v Singh*, the claim of invincible repugnance was rejected on the evidence: mere lack of desire to consummate did not suffice, and might instead amount to wilful refusal.[321] However, psychological incapacity can be specific to one person, so the aversion need not relate to sexual relations per se.[322]

Wilful refusal

Not any refusal to have intercourse suffices. Since consummation need occur only once, refusal to repeat the exercise will not render the marriage voidable, though it might give grounds for divorce. 'Wilful refusal' was described in *Horton v Horton* as a 'settled and definite decision reached without just excuse', viewed in light of the whole history of the marriage.[323] Here, consummation had been delayed by the war, and an unsuccessful attempt subsequently made. The court acknowledged that in such 'false start' cases, one or both parties would frequently be reluctant and hesitant to try again, and in light of the wife's evident anxiety to resolve the problem, she could not be said to be wilfully refusing. Nor, according to *Potter v Potter*, is natural loss of ardour to be equated with wilful refusal.[324] The parties in *Ford v Ford* were frustrated by the husband's imprisonment in an institution with no facilities for conjugal visits, and rules specifically prohibited intercourse during prison visits. Whilst other prisoners and their spouses were apparently content to take their chances, the husband's disinclination to do so did not constitute wilful refusal.[325] The concept of wilful refusal has acquired a special meaning in the context of marriages between parties whose faith demands that a religious ceremony be performed, as well as a civil marriage ceremony, before intercourse is permitted. In *Kaur v Singh*, the husband's refusal to perform his obligation to arrange such a ceremony was itself interpreted as a wilful refusal to consummate.[326]

Why consummation? Different conceptions of 'marriage'

Consummation has always been regarded as integral to the traditional definition of marriage, that is, in its opposite-sex form. Lord Denning once remarked, 'No one can call a marriage a real marriage when it has not been consummated'.[327] So

---

[319] *D v D (Nullity: Statutory Bar)* [1979] Fam 70.
[320] [1943] 2 All ER 540.
[321] [1971] P 226.
[322] *G v M* (1885) 10 App Cas 171.
[323] [1947] 2 All ER 871.
[324] (1975) 5 Fam Law 161.
[325] (1987) 17 Fam Law 232.
[326] [1972] 1 WLR 105.
[327] *Ramsay-Fairfax (orse Scott-Gibson) v Ramsay-Fairfax* [1956] P 115, 133.

important is consummation that express pre-marital agreements not to have sex have been struck down as being void on grounds of public policy, though the courts' views seem to depend upon the parties' age or situation. As the court observed in *Morgan v Morgan*,[328] while agreements between young couples never to cohabit and have sexual relations have been struck down on grounds of public policy,[329] an agreement between an elderly or infirm couple who wish to marry purely for companionship is a different matter. It would be unjust for one to be permitted subsequently to have the marriage annulled for incapacity to consummate when it had never been intended that it should be consummated.

Further evidence of the seriousness of marriage—and the consummation requirement—is provided by the intervention in *Morgan* of the Queen's Proctor,[330] a Crown officer statutorily empowered to intervene in matrimonial and civil partnership proceedings to represent the public interest in the interpretation of the legislation, and to guard against fabrication of evidence by the parties. The court in *Morgan* observed that it 'must always treat nullity cases as of national importance irrespective of the wishes of the parties'.[331] However, the importance of consummation is easily overstated: its location amongst the voidable grounds necessarily confers substantial privacy in the matter, letting the parties decide whether they want a purely companionate marriage; and the estoppel bar may then prevent nullity actions from succeeding in such cases: see s 13(1), discussed above.

And yet, even if a matter for the parties, it is still there as a matter identified by the state as sufficiently grave to warrant nullity proceedings. So what does it signify? Surprisingly to the layperson, consummation clearly has nothing to do with procreation.[332] Yet procreation has extraordinary persistence even in some judicial accounts of marriage, forming a key plank, for example, in *Wilkinson v Kitzinger*,[333] even though the European Court has removed it from its conceptualization of the relationship protected by Article 12.[334] The concept of consummation may also seem perplexing given its one-off nature, again an aspect which substantially detracts from any procreative purpose. A historical view may throw light on the matter: until 1991, husbands were permitted to have sexual intercourse with their wives regardless of whether they were then consenting, the original act of consummation (itself consensual) entitling the husband to sexual relations thereafter.[335]

Consummation and the (now historical) marital rape exemption—and what they imply about the (traditional) institution of marriage—have inevitably attracted academic comment, in particular from law and gender scholars:[336]

---

328 [1959] P 92, 101.

329 *Brodie v Brodie* [1917] P 271.

330 MCA 1973, ss 8 and 15; CPA 2004, s 39.

331 [1959] P 92, 96.

332 *Baxter v Baxter* [1948] AC 274.

333 [2006] EWHC 2022; see also *Bellinger v Bellinger* [2003] UKHL 21, [46]–[47] and [64].

334 *Goodwin v United Kingdom* (App No 28957/95, ECHR) (2002); *Schalk and Kopf v Austria* (App No 30141/04, ECHR) (2010).

335 See now *R v R* [1992] 1 AC 599. While the point is unclear, some sources indicate or assume that consummation did have to be consensual: see O'Donovan (1993), 46–7.

336 E.g. Collier (1995), ch 4; O'Donovan (1993), 66–8.

K. O'Donovan, *Family Law Matters* (London: Pluto Press, 1993), 46–8

The marriage contract establishes the possession of the wife's body by her husband, but she has no corresponding right. After consummation further heterosexual acts are assumed to take place in accordance with male desire. It is evident that the law approves heterosexuality in marriage but withholds its constitutive power from other relationships not legally approved.

The requirement of consummation places primacy on penetrative sex, an act constitutive of masculinity.... Reported cases reveal bizarre knowledge against which questions were asked about 'how long, and how wide, and how far, and whether, and what'. Determination of the standard, the norm, against which to measure the answers created a 'knowledge' of male sexuality and a discourse of normal masculinity. Law's insistence on consummation as the final performative act constituting marriage marginalises other sexual practices. The missionary position, in which the woman lies under the man and facing him in readiness for coition, has been privileged in this discourse...

... The story of marriage as an institution in which the sexes are united and opposed relates to the uncovering of the sexual contract. Not only is a particular form of marriage constituted, with a delineation of social roles and hierarchy, but marriage has much to say about the meaning of masculinity and femininity. Marriage establishes 'orderly access by men to women's bodies' according to Pateman. This law of male sex-right embodies women as sexual beings. Although personal autonomy over sexuality has largely been won by women today, elements of the history of marriage remain. The story helps to understand what it is to be masculine or feminine in modern civil society. No matter how much we try to avoid replicating patriarchal marital relations, these are reproduced in the institution of marriage...

Opposite-sex marriage (at least) also has a religious aspect, again evidenced by consummation:

The sacred character of marriage as an institution calls on a past, understood and shared tradition, and on an eternal future, a perpetuity. Marriage is an emblem of continuity, of reproduction of the race... Not only are sexual needs to be met but marriage is the place for the veneration of motherhood, for deference to patriarchy, for the continuance of tradition, learned yet known anew by each generation and in each generative act.

Through marriage the couple become one flesh, one body. In legal terms, this biblical notion takes form in the constitution of the couple as a unit headed by the husband.... The 'consummation most devoutly to be wished for' is the final performative act of consecration of the marriage....

It is 'doubtful that any intelligible secular principle can be wrought from the "one-flesh" dogma'.[337] However, despite this patriarchal reading of marriage, as we have seen, those historically excluded from marriage (trans persons, same-sex couples) sought access to the institution, and have finally been admitted. Those individuals clearly identified something in marriage that they wanted to obtain, without necessarily endorsing its traditional form. As we saw at 2.3 above, there are many benefits that flow from marriage—from the legal and social recognition of the relationship—which have nothing to do with the parties' genders or whether they have any sort of sexual relationship. This opening up of marriage, taking it

---

[337] Green (2011), 15.

definitively away from its traditional roots, makes the retention of non-consummation as a ground of nullity even more peculiar.

The admission of non-traditional partnerships into marriage may have a transformative effect on our view of the institution and its functions. But minority cultures in England and Wales also take a very different view of the function of marriage. This is highlighted in a case concerning the marriage of a severely mentally disabled young Muslim man, IC (who patently lacked capacity to marry as a matter of English law), which was not recognized by the English court:

KC and NNC v City of Westminster Social and Community Services Department [2008] EWCA Civ 198

WALL LJ:

44. The appeal throws up a profound difference in culture and thinking between domestic English notions of welfare and those embraced by Islam. This is a clash which...this court cannot side-step or ignore. To the Bangladeshi mind,...the marriage of IC is perceived as a means of protecting him, and of ensuring that he is properly cared for within the family when his parents are no longer in a position to do so.

45. To the mind of the English lawyer, by contrast, such a marriage is perceived as exploitative and indeed abusive. Under English law, a person in the position of IC is precluded from marriage for the simple reason that he lacks the capacity to marry....Furthermore, as IC is incapable of giving his consent to any form of sexual activity, NK [the wife] would commit a criminal offence in English law by attempting...any form of sexual contact with him.

46. To the mind of the English lawyer, the marriage is also exploitative of NK, although the evidence is that she entered into it with a full knowledge of IC's disability. The English lawyer inevitably poses the theoretical question: what young woman of marriageable age, given a free choice, would ally herself for life in marriage to a man who she will have to care for as if for a child; with whom, on the evidence, she will be unable to hold a rational conversation, let alone any form of normal social intercourse; by whom she cannot have children, and indeed with whom any form of sexual contact will, under English law...constitute a criminal offence?[338]

Opening the door to other types of formalized relationship?

The curiosity of consummation and its omission from civil partnership law (in particular) have invited questions about why the legal privileges of marriage and civil partnership attach only to particular relationships. The government struggled to articulate during the passage of the Civil Partnership Bill why no sexual relationship should be required between the parties, even though the prohibited degrees would bar civil partnership between blood relatives.[339] The Church of England's observations on civil partnership are thought-provoking, both about the (lack of) analogy with marriage, and what that

---

[338] Probert (2008a), 403–4.
[339] See, e.g., the exchange between Baroness Scotland and Lord Tebbit, Hansard HL Deb, vol 666, col 1479, 17 November 2004.

implied about who should be eligible to acquire the legal status associated with marriage and civil partnership. This debate would be reopened by the Burden sisters,[340] whose case we consider later in this chapter, and arose again during the passage of the same-sex marriage legislation:

Church of England, *Response to Civil Partnership Consultation* (2003)

12.... [T]here is an ambiguity at the heart of the Government's proposals about the nature of the proposed partnerships and about what precisely the couple are promising to be to each other. This is reflected in the shifting language in the document between 'gay, lesbian and bisexual' couples in some places and 'same sex partnerships' (potentially a wider category) in others. In a matter of this kind clarity is crucial.

13. The extremely close parallel between the new arrangements and the legal framework for marriage is likely to deter some people who might otherwise register—for example those who choose to share a home with others for a substantial period and may wish to benefit from the new partnership provisions in relation to successor tenancy rights but are not homosexual. Conversely, gay and lesbian couples will receive less protection than they might expect from a legal framework so akin to marriage—... no equivalent to a nullity process should a sexual relationship be wilfully refused...

14.... Is the primary aim to remedy injustice and create some new legal rights and safeguards for those who are not married but who may wish to share important parts of their lives with each other, whether or not within a sexual relationship? If so, the logical approach would be to remove the prohibited degrees of relationship, thereby enabling, say, two brothers or two sisters to access the new set of rights. Indeed, if this is the primary aim it could be argued that they should not be confined to same-sex couples.

15. If, on the other hand, the Government's primary aim is to confer rights on gay and lesbian people in long-term, committed relationships, the logic would be for the legal framework to acknowledge the sexual nature of the relationship.

Several attempts were made to amend the Civil Partnership Bill to allow registration of non-conjugal relationships between blood relatives.[341] Although unsuccessful, the debates increased awareness that marriage itself is a legal concept, as well as an important social, cultural, and religious institution.

But why do particular legal rights and duties attach to marriage and civil partnership at all, and only to those institutions and not other relationships? If the legal consequences are justified simply on the basis that the parties have elected to form a legal union, why cannot any two people do so? The fact that the law only permits certain pairings to become spouses and civil partners suggests that there is more to it than party autonomy. So what is the justification for confining marriage and civil partnership to presumptively sexual/intimate relationships between legal strangers? Nothing in law prevents *unrelated* platonic pairs from forming a marriage or civil partnership. But the cultural aura of romantic love surrounding both institutions, and implied by the prohibited degrees, inevitably inhibits this. Should there be some mechanism whereby related or unrelated

---

[340] *Burden and Burden v United Kingdom* (App No 13378/05, ECHR) (2008).

[341] See Glennon (2005), Stychin (2006); e.g. Hansard HL Deb, vol 660, cols 405 et seq, 22 April 2004, Baroness O'Cathain.

individuals could register their relationships in order to acquire a legal status akin to marriage, or to nominate particular individuals to benefit in specific legal contexts? In the absence of any registration option, such relationships can only be recognized on a non-formal basis. It is to those relationships that we now turn.

2.8 NON-FORMALIZED RELATIONSHIPS: COHABITANTS AND OTHER 'FAMILY'

Many people have 'family' relationships outside marriage or civil partnership. In matters relating to children, the nature of the parents' relationship is now largely irrelevant. But in the law dealing with the relationship between the adults, relationships other than marriage and civil partnership are only recognized in relatively limited circumstances and with limited consequences. This is even the case for blood relatives, who are undoubtedly 'family' but whose relationships rarely attract specific legal consequences. In the absence of family law provision, parties are left to use the general law (of property, contract, trusts, etc) to ascertain their legal position. As we shall see in later chapters, that law is not often suited to family disputes.

Where they are recognized, there is no uniformly defined set of 'second-tier', non-formalized relationships. Various formulae are used in different areas of the law to describe family relationships to which rights and duties attach. The most commonly recognized non-formalized family type is 'cohabitation': the relationship of couples who live together in circumstances akin to marriage and civil partnership. Ironically, in order to gain legal recognition, such couples have to work rather 'harder' than spouses and civil partners to get it, even though the rewards are usually less generous. Spouses and civil partners are recognized simply by virtue of their legal status. Even parties to void marriages and civil partnerships achieve quite substantial recognition and potential protection. This basic recognition flows regardless of how the parties actually live their lives, as *Vervaeke v Smith*[342] illustrates: the parties' relationship in that case was non-existent in social and functional terms, yet they had the status of spouses, and so held the passport to a wide range of legal rights and duties. By contrast, those seeking recognition as cohabitants must demonstrate that their relationship actually functions in the way that we imagine many marriages in fact do (but legally need not).

However, although spouses are not subjected to such scrutiny as a precondition of legal recognition, many legal remedies depend on the exercise of the courts' discretion, and they examine all the circumstances before making any order. If, as in *Vervaeke v Smith*, a marriage is in fact just an empty legal shell, a remedy is likely to be unnecessary or inappropriate, and none is likely to be granted. Moreover, although formalized and non-formalized relationships are still treated differently in many respects, there has been some convergence. Many of the traditional rights and duties of husband and wife have been eroded and divorce is easier, making status per se less significant as a source of automatic rights and duties, while non-formalized relationships are increasingly recognized in some areas. The logical conclusion of these developments might be that marriage and civil partnership should no longer have automatic legal implications: as Eric Clive put it, that marriage is unnecessary as

---

[342] See above p 85.

a legal concept.[343] Instead, the law should adopt an entirely functionalist or 'de facto' model, providing rights, duties, and remedies for parties to relationships that in fact need them, for example because of the parties' economic interdependence, not purely because of their legal ('de jure') form.[344]

England and Wales is currently a long way from adopting a thoroughgoing functional approach. Lisa Glennon argues that the inception of civil partnership—and now recognition of same-sex marriage—re-emphasizes formal conceptions of family.[345] The marriage/civil partnership passport remains important to many areas of law. This may seem ironic at a time when marriage rates are near their historical low and cohabitation rising.[346] However, any move to reduce the legal significance of marriage would face stiff opposition; indeed, the Conservative Party is keen that the position of marriage be enhanced, particularly in the tax system.[347] Increasing the legal consequences automatically attaching to non-formalized relationships would also be opposed by those who wish to preserve personal autonomy outside marriage.[348] Nevertheless, recent years have seen growing recognition of non-formalized family relationships, and so we address them here.

2.8.1 IDENTIFYING 'FAMILY'

A panoply of tests

The term 'family' itself appears infrequently in domestic legislation, mainly appearing in statutes governing tenancy succession. The Human Rights Act 1998 (HRA 1998) has required English courts to consider the scope of 'family life' for the purposes of Article 8. Same-sex couples and opposite-sex couples, with[349] or without children[350] are now regarded by the Strasbourg Court as having 'family life', even if they are not actually cohabiting, provided the relationship is stable.[351] As we saw in 2.3.2, before the European Court reached that position, both domestic case law interpreting 'family' under tenancy succession legislation and recently enacted legislation had already accommodated a wide range of non-traditional family forms.[352] But there remain limits to what English courts regard as constituting 'family' for these purposes, and little legislation extends beyond 'cohabitants' to confer rights on other forms of relationship.

The parliamentary draftsman has produced a panoply of terms, many of which are undefined and have yet to receive judicial attention. The concept of 'associated person' governs eligibility to access remedies regarding domestic violence, forced marriage, and occupation of the home.[353] It covers a broad range of relationships, exhaustively listed by the legislation, including spouses, civil partners, cohabitants, relatives, and platonic home-sharers. It also covers 'intimate personal relationships... of significant duration': this does not

---

343 (1980).
344 See also Bailey-Harris (1996); Probert and Barlow (2000); Dewar (2003).
345 (2008).
346 Auchmuty (2008); see data at 2.2 above.
347 Conservative Party (2010): see Probert (2012a).
348 See, e.g., discussion in Law Com (2006), Part 5; Deech (2009b).
349 *Saucedo Gomez v Spain* (App No 37784/97, ECHR) (1999).
350 *Schalk and Kopf v Austria* (App No 30141/04, ECHR) (2010).
351 *Vallianatos v Greece* (App Nos 29381/09 and 32684/09 ECHR) (2013), [73].
352 Though the 'home' rather than 'family' aspect of Art 8, in conjunction with Art 14 ECHR was key to many of these cases.
353 Family Law Act 1996 (FLA 1996), s 62: see chapter 4.

require cohabitation by the parties, or a blood or formalized relationship, but its scope is unclear.[354] It will be interesting to see whether 'intimate' is held to encompass non-sexual relationships, such as between carers and their dependants. 'Partners [living] in an enduring family relationship' are eligible to adopt[355] and to acquire parenthood via surrogacy;[356] certain blood relations are specifically excluded from the scope of this expression, but the terms are otherwise undefined. It remains to be seen how 'enduring' will be interpreted and proved, and whether 'partner' will receive similar interpretation to 'cohabitant', discussed below, save that parties to such a relationship need not cohabit.[357]

Sharing a household

Some statutes, either expressly or as a result of judicial interpretation, require the parties to share a 'household'. Merely living under the same roof does not mean that you share a household: the latter requires a degree of domestic interaction. But you may be a member of a household despite periodical absence from it. *Kotke v Saffarini* concerned a compensation claim under the Fatal Accidents Act 1976. The applicant had to show that she had been living with the deceased in the same household as (if) husband and wife for two years immediately before his death. But what is a 'household' for these purposes?

Kotke v Saffarini [2005] EWCA Civ 221

POTTER LJ:

28. . . . Use of [the word 'household'] embodies a concept somewhat elusive of definition, combining as it does both the physical connotation of a place i.e. a particular house or home and personal connotations of association i.e. the family or household resident within it. Both aspects are covered by the various dictionary definitions available. . . .

29. In the context of matrimonial law . . . ([MCA 1973, s 2(6):] "For the purposes of this Act a husband and wife shall be treated as living apart unless they are living with each other in the same household") it has been said:

"First, it does not use the word 'house', which relates to something physical, but 'household', which has an abstract meaning. Secondly, that the words 'living with each other in the same household' should be construed as a single phrase . . . On the contrary, use is again made of words with a well settled matrimonial meaning—'living together', a phrase which is simply the antithesis of living apart, and 'household', a word which essentially refers to people held together by a particular kind of tie, even if temporarily separated . . . " (per Sachs LJ in *Santos v Santos*) . . . .

31. [In *Gully v Dix* [2004] EWCA Civ 139, the] issue . . . was whether Mrs Gully, who, without marrying the deceased, had co-habited with him for many years, but had left the deceased and lived apart from him for the last three months of his life, was yet able to demonstrate that she was living in the same household as the deceased during the whole of the period of two years immediately before the date of his death [under s 1(1A), Inheritance (Provision for

---

354 FLA 1996, s 62(3)(ea).
355 ACA 2002, s 144(4)–(7): see chapters 9 and 13.
356 Human Fertilisation and Embryology Act 2008, s 54.
357 *T and M v OCC and C* [2010] EWHC 964.

Family and Dependants) Act 1975]. The judgment of Ward LJ...referred...to the observations of Sachs LJ in *Santos v Santos* quoted above and stated:

"24. In my judgment, similar considerations must apply to the meaning to be given to the statute with which we are presently concerned. Thus the claimant may still have been living with the deceased in the same household as the deceased at the moment of his death even if they had been living separately at that moment in time. The relevant word is 'household' not 'house', and 'household' bears the meaning given to it by Sachs LJ. Thus they will be in the same household if they are tied by their relationship. The tie of that relationship may be made manifest by various elements, not simply their living under the same roof, but the public and private acknowledgment of their mutual society, and the mutual protection and support that binds them together. In former days one would possibly say one should look at the whole consortium vitae." ...

41....It is clear from the authorities that in principle a person may be a member of household A, albeit he has a second house or home elsewhere at B to which he departs temporarily from time to time....

Two years before the death, the deceased had owned a house in Doncaster where he slept several nights a week and kept most of his belongings, from which he commuted to work in London, and which he retained as his official address. The applicant lived in Sheffield. The deceased stayed with her there and shared shopping expenses at weekends, 'living out of an overnight bag'. They discussed buying a house together, but the deceased's negative equity problem delayed their plans. Were they sharing a household at this point? The applicant subsequently became pregnant, and was left with a young baby when the deceased died, having only recently moved in. But this was not enough:

59....We consider the judge was correct in drawing a distinction between wanting and intending to live in the same household, planning to do so, and actually doing so.... [The] relationship of these parties [as described in the text above] did not cross the statutory threshold into the final stage.... [The] situation only changed after the pregnancy when...the deceased's centre of gravity began to move and they really began to make plans. The mere sharing of the shopping expenses when the claimant and the deceased were together [in Sheffield] was evidence of a sharing relationship, but one which fell short of the establishment of a joint household.

The functional approach in action

Most of the tests for identifying non-formalized relationships turn on 'functional' criteria. The case law interpreting the 'family' concept in the tenancy succession legislation shows a clear evolution as courts' perception of the 'ordinary meaning' and the 'ordinary man's view' of family evolved. A decision in the 1950s refused to characterize an opposite-sex cohabiting couple as 'family': only a marital, parental, or quasi-parental relationship would suffice.[358] But by the 1970s, the courts accepted that an 'ordinary person' would regard such a relationship as familial, provided it was sufficiently permanent.[359] In the 1980s, a similar relationship between a same-sex couple was denied 'family' status.[360]

---

[358] *Gammans v Ekins* [1950] 2 KB 328; see Probert (2004c); cf *Sheffield City Council v Wall* [2010] EWCA Civ 922.

[359] *Dyson Holdings Ltd v Fox* [1976] QB 503; cf *Helby v Rafferty* [1979] 1 WLR 13.

[360] *Harrogate BC v Simpson* (1985) 17 HLR 205.

The issue arose again in relation to a same-sex relationship in *Fitzpatrick*. Mr Fitzpatrick's case could not have had stronger factual merits. The deceased, Mr Thompson, and the appellant had lived together in a 'close, loving and faithful' relationship in Mr Thompson's rented flat for ten years when the deceased was rendered tetraplegic after an accident. Mr Fitzpatrick personally provided the constant care which Mr Thompson needed until his death eight years later. Could Mr Fitzpatrick succeed to the tenancy? The relevant statutory provision offered him two arguments, one of which was to show that he had been a 'member of [Mr Thompson's] family'.[361] Crucially, 'family' was undefined, leaving the matter to judicial interpretation. Ward LJ in the Court of Appeal provided a nice account of the functional approach:

Fitzpatrick v Sterling Housing Association Ltd [1998] Ch 304 (CA), 336–9

WARD LJ (dissenting):

Since the inception of the Rent Acts in or before 1920, the home of members of the tenant's family has been preserved for them. As the decided cases show, the meaning of family has been progressively extended. The movement has been away from the confines of relationships by blood and by marriage to the reality of family life, and from de jure to de facto relationships.... The trend in the cases, as I see them, is to shift the focus, or the emphasis, from structure and components to function and appearance—what a family does rather than what it is, or, putting it another way, a family is what a family does. I see this as a functionalist approach to construction as opposed to a formalist approach. Thus whether the *Joram Developments Ltd. v. Sharratt* [1979] 1 WLR 928 test is satisfied, i.e. whether there is "at least a broadly recognisable de facto familial nexus," or a conjugal nexus, depends on how closely the alternative family or couple resemble the traditional family or husband and wife in function if not in precise form...

A family unit is a social organisation which functions through linking its members closely together. The functions may be procreative, sexual, sociable, economic, emotional. The list is not exhaustive. Not all families function in the same way.

...Whilst there clearly is no right of self-determination it cannot be immaterial to have regard to the view the parties have of their own relationship. If the officious commuter on the Clapham omnibus had paid a visit to the deceased's household, asked all the relevant questions about their relationship and asked the deceased finally, "What is Mr. Fitzpatrick to you? Is he one of the family?," it seems to me to be inconceivable that the deceased would not have testily suppressed him by replying, "Of course he is." I doubt whether the ordinary man would be surprised by the answer...I am quite certain that he would not treat the answer as an abuse of the English language. Indeed I am satisfied that the ordinary man is liberated enough to accept in 1997..., looking broadly at the plaintiff's life and comparing it with the other rich patterns of family life he knows, that the bond between the plaintiff and the deceased was de facto familial.

Ward LJ was dissenting in the Court of Appeal. When the case reached the House of Lords, as we saw at 2.3.2, the majority were persuaded that the relationship was familial. Lord

---

361 Rent Act 1977, Sch 1, para 3(1).

Slynn's judgment reflects the functional character of the majority's reasoning, focused on the purpose of the housing legislation:

Fitzpatrick v Sterling Housing Association Ltd [2001] 1 AC 27, 34–40, 48–9, 51

LORD SLYNN:

[I have found this question] difficult largely because of preconceptions of a family as being a married couple and, if they have children, their children; difficult also because of the result in some of the earlier cases when applying the law to the facts. It is, however, obvious that the word "family" is used in a number of different senses, some wider, some narrower. "Do you have any family?" usually means "Do you have children?" "We're having a family gathering" may include often distant relatives and even very close friends. "The family of nations", "the Christian family" are very wide. This is no new phenomenon. Roman law, as I understand it, included in the familia all members of the social unit though other rights might be limited to spouses or heirs...

Given... that the word ["family"] is to be applied flexibly, and does not cover only legally binding relationships, it is necessary to ask what are its characteristics in this legislation and to answer that question to ask further what was Parliament's purpose. It seems to me that the intention in 1920 was that not just the legal wife but also the other members of the family unit occupying the property on the death of the tenant with him should qualify for the succession...

The hall marks of the relationship were essentially that there should be a degree of mutual interdependence, of the sharing of lives, of caring and love, of commitment and support. In respect of legal relationships these are presumed, though evidently are not always present as the family law and criminal courts know only too well. In de facto relationships these are capable, if proved, of creating membership of the tenant's family. If, as I consider, this was the purpose of the legislation, the question is then who...today...are capable in law of being members of the tenant's family. It is not who would have been so considered in 1920....

In particular if the [amendment which introduced a specific provision for cohabitants] had not been made I would have had no hesitation in holding today when, it appears, one-third of younger people live together unmarried, that where there is a stable, loving and caring relationship which is not intended to be merely temporary and where the couple live together broadly as they would if they were married, that each can be a member of the other's family for the purpose of the 1977 Act.

If, as I think, in the light of all the authorities this is the proper interpretation of the Act of 1920 I hold that as a matter of law a same-sex partner of a deceased tenant can establish the necessary familial link. They are capable of being in Russell LJ's words in *Ross v Collins*...: "A broadly recognisable de facto familial nexus." It is then a question of fact as to whether he or she does establish the necessary link...

It seems to be suggested that the result which I have so far indicated would be cataclysmic. In relation to this Act it is plainly not so. The onus on one person claiming that he or she was a member of the same-sex original tenant's family will involve that person establishing rather than merely asserting the necessary indicia of the relationship. A transient superficial relationship will not do even if it is intimate. Mere cohabitation by friends as a matter of convenience will not do...Far from being cataclysmic it is...in accordance with contemporary notions of social justice.

In the following extract, Jenni Millbank describes the feminist roots of the functional approach, comparing it with normative alternatives:

J. Millbank, 'The Role of "Functional Family" in Same-Sex Family Recognition Trends', (2008) 20 *Child and Family Law Quarterly* 155, 156

Functional family approaches accord with a core objective of feminist legal scholarship and law reform projects – to centre 'lived lives' rather than legal doctrine or formal legal categories. Not coincidentally, therefore, many of the proponents of functional family approaches in relationship law are feminist and progressive scholars who embrace the idea of dynamic change in law to reflect changing social practices. By positing law's role as reflecting and assisting actual families' experiences and needs, rather than as encouraging or mandating a particular family form, functional family approaches run directly counter to normative approaches to law such as the so-called 'channelling' purpose of family law. The 'channelling function' has been expressed as one which 'supports social institutions which are thought to serve desirable ends', such as marriage, by 'channelling' people towards them. In this competing view, law's role is to tell people, both individually and collectively, how they should form families (and, to a greater or less extent, to provide inducements for those who listen to these messages, and impose punitive consequences on those who do not). Not coincidentally, proponents of the normative or channelling approach to family law are often conservative scholars and religious organisations, who wish to maintain established legal traditions and use them to (attempt to) stem or reverse changing social practices.

However, the functional approach, as applied by the judges, has been criticized by some commentators for its tendency to make legal recognition contingent upon compliance with one particular model of 'family' relations to the exclusion of others.[362] Conversely, Probert has argued that we should be wary of too quickly assuming the functional equivalence of certain relationships: some family forms might function more effectively and there may consequently be a case for privileging them in law: we need to examine the evidence.[363]

2.8.2 COHABITANTS

The functional family most frequently recognized in law is cohabitation, opposite-sex, and same-sex.[364] The law has not always been as accommodating of unmarried couples as it is today.[365] But since the 1970s, both courts and Parliament have become increasingly aware of the needs of the growing number of cohabitants.

The legal definitions

Many statutory provisions refer to couples who 'live together as if they were husband and wife',[366] or 'as if they were civil partners', expressly drawing an analogy between them and marriage/civil partnership in a way some commentators find restrictive. In some contexts

---

362 See Diduck (2001) above p 51; Leckey (2013).
363 Probert (2009c), 322.
364 See 2.3.2.
365 See Probert (2004c) for a discussion of the varied history of cohabitants in law.
366 Now to be read as referring equally to same-sex spouses: M(SSC)A 2013, Sch 3, para 2.

(like *Kotke v Saffarini*, above), parties must have lived together in this manner for a minimum period before acquiring the relevant legal protection; this may need investigation, since cohabiting relationships do not always have firm start and end dates, unlike marriage and civil partnership. Cohabitation is not defined uniformly throughout the law. Given the range of formulae now used to describe non-formalized relationships, it may not be immediately obvious to any couple what all their legal rights and duties are.

As we shall see in later chapters, the courts' willingness to accept a given relationship as cohabitation may be conditioned by the context and the remedy sought. Here, we outline the test commonly used throughout family law to ascertain whether a couple are 'living together as husband and wife'. The test is borrowed from social security law, which treats cohabitants in the same way as spouses for certain purposes.[367] Like *Fitzpatrick*'s approach to defining 'family', it focuses on the way in which the couple functions as a unit.

Crake v Supplementary Benefits Commission [1982] 1 All ER 498, 502–3, 505

WOOLF J:

...[For the purposes of the social security rule] it is not sufficient, to establish that a man and woman are living together as husband and wife, to show that they are living in the same household. If...they are living together in the same household, that may raise the question whether they are living together as man and wife, and, indeed, in many circumstances may be strong evidence to show that they are living together as man and wife; but in each case it is necessary to go on and ascertain, in so far as this is possible, the manner in which and why they are living together in the same household; and if there is an explanation which indicates that they are not there because they are living together as man and wife, then...they are not two persons living together as husband and wife.

It is impossible to categorise all the explanations which would result in [the rule] being inapplicable but it seems to me that if the reason for someone living in the same household as another person is to look after that person because they are ill or incapable for some other reason of managing their affairs, then that in ordinary parlance is not what one would describe as living together as husband and wife....

Quite clearly if that were not the position, housekeepers performing no other functions, other than those of housekeepers, could be regarded as falling within this paragraph. A couple who live together because of some blood relationship could be treated as falling within this paragraph. In my view it was not the intention of Parliament that they should. What Parliament had in mind was...that where a couple live together as husband and wife, they shall not be in any different position whether they are married or not...

Woolf J then adopted the 'six signposts' which have become a standard set of criteria for identifying a cohabiting relationship:

[They] are admirable signposts to help a tribunal...to come to a decision whether in fact the parties should be regarded as being within the words 'living together as husband and wife'. They are: whether they are members of the same household; then there is a reference to stability; then there is a question of financial support; then there is the question of sexual relationship; the question of children; and public acknowledgment...

---

[367] See 3.8.2.

It has been said that it is most important to evaluate the parties' 'general relationship', in light of six signposts, rather than just ticking off those boxes, but that had the parties never had a sexual relationship, it might be difficult to classify them as cohabitants.[368]

Despite the diversity of couple-relationships, there are limits to what will be recognized:

Re Watson (Decd) [1999] 3 FCR 595 (Ch Div), 601

NEUBERGER J:

[O]ne must beware of indulging in too much over-analysis. Anyone who reads newspapers or law reports does not need to be told that marriages, like, perhaps even more than, other human relationships, can vary from each other in multifarious ways. However, in my judgment, when considering whether two people are living together as husband and wife, it would be wrong to conclude that they do so simply because their relationship is one which a husband and wife could have. If the test were as wide as that, then, bearing in mind the enormous variety of relationships that can exist between husband and wife, virtually every relationship between a man and a woman living in the same household would fall within s 1(1A). It seems to me that, when considering the question, the court should ask itself whether, in the opinion of a reasonable person with normal perceptions, it could be said that the two people in question were living together as husband and wife; but, when considering that question, one should not ignore the multifarious nature of marital relationships.

The Court of Appeal has approved the suggestion that the parties must have made a 'lifetime commitment to permanence', and the relationship must be 'openly and unequivocally displayed to the outside world' for the parties to be regarded as 'living together as husband and wife' in the context of tenancy succession.[369] But the fact that one party remains formally married to someone else may not automatically prevent cohabitants from being found to constitute a family.[370]

Couples who 'live apart together', perhaps *unable* to reside permanently together in one location owing to the constraints of their respective employments and so who maintain separate homes (as in *Kotke v Saffarini*[371]), will not be regarded as cohabiting. They may be economically interdependent to some extent, and be as intimate and committed as many cohabitants. Yet lack of a shared household precludes their legal recognition in many domestic contexts, even though they may now be regarded as having 'family life' under Article 8 ECHR if the relationship is sufficiently stable.[372] But it is clear both that there is huge variation in the types of relationship that fall into this category, particularly in the degree of interdependence and support between them, and that the views of parties to such relationships on the question of legal recognition also vary considerably.[373]

---

[368] *Re J (Income Support: Cohabitation)* [1995] 1 FLR 660, 665–6.

[369] *Nutting v Southern Housing Group Ltd* [2004] EWHC 2982; *Helby v Rafferty* [1979] 1 WLR 13; see also *Lindop v Agus* [2009] EWHC 1795.

[370] *Watson v Lucas* [1980] 1 WLR 1493: applying the 'member of the tenant's family' Rent Act test.

[371] [2005] EWCA Civ 221, see extract above; cf *Kaur v Dhaliwal* [2014] EWHC 1991.

[372] *Vallianatos v Greece* (App Nos 29381/09 and 32684/09, ECHR) (2013), [73].

[373] Duncan et al (2012).

Some policy questions

The legal regulation of cohabitants—couples who (given the ready availability of divorce) are generally free to marry or form civil partnerships—is a hotly contested area of family policy. These debates have particularly focused on whether cohabitants should have access to financial remedies on relationship breakdown, a topic we address in chapter 7.

As we noted at 2.2 above, the cohabiting population is heterogeneous: people cohabit at different life stages for different reasons. Cohabitation is increasingly used as a prelude or alternative to marriage, and is lasting longer. Social attitudes towards relationships are becoming more liberal, especially amongst younger cohorts of the population.[374] Two-thirds of people consider that there is little social difference between marriage and cohabitation, and only one in four think spouses make better parents than cohabitants.[375] But the important *legal* differences between marriage and cohabitation are not fully appreciated. While some deliberately do not formalize their relationship in order to avoid the legal consequences of doing so, the British Social Attitudes (BSA) survey in 2000[376] made startling revelations about the so-called 'common law marriage myth'—the erroneous belief that couples who live together have the same legal status as spouses:[377]

A. Barlow, 'Regulation of Cohabitation, Changing Family Policies and Social Attitudes: A Discussion of Britain within Europe', (2004) 26 *Law and Policy* 57, 72–3

That people see cohabitation or marriage as personal lifestyle choices was underlined by their surprising lack of awareness about the different legal consequences of these relationships. Fifty-six percent of the BSA national survey believed that cohabiting for a period of time gave rise to a common-law marriage giving them the same legal rights as married couples. Among cohabitants, this false belief rose to 59 percent and the in-depth sample found that the source of this was most often family and friends although the media and official social security application forms had also informed a significant number of views. None of the interviewees had sought legal advice specifically in relation to their position as cohabitants...When you add to this the finding by another research team, that 41 percent of their sample of 173 engaged couples (73 percent of whom were cohabiting) thought that marriage would not change the legal nature of their relationship (Hibbs, Barton and Beswick 2001), a disturbing picture of legal misperceptions emerges. What is more worrying still to policymakers, is that consciously at least, in most cases people's perceptions of the legal consequences had no impact on their decision to cohabit or marry.

Such misconceptions about the law are concerning if they mean that individuals are organizing their lives oblivious of the legal implications of their arrangements. Moreover, public ignorance of the law will impair attempts by government to encourage marriage by withholding key legal rights from other relationships.[378]

---

[374] Haskey (2001a), 5–7.
[375] Duncan and Phillips (2008).
[376] Barlow et al (2001).
[377] Rebecca Probert has demonstrated the lack of historical foundation for this belief: see Probert (2009b), (2011b), (2012b), discussed on the Online Resource Centre.
[378] Barlow and Duncan (2000).

How should the law respond? Many—particularly those keen to promote marriage—consider that, rather than change the law to match people's beliefs, we should better educate the public about the law in the hope that they will then take 'legally rational' decisions.[379] A government-funded campaign accordingly sought to dispel the 'common law marriage myth'. The campaign to some extent improved legal knowledge (at least amongst those who accessed the information) and a later survey indicates that most people do believe marriage offers greater financial security than cohabitation.[380] But for many reasons the campaign did little to change most couples' behaviour, whether by prompting them to marry or to take other steps to secure their legal position, for example by drafting wills or 'living together' agreements.[381]

However, while non-marital relationships are now increasingly common and socially acceptable, marriage is not regarded as irrelevant: only a small minority—9 per cent of all BSA respondents, 19 per cent of cohabitants—think that marriage is 'just a piece of paper'.[382] Surveys find that a large majority of young people aspire to marry.[383] This will please commentators and policy-makers who wish actively to encourage marriage, considering that marriage ensures a more stable, committed relationship than cohabitation.[384] However, the empirical basis for such views is doubtful. Cohabiting relationships are more susceptible to breakdown than marriages. But it is important to compare like with like: for example, many cohabiting relationships involve young couples, and youth is known to be a predictor of relationship instability, married or not; meanwhile, many long-term cohabitations are indistinguishable from marriages. While spouses may generally report higher levels of commitment, it is hard to disentangle cause and effect, as the following extract—which focuses on the impact of relationship form for children—explains.[385] While the process of making the promises entailed in marriage may have some stabilizing effect,[386] overall, marriage may be the product of pre-existing commitment, rather than a creator of commitment:[387]

British Academy Working Group, *Social Science and Family Policies*
(London: British Academy, 2009), 48–50

But is marriage the cause or consequence of that commitment? There are no studies to date that adequately deal with that issue...

[Another] consideration involves the major factors involved in 'selection effects', meaning the fact that those who marry before they have children are likely to be rather different sorts of people from those who have children while cohabiting. The factors predisposing childbirth outside marriage include being economically worse off, lower educational attainments, less religious commitment, the experience of sex before 16, having a widowed mother, black ethnicity, having been a teenage parent, and having a low income.... Accordingly, it is quite possible that the disadvantages experienced by children born to those who are unmarried

379 Cf Reece (2014).
380 See also Barlow et al (2008): 2006 BSA findings.
381 Barlow and Smithson (2010).
382 Barlow et al (2008).
383 De Waal (2008); Coast (2009).
384 E.g. Centre for Social Justice (2009).
385 See also Goodman and Greaves (2010), Crawford et al (2012).
386 Probert (2009c), 325, (2012a), 78–9.
387 De Waal (2008); see also Garrison (2014), Fahey (2014), 106–8.

but living together have more to do with the characteristics of the people concerned than with whether or not they are legally married...Bearing in mind these findings, a thought experiment can be carried out. If legal steps were taken to ensure that more people in the high risk group married, what would happen to marriage stability? The evidence suggests that probably it would lessen and that the differences between the married and the cohabiting would diminish....[I]t cannot be claimed that we have adequate evidence on the pros and cons of marriage versus non-marital cohabitation....Also, the scientific findings make it very clear that any conclusions on the benefits of marriage must be based on considerations that include differences between people who do, and who do not, choose to marry. In other words, people choose whether or not to marry, and the differences in child outcomes between groups of married and cohabiting couples with children may reflect the sorts of people who choose to marry, rather than the effects of the marital situation as such. That is not to say that marriage does not engender commitment. But we cannot ascribe all the differences between the married and non-married to the degree of commitment between partners (either as a cause or consequence of marriage).

Human rights issues

ECHR case law currently offers limited support for equal treatment of cohabitants with spouses and civil partners under Article 14. The European Court has endorsed the UK's maintenance of 'bright-line rules', excluding cohabitants from various legal protections, based on support for the traditional family based on marriage or, in the civil partnership era, on the parties having undertaken public, legally binding commitments towards each other.[388] The issue has generally arisen in the context of welfare benefits or taxation[389] in relation to which the Court has consistently held that spouses' distinctive legal status means that spouses and cohabitants are not analogous, so the different treatment does not require justification. Case law involving other states has considered access to financial remedies on separation and death. It has been held that while a cohabiting couple with children have 'family life' under Article 8, the state has no positive duty under that Article to provide access to such remedies.[390] In *Saucedo Gomez v Spain*, the Commission considered whether failure to provide remedies violated Article 14 in conjunction with Article 8. But while it seemed prepared to accept that cohabitants and spouses might be regarded as analogous in that context, it held that states were justified in distinguishing between marriage and cohabitation to promote the traditional concept of family.[391]

English courts and the Privy Council have also usually declined to find any discrimination in these cases, at least where the couple in question could have formalized their relationship in law.[392] However, the House of Lords held in *Re P*[393] that Northern Irish

---

[388] E.g. *Courten v United Kingdom* (App No 4479/06, ECHR) (2008); *MW v United Kingdom* (App No 11313/02, ECHR) (2009); *Burden and Burden v United Kingdom* (App No 13378/05, ECHR) (2008), *Shackell v United Kingdom* (App No 45851/99, ECHR) (2000). The one exception related to the taxation of unmarried fathers' child maintenance payments: *PM v United Kingdom* (App No 6638/03, ECHR) (2006).

[389] See 3.8.2.

[390] *Johnson v Ireland* (A-112, ECHR) (1987).

[391] (App No 37784/97, ECHR) (1999).

[392] E.g. *Ratcliffe v Secretary of State for Defence* [2009] EWCA Civ 39; cf *Rodriguez v Minister of Housing of the Government of Gibraltar* [2009] UKPC 52.

[393] [2008] UKHL 38,

adoption law was incompatible with Article 14 in conjunction with Article 8 by refusing to permit unmarried couples to be considered as potential adopters. In this context, where the child's best interests are paramount, the law could not rationally exclude an entire class of potential adopters simply because of their marital status. However, the House acknowledged that in other contexts maintaining a bright-line rule distinguishing married from unmarried couples could be lawful, certainly where the parties were free to marry.[394] The question must be considered in relation to specific issues rather than as a blanket rule. But where cohabitants are recognized, the inclusion in the eligibility criteria of a minimum duration requirement is unlikely to violate the Convention: such a requirement, if arbitrary, 'is a simple way of demonstrating a real relationship of constancy and permanence' that merits protection which the state is entitled to impose.[395]

2.8.3 THE PLATONIC, NON-CONJUGAL FAMILY

Another set of families that has attracted recent attention, particularly during the Civil Partnership Bill debates,[396] is platonic relationships, often between legal strangers (i.e. those not already related by blood or formalized relationship). Few laws expressly apply, or have been interpreted as applying, to platonic home-sharers and friends, or even blood relationships. Relationships with a sexual aspect are readily classified as quasi-conjugal and so fall within the scope of laws applying to cohabitants. But the absence of sexual intimacy probably excludes platonic relationships from laws applicable to 'cohabitants'. Just as marriage (in particular) is based on sex, so too, it seems, must its analogues, however central a platonic friendship may be to the lives of those concerned.[397] Platonic home-sharers who are not blood or adoptive relatives have also even been excluded from judicial interpretations of the ambit of 'family' in the tenancy succession statutes, however long-standing and close the relationship.[398] But they do fall within some of the more broadly framed concepts used by family law statutes. For example, the mere sharing of a household in a non-commercial context makes parties 'associated persons' for the purposes of domestic violence legislation.[399] By contrast, some jurisdictions have brought non-sexual, caring domestic relationships within the scope of family law more generally,[400] in the case of Tasmania, including where the parties are related by family,[401] creating both opportunities to register the relationship and to be recognized on a de facto basis.

One reason for English law's reluctance to extend beyond conjugal and quasi-conjugal couples, certainly to parties not related by blood, might be the perceived difficulties of defining family beyond those examples and so of drawing a clear line (assuming that such

---

394 Ibid, at [13]–[16] and [108]–[110].

395 *Swift v Secretary of State for Justice* [2013] EWCA Civ 193: no breach in the context of the Fatal Accidents Act 1976 requirement of two years' cohabitation.

396 Glennon (2005).

397 See Westwood (2013).

398 *Ross v Collins* [1964] 1 WLR 425, 432; *Sefton Holdings Ltd v Cairns* (1987) 20 HLR 124.

399 FLA 1996, s 62(3)(c): see chapter 4.

400 See Australian states' experience, e.g. Property (Relationships) Act 1984 (NSW), as amended; Domestic Relationships Act 1994 (ACT).

401 Relationships Act 2003 (Tas), s 5.

relationships cannot be formalized in law). However, some would say that the line drawn by the *present* law is unsustainable:

Fitzpatrick v Sterling Housing Association Ltd [2001] 1 AC 27, 64, 67

LORD HUTTON (dissenting):

A further difficulty which confronts the argument on behalf of [Mr Fitzpatrick] is that if it is correct and if the underlying purpose of the legislation is to provide a secure home for a person who shares his or her life with the tenant in a relationship of mutual affection, commitment and support, it is difficult to see why two elderly spinsters who live together for mutual support and companionship in old age without any sexual element in their relationship and who give each other devoted care should not qualify as members of the same family. I do not consider that the absence of a sexual relationship distinguishes such a case from the present one. The sexual relationship between a couple is a very important and enriching part of their life together, but I am unable to accept that there is such a distinction between an elderly homosexual couple who once had an active sexual relationship and two elderly spinsters who never had a sexual relationship that the homosexual couple should be regarded as members of each other's family and the spinsters should not. If the courts depart from the requirement of . . . [a broadly recognisable familial nexus, which the dissenting judges in *Fitzpatrick* take to require a heterosexual, (and so) marriage-like relationship] it is difficult to discern what criterion would include one person residing with the tenant and exclude another.

English law's exclusion of such relationships from various legal rights and duties raises difficult and interesting questions. It can be argued that if the law's purpose is to assist those in practical need, the presence or absence of a sexual or blood relationship should be irrelevant to legal recognition. For example, in the context of financial and property rights and remedies, the existence of economic interdependence, or dependence, might be felt the more obvious criterion for identifying relationships eligible for legal recognition.[402] The restrictions on access to marriage and civil partnership, particularly the rules regarding prohibited degrees, combined with the absence of legal protection for non-formalized relationships, leave some deserving parties with no mechanism for acquiring the legal protection they might be thought to need or deserve. While parties can protect themselves to some extent through contract, declarations of trust, and wills, that will not solve all of their problems, particularly where the complaint involves an issue of public law such as taxation.

The Burden sisters' case

These issues hit the headlines when the Burden sisters unsuccessfully challenged English tax law before the European Court of Human Rights.[403] The unmarried Burden sisters have lived together all their lives, for the last 30 years in a jointly-owned house worth £875,000, built by their brother on land inherited from their parents. When one dies, the survivor will have to pay inheritance tax on the deceased sister's share of the house.[404] Spouses or civil partners in

---

[402] Bailey-Harris (1998), 85.
[403] *Burden and Burden v United Kingdom* (App No 13378/05, ECHR) (2008).
[404] Despite suggestions that this would mean selling the house, this appears unlikely to be necessary: see Auchmuty (2009).

the same position would be exempt from inheritance tax. And that was the basis of the sisters' complaint: why should they not be able to enjoy a similar exemption, having lived interdependently for decades? Being related within the prohibited degrees, they cannot arrange their affairs to avoid the liability by forming a civil partnership. The case provoked debate on why only spouses and civil partners should be able to enjoy the exemption—and why marriage and civil partnership are open only to pairs unrelated by family within the prohibited degrees.

The sisters formulated their complaint as a breach of Article 14 taken in conjunction with Article 1 of Protocol 1 to the ECHR (the right to peaceful enjoyment of possessions), marshalling an impressive range of arguments. They argued that their position is analogous to spouses or civil partners, having 'chosen to live together in a loving, committed and stable relationship for several decades, sharing their only home, to the exclusion of other partners'.[405] The fact that their relationship is not sexual could not be relevant, as civil partnership law has no sexual aspect. They argued that they should not be prejudiced by the fact that their relationship arose initially by accident of birth and that it entails no legally enforceable financial obligations expressly elected by them by formalizing their relationships: being unable in law to form a civil partnership, their decision to live together should itself be regarded as an equivalent exercise of self-determination to assume responsibility for each other.[406] If the purpose of the tax exemption, as described by the government, is to promote stable and committed relationships, that purpose applies equally to adult siblings who live together in such circumstances, so denying them the same exemption serves no legitimate aim.[407] They argued that English law should reach beyond conjugality by introducing a statutory scheme conferring certain fiscal benefits on pairs of siblings or other close relations who had lived together for a minimum period and not married or formed civil partnerships with third parties. In response to the suggestion that extending such a tax exemption would deprive the public purse of revenue, they argued that this would potentially be offset by gains in other areas: for example, people would be encouraged to care for disabled and elderly relations and so avoid the need for state-funded care.[408]

Their case failed both at first instance and on appeal. The court of first instance reached no decision on whether the sisters' position was analogous to that of spouses and civil partners, who are exempt from inheritance tax. Instead, it found that the difference in treatment could in any event be justified within the state's margin of appreciation. Two dissenting judges noted that while the state might have been able to justify its position by reference to Article 12 had the tax exemption been confined to spouses, the position changed once it was extended to civil partners: 'once the legislature decides that a permanent union of two persons could or should enjoy tax privileges, it must be able to justify why such a possibility has been offered to some unions while continuing to be denied to others'.[409] This meant that it was important to examine the point left undecided by the majority. While earlier case law had compared the treatment of spouses with cohabitants—that is, people who were free to acquire the privileged legal status but had not done so[410]—the sisters' position was quite different, being barred by their blood relationship from formalizing their relationship and so acquiring the tax exemption.[411]

405 Judgment of first instance ECtHR, [50].
406 Cf the government's argument, [46] and [48].
407 Ibid, [51]. Cf the government's argument, [47].
408 Ibid, [52].
409 Dissenting judgment of Judges Bonello and Garlicki, [2].
410 E.g. *Shackell v United Kingdom* (App No 45851/99, ECHR) (2000).
411 Judges Bonello and Garlicki, [3].

By contrast, the majority of the Grand Chamber considered that the sisters fell at the first hurdle: their position is not analogous to that of spouses and civil partners. The majority's reasoning here is generally regarded as somewhat weak. They took what may be called a formalistic (and somewhat circular) approach, failing to engage with arguments about the functional similarity between the sisters and spouses in relation to the issue of inheritance tax and possible loss of a shared home:

Burden and Burden v United Kingdom (App No 13378/05, ECHR) (2008)

62....[T]he relationship between siblings is qualitatively of a different nature to that between married couples and homosexual civil partners...The very essence of the connection between siblings is consanguinity, whereas one of the defining characteristics of a marriage or [civil partnership] is that it is forbidden to close family members...The fact that the applicants have chosen to live together all their adult lives, as do many married and Civil Partnership Act couples, does not alter this essential difference between the two types of relationship.

63. Moreover, the Grand Chamber notes that it has already held that marriage confers a special status on those who enter into it. The exercise of the right to marry is protected by Article 12 of the Convention and gives rise to social, personal and legal consequences...

65. As with marriage, the Grand Chamber considers that the legal consequences of civil partnership..., which couples expressly and deliberately decide to incur, set these types of relationship apart from other forms of co-habitation. Rather than the length or the supportive nature of the relationship, what is determinative is the existence of a public undertaking, carrying with it a body of rights and obligations of a contractual nature. Just as there can be no analogy between married and Civil Partnership Act couples, on the one hand, and heterosexual or homosexual couples who choose to live together but not to become husband and wife or civil partners, on the other hand (see *Shackell v UK*), the absence of such a legally binding agreement between the applicants renders their relationship of co-habitation, despite its long duration, fundamentally different to that of a married or civil partnership couple.

The weaknesses of the majority reasoning were recognized by two other judges who, while also dismissing the appeal for reasons similar to those of the first instance court, were expressly critical of the majority's approach to whether the sisters are in an analogous position to spouses and civil partners:

JUDGE BJÖRGVINSSON:

The reasoning of the majority...is in my view flawed by the fact that it is based on comparison of factors of a different nature and which are not comparable from a logical point of view. It is to a large extent based on reference to the specific legal framework which is applicable to married couples and civil partnership couples but which does not, under the present legislation, apply to the applicants as cohabiting sisters. However, although in the strict sense the complaint only relates to a difference in treatment as concerns inheritance tax, in the wider context it relates, in essence, to the facts that different rules apply and that consanguinity between the applicants prevents them from entering into a legally binding agreement similar to marriage or civil partnership, which would make the legal framework applicable to them, including the relevant provisions of the law on inheritance tax.

I believe that in these circumstances any comparison of the relationship between the applicants, on the one hand, and the relationship between married couples and civil partnership couples, on the other, should be made without specific reference to the different legal frame-work applicable, and should focus only on the substantive or material differences in the nature of the relationship as such. Despite important differences, mainly as concerns the sexual nature of the relationship between married couples and civil partner couples, when it comes to the decision to live together, closeness of the personal attachment and for most practical purposes of daily life and financial matters, the relationship between the applicants in this case has, in general and for the alleged purposes of the relevant inheritance tax exemp-tions in particular, more in common with the relationship between married or civil partner-ship couples, than there are differences between them. Despite this fact, the law prohibits them from entering into an agreement similar to marriage or civil partnership and thus take advantage of the applicable rules, including the inheritance tax rules. That being so, I am not convinced that the relationship between the applicants as cohabiting sisters cannot be com-pared with married or civil partner couples for the purposes of Article 14 of the Convention. On the contrary there is in this case a difference in treatment of persons in situations which are, as a matter of fact, to a large extent similar and analogous.

Taking functionalism to its logical conclusion

In the following extract, Alison Diduck outlines how a purely functional approach can be taken to determining the proper reach of legal regulation. It is worth considering how this approach might be applied to a situation such as the Burdens':

A. Diduck, 'Shifting Familiarity', (2005) 58 *Current Legal Problems* 235, 249

In 2001, the Law Commission of Canada... observed the growing diversity in family life and it concluded that recognising and supporting the great variety of caring personal adult relation-ships is 'an important state objective'. It identified certain basic principles and values that the state must attend to when it devises a principled and comprehensive approach to the needs of all in relationships. It concluded that the state must value equality and autonomy, personal security, privacy, freedom of conscience and religion and coherence and efficiency. It further concluded that the distinction between conjugal and non-conjugal is inconsistent with the value of equality, since conjugality 'is not an accurate marker of the qualitative attributes of personal adult relationships that are relevant to practical legislative [and policy] objectives'. It said that 'the state's role should be neutral regarding the roles that people assume in their personal relationships'.

Instead, then, of simply arguing that some relationships currently excluded should be included in legal recognition, it proposed that we start from scratch and 'look at the way governments have relied upon relational status in allocating rights and responsibilities', and try to design a legislative regime that accomplishes its goals by relying less on whether people are living in certain kinds of relationships. Sometimes some characteristics of the relationship will be important, other times they would not be, but conjugality would never be important.

On the one hand this approach runs the risk of even broader familialisation,[412] yet on the other, it eschews the word family completely in these contexts, and focuses on the variety

---

412 Diduck is concerned that apparently liberal designation of a relationship as 'family' is a way to enforce and privatize particular *obligations*: see extract at 2.3.2.

of personal and caring relationships in which people live. Instead of being concerned about families, then, it is concerned about the individual rights and responsibilities that accrue from different relationships and about how the law can help distribute them among people more equitably. For me the change in language is important. It allows us to think outside the 'family' box.

2.9 CONCLUSION

Whether individuals have the legal status of spouse or civil partner—and whether they are legally permitted to acquire that status—still makes a considerable difference to their treatment in many areas of the law. Other family relationships between adults are acknowledged in some areas, but not others. Extending legal rights and duties beyond marriage is often politically controversial, many fearing that such developments undermine the institution of marriage. We shall consider in later chapters what practical impact continued difference of treatment has on the individuals involved, and whether it can be justified.

ONLINE RESOURCE CENTRE

Questions, suggestions for further reading, and supplementary materials for this chapter (including updates on developments in this area of family law since this book was published) may be found on the Online Resource Centre at **www.oxfordtextbooks.co.uk/orc/familytcm3e/**.

3

FAMILY PROPERTY AND FINANCES

CENTRAL ISSUES

1. The ownership, occupation, and use of the family home, other property, and resources within families are principally governed by the general law of property. That law has been criticized for failing adequately to deal with the particular needs of the family context. The recent judicial development of specific principles for 'domestic' cases is controversial, creating new problems and uncertainties.

2. By contrast with many European jurisdictions and despite various reform recommendations, English family property law is based on the notion of 'separate property'. No property is jointly owned or held in 'community' simply because of marital or other family status. Each individual's property rights must therefore be addressed separately.

3. Most of the few statutory provisions creating specific 'family' rules apply only to spouses and civil partners, and deal with occupation of the family home rather than its ownership. Family members with no right of ownership have only limited power to influence the owner's decisions regarding sale or mortgage of the home.

4. The law imposes a mutual duty of support between spouses and civil partners, enforceable in private law. The public law of welfare benefits and tax credits assumes that cohabitants also support each other, even though they have no means of securing support from their partner.

5. The law relating to welfare benefits, tax credits, and taxation of the family sheds interesting light on law's concept of family, adopting different definitions of family according to the particular policy goals at stake.

3.1 INTRODUCTION

Much of family law deals with family 'pathology': the consequences of family breakdown. But the law addressed in this chapter applies as much to happy families as it does to those in trouble. However, much of this law is not 'family' law, in the sense of law devised specifically for the family. Indeed, it has been said that 'there is really no such thing in English law as "family property"', despite the social importance of family.[1]

But if the family is together, does it matter who technically owns what, who has a legal right to occupy the home, or who earns the money used to support the family? Yes, it does. For example, if the family home and mortgage used to purchase it are in the name of one spouse, who defaults on the repayments, what rights do the other spouse and any other occupants have to resist the mortgagee which wishes to realize its security by repossessing the property? What if one family member is bankrupt—can the home and other property be preserved for the rest of the family? If one party dies, what property was his and so available is to be inherited by others, and what in fact already belongs to some of those other family members?

While there is no coherent family property law, a limited corpus of legislation touches on various aspects of family property and finances. Those 'family law' provisions are based on a narrow view of what counts as 'family'. Most statutory provisions deal exclusively with spouses and civil partners. The position of other family members—including children, blood relatives, cohabitants, and other home-sharers—remains governed almost entirely by the general law, though some aspects of the 'public law' of family finances—relating to welfare benefits and tax credits—apply to cohabitants. However, even the special provisions applicable during marriage and civil partnership have fairly limited effect. So to determine the property and financial rights of family members, we must examine the general law. By contrast, as we shall see in chapters 6 and 7, there are substantial 'family law' provisions dealing with economic consequences of family breakdown. Those laws focus principally on support of minors and on financial remedies between separating spouses and civil partners. Save in relation to children (and on death), little family law currently deals with the end of cohabiting and other 'family' relationships. Much of the general law discussed in this chapter therefore determines the outcomes of property disputes when those relationships end.

It has been said that 'so far as possible the law should be kept out of the intimate life of the family'.[2] That perhaps explains why there is so little specific family law in this area. However, 'family privacy' may be counterproductive for economically weaker family members. It is important to examine the implications of the law for *individuals*, some of whom it may serve better than others. An unequal division of assets and income may create or sustain dependency and poverty within the family, particularly for women in opposite-sex relationships.[3] Those with no rights to occupy the home and to contribute to decisions about transactions such as sale or mortgage may be powerless to influence one of the most fundamental aspects of family life—the place in which it is carried on.

The law regarding family property and finances also reveals something about the law's understandings of different types of relationships and the roles of individuals within them, as Kevin Gray has suggested:

---

[1] Law Com (1971), para 0.1.

[2] Royal Commission on Marriage and Divorce (1956), para 647.

[3] See generally O'Donovan (1985), various chapters in Miles and Probert (eds) (2009).

K. Gray, *Reallocation of Property on Divorce* (Abingdon: Professional Books, 1977), 1

> Family law uniquely represents a conjunction of law, sociology, ethics, religion and economics. This statement is particularly true of that part of family law which touches upon the property relations of husband and wife. There is a sense in which the law of matrimonial property is concerned, not with property at all, but with human relations and ideologies in respect of property. Just as the general law of property provides "the basis for a broad range of social and economic assessments that are intrinsic to the way in which the community defines its culture," the law of matrimonial property "comprises a substantial portion of the secular definition of marriage." The law regulating the spouses' property relations is fundamentally an index of social relations between the sexes, and, for this reason, affords a peculiar wealth of commentary on such matters as the prevailing ideology of marriage, the cultural definition of marital roles, the social status of married women, and the role of the state *vis-à-vis* the family.

This last sentence prompted the following response from Carol Smart:

C. Smart, *The Ties that Bind* (London: Routledge, 1984), 101–2

> This statement written by an academic lawyer, rather than a sociologist, reveals the extent to which law has been increasingly conceptualised as a social construct which is profoundly imbued with ideological content. However, there still appears to be a tendency to identify the law as both passive (i.e. as an index) and homogenous. The law relating to family structure is neither of these; it actively regulates the behaviour of family members and through a variety of methods encourages marriage and reproduces the 'social relations between the sexes'. It is not homogenous because different fields of law advocate different principles even where the family is concerned, and family law itself 'speaks' with a variety of different voices.... None the less Gray is correct when he argues that an analysis of law and its implementation is a valuable site of analysis of—or peculiar wealth of commentary on—the social organisation of households and the sexual division of labour.

3.2 THE SOCIAL CONTEXT

In order to evaluate the suitability and fairness of the law governing family property and finances, it is helpful to note the current position of different families and family members in relation to housing and employment.[4]

3.2.1 THE FAMILY HOME

Key questions considered in this chapter concern the family home: who owns it, and what rights, if any, other family members have in it. Data for 2012–13 reveal that 65 per cent of English households are in owner-occupied homes, 18 per cent privately rented, and

---

4 We consider single parents at the start of chapter 6.

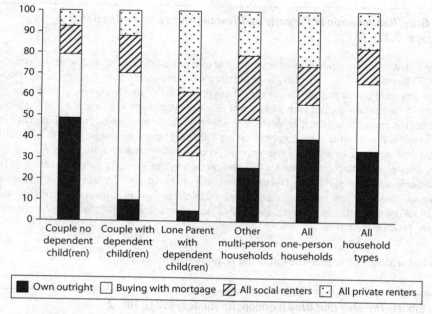

Chart 3.1 Household type by tenure, based on DCLG (2014), table 1

17 per cent in socially rented accommodation (local authority, housing association properties); this was the first time that the private rental sector was larger than the social sector.[5] Housing tenure varies both by marital status and by whether the family includes dependent children. In 2007–8,[6] while 83 per cent of spouses lived in owner-occupied property, only 62 per cent of cohabitants, 56 per cent of single people, and 54 per cent of divorced and separated people did so. Conversely, 29 per cent of divorced and separated individuals lived in social housing, 21 per cent of single people, 16 per cent of cohabitants, and 9 per cent of spouses.[7] Chart 3.1 shows the prevalence of each tenure type for different types of households in 2012–13.

3.2.2 THE FAMILY ECONOMY

The law attaches great significance to property ownership, which usually derives from purchasing that property or contributing financially to its acquisition. Each family member's economic power is therefore important. Women's employment patterns, particularly following motherhood, have changed markedly over the last 30 years, as increasing numbers of women, including mothers, have entered the workforce. However, 74 per cent (over six million) of the 8.27 million part-time employees in 2013–14 were women, whereas 63 per cent (over 14 million) of the 22.5 million full-time employees were men.[8] More female than male employees have opted for flexible working patterns to accommodate

---

[5] DCLG (2014), 1.4–1.6.
[6] This appears to be the last year in which data was recorded by marital status.
[7] DCLG (2009), table 1.7; for equivalent Welsh data, see Welsh Assembly Government (2009), ch 12.
[8] ONS (2014h), 10.

child-care.[9] While nearly 900,000 women (over one million men) were unemployed in the third quarter of 2014,[10] nearly 5.7 million working age women (3.4 million working age men) were 'economically inactive'. The most common reason for this is that they are looking after family or home: 36 per cent of working age women who were economically inactive (over two million women) gave that reason in 2014, compared with only 7 per cent of men (234,000 men); the most common reason for male economic inactivity is long-term sickness.[11] Indeed, while being a mother of dependent children makes a woman less likely to be employed, the opposite is true for men: a higher proportion of fathers of dependent children are in paid employment than other men. And the younger the child, the less likely the mother is to work, especially if she is a single parent.[12]

Some parents positively choose a traditional division of roles. However, for mothers who want to play a greater role in the workforce, labour law rights are crucial. Recent years have seen an increase in family-friendly employment legislation and registered child-care places, though complaints about the lack of accessible and affordable child-care places persist.[13] However, emphasis on encouraging and enabling women to work, creating a 'dual earner family model', may come at the expense of exploring more fully what can be done to encourage and enable *men* to shoulder more caring responsibilities, achieving better work/life balance for both parents.[14] Many men would like to work fewer hours to care for children, but encounter obstacles to doing so.[15] New rules for shared parental leave from 2015 will enable parents to share the leave entitlement, but the pay beyond the initial period is very low, which may prevent many fathers from taking it up.[16] Unlike some other jurisdictions, English law does not create a 'daddy quota' that has to be taken by the father or lost.[17] Until men's ability to take time off work to care for children is properly realized, the burden of juggling work and family responsibilities is likely to rest predominantly with women. Recent survey data reveal that UK wives on average still undertake three-quarters of housework.[18]

So although far more women are working now than in the 1960s, men's and women's engagement with the labour market remain very different. Women's employment patterns over their lifetime are substantially affected by child-care, home-making, and other unpaid caring responsibilities (e.g. for older relatives).[19] This places many women in an inferior economic position in their relationships, with less money at their disposal for personal spending and saving,[20] pension building,[21] and contribution to household expenses and acquisition of the family home. This potentially disadvantages them significantly in property law and, if the parties are not spouses or civil partners, on relationship breakdown.

9 ONS (2010e), table 4.11.
10 ONS (2014h), table A01.
11 Ibid, table INAC01.
12 ONS (2013f), 9–10.
13 DFE (2014c), fig 6.4.
14 EHRC (2009), Scott and Dex (2009), Lewis (2009), James (2009).
15 Hobson and Fahlén (2011).
16 Children and Families Act 2014, Part 7 and associated regulations.
17 See Hobson and Fahlén (2011).
18 McFall et al (eds) (2012), 7–8.
19 On patterns of unpaid work in the home and its impact on earnings, see ibid; ONS (2007), ch 2; Bryan and Sanz (2008); Scott and Dex (2009).
20 Vogler et al (2008).
21 Price (2009).

3.3 FAMILY PROPERTY SYSTEMS: SEPARATE PROPERTY

English law operates a system of 'separate property': there is no such thing as 'family property' which is jointly owned and controlled by family members by virtue of their relationship. Instead, each individual has whatever rights of ownership he or she enjoys under the general law of property and trusts.

Historically, this was not so for spouses. The law of husband and wife imposed special rules on the capacity of each spouse to hold property. It is helpful to consider those rules before we examine the current law (which applies in almost[22] exactly the same way to spouses, civil partners, cohabitants, and any other person seeking to assert an interest in property), in order to see how and why English law has reached its current position.

3.3.1 THE OLD LAW OF HUSBAND AND WIFE

As we noted in chapter 2, at common law, the doctrine of unity prescribed that husband and wife were one person in law, represented by the husband.[23] This had profound implications for wives' property:[24] in principle, wives were disabled from owning property so all personal property of the wife owned prior to marriage or acquired during it, including any earnings, were the husband's. The position regarding the wife's real property (land) was more complicated: the husband took control of that property during the marriage; if a child was born, the husband would have a life interest in the property; but if he predeceased the wife, she would be able to recover any land that he had disposed of without her consent.[25] As a result of these laws, and wives' disabilities in contract and tort law, Cretney concludes that 'it is not a great exaggeration to say that the common law robbed the married woman of full human personality'.[26] Equity, however, took a different view, and so wealthy parents would ensure that their daughters' property was protected by trust before they married. But that avenue was not practically available to the poorer classes and—crucially for working class wives—could not protect a wife's earnings. As John Stuart Mill put it in his powerful essay of 1869, *The Subjection of Women*: 'The two are called "one person in law", for the purpose of inferring that whatever is hers is his, but the parallel inference is never drawn that whatever is his is hers; the maxim is not applied against the man, except to make him responsible to third parties for her acts, as a master is for the acts of his slaves or of his cattle.'[27]

There were limited compensations for the wife's disabilities: for example, she had a right at common law to be maintained by her husband and would be presumed to be acting as his agent in the purchase of 'necessaries', so could pledge his credit with tradesmen;[28] he would be liable for any tort she committed.[29] But her essential disability remained, while her unmarried sister enjoyed the same rights to own property as men.

[22] A few statutory rules apply to spouses and civil partners.

[23] See 2.4.2.

[24] This summary is taken from Cretney (2003a), 90–3.

[25] See Doggett (1992), 36–59; Kahn-Freund (1955); O'Donovan (1985), ch 2.

[26] Cretney (2003a), 91.

[27] Mill (1869), 463.

[28] Since she could own no property, a wife could not make a contract herself, having no means of fulfilling it.

[29] These were necessary results of wives' incapacity regarding property: Kahn-Freund (1955), 271–2.

Katherine O'Donovan has argued that the common law was largely based on ideological and economic rationales.[30] The ideological basis was the doctrine of unity and the wife's consequent subjection to the husband's control. But the common law also served an economic function: by denying them economic power and rendering them dependent on their husbands, wives were pushed into motherhood and unpaid domestic service in the home, while husbands went out into the market to earn a 'family wage'. The law therefore sustained the traditional division of labour between spouses and the separation of the public world inhabited by men from the private world of women.[31]

3.3.2 REFORM: SEPARATE PROPERTY AND SEPARATE LIABILITY FOR SPOUSES

The Married Women's Property Acts of 1870 and 1882 brought key reform. This legislation followed sustained campaigns by the early women's movement, with the support of sympathetic (male) parliamentarians, moved by the injustice experienced in particular by working class wives.[32] The current law is found in early twentieth-century legislation:

Law of Property Act 1925, s 37

A husband and wife shall, for all purposes of acquisition of any interest in property...be treated as two persons.

Law Reform (Married Women and Tortfeasors) Act 1935

1 Capacity of married women

Subject to the provisions of this Act, a married woman shall—

(a) be capable of acquiring, holding, and disposing of, any property; and

(b) be capable of rendering herself, and being rendered, liable in respect of any tort, contract, debt, or obligation; and

(c) be capable of suing and being sued, either in tort or in contract or otherwise;

(d) be subject to the law relating to bankruptcy and to the enforcement of judgments and orders,

in all respects as if she were a feme sole [single woman].

---

[30] O'Donovan (1985), 30–5.

[31] Until the early twentieth century, women (married or not) had no vote and were excluded from professional occupations, public office, and reading for university degrees: Representation of the People Acts 1918 and 1928 and Sex Disqualification (Removal) Act 1919.

[32] Holcombe (1983).

2 Property of married women

(1) Subject to the provision of this Part of this Act all property which—

    (a) immediately before the passing of this Act was the separate property of a married woman or held for her separate use in equity; or

    (b) belongs at the time of her marriage to a woman married after the passing of this Act; or

    (c) after the passing of this Act is acquired by or devolves upon a married woman,

shall belong to her in all respects as if she were a feme sole and may be disposed of accordingly.

3 Abolition of husband's liability for wife's torts and ante-nuptial contracts, debts and obligations

Subject to the provisions of this Part of this Act, the husband of a married woman shall not, by reason only of his being her husband, be liable—

    (a) in respect of any tort committed by her whether before or after the marriage, or in respect of any contract entered into, or debt or obligation incurred, by her before the marriage; or

    (b) be sued, or made a party to any legal proceeding brought, in respect of any such tort, contract, debt, or obligation.

4 Savings...

(2) For the avoidance of doubt it is hereby declared that nothing in this Part of this Act—...

    (c) prevents a husband and wife from acquiring, holding, and disposing of, any property jointly or as tenants in common, or from rendering themselves, or being rendered, jointly liable in respect of any tort, contract, debt or obligation, and of suing and being sued either in tort or in contract or otherwise, in like manner as if they were not married;...

In the middle of the last century, a series of decisions involving Lord Denning MR sought to establish a doctrine of 'family assets' under which spouses would readily be found to co-own their home and other property central to family life.[33] Lord Denning's initiative was quashed by the House of Lords in *Pettitt v Pettitt*, which firmly established that the general law of property applies between husband and wife, 'while making full allowances in view of that relationship'.[34]

So the general law applies to determine all family members' property rights. Under that law, the question for the judge is 'whose is this?' and not, as on divorce, 'to whom shall this be given?'.[35] But despite the suggestion that 'allowances' would be made for the parties' relationship and recent case law developments explored below, the general law of property can still be regarded as an inadequate tool for the protection of economically weaker family members. 'Separate property' is in that respect not all that its proponents might have hoped

[33] See Hayward (2012).
[34] [1970] AC 777, 813.
[35] *Pettitt v Pettitt* [1970] AC 777, 798.

as a measure for wives' economic emancipation. The nineteenth-century reformers, motivated by a political philosophy of individualism, sought formal equality: married women should have the same rights as any other person to own property. The basic appeal of that claim seems irresistible. However, while wives now had the legal *power* to own property, many were in *practice* unable to acquire any property owing to their confinement to the domestic sphere and the basis on which the general law allows interests in property to be acquired.[36] As Katherine O'Donovan put it, 'So long as equality remains a formal notion, like the Ritz hotel which is open to all, structural obstacles will prevent those for whom opportunities are opened from taking advantage of them.'[37] Despite the increasing numbers of wives and mothers who engage in paid employment, these problems remain.

It is important, however, to remember the statutory remedies available between spouses and civil partners on relationship breakdown; for the benefit of children who live apart from one or both parents; and for a wide range of family members in the event of death, under the laws of intestacy and family provision.[38] Given the scope for property sharing entailed in these schemes, it is misleading to describe English family property law as a separate property regime.[39] But for those not covered by such a scheme—notably, cohabitants—the general law can create results which may appear harsh. We consider possible statutory reform for such cases at the end of chapter 7.

3.4 THE CURRENT LAW: ASCERTAINING OWNERSHIP OF LAND

Different rules apply to determine the ownership of land and other assets. The law ordinarily insists on compliance with certain formal requirements for the creation and transfer of interests in land, whereas interests in other forms of property can be created and transferred orally. However, interests in land may arise informally under the laws of implied trust, in particular the 'common intention' constructive trust, and proprietary estoppel. Those areas of law have received particular attention from commentators and law reformers, and we give them most attention here.

It is impossible here to provide a full account of this complex area of law; readers are advised to refer to a specialist textbook on land law.[40] The following discussion assumes basic understanding of English law's concepts of land, estates, and interests in land; the distinction between legal and equitable ('beneficial') ownership; the concepts of joint tenancy and tenancy in common; the system of land registration; and the concept of overreaching.

3.4.1 TRANSFERS AND EXPRESS TRUSTS: FORMAL REQUIREMENTS

Interests in land can be expressly created and transferred only by signed writing. A declaration of trust in relation to land must ordinarily be manifested and proved by some

---

[36] See Smart (1984), 29–30, 47–9.
[37] O'Donovan (1985), 167.
[38] See chapters 6 and 7.
[39] Kahn-Freund (1955), 284–6; Simon (1964), 18.
[40] Gray and Gray (2009), (2011).

signed writing of the settlor(s).[41] All transfers of land and interests in land are void unless made by deed.[42] If the property is transferred into the name of one person, prima facie that individual becomes both legal and beneficial owner. If property is owned by two or more people, it is held on trust. Usually, the property is transferred into the parties' joint names so that they are both legal owners (once registered as proprietors).[43] The legal owners should, ideally, also declare (in writing) the basis on which they, and any others, hold the beneficial interest in the property: do they all have beneficial shares; if so, as joint tenants or tenants in common; and if as tenants in common, what size share does each party have?[44] Any such express declaration of trust determines the shares in which the beneficial interest is held.[45] Express joint ownership of homes is now common amongst spouses, but rather less so amongst cohabiting couples.[46]

The law permits some important exceptions to these formal requirements, allowing beneficial interests to arise by implied (resulting and constructive) trusts and proprietary estoppel.[47] These allow someone (who may or may not be on the legal title) to acquire a beneficial share in property, even if there is no valid express declaration of trust in his or her favour. Because the application of implied trust and estoppel law is notoriously complicated and uncertain, it is preferable that parties think specifically about how the beneficial title of property is to be held and declare an express trust. The courts' exasperation with those who fail to do so is exemplified in *Carlton v Goodman*. Mr Goodman and Ms Carlton had bought a house in joint names and with a joint mortgage, to be occupied only by Mr Goodman, he alone paying the mortgage instalments. They had not expressly declared how the beneficial title was to be held, so the case was decided by reference to the law of resulting trust (a complex exercise in cases of mortgage-financed purchase):

Carlton v Goodman [2002] EWCA Civ 545

WARD LJ:

44. I would add only this. The conveyancer who acted for these parties thought at one time that she had discussed with Mr Goodman whether or not he wished to declare their beneficial interest in the conveyance and record that they held as joint tenants, the rules of survivorship having been explained to him [i.e. that where property is held on a joint tenancy, in the event of the death of one of two joint tenants, the survivor is immediately sole owner of the whole property]. When she gave evidence she eventually concluded that she did not have any such discussion with Mr Goodman and the judge had no hesitation in concluding that no such discussion had taken place. It was common ground that Anita [Carlton] was not

---

[41] Law of Property Act 1925 (LPA 1925), s 53(1)(a) and (b).

[42] Ibid, s 52.

[43] Land Registration Act 2002 (LRA 2002), s 27. The legal title may be held by up to four people: Trustee Act 1925, s 34(2), LPA 1925, s 34(2).

[44] A clause providing that the survivor of the trustees can give a valid receipt for the proceeds of sale or other disposition of the property does not constitute an express declaration of a beneficial joint tenancy: *Stack v Dowden* [2007] UKHL 17.

[45] *Goodman v Gallant* [1986] Fam 106; subject, e.g., to vitiating grounds such as fraud; the possibility of a subsequent express variation of their interests: *Singla v Browne* [2007] EWHC 405; or a supervening constructive trust arising: *Qayyum v Hameed* [2009] EWCA Civ 352.

[46] Haskey (2001b), table 2.

[47] LPA 1925, s 53(2).

involved in any such discussion. I ask in despair how often this court has to remind conveyancers that they would save their clients a great deal of later difficulty if only they would sit
the purchasers down, explain the difference between a joint tenancy and a tenancy in common, ascertain what they want and then expressly declare in the conveyance or transfer how
the beneficial interest is to be held because that will be conclusive and save all argument.
When are conveyancers going to do this as a matter of invariable standard practice? This
court has urged that time after time. Perhaps conveyancers do not read law reports. I will try
one more time: ALWAYS TRY TO AGREE ON AND THEN RECORD HOW THE BENEFICIAL
INTEREST IS TO BE HELD. It is not very difficult to do.

The Land Registry process prompts parties to think about beneficial ownership: the purchasers must complete a form on which they are invited to state how the beneficial interest
is to be held.[48] It had been assumed, not least given the language on the form itself, that purchasers were required to complete that part of the form.[49] However, Baroness Hale in *Stack v
Dowden* suggested otherwise, whilst observing that many of the problems we are about to
examine would disappear if it were compulsory.[50] This led to a review to determine whether
the rules ought to make its completion compulsory—the review team concluded that it
should become a requirement, but Land Registry declined to act on that recommendation.[51]

This is a difficult area. As matters stand, Land Registry will register transfers without
completion of that part of the form; as a default measure, it enters a restriction on the register, a step which (whilst not conclusive) tends incorrectly to be interpreted by others as
meaning that the parties wish to be beneficial tenants in common, rather than joint tenants.
The parties are then left to thrash out their respective rights under the law of implied trusts.
However, recent research suggests that many purchasers who currently do complete and
execute the form (thereby making a binding express declaration of trust) do not fully appreciate the significance of their choice and so may get an unpleasant surprise should their
relationship break down. In particular, it seems that many couples select a beneficial joint
tenancy on the basis that, in the event of their relationship ending by death, the survivor
will automatically acquire title to the whole property under the doctrine of survivorship.[52]
However, it is less well appreciated that if a cohabiting relationship instead ends by separation, on severance of the beneficial joint tenancy the equity in the property (the capital value
remaining after the mortgage loan has been repaid) will be divided 50:50, however much
each party contributed financially to the property's acquisition. With a tenancy in common,
by contrast, the parties must draft wills to ensure that the survivor inherits, but can specify
whatever lifetime shares in the property they like.[53]

At the very least, purchasers should be alerted to the significance of their choices by
information and legal advice provided at the point of conveyancing, particularly where

---

[48] LRA 2002, s 44(1), and Land Registration Rules 2003, r 95(2)(a); Form FR1 in the case of first registration, and Form TR1 in the case of a transfer of registered land.

[49] See Dixon (2007a).

[50] [2007] UKHL 17, [52].

[51] Cf Cooke (2011a).

[52] Douglas, Pearce, and Woodward (2007a), (2007b).

[53] Cf the construction placed on the declaration of trust in *Chopra v Bindra* [2009] EWCA Civ 203, which
purported to create survivorship in what was otherwise a tenancy in common: the court construed the survivorship clause as conferring a contingent remainder interest on the survivor in the other party's share. The
parties thus achieved separate, unequal interests during their joint lives, but with survivorship (in effect) on
death. For comment, see (2009) FL 584.

potentially conflicting interests mean that parties should receive independent advice.[54] Private ordering—parties deciding at the outset how they wish to deal with their property—has many advantages, not least the avoidance of protracted subsequent litigation under the law of implied trusts. But private ordering can only be as good as the knowledge with which the parties act. Moreover, the Land Registry form and associated advice is only likely to draw people's attention to the question of beneficial ownership if they purchase land together. It does not help where the property is bought in the name of one party only, or where one party moves into property already acquired by the other. There therefore remain many cases where resort must be had to the law of implied trusts and estoppel in order to decide whether that other party has an interest in the property.

3.4.2 IMPLIED TRUSTS OF LAND AND PROPRIETARY ESTOPPEL: INTRODUCTION

Whether the legal title is held solely or jointly, if there is no express declaration of trust, a trust may be implied by law. The law of implied trusts identifies the extent of the beneficial interests, if any, held by joint legal owners who failed to declare an express trust, and enables individuals who are not on the legal title to acquire a beneficial interest. The law of proprietary estoppel may also generate an interest in property for a claimant. Before embarking on an examination of this area, comments from a Court of Appeal judge—prompted by the morass of complex and often apparently contradictory case law—deserve repetition:

Stack v Dowden [2005] EWCA Civ 857

CARNWATH LJ:

75. To the detached observer, the result [of this case law] may seem like a witch's brew, into which various esoteric ingredients have been stirred over the years, and in which different ideas bubble to the surface at different times. They include implied trust, constructive trust, resulting trust, presumption of advancement, proprietary estoppel, unjust enrichment, and so on. These ideas are likely to mean nothing to laymen, and often little more to the lawyers who use them.

3.4.3 IMPLIED TRUSTS OF LAND: THE PRESUMPTIONS OF RESULTING TRUST AND ADVANCEMENT

We must first examine two presumptions, one of which (resulting trust) is less relevant in family cases than formerly, the other of which (advancement) is due to be abolished by statute. Both presumptions are (or were) based on what the courts assume—in the absence of evidence—to be the 'commonsense' view of what parties would intend in particular circumstances.

---

[54] See findings of Douglas, Pearce, and Woodward (2007a), (2007b).

The presumption of resulting trust

Generally, if property is transferred into the name of A, but B funded the purchase, the law will presume that the parties intended that A would hold the land on a resulting trust for B to the extent of B's contribution. So if A and B buy property, whether in A's name or in A and B's joint names, and they contribute 40 per cent and 60 per cent of the purchase price respectively, A (or, if in joint names, A and B) hold the property on trust for A and B in shares of 40:60. Such a resulting trust only arises where B makes some direct financial contribution to the acquisition of the property, for example by paying a deposit, assuming personal liability under a mortgage,[55] or—depending on the circumstances and type of mortgage—paying mortgage instalments.[56] Indirect financial contributions (e.g. paying other household bills or contributing to a common pool from which household expenses are met) and non-financial contributions to the parties' relationship (e.g. home-making and child-rearing) are irrelevant.[57] Where there is evidence that B's financial contribution was intended as a gift or a loan to A, the presumption is rebutted so B acquires no share.[58]

This exclusive focus on financial contributions makes it difficult for some family members to acquire a share in land under this presumption. However, although the presumption of resulting trust remains part of the law, it has been said that:

> 53. The assumptions as to human motivation, which led the courts to impute particular intentions by way of resulting trust, are not appropriate to the ascertainment of beneficial interests in a family home....[59]

The presumption of advancement

The presumption of advancement, due to be abolished prospectively by s 199 of the Equality Act 2010,[60] was an interesting relic of the law's historical treatment of certain family relationships.[61] It remains good law for cases arising from events occurring or obligations arising before the Act comes into force. Where a husband or father made a transfer to his wife or child—but not where a wife or mother did so[62]—the law initially presumed not a resulting trust, but a gift.[63] This presumption was not replicated in the civil partnership legislation (unsurprisingly, given its gendered nature), nor did it apply between cohabitants.[64]

The presumption was based on an increasingly dubious assumption that a husband or father would intend to make a gift, given his natural and moral obligation to his wife or child[65] and

---

55 Cf *Stack v Dowden* [2007] UKHL 17, [120] per Lord Neuberger.

56 *Huntingford v Hobbs* [1993] 1 FLR 736; *Carlton v Goodman* [2002] EWCA Civ 545; *Curley v Parkes* [2004] EWCA Civ 1515; *McKenzie v McKenzie* [2003] 2 P&CR DG6.

57 *Gissing v Gissing* [1971] AC 886.

58 *Re Sharpe (A Bankrupt)* [1980] 1 WLR 219; *Chapman v Jaume* [2012] EWCA Civ 476.

59 *Jones v Kernott* [2011] UKSC 53.

60 Not in force December 2014; see Glister (2010).

61 See generally Gray and Gray (2009), from 7.2.33.

62 Gender inequality in the parental context was questioned in *Gross v French* (1976) 238 EG 39; note also developments in some Commonwealth jurisdictions: Gray and Gray (2009), 7.2.37.

63 *Dyer v Dyer* (1788) 2 Cox Eq Cas 92; it was extended by statute to fiancés: Law Reform (Miscellaneous Provisions) Act 1970, s 2(1), *Mossop v Mossop* [1989] Fam 77; cf *Mercier v Mercier* [1903] 2 Ch 98.

64 *Soar v Foster* (1858) 4 K&J 152, 162.

65 *Bennet v Bennet* (1879) 10 Ch D 474, 477.

their economic dependence on him.[66] By contrast, a wife or mother would not be taken to intend to make a gift in such cases, but rather to retain an interest under resulting trust. As early as 1970, the House of Lords in *Pettitt* considered that the force of the presumption was much weakened in contemporary conditions.[67] In any event, there was almost always evidence, however slight, from which the parties' actual intentions could be deduced, readily rebutting the presumption.[68]

The presumption of advancement was widely thought to be incompatible with human rights law.[69] Its retention prevented the UK's ratification of a Protocol to the European Convention on Human Rights (ECHR):

Article 5 of the Seventh Protocol of the European Convention on Human Rights

Equality between spouses

Spouses shall enjoy equality of rights and responsibilities of a private law character between them, and in their relations with their children, as to marriage, during marriage and in the event of its dissolution.

Once the Equality Act 2010 provision is implemented, ratification should be possible.

3.4.4 IMPLIED TRUSTS OF LAND: 'COMMON INTENTION' CONSTRUCTIVE TRUSTS

Following *Stack v Dowden*[70] and *Jones v Kernott*,[71] the common intention constructive trust is the principal form of implied trust in the 'domestic' context[72] where parties acquire a home together in joint or sole names, or where one moves into the other's home and claims a beneficial interest. The voluminous case law in this area gives property and trust lawyers considerable doctrinal difficulty and has generated a vast literature. It is not easy to state the law. Many commentators consider that *Stack* and *Jones* have significantly relaxed the requirements of the common intention constructive trust, increasing its ability to produce 'fair' outcomes in family cases.[73] However, it is far from clear whether that is the effect of those decisions (or, on key points, of obiter remarks in those decisions), and few if any subsequent cases have reached outcomes strikingly different from those that would previously have been expected. Moreover, it is questionable whether it is appropriate for trusts law to be used to reach the 'fair' outcomes that are sought: a specifically tailored statutory scheme may be far safer, doctrinally, as a means of achieving this.[74]

---

[66] *Pettitt v Pettitt* [1970] AC 777, 793.
[67] For criticism, see Auchmuty (2007), 180–3.
[68] *Pettitt v Pettitt* [1970] AC 777, 793, 811, 814, and 824.
[69] See Andrews (2007); cf Glister (2010).
[70] [2007] UKHL 17.
[71] [2011] UKSC 53.
[72] Contrast 'commercial' cases: *Stack v Dowden*, ibid, [57]–[58]. We explore this distinction below at p 146.
[73] Most enthusiastic are Gardner (2013), and Gardner and Davidson (2012).
[74] See Mee (2011), (2012).

On an orthodox understanding of the law, there are three inter-related ingredients to be proved in establishing a common intention constructive trust: (i) a common or shared intention between the parties that the claimant should have a beneficial share in the property; on which (ii) the claimant has detrimentally relied, such that it would be unconscionable for the owner to deny the claimant's interest; and finally (iii) quantification of that interest. The detailed discussion of these ingredients below is organized around the categories of case identified in *Stack/Jones* in which those three ingredients are differently interpreted and applied: first, cases in which the legal title is held jointly (joint-names cases); and secondly, those in which it is held by one party (sole-name cases).

The law applicable to 'domestic cases'

The leading statement of the law, at a high level of generality, that applies in 'domestic' cases[75] is found in *Jones v Kernott*, supplemented by key passages of Lady Hale's judgment in *Stack v Dowden*:

Jones v Kernott [2011] UKSC 53

LORD WALKER AND LADY HALE:

51. In summary, therefore, the following are the principles applicable in a case such as this, where a family home is bought in the joint names of a cohabiting couple who are both responsible for any mortgage,[76] but without any express declaration of their beneficial interests.

(1) The starting point is that equity follows the law and they are joint tenants both in law and in equity.

(2) That presumption can be displaced by showing (a) that the parties had a different common intention at the time when they acquired the home, or (b) that they later formed the common intention that their respective shares would change. [see further below]

(3) Their common intention is to be deduced objectively from their conduct: "the relevant intention of each party is the intention which was reasonably understood by the other party to be manifested by that party's words and conduct notwithstanding that he did not consciously formulate that intention in his own mind or even acted with some different intention which he did not communicate to the other party" (Lord Diplock in *Gissing v Gissing* [1971] AC 886, 906). Examples of the sort of evidence which might be relevant to drawing such inferences are given in *Stack v Dowden*, at para 69. [extracted immediately below]

(4) In those cases where it is clear either (a) that the parties did not intend joint tenancy at the outset, or (b) had changed their original intention, but it is not possible to ascertain by direct evidence or by inference what their actual intention was as to the shares in which they would own the property, "the answer is that each is entitled to that share which the court considers fair having regard to the whole course of dealing between them in relation to the property": Chadwick LJ in *Oxley v Hiscock* [2005] Fam 211, para 69. In our judgment, "the whole course of dealing…in relation to the property" should be given a broad meaning, enabling a similar range of factors to be taken into account as may be relevant to ascertaining the parties' actual intentions.

(5) Each case will turn on its own facts. Financial contributions are relevant but there are many other factors which may enable the court to decide what shares were either intended (as in case (3)) or fair (as in case (4)).

---

[75] We explore this concept below at p 146.

[76] It seems clear that a joint mortgage is not an essential feature of a case being classed as 'domestic' for these purposes. We discuss the scope of 'domestic' further below.

52. This case is not concerned with a family home which is put into the name of one party only. [There the] starting point is different. The first issue is whether it was intended that the other party have any beneficial interest in the property at all. If he does, the second issue is what that interest is. There is no presumption of joint beneficial ownership. But their common intention has once again to be deduced objectively from their conduct. If the evidence shows a common intention to share beneficial ownership but does not show what shares were intended, the court will have to proceed as at para 51(4) and (5) above.

Stack v Dowden [2007] UKHL 17

BARONESS HALE:

68. The burden will...be on the person seeking to show that the parties did intend their beneficial interests to be different from their legal interests, and in what way. This is not a task to be lightly embarked upon. In family disputes, strong feelings are aroused when couples split up. These often lead the parties, honestly but mistakenly, to reinterpret the past in self-exculpatory or vengeful terms. They also lead people to spend far more on the legal battle than is warranted by the sums actually at stake. A full examination of the facts is likely to involve disproportionate costs. In joint names cases it is also unlikely to lead to a different result unless the facts are very unusual...It cannot be the case that all the hundreds and thousands, if not millions, of transfers into joint names using the old forms[77] are vulnerable to challenge in the courts simply because it is likely that the owners contributed unequally to their purchase.

How is the court to ascertain what the parties intended? Having indicated that the presumption would rarely be rebutted, the range of relevant factors appear to provide considerable room for parties to attempt to do just that:

69. In law, "context is everything" and the domestic context is very different from the commercial world. Each case will turn on its own facts. Many more factors than financial contributions may be relevant to divining the parties' true intentions. These include: any advice or discussions at the time of the transfer which cast light upon their intentions then;[78] the reasons why the home was acquired in their joint names; the reasons why (if it be the case) the survivor was authorised to give a receipt for the capital monies; the purpose for which the home was acquired; the nature of the parties' relationship; whether they had children for whom they both had responsibility to provide a home; how the purchase was financed, both initially and subsequently; how the parties arranged their finances, whether separately or together or a bit of both; how they discharged the outgoings on the property and their other household expenses. When a couple are joint owners of the home and jointly liable for the mortgage, the inferences to be drawn from who pays for what may be very different from the inferences to be drawn when only one is owner of the home. The arithmetical calculation of how much was paid by each is also likely to be less important. It will be easier to draw the

---

[77] I.e. forms containing the 'valid receipt' clause, discussed at n 44 above, which was held in *Stack* not to constitute an express declaration of trust, hence the resort to implied trust law.

[78] E.g. the draft declaration of trust considered in *Williamson v Sheikh* [2008] EWCA Civ 990; the claimant was a minor at the date of purchase, so could not appear on the legal title.

inference that they intended that each should contribute as much to the household as they reasonably could and that they would share the eventual benefit or burden equally. The parties' individual characters and personalities may also be a factor in deciding where their true intentions lay. In the cohabitation context, mercenary considerations may be more to the fore than they would be in marriage, but it should not be assumed that they will always take pride of place over natural love and affection. At the end of day, having taken all this into account, cases in which the joint legal owners are taken to have intended that their beneficial interests should be different from their legal interests will be very unusual.

70. This is not, of course, an exhaustive list. There may also be reasons to conclude that, whatever the parties' intentions at the outset, these have now changed. An example might be where one party has financed (or constructed himself) an extension or substantial improvement to the property, so that what they have now is significantly different from what they had then.

In relation to cases where intentions are claimed to have changed over time, Baroness Hale said:

62....[A]lthough the parties' intentions may change over the course of time, producing...an "ambulatory" constructive trust, at any one time their interests must be the same for all purposes. They cannot at one and the same time intend, for example, a joint tenancy with survivorship should one of them die while they are still together, a tenancy in common in equal shares should they separate on amicable terms after the children have grown up, and a tenancy in common in unequal shares should they separate on acrimonious terms while the children are still with them.

An important point to note from this exposition of the law and other passages extracted below is the conspicuous absence of any reference to detrimental reliance, the second of the three ingredients required on the orthodox understanding of the law. It would be extremely curious if this requirement were dispensed with in common intention constructive trust cases—certainly without any justifying commentary—not least since it clearly remains a requirement in proprietary estoppel where, as discussed below, the claimant may be asserting a much *less significant* claim over the property than the shared beneficial interest claimed in the trusts cases. In *Stack*, at least, the court was not called on to consider whether the claimant had a beneficial share *at all*—the focus was on quantification, so the issue of detrimental reliance did not arise for decision.[79] And both decisions were entirely obiter regarding sole-name cases; there, at least, the requirement retains an important function.

Inferring intention, imputing intention, and the role of 'fairness'

Jones v Kernott identifies two stages: (i) the *acquisition* stage—do the parties have a common intention to have interests different from those which the relevant presumption supplies?;[80] if so, (ii) the *quantification* stage—in what other shares do the parties hold the beneficial title? Although there is some ambiguity elsewhere in the lead judgment,[81] it is clear that

---

79 *Stack v Dowden* [2007] UKHL 17, [63].
80 Note lack of reference to detrimental reliance.
81 [2011] UKSC 53, end of [31], opening of [48]; cf views of Lords Collins [64], Kerr [68], and Wilson [84].

the Supreme Court requires stage (i) to be answered by reference to the parties' actual intentions, either evidenced directly or inferred from their conduct. It is not open to the courts at this stage to 'impute' to the parties an intention that they never had or to impose the answer it regards as 'fair'.[82] In *Midland Bank v Cooke*, Waite LJ had suggested that a constructive trust could be found even where the parties 'had been honest enough to admit that they never gave ownership a thought or reached any agreement about it', thinking it 'unrealistic' to expect them to have had such conversations.[83] True as his view of the world may be, the orthodox position rejects use of imputed intentions at stage (i). Lord Neuberger, dissenting in *Stack*, rejected *any* resort to imputation:

Stack v Dowden [2007] UKHL 17

LORD NEUBERGER:

126. An inferred intention is one which is objectively deduced to be the subjective actual intention of the parties, in the light of their actions and statements. An imputed intention is one which is attributed to the parties, even though no such actual intention can be deduced from their actions and statements, and even though they had no such intention. Imputation involves concluding what the parties would have intended, whereas inference involves concluding what they did intend.

127. To impute an intention would not only be wrong in principle and a departure from [*Pettitt v Pettitt* [1970] AC 777 and *Gissing v Gissing* [1971] AC 886] in this very area, but it would also involve a judge in an exercise which was difficult, subjective and uncertain.... It would be difficult because the judge would be constructing an intention where none existed at the time, and where the parties may well not have been able to agree. It would be subjective for obvious reasons. It would be uncertain because it is unclear whether one considers a hypothetical negotiation between the actual parties, or what reasonable parties would have agreed. The former is more logical, but would redound to the advantage of an unreasonable party.

However, despite Lord Neuberger's reservations, once we reach quantification at stage (ii), *Jones* clearly decides that if the parties' actual intentions regarding the size of their respective beneficial interests cannot be ascertained, or were non-existent, the court must substitute an answer based on what is fair. Earlier in their judgment,[84] Lord Walker and Lady Hale had used the language of 'imputed intention' to describe this decision. It is hard to see how a decision described in terms of 'imputed intention' is different from one expressed in terms of what is fair in the circumstances. Where the parties' *actual* intention requires a result that is considered objectively *unfair*, the court must follow it.[85] By contrast, where no actual intention can be found, it is hard to imagine a court imputing to the parties an objectively unfair intention, certainly not if they treat the

---

[82] *Geary v Rankine* [2012] EWCA Civ 555, [19]; *Thompson v Hurst* [2012] EWCA Civ 1752, [22]; cf imprecision in *Aspden v Elvy* [2012] EWHC 1387, [93.4] and obiter remarks in *Bhura v Bhura (No 2)* [2013] EWHC 727, [8(vii)].

[83] [1995] 4 All ER 562, 575; *Kernott v Jones* [2010] EWCA Civ 578, [90].

[84] E.g. [2011] UKSC 53, [31].

[85] See *James v Thomas* [2007] EWCA Civ 1212, [38].

parties as 'reasonable people' for these purposes.[86] But the language of fairness is more transparent:[87]

Jones v Kernott [2011] UKSC 53

LORD KERR:

74. The reason that I question the aptness of the notion of imputing an intention is that, in the final analysis, the exercise is wholly unrelated to ascertainment of the parties' views. It involves the court deciding what is fair in light of the whole course of dealing with the property. That decision has nothing to do with what the parties intended, or what might be supposed would have been their intention had they addressed that question. In many ways, it would be preferable to have a stark choice between deciding whether it is possible to deduce what their intention was and, where it is not, deciding what is fair, without elliptical references to what their intention might have – or should have – been. But imputing intention has entered the lexicon of this area of law and it is probably impossible to discard it now.

But however described, the greater difficulty is the lack of criteria for deciding *what* is 'fair'. In a related sphere, the courts have conceded that 'fairness is an elusive concept', and that in order to achieve consistency 'the courts must…articulate, if only in the broadest fashion, what are the applicable if unspoken principles guiding the court's approach'.[88] We await any such principles for the operation of trusts law in these cases.

In the next two sections, we look more closely at how the *Stack/Jones* approach has been applied, first in 'joint-names' cases and then in the cases where legal title is in the name of one party.

Cases where the legal title is in joint names

Mr Stack and Ms Dowden, parents of four children, were legal co-owners of a home purchased ten years into their 20-year cohabiting relationship. The purchase was funded by capital from Ms Dowden, the proceeds of sale of their previous home held in her name, and a joint mortgage. Throughout the relationship, she was the higher earner. They had separate bank and savings accounts. He paid off the mortgage interest; she paid all other household bills; both helped pay off the capital sum due under the mortgage. Overall, her financial contribution to the acquisition of this property and their previous home had been the greater. There was, of course, no express declaration of the parties' beneficial shares in the property.

The House of Lords held that in 'domestic' cases where the property is held in the parties' joint names (which means that there must be *a* trust) but no beneficial interests have been expressly created, the fact of putting title in joint names will 'at least in the vast majority of cases' demonstrate that the parties intended that both would have a beneficial share.[89] The majority, not called on to make a decision regarding the acquisition stage, appear to assume

---

86 *Jones v Kernott* [2011] UKSC 53, [48].
87 Not least to keep the distinction clear: cf the view of Lord Walker and Lady Hale that there may be little practical difference between inferring and imputing intention, ibid, [38].
88 *Miller; McFarlane* [2006] UKHL 24, [4]–[6]: see 7.5 below.
89 *Stack v Dowden* [2007] UKHL 17, [55], [63].

detrimental reliance on this presumed intention by whichever party most benefits from it.[90] As to the size and nature of those shares, it is *strongly* presumed in such cases that the parties intended to create a beneficial joint tenancy.[91] This would give the parties equal shares on sale of the property following their separation (at which point the joint tenancy would in practice be severed), and the survivor would take all when the other owner(s) died. This effectively creates a highly valuable, gender- and relationship status-neutral presumption of advancement in favour of whichever party made the lesser (or even no) financial contribution to the purchase.[92] The basis of this presumption was further explained in *Jones v Kernott*:

Jones v Kernott [2011] UKSC 53

LORD WALKER AND LADY HALE:

19. The presumption of a beneficial joint tenancy is not based on a mantra as to "equity following the law" ... There are two much more substantial reasons (which overlap) why a challenge to the presumption of beneficial joint tenancy is not lightly to be embarked upon. The first is implicit in the nature of the enterprise. If a couple in an intimate relationship (whether married or unmarried) decide to buy a house or flat in which to live together, almost always with the help of a mortgage for which they are jointly and severally liable, that is on the face of things a strong indication of emotional and economic commitment to a joint enterprise. That is so even if the parties, for whatever reason, fail to make that clear by any overt declaration or agreement...

22. The notion that in a trusting personal relationship the parties do not hold each other to account financially is underpinned by the practical difficulty, in many cases, of taking any such account, perhaps after 20 years or more of the ups and downs of living together as an unmarried couple. That is the second reason for caution before going to law in order to displace the presumption of beneficial joint tenancy...

The onus lies with whichever party wishes to claim a larger share to rebut the presumption of beneficial joint tenancy by bringing evidence to show that the parties had an different common intention (on which, orthodoxy would add, the claimant had relied to her detriment[93]). One might have thought it could be rebutted where parties had made different levels of financial contribution to the acquisition of the property, triggering the presumption of resulting trust instead.[94] However, the majority rejected this approach, arguing that in contemporary circumstances 'the importance to be attached to who paid for what in a domestic context may be very different from its importance in other contexts or long ago'. Baroness Hale, for the majority in *Stack v Dowden*, claimed that only rarely would the presumption be rebutted by a finding that other beneficial shares were

---

90 Ibid, [63]; Gray and Gray (2009), 7.3.37, 7.3.66; Gardner (2008) and Etherton (2009) may go too far in suggesting that detrimental reliance is no longer required given the absence of any express discussion of the point.

91 [2007] UKHL 17, [53]–[56].

92 Ibid, [112].

93 Ms Dowden's greater financial contribution was the classic form of detriment.

94 Lord Neuberger would take this approach where the only additional evidence is different levels of financial contribution: [2007] UKHL 17, [110]–[122].

intended; but such a finding turns on the parties' 'whole course of conduct in relation to the property', by reference to the factors set out in paragraph 69, extracted above.[95] If a common intention to hold the beneficial interest other than as joint tenants can be found, the court then quantifies the shares by references to the parties' intentions or, after *Jones v Kernott*, absent such intentions, by reference to what is 'fair'.

Far from discouraging arguments attempting to rebut the presumption, the wide range of relevant factors identified in *Stack* and the result itself encouraged practitioners to suggest that it might be worth trying to rebut the presumption quite regularly.[96] Stack and Dowden emerged with 35:65 shares, essentially reflecting their respective financial contributions to the purchase. Baroness Hale concluded that they intended to hold in those proportions because they had: contributed unequally to the purchase price;[97] kept their money in separate accounts, not pooled it; and divided responsibility for household outgoings rigidly: he paid the mortgage interest and endowment policy instalments, she all other household bills. This financial separation, and Mr Stack's apparent failure to commit at least 'to do what he could' towards family expenditure,[98] persuaded Baroness Hale that this relationship was not a 'partnership' in which a beneficial joint tenancy was intended. This despite the parties' having chosen to put *this* asset in joint names, the length of their relationship, their raising four children together, and the fact that they contributed equal proportions of their earnings to the purchase.[99] We examine below empirical evidence about cohabitants' money management practices which suggests that such cases are less unusual than Baroness Hale supposes.[100]

The outcome suggests that the presumption of resulting trust, formally abandoned, remains close by:[101] the presumption of beneficial joint tenancy seems to yield quickly to unequal financial contributions. As Lord Neuberger has observed extra-judicially, 'If the presumption of equality is to be rebutted because the contributions are significantly different, it is a pretty useless presumption: the only time you need it, it isn't there'.[102]

Applying Stack v Dowden

One later case paints a different picture. In *Fowler v Barron*,[103] the parties had cohabited for 23 years and had two children. Mr Barron, a retired fireman on a pension, looked after the children while Ms Fowler worked. Without any legal advice or express discussion, they put their house in joint names (with no declaration of trust) and took out a joint mortgage, despite having no intention that Ms Fowler would help repay the debt. Mr Barron contributed the deposit and paid the mortgage, and all of the utility, council tax, and other general household bills. Ms Fowler made no financial contribution to the house or general household costs. Her wages were used to buy her clothes and to meet the

---

95 Ibid, [60].

96 See, e.g., Barnes (2007).

97 This appeared to be sufficient for Lord Hope, [11], which indicates, despite his approval of Baroness Hale's reasoning, sympathy for Lord Neuberger's minority approach.

98 [2007] UKHL 17, [91].

99 George (2008a).

100 See also *Kernott v Jones* [2010] EWCA Civ 578, [75].

101 See in particular Lord Hope: [2007] UKHL 17, [11]; *Jones v Kernott* [2011] UKSC 53, [25].

102 Neuberger (2008), para 15.

103 [2008] EWCA Civ 377.

children's various expenses. When they separated, Ms Fowler sought to establish that she had an interest in the property, but the trial judge found that the beneficial title was Mr Barron's alone under the presumption of resulting trust, having found that the parties had no intention about beneficial ownership at all. The Court of Appeal, overturning that decision, set out its general approach to *Stack*'s presumption of beneficial joint tenancy as follows:

Fowler v Barron [2008] EWCA Civ 377

ARDEN LJ:

35. In determining whether the presumption [of beneficial joint tenancy] is rebutted, the court must in particular consider whether the facts as found are *inconsistent* with the inference of a common intention to share the property in equal shares to an extent sufficient to discharge the civil standard of proof on the person seeking to displace the presumption arising from a transfer into joint names. [emphasis added]

This elaboration of how the presumption works is important. Evidence *consistent* with a beneficial joint tenancy does *not necessarily* mean that parties *intended* a beneficial joint tenancy—the facts may be equally consistent with a tenancy in common (quite possibly in shares other than 50:50) or sole beneficial ownership. But that will not displace the presumption. The party seeking to rebut the presumption, here Mr Barron, must establish facts positively *inconsistent* with a beneficial joint tenancy. Viewed in this way, Mr Barron's task looks daunting (and *Stack*'s outcome perhaps too favourable to Ms Dowden).

In *Fowler*, there was only circumstantial evidence of the parties' common intention regarding ownership of the property. The trial judge found that Mr Barron had intended that Ms Fowler should become sole owner of the property on his death: this is consistent with joint tenancy's doctrine of survivorship. But the judge also found that he had not intended that she should get an equal share should they separate: this is evidently inconsistent with a beneficial joint tenancy. However, this 'secret' intention had not been communicated to Ms Fowler, so could not form the basis of a *common* intention.[104] The parties had executed mutual wills, leaving each other their interests in the property: this implied that both thought each had *a* share (at least) during their lifetime.[105] But despite being party to the mortgage, Ms Fowler, unlike Mr Stack, had made no financial contribution to the mortgage or other regular household expenditure. Like Stack and Dowden, the parties had no joint bank account. *Perhaps* like Mr Stack (we know little about these aspects of *Stack v Dowden*), Ms Fowler had not been the children's primary carer since she was working. Nevertheless, the Court of Appeal upheld the presumption of beneficial joint tenancy,[106] giving each party an equal share after severance.

---

[104] Ibid, [36]–[37].
[105] Ibid, [6], [42].
[106] With no reference to detrimental reliance, though Ms Fowler was liable on the mortgage.

Fowler v Barron [2008] EWCA Civ 377

ARDEN LJ:

41. ... Mr Barron paid some items properly described as household expenses, such as the council tax and utilities bills, whereas she paid for other such items. The division was perfectly logical if ... she did most of the shopping for the children. The further inference that ... it is appropriate to draw is that the parties intended that it should make no difference to their interests in the property which party paid for what expense. Those payments also throw light on their intentions in this respect. The inference from this, especially when taken with the evidence as to mutual wills ... was that the parties simply did not care about the respective size of each other's contributions. ...

45. In a case where the parties have made unequal contributions to the cost of acquiring their home, it is obvious that in some cases there may be a thin dividing line between the case where the parties' shared intention is properly inferred to be ownership of the home in equal shares, and the case where the parties' shared intention is properly inferred to be that the party who has contributed less should have a smaller interest than the other. The resolution of such cases must however all depend on the facts. In my judgment it is important to return to the ratio in *Stack*. The essential reasoning of the House was (1) that, where parties put their home in joint names, the burden is on the one asserting that they own the property other than in equal shares to rebut the presumption of beneficial joint ownership that arises from their legal co-ownership, and (2) that the court must have regard to all the circumstances which would throw light on their shared intentions and not just their financial contributions to the cost of acquiring the property. It is necessary to consider the resolution of the facts in *Stack* with these principles in mind. In other words, it was not the fact that the parties made unequal contributions to the cost of acquiring their property ... that mattered so much as the inferences as to their shared intentions to be gleaned from the evidence overall.

Arden LJ sought to justify upholding the presumption of beneficial joint tenancy on the basis of factual differences from *Stack* that, with respect, do not obviously *favour* Ms Fowler: for example, the mutual wills; the lack of other substantial assets; the fact that she had made no financial contribution (why should that give her more rather than less than Mr Stack?); that, without a share, she might become reliant on state support, which—in Arden LJ's view—the parties could not reasonably be inferred to have intended;[107] and their treatment of their money as a common pool (despite the lack of joint account).[108]

The outcome is perhaps more convincing without attempting to distinguish it in detail from *Stack*:

TOULSON LJ:

53. In *Stack v Dowden* the House of Lords regarded the facts as very unusual. In the present case there was nothing at all unusual about the circumstances in which the property was acquired. It was bought and conveyed into the parties' joint names ... at a time when

---

107 See Miles (2011a), 101.
108 [2008] EWCA Civ 377, [46].

they had a 9 month old baby...They had been in a relationship for 4 years. They had not been cohabiting, but Miss Fowler said...that the birth..."was the spur for us to become a proper family unit". The judge found that the property was bought in order to provide a home for themselves and their son....They were joint borrowers and jointly liable [on the mortgage]. The judge found that whatever either of them thought about the question of ownership of the property at the time of the transfer, nothing was ever said. Looking at the matter at the time of acquisition, there was in my judgment nothing to rebut the ordinary presumption in such circumstances that the parties were intended to be joint beneficial owners in equal shares....

56....[He summarizes the factors listed in [69] of Baroness Hale's judgment in *Stack*, and goes on:] The judge in his analysis of the facts looked only at financial matters. That is too narrow an approach when addressing issues of inferred common intention. In this case the property served as a family home for the parties and their children from the time of its acquisition until the time of the breakdown of the relationship. During those 17 years Miss Fowler contributed to the life and wellbeing of the family in financial and other ways...In that family context I would reject any argument that a common silent intention should be inferred from the parties' conduct that their property interests were to be varied so as to reduce Miss Fowler's original share.

If anything, therefore, the difficulty lies not in Ms Fowler having a half-share, but in Mr Stack not doing so. The analysis in *Fowler v Barron* may prove to be more typical, and *Stack extremely* unusual.[109]

Jones v Kernott proved to be another unusual case, but here the question of beneficial ownership arose 14 years after the parties' separation, during which time Ms Jones alone had funded the mortgage without any significant child support payments from Mr Kernott, who had acquired his own home and shown no interest in the property at all.[110] The Supreme Court reinstated the trial judge's decision that the presumption of beneficial joint tenancy could be rebutted. While the presumption would have held had the issue arisen on separation, it was inferred that the parties' intentions had changed over the intervening period—*Jones* thus exemplifies a so-called 'ambulatory trust' which changes over time. By majority, it was further inferred[111] that the parties intended that Mr Kernott's share in the property should crystallize *in value* on separation: they liquidated some other assets at that point to help him buy a new home, which had since increased in value. The value of his crystallized share on a rough-and-ready basis justified 90:10 shares of the current value in favour of Ms Jones.[112]

Not applying Stack *and* Jones: *what is a 'domestic' case?*

Other cases have addressed the more fundamental question whether the presumption of beneficial joint tenancy applies at all. The *Stack/Jones* approach is predicated on a distinction

---

[109] See *Kernott v Jones* [2010] EWCA Civ 578, [72] and [75].

[110] [2010] EWCA Civ 578. Cf the sole-name case, *Holman v Howes* [2007] EWCA Civ 877.

[111] Lords Kerr and Wilson reached the same outcome via imputation.

[112] See also *Quaintance v Tandan* [2012] EWHC 4416: 100:0 where no contribution from the other party at all, having left very shortly after purchase of the property.

between the 'domestic'/'consumer' and 'commercial' contexts. Early in *Stack*, Baroness Hale noted:

Stack v Dowden [2007] UKHL 17

42. ... the recognition in the courts that, to put it at its lowest, the interpretation to be put on the behaviour of people living together in an intimate relationship may be different from the interpretation to be put upon similar behaviour between commercial men. To put it at its highest, an outcome which might seem just in a purely commercial transaction may appear highly unjust in a transaction between husband and wife or cohabitant and cohabitant.

Lord Hope agreed:

3. ... Where the parties have dealt with each other at arms' length it makes sense to start from the position that there is a resulting trust according to how much each party contributed. ... But cohabiting couples are in a different kind of relationship. The place where they live together is their home. Living together is an exercise in give and take, mutual co-operation and compromise. Who pays for what in regard to the home has to be seen in the wider context of their overall relationship. A more practical, down-to-earth, fact-based approach is called for in their case. ...

Baroness Hale built on this analysis in identifying the appropriate starting point for joint-names cases, arguing that the presumption of beneficial joint tenancy had 'even more force...in the consumer context'.[113] From this flowed the very strong presumption in *domestic* joint-names cases of beneficial joint tenancy, and the holistic search for the parties' alternative common intention.

Stack thus exemplifies what Dewar has called the 'familialization' of trusts law: developing trust law doctrine in a way that better accommodates the family context.[114] But Lord Neuberger, dissenting, doubted the wisdom, propriety, and necessity of judges developing specific principles for 'domestic' cases:

101. The determination of the ownership [of] the beneficial interest in a property held in joint names primarily engages the law of contract, land and equity. The relevant principles in those areas have been established and applied over hundreds of years, and have had to be applied in all sorts of circumstances. While both the nature and the characteristics of the particular relationship must be taken into account when applying those principles, the court should be very careful before altering those principles when it comes to a particular type of relationship ...

102. ... A change in the law, however sensible and just it seems, always carries a real risk of new and unforeseen uncertainties and unfairnesses. That is a particular danger when the change is effected by the court rather than the legislature, as the change is influenced by, indeed normally based on, the facts of a particular case, there is little room for public consultation, and there is no input from the democratically elected legislature.

---

113 [2007] UKHL 17, [54]; contrast various business contexts where, especially, the parties would presumably not wish the doctrine of survivorship to apply: ibid, [57].

114 Dewar (1998b), Hayward (2012).

What is the scope of this 'familial' trusts law?[115] *Stack* involved a long-term cohabiting couple with four children and their shared home. What about: the purchase of a holiday home, or of a pied-à-terre occupied by only one party during the working week; blood relatives who live together; the joint purchase by an adult child and his or her parent of a home to be occupied for the foreseeable future by the parent alone;[116] or a purchase by friends?[117] What if cohabitants or spouses are business partners—is the case nevertheless 'domestic'?[118]

In *Adekunle v Ritchie*,[119] the presumption of beneficial joint tenancy was *applied* to a mother and son who had purchased a property in joint names which both occupied for some years until the mother's death. But the judge held that the circumstances were sufficiently unusual to *depart* from the presumption, suggesting that outside the context of cohabiting couples, it may be easier to conclude that the parties did not intend a beneficial joint tenancy.[120] The primary purpose of this purchase had been to acquire a home for the mother, who could not use the 'right to buy' option over her council house without the son's help in obtaining a mortgage; the parties had kept their finances separate; the mother had nine other children with whom she had good relations, and so it was inconceivable that she would have intended to have a beneficial joint tenancy with the son, with the effect that he would take the house (her only sizeable asset) on her death under the doctrine of survivorship.[121] However, the son was clearly intended to have some interest, since the property had been put in joint names with a joint mortgage; he had lived in the house when it was bought; he had made some financial contribution to the mortgage payments. The judge found that the parties' financial contributions justified at most a 25 per cent share for the son, but (for reasons that were not closely articulated) increased his share to a third pursuant to the 'holistic' examination required by *Stack*. Judge Behrens was clearly less than comfortable in conducting that exercise, acknowledging the 'subjectivity and uncertainty' of the task highlighted by Lord Neuberger.[122]

By contrast, in *Laskar v Laskar*,[123] the Court of Appeal held that the presumption of beneficial joint tenancy *did not apply at all* where mother and daughter purchased the mother's former council house in joint names with a joint mortgage as an investment: the property was let (the rent covering the mortgage) and the mother moved to live with another daughter. A family relationship does not of itself attract the presumption:

Laskar v Laskar [2008] EWCA Civ 347

LORD NEUBERGER:

15. . . . It is by no means clear to me that the approach laid down by Baroness Hale . . . in [*Stack*] was intended to apply in a case such as this. In this case, although the parties were

---

[115] Cf Law Com (2002).

[116] Cf *Abbey National Bank v Stringer* [2006] EWCA Civ 338; *Ledger-Beadell v Peach and Ledger-Beadell* [2006] EWHC 2940.

[117] Cf the sole-name case, *Gallarotti v Sebastianelli* [2012] EWCA Civ 865.

[118] Lord Walker suggested that the doctrine of resulting trust might remain relevant here: [2007] UKHL 17, [32].

[119] [2007] EW Misc 5 (EWCC).

[120] Ibid, [65]. Dixon suggests that rather than being unusual this may simply feel 'unfair': (2007b), 459–60.

[121] At [66]–[67].

[122] At [68].

[123] [2008] EWCA Civ 347.

mother and daughter and not in that sense in an arm's length commercial relationship, they had independent lives, and...the purchase of the property was not really for the purpose of providing a home for them....

17. It was argued that this case was a midway between the cohabitation cases of co-ownership where property is bought for living in, such as *Stack*, and arm's length commercial cases of co-ownership, where property is bought for development or letting. In the latter sort of case, the reasoning in *Stack v Dowden* would not be appropriate and the resulting trust presumption still appears to apply. In this case, the primary purpose of the purchase of the property was as an investment, not as a home. In other words this was a purchase which, at least primarily, was not in "the domestic consumer context" but in a commercial context. To my mind it would not be right to apply the reasoning in *Stack v Dowden* to a case such as this, where the parties primarily purchased the property as an investment for rental income and capital appreciation, even where their relationship is a familial one.

He further held that even if the presumption *did* apply, it would readily be rebutted for various reasons, several similar to those relied on in *Adekunle*.[124] The case was therefore decided, in the absence of any agreement between the parties, on the basis of the parties' financial contributions to the property, yielding a one-third share for the daughter. Such a strictly mathematical approach to the parties' shares (by contrast with the wider range of factors considered in *Adekunle*) was said to be not unreasonable, since the purchase was an investment.[125]

These cases show that even if the presumption of beneficial joint tenancy is prima facie applicable, it may readily be rebutted in non-conjugal cases, and the case will then proceed as if the presumption had not applied. More generally, these cases may indicate that it is *use of property as a home by the parties together* that attracts both the presumption of beneficial joint tenancy and holistic analysis in quantifying the beneficial interests.

Cases where the legal title is in the sole name of one party

The starting point again is that 'equity follows the law'. But here, that means that equity presumes sole beneficial ownership from sole legal ownership. The onus is therefore on the party not on the legal title to prove he or she has a beneficial interest.[126] It is here that the three analytical stages of orthodox common intention constructive trust doctrine—intention, detrimental reliance, quantification—are more clearly evident. The first two map on to the 'acquisition' stage in *Stack/Jones*.

Acquisition: finding a 'common intention' to share beneficial ownership

The first stage on the *Stack/Jones* approach is to establish a common intention—express or inferred—that the claimant should have a beneficial share at all. The leading case on sole-name cases remains the House of Lords decision in *Lloyds Bank v Rosset*:

---

124 Ibid, [19].
125 Ibid, [33].
126 *Stack v Dowden* [2007] UKHL 17, [56].

Lloyds Bank v Rosset [1991] 1 AC 107, 132–3, 131

LORD BRIDGE:

The first and fundamental question which must always be resolved is whether, independently of any inference to be drawn from the conduct of the parties in the course of sharing the house as their home and managing their affairs, there has at any time prior to acquisition, or exceptionally at some later date, been any agreement, arrangement or understanding reached between them that the property is to be shared beneficially. The finding of an agreement or arrangement to share in this sense can only, I think, be based on evidence of express discussions between the partners, however imperfectly remembered and however imprecise their terms may have been. Once a finding to this effect is made it will only be necessary for the partner asserting the claim to a beneficial interest against the partner entitled to the legal estate to show that he or she has acted to his or her detriment or significantly altered his or her position in reliance on the agreement in order to give rise to a constructive trust or a proprietary estoppel.

Some judges have generously been prepared to find an express common intention where the owner has given some excuse for not putting the claimant on the legal title. Whilst those owners clearly had no intention that their partners should have any share, the reasonable understanding by the claimants of what was said supported the objective finding of a common intention to share.[127] Gardner considers that finding a common intention to share the beneficial ownership here may recognize the owner's moral obligation, but is nonetheless problematic: as he puts it, someone who gives a bogus excuse for declining an invitation to a boring party does not thereby indicate an intention to attend.[128] Sometimes, by contrast, it will be clear from the parties' discussions that the owner has no intention that the other should have a share at all, so no *common* intention will be found.[129]

Lord Bridge's exposition in *Rosset* continued with the 'inferred' finding of intention:

In sharp contrast with this situation is the very different one where there is no evidence to support a finding of an agreement or arrangement to share, however reasonable it might have been for the parties to reach such an arrangement if they had applied their minds to the question, and where the court must rely entirely on the conduct of the parties both as the basis from which to infer a common intention to share the property beneficially and as the conduct relied on to give rise to a constructive trust. In this situation direct contributions to the purchase price by the partner who is not the legal owner, whether initially or by payment of mortgage instalments, will readily justify the inference necessary to the creation of a constructive trust. But, as I read the authorities, it is at least extremely doubtful whether anything less will do.

This was bad news for Mrs Rosset. She had been married to Mr Rosset for 12 years and had two children. The newly acquired home was in his sole name, there was no evidence of an express common intention to share, and she had made no direct financial contribution to the acquisition or renovation of the property. What she had done was to supervise

---

[127] E.g. *Eves v Eves* [1975] 1 WLR 1338; *Grant v Edwards* [1986] Ch 638.
[128] Gardner (1993), 265.
[129] E.g. *Geary v Rankine* [2012] EWCA Civ 555.

the renovations, carried out decorating work herself daily, and obtained building materials while her husband was working abroad:

> [T]he judge based his inference of a common intention that Mrs Rosset should have a beneficial interest...essentially on the basis of what Mrs Rosset did in and about assisting the renovation of the property...Yet by itself this activity...could not possibly justify any such inference. It was common ground that Mrs Rosset was extremely anxious that the new matrimonial home should be ready for occupation before Christmas if possible. In these circumstances it would seem the most natural thing in the world for any wife, in the absence of her husband abroad, to spend all the time she could spare and to employ any skills she might have, such as the ability to decorate a room, in doing all she could to accelerate progress of the work quite irrespective of any expectation she might have on enjoying a beneficial interest in the property. The judge's view that some of this work was work "upon which she could not reasonably have been expected to embark unless she was to have an interest in the house" seems to me, with respect, quite untenable.

In *Stack v Dowden*, Lord Walker opined that whether or not Lord Bridge's doubts about the adequacy of anything other than direct financial contributions were rightly held at that time, 'the law has moved on'.[130] Baroness Hale acknowledged that it could be argued that Lord Bridge had set the hurdle 'rather too high'.[131] They did not directly revisit the issue in *Jones v Kernott*, but commentators seized upon the fact that the exposition of the law in paragraphs 51–52 of their judgment, extracted above, simply states that the parties' common intention may be inferred from their *conduct*, noting Baroness Hale's expansive list of factors in paragraph 69 of *Stack*, to herald the era of a newly liberalized trusts regime.[132] Yet neither *Stack* nor *Jones* was a sole-name case, so the matter did not fall for decision, and so the remarks provide slim foundations for reversing the well-established *Rosset* position.

Although later sole-owner cases appear to accept that it is appropriate to look at the parties' wider conduct—not just direct financial contributions—in seeking to infer their common intention at the acquisition stage, the *results* of those cases provide little evidence that the law has really loosened up: successful claimants have made direct financial contributions to the acquisition of the property[133] or something very close to it, such as the significant financial and labour contribution towards the creation of a dwelling from the barn in *Aspden v Elvy*, which are of a rather different order of magnitude from Mrs Rosset's activities.[134] There can be very little hope that *purely* domestic contributions, such as looking after the home and caring for children,[135] or general financial contributions to some household costs,[136] will generate a beneficial share. Indeed, the sole-name cases are as strict

---

130 [2007] UKHL 17, [26]; see also [34]–[36].

131 Ibid, [63]; see also dicta in *Abbott v Abbott* [2007] UKPC 53.

132 E.g. Gardner (2008), (2013), Dixon (2012), Sloan (2015), who expresses some caution, Lees (2012), Newnham (2013).

133 E.g. *Abbott v Abbott* [2007] UKPC 53, *CPS v Piper* [2012] EWHC 3570, *Rubin v Dweck* [2012] BPIR 854.

134 [2012] EWHC 555.

135 *Burns v Burns* [1984] Ch 317. Cf the optimism of Gardner (2013) and the view of Mee (2011). *Bank of Scotland v Brogan* [2012] NICh 21 is best viewed as a case of express intention, essentially corroborated by other factors, including significant financial contribution to extension of the property. Thanks to John Mee for discussion of this point.

136 Cf *Webster v Webster* [2008] EWHC 31, [33]: common intention to share inferred, without close analysis, from indirect contributions to general family expenditure; cf *Le Foe v Le Foe and another* [2001] 2 FLR 970: such contributions sufficing if they *enable* the other to pay the mortgage.

as *Fowler v Barron*—here to the *disadvantage* of the party who made little or no financial contribution—in identifying evidence from which a common intention rebutting the relevant presumption may be inferred.[137]

For example, in *James v Thomas*,[138] the parties had cohabited for 15 years in a property previously acquired in his sole name by Mr Thomas with mortgage finance. Miss James worked unpaid in his business throughout the relationship (that work including heavy labour[139]), only latterly becoming a formal business partner. The parties were reliant on the business for their livelihood; the mortgage and all outgoings on the property were paid from the business profits. When their relationship ended, the claimant claimed a beneficial share of the home.[140] The court found no evidence of an express common intention to share the beneficial title: Mr Thomas' remarks (regarding improvement to the property) that 'this will benefit us both' were construed as statements regarding shared use and enjoyment of the property, not shared beneficial ownership.[141] And, despite accepting that it was entitled to survey the parties' whole course of dealing for this purpose, the court declined to infer an intention, despite Miss James' substantial non-financial contribution to the business (and so, it might be argued, indirectly to the mortgage repayments) and to the property's renovation.[142]

James v Thomas [2007] EWCA Civ 1212

SIR JOHN CHADWICK:

27. Although it is possible to envisage circumstances in which the fact that one party began to make contributions to capital repayments due under a mortgage might evidence an agreement that that party was to have a share in the property, the circumstances of this case are not of that nature. On the facts found by the judge, the only source of funds to meet Mr Thomas' commitments under the mortgage, as well as all other household and personal expenses, was the receipts of the business. While the parties were living together they were dependent on the success of the business to meet their outgoings. It was not at all surprising that, in the early days of their relationship, Miss James should do what she could to ensure that the business prospered. That is not to undervalue her contribution, which, as Mr Thomas recognised, was substantial. But it is to recognise that what she was doing gives rise to no inference that the parties had agreed (or had reached a common understanding) that she was to have a share in the property: *what she was doing was wholly explicable on other grounds*. [emphasis added]

Similarly, in *Morris v Morris*[143] a wife unsuccessfully claimed a beneficial interest in the family farm, owned at law by the husband's mother.[144] Here too the Court of Appeal emphasized

---

137 Piska (2009), 229.

138 [2007] EWCA Civ 1212. See also *Morris v Morris* [2008] EWCA Civ 257.

139 Cf *Eves v Eves* [1975] 1 WLR 1338.

140 She was in any event entitled to her share of the business assets on dissolution of the partnership.

141 [2007] EWCA Civ 1212, [33].

142 Ibid, [19]. This same caution denied the woman's claim in *Aspden v Elvy* [2012] EWHC 1387, [110]–[112]. The adequacy, in principle, of the woman's activities to infer an intention in *Geary v Rankine* [2012] EWCA Civ 555 was not argued, the case failing on the basis that the man clearly had no intention that she should share.

143 [2008] EWCA Civ 257.

144 The wife's case was made more difficult to sustain by the various business and property-holding structures between the parties.

the need for 'exceptional circumstances'[145] before any common intention to share beneficial ownership could be inferred from conduct, particularly conduct after the property
had already been acquired. Sir Peter Gibson talked in terms of conduct which 'can only be
explained on the footing that [the claimant] believes that she was acquiring an interest in
the land'.[146] The wife's apparently full (and unpaid) involvement in a joint business venture
on the farm was insufficient.

The courts have also been reluctant to infer a common intention to share beneficial ownership where the parties were cohabiting when the property was purchased. In *Thomson v
Humphrey*,[147] the court emphasized that previous properties had also been held in the
defendant's sole name, and attached significant weight to a cohabitation agreement confirming that the claimant had no interest but which she had refused to sign; the unsigned
agreement made it harder to show that her partner, the legal owner, intended that she
should have a share at all. But even without that striking feature, for a home to be bought
during a relationship in the name of just one party strongly suggests they do not intend
shared beneficial ownership. Even if that legal sole-ownership is imposed by external
circumstances—for example, a mortgagee's insistence that only the creditworthy party take
on the responsibility—the courts will not readily make assumptions about what the parties
would have intended about the beneficial ownership in other circumstances in order to infer
an intention to share after all.[148]

Acquisition: detrimental reliance

If a common intention to share beneficial ownership can be found, the claimant must then
show detrimental reliance on that intention. While some decisions, in which the claimants had made financial contributions that would readily suffice, are silent on the issue,
the continuing need (in the absence of formal requirements for a declaration of trust having been executed) for detrimental reliance to secure the intention to share is confirmed
in Court of Appeal cases.[149] As noted earlier, it would be extraordinary—particularly
perhaps in a sole-name case—if the requirement had evaporated from the law without
explanation.

Where common intention is inferred from direct financial contributions to acquisition
of the property or something akin to it, those contributions also readily constitute detrimental reliance. In express common intention cases, the claimant must show detrimental
reliance separately. A wider range of conduct has sometimes been admitted as detrimental
reliance in express intention cases than would provide a basis for inferring an intention to
share.[150] But while financial contribution, direct or indirect, to the purchase is not required,

145 At [23].

146 [2008] EWCA Civ 257, [25]; see also *Walsh v Singh* [2009] EWHC 3219.

147 [2009] EWHC 3576.

148 Cf *Thompson v Hurst* [2012] EWCA Civ 1752: an express common intention to share was found, but
the court would not infer an intention to share *equally*, despite the mortgagee's position having prevented
joint-names purchase.

149 *James v Thomas* [2007] EWCA Civ 1212; *Smith v Bottomley* [2013] EWCA Civ 953, though neither
Stack nor *Rosset* referred to, case complicated by interposition of company; *Agarwala v Agarwala* [2013]
EWCA Civ 1763, though *Stack* said to be inapplicable as 'not a cohabiting couple or joint names case', [13], so
focus on 'underlying principles' instead. See generally, Mee (2011), 192.

150 E.g. *Grant v Edwards* [1986] Ch 638, 657A–B, per Browne-Wilkinson V-C; cf the stricter approach of
Nourse LJ, at 648G–H; *Hammond v Mitchell* [1991] 1 WLR 1127; *Eves v Eves* [1975] 1 WLR 1338; *Cox v Jones*
[2004] EWHC 1486.

the courts have commonly required that the conduct constituting detrimental reliance be 'referable' to the acquisition of an interest in the property, and not something which the claimant would have done anyway. This approach effectively excludes 'normal' domestic contributions to family life from consideration. Recent cases have taken this harder line, excluding even quite extensive domestic and business conduct that was explicable for other reasons:

James v Thomas [2007] EWCA Civ 1212

36. It would unreal to think that Miss James did what she did in reliance on such a promise. The true position...is that she worked in the business, and contributed her labour to the improvements to the property, because she and Mr Thomas were making their life together as man and wife. The Cottage was their home: the business was their livelihood. *It is a mistake to think that the motives which lead parties in such a relationship to act as they do are necessarily attributable to pecuniary self-interest.* [emphasis added]

This approach may be said to privilege the mercenary-minded over those who simply get on with life.[151]

Quantification

If intention and detrimental reliance are proved, the court moves to stage (ii), quantifying the parties' beneficial shares. Here the *Stack/Jones* approach prescribes that if the parties have no actual intention (expressed or inferred) the court may impute an intention or, in other words, impose a fair outcome. The outcomes in the recent cases suggest that there is a spectrum from the full partnership of marriage where a 50:50 outcome is likely,[152] through cases where the parties' domestic relationship is considered less of a joint venture,[153] to increasingly more business-like cases where the property is purchased as an investment and the 'domestic' character of *Stack/Jones* is held to be inapplicable.[154] The closer the case to this end of the spectrum, the closer the outcomes to parties' financial contributions, even to the point of finding sole beneficial ownership in the legal non-owner who provided all of the funding.[155] The judge in *Aspden v Elvy* can be forgiven for regarding the outcome of his deliberations somewhat 'arbitrary',[156] given the absence of guiding principles determining the content of 'fairness' at this stage.

Before exploring criticisms of the common intention constructive trust, we complete the picture of land ownership by examining two other claims that may be available in these cases.

---

[151] Compare Gray and Gray's analysis of more generous, earlier case law: (2009), 7.3.46.
[152] E.g. *Abbott v Abbott* [2007] UKPC 53, *CPS v Piper* [2012] EWHC 3570, *Rubin v Dweck* [2012] BPIR 854, *Bank of Scotland v Brogan* [2012] NICh 21.
[153] E.g. the platonic flat-sharers in *Gallarotti v Sebastianelli* [2012] EWCA Civ 865; but see also the cohabitants in *Thompson v Hurst* [2012] EWCA Civ 1752, and the on-off cohabitants in *Aspden v Elvy* [2012] EWHC 1387.
[154] *Agarwala v Agarwala* [2013] EWCA Civ 1763, [13]. Contrast the investment joint-names cases discussed above at p 148.
[155] Ibid.
[156] [2012] EWHC 1387, [128].

3.4.5 PROPRIETARY ESTOPPEL

The ingredients of a proprietary estoppel claim are superficially similar to common intention constructive trusts, and the courts often elide the two,[157] but there are key differences. Indeed, it has been remarked that proprietary estoppel is generally the lesser remedy, in terms of the likely outcome for the claimant.[158] It must be shown that the legal owner has made some representation or assurance to the claimant that the latter has or will have an interest in property. The claimant must have relied on that to his or her detriment, in circumstances making it unconscionable for the legal owner to deny the claimant an interest. In deciding whether the necessary unconscionability exists, the court should take a broad approach, looking at the matter 'in the round'.[159] It then determines what remedy is 'necessary to satisfy the equity' that has arisen.

As in the constructive trust context, the House of Lords has distinguished between 'domestic' and 'commercial' proprietary estoppel cases:[160]

Yeoman's Row Management Ltd v Cobbe [2008] UKHL 55

LORD WALKER:

68. . . . In the commercial context, the claimant is typically a business person with access to legal advice and what he or she is expecting to get is a *contract*. In the domestic or family context, the typical claimant is not a business person and is not receiving legal advice. What he or she wants and expects to get is an *interest* in immovable property, often for long-term occupation as a home. The focus is not on intangible legal rights but on the tangible property which he or she expects to get. The typical domestic claimant does not stop to reflect (until disappointed expectations lead to litigation) whether some further legal transaction (such as a grant by deed, or the making of a will or codicil) is necessary to complete the promised title.[161]

The nature of domestic cases is such that it is more likely to be reasonable for parties to rely on informal assurances where a business person should insist on legal formality. Writing extra-judicially, Lord Neuberger has noted that emotional or social factors in domestic relationships in which such assurances are made may impede parties from insisting that those assurances be formalized, and that it would be 'unreal' to expect that they should. He argues that there is therefore more room for proprietary estoppel to operate in domestic cases than in the commercial context, where parties can be expected formally to protect their legal position rather than rely on informal assurances.[162]

It is clear that the assurance or representation underpinning a proprietary estoppel claim must actually exist.[163] However, in domestic cases the courts may more readily find that

---

[157] Lord Walker in *Stack v Dowden* [2007] UKHL 17 retracted from that position: [37].

[158] Ibid; *Q v Q* [2008] EWHC 1874, [113].

[159] *Gillett v Holt* [2001] Ch 210; *Jennings v Rice* [2002] EWCA Civ 159.

[160] For criticism, see Mee (2009), 374.

[161] See also Lord Neuberger, *Thorner v Major* [2009] UKHL 18, [96]–[97].

[162] Neuberger (2009), 542, contrasting the decisions in *Yeoman's Row Property Ltd v Cobbe* [2008] UKHL 55 and *Thorner v Major* [2009] UKHL 18.

[163] Cf unorthodox suggestions that the intention at stage (i) of the constructive trust case could be imputed: e.g. *Bhura v Bhura (No 2)* [2014] EWHC 727.

an assurance was intended to be taken seriously and that the claimant's reliance on it was therefore reasonable. As Lord Walker remarked in *Thorner v Major*, whether an assurance has sufficient clarity is 'hugely dependent on context': it need only be 'clear enough'.[164] In *Thorner*, the claimant had worked unpaid for decades on his taciturn cousin's farm, the cousin having given several somewhat oblique, allusive indications that he would leave the farm to the claimant. He died without a will, leaving the claimant with nothing. In the context of the parties' relationship and the deceased's character, his remarks and conduct were regarded as sufficiently clear to underpin a claim to the farm in proprietary estoppel, a finding that would never be made in a commercial case. Proprietary estoppel, like the common intention constructive trust, is therefore responsive to the familial context. Nevertheless, even in a domestic case the assurance must relate to a particular asset or ascertainable pool of assets.[165] A general promise that the respondent will support the claimant or that the claimant will be 'financially' secure in the future is not enough.[166] Though an assurance that the claimant 'would always have a home and be secure in this one' was.[167]

The detrimental reliance requirement raises problems similar to those experienced in constructive trust cases for claimants who have made only domestic contributions to family life. While domestic contributions are not ruled out entirely,[168] it may be difficult to show that such actions were not explicable as a normal aspect of family life; if so, they will not constitute detrimental reliance on the assurance.[169] However, such contributions may suffice if, the assurance having been made, the claimant would not then continue to make them if the assurance were then withdrawn.[170]

But proprietary estoppel again diverges from constructive trust on deciding what remedy is necessary to satisfy the equity. The basis of the remedy is uncertain: should the court be seeking to meet the claimant's expectation in full, or simply to compensate losses incurred in reliance on it, or something in between? Some cases emphasize that the remedy must be proportionate to the detriment sustained and the claimant's expectation.[171] But recent cases have involved awards meeting the claimant's expectation despite the gross disproportion between that expectation and the detriment incurred.[172] The court has considerable remedial flexibility. It is not confined to awarding a beneficial share in the relevant property. It can instead award some other sort of interest in the property[173] or monetary compensation,[174] or even conclude that no remedy is required because benefits enjoyed by the claimant during the relationship counterbalance any disadvantage sustained.[175] The claimant's expectation may therefore not be met, distinguishing proprietary estoppel from the intention-based outcome of the constructive trust.

---

[164] [2009] UKHL 18, [56].

[165] *Jennings v Rice* [2002] EWCA Civ 159; *Thorner v Major* [2009] UKHL 18.

[166] *Lissimore v Downing* [2003] 2 FLR 308; *Layton v Martin* [1986] 2 FLR 227.

[167] *Southwell v Blackburn* [2014] EWCA Civ 1347.

[168] *Greasley v Cooke* [1980] 1 WLR 1306; *Campbell v Griffin* [2001] EWCA Civ 990.

[169] *Lissimore v Downing* [2003] 2 FLR 308; *Coombes v Smith* [1986] 1 WLR 808; cf *Grant v Edwards* [1986] Ch 638, 656; *Henry v Henry* [2010] UKPC 3.

[170] *Wayling v Jones* [1995] 2 FLR 1029.

[171] *Jennings v Rice* [2002] EWCA Civ 159; *Gillett v Holt* [2001] Ch 210.

[172] E.g. *Suggitt v Suggitt* [2012] EWCA Civ 1140, criticized by Mee (2013).

[173] E.g. the entire freehold: *Pascoe v Turner* [1979] 1 WLR 431; a life interest: *Greasley v Cooke* [1980] 1 WLR 1306.

[174] *Dodsworth v Dodsworth* (1973) 228 EG 1115; *Jennings v Rice* [2002] EWCA Civ 159.

[175] *Sledmore v Dalby* (1996) 72 P&CR 196.

3.4.6 IMPROVEMENT TO PROPERTY BY SPOUSE OR CIVIL PARTNER

Statute provides another basis on which (specifically) a spouse, civil partner, or fiancé(e) may acquire a beneficial interest in property belonging to the other.[176] Where one party makes a substantial contribution in 'money or money's worth' to the improvement of land or other property beneficially owned by one or both parties, the contributor will (absent contrary agreement) be found to have acquired a share, or an enlarged share, in that property. The size of that share is as agreed by the parties or, absent any agreement, as seems just in all the circumstances. Unlike the common intention constructive trust or proprietary estoppel, this provision enables certain domestic contributions (contributions of 'money's worth') to generate a beneficial interest without having to prove any intention or assurance that the contributor will thereby acquire a share.[177] The status of the parties' relationship is effectively substituted for that requirement. But it applies only where the contributions 'improve' the property; day-to-day housekeeping and maintenance, acquisition of furnishings and domestic appliances for the home do not suffice.[178]

3.4.7 CRITICISMS OF THE CURRENT LAW RELATING TO OWNERSHIP OF LAND

Many commentators have criticized the law as unfair and uncertain, both in terms of the substantive requirements and their application in individual cases.[179] Property ownership is now theoretically equally open to all, but the preconditions required for property ownership to arise where there is no express declaration of trust often—particularly in sole-name cases—prevent family members not engaged in paid employment from acquiring ownership of assets on which family life is based. Particular problems arise with common intention constructive trusts from the need to base the trust on the parties' intentions regarding property ownership, and the courts' continuing reluctance (in sole-name cases) to infer such intentions from anything other than financial contributions to the acquisition of the property. As more couples cohabit outside marriage, the law discussed here is becoming increasingly significant in practice because cohabitants who separate depend principally on the general law to divide their property. We address five problems relating particularly to constructive trusts: (i) the empirical basis for the approach developed in *Stack v Dowden*; (ii) the problems surrounding 'intention'; (iii) the understanding of detrimental reliance; (iv) the situation of the homemaker; and (v) the uncertainty of the law and its outcomes.

The empirical basis for *Stack v Dowden*

Legal presumptions fill the gaps where there is no actual evidence of what parties intended, on the basis that, given circumstance *y*, individuals can (the courts think) generally be expected to

---

[176] Matrimonial Proceedings and Property Act 1970, s 37; Civil Partnership Act 2004 (CPA 2004), s 65; Law Reform (Miscellaneous Provisions) Act 1970, s 2; CPA 2004, s 74(2); *Dibble v Pfluger* [2010] EWCA Civ 1005. The provision originates in Law Com (1969), paras 56–8.

[177] Cf *Stack v Dowden* [2007] UKHL 17, [70].

[178] *In re Nicholson (Deceased)* [1974] 1 WLR 476.

[179] For a useful survey pre-*Stack v Dowden*, see Law Com (2006), Part 4. The extent of the post-*Stack* and *Jones* literature does not suggest certainty has been achieved.

intend *x*. We start these cases with one presumption and rebut it with evidence that the parties actually intended *something* else. If we do not know precisely what that 'something else' was (or they did not get as far as thinking about that detail), we fill the resulting gap with an imputed intention—or decision about what is fair—based on the wider circumstances of the case, looking beyond the basic facts which generated the starting presumption. In *Stack v Dowden*, both Baroness Hale and Lord Neuberger sought to describe what people may, or may not, be taken to intend in particular circumstances. But, crucially, they offered rather differing assessments of the same facts.[180] The majority's presumption of beneficial joint tenancy, reinforced in *Jones v Kernott* in the extract above at p 142 assumes that putting the house in joint names is a meaningful and conscious[181] decision denoting a 'joint enterprise' between parties in a 'materially communal relationship'.[182] But as Baroness Hale acknowledged in *Stack*, parties' actions regarding house purchase are not necessarily as deliberate or even voluntary as we might assume:

Stack v Dowden [2007] UKHL 17

67. This is not to say that the parties invariably have a full understanding of the legal effects of their choice: there is recent empirical evidence from a small scale qualitative study to confirm that they do not [(Douglas, Pearce, and Woodward (2007b)]. But that is so whether or not there is an express declaration of trust and no-one thinks that such a declaration can be overturned, except in cases of fraud or mistake...Nor do they always have a completely free choice in the matter. Mortgagees used to insist upon the home being put in the name of the person whom they assumed would be the main breadwinner. Nowadays, they tend to think that it is in their best interests that the home be jointly owned and both parties assume joint and several liability for the mortgage. (It is, of course, a matter of indifference to the mortgagee where the beneficial interests lie.) Here again, this factor does not invalidate the parties' choice if there is an express declaration of trust, nor should it automatically count against it where there is none.

However, it is one thing not to ignore the fact of purchase in joint names, quite another to erect a strong presumption that the parties thereby intended a beneficial joint tenancy. If parties who *expressly* declared a beneficial joint tenancy fail to appreciate its significance, it is difficult to presume that parties who bought a home together without making such a declaration nevertheless intended to create a beneficial joint tenancy, particularly (perhaps) where they contributed different amounts to the purchase.[183] In practice, evidence of clear, *common* intention about property ownership seems scarce:

G. Douglas, J. Pearce, and H. Woodward, 'Money, Property, Cohabitation and Separation: Patterns and Intentions', in J. Miles and R. Probert (eds), *Sharing Lives, Dividing Assets* (Oxford: Hart Publishing, 2009)

In our study, we found that the type of ownership of property – joint or sole, joint tenancy or (rarely) tenancy in common – established at the point of purchase was selected for a

---

180 Contrast [2007] UKHL 17, [66]–[67], Baroness Hale with [113]–[116], Lord Neuberger.
181 *Stack v Dowden* [2007] UKHL 17, [66].
182 [2011] UKSC 53, [19] and quoting Gardner and Davidson (2011) at [21].
183 Lord Neuberger: [2007] UKHL 17, [113].

variety of reasons or no conscious reason at all. Whilst one would expect that cohabitants might have poor recollections of conversations and advice which had taken place several years before they were interviewed, our discussions with practitioners confirmed that, even at the time, most couples are not interested in such matters. Moreover, as some cohabitant respondents explained, a joint meeting with a conveyancer may not be the right time or setting in which to consider coolly how to protect one's individual interests. At the same time, other, more wily (or more astute) cohabitants may be able to mislead partners so that they fail to assert their own interests or may not have any to protect. The complexity of the law and the opacity of the legal jargon may contribute to the parties' lack of understanding of their positions, and explanations written by lawyers for whom such language is commonplace may not be sufficiently clear to overcome the difficulties.

Baroness Hale and Lord Neuberger also attached different significance to parties' money management practices as a reflection of their intentions regarding beneficial ownership of the home.[184] Empirical research into couples' money management shows that more spouses than cohabitants pool their resources, but that cohabiting *parents* act more like spouses in their money management than childless cohabitants.[185] That Stack and Dowden, long-term cohabiting parents, did *not* pool their resources may thus seem 'unusual'. However, researchers caution against making assumptions about the nature and commitment of couples' relationships, never mind their intentions regarding ownership of their *home*, from simplistic analysis of their general money management.[186] There are many pragmatic reasons for keeping money separate (e.g. access to extra credit and tax-free allowances, management of personal debts, even sheer inertia) which do not necessarily indicate that parties regard themselves as separate financial entities; as in *Fowler v Barron*, separate bank accounts may conceal a de facto pooling arrangement.[187] Lord Neuberger remarked that 'there is a substantial difference, in law, in commercial terms, in practice, and almost always in terms of value and importance, between ownership of a home and the ownership of a bank account or, indeed, furniture, furnishings and other chattels'.[188] For him, parties' treatment of their household finances, whether pooled or separate, does not necessarily cast light on their intentions regarding home ownership where the parties have made different financial contributions to its purchase. Conversely, if they generally keep their finances separate but put the *home* into joint names (as Stack and Dowden did), that might suggest they had different intentions regarding the home. But even there, he would be cautious about drawing any inference about joint ownership;[189] as Baroness Hale notes in the extract above, the selection of joint names may have been dictated by the lender.

Empirical research can improve our understanding of how people behave in relation to their property and finances, and what they think about them, in order to inform courts and policy-makers. Real life is more complicated than neat legal presumptions can accommodate. Gillian Douglas and colleagues drew the following conclusions from their study

184 Compare [2007] UKHL 17, [86]–[92] and [131]–[137], [143].
185 Vogler (2009).
186 Barlow, Burgoyne, and Smithson (2007), 62–3.
187 Burgoyne and Sonnenberg (2009).
188 [2007] UKHL 17, [133].
189 Ibid, [134].

of cohabitants' property disputes, having analysed their data in light of Baroness Hale's 'paragraph 69' factors:

G. Douglas, J. Pearce, and H. Woodward, 'Money, Property, Cohabitation and Separation: Patterns and Intentions', in J. Miles and R. Probert (eds), *Sharing Lives, Dividing Assets* (Oxford: Hart Publishing, 2009), 159

Couples' relationships vary infinitely, in terms of why they cohabit initially and why they remain cohabiting, their economic and domestic positions, their personalities, the dynamics of their relationship, the changes they undergo as life proceeds, and how far they can or do make financial contributions to keeping the relationship going and acquiring property during it. The way they hold property, and the way they organise their finances, as our study and others' demonstrate, may in turn reflect this myriad of circumstances and does not always conform to what one might logically or rationally predict or assume. It is arguable whether, on the breakdown of their relationship, a couple should be held to arrangements which have arisen during their relationship in response to circumstances as if they were by common intention.

Baroness Hale's list of factors was intended to capture and encapsulate this variety and to indicate which elements might be relevant to establishing the parties' 'true intentions', but our study gives little encouragement to the belief that it will provide a clear pointer towards those cases which are 'unusual' enough to warrant departure from the legal title. On the basis of our findings, we are more inclined to agree with the view of Lord Neuberger:

'To say that factors such as a long relationship, children, a joint bank account, and sharing daily outgoings of themselves are enough, or even of central importance, appears to me not merely wrong in principle, but a recipe for uncertainty, subjectivity, and a long and expensive examination of the facts.'

The problem of intention

As Douglas et al's research suggests, ascertaining parties' intentions regarding beneficial ownership is difficult. It is hard enough to discern what each individually might have intended, harder to divine commonly held intentions, assuming that they ever existed.[190] But simply abandoning that inquiry, as some would wish,[191] in favour of 'imputing' to the parties an intention that they never had, or simply deciding for them what is 'fair', would take us into doctrinally troubling waters.[192]

Finding express evidence of common intention

Happy families rarely think about what each individual's entitlements in relation to the home may or may not be, and are even less likely to discuss them expressly:

---

[190] Probert (2008b), 345.
[191] Notably Gardner (2013) and, in relation to estoppel, (2014).
[192] Mee (2011), (2013).

Lloyds Bank v Rosset [1991] 1 AC 107, 127–8

LORD BRIDGE:

Spouses living in amity will not normally think it necessary to formulate or define their respective interests in property in any precise way. The expectation of parties to every happy marriage is that they will share the practical benefits of occupying the matrimonial home whoever owns it. But this is something quite distinct from sharing the beneficial interest in the property asset which the matrimonial home represents. These considerations give rise to special difficulties for judges who are called on to resolve a dispute between spouses who have parted and are at arm's length as to what their common intention or understanding with respect to interests in property was at a time when they were still living as a united family and acquiring a matrimonial home in the expectation of living in it together indefinitely.

One judge has described as 'grotesque' the idea of 'a normal married couple spending the long winter evenings hammering out agreements about their possessions'.[193] But failure to devote at least one or two evenings to that exercise may cause uncertainty and insecurity in the longer term. These cases can devolve into a 'painfully detailed retrospect':

Hammond v Mitchell [1991] 1 WLR 1127 (Fam Div), 1139

WAITE J:

The primary emphasis accorded by the law in cases of this kind to express discussions between the parties ("however imperfectly remembered and however imprecise their terms") means that the tenderest exchanges of a common law courtship may assume an unforeseen significance many years later when they are brought under equity's microscope and subjected to an analysis under which many thousands of pounds of value may be liable to turn on fine questions as to whether the relevant words were spoken in earnest or in dalliance and with or without representational intent. This requires that the express discussions to which the court's initial inquiries will be addressed should be pleaded in the greatest detail, both as to language and as to circumstance.

This undertaking is now bypassed in joint-names cases to the extent that a common intention to hold a beneficial joint tenancy will be presumed. But it remains key to sole-name cases, unless intention can instead be inferred.

The subjective and gendered nature of intention

But inferring an actual common intention is not straightforward. Several items on Baroness Hale's paragraph 69 list are inherently subjective: for example, the 'nature of the parties' relationship'; the parties' 'individual characters and personalities'. In neither case is it clear what specific issue she has in mind and what, if anything, each might suggest about the

---

[193] *Pettitt v Pettitt* [1970] AC 777, 810.

parties' intentions about the ownership of their home.[194] All depends on the judge's analysis of the facts and his or her decision regarding inferences about the parties' intentions which may properly be drawn from them, rendering outcomes unpredictable, and quite possibly unrelated to whatever the parties did actually intend.[195]

Anne Bottomley has argued that 'intentions' are often construed differently by men and women. She bases her argument on an analysis of reported cases:[196]

A. Bottomley, 'Self and Subjectivities: Languages of Claim in Property Law', (1993) 20 *Journal of Law and Society* 56, 61–3

Evidence given in [*Lloyds Bank v Rosset*] is not, in my opinion, unusual and illustrates this point:

As soon as we heard he was likely to get the money, we looked round, looked for a suitable home for us and children. I always understood we were going to share whatever we had, big or little. We always discussed it as being ours. The only discussion was in very general terms. We needed a house; we would go out and look for one we could own as a couple for a family. When we found [the house], he said he was glad he would be able to provide a proper home, a place where we could be secure. I understood it would be jointly ours. He'd always indicated it would be a joint venture. Everything we did in the past had been jointly done. If you live with someone, you don't 'dissect'. It was the accepted thing.

This was enough for the trial judge and Court of Appeal, but the more 'orthodox' Lord Bridge was not so easily satisfied:

He wanted explicit evidence that there was an agreement about ownership.

I pause to observe that neither a common intention by spouses that a house is to be renovated as a 'joint venture' nor a common intention that the house is to be shared by parents and children as the family home throws any light on their intentions with respect to beneficial ownership of the property.

[She also quotes the extract from pp 127–8 of Lord Bridge's judgment, set out above.]

...It seems to me that this is not only a requirement of a certain jurisprudential approach but also a mode of reasoning and language use which is more conducive to men than women. This may in part be due to material factors and differences in socio-economic strengths and roles, but evidence drawn from psychoanalytical material would suggest that this division derives from the construction of gender identity. In other words, it is far more deeply embedded than a simple analysis of economic difference and consequent relative power relations would reveal.

...There is some evidence from the case material to suggest that women too often read silence as positive assent and lack of specificity as covering a number of issues with equal firmness rather than evading the particular issue.

There is also evidence of the great difficulty some women experience in raising issues about property as well as their difficulty in persuading their partners to confront the issue through discussions.

---

[194] See Lord Neuberger's analysis: [2007] UKHL 17, [131]–[139]; and Douglas et al (2009).
[195] See Mee (2012), 176–7 criticizing this process.
[196] Probert (2001) argues that it may not be safe to draw generalizations from this source.

The high hurdle for claimants in sole-name cases

Despite commentators' enthusiasm for the *Stack/Jones* approach, the courts continue to be conservative in finding a common intention that the claimant should have a share in sole-name cases. Yet as Simon Gardner once observed,[197] what is odd is not so much the refusal to infer a common intention to share from non-financial contributions in those cases, but rather that the courts should be so quick to assume the existence of such an intention where there is a direct financial contribution to property acquisition. Such contributions might equally be motivated by other intentions, yet there the law assumes 'pecuniary self-interest'.[198] This approach deprives many claimants of a share where either the intention to share might well have existed (albeit unexpressed and not evidenced by the required sort of conduct) or where no intention was held at all, because people in intimate relationships seldom consider ownership of their home. It may be that we cannot expect property law to provide 'fair' outcomes, but these cases fuel further the calls for statutory reform, not least to provide financial relief at the end of non-marital relationships.[199]

Abandoning intention?

While Bottomley would nevertheless retain a concept of intention in this context, other commentators have argued that intention provides the wrong starting point in the family sphere. The focus should instead be on the parties' relationship:

S. Gardner, 'Rethinking Family Property', (1993) 109 *Law Quarterly Review* 263, 282–3

A doctrine centred on the parties' own thinking ostensibly takes its stand on the recognisable individualist platform that the law should not impose obligations on persons other than by their consent. However, it has long been a commonplace that palpable thinking on the subject of property rights is unlikely to be forthcoming on the part of those who are emotionally committed to one another. So if the true facts are adhered to, it is natural that individualist doctrines will give a remedy only infrequently in such cases.

A doctrine centred on the fact of the relationship would allow the law to bypass such specific reference to the parties' thinking, and so give remedies more freely—as indeed seems to be the courts' instinct. The challenge now is to point to some defensible analysis which proceeds on the strength of the parties' relationship rather than of their thinking. . . . [One] possible analysis . . . argues that in at least some cases, the intrinsic logic of trust and collaboration is that the parties should be seen not as keeping separate accounts, . . . but as pooling their efforts and their rewards: each operating on joint behalf of both. Being thus in effect mutual fiduciaries, they would hold the relevant property on a trust whose obligations follow from the ideas of trust and collaboration: either, simply, to share the property equally, or to provide for the adequate future support of each.

---

[197] Gardner (1993), 264–5; cf his more recent writing.
[198] *James v Thomas* [2007] EWCA Civ 1212.
[199] See chapter 7.

Following *Stack v Dowden*, Gardner refined this approach to argue that the court's task is to 'effectuate the implications of the parties' relationship'. Thus, where the relationship is found to be 'materially communal', as it was in *Fowler v Barron*,[200] the parties pooling their financial and other resources in a common endeavour in life, the outcome should be equal sharing of the beneficial interest; in other circumstances, as in *Stack v Dowden*, a resulting trust analysis should determine the parties' shares.[201] Attractive as this approach may seem, it suffers from similar empirical and evidential problems as the intention-based test in relying on judicial characterization of the parties' relationship. And as John Mee has observed:[202]

> The essential problem is that an approach which conscientiously focuses on genuine intentions would provide a remedy in a very limited set of circumstances, while an approach which moves beyond real intentions seems to involve impermissible judicial law-making.

The problem of detrimental reliance

Assuming that it remains a requirement at least in sole-name and estoppel cases, the law regarding detrimental reliance in both areas has been accused of gender bias, to the potential disadvantage of both female and male claimants, in generally requiring 'conduct on which the [claimant] could not reasonably have been expected to embark, unless she was to have an interest in the house'.[203] So how do the courts construe parties' conduct?

L. Flynn and A. Lawson, 'Gender, Sexuality and the Doctrine of Detrimental Reliance', (1995) 3 *Feminist Legal Studies* 105, 116–18

> In their construction of normality, the decisions of the courts display the tenacious hold of the 'separate spheres' ideology [i.e. that woman's place is in the home, and man's place out in the labour market]. All the behaviour which is placed in the realm of the domestic, no matter how arduous, will not amount to detriment because it can be expected of any woman in an intimate relationship with a man. Behaviour which takes the [female] claimant outside the domestic realm is categorised as abnormal, and, in order to explain it, must be placed in the context of a market-like transaction giving rise to a property interest [rather than the product of love or desire to live in a comfortable home]. According to the authorities one cannot expect women, out of the love they have for their partners or of the desire to live in a comfortable place, to pay towards mortgage instalments.[204] Nor is it reasonable to expect to them to spend small sums on improvements, at least when those small sums represent a quarter of all their worldly wealth and their partner

---

200 [2008] EWCA Civ 377.

201 Gardner (2008) and (2013), and with Davidson (2011), (2012); see also Harding (2009) on the communitarian aspects of *Stack v Dowden*, Newnham (2013).

202 (2012), 179; see also (2011), 191–2.

203 *Grant v Edwards* [1986] Ch 638, 648G–H per Nourse LJ; cf the more generous test at 657A–B, per Browne-Wilkinson LJ and the reasoning in *Wayling v Jones* [1995] 2 FLR 1029.

204 *Grant v Edwards* [1986] Ch 638.

is a comparatively rich man.[205] A woman cannot be reasonably expected to wield 14-lb. sledge-hammers[206] or work cement mixers[207] out of love or the desire for more pleasant surroundings. Prompted by such motives, however, it is reasonable to expect women to leave their husbands, move in with their lovers, bear their babies, refrain from seeking employment,[208] wallpaper, paint and generally decorate and design their lovers' houses, and to organize builders working on those same houses, even when this includes the purchase and delivery of building materials.[209] In order to succeed, female claimants must show that they "did much more than most women would do",[210] or rather that they did more than the judges would expect most women to do. If the claimant's conduct is of a type regarded by judges as "the most natural thing in the world for a wife"[211] to have done, she will not succeed. The use of the stereotype as a norm, from which deviation has to be established, is an almost inevitable consequence of adopting Nourse LJ's test. [footnotes from the original]

Similarly, as Lawson observes,[212] men may not be regarded as incurring detriment by undertaking stereotypically 'male' tasks, such as gardening, DIY, and house-decoration.[213] How the courts would react to the male partner in an opposite-sex relationship who undertook child-care and looked after the house while his partner went out to work remains to be seen.[214] More problematic and revealing for this test are same-sex relationships. *Wayling v Jones*,[215] a proprietary estoppel case, involved a 20-year-long gay partnership, in which the younger man (Wayling) acted as the other's companion and gave him substantial professional assistance (as a trained chef) in running his hotel and restaurant businesses.

L. Flynn and A. Lawson, 'Gender, Sexuality and the Doctrine of Detrimental Reliance', (1995) 3 *Feminist Legal Studies* 105, 118–19

Homosexuality is a troubling presence in such a scheme. One of the problems with same-sex sexual relations is that they call into question the inevitability of basic social norms which underlie patriarchy. While this is not to suggest that homosexuality cannot be appropriated by patriarchal modes of representation, homosexuality is always, to some extent, a challenge. At a basic level it upsets the images of the 'real man' or the 'authentically feminine', disrupting strongly held codes of masculinity and femininity. For the most part, the anxiety which this provokes results in hostility to lesbians and gay men. But when the normalcy-dependent test of detriment is applied to male-male relationships the

---

205 *Pascoe v Turner* [1979] 1 WLR 431.
206 *Eves v Eves* [1975] 1 WLR 1338.
207 *Cooke v Head* [1972] 1 WLR 518.
208 *Coombes v Smith* [1986] 1 WLR 808.
209 *Lloyds Bank v Rosset* [1991] 1 AC 107.
210 *Cooke v Head* [1972] 1 WLR 518, 519.
211 *Lloyds Bank v Rosset* [1991] 1 AC 107, 131.
212 Lawson (1996).
213 *Pettitt v Pettitt* [1970] AC 777.
214 The female claimant in *Fowler v Barron* [2008] EWCA Civ 377 benefited from the joint-names case presumption.
215 [1995] 2 FLR 1029.

unnatural qualities of these relations between men can operate in favour of the cohabiting claimant. In the separate spheres ideology which resurfaces in this field, it is not normal for a man to undertake caring, domestic duties. As a result, it is necessary for Balcombe LJ to explain (and to elevate) Wayling's domestic behaviour in the description of him acting as companion and chauffeur in exchange for monetary support. Wayling's activities have a visibility here which no woman's would possess. However, the Court of Appeal does not dwell on this aspect of the case because it can turn to a more conventional pattern of behaviour. Wayling has also engaged in non-domestic activity with Jones, and his work in the various hotels and restaurants which they ran is deemed to constitute detrimental behaviour. Wayling, a man who lives with another gay man, who works inside and outside the domestic sphere, is visible in a way in which a woman living with Jones would not have been. All of his private behaviour is unnatural and so could amount to detriment in the eyes of a court. All of his public behaviour in the market is conventional and familiar; he does the type of things which men do which are the foundations of contracts and property transactions.

The position of the homemaker

Where legal title to the home is in joint names, family members who have devoted themselves to raising children and looking after the home now benefit from the strong presumption of beneficial joint tenancy that arises following *Stack v Dowden*. Should the other party seek to rebut that presumption, the apparent magnetism that financial contributions had in *Stack* itself and the lack of attention to the issue of responsibility for child-care in that case may suggest that the homemaker is vulnerable to losing the benefit of the presumption.[216] But *Fowler v Barron* augurs favourably.[217] More problematic is the position of the homemaker whose partner is the sole legal owner and so presumptive sole beneficial owner. Without an express common intention to share, despite some commentators' optimism, she will struggle to establish any share in the property for want of both evidence of common intention and proof of detrimental reliance.

The case most commonly used to illustrate the law's perceived unfairness is *Burns v Burns*,[218] which would be decided identically today.[219] Mrs Burns and her partner, who were unmarried although she had taken his name, lived together for nearly 20 years in a house purchased in his name. Mrs Burns raised their children and looked after the home. When the children were older, she took up employment, but did not earn significant income until 15 years into their relationship. From her earnings, she paid some household bills and bought items for the house, including a washing machine, tumble dryer, and furniture. Her partner paid the mortgage instalments. When they separated, she was able to keep the washing machine and other goods that she had bought, but was held to have no share in the home. There was no express common intention to share the beneficial interest,

---

[216] Probert (2008b), 349 is concerned that this augurs badly for homemakers.

[217] Cf the unusual division of responsibilities in *Fowler v Barron* [2007] EWCA Civ 377; *Abbott v Abbott* [2007] UKPC 53, a sole-name case.

[218] [1984] Ch 317.

[219] E.g. Gardner (2013), who fails to acknowledge *James v Thomas* [2007] EWCA Civ 1212 or *Morris v Morris* [2008] EWCA Civ 257; cf the orthodox view of Mee (2011) and Lady Hale's own view regarding the continuing need for reform, referring to *Burns: Gow v Grant* [2012] UKSC 29, [50].

and in the absence of any financial contribution to the acquisition of the house, no such intention could be inferred. She had little to show for nearly 20 years' contribution to her family, despite her having 'worked just as hard as the man' in her domestic sphere.[220] But Fox LJ concluded that 'the unfairness of that is not a matter which the courts can control. It is a matter for Parliament'.[221]

As Rebecca Probert has observed, the world has changed both legally and socially since Mrs Burns' case. Many family homes are now expressly jointly owned, legally and beneficially, so most couples do not need to rely on the law of implied trusts and estoppel. *Stack v Dowden* potentially offers much to homemakers in joint-names cases. Sex equality legislation, more family-friendly employment law, and increased child-care provision have opened up the labour market to many more women, who are therefore more likely to make financial contributions of a sort that will generate an interest in sole-name cases.[222] But, as the data at 3.2.2 above indicate, full economic equality between the genders has not yet been achieved.

John Eekelaar has strongly criticized the law:

J. Eekelaar, 'A Woman's Place—A Conflict Between Law and Social Values', (1987) 51 *Conveyancer and Property Lawyer* 93, 94

What is significant is that the fact that a woman bears a man a child, that she and the child move into a house with him in the clear expectation that this will constitute the environment in which the child will be nurtured and protected and that she devotes her time fully to the child and the house, cannot together be counted as evidence of an intention that the woman should have an interest in the house, with the relative security of occupation it can bring and the expectation of a share in its capital value should the relationship terminate. Only a person's "financial behaviour" can be considered in deciding what the original intentions might have been.

...Mrs. Burns (as she called herself) was held to have acquired no beneficial interest whatever in the home. No intention that she should do so could be spelt out of her activities after the house was bought. In looking for evidence of such intention, the court confined itself entirely to her income-generating pursuits. Her domestic duties were thought incapable of showing such an intention. "The mere fact that the parties live together and do the ordinary domestic tasks is, in my view, no indication at all that they intended to alter the existing property rights of either of them." The "mere" fact that the bearing and upbringing of a child is the decisive event which for most women permanently reduces their earning capacity, throwing them into dependency on men for their security in both the short and long term is to count as nothing when considering whether the parties may have intended that some form of such security may have been provided. The very activity which deprives a woman of her independent means of acquiring security and saving capital is excluded when deciding whether an alternative form of security was intended. A woman's place is often still in the home, but if she stays there, she will acquire no interest in it.

[220] [1984] Ch 317, 345, per May LJ.
[221] Ibid, 332.
[222] Probert (2001).

The uncertainty of the law in practice

Both constructive trust and proprietary estoppel cases are fraught with uncertainty. This is particularly so where the court now has a broad discretion to identify a 'fair' quantum for the beneficial interest in constructive trust cases and when the court decides how to satisfy the equity in proprietary estoppel cases. But there is also uncertainty at earlier stages of both types of claim, making it unclear whether and on what basis any interest will be found. In the case of the common intention constructive trust, there is ample scope for argument, not least about whether the case is a 'domestic' one to which the *Stack v Dowden* approach applies at all, and then in undertaking the wide-ranging factual survey necessary to identify the parties' intentions and anticipating whether and when a court might be prepared to infer a common intention to share the beneficial interest differently from the result presumed by the applicable starting point. It may be impossible to know whether the case in front of you is a 'very unusual' one, in which the presumption of beneficial joint tenancy may be rebutted, unless and until you have examined the 'paragraph 69 factors'.[223] Contrary to Baroness Hale's hopes, this simply promotes litigation.

It is tempting to try to use trusts law to rescue economically vulnerable ex-cohabitants from their predicament. But as John Mee cogently argues, that should not be done at the expense of sacrificing the doctrinal coherence and increasing uncertainty:

J. Mee, '*Burns v Burns*: The Villain of the Piece?', in S. Gilmore et al (eds), *Landmark Cases in Family Law* (Oxford: Hart Publishing, 2011), 194

The creation of more sweeping (and more invasive) rules, involving a higher level of discretion, has the effect of diminishing predictability, potentially involving more people in litigation and the threat of litigation, setting family members against each other in a context of heightened tension, and risking remedies being unjustly granted in favour of claimants who can exploit the open-endedness of the law to present an unmeritorious claim in a plausible way.

3.5 THE CURRENT LAW: ASCERTAINING OWNERSHIP OF OTHER PROPERTY

Title to most forms of property other than land can be acquired without completing onerous formalities. The discussion in the following extract applies as much to non-spouses as to husband and wife.

Law Commission, *Family Law: Matrimonial Property*, Law Com No 175 (London: HMSO, 1988b)

2.1 In deciding who owns property acquired by the spouses during the marriage the law at present places great weight on who paid for the property. Superficially this may seem

---

[223] Probert (2008b), 345.

reasonable but two examples may serve to show how the results may not reflect the spouses' wishes.

(i) Husband and wife decide to buy a washing machine; one Saturday they look together at various makes and decide to discuss it over the weekend. They decide upon the make they want and on Monday, the husband, who happens to pass on his way to work a shop which has the particular machine in stock, goes and buys the machine. On sale, ownership of the machine passes to the husband.

(ii) A husband is paid in cash, and his wife receives a monthly salary cheque. Because of this, they use his money for rent, food and other day to day necessities, and her money for bills and larger purchases. Consequently all the furniture in the house belongs to her.

Further, the emphasis on who pays creates great disadvantage for a non-earning spouse, who, whatever other contributions he or she may be making to the couple's life together, is likely to end up owning very little of the property which both of them may well regard as "joint".

2.2 It might be thought that the couple could avoid these results by choosing co-ownership. However, co-ownership cannot arise simply because the parties intend to own property in this way. Intention alone is insufficient; there must be some act which is effective to create the co-ownership. . . .

There are various ways—in the vast majority of cases, determined by the general law—in which ownership or co-ownership of property other than land can arise within a family.[224] First, unless the presumption of advancement applies, paying for an item generates beneficial ownership under the doctrine of resulting trust. The common intention constructive trust and proprietary estoppel can also be used outside the land context to create beneficial ownership of chattels and other property.[225] One party purchasing an item for joint use does not of itself generate joint ownership.[226] But property purchased using funds pooled, either in cash or in a bank account held jointly both legally and beneficially,[227] will belong to both parties. Secondly, ownership of chattels can be transferred either by using a deed or by the property being delivered to the new (co-)owner with an intention to transfer ownership. But it can be difficult to prove delivery between spouses,[228] especially in such a way as to create co-ownership. Thirdly, an owner of property can orally[229] declare himself to hold the asset on trust for another, provided it is made clear that he intends to become a trustee and does not just indicate a wish that the other party should have an interest. Fourthly, special statutory rules determine the ownership of property bought with savings made from a housekeeping allowance.[230]

The Law Commission's view of the current law is that creating co-ownership (specifically) can be difficult:

2.4 . . . [E]ven when a married couple have thought about it and wish their property to be co-owned, creating co-ownership may present difficulties. In what we suspect is the more usual case, where the couple have not thought about it at all, but if asked would say that they *assumed* much of their property was co-owned, they would be wrong.

224 The following discussion is taken largely from Law Com (1988b), para 2.2.
225 E.g. *Parrott v Parkin* [2007] EWHC 210, in relation to a boat.
226 Law Com (1988b), para 2.3 considers how the law of agency might apply.
227 See further below.
228 *Re Cole* [1964] Ch 175.
229 Cf the writing requirement for land: 3.4.1 above.
230 See 3.8.1 below: Married Women's Property Act 1964, now the Matrimonial Property Act 1964.

In the next two sections, we focus on two specific issues: express trusts and bank accounts.

3.5.1 EXPRESS TRUSTS OF OTHER PROPERTY

As noted above, express trusts of property other than land can be created orally, provided that the speaker manifests a clear intention to create or transfer the relevant interest. As with express common intention constructive trusts of land, this creates scope for litigation over conversations held long ago. In one case, a yacht (bought with the man's funds and in which the parties intended to sail the world following his divorce) was found to be owned by the parties in half-shares, owing to conversations in which he had repeatedly referred to the boat as 'ours':

Rowe v Prance [1999] 2 FLR 787 (Ch Div), 792–5

NICHOLAS WARREN QC (sitting as a deputy judge of the High Court):

In his witness statement, [Mr Prance] says that he meant this in the sense that people might refer to the hotel or restaurants they visit together as 'our' hotel or restaurant; and that he would refer to the previous boats he had owned as 'our' boat to the crew he had on board. In oral evidence, he gave a rather different explanation. He said he did not like to boast, and preferred to refer to the boat as 'our' boat so as to remove the spotlight—my word not his—as it were from him. . . . I found all that very unconvincing. I consider that Mr Prance's use of the word 'our' on many occasions was a reflection of how he wanted Mrs Rowe to think things were. It was the only expression of his intention and it is the effect of those words with which I am concerned. . . .

. . . There was . . . a conversation in which Mrs Rowe raised the issue of her security [She had given up her rented accommodation and put her furniture in storage to live on the boat.] . . . [The] response from Mr Prance . . . was that her security was his ability to sail the boat *and her interest in it.*

Unlike many assets, ownership of boats has to be registered. In this case, the boat was registered in Mr Prance's sole name. What bearing did that have?

[Ms Rowe] asserts that she was told by Mr Prance that the boat could not be registered in their joint names because she did not hold an Ocean Master's certificate. . . . Of course, no such certificate is necessary for yacht ownership at all. But if Mr Prance *did* say something to that effect, it is strong evidence of ownership on the part of Mrs Rowe: otherwise Mr Prance would not have made such a statement but would have said—if there was an occasion for him to need to say anything at all—that the boat was entirely his. . . .

I am satisfied that Mr Prance effectively constituted himself an express trustee of the boat. . . .

The judge then turned to the size of the parties' shares:

Nothing express was said to that effect, but the regular use of the word 'our' indicates to me an intention that there was no distinction to be drawn by Mr Prance between himself and Mrs Rowe so far as concerned ownership of the boat. Moreover, the discussion about

> security indicates that Mrs Rowe was intended to have a substantial interest. If I am reading too much into the first of these factors (the use of 'our') in deciding that it points to equality, and given also that the second factor (the reference to security) does not necessarily require equality, I consider that I should apply the maxim that equality is equity and hold that the shares are equal.

Since the property at stake was not land, Mrs Rowe did not need to prove any detrimental reliance on Mr Prance's oral statements about ownership of the boat in order to make them binding as an express trust. Those who live in houseboats and caravans[231] may therefore acquire a stake in their homes more readily than those who live between bricks and mortar.

3.5.2 BANK ACCOUNTS

Like land held in the name of one party, the credit balance of a sole-name bank account may be subject to a trust giving rise to a beneficial interest in favour of another person. Since a bank account is personal property, an express trust over the credit balance may arise orally. In *Paul v Constance*, the repeated statement that 'the money is as much yours as mine', made in relation to funds in a bank account held in the name of the man but on which his partner had the right to draw, was held to confer on her a half interest in those funds.[232] Conversely, the fact that an account is held in joint names does not necessarily mean that both parties are beneficially entitled to the funds, either at all or to the same degree. This depends on the parties' intentions:

Law Commission, *Cohabitation: The Financial Consequences of Relationship Breakdown*, Law Com CP 179 (London: TSO, 2006)

Ownership of funds in bank accounts

3.38...If the account is fed from the resources of one party, A, but is held in joint names with B merely for convenience—for example, to give B access to funds—B has no beneficial interest in the money in the account until he or she actually exercises the right to draw funds from it. While it remains in the account, the money will belong, under resulting trust principles, to A as the party who fed the account. If B has made no contribution to the account, A will be entitled to terminate B's access to the funds at any time.[233]

3.39 Where both parties contribute to the account, pooling their resources, they will at least be found to own the funds on a resulting trust basis in accordance with their contributions. However, both in pooling cases and in cases where A has provided all the funds, the presumption of resulting trust might be displaced, for example, where there is an express declaration of trust or common intention to the effect that the parties should share the account in some other proportions. Indeed, the court might find that the parties intended to be joint tenants of the beneficial interest, each equally entitled to the whole of the fund.

---

[231] Unless the caravan constitutes a fixture: see Gray and Gray (2011), 1-023 et seq.
[232] [1977] 1 WLR 527.
[233] *Stoeckert v Geddes (No 2)* [2004] UKPC 54.

> 3.40 Property purchased with funds from a joint account will ordinarily belong to whoever acquires title to that property, even if that person had no or only a part-share in the funds when they were in the account.[234] If, unusually, there is evidence that the assets acquired were intended to be held in the same way as the funds in the account, then that property will be held accordingly.[235] [some footnotes retained from original]

In this context, as with land, the courts may be quicker in the case of spouses and civil partners than with others to imply an intention to pool both funds in the account and property acquired from those funds.[236]

3.6 FAMILY PROPERTY SYSTEMS: OPTIONS FOR REFORM

The law currently picks its way through the parties' intentions and contributions in order to establish whether a given asset is 'his', 'hers', or 'theirs', and if the last, in what shares, resorting to a general 'fairness' inquiry if evidence of intention runs out at that stage. But there has long been wide public support for the proposition that the matrimonial home should be jointly owned automatically.[237] Ought the law prescribe that particular assets are, by law, automatically 'theirs' in equal shares?[238]

3.6.1 BASIC QUESTIONS FOR REFORM OF FAMILY PROPERTY LAW

Any 'family property' regime must address three basic questions: (i) to whom should the scheme apply? (ii) to what property should it apply? (iii) on what basis should property be shared, and what other rights should each party have in relation to it? Major reform is properly a matter for the legislature, rather than judicial development,[239] so that the scheme can be confined to clearly identified situations for which it would be appropriate, and tailored accordingly. So what we are principally contemplating here are options for a family property law, created by statute specifically for the family context, not an evolution of general property law.

The various answers which can be given to the three questions above reflect differing views about the purpose of the law, ideological views about the family relationships involved, and the implications they should have for the property relations between the parties. Reform could be driven by various goals, alone or in combination, for example: to provide more certain determination of property rights; to recognize the economic value of

---

234 Ibid.

235 *Jones v Maynard* [1951] Ch 572.

236 E.g. *Jones v Maynard* [1951] Ch 572.

237 Law Com (1973b), paras 4 and 22; public support for joint ownership may not be based on legally relevant reasons: Cooke, Barlow, and Callus (2006), 25.

238 Kahn-Freund (1952), 135.

239 *Pettitt v Pettitt* [1970] AC 777, 794–5; *Burns v Burns* [1984] Ch 317, 332 per Fox LJ, and 345 per May LJ; *Stack v Dowden* [2007] UKHL 17, contrast Baroness Hale at [47]–[48], and Lord Neuberger at [101]–[107]. Cf Gardner (2013) and Mee (2011).

domestic contributions; to protect the position of economically weaker family members; to align the law with public beliefs about what the law is or should be, and so better reflect parties' likely intentions; to promote a particular ideological view about marriage or other family relationships.

None of the three questions can be answered independently from each other. Lorna Fox has developed a useful pair of spectrums on which to evaluate family property regimes.[240] First, does the scheme apply 'broadly' or 'narrowly': to various relationships, or only to a limited class, such as spouses and civil partners? Secondly, is the level of protection 'deep' or 'shallow': do the rights take effect against third parties, or merely bind other family members? Viewed in these terms, a 'deeper' answer to question (iii) above might merit a 'narrower' answer to question (i): if a scheme confers substantial entitlements (such as automatic co-ownership of a pool of assets), it is likely to be appropriate for a more limited range of relationships.

It is impossible wholly to detach discussion of the position during relationships from the position when they end. For all except spouses and civil partners, the law currently applicable during the relationship largely dictates the division of assets on separation. Moreover, some of the options that have been mooted in this area for spouses (and civil partners) would apply both during and following marriage. For example, the law could provide that certain property is co-owned in equal shares during marriage and that spouses retain those shares when it ceases; there might be separate rules governing the question of maintenance (income provision) following divorce, but the basic property rights could be fixed. A fourth question could therefore be added to our list: at what point in the relationship should family property rights conferred by the scheme arise: only during the relationship, when it ends, or throughout?

We shall see later in this chapter that various rights, short of full ownership, can be and to some extent have been conferred by legislation on some family members, in particular in relation to the home. Some argue that, given these rights and the statutory remedies available on divorce and death, there is no need to amend the law of property ownership during marriage. However, it has been said that 'it is a poor and incomplete kind of marital justice which is excluded from continuing marriage relationships and allowed to operate only when those relationships end'.[241] Various proposals have therefore been made to confer property rights on family members during relationships. The Law Commission during the 1970s and 1980s sought to devise co-ownership schemes that could operate during marriage, but none was implemented.[242] More recently, its *Sharing Homes* project considered ownership of the shared home in a wider range of domestic situations, not just marriage.[243] Renewed interest in joint ownership has arisen following comparative studies of laws applying elsewhere in Europe.[244] Some reform options, modelled on the matrimonial property laws of some European and other jurisdictions, involve 'community' or sharing in wider pools of property and debts. Some propose joint ownership of the home and essential household goods. Others, like the *Sharing Homes* project, simply seek to make the law of trusts better suited to the social and economic realities of family life.

---

[240] Fox (2003).
[241] Law Com (1978), para 0.11.
[242] Law Com (1971), (1973), (1978), (1982a), (1988b).
[243] Law Com (2002).
[244] Cooke, Barlow, and Callus (2006), 2; Pintens (2011); Boele-Woelki et al (2014), Part 1.

3.6.2 COMMUNITY OF PROPERTY REGIMES

Many jurisdictions have systems of community property for spouses. The range of property covered varies. For example, the Netherlands operates a 'full' or 'universal' community of property; France operates a 'community of acquests', defined in the extract below.[245] Community systems operate on an 'opt-out' basis, allowing couples to choose either separation of property or a form of community different from the default regime. One important characteristic of these systems is that they create an 'immediate' community from the point of marriage. By contrast, systems of 'deferred' community, such as those in Sweden and Canada, only arise when the relationship ends; separate property applies during the relationship. The basic precepts of 'immediate' community schemes have been evaluated by the Scottish Law Commission:

Scottish Law Commission, *Matrimonial Property*, Scot Law Com No 86
(Edinburgh: HMSO, 1984)

A "full community property" system

3.2 In a "full community property" system practically all the property of a married couple, including property owned by one of them before the marriage or inherited during it, would be automatically subject to a special form of joint ownership. It would not belong to one spouse or the other but would become "community property". Special rules would be necessary to regulate the management of the community property [by the couple jointly]...Among the usual consequences of a full community system are these:

(a) The community property is liable for the debts of both spouses. So one spouse may lose all the property he or she brings into the marriage if the other is a spendthrift or becomes bankrupt.

(b) The community property is divided equally on divorce. So one spouse may lose half of the property he or she brings into the marriage, even after a very short marriage.

(c) The community property is divided equally on the death of *either* spouse. So if one spouse dies after, say, a year of marriage, the surviving spouse may have to pay half of the property he or she brought into the marriage to the heirs of the other...

A law introducing a full community system would be extremely complex. In countries with such systems many couples contract out of them. In our view the effect of introducing such a system...would be that many couples would be put to the expense and inconvenience of opting out of it by marriage contract....

A "community of acquests" system

3.3 Under most "community of acquests" systems the only property which becomes community property is that which is acquired by the spouses during the marriage otherwise than by gift or inheritance. There will usually be an equal division of such property on the dissolution of the marriage by death or divorce and joint liability for at least some debts. The advantage of such systems is that they give expression to the idea of marriage as an equal partnership. The disadvantages are complexity and r[i]gidity.

---

[245] See Pintens (2011), for an overview.

3.4...[T]he important question is whether a community of acquests system would have significant advantages in practice, on the dissolution of a marriage or during its subsistence, over a rule of separate property during marriage with rules for a division of property on dissolution of the marriage by death or divorce...So far as the position on death or divorce is concerned, there is no reason why a rule of separate property during marriage should not co-exist with satisfactory rules for the division of property on death or divorce...So far as the position during marriage is concerned, we do not believe that a community of acquests system would bring about significant benefits for many people. We know from the family property survey that there is already a great deal of voluntary sharing of property by married couples under our system. A community of acquests system would not make very much, if any, practical difference in cases where there already is considerable voluntary sharing and it would be unlikely to make very much practical difference, during the marriage, in those cases where there is little or no sharing. The crucial problem here is the day to day management of the community funds...To require the consent of *both* spouses to any dealing with community assets would be unwieldy. That leaves two solutions—to allow either spouse to deal with any part of the community property, or to allow each spouse to deal with the property he or she brought into the community. The first solution leaves both spouses at risk, while neither protects the non-earning spouse. Of course, the general rules on the management of the spouses' property could be qualified by special rules for the protection of the non-earning spouse, but that is also the case in separate property systems. The aspect of a community of acquests system which appealed to the minority of commentators supporting this type of system was the governing principle itself. In our view, any advantage of adopting this governing principle would, during the marriage, be more symbolic than real and would be outweighed by the disadvantages of introducing a community of acquests system.

The Scottish Law Commission felt that the principal disadvantage of community property was the 'excessive legal complexity' it might entail. Some spouses would fall within the scheme, others would opt out; third parties would need to know who was in and who was out, and that might require a register. For those within the scheme, detailed rules would have to prescribe what assets fell within the community: how should gifts, inheritances, compensation for injury, and so on be categorized? Even within the scheme, unless universal community were adopted, each marriage would have three pots of property—his, hers, and theirs—and further rules would have to deal with the relationship between these three pots. For example, if the wife sold an asset acquired before marriage and used the proceeds to buy something during the marriage, should that new asset be hers or theirs? What if the wife spent money restoring a painting belonging to the husband: should his fund have to compensate hers? On balance, the Commission felt that it would be easier and cheaper simply to let those who wished to share particular assets do so under the general law, rather than to erect a complex scheme of community property from which the process of opting-out might be rather more elaborate and costly.[246]

In researching some European systems, Cooke, Barlow, and Callus[247] found lawyers and notaries were broadly satisfied with the law, though the degree of public awareness and understanding of the law was questioned. The simplicity of the 'universal' Dutch community system was appreciated: all property is included. Nevertheless, the researchers did not advocate the adoption of any form of immediate community of property in England and

246 Scot Law Com (1984), paras 3.5–3.6.
247 Cooke, Barlow, and Callus (2006), ch 3.

Wales. They considered that the original rationale of such schemes—to protect the interests of wives who looked after home and family rather than undertaking paid employment—sits uneasily with contemporary women's independence, and noted that the trend within Europe is to move away from full and immediate community in favour of more limited and deferred systems. Moreover, the results of their English attitudinal survey suggested that the key *debt*-sharing feature of community systems would be unacceptable, even given the option to opt out.[248] The traditional marriage vow—'for better, for worse, for richer, for poorer'—may not translate comfortably into law.

3.6.3 JOINT OWNERSHIP OF HOME, CONTENTS, AND OTHER ASSETS

Automatic co-ownership

The Law Commission has focused on joint ownership of key family assets, particularly the home, rather than wider-ranging community property schemes. The following remarks still have some force, despite *Stack* and *Jones*, especially in sole-name cases.

Law Commission, *Third Report on Family Property: The Matrimonial Home (Co-ownership and Occupation Rights) and Household Goods*, Law Com No 86 (London: HMSO, 1978)

0.9...The present law about the ownership of the matrimonial home during marriage is not only highly technical and sometimes uncertain in application, but inappropriate in substance. The rules now applied to determine the ownership of the home are essentially the same as those which determine the ownership of a commercial or investment property: they ignore the fact that the home is the residence of a family as well as being, in many cases, its major capital asset. Husband and wife each contribute to the home in their different ways—the wife's contributions are no less real because they may not be financial—and the home is essential to the well-being of the family as a whole. In our view these factors make the matrimonial home a unique item of property, and one to which a unique law of co-ownership should apply...

The Commission accordingly developed a scheme whereby spouses would enjoy statutory co-ownership of the matrimonial home as joint tenants. The scheme would not apply where they were express co-owners under the general law or in other prescribed circumstances. The courts would retain their powers on divorce and death to adjust spouses' property rights under the scheme. The Matrimonial Homes (Co-ownership) Bill 1980 was put before Parliament but withdrawn before being fully debated.[249] The Commission later took the view that, since joint ownership of the matrimonial home had become standard practice, there was no pressing need for its controversial scheme.[250] Instead, it advocated statutory joint ownership of certain other property (not acquired for business purposes), including household goods and cars:[251]

---

[248] See also Law Com (1988b), paras 4.17–4.18 on debt-sharing.

[249] See Fox (2001) and Cretney (2003a), 136–41 on the parliamentary history of the Bill and its collision with *Williams & Glyn's Bank v Boland* [1981] AC 487; Law Com (1982a).

[250] Law Com (1988b), para 4.3.

[251] On the importance of these assets, see Kahn-Freund (1971), 503.

Law Commission, *Family Property: Matrimonial Property*, Law Com No 175
(London: HMSO, 1988b)

2.8 The present law [of ownership of property other than land] is unsatisfactory because its application may not result in co-ownership of property even when a married couple desire this. Actual ownership may be held to depend on factors which neither party considered significant at the time of acquisition. In its treatment of money allowances and gifts of property the law discriminates between husband and wife.[252]

...

4.1 Money may be spent by spouses for many different purposes. However we believe that it is possible to distinguish two main purposes; first the use or benefit of the spouses jointly and, secondly, other uses or benefits. There is evidence to suggest that spouses regard much of their property as jointly owned even when in law it is probably not. Dissatisfaction with the present law arguably stems from the fact that ownership of the money used and property acquired with it is quite unconnected with the purposes for which it is to be used. The policy of our reform is to create a direct connection between the purposes for which money is spent and its ownership. Accordingly our proposal has two main limbs:

(i) where money is spent to buy property, or property or money is transferred by one spouse to the other...for their joint use or benefit[,] the property acquired or money transferred should be jointly owned.

(ii) where money or property is transferred by one spouse to the other for any other purpose, it should be owned by that other.

In both cases, the general rule should give way to a contrary intention on the part of the paying or transferring spouse, provided that the contrary intention is known to the other spouse....

4.11 ...the proposals apply to purchases by a spouse or transfers by a spouse, anything owned before the marriage will necessarily be excluded. Likewise gifts or inheritances received by one spouse during the marriage are excluded, although the spouse who has received them may still make a transfer to the other spouse or to both of them jointly, in which case the new rules will apply. Most importantly, our proposals are designed for the property bought or transferred for the purposes of the couple's domestic life together...

Various forms of joint ownership have occasionally resurfaced in reform proposals.[253] But joint ownership schemes have been subject to criticism:

Scottish Law Commission, *Matrimonial Property*, Scot Law Com No 86
(Edinburgh: HMSO, 1984)

3.10 There appear to be four arguments for a scheme of statutory co-ownership of the matrimonial home:

(i) It would give expression to the idea of marriage as an equal partnership.

(ii) It would reward the contributions in unpaid work by a non-earning spouse, particularly a housewife.

---

252 See now the Equality Act 2010, ss 198–200; not in force at December 2014.
253 Law Reform Advisory Committee for Northern Ireland (2000); Barlow and Lind (1999); Lord Lester's Civil Partnership Bill (HL), cl 9; Cooke, Barlow, and Callus (2006).

(iii) It would bring the law more into line with the views of most married people.

(iv) It would give effect to the view that the matrimonial home should be owned in common because it is used in common.

These arguments can, however, be met by the following arguments:

(i) Statutory co-ownership of the matrimonial home would not be a good way of giving expression to the idea of marriage as an equal partnership. In some cases it would go too far, particularly if it applied to a home owned before marriage, or acquired by gift or inheritance during the marriage. These are not the results of the spouses' joint efforts. In other cases it would not go far enough and could produce results which were unfair as between one spouse and another. If the wife, say, owned the home and the husband owned other property, he could acquire a half share in the home without having to share any of his property. A spouse with investments worth thousands of pounds could allow the other to buy a home and then claim half of it without contributing a penny. The scheme would also work very unevenly as between different couples. If Mr A had invested all his money in the matrimonial home while his next-door neighbour Mr B had mortgaged his home to its full value in order to finance his business, the law would operate very unevenly for the benefit of Mrs A and Mrs B.[254] It would, in short, be a hit or miss way of giving effect to the partnership ideal.

(ii) Statutory co-ownership of the matrimonial home would not be a good way of recognising contributions in unpaid work by a non-earning spouse. It would benefit the undeserving as well as the deserving. Extreme cases can be imagined. A man might marry a wealthy widow, encourage her to buy an expensive house, claim half her house and leave her. Even in less extreme cases statutory co-ownership would be a poor way of rewarding unpaid work. [Some] housewives would get nothing from the new law because its effects would be confined to owner-occupiers [excluding tenants[255]] . . . Even where the new law did apply, its effects would be totally arbitrary. Not only would the net value of the home vary enormously from case to case, and from time to time, but so too would the respective values of the spouses' contributions.

(iii) Statutory co-ownership would not necessarily bring the law into line with the views of most married people. . . .

As to this, the English Law Commission public survey asked whether the home should be legally jointly owned, but did not ask whether that outcome should be achieved by way of a default statutory rule to that effect—Law Com (1973), para 22.

(iv) It is not self-evident that property which is used in common should be owned in common. Even if this proposition were accepted, it would lead further than co-ownership between spouses. It would lead to co-ownership between the members of a household, including for example, children and parents.

There were further objections. As with community property, the scheme would be complex, potentially requiring detailed legal advice to protect each spouse's interests, in turn

---

[254] Though both spouses' consent could be required for mortgaging.
[255] Law Com (1982a) recommended co-ownership of most leases too.

potentially fomenting dispute between otherwise happy spouses, and not necessarily yielding fairer outcomes in return:

> (v) A scheme for statutory co-ownership of the matrimonial home would be very complex...Should, for example, co-ownership come about automatically by operation of law (in which case how would third parties, such as people who have bought the house in good faith, be protected) or should it come about, say, on registration of a notice [on the land register] by the non-owner spouse (in which case would non-owner spouses bother to register before it was too late)? Should co-ownership apply to a house owned by one spouse before the marriage? Should it apply to a home which is part of a commercial or agricultural property? Should it apply to a home bought by one spouse after the couple have separated? If not, should it make any difference if the spouses resume cohabitation for a short period? Should the spouses become jointly liable for any debts secured on the home? When should it be possible for one spouse, or both, to opt out of co-ownership and how should this be done? Should a spouse be able to claim half of the sale proceeds of one home, refuse to contribute to the purchase price of a new home, and then claim half of that one too? If not, how can this be remedied without forcing a spouse to invest in a home he or she does not want to invest in? These are just some of the less technical questions that would have to be answered....[A]lthough statutory co-ownership of the matrimonial home seems attractively simple in general terms, it turns out to be surprisingly complicated...

It was also doubted, given the predominance of joint ownership by spouses under the general law, whether many would want to take advantage of a new scheme. Moreover, since death or divorce would trigger the specific rights and remedies available following those events, superseding the parties' interests under the joint ownership regime, it was felt that little practical benefit would arise from the scheme at all.

Automatic co-ownership would at least avoid the need that arises in some cases in England and Wales[256] to grapple with the law of implied trusts in order to establish parties' beneficial interests in the absence of an express declaration of trust. But because it would have to take effect as joint *equitable* ownership only, Cooke, Barlow, and Callus have argued[257] that very little would be gained in practice. The interest would presumably be overreachable (though overreaching would only occur if there were two trustees). Third parties dealing with the property would in any event seek waivers from all adult occupiers to prevent an overriding interest being asserted. Conferring a share in the property would therefore give no extra power or protection to the non-owner. At the same time, they argued, the increased possibility of an unknown occupier 'coming out of the woodwork' with an overriding interest would cause lending institutions and other third parties to oppose such reform. The only way to guard against this—to bar statutory co-ownership interests from being overriding and to require registration, as the Law Commission recommended[258]—would seriously weaken the theoretical protection for the non-owning spouse: experience from the use of statutory home rights, addressed below, suggests registration would be very unlikely.

---

[256] The Scottish Law Commission's views must be assessed in light of the different general law of property that applies there, in particular, the lack of implied trusts law.

[257] Cooke, Barlow, and Callus (2006), 25–6.

[258] Law Com (1982a).

Presumption of joint ownership

An alternative might be to presume joint ownership of certain assets, rather than impose it automatically, in an effort to reduce the complexity and uncertainty involved in seeking to establish ownership of property under the general law. This approach is taken in Scotland in relation to some types of money and property for both spouses and civil partners[259] and (with rather weaker presumptions, applying in some respects to a narrower range of property) cohabitants.[260] The Law Commission rejected this technique for English law. As a rule of evidence, presumptions only assist where there is no evidence supporting a finding of legal ownership, or the evidence is finely balanced, and do not supply the certainty of a rule.[261] Of course, *Stack v Dowden* created precisely this presumption—in supposedly strong form—where land is bought in joint names. Readers should revisit the discussion and criticism of that decision and subsequent case law above to decide whether the Law Commission's scepticism about the utility of such a presumption was well founded.

3.6.4 BUT IS COMMUNITY OR JOINT OWNERSHIP APPROPRIATE?

Technical problems aside, there is considerable disagreement about whether it is socially and ideologically appropriate to translate the equal partnership of marriage (and now civil partnership) into equal sharing of family property where that is not expressly chosen by the parties.[262]

Calls for joint ownership of key family assets by spouses emerged powerfully in the 1950s, when spouses were expected to perform distinct roles in marriage and there was no capital redistribution following divorce. Automatic joint co-ownership would ensure that wives' contributions were valued and their economic position protected. As noted at 3.2.2, female labour market participation has increased substantially since then, but many women are still not employed, and many work only part-time. There may therefore remain a case for automatic joint ownership to provide greater economic equality between spouses.

Alternatively or additionally, automatic sharing or community of property (and of liabilities) could be regarded as a contemporary manifestation of the 'community' that marriage or civil partnership should be understood to create. This could be thought to flow from the parties' express commitment to their legal status, without implying that either party is economically dependent.[263] The parties' chosen legal status could be treated as at least presumptive evidence that they intend to share certain assets. The idea of equal partnership has become a powerful factor shaping financial settlements on divorce,[264] and it may be desirable that it should also shape entitlements during marriage. Indeed, if most spouses use their property as if it were jointly owned, regardless of

---

[259] Family Law (Scotland) Act 1985, ss 25–6. Scot Law Com (1984), paras 4.2–4.8.
[260] Family Law (Scotland) Act 2006, ss 26–7. Scot Law Com (1992), paras 16.7–16.13.
[261] Law Com (1988b), para 3.2; compare Scot Law Com (1992), para 16.9 on the practical effect of the spouses' presumption.
[262] E.g. Zuckerman (1978), 51–7; Deech (1980a).
[263] E.g. Kahn-Freund (1955), 267–8; (1959), 248–9.
[264] *Miller v Miller; McFarlane v McFarlane* [2006] UKHL 24: see chapter 7.

the technical position, why not reflect that in law? Or should property ownership be left for the parties to arrange as they wish, from a starting point of separate property? The following discussion by Mary Ann Glendon was written in the mid-1970s, but much of her analysis remains relevant:

M. Glendon, 'Is There a Future for Separate Property?', (1974) 8 *Family Law Quarterly* 315, 323–7

There is an eternal tension in matrimonial law, in social attitudes, and in every marriage between the community of life that marriage involves and the separate, autonomous existence of the individuals who are associated in this community of life. Emphasis on one or other aspect varies from time to time in the law, in societies and in the lives of couples. John Stuart Mill's idea that marriage ought to be likened to a partnership, and its expression in [marital property regimes that involve sharing] emphasizes the community aspect of marriage.

But there is another idea that has regained great currency in contemporary society and which is in conflict with the ideology of community. This is the notion that marriage exists primarily for the personal fulfillment of the individual spouses and that it should last only so long as it performs this function to the satisfaction of each. [Hence the introduction in many jurisdictions of no-fault, unilateral divorce and clean break divorce settlements.[265]] . . .

. . . [However,] [t]he increased labor force participation of married women includes so much intermittent and part-time work that it cannot be seen as a move towards imminent economic [in]dependence of most married women. Thus, from one point of view, the stage is set for the introduction of more mechanisms to enable each spouse to share in the other's acquests. However, three additional questions must be asked at this point.

In the first place, the factual economic dependence of great numbers of married women must be distinguished from their potential for being economically independent. . . . Therefore, we must ask whether their potential, rather than their actual, status should be emphasized in framing laws affecting the economic relations of spouses.

Secondly, how much weight should be given to the fact that laws emphasizing and responding to the factual dependence of married women may tend to perpetuate dependence and to discourage the acquisition of skills and seniority needed to make married women economically independent and equal in the labour market?

Finally, . . . [c]onceding the compatability of sharing mechanisms with current economic behavior of spouses, how can we assess their compatability with current marriage behavior and ideologies? Is ideology at cross-purposes, in the short run at least, with economic reality? A leading French writer, Dean Savatier, advises married women that their choice is between "la finance" and "la gloire", and counsels them to take the bucks. Others think it is not just a question of choosing between financial security here and now and an illusion of glory later. They feel that opting for devices which shore up the economic role of housewife will, in the long run, work to the economic detriment of women. Certainly a factor to be considered here is the question of whether the role of housewife should be discouraged before a solution to the problem of child care can be seen.

---

265 See chapters 5 and 7.

These questions are thorny but cannot be overlooked by law reformers. Many different conceptions of marriage coexist in society at the present time. It is impossible to say which predominates. But when the widespread expectation that marriage will last only so long as it performs its function of providing personal fulfillment is put together with the reality of unilateral divorce, a diminished sense of economic responsibility after divorce, the increasing economic independence of married women, and the expansion of social welfare, the resulting state of affairs does not lead inevitably to the sharing of worldly goods . . .

Seen in this light, the system of separation of assets with the possibility it has always offered for purely voluntary co-ownership may come to have the most appeal for the greatest number of people.

Whatever the rationale for joint ownership might be, ought such a scheme extend to cohabitants? The Scottish Law Commission thought not:[266]

Scottish Law Commission, *Matrimonial Property*, Scot Law Com No 86 (Edinburgh: HMSO, 1984)

4.23 We expressed the provisional view . . . that a scheme of statutory co-ownership of the matrimonial home could not apply to unmarried couples cohabiting as man and wife. Such a scheme would involve fixed property rights and this would be inappropriate for a relationship as varied as cohabitation. It would presumably be unacceptable to allow a half share in a person's house to be acquired by a person of the opposite sex after, say, one week of cohabitation as man and wife. A minimum duration of two or three years would probably have to be required. Even then, however, there would be practical difficulties in deciding whether a couple came within the definition, and in applying any provisions allowing "opting out" before marriage. Third parties dealing with one of the parties would be placed in an impossible position. Similar objections applied, in our view, to extending a scheme for statutory co-ownership of household goods to unmarried cohabiting couples. They would apply *a fortiori* to any more general community property scheme.

By contrast, the Law Reform Advisory Committee for Northern Ireland, while recognizing the diversity of cohabiting relationships, recommended that automatic co-ownership of the home,[267] housekeeping money, and household goods should apply to those cohabiting either for two years or who have a child.[268] But their recommendation was based on the empirically doubtful presumption that the intentions and financial arrangements of cohabitants do not significantly differ from those of spouses. Some cohabitants, particularly those with children, do pool their resources like spouses do, but many others do not.[269] The mere fact of cohabitation may not warrant conferring substantial property rights on the non-owner, particularly if that party has made no particular contribution to or economic sacrifice for the relationship.[270]

---

[266] See also Law Com (1982a), para 111; cf Law Com (1988b), para 4.21.
[267] See also Barlow and Lind (1999).
[268] For criticism see Fox (2001).
[269] Vogler (2009).
[270] Cf Scot Law Com (1984), para 3.10(ii), extracted above at p 178.

3.6.5 MODIFIED TRUSTS LAW FOR THE 'SHARED HOME'

Instead of creating automatic co-ownership, one might attempt to adapt the law of trusts to deal more predictably and fairly with family situations. Many commentators have pointed to how other Commonwealth courts (notably in Australia, Canada, and New Zealand) have developed more flexible laws of remedial constructive trust, which are not dependent on finding (or creating) a common intention by the parties that ownership be shared.[271] John Mee has questioned the democratic legitimacy of radical judicial development of trusts law to protect economically vulnerable parties and cautioned about the doctrinal incoherence that results from attempts to do so:

J. Mee, '*Burns v Burns*: The Villain of the Piece?', in S. Gilmore et al (eds), *Landmark Cases in Family Law* (Oxford: Hart Publishing, 2011), 191

In thinking about the role of the law of trusts as a possible location for law reform in this area, it is crucial to remember that the law of trusts, like all areas of the law, has its own function to perform within the legal system. Like impatient visitors to a distant country, irritated at the locals' inability to speak the visitors' language, lawyers concerned only with the achievement of the goal of affording cohabitants greater remedies may chafe at the limitations of equity and trusts. The problem is that the law of trusts is important for reasons other than its role in respect of resolving disputes between cohabitants. We are not talking here about abstract theoretical purity and logic which could appeal only to anorak-clad property-law scholars. Rather, having a sensible law of equity and trusts is important because it impacts on people's lives (as do all areas of law).

Democratic legitimacy, at least, could be achieved by statutory reform, and so the Law Commission's *Sharing Homes* project sought to develop a new statutory trust of the 'shared home', to displace the general law of implied trusts and estoppel. The ownership of 'shared homes' would be determined by reference to the parties' various financial and non-financial contributions to their shared life. To use Lorna Fox's terminology, the scheme was confined narrowly to just one asset (the home), but otherwise both wide and deep:[272] it covered all domestic home-sharers, including relatives and platonic friends, and conferred full property rights, rather than lesser rights (e.g. to occupy). This breadth and depth was the project's downfall. The Commission felt unable to devise a scheme that would: (i) release cases from the strictures of the current law (particularly the need to prove a common intention about ownership); whilst also (ii) producing appropriate outcomes for the full range of relationships. For example, an outcome which would be fair between a married or cohabiting couple may not be fair between an adult child and the parents to whose home he has returned. Parties in those situations are likely to have differing (if often unarticulated) views about whether and when certain contributions should give rise to shared ownership of the property.[273]

---

271 See Gray and Gray (2009), 7.3.77 et seq; Rotherham (2004); Mee (1999); Gardner (1993).
272 Fox (2003).
273 Law Com (2002), paras 3.55–3.74. See Miles (2003); Fox (2003); Mee (2004).

In another sense, however, the *Sharing Homes* project could be regarded as having been too *narrow*. Rebecca Probert has argued that if the justification for reform is to ensure that domestic and other non-financial contributions to inter-personal relationships are properly valued, another raft of candidates for a new scheme emerge:

R. Probert, 'Trusts and the Modern Woman—Establishing an Interest in the Family Home', (2001) 13 *Child and Family Law Quarterly* 275, 285

A...justification for reform might be that, on principle, domestic contributions should be treated in the same way as financial contributions. This would require reform to embrace both married and cohabiting couples. However, it should also be noted that those who share a home are not the only ones who make contributions to each other's welfare. Recent statistics on the extent to which informal care is being provided found that while 4% of adults were caring for someone who lived with them, 7% were providing equally significant levels of care for someone who lived in another household.[274] The only justification for excluding the latter from consideration would be the assumption that their services are provided out of 'love and affection', which would merely perpetuate one of the major deficiencies of the current law.[275]

3.6.6 SHOULD WE FOCUS ON 'OWNERSHIP' DURING RELATIONSHIPS AT ALL?

Many proposals relating to intact families have focused on ownership. But ownership may not be the most helpful 'conceptual starting point'.[276]

J. Dewar, 'Land, Law and the Family Home', in S. Bright and J. Dewar (eds), *Land Law: Themes and Perspectives* (Oxford: OUP, 1998b), 353–4

I want to suggest that, in devising a legislative strategy in this context, we need not think exclusively in terms of ownership; and that ownership thinking may have become something of a strait-jacket. Instead, I want to suggest that, in line with the English tradition of pragmatism in this area, we should think functionally. Thinking functionally about the family home means asking what rights family members need in relation to it. If we can identify what those are or might be, we can set about conferring them directly, without necessarily invoking the language of ownership. This means avoiding the Law Commission's strategy [in pre-*Sharing Homes* projects] of creating equal ownership in order to confer rights incidental to that ownership. The focus would be on status as the mechanism for conferring the necessary rights, not on property. Of course, this begs the question of what we mean by familial 'status' for these purposes, who would qualify for it, and how the different interests of family members and third parties would be weighed against each other: but at least the strategy would be clear.

In order to get discussion going on these lines, I suggest that there are four broad rights that family members need in relation to the family home: a right of *control over dealings* (such

---

[274] See now data from ONS (2010d), 113 et seq.
[275] See extract from Flynn and Lawson (1995), p 164 above.
[276] See also Deech (1984); Miles (2003).

as mortgages or sales); a right of *occupation or enjoyment*; a right of *capital entitlement on sale*, and a right, on the termination of the relationship, to have *basic needs met out of the family resources represented by the family home*.

...[T]he incidents of property ownership have been developed judicially in such a way that co-owners of a family home already have many of these rights secured to them—through what I have called the 'familialization' of property law. An equitable interest in land, for example, can form the basis of securing the first two rights of consent to dealings and enjoyment through occupation; and ownership remains pre-eminent in determining the third right, at least where there are no statutory alternatives available for doing so. But, in a family context, or more specifically a context of gender inequality, it needs to be asked whether ownership is a sufficient or necessary basis for securing these rights.

I would suggest that it is neither. It is not necessary, because there are existing instances in which some of these rights are secured to family members *as such*, regardless of their rights of ownership (for example, occupation orders under the Family Law Act 1996,[277] or property distribution orders under the Matrimonial Causes Act 1973[278]); and there is no reason why a status-based logic, which bypasses ownership, could not be extended to securing the other rights mentioned.

Nor is it sufficient, given the weight of evidence suggesting that, despite judicial development, the rules of ownership acquisition operate unfavourably in a family context, especially against women, by according pre-eminence to money contributions to acquisition; and in the light of the fact that ownership is a very crude device for securing all four of the rights mentioned above, especially the fourth. For example, an a priori assumption of equal ownership would translate into a principle of equal division on separation, yet that is a rule that legislatures have generally avoided, on the basis that equal division can lead to serious post-separation inequalities. Instead, distribution of property has to be seen in the light of the parties' post-relationship needs and of other powers concerning maintenance for spouses and children. Vindication of the fourth right therefore requires more than a simple rule about ownership.

...[T]here is a sense in which all four of the rights mentioned are already secured, to some degree, by means of existing legislation... To that extent, we might say that ownership is in any case fast becoming obsolete as a significant conceptual category in this area; and that, in its pragmatic way, English statute law is groping towards a satisfactory regime for the family home, despite its continuing theoretical attachment to the doctrine of separation. But...that statutory regime has arisen piecemeal, and varies significantly in its application according to status or the procedural context in ways that are not obviously justified.

If, instead, we were to view the current maze of the law relating to the family home through the grid of the four rights mentioned above, and at the same time reduce our attachment to ownership as the sole vehicle for attaining these rights, we might get some greater clarity about the proper policy in this important area of social and economic life.

Some commentators advocate family ownership schemes, in preference to reliance on the exercise of judicial discretion in favour of economically vulnerable individuals.[279] They emphasize the 'symbolic' value of property ownership,[280] and the psychological security

---

[277] Chapter 4.
[278] Chapter 7.
[279] See Bottomley (1998); Law Com (1971), para 22.
[280] O'Donovan (1985), 112.

it can provide. However, addressing more specific issues—such as the right to occupy the home, and financial remedies on relationship breakdown—rather than, or alongside, ownership helps us to focus clearly on our objectives. While property ownership itself may seem too substantial an entitlement for some categories of family members, any or all of the 'sub-rights' identified by John Dewar might be appropriate. Unpacking the question in this way may offer a more productive strategy for dealing with today's diverse family relationships.

John Mee observed that the *Sharing Homes* project could be said to have tried to 'treat the symptom of disputes over the ownership of houses rather than address the underlying problem of the fall-out from the breakdown of informal relationships'.[281] Indeed, in concluding its project, the Law Commission diagnosed:

> ...a wider need for the law to recognise and to respond to the increasing diversity of living arrangements in this country. We believe that further consideration should be given to the adoption, necessarily by legislation, of new legal approaches to personal relationships outside marriage, following the lead given by other jurisdictions...[282]

A flexible scheme of remedies on relationship breakdown may indeed be preferable to a system of fixed property rights. The reform agenda has accordingly shifted from property ownership during relationships to providing fairer outcomes via court-based remedies at the *end* of non-marital relationships, tailored specifically to the type of relationship involved. In the following sections of this chapter, we examine the first two 'rights' suggested by Dewar—occupation rights and control over dispositions of the home—which have to some extent been conferred by legislation independently of ownership. We address the financial remedies provided by English law on relationship breakdown in chapters 6 and 7.

3.7 RIGHTS IN RELATION TO THE FAMILY HOME AND ITS CONTENTS

Although English law confers no automatic joint or community ownership on any family members, there are some basic 'mitigations'[283] to the separate property regime, conferring limited rights and protections short of ownership on some family members. The current law in this area is limited in its scope and application. To adopt Fox's typology again, English law can be regarded as both narrower and shallower than that of many other jurisdictions.[284] The rights are largely confined to spouses and civil partners, and even they enjoy relatively limited protection. Our focus in this chapter is on the basic rights of members in the intact family. We reserve detailed discussion of disputes between family members regarding occupation of the home to chapters 4, 6, and 7.[285]

---

[281] Mee (2004), 417.

[282] Law Com (2002), 86; see now Law Com (2006) and (2007).

[283] Kahn-Freund (1959), 247.

[284] Fox (2003).

[285] Under Children Act 1989 (CA 1989), Sch 1, Family Law Act 1996 (FLA 1996), and Trusts of Land and Appointment of Trustees Act 1996 (TOLATA 1996).

3.7.1 RIGHTS TO OCCUPY THE FAMILY HOME

The general law

The right to occupy property is ordinarily governed by the law of property or contract. Whether the right is proprietary or merely contractual is important if it becomes necessary to assert the right against someone other than the individual who granted it.

Where property is co-owned and so subject to a trust, the beneficial owners have a statutory right to occupy the trust property if a purpose of the trust is to make the property available for their occupation and the property is in fact available and suitable for their occupation.[286] Since the right to occupy flows from ownership of an estate in the land, anyone claiming that right must be able to demonstrate that he or she is a beneficial freehold owner or tenant under a lease. A proprietary estoppel claim may also generate a right to occupy.[287] As a proprietary right, the beneficial owner's or estoppel claimant's right can bind third parties.

A right to occupy property may also be conferred by written or oral, express or (more problematically) implied contract.[288] If the contract does not grant a lease, it takes effect simply as a personal right and so does not ordinarily bind third parties. There are statutory constraints on terminating contractual licences, but these do not apply to licences to share property with the resident owner or a member of the owner's family.[289] While a contractual licence cannot lawfully be terminated other than in accordance with the agreement,[290] the court will not enforce by injunction a licence of a shared home;[291] the wrongfully ejected licensee will be left to a remedy in damages.

A licence to occupy may be granted, expressly or impliedly, on a gratuitous basis (without the intention to create legal relations and valuable consideration necessary to create a contract). This is the most tenuous basis for occupation, easily terminated by the licensor withdrawing the permission. It has been said that the right to respect for the home under Article 8 ECHR requires that reasonable notice be given to terminate a licence to occupy property as a home,[292] but the owner's right to terminate a bare licence is otherwise unqualified; no reason need be given.

Since many spouses now elect to own or lease their homes jointly, most spouses enjoy rights to occupy as a matter of property law. Spouses and other family members who do not have a beneficial interest in the shared home may at best—in terms of the general law—occupy by virtue of a bare licence. However, some family members enjoy special occupation rights by virtue of their family status.

---

[286] TOLATA 1996, s 12; Gray and Gray (2011), 7-165 et seq.

[287] E.g. *Greasley v Cooke* [1980] 1 WLR 1306.

[288] E.g. *Tanner v Tanner* [1975] 1 WLR 1346; cf *Horrocks v Foray* [1976] 1 WLR 230. *Coombes v Smith* [1986] 1 WLR 808. On the various categories of licensee, see Gray and Gray (2011), 10-021 et seq; (2009), 10.3.12 et seq on contractual licences in family cases.

[289] Protection from Eviction Act 1977, s 3A(2)–(3).

[290] The court may have to imply terms regarding termination, e.g. reasonable notice: *Chandler v Kerley* [1978] 1 WLR 693.

[291] *Thompson v Park* [1944] KB 408.

[292] *Parker v Parker* [2003] EWHC 1846, para 276. 'Home' rights under Art 8 can be asserted even by those with no legal right to occupy the property: *Prokopovich v Russia* (App No 58255/00, ECHR) (2006).

Spouses and civil partners: statutory 'home rights'

The rights of the wife at common law

At common law, a wife with no right to occupy the matrimonial home under the general law enjoys a personal right to occupy it[293] simply by virtue of being a wife. This is an aspect of the wife's common law right to be maintained by the husband.[294] The nature and scope of this right has been explored by the House of Lords:

National Provincial Bank Ltd v Ainsworth [1965] AC 1175, 1229–30, 1232–3

LORD UPJOHN:

[T]he law has never adjudicated between the parties where or how they are to live. It is for the spouses to decide where and in what state they and the family are to live, be it in the Ritz or a caravan. The choice from time to time of the matrimonial home is entirely a matter for decision within the domestic forum; though, no doubt...where there is a difference of opinion between the spouses as to the place of the matrimonial home someone must have the casting vote. A wife on entering a matrimonial home, the property of her husband, has no rights, even inchoate, in that home which the law will recognise or protect...But, on the other hand, having regard to the duty of the spouses to live together the court does not, during the subsistence of the marriage, merely give effect to the strict legal and equitable rights of a spouse qua owner of the property as though the spouses were strangers. Recognising the obligations of the spouses to live together[295] the court will only make orders with regard to the occupation of the matrimonial home subject to those obligations...

[A] wife does not remain lawfully in the matrimonial home by leave or licence of her husband as the owner of the property. She remains there because as a result of the status of marriage it is her right and duty so to do and if her husband fails in his duty to remain there that cannot affect her right to do so. She is not a trespasser, she is not a licensee of her husband, she is lawfully there as a wife, the situation is one sui generis...

But apart from authority, what is the extent and ambit of her right to continue in occupation? I have already pointed out that...she has no special rights in the particular house where the spouses are living...[If the husband deserts the wife, her] rights as a wife continue as before, they are not increased by breach of duty on the part of the husband, but being in breach himself he may find it difficult to turn her out of the house where she is lawfully living awaiting his return and the court may prevent the husband by injunction from dealing with his property to the prejudice of the wife without safeguarding her position...But then many things may happen: he may offer alternative accommodation to the wife: he may offer her substantial maintenance to go and live elsewhere...[P]rovided the wife's marital rights are adequately safeguarded in some such way the court would not normally refuse to evict a wife if the husband wants to deal with his property. Or he may return and resume cohabitation [at which point] the domestic forum resumes exclusive jurisdiction. Or the wife may change her position. She may commit a matrimonial offence which may lead the court to refuse her the

---

[293] The right only applies to property which is or has been the matrimonial home: *Hall v King* [1988] 1 FLR 376; in relation to other property, the wife may have only a bare licence. It is unenforceable if the home is owned by or with third parties: *Chaudhry v Chaudhry* [1987] 1 FLR 347

[294] Query whether it may therefore be abolished by the Equality Act 2010: see 3.8.1.

[295] See the concept of consortium, at p 57 above; the action for restitution of conjugal rights was abolished in 1970: see Cretney (2003a), ch 4.

right to continue under her husband's roof;[296] she may obtain (as in this case) a decree of judicial separation which at all events brings the husband's desertion to an end...Such a decree must necessarily be an important though not conclusive factor if the husband is seeking to turn his wife out of occupation. Finally, any right on the part of the deserted wife to remain in occupation terminates when the marriage terminates.

It is unclear whether a husband enjoys equivalent rights against a property-owning wife.[297] Civil partnership, a creature of statute, confers no such common law entitlements (which presumably do not apply to same-sex marriage either). However, the significance of any common law right to occupy is superseded by statutory 'home rights' which are enjoyed equally by spouses and civil partners.

Statutory 'home rights'

In order to appreciate the significance of home rights (formerly called 'matrimonial home rights'), it is necessary to review the background to their creation. One of Lord Denning's initiatives to protect wives' interests in the family home was the 'deserted wife's equity': could the wife's common law right to occupy the matrimonial home (as wife rather than co-owner) be enforced both against the husband who had deserted her and against a third party to whom the deserting husband had sold or mortgaged the property? Several Court of Appeal decisions held that it could. However, while a wife may still be able to assert her common law right to occupy as against a landlord in leasehold cases,[298] the House of Lords in *Ainsworth* held that no such right was enforceable against third parties in the context of freehold land:

National Provincial Bank Ltd v Ainsworth [1965] AC 1175, 1233–4, 1242

LORD UPJOHN:

The right of the wife to remain in occupation even as against her deserting husband is incapable of precise definition, it depends so much on all the circumstances of the case, on the exercise of purely discretionary remedies, and the right to remain may change overnight by the act or behaviour of either spouse. So as a matter of broad principle I am of opinion that the rights of husband and wife must be regarded as purely personal inter se and that these rights as a matter of law do not affect third parties [even if they have full notice of the desertion].

In this case your Lordships are dealing with essentially conveyancing matters. It has been the policy of the law for over a hundred years to simplify and facilitate transactions in real property. It is of great importance that persons should be able freely and easily to raise money on the security of their property. Of course an intending purchaser is affected with notice of all matters which would have come to his notice if such inquiries and inspections had been made by him as ought reasonably to have been made (section 199 of the [LPA] 1925[299]). But surely any inquiry, if it is to be made reasonably, must be capable of receiving a positive answer as to the rights of the occupier and lead to a reasonably clear conclusion as to

---

296 Cf the regulation of statutory home rights under FLA 1996, s 33; see 4.5.3.
297 *Seel v Watts and Butterworth* [1954] CLY 2861 concluded not; but compare *Harman v Glencross* [1985] Fam 49, 58.
298 E.g. *Metropolitan Properties Co Ltd v Cronan* (1982) 44 P&CR 1. The position is now covered by FLA 1996, s 30(4).
299 Cf registered land: LRA 2002.

what those rights are? The answer "I am a deserted wife" (if given) only gives notice of a right so imprecise, so incapable of definition, so impossible of measurement in legal phraseology or terms of money that if he is to be safe the mortgagee will refuse to do business and much unnecessary harm will be done...It does not seem to me that an inquiry as to the marital status of a woman in occupation of property is one which the law can reasonably require to be made; it is not reasonable for a third party to be compelled by law to make inquiries into the delicate and possibly uncertain and fluctuating state of affairs between a couple whose marriage is going wrong. Still less can it be reasonable to make an inquiry if the answer to be expected will probably lead to no conclusion which can inform the inquirer with any certainty as to the rights of the occupant. These considerations give strong support to the opinion I have already expressed that the rights of the wife must be regarded as purely personal between herself and her husband.

LORD WILBERFORCE:

The ultimate question must be whether such persons can be given the protection which social considerations of humanity evidently indicate without injustice to third parties and a radical departure from sound principles of real property law.

The House of Lords held they could not. However, Parliament promptly filled the gap with 'matrimonial home rights', originally in 1967; the relevant provisions are now consolidated in the FLA 1996. That legislation, unlike the common law, is gender neutral, and applies to civil partners. These rights are enforceable against the other spouse or partner, provide eligibility to apply for an occupation order against the other spouse or partner, and (if registered on the appropriate land register) are enforceable against third parties as a charge:

Family Law Act 1996

30 Rights concerning home where one spouse or civil partner has no estate etc.

(1) This section applies if—

    (a) one spouse or civil partner ("A") is entitled to occupy a dwelling-house by virtue of—

        (i) a beneficial estate or interest or contract; or

        (ii) any enactment giving A the right to remain in occupation; and

    (b) the other spouse or civil partner ("B") is not so entitled.

(2) Subject to the provisions of this Part, B has the following rights ("home rights")—

    (a) if in occupation, a right not to be evicted or excluded from the dwelling-house or any part of it by A except with the leave of the court given by an order under section 33;

    (b) if not in occupation, a right with the leave of the court so given to enter into and occupy the dwelling house.

(3) If B is entitled under this section to occupy a dwelling-house or any part of a dwelling-house, any payment or tender made or other thing done by B in or towards satisfaction of any liability of A in respect of rent, mortgage payments or other outgoings affecting the dwelling-house is...as good as if made or done by A.

(4) [Provisions regarding security of leasehold tenure—see n 298 above]

(5) If B—

(a) is entitled under this section to occupy a dwelling-house or any part of a dwelling-house, and

(b) makes any payment in or towards satisfaction of any liability of A in respect of mortgage payments affecting the dwelling-house,

the person to whom the payment is made may treat it as having been made by A, but the fact that that person has treated any such payment as having been so made does not affect any claim of B against A to an interest in the dwelling-house by virtue of the payment.

(6) [Provision regarding the operation of (3)–(5) where A is a beneficiary of trust property—rights bind trustees as they bind A]

(7) This section does not apply to a dwelling-house which—

(a) in the case of spouses, has at no time been, and was at no time intended by them to be, a matrimonial home of theirs; and

(b) in the case of civil partners, has at no time been, and was at no time intended by them to be, a civil partnership home of theirs.

(8) B's home rights continue—

(a) only so long as the marriage or civil partnership subsists, except to the extent that an order under section 33(5) otherwise provides; and

(b) only so long as A is entitled as mentioned in subsection (1) to occupy the dwelling-house, except where provision is made by section 31 for those rights to be a charge on an estate or interest in the dwelling-house.

(9) It is hereby declared that a person—

(a) who has an equitable interest in a dwelling-house or in its proceeds of sale, but

(b) is not a person in whom there is vested (whether solely or as joint tenant) a legal estate in fee simple or a legal term of years absolute in the dwelling-house,

is to be treated, only for the purposes of determining whether he has home rights, as not being entitled to occupy the dwelling-house by virtue of that interest.

31 Effect of home rights as a charge on dwelling-house

(1) Subsections (2) and (3) apply if, at any time during a marriage or civil partnership, A is entitled to occupy a dwelling-house by virtue of a beneficial estate or interest.

(2) B's home rights are a charge on the estate or interest.

(3) The charge created by subsection (2) has the same priority as if it were an equitable interest created at whichever is the latest of the following dates—

(a) the date on which A acquires the estate or interest;

(b) the date of the marriage or the formation of the civil partnership; and

(c) 1st January 1968 (the commencement date of the Matrimonial Homes Act 1967).

[(4)–(7) Provisions regarding trusts—where only A and B are or could be beneficiaries, B's interest is a charge binding on the trustees]

(8) Even though B's home rights are a charge on an estate or interest in the dwelling-house, those rights are brought to an end by—

(a) the death of A, or

(b) the termination (otherwise than by death) of the marriage or civil partnership, unless the court directs otherwise by an order made under section 33(5)....

(10) If the title to the legal estate by virtue of which A is entitled to occupy a dwelling-house (including any legal estate held by trustees for A) is registered under the Land Registration Act 2002 or any enactment replaced by that Act—

    (a) registration of a land charge affecting the dwelling-house by virtue of this Part is to be effected by registering a notice under that Act; and

    (b) B's home rights are not to be capable of [operating as an overriding interest by virtue of B's actual occupation of the property under]...paragraph 2 of Schedule 1 or 3 to that Act.

    ...

[(12)–(13) Provision regarding the priority of home rights in unregistered land: home rights are registrable as a Class F land charge under the Land Charges Act 1972, s 2]

63 Interpretation...

(5) It is hereby declared that this Part applies as between the parties to a marriage even though either of them is, or has at any time during the marriage been, married to more than one person.[300]

Statutory home rights are 'purely personal': they do not entitle that spouse to give any other person a right to occupy the property, and cannot be assigned or disposed of.[301] However, home rights are more concrete than wives' old common law right: they do not depend for their continued existence on the parties' conduct (e.g. there is no need for the owning spouse to have deserted the other), but they may be terminated by court order.[302] The rights may be asserted against the other spouse over more than one property and against property co-owned by the other spouse with third parties,[303] but can only be registered and so bind third parties in relation to one.[304] In order to bind a third party, they must be appropriately registered.

Children

With the exception of those who have a right to occupy by virtue of a beneficial interest in the property,[305] the status of children is unclear. Statutory home rights confer no right to occupy on any children (or anyone else) who lives with the spouse.[306] Case law, perhaps surprisingly, suggests that even minor children occupy their parents' home under

---

[300] Presumably meaning 'validly married': cf *Ramsamy v Babar* [2003] EWCA Civ 1253.

[301] *Wroth v Tyler* [1974] Ch 30.

[302] See FLA 1996, s 33; conduct is a relevant factor: s 33(6); see 4.5.3.

[303] *Abdullah v Westminster CC* [2011] EWCA Civ 1171.

[304] FLA 1996, Sch 4, para 2.

[305] Such interest must be registered to bind third parties, since a minor cannot be in 'actual occupation' for the purposes of establishing an overriding interest under LRA 2002, Sch 3, para 2: *Hypo-Mortgage Services Ltd v Robinson* [1997] 2 FLR 71; Gray and Gray (2011), 8-108. A minor cannot hold a legal estate in land: LPA 1925, s 1(6): Gray and Gray (2011), 1-052. In the leasehold context, see *Kingston upon Thames BC v Prince* [1999] 1 FLR 593.

[306] *Wroth v Tyler* [1974] Ch 30, though the interests of certain children are relevant to decisions of the court regulating home rights under FLA 1996, s 33; see 4.5.3.

only a bare licence.[307] Parents could in theory therefore withdraw permission for their own children to live with them. While that may be appropriate in the case of adult children, it would sit somewhat incongruously alongside parents' ordinary responsibilities to children under 18; a parent who evicts his or her minor child may be guilty of child neglect and attract child protection proceedings.[308] It has accordingly been argued that these obligations, together with Article 8 ECHR and Article 16 of the United Nations Convention on the Rights of the Child (UNCRC) (no child 'shall be subjected to arbitrary or unlawful interference with his or her ... home'), demand that children attract a protected occupation status in their home, at least vis-à-vis their parents or de facto carers, if not against third parties.[309]

Other family members with no right to occupy under the general law

All other family members—cohabitants, adult children, parents, relatives, and non-commercial[310] home-sharers—who cannot establish a proprietary or contractual right to occupy the property under the general law have only limited rights. Most are bare licensees, who need only be afforded 'reasonable' notice if required by the owner to leave,[311] and who have no right that will bind a third party. The only extra family law protection is for cohabitants (and former spouses and civil partners with no home rights), who may be able to obtain relatively short-term occupation orders under the FLA 1996.[312] The Law Society's recommendation that cohabitants with children or whose relationships have lasted two years should also have home rights has not been adopted.[313]

3.7.2 DECISION-MAKING ABOUT SALE AND OTHER TRANSACTIONS RELATING TO THE FAMILY HOME

The general law

Under the general law, decisions about sale, mortgage, and other dispositions of property are for the legal owner(s). Where all occupiers of the property are legal owners, all must consent to any disposition, so each has a right of veto. Since most spouses jointly own their homes, the general law therefore gives both an equal say.

Adults who are not on the legal title but who have beneficial shares in the property have no right of veto, unless the trust specifically requires that their consent be obtained.[314] A beneficiary of property held by a sole trustee can at least delay a disposition by registering a restriction which, in effect, will prevent the disposition from going ahead without a second trustee being appointed.[315] But if the owner can find someone else willing to become

---

307 E.g. *Metropolitian Properties Co Ltd v Cronan* (1982) 44 P&CR 1.
308 E.g. Children and Young Persons Act 1933, s 1; on child protection, see chapter 12.
309 Gray and Gray (2009), 10.2.16.
310 Lodgers, tenants, and employees of the owner are subject to relevant housing and employment law.
311 E.g. *Hannaford v Selby* (1976) 239 EG 811.
312 See 4.5.3.
313 Law Society (2002).
314 TOLATA 1996, s 10, likely only to be the case with express trusts. In registered land, such a right will operate only as a personal right against the trustees unless reflected in a restriction on the register: LRA 2002, s 40.
315 LRA 2002, s 40.

a trustee, the disposition may proceed, overreaching the beneficiary's interest.[316] In the case of trusts created after 1996, beneficiaries have a right to be consulted, so far as is practicable. Trustees must give effect to the majority view, so far as that is consistent with the general interest of the trust.[317] Failure to comply with the statutory duty to consult will not, of itself, affect any purchaser of the property.[318] In case of dispute regarding transactions over the property, one or other party can refer the case to the court under TOLATA 1996, which we discuss in chapter 7.[319]

Family law protection?

No right as family member to be consulted about or veto transactions

English law does not straightforwardly provide any family member with a right to be consulted about transactions regarding the family home, in that capacity, rather than as a co-owner of the property. Lord Wilberforce in *National Provincial Bank Ltd v Ainsworth* considered that such a requirement would 'create impossible difficulties for those dealing with the property of a married man', requiring, as it would, the wife's consent to all dealings affecting the home.[320] Nor does English law prevent or limit use of the family home as security for business loans, preferring instead to maximize the marketability of that asset.[321] Such loans may be essential for the livelihood of a family dependent on that business. But that may not of itself justify depriving family members of a say in whether their home should be used for that purpose, given the risks involved.[322]

The FLA 1996 provisions regarding home rights give spouses and civil partners some leverage over such decisions if they have registered their rights.[323] But it has been asked whether the owner-spouse should be obliged to give the other advance notice of any proposed transaction which would affect the latter's right of occupation, alerting the other to the need to take steps to protect his or her home rights. The law could even require that the latter's active consent to any such transaction be obtained, so that any purported sale or mortgaging of the family home would be void without it.

The Law Commission's proposals for statutory co-ownership of the matrimonial home would have provided the 'incidental advantage' of giving the otherwise non-owning spouse control over dispositions of the property: a disposition without the spouse's consent (or without having dispensed with it by court order) would have no legal effect. However, consistent with the approach to statutory home rights, the right would in most cases have been enforceable against third parties only if the co-ownership interest had been registered.[324] The Commission rejected the view that a spouse should be entitled to prevent any disposition of the matrimonial home, regardless of whether he or she

---

[316] See Hopkins (2009), 320–1: overreaching conceptualizes the home as an investment.

[317] TOLATA 1996, s 11. The 'majority' is calculated by the size of the parties' interests.

[318] Unless an appropriate restriction has been entered to prevent the registration of a disposition unless consultation has taken place: LRA 2002, s 40. In relation to unregistered land: TOLATA 1996, s 16(1).

[319] See 7.8.3.

[320] [1965] AC 1175, 1248.

[321] See *Barclays Bank v O'Brien* [1994] 1 AC 180, 188. Compare the 'homestead' legislation of some Canadian provinces and US states, and New Zealand's Joint Family Homes Act 1964, which to a greater or lesser extent puts the home 'off limits' to creditors: Fox (2005).

[322] Even if those family members would not think twice about consenting: Fehlberg (1997).

[323] See discussion on the Online Resource Centre.

[324] Law Com (1978), paras 0.12 and 1.417(79)–(116); Law Com (1982a), paras 90–105.

co-owned it: such a right 'would represent a drastic inroad into accepted concepts of property'.[325]

By contrast, many other jurisdictions give spouses statutory rights of consultation and veto which are enforceable without prior registration. Some of those countries operate full community of property during marriage, but, as Dewar suggests, there is no reason why the right to control dispositions of key assets cannot be enjoyed independently of ownership.[326] Since the right attaches only to spouses (and, if adopted in England, to civil partners), third parties can easily check the legal status of the person with whom they wish to transact (marital status being a matter of public record) and so ascertain whether there is a spouse whose consent must be obtained. Commonly, non-compliance with such requirements renders the relevant transaction voidable for a given period,[327] or even void (unless the third party is a purchaser for value in good faith, who is unaware that the vendor or mortgagor is married).[328] In practice, most purchasers and mortgagees check whether there are any other adults occupying the property in order to get them to waive whatever rights they may have (whether as co-owners, home rights holders, or otherwise). But English law would arguably benefit from a more formalized mechanism for obtaining consent, at least from spouses and civil partners, if not also from other family members.

Can the court prevent a disposition?

If a non-owning spouse or other family member cannot prevent the disposition privately, can he or she do so via court order?[329] The law here is not entirely clear. The fact that someone has statutory home rights (even if registered) or the benefit of an occupation order under the FLA 1996 does not prevent the owner from selling or mortgaging the property[330] or, probably, terminating a tenancy of it.[331] However, it may be possible to obtain an injunction prohibiting dispositions of the property. Where divorce proceedings are in progress, the courts have specific powers to prevent certain types of transaction.[332] It has also been held that s 17 of the Married Women's Property Act 1882 empowers the court to grant an injunction barring sale unless the husband provides alternative accommodation for the wife, as an aspect of the common law duty to provide a home for the wife; the courts might now regard wives as being subject to this duty as well as husbands. This power seems to survive the creation of statutory home rights.[333] Even outside the context of marriage, it might also be possible to use s 37 of the Senior Courts Act 1981 to restrain a disposition which would prejudice rights enjoyed under an occupation order or home rights.[334] Such an injunction could not bar dispositions of the property for any period longer than the underlying occupation order or home rights endured. Otherwise, however, the owner is free to do as he or she wishes with the property.

---

325 Law Com (1982a), para 110(iii). See also Law Com (1978), paras 2.87–2.89.

326 Dewar (1998b); e.g. in Sweden, where there is no community of property during marriage.

327 E.g. Swedish Marriage Code, ch 7, s 5: see generally Cooke, Barlow, and Callus (2006), ch 5.

328 Irish Family Home Protection Act 1976, s 3.

329 Royal Commission on Marriage and Divorce (1956) thought he or she should be able to: para 670.

330 Law Com (1992), para 4.19; *Davis v Johnson* [1979] AC 264, 343 and 349. Even though the owner might be required by order to continue to pay the mortgage or rent: FLA 1996, s 40.

331 *Harrow LBC v Johnstone* [1997] 1 WLR 459; Lowe and Douglas (2007), 255 query whether an order under the FLA 1996 might prohibit the respondent from giving notice to quit.

332 Matrimonial Causes Act 1973 (MCA 1973), s 37; CPA 2004, Sch 5, Part 14: see p 496.

333 *Lee v Lee* [1952] 2 AC 489; *Halden v Halden* [1966] 1 WLR 1481; *Gurasz v Gurasz* [1970] P 11.

334 Cf *Moore v Moore* [2004] EWCA Civ 1243.

3.7.3 PROTECTING OCCUPATION AGAINST THIRD PARTIES

Suppose that the legal owner mortgages the home and defaults on the payments, or sells the property. Can a family member with beneficial ownership or a statutory home right defend an action for possession of the home by a third party? To answer this question, we must first ask whether the third party is bound by the family member's interest under the general law or pursuant to the statutory home rights regime. Even if the third party *is* bound by a family member's proprietary interest, it may still be able to secure the family's eviction from the home by forcing a sale to realize its interest; different legal provisions apply depending on whether the third party is a purchaser, secured creditor, or trustee in bankruptcy. In the case of binding home rights, the third party can apply for an occupation order under the FLA 1996 scheme. The law in this area and its application in practice have been criticized for giving too much weight to the commercial interests of the third parties and insufficient weight to the use value of the property as a family home.

ONLINE RESOURCE CENTRE

Readers wishing to learn more about this area of the law should visit the Online Resource Centre for chapter 3, where the law and critical commentaries are explained.

3.7.4 RIGHTS REGARDING THE CONTENTS OF THE FAMILY HOME

Ownership of the contents of the family home—furniture, furnishings, kitchen equipment, crockery and cutlery, household linen, and so on—is entirely a matter for the general law. Ordinarily, the use and possession of that property flows from ownership. In the course of normal family life, of course, the technical owner of the spoons, towels, and sofa, whoever he or she may be (the parties may have no idea), will give implicit permission to all other family members to use that property.

The only family law specifically addressing use of such property is an adjunct to the occupation order regime discussed in chapter 4. When making an occupation order under the FLA 1996, the court can include additional provisions granting either party possession or use of furniture or other contents.[335] The 'width' of this protection is governed by the width of the FLA 1996 regime—only those eligible to apply for and who have obtained an occupation order benefit from it. So, save for those family members who have a beneficial interest in the home, only current and former spouses, civil partners, and cohabitants can access this provision.

No other property, such as the family car,[336] attracts similar protection, and there is no protection where occupation of the home is not in issue. The Law Commission's recommendation that the courts have power to make orders between spouses regarding the use

---

[335] FLA 1996, s 40; see generally 4.5.3.
[336] Occupation orders can be made over caravans or houseboats used as the family home: ibid, s 63.

and possession of 'household goods' (including cars), and independently of disputes over occupation, has not been enacted.[337]

3.8 FAMILY FINANCES

An examination of family finances involves both private law and two aspects of public law, welfare benefit/tax credit and tax law. The state's role in regulating and supporting families through these avenues is significant not only for its practical impact. The scope of these laws also reflects interestingly on the law's conception of 'family', in terms both of the breadth of family and the presumed roles of individuals within it.

Research about couples' money management practices is important for evaluating the law. Times have changed significantly from the days of the man's 'family wage', which supported a male breadwinner/female homemaker model of marriage. But economic inequalities remain.

J. Pahl, 'Individualisation in Couple Finances: Who Pays for the Children?', (2005) 4 *Social Policy and Society* 381, 381–4

Patterns of money management within the household have changed dramatically over the past half century. Fifty years ago in the UK there were widespread and commonly shared notions about the allocation of money within the family, about the form which 'proper' families should take and about the ways in which the welfare state should cater for the needs of individuals within families. The Beveridge Report [(1942), on which the modern welfare state, introduced by the National Assistance Act 1948, was based] argued that,

All women by marriage acquire a new economic and social status with risks and rights different to those of the unmarried. On marriage a woman gains a legal right to maintenance by her husband as a first line defence against risks which fall directly on the solitary woman; she undertakes at the same time to perform vital but unpaid service and becomes exposed to new risks, including the risk that her married life may be ended prematurely by widowhood or separation.... Beveridge, 1942: 49

This statement encapsulates the idea that the married couple should be a financial unit, within which the man would be the breadwinner and a woman would accept financial dependence in exchange for financial security. This idea was translated into social security legislation which gave married women a right to a pension on the basis of their husbands' contributions and a widow's pension if he died before she did. It reflected a situation in which less than half of women aged 16 to 59 were in paid work in 1961, compared with 68 per cent in 2000...

Studies carried out at the time showed that the ways in which couples organised their finances reflected the idea of the male breadwinner. Zweig's study [in 1961] of 337 men in south and central England showed that 70 per cent gave their wives a housekeeping allowance, while 16 per cent handed over the whole wage packet, either keeping back a sum for themselves or receiving a sum back from the wife for their pocket money. Only 16 per cent of couples pooled their income, and Zweig commented that this system was particularly common among younger couples and when both partners were earning. He also noted 'a

---

337 Law Com (1978), Book Three.

very peculiar arrangement' which was described by one respondent as 'What she makes is hers, what I make is mine'...

By the 1980s the situation had changed. From being a minority way of managing money, pooling had become the most common system. My first study, which reported on interviews with 102 couples and used data collected in 1982–84, found that 56 per cent of couples pooled their money, typically in a joint bank account; in 22 per cent of couples the husband gave his wife a housekeeping allowance; 14 per cent used a whole wage system; and 9 per cent were classified as maintaining independence in financial matters...

Changing patterns of money management reflected changing ideologies about marriage. The Beveridge acceptance of economic inequality within marriage was being challenged, not least by feminists, and there was a new reluctance, among some couples at least, to seeing one partner as the breadwinner and the other as financially dependent...The classic statement by couples who pool their money is, 'It's not my money; it's not his/her money; it's our money'. This would seem to perpetuate the idea that the couple is a financial unit, but it also implies an ideal of equality between the two individuals making up the couple. Many of those interviewed in the 1980s expressed anxiety about the differences in earning power between men and women and saw the pooling of money as a way to diminish its impact....

...[T]he fastest growing [money management] system...is 'partial pooling'. This depends on each partner having their own personal income, so that each can keep some money under their own personal control, while contributing some to a common pool; the system also relies on the couple agreeing a distinction between joint and personal spending....[Both partial pooling and independent management] express an essential individualism. If couples do not pool their money or maintain a common kitty, this is often because one or both want to maintain a degree of autonomy or privacy in their money management practices....[Research from the late 1990s showed that] independent management of money was particularly characteristic of younger couples, of those without children and of those where the woman was in full time paid work.

Research has found that the system adopted varies by relationship status. While spouses are more likely to operate as a single economic unit, cohabitants are more likely to operate independently. However, cohabiting *parents* are much more likely to pool: they appear to behave more like spouses in their financial practices.[338] While this similarity between spouses and some cohabitants is reflected to an extent in welfare benefit and tax credit law, private law treats the two types of relationship very differently.

3.8.1 PRIVATE LAW

The law in this area is important owing to the continued imbalance in earning power between many parents, married or not, described at 3.2.2 above. Where one parent (usually the mother, in opposite-sex couples) gives up or reduces paid employment to take on the role of primary carer, that person is rendered to some extent dependent on the wage-earner. However, private law relating to income and savings from earnings is similar to that governing ownership and use of property. Ownership of such funds is largely determined by the general law: the earner is exclusively entitled to his or her income, and is under no general obligation to share it with any family member. Nor does any family member have a right

---

[338] Vogler (2009).

to know what others' income is.[339] The general position is mitigated by basic 'maintenance' obligations. But, save in relation to minors, they arise only between spouses and civil partners.[340] English law does not impose wider family duties of support. Even between spouses, the practical significance of the obligation is limited.

The common law duty of husbands to support wives

Having disabled wives from owning property, including any wages that they might earn through paid employment, the common law obliged husbands to maintain their wives. But the obligation was not directly enforceable:

R (Kehoe) v Secretary of State for Work and Pensions [2005] UKHL 48

BARONESS HALE:

53. The common law courts would not intrude into the matrimonial relationship, or trespass upon the jurisdiction of the ecclesiastical courts over that relationship, by ordering the husband to make payments to his wife. But a wife who was living with her husband did have the apparent authority to contract as his agent for the expenses of the household. And if they were living apart, the common law recognised her agency of necessity, the right to pledge her husband's credit for necessaries according to her station in life. Unlike the housekeeping authority, this could not be countermanded by the husband. But the agency of necessity subsisted only if the wife was justified in living apart from her husband. Hence she would lose it for ever if she was guilty of adultery, no matter how badly her husband had behaved;...it would be suspended while she was in desertion...; but if they were obliged to live apart through no fault of hers, for example because of illness, the obligation continued.

The wife's agency of necessity was abolished in 1970, when the court's modern-day powers to order financial provision on divorce, judicial separation, and nullity were created.[341] The common law duty to maintain was superseded in practice by gender-neutral legislation empowering the courts to make enforceable maintenance orders between spouses and civil partners, and is due to be abolished by the Equality Act 2010.[342]

Statutory maintenance obligations

The courts can order payment of maintenance *during* marriage and civil partnership under various statutes.[343] In practice, the power is exercised, if at all, only where the relationship has broken down (but is not subject to dissolution, separation, or nullity proceedings[344]). In order to preserve 'family privacy', the law is reluctant to intervene in the intact family.[345]

---

[339] Cf the old law which required married couples to complete a single tax return, completed by the husband, which would ensure that he knew her income, but not vice versa.

[340] See chapters 6 and 7; contrast the public law of welfare benefits, 3.8.2.

[341] Matrimonial Proceedings and Property Act 1970, s 41.

[342] S 198; not in force December 2014.

[343] Domestic Proceedings and Magistrates' Courts Act 1978 (DPMCA 1978), CPA 2004, Sch 6; MCA 1973, s 27, CPA 2004, Sch 5, Pt 9: Cretney (2003a), ch 11.

[344] As to that, see chapter 7.

[345] Boden and Childs (1996), 114; O'Donovan (1985), 112, 182.

Although orders may be made and enforced while the parties are living together, some orders for maintenance automatically expire after six months' continuous cohabitation by the parties.[346] The basis on which these orders may be made and enforced is very similar to that governing equivalent powers on dissolution, judicial separation, and nullity, so we shall not examine them in detail here.[347] Where there are minors, child support is payable in the event of parental separation (whether married or not); that is far more significant than maintenance for the benefit of the spouse, which is rare.[348]

The courts can also make financial orders to secure payments relating to property subject to an occupation order under the FLA 1996,[349] but these powers are 'not intended as a disguised form of maintenance for those who are not entitled to it'.[350] Although the power is exercisable in favour of a cohabitant, it therefore cannot be used as a means of requiring the respondent to support that individual, to whom no duty to maintain is owed.

One special rule of ownership: savings from housekeeping money

One statutory provision creates co-ownership of a specific pool of money, originally only within marriage. Like the presumption of advancement, the statutory rule about ownership of savings made from housekeeping money, in its original form, was something of an historical curio and raised human rights problems. It cast interesting light on historical understandings of the family and family members' roles. As originally enacted, it read as follows:

Married Women's Property Act 1964, s 1

If any question arises as to the right of a husband or wife to money derived from any allowance made by the husband for the expenses of the matrimonial home or for similar purposes, or to any property acquired out of such money, the money or property shall, in the absence of any agreement between them to the contrary, be treated as belonging to the husband and wife in equal shares.

This explicitly gendered provision—husbands earn wages from which an 'allowance' for housekeeping is made to housewives (who receive no personal income)—was introduced to protect the interests of the thrifty housewife who made savings from the housekeeping money.[351] It followed a case which held that, in the absence of any other agreement, the husband solely owned that money or any property acquired with it, in that case, a winning football pools coupon.[352] Although applauded for treating marriage as a partnership which should give rise to joint ownership of property, the provision was criticized as far

---

[346] DPMCA 1978, s 25; CPA 2004, Sch 6, para 29.

[347] But note the particular 'grounds' on which maintenance orders may be made in this context: DPMCA 1978, s 1; MCA 1973, s 27(1); CPA 2004, Sch 6, para 1; Sch 5, para 39. For case law examples see *Barnes v Barnes* [1972] 1 WLR 1381; *Blower v Blower* [1986] 1 FLR 292; *Robinson v Robinson* [1983] Fam 42; *Vasey v Vasey* [1985] FLR 596.

[348] There are no data on use of this jurisdiction: Cretney (2003a), 472–3.

[349] FLA 1996, s 40.

[350] Law Com (1992), para 4.41.

[351] Cf the gender-neutral Scottish presumptions: Family Law (Scotland) Act 1985, ss 25–6, and Family Law (Scotland) Act 2006, ss 26–7.

[352] *Hoddinott v Hoddinott* [1949] 2 KB 406.

too narrow. Why, for example, should joint ownership only arise from housekeeping money, and not from savings made directly by the husband from his wage for expenditure on items for the family's use?[353]

Like the presumption of advancement, this provision appeared to be incompatible with Article 5 of the Seventh Protocol. The Equality Act 2010 accordingly amends the provision prospectively (relabelling it 'Matrimonial Property Act 1964') to make it gender neutral—so it applies equally to savings made by a husband to whom an allowance is made by the wife—and to extend it to civil partners.[354] Whether many, if any, couples will ever rely on it is doubtful, given the substantial decline of the housekeeping allowance money management system, particularly among young couples.[355]

Leaving it to the parties

In the absence of any effective legal regulation of family finances during the currency of relationships, the matter is left to the parties.[356] This raises concerns that by keeping out of the family, the law simply protects the more economically powerful, who can decide whether to share their money with the rest of the family. Research on money management in opposite-sex relationships suggests that where couples do not pool their resources and give each party equal decision-making power over and access to the funds, there can be marked imbalances between the parties, prejudicing the lower earning party (often the woman). The resulting strain on the relationship may even precipitate separation.[357]

It has been argued that the failure to give an entitlement to share in the family finances (and the family home) to those undertaking unpaid work in the home encourages the perception that that work is of no value.[358] One campaigning organization seeks 'wages for housework' from the state. In 2000, gross unpaid household production (including the provision of housing) was worth £877 billion to the national economy.[359] In 2012, household clothing and laundry services alone were worth £97 billion, equivalent to 5.9 per cent of GDP.[360] A state-paid wage for housework seems unlikely. But the value of this work—and the economic sacrifices made by those who devote themselves to home and family, in terms of lost opportunity to develop and maximize earning capacity—needs to be recognized. We shall see in chapter 7 that they are acknowledged on divorce. The question here is whether they ought to receive firmer recognition *during* relationships by the conferment of further private law entitlements.

3.8.2 FAMILIES IN THE TAX AND BENEFIT SYSTEMS

We turn finally to the law relating to welfare benefits/tax credits and tax.[361] This area of law is important for what it reveals about the relative responsibilities of family and

---

353 Kahn-Freund (1959), 250–1.
354 Ss 200–1: not in force December 2014.
355 On the practices of under-35s, see Vogler (2009).
356 We consider the law relating to maintenance agreements in 7.7.2.
357 Vogler (2005).
358 Taub and Schneider (1998), 334.
359 ONS (2006b), table 5.27.
360 Fludger and Dougherty (2014).
361 For detailed discussion of particular benefits, tax credits, and taxes, see CPAG (2014), Douglas (2000a), Wikeley (2007c); on tax law, Lee (2014), Salter (2007). Universal Credit would replace most existing means-tested benefits and tax credits with one payment; its fate is uncertain, so not discussed here.

state to support economically weaker individuals.[362] Rather than examine this very complex law in detail, we briefly address three broad issues: family members' liability to support each other; 'aggregation' provisions, which assume the existence of economic support within families; and use of welfare benefits and tax credits to alleviate the relative poverty of individuals *within* the family unit. We also consider whether and how this law can be used to try to incentivize particular behaviour, for example by providing tax advantages for spouses. We shall see that broader and narrower concepts of family are used in different areas: as Nick Wikeley has observed, welfare benefit law has 'always treated "the family" as a protean term, depending on the respective policy goals of the benefits schemes in question'.[363]

Public law liability of family members to support each other

Historically, the scope of state-enforced family responsibility was wider than it is today:

R (Kehoe) v Secretary of State for Work and Pensions [2005] UKHL 48

BARONESS HALE:

56. Statutory recognition of the parental duty to maintain dates back to the Elizabethan poor laws, culminating in the Poor Relief Act of 1601 . . . , s 7 of which provided that

". . . the father and grandfather, and the mother and grandmother, and the children of every poor . . . person . . . being of a sufficient ability, shall, at their own charges, relieve and maintain every such poor person in that manner, and according to that rate, as by the justices of peace of that county where such sufficient persons dwell, or the greater number of them, at their general quarter sessions shall be assessed; upon pain that every one of them shall forfeit 20s for every month which they shall fail therein."

The practice was to order, not only payment for the future, but also repayment of money already spent by the overseers of the poor. . . . Thus the principle of family responsibility or solidarity was laid down. . . .

60. There is [now] . . . a system, descended from the Poor Law, for recovering the costs of public assistance from 'liable relatives'. We have already seen the extent of the family obligations between parents, grandparents and children . . . Obligations towards wives, and then husbands, came later [in 1834] . . .

61. The Poor Law was abolished by the National Assistance Act 1948. In the post war welfare state, it was expected that most areas of need would be covered by national insurance benefits [paid for via contributions made from employees' earnings] and that means-tested benefits would be a safety net for the few who were not covered by the national insurance scheme. The 1948 Act retained the possibility of recovery from a 'liable relative' but reduced those liable: under section 42, a man was liable to maintain his wife and children . . . and a woman was liable to maintain her husband and children. Neither was liable to maintain a *former* spouse.

Wikeley argues that the law here had a 'preventative' rather than 'restorative' function, seeking to encourage intra-family responsibility and so avoid the need to enforce it.[364] But the

---

[362] Miles (2011a).
[363] Wikeley (2007c).
[364] Ibid.

law's view of family responsibility for these purposes is now narrow and based on formal-ized, conjugal relationships rather than, as formerly, kin-based relationships.[365] The liable relative procedure, now chiefly confined to spouses and civil partners,[366] in practice applies only where they are living apart; where they share a household, any means-tested benefit payments are reduced by aggregating the parties' income and capital for means-testing. Where one spouse or civil partner living apart from the other makes a claim for a relevant means-tested benefit, the Department for Work and Pensions (DWP) may seek a voluntary contribution from the other, or apply to the court to recover sums paid out; the court has a discretion about how much, if anything, to require liable persons to pay, on pain of criminal prosecution.[367]

Assumptions about economic roles and support within families

Historically, at least, the gendered model of breadwinner/homemaker family has been dom-inant in welfare benefit law. Contribution-based benefits were originally set up following the Beveridge Report in 1942 such that a wife's entitlement to contribution-based benefits depended upon her husband's contributions, rather than her own.[368] Spouses and civil part-ners are now largely treated individually for the purposes of contribution-based benefits (such as contribution-based jobseeker's allowance).[369] But, though the law is now gender neutral, spouses and civil partners can still base some claims, such as bereavement benefits, on their spouse or partner's contribution record; the exclusion of cohabitants from these benefits does not violate the ECHR.[370]

While the family is intact, some welfare benefits adopt a rather wider view of 'family' than the liable relative procedure. This sometimes advantages claimants, by recognizing de facto support provided within families by those under no legally enforceable obligation to do so: for example, if a claimant of means-tested benefits is supporting an elderly or inca-pacitated relative by letting them occupy a dwelling owned (and previously occupied) by the claimant, the value of that property can be excluded from means-testing.[371] But elsewhere, the rules make *assumptions* about economic roles and support within intact families which *reduce* the benefits payable. This is relatively uncontroversial for spouses and civil partners since they have private law obligations to support each other. However, public law goes fur-ther, assuming support where there is no corresponding private law remedy to enable the individual affected to secure it. The main example of this is cohabitants,[372] who, for the two key means-tested benefits (income support and income-based jobseeker's allowance, 'JSA'), are treated as an economic unit: only one of them may bring a claim, a cohabitant whose partner is in full-time work cannot claim income support, and their income and capital are aggregated for means-testing.[373]

---

[365] See generally Maclean and Eekelaar (1997), ch 3, and 42–3; Oldham (2001).
[366] See generally Wikeley (2008).
[367] Social Security Administration Act 1992, ss 105–8.
[368] Douglas (2000a), 261.
[369] See generally CPAG (2014), ch 33.
[370] *Shackell v United Kingdom* (App No 45851/99, ECHR) (2000).
[371] Wikeley (2007c); CPAG (2014), 353.
[372] For other examples, e.g. treatment of adult children at home under the age of 25 and other close 'non-dependent' relatives in relation to housing benefit, see Wikeley (2007c); CPAG (2014), 116–20.
[373] Social Security Contributions and Benefits Act 1992, ss 124(1)(c), 134(2), 136(1), 137.

Much of the case law exploring the meaning of 'cohabitation' and 'living together as husband and wife' (and 'as civil partners'[374]) has arisen in this context.[375] The cohabitation rule has been controversial, not least because the DWP may have to inquire about the couple's intimate life and sleeping arrangements in order to establish whether they are 'cohabiting' rather than, for example, living together because one party is ill or disabled and the other is caring for him or her.[376] It has been suggested that investigating parties' sexual relationships may raise issues under Article 8 ECHR.[377] Is the rule as it applies to cohabitants justifiable?

N. Harris, 'Unmarried Cohabiting Couples and Social Security in Great Britain', (1996) 18 *Journal of Social Welfare and Family Law* 123, 127–8

The basic argument used to justify the rule has been that it would be unfair if an unmarried partner was entitled to receive benefit that would be denied to a married person whose partner was in employment...This equity principle led the Finer Committee [DHSS (1974)]...to conclude that the rule should continue. It is also argued that if the law places unmarried partners in a more advantageous position than married couples in this way, it might serve to discourage marriage...(However, it has always been argued that the cohabitation rule discourages stable relationships between unmarried partners.) The Supplementary Benefits Commission (SBC) also argued that discouraging marriage in this way might 'present an obstacle to the legitimation of children'...The rule was, it was claimed, in tune with contemporary social attitudes—most people, the SBC argued, considered such a rule to be fair and equitable.

The rule's retention also reflects the lack of feasible alternative:

One possibility that has been discussed, in relation to income-related benefits, is assessment of each partner's actual contribution to the household, and especially that of the working partner. The SBC...considered that the administrative difficulties and expense in assessing entitlement on this basis made it unworkable. Lister,...however, argued that rather than complete aggregation of each partner's resources there might be 'possible reduction of benefit according to the resources actually at the woman's disposal in relation to her needs as defined by the statutes'. This would have been consonant with an argument used to justify differential treatment of married and cohabiting couples under the law generally, namely that a decision not to marry may imply an intention, by the parties, to have a relationship which is truly different in character (e.g. looser) than marriage...It would also weaken the broad dependency assumption, under which women have traditionally been faced with a loss of independent income as a result of being forced to rely on a joint payment made to the man..., although since 1983 either party can be the claimant...It has also been argued that the rule 'assumes...a support obligation which the law does not recognise'...(unmarried partners owe no legal obligation to support each other under English law) and 'ignores the unequal distribution of income within the family which disadvantages women'...

---

[374] Jones (2007).

[375] See *Crake v Supplementary Benefits Commission* [1982] 1 All ER 498; *Re J (Income Support: Cohabitation)* [1995] 1 FLR 660; CPAG (2014), 206–10; DWP (2014c), vol 3, ch 11.

[376] Harris (1996); *Butterworth v Supplementary Benefits Commission* [1982] 1 All ER 498.

[377] Harris (1996), 137.

> The question of how the practical difficulties and high administrative costs...can be overcome remains unanswered. Nevertheless, there continues to be discussion about 'individualisation', which involves assessing each partner's benefit entitlement, and paying them, independently. Because members of married and unmarried couples would be treated the same way, the principle behind the cohabitation rule would continue to apply, but the disadvantages to women in particular would be reduced...

Research[378] examining how couples manage money received by one of them as income support or JSA has found that, although benefits are less commonly regarded as 'belonging' to one party than earnings, there remains evidence of a 'breadwinner' stereotype:

A. Morris, 'Couples and Benefits Claims: A Comment on *Relying on the State, Relying on Each Other'*, (2000) 7 *Journal of Social Security Law* 228, 233–5, 239–40

> For example, [most] JSA claimants were men, and only the man's name appeared on the cheque. This was taken to reflect "state recognition and validation of the role of males as head of the household". Bearing in mind that JSA requires the claimant to be actively seeking work, this can be explained (in the light of societal expectations) by the fact that in-work patterns are replicated in benefit management and perception. In other words, unemployment alone does not disrupt the idea that the man is responsible for fulfilling the role of the provider...
>
> Traditional gender roles are also apparent in the way in which one particular benefit is generally perceived and treated. Child benefit is seen as "belonging" to the mother rather than the father. This raises interesting questions as to the role played by the benefits system in reinforcing stereotypical gendered views. Child benefit is not only payable by default to the mother [an example of a benefit directed "at the purse not the wallet"] it also appears to be regarded as particularly appropriate that women should claim it because it is their role to "look after" the children...

However, while benefit claims might be made in the name of the man, the man would not necessarily manage the money once it arrived, though money management patterns and their practical and psychological implications can be complex:

> [E]arlier research...has already established that the lower the income, the more likely it is that there will be a system of female management....[T]he fact that one partner set the budget and allocated expenditure did not necessarily mean that they had *physical* control of the money. The issue of control is especially problematic—even where financial management is handed over to a woman, her partner may still question her allocation or request additional personal money...
>
> However, it is a central finding that there was nothing in the data "to indicate that women were financially deprived in couples using the less equitable systems [of money management]. Indeed,...there was generally a shared sense that household income had to be pooled in order to survive on the amount received..."...Nevertheless, there was an

---

378 Snape and Molloy (1999).

identifiable feeling of psychological dependency where men were named claimants. Women could then feel that they were invisible within the system. There was a view that dependency was reinforced by the fact that only one name appeared on the benefit cheque...The idea of benefit-splitting (each receiving half the benefit in their own name) was not favourably received by couples who felt it would run counter to the idea of sharing which is the basis of the way benefits are allocated to couples. The result of splitting would be to give each individual a sum which would probably be insufficient and necessitate pooling in any event. Women also felt that their role as manager of the household budget could be undermined by splitting....One reform which is suggested is that naming both partners as entitled to access [the money by being entitled to cash the benefit cheque] might be sufficient to counter feelings of psychological dependency and anonymity.

Benefits are now usually paid directly into bank accounts—but that then makes access to funds dependent on access to that account.

Alleviating child poverty and poverty within working families

Alleviating child poverty is an important governmental objective. Children's needs are currently dealt with separately from their carers' via child benefit (CB),[379] child tax credit (CTC), and working tax credit (WTC).[380] These are available more widely than means-tested welfare benefits as the means-ceiling is higher and related only to income (not capital), and they can be claimed by those in full-time work. The credits are intended to supplement earned income (and/or benefits), encouraging claimants to enter or stay in the labour market. They pursue two key policies: supporting families and tackling child poverty, and 'making work pay'.[381] WTC may be claimed by couples without children and by single people, as well as by parents.

Both tax credits and child benefit are payable to those with 'responsibility' for a child, whether or not that person is the child's parent or in a couple. The law here takes a functional approach, recognizing de facto responsibility for raising children, regardless of legal or relationship status.[382] A 'child' is someone under 16, or 20 if criteria regarding educational and employment status as a 'qualifying young person' are met.[383] Only one CTC and CB payment is available per child. A person is responsible for a child if he or she 'normally lives with' that person, or that person has the main responsibility for the child.[384] A claim by someone living in a couple must be made jointly, and the aggregation rule applies for means-testing. The amount of credit payable depends on family circumstances (including number and age of children, whether lone parent or a couple) and income (not capital). WTC also covers a set proportion of child-care costs, to help parents pursue paid employment. But it is only available for registered/approved childminders and child-care facilities, and cannot meet the costs incurred by relatives and others caring for the child informally. Ann Mumford has argued that this, together with tax credits' drive to get more mothers working, devalues care provided by families for their own members.[385]

---

[379] CPAG (2014), ch 26.
[380] Ibid, chs 8–9, Part 11.
[381] HM Treasury and Inland Revenue (2002), 2.2.
[382] Wikeley (2007c).
[383] CPAG (2014), 551–6.
[384] Ibid, and 153–6.
[385] Mumford (2007), 206.

CB, CTC, and the child-care component of WTC are paid directly to the child's 'main carer', a payment to 'purse rather than wallet'. Where the parents are living together, the mother will receive CB. In the case of a joint claim by a couple for tax credit, the 'main carer' will either be nominated by them or, if they cannot agree, identified by HMRC.[386] This is intended to ensure that some money reaches women, who may otherwise receive no funds directly, and who, research suggests, are more likely to spend it for the benefit of the children.[387] However, since means-testing is based on aggregated income, a woman with a wealthy partner may not be eligible for any tax credit, or even CB.[388]

Where parents are separated, the main carer is generally the mother. There is no facility for payments to be split pro rata where care is shared, and it has been held that no Article 14 discrimination on grounds of gender arises against fathers with whom the child spends a substantial part (but not most) of the week who accordingly receive no payment.[389] This 'no-splitting' approach sits uneasily alongside the government's policy of promoting involvement by both parents following separation,[390] but is aimed to ensure that the household of the child's main carer is lifted out of poverty.[391]

Tax law and the family

Key questions for tax law are whether the family is to be treated as a unit for tax purposes, and if so, how that unit should be defined, or whether family members should be taxed individually.[392] As David Salter has observed, answers to these questions depend on political judgement and may be culturally specific.[393] We briefly outline two key themes: historical treatment of wives by income tax law; and the treatment of different family forms for tax purposes.[394]

Tax law took over one hundred years to catch up with the implications of wives' separate property and income.[395] Until relatively recently, married couples[396] were treated as a unit for income tax purposes: the husband completed the tax return on which any income of the wife would be deemed to be the husband's, and he was liable to pay the resulting tax. This rule reflected wives' subordination to their husbands,[397] and deprived wives whose income was not taxed at source of financial privacy within their marriages. But the rule also prejudiced poorer husbands whose income-rich wives declined to contribute towards payment of the resulting tax bill.[398] The rules were gradually relaxed, until entirely separate income taxation for spouses was introduced in the late 1980s. For income tax purposes, spouses are therefore treated largely like any other individuals.[399] But it has been observed that there is

---

[386] CPAG (2014), 154.

[387] Lundberg, Pollak, and Wales (1997).

[388] See Douglas (2000a); Pahl (2005), 9; and note 'High Income Child Benefit charge', effectively excluding CB where one parent has income above £50,000.

[389] *Humphreys v Revenue and Customs Commissioners* [2012] UKSC 18.

[390] See chapter 11.

[391] [2012] UKSC 18, [9]–[10].

[392] Salter (2007).

[393] Ibid.

[394] See more generally Mumford (2007), Young (2009).

[395] Deech (1984), 256.

[396] *Rignell v Andrews* [1991] 1 FLR 332: not cohabitants.

[397] Cf the view of the Royal Commission on Income Tax (1920), cited in *Lindsay v United Kingdom* (App No 11089/84, ECHR) (1986).

[398] Williams (1947), 29.

[399] Cf the litigation in *Jones v Garnett*, discussed by Salter (2007).

some incongruity in spouses and others being treated individually for tax purposes while their incomes are aggregated for the purposes of welfare benefit and tax credit law, compromising the financial privacy that independent taxation was intended to provide.[400]

Historically, husbands also received a special tax allowance, worth one and a half times the ordinary personal allowance, a rate which assumed that the wife was not in paid employment and was being supported by the husband. As Claire Young has argued, this sort of allowance reinforced spouses' traditional roles, encouraging and privatizing wives' dependency within the family, and failing to reward them personally for the economic value of their work.[401] If the wife was working, and well paid, spouses risked being taxed more highly than an unmarried couple, each of whom enjoyed a full personal allowance.[402] Independent taxation of wives ensured that spouses were no longer *penalized* by the taxation system. Not long after, the married person's tax allowance was withdrawn in favour of the tax credit system, which is targeted more widely at families with children, including cohabiting and lone-parent families. However, spouses and civil partners[403] still receive some special tax treatment. The most high-profile example is their exclusive enjoyment of exemption from inheritance tax, which has been held not to violate the Convention rights of cohabiting couples.[404] As we discussed at 2.8.3, the Burden sisters unsuccessfully sought to assert a wider concept of 'family' for this purpose.[405]

Some current questions

Fiscal policy is controversial. Concerns have been expressed about two features of current tax and benefit laws: (i) the so-called 'couple penalty' that can arise from the aggregation rule that applies to couples claiming welfare benefits and tax credits; and (ii) the limited specific recognition of marriage (and civil partnership) in the tax system.

The 'couple penalty' argument focuses on the fact that, given certain characteristics (notably income level and whether both parties are working), some couples would be better off in terms of their benefits and tax credit entitlement were they to live separately.[406] The aggregation rule, it is said, may discourage some couples from living together in order to maximize benefits entitlements, destabilizing family life.[407] Conversely, however, failure to *disclose* the fact of cohabitation is a common benefit fraud.[408] Of course, one function of the aggregation rule is to recognize the economies of scale that couples can achieve, reducing the per capita spend, compared with a single person. Nevertheless, there has been political pressure to remove the 'couple penalty' in order to encourage the formation and maintenance of co-residential relationships, not least for the benefit of children. However, a recent review of international research in this area concluded that there is only mixed evidence of the couple penalty having this effect in practice, noting in particular the impact of factors other than financial incentives

---

[400] Salter (2007), Wikeley (2007c).

[401] Young (2009).

[402] Complaint that Art 1 of Protocol 1 and Art 8, in conjunction with Art 14, ECHR were violated where spouses attracted higher tax than cohabitants was held inadmissible: *Lindsay v United Kingdom* (App No 11089/84, ECHR) (1986).

[403] Inland Revenue (2004).

[404] *Holland v IRC* [2003] STC (SCD) 43.

[405] *Burden and Burden v United Kingdom* (App No 13378/05, ECHR) (2008).

[406] E.g. Centre for Social Justice (2009), 6.3.

[407] Smart and Stevens (2000), 36.

[408] DWP (2010), table 4.1.

and disincentives; where there is an impact, it tends to be small and vary considerably between different groups of the population.[409] Given the evidence of the penalty having only marginal impact within a complex picture, researchers have cautioned against attempts to 'fix' the system, not least on grounds of likely cost to the state (simply removing the penalty by assessing everyone individually would cost around £34 billion on current figures) and the potential of new rules to create new, unwanted impacts on individuals' behaviour.[410]

So, if penalties are not the problem (or cannot readily be fixed), what about the lack of premium for spouses? The withdrawal of the married person's allowance and introduction of marriage-neutral tax credits has been criticized by those who consider the tax and benefit system should be used to encourage marriage, and child-rearing within marriage, instead of cohabitation or lone parenthood.[411] But as John Eekelaar argues, tax incentives must be carefully designed if they are to be effective, particularly as society changes—even assuming that fiscal policy has the power to affect social behaviour at all:[412]

J. Eekelaar, 'Uncovering Social Obligations: Family Law and the Responsible Citizen', in M. Maclean (ed), *Making Law for Families* (Oxford: Hart Publishing, 2000), 22–3

It is not difficult to see how fiscal policy may affect family life. Financial measures may be a clear expression of a wish to reward or deter certain behaviour patterns. These also operate against a backdrop of legal and social norms. Where there is a social norm that cohabiting adults "ought to" be married, for example, a tax allowance for married couples will support that norm. But failure to keep track of evolving norms can be self-defeating. For example, the "old" system whereby a husband and wife's incomes were aggregated for taxation purposes, the "married allowance" deducted and the tax levied on the husband, assumed that ordinarily the husband will have far greater income than the wife: that is, that the domestic role will be assumed by her. Indeed, it could be seen as a measure in support of a norm that she *should* assume that role because, if she had high earned or unearned income, depending on the size of any allowance permitted for the wife's earned income, the total tax liability would be greater than it would be if the couple were taxed separately (at lower rates). However, changes in the social norm that women should adopt the domestic role were too rapid and the application of that taxation regime began (at least theoretically) to threaten another social norm: that adults who cohabit should be married. For, if the woman's income was above a certain level, it would be financially better for the couple to live together without marrying and be taxed separately. That was the position in the UK until separate taxation was allowed for earned income in 1972, and for unearned income in 1990. However, there is no evidence that these factors affected the marriage rate, which declined steadily throughout that period, and although there is now a modest tax benefit to be obtained from marrying (soon to be removed [the married person's allowance]), this seems to have done little (if anything) to arrest the decline in the marriage rate.[413] Perhaps the experience of taxation and family life shows the relatively weak influence even fiscal measures can have when confronted by deep-seated changes in social norms.

---

[409] Stafford and Roberts (2009).
[410] Adam and Brewer (2010).
[411] O'Neill (2005); Centre for Social Justice (2009), 6.3.
[412] See Henshaw (2006), paras 31–5 on incentive effects of child support rules.
[413] See Probert (2013b) for analysis.

Taxation rules can also be used for symbolic reasons: to signify relationships, behaviours, or transactions that are valued by the state. In 2010, the Conservative Party proposed an allowance for basic rate taxpaying spouses that would net up to £150 per year. Considerably less valuable than the previous married person's tax allowance, it would be costly for the state and it is doubtful whether such a low rate would send the strong message that its proponents intend. It would surely not encourage many couples to marry—or to stay together.[414]

3.9 CONCLUSION

English law of family property and finances is complex, drawn from a variety of general law and statutory sources. The general law still gives inadequate attention to the needs of the family context, potentially leading to unfair outcomes. Welfare benefit laws recognize a wide range of family relationships; but here the law is at its most complicated, different relationships being recognized in different contexts in order to advance particular policy goals. Thorough-going review of private law in this area seems unlikely in the foreseeable future. Attention is instead currently focused on the situation on family breakdown, where the unfairness generated between ex-cohabitants by implied trusts law is of most concern. The next four chapters examine the specialist statutory rights and remedies that apply on relationship breakdown.

ONLINE RESOURCE CENTRE

Questions, suggestions for further reading, and supplementary materials for this chapter (including updates on developments in this area of family law since this book was published) may be found on the Online Resource Centre at **www.oxfordtextbooks.co.uk/orc/familytcm3e/**.

---

[414] Ibid; IFS (2010); on promotion of marriage, see generally 2.8.2 above.

4

DOMESTIC VIOLENCE

CENTRAL ISSUES

1. Domestic violence is a widespread problem, experienced particularly by women in opposite-sex couples.

2. Historically, domestic violence was regarded as a 'private' problem, and the state failed to protect victims. Government policy now clearly aims to prevent, reduce, and punish domestic violence, and to support victims. States' duties towards victims under human rights law are increasingly well understood.

3. A key issue for current policy is how to provide an integrated response to domestic violence, involving criminal, civil, and family law, providing material and emotional support to victims, and giving appropriate weight to victims' wishes and interests.

4. The civil law provides remedies principally under the Family Law Act 1996 (FLA 1996). The family courts can make non-molestation orders and occupation orders between parties to a wide range of domestic relationships.

5. The family courts have strong powers to enforce orders made under the FLA 1996. Controversially, breach of a non-molestation order is also a criminal offence.

6. Police powers under the Crime and Security Act 2010 (CSA 2010) to require alleged perpetrators to leave the home and then to apply for a court order to extend that removal for up to 28 days without victims' consent raise questions about how best to prevent violence whilst respecting victim autonomy.

4.1 INTRODUCTION

Every 30 seconds, someone contacts the police for assistance regarding domestic violence.[1] Domestic violence destroys many relationships, impairs the emotional, social, and psychological development of children who witness it, and can have devastating, long-term effects on the immediate victims. It has been estimated that domestic violence

---

[1] HMIC (2014), 38.

costs public services and the wider economy over £5.7 billion a year. The pain and suffering of victims is calculated to cost £10 billion a year.[2]

Domestic violence impacts on many areas of family law. Should a court make an order
allowing contact between parent and child if that parent has abused the other? Should the
state intervene to protect children who are not the primary victims of violence between
adults in their household? Should domestic violence affect financial remedies on divorce?
Can mediation safely be used where there has been domestic violence? We address these
specific questions elsewhere. The presence of domestic violence is now also a key route to
obtaining legal aid for lawyers' services for all private family law matters, for which legal aid
is now otherwise generally unavailable. That makes it increasingly important for victims
to take action in relation to the violence in order to obtain the evidence required to access
legal aid.[3] This chapter focuses on what the law can do directly to punish and rehabilitate
perpetrators and to protect victims.

Central to any discussion of domestic violence is the dichotomy between the public and
private spheres. Domestic violence used to be regarded as a private problem, ignored by the
state and society. Since the 1970s, the state has increasingly recognized its responsibility to
tackle domestic violence. Its role might initially appear obvious: domestic violence is criminal conduct. We might therefore expect offences committed in the domestic context to be
treated like any other crime. Recent initiatives seek to improve the criminal justice system's
response, both in dealing with perpetrators and supporting victims. However, the dynamics
of domestic violence raise complicated issues, particularly in relation to the extent to which
victims can, or should be able to, control any criminal proceedings. While domestic violence has rightly emerged from the privacy of the family home, victims still have legitimate
private interests that might affect how the state should deal with perpetrators.

This chapter focuses mainly on the family courts' powers. 'Non-molestation orders'
can be used to prohibit a wide range of abusive conduct. 'Occupation orders' can secure
the victim's right to occupy a home shared by the parties and exclude the abuser. We discuss occupation orders principally here in the context of domestic violence, but they have
wider significance: see chapter 3, regarding family members' rights to occupy the home;
and chapter 7, regarding the financial and property implications of separation, particularly for family members other than spouses and civil partners. Here too, recent developments pose new questions for the public/private dichotomy: the criminalization of breach
of non-molestation orders blurs the boundaries between civil and criminal justice, with
implications for victims' ability to control their family's fate. So too does the introduction
of police powers to obtain domestic violence prevention orders without victim consent.
Determining the proper legal response to domestic violence is not easy.

ONLINE RESOURCE CENTRE

We discuss the civil and criminal laws' responses to forced marriage on the
Online Resource Centre.

---

[2] Walby (2009).
[3] Legal Aid, Sentencing and Punishment of Offenders Act 2012, Sch 1, paras 11 and 12, and Civil Legal
Aid (Procedure) Regulations, SI 2012/3098, reg 33; see Emmerson and Platt (2014).

4.2 BACKGROUND ISSUES: DOMESTIC VIOLENCE AND KEY POLICY QUESTIONS

4.2.1 DEFINING 'DOMESTIC VIOLENCE'

The term 'domestic violence' has no general legal meaning,[4] but all government agencies dealing with the problem now use this definition:

Home Office, *Cross-Government Definition of Domestic Violence – A Consultation. Summary of Responses* (2012), 19

Any incident or pattern of incidents of controlling, coercive, threatening behaviour, violence or abuse between those aged 16 or over who are or have been intimate partners or family members regardless of gender or sexuality. The abuse can encompass but is not limited to:

- psychological
- physical
- sexual
- financial
- emotional

Controlling behaviour is: a range of acts designed to make a person subordinate and/or dependent by isolating them from sources of support, exploiting their resources and capacities for personal gain, depriving them of the means needed for independence, resistance and escape and regulating their everyday behaviour.

Coercive behaviour is: an act or a pattern of acts of assault, threats, humiliation and intimidation or other abuse that is used to harm, punish, or frighten their victim.

The inclusion of family members as perpetrators (as well as partners in couple-relationships) brings activities such as elder abuse,[5] forced marriages, and 'honour crimes' within domestic violence policy.[6] The inclusion of controlling and coercive, as well as physically violent, behaviour acknowledges the many abusive activities used to exercise power in relationships, a feature highlighted by feminist analysis of domestic violence.[7]

As we discuss below, domestic violence is widely regarded as a gender-based problem:[8] most victims are women in opposite-sex relationships. 'Domestic violence' may therefore be misleadingly gender neutral. The expression 'violence against women' is sometimes preferred, though it may inhibit other victims—in same-sex relationships or heterosexual men—from coming forward.[9] However, family law's remedies for domestic violence—and the government's definition—apply to a broader range of more or less loosely 'familial' relationships, characterized by physical, emotional, and often financial closeness. The parties'

---

4 Cf Housing Act 1996, s 177: *Yemshaw v Hounslow LBC* [2011] UKSC 3.
5 See Herring (2011).
6 HO (2012), 19.
7 See 4.2.3 below.
8 HM Government (2010).
9 Donovan et al (2006).

proximity poses potential difficulties: it can make victims reluctant or unable to pursue remedies that objectively appear best suited to ending the violence.

The word 'domestic' is controversial, associated with historical trivialization of the problem. Police were particularly criticized: their expression 'it's just a domestic' betrayed a failure to take violence in the home as seriously as violence committed in public.[10] Some commentators object to 'victim', preferring 'survivor'. Hoff described the women she met when researching domestic violence as:

> knowledgeable, capable people who developed strategies for coping within the violent relationship, as well as for eventually leaving it. Their ability to cope with life-threatening crises in spite of self-blame and intimidations from others that they were somehow responsible for their plight, reveals them more as survivors than as helpless victims.[11]

Throughout this chapter, we use various terms, including 'victim', the word used by the criminal justice system. In discussing civil remedies, we use 'applicant' and 'respondent'.

4.2.2 EVIDENCE ABOUT DOMESTIC VIOLENCE

The prevalence of domestic violence

It is difficult accurately to measure the prevalence of domestic violence, not least because agencies have used differing definitions for data collection.[12] There are particular gaps in our knowledge about violence against groups who are inhibited for various reasons from coming forward: men, members of black and ethnic minority communities, and those in same-sex relationships.[13] But domestic violence is clearly under-reported and under-recorded, and so its contribution to administrative and court data is misleadingly small.[14] Many victims do not regard themselves as victims of a criminal offence.[15] Researchers are often the first people—and the police the last—to whom the abuse has been disclosed, if it is disclosed at all.[16] The Crime Survey for England and Wales (CSEW)[17] provides important data on 'intimate violence'. It collects information about incidents which never reach the legal system, and the additional privacy of its self-completion questionnaire has yielded ten times more reports of abuse than face-to-face interviews.[18] Since the CSEW is based on private households, those living in refuges, who might have experienced the worst abuse, are unrepresented. But even with these and other limitations,[19] the figures gathered are high.

In evaluating the data, particularly when analysing the prevalence of abuse against women and men respectively, we must distinguish between the different categories of abuse covered by the survey. It counts not just the use and threat of physical violence,[20] but also financial and emotional abuse: preventing the victim from having a fair share of the

---

[10] Mullender and Morley (1994), 11.
[11] Hoff (1990), 229.
[12] HM CPS Inspectorate and HMIC (2004), 8.
[13] HO (2006), 45.
[14] Smith (1989).
[15] Roe (2010), table 3.17.
[16] ONS (2014d), ch 4, 23.
[17] Formerly the British Crime Survey.
[18] ONS (2014d), ch 4, 3; this partly reflects the definitions of abuse used in each method.
[19] Mirlees-Black (1999) describes various methodological problems; see also Walby and Allen (2004).
[20] Cf the earlier survey reported by Mirlees-Black (1999).

household money; stopping the victim from seeing friends and relatives; repeatedly belittling the victim so that he or she felt worthless. Sexual violence and stalking by current and former partners and other family members are also counted. Abuse by a current or former partner and other 'family' abuse are distinguished. The headline findings from the most recent survey on the extent of 'intimate violence' of all types were as follows:

ONS, *Crime Statistics, Focus on Violent Crime and Sexual Offences* (2014d), ch 4, 4, 6, and fig 4.1

The CSEW 2012/13 found that, overall, 30.0% of women and 16.3% of men had experienced any domestic abuse since the age of 16...These figures were equivalent to an estimated 4.9 million female victims of domestic abuse and 2.7 million male victims...

Partner abuse (non-sexual) was the most commonly experienced type of intimate violence, covered by the survey, among both women and men since the age of 16. However, twice as many woman (23.8% compared with 11.1% of men) reported having experienced such abuse since the age of 16...

Figure 4.1 Percentage of adults aged 16 to 59 who experienced intimate violence since the age of 16, by sex and headline category, 2012/13 CSEW

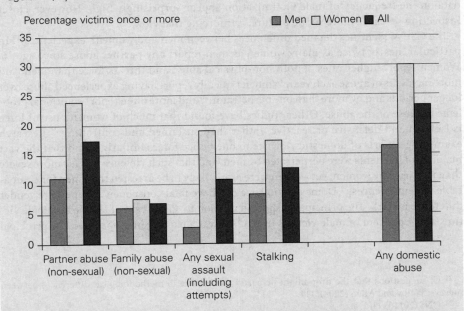

Source: Crime Survey for England and Wales, Office for National Statistics.

There were 7.1% of women and 4.4% of men who reported having experienced any type of domestic abuse in the last year, equivalent to an estimated 1.2 million female victims of domestic abuse and 700,000 male victims.

In the last year, partner abuse (non-sexual) and stalking were the most common of the separate types of intimate violence: 4.0% of women and 2.8% of men reported having experienced partner abuse (non-sexual); 4.1% of women and 2.9% of men reported having experienced stalking.

Although reports of domestic violence to the Survey decreased substantially after the mid-1990s,[21] domestic violence remains a 'volume crime', constituting about 20 per cent of all violent crime reported in CSEW interviews (which, remember, have lower reports of domestic violence than the self-completion questionnaire)[22] and a third of all police-recorded assaults with injury.[23] It is the highest offence for repeat victimization: in 2012/13, 75 per cent of all domestic violence was a repeat incident;[24] nearly 22 per cent of victims reported abuse on three or more occasions, but over half declined to answer or did not know how often they had been abused.[25] It has been estimated that nearly one million children in the UK could be living with domestic violence.[26]

The gender dimension

The orthodox view is that most victims are women, and most perpetrators male. However, it is difficult accurately to identify the pattern and frequency of abuse by gender. Researchers using different methodologies have reached apparently contradictory conclusions about the incidence of women's violence against men. Gathering reliable evidence of male victimization through official records is especially problematic: in the 2012/13 CSEW, 29 per cent of male victims of partner abuse (in the broad sense) reporting abuse in the last year had told no one about it.[27] Given the orthodox view, CSEW data on the frequency of male victimization appear surprisingly high. However, closer inspection reveals a more subtle picture, reinforcing that view.[28]

The CSEW identifies detailed differences between men and women's experiences.[29] In particular, nearly twice as many women as men report any partner abuse since age 16. Women report higher rates of both non-physical abuse and threats/force than men, and more incidents of abuse each year. Women typically report having experienced abuse over longer periods and by more than one perpetrator,[30] and more often report emotional problems because of the abuse. Other studies have found that much of women's use of force is isolated and defensive or reactive, rather than sustained and controlling.[31] Research examining reports of domestic violence to one police force similarly found that the vast majority of incidents were perpetrated by men, and that such violence was far more severe than that used by women; yet women were more likely to be arrested than men for comparable violent offences.[32] Domestic violence can have fatal consequences, and here gender difference is stark. The principal suspect in relation to 45 per cent of female homicide victims and 4 per cent of male victims in 2012/13 was a partner or ex-partner; the principal

---

[21] Cf suggestions that the drop might be partly attributable to methodological differences between surveys: Walby and Allen (2004), 114.

[22] ONS (2014d), ch 1, 8.

[23] HMIC (2014), 5.

[24] ONS (2014d), ch 1, table D7.

[25] Ibid, ch 4, 16 and table 4.12.

[26] UNICEF (2006).

[27] ONS (2014d), 23. For discussion of reasons for this under-reporting, see Walby and Allen (2004).

[28] Mirlees-Black (1999), Walby and Allen (2004), Dobash and Dobash (2004); discussed by Kaganas (2007), 144–6.

[29] See various tables for ONS (2014d), ch 4.

[30] Roe (2010), tables 3.08 and 3.09; this issue not covered by ONS (2014d) data.

[31] Dobash and Dobash (2004).

[32] Hester (2009).

suspect in relation to 23 per cent of female victims and 10 per cent of male victims was another family member.[33]

Causes and risk factors

If gathering reliable statistical evidence about the prevalence and experience of domestic violence is difficult, reliably identifying its causes is harder. Several suggested causal explanations, each controversial, indicate different strategies for dealing with domestic violence.[34] Some theories focus on the psychology of the individuals involved: perpetrators having unusually aggressive or jealous personalities, victims being unusually insecure or masochistic. Some theories suggest abuse may be explained inter-generationally, parties repeating behaviour witnessed by them as children in their own families.[35] Some focus on social and economic deprivation; others on alcohol and other substance abuse. Feminist theories, explored in 4.2.3, view domestic violence as a manifestation of patriarchy, of male power being systematically exercised over women.

In reality, no one theory can explain any one incident of domestic violence. Theories which in some way blame victims are controversial and inconsistent with findings about survivors' determination to escape.[36] It is easier to identify correlations or risk factors that heighten the probability of abuse than to isolate specific causes.[37] Various factors have been found to increase the likelihood of victimization, including: being female; of young age (16–24); being separated, divorced, or single; being pregnant; living as a single parent; suffering long-term illness or disability; having low household income and living in rental accommodation.[38] Perpetrators tend to: be male, have a history of criminal and delinquent behaviour, unemployment, frequent substance abuse; have low income and education; inadequate social networks; stress and other negative consequences of low income and poor accommodation; and various psychological traits, such as a tendency to deny personal responsibility for one's circumstances, jealousy and heightened dependence, lack of empathy.[39]

However, whilst certain characteristics increase the risk, abuse is not confined to any social or economic class or ethnic group, age, or gender pattern.[40] The perception that domestic violence is particularly prevalent in lower socio-economic classes may reflect such groups' greater visibility to public agencies. Victims in more affluent households may have better support networks that enable them to keep abuse private,[41] and may be less likely to report abuse to official agencies.[42] Other studies have found no differences in the incidence of violence by reference to socio-economic status[43] or ethnicity, though poverty and social exclusion may be *consequences* of abuse.[44]

---

33 ONS (2014d), ch 2, 9–10 and table 2.05.
34 Law Com (1992), from para 2.6.
35 Morley and Mullender (1994), 6–7.
36 Edwards (1989), 164–72; Hoff (1990); Dobash and Dobash (1992), ch 7.
37 Walby and Myhill (2001); see ONS (2014d), ch 4, 19–22 on example of substance abuse.
38 HO (2006), 56–8; ONS (2014d), ch 4, 11–13.
39 HO, ibid.
40 See ONS (2014d), tables.
41 Law Com (1992), para 2.2; Select Committee (1975), para 7.
42 Walby and Allen (2004), 98.
43 Finney (2006).
44 Walby and Allen (2004), 90.

R. Morley and A. Mullender, *Preventing Domestic Violence to Women*
(London: Home Office, 1994)

Attempting to isolate particular groups of people prone to domestic violence may be defended as a way of furthering an understanding of the causes and hence cures of the problem. However, the message from research is clear. While class, ethnicity, drinking, childhood experiences and indeed other psychological/social factors may in some cases contribute to the establishment of violent relationships and/or their continuation, domestic violence to women is far too common throughout society to isolate specific groups as constituting *the* problem.

Why not just leave?

Ending the relationship does not always stop the violence, and may even precipitate or escalate abuse.[45] Many victims are abused in the context of contact arrangements for children of the family and the now ex-partner.[46] Separation can make abusers increasingly serious and obsessive, exposing some victims to greater risk of homicide.[47] Fear of abuse commencing or worsening, together with family responsibilities and cultural, physical, or economic barriers may therefore inhibit victims, particularly women,[48] from leaving their relationship or even reporting the abuse:

C. Humphreys and R. Thiara, 'Neither Justice nor Protection: Women's Experiences of Post-Separation Violence', (2003) 25 *Journal of Social Welfare and Family Law* 195, 196

'Why doesn't she leave?' is probably one of the most frequently asked questions for those who witness a woman suffering domestic violence. Implicit in this question is frustration and mystification that women are failing to 'look after themselves', and often their children, by remaining caught in a web of violence and abuse. This individualizing discourse places the responsibility on the woman for leaving herself open to continued violence and abuse. It further implies that there is a clear line separating her life in the abusive relationship and the safety and security which awaits her once she separates.

Post-separation violence is a fear and frequently a reality for women and children who attempt to escape from abusive and violent relationships. However, it is often over-looked as a danger and remains an area where the failure of effective intervention leaves women and children vulnerable and unprotected. The effect of this failure is not neutral, but compounds the abuser's control and the woman's sense of entrapment.

The justice gap

Taking even modest estimates of the prevalence of domestic violence, there is a vast 'justice gap' between the number of cases in the legal system and the estimated 1.9 million victims

---

[45] Ibid, 62–9.
[46] See 11.7.2.
[47] See work discussed by Paradine and Wilkinson (2004), 14.
[48] ONS (2014d) found no difference in women and men's likelihood of leaving for at least one night—but that gives no insight into longer-term outcomes.

each year, with an estimated 574,000 victims experiencing severe force in 2012/13. Many are repeat victims who between them experience many more individual *incidents* of abuse.[49] By contrast, in 2013/14, the CPS brought just over 78,000 prosecutions and secured around 58,300 convictions for domestic abuse.[50] Meanwhile, only about 20,000 cases involving applications for civil orders relating to domestic violence occur each year.[51]

4.2.3 FEMINIST CRITIQUES OF DOMESTIC VIOLENCE LAW, POLICY, AND PRACTICE

The statistical evidence explored above indicates that domestic violence may be principally viewed as a problem of violence against women. Feminist scholars have accordingly been at the forefront of critiques of the law and domestic violence. While feminist theories classically offer an explanation of the abuse of women by men, they can be applied more widely to abuse of power by dominant parties in any unequal relationships, such as the abuse of vulnerable older people by family members or 'carers'.[52] Michelle Madden Dempsey has argued that in order properly to understand the phenomenon and so tailor appropriate responses, it is important to distinguish instances of domestic violence in its 'strong sense'—where it carries this aspect of control and abuse of power in an unequal relationship—from other instances of violence between family members.[53]

Central to feminist analysis of domestic violence is the dichotomy between the public and private spheres. The law and its agents have been accused of regarding domestic violence as a private matter, not a concern for the state. The state and wider society have thus enabled abuse to continue free from outside interference, and so condoned it. Historically, those charges are unanswerable. Until relatively recently, the law paid no special attention to domestic violence, instead placing wives in an inferior position. The common law permitted husbands to use 'reasonable' chastisement on their wives and to confine them in order to control their behaviour and to enforce the right to consortium.[54] These rights flowed from the law's understanding of the marital relationship:

W. Blackstone, *Commentaries on the Laws of England*, vol 1 (1765, Facsimile edn: Chicago: University of Chicago Press, 1979), 430, 432–3

By marriage, the husband and wife are one person in law: that is, the very being or legal existence of the woman is suspended during the marriage, or at least is incorporated and consolidated into that of the husband: under whose wing, protection, and *cover*, she performs every thing... Under this principle, of an union of person in husband and wife, depend almost all the legal rights, duties, and disabilities, that either of them acquire by marriage....

The husband also (by the old law) might give his wife moderate correction. For, as he is to answer for her misbehaviour, the law thought it reasonable to intrust him with this power of

---

49 Roe (2010), 64.
50 CPS (2014a).
51 MOJ (2014a), table 2.7.
52 Freeman (1989), 743–5. Cf concerns that an exclusively feminist focus may exclude atypical victims: Centre for Social Justice (2012).
53 Madden Dempsey (2006).
54 See Cretney (2003a), ch 4.

restraining her, by domestic chastisement, in the same moderation that a man is allowed to correct his servants or children; for whom the master or parent is also liable in some cases to answer. But this power of correction was confined within reasonable bounds...But...this power of correction began to be doubted: and a wife may now have security of the peace against her husband; or, in return, a husband against his wife. Yet the lower rank of people, who were always fond of the old common law, still claim and exert their antient privilege: and the courts of law will still permit a husband to restrain a wife of her liberty, in case of any gross misbehaviour....[55]

The law also granted husbands immunity from liability for rape:

M. Hale, *The History of the Pleas of the Crown* (1736, London: Professional Books, 1971), 629

...the husband cannot be guilty of a rape committed by himself upon his lawful wife, for by their mutual matrimonial consent and contract the wife hath given up herself in this kind unto her husband, which she cannot retract.

These rights were eroded over time, but it was not until 1891 and 1991 that the courts definitively declared each right no longer to exist.

The Queen v Jackson [1891] 1 QB 671, 678–9, 680

LORD HALSBURY LC:

I confess that some of the propositions which have been referred to during the argument are such as I should be reluctant to suppose ever to have been the law of England. More than a century ago it was boldly contended that slavery existed in England; but, if any one were to set up such a contention now, it would be regarded as ridiculous. In the same way, such quaint and absurd dicta as are to be found in the books as to the right of a husband over his wife in respect of personal chastisement are not, I think, now capable of being cited as authorities in a court of justice in this or any civilized country...The [case] seems to me to be based on the broad proposition that it is the right of the husband, where his wife has wilfully absented herself from him, to seize the person of his wife by force and detain her in his house until she shall be willing to restore to him his conjugal rights. I am not prepared to assent to such a proposition.

Regina v R [1992] 1 AC 599, 616

LORD KEITH OF KINKEL:

The common law is...capable of evolving in the light of changing social, economic and cultural developments. Hale's proposition reflected the state of affairs in these respects at the

---

[55] Doggett (1992), ch 2, argues that husbands' right to control wives was the very *essence*, not the mere consequence, of the doctrine of coverture.

time it was enunciated. Since then the status of women, and particularly of married women, has changed out of all recognition in various ways...Apart from property matters and the availability of matrimonial remedies, one of the most important changes is that marriage is in modern times regarded as a partnership of equals, and no longer one in which the wife must be the subservient chattel of the husband. Hale's proposition involves that by marriage a wife gives her irrevocable consent to sexual intercourse with her husband under all circumstances and irrespective of the state of her health or how she happens to be feeling at the time. In modern times any reasonable person must regard that conception as quite unacceptable.

However, even once all adults *theoretically* enjoyed equal protection under the law, commentators continued to highlight the legal system's failure to treat domestic violence as seriously as other offences. This failure to intervene was attributed to a widespread perception that domestic violence is a 'private' matter:[56]

J. Pahl, *Private Violence and Public Policy: The Needs of Battered Women and the Response of Public Services* (London: Routledge and Kegan Paul, 1985), 13–15

In a culture which, both explicitly and implicitly, assumes fundamental linkages between such concepts as 'woman', 'wife', 'family', 'home' and 'private', it is no accident that violence against a woman, perpetuated by her husband within their family home, is somehow seen as a different sort of crime from violence against a stranger in a public place. We can see these linkages exemplified in many different statements which have been made on the subject, most especially in the justifications for non-intervention given both by violent husbands, and also by people who might well have intervened had the violence occurred between strangers in a public place.

Pahl drew on two examples from evidence given to the 1975 Parliamentary Select Committee on Violence in Marriage. The first was from the Association of Chief Police Officers:

It is important to keep 'wife battering' in its correct perspective and realise that this loose term is applied to incidents ranging from a very minor domestic fracas where no Police action is really justified, to the more serious incidents of assaults occasioning grievous bodily harm and unlawful woundings. Whilst such problems take up considerable Police time during say, 12 months, in the majority of cases the role of the Police is a negative one. We are, after all, dealing with persons 'bound in marriage', and it is important for a host of reasons, to maintain the unity of the spouses. (Select Committee Report, 1975, 366).

The second example came from the Home Office, addressing the scope of criminal injuries compensation:

It can perhaps be argued that the Government (or the police) cannot have the same day to day responsibility for the day to day behaviour of members of a household within their own walls. Some disagreement may be inevitable within a family. Even a degree of minor violence

---

[56] Pizzey (1974); Pahl (1985); Edwards (1989); Hoff (1990); Dobash and Dobash (1992).

may be normal in some homes. It can perhaps be argued that the point at which the State should intervene in family violence should be higher than that which is expected in the case of violence between strangers. Or even that the State has no particular responsibility for compensating those who suffer violence in circumstances which are largely (in the case of adult members of a family) under their own control. (Select Committee Report, 1975, 418)

According to Pahl:

Both these statements suggest that the intervention of the state is less appropriate when the individuals concerned are linked by family ties as opposed to being strangers, and when the incident takes place in a private rather than a public place. To question this is not to advocate that there should be a policeman in every bedroom nor is it to argue for the abolition of privacy or domestic life. However, for our topic it is important to consider more carefully the ways in which the public-private boundary is defined; more specifically, it is important to consider *whose* privacy is being respected or violated in particular circumstances. . . . [T]he notion of privacy is not an absolute value, . . . some people's privacy appears to be more inviolate than other people's privacy, and . . . by looking at how 'the private' is defined and maintained we can understand a great deal about the power relations in a particular society.

E. Schneider, 'The Violence of Privacy', in M. Fineman and R. Mykitiuk (eds), *The Public Nature of Private Violence* (New York: Routledge, 1994), 44

Although social failure to respond to problems of battered women has been justified on grounds of privacy, this failure to respond is an affirmative political decision that has serious public consequences. The rationale of privacy masks the political nature of the decision. Privacy thus plays a particularly subtle and pernicious ideological role in supporting, encouraging, and legitimating violence against women. The state plays an affirmative role in permitting violence against battered women by protecting the privileges and prerogatives of battering men and failing to protect battered women, and by prosecuting battered women for homicide when they protect themselves.

Domestic violence and the concept of privacy which allowed it to flourish are the product of deep-seated, patriarchal ideology, present throughout law and society:

M. Freeman, 'Legal Ideologies, Patriarchal Precedents, and Domestic Violence', in M. Freeman (ed), *State, Law, and the Family: Critical Perspectives* (London: Tavistock, 1984), 72

[G]iven the position of women in society the behaviour of violent husbands is rational, if extreme. It is not necessary for husbands to have formal rights such as to chastise their wives. That they once had this right and exercised it is sufficient. It helped to form and then to reinforce an ideology of subordination and control of women. The ideology remains imbricated in the legal system even if one of its grosser manifestations has virtually disappeared. Wife battering remains one of its legacies and if this too is to go the ideology must be dismantled. The legal system has been committed to a patriarchal ideology. It is this that must be challenged if violence against women is to diminish and ultimately to cease.

L. Hoff, ***Battered Women as Survivors*** (London: Routledge, 1990), 234, 241

> Terms such as the 'battered wife syndrome' and 'domestic violence' reveal an interpretation of wife battering as only a 'family' or medical problem and tend to mask the political and broader social ramifications of the more explicit term 'violence against women'...
>
> [W]oman abuse is more than a personal crisis. It is a public health problem which arises from traditional values that regard women as appropriate objects of violence and male control; from the chronic problem of women's continued economic disparity in a wealthy industrialized society; and from the gender-based division of labour regarding child-care.

On this view, improving the law's response to individual perpetrators may alleviate a symptom, but it will not destroy the underlying infection. Domestic violence will not be rooted out until the structural inequality of women in society is removed, for example through fundamental reform of employment law and child-care practices, yielding a more equal division of responsibilities within the home, to give men and women more equal economic power; and through initiatives designed to educate children and the public generally about healthy relationships and appropriate inter-personal behaviour, and to raise awareness of domestic violence.[57]

4.2.4 THE HUMAN RIGHTS DIMENSION

One relatively new arrival in legal discourse about domestic violence is human rights law.[58] Until recently, human rights arguments in this sphere tended to focus on proportionate and fair treatment of perpetrators (especially under Articles 6 and 8 of the European Convention on Human Rights (ECHR)). However, the European Court of Human Rights was invited to consider domestic violence itself as a human rights violation in several recent cases, notably *Opuz v Turkey*.[59] In this section, we outline the law set out in *Opuz* and other human rights arguments that may be made to protect victims of domestic violence. We shall pick up on particular issues in the English context throughout the chapter.

The applicant's husband in *Opuz* had over several years perpetrated serious attacks on the applicant and her mother, threatening to kill them. Despite arresting the husband, the police released him, the women withdrew their complaints (under threat from the husband), and the prosecutor dropped the charges. He was later convicted for a multiple stabbing of the applicant, but sentenced only to pay a fine. Despite the women's appeals for further action, nothing was done. Shortly afterwards, the husband killed the mother, claiming that he had to do so to protect his 'honour'. He was again released pending an appeal, going on to threaten again to kill the applicant and her new partner. The police responded simply by circulating his picture and fingerprints to facilitate an arrest should he appear again near the applicant's home.

---

[57] E.g. Hoff (1990); Law Com (1992), para 2.8; HM Government (2010).
[58] See generally Choudhry and Herring (2006a), (2006b), (2010), ch 9; Council of Europe (2011).
[59] (App No 33401/02, ECHR) (2009); *Kontrova v Slovakia* (App No 7510/04, ECHR) (2007).

The applicant successfully claimed violations of Articles 2, 3, and 14 ECHR, arguing that the Turkish state had breached its positive obligations to protect her and her mother, and that its lacklustre policing, prosecution, and sentencing of domestic violence constituted discrimination against women, the principal victims of that official inactivity. The Court took a robust approach, drawing on its own case law concerning the state's obligations regarding child protection, and referring extensively to other international conventions and policies regarding the prevention of violence and discrimination against women. Turkish law and practice were found wanting. It should have been possible to prosecute the husband despite the victims' withdrawal given the seriousness of his offences and the continuing threat posed. The response of police and prosecutors was found 'manifestly inadequate', having no impact on the husband's behaviour; the few judicial interventions were chastised for exhibiting 'a certain degree of tolerance' of his conduct.[60]

Article 2

The following passage sets out the Court's approach to Article 2, the right to life, breached in *Opuz*:

Opuz v Turkey (App No 33401/02, ECHR) (2009)

128. . . . Article 2§1 enjoins the State . . . to take appropriate steps to safeguard the lives of those within its jurisdiction . . . This involves a primary duty on the State to secure the right to life by putting in place effective criminal law provisions to deter the commission of offences against the person backed up by law enforcement machinery for the prevention, suppression and punishment of breaches of such provisions. It also extends in appropriate circumstances to a positive obligation on the authorities to take preventive operational measures to protect an individual whose life is at risk from the criminal acts of another individual . . .

129. Bearing in mind the difficulties in policing modern societies, the unpredictability of human conduct and the operational choices which must be made in terms of priorities and resources, the scope of the positive obligation must be interpreted in a way which does not impose an impossible or disproportionate burden on the authorities. Not every claimed risk to life, therefore, can entail for the authorities a Convention requirement to take operational measures to prevent that risk from materialising. For a positive obligation to arise, it must be established that the authorities knew *or ought to have known* at the time of the existence of a real and immediate risk to the life of an identified individual from the criminal acts of a third party and that they failed to take measures within the scope of their powers which, judged reasonably, *might have been expected to avoid* that risk. Another relevant consideration is the need to ensure that the police exercise their powers to control and prevent crime in a manner which fully respects the due process and other guarantees which legitimately place restraints on the scope of their action to investigate crime and bring offenders to justice, including the guarantees contained in Articles 5 and 8. [emphasis added]

---

[60] *Opuz*, [170].

The second set of italicized words are significant: the applicant is not required to prove causation, that prompt action by the state *would have prevented* the death. It is enough that it *might* have done.[61] However, in other respects the test set out in *Opuz* may be difficult to satisfy. Considerable operational discretion was afforded to the police by the House of Lords in *Van Colle* (a case brought under the Human Rights Act 1998 (HRA 1998)) and the joined appeal in *Smith* (brought in negligence) in relation to police inaction in the face of threats which culminated in fatal and near-fatal assaults.[62] Mandy Burton has expressed concern that what police 'ought to have known' for the purposes of Article 2 may now be assessed on the basis of information already available to them, and not on the basis of further information they might have discovered had they investigated more actively.[63] If so, victims must ensure that they put as much information as possible about the history of their case before the police in requesting action.[64]

Article 3

The Court in *Opuz* recognized that sufficiently serious domestic violence can constitute 'ill-treatment' within the scope of Article 3, whether it entails physical injury or psychological pressure, and so potentially trigger the state's positive duty under that Article to protect 'vulnerable individuals'.[65] The applicant here was vulnerable, not least because of the history of violence and fear of further violence from the husband.[66] States have some discretion in deciding how to act given local conditions, but must operate within the ambit of common international values and understandings of states' duties 'relating to the eradication of gender-based violence'.[67] This the Turkish state had lamentably failed to do.[68]

Article 14

The Court turned finally to the charge of discrimination on grounds of gender under Article 14 in conjunction with Articles 2 and 3. The Court here particularly drew on growing international legal and political measures to combat violence against women:

Opuz v Turkey (App No 33401/02, ECHR) (2009)

186.... The [UN Convention on the Elimination of All Forms of Discrimination Against Women (CEDAW)] defines discrimination against women under Article 1 as '... any

---

[61] See *DSD v Commissioner of Police for the Metropolis* [2014] EWHC 436.

[62] *Chief Constable of the Hertfordshire Police v Van Colle* and *Smith v Chief Constable of Sussex Police* [2008] UKHL 50, applying *Osman v United Kingdom* (App No 23452/94, ECHR) (1998); cf *Michael v Gwent Police* [2012] EWCA Civ 981.

[63] Ibid, [86].

[64] Burton (2010), (2009a); Choudhry and Herring (2010), 356–62.

[65] *Opuz v Turkey* (App No 33401/02, ECHR) (2009), [158]–[161].

[66] The Court also referred to the inferior position of women generally in the particular region of Turkey: ibid, [160].

[67] Ibid, [164]–[165].

[68] See also *DSD v Commissioner of the Police for the Metropolis* [2014] EWHC 436 for full analysis of the positive obligation to investigate.

> distinction, exclusion or restriction made on the basis of sex which has the effect or purpose of impairing or nullifying the recognition, enjoyment or exercise by women, irrespective of their marital status, on a basis of equality of men and women, of human rights and fundamental freedoms in the political, economic, social, cultural, civil or any other field.'
>
> 187. The CEDAW Committee has reiterated that violence against women, including domestic violence, is a form of discrimination against women . . .
>
> 188. The UN Commission on Human Rights expressly recognised the nexus between gender-based violence and discrimination by stressing in resolution 2003/45 that 'all forms of violence against women occur within the context of *de jure* and *de facto* discrimination against women and the lower status accorded to women in society and are exacerbated by the obstacles women often face in seeking remedies from the State.' . . .
>
> 191. . . . [T]he State's failure to protect women against domestic violence breaches their right to equal protection of the law and . . . this failure does not need to be intentional.

The Court went on to find that while the legislative framework in Turkey was not itself discriminatory, discrimination nevertheless arose from:

> 192. . . . the general attitude of the local authorities, such as the manner in which the women were treated at police stations when they reported domestic violence and judicial passivity in providing effective protection to victims.

It concluded that:

> 198. . . . the applicant has been able to show, supported by unchallenged statistical information, the existence of a prima facie indication that the domestic violence affected mainly women and that the general and discriminatory judicial passivity in Turkey created a climate that was conducive to domestic violence.[69]

Article 8

Balancing rights

Owing to the seriousness of the abuse in that case, *Opuz* did not address the state's obligation to protect victims under Article 8. However, less serious abuse may fall within the scope of victims' right to respect for private and family life, and state inactivity may accordingly violate Article 8 (and Article 14 in conjunction with it).[70] The key difference between Article 8 and Articles 2 and 3, however, is that Article 8 is a qualified right. Respondents might seek to assert their rights under Article 8 to resist, for example, removal from the parties' home, or civil injunctions or bail conditions which inhibit their relationship with the parties' children. We explore the potential impact of Article 8 in the English context when we examine occupation orders at 4.5.4 below. However, two points raised by Choudhry and Herring should be noted here.[71] First, they have argued that Article 17 may preclude respondents from asserting their Convention rights in these cases:

---

[69] Cf on the facts, *A v Croatia* (App No 55164/08, ECHR) (2010).

[70] *Bevacqua v Bulgaria* (App No 71127/01, ECHR) (2008); *Hadjuova v Slovakia* (App No 2660/03, ECHR) (2010); *R (Waxman) v CPS* [2012] EWHC 133, from [21].

[71] Choudhry and Herring (2006a).

Article 17

> Nothing in this Convention may be interpreted as implying for any State, group or person any right to engage in any activity or perform any act aimed at the destruction of any of the rights and freedoms set forth herein or at their limitation to a greater extent than is provided for in the Convention.

M C Q

On this basis, they argue, perpetrators of domestic violence should forfeit their right to respect for private life and home where necessary to protect victims and their Article 8 rights from the threat posed by the abuse. Some support for this approach may be drawn from the remark in *Opuz* (made without reference to Article 17) that 'in domestic violence cases perpetrators' rights cannot supersede victims' human rights to life and to physical and mental integrity',[72] the latter falling within Article 8. Secondly, where children are affected by the violence, their rights will often be determinative or at least highly influential in an Article 8 balancing exercise.

Balancing rights and victim withdrawal

One other aspect of Article 8 was explored in *Opuz*. The Turkish state argued that its relative inactivity following the withdrawal of the victims' complaints was intended to respect their family life under Article 8. If individuals do not want the state to intervene in their lives, can the state ignore those wishes? The problem of victim withdrawal divides commentators,[73] particularly once—as in England and Wales—the state adopts a more rigorous approach to tackling domestic violence. Should the criminal or civil law be used, or both? Should legal proceedings be taken even where the victim opposes such intervention? Is a *legal* response necessarily the most constructive one? Improvements to the *civil* justice response to domestic violence might reinforce the idea of domestic violence as a *private* problem, when perpetrators should instead be subject to the public condemnation of criminal justice.[74] On the other hand, victims may wish to retain the control that the civil justice system (on the face of it) allows them. Many victims seem reluctant to bring or cooperate with any legal proceedings, often for negative reasons: they may not perceive themselves as victims of criminal or even wrongful behaviour;[75] they may blame themselves for their predicament;[76] they may fear reprisals; indeed—as in *Opuz*—they may have been directly threatened. Some victims view legal intervention, particularly criminal justice, as detrimental to their and their family's interests. While it is important to help victims overcome these barriers to taking remedial action, the state cannot simply ignore their aversion to using the law. It is said that the state should aim to empower victims to make informed choices about whether and how to engage with the legal system, thus preserving their autonomy.[77] Otherwise, victims escape the patriarchal control of their abusers only to be subjected to control by the state.[78] However, others caution against

---

[72] *Opuz v Turkey* (App No 33401/02, ECHR) (2009), [147].
[73] Morris and Gelsthorpe (2000), 412.
[74] E.g. Edwards (1989).
[75] Roe (2010), table 3.17.
[76] Hoff (1990).
[77] Hoyle and Sanders (2000).
[78] Schneider (1994).

placing inappropriate weight on 'victim autonomy', given the difficulties some victims have in exercising truly free choice. The independent interests of children affected by the violence, and of wider society, may also mean that victims' wishes cannot invariably be prioritized.[79]

In *Opuz*, the Turkish authorities were found to have breached both Articles 2 and 3 through their approach to victim withdrawal: they had failed to explore why the victims withdrew their complaints, had not weighed up countervailing factors which favoured continuing the prosecution without them, and had instead 'given exclusive weight to the need to refrain from interfering in what they perceived to be a "family matter"'.[80] The Court specifically endorsed the approach of the English prosecuting authority, the CPS, to victim withdrawal. This involves weighing up a number of factors in deciding whether it is in the public interest to prosecute: the seriousness of the offence, the nature of any injuries, whether the attack was planned and armed, its effect on any children in the household, the risk of recurrence, the history and current state of the parties' relationship and the likely impact on it of any prosecution, and so on. A key factor for the CPS is the safety of the victim and any children.[81] The Court supported this approach on the basis that:

> 144. ...in some instances, the national authorities' interference with the private or family life of the individuals might be necessary in order to protect the health and rights of others or to prevent commission of criminal acts.

Indeed, the victim's Article 2 rights might take precedence over her *own* Article 8 right to respect for private and family life.[82]

4.3 THE CRIMINAL LAW AND DOMESTIC VIOLENCE

While its response to domestic violence is far from unimpeachable, the UK is considerably further along the road mapped by the European Court in *Opuz* than Turkey. For example, the CPS policy endorsed by the European Court explicitly identifies domestic violence not just as a crime of violence but of coercive control, reflecting a feminist-inspired, 'strong sense' of domestic violence of the sort described by Madden Dempsey.[83] In this section, we outline the principal features of English criminal law and justice applicable to domestic violence. At 4.6.2 we examine the increasing interaction between criminal and civil law in this field, and the problems that raises.

4.3.1 THE CRIMINAL LAW

The criminal law now protects all adults, regardless of marital status. The general criminal law is fairly well equipped to deal with the various physical, sexual, psychological, and

---

[79] Choudhry and Herring (2006a); see Miles (2001), Dobash and Dobash (1992), ch 4.
[80] *Opuz v Turkey* (App No 33401/02, ECHR) (2009), [143].
[81] See CPS (2009), para 6.3.
[82] *Opuz v Turkey*, [140].
[83] CPS (2009), para 2.1; Madden Dempsey (2006).

financial manifestations of domestic violence. Relevant charges include assault, wounding, grievous bodily harm, homicide offences, sexual offences, false imprisonment, kidnap, blackmail, criminal damage, witness intimidation, breach of the peace, and other public order offences.[84] Less severe forms of abuse, such as stalking and other forms of harassment, are covered by the Protection from Harassment Act 1997 (PHA 1997) and offences relating to misuse of computers and telecommunications. Domestic cases constitute half of all harassment crimes reported to the police,[85] and the largest category of prosecutions under the PHA 1997.[86] The PHA 1997 also empowers the criminal courts to issue restraining orders, both following conviction for any offence (not just harassment) or even on acquittal, breach of which constitutes an offence.[87] These orders closely resemble civil law injunctions, designed to protect victims by prohibiting specified behaviour by the offender.

In addition to these general offences, the criminal law has recently been expanded to include some offences specific to the domestic violence context. Breach of a non-molestation order granted by a *civil* court under the FLA 1996, discussed at 4.6.2 below, is also now a criminal offence. Following a consultation exercise in 2014, the government introduced a clause in the Serious Crime Bill 2015 which would create a new offence of 'coercive and controlling behaviour' within intimate or family relationships.[88]

Some victims of domestic violence find themselves on the wrong side of the criminal law, notably women who have killed abusive partners. The law's response to these cases has long been questioned, and the law of homicide, particularly the defences available to murder, has been reformed, though whether to the benefit of these women is not yet clear.[89]

4.3.2 THE CRIMINAL JUSTICE SYSTEM

Despite the criminal law's potential, the criminal justice system has been accused of dismissing domestic violence as a trivial, private matter. Police have been reluctant to intervene, particularly if victims do not demonstrate a clear commitment to pursue the case; arrest and charge rates have been low; even where charges have been brought, incidents have been 'down-crimed', that is, the abuser merely cautioned or charged with a less serious offence than that committed; courts have been criticized for lenient sentencing.[90] Women have reported feeling 'more endangered than protected by the prosecution process',[91] their experience of using the system described as 'double victimization'.[92] Even quite recently it has been suggested that domestic violence has been 'decriminalized' in some areas.[93]

---

84 See CPS (2009), Annex A; Ormerod (2011).
85 HO (2014a), (2014b).
86 Harris (2000).
87 PHA 1997, ss 5–5A.
88 HO (2014a), (2014b); cf Tadros (2005); HO (2003).
89 Coroners and Justice Act 2009, ss 54–6; Norrie (2010), 285.
90 See generally Pahl (1985); Edwards (1989); Grace (1995); Dobash and Dobash (1992); Rumney (1999) on rape; Harris (2000) on the PHA 1997.
91 Humphreys and Thiara (2003), 203.
92 Edwards (1989), 153.
93 Humphreys and Thiara (2003), 211, referring to research in Surrey in 2001.

However, in recent years, government is committed to tackling domestic violence on all fronts, with strategies underpinned by research identifying more effective responses to domestic abuse.[94] And the courts are clear that:

> [T]he days when courts sought to distinguish between violence within the home from violence on the streets are...long gone. Cases...[which attempted] to distinguish between situations of violence and breach of the peace in a domestic context and elsewhere are...not to be relied upon and hopelessly out of date.[95]

Government strategy has multiple components: prevention of violence, through education and early intervention; provision of support to victims through a coordinated multi-agency response in partnership with victims; and protection and justice through the legal system, with criminal justice at the forefront and regular monitoring of arrest and conviction rates.[96]

New initiatives aim to ensure a robust, effective, and consistent criminal justice response, designed to protect victims from repeat abuse, and to hold perpetrators responsible. Domestic violence is emphatically regarded as criminal; if anything, the domestic context may be an aggravating factor.[97] Police and CPS policies are pro-arrest and pro-prosecution, with or without victims' agreement.[98] Police powers in the criminal justice arena have been significantly enlarged: an arrest may now be made for any offence,[99] including now breach of family courts' non-molestation orders under the FLA 1996 and breach of civil injunctions and restraining orders made under the PHA 1997. We discuss at 4.7.1 a novel civil justice power given to police to secure perpetrators' removal from the home on an interim basis. Since the victim is often the only witness, police are encouraged to gather as much other evidence as possible to reduce reliance on victim testimony.[100] Decisions about charges are for the CPS, not the police or the victim. Where victims wish to retract their evidence, pursuant to the policy endorsed in *Opuz v Turkey*,[101] prosecution will proceed if there is enough evidence and it is in the public interest. Decisions to retract should also be closely investigated to ensure they are not the product of pressure or threats. Where defendants are bailed pending trial, appropriate bail conditions should be used to protect victims. Specific sentencing guidelines seek to ensure that domestic offences are properly penalized. Their starting point is that domestic violence is no less serious than other crime; several aggravating features are identified as meriting stiffer penalties.[102] Sentencing under community rehabilitation orders may now include referral to 'perpetrator programmes', designed to reform offenders' attitudes and behaviour through counselling and group work, though the effectiveness of such programmes—and their funding—remains doubtful.[103]

---

[94] Hester and Westmarland (2005).

[95] *Demetriou v DPP* [2012] EWHC 2443, [8].

[96] HM Government (2010), HMIC (2014), CPS (2014b).

[97] CPS (2009), para 1.2.

[98] See generally: HO (2000); ACPO (2008); CPS (2009)—currently under review, (2014c); Ellison (2003).

[99] Serious Organised Crime and Police Act 2005, amending the Police and Criminal Evidence Act 1984, s 24.

[100] *Re C* [2007] EWCA Civ 3463.

[101] Discussed above at 4.2.4.

[102] Sentencing Guidelines Council (2006a), (2006b); Burton (2008a), 63–6; *R v McNaughten* [2003] EWCA Crim 3479; *R v Liddle* [2000] 1 Cr App R (S) 131.

[103] HMIC (2014), 108–9; NAPO (2012).

If victims are to be encouraged, or even required,[104] to participate in criminal justice, they need support and protection. Where victims attend court, that ordeal can be alleviated to some extent through protections for 'vulnerable and intimidated' witnesses.[105] All crime victims now have rights to information about the progress of their case and within court proceedings.[106] Specialist Domestic Violence Courts have become central to the new strategy. Hearings in these courts are conducted with specially trained police, prosecutors, and magistrates, and can offer a fast-track procedure, minimizing delays. They also provide the hub of a multi-agency response to domestic violence[107] and independent domestic violence advisers for high-risk victims who: support victims through the criminal justice process; liaise between police, prosecutors, courts, other agencies, and victims; and help victims access material and emotional resources to start a new life free from abuse.[108]

However, entrenched working practices, attitudes, and cultures within the police and CPS make it difficult to ensure effective implementation of official policy on the ground.[109] There remains considerable room for improvement and the risk of ECHR violation in individual cases therefore remains.[110]

HMIC, *Everyone's Business: Improving the Police Response to Domestic Violence* (2014), 6–7

The overall police response to victims of domestic abuse is not good enough. This is despite considerable improvement in the service over the last decade, and the commitment and dedication of many able police officers and police staff. In too many forces there are weaknesses in the service provided to victims; some of these are serious and this means that victims are put at unnecessary risk. Many forces need to take action now.

Domestic abuse is a priority on paper but, in the majority of forces, not in practice.... Tackling domestic abuse too often remains a poor relation to acquisitive crime and serious organised crime. The factors that contribute to this in many forces are:

- a lack of visible leadership and clear direction set by senior officers
- alarming and unacceptable weaknesses in some core policing activity, in particular the collection of evidence by officers at the scene of domestic abuse incidents;
- poor management and supervision that fails to reinforce the right behaviours, attitudes and actions of officers;
- failure to prioritise action that will tackle domestic abuse when setting the priorities for the day-to-day activity of frontline officers and assigning their work;
- officers lacking the skills and knowledge necessary to engage confidently and competently with victims of domestic violence; and
- extremely limited systematic feedback from victims about their experience of the police response.

---

104 Victims can be compelled to give evidence: but victim retraction has commonly marked discontinuation of the case: Cretney and Davis (1997); cf CPS (2009), Part 5.

105 Youth Justice and Criminal Evidence Act 1999, Part II, Chapter I; CPS (2009), Part 11.

106 DVCVA 2004; MOJ (2013).

107 Cook et al (2004); Vallely et al (2005); Burton (2008a), ch 7.

108 Hester and Westmarland (2005); HMIC (2014), from 95.

109 Grace (1995); Kelly (1999).

110 Choudhry and Herring (2006a), 107; Burton (2010), 136–7. For a survey of recent research, see Burton (2008a), ch 6.

HMIC found that arrest rates vary wildly between forces: some arrest in just 45 per cent of domestic abuse cases, others in as many as 90 per cent. Some forces rely excessively on cautioning rather than charging offenders. Nearly a third of victims retract their statements, and while the proportion of such cases which nevertheless continue to conviction has risen,[111] HMIC found very few cases taken without victim testimony or support, not least because of inadequate evidence-gathering. HMIC's own victim survey found that a third felt no safer—or less safe—after the police's initial response.

The picture is not entirely gloomy. The CPS is prosecuting more cases of domestic abuse, and national conviction rates for domestic abuse were the highest ever in 2013/14 at 75 per cent, with over 90 per cent of convictions following a guilty plea, thereby sparing victims from having to testify.[112] Areas with Specialist Domestic Violence Courts have been performing most strongly.[113] But the vast 'justice gap' remains: in the CSEW 2012/13, police were reported to have taken no action in 21 per cent of the incidents to which they were called, with only a quarter of cases in which police had taken some action reaching court. The attrition rate from police call, to arrest, to charge, and on to conviction is still too high.

However, 'improvement' of the criminal justice response may not be best, or solely, measured by reference to arrest and conviction rates. Nor is victim retraction necessarily a failure, provided the victim was properly supported. Not all victims measure success in these terms.[114] The goal must be for victims to become 'domestic violence free', something which arrest, victim retraction, and conviction rates cannot reliably measure.[115] Some victims may not view prosecution and conviction as constructive steps towards that goal, particularly if they want the relationship to continue in some form. But whether and when the system should respect victims' opposition to arrest or prosecute is controversial. The importance of victim choice is recognized in the current policy framework,[116] but ultimately, the public interest and affected children's interests may be determinative.[117]

On any view, however, the criminal justice system is only one, and perhaps not always the best, option, alongside housing, welfare, counselling, and other social tools—and the civil law, to which we now turn.[118]

4.4 THE CIVIL LAW AND DOMESTIC VIOLENCE: INTRODUCTION

By contrast with criminal justice, the principal purpose of civil law is protection of the victim rather than punishment of the abuser.[119] Civil law remedies are dispensed on a lower

---

[111] CPS (2006), (2014b).
[112] CPS (2014a), (2014b).
[113] HMCS, HO, and CPS (2008).
[114] Kelly (1999), Hoyle (1998); cf Hester (2005).
[115] Women's Aid (2005); Robinson and Cook (2006).
[116] HO (2005), para 21.
[117] CPS (2009).
[118] Hoyle and Sanders (2000); Robinson and Cook (2006); cf Lewis, R. (2004).
[119] Law Com (1992), para 2.11.

standard of proof[120] in private hearings. The general civil law is available to victims of domestic violence. However, the laws of tort and property both in theory and in practice have only limited ability to protect victims from abuse and provide them with a safe and secure home, particularly for applicants who have no right to occupy the family home.[121] The civil courts' enforcement powers are also limited, and civil procedures different from those of the family courts.[122] Courts issuing injunctions at common law cannot attach powers of arrest to apprehend defendants in the event of breach.

These limitations of the general law contributed to calls for reform to deal directly and appropriately with domestic violence as a specific social problem. The Women's Aid Movement in the 1970s brought domestic violence to public attention,[123] prompting a Parliamentary Select Committee to examine the matter.[124] Two important statutes designed to improve protection of victims were enacted: the Domestic Violence and Matrimonial Proceedings Act 1976 and the Domestic Proceedings and Magistrates' Courts Act 1978.[125] These created special statutory remedies for spouses and cohabitants: non-molestation orders and 'ouster' orders regulating occupation of the matrimonial and quasi-matrimonial home,[126] and empowered family courts to attach powers of arrest to their orders.

However, the implementation of these Acts was heavily criticized. The schemes were complex, incoherent, and of limited scope. Different levels of court had powers to make different types of order between different categories of party under different criteria.[127] Judges were reluctant to make ouster orders and to attach the new powers of arrest.[128] Solicitors, the gatekeepers of the civil justice system, discouraged many victims from taking action.[129] The Law Commission re-examined the civil law remedies,[130] and, after one abortive effort in 1995,[131] Parliament passed the FLA 1996, amended by the Domestic Violence, Crime and Victims Act 2004 (DVCVA 2004). Meanwhile, the general law of tort was expanded by the PHA 1997, regardless of the nature of the relationship (if any) between the parties. But the main focus of this chapter is the FLA 1996.

4.5 THE FAMILY LAW ACT 1996, PART IV

The FLA 1996 is the principal source of family law remedies for domestic violence. It provides two types of order: non-molestation orders and occupation orders. These respectively protect victims from physical and other forms of abuse, and offer victims security in

---

120 Cf Edwards and Halpern (1991), 98–9.

121 Law Com (1992), paras 3.13–3.17; see 3.7.1 and 7.8.3 on the position of non-owners.

122 Ibid, para 3.15.

123 Pizzey (1974).

124 Select Committee (1975).

125 Note also the Homeless Persons Act 1977: housing law and domestic violence are discussed in a supplement to this chapter on the Online Resource Centre.

126 See also the Matrimonial Homes Act 1967: 3.7.1–3.7.2.

127 Law Com (1992), paras 1.2, 2.21–2.30.

128 McCann (1985); Edwards (1989).

129 See Burton (2008a), ch 3.

130 Law Com (1992).

131 See Cretney (1998), 2.

the home. The Act's procedures and enforcement provisions are designed for the domestic violence context.

4.5.1 THE RANGE OF RELATIONSHIPS COVERED: 'ASSOCIATED PERSONS'

Unlike the 1970s legislation, which applied only to spouses and cohabitants, the FLA 1996 protects a wide range of 'associated persons'. Non-molestation orders are equally available to all categories of associated person. But the nature of the parties' relationship affects whether occupation orders are available at all, and, if so, the basis on which they are made. This makes identifying the type of 'associated person' relationship between the parties, particularly whether or not they are 'cohabiting', crucial.

Family Law Act 1996

62 Meaning of . . . 'associated persons'

(3) For the purposes of this Part, a person is associated with another person if—

    (a)   they are or have been married to each other;

    (aa)   they are or have been civil partners of each other;

    (b)   they are cohabitants or former cohabitants;

    (c)   they live or have lived in the same household, otherwise than merely by reason of one of them being the other's employee, tenant, lodger or boarder;

    (d)   they are relatives;

    (e)   they have agreed to marry one another (whether or not that agreement has been terminated);[132]

    (eza)   they have entered into a civil partnership agreement (as defined by section 73 of the Civil Partnership Act 2004) (whether or not that agreement has been terminated);[133]

    (ea)   they have or have had an intimate personal relationship with each other which is or was of significant duration;

    (f)   in relation to any child, they are both persons falling within subsection (4); or

    (g)   they are parties to the same family proceedings (other than proceedings under this Part).

(4) A person falls within this subsection in relation to a child if—

    (a)   he is a parent of the child; or

    (b)   he has or has had parental responsibility for the child.

One other individual whom the courts must consider, and in favour of whom a non-molestation order may be made, is the 'relevant child'. A child is any person under the age of 18;[134] a 'relevant child' is defined in s 62(2) as:

---

[132] See FLA 1996, ss 44, 42(4), 33(2).
[133] Ibid, ss 44, 42(4ZA), 33(2A).
[134] Ibid, s 63.

(a) any child who is living with or might reasonably be expected to live with either party to the proceedings;

(b) any child in relation to whom an order under the...Adoption and Children Act 2002 or the Children Act 1989 is in question in the proceedings; and

(c) any other child whose interests the court considers relevant.

Some of the terms used in s 62(3) to define 'associated person' themselves require definition. 'Relatives' is broadly defined:

63 Interpretation of Part IV

(1) In this Part—...

'relative', in relation to a person, means–

(a) the father, mother, stepfather, stepmother, son, daughter, stepson, stepdaughter, grandmother, grandfather, grandson, granddaughter of that person or of that person's spouse, former spouse, civil partner or former civil partner, or

(b) the brother, sister, uncle, aunt, niece, nephew or first cousin (whether of the full blood or of the half blood or by marriage or civil partnership) of that person or of that person's spouse, former spouse, civil partner or former civil partner,

and includes, in relation to a person who is cohabiting or has cohabited with another person, any person who would fall within paragraph (a) or (b) if the parties were married to each other or were civil partners of each other.

The definition of 'cohabitant' adopts the marriage analogy commonly used to identify such relationships:

62 Meaning of 'cohabitants'...

(1) For the purposes of this Part—

(a) 'cohabitants' are two persons who are neither married to each other nor civil partners of each other but are living together as husband and wife or as if they were civil partners; and

(b) 'cohabit' and 'former cohabitants' are to be read accordingly, but the latter expression does not include cohabitants who have subsequently married each other or become civil partners of each other.

We considered the general interpretation of this and similar concepts in chapter 2, but here we examine the courts' approach in the context of the FLA 1996.

The leading case is *G v F (Non-Molestation Order: Jurisdiction)*,[135] the facts of which demonstrate the difficulties of categorizing relationships which are neither formalized in marriage or civil partnership nor based on blood relationship. When the parties' sexual relationship began, they had separate homes but spent most nights together. Two years later, they discussed marriage. When the man had to sell his home, he deposited the proceeds in the parties' joint account and most of that money was spent improving the woman's house,

---

135 [2000] Fam 186.

the anticipated matrimonial home. Initially, they continued to maintain separate homes, the man renting a flat, but he subsequently moved in with her. Only weeks later, he moved out, withdrawing his funds (and his name) from the joint account. The relationship ended shortly afterwards, having lasted just over three years. The woman sought a non-molestation order, arguing that the parties were 'associated persons' by virtue of being 'cohabitants'. The magistrates concluded that the parties were not 'cohabitants', applying the 'six signposts' from social security law.[136] Their decision was overturned:

G v F (Non-Molestation Order: Jurisdiction) [2000] Fam 186, 196

WALL J:

In my judgment, the evidence is sufficient to support the proposition that the applicant and the respondent were cohabitants within the meaning of section 62(3)(b) of the Act. Of the "admirable signposts" set out in *Crake v Supplementary Benefits Commission*..., three are present. There was plainly a sexual relationship; there is evidence that they lived in the same household, and there was substantial evidence... that the applicant and the respondent operated a joint account into which the proceeds of sale of the respondent's previous property were paid. The respondent asserts also that money was spent on the applicant's property. In my judgment... the respondent's evidence taken as a whole is sufficient to demonstrate that he and the applicant were, indeed, cohabitants. It is true that the relationship was not stable, although in one way or another it appears to have lasted [for three years]...

[T]he message of this case...is that where domestic violence is concerned, [courts] should give the statute a purposive construction and not decline jurisdiction, unless the facts of the case...are plainly incapable of being brought within the statute. Part IV of the Family Law Act 1996 is designed to provide swift and accessible protective remedies to persons of both sexes who are the victims of domestic violence, provided they fall within the criteria laid down by section 62. It would, I think, be most unfortunate if section 62(3) were narrowly construed so as to exclude borderline cases where swift and effective protection for the victims of domestic violence is required. This case is, after all, about jurisdiction; it is not about the merits. If on a full inquiry the applicant is not entitled on the merits to the relief she seeks, she will not get it.

This case signals a generous approach to the interpretation and application of the 'associated person' categories. But the relationship must still fall within one of those categories. When the case was decided, had the parties not been regarded as 'cohabitants' or as having 'lived in the same household' (s 62(3)(c)), and if the court had found no evidence of an agreement to marry, that would have been the end of it; the applicant would have been left to the general law, including the PHA 1997. However, s 62(3)(ea) now brings non-cohabiting but intimate relationships within the Act. It is unclear how 'intimate personal relationship of significant duration' will be interpreted. The Explanatory Notes to the amending Act state that:

It will be for the court to decide on whether the relationship meets these criteria. This covers a long-standing relationship which may, or may not, be a sexual relationship, but which is an intimate and personal one. It does not include long-term platonic friends or "one-night stands".[137]

---

[136] *Crake v Supplementary Benefits Commission* [1982] 1 All ER 498; see 2.8.2.
[137] Explanatory Notes to the Domestic Violence, Crime and Victims Act 2004, para 24.

It might be interpreted to include relationships between vulnerable adults and non-residential carers, as well as sexual relationships.[138]

The concept of 'associated person' is the widest concept of 'family' in law. Some of the relationships necessarily involve the parties living together: paras (b) and (c). Many others do not: paras (a), (aa), and (d)–(g). Some involve blood or other legal relationship: paras (a), (aa), (d), (e), (eza), and (f). Some categories turn on factual rather than legal factors: paras (b), (c), and (ea). The definition of 'relative' is particularly wide, not least given the inclusion of 'in-law' relationships based on cohabitation rather than marriage or civil partnership. However, there are arguable omissions. For example, the Act does not protect new partners of those whose former partners resent the new relationship and direct their frustration at the new partner. Although undoubtedly 'associated' with the person on the third side of this love triangle, the new and ex-partners have no associated person relationship with each other so no order can be made between them; resort must be had to the general law.

The rationale for the Act's initial coverage was described by the Law Commission, on whose recommendations the Act is largely based:

Law Commission, *Family Law: Domestic Violence and Occupation of the Family Home,* Law Com No 207 (London: HMSO, 1992)

3.17 The need to extend the scope of injunctions in family proceedings beyond the scope of the law of tort has been explained by reference to the special nature of family relationships. When problems arise in close family relationships, the strength of emotions involved can cause unique reactions which may at times be irrational or obsessive. Whilst these reactions may most commonly arise between spouses and cohabitants, they can also occur in many other close relationships which give rise to similar stresses and strains and in which the people concerned will often continue to be involved with one another...

3.19...As we see it, there are three possible choices:

(i) [to extend the law to include *former* spouses and cohabitants, and possibly people with parental responsibility for the same child];

(ii) to remove all restrictions on applicants and throw the jurisdiction open to all as has been done in some Australian states; or

(iii) to choose a middle path and widen the range of applicants to include anyone who is associated with the respondent by virtue of a family relationship or something closely akin to such a relationship.

On reflection, we have concluded that the third is the best alternative. The first might exclude people who have a genuine need for protection in circumstances which most people would regard as a family relationship in the broader sense... [for example] people who lived together on a long term basis whether as close friends or in a homosexual relationship. We think that the second alternative goes too far. We do not think it is appropriate that this jurisdiction should be available to resolve issues such as disputes between neighbours, harassment of tenants by landlords or cases of sexual harassment in the workplace. Here there is no domestic or family relationship to justify special remedies or procedures and resort should properly be had to the remedies provided under property or employment law. Family relationships can, however, be appropriately distinguished from other forms of association. In practice,

---

138 Such as *JM v CZ* [2014] EWHC 1125.

many of the same considerations apply to them as to married or cohabiting couples. Thus the proximity of the parties often gives unique opportunities for molestation and abuse to continue; the heightened emotions of all concerned give rise to a particular need for sensitivity and flexibility in the law; there is frequently a possibility that the relationship will carry on for the foreseeable future; and there is in most cases the likelihood that they will share a common budget, making financial remedies inappropriate.

On the face of it, the breadth of 'associated person' exemplifies 'functional' approaches to family, extending family law beyond its traditional confines. But critics are concerned about diluting the concept of domestic violence as a phenomenon particularly experienced by women in marital and cohabiting relationships:[139]

H. Reece, 'The End of Domestic Violence', (2006) 69 *Modern Law Review* 770, 782, 790–1

Contrary to the Law Commission's rendition, the four features of proximity, heightened emotions, the possibility of a continuing relationship and the likelihood of a common budget had little to do with special protection against domestic violence for wives and female heterosexual cohabitants. Such protection was primarily associated with proximity only when coupled with isolation, controlled rather than heightened emotions in the context of unequal power, barriers to leaving the relationship rather than the mere possibility that the relationship would continue and financial dependence as opposed to a common budget...

In many contexts, there are progressive aspects to expanding our understanding of the concept of family. But if the boundaries of the family are also treated as the boundaries for enhanced protection against domestic violence then in this context expanding the boundaries of the family is regressive, because expansion endangers the specificity of the category of domestic violence. Domestic violence used to be treated as a problem specific to the traditional marital or quasi-marital union, caused partly by women's inferior position within the home and family, 'but now the violence between those in close emotional relationships is seen as a wider problem, being restricted not just to wives nor even to domestic situations'. Intimacy is replacing inequality as the touchstone of domestic violence law...

Feminist commentators have commonly interpreted the state's *apparent* concern to protect women from domestic violence as motivated by a *real* concern to preserve the status of the traditional nuclear family. They have suggested that the state achieves this objective by minimising domestic violence in various connected ways. The claim that domestic violence occurs in every type of relationship seems to be the reverse of minimising domestic violence, but in fact it is another method, because if domestic violence occurs everywhere then domestic violence occurs nowhere...

However, structural inequalities can be found outside spousal and quasi-spousal relationships.[140]

---

[139] See also views collected by HMIC (2014), 36–7, re the breadth of the government's definition of domestic abuse

[140] Burton (2008), 19.

4.5.2 NON-MOLESTATION ORDERS

Family Law Act 1996

42 Non-molestation orders

(1) In this Part a "non-molestation order" means an order containing either or both of the following provisions—

(a) provision prohibiting a person ("the respondent") from molesting another person who is associated with the respondent;

(b) provision prohibiting the respondent from molesting a relevant child.

...

(5) In deciding whether to exercise its powers under this section and, if so, in what manner, the court shall have regard to all the circumstances including the need to secure the health, safety and well-being—

(a) of the applicant...; and

(b) of any relevant child.

(6) A non-molestation order may be expressed so as to refer to molestation in general, to particular acts of molestation, or to both.

(7) A non-molestation order may be made for a specified period or until further order....

63 Interpretation of Part IV...

'health' includes physical or mental health

Non-molestation orders are available on the same basis between all categories of associated person. They can be obtained by an applicant for the protection of a relevant child without also protecting the applicant herself.[141] In this section, we examine the concept of molestation and the court's discretion to make an order. We address issues relating to applications for and enforcement of non-molestation orders below.

Molestation

'Molestation' is undefined, as the Law Commission recommended.[142] It is implicit from s 42(5) that molestation may prejudice the health, safety, and well-being of victims. Case law provides further guidance, cases decided under the 1970s legislation remaining instructive. Neither actual nor threatened violence is required.[143] Molestation, or its close cousin harassment, 'includes within it an element of intent, intent to cause distress or harm'.[144]

---

[141] *Re A (Non-Molestation Proceedings by a Child)* [2009] NI Fam 22.
[142] Law Com (1992), para 3.1.
[143] *Horner v Horner* [1982] Fam 90, 93.
[144] *Johnson v Walton* [1990] 1 FLR 350, 352.

In *Vaughan v Vaughan*,[145] after the wife had successfully petitioned for divorce on grounds of cruelty,[146] the husband followed her between home and workplace, despite constant requests not to and his knowing that she was frightened of him owing to his past violence; her health consequently suffered. The husband claimed that he simply wanted to ask her to see and speak to him. The court resorted to the dictionary:

Vaughan v Vaughan [1973] 1 WLR 1159 (CA), 1162–3, 1165

DAVIES LJ:

There are two different definitions...: "meddle hostilely or injuriously"..."to cause trouble to; to vex, annoy, put to inconvenience". It seems to me that, in the circumstances of this case, taking into consideration this lady's health, of which the husband was to some degree aware, and taking into consideration the fact that he knew she was frightened of him, molestation has plainly been made out in the present case.

STEPHENSON LJ:

"Molest" is a wide, plain word which I should be reluctant to define or paraphrase. If I had to find one synonym for it, I should select "pester". Whether communication amounts to molestation is a question of fact and degree. I have no doubt that what this man did...to this woman, with the knowledge of his past conduct which both of them had, was to molest her.

Molestation was also found in *Horner v Horner*, where the husband accosted the wife in public, repeatedly telephoned the school where she worked and made demeaning comments about her to the school secretary, and displayed abusive posters about her on the school railings in sight of her pupils' parents.[147] The aggrieved ex-partner in *Johnson v Walton* was alleged to have instigated articles about the parties' relationship in the press illustrated by semi-nude photographs of the applicant. The court held that, if done with intent to distress the applicant, this was clearly molestation.[148]

Molestation was not found in *C v C (Non-Molestation Order: Jurisdiction)*. The respondent instigated articles in the press critical of the applicant's behaviour during the marriage and previous relationships. The applicant was concerned that these articles would damage his reputation, and that of the charity for which he worked, with adverse financial consequences.

C v C (Non-Molestation Order: Jurisdiction) [1998] Fam 70, 73

STEPHEN BROWN P:

[Counsel for the husband] submits that although in this case there is no direct threat to, or "molestation" of [the husband] in the physical sense by his former wife, nor is there any direct interference by telephoning or by sending letters or communications directly to [him],

---

[145] [1973] 1 WLR 1159.
[146] This was one of the grounds for divorce before 1969: 5.4.
[147] [1982] Fam 90.
[148] [1990] 1 FLR 350.

nevertheless, on the basis of the fact that she has given information to newspaper reporters resulting in the publication of...articles [offensive to him] in the newspapers, that amounts to conduct which would justify the application of section 42...

...[T]here is no legal definition of "molestation"....It is a matter that has to be considered in relation to the particular facts of particular cases. It implies some quite deliberate conduct that is aimed at a high degree of harassment of the other party, so as to justify the intervention of the court. There is no direct communication...between the former wife and the former husband in this case...

Endeavours have been made...to widen the concept of molestation. It does not include enforcing an invasion of privacy per se. There has to be some conduct which clearly harasses and affects the applicant to such a degree that the intervention of the court is called for.

It is further significant that in section 42(5) the [FLA 1996] provides...[The judge then sets out s 42(5)]

It is significant...that section 42 is to be found in Part IV of the Family Law Act 1996, which is concerned with the general topic of domestic violence. In this particular case the marriage between these parties has been finally ended; they are quite separate individuals, and the material complained of is some alleged revelations by the former wife of what she regarded as her former husband's misconduct. In my judgment it comes nowhere near molestation as envisaged by section 42...I believe this is a misconceived endeavour to seek to impose what might be called a gagging order...It is not "molestation" as much as damage to his reputation with which [the husband] is concerned.

Stephen Brown P did not refer to *Johnson v Walton*, which had been cited in argument. It seems hard to distinguish these cases, unless the wife in *C v C (Non-Molestation Order: Jurisdiction)* did not intend to cause distress. The suggestion that the FLA 1996 is unsuited to cases between ex-partners overlooks the reality that much abuse arises on relationship breakdown; 'associated person' is defined specifically to include former relationships. However, it is important to police the limits of molestation. 'Molestation' should be broadly defined in order to attract remedies where the general law cannot. But in some situations there are good reasons why the general law—of harassment, defamation, privacy, breach of confidence, and so forth—denies a remedy, for example to protect freedom of expression where there is no sufficiently strong countervailing interest to be protected.[149] The mere fact that the parties have a relationship falling within the scope of the FLA 1996 does not invariably warrant overriding limitations of the general law.

The suggestion that 'molestation' includes a mental element—an 'intent to cause distress or harm'; 'deliberate' conduct 'aimed' to harass—raises interesting questions where the behaviour derives from mental health problems over which the respondent has no control. The wife's mental illness in *Banks v Banks*[150] caused her to abuse her husband verbally and physically. A non-molestation order was refused. It is unclear whether that was because the wife's behaviour could not be regarded as molestation, or because the judge simply exercised his discretion to refuse an order.[151]

149 Art 10 ECHR; cf *R v Debnath* [2005] EWCA Crim 3472; *Hipgrave v Jones* [2004] EWHC 2901, [21].
150 [1999] 1 FLR 726.
151 Cf the less serious mental condition of the respondent in *Gull v Gull* [2007] EWCA Civ 900.

Research suggests that it is harder to get non-molestation orders where the abuse is not physical.[152] The criminalization of breach of non-molestation orders (discussed below) may further raise the bar if courts are reluctant to expose respondents to the risk of criminal sanction.[153]

The court's discretion

Even if molestation is found, the court has a discretion whether to make an order and, if so, in what terms and for what duration. Section 42(5), set out above, lists some factors to which the court must have regard, but, as usual, it is directed to have regard to 'all the circumstances'.

Banks v Banks arguably supplies an example of the judge simply declining to make an order. *Chechi v Bashir*[154] provides another, rather unusual example. A family feud over land led to cross-allegations of violence to person and property, some attracting criminal charges. One brother sought a non-molestation order against other relatives. The trial judge refused an order on various grounds, two of which were upheld. But the Court of Appeal rejected his first objection: that the existence of the family relationship was incidental to the dispute. Butler-Sloss LJ noted the Law Commission's rationale for covering a wide range of relationships, remarking that:

> Although the dispute between the parties is in origin about land, it is patently overlaid and magnified by the family relationship...The depth of the dissension and the violent reaction on both sides must owe a great deal to family ill-feeling.[155]

Where molestation is found, the court will usually grant an order. The order may prohibit 'molestation' generally, the use or threat of violence, intimidation, pestering, and harassment, or the encouragement or instruction of anyone else to do so. It may include specific prohibitions: for example, from coming within a defined area around the applicant's home or workplace;[156] from telephoning, writing to, or otherwise communicating with the applicant, except for defined purposes or through defined routes, for example through a solicitor. The potentially criminal consequences of breach may now encourage courts to draft orders more tightly, to try to avoid any ambiguity about the conduct prohibited: it is better to prohibit specific behaviour rather than 'molestation' generally.[157] Where the parties are parents, the order may need to be carefully drafted to facilitate contact between the respondent and child, without jeopardizing the applicant's safety and well-being.[158] The principal objective is to protect victims whose rights under Articles 3 and 8 (or even Article 2) are at stake. But, whilst those rights under Articles 2 and 3 are unqualified, the court must otherwise be careful not to impose any greater restriction on respondents' rights under Articles 8 and 10 than is necessary

---

[152] Burton et al (2002), discussed by Burton (2008a) from 39.
[153] Cf *Majrowski v Guy's and St Thomas' NHS Trust* [2005] EWCA Civ 251, [83]; Noon (2008).
[154] [1999] 2 FLR 489.
[155] Ibid, 493.
[156] E.g. *Re T (A Child: Murdered Parent)* [2011] EWHC 1185, [79].
[157] See Platt et al (2009), 6.69.
[158] See 11.7.2.

and proportionate to the objective of protecting applicants' and any relevant children's rights and interests.[159]

Orders may last for a specified time or indefinitely. In *Re B-J (Power of Arrest)*, a non-molestation order was made indefinitely in the context of ongoing disputes regarding contact between the respondent father and the parties' ten-year-old child, C, who no longer wanted contact with her father and his new family:

In re B-J (A Child) (Non-Molestation Order: Power of Arrest) [2001] Fam 415 (CA)

HALE LJ:

28 [Counsel for the father] argues that an indefinite order was wrong. [He relied on *M v W (Non-Molestation Order: Duration)* [2000] 1 FLR 107, in which Cazalet J said]:

"...the object of non-molestation orders is designed to give a breathing space for the parties and, unless there are exceptional or unusual circumstances, it should be for a specified period of time. If this latter course is not taken then many years may go by and a party may find himself or herself suddenly arrested under an order made many years previously when much has since changed and the original order has lost the substance of its main purpose."

29 In my judgment, that passage both underestimates the range of purposes for which non-molestation orders were designed and contains a serious fallacy. A non-molestation order is indeed sometimes, even often, designed to give a breathing space after which the tensions between the parties may settle down so that it is no longer needed. But in other cases it may be appropriate for a much longer period, and it is not helpful to oblige the courts to consider whether such cases are "exceptional" or "unusual". [The judge then set out s 42(5) and (7) and went on:]...

31 These provisions implemented the recommendations of the Law Commission [(1992) para 3.28]:

"...protection should be available when and for as long as it is needed. Fixed time limits are inevitably arbitrary and can restrict the courts' ability to react flexibly to problems arising within the family. In particular, it is important that non-molestation orders should...be capable of enduring beyond the end of a relationship, although in some cases, short term relief will be all that is necessary or desirable."

Earlier, the Commission had rejected the idea of a two-tier system of short- and long-term remedies, with different criteria, at para 2.43:

"The distinction between short and long term remedies certainly arises in practice...But this distinction does not always correspond to the requirements of particular categories of applicant and is not therefore a justification for requiring the courts to distinguish between short and long term orders in each case. Sometimes the need for a long term order may be apparent from the outset. Often, having solved the immediate problem the parties do not need to return....In principle the criteria upon which a decision is based should be appropriate to the nature of the remedy sought: the duration of the remedy is simply a matter of judgment according to the circumstances of the particular case."

...

---

[159] Cf *R v Secretary of State for the Home Department, ex parte Craven* [2001] EWHC Admin 850.

33 A non-molestation order rarely prohibits a person from doing something which would otherwise be completely unobjectionable. It is not usually appropriate to use or threaten violence, or to harass, pester or molest another person. There are obviously cases, of which this is one, in which the continuing feelings between parties who separated long ago are such that a long-term or indefinite order is justified. The order in this case was made for the benefit of C as much as for her mother: it is to C's benefit that her mother is not threatened or pestered.

Since a non-molestation order 'rarely prohibits...something...completely unobjectionable', it is unlikely that long-term orders, simply by reason of their duration, violate respondents' rights under the ECHR. But indefinite orders are less likely to be made if they prohibit everyday activity.[160]

4.5.3 OCCUPATION ORDERS

Occupation orders can be made in relation to a dwelling-house in which the parties have lived or do live together as their home or, in some cases, in which they intended to live together.[161] They can perform two basic functions: (i) confer a personal right to occupy on someone otherwise not entitled to (under contract or property law), or enforce a pre-existing right to occupy; and (ii) exclude from the property another party, or otherwise regulate that party's occupation of the home, even if that party is the sole owner. They can support non-molestation orders, physically separating the parties and so reducing opportunities for abuse.

The rules governing occupation orders are more complex than those for non-molestation orders, since the FLA 1996, departing to some extent from the Law Commission's scheme, differentiates sharply between different categories of applicant, depending on their marital status and entitlement to occupy the property. In consequence, five sections deal with five types of case:

- s 33: associated persons (of any category), where the applicant is 'entitled to occupy' the property or has 'home rights' under s 30;[162]
- s 35: former spouses or former civil partners, where the applicant is not entitled to occupy the property, but the respondent is entitled;
- s 36: cohabitants or former cohabitants, where the applicant is not entitled to occupy the property, but the respondent is entitled;
- s 37: current and former spouses and civil partners, where neither party is entitled to occupy the property;
- s 38: cohabitants or former cohabitants, where neither party is entitled to occupy the property.

Entitlement to occupy for these purposes flows from 'a beneficial estate or interest or contract or...any enactment giving...the right to remain in occupation'.[163]

---

[160] James (2007).
[161] FLA 1996, ss 33, 35–6; contrast ss 37–8. Law Com (1992), para 4.4.
[162] See 3.7.1.
[163] E.g. FLA 1996, s 33(1)(a)(i).

Figure 4.1 Features of different categories of occupation order

We discussed the relevant law for these purposes in chapter 3. Beneficial owners or co-owners of property, contractual licensees, and statutory tenants all have relevant rights to occupy and so fall within s 33. So do spouses and civil partners (and some ex-spouses/civil partners) with home rights under s 30. Those occupying merely under a bare licence are not entitled for these purposes, so may only apply under ss 35–8.

Figures 4.1 and 4.2 provide an overview of the five categories. Features on these diagrams such as the 'balance of harm' test are explained in the text below.

It is important to select the appropriate section, as each:

- has different qualifying criteria;
- confers different powers regarding the types of order that can be made and the terms that can be included;
- allows for different maximum duration of orders;
- requires the court to consider different factors in exercising its discretion to make an order, to define the order's terms, and to determine its duration;
- in some cases, constrains the court's discretion by *requiring* it to make an order in certain circumstances, under the 'balance of harm test'.

A hierarchy of property-ownership and family forms emerges from the occupation order scheme. The best protection is enjoyed by applicants who are entitled to occupy the property, whatever sort of 'associated person' relationship they have with the respondent, and to spouses/civil partners with home rights under s 30. Applicants who are not entitled to occupy the property are ranked according to the type of relationship they have with the respondent: spouses and civil partners (current and former) secure the better treatment under ss 35 and 37; cohabitants (current and former) have a lesser measure of protection under ss 36 and 38. Other non-entitled

Figure 4.2 FLA 1996: choosing the right section

individuals—such as adult children living at home with their parents, other 'home-sharers', even if they are related—cannot apply for an occupation order at all. They are left to remedies under the general law discussed in chapter 7 and non-molestation orders.

We next examine the components of each section closely: qualifying criteria; terms that the order may contain and its potential duration; and factors bearing on the court's discretion. Having set out the framework for each section, we examine a key feature of the FLA 1996 scheme: the balance of harm test.

Section 33: entitled applicants—associated persons

The qualifying criteria

Section 33 is in one sense the widest category, covering any type of 'associated person' relationship. However, that generosity is limited since this section is available only to applicants who are entitled to occupy the property or who have s 30 home rights over it. The order must relate to a dwelling that has been or is or has at any time been intended by both parties to be their home together.[164]

The order's terms and duration

Because the applicant already has the right to occupy the property, the order need not confer such a right, though the court might be asked to declare that the right exists.[165] The applicant may have been ejected from the property by the respondent or otherwise wish to enforce his or her right to occupy. The applicant may also want the respondent's occupation to be regulated, even terminated.

Family Law Act 1996, s 33

...

(3) An order under this section may—

   (a) enforce the applicant's entitlement to remain in occupation as against the [respondent];

   (b) require the respondent to permit the applicant to enter and remain in the dwelling-house or part of the dwelling-house;

   (c) regulate the occupation of the dwelling-house by either or both parties;

   (d) if the respondent is entitled [to occupy, as defined above p 244], prohibit, suspend or restrict the exercise by him of his right to occupy the dwelling-house;

   (e) if the respondent has home rights in relation to the dwelling-house and the applicant is the other spouse or civil partner, restrict or terminate those rights;

   (f) require the respondent to leave the dwelling-house or part of the dwelling-house; or

   (g) exclude the respondent from a defined area in which the dwelling-house is included.

...

(10) An order under this section may, in so far as it has continuing effect, be made for a specified period, or until the occurrence of a specified event or until further order.

It has been suggested that the power under para (c) to regulate the parties' occupation can govern specific details of their use of the home: allowing each party exclusive use of one bedroom; prohibiting communication by notes; requiring decision-making via consultation and not by dictation; requiring each party to give the other advance notice of intended overnight absences.[166] An exclusion zone can be obtained under para (g), but is also commonly made through non-molestation orders.[167] Given the criminal consequences of breaching the latter type of order, careful consideration should be given before using a non-molestation order to create an exclusion zone.[168]

---

[164] Ibid, s 33(1).
[165] Ibid, s 33(4).
[166] *G v G (Occupation Order)* [2000] 3 FCR 53, 59.
[167] *Re T (A Child: Murdered Parent)* [2011] EWHC 1185.
[168] Soni (2007).

The court's discretion to make s 33 orders and the balance of harm

The court's discretion is guided by a statutory checklist and constrained by the 'balance of harm' test.

Family Law Act 1996, s 33

...

(6) In deciding whether to exercise its powers under subsection (3) and (if so) in what manner, the court shall have regard to all the circumstances including—

    (a) the housing needs and housing resources of each of the parties and of any relevant child;

    (b) the financial resources of each of the parties;

    (c) the likely effect of any order, or of any decision by the court not to exercise its powers under subsection (3)...on the health, safety or well-being of the parties and of any relevant child; and

    (d) the conduct of the parties in relation to each other and otherwise.

(7) If it appears to the court that the applicant or any relevant child is likely to suffer significant harm attributable to conduct of the respondent if an order under this section containing one or more of the provisions mentioned in subsection (3) is *not* made, the court *shall make* the order *unless* it appears to it that—

    (a) the respondent or any relevant child is likely to suffer significant harm if the order *is* made; and

    (b) the harm likely to be suffered by the respondent or child in that event is as great as, or greater than, the harm attributable to conduct of the respondent which is likely to be suffered by the applicant or child if the order is not made. [emphasis added]...

The effect of the balance of harm test in subsection (7) is that where the applicant 'wins' that test, the court has *no* discretion as to *whether* to make an order, but retains discretion regarding the order's precise terms and duration. In *Chalmers v Johns*, it was said that the court should first check whether the test in subsection (7) was met, before addressing the subsection (6) factors. If the test in (7) is satisfied, the court knows it must make an order. If not, it has a broad discretion under (6).[169] This suggests that subsection (6) has no function unless and until that balance of harm test has been applied. If the applicant wins the test, subsection (6) simply guides the court's decision as to the terms and duration of the order; if the applicant loses, subsection (6) helps the court to decide whether nevertheless to make an order, and (if so) in what terms and for how long. However, the balance of harm test cannot be conducted in a vacuum. Assessing likely harm may require an examination of the subsection (6) factors, such as the parties' housing resources. It is also clear that an application may be made where there is no question of the balance of harm test being satisfied in favour of the applicant, but an occupation order is nevertheless desirable.[170]

---

[169] [1999] 2 FCR 110, 114.
[170] *Grubb v Grubb* [2009] EWCA Civ 976; *Dolan v Corby* [2011] EWCA Civ 1664.

Section 35: non-entitled former spouse or civil partner; entitled respondent

The qualifying criteria

Section 35 applies to former spouses and civil partners where the respondent is entitled to occupy but the applicant need not be.[171] It applies only to *former* spouses and civil partners because *current* spouses or civil partners of respondents who are entitled to occupy the property enjoy home rights under s 30, and so fall within s 33. Since home rights ordinarily terminate on divorce, such individuals may require an alternative basis on which to seek occupation orders: hence s 35. The order must relate to a dwelling that has been or is or has at any time been intended by both parties to be their home together.[172]

The order's terms and duration

Section 35 cases involve non-entitled applicants and entitled respondents. Unlike applicants under s 33, these applicants have no right to be in the property themselves, never mind a right to exclude the entitled party. So, if any order is made at all, it must first confer on the applicant a right to occupy. Different subsections apply according to the applicant's situation at the date of the hearing:

Family Law Act 1996, s 35

. . .

(3) If the applicant is in occupation, an order under this section must contain provision—

   (a) giving the applicant the right not to be evicted or excluded from the dwelling-house or any part of it by the respondent for the period specified in the order; and

   (b) prohibiting the respondent from evicting or excluding the applicant during that period.

(4) If the applicant is not in occupation, an order under this section must contain provision—

   (a) giving the applicant the right to enter into and occupy the dwelling-house for the period specified in the order; and

   (b) requiring the respondent to permit the exercise of that right. . . .

If the court decides to make an order in those terms, it additionally has the power under s 35(5) to regulate the respondent's occupation of the property. Its powers here match those under paras (c), (d), (f), and (g) of s 33(3), set out above. The duration of any order made under s 35 is limited to six months, but it may be extended on one or more unlimited occasions for further specified periods not exceeding six months each.[173]

---

171 Note s 35(11)–(12) and equivalent provisions in s 36 allow applicants to use these sections without prejudicing any future claim they might wish to make regarding their entitlement to occupy and a consequent s 33 application.

172 FLA 1996, s 35(1).

173 Ibid, s 35(10).

The court's discretion to make s 35 orders and the balance of harm

There are potentially two stages to any case under s 35: first, the court must consider whether to make an order giving the applicant a personal right to occupy the property for the order's duration; if it does that, the court must then consider whether to attach a provision regulating the respondent's occupation. Different considerations apply at each stage. Subsection (6) sets out the criteria for the first stage, determining whether it is appropriate to give a right to occupy to the non-entitled former spouse or civil partner:

Family Law Act 1996, s 35

...

(6) In deciding whether to make an order under this section containing provision of the kind mentioned in subsection (3) or (4) and (if so) in what manner, the court shall have regard to all the circumstances including—

  (a) the housing needs and housing resources of each of the parties and of any relevant child;

  (b) the financial resources of each of the parties;

  (c) the likely effect of any order, or of any decision by the court not to exercise its powers under subsection (3) or (4), on the health, safety or well-being of the parties and of any relevant child;

  (d) the conduct of the parties in relation to each other and otherwise;

  (e) the length of time that has elapsed since the parties ceased to live together;

  (f) the length of time that has elapsed since the marriage or civil partnership was dissolved or annulled; and

  (g) the existence of any pending proceedings between the parties—

    (i) for an order under section 23...or 24 of the Matrimonial Causes Act 1973 (property adjustment orders in connection with divorce proceedings, etc.);

    (ia) for a property adjustment order under Part 2 of Schedule 5 to the Civil Partnership Act 2004;[174]

    (ii) for an order under paragraph 1(2)(d) or (e) of Schedule 1 to the Children Act 1989 (orders for financial relief against parents);[175] or

    (iii) relating to the legal or beneficial ownership of the dwelling-house.[176]...

If the parties separated and divorced years ago, the case for giving the ex-spouse the right to occupy a dwelling that had been intended to be, but in the event never was, the matrimonial home is not obviously strong. However, orders will sometimes be appropriate, in particular where the children's needs require it. *S v F (Occupation Order)*[177] provides an interesting example in a non-violent case. The parties had divorced and both remarried. Their teenage children lived with the mother in the former matrimonial home. She

---

[174] See 7.3.2.
[175] See 6.5.1.
[176] See 3.4 and 7.8.3.
[177] [2000] 3 FCR 365.

decided to move to Somerset, without consulting the children or the father, then living in Malaysia. The son insisted on staying in London to complete his education. The mother (it might be said) effectively abandoned him, and he went to live with an aunt. The father applied for an occupation order to provide a home for his son in the former matrimonial home. He also sought financial provision from the mother under the Matrimonial Causes Act 1973 (MCA 1973); those proceedings were pending at the time of the occupation order application:

S v F (Occupation Order) [2000] 3 FCR 365 (Fam Div), 372

JUDGE CRYAN:

I must have regard to the length of separation, seven years, and the time since [the divorce], five years, and take those factors into account.... They are long periods and are together factors which have caused me to pause. But it seems to me that I have to see the timescale in the context of a continuing common parental responsibility and the use to which this property is put. It was still the children's home until they went to [Malaysia this summer].

I must also have regard to the present applications for ancillary relief.

Balancing all these [and other] factors I take the view that I should make an order permitting the father to return to the property forthwith for a period of six months, or until the ancillary relief proceedings between the parties have been resolved, whichever is the shorter.

Turning to the second stage, the court may then be invited to regulate the respondent's occupation by making provision under s 35(5). From this point, the case proceeds as under s 33: the court must first apply the balance of harm test in s 35(8). As in s 33, if the applicant wins that test, provision regulating the respondent's occupation *must* be included, leaving the court with discretion only as to the order's particular terms and duration. Again, as in s 33, should the applicant *not* win the test, the court retains a discretion to make provision regulating the respondent's occupation. Wherever the court has a discretion, it must have particular regard to paras (a)–(e) of s 35(6).[178]

Section 36: non-entitled current or former cohabitant; entitled respondent

The qualifying criteria

Like s 35, this section is available between applicants who are not entitled to occupy the property and respondents who are.[179] It too is limited to a particular class of 'associated person': current and former cohabitants. The order must relate to a dwelling that has been or is or has at any time been intended by both parties to be their home together.[180]

The order's terms and duration

As under s 35, cases under s 36 have two potential stages: first, securing the applicant's occupation; and secondly, regulating the respondent's occupation. The types of order

---

178 FLA 1996, s 35(7).
179 See n 171.
180 FLA 1996, s 36(1).

that may be made are the same as under s 35. However, the duration of s 36 orders differs: in the first instance, it may be made for a period not exceeding six months, but only *one* extension (again of up to six months) is permitted.[181]

The court's discretion to make s 36 orders and the balance of harm

The two-stage pattern for orders under s 36 means that again there are different sets of criteria for the two stages. The subsection (6) criteria for the first stage—giving the applicant the right to occupy—are different in some respects from those applying under s 35:

Family Law Act 1996, s 36

...

(6) In deciding whether to make an order under this section containing provision of the kind mentioned in subsection (3) or (4) and (if so) in what manner, the court shall have regard to all the circumstances including—

(a) the housing needs and housing resources of each of the parties and of any relevant child;

(b) the financial resources of each of the parties;

(c) the likely effect of any order, or of any decision by the court not to exercise its powers under subsection (3) or (4), on the health, safety or well-being of the parties and of any relevant child;

(d) the conduct of the parties in relation to each other and otherwise;

(e) the nature of the parties' relationship and in particular the level of commitment involved in it;

(f) the length of time during which they have cohabited;

(g) whether there are or have been any children who are children of both parties or for whom both parties have or have had parental responsibility;

(h) the length of time that has elapsed since the parties ceased to live together; and

(i) the existence of any pending proceedings between the parties—

(i) for an order under paragraph 1(2)(d) or (e) of Schedule 1 of the Children Act 1989 (orders for financial relief against parents);[182] or

(ii) relating to the legal or beneficial ownership of the dwelling-house.[183] ...

At the second stage—regulating the respondent's occupation—there is another major difference between this section and ss 33 and 35. In those sections, the balance of harm can *require* the court to include provision regulating the respondent's occupation. By contrast, under s 36(7) and (8), the court is directed only to 'have regard to' the balance of harm 'questions', along with the first four factors in subsection (6). So, the court must consider whether the applicant or any relevant child is likely to suffer

---

[181] Ibid, s 36(10).
[182] See 6.5.1.
[183] See 3.4 and 7.8.3.

significant harm attributable to the respondent's conduct if such provision is not made; and whether the respondent or any relevant child is likely to suffer significant harm if such provision is made; and it must ascertain which side of the balance weighs more heavily. But even if the applicant's likely harm is clearly greater than the respondent's, the court is not obliged to regulate the respondent's occupation; it retains full discretion.

Sections 37 and 38: current and former spouses, civil partners, and cohabitants, where neither party is entitled to occupy

The qualifying criteria

Both sections deal with cases where *neither* party is entitled to occupy the property in relation to which the order is sought. They may, for example, be living by personal licence in a third party's property, or even be squatting. The sections are limited to current and former spouses and civil partners (s 37), and current and former cohabitants (s 38). The property must be or have been the matrimonial or civil partnership home (s 37) or one in which the parties cohabit or have cohabited (s 38); no order can be made in relation to property merely intended to be a joint home.[184]

The order's terms and duration

Since neither party is entitled to occupy the property, that limits the type of order available:

Family Law Act 1996, ss 37(3) and 38(3)

. . .

(3) An order under this section may—

    (a) require the respondent to permit the applicant to enter and remain in the dwelling-house or part of the dwelling-house;

    (b) regulate the occupation of the dwelling-house by either or both of the parties;

    (c) require the respondent to leave the dwelling-house or part of the dwelling-house; or

    (d) exclude the respondent from a defined area in which the dwelling-house is included. . . .

The duration of orders under each section differs as it does in ss 35 and 36: under s 37 (spouses and civil partners), an unlimited number of six-month orders may be made; under s 38 (cohabitants), only two six-month orders are available.[185]

The court's discretion in ss 37 and 38 and the balance of harm

Here too, the position largely corresponds with that under ss 35 and 36 respectively. Under s 37 (spouses and civil partners), the court is bound by the balance of harm test, and its remaining discretion is guided by the factors set out in s 33(6). Under s 38 (cohabitants), the

---

184 FLA 1996, ss 37(1) and 38(1).
185 Ibid, ss 37(5) and 38(6).

court must merely have regard to the balance of harm 'questions' and a checklist matching that in s 33(6).[186]

Ancillary orders under s 40

Section 40 empowers the court to attach additional provisions dealing with incidental matters on making an occupation order under ss 33, 35, and 36 (only):

Family Law Act 1996, s 40

(1) The court may on, or at any time after, making an occupation order under section 33, 35 or 36—

   (a) impose on either party obligations as to—

      (i) the repair and maintenance of the dwelling-house; or

      (ii) the discharge of rent, mortgage payments or other outgoings affecting the dwelling-house;

   (b) order a party occupying the dwelling-house or any part of it (including a party who is entitled to do so [as defined above, p 244] to make periodical payments to the other party in respect of the accommodation, if the other party would (but for the order) be entitled to occupy the dwelling-house [as defined above];

   (c) grant either party possession or use of furniture or other contents of the dwelling-house;

   (d) order either party to take reasonable care of any furniture or other contents of the dwelling-house;

   (e) order either party to take reasonable steps to keep the dwelling-house and any furniture or other contents secure.

(2) In deciding whether and, if so, how to exercise its powers under this section, the court shall have regard to all the circumstances of the case including—

   (a) the financial needs and financial resources of the parties; and

   (b) the financial obligations which they have, or are likely to have in the foreseeable future, including financial obligations to each other and to any relevant child.

(3) An order under this section ceases to have effect when the occupation order to which it relates ceases to have effect.

To think that this appears to be rather petty detail would be to misunderstand the nature of domestic abuse:

H. Conway, 'Money and Domestic Violence—Escaping the *Nwogbe* Trap', (2002) 32 *Family Law* 61

The predominant feature of domestic violence is less physical assault than the exercise and maintenance of power held by one party over the other.... Often ill-treatment is manifested in a financial way, with the income and monetary arrangements for the family being in the

---

186 Ibid, s 38(4).

sole domain of one of the parties, thus leading to unacceptable levels of control over the life of the other partner.

It is a further feature of domestic violence that in many cases an abuser will be imaginative and vindictive in seeking ways around the law to continue his abuse. Unless orders are drafted carefully, using the ability to specify particular forms of behaviour as molestation, a level of abuse may continue, although it might not legally form the basis for a power of arrest being activated or a committal application being founded.

[Hence s 40, which was] partly intended to prevent the undermining of occupation orders by such actions that would make continued occupation of the home under an order either impossible (for example, because of repossession) or intolerable (for example, because the property is stripped of all the furniture).

We shall see at 4.6.1 that insofar as it involves ordering payment of outgoings to third parties (e.g. landlords, local authorities, etc), the effectiveness of s 40 is seriously limited by problems surrounding its enforcement.

The balance of harm test and questions

Under the 1970s legislation, judges appeared reluctant to take what they regarded as the 'Draconian step' of excluding respondents from their own homes. Lower courts initially held that occupation orders could not be made at all in favour of non-entitled cohabitants against their property-owning partners. The House of Lords in *Davis v Johnson*, by majority, overturned those decisions.[187] Lord Scarman's powerful speech emphasized the importance of ensuring that property rights should not be allowed to undermine the protection offered to victims whose fundamental rights to integrity and safety of the person were at stake, whether as a result of the property owner's violence or the risk of homelessness should an order not be made.[188] However, many courts continued to emphasize the 'Draconian' nature of occupation orders and the need for strong justification for ejecting property owners.[189] Even the House of Lords regarded occupation orders as a 'first aid' measure rather than a long-term solution.[190]

The balance of harm test and the corresponding 'questions' that apply to ss 36 and 38 were intended to ensure that applicants needing protection receive it. Research suggests that occupation orders are made more frequently than under the old legislation.[191]

Breaking the test into separate steps helps us to see more clearly what it involves and how it is 'won' or 'lost' in sections 33, 35, and 37. We examine next the key components of the test, indicated below in square brackets.

- Is the applicant or any relevant child [likely] to suffer [significant harm] [attributable to the respondent's conduct] if the relevant type of order is *not* made? If not, the test has not been satisfied, so the court is not *required* to make the order but may *choose* to do so.

---

[187] [1979] AC 264.

[188] Ibid, 348.

[189] Cases treating children's interests as the first consideration were overruled in *Richards v Richards* [1984] 1 AC 174; Burton (2008a), 35.

[190] *Davis v Johnson* [1979] AC 264, 343, and 349.

[191] Edwards (2001).

- If such harm is likely, is the respondent or any relevant child [likely] to suffer [significant harm] if the order *is* made? If not, the applicant wins by default and so the court must, under ss 33, 35, and 37, make an order.
- If such harm is likely, the court must weigh the respective harm on each side of the balance.
- If the harm on the applicant's side of the balance is *greater than* the harm on the respondent's side, then an order *must be made*.
- If the harm on the respondent's side is greater, *or if the scales are evenly balanced*, then the court is not obliged to make an order, but may choose to do so.

In ss 36 and 38 (applications by non-entitled cohabitants), the court simply asks these questions, but is never obliged to make an order, retaining full discretion.

'Significant harm'

The core concept, 'harm', is more serious than mere 'hardship':

Family Law Act 1996, s 63(1)

... "harm"—

(a) in relation to a person who has reached the age of eighteen years, means ill-treatment or the impairment of health; and

(b) in relation to a child, means ill-treatment or the impairment of health or development; ...

"development" means physical, intellectual, emotional, social or behavioural development; "health" includes physical or mental health; "ill-treatment" includes forms of ill-treatment which are not physical and, in relation to a child, includes sexual abuse ...

The harm must be 'significant', which is taken here, as in the context of child protection law, to mean 'considerable, noteworthy or substantial'.[192] Harm in relation to children can include emotional harm suffered as a result of non-violent but acrimonious verbal feuding between separating parents.[193]

Likely

The significant harm must be 'likely'. By analogy with child protection law, this does not mean that the harm must be 'more likely than not' to occur—a greater than 50 per cent chance. It is sufficient that there is a 'real possibility' of that harm occurring. But that prognosis must be based on facts that have themselves been proved on the balance of probabilities, and not on mere suspicions.[194] By contrast with child protection law, the test is concerned only with the likelihood of harm in the future. The fact that harm may have occurred in the past or present is irrelevant if it is unlikely to endure.

---

[192] *Chalmers v Johns* [1999] 2 FCR 110, 117, adopting *Humberside County Council v B* [1993] 1 FLR 257. See 12.5.3.

[193] *Re L* [2012] EWCA Civ 721, [26].

[194] *Re H and others (Minors) (Sexual Abuse: Standard of Proof)* [1996] AC 563.

It has been argued that this focus on the future and the courts' particular interpretation of the likelihood test in the FLA 1996 may deny remedies to worthy applicants. In *B v B (Occupation Order)*,[195] the respondent's serious violence caused the applicant to flee the parties' home with their baby. At the time of the application, they were safely (though unsatisfactorily) housed elsewhere. In asking whether the applicant and child were likely to suffer significant harm in the future, the court focused on their housing situation, not on the respondent's violence. Felicity Kaganas has criticized the court's approach: Parliament can hardly have intended that victims should be deprived of the protection of an occupation order by fleeing their home.[196] At what point should the likelihood of harm be assessed: the time of the hearing or some earlier point? Kaganas advocates an approach similar to that used for the threshold test in child protection cases,[197] whereby the court would ask whether significant harm was likely when the applicant took steps to protect herself, by calling the police, leaving the home, etc. Alternatively, she suggests that the courts should consider whether harm is likely should the applicant return home. Applicants otherwise face an invidious choice: they could remain in a violent home in order to satisfy the balance of harm test; or they could escape to safety, but thereby fail the test and so perhaps fail to secure an occupation order.

One further difficulty with the test is its hypothetical nature: the court must consider what is likely to happen should it make, or not make, an order. At that stage, the court does not know what precise terms any order that it might make would contain. For the test to make practical sense, the court should consider the harm in the light of specific possibilities. For example: what harm is the applicant likely to suffer if we do not regulate the respondent's occupation or, alternatively, suspend the respondent's right to occupy; and what harm is the respondent likely to suffer if we do make either sort of provision? In almost all cases, a non-molestation order will also be sought and made. The court will then have to predict how effective that order will be. If a non-molestation order has been made, will that stop the violence and remove any real possibility of further harm?

'Attributable to the conduct of the respondent'

A further limitation is that it must be shown that the likely harm on the applicant's side of the scales is 'attributable to the conduct of the respondent'. This makes the test harder for the applicant to win; it formed no part of the Law Commission's recommendations, which focused on need rather than conduct.[198] What sort of link between the conduct and the harm is required?

The first question is whether it must be shown that the respondent *intends* to harm the applicant or relevant child. In *G v G (Occupation Order)*,[199] the parties were divorcing but still living in the same household with their children. The wife sought an occupation order. The strain between the parents was found by the judge to be causing significant harm to the wife and children, but was it attributable to the husband's conduct? The first instance judge thought not. His remarks could describe the ending of many relationships:

---

195 [1999] 2 FCR 251.
196 Kaganas (1999a), 201.
197 Ibid; Children Act 1989 (CA 1989), s 31(2); see 12.5.3.
198 Law Com (1992), para 4.34.
199 [2000] 3 FCR 53.

G v G (Occupation Order: Conduct) [2000] 3 FCR 53 (CA), 57

Quoting the first instance judge:

... [T]o a great extent the conduct of the father is ... unintentional. I do not believe ... that this is a father who sets out to be unpleasant ... [M]uch of the present strain and worry is the result of the meeting of two apparently incompatible personalities, and that the great differences between them are aggravated by this awful no-man's land in which they have now been living for a year. ...

... [I]n all the circumstances of this thoroughly difficult case, bearing in mind the length of the marriage [15 years] and that much of the difficulties are to do with character and temperament and other factors unavoidable on an adult relationship breakdown, I am not persuaded that it would be appropriate ... to make an occupation order.

On appeal, the wife successfully argued that unintended conduct and resulting harm should be considered:

THORPE LJ:

13. ... Plainly, the word attributable on its proper construction could not dissociate the tension that the judge found evident in the complaint from the conduct by the husband that he had found proved. Plainly, the court's concentration must be upon the effect of conduct rather than on the intention of the doer. Whether misconduct is intentional or unintentional is not the question. An applicant under s 33 is entitled to protection from unjustifiable conduct that causes harm to her or the children of the family. The effect is what the judge must assess. Tiny wounds may be inflicted with great malice: great blows may be struck unintentionally. Of course, lack of intent might support a plea of accidental injury. But where something is not done accidentally it is not to be dismissed on the grounds that it was not done deliberately.

In *Re L (Children)*, the judge had found that the applicant could not satisfy the test because *both* parents were responsible for the harm being caused to the children by the acrimony accompanying the end of their relationship, a conclusion not challenged on appeal.[200]

Secondly, 'attributable' implies some causal relationship between conduct and harm. But how far can the 'chain of causation' stretch before harm can no longer be attributed to the respondent's conduct?

F. Kaganas, '*B v B (Occupation Order)* and *Chalmers v Johns:* Occupation Orders under the Family Law Act 1996', (1999) 11 *Child and Family Law Quarterly* 193, 198

Section 33(7) does not prevent the courts, in assessing the harm to a respondent or relevant child, from taking cognisance of factors such as their housing needs and resources; the provision does not limit the types of harm that are relevant here and it appears that any harm that would be likely to stem from the making of an order can be taken into account. Indeed, in explaining the operation of the balance of harm test, the Law Commission, while suggesting that this would not normally constitute significant harm, specifically cited as

---

200 [2012] EWCA Civ 721, [18].

an example of potential hardship to a respondent difficulty of finding alternative accommodation. But doubts have been expressed as to whether considerations of this nature can be taken into account when determining whether there is a risk of significant harm to the applicant or child. In relation to the applicant or child, subsection 7 provides that it is only the likelihood of harm attributable to the conduct of the respondent that can be considered. It has accordingly been suggested that the harm suffered by an applicant or child as a result of having to flee to overcrowded or unsuitable accommodation because of the respondent's violence may be attributable to the inadequate provision of refuges and housing rather than to the conduct of the respondent. Against this, however, it could be argued that such harm can be attributed to both factors; although it is not the respondent's conduct that renders the available accommodation unsatisfactory, it is his conduct that forces the applicant and the child to occupy it. On this reasoning, the harm suffered by the applicant and child as a result of the move whether caused by inhabiting a dangerous environment or, say, by the disruption for a child of having to change schools, would fall within the purview of subsection 7.

This was the approach taken in *B v B (Occupation Order)*.[201] Having fled the family home owing to the husband's violence, the wife and baby were housed by the local authority in temporary, extremely poor, bed and breakfast accommodation: mother and child occupied one room with a shower and shared a bed; 12 other people lived in the house, with only one kitchen, one toilet, and two bathrooms; there was no garden, but a park ten minutes away. The judge found that, particularly in winter when poor weather would confine them to their room, this accommodation was likely significantly to impair the baby's health and development. The appeal court agreed that this was attributable to the father's conduct.

Illustrations from the case law: applying the balance of harm test and statutory discretion

The appellate courts have been reluctant to make even short-term orders excluding a violent party who is entitled to occupy the property, particularly where there are ongoing family proceedings with implications for the home's future occupation. In *Chalmers v Johns*, the parties had had a long relationship, were joint tenants of their home, and had a child aged seven. Each party had assaulted the other over the years, causing no more than minor injury. The mother, in particular, had problems with alcohol. The father had called out the police on three previous occasions in the last year, but although the mother had been arrested each time, she had not been charged.

Chalmers v Johns [1999] 2 FCR 110 (CA), 112, 115–16

THORPE LJ:

The final call out came on 5 May. On this occasion it was the mother who called the police. On this occasion she was observed to have minor injury. On this occasion the police seemed to have taken a more robust line, for they arrested the father and charged him with common assault. Apparently he was bailed on condition that he vacated the family home pending trial.

---

[201] [1999] 2 FCR 251.

That trial took place on 5 June. The justices acquitted the father and so he was free to return to the family home.

The mother's emotional reaction is not established but can be imagined. She exercised her right to leave, taking the youngest child with her and sadly that has to date constituted a final separation. I say that because it does seem very sad that this couple after 25 years of shared family life and obvious attachment each to the other should have determined, at least on one side, that a continuing relationship is impossible.

There have been a welter of applications to the court following the mother's departure. On 11 June she applied for a non-molestation and an occupation order. On 19 June the father applied for a residence order and an occupation order. On 13 July she applied for a transfer of tenancy and for a residence order. Those applications have been before the court either for directions, or for conciliation or for interlocutory application. . . . [At one hearing an order was made allowing regular staying contact between the youngest child and the father in the family home.]

When with her mother [that child, A] is in unsatisfactory temporary council accommodation, which is said to be a mile and a half from school. The family home is about ten minutes' walk from the school . . .

The Children Act 1989 order determining which parent A would live with had not yet been made. The instant appeal had been brought by the father against an interim occupation order excluding him from the family home and allowing the mother to return with the daughter. Thorpe LJ overturned the judge's finding that the balance of harm test was satisfied, and turned to the exercise of the discretion. He remarked that this was 'a very slight' case as domestic violence cases go, such that it did not fall within the scope of the balance of harm test at all. That left the question whether to make an order to the court's discretion. The fact that the Children Act hearing was just a month away was considered highly relevant:

On that occasion the court will have before it all the issues and principally which of these two parents, if they have to remain separate, should have the primary responsibility for A's care; which of the two, if they must be separate, should have the sole tenancy of the family home; and whether there should be orders of a more permanent character under the Family Law Act 1996. . . . As a matter of generality, . . . a court should be cautious to make a definitive order at an interlocutory stage with a final hearing only six or seven weeks distant. The gravity of an order requiring a respondent to vacate the family home, an order overriding proprietary rights, was recognised in cases under the [1970s legislation] and a string of authorities in this court emphasise the draconian nature of such an order, and that it should be restricted to exceptional cases. . . . [T]he wider statutory provisions contained in the Family Law Act [do not] obliterate that authority. The order remains draconian, particularly in the perception of the respondent. It remains an order that overrides proprietary rights and it seems to me that it is an order that is only justified in exceptional circumstances. Of course there will be cases where the character of the violence or the risk of violence and the harm to the victim or the risk of harm to the victim is such that the draconian order must be made, must be made immediately, and must be made at the earliest interlocutory stage. But I simply do not see this case on its facts approaching anywhere near that category. Conventionally the court has given careful consideration to the control of domestic disharmony by the imposition of [non-molestation] orders before resorting to the draconian order. It is to be noted that in the history of this case, there is clear evidence of such judicial management having proved highly effective . . .

It may have been difficult to satisfy the balance of harm test on these facts, and the violence was being controlled by non-molestation orders. But there is something to be said for enabling the parties to live apart pending the final hearing and so removing the tension that would otherwise exist (even if non-molestation orders are made). An order would also have enabled the mother and daughter to return to the family home and so closer to the child's school. Kaganas considers that Thorpe LJ's focus on violence (specifically) and property rights undermines Parliament's intention to emphasize the broader interests of victims and children and to give the courts power to achieve 'sensible' solutions to the problems associated with relationship breakdown.[202]

G v G (Occupation Order)[203] is open to similar criticism. There had been no violence, but the husband's conduct and the tense atmosphere over the divorce were making the home miserable, particularly for the children. Again the court refused an interim order pending the final hearing of the child arrangements and financial applications: those proceedings had been accelerated, the husband would be away on business much of the time, and the judge had prescribed detailed rules regarding the parties' occupation of the property and their behaviour towards each other until the hearing. The judge considered that 'the friction between the parties was only the product of their incompatible personalities and the heightened tensions that any family has to live with whilst the process of divorce and separation is current'.[204]

The reluctance to use occupation orders as a matter of course on relationship breakdown was also shown in another case:

Re Y (Children) (Occupation Order) [2000] 2 FCR 470 (CA), 478, 480

SEDLEY LJ:

The purpose of an occupation order, however large its grounds may be, is not to break matrimonial deadlocks by evicting one of the parties ... To use the occupation order as a weapon in domestic warfare is wholly inappropriate. Parliament has made provision for it as a last resort in an intolerable situation, not as a move in a game of matrimonial chess.[205]

By contrast, *B v B (Occupation Order)*,[206] aspects of which we have already considered, was an unusual case in which an order was withheld despite serious violence, and illustrates the importance of housing law to occupation order cases. The wife and baby had fled to temporary bed and breakfast accommodation following serious violence by the husband against the wife. He remained in the home with his six-year-old son from a previous marriage. Having fled the home because of domestic violence, the wife was entitled to permanent rehousing by the local authority, as someone having a 'priority need' for accommodation and not 'intentionally homeless'.[207] The husband would also have priority need by virtue of having his son with him, but, if ejected from the home by an occupation order because of his violence, he would be regarded as intentionally homeless. As such, he and his son would

---

202 Kaganas (1999a), 197.
203 [2000] 3 FCR 53.
204 Ibid, 58.
205 [2000] 2 FCR 470, 478, and 480.
206 [1999] 2 FCR 251.
207 Housing Act 1996, s 193.

be given only temporary accommodation and advice and assistance in seeking a home.[208] Since the husband was caring full-time for his son, he could not afford to rent private sector accommodation:

B v B (Occupation Order) [1999] 2 FCR 251 (CA), 258–61

BUTLER-SLOSS LJ:

The respective housing needs of the parties are, in one sense, equal. Each needs two-bedroom accommodation provided by the local authority; but the 'housing resources', using that term to include the duty owed to each by the local authority, were quite different. Unsatisfactory as [the wife's] current temporary accommodation is, there is every prospect that in the reasonably foreseeable future she and [the baby] will be rehoused by the local authority in suitable two-bedroomed accommodation. There is no such prospect for [the husband and his son, MB] if the occupation order stands.

As we discussed above, the judge had found, and the Court of Appeal agreed, that the baby was likely to suffer significant harm in the poor accommodation and that this could be attributed to the respondent's conduct. However, the Court of Appeal also found that were the husband and his son evicted to allow the wife and baby to return home, the son would suffer significant harm: he had already suffered from his parents' separation and would have to change schools for the fifth time in 18 months, further impairing his social, educational, and emotional development.

In our judgment, and whilst in no sense under-estimating the difficulties and frustrations of living with and caring for a toddler in bed and breakfast accommodation, the essential security for a child of [the baby's] age is being where her mother is. Furthermore, . . . on the evidence, Mrs B's residence in bed and breakfast accommodation is likely to be temporary.

For MB the position is much more complex. His security depends not just on being in the care of his father, but on his other day-to-day support systems, of which his home and his school are plainly the most important . . .

In our judgment, if, on the facts of this case, the respective likelihoods of harm are weighed so far as the two children are concerned, the balance comes down clearly in favour of MB suffering the greater harm if an occupation order is made.

However, Butler-Sloss LJ emphasized that this was an unusual case, and that the husband should not think that the court condoned his behaviour:

. . . This case turns on its own very special facts. We have no sympathy for Mr B. He has behaved towards his wife in a manner which the judge found to be disgraceful. He treated her with serious domestic violence. Such conduct is unacceptable, and plainly falls to be considered within s 33(6)(d). Thus, were it not for the fact that he is caring for MB, and that MB has particular needs which at present outweigh those of [the baby], an occupation order would undoubtedly have been made.

---

208 Ibid, s 190.

The message of this case is emphatically *not* that fathers who treat their partners with domestic violence and cause them to leave home can expect to remain in occupation of the previously shared accommodation. Equally, such fathers should not think that an application for a residence order in relation to a child or children of the relationship will prevent occupation orders being made against them.

Part IV of the 1996 Act is designed to protect cohabitants from domestic violence and to secure their safe occupation of previously shared property. Nothing in this judgment should be read as weakening that objective.

Each case will, of course, turn on its facts. The critical, and highly unusual facts of this case are (1) that MB is not a child of the parties; (2) that there is no question of MB being cared for by Mrs B or anyone other than Mr B; (3) that Mr B is thus the full-time care of a child who is likely to suffer greater harm that the harm which will be suffered by Mrs B and [the baby] if an occupation order is made. It is the position of MB alone which...makes it inappropriate for an occupation order to be made on the facts of this case.

The courts are alert to what they regard as undue reliance on public housing entitlements. In *Re Y (Children) (Occupation Order)*,[209] it had been suggested that the local authority would find it easier to rehouse the wife than the husband, who had special accommodation needs associated with his disability. But the authority might find the wife intentionally homeless if she were evicted by an occupation order and regard the husband as having a greater need. In any event, the Court of Appeal held that an occupation order was not merited: the home was large enough to share, and mutual undertakings made by the parties seemed to have brought their behaviour under control. The local authority's ability to reduce tension by housing one party was not regarded as a reason either to require that party to leave or to refuse to make an order in favour of that party. If a home can safely be shared, or if the applicant for an occupation order can make a good case for evicting the other party, the court considered that it should not engineer an outcome that throws the party with stronger housing entitlements on the local authority. As Sedley LJ pithily put it, 'the purpose of an occupation order... [is not] to use publicly-funded emergency housing as a solution for domestic strife'.[210]

Difficult issues may arise where the parties' home is shared with the extended family, a situation not uncommon in certain minority ethnic communities. In a pre-FLA 1996 case, *Chaudhry v Chaudhry*, the judge declined to make an occupation order in favour of a blameless wife where the matrimonial home was owned by the husband and his father, and occupied by several members of his family who had allegedly attacked the wife. The judge found that requiring the husband to permit the wife to occupy the property would create a 'miserable situation which would lead to violence and...an impossible situation'. Divorce proceedings were in any event pending, and these would resolve the issue of the wife's accommodation in the longer term.[211] Under the FLA 1996, the court could now make non-molestation orders against the husband's family and, provided that the applicant had home rights or was otherwise entitled to occupy the property, could also make an occupation order against them under s 33. Were the balance of harm test satisfied, an occupation order would now have to be made. But where the applicant cannot invoke s 33, no occupation

---

[209] [2000] 2 FCR 481.
[210] Ibid, [30].
[211] [1987] 1 FLR 347.

order interfering with the wider family's occupation of the home would be possible: ss 35–8 only permit orders to be made against the applicant's spouse, civil partner, or cohabitant, not other 'associated persons'.

Mary Hayes long ago advocated a more expansive use of occupation orders:

M. Hayes, 'The Law Commission and the Family Home', (1990) 53 *Modern Law Review* 222, 223–4

...[I]t is a dangerous social policy which regulates the right to occupy the matrimonial home...only where there is proof of violence....Such a rigid approach could provoke a wife, desperate to live apart from her husband, but needing to stay in the family home (perhaps because of the children) either falsely to accuse him of violence or, in an extreme case, to precipitate an act of violence against herself...

[I]s it reasonable to expect spouses to remain together under the same roof, where one of them has decided that the marriage has broken down to such a degree that he or she wants the other spouse to leave the home and is prepared to apply to a court to achieve this purpose?...[W]here one spouse is in an economically weak position, and especially where housing must be provided for the children, that spouse...may not be able to separate from her husband without recourse to, and the assistance of, the courts.

The decisions in *G v G* and *Re Y* have also been criticized for underestimating the impact on children of living in a high-tension household.[212]

However, the tide may be turning, following a series of recent non-violent cases in which orders were made to alleviate pressures experienced by families on relationship breakdown. In *Grubb v Grubb*,[213] an occupation order was made in favour of the wife pending the resolution of the parties' financial issues following their stressful, defended divorce. Crucially, the husband had adequate alternative accommodation and the wife was prepared to vacate the family home as soon as he provided somewhere else for her to live. *Re L (Children)* provides a similar example, where it had been found that the children were likely to suffer significant emotional harm as a result of their parents' non-violent but acrimonious verbal feuding. The balance of harm test was not satisfied on the basis that both parents were responsible for the harm, but the court exercised its discretion to make an order excluding the husband from the home for just three months. That order was upheld on appeal:

Re L (Children) [2012] EWCA Civ 721

BLACK LJ:

21. There is nothing in section 33(6) to limit the discretion to make an occupation order to cases in which there has been physical violence. Even in section 33(7), which deals with "significant harm", physical harm is not required as we can see from the definition of harm in section 63..., which is wide. Section 33(6) requires the court to look at all the

---

[212] Choudhry and Herring (2010), 370.
[213] [2009] EWCA Civ 976.

circumstances and by section 33(6)(c) it is directed to include in these "the likely effect of any order, or of any decision by the court not to exercise its powers under subsection (3), on the health, safety or well-being of the parties and any relevant child." This is broadly drafted covering not just cases in which there is violence but also all manner of other problems that can occur when a relationship has run into difficulties. This court dealt with this issue recently in *Dolan v Corby*, paragraph 27 of which includes the following passage.

"No finding of violence had been made by the [judge] against Mr Corby and the [judge] had that in mind. I do not read *Chalmers v Johns* or *G v G* as saying that an exclusion order can only be made where there is violence or a threat of violence. That would be to put a gloss on the statute which would be inappropriate. *Chalmers v Johns* and *G v G* stress that it must be recognised that an order requiring a respondent to vacate the family home and overriding his property rights is a grave or draconian order and one which would only be justified in exceptional circumstances, but exceptional circumstances can take many forms and are not confined to violent behaviour on the part of the respondent or the threat of violence, and the important thing is for the judge to identify and weigh up all the relevant features of the case whatever their nature."

22. There is equally no authority establishing that a spouse can only be excluded from the home if reprehensible conduct on his or her behalf is found. It would be surprising if there were such an authority given the general terms of the relevant provisions of the Act and in particular the requirement of section 33(6) that there be consideration of all the circumstances.

Black LJ noted that the judge did not appear to have contemplated alternatives to exclusion, such as the parties being confined to separate areas of the large house, or—interestingly—an arrangement (facilitated by the husband's occasional absences) for a 'Box and Cox situation where the children lived in the house at all times but the parents alternated in the time they spent there with them'.[214] But the short-term order was upheld, such alternatives perhaps having already been ruled out by the parties as impractical.

In *Dolan v Corby*, the female partner was permitted to remain in the parties' rented home to the exclusion of the male partner under s 33 where there had been only verbal abuse, but the woman's greater vulnerability arising from her psychiatric condition made her less well able to find alternative accommodation.

Dolan v Corby [2011] EWCA Civ 1664

BLACK LJ:

28. Exercising discretion under Section 33(6) is not a matter of considering the behaviour of the parties and awarding occupation of the property in question to the one who has behaved less inappropriately. All the circumstances must be considered, of which conduct is only one. The end of the relationship between these parties had given rise to a situation in which the [judge] had no choice but to exclude one of them from the house as it was clearly unworkable for them both to live there together...

214 [2012] EWCA Civ 721, [30].

4.5.4 A HUMAN RIGHTS AUDIT OF THE OCCUPATION ORDER SCHEME

Unlawful discrimination contrary to Article 14?

A striking feature of the occupation order scheme is its differential treatment of different types of applicant. Can this be justified, or does it constitute discrimination contrary to Article 14 ECHR, in conjunction with Articles 2, 3, and 8? The Law Commission's original recommendations had distinguished between applicants by reference to their property entitlement, but not their marital status.[215] This was unacceptable to parliamentarians who feared that marriage would be undermined (apparently oblivious that cohabitants had been included in the legislation since the 1970s), and who forced the insertion of the distinctions between spouses (and now civil partners) and cohabitants. There are four key differences: (i) the applicability of the balance of harm test; (ii) the checklists; (iii) the duration of orders; and (iv) the fact that non-entitled individuals in other forms of 'associated person' relationship cannot apply at all.

The differences regarding the balance of harm and duration of orders in ss 35 and 36 seem hard to explain. The parties in s 35 made a formal legal commitment (now dissolved) to each other, which the s 36 cohabitants never have. That lack of legal commitment does not inhibit cohabitants applying under s 33, though there they are entitled to occupy the property, which s 36 applicants are not. Property entitlement is clearly important. That may explain the difference between ss 35 and 36: since the respondent is entitled to occupy and the applicant not, the applicant needs particular justification for invading the respondent's right, and the s 35 parties' (former) marital status arguably provides that. But protection of property rights cannot explain the difference between ss 37 and 38. Here both parties are non-entitled, so it is not obvious why spousal applicants should be in a better position than cohabitants. Section 36 requires the courts to examine the degree of commitment in the cohabitants' relationship when deciding whether to give the applicant a right to occupy.[216] But even marriage-like relationships of 20 years that easily clear that hurdle are still denied the balance of harm test available to the divorced applicant, even after a short marriage. Can it plausibly be argued that protection of the traditional family based on marriage provides sufficient justification for the different treatment of otherwise similarly situated victims of domestic violence? Bright-line rules distinguishing spouses/civil partners from others may be tenable in the welfare, fiscal, and financial context to signal the state's approval of formal commitment and so to attempt to encourage it. But it is not clear that such distinctions should be made where fundamental rights to personal security are at stake.[217]

The importance attached to property rights—and even to sex—is evident in the exclusion of non-entitled individuals in 'other' associated person relationships from the occupation order scheme. It is not clear (from a functional perspective) why the

---

[215] Law Com (1992), Part IV; spouses and cohabitants were treated identically, but the Law Commission did not extend occupation orders to 'other' non-entitled associated persons.

[216] FLA 1996, s 36(6)(e).

[217] See 2.8.2 on relevant human rights case law, none of it dealing with domestic violence.

existence of a relationship formalized by marriage or civil partnership or one that functions similarly (in sexual terms[218]) should be a prerequisite for non-entitled applicants to seek an occupation order, particularly where a principal aim is to secure protection from violence in the domestic sphere.[219] The standard requirement that the property be one that is, was, or was intended to be lived in by the parties together might be adequate justification. As Wall J emphasized in *G v F (Non-Molestation Order: Jurisdiction)*,[220] the courts can always refuse to make orders where the merits of individual cases are weak.

These features of the occupation order scheme may not withstand close scrutiny under Article 14. But, at least for those falling within the scope of the scheme, the *theoretical* difference of legal treatment may not yield very different outcomes in practice: that may cure any discrimination on the face of the legislation. The balance of harm issue does not become relevant in applications between cohabitants unless and until the court has made an order giving the applicant the right to occupy. In making that order under s 36, the court has determined that the parties' relationship is sufficiently serious that it should attract remedies of this nature. That being so, and if the balance of harm 'questions' are answered in the applicant's favour, it is hard to imagine a court then refusing to make such an order. The court could do nothing to overcome the different rules concerning the duration of orders for cohabitants, but it could at least ensure that an order was made.

The implications of Articles 2, 3, and 8 ECHR

Indeed, applicants' rights under Articles 2, 3, and 8 ECHR may limit the courts' discretion under the FLA scheme.[221] The conflict between victims' rights to personal protection and respondents' property rights has always been prominent in debates about the legal response to domestic violence. The ECHR provides a new framework within which the balance between the rights of victim and perpetrator must be struck, presaged by Lord Scarman's remarks in *Davis v Johnson*, described above.[222] As we noted at 4.2.4, where Article 2 or 3 applies, there is no balancing to be done: these rights are absolute—victim protection is paramount, and the state is under a duty to take reasonable steps to protect victims' rights. No case has yet addressed the implications of parties' Convention rights for occupation orders, but we can formulate the likely arguments.

Under the HRA 1998, s 6, the courts must act compatibly with parties' Convention rights. Choudhry and Herring argue that 'significant harm' in the balance of harm test should be found wherever the abuse or its impact on children in the household reaches the Article 3 threshold.[223] This would ensure that orders are made wherever, as in s 33, satisfaction of the balance of harm test mandates an order. However, it can further be argued that Articles 2 and 3 effectively require a court to exercise its discretion in

---

218 Cf 2.7.5 and 2.7.6 on the curious nature of civil partnership in this regard.
219 Though see Reece (2006).
220 [2000] Fam 186, extracted above.
221 See also Choudhry and Herring (2006a).
222 [1979] AC 264.
223 (2006b).

cohabitants' cases to make an order where not doing so might expose the applicant to a risk of death or ill-treatment bad enough to fall within Article 3.[224]

In less serious cases, Article 8 requires the courts to balance parties' competing rights: victims' rights to respect for family, private life, and home, in the form of their personal integrity and residential security (even in a home in which they have no property right, provided they have sufficient and continuing links with the property[225]); respondents' rights to respect for their home and to family life with their children; and children's competing rights to safety and a relationship with both parents. As in *B v B (Occupation Order)*, the rights of another child may also need to be considered.[226] In cases under s 36, the respondent's rights could be asserted as a legitimate reason for the court to decline to make an order or to limit its duration. However, wherever the applicant or any relevant child stands to suffer the greater harm, that should—as Lord Scarman argued as a matter of purely domestic law—arguably determine the balancing exercise under Article 8. As discussed above at 4.2.4, this argument may be reinforced by reference to Article 17, discounting the respondents' rights.

If these arguments are accepted, non-entitled cohabitants under ss 36 and 38 may find that the differences on the face of the statute rarely result in different treatment in practice, save in relation to the duration of orders.[227] Any incompatibility with the Convention may therefore largely be avoided. In light of these arguments, the Court of Appeal may have taken an inappropriately reserved starting point in suggesting that an occupation order will only be justified in 'exceptional' circumstances.[228]

4.5.5 APPLICATIONS, ORDERS, AND UNDERTAKINGS

The number of applications and orders made each year under the FLA 1996 has fluctuated over the years. In 2003, there were 30,986 applications for both types of order, and over 25,000 non-molestation orders and nearly 11,000 occupation orders were made. Numbers steadily declined over the following decade, but 2013 saw the first rise in numbers, with nearly 24,000 applications and 25,000 orders, of which around 22,300 were non-molestation orders.[229] Various factors may influence the number of applications in any year, aside from changes in the prevalence of domestic violence, including changes in the availability of public funding for legal proceedings and changes in the enforcement options available for non-molestation orders (discussed at 4.6.2 below). It seems likely that one key factor in the recent rise in applications is the importance of FLA 1996 orders as one of the keys for unlocking legal aid for all other types of private family law application.[230]

---

[224] Such a 'reading down' of the legislation would be possible under HRA 1998, s 3: *R (Friends Provident Life and Pensions Ltd) v Secretary of State for Transport, Local Government and the Regions* [2001] EWHC (Admin) 820. Cf Choudhry and Herring (2006b), 779–80, 783.

[225] *Harrow LBC v Qazi* [2003] UKHL 43.

[226] [1999] 2 FCR 251.

[227] A court cannot 'interpret' the duration provisions under the HRA 1998, s 3 to remove any limitation that was held incompatible with Art 2, 3, 8, or 14. A declaration of incompatibility would be required.

[228] *Chalmers v Johns* [1999] 2 FCR 110, extracted above, p 260.

[229] MOJ (2014a), table 2.7.

[230] Civil Legal Aid (Procedure) Regulations, SI 2012/3098, reg 33; Emmerson and Platt (2014).

Orders on application by one party or of the court's own motion

Usually, orders are made on the application of a qualifying 'associated person'. Leave is required for applications by children under 16 years old, which may only be granted if the court 'is satisfied that the child has sufficient understanding to make the proposed application'.[231] The more usual course, wherever possible, would be for an adult associated person to apply on the child's behalf.[232] However, the court can make a non-molestation order in someone's favour even though no application has been made, which is why more such orders are made than there are applications.

Family Law Act 1996, s 42

. . .

(2) The court may make a non-molestation order—. . .

   (b) if in any family proceedings to which the respondent is a party the court considers that the order should be made for the benefit of any other party to the proceedings or any relevant child even though no such application has been made. . . .

(4A) A court considering whether to make an occupation order shall also consider whether to exercise the power conferred by subsection (2)(b). . .

'Family proceedings'[233] encompass proceedings under the inherent jurisdiction and under various statutes including: the FLA 1996; proceedings for financial remedies on divorce;[234] private and public law proceedings in relation to children,[235] including (in this context) cases in which the court has made an emergency protection order in relation to a child with an exclusion requirement;[236] adoption cases;[237] and applications for parental orders in surrogacy cases.[238]

Third party applications?

Section 60 of the Act potentially allows both non-molestation orders and occupation orders to be made on the application of a third party. However, rules of court that would permit this have never been made for the FLA 1996 and there are no plans to do so, policy attention having shifted to criminal justice. Such applications are possible in cases of forced marriage[239] and new police powers under the Crime and Security Act 2010 to evict alleged perpetrators and apply for orders from the magistrates' court have similar effect and raise similar concerns. We discuss the general controversy surrounding such applications below at 4.7.

---

[231] FLA 1996, s 43(2): see 8.5.4.

[232] *Re A (Non-Molestation Proceedings by a Child)* [2009] NI Fam 22.

[233] FLA 1996, s 63.

[234] MCA 1973, Civil Partnership Act 2004 (CPA 2004), Schs 5–7, Domestic Proceedings and Magistrates' Court Act 1978 (DPMCA 1978).

[235] CA 1989, Pts I, II, and IV.

[236] Ibid, s 44A; FLA 1996, s 42(3).

[237] Adoption and Children Act 2002.

[238] Human Fertilisation and Embryology Act 2008, s 54.

[239] FLA 1996, s 63C.

Ex parte orders

Ordinarily, respondents must have at least two days' notice of proceedings. But cases involving domestic violence are often urgent. In 'exceptionally urgent' cases, where the victim's safety requires it,[240] the court must be able to provide immediate protection without the respondent being tipped off about the application. Orders can therefore be obtained without giving notice:

Family Law Act 1996, s 45

Ex parte orders

(1) The court may, in any case where it considers that it is just and convenient to do so, make an occupation order or a non-molestation order even though the respondent has not been given such notice of the proceedings as would otherwise be required by rules of court.

(2) In determining whether to exercise its powers under subsection (1), the court shall have regard to all the circumstances including—

    (a) any risk of significant harm to the applicant or a relevant child, attributable to conduct of the respondent, if the order is not made immediately

    (b) whether it is likely that the applicant will be deterred or prevented from pursuing the application if an order is not made immediately; and

    (c) whether there is reason to believe that the respondent is aware of the proceedings but is deliberately evading service and that the applicant or a relevant child will be seriously prejudiced by the delay involved [in commencing the proceedings].

(3) If the court makes an order by virtue of subsection (1) it must afford the respondent an opportunity to make representations relating to the order as soon as just and convenient at a full hearing [i.e. a hearing of which notice has been given to all parties in accordance with the rules of court]....

Many applications are made on an ex parte basis, but research suggests that *occupation* orders are particularly difficult to obtain ex parte.[241] These applications do have drawbacks:

Law Commission, *Family Law: Domestic Violence and Occupation of the Family Home*, Law Com No 207 (London: HMSO, 1992)

5.6 The danger of a misconceived or malicious application being granted or the risk of some other injustice being done to the respondent is inevitably greater where the court has only heard the applicant's side of the story and the respondent has had no opportunity to reply. Also, on ex parte applications, the judge has no opportunity to try to resolve the

---

240 *JM v CZ* [2014] EWHC 1125.
241 Barron (2002); Burton et al (2002).

parties' differences by agreed undertakings or otherwise to reduce the tension of the dispute. Equally, there is no opportunity to bring home the seriousness of the situation to the respondent and to underline the importance of complying with the order...

In many cases involving violence, 'reducing tension' is an inadequate response and an ex parte order will be appropriate.[242] But it is important that the procedure *as a whole* is fair to the respondent and complies with Article 6 ECHR. Compliance should be ensured by the fact that the legislation entitles the respondent to an inter partes hearing and to have an ex parte order set aside.[243] New practice guidance requires that ex parte orders be of fixed duration, normally no more than 14 days.[244]

Undertakings

Instead of making an order, courts can accept undertakings from one or both parties: a voluntary promise to the court, commonly to do what an order would otherwise have required. Before the FLA 1996, undertakings were popular amongst some applicants and professionals—and still are[245]—but their use is not uncontroversial:

A. Kewley, 'Pragmatism before Principle: The Limitations of Civil Law Remedies for the Victims of Domestic Violence', (1996) 18 *Journal of Social Welfare and Family Law* 1, 3–6

[An applicant] who accepts...an undertaking in lieu of a court injunction, will not have to testify in court, an experience which the evidence suggests many women would prefer to avoid if an alternative option is available to them.

Undertakings appear to be popular with judges and lawyers...because the practice of accepting them means that an expensive, protracted and difficult hearing of the case is avoided and that the practical effect—[with the exception of the power of arrest: see below]—is much the same as if an...order is granted in that breach of the undertaking may theoretically be punishable [as] contempt of court. Some practitioners consider that in some ways such undertakings are likely to be more effective than orders...because they are given freely and voluntarily by the respondent to the judge rather than to an estranged ex-partner and that, having been given to the court, are the more likely to be honoured, because the judge has the authority to punish any future non-compliance. It is apparent that domestic violence victims may sometimes be subject to considerable pressure from their lawyers to accept an undertaking instead of a court order because lawyers' training and practical experience are characterized by the need to avoid lengthy and expensive disputes if at all possible by a process of negotiation and compromise between the parties. Moreover, there is evidence that a complainant may be subject to pressure to accept an undertaking from the respondent even where there has been a breach of a previous undertaking or court order...and where the woman has understandable doubts about the probable effectiveness of accepting the undertaking offered to her....

---

[242] Kaganas (1999a), 196–7.
[243] See generally *JM v CZ* [2014] EWHC 1125 on the procedure for such cases.
[244] Practice Guidance (2014), though this guidance is currently being reviewed.
[245] Burton (2008a), 40.

It is one thing to accept an undertaking from the respondent instead of getting the vindication and protection of an order. But in some cases, the victim might even be required to give a 'cross-undertaking' in return:[246]

> [I]t is viewed by some courts as a 'sensible' or 'fair' way of keeping the domestic peace in that blame is not being attached to either party's conduct but that each of the parties undertakes to behave reasonably in the future....A victim of violence may feel understandably aggrieved in such a case where she infers that she is being held partly to blame for the abuse that she has had to endure.
>
> Finally, the acceptance of an undertaking denies the victim of violence a chance for the court formally to find fault and to condemn, through the granting of the injunction, the violence that has taken place....By giving an undertaking on a purely voluntary basis, the respondent has not been required to accept any responsibility for his or her actions nor has he or she been required to acknowledge having been culpable of any wrongdoing. In such circumstances, failure to obtain the required court order...may also leave the [victim] understandably disillusioned with the whole legal process and reluctant to seek to obtain legal redress if, as experience has shown, it is likely that the violence or harassment will be repeated in the future.

While an undertaking can be enforced as if it were a court order, it is not possible to attach a power of arrest to an undertaking. The court may be unable to accept an undertaking in lieu of an order for that reason, as we discuss in the next section.

4.6 ENFORCEMENT OF ORDERS UNDER THE FLA 1996

Research since the FLA 1996 came into force suggests that the family justice system has still failed victims in relation to enforcement.[247] The enforcement of non-molestation orders has controversially been reformed to bring the weight of the criminal justice system behind the family court. This creates the potential for family, criminal, and civil courts (e.g. under the PHA 1997) to have parallel jurisdiction in the same case.

4.6.1 OCCUPATION ORDERS

Breach of an occupation order is a contempt of court, exclusively a matter for the family court. There are two routes to arrest: either the applicant may return to court for a warrant; or the family court can attach a power of arrest to the original order. The latter power permits the police to arrest the respondent without returning to court for a warrant where the officer has reasonable cause to suspect a breach.[248] Where a warrant is sought, the court must be satisfied on evidence given under oath that there are reasonable grounds for believing that a breach has occurred.[249] Whether arrested under an original power of arrest or

---

[246] If a cross-undertaking is given, then the applicant will not be eligible for legal aid: cf SI 2012/3098, reg 33(2)(e).

[247] Barron (2002); Burton et al (2002); Humphreys and Thiara (2003).

[248] FLA 1996, s 47(6).

[249] Ibid, s 47(9).

pursuant to a warrant, respondents must be brought to court within 24 hours of arrest; either the matter is dealt with then, or the respondent is remanded or released on bail until a later hearing.[250]

It has been argued that since the court has no substantial power to penalize minors for contempt, it should not be able to attach powers of arrest to orders made against minors. This argument has been rejected in view of s 47's mandatory language and the functions of powers of arrest:

Re H (Respondent under 18: Power of Arrest) [2001] 1 FCR 370 (CA)

HALE LJ:

16. . . . [I]t is not the sole purpose of a power of arrest to provide a convenient short route to the court's power to commit for contempt of court. That is one of its purposes and a very helpful one, but it also has the purpose of taking the person concerned away from the scene. In a case such as this, the immediate object was to ensure that the young man did indeed leave the family home and that objective can readily be secured by a power of arrest.

Under the 1970s legislation, powers of arrest were rarely attached to orders,[251] but the FLA 1996 requires their use in certain situations:

Family Law Act 1996

47 Arrest for breach of order

. . .

(2) If—

    (a) the court makes an occupation order; and

    (b) it appears to the court that the respondent has used or threatened violence against the applicant or relevant child,

    it shall attach a power of arrest to one or more provisions of the order unless satisfied that in all the circumstances of the case the applicant or child will be adequately protected without such a power of arrest.

(3) Subsection (2) does not apply [to ex parte orders], but in such a case the court may attach a power of arrest to one or more provisions of the order if it appears to it—

    (a) that the respondent has used or threatened violence against the applicant or a relevant child; and

    (b) that there is a risk of significant harm to the applicant or child, attributable to conduct of the respondent, if the power of arrest is not attached to those provisions immediately. . . .

---

250 Ibid, s 47(7).
251 Law Com (1992), para 5.11.

Powers of arrest and undertakings

Since undertakings are voluntary, no power of arrest can be attached to them.[252] In order to ensure that a power of arrest is available wherever one would be appropriate, the court cannot accept an undertaking instead of making an occupation order if, were it to make an order, it would be obliged to attach a power of arrest.[253] Wherever courts consider accepting undertakings, they must therefore ensure that a power of arrest is unnecessary. Official data last reported for 2005 suggests that undertakings are accepted in only a minority of cases.[254] But the reliability of these figures depends on courts' record-keeping: often no formal record was made of undertakings prior to the FLA 1996.[255] The use of orders and undertakings has been found to vary regionally.[256]

Lawyers and courts must ensure that those needing the full protection of a court order are not left in a vulnerable position. It has often been observed that the effectiveness of legislation can be, and has been, undermined by the attitudes of those responsible for implementing it.[257] Nevertheless, some of the concerns expressed by Kewley[258] may be alleviated by the FLA 1996. For example, it is questionable whether a proper hearing can now be avoided, for without testing the evidence the court cannot decide—as it is required to—whether a power of arrest (and so an order) is necessary and so whether an undertaking may be lawfully accepted. Where a power of arrest is required, victims ought now to obtain a court order.

Duration of powers of arrest

Where a power of arrest is attached to an occupation order, the court must decide how long that power should last. The Act specifically provides that the power of arrest attached to an ex parte order may last a shorter period than the order itself[259] but says nothing about orders made at an inter partes hearing. Before the introduction of s 42A (discussed below), powers of arrest would very often be attached to non-molestation orders of indefinite duration. Is it necessary or might it be inappropriate for the power of arrest to be similarly unlimited in time? The Court of Appeal, mindful of respondents' rights, decided that powers of arrest can operate for a shorter period than the inter partes order to which they are attached:

In re B-J (A Child) (Non-Molestation Order: Power of Arrest) [2001] Fam 415 (CA)

HALE LJ:

43 There is nothing inherently incompatible between the mandatory duty contained in section 47(2) and [the flexibility of allowing powers of arrest shorter than the order to which they are attached]. The court would have to be satisfied that the victim would be adequately protected with only a shorter power of arrest. The cases in which the court could be satisfied

---

252 FLA 1996, s 46(2).
253 Ibid, s 46(3).
254 DCA (2006a), table 5.9.
255 Kewley (1996), 3.
256 Edwards (2001); Burton et al (2002).
257 Smart (1989), 164; Kewley (1996), 7.
258 Ibid, and extracted above, p 271.
259 FLA 1996, s 47(4).

of this might be difficult but are not impossible to imagine....The great variety of circumstances in which Part IV orders, especially perhaps occupation orders, may be required make this by no means impossible, although it may not be common. One thing, however, is clear from section 47(2): the criterion is whether or not the applicant or child will be adequately protected without the power of arrest, not whether its continued existence will be inconvenient for others.

44 Given the inherent difficulties of predicting the future, and in particular when people will be safe, however, it would usually be preferable to attach the power for the same time as the order. Once it can be shown that the victim will be adequately protected without it, or without a different power, the obvious course is to vary the order [under s 49] so as to remove the power of arrest or reduce its scope....

47...If there is a case in which an order is appropriate but the court is indeed satisfied that the victim will be adequately protected by a time-limited power of arrest, an order which gives a larger power of arrest without warrant might...be incompatible with Convention rights. The court would then have to read section 47(2) [under s 3 of the HRA 1998] so as to permit this.

49...In the context of the liberty of the subject, statutes are normally to be construed in such a way as to limit rather than enlarge the powers of the state. Powers of arrest for breach of the orders of a civil court are themselves unusual, although amply justified by the need effectively to secure the performance of the obligations contained in the order....[T]o require the court to attach a power of arrest for a longer period than the court is satisfied is required for the protection of victims is manifestly unjust to the respondent; it may also indirectly lead to injustice to the victims if the court is thereby deterred, either from making an order for the appropriate period, or from attaching a power of arrest....

Similar arguments may be made when deciding the *parts* of the order to which a power of arrest should be attached; a power necessary only for some types of breach should not be applied to the whole order.

Use of powers of arrest

Under earlier legislation, a power of arrest was attached to only one-third of all orders. The FLA 1996 has ensured that powers of arrest are more frequently attached. Edwards reported a considerable increase in the attachment of a power of arrest in 2001: they were made in 75 per cent of occupation order cases and, when the courts had the power to do so (see below), in 80 per cent of non-molestation order cases.[260] More recent data show a rapidly declining number of occupation orders, though a greater proportion of those orders that are made have powers of arrest attached.[261]

Enforcement of provisions ancillary to occupation orders under s 40

An important limitation on the courts' powers was exposed in *Nwogbe v Nwogbe*.[262] The court had made an occupation order with s 40 provisions requiring the respondent to pay the rent and other outgoings on the property from which he had been excluded.

---

260 Edwards (2001).
261 MOJ (2010a), table 2.9.
262 [2000] 2 FLR 744.

He failed to pay. The wife brought contempt proceedings. The Court of Appeal reluctantly found itself powerless. The maze of relevant statutes offers no way of enforcing payment of money to a third party in this context, whether by imprisonment or less serious measures, such as attachment of earnings. Without some other basis on which the respondent can be ordered to pay money directly to the applicant, who can then pass it on to the third party, this form of s 40 provision is useless. Where the parties are spouses or civil partners, the problem might be avoided by relying on the various matrimonial financial orders.[263] But cohabitants and other associated persons may have no such alternative. Parliament has yet to remedy this deficiency, despite strong criticism from the court.

4.6.2 NON-MOLESTATION ORDERS

Breach of non-molestation orders is no longer exclusively a matter for the family court which made them. The PHA 1997 introduced a novel combination of civil and criminal law for the enforcement of its injunctions against harassment that was replicated in a reform of the FLA 1996. This development raises controversial questions of policy and practice, in particular about the treatment of domestic violence as a public or private issue.

Criminalizing breach of non-molestation orders

The FLA 1996 was amended by the DVCVA 2004 to enhance, and dramatically alter, the enforcement of non-molestation orders. Non-molestation orders were originally enforced like occupation orders. Now, although breach of a non-molestation order is still a contempt of the family court which made it, that court cannot attach a power of arrest to its order (though a warrant can later be issued). Crucially, breach of a non-molestation order is now also a criminal offence:

Family Law Act 1996

42A Offence of breaching non-molestation order

(1) A person who without reasonable excuse[264] does anything that he is prohibited from doing by a non-molestation order is guilty of an offence.

(2) In the case of an [ex parte order], a person can be guilty of an offence under this section only in respect of conduct engaged in at a time when he was aware of the existence of the order.

(3) Where a person is convicted of an offence under this section in respect of any conduct, that conduct is not punishable as contempt of court.

(4) A person cannot be convicted of an offence under this section in respect of any conduct which has been punished as a contempt of court.

---

[263] See 7.3.

[264] The burden lies with the prosecution to prove there was no such excuse: *R v Richards* [2010] EWCA Crim 835; cf *R v Nicholson* [2006] EWCA Crim 1518 on the contents of the defence.

(5) A person guilty of an offence under this section is liable—

    (a) on conviction on indictment, to imprisonment for a term not exceeding five years, or a fine, or both; and

    (b) on summary conviction, to imprisonment for a term not exceeding twelve months, or a fine..., or both....

46 Undertakings...

(3A) The court shall not accept an undertaking...instead of making a non-molestation order in any case where it appears to the court that—

    (a) the respondent has used or threatened violence against the applicant or a relevant child; and

    (b) for the protection of the applicant or child it is necessary to make a non-molestation order so that any breach may be punishable under section 42A.

The Explanatory Notes accompanying the 2004 Act explained that the purpose of the reform was to permit police to arrest for breach of an order without needing a power of arrest to have been attached to the order or a warrant subsequently issued.[265] Victims therefore no longer need to rely on family courts deciding to attach a power of arrest to the order in order to secure the respondent's immediate arrest. The power to arrest a respondent endures for the lifetime of the order.

The CPS guidance states that the offence 'aims to place complainants at the heart of the criminal justice system' and so 'gives complainants a choice' about whether breach of a non-molestation order will be dealt with criminally or as a contempt of the family court.[266] It suggests that where the conduct which breached the non-molestation order was not otherwise criminal in nature, the public interest may be better served by leaving the matter to be dealt with by application from the victim to the family court, rather than by criminal prosecution. But the possibility of parallel criminal and civil (family) proceedings is also contemplated. Breach of an order may be prosecuted either for that specific offence only, for a substantive criminal offence (e.g. assault), or both. Whatever offence is charged, the fact that a court order has been breached should be regarded as an aggravating feature.[267] Where both breach of the order and a substantive offence are charged, consecutive sentences should be considered to reflect the seriousness of the conduct.[268] Sentencing guidelines also emphasize that since the purpose of the non-molestation order was to protect the victim from harm, the primary aim of sentencing should be achieving compliance with the order and protecting the victim.[269]

Evidently, the criminal justice system is only useful as an enforcement mechanism for family court orders if the police know about those orders' existence and their terms, particularly where the behaviour they proscribe would not otherwise constitute an offence. Since harassment is an offence under the PHA 1997, there may be few cases in which breaches of *non-molestation* orders will not, independently of the order, involve an offence. However, 'harassment' and 'molestation' are amorphous concepts: matters would be far clearer for the

---

265 Para 15.
266 CPS (2008).
267 Sentencing Guidelines Council (2006b), para 2.2.
268 Ibid, para 2.1.
269 Ibid, paras 3.3–3.4.

police if they knew what specific behaviour had been prohibited. Where a non-molestation order has been made and where the applicant has no lawyer representing her, the court is responsible for delivering the relevant documentation to the police on the applicant's request. Otherwise, the duty to notify the police formally rests with the applicant,[270] though internal guidance instructs court staff to send the police copies of orders in relation to which an arrest may be made.

The government strongly promoted criminalization, arguing that it brought several advantages:

Hansard, *Official Report*—Domestic Violence, Crime and Victims Bill Debates, Hansard HL Deb, cols GC237–8, 240, 19 January 2004

Baroness Scotland of Asthal, Minister of State:

There are a number of reasons why contempt of court is not a sufficient or effective sanction. Contempt of court is of course a very serious matter and has always been so. However, many victims with whom we have spoken have stressed to us the disdain in which the offender holds the non-molestation order—even where a power of arrest is attached to that order. We are concerned that the sanction for breach of a non-molestation order must bring home to the respondent the seriousness of that breach. That is why we wish to make breach a criminal offence. . . .

Making breach a criminal offence would also extend the range of sanctions available to the courts to punish the offender. Contempt of court limits the sanctions to imprisonment or fine. Where a breach is a criminal offence, the courts would also be able to impose the usual range of community sentences. Sections 189 and 190 of [the Criminal Justice Act 2003] provide that, on conviction, conditions can [in certain cases] be imposed to do with curfew, mental health, drug treatment, voluntary activities, residence and supervision. If the person does not comply with those conditions, a suspended sentence can take effect. . . .

That gives the court an opportunity to deal with the offending behaviour. Many partners who find themselves involved in domestic violence are in need of anger management, drug treatment and a whole series of other interventions that will inure to the benefit not only of that partner, but of partners who may come afterwards. . . . [In] the analysis of partners who kill, it is very unusual indeed if those persons have not had a series of partners whom they have abused on the way to the murder that they eventually commit. It is not simply the complainant on the day whom we have to protect, but all the other partners who may come afterwards. That should exercise our attention, because of the nature of domestic violence. . . .

. . . Some women do not wish to criminalise their husbands but wish to have the abuse stopped. It will be possible to continue to do that through the civil route. But we should also take on board that the very abusive nature of domestic violence often erodes the will of the woman, who may need the greater support offered by the criminal court as well as that of the civil court, and that an intervention of that nature may prove necessary.

Many have said that they have benefited from having a police officer come to the door to arrest and remove the assailant. The courts can apply those provisions with flexibility and speed. We do not accept that they will be longer drawn-out as a result of the procedures.

---

[270] Family Proceedings Rules 2010 (FPR 2010), SI 2010/2955, r 10.10.

We will be assisted greatly by the way in which case management is currently dealt with and the fact that the CPS is working very closely with the police and the courts to get together protocols so that we have a holistic approach to domestic violence.

Hansard HC Deb, Proceedings of Standing Committee E, col 45, 22 June 2004

The Parliamentary Under-Secretary of State for the Home Department, Paul Goggins MP:

[Introducing s 42A would involve] a rebalancing between civil and criminal in the system. That is entirely in keeping with the spirit of this legislation, which is to empower and protect the victim on the one hand while also sending out a very clear message that Parliament—and the country—regards with increasing seriousness crimes associated with domestic violence and intends the penalties to be heavy and the protection to be stronger. There may be some rebalancing, and that would be entirely right.

The meaning of 'rebalancing' here is somewhat unclear and its wisdom debatable. The reforms tend to push domestic violence towards the public realm of the criminal justice system, whilst 'further blur[ring] already muddied waters regarding the objectives of sanctions for breach of civil orders and criminal sanctions'.[271] The policy objectives need to be clarified. The choice between criminal and civil/family proceedings has many implications: for the sanctions available; for the degree of victim involvement in and control over the proceedings; for evidential rules; and for the public and police perception of these cases. Is the objective to protect the victim for the future, or to punish the abuser? Criminal law has traditionally focused on the latter, family law on the former.

Criminalization of breach relieves victims of the financial and psychological burden of bringing enforcement proceedings themselves. Moreover, increased use of the criminal law sends out strong messages about society's disapproval of domestic abuse. However, criminalizing breach of civil orders as such may—ironically—undermine this aim. Charging the new offence under s 42A of the FLA 1996, instead of an ordinary criminal offence applicable to the facts, may downgrade domestic violence by giving the impression that it is not 'real crime'. Indeed, police and prosecutors might feel encouraged to require victims to pursue civil remedies before the criminal law steps in at all. Much will depend upon prosecutors' practice.

Opponents also raised questions about victim control.[272]

M. Burton, 'Criminalising Breaches of Civil Orders for Protection from Domestic Violence', [2003] *Criminal Law Review* **301, 305–6**

Domestic violence is not just an individual matter but an offence against the state. The onus should not be on the victim to seek enforcement of the order, rather through criminal proceedings the state should mark society's disapproval of the defendant's conduct in breaching the order. The difficulty with this model is that the victim's interests may become supplanted

---

271 Burton (2003b), 305–8.
272 See in particular Hansard HL Deb, vol 656, cols GC229–30, 19 January 2004, Lord Thomas of Gresford.

by a wider public interest and the victim's views may become marginalised in relation to any decisions that may be taken by the prosecuting authorities about whether to prosecute for breach of a non-molestation order. If the conduct is grave enough to warrant criminalisation then it has been argued that it is right that the victim should lose control over the prosecution process, albeit that they should be kept informed of its progress. However, it can be questioned whether breach of a non-molestation order should result in the victim's wishes being subordinated to a wider public interest. It may be in practice that the police and CPS would not prosecute for breaches of a non-molestation order where the victim did not want them to, however, the possibility remains....Perhaps prosecutors would feel that the victim should have more influence in relation to cases which came to them by the indirect route of breach of a civil order rather than the direct route of the police charging the defendant for assault or other general offences related to domestic violence. However, as far as victim decision-making in legal interventions is concerned, the victim has a more prominent role in civil interventions. There may be value in preserving that role and not, even theoretically, subordinating it to a wider public interest.

Victims preferring to take civil proceedings cannot elect from the outset to have a power of arrest attached to the order, so they have to return to the family court to obtain a warrant if they wish to enforce the order through that route. If victims call the police when a breach occurs, the case is likely to be taken through the criminal justice system. Unless the victim brings enforcement proceedings in the family courts before the criminal process has concluded, civil enforcement is barred by the rules against double punishment.[273] Victims have no party status in criminal proceedings, so are not directly represented by their own lawyer. Victims might be deterred from seeking non-molestation orders at all if they know that their partners might gain a criminal record as a result of any breach and that decisions regarding charge and prosecution, in the public criminal courts, will be beyond their control.

Concerns were also expressed that the courts might start applying a more stringent standard of proof when making a non-molestation order, by analogy with anti-social behaviour orders (ASBOs). Although the wider rules of civil evidence apply to ASBOs, it has been held that the potential criminal consequences of breach mean that the *criminal* standard of proof applies not only to adjudication on alleged breaches, but also to the *making* of these orders.[274] These fears may be alleviated by *Hipgrave v Jones*, which held that the civil standard of proof applies to the making of injunctions under the PHA 1997, breach of which is also criminal.[275] It seems highly likely that the same approach will be taken to non-molestation orders. However, the fact that breach constitutes an offence might make the courts reluctant to make some orders at all. The prospect of a power of arrest instigating *contempt* proceedings being invoked dissuaded the court from making a non-molestation order in *Chechi v Bashir*, the case involving brothers feuding over a land dispute.[276] It was felt that this would put too much power into the hands of the applicant. The prospect of *criminal* proceedings might weigh even more heavily against making an order, though it may be hoped that in paradigm domestic violence cases these sorts of considerations would not influence courts' decisions.

---

[273] FLA 1996, s 42A(3), (4); PHA 1997, s 3.
[274] *R (McCann) v Manchester Crown Court; Clingham v Kensington and Chelsea RLBC* [2002] UKHL 39.
[275] [2004] EWHC 2901.
[276] [1999] 2 FLR 489.

However, criminal punishment—if not very carefully managed—may be counterproductive, prejudicing victims' safety rather than protecting them. Short prison sentences may simply aggravate the situation. Fines are problematic where victim and abuser live in the same household; it has even been known for victims to pay fines themselves.[277] An alternative approach, preferred by opponents of criminalization, would enhance the family courts' enforcement and sentencing powers. Family courts already hold many attractions with their more accommodating rules of evidence, the opportunity for proceedings to be held in private, and their speed of action. The currently limited menu of family court sanctions may not best serve victims' interests. Notably, family courts cannot order participation in a perpetrator programme or other community sentences.

Early evidence of the impact of change

Early anecdotal and survey-based evidence suggested that concerns about criminalization deterring victims (or even courts) from making orders might have been well founded.[278] It has been suggested that police are not treating these breaches seriously, not arresting or not charging, and issuing cautions inappropriately.[279] Breach of a non-molestation order could be dealt with by family courts in a matter of hours: the police were obliged to bring respondents to court within 24 hours of arrest. By contrast, the criminal justice system can take weeks to act, and at rather greater cost; and the CPS has a discretion whether to charge the defendant at all. Delay increases the chances of victim withdrawal.[280] Information-transfer to the criminal justice agencies has also proved problematic.[281]

Judges reported that fewer victims seemed to be applying for non-molestation orders in the first place,[282] concerns corroborated by two surveys based on court data.[283] One of those surveys, by Judge Platt, found an average drop of 25 per cent in applications for non-molestation orders, comparing the two six-month periods before and after the new law, suggesting that some applicants may be applying for occupation orders to achieve the effects of a non-molestation order without the threat of criminalization. He suggested three other possible explanations, operating alone or together. The first, highly unlikely, is that the risk of criminalization has suddenly reduced the occurrence of domestic violence. Secondly, some victims might be bypassing family proceedings and going straight for criminal proceedings, an explanation supported by the increase in prosecutions in that year. Finally, victims might be deterred from using the family courts now that the threat of criminal sanctions hangs over respondents. Platt strongly suspects this to be a factor, though Burton has suggested that the problem may be the opposite: that victims' groups had welcomed criminalization of breach, but had since been disappointed by police inaction.[284] A number of other practical factors are hampering victims' access to the family courts (notably

---

277 Pizzey (1974).

278 See generally Burton (2009b).

279 Home Affairs Select Committee (2008).

280 Minute of evidence given by District Judge Mornington to the Home Affairs Select Committee (2008), Q55, 22 January 2008.

281 Hester et al (2008) report several further practical problems with implementation of the new law.

282 Gibb (2008); Millward (2008).

283 Platt (2008); Hester et al (2008). See also Burton's review for the Legal Services Commission (2008b).

284 Burton (2009b), 117.

reduced availability of legal aid[285]) and impeding the successful implementation of the new provisions. However, as Burton points out:

M. Burton, 'Civil Law Remedies for Domestic Violence: Why are Applications for Non-Molestation Orders Declining?', (2009) 31 *Journal of Social Welfare and Family Law* **109**

Victims' help-seeking behaviour is influenced by a range of factors, not all of which are related to their perceptions about the relevance or potential usefulness of the legal process and civil remedies. Many victims do not even consider the legal system, so the idea that they would be 'encouraged' or 'put off' by changes to legal criteria, the attitudes of legal personnel or the availability of [legal aid] funding seems unlikely. Nevertheless, for those who do wish to use civil remedies, or could be encouraged to do so, some improvements could be made. These include a greater level of specialisation in the civil justice system to ensure that those using the FLA are well informed about the legal framework, the funding criteria and, most importantly, the dynamics of domestic abuse and how to respond sympathetically and appropriately to victims.

Hester et al caution that research over a longer period than they were able to undertake (only July–Nov 2007) is needed to discern whether the drop in applications is a product of the new Act rather than a consolidation of longer term trends predating the change.[286] After a small rise in applications in 2009, however, numbers declined again markedly until the recent spike widely attributed to the legal aid reform.[287] This issue will have to be revisited as more data become available.

4.6.3 SANCTIONS FOR BREACH IN THE FAMILY COURT

If the criminal route is not used,[288] the respondent in breach of an FLA 1996 order will be brought to the family court under a power of arrest or warrant. Contempt proceedings in the family court are 'criminal proceedings' for the purposes of Article 6 ECHR, carrying the rights to legal representation and against self-incrimination.[289] If the respondent is found guilty of contempt (on a criminal standard of proof), the court must decide what sanction to impose. Family courts had been criticized for imposing nominal sanctions. The suggestion in *Ansah v Ansah*[290] that in most cases 'stern warnings' will suffice was said to downgrade the seriousness of domestic violence.[291] Recent decisions have emphasized the importance of proper penalties. When assessing these cases, it is important to remember that the maximum penalty available to the family court when sentencing for contempt is only two years' imprisonment.[292] In *A-A v B-A*,[293] the husband's rape was punished by 12 months'

---

[285] Cf HO (2008), 27. Legal aid criteria require victims to cooperate with criminal prosecution before they can obtain legal aid for civil remedies.

[286] Hester et al (2008), 27

[287] MOJ (2014a), table 2.7.

[288] For early sentencing decisions in the criminal courts for breach of non-molestation orders, see *R v Briscoe* [2010] EWCA Crim 373; *R v Franks* [2010] EWCA Crim 1030.

[289] *Hammerton v Hammerton* [2007] EWCA Civ 248.

[290] [1977] Fam 138, 144, per Ormrod J.

[291] McCann (1985), 83–4.

[292] Contempt of Court Act 1981, s 14. Minors cannot be imprisoned for contempt: see *Re H (Respondent Under 18: Power of Arrest)* [2001] 1 FCR 370.

[293] [2001] 2 FLR 1.

imprisonment. In a case where the respondent seriously assaulted the applicant at midday outside her solicitors' offices, the trial judge's 'wholly inadequate' sentence of 14 days was increased on appeal to three months:[294]

Wilson v Webster [1998] 2 FCR 575 (CA), 578–9

THORPE LJ:

There is an element in this matter of public confidence. Domestic violence is a serious matter. It would appear that Parliament has taken particular note of the incidence of domestic violence and the courts who have to deal with incidents of domestic violence must take it very seriously indeed. This was, in my judgment, an exceptional case. This was a quite deliberate attack on this lady in breach of the undertaking at midday in the centre of a city when she had just left her solicitor's offices. He punched her, he punched her to the ground and continued punching her and desisted, it would seem, when he was finally pulled away from her. This is not a matter which could receive a mere caution, it was certainly a matter which required serious punishment...

Each case will be dealt with on its own merits but I hope that county court judges will take seriously the views of this court that matters of this kind are to be dealt with seriously.

Recent Court of Appeal cases have sought to provide guidance on sentencing for contempt under the FLA 1996, seeking to work out what the parallel jurisdictions of the criminal courts and the civil courts under the PHA 1997 mean for family courts' sentencing:

Hale v Tanner [2000] 1 WLR 2377 (CA)

HALE LJ:

Family cases, it has long been recognised, raise different considerations from those elsewhere in the civil law. The two most obvious are the heightened emotional tensions that arise between family members and often the need for those family members to continue to be in contact with one another because they have children together or the like. Those two factors make the task of the court, in dealing with these issues, quite different from the task when dealing with commercial disputes or other types of case in which...sanctions have to be imposed for contempt of court. Having said that:

(1) These cases have to come before the court on an application to commit. That is the only procedure which is available. Not surprisingly, therefore, the court is directing its mind to whether or not committal to prison is the appropriate order. But it does not follow from that that imprisonment is to be regarded as the automatic consequence of the breach of an order. Clearly it is not. There is, however, no principle that imprisonment is not to be imposed at the first occasion...Nevertheless, it is a common practice, and usually appropriate in view of the sensitivity of the circumstances of these cases, to take some other course on the first occasion.

(2) There is the difficulty...that the alternatives are limited. The full range of sentencing options is not available for contempt of court. Nevertheless, there is a range of things that the

---

294 Cf *Gull v Gull* [2007] EWCA Civ 900; *Nicholls v Nicholls* [2008] EWCA Civ 121 where longer sentences were passed for non-violent but serial breaches.

court can consider. It may do nothing—make no order. It may adjourn, and in a case where the alleged contemnor has not attended court, that may be an appropriate course to take, although I would not say so in every case; it depends on the reasons that may be thought to lie behind the non-attendance. There is a power to fine. There is a power of sequestration of assets and there are mental health orders. All of those may, in an appropriate case, need consideration, particularly in a case where the court has not found any actual violence proved.

(3) If imprisonment is appropriate, the length of the committal should be decided without reference to whether or not it is to be suspended. A longer period of committal is not justified because its sting is removed by virtue of its suspension.

(4) The length of the committal has to depend upon the court's objectives. There are two objectives always in contempt of court proceedings. One is to mark the court's disapproval of the disobedience to its order. The other is to secure compliance with that order in the future. Thus, the seriousness of what has taken place is to be viewed in that light as well as for its own intrinsic gravity.

(5) The length of the committal has to bear some reasonable relationship to the maximum of two years which is available.

(6) Suspension is possible in a much wider range of circumstances than it is in criminal cases. It does not have to be the exceptional case. Indeed, it is usually the first way of attempting to secure compliance with the court's order.

(7) The length of the suspension requires separate consideration, although it is often appropriate for it to be linked to continued compliance with the order underlying the committal.

(8) Of course, the court has to bear in mind the context. This may be aggravating or mitigating. The context is often the break-up of an intimate relationship in which emotions run high and people behave in silly ways. The context of having children together, if that be the case, cannot be ignored. Sometimes that means that there is an aggravation of what has taken place, because of the greater fear that is engendered from the circumstances. Sometimes it may be mitigating, because there is reason to suppose that once the immediate emotions have calmed down, the molestation and threats will not continue.

(9) In many cases the court will have to bear in mind that there are concurrent proceedings in another court based on either the same facts or some of the same facts which are before the court on the contempt proceedings. The court cannot ignore those parallel proceedings. It may have to take into account their outcome in considering what the practical effect is upon the contempt proceedings. They do have different purposes and often the overlap is not exact, but nevertheless the court will not want, in effect, the contemnor to suffer punishment twice for the same events.

(10) It will usually be desirable for the court to explain very briefly why it has made the choices that it has made in the particular case before it.... [I]t would be appropriate in most cases for the contemnor to know why he or she was being sentenced to a period of imprisonment; why it was the length that it was; if it was suspended, why the suspension was as it was, but only very briefly.

An important part of the exercise is that the contemnor should understand the importance of keeping court orders, of not breaking them and the likely consequences if they are so broken.

In *H v O*, it was said that the fact that breaches occurred in the context of a contact dispute should be regarded as an aggravating rather than mitigating factor.[295] But what should

---

[295] [2004] EWCA Civ 1691, [38].

the court do where there are parallel or prior proceedings in another court concerning related conduct?

Lomas v Parle [2003] EWCA Civ 1804, [2004] 1 WLR 1642

THORPE LJ:

47....[A] perpetrator may face sentence for the same act which amounts to both a breach of an injunction made in family proceedings and also a crime under the Protection from Harassment Act 1997. Of course, the sentencing courts do not share the same objective and operate in different ranges. The judge in the family proceedings has to fit a custodial sentence within a range of 0–24 months. An important objective for him is to uphold the authority of the court by demonstrating that its orders cannot be flouted with impunity. Nevertheless there will be a shared deterrent objective in the punishment of domestic violence by imprisonment.

48....[T]he first court to sentence must not anticipate or allow for a likely future sentence. It is for the second court to sentence to reflect *the prior sentence* in its judgment in order to ensure that the defendant is not twice punished for the same act. It is essential that the second court should be fully informed of the factors and circumstances reflected in the first sentence. The defendant is often publicly funded to defend the proceedings in each court and may well have different solicitors and counsel in each justice system. There is, therefore, an obligation on the first court to ensure that the basis of its sentence is fully expressed, and that a transcript of its judgment is made available to the second court...

50. Within the constraints of the two-year limit on sentences for harassment in breach of [non-molestation orders] and the different scale which this necessarily involves, judges should as far as possible ensure that sentences passed under section 42 [FLA 1996] are not manifestly discrepant with sentences for harassment charged under sections 3, 4 or 5 of the Protection from Harassment Act 1997. The experience of counsel before us is that the level of sentencing under the [PHA 1997] is very significantly higher than the present level of sentencing for comparable incidents leading to committal for breach of [non-molestation orders under FLA 1996]. Of course, domestic violence may also be the subject of other criminal charges varying from common assault to murder. The more serious the offences, the less scope there will be, in view of the two-year limit, to maintain any relationship between family and criminal court sentences—if indeed such cases are brought before the family court at all. [emphasis added]

The recommendation that family courts endeavour to issue sentences corresponding with those that might be issued by a criminal court under the PHA 1997 is problematic. Since the PHA 1997, and now the FLA 1996, s 42A, permit a maximum of five rather than just two years' imprisonment in criminal cases, and many other criminal offences carry higher penalties than the family courts can impose, it will often be impossible for the family court to 'keep up'. One answer may be to bring proceedings under the PHA 1997 or to prosecute breach of the non-molestation order instead of using contempt proceedings.[296]

---

[296] *Robinson v Murray* [2005] EWCA Civ 935, [13]. Since PHA 1997 proceedings are not 'family proceedings', a court faced with an application under that Act or under the FLA 1996 cannot simply elect to make an order under the other Act instead.

Where the respondent has already been sentenced in criminal proceedings for overlapping and other related incidents, the second court must tread carefully to avoid punishing the respondent twice for the same conduct.[297] How should such parallel proceedings be managed? Wilson LJ refined Thorpe LJ's remarks in *Lomas v Parle* to deal with this issue, on the basis that it is the *conduct* which cannot be punished twice:

Slade v Slade [2009] EWCA Civ 748

WILSON LJ:

21.... Thus in my view we should not be misled by the words in [48] of *Lomas v Parle* [italicized above]: the second court should not so much reflect "the prior sentence" in its judgment as to decline to sentence for such of the conduct as has already been the subject of punishment in the criminal court. It follows that, even if a civil judge were to regard the punishment given by the criminal court for certain conduct as too lenient, it would be improper for him to use his power of committal in respect of that self-same conduct in order to top up the punishment to what he regards as a proper level. What he must do is to sentence only for such conduct as was not the subject of the criminal proceedings...

He went on to consider how the family court should sentence as contempt conduct which, in breach of the family court's order or an undertaking made to the court, had already been punished in criminal proceedings. Here, the court must focus on the *contemptuous aspect* of the conduct and, save for its gravity, not the basic conduct itself. The latter will already have been dealt with by the criminal sanction, so the family court must instead weigh the seriousness of the contempt, given the context of the breach: for example, whether this was a first contempt or one of a series, and how quickly the breach followed the making of the order.[298]

4.7 THIRD PARTY ACTION TO PROTECT VICTIMS

The power to permit third party applications under the FLA 1996, s 60, has not been exercised. But the question of others acting on victims' behalf, with or without their consent to proceedings, remains live, not least given new police powers under the Crime and Security Act 2010 (CSA 2010). The issue is also highlighted by *DL v A Local Authority*, in which a local authority were permitted to seek injunctions under the inherent jurisdiction to protect a vulnerable but competent elderly couple, against their wishes, from their allegedly abusive adult son.[299] These cases raise in more acute form the difficulty entailed in taking action without victim consent, considered at 4.6.2 above: there, the order being enforced by the state had at least been made on the application of the victim; here, by contrast, the state is instigating the entire matter.

---

[297] FLA 1996, s 42A(3), (4); PHA 1997, s 3. *Chechi v Bashir* [1999] 2 FLR 489: parallel civil proceedings for damages for assault, trespass to land, and damage to property contributed to the refusal to make a non-molestation order.

[298] [2009] EWCA Civ 748, [23].

[299] [2012] EWCA Civ 253.

4.7.1 THE CSA 2010: DOMESTIC VIOLENCE PROTECTION NOTICES AND ORDERS

Section 24 of the CSA 2010 empowers a senior police officer (without court proceedings) to issue a domestic violence protection notice[300] (DVPN) to 'P', prohibiting P from molesting another individual with whom P is 'associated' (in the FLA 1996 sense), and potentially excluding P from property shared with the person to be protected by the notice.[301] The scope of the notice and factors relevant to the officer's discretion are similar to those applicable to domestic violence protection orders (DVPO), set out below, save that the authorizing officer need only have reasonable grounds to believe that the criteria are met.[302] Crucially, the victim's consent to the DVPN is not required, but the police must take reasonable steps to ascertain, and then have regard to, her opinions and any representations made about the proposed notice.[303]

The police must then apply for a DVPO from the magistrates' court. That hearing must take place within 48 hours of the DVPN being issued (but may be adjourned with P remanded if he has breached the DVPN),[304] and P must ordinarily be given notice of the hearing.[305]

Crime and Security Act 2010

28 Conditions for and contents of a domestic violence protection order

(1) The court may make a DVPO if two conditions are met.

(2) The first condition is that the court is satisfied on the balance of probabilities that P has been violent towards, or has threatened violence towards, an associated person.

(3) The second condition is that the court thinks that making the DVPO is necessary to protect that person from violence or a threat of violence by P.

(4) Before making a DVPO, the court must, in particular, consider–

    (a) the welfare of any person under the age of 18 whose interests the court considers relevant to the making of the DVPO (whether or not that person is an associated person), and

    (b) any opinion of which the court is made aware–

        (i) of the person for whose protection the DVPO would be made, and

        (ii) in the case of provision included by virtue of subsection (8), of any other associated person who lives in the premises to which the provision would relate.

(5) But the court may make a DVPO in circumstances where the person for whose protection it is made does not consent to the making of the DVPO.

(6) A DVPO must contain provision to prohibit P from molesting the person for whose protection it is made.

---

300 CSA 2010, s 25.
301 Ibid, s 24(1), (2), (6), (9).
302 Ibid, ss 24(2)–(8), 25.
303 Ibid, s 24(3), (5).
304 Ibid, ss 27(8), 26, 30.
305 Ibid, s 26(1)–(3).

(7) Provision required to be included by virtue of subsection (6) may be expressed so as to refer to molestation in general, to particular acts of molestation, or to both.

(8) If P lives in premises which are also lived in by a person for whose protection the DVPO is made, the DVPO may also contain provision—

(a) to prohibit P from evicting or excluding from the premises the person for whose protection the DVPO is made,

(b) to prohibit P from entering the premises,

(c) to require P to leave the premises, or

(d) to prohibit P from coming within such distance of the premises as may be specified in the DVPO . . .

The DVPO may last a specified period between 14 and 28 days.[306] Breach of either the notice or the order may lead to arrest without warrant[307] and be dealt with as a civil breach (not a criminal offence), with penalties of £50 for each day in default, up to a maximum of £5,000 or two months' imprisonment.[308]

This regime may be regarded as a 'mini' version of what the unimplemented s 60 of the FLA 1996 would have permitted: third party applications for an order having the effect of a non-molestation and occupation order. The key differences are that the process under the CSA 2010 is initiated by the police without court involvement, but then that the ultimate order can last no more than 28 days.[309]

4.7.2 PROS AND CONS OF THIRD PARTY ACTION

Should third party applications be allowed and, if so, in what form? Are the police the right agency to be empowered to act in this way? Given the CSA 2010 scheme, should local authorities also be able to obtain injunctions under the inherent jurisdiction, as they did in *DL v A Local Authority*?[310] Does the CSA 2010 scheme jeopardize the rights of either party?[311] Should victims' consent to the application be required?

The CSA 2010's rationale was articulated in guidance for its pilot scheme:

Home Office, *Domestic Violence Protection Notices and Domestic Violence Protection Orders: Interim Guidance Document for Police Regional Pilot Schemes* (2011)

1.3 Research has highlighted that a large proportion of cases involving domestic violence incidents 'fall out' as they progress through the criminal justice system. Initiatives aimed at decreasing such attrition include a focus on positive action by the police and an increase in prosecution and conviction. None the less, about a quarter of incidents

---

306 Ibid, s 28(10)–(11).
307 Ibid, ss 25(1)(b), 28(9).
308 Magistrates' Court Act 1980, s 63.
309 For evaluation of the pilot project, see Kelly et al (2013).
310 [2012] EWCA Civ 253; Miles (2011b), on the first instance decision.
311 See Crompton (2013).

recorded by the police result in arrest, while only 1.5–5% of incidents result in conviction. Research indicates that from a victim's perspective, the ability of the [criminal justice system] to provide safety is key to the decision about 'staying in' or 'dropping out' of the system.

1.4 It is not unusual for situations to arise in which a suspected offender, who is neither charged or otherwise on bail at the time of release from police custody, is free to return to the scene of abuse sometimes within hours of arrest. Research shows us that this is a time of increased risk to a victim. Where a risk assessment is undertaken it is frequently deemed necessary for the victim to consider leaving the address (with depend[a]nts where applicable) and/or for an injunction to be sought to prevent further abuse or harassment by the alleged perpetrator. Leaving home can have a negative impact on the victim's well-being and causes disruption to the victim's children and could well be another factor in the prosecution attrition rate.

1.5 There is no readily available, consistent, affordable and timely access to civil court orders in the immediate aftermath of a domestic violence incident and therefore a gap exists between how the criminal justice system and civil law processes interact to provide immediate safety and a seamless service to victims at on-going risk of violence.

1.6 There is evidence that specific groups of vulnerable victims, such as those persons with insecure immigration status and people with disabilities find it difficult to get access to refuge provision for a number of complex reasons.... The DVPN and subsequent DVPO provide a further opportunity to enhance the safety of diverse groups of victims of domestic violence.

The scheme aims to give victims space in which to decide, with support services, what steps to take to protect themselves longer term, for example by seeking orders under the FLA 1996. The potential benefits are identified by domestic violence professionals who participated in a study evaluating possible implementation of s 60 of the FLA 1996, which could have involved orders obtained by third parties far longer than the CSA 2010's 28 days; an important question is whether the benefits identified here have the same force given the short duration of DVPO protection. The principal advantage is relieving victims of the need to protect themselves:

M. Burton, 'Third Party Applications for Protection Orders in England and Wales: Service Provider's Views on Implementing Section 60 of the Family Law Act 1996', (2003) 25 *Journal of Social Welfare and Family Law* **137, 139–41, 146**

First, respondents felt that the confidence of some survivors may be so eroded by their experience of domestic violence that they would be unable to recognise that their situation called for a remedy, let alone undertake the daunting task of pursuing an order from a position of such low self-esteem. It was thought that the support of the third party could be beneficial in rebuilding the confidence of the survivor. Second, the survivor would know that she was believed by the third party, a boost to confidence in addition to that accruing from the order itself. Third, respondents also argued that third party applications would remove any blame attributed to the survivor for invoking the protection offered by the legal system against the perpetrator. It was felt that the survivor would be able to simply tell the perpetrator that the application had nothing to do with her; she could 'hide behind' the third party. Thus third party applications could deflect the blame coming from the perpetrator and also, in some situations, the extended family and wider community. This latter factor was considered to be particularly important for survivors in ethnic minority communities, where pursuing redress for domestic violence can lead to being ostracized by the whole community...An important consideration for women, in deciding whether to pursue a civil remedy, is weighing up the prospect of the remedy being effective against the chances that pursuing it may result in further violence. Many respondents in this study commented that women were put off pursuing civil protection by fear of reprisals. Respondents who favoured implementation of Section 60 saw third party applications as beneficial in reducing a survivor's fear of reprisals. It was thought that women would be less likely to be subjected to pressure by the respondent if a third party application was being made, because there would be no point in the respondent intimidating his partner with a view to getting her to withdraw the case.

However, the victim may remain at risk of reprisals:

Respondents who opposed implementation, about a quarter (16/60) of those interviewed, pointed out that third party applications might not reduce the survivor's fear of reprisals. The perpetrator would still believe the woman to have played some part in the application being made, even if the extent of her involvement was merely alerting an outside agency to the existence of violence. Thus, the woman would still be blamed for the application.

Since the CSA 2010 does not require the victim's consent to action, perhaps most important are Burton's findings that:

the main objection...was that third party applications would reinforce a survivor's low self-esteem and confidence. It would reaffirm a survivor's belief that they are unable to obtain remedies themselves and deprive them of the benefits that may be gained by actively and fully engaging in the process of successfully pursuing a remedy. On the other hand, this objection to implementation does not address the argument that women may need third party applications not because they lack confidence to pursue remedies but because they lack financial resources...

Most respondents opposed applications made without consent. This would:

reinforce the lack of power and control that the survivor had already experienced due to the domestic violence. A comparison was...made with mandatory prosecutions...Even amongst respondents who supported mandatory prosecution, there were some who felt that there was a difference between pursuing a prosecution without the victim's consent and obtaining a protective order without her consent and cooperation.

Consent was considered important principally for pragmatic reasons—lack of victim cooperation may hamper collection of evidence and enforcement. But there are also important human rights considerations. The CSA 2010 does at least require that victims' wishes are considered, where known,[312] but acting against victims' wishes arguably breaches their

---

[312] CSA 2010, ss 24(3)–(4), 28(4).

rights under Article 8 ECHR.[313] However, the concept of victim autonomy in this area is complex, as remarks in *DL v A Local Authority* indicate:

DL v A Local Authority [2012] EWCA Civ 253

MACFARLANE LJ:

54. The appellant's submissions [against intervention] rightly place a premium upon an individual's autonomy to make his own decisions. However this point, rather than being one against the existence of the inherent jurisdiction in these cases, is in my view a strong argument in favour of it. The jurisdiction...is in part aimed at enhancing or liberating the autonomy of a vulnerable adult whose autonomy has been compromised by a reason other than mental incapacity because they are...:

a) Under constraint; or

b) Subject to coercion or undue influence; or

c) For some other reason deprived of the capacity to make the relevant decision or disabled from making a free choice, or incapacitated or disabled from giving or expressing a real and genuine consent.

Moreover, where children or other vulnerable individuals are affected by the violence, state intervention might still be justified.[314] And, as discussed at 4.2.4, victims' own need for protection may justify intervention against their wishes.[315] Insisting on victim consent might deprive third party action of its chief advantage: protection of victims too petrified to protect themselves. The difficult task is to find the right balance such that victims are empowered overall, rather than victimized a second time by being deprived of control by the state. Most victims in the evaluation of the CSA 2010 pilots reported relief that the police could remove perpetrators, but some were critical of action taken without their participation. But few victims apparently went on to obtain their own FLA orders after the DVPO expired.[316] That may reflect the DVPO itself having had the desired effect by chastening the perpetrator—providing a 'wake up call' in chronic cases[317]—but it will be important to monitor how far DVPOs really do empower victims and reduce re-victimization.

A quarter of Burton's respondents also identified a potential symbolic virtue of s 60 applications, shared by the CSA 2010:

[I]t would affirm the responsibility of the state, through public bodies, to provide protection for survivors of domestic violence....[A] clear message would be sent out by third party applications that domestic violence is a public matter not a private matter; it is a legitimate sphere of state intervention in the interests of society as a whole.[318]

---

[313] Cf findings re victims' views of the CSA 2010 pilot project: Kelly et al (2013), 26–8.

[314] Cf the exclusion requirements that can be attached to emergency protection and interim care orders, CA 1989, ss 38A and 44A: 12.6.2 and 12.7.

[315] Choudhry and Herring (2006a).

[316] Kelly et al (2013), 26.

[317] Ibid, 35.

[318] Burton (2003a), 141.

However, empowering police in the civil arena risks further 'decriminalizing' domestic violence, here by avoiding using the criminal law entirely, by contrast with use of the (arguably) less serious offence in the cases discussed at 4.6.2 above.[319] The interim guidance for the CSA 2010 pilot required that consideration be given to:

> identification and prosecution for substantive criminal offences. If CPS advice is to charge for a domestic related offence then a DVPN may not be necessary or proportionate where there is a remand in custody. . . or when strict bail conditions [are] in place.[320]

The use of DVPNs and DVPOs must be monitored to ensure that both parties' rights are protected and that the scheme is not re-privatizing domestic violence.[321] The CSA 2010 evaluation has already queried whether breach should be criminalized, to underline the seriousness of DVPOs and increase sentencing powers.[322]

4.8 THE FUTURE: INTEGRATED DOMESTIC ABUSE PROCEEDINGS?

Recent reforms blurring the criminal, civil, and family jurisdictions—not least the criminalization of breach of non-molestation orders and police applications under the CSA 2010—have introduced complexity and fragmentation into the legal response to domestic violence.[323] Short-term DVPOs in theory free victims to bring their own application under the FLA 1996, so one would not ordinarily expect to have a DVPO and a non-molestation order in force at the same time. And it is usual for just one legal strategy to be pursued, not least because of the lack of integration between the civil/family and criminal justice systems. However, as we saw at 4.6.3, the overlapping criminal, civil, and family court jurisdictions potentially cause wasteful duplication of effort, penalties from different courts dealing with the same basic facts, and various orders pursuing different objectives in relation to different aspects of the parties' lives.[324]

Victims are not represented directly before the court in criminal or CSA 2010 proceedings, and family solicitors retained to deal with family proceedings may lack the expertise, or funding, to advise on related criminal proceedings. But proceedings dealing directly with domestic violence are often only part of the picture. Many cases involve disputes about child arrangements, for example regarding contact with children of the family. A criminal court may be ignorant of these proceedings, their outcome, and their implications for the matter before it: it might issue a restraining order in terms which preclude contact ordered by a family court; or, a restraining order having been made by a criminal court, a family court might wish to order contact in a manner barred by the restraining order; or the parties themselves might wish to agree such contact. As matters stand, parties would have to return to the criminal court to seek variation of its restraining order

---

[319] Humphreys and Kaye (1997), 410–12; Burton (2003a), 142–3; Crompton (2014).
[320] HO (2011), para 2.5; see also para 5.4.4.
[321] Cf Kelly et al (2013).
[322] Ibid, 46–7.
[323] Burton (2004a).
[324] Humphreys and Thiara (2003), 202.

before contact could proceed. Important safeguarding and other welfare issues might get lost in the process.[325]

The answer may be to combine all relevant jurisdictions regarding domestic violence within one integrated court, ideally on a 'one family, one judge' model enabling one judge to deal with all aspects of the family's legal problems, whether cast in criminal, civil, or family law terms. This option was highlighted in *Lomas v Parle*,[326] in light of US experience:

M. Burton, 'Domestic Violence—From Consultation to Bill: Closer Integration of the Civil and Criminal Justice Systems', (2004) 34 *Family Law* 128, 131–2

The coordination of the civil and criminal functions in the new court has been evaluated as the single most important aspect of the process. The researchers note that, prior to the formation of the new court, victims of domestic violence were shuttled between various courts seeking different relief. In the integrated court, victim safety had increased because victims could obtain all forms of relief from the one court. And the situation in the past, where conflicting orders were sometimes made in criminal and civil proceedings, has been resolved. . . .

It appears . . . that an integrated specialist domestic violence court has the potential to resolve not only any information-sharing problems that exist in the traditional judicial system but also 'evidence-sharing' problems. Specially trained judges in integrated domestic violence courts have no difficulties applying the different evidential burdens and tailoring relief to the whole case before them. Rather than compromising neutrality, specialisation, it seems, creates judicial expertise and promotes continuity and consistency in decision-making.

It should not be thought that the integration of civil and criminal matters in a single specialist court is completely without detriment to victims. Kellitz observes that integrated systems that include family proceedings, or systems where there is a high level of information sharing, may deter some women from accessing the system for fear of losing their children . . . Epstein has also commented that integration may maximise women's access to services but also 'can reduce their ability to decline such services if they wish to do so' . . . Women who want help with the civil justice route may be pushed into pursuing the criminal justice route as well. Implementation of a specialist domestic violence court has to remain responsive to the individual victim's needs and wishes. Judicial burnout has been identified as a further potential problem . . . Nevertheless, the benefits of specialisation on the fully integrated model, seem to outweigh the problems to the extent that it has become the preferred model for new courts in the US.

The increasing overlap between jurisdictions and the implications of domestic violence for other aspects of family life before the courts demand a holistic approach of the sort that integrated courts could provide. Very disappointingly, however, a pilot project of an integrated court in Croydon ended in failure, and the idea has been dropped.[327]

---

[325] See Hansard HC Proceedings of Standing Committee E on the Domestic Violence, Crimes and Victims Bill, 29 June 2004: discussion of amendments to cl 10.

[326] [2003] EWCA Civ 1804, [52].

[327] Hester, Pearce, and Westmarland (2008); HO (2009), 24.

4.9 CONCLUSION

A poor response from the legal system to domestic violence can be worse than the victim not using the law at all.

C. Humphreys and R. Thiara, 'Neither Justice nor Protection: Women's Experiences of Post-Separation Violence', (2003) 25 *Journal of Social Welfare and Family Law* 195, 210

[In their research sample there was] a smaller group of chronic and serious offenders [who] were unresponsive to normative frameworks. 'Brushes' with the law which result in being charged with minor offences, cautions, binding over or short custodial sentences had no effect and in fact served to reinforce the abuser's belief that there are no effective constraints or sanctions on his behaviour. They can increase the dangers to women, who will be seen to have 'transgressed' having called the police or given evidence against the abuser. Moreover, poor and ineffective action from law enforcement and prosecution services may serve to confirm a woman's belief that she is outside help and, therefore, has no option other than to seek to appease the abuser.

The legal system must provide effective and timely protection for victims. However, the law's ability to deal with domestic violence is limited. The vast majority of victims never reach a courtroom. The activities of other government and voluntary sector agencies are vital to victims' safety. Current policy emphasizes an integrated, multi-agency approach to secure prevention and support, justice and protection. Education, particularly of young people, is important to root out attitudes which tolerate or even support domestic abuse, and to encourage victims and others to speak out. Proper resourcing and training for all agencies involved with families experiencing domestic violence are essential. Social exclusion and other risk factors associated with domestic violence must be tackled. Only these non-legal measures will secure a significant reduction in the prevalence of domestic violence.

ONLINE RESOURCE CENTRE

Questions, suggestions for further reading, and supplementary materials for this chapter (including updates on developments in this area of family law since this book was published) may be found on the Online Resource Centre at www.oxfordtextbooks.co.uk/orc/familytcm3e/.

5

ENDING RELATIONSHIPS: DIVORCE AND SEPARATION

CENTRAL ISSUES

1. The law of divorce has always been controversial owing to its implications for the institution of marriage and the family. Attempts to reform the law trigger heated political debate amongst those who wish to retain state control over divorce and those who wish to promote party autonomy.

2. Divorce used to be fault-based, available only if the respondent had committed a 'matrimonial offence'. Since 1969, divorce has been available on the basis that the marriage has irretrievably broken down. But that ground can be satisfied only by proving one of five 'facts', three of which (adultery, behaviour, and desertion) are generally fault-related, two of which (based on separation) do not require proof of fault.

3. The law of civil partnership dissolution is largely identical to the law of divorce, save that there is no 'fact' based on 'adultery'. Like the omission of sex-related grounds from the law of nullity, this raises interesting questions about the nature of civil partnership.

4. In practice, the simple, largely administrative procedure for undefended cases severely limits the extent of any real adjudication on questions of fault on divorce, such that it may be said that in reality we have divorce by mutual consent or even on demand.

5. There are continued calls for reform of divorce law, in the wake of a failed attempt at reform in 1996. The introduction of no-fault divorce would be compatible with the emphasis in current family policy on 'divorcing responsibly' and resolving disputes on family breakdown by agreement.

5.1 INTRODUCTION

Thousands of families are touched by divorce every year. That sad fact attracts a range of responses. Some see divorce as the death of family, symptomatic of moral decay, a cause of social dislocation, economic cost to society, and damage to children. Divorce and separation must therefore be curtailed and marriage promoted as the functional and ideological 'gold standard'. Others are more sanguine, seeing divorce as a common stage in contemporary family life beyond which family continues, albeit reconfigured across two households. On this view, the issue is how law can enable families to adjust and maintain good relationships after relationship breakdown, particularly where the couple have children.[1] These concerns apply equally to couples who cohabit and become parents without marrying. Issues surrounding parenting and property arrangements on separation are as pressing for them as they are for divorcing spouses. But while separating spouses and cohabitants share many practical problems, spouses and civil partners may wish (and need) to end their relationship not only in fact but also in law. Simply separating does not extinguish the legal status of marriage or civil partnership. The legal rights and duties attaching to the status continue, and, while they may cohabit with another, the parties are unable to marry or form a civil partnership with anyone else. Releasing the parties from their legal status is the job of the law of divorce, the principal focus of this chapter.

There is a human right to marry, but the European Convention on Human Rights (ECHR) does not recognize a right to divorce.[2] Nevertheless, all European states now permit divorce and Article 12 ECHR entitles divorcees to remarry without unreasonable restrictions.[3] However, each state is free to determine the basis on which divorce is granted and there is considerable variety across Europe.[4] Divorce in England and Wales is governed by the Matrimonial Causes Act 1973 (MCA 1973) and equivalent provisions of the Civil Partnership Act 2004 (CPA 2004). Unless clear from the context, references here to 'divorce' and associated terminology include civil partnership dissolution. The MCA 1973 provides a 'mixed economy' divorce system, combining fault-based and 'no-fault' elements. It had been expected that the MCA 1973 would be replaced by the Family Law Act 1996 (FLA 1996), which would have placed divorce on an entirely no-fault basis and transformed the procedure for obtaining divorce. For reasons that we shall explore later, the relevant Parts of that Act were repealed without being brought into force, but the FLA 1996 continues to provide a useful model for possible reform.

Like its law of nullity,[5] a society's divorce law (or its absence) reveals something about that society's understanding of the nature and significance of marriage, and about the boundaries between public and private, between community interest and individual interest. It involves basic questions about the role of the state and the law in regulating adults' private lives and the nature that that regulation should take. If the law makes no provision for divorce, then marriage is a lifelong status. If divorce is permitted, on what basis? Is marriage a status terminable only if one party commits some 'offence' regarded by the state as sufficiently grave to excuse the innocent party from continued

---

[1] Hasson (2006). Lewis (2001a), 162 observes that it is difficult to prove the cause and effect relationship between divorce and outcomes for children, since it is hard to disentangle the impact of divorce (specifically) on children's outcomes from other factors affecting families before, during, or after separation.

[2] *Johnson v Ireland* (App No 9697/82, ECHR) (1986); *Ivanov and Petrova v Bulgaria* (App No 15001/04, ECHR) (2011).

[3] *F v Switzerland* (App No 11329/85, ECHR) (1987), [32]: three-year ban on remarriage by a serial divorcee and adulterer was unreasonable; *VK v Croatia* (App No 38380/08, ECHR) (2012).

[4] Boele-Woelki et al (2004).

[5] 2.6, 2.7.

participation in the marriage? Is it a contract dissoluble by mutual consent, its terms (to that extent) implicitly agreed by the parties, rather than the state? Or can marriage last only for so long as both parties assent to its continuation, allowing one party to end it unilaterally? Even if divorce is freely available in this sense, might the law seek in other ways to influence parties' behaviour surrounding divorce, for example by imposing waiting periods?

5.2 THE RISE IN DIVORCE

Most marriages end by death, but the number and proportion of marriages ending by divorce increased dramatically during the last century. This overall trend is matched across much of the developed world, although differences in laws and social, cultural, and religious factors are reflected in countries' divorce rates.[6] In one sense at least, changes in the substantive and procedural law governing divorce contributed to this increase: it is now legally possible for many of those who wish to divorce to do so when previously they could not. But this does not itself mean that more marriages now fail: before the law permitted divorce, many couples in unhappy marriages physically separated.[7] Some formed new relationships which, without a divorce from the earlier marriage, could not be formalized by marriage. A restrictive divorce law may therefore not have kept unhappy couples together, but simply prevented them from terminating their legal relationship.[8]

The huge social changes of the twentieth century were also major contributing factors to increasing divorce, especially those regarding women's position in the home and their increased participation in the labour market, birth control, sexual morality, declining levels of religious adherence, and the transformation of home and family from a unit of production to a haven from the outside world. These changes affected people's expectations of marriage, now principally regarded as a source of companionship through life.[9] Moreover, greater longevity has exposed more marriages to the test of time: in 1820, the same proportion of marriages ended by death within 15 years of marriage as ended by divorce in 1980.[10] However, the relationship between social behaviour and law reform is complex. Commentators and researchers have disagreed about whether and to what extent reforms liberalizing divorce either responded to social demand or increased the divorce rate amongst couples who would otherwise have stayed together, but the better view seems to be that they have probably had only a modest and short-term impact on divorce rates.[11]

5.2.1 DIVORCES IN ENGLAND AND WALES

In the early 1900s, around 500 divorces were granted each year in England and Wales. Thereafter, the numbers rose after each reform enlarging the grounds on which divorce

---

6 Fahey (2014).
7 Ibid.
8 Law Com (1988a), paras 2.15–2.16.
9 Rheinstein (1972), 273–6; Phillips (1991), ch 9.
10 Walker (1991).
11 Fahey (2014), 103, citing in particular Allen and Gallagher (2007); González and Viitanen (2006).

could be obtained.[12] After 1923, there were about 2,500 divorces annually, from 1937, around 7–8,000. Social upheaval during and following the Second World War unsurprisingly generated an exceptional 60,300 divorces in 1947, but otherwise around 25–30,000 divorces were granted per year post-war until the 1960s.[13] This increase was partly attributable to the availability of public funding for legal services, ('legal aid') from 1948 until the mid-1970s, which made divorce accessible to those who had previously been unable to afford it. During the 1960s, the number of divorces doubled independently of any major substantive legal change.[14] Following reform in 1969—which introduced the law in force today—the number of divorces each year spiked, quickly exceeding 100,000 per year and peaking at 165,018 in 1993. But numbers have, on the whole, declined markedly since the early 2000s. In 2012, 118,140 divorces were granted in England and Wales.[15] It is anticipated that the *numbers* of divorces will drop over the coming decades as fewer people marry. Those who do marry increasingly do so later in life, reducing the number of youthful marriages which are more prone to divorce.[16]

Another useful measure is the divorce *rate*: how many people each year divorce per 1,000 members of the married population: see fig 5.2. This statistic is unaffected by changes in the overall population or the number of marriages and so more accurately indicates the frequency of divorce. In England and Wales, the divorce rate in 1961, before the 1969 reforms, was 2.1 per 1,000 of the married population.[17] By 1971, it was 6.0; it peaked at 14.1 in 2004, but since then has dropped away and in 2010 was 10.8, a rate

Figure 5.1 Number of marriages and divorces, 1932–2012, England and Wales: ONS 2014
Source: Reproduced from ONS (2014a), by Crown copyright ©.

---

[12] See 5.4.
[13] Stone (1990), table 13.1.
[14] The Matrimonial Causes Act 1963 amended the laws of condonation and collusion: Cretney (2003a), 349–51; there was also some liberalization in the case law during the 1960s: ibid, 352–3.
[15] ONS (2014a), 2.
[16] ONS (2010c), tables of projected numbers of marriages and divorces.
[17] Law Com (1988a), Appendix A.

Figure 5.2 Divorce rates by sex, 1972–2012, England and Wales: ONS 2014

Source: Reproduced from ONS (2014a), by Crown copyright © Readers should refer to the source for information regarding the data for 2002–10.

last seen in the late 1970s.[18] This drop suggests that the current married population are more likely to stay married. Indeed, while the divorce rate and numbers of divorces have declined, so too has the marriage rate, and with the age af first marriage rising, many of those who do marry are more likely to stay together.[19] Nevertheless, around 42 per cent of marriages are estimated to end in divorce, almost half of divorces occurring before the tenth wedding anniversary.[20]

Divorce statistics tell us nothing about marital breakdown that does not culminate in divorce.[21] But nor, of course, can they tell us about the breakdown of cohabiting relationships. Owing to the informal nature of these relationships, gathering data about them is challenging, but survey evidence indicates that their breakdown rate is higher than that of spouses.[22] There are now statistics on the dissolution of civil partnership, but the numbers unsurprisingly, given the youthfulness of the institution, remain low.[23]

5.2.2 WHO DIVORCES?

Twice as many divorces are granted to wives as to husbands,[24] which presumably indicates that twice as many divorce petitions are presented by wives; however, it is important to bear in mind that the petitioner is not necessarily the spouse who instigated the separation.[25] Just

---

18 ONS (2014), 3.
19 See 2.2. Beaujouan and Ní Bhrolcháin (2011), 14–15.
20 ONS (2014a), 10.
21 See Fahey (2014).
22 See discussion at 2.8.2.
23 ONS (2013b), 7–10.
24 ONS (2014a), 8.
25 Davis and Murch (1988), 64–6.

over half of couples divorcing today have at least one child aged under 16. In 2012, nearly 100,000 children under 16 experienced parental divorce;[26] of course, many others will have experienced the breakdown of their parents' non-marital relationships. Just as an increasing proportion of marriages are remarriages, so an increasing proportion of those divorcing are doing so for the second time: since 1981, the proportion has doubled to one in five.[27] Just as mean age at first marriage is rising,[28] so is mean age at divorce. In 2012, the mean age of divorcees was 44.7 for men and 42.2 for women. The median duration of marriage at divorce in 2012 was 11.5 years;[29] many couples will have separated some time before divorce is obtained, so the duration of their 'live' relationships will have been shorter. The divorce rate is considerably higher for younger couples (those under 30) than for older ones, especially those over 60.[30]

Various factors are associated with an increased likelihood of divorce, including: early (especially teenage) marriage; premarital cohabitation, whether with the spouse or another; prior relationship breakdown; premarital births; parental divorce; poor economic circumstances (also associated with young marriage); poor psychological and physical well-being.[31] Similar characteristics are associated with separation by unmarried couples.

5.3 THE NATURE, FUNCTION, AND LIMITS OF DIVORCE LAW

Before examining current divorce law and reform options, we sketch some inter-related themes which have been debated since judicial divorce was introduced in 1857. It is striking how timeless many of the political concerns about marriage and divorce seem to be, despite massive social and legal change. A law of divorce can assume various shapes, depending on the chosen degree, nature, and purpose of state intervention and the state's view of marriage. How can and should the law be used in relation to divorce?

5.3.1 REGULATION OR REGULARIZATION?

Divorce law can have more or less substantial roles, described by John Eekelaar as 'regulation' and 'regularization'. Regularization:

accepts, fatalistically, that separation and divorce will occur whatever the legal process does. It wishes to ensure that that process does not add to its harms, and leaves it largely to the people involved to settle the consequences. The legal process is therefore largely confined to ensuring that cases are processed efficiently and formalities attended to properly.[32]

---

[26] ONS (2014a), 8.
[27] ONS (2014a), 8.
[28] See 2.2.
[29] ONS (2014a), 6.
[30] Ibid, tables 3a and 3b.
[31] Clarke and Berrington (1999); Kiernan and Mueller (1998); Coleman and Glenn (2010); Beaujouan and Ní Bhrolcháin (2011); ONS (2014a).
[32] Eekelaar (1991b), 142.

Marriage and civil partnership can be created by a relatively straightforward, low-cost administrative process. The law could adopt a similarly hands-off stance at the end, effecting divorce by an administrative, rather than judicial, process instigated by both parties, or even (unlike marriage) by one of them. Divorce would thus be the product of private decision. There may be disputes about *consequences* of divorce, for example regarding children or finances in which the state might assert an interest to protect vulnerable family members or the public purse. But judicial determination of these ancillary issues would not detract from the essentially private, administrative nature of the underlying divorce.

By contrast, 'regulation' implies some more substantial role for the law, imposing restrictions on divorce which reflect the seriousness of that step and, by implication, the importance of marriage to the welfare of the parties, any children of the marriage, and society at large. The precise *nature* of that role and those restrictions would depend upon the state's view of marriage and its interest in it. But it would be more paternalistic, interventionist, and directive than mere 'regularization'.

5.3.2 FAULT OR 'NO-FAULT'?

The legal system characteristically dispenses justice, adjudicating on right and wrong. Divorce law could do the same, providing 'justice' for a wronged party and enforcing responsibility for wrongdoing. A fault-based divorce law identifies various 'matrimonial offences', commission of which render the 'guilty' spouse vulnerable to the penalty of being divorced on the other's application. This to some extent reflects a contractual view of marriage,[33] the guilty party's breach excusing the other from continued performance of the contract and entitling that party to some form of compensation. But, undermining the contract analogy, the couple do not decide what constitutes a breach: that is determined for them by the law of divorce (though it is for the innocent party, once a breach has occurred, to decide whether to instigate divorce). A fault-based law also performs an exhortatory function, establishing a moral code for marriage. However, there are various problems with administering fault-based divorce, and most—though not all—options for reform remove fault, leaving parties a greater or lesser degree of freedom to divorce simply because one or both of them consider that the marriage has broken down.[34]

5.3.3 'EASIER' OR 'HARDER' DIVORCE AND SUPPORTING THE INSTITUTION OF MARRIAGE

A perennial theme is whether the law makes divorce too easy or too hard, and whether any reform would make divorce easier or harder. This is linked to the degree of support which the law appears to offer the institution of marriage: easy divorce is said to undermine it, hard divorce to support it. These political debates continue despite Otto Kahn-Freund's observation nearly 50 years ago that 'it is a hopeless quest to promote the stability of marriage by making divorce "difficult" and... the problem is far more complex and more profound than the crude question whether divorce should be a little more or a little less "easy".'[35] Davis and Murch expand on this theme:

---

[33] See discussion at 2.4.1.
[34] See 5.7, and compare Rowthorn (1999) and Ellman (1997).
[35] Kahn-Freund (1967), 181.

G. Davis and M. Murch, *Grounds for Divorce* (Oxford: Clarendon Press, 1998), 148

It is tempting to view this debate in light of a liberal/conservative battleground, with the liberals seeking 'easier' divorce through shorter time periods or the abandonment of fault, whilst the conservatives struggle to maintain some disincentive to ill-considered termination of marriage through longer time periods or the maintenance of fault. But 'fault' and time constraints, whilst they may each be thought to make divorce more difficult, make it more difficult *in different ways*—and for different people. In other words, there are arguments for and against delay; there are also arguments for and against fault; but they are not the *same* arguments and they should not be lumped together under the heading of 'easier' or 'more difficult' divorce.

For example, a law which allows a spouse to obtain a divorce in under six months because of the other's adultery would be rendered considerably 'harder' if fault were replaced by a uniform one-year separation requirement. On the other hand, such a reform would make divorce 'easier' for a spouse who currently has to be separated for *two* years before divorce is permitted. But that same reform would be 'harder' for those individuals if it required them to use the one-year period to resolve all issues regarding their children and finances. All of this overlooks the emotional pain of divorce, even for those who ostensibly desire it, which the law can do little to alleviate.[36] Divorce in that sense is never 'easy'.

It is often said that the law of divorce should seek to support the institution of marriage, but again what this implies for the ease or difficulty of divorce is ambiguous. A restrictive divorce law, for example requiring proof of grave fault by the respondent, could be said to support marriage by emphasizing the seriousness of matrimonial obligations and requiring people to remain married, however dissatisfied they may be, unless one partner commits a relevant offence. The same law could be said to undermine marriage by insisting that marriages of poor quality be upheld, even if the parties have long since separated. By contrast, an 'easy' divorce law which released those who were dissatisfied with their marriages could be said to support the institution by reserving marriage and its legal consequences for 'good quality' relationships.[37] Might such a law encourage people to adopt a 'throw-away' approach to marriage and give up too soon? But is the law the, or even a, principal determinant of people's behaviour in this arena? And, if it is, how might it best seek to influence them?

5.3.4 CAN DIVORCE LAW AFFECT MARITAL AND DIVORCING BEHAVIOUR?

Commentators disagree on whether divorce law should simply provide a mechanism for individuals to terminate their marriage, or whether it can or should go further, seeking to influence relationship behaviour. We have noted the arguments about whether liberal divorce causes more marriages to fail. But other questions arise. Can and should divorce law be based on fault to deter whatever behaviour gives grounds for divorce?

---

[36] See Law Com (1990), paras 3.46–3.47; LCD (1993), 6.51–6.53.
[37] Cf *Reiterbund v Reiterbund* [1974] 1 WLR 788, extract below p 331; *Vervaeke v Smith* [1983] 1 AC 145, extract above p 85; Smart (2000), 371.

Does divorce law affect parties' willingness to invest in their marriages, easier divorce reducing parties' reliance on marriage?[38] If divorce is hard, might some be dissuaded from marrying at all? If so, would that be a good or bad thing? Can the law rescue couples from divorce by helping them to save saveable marriages? It has been said that the notion that divorce law can save individual marriages (as opposed to the institution more generally) is one that 'conventional wisdom has long firmly rejected'.[39] Nevertheless, the idea that something should be done to 'save saveable marriages' has persistent political appeal.[40] The law might also encourage parties to divorce in a particular manner—or at least make it easier for them to do so in a way that limits any bitterness and hostility. Government publications in recent decades have emphasized 'responsibility' on divorce and in dealing with the consequences of relationship breakdown.[41] The concern here is not with responsibility to respect the lifelong commitment of marriage or a guilty party's duty to accept responsibility (blame) for its breakdown. Rather, the new concept of responsibility requires *both* parties to 'divorce responsibly';[42] in particular, 'responsible' couples resolve their differences by way of mediation rather than via lawyers and the courts. However, whether law can steer parties' behaviour in this manner is questionable. Evidence that such attempts would fail caused major divorce reforms to be abandoned,[43] and recent legal aid reforms have—at least initially—seen mediation numbers plummet rather than rise as hoped.[44]

5.3.5 A LEGAL OR NON-LEGAL APPROACH?

While terminating spousal status is inevitably a legal process, the legal system need not have a monopoly over resolving the practical issues that arise on divorce (regarding children and financial settlements) or over determining whether the spouses' relationship has ended. Non-legal disciplines may have roles here: education and information provision, therapeutic intervention such as marriage counselling and social work, and mediation[45] may be able to perform some of those functions that the state is keen to pursue but which the *legal system* cannot fulfil. In particular, the legal system may be unable to save marriages or to help parties to cope psychologically with divorce. But the law could provide a framework for the delivery and funding of such services when divorce is sought or earlier. Whether the legal system can help couples to cooperate in resolving the practical consequences is hotly contested by lawyers and mediators.[46] Non-legal approaches to relationship support and breakdown have become increasingly prominent. However, the current substantive law of divorce, experienced by most couples as a fault-based process, sits somewhat uneasily alongside the outlook of non-legal disciplines and the forward-looking focus of the law in dealing with financial remedies and arrangements for children on divorce.

---

[38] See 5.7.1.
[39] Cretney (1996a), 45.
[40] E.g. LCD (1993), (1995). See Hasson (2006).
[41] LCD (1993), (1995); HO (1998); MOJ (2010a).
[42] Reece (2003).
[43] See 5.8.1.
[44] See 1.2.7.
[45] Mediation is not to be confused with counselling and reconciliation: see 1.2.7.
[46] Ibid.

5.4 A BRIEF HISTORY OF DIVORCE LAW TO 1969

Until 1857, divorce by way of court order terminating marriage did not exist.[47] The ecclesiastical courts issued decrees of nullity and various remedies short of divorce. A valid marriage could only be ended by Private Act of Parliament, a route open only to the wealthy.[48] Following a Royal Commission, the ecclesiastical courts' jurisdiction was replaced by a new civil court with the power to dissolve marriages. Under the Matrimonial Causes Act 1857, divorce could be obtained by the husband on the ground of his wife's adultery, and by the wife on the ground that her husband had been guilty of incestuous adultery, bigamy with adultery, rape (of someone other than the wife[49]), sodomy, bestiality, or adultery coupled either with desertion for two years or with cruelty. The lack of gender equality persisted until 1923, when wives were permitted to petition on grounds of adultery alone.[50] Adultery was effectively the sole ground for divorce until 1937:

Law Commission, *Facing the Future: A Discussion Paper on the Ground for Divorce*, Law Com No 170 (London: HMSO, 1988a)

2.1 Before the Divorce Reform Act 1969, a divorce could only be obtained [under the Matrimonial Causes Act 1937] by proving that the respondent had committed a matrimonial offence (the only material offences were adultery, cruelty and desertion for three years). A petitioner who was himself guilty of such an offence, or had somehow contributed to the offence of the other, or had condoned it, might be refused relief.[51] No divorce could be granted within three years of marriage, unless special leave was given on the ground that the petitioner would suffer exceptional hardship or that the respondent was guilty of exceptional depravity.

2.2 Since the 1950s there had been increasing disillusionment with the operation of the fault-based law.[52] It was clear that there was no real barrier to consensual divorce where both parties wanted it and one was prepared to commit, or perhaps appear to commit, a matrimonial offence to supply the necessary ground [though technically collusion was an absolute bar to divorce until 1963]. On the other hand, where parties were not prepared to resort to such expedients, there was often no remedy, even though the marriage had irretrievably broken down. It was argued by the proponents of reform that the court was in no position to allocate blame; that in many cases both parties were at fault, and that matrimonial offences were often merely symptomatic of the breakdown of the marriage rather than the cause. However, the majority of the Royal Commission on Marriage and Divorce (the Morton Commission of 1956) affirmed the matrimonial offence as the sole basis of divorce because they saw this as the only means to ensure the stability of the institution of marriage. Three attempts, in Private Members' Bills, to introduce a provision allowing for divorce after long

---

[47] For the long history, see Stone (1990) and Cretney (2003a), Part II.

[48] Probert (2011a).

[49] At that time, husbands could not be guilty of raping their wives: see 4.2.3.

[50] Probert (1999).

[51] The law barred divorce (absolutely or on a discretionary basis) where the petitioner had colluded with the respondent in drafting the petition, condoned or connived in the respondent's offence, or had also committed a matrimonial offence: see Cretney (2003a), 176–7.

[52] See Law Com (1966), paras 19 et seq.

periods of separation were unsuccessful. Finally, the publication in 1966 of the report of the Archbishop of Canterbury's Group [Mortimer Commission], entitled *Putting Asunder—A Divorce Law for Contemporary Society*, paved the way for reform. The report found the existing law concentrated exclusively on making findings of past delinquencies, whilst ignoring the current viability of the marriage. It therefore recommended that the matrimonial offence be abolished and be replaced by the principle of breakdown as the sole ground for divorce. It was envisaged that the court would determine whether the marriage had broken down after considering all the evidence.

2.3 The Lord Chancellor referred *Putting Asunder* to the Law Commission, whose response was published later in the same year, entitled Reform of the Grounds of Divorce—the Field of Choice. The Commission agreed with the Archbishop's Group's criticisms of the existing law. In particular, it found that the need to prove a matrimonial offence caused unnecessary bitterness and distress to the parties and their children. The law did not accord with social reality, in that many spouses who could not obtain a divorce simply left the "empty shells" of their marriages and set up "stable illicit unions" with new partners.[53] The Commission also agreed that where both parties wanted to end the marriage, divorce was easily available if they were prepared to commit or appear to commit a matrimonial offence. The Commission considered the objectives for a good divorce law to be:

(i) To buttress, rather than to undermine, the stability of marriage; and

(ii) When, regrettably, a marriage has irretrievably broken down, to enable the empty legal shell to be destroyed with the maximum fairness, and the minimum bitterness, distress and humiliation. . . .

2.4 Thus, both bodies agreed that the fault principle was unsatisfactory and that the law should be reformed to allow marriages which had irretrievably broken down to be dissolved in a humane fashion. The difficulty, of course, was how to identify those marriages which had irretrievably broken down. The Law Commission did not favour the solution advocated by the Archbishop's Group. First, it considered the proposed inquest impracticable partly because breakdown was not a justiciable issue. Secondly, it was concerned that such an inquest into the conduct of the parties in order to determine breakdown would cause unnecessary bitterness and humiliation and prevent the marital ties being dissolved with decency and dignity. After consultations between the various interested bodies, a compromise solution was reached whereby breakdown would become the sole ground for divorce, but would be inferred from the existence of one of a number of facts rather than by judicial inquest. This solution was enacted in the Divorce Reform Act 1969.

5.5 THE PRESENT LAW OF DIVORCE AND JUDICIAL SEPARATION

The present law of divorce, found in the MCA 1973, is largely as enacted in 1969, though recently amended by the Marriage (Same Sex Couples) Act 2013. The corresponding law

---

[53] Ibid, paras 33 et seq.

applying to civil partnerships is modelled on divorce law, with some difference of terminology, for example 'dissolution' rather than 'divorce' and 'applicant' rather than 'petitioner'. We use the traditional terminology of divorce here, only mentioning civil partnership separately where necessary to highlight a difference in the applicable law.[54] We look first at the substantive law under which divorce must be obtained. But it is essential also to understand divorce procedure, which largely shapes the parties' experience of contemporary divorce in operation.

5.5.1 THE GROUND FOR DIVORCE: IRRETRIEVABLE BREAKDOWN OF MARRIAGE

There is now only one ground for divorce and it is not fault-based: that the marriage has irretrievably broken down. This must be established at the date of the hearing, not at the date of filing the petition.[55] But one or both parties cannot simply assert that that is the case, however clear it may be. It is also necessary to prove one of five 'facts'.

Matrimonial Causes Act 1973, s 1[56]

(1) ...[A] petition for divorce may be presented to the court by either party to a marriage on the ground that the marriage has broken down irretrievably.

(2) The court hearing a petition for divorce shall not hold the marriage to have broken down irretrievably unless the petitioner satisfies the court of one or more of the following facts...

Three of those facts—adultery, desertion, and behaviour by the respondent—appear principally fault-based, though the behaviour fact can apply in situations that involve no fault, as such, by the respondent. Petitioners need not have 'clean hands'.[57] The other two—based on separation, for two years if the respondent consents to the divorce, for five years without that consent—are no-fault facts. English law therefore operates a 'mixed system' of divorce, comprising both fault-based and no-fault elements. The only difference of *substance* between divorce and civil partnership dissolution is that civil partnership may not be dissolved on the basis of 'adultery', though sexual infidelity by a civil partner would probably satisfy the 'behaviour' fact.[58]

The requirement that the petitioner must prove a 'fact' means parties cannot divorce immediately by mutual consent, a right which might have been thought implicit in the irretrievable breakdown test. Something more substantial must also be proved. In *Buffery v Buffery*, for example, the parties had grown apart and could no longer communicate, but would have to wait to obtain their divorce on a separation fact.[59] Divorce is in that sense a

---

[54] The Family Procedure Rules 2010 (FPR 2010) were supposed to modernize the language of divorce, but key parts of the old language have been retained because of the IT costs for the court service that would have been involved in changing it: Norgrove (2011), para 4.168.

[55] *Pheasant v Pheasant* [1972] Fam 202.

[56] CPA 2004, s 44.

[57] Contrast the old discretionary bars to divorce: Cretney (2003a), 188–95.

[58] Cf 2.7.6 on the omission of consummation from the nullity grounds in the CPA 2004.

[59] [1988] 2 FLR 365.

public, not a private matter. Conversely, even if it is accepted on all sides that the marriage has broken down irretrievably, the party with grounds to petition is entitled *not* to instigate proceedings.[60]

The fact-based approach to breakdown seeks to overcome the problem that, 'except in the clearest of cases, [whether a marriage has broken down irretrievably] is not a justiciable issue'.[61] What courts can adjudicate upon are more specific allegations of the sort comprised in the 'facts'. Curiously, however, there is no need to prove that the 'fact' *caused* the breakdown.[62] Once the 'fact' is proved, the court must grant a decree of divorce, *unless* it is satisfied on all the evidence that—notwithstanding proof of the 'fact' and the petitioner's wish to be divorced—the relationship has *not* irretrievably broken down.[63] This effectively requires petitioners to prove their 'fact', and leaves respondents with the uphill task of trying to persuade the court that the relationship remains viable.[64]

5.5.2 THE FACTS: ADULTERY BY THE RESPONDENT

Matrimonial Causes Act 1973, s 1(2)(a) and s 1(6)

(2) (a)... the respondent has committed adultery and the petitioner finds it intolerable to live with the respondent.

(6) Only conduct between the respondent and a person of the opposite sex may constitute adultery for the purposes of this section.

The proscribed behaviour

This fact applies only to marriages. It is not available as a fact for dissolution of civil partnership, even though it applies to same-sex marriages. However, even in the case of same-sex marriages, adultery entails voluntary intercourse by one spouse with a third party of the opposite sex.[65] Sexual activity between one spouse and someone of the same sex does not constitute adultery, though it may satisfy the behaviour fact (as it may for civil partnerships). No reported case has considered whether artificial insemination by another man without the husband's consent constitutes adultery.[66]

---

[60] E.g. they might delay for tactical reasons, such as to preserve matrimonial home rights (3.7.1): *Stevens v Stevens* [1979] 1 WLR 885.

[61] *Pheasant v Pheasant* [1972] Fam 202, 206.

[62] *Buffery v Buffery* [1988] 2 FLR 365, 366.

[63] Notwithstanding *Cotterell v Cotterell* [1998] 3 FCR 199, the court must examine the fact before assessing whether the marriage has broken down irretrievably.

[64] MCA 1973, s 1(4); CPA 2004, s 44(4). Cretney (2003a), 367 records that in no reported case has a respondent succeeded, though many apparently try, at least initially: Davis and Murch (1988), 102.

[65] Presumably including someone with a full gender recognition certificate and appropriate constructive surgery (Gender Recognition Act 2004); cf case law regarding consummation in such cases: see 2.7.5.

[66] Cretney (2003a), 254, n 28.

The old case law still offers guidance on the scope of adultery. The wife's lover in *Dennis v Dennis*, Mr Spillett, was found to be 'unable to effect his purpose', owing to nerves:

Dennis v Dennis (Spillett cited) [1955] P 153, 160

SINGLETON LJ:

I do not think that it can be said that adultery is proved unless there be some penetration. It is not necessary that the complete act of sexual intercourse should take place. If there is penetration by the man of the woman, adultery may be found, but if there is no more than an attempt, I do not think that a finding of adultery would be right.

Attempts at intercourse and the actual commission of lesser sexual acts, even those that might result in conception, were therefore held to be insufficient. Intercourse is not regarded as voluntary where the respondent is raped.[67] The effect of intoxicants on the respondent may not be so serious as to render intercourse involuntary. If voluntarily consumed alcohol disinhibits the respondent, causing him or her to have sex when he or she would not have done so sober, and even to have no memory of the event, the intercourse may still be adulterous. Contrast the case where intoxication deprives the respondent of the power to give any valid consent to intercourse.[68] Special issues arise where the respondent has validly contracted a polygamous marriage in another jurisdiction.[69]

The intolerability requirement

It is not enough to prove adultery. Petitioners must also prove that they find it intolerable to live with the respondent. But must the adultery and intolerability be connected—must the latter arise in consequence of the former? It was held in *Roper v Roper* that it must, otherwise a wife could take the chance occurrence of her husband's adultery to get the divorce that she had always wanted because of the irritating way in which he blew his nose. Nor could the petitioner simply *say* that she found it intolerable to live with the respondent: she might actually want a divorce because she was sexually attracted to another man.[70] However, the Court of Appeal subsequently took another view, which now represents the law:

Cleary v Cleary and Hutton [1974] 1 WLR 73 (CA), 76, 78

DENNING LJ:

As a matter of interpretation. I think the two facts in section [1(2)(*a*)] are independent and should be so treated. Take this very case. The husband proves that the wife committed adultery and that he forgave her and took her back. That is one fact. He then proves that, after she comes back, she behaves in a way that makes it quite intolerable to live with her. She corresponds with the other man and goes out at night and finally leaves her husband, taking the children with her. That

---

[67] *Redpath v Redpath* [1950] 1 All ER 600: unclear whether the burden of proving lack of consent falls on the respondent.

[68] *Goshawk v Goshawk* (1965) 109 SJ 290.

[69] Collins (2000), 18-021; Law Com (1985a), para 4.16; *Onobrauche v Onobrauche* (1978) 8 FL 107; *Quoraishi v Quoraishi* [1985] FLR 780.

[70] [1972] 1 WLR 1314, 1317.

is another fact. It is in consequence of that second fact that he finds it intolerable—not in consequence of the previous adultery. On that evidence, it is quite plain that the marriage has broken down irretrievably. He complies with section [1(2)(a)] by proving (a) her adultery which was forgiven; and (b) her subsequent conduct (not adultery), which makes it intolerable to live with her.

I would say one word more. In *Rayden on Divorce*...it is suggested...: "It may even be his own adultery which leads him to find it intolerable to live with the respondent." I cannot accept that suggestion. Suppose a wife committed adultery five years ago. The husband forgives her and takes her back. He then falls in love with another woman and commits adultery with her. He may say that he finds it intolerable to live with his wife, but that is palpably untrue. It was quite tolerable for five years: and it is not rendered intolerable by his love for another woman. That illustration shows that a judge in such cases as these should not accept the man's bare assertion that he finds it intolerable. He should inquire what conduct on the part of the wife has made it intolerable. It may be her previous adultery. It may be something else. But whatever it is, the judge must be satisfied that the husband finds it intolerable to live with her.

Scarman LJ agreed, noting s 1(3) of the MCA which requires the court 'so far as it reasonably can' to 'inquire...into the facts alleged' by each party. The judge must therefore be satisfied on the balance of probabilities that the petitioner is telling the truth in claiming that he or she finds it intolerable to live with the respondent. Yet he appreciated that in undefended cases there may be rather little evidence on which the judge could base his finding other than the petitioner's own statements. We shall see later that this problem has been exacerbated by the procedure now adopted in undefended cases.[71]

The relevance of continued cohabitation

A final issue is the relevance of continued cohabitation by the parties after the petitioner discovered the adultery:

Matrimonial Causes Act 1973, s 2(1)

One party to a marriage shall not be entitled to rely for the purposes of section 1(2)(a) above on adultery committed by the other if, after it became known to him that the other had committed that adultery, the parties have lived with each other for a period exceeding, or periods together exceeding, six months.

We explore the meaning of 'lived with each other' for these purposes when we examine the two separation facts. Essentially, it has been interpreted to mean sharing a household as husband and wife. Living under the same roof, even sharing a household, may therefore not prevent reliance on adultery, provided that the parties are not living 'as husband and wife'. The clock starts running from discovery of the last incident; so where there are multiple adulterous liaisons, petitioners who have continued to live with their spouse for over six months from the last known incident will not be prevented subsequently from relying on *later* adultery once it is discovered.[72] Cohabitation of less than six months is disregarded.[73] But if the parties cohabit for more than six months from the discovery of the adultery at any

---

[71] 5.5.7.
[72] *Carr v Carr* [1974] 1 WLR 1534.
[73] MCA 1973, s 2(2).

stage before the divorce is finally granted, the petitioner cannot rely on that adultery—the cohabitation effectively negates the intolerability requirement and so the claim that the marriage has broken down irretrievably.[74]

The proof of adultery

Respondents usually concede guilt in the relevant court forms. Otherwise, proof must be found elsewhere. It has been said that 'being a secret matter, as a rule [adultery] has to be inferred from evidence of inclination and opportunity, and if evidence is given of a guilty intention and of acts of gross indecency, adultery itself may readily be inferred'.[75] Evidence that a third party is the father of a child conceived by the wife after marriage may evidence adultery. So too would conviction of the husband for rape. The standard of proof has never been formally settled,[76] and in practice now the issue seldom arises, since the vast majority of divorces are undefended.

5.5.3 THE FACTS: BEHAVIOUR OF THE RESPONDENT

Matrimonial Causes Act 1973, s 1(2)(b); Civil Partnership Act 2004, s 44(5)(a)

...the respondent has behaved in such a way that the [petitioner/applicant] cannot reasonably be expected to live with the respondent.

This fact is frequently—but erroneously—referred to as 'unreasonable behaviour'. It is not the behaviour that must be unreasonable (though it may often be so) but the expectation that the petitioner should live with the respondent.[77] It has been said that this is an 'increasingly low' bar.[78]

The behaviour

The case law has considered a wide range of behaviour. The most serious cases involve violence and sexual assault. Others involve emotional abuse (e.g. a campaign of attrition by the husband designed to secure the wife's departure from the shared home);[79] financial irresponsibility causing problems for the family;[80] overambitious home improvement projects (inter alia, lifting all the floorboards and not replacing them for a two-year period, depositing 30 tons of rubble from beneath the floorboards in the garden, and leaving the lavatory without any door for eight months, all of which prevented the petitioner and children from

---

[74] *Kim v Morris* [2012] EWHC 1103, where cohabitation was treated primarily as an absolute bar to grant of divorce, or alternatively as a matter for the court's discretion, having regard to the reasons for, timing, and duration of the continued cohabitation, in that case after grant of the decree nisi (see p 338 below).

[75] *Dennis v Dennis (Spillett cited)* [1955] P 153, 161.

[76] See divergent views expressed in *Blyth v Blyth* [1966] AC 643.

[77] *Bannister v Bannister* (1980) 10 FL 240.

[78] *Miller Smith v Miller Smith* [2009] EWCA Civ 1297, [15].

[79] *Stevens v Stevens* [1979] 1 WLR 885; see also the boorish behaviour in *Livingstone-Stallard* [1974] Fam 47; *Birch v Birch* [1992] 1 FLR 564.

[80] *Carter-Fea* (1987) 17 FL 131.

conducting any sort of social life from the house);[81] questioning the children's paternity;[82] and various complaints regarding the couple's lack (usually) of sexual and intimate life.[83] Behaviour extraneous to the marriage—such as the commission of criminal offences by the respondent—might also suffice, though some dicta suggest that it must 'have some reference to' the marriage.[84] 'Behaviour' preceding desertion and desertion itself cannot provide a basis for this fact; petitioners could otherwise avoid the two-year requirement of the desertion fact.[85]

Difficult questions arise regarding respondents with mental health problems or other disabilities who are not responsible for their actions, or who may be entirely inactive owing to their problems. The issues were fully explored in *Thurlow v Thurlow*. The wife for many years suffered from epilepsy and a severe, worsening, neurological disorder which ultimately required full-time institutional care. The husband, who knew about the wife's condition before the marriage and that it might deteriorate, had done his best to care for her at home; their relationship had become 'more like a nurse and a patient'. Rees J concluded that 'negative' behaviour (i.e. inactivity) could suffice; so too could 'involuntary' behaviour caused by physical or mental illness:

Thurlow v Thurlow [1976] Fam 32 (Fam Div), 40–5

REES J:

The husband's case therefore consists of allegations of both negative and of positive behaviour on the part of the wife. The negative behaviour alleged and proved is that [over three years]...she gradually became a bedridden invalid unable to perform the role of a wife in any respect whatsoever until she reached a state in which she became unfitted even to reside in an ordinary household at all and required to be removed to a hospital and there reside for the rest of her life. The positive behaviour alleged and proved is that during the same period she displayed bad temper and threw objects at her mother-in-law and caused damage by burning various household items such as towels, cushions and blankets. From time to time she escaped from the home and wandered about the streets causing alarm and stress to those trying to care for her.

I am satisfied that by July 1972 the marriage had irretrievably broken down and since the wife, tragically, is to spend the rest of her life as a patient in a hospital the husband cannot be expected to live with her. But the question remains as to whether the wife's behaviour has been such as to justify a finding by the court that it is unreasonable to expect him to do so....[I]t is not sufficient to identify a state of affairs wherein there is a dead marriage coupled with an impossibility of cohabitation. It must be shown that it is the behaviour of the respondent which justifies a conclusion by the court that the petitioner cannot reasonably be expected to endure cohabitation. A state of affairs in which there is merely a dead marriage and inevitable separation of the parties can be dealt with under section 1(2)(e) [MCA 1973] by obtaining a decree after five years....It is worth observing that in cases in

---

[81] *O'Neill v O'Neill* [1975] 1 WLR 1118.
[82] Ibid.
[83] *Dowden v Dowden* (1978) 8 FL 106; *Mason v Mason* (1980) 11 FL 143; *Pheasant v Pheasant* [1972] Fam 202.
[84] *Katz v Katz* [1972] 1 WLR 955, 960, quoted in the extract from *Thurlow* below.
[85] *Morgan v Morgan* (1973) 117 SJ 223; *Stringfellow v Stringfellow* [1976] 1 WLR 645.

> which a respondent is mentally ill it will rarely, if ever, be possible to make use of section 1(2)
> (d) [two year separation with respondent's consent to divorce] because of doubt as to the
> capacity to give a valid consent....

Rees J then asked himself whether behaviour which is wholly or mainly negative in character would suffice:

> As to the distinction which has been made between "positive" and "negative" behaviour
> I can find nothing in the statute to suggest that either form is excluded. The sole test pre-
> scribed as to the nature of the behaviour is that it must be such as to justify a finding that the
> petitioner cannot reasonably be expected to live with the respondent. It may well be that in
> practice such a finding will more readily be made in cases where the behaviour relied upon is
> positive than those wherein it is negative. Spouses may often, but not always, be expected
> to tolerate more in the way of prolonged silences and total inactivity than of violent language
> or violent activity...
>
> But there remains for consideration the kind of case in which the conduct or behaviour
> relied upon is total passivity (sometimes described as a "cabbage" existence). I do not pause,
> at this stage, to consider whether the behaviour stems from mental illness or from a sudden
> accidental physical injury or from a malicious campaign of withdrawal from all aspects of
> matrimonial life with an intention of injuring the other spouse....

He concluded that whilst such conduct would not have amounted to 'cruelty' under the old law when it stemmed from illness, it could sometimes be proper to find that a petitioner could not reasonably be expected to live with such behaviour:

> I have found support for this view in a recent succinct statement of the law by Sir George
> Baker P. in *Katz v. Katz* [1972] 1 W.L.R. 955 ...:
>
> "Section 2 (1) (b) of the Divorce Reform Act 1969, under which this petition is brought, requires
> first that the husband 'has behaved.' Behaviour is something more than a mere state of affairs or
> a state of mind, such as for example, a repugnance to sexual intercourse, or a feeling that the wife
> is not reciprocating his love, or not being as demonstrative as he thinks she should be. Behaviour
> in this context is action or conduct by the one which affects the other. Such conduct may either
> take the form of acts or omissions or may be a course of conduct and, in my view, it must have
> some reference to the marriage."
>
> Accordingly upon principle and authority I conclude without hesitation that "negative" as
> well as "positive" behaviour is capable of forming the basis of a decree of divorce under
> section 1(2)(b)...

Rees J then considered whether behaviour stemming specifically from mental illness, which might be involuntary, fell within the statute. The wife had argued that for a respondent who had become a 'human vegetable' following an accident to be divorced on the basis of their 'behaviour' would be contrary to Parliament's intention and unjustly impute wrongdoing where none could be found. Divorce in such cases should instead be available only following five years' separation, which would give the respondent the additional protection of the safeguards applicable to separation cases (under ss 5 and 10).[86] But the

---

[86] See 5.5.5 and 5.5.6 below.

judge concluded that the behaviour fact could be satisfied in such cases, provided it was unreasonable to expect the petitioner to live with the respondent. Importantly, Rees J had emphasized that:

> The granting of the decree to the petitioner does not necessarily involve any blameworthiness on the part of the respondent, and, no doubt, in cases of misfortune the judge will make this clear in his judgment.

He focused on the need to protect the other spouse:

> There is no completely satisfactory answer to [the wife's] submissions but what may properly be said is that the law as laid down in *Williams v. Williams* [1964] A.C. 698 does provide a remedy by divorce for a spouse who is the victim of the violence of an insane respondent spouse not responsible in law or fact for his or her actions and in no respect blameworthy. The basis for that decision is the need to afford protection to the petitioner against injury. So also in the insanity cases where the behaviour alleged is wholly negative and no violence in deed or word is involved but where continuing cohabitation has caused, or is likely to cause injury to health, it should be open to the court to provide a remedy by divorce. Before deciding to grant a divorce in such cases the court would require to be satisfied that the petitioner could not reasonably be expected to live with the respondent and would not be likely to do so in the cases referred to by [counsel for the wife] unless driven to it by grave considerations which would include actual or apprehended injury to the health of the petitioner or of the family as a whole....The safeguard provided for the interests of respondents is that it is the judge and not the petitioner who must decide whether the petitioner can reasonably be expected to live with the respondent; and that decision is subject to review upon appeal.
>
> I do not propose to state any concluded view upon the case postulated in which a spouse is reduced to a human vegetable as the result of a road traffic accident and is removed at once to hospital to remain there for life. When that case does arise for decision I apprehend that the petitioner may face very considerable difficulties in establishing that there was any, or any sufficient, behaviour towards him or her or alternatively that such behaviour as there was justified a conclusion that the petitioner could not reasonably be expected to live with him or her.

Whether, given that behaviour, the petitioner can reasonably be expected to live with the respondent

Like the adultery fact, the behaviour fact has two parts, but as the extract from *Thurlow* shows, here they are linked: the behaviour and an evaluation of its impact on the petitioner. Moreover, while the intolerability test in adultery cases is simply a question of subjective fact, the 'reasonableness' test is more complex and on the face of it objective. It has been said that reference to the Book of Common Prayer and its 'for better, for worse' test is misplaced.[87] But the courts are—rightly or wrongly—required to identify the acceptable limitations and burdens of married life.

---

[87] *O'Neill v O'Neill* [1975] 1 WLR 1118, 1121.

One question is how far the apparently objective test of reasonableness is conditioned by the parties' characteristics. In *Pheasant v Pheasant*, Ormrod J noted the ambiguity of the word 'expected'. One interpretation, focusing on the petitioner's 'expected' future conduct—is there any prospect of the petitioner staying with the respondent?—would, it was conceded, make the other facts 'superfluous':

Pheasant v Pheasant [1972] Fam 202 (Fam Div), 207–9

ORMROD J:

[Counsel for the petitioner] concedes that the word "expected" is used in its other sense, which approximates to "required". He submits that the matter should be approached very largely, if not entirely, from the point of view of the petitioner, and that the court should consider . . . whether it is reasonable to require this petitioner to go on living with this respondent, having regard to her behaviour, giving that word its widest meaning and including both acts and omissions. This is sometimes called the subjective, in contrast to the objective approach, but so stated the antithesis is, in my opinion, misleading. In matrimonial cases there are two subjects to be considered . . . whose personalities are constantly interacting with one another throughout their relationship.

In my judgment, this construction is untenable for several reasons. It places the primary emphasis upon the petitioner and his personal idiosyncrasies, whereas the paragraph clearly places the primary emphasis on the behaviour of the respondent. A respondent whose behaviour is beyond reproach by any standards other than the petitioner's would be liable to be divorced without any possibility of resistance except to rely on section [1(4)] and try to show that the marriage has not finally broken down. [Counsel for the petitioner] faces this and says that under the modern law the court is concerned only to crush empty shells. Had this been the intention of the statute, paragraph (b) need only have provided that a decree could be granted if the court is satisfied that the petitioner finds life with the respondent unbearable. Once again the other four paragraphs would be surplusage and the court would be faced with an untriable issue. The experience of this particular trial which proceeded on [counsel for the petitioner's] assumption, should have convinced any doubters of the utter impracticality of such an inquiry. In the end it became reduced to a series of almost hysterical assertions by the petitioner and calm rebuttals by the respondent. So far from saving "bitterness, distress and humiliation" it produced a degree of humiliation of the petitioner which is unique in my experience . . .

[My preferred approach is to] consider whether it is reasonable to expect this petitioner to put up with the behaviour of this respondent, bearing in mind the characters and the difficulties of each of them, trying to be fair to both of them, and expecting neither heroic virtue nor selfless abnegation from either. It would be consistent with the spirit of the new legislation if this problem were now to be approached more from the point of view of breach of obligation than in terms of the now out-moded idea of the matrimonial offence.[88] It must also be borne in mind that the petitioner is still free to make his own decision whether to live with his wife or otherwise. The court is only concerned with the next stage, i.e. whether he is entitled to have his marriage dissolved.

---

[88] Whilst the matrimonial offence doctrine certainly has no place in the modern law, the concept of breach of obligation may be problematic, particularly in cases of mental health problems: see *Katz v Katz* [1972] 1 WLR 955, 961.

The courts have considered the reasonableness test several times.[89] In assessing what is reasonable, regard will be had to the particular individuals involved:

Ash v Ash [1972] Fam 135 (Fam Div), 140

BAGNALL J:

In order, therefore, to answer the question whether the petitioner can or cannot reasonably be expected to live with the respondent, in my judgment, I have to consider not only the behaviour of the respondent as alleged and established in evidence, but the character, personality, disposition and behaviour of the petitioner. The general question may be expanded thus: can this petitioner, with his or her character and personality, with his or her faults and other attributes, good and bad, and having regard to his or her behaviour during the marriage, reasonably be expected to live with this respondent? It follows that if a respondent is seeking to resist a petition on the first ground upon which Mr Ash relies, he must in his answer plead and his evidence establish the characteristics, faults, attributes, personality and behaviour on the part of the petitioner upon which he relies....

[I]t seems to me that a violent petitioner can reasonably be expected to live with a violent respondent; a petitioner who is addicted to drink can reasonably be expected to live with a respondent who is similarly addicted; a taciturn and morose spouse can reasonably be expected to live with a taciturn and morose partner; a flirtatious husband can reasonably be expected to live with a wife who is equally susceptible to the attractions of the other sex; and if each is equally bad, at any rate in similar respects, each can reasonably be expected to live with the other.

The Court of Appeal has twice endorsed the following test:[90]

Livingstone-Stallard v Livingstone-Stallard [1974] Fam 47, 54

DUNN J:

Would any right-thinking person come to the conclusion that this husband has behaved in such a way that this wife cannot reasonably be expected to live with him, taking into account the whole of the circumstances and the characters and personalities of the parties?

In *Birch v Birch*, the Court of Appeal added that, in judging the behaviour by reference to the petitioner's capacity to tolerate it, 'the court would consider to what extent the respondent knew or ought reasonably to have known of that capacity'.[91] However, the dicta in *Ash v Ash*[92] perhaps go too far in suggesting that violence is acceptable, even if reciprocated, and should perhaps be read in their historical context, predating the 1975 parliamentary Select

---

[89] For recent Court of Appeal decision, see *Birch v Birch* [1992] 1 FLR 564, which endorsed the extracts set out above.

[90] See *O'Neill v O'Neill* [1975] 1 WLR 1118; *Birch v Birch* [1992] 1 FLR 564.

[91] Ibid, 568.

[92] [1972] Fam 135, 140.

Committee inquiry on domestic violence in marriage. Bagnall J sought to support his view by reference to the Law Commission's aim 'to buttress, rather than undermine, the stability of marriage'. But the institution of marriage would scarcely be supported by divorce law apparently condoning domestic violence. The court in *Birch* made no direct comment on the *Ash* dicta, but did endorse a test that conduct must be judged only 'up to a point' by the capacity of the petitioner to endure it.[93]

In *Thurlow*, the court found the fact to be satisfied on the following test:

Thurlow v Thurlow [1976] Fam 32 (Fam Div), 44, 46

REES J:

...If the behaviour stems from misfortune such as the onset of mental illness or from disease of the body, or from accidental physical injury, the court will take full account of all the obligations of the married state. These will include the normal duty to accept and to share the burdens imposed upon the family as a result of the mental or physical ill-health of one member. It will also consider the capacity of the petitioner to withstand the stresses imposed by the behaviour, the steps taken to cope with it, the length of time during which the petitioner has been called upon to bear it and the actual or potential effect upon his or her health. The court will then be required to make a judgment as to whether the petitioner can fairly be required to live with the respondent....

...It will be for the judge to decide subject to review on appeal whether the behaviour is sufficiently grave to make it unreasonable to expect the petitioner to endure it. In reaching the decision the judge will have regard to all the circumstances including the disabilities and temperaments of both parties, the causes of the behaviour and whether the causes were or were not known to the petitioner, the presence or absence of intention, the impact of it upon the petitioner and the family unit, its duration, and the prospects of cure or improvement in the future.

Since no causal connection between the fact relied on and the breakdown of the marriage is required, the behaviour relied on may post-date a breakdown caused by the *petitioner's* earlier behaviour. Such circumstances are taken into account in applying the reasonableness test. We might expect both parties in such cases to be keen to divorce, so, save where the respondent seeks some tactical advantage from keeping the marriage formally alive, this point will rarely arise.[94]

The relevance of continued cohabitation

As in the case of adultery, the Act instructs the court what relevance to attach to cohabitation following the last behaviour complained of. The relevance of cohabitation here is different from the adultery cases. Under s 2(3)[95] continued cohabitation of under six months since the last event relied on as behaviour is disregarded in deciding whether

---

[93] *Birch v Birch* [1992] 1 FLR 564, 568.
[94] *Stevens v Stevens* [1979] 1 WLR 885.
[95] CPA 2004, s 45(1), (2).

the petitioner can reasonably be expected to live with the respondent. Unlike adultery, there is no bar on use of the behaviour fact where the cohabitation lasts beyond six months; but nor is that irrelevant to the reasonableness test. In extreme cases the petitioner may have had no choice but to remain in the home, even the same bed, as the respondent:

Bradley v Bradley [1973] 1 WLR 1291 (CA), 1295

SCARMAN LJ:

There are many, many reasons why a woman will go on living with a beast of a husband. Sometimes she may live with him because she fears the consequences of leaving. Sometimes it may be physical duress, but very often a woman will willingly make the sacrifice of living with a beast of a husband because she believes it to be in the true interest of her children. Is such a woman to be denied the opportunity...of calling evidence to show that, although she is living with him, yet the family situation is such and his behaviour is such that she cannot reasonably be expected to do so? It seems to me...that there is no logical difficulty in the way of the wife; and the Act plainly envisages that she should have the opportunity of placing her case before the court.

The behaviour fact and civil partnership 'adultery'

Since the adultery fact is unavailable in civil partnership cases, civil partners wishing to complain of sexual infidelity must rely instead on the behaviour fact. This was the government's intention.[96] Indeed, given the narrowness of the adultery test, many forms of sexual infidelity practised by spouses also have to proceed under this fact, including all forms of same-sex infidelity. It may be that the outcome will not be different, though use of the behaviour fact involves the ostensibly more stringent 'reasonableness' test, instead of the subjective 'intolerability' test. Conversely, applicants using this fact enjoy the more generous approach to continued cohabitation.

However, all of this depends upon judicial evaluation of whether sexual infidelity is something that makes it unreasonable to expect the applicant to live with the respondent. This requires an examination of what civil partnership is for. As we saw in chapter 2, the law of nullity studiously avoids referring expressly to any sexual relationship between civil partners, even though many civil partners do have sexual relationships. In dealing with dissolution cases based on this fact, the judges will have to decide whether that cultural expectation of sexual intimacy and the applicant's expectation of exclusivity is enough to justify dissolution on this basis.[97]

---

96 Women and Equality Unit (2003b), 35.
97 Cretney (2006a), 32–8.

5.5.4 THE FACTS: DESERTION FOR TWO YEARS BY THE RESPONDENT

Matrimonial Causes Act 1973, s 1(2)(c); Civil Partnership Act 2004, s 44(5)(d)

...the respondent has deserted the [petitioner/applicant] for a continuous period of at least two years immediately preceding the [presentation of the petition/making of the application]

Desertion and the separation facts compared

Desertion is the last of the facts originating in the old law of divorce. Some of its basic ingredients are similar to the no-fault separation facts introduced in 1969. The features which distinguish it from separation are: (i) the deserter must have no justification for leaving; and (ii) the party not in desertion must not consent to the other's absence, although now wishing to divorce the deserter. Where, as is likely, the deserter also wants to divorce, the parties may proceed under the next fact: two years' separation with the respondent's consent to divorce. Desertion is therefore likely to be used only where two-year separation (or some other fact[98]) is unavailable because the deserter refuses to consent to divorce, or where the petitioner perceives that some tactical advantage is to be gained by relying on desertion. The deserter may only petition for divorce without the other's consent if the desertion last five years, on the basis of five years' separation.

The basic elements of desertion

The essence of desertion lies in destroying the 'consortium vitae' of marriage without consent or other justification. It consists of two elements, one physical—de facto separation—and the other mental—the 'animus deserendi', that is, the intention to bring the matrimonial union to an end.[99] Both must be present throughout a two-year period without consent or other justification. If the original separation is unaccompanied by the requisite intention, it is enough that that intention arises later, provided both separation and intention are present together for two years.[100] The two-year clock may be stopped for up to six months in total during attempted reconciliations.[101]

Physical separation

The physical separation required for desertion is not as complete as the word might suggest. A mere refusal of sexual intercourse will not suffice.[102] However, one spouse may desert the other even though they remain living under the same roof. At various points in history,

---

[98] Desertion will often be accompanied by adultery, but not necessarily by behaviour: *Stringfellow v Stringfellow* [1976] 1 WLR 645.

[99] *Lang v Lang* [1955] 1 AC 402, 417.

[100] *Hopes v Hopes* [1949] P 227, 231.

[101] MCA 1973, s 2(5); CPA 2004, s 45(6).

[102] *Weatherley v Weatherley* [1947] AC 628.

notably in the aftermath of the Second World War and during housing market slumps, this has been important for those unable to find alternative accommodation. The key here is the concept of the shared 'household':

Hopes v Hopes [1949] P 227 (CA), 235–6

DENNING LJ:

One of the essential elements of desertion is the fact of separation. Can that exist whilst the parties are living under the same roof? My answer is: "Yes". The husband who shuts himself up in one or two rooms of his house, and ceases to have anything to do with his wife, is living separately and apart from her as effectively as if they were separated by the outer door of a flat. They may meet on the stairs or in the passageway, but so they might if they each had separate flats in one building. If that separation is brought about by his fault, why is that not desertion? He has forsaken and abandoned his wife as effectively as if he had gone into lodgings. The converse is equally true. If the wife ceases to have anything to do with, or for, the husband and he is left to look after himself in his own rooms, why is not that desertion? She has forsaken and abandoned him as effectively as if she had gone to live with her relatives....I find myself in agreement with all the decisions of the Divorce Division except perhaps *Wanbon v. Wanbon*...where the parties were said to be still in one household. If that means that, although living at arms length, they were still sharing the same living room, eating at the same table and sitting by the same fire, then I cannot agree with the finding of desertion....[Desertion exists] where the parties are living separately and apart. In cases where they are living under the same roof, that point is reached when they cease to be one household and become two households; or, in other words, when they are no longer residing with one another or cohabiting with one another.

Parties may sometimes be prevented from physically cohabiting, for example because one spouse has been hospitalized. Desertion can occur here even though the parties had no common home which could be left: 'desertion is not the withdrawal from a place, but from a state of things...The law does not deal with the mere matter of place. What it seeks to enforce is the recognition and discharge of the common obligations of the married state'.[103] So a husband could be in desertion by leaving the district and setting up home with another woman while his wife was in hospital, despite continuing to support the wife financially.[104]

Intention, communication, and consent

It has been said that it is not necessary that the deserting spouse should communicate his or her intention to desert to the other.[105] However, it must be shown that the innocent spouse does not consent to the deserter's absence. Suppose that, at the outset, the innocent spouse consents to the other's physical absence on the understanding that it is for some temporary purpose, but the other—without the innocent spouse's knowledge—subsequently forms an intention to desert. It has been held that unless and until the remaining spouse

---

103 *Pulford v Pulford* [1923] P 18, 21–2.
104 *Yeatman v Yeatman* (1868) 1 P&D 489.
105 *Nutley v Nutley* [1970] 1 WLR 217, 221.

withdraws consent to the other's absence, desertion cannot be found. Surprisingly, perhaps, that spouse's lack of knowledge of the other's intention to desert seems not automatically to vitiate consent to the other's continued absence.[106]

Respondents experiencing mental health problems may leave without intending to desert. Capacity to form, and actual formation of, intention must be proved, and the respondent will be judged on the facts as he or she honestly believes them to be.[107] Where the respondent has fluctuating capacity and had the required intention at some point, the court may treat desertion as continuing during periods of incapacity if it would (without the incapacity) have inferred from the evidence that the desertion continued at that time.[108]

Justification and constructive desertion

A party is only in desertion where there is no justification for his or her departure. That justification may be actual, reasonably believed,[109] or, in case of delusion at least, honestly believed.[110] For such justification to be found, the cause must be 'grave and weighty'.[111] In such cases, the tables may be turned and the party who left may be entitled to petition for divorce on the basis of 'constructive desertion': where one spouse's conduct drives the other party away and the latter is justified in leaving.

Lang v Lang [1955] AC 402 (PC), 417–18

LORD PORTER:

[T]he party truly guilty of disrupting the home is not necessarily or in all cases the party who first leaves it. The party who stays behind (their Lordships will assume this to be the husband) may be by reason of conduct on his part making it unbearable for a wife with reasonable self-respect, or powers of endurance, to stay with him, so that he is the party really responsible for the breakdown of the marriage. He has deserted her by expelling her: by driving her out. In such a case the factum is the course of conduct pursued by the husband—something which may be far more complicated than the mere act of leaving the matrimonial home. It is not every course of conduct by the husband causing the wife to leave which is a sufficient factum. A husband's irritating habits may so get on the wife's nerves that she leaves as a direct consequence of them, but she would not be justified in doing so. Such irritating idiosyncrasies are part of the lottery in which every spouse engages on marrying, and taking the partner of the marriage "for better, for worse." The course of conduct—the "factum"—must be grave and convincing.

This involves determining what behaviour the departing spouse is expected to tolerate before his or her departure will be justified and constructive desertion by the remaining spouse found. Like the behaviour fact, this requires the courts to make value judgements

---

[106] Ibid; cf *Santos v Santos* [1972] Fam 247, below at 5.5.5, which assumes that communication is required for desertion.

[107] *Perry v Perry* [1964] 1 WLR 91.

[108] MCA 1973, s 2(4); CPA 2004, s 45(5).

[109] *Everitt v Everitt* [1949] P 374.

[110] *Perry v Perry* [1964] 1 WLR 91.

[111] *Yeatman v Yeatman* (1868) 1 P&D 489, 494.

about married life which are likely to change as social conditions and understandings of the nature of those relationships alter.[112] Most of the case law predates introduction of the behaviour fact, but at a time when its forerunner—'cruelty'—afforded grounds for divorce. Cruelty was a stricter concept than 'behaviour', and conduct not amounting to cruelty could justify departure and so create constructive desertion.[113] It is hard now to imagine conduct justifying desertion which would not itself satisfy the 'behaviour' fact. But if one party simply orders the other to leave, it will still be dealt with as desertion.[114]

Intention to desert in cases of constructive desertion will be inferred where the other spouse's departure is the natural and probable consequence of the respondent's behaviour, but that inference can be rebutted where the evidence shows that the respondent did not intend the petitioner to leave. As in the criminal law, it is necessary to distinguish between intention and desire: the respondent may not want the petitioner to go, but nevertheless know that that will be the effect of his or her conduct and so intend it.[115]

Refusal to accept the deserter's return

Desertion ends if the parties are reunited. If the hitherto innocent unreasonably refuses to let the respondent back, that spouse will now be in desertion. However, petitioners are sometimes justified in refusing respondents' offers to return and the original desertion is deemed to continue. This was the outcome in *Everitt*, where the wife's reasonable (though, as it turned out, erroneous) belief that the husband had committed adultery during his desertion justified her refusing his offer to return, even though she knew that such adultery could not now be continuing.[116] If the respondent had committed domestic violence against the petitioner prior to desertion (actual or constructive), that too would justify a refusal to resume cohabitation.

5.5.5 THE SEPARATION FACTS

Matrimonial Causes Act 1973, s 1(2)(d)(e); Civil Partnership Act 2004, s 44(5)(b)(c)

...the parties...have lived apart for a continuous period of at least two years immediately preceding the presentation of the petition (..."two years' separation") and the respondent consents to a decree being granted.
...the parties...have lived apart for a continuous period of at least five years immediately preceding the presentation of the petition (..."five years' separation").[117]

These two facts were introduced in 1969, providing the first no-fault bases for divorce in English law. The five-year separation fact is the sole fact available to a 'guilty' party whose

---

112 *Hall v Hall* [1962] 1 WLR 1246.
113 *Timmins v Timmins* [1953] 1 WLR 757.
114 *Morgan v Morgan* (1973) 117 SJ 223.
115 *Lang v Lang* [1955] AC 402.
116 [1949] P 374.
117 The CPA provisions reflect the different procedural terminology.

spouse does not want to divorce.[118] The introduction of these facts contributed to the sudden rise in divorces shortly after the legislation came into force, as the 'backlog' of long-dead marriages in which neither party had committed—or wished to plead—any fault could finally be dissolved.[119]

Separation shares some ground with the basic concepts underpinning desertion, but there is no need here to prove that one party had left without the other's consent or that the departure was unjustified. As in the case of desertion, the clock can stop running for a period or periods of time adding up to no more than six months of resumed cohabitation.[120] The Court of Appeal considered the essential ingredients of separation in *Santos v Santos*. A key question was whether the concept of 'living apart', which is central to the separation facts, was a purely physical state or included some sort of mental element, bearing in mind that the meaning of the term must be the same for both separation facts, but distinctive from desertion. Sachs LJ took the view that 'living apart' required something more than physical separation:

Santos v Santos [1972] Fam 247 (CA), 259–63

SACHS LJ:

"Living apart": prima facie meaning

[T]he phrase "living apart" when used in a statute concerned with matrimonial affairs normally imports something more than mere physical separation [namely a recognition by one or both spouses that the marriage is no longer subsisting]. . . . It follows that its normal meaning must be attributed to it in the 1969 Act, unless one is led to a different conclusion either by the general scheme of the statute coupled with difficulties which would result from such an interpretation or alternatively by some specific provision in that statute.

The 1969 Act: general scheme: questions for consideration

[The lack of express provisions for dealing with the hospitalization of mentally ill spouses, long-term imprisonment etc.] tend to highlight some linked problems bearing on the meaning of "living apart" which have caused us concern.

He then posed himself three questions:

If these words import an element additional to physical separation, can that element depend on a unilateral decision or attitude of mind; if so, must its existence be communicated to the other spouse; and, in any event, how can it be identified so that it is in practice capable of judicial determination?

Obviously this element is not one which necessarily involves mutual consent, for otherwise the new Act would not afford relief under head (e) in that area where it was most plainly intended to be available—where the "innocent" party adheres to the marriage, refusing to

---

[118] See Law Com (1966), paras 85 et seq.
[119] Richards (1996), 152. Cretney describes witnessing such divorces being granted: (1996a), 41.
[120] MCA 1973, s 2(5); CPA 2004, s 45(6).

recognise that in truth it has ended, often despite the fact that the "guilty" one has been living with someone else for very many years. So it must be an element capable of being unilateral: and it must in our judgment involve at least a recognition that the marriage is in truth at an end—and has become a shell, to adopt a much-used metaphor.

If the element can be unilateral in the sense of depending on the attitude of mind of one spouse, must it be communicated to the other spouse before it becomes in law operative? That is a question that gave particular concern in the course of the argument. There is something unattractive in the idea that in effect time under head (e) can begin to run against a spouse without his or her knowledge. Examples discussed included men in prison, in hospital, or away on service, whose wives, so far as they knew, were standing by them: they might, perhaps, thus be led to fail to take some step which they would later feel could just have saved the marriage. On the other hand, communication might well be impossible in cases where the physical separation was due to a breakdown in mental health on the part of the other spouse, or a prolonged coma such as can occasionally occur. Moreover, need for communication would tend to equate heads (d) and (e) with desertion... something unlikely to be intended by the legislature.[121] Moreover, bowing to the inevitable is not the same thing as intending it to happen.

In the end we have firmly concluded that communication by word or conduct is not a necessary ingredient of the additional element.

On the basis that an uncommunicated unilateral ending of recognition that a marriage is subsisting can mark the moment when "living apart" commences, "the principal problem becomes one of proof of the time when the breakdown occurred".... How, for instance, does a judge in practice discharge the unenviable task of determining at what time the wife of a man immured long term in hospital or one serving a 15 year sentence changes from a wife who is standing by her husband (in the sense of genuinely keeping the marriage alive until he recovers or comes out) to one who realises the end has come but visits him merely from a sense of duty arising from the past? Sometimes there will be evidence such as a letter, reduction or cessation of visits, or starting to live with another man. But cases may well arise where there is only the oral evidence of the wife on this point.... In some cases, where it appears that the petitioning wife's conduct is consistent with a continuing recognition of the subsistence of the marriage, automatic acceptance of her uncorroborated evidence inconsistent with such conduct would not be desirable. On the other hand, there can be cases where a moment arrives as from which resumption of any form of married life becomes so plainly impossible, e.g. on some grave disability becoming known to be incurable, that only slight evidence is needed—for the nature of the breakdown is so patent.

The difficulties arising from some of these problems at one stage led to hesitation as to whether after all "living apart" in this particular Act might not refer merely to physical separation.... [But] injustices and absurdities... could result from holding that "living apart" refers merely to physical separation; these... outweigh any hard cases or difficulties that can arise from the standard interpretations.

One category under head (e) is exemplified by the case of a long-sentence prisoner whose wife has, with his encouragement, stood by him for five years—only for her to find that when he comes out he files a petition for divorce relying on ground (e). But the more usual categories relate to men who could unjustly find time running against them through absences on public service or on business in areas where, out of regard for the welfare of

---

121 Cf *Nutley v Nutley*, n 105 above and associated text.

the wife or the children of the family, the former remains in this country: particularly hardly could this bear on men whose home leave did not for some years total the six months referred to in [s 2(5) MCA 1973].

Turning from hardships under head (e) to absurdities under head (d), read in conjunction with [s 2(5) MCA 1973], it is plain that in cases arising under the latter head the spouses can spend up to 20 per cent. of their time together without interrupting the continuity of the separation (i.e. six months in two years and six months). Thus if living apart means mere physical separation, a man who got home on leave for less than 20% of the two to two-and-a-half years immediately preceding the filing of the petition would be in a position to satisfy the court under head (d), even though he and his wife had been on excellent terms until they had a row on the last day of his last leave. As petitions under head (d) are normally undefended, there would be no evidence to rebut this presumption that the breakdown of the marriage was irretrievable and the decree would be granted. Unless—contrary to our view—the Act intended to permit divorce by consent simpliciter such a result would be absurd. On the contrary the tenor of [s 1(2) MCA 1973] is to ensure that under heads (c), (d) and (e) a breakdown is not to be held irretrievable unless and until a sufficiently long passage of time has shown this to be the case...

[S 2(6) MCA 1973]...makes it clear beyond further debate that when two spouses are living in the same house, then, as regards living apart, a line is to be drawn, in accordance with the views of Denning LJ [in *Hopes v Hopes*, see above], and they are to be held to be living apart if not living in the same household.

And so he concluded that *in the vast majority of cases*, it would be necessary to prove more than mere physical separation: it cannot be said that the parties are living apart 'where both parties recognise the marriage as subsisting'. Where a separation started on a 'voluntary' basis, the judge would have to determine at what point either or both parties no longer regarded the marriage as subsisting, but rather a 'mere shell'. However:

We have deliberately refrained from speaking unequivocally of "all cases" (as opposed to "the vast generality of cases") arising under heads (d) and (e) for the same reason that we have not sought to attempt any definition either of "consortium" or of "absence of consortium"; similarly we have gone no further than to specify the attitude of mind that precludes its being said that the parties are living apart. This is because there may arise wholly exceptional cases: to take an extreme and one hopes a particularly unlikely example, there may one day fall to be dealt with a case were some misfortune has caused both spouses to be of unsound mind for more than five years. Such cases can only be dealt with when they arise—and it can then be decided whether resort can be had to inferences to be drawn from the hopelessness of the situation in which the parties find themselves.

Sachs LJ was concerned that judges should carefully investigate the facts, and not simply rubber-stamp applications on the basis of written evidence. However, we shall see that the procedure now used for undefended divorces effectively leaves the judge in no position to do much more than rubber-stamping.[122]

The issue addressed by Denning LJ in *Hopes* had received some attention in relation to separation prior to *Santos*. The 'living apart' requirement can be difficult for couples who continue living in the same house for laudable reasons. In *Mouncer v Mouncer*, the parties

---

[122] 5.5.7.

stayed under the same roof and tried to carry on a semblance of normal domestic life for the benefit of their two children. They slept in separate rooms, but usually ate all together (the wife having cooked) and, bedrooms aside, shared use of the other rooms; they both worked part-time, each doing chores while the other was at work; the wife no longer did the husband's laundry. Could they be said to be 'living apart'? The judge found such a conclusion impossible where they were—as here—still living 'in the same household':

Mouncer v Mouncer [1972] 1 WLR 321 (Fam Div), 322–3

WRANGHAM J:

There have, of course, been many cases in which it has been held under the former law that husband and wife were living apart even though they lived under the same roof ... It is, however, to my mind plain that if this case were being considered under the old law it would be held that this husband and wife were living together ...: see *Hopes v Hopes*. It is contended on the part of both the husband and the wife that the test under the new legislation is wholly different. [The first part of section 2(6) MCA 1973] provides that for the purposes of the Act, a husband and wife shall be treated as living apart unless they are living with each other in the same household. It is argued that the effect of this subsection is that spouses are to be treated as living apart unless they fulfil two separate requirements. First they must be living with each other; second, they must be living in the same household. On the facts of this case it is said the parties may be said to be living in the same household but they were not in any real sense living with each other. The wife had done all she could to reject her husband as a husband and to break the matrimonial relation between them by refusing to share his bedroom. It is hard to see how husband and wife who share a household could ever be said not to be living with each other unless rejection of a normal physical relationship coupled with the absence of normal affection is sufficient for this purpose. But if the effect of [s 2(6)] is that spouses are to be treated as living apart whenever one spouse has refused the right of intercourse, and they are (as of course they naturally would be in such circumstances) on bad terms, that would mean that the law ... has been altered, and I think that if Parliament had intended to do that, it would have done so specifically.

The truth, in my opinion, is that [the first part of s 2(6)] does not lay down two separate requirements at all. A clue to the true meaning of the subsection can be discovered from comparison with [the second part of s 2(6)] which provides: "References in this section to the parties ... living with each other shall be construed as references to their living with each other in the same household." It is plain that in that subsection the words "in the same household" are words of limitation. Not all living with each other is sufficient for the purposes of [that part of s 2(6)], only living with each other in the same household. And in my view the same applies to [the first part of s 2(6)]. What it means is that the husband and wife can be treated as living apart, even if they are living with each other, unless that living with each other is in the same household. It follows that in my judgment the draftsman ... was not providing for a case where parties live in the same household but do not live with each other. Indeed I do not think that there is such a case. ... For these reasons I have come to the conclusion that it is not proved that these spouses were living apart.

However, contrary to Wrangham J's opinion, it may be possible for spouses to live in the same household without living 'with each other'. It could have been argued in *Mouncer* that they were living in the same household not 'with each other' as spouses, but in some other capacity, there as co-parents. *Fuller v Fuller* provides a rather different illustration of such a case:

Fuller v Fuller [1973] 1 WLR 730 (CA), 732

LORD DENNING MR:

From 1964 to 1968 the parties were undoubtedly living apart. The wife was living with [Mr Penfold as his] wife in that household, and the husband was separate in his household. From 1968 to 1972 [after having suffered a coronary thrombosis and being advised that he ought not to live alone] the husband came back to live in the same house but not as a husband. He was to all intents and purposes a lodger in the house. [Section 2(6)] says they are to be treated as living apart "unless they are living with each other in the same household". I think the words "with each other" mean "living with each other as husband and wife". In this case the parties were not living with each other in that sense. The wife was living with Mr Penfold as his wife. The husband was living in the house as a lodger. It is impossible to say that husband and wife were or are living with each other in the same household. It is very different from *Mouncer v Mouncer* . . . where the husband and wife were living with the children in the same household—as husband and wife normally do—but were not having sexual intercourse together. That is not sufficient to constitute "living apart". I do not doubt the correctness of that decision. But the present case is very different. . . . I would allow the appeal and pronounce the decree nisi of divorce.

Although Lord Denning attempts to distinguish *Mouncer*, the contrary argument can be made. If the Fullers were not living 'with each other' by virtue of their new status as landlady and lodger, could the Mouncers not similarly be regarded as not living with each other now that they did so as co-parents? Indeed, parties who behave like the Mouncers—sharing the task of parenting following relationship breakdown—act compatibly with contemporary notions of good parenting post-divorce. It would be unfortunate for such responsible behaviour to disqualify couples from divorcing on this no-fault basis.

Two-year separation and the consent requirement

The separation facts are differentiated by the requirement in the two-year cases that the respondent consents to the divorce. That consent must exist at the time of the decree,[123] must be made positively, rather than simply inferred from lack of protest,[124] and is ordinarily supplied by the respondent completing the relevant court form. Consent must be full and informed: the respondent must have had the information necessary to understand the consequences of consenting to the decree.[125]

---

[123] *Beales v Beales* [1972] Fam 210.

[124] *McGill v Robson* [1972] 1 WLR 237.

[125] MCA 1973, s 2(7); CPA 2004, s 45(3)–(4). The court can rescind a decree nisi (before the decree absolute has been granted—see p 337 below) if the petitioner is found to have misled the respondent, intentionally or not, about any matter which the respondent took into account in deciding to consent: MCA 1973, s 10(1); CPA 2004, s 48(1).

5.5.6 BARS AND OTHER RESTRICTIONS ON DIVORCE

There are several bars and restrictions on divorce, some of which apply to all facts, others to just one or both of the separation facts. In practice, the principal function of most of these bars is to provide bargaining power to one party: to hold up the divorce (and so the opportunity to remarry) pending a desirable settlement of ancillary matters, particularly financial issues. Divorce is rarely delayed substantially, let alone barred outright, by a bar or restriction being invoked.

Time bar on divorce

It is not possible to petition for divorce or apply for dissolution of a civil partnership during the first year of the union.[126] However, it is possible to rely on events during that first year to prove the fact relied on. For example, parties could separate immediately after the wedding and petition for divorce on the basis of two years' separation on their second wedding anniversary. The remedy of judicial separation provides relief, including access to financial remedies, where necessary during that first year.[127] Nullity proceedings can also be brought immediately where grounds to do so apply.[128] Occupation and non-molestation orders under the FLA 1996 can provide protection from domestic violence.[129]

This bar delays divorce and so delays remarriage. To that extent, it might be argued that it breaches the right to marry under Article 12 ECHR. In *F v Switzerland*,[130] it was briefly asserted that this sort of rule does not violate the Convention. Although the Court offered no reasoning, it may be inferred that since the rule operates during a marriage, and as a condition of divorce, it can be distinguished from the bar on remarriage arising *after* divorce which was successfully challenged in that case. Since the Convention does not confer a right to divorce, it cannot restrict the terms on which divorce may be granted, so a time bar of this sort is legitimate. But once a divorce has been granted—as in *F*—the state must not disproportionately restrict the right to remarry.

Financial protection for respondents in separation cases

Respondents in separation cases against whom no 'fact' has been found are entitled to apply under s 10 to have their financial position post-divorce considered by the court before the divorce is finalized.[131] In cases involving middle-aged clients, the respondent's solicitor (unless instructed otherwise) may be negligent if he or she does not file a s 10 application to enable a proper investigation of the financial circumstances, particularly regarding pension rights, to be made prior to grant of the decree absolute.[132] If loss of potential pension rights associated with ongoing marital status—principally a widow's pension—could put

---

126 MCA 1973, s 3; CPA 2004, s 41.
127 MCA 1973, ss 17–18; CPA 2004, ss 56–7; see 5.5.9 below.
128 See 2.5–2.7.
129 See chapter 4.
130 (App No 11329/85, ECHR) (1987).
131 MCA 1973, s 10(2)–(4); CPA 2004, s 48(2)–(5). It may be used to seek compensation for arrears accrued under past financial obligations: *Garcia v Garcia* [1992] Fam 83.
132 *Griffiths v Dawson & Co* [1993] 2 FLR 315.

the respondent in financial difficulty, the divorce should be delayed until suitable financial remedies have been explored.[133]

Where such an application has been made, the court may not ordinarily grant the decree absolute unless satisfied in all the circumstances either that: (i) no financial provision ought to be made by the petitioner; or (ii) the financial provision that has been made[134] is reasonable and fair or the best that can be made in the circumstances. The low standard of 'the best [financial provision] that can be made in the circumstances' recognizes that where resources are limited financial hardship may be unavoidable, yet divorce should still be permitted. This test must be compared with the hardship bar, below. Even if *not* satisfied that the best possible provision has been made (or that no provision should be made), the court may still finalize the divorce if: (i) it is desirable to do so in the circumstances without delay; and (ii) the petitioner has made satisfactory undertakings to make provision approved—in fairly firm and achievable outline[135]—by the court. Courts are wary of allowing cases to proceed with mere undertakings if, having obtained the desired divorce, the petitioner might fail to cooperate further in financial remedy proceedings.[136]

The hardship bar in five-year separation cases

The introduction of the five-year separation fact was highly controversial. For the first time, blameless spouses could be divorced against their wishes, even on the petition of a spouse guilty of adultery, desertion, and worse. This was a seismic shift: the old law of matrimonial offences was clearly being supplanted by no-fault divorce. There was particular concern about the plight of older wives abandoned by mid-life-crisis husbands seeking younger models, leaving the wives in financial difficulty. In order to prevent the new law becoming a 'Casanova's charter', under s 5 the grant of the decree nisi can be barred in some five-year separation cases. In the event, the five-year separation fact has been used as much by women as men,[137] and the facts and judgements required to invoke the bar are so demanding that it rarely prevents divorce. But it might be deployed successfully as a delaying tactic to help secure good financial settlements:[138]

Matrimonial Causes Act 1973, s 5[139]

(1) The respondent to a petition for divorce in which the petitioner alleges five years' separation may oppose the grant of a decree on the ground that the dissolution of the marriage will result in grave financial or other hardship to him and that it would in all the circumstances be wrong to dissolve the marriage.

---

[133] See 7.3.3.

[134] Not merely proposed: *Wilson v Wilson* [1973] 1 WLR 555.

[135] *Grigson v Grigson* [1974] 1 WLR 228.

[136] Cf *Wickler v Wickler* [1998] 2 FLR 326, regarding the court's power to permit a respondent to apply for decree absolute under s 9(2).

[137] Gibson (1994), 173; for most recent data, ONS (2014a), table 8.

[138] Law Com (1988a), para 3.29.

[139] CPA 2004, s 47.

(2) Where the grant of a decree is opposed by virtue of this section, then—

   (a) if the court finds that the petitioner is entitled to rely in support of his petition on the fact of five years' separation and makes no such finding as to any other fact [under s 1(2)], and

   (b) if apart from this section the court would grant a decree on the petition,

the court shall consider all the circumstances, including the conduct of the parties to the marriage and the interests of those parties and of any children or other persons concerned, and if of opinion that the dissolution of the marriage will result in grave financial or other hardship to the respondent and that it would in all the circumstances be wrong to dissolve the marriage it shall dismiss the petition.

(3) For the purposes of this section hardship shall include the loss of the chance of acquiring any benefit which the respondent might acquire if the marriage were not dissolved.

Grave financial or other hardship arising from dissolution of the union

It must be proved that hardship 'will' arise; a mere risk of hardship is not sufficient. Moreover, the hardship—financial or otherwise[140]—must be 'grave'. This may be contrasted with 'substantial' and 'significant', generally interpreted to mean 'more than trivial'. 'Grave' is a much higher threshold: 'important', or 'very serious'.[141]

The hardship must result specifically from the change of legal status effected by the divorce.[142] Much of the hardship arising on divorce is attributable to the physical, rather than legal, separation of the parties, in particular the need to maintain two households, rather than one, from the same pool of resources. That sort of hardship is irrelevant to s 5. Most of the reported cases instead concern loss of pension rights, in particular widows' pensions, where it is clearly loss of spousal status that would cause the hardship: if not married to the deceased at his death, the respondent will not be his widow and so not qualify for the pension. However, 'grave' financial hardship of that sort now arises less frequently because the courts have substantial powers to adjust the parties' property and pension rights and to order periodical payments from income.[143] The courts' powers regarding pensions are much greater than they were when many of the reported cases considering s 5 were decided. Many cases can therefore now proceed under s 10 (see above) for proper pension or alternative compensatory provision to be made, rather than be barred absolutely under s 5.[144] Only where the rules of the particular pension scheme preclude sharing and there are insufficient other assets available to compensate the spouse is grave financial hardship likely to be proved. If the hardship can be alleviated only by steps which the courts have no power to order, the petitioner will have to implement satisfactory proposals to mitigate it.[145] Welfare benefits might also alleviate potential hardship.[146]

---

[140] *Rukat v Rukat* [1975] Fam 63.

[141] *Reiterbund v Reiterbund* [1975] Fam 99, 107; *Archer v Archer* [1999] 1 FLR 327.

[142] Contrast s 10: *Garcia v Garcia* [1992] Fam 83, 89.

[143] 7.3.

[144] Cf *Le Marchant v Le Marchant* [1977] 1 WLR 559, 562; though 'the best that can be done' under s 10 may not be enough to alleviate the hardship: *Parker v Parker* [1972] Fam 116, 118.

[145] *Le Marchant v Le Marchant* [1977] 1 WLR 559; *K v K (Financial Relief: Widow's Pension)* [1997] 1 FLR 35.

[146] *Reiterbund v Reiterbund* [1975] Fam 99; *Jackson v Jackson* [1993] 2 FLR 848.

Cases of financial hardship are perhaps relatively easy to decide as the hardship claimed is objectively measurable. Cases of 'other' grave hardship have generally involved claims regarding social stigmatization following divorce as a result of religious or cultural mores in the respondent's home country or community.[147] These claims are more intangible. None of the reported cases has succeeded. The wife in *Rukat v Rukat* was of Roman Catholic Sicilian extraction, for whom divorce was anathema on moral and religious grounds. She felt that if she were divorced she and her child would not be able to return to Sicily because of community attitudes. However, there was no evidence that anyone would know she had been divorced, or (if they did) that her fears of social ostracism would be realized once it were understood that the divorce involved no fault on her part, not least since it was known that she and her husband had been living apart for over 25 years. The Court of Appeal found that no grave hardship had been proved. Lawton LJ considered the nature of the test to be applied:

Rukat v Rukat [1975] Fam 64 (CA), 73–4, 75–6

LAWTON LJ:

The [MCA 1973]...has now been in operation a few years. As far as counsel knows, and as far as I know, no one has yet succeeded in a defence under that part of section [5] under which this wife comes to this court for help; and I have asked myself the question whether the courts may not have whittled away the defence provided by Parliament by setting far too high a standard of proof.

One has to start, I think, by looking at the context in which the phrase "grave financial or other hardship" occurs. The word "hardship" is not a word of art. It follows that it must be construed by the courts in a common-sense way, and the meaning which is put upon the word "hardship" should be such as would meet with the approval of ordinary sensible people. In my judgment, the ordinary sensible man would take the view that there are two aspects of "hardship"—that which the sufferer from the hardship thinks he is suffering and that which a reasonable bystander with knowledge of all the facts would think he was suffering. That can be illustrated by a homely example. The rich gourmet who because of financial stringency has to drink vin ordinaire with his grouse may well think that he is suffering a hardship; but sensible people would say he was not.

If that approach is applied to this case, one gets this situation. The wife undoubtedly feels that she has suffered a hardship; and the judge...found that she was feeling at the time of the judgment that she could not go back to Sicily. That, if it was genuine and deeply felt, would undoubtedly be a "hardship" in one sense of that word. But one has to ask oneself the question whether sensible people, knowing all the facts, would think it was a hardship. On the evidence, I have come to the conclusion that they would not.

Ormrod LJ agreed, remarking that:

Making all allowances for the sacramental views of some people, to keep in existence a marriage which has been dead for 25 years requires, in my judgment, a considerable amount of justification.

---

[147] Several cases involve Hinduism: *Banik v Banik* [1973] 1 WLR 860; *Parghi v Parghi* (1973) 117 SJ 582; *Balraj v Balraj* (1981) 11 FL 110.

And it would be wrong in all the circumstances to dissolve the union

These last words of Ormrod LJ bring us to the second limb of the test: even if the court finds that grave hardship will arise, it may nevertheless grant the divorce because the bar can only succeed if it would be 'wrong' to dissolve the marriage or civil partnership.

Reiterbund v Reiterbund [1974] 1 WLR 788 (Fam Div), 797–8[148]

FINER J:

It seems to me that the word "wrong" must there be construed to mean "unjust." However, in determining whether in all the circumstances it would be wrong, or unjust, to dissolve the marriage, it seems to me that the court must be careful to avoid subverting the policy which led to the inclusion of section 1(2)(e)...as one of the facts establishing irretrievable breakdown by, so to speak, treating the paragraph (e) "fact" as of a lower order than the other four. Irretrievable breakdown is now the sole ground for divorce, and it may be established through any one of the matters set out in section 1(2), all of which carry equal weight in expressing the object of the legislation. It seems to me, therefore, that in considering the section 5 defence, the court has to exclude from its consideration that a petition based on five years' separation is brought by a "guilty" husband (in the phraseology of the old law) against a non-consenting wife, for this would be tantamount to striking section 1(2)(e) out of the Act altogether.... The parties in this case are not young, but even if there were no prospect at all of the husband marrying again (and there is at least a hint that he may) I do not consider that it would be wrong to dissolve this marriage. On the contrary, I think it is a case which is well within the policy embodied in the new law which aims, in all other than exceptional circumstances, to crush the empty shells of dead marriage.

Where the parties are young, it will be extremely difficult to satisfy this test:

Mathias v Mathias [1972] Fam 287 (CA), 300, 301

DAVIES LJ:

On the second part of the subsection, I would say,...that, so far from its being wrong to dissolve this marriage, I am absolutely satisfied that it would be wrong not to do so. The ages of the parties are about 35 and 32 respectively. We do not know the age of [the husband's fiancée], but no doubt she is a young woman. All three of the parties, the husband, the wife and [the husband's fiancée], would, in the ordinary course of events, have many years to live; and in my view, unless there were strong reasons to the contrary, it would be ridiculous to keep alive this shell of a marriage and prevent perhaps all three of the parties settling down to a happier life in happier circumstances. The cohabitation lasted for some two and three-quarter years. They have been living apart now for some seven and three-quarter years. I should have thought that the sooner that latter situation is put an end to the better.

---

[148] Aff'd [1975] Fam 99.

The relevance of conduct

Section 5 requires the court to consider the parties' conduct in deciding whether to apply the bar. Although divorce law and financial settlements on divorce are no longer fault-based, it has been held that conduct, good or bad, must be taken into account here.[149]

Special protection for parties to some religious marriages

Some marriages cannot be wholly dissolved by civil divorce. Although the state recognizes the divorce for all purposes, the religious law under which a marriage was contracted may not recognize civil divorce, and further procedures may have to be completed before the parties will be free to remarry in accordance with their religious rites.[150] Conversely, religious divorces obtained in the UK will not dissolve marriage for civil law purposes; there must be a civil divorce.[151] This perhaps contrasts oddly with the recognition of certain religious marriage ceremonies as being competent to create a marriage for civil law purposes.[152]

Difficulty arises where only one spouse wishes to remarry under religious law but cannot do so without the other's cooperation. For example, under Jewish law the parties are only divorced if the husband gives and the wife accepts a formal document issued under the auspices of a rabbinic court called a 'Get'. If the husband is content to remarry outside the faith, he has no incentive to fulfil this procedure, and that leaves the wife effectively unable to remarry within her faith, and any children she might have will be illegitimate under Jewish law.

Following a series of cases[153] highlighting the problem faced by some Jewish wives, a new provision designed expressly to deal with the problem—s 10A—was introduced in 2002.[154] This empowers the court, if it is just and reasonable to do so, to withhold the decree absolute until both parties have taken any steps required to dissolve the marriage under their religious law. In many cases (assuming that the intransigent party wants a civil divorce), the threat of invoking s 10A may produce the desired result. Evidently, no equivalent issue arises for civil partners.

5.5.7 THE PROCEDURE FOR DIVORCE

The nature of the judge's task under the MCA 1973 has been described thus:

Ash v Ash [1972] Fam 135 (Fam Div), 141

BAGNALL J:

The only circumstances in which the court will have to decide…whether the marriage has broken down irretrievably must be when one of the spouses is asserting the affirmative of

---

[149] *Brickell v Brickell* [1974] Fam 31.

[150] See Morris (2005); Schuz (1996), writing before the reform discussed in the text; see also Douglas et al (2012) for recent research into the practices of religious tribunals.

[151] Family Law Act 1986, s 44; *Sulaiman v Juffali* [2002] 1 FLR 479.

[152] Schuz (1996); see 2.5.3, particularly in relation to Jewish and Quaker marriages, which proceed entirely under their own rites without any additional civil requirements save registration.

[153] See, e.g., *N v N (Divorce: Ante-Nuptial Agreement)* [1999] 2 FCR 583; *O v O (Jurisdiction: Jewish Divorce)* [2000] 2 FLR 147, in which s 9(2) was used to delay granting a decree absolute to the respondent husband.

[154] Divorce (Religious Marriages) Act 2002: it currently applies only to Jewish marriages.

that proposition and the other is asserting the negative. Simple assertion either way, it seems to me, cannot suffice. What I have to do is to examine the whole of the evidence placed before me, including and giving not inconsiderable weight to the assertions of the parties, and make up my mind, quite generally, whether it can be said that in spite of the behaviour of the husband, and the reaction to that behaviour of the wife, the marriage has not broken down irretrievably. In my opinion, in performing that general exercise on a survey of the evidence, only a general answer is appropriate and no useful purpose would be served by seeking to place quantitative weight on one consideration or another. Performing the best survey that I can of the evidence, and having regard to the personalities of the parties as displayed in the witness box, I have concluded that I cannot be satisfied on all the evidence that the marriage has not broken down irretrievably and accordingly I must pronounce a decree nisi.

However, the judge's job is rather different in undefended divorces, which are now decided without any substantive court hearing and with increasingly minimal involvement of the judge. The reality of modern divorce law cannot be appreciated without reference to this procedure. That reality is far from what we might expect from the face of the substantive law that we have just discussed, and raises fundamental questions about the relevance of that law.

The judicial duty to inquire and the procedure for undefended divorces

Since 1857, statute has required divorce judges to perform an inquisitorial function.[155] When reform was being considered during the 1960s, the Archbishop's Group desired a thorough judicial investigation into the end of couples' relationships. For practical reasons, that approach was rejected.[156] However, although not required to conduct a wide-ranging inquiry into the various causes of the claimed irretrievable breakdown, the judges still have a limited inquisitorial role:

Matrimonial Causes Act 1973, s 1[157]

(3) On a petition for divorce it shall be the duty of the court to inquire, so far as it reasonably can, into the facts[158] alleged by the petitioner and into any facts alleged by the respondent.

(4) If the court is satisfied on the evidence of any [of the five facts set out in s 1(2)], then, unless it is satisfied on all the evidence that the marriage has not broken down irretrievably, it shall, subject to section 5 [the hardship bar, see above p 328], grant a decree of divorce.

Even pre-1969 when the concept of the matrimonial offence still prevailed, the reality of divorce trials, which were heard in the High Court, had long since failed to live up to the image projected by the substantive law.

---

155 See generally Booth Committee (1985), paras 2.13 et seq and Eekelaar (1994).
156 Law Com (1966), paras 60 et seq.
157 CPA 2004, s 44(2).
158 *Darnton v Darnton* [2006] EWCA Civ 1081, [8]–[9].

C. Gibson, *Dissolving Wedlock* (London: Routledge, 1994), 175–80

It is not known whether the guardianship of High Court divorce judges made couples more decorous within their marital relationships. But it is clear that the vast majority of divorces were undefended petitions which were speedily processed by Special Divorce Commissioners masquerading as High Court judges.[159] Undefended cases, as Mr Harvey QC explained in a caustic exposition of the post-war divorce procedure, 'works almost on the slot machine principle'....Sir Hartley Shawcross, the Attorney-General, recalled to the House of Commons in 1951: 'One used to handle these undefended cases at the rate of about one in two minutes...it did not impress me at the time that there was any real principle operating in practice in the administration of our divorce laws'.

When the 1969 legislation came into force, that inquiry ostensibly remained the function of the senior judiciary, and appellate decisions emphasized the importance of judges making factual findings even in undefended cases, rather than merely rubber-stamping the petition.[160] However, the distance between substance and procedure would soon become greater with the introduction of what until 2011 was called the 'special procedure'.[161]

[By] 1977 the divorce process had been changed into a private arrangement validated within an administrative setting. This most radical transformation in the approach to, and meaning of, divorce took place without serious Parliamentary debate. The new process was essentially the outcome of a cost-saving exercise rather than a purposeful Parliamentary rethinking of what the legislative, administrative and social needs of a modern divorce policy should be.

When introduced in 1973 the new arrangements were properly termed 'special procedure', for availability was restricted to petitioners without dependent children who sought divorce on the fact of two years'...separation. Two further extensions have meant that since April 1977 all undefended divorces are dealt with by special procedure. And this, in fact, is the general everyday procedure used by 99.9 per cent of all petitioners. The parties are not required to appear before a judge unless there are dependent children or...there are ancillary matters to be resolved. The district judge examines the papers in his office for both conformity to administrative requirements and assurance that the petition and its supporting affidavit evidence meets the substantive requirements for divorce. When satisfied on these two counts the district judge certifies his approval. This is the crucial decision, for with this certificate to hand the divorce judge must pronounce the decree nisi.

As Gibson goes on to explain, the extension of what had been a 'special' procedure to all undefended cases, regardless of the fact relied on, effected a 'fundamental change...to the administration and regulation of divorce':

The Bishop of Durham could write to *The Times* (4 April 1977):

I am disturbed at the implications of divorce by post, and even more disturbed by the apparently casual manner in which such a fundamental change has been made...To avoid public action tilts the concept of marriage breakdown dangerously in the direction of divorce by consent, and in

---

[159] County court judges had been designated as High Court judges for the purposes of granting divorces locally to help process the otherwise unmanageable numbers of cases.

[160] See, e.g., *Santos v Santos* [1972] Fam 247, 263–4.

[161] See Black et al (2012), ch 8; *Pounds v Pounds* [1994] 1 FLR 775, 778.

doing so widens the gulf between Christian and purely contractual understandings of marriage. I believe it would be an immeasurable loss if those who, from both sides, wish to widen this gulf were given encouragement to do so by a piece of administrative convenience.

But executive endorsement of special procedure was not governed by a radical belief that divorce should now be seen as an essentially administrative process that no longer required a court hearing. Rather, at a time of economic crisis, causing the Treasury to insist on major cuts in public spending and the government to announce that there was to be little or no increase in expenditure on legal aid for the next five years, the Lord Chancellor concluded that there was only one area within civil legal aid where sizeable savings could justifiably be made. This was the field of divorce...

When Lord Chancellor Elwyn-Jones announced in 1976 the extension of the special procedure to all undefended divorces he also declared that legal aid would no longer be available in such proceedings. The rationale behind this change was that as determination of the undefended petition would not now require a court hearing there was no longer need for a lawyer's attendance at court. However, legal aid would still be available where the need for a hearing arose for which legal representation was necessary. This covered contested petitions and such matters as disputes over ancillary questions involving maintenance, property or arrangements for children. Ancillary proceedings were, in the words of the Lord Chancellor, 'the areas of real contest between the parties to divorce proceedings today, not the question whether the petitioner should get a decree'...

The divorce process has been radically transformed from a public judicial inquest titularly undertaken by High Court judges to a private administrative ratification of the spouses' decision to divorce.

Given the near-universal application of the procedure, the label 'special' was a 'complete misnomer',[162] and it was dropped from the most recent rules.[163] It has been said that the objectives of this procedure for undefended divorces are 'simplicity, speed and economy', so that, whilst the essentials of the petition must be satisfactory and its contents proved, 'there should be no room for over-meticulousness and over-technicality in approach'; substance should be preferred over form.[164] It has also been said that 'the judge's duty pursuant to s 1(3)...to enquire, so far as he reasonably can, into the facts alleged by the petitioner is...emasculated almost into invisibility'.[165] One study did find that even within the narrow boundaries of the procedure for undefended divorces, there remained some room for strict judicial control, if only over form and procedure, if the judge wished to exert it.[166] However, the latest rule change means that the s 1(3) duty is now ordinarily performed by court officers who check the paperwork, rather than by a judge, rendering the procedure even less 'special' and more administrative than ever.[167] The judge in most cases just formally grants the decrees on the back of the officials' assessment of the forms.

Stephen Cretney has suggested that 'in relation to divorce, procedural change has over the years often had more impact than changes in the substantive law', and certainly affected

---

162 *Day v Day* [1980] Fam 29, 32, per Ormrod LJ.
163 See FPR 2010, r 7.20(2).
164 *R v Nottingham County Court, ex parte Byers* [1985] 1 WLR 403, 406.
165 *Bhaji v Chauhan* [2003] 2 FLR 485, 487, per Wilson J.
166 Ingleby (1989), 240.
167 The Justices' Clerks and Assistants Rules 2014, SI 2014/603.

public perceptions of the law.[168] The 'special' procedure for undefended divorce necessarily radically reduced the courts' ability to make any effective inquiry in these divorces and so reduced the influence of the substantive law.[169] This must be borne in mind when considering the case law on the 'facts'. Many of those cases were decided before the special procedure arrived, or were defended. The judges were therefore able to conduct a far deeper inquiry than the current procedure permits. Indeed, some of the instructions given to the judge by that case law are effectively impossible to implement. Of course, the substantive law is not irrelevant to undefended cases, as the evidence submitted must fulfil the substantive requirements. However, it is only in defended cases that the judge has room to operate in the way envisaged by the case law. Divorce is therefore more easily obtained than the face of the legislation and case law may suggest.

Davis and Murch conclude that 'we have...moved to a position where the *state*'s interest in the breakdown of marriage has receded almost to vanishing point...in favour of an increased emphasis on private agreement'.[170] Ruth Deech has observed that 'conceptually and procedurally, it is far more difficult to terminate those other pillars of a stable life, employment and a tenancy, than marriage'.[171] The grant of divorce may ultimately rest with a judge, but that judge is essentially discharging an administrative responsibility rather than adjudicating in any substantial sense. English law may be said to have reached a 'hypocritical compromise',[172] whereby the law on the face of the statute promises state control over divorce whilst the law in practice deprives the state of any real possibility of control in most cases.

Defended cases

Defended divorces are now extremely rare. Even by 1966—before the current law came into force—93 per cent of divorces were undefended.[173] Statistics on defended divorces have not been collected centrally since 1991. In that year, 153 defended divorces were listed for trial in the High Court, of which 82 went to trial; in none was a decree granted. Figures for defended divorces in the county courts were last reported for 1989, when 511 cases were listed for trial and 259 resulted in divorce decrees.[174] To put these figures in perspective, in 1991 over 153,000 divorce decrees were granted.[175]

However, the relatively tiny number of defended cases does not indicate that all cases passing via the procedure for undefended divorces are factually undisputed. Davis and Murch describe defended divorce as a 'seriously underestimated problem'.[176] Many respondents may wish to defend the petition, particularly where it is based on the behaviour fact and the detailed allegations are disputed. Or the respondent may agree that the marriage has irretrievably broken down, but vehemently deny the allegation that

---

[168] Cretney (2003a), 165. The different procedures under the Divorce (Scotland) Act 1976 are probably a cause of most Scottish divorces' reliance on separation rather than fault-based facts: Law Com (1990), para 3.17; Harvie-Clark (2005).

[169] Booth Committee (1985), para 2.8.

[170] Davis and Murch (1988), 13.

[171] Deech (2009a).

[172] Antokolskaia (2014), 94.

[173] Law Com (1966), para 20.

[174] LCD (1990), table 5.6.

[175] LCD (1992), table 5.3.

[176] Davis and Murch (1988), 100.

his or her behaviour is the problem. However, public funding is now rarely available to pay for legal advice and representation to defend a divorce: only in cases involving domestic violence or in exceptional cases might public funding be available.[177] Only the most persistent respondents with private means or the confidence to act without a lawyer are therefore likely to defend. The vast majority of respondents who might have wished to defend will reluctantly concede defeat rather than see the case go to trial.[178] It has been held to be unarguable that lack of legal representation or advice in divorce proceedings, whether that be the result of the litigant's choice or not, breaches Article 6 ECHR.[179]

Where a defence does proceed, the respondent is entitled to a proper hearing.[180] The petition must provide adequate detail regarding the facts alleged; specific findings of fact should be made; and a more senior level of judge should hear the case. That did not occur in *Butterworth*, where the respondent, who was acting as a litigant in person, was faced with 'hopelessly general' allegations:

Butterworth v Butterworth [1997] 2 FLR 336 (CA), 339

BUTLER-SLOSS LJ:

At the end of the day, looking at this case, although I am sure that the recorder did his best to hear the evidence and to try to come to a decision between the parties, the impression given, even if incorrect, is that it is unreasonable for husbands to object to divorces and that the evidence in support of the petition is somewhat of a formality. That is far from the truth. All courts hope that spouses whose marriages fail will bury them decently and will not litigate the divorce in public with the consequential adverse effect upon each of the parties and upon their children. But the present state of the English law of divorce gives the respondent to a divorce petition the right to oppose it and to have the allegations made in the petition against him properly proved to the satisfaction of the court to the civil standard of the balance of probabilities.

These are potentially serious allegations [of violence, alcoholism etc]. They are allegations that this respondent does not wish to have made against him. The fact that most other respondents do not bother too much does not prevent him having the right to say: 'I do not agree with them. Prove them', and I have to say that the allegations made in this petition were not proved.

The two-stage process

Whether defended or not, divorce proceeds in two stages. Once the papers have been examined, or the defended trial heard, and the judge is satisfied that the ground for divorce is made out, he or she initially issues a decree nisi.[181] After six weeks, the petitioner may apply

---

177 Legal Aid, Sentencing and Punishment of Offenders Act 2012, s 10 and Sch 1, para 12.
178 Davis and Murch (1988), chs 7–10.
179 *Darnton v Darnton* [2006] EWCA Civ 1081, [16], though note that no case law was cited, the applicant was unrepresented, and the respondent failed to appear.
180 *Price v Price* [2014] EWCA Civ 655.
181 MCA 1973, s 1(5); in civil partnership law: 'conditional order', CPA 2004, s 37(2).

for the decree absolute.[182] If the petitioner has not done this within three months of the six-week point, the respondent may apply for the decree absolute to be made, or for the decree nisi to be rescinded.[183] If the application is made over 12 months from the first possible date, the court may require evidence to account for the delay before deciding whether to grant the decree absolute, not least to ascertain whether recent events cast doubt on the findings made to support the decree nisi.[184] If dissatisfied, the court can rescind the decree nisi.[185] The eventual grant of the decree absolute has been described as an administrative rather than judicial procedure.[186] But only at that point are the parties divorced and so free once more to marry or form a civil partnership.

Fraud unravels everything, so a decree absolute may be rescinded if it is discovered that the divorce was obtained on false evidence.[187] Procedural errors, whether committed by the parties or the court itself, may also render a decree absolute void. This may have adverse implications for a party who has, on the faith of the decree absolute, since remarried. In *Dennis v Dennis*, the petitioner wife was not sent notice of the husband's application for the decree absolute, which was in any event made earlier than it ought to have been, and the court then failed to send the wife a copy of the decree. When the errors came to light, the court of its own motion reopened the case to declare the decree void, a result which neither party wanted, but in relation to which there was no discretion. This rendered void the husband's remarriage. The husband argued that this breached his rights under Articles 8 and 12 ECHR, but the court found no prima facie violation of either Article.

Dennis v Dennis [2000] Fam 163 (Fam Div), 180–1

WALL J:

Regulation of marriage and divorce is clearly a function of the state. Freedom to marry, in a society which practi[s]es monogamy, depends upon capacity to marry. There is nothing, in my judgment, in Part I of the Matrimonial Causes Act 1973 which is ambiguous, or which cannot be said to be Human Rights Act compliant...The statute sets out a scheme to enable spouses to divorce each other by means of clear and well-recognised procedures...[T]he provision...of a two-stage process leading to the final decree of divorce is not only unexceptionable, but is designed to protect the status and rights of both parties. Divorce affects not only personal status and capacity to remarry, but also inheritance and pension rights. A woman in the petitioner's position is plainly entitled at all times to know what her marital status is; and, if that status is to be changed, she is entitled to have notice of and to be heard on the question. These, in my judgment, are as much rights under articles 8 and 12 as the respondent's rights under the same articles. As it happens, on the facts of this case, the petitioner's inheritance and pension rights in the context of her marital status would not have

---

[182] MCA 1973, s 1(5); 'final order': CPA 2004, s 38(1); Matrimonial Causes (Decree Absolute) General Order 1972.

[183] MCA 1973, s 9(2); CPA 2004, s 40(2). The court has a discretion whether to make the final order on the respondent's application, and may decline to do so if it might prejudice the petitioner, in particular in relation to ongoing ancillary relief proceedings: *Wickler v Wickler* [1998] 2 FLR 326; *Darnton v Darnton* [2006] EWCA Civ 1081.

[184] See, e.g., *Kim v Morris* [2012] EWHC 1103.

[185] *Court v Court* [1982] Fam 105; FPR 2010, r 7.32(3).

[186] *Dennis v Dennis* [2000] Fam 163, 183.

[187] *Moynihan v Moynihan* [1997] 1 FLR 59.

been affected if I had been able to hold that the decree absolute was voidable rather than void; however, the position might well have been different if, for example, the respondent had died in the intervening period.

The role of the Queen's Proctor

The delay between decrees nisi and absolute also provides an opportunity for intervention by the Queen's Proctor, the Crown officer charged with representing the public interest in the law and practice of divorce against manipulation by private individuals who wish to evade the substantive law and effectively divorce on their own terms.[188] The Queen's Proctor may be called upon to act as amicus curiae in cases raising difficult points of law, where it may be in neither party's interests to oppose the divorce. When divorce was based on the concept of matrimonial offence, divorce was prohibited where the parties had colluded to create the grounds for divorce or the petitioner had connived at or condoned the respondent's offence (notably where the husband undertook to commit adultery—or to give the impression of having done so—with another woman in a hotel). The Queen's Proctor would investigate where it was suspected that such activities were afoot.[189] His evidence could deprive spouses who both wished to be divorced of the decree they sought. These bars and the role of the Queen's Proctor emphasized the public interest in the sacrosanct nature of the marriage bond.[190]

Nowadays, opportunities for proctorial intervention are more limited, the old bars of collusion, connivance, and condonation having gone. However, there may still be situations—particularly in undefended cases where a quick divorce is wanted—where parties falsely assert the facts required to obtain the desired outcome. Under the procedure for undefended cases where the paperwork appears satisfactory, suspicion of perjury may rarely arise. But once suspicions are aroused, an oral hearing of the undefended petition may follow, the Queen's Proctor intervening to oppose the divorce.[191] In *Bhaji v Chauhan*, five almost identically worded petitions crossed the same judge's desk. In each case, one party was a UK national, the other an Indian national who was given leave to enter the UK because of the marriage. In each case, the marriage was alleged to have broken down shortly after indefinite leave to remain in the UK had been obtained. The papers were sent to the Queen's Proctor who then intervened to prove that the petitions were a sham:

Bhaji v Chauhan, Queen's Proctor Intervening (Divorce: Marriages Used for Immigration Purposes) [2003] 2 FLR 485 (Fam Div)

WILSON J:

[20] This hearing may serve to bring to public attention the opportunity which exists for serious abuse both of our immigration rules and of our divorce laws; and inevitably one wonders whether the abuse is more widespread than is reflected in this handful of five petitions presented in the county court in Bolton.... The opportunity for abuse of our divorce laws is the opportunity to

---

188 The Queen's Proctor may also intervene in nullity and judicial separation cases.
189 The lengths to which these inquiries might go are vividly portrayed in A.P. Herbert's *Holy Deadlock*.
190 Cretney (2003a), 176–7.
191 For an egregious example, see *Rapisarda v Colladon (No 2)* [2014] EWFC 35.

procure an immediate divorce by the inclusion of false allegations of unreasonable behaviour in a petition presented once the marriage has been successfully used in securing indefinite leave. I am well aware that, after 2 years of separation, one spouse can, with the other's consent, lawfully obtain a divorce. Indeed it was submitted to me that there is no point in my dismissing the petitions because the parties to all the marriages will within the next year have become separated for 2 years and will thus be entitled to a divorce by consent. With respect, that argument entirely misses the point. In England and Wales divorce is not yet available simply upon joint demand following separation. This unusual hearing has exposed a concerted attempt to bypass the requirements of the present law and, by use of bogus allegations of behaviour, to secure the immediate dissolution of marriages which have outlived their perceived usefulness.

Encouraging reconciliation

Several statutory provisions seek to encourage reconciliation before the parties reach the point of no return. Whether any of these provisions do—or ever could—save saveable marriages is doubtful; indeed, they were not introduced with any great hopes that they would.[192]

The bar on initiating divorce proceedings in the first year of marriage may be viewed as an attempt to encourage spouses to make a go of a new union.[193] If at any point during the divorce proceedings, the court considers that reconciliation might be reasonably possible, it can adjourn proceedings to allow efforts to be made in that direction.[194] But, given the essentially administrative procedure for undefended divorces, it is difficult to see how the court can make that judgement. If the petitioner has sought legal advice in connection with the divorce, the solicitor must certify *whether* he or she has discussed the possibility of reconciliation with the petitioner and supplied details of appropriate couple counselling services.[195] But since many petitioners act in person rather than with legal advice there may be no solicitor on hand to perform even this limited duty.[196]

The substantive law also seeks to facilitate reconciliation by allowing the clock running in desertion and separation cases to stop for up to six months in total should the parties cohabit again, and by permitting some degree of continued cohabitation in adultery and behaviour cases.[197] The policy of promoting reconciliation has also shaped interpretation of the substantive law. It has been held that it is necessary only to prove irretrievable breakdown at the date of the hearing, not on the date of filing the petition. Were it otherwise, the court's power to adjourn pending a possible reconciliation would be of no value, and 'petitioners would be discouraged by their legal advisers from making or accepting any overtures for reconciliation while the proceedings were pending', a result which 'would clearly be contrary to the policy of the Act'.[198]

5.5.8 THE FACTS IN PRACTICE

The five facts are used to differing extents by the divorcing population as a whole and by husband and wife petitioners respectively. The most relied upon fact (both overall and amongst

---

[192] See Law Com (1966), paras 29–32.
[193] See 5.5.6 above.
[194] MCA 1973, s 6(2); CPA 2004, s 42(3).
[195] MCA 1973, s 6(1); CPA 2004, s 42(2); see Eekelaar, Maclean, and Beinart (2000), ch 8.
[196] Law Com (1988a), para 3.9; Booth Committee (1985), para 4.42.
[197] MCA 1973, s 2; CPA 2004, s 45.
[198] *Pheasant v Pheasant* [1972] Fam 202, 205–6.

wives) is behaviour, accounting for nearly half of divorces today. The separation facts, in particular the two-year fact, have been more popular than adultery. But the hope that the separation facts would be the most popular has proved unfounded.[199] Desertion cases are extremely rare.

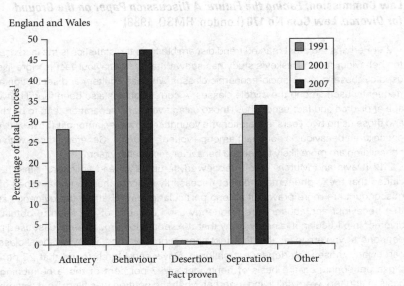

¹ This excludes cases where divorces were granted to both parties and annulments.

Figure 5.3 Facts proven at divorce as percentage of total divorces, 1991, 2001, and 2007

Source: Reproduced from *Population Trends* No 133 by the Office for National Statistics, by Crown copyright © 2008 (ONS (2008), figure 1).

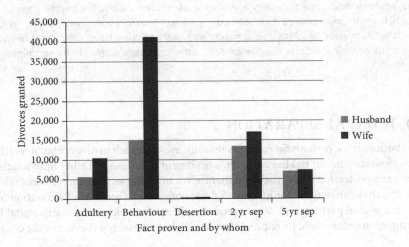

Figure 5.4 Facts proven at divorce and to whom granted, 2012

Source: Based on data reported in ONS (2014a), table 8.

---

¹⁹⁹ Law Com (1966), paras 92–3. Compare the position in Scotland: n 168 above.

Studies conducted in the 1980s sought to investigate the use of particular facts. The Law Commission reported their findings:

Law Commission, *Facing the Future: A Discussion Paper on the Ground for Divorce*, Law Com No 170 (London: HMSO, 1988)

2.11 Perhaps the most marked trend discernible from the statistics is the increased use of the behaviour fact...Haskey's study has shown that the behaviour fact is more likely to be used by those in lower socio-economic classes whereas adultery and separation are more frequently used among the middle classes. A correlation has also been found between the age at divorce and fact used. Thus, those using five years' separation tend to be the oldest and those using two years' separation the youngest. However, amongst those with dependent children behaviour is dominant among "young" divorces. Generally, those with dependent children are more likely to use the behaviour and adultery facts.

2.12 [Davis and Murch, who interviewed parties and read solicitors' files] have concluded that these phenomena do not necessarily indicate that particular types of marital misconduct are more prevalent among particular groups. Rather, the evidence suggests that behaviour and adultery are frequently used because of the need to obtain a quick divorce. In particular, it is noteworthy that the separation grounds are least used by those petitioners who are least able to effect separation—women, in lower social classes, and particularly those with dependent children. Davis and Murch found that 28 per cent of those petitioning on the basis of behaviour and 7 per cent of those petitioning on the basis of adultery were still living together when the petition was filed. These same groups are also more likely to need to have ancillary issues relating to [child residence], maintenance and housing determined quickly. This is most likely to occur once the petition has been filed.

2.13 The choice between adultery and behaviour seems to depend on social mores and on the state of the relations between the parties, as much as upon their marital history. Thus, adultery would seem to carry less stigma particularly among the middle classes and is more likely to be employed than behaviour where the parting was consensual or at least amicable. Behaviour petitions seem much less likely to have been discussed between the parties or their solicitors in advance and sometimes take respondents completely by surprise.

5.5.9 JUDICIAL SEPARATION

One or both parties, perhaps for religious reasons, may not wish to divorce but nevertheless wish to separate without risking an adverse finding of desertion.[200] Other individuals may require early protection where they find themselves in an impossible, even violent relationship before they can petition for divorce. A decree of judicial separation ('separation order', in the case of civil partnership) cannot require either party to leave the matrimonial home (an occupation order would be required for that[201]), but on making the decree the court can

---

[200] Cf MCA 1973, s 18(1); there is no equivalent provision in the CPA, but absence pursuant to an order for separation clearly provides justification under the law of desertion.
[201] See 4.5.3.

make financial orders, as it can on divorce and annulment.[202] The decree releases spouses from the duty to cohabit without effecting any change of status, save in relation to inheritance on intestacy.[203]

In order to obtain a decree, it is necessary to prove that one of the five (or, in the case of civil partnership, four) facts applies. But the court is not required to find that the union has irretrievably broken down. Should the parties wish subsequently to divorce, the same fact can be relied on, but judicial separation cannot simply be converted into a divorce; it is necessary to petition and produce evidence again.[204] Comparatively small numbers of judicial separation orders are now made each year—in 2012, there were just 670 petitions and 416 concluded cases of annulment and judicial separation combined, figures dwarfed by the 120,702 divorces.[205]

5.6 EVALUATION OF THE CURRENT LAW

The original objectives of the current law were first set out in 1966:

Law Commission, *Reform of the Grounds of Divorce: The Field of Choice*, Law Com No 6 (London: HMSO, 1966)

15. . . . [A] good divorce law should seek to achieve the following objectives:

(i) To buttress, rather than to undermine, the stability of marriage; and

(ii) When, regrettably, a marriage has irretrievably broken down, to enable the empty legal shell to be destroyed with the maximum fairness, and the minimum bitterness, distress and humiliation.

. . .

18. In addition to these two main objectives, another important requirement is that the divorce law should be understandable and respected. It is pre-eminently a branch of law that is liable to affect everyone, if not directly at any rate indirectly. Unless its principles are such as can be understood and respected, it cannot achieve its main objectives. If it is thought to be hypocritical or otherwise unworthy of respect, it will not only fail to achieve those objectives but may bring the whole of the administration of justice into disrespect.

The defects of the current law, assessed against those criteria and others, have been catalogued many times: by the Law Commission,[206] the government,[207] and academic researchers.[208] The criticisms reported by the Law Commission a quarter of a century ago hold good today.

---

[202] See 7.3.4.
[203] MCA 1973, ss 17–18; CPA 2004, ss 56–7; Law Com (1990), paras 4.2–4.11; Cretney (2003a), 149 et seq.
[204] MCA 1973, s 4; CPA 2004, s 46.
[205] MOJ (2014a), table 2.1.
[206] Most fully, Law Com (1988a), Part III.
[207] LCD (1993), (1995).
[208] E.g. Davis and Murch (1988), Eekelaar (1991b), Gibson (1994).

Law Commission, *The Ground for Divorce*, Law Com No 192
(London: HMSO, 1990)

Criticisms of the present law and practice

2.7 The criticisms of the present law...add up to a formidable case for reform.

(i) It is confusing and misleading

2.8 There is a considerable gap between theory and practice, which can only lead to confusion and lack of respect for the law. Indeed, some would call it downright dishonest. There are several aspects to this. First, the law tells couples that the only ground for divorce is irretrievable breakdown, which apparently does not involve fault. But next it provides that this can only be shown by one of five "facts", three of which apparently do involve fault. There are several recent examples of divorces being refused despite the fact that it was clear to all concerned that the marriage had indeed irretrievably broken down. The hardship and pain involved for both parties can be very great.

2.9 Secondly, the fact which is alleged in order to prove the breakdown need not have any connection with the real reason why the marriage broke down. The parties may, for example, have separated because they have both formed different associations, but agree to present a petition based on the behaviour of one of them, because neither wishes their partner to be publicly named [see MCA 1973, s 49]. The sex, class and other difference in the use of the facts make it quite clear that these are chosen for a variety of reasons which need have nothing to do with the reality of the case. This is a major source of confusion, especially for respondents who do not agree with the fact alleged. As has long been said, "whatever the client's reason for wanting divorce, the lawyer's function is to discover grounds".

2.10 The behaviour fact is particularly confusing. It is often referred to as "unreasonable behaviour", which suggests blameworthiness or outright cruelty on the part of the respondent; but this has been called a "linguistic trap", because the behaviour itself need be neither unreasonable nor blameworthy: rather, its effect on the petitioner must be such that it is unreasonable to expect him or her to go on living with the respondent, a significantly different and more flexible concept which is obviously capable of varying from case to case and court to court....

2.11 Finally, and above all, the present law pretends that the court is conducting an inquiry into the facts of the matter, when in the vast majority of cases it can do no such thing [owing to the procedure for undefended divorce]. This is not the fault of the court, nor is it probably any more of a problem under the present law and procedure than it was under the old. It may be more difficult to evaluate the effect of the respondent's behaviour from the papers than from the petitioner's account in the witness box, but it has always been difficult to get at the truth in an undefended case. Moreover, the system still allows, even encourages, the parties to lie, or at least to exaggerate, in order to get what they want. The bogus adultery cases of the past may have all but disappeared, but their modern equivalents are the "flimsy" behaviour petition or the pretence that the parties have been living apart for a full two years. In that "wider field which includes considerations of truth, the sacredness of oaths, and the integrity of professional practice", the present law is just as objectionable as the old.

(ii) It is discriminatory and unjust

2.12 83% of respondents to our public opinion survey thought it a good feature of the present law that couples who do not want to put the blame on either of them do not have to do so, but these couples have to have lived apart for at least two years. This can be extremely difficult to achieve without either substantial resources of one's own, or the co-operation of the other spouse at the outset, or an ouster order from the court.[209] ...The law does recognise that it is possible to live apart by conducting two separate households under the same roof. In practice, this is impossible in most ordinary houses or flats, especially where there are children: it inevitably requires the couple to co-operate in a most unnatural and artificial lifestyle. It is unjust and discriminatory of the law to provide for a civilised "no-fault" ground for divorce which, in practice, is denied to a large section of the population. A young mother with children living in a council house is obliged to rely upon fault whether or not she wants to do so and irrespective of the damage it may do.

2.13 The fault-based facts can also be intrinsically unjust. "Justice" in this context has traditionally been taken to mean the accurate allocation of blameworthiness for the breakdown of the marriage. Desertion is the only fact which stills attempts to do this...Desertion, however, is hardly ever used, because its place has been taken by the two separation facts. A finding of adultery or behaviour certainly need not mean that the respondent is any more to blame than the petitioner for the breakdown of the marriage....

2.14 This inherent potential for injustice is compounded by the practical problems of defending or bringing a cross-petition of one's own. It is extremely difficult to resist or counter allegations of behaviour. Defending them requires time, money and emotional energy far beyond the resources of most respondents. Even if the parties are prepared to go through with this, what would be the point? If the marriage is capable of being saved, a long-fought defended divorce, in which every incident or characteristic that might amount to behaviour is dragged up and examined in detail, is not going to do this. It can only serve to make matters worse and to consume resources which are often desperately needed elsewhere, particularly if there are children....Small wonder, then, that lawyers advise their clients not to defend and that their clients feel unjustly treated.

(iii) It distorts the parties' bargaining positions

2.15 Not only can the law be unjust in itself, it can also lead to unfair distortions in the relative bargaining power of the parties. When a marriage breaks down there are a great many practical questions to be decided: with whom are the children to live, how much are they going to see the other parent, who is to have the house, and what are they all going to live on? Respondents to [the Law Commission's earlier discussion paper] told us that the battles which used to be fought through the grounds for divorce are now more likely to be fought through the so-called ancillary issues which in practice matter so much more to many people. The policy of the law is to encourage the parties to try and resolve these by agreement if they can, whether through negotiation between solicitors or with the help of a mediation or conciliation service. Questions of the future care of children, distribution of family assets, and financial provision are all governed by their own legal criteria. It is not unjust for negotiations to be affected by the relative merits of the parties' cases on these matters. Yet negotiations may also be distorted by whichever of the parties is in a stronger position in relation to the divorce itself. The strength of that position will depend upon a combination of how anxious or reluctant that party is to be divorced and how easy or difficult he or she will find it to prove or disprove one of the five facts. That might not matter if these represented a coherent set of principles, reflecting the real reasons why the marriage broke down; but as

---

[209] See 4.5.3 on occupation orders under the FLA 1996.

we have already seen, they do not. The potentially arbitrary results can put one party at an unfair disadvantage.

(iv) It provokes unnecessary hostility and bitterness

2.16 A law which is arbitrary or unjust can exacerbate the feelings of bitterness, distress and humiliation so often experienced at the time of separation and divorce. Even if the couple have agreed that their marriage cannot be saved, it must make matters between them worse if the system encourages one to make allegations against the other. The incidents relied on have to be set out in the petition. Sometimes they are exaggerated, one-sided or even untrue. Allegations of behaviour or adultery can provoke resentment or hostility in a respondent who is unable to put his own side of the story on the record. We are not so naive as to believe that bitterness and hostility could ever be banished from the divorce process. It is not concerned with cold commercial bargains but with the most intimate of human relations. The more we expect of marriage the greater the anger and grief when marriage ends. But there is every reason to believe that the present law adds needlessly to the human misery involved. . . .

(v) It does nothing to save the marriage

2.17 None of this is any help with the law's other objective, of supporting those marriages which have a chance of survival. The law cannot prevent people from separating or forming new relationships, although it may make it difficult for people to get a divorce. The law can also make it difficult for estranged couples to become reconciled. The present law does make it difficult for some couples—in practice a very small proportion—to be divorced, but it does so in an arbitrary way depending upon which facts may be proved. It also makes it extremely difficult for couples to become reconciled. A spouse who wishes to be divorced is obliged either to make allegations against the other or to live apart for a lengthy period. If the petitioner brings proceedings based on behaviour, possibly without prior warning, and sometimes while they are still living together, the antagonism caused may destroy any lingering chance of saving the marriage. The alternative of two or five years' separation may encourage them to part in order to be able to obtain a divorce, when their difficulties might have been resolved if they had stayed together. From the very beginning, attention has to be focussed on how to prove the ground for divorce. The reality of what it will be like to live apart, to break up the common home, to finance two households where before there was only one, and to have or to lose that day-to-day responsibility for the children which was previously shared, at least to some extent: none of this has to be contemplated in any detail until the decree nisi is obtained. If it had, there might be some petitioners who would think again.

2.18 It is a mistake to think that, because so few divorces are defended, the rest are largely consensual. There are many, especially behaviour cases, in which the respondent indicates an intention to defend, but does not file a formal answer, or files an answer which is later withdrawn. Some of these are a reaction to the unfairness of the allegations made against them, but some reveal a genuine desire to preserve the marriage. A defended suit is not going to do this, and if a case is, or becomes, undefended, there is little opportunity to explore the possibility of saving the marriage. An undefended divorce can be obtained in a matter of weeks. If both parties are contemplating divorce, the system gives them every incentive to obtain a "quickie" decree based on behaviour or separation [sic, presumably adultery was meant, rather than separation], and to think out the practical consequences later.

(vi) It can make things worse for the children

2.19 The present system can also make things worse for the children. The children themselves would usually prefer their parents to stay together. But the law cannot force parents to live amicably or prevent them from separating. It is not known whether children suffer more from their parents' separation or from living in a household in conflict where they may be blamed for the couple's inability to part. It is probably impossible to generalise, as there are so many variables which may affect the outcome, including the age and personality of the particular child. But it is known that the children who suffer least from their parents' break-up are usually those who are able to retain a good relationship with them both. Children who suffer most are those whose parents remain in conflict.

2.20 These issues have to be faced by the parents themselves, as they agonise over what to do for the best. However regrettably, there is nothing the law can do to ensure that they stay together, even supposing that this would indeed be better for their children. On the other hand, the present law can, for all the reasons given earlier, make the conflict worse.... It is often said that couples undergoing marital breakdown are too wrapped up in their own problems to understand their children's needs. There are also couples who, while recognising that their own relationship is at an end, are anxious to do their best for their children. The present system does little to help them to do so.

Conclusion

2.21 These defects alone would amount to a formidable case for reform. The response to Facing the Future very largely endorsed its conclusion that "Above all, the present law fails to recognise that divorce is not a final product but part of a massive transition for the parties and their children."

And so the Law Commission concluded that the most suitable role for the law on divorce lay in adjudicating not on the breakdown of the marriage itself, but instead on the practical issues—arrangements for children, financial remedies—that inevitably flow from divorce where agreement cannot be reached. While the law may not itself be the source of the bitterness and hostility so often seen on divorce, the current law does nothing to help the parties come to terms with the life-changes associated with divorce.

Divorcing couples, lawyers, and government have also expressed the concern that for many people divorce is too quick and 'easy' and so might encourage precipitate divorce where a marriage could be saved.[210] The median duration of divorce proceedings under the two principal fault-based facts is under six months; some couples get from petition to decree absolute in as little as three months.[211] In one sense, this appears to undermine suggestions that divorce is made 'harder' by requiring that it be based on fault. Given the ease with which fault may be alleged and the briskness of the procedure for undefended divorces, the 'quickie' divorce may seem rather attractive to prospective divorcees, even enabling divorce very nearly on the basis of unilateral demand where the respondent feels little practical choice but to accede to the other spouse's wish to divorce. But the fact that divorce may be readily available does not necessarily encourage irresponsible behaviour;

---

[210] Davis and Murch (1988), 66–70.
[211] LCD (1995), para 2.7.

divorce is rarely entered into lightly.[212] Indeed, it has been said that where it is clear that a marriage has irretrievably broken down, spouses who are forced to rely on the five-year separation fact are made to wait too long for their divorce and so for access to the full powers of the court to make financial orders.[213] Nor does the law systematically protect the economically weaker party. The Law Commission found it anomalous that the special protection of ss 5 and 10 should be available only to respondents in separation cases. Reliance on a separation fact does not necessarily mean that the respondent is blameless; nor, given the difficulty of clearly ascribing blame for marital breakdown, does the selection of a fault-based fact necessarily indicate that the respondent is undeserving of the court's protection.[214]

But the case for reform is not universally accepted:

R. Deech, 'Divorce Law and Empirical Studies', (1990) 106 *Law Quarterly Review* 229, 242–3

As far as the divorce grounds go, there is certainly no public or professional clamour for reform. And if the rate of divorce is really levelling off, then also there is no need for reform because it is evident that we have exhausted the possibilities of *de jure* ending all *de facto* breakdowns. If all those people whose marriages have broken down can obtain divorces under existing law, there is no need to liberalise it...[Deech then argues that further liberalization of divorce law would only further increase divorce rates.]

[Insofar as research suggests that the long-term harm caused to children occurs at the point of separation,] any alteration to divorce law is irrelevant to children's post-divorce suffering and...we should not delude ourselves that the nature of the divorce petition can make a real improvement...

Even the widely held perception of the grounds of adultery, behaviour and desertion as acrimonious and unfair may be overstated. It is not usually the spouses who choose the grounds relied on but their solicitors, and there may well be more long drawn out legal difficulties [e.g. occupation orders, interim maintenance, child arrangements] in the lapse of separation periods than where the quick grounds are relied on. It is also probably not the case...that immediate consensual divorces are available. There is always a waiting period, currently of seven or eight months on average between service of petition and decree absolute. So it is the *grounds* that are immediate, not the decree, and some studies report that petitioners do not take sudden decisions to divorce.

5.7 OPTIONS FOR REFORM OF DIVORCE LAW AND THE PROCESS OF DIVORCE

Given the many criticisms of current law and procedures for divorce, now replicated for dissolution of civil partnership,[215] anxiety about the rising divorce rate, the apparent 'ease'

---

[212] Walker (1991).
[213] Law Com (1988a), para 3.12.
[214] Ibid, paras 3.19 and 3.31.
[215] See Hasson (2006), 285–90.

of divorce, and the claimed effects of divorce on children and society, ought the law to be reformed, and if so how?[216] There are a number of perspectives from which reform might be approached, between them suggesting different models for divorce law which may in turn suggest different understandings about the nature of marriage.[217] The first focuses on the role of fault. The others are all forms of no-fault divorce. The options are not mutually exclusive, and many reform proposals—like current English law—offer several alternative routes to divorce.[218]

5.7.1 REAFFIRMING THE CENTRALITY OF FAULT?

The Morton Commission of 1956 considered that the role of divorce law was to give relief where wrong had been done.[219] There is still popular support for fault: 84 per cent of respondents to a public opinion survey for the Law Commission conducted in the late 1980s supported divorce for fault, though not as the sole basis for divorce.[220] But jurisdictions worldwide have been retreating from fault. It has been said that the legal concept of marriage which requires spouses to be subservient to a particular view of moral duty has been replaced by a concern for the quality of individual relationships and the psychological well-being of the individuals involved.[221]

Some commentators and legislators seek to resist this trend, considering that fault should remain a central feature of divorce law and family justice more generally. Ruth Deech makes the case for fault in these terms:

R. Deech, 'Divorce Law – A Disaster?', (2009a) Gresham lectures 2009–10

It seem[s] to me to be clear that [the lack of morality in public life] is because over the last forty years or so we have abandoned, in terms of approbation/disapprobation, law and categorisation, any pressure to conform to basic, long unchallenged tenets of private morality. At the time I applauded the liberalising laws of the 1960s and still think that on balance they did more good than harm – the legalisation of abortion and homosexuality, the ending of the criminalisation of suicide, [ending] the stigmatising of illegitimacy, and the liberalising of contraception and divorce. Yet the effect, when taken all together a few decades on, is to live in a society where there are no constraints on private morality, no judgmentalism, no finger wagging or name calling, only acceptance of anything that anyone does, short of the criminal law, in the name of the pursuit, if not of individual happiness, then at least individual choice.... So individual happiness is pitted against, and prevails over the good of one's family and others.

Contemporary debate about fault was first stimulated by the divorce reforms in Part II of the Family Law Act 1996, which (we shall see below) was never brought into force. It

---

[216] See generally Harvie-Clark (2005); Boele-Woelki et al (2004); Law Com (1988a) and (1990).

[217] See the themes considered earlier: 5.3.

[218] Including those of the Commission for European Family Law: Boele-Woelki et al (2004).

[219] Royal Commission on Marriage and Divorce (1956), para 69(xii).

[220] Law Com (1990), 183.

[221] Ellman (2000), 344; this is not to say that people no longer feel a sense of obligation and commitment within their intimate relationships: see Lewis (2001b).

would have removed fault entirely from English divorce law. Concerns were expressed during the passage of the Act about what opponents saw as the removal of individual responsibility from marriage. As Lord Stallard put it, 'No fault, to me, means no responsibility, no commitment and no security'.[222] Economist Robert Rowthorn later offered the following analysis:

R. Rowthorn, 'Marriage and Trust: Some Lessons from Economics', (1999) 23 *Cambridge Journal of Economics* 661, 662–3

[M]arriage should be seen as an institution for creating trust between individuals in the sphere of family life, and...legal and social policy should be fashioned so as to allow this function to be effectively performed. Many of the legal and social reforms which have been implemented in modern times have undermined the ability of marriage to perform its basic role as a trust-creating institution. To get married is no longer such a major commitment and no longer offers the degree of security which it once did, since divorce is now relatively easy and the responsibilities and rights of the married and the unmarried are increasingly similar. These developments are often presented as an advance in human freedom since they allow individuals to exit unilaterally from unhappy relationships at minimum cost to themselves and with minimum delay. However, this is a one-sided view, since it ignores the benefits and freedoms associated with trust and security. The fact that individuals can now exit easily, and unilaterally, from a relationship makes it difficult for couples to make credible commitments to each other. They can promise anything they want, but many of these promises are no longer legally enforceable, and many are undermined by social policies which reward those who break their promises. By eroding the ability of couples to make credible commitments to each other, modern reforms have deprived them of an important facility which, for all its defects, the old system provided.

...The marriage contract has been diluted to the point that it is now much less binding than the average business deal. While employment law has increased job security and protection for workers, legal security in the family has been weakened and in many Western countries the marriage contract can now be terminated at will virtually without penalty. Marriage is now one of the few contracts where the law and government policy frequently protect the defaulting party at the expense of his or her partner.

The debate about fault and no-fault divorce has been particularly strong in the United States, where no-fault divorce was introduced during the 1970s. Many states permit divorce on unilateral demand after six months' separation, often alongside traditional fault-based grounds.[223] A guilty party can therefore divorce fairly easily. In reaction to this, rather than advocate a wholesale return to fault-based divorce, some commentators devised a special class of marriage with more restrictive grounds for divorce which couples can select at the outset: 'covenant marriage'. The concern is principally to secure the position of the spouse who is unwilling to divorce, so covenant marriage adopts a private contract view of marriage, rather than a public interest model that seeks to uphold marriage by keeping parties together in the absence of fault, even where both wish to part. Under covenant marriage, an innocent party can instigate divorce immediately on fault-based grounds, but divorce is

---

222 Hansard HL Deb, vol 569, col 1651, 29 February 1996.
223 See Ellman (2000).

also available on no-fault grounds which are less generous than the US norm; for example, Louisiana's covenant marriage law permits unilateral divorce following a more onerous two years of separation. So even under this scheme, to English eyes, divorce is not drastically restricted. Three states have enacted covenant marriage laws, but the take-up has been very low.[224] The principal architect of the Louisiana covenant marriage statute makes the case for this new form of marriage:

E. Spaht, 'Louisiana's Covenant Marriage Law: Recapturing the Meaning of Marriage for the Sake of the Children', in A. Dnes and R. Rowthorn (eds), *The Law and Economics of Marriage and Divorce* (Cambridge: CUP, 2002), 110–11

Restoration of "moral discourse" to divorce law...troubles most critics of the covenant marriage law more than any other aspect of the legislation. The "moral discourse" consists of society's collective condemnation of certain conduct within the marital relationship. Returning to objective moral judgments about a spouse's conduct threatens the notion that morality cannot be legislated. Congress and legislatures do it every day. Only when the morals to be legislated have the potential of impeding the affected person's "liberty" to leave his or her family when he or she so chooses and be considered legally "a single person" do we hear objections. In matters of breach of contract, no one has objected to assigning *blame* for failure to perform a contract, requiring that contracts be performed in good faith, and assessing damages based upon whether the party breached the contract in good faith or bad faith. If principles of contract law involve moral judgments in the context of a relationship between strangers,[225] why should the law hesitate to make a moral judgment about spouses who have been married for thirty years and have three children?

Another argument against the restoration of fault to divorce law is the assertion that fault cannot be proven, thus, those who desire divorce will be relegated to perjury, allegedly a widespread practice prior to no-fault divorce. Fault in the nature of adultery or physical abuse sufficient for an immediate divorce [under covenant marriage law] may be proven by mere preponderance of the evidence (more likely than not), and that evidence need only be circumstantial, not direct. Surely, it is no more difficult to prove adultery by a spouse than to prove which driver's fault, and the degree of that fault expressed in a percentage, caused a car accident. As a response to the expressed concern about widespread perjury, the answer is that the judiciary and attorneys bear responsibility. Even though perjury should surely be condemned, the fraud upon the court did at least require *cooperation of both spouses* and precluded the current practice [under no-fault divorce] of legalized desertion by one spouse.

Arguments about fault in divorce law are hotly contested. Some view fault-based divorce as a tool for influencing behaviour: to deter divorce and to deter bad behaviour during marriage (i.e. whatever behaviour would give the other spouse grounds for divorce).[226] It

---

[224] Louisiana (La Rev Stat Ann Sect 9:272–275, 307–9), Arizona (Ariz Rev Stat Ann Sect 25-901–906), Arkanas (Covenant Marriage Act of 2001); Bills have been introduced in several other states, but not yet been passed.

[225] By contrast with many other legal systems, English contract law has no general good faith doctrine.

[226] E.g. Royal Commission on Marriage and Divorce (1956), para 69(xxxvii).

is also argued that the knowledge that divorce may only occur if each party misbehaves (or consents to divorce, where divorce is also available on the basis of mutual consent) would encourage spouses to 'invest' in the marriage for their mutual benefit (e.g. by one spouse reducing paid employment in order to raise the children), safe in the knowledge that their investments are protected for so long as the other party has no grounds for divorce.[227]

But others question whether deterrence of bad behaviour is properly or realistically the role of divorce law, rather than criminal or tort law. If conduct is not sufficiently grave to warrant the intervention of criminal or tort law, or cannot be defined sufficiently clearly for those purposes, that may suggest that it is not something that should be adjudicated on even by the divorce courts.[228] And, while proponents of fault contest their validity,[229] the practical difficulties outlined by the Law Commission for rejecting fault remain.[230] Ascribing guilt and innocence in intimate relationships is often far from straightforward, and the legal system is said to be ill-equipped to identify correctly the causes of a marriage's demise. If done properly (assuming even that it could be), it would be extremely costly both for the parties and the family justice system.

Even if fault is properly a matter for family law, it may be also doubted whether spouses invest in marriage because the law places barriers in the way of divorce: most couples are affected by 'optimism bias'—few spouses enter marriage thinking that theirs might be one of the many marriages that will end badly—and most people have no detailed knowledge of family law.[231] Many also question whether law is a sufficiently sophisticated mechanism for influencing conduct within marriage and encouraging commitment; social norms may be more potent.[232]

Moreover, the strength of the 'sanction' of divorce as a deterrent to bad behaviour will only be as strong as the guilty party's desire not to be divorced and that party's unwillingness to satisfy the terms that the innocent party may demand as a condition for agreeing to divorce.[233] Proponents of fault say that a guilty party who *wants* divorce can be punished under fault-based law by the innocent party withholding divorce. But critics have argued that this course of action may rarely be in the interests of the innocent party, who may be rather better protected by the courts' powers to make financial orders which arise on divorce.[234] And the spouse wishing to leave may simply do so, without bothering about a divorce.[235]

In making the case for covenant marriage, Spaht argues that, logically, the revival of fault should extend to the determination of child arrangements and financial remedies. If fault-based divorce law is to achieve its aims, it may indeed be logical to ensure that a finding of fault is reflected in decisions about the future arrangements for any children and the distribution of the parties' assets: the children would live with the 'innocent' party, who

---

[227] E.g. Rowthorn (1999).

[228] E.g. Ellman (1997), 226.

[229] Rowthorn (1999), 684–5.

[230] See extract above pp 344–5 and Law Com (1990), paras 3.6–3.9, 3.40; O'Donovan (1993), 110–15; Scott (2002), 50–1.

[231] Herring, Probert, and Gilmore (2012), 178.

[232] Contrast Deech (1990); Schuz (1993); Eekelaar (2000).

[233] Ellman (1997), 226.

[234] Eekelaar (2006b), 105–11. One response to this would be to open up wider remedies outside the divorce context.

[235] See Fahey (2014) on the prevalence of marital separation in jurisdictions with restrictive divorce laws.

could claim financial recompense from the 'guilty' party for lost expectations on divorce.[236] But adopting fault as the key criterion for these decisions would entail a major reversal in policy, prioritizing 'justice' between the spouses over the welfare and rights of individual children. This proposal has therefore been criticized by Carol Smart for returning children to the status of 'trophies in the adversarial system'.[237] Moreover, John Eekelaar and others have argued that financial settlements on divorce can promote 'responsibility' on divorce and protect parties' investments in marriage via mechanisms other than fault.[238] Indeed, simply adjudicating fault—even without that having direct implications for the children and finances—can only be damaging to the parties' future relations as joint parents of their children.

Finally, there is another psychological angle to consider. Other commentators have cautioned against attempts to 'sanitize' divorce by removing any opportunity for parties to express their sense of grievance. From a psychological perspective, the emotional conflict accompanying divorce is neither trivial nor pathological, but a normal part of the process of bereavement experienced on divorce.[239] It may be desirable for the divorce process to contain that conflict, rather than simply try to deny or reduce it,[240] and to recognize that current norms associated with 'good' divorce, such as the importance of joint parenting following separation, may actually fuel conflict.[241] The question is whether the *legal* forum, whether via the grounds for divorce or otherwise, provides the environment or context in which the emotional consequences of divorce can be most satisfactorily addressed. But providing at least some facility for divorce on the ground of fault (perhaps alongside no-fault options) may also send a valuable signal that fault is sometimes unequivocally present on one side, for example in cases of domestic abuse: 'To deny the existence of fault . . . would reinforce the feeling of many victims that the abuse is in some way *their* fault'.[242]

5.7.2 DIVORCE BY MUTUAL CONSENT?

The Law Commission found substantial support for divorce on the basis of mutual consent: 90 per cent of survey respondents thought that divorce should be available on this basis.[243] Long gone are the days when the public interest demanded that parties be prevented from reaching agreements regarding divorce. It is probably no exaggeration to say that many of today's divorces are now effectively obtained on this 'ground', albeit that the petition will be framed in terms of one of the fault-based facts (in order to secure a quick divorce) or two years' separation. If so, adopting mutual consent as an immediate ground for divorce could be viewed simply as 'a technical fix aimed at improving the functioning of the judicial

---

236 Rowthorn (1999), 671; Dnes (1998), 345 argues instead that, rather than find fault in a tradition sense, a party who unilaterally seeks divorce without good cause should be regarded as being 'in breach', and so treated as the guilty party. Determining whether 'good cause' exists might, however, reintroduce traditional fault arguments.

237 Smart (2000), 380.

238 Eekelaar (2006b), 105–11; Ellman (1997); see 7.5.6 on the marginal relevance of fault in English law of financial remedies on divorce.

239 Day Sclater (1999), 180.

240 Brown and Day Sclater (1999), 158; Walker (1991), 236.

241 Collier (1999), 262.

242 Herring, Probert, and Gilmore (2012), 192.

243 Law Com (1990), 183.

system rather than...a fundamental change in family policy'.[244] Whether it would be perceived that way is another matter: like any no-fault option, this purely *private* view of marriage which removes the state from any adjudicative role over its dissolution might attract opposition. But it would certainly be readily comprehensible.[245]

Current English law expressly contemplates divorce by mutual consent only where the parties have been separated for two years. There are significantly fewer cases of divorce on this basis than on the fault-based facts. If it were thought desirable that more cases should proceed on a no-fault basis, but that a separation requirement remained appropriate (rather than allowing immediate divorce by consent), the law could try to encourage reliance on the 'separation with consent' fact by reducing the period of separation required. The time periods for the separation facts in Scotland are now one and two years respectively.[246]

If mutual consent were to become a ground for divorce, increased procedural safeguards would be needed to ensure that consent had been given in a free and informed way.[247] Mutual consent could not, however, serve as the sole ground for divorce. There are situations in which one party should be free to instigate divorce without consent (especially where the respondent is guilty of some grave fault), and an exclusive mutual consent ground could replicate the 'distortions' of bargaining position for which the current law is criticized.[248] The question is whether the law should identify specific circumstances in which one party should be able to instigate divorce (whether based on specific categories of fault or on a period of separation), or whether divorce on unilateral demand should be adopted.

5.7.3 DIVORCE ON UNILATERAL DEMAND?

If divorce should be available where a marriage has irretrievably broken down, the corollary may be to accept that divorce should be available not only where the parties agree on that course, but wherever *one* party desires it. On this view, consent of both parties to divorce ought not to be a necessary precondition: the consent of both parties ought to be necessary for marriage to *continue*. Moreover, it might be safe to assume that those best placed to determine whether a marriage has irretrievably broken down are the parties themselves—if one party wishes to divorce, that is surely the best evidence available that divorce is appropriate. Many believe that the legal system cannot undertake that evaluation—the issue is not justiciable.[249] The wish to make the notion of lifelong obligation meaningful by subjecting the dissolution of marriage 'to an authority that is independent of the will of the parties...a real exercise of judgment by the Court, acting on the community's behalf'[250] may simply be unrealizable. Given the difficulty of defending divorce petitions and the lack of serious scrutiny under the procedure for undefended divorces, many divorces are already effectively granted on this basis, not only those based on the one no-fault unilateral fact, five-year separation.[251]

However, the public may be less willing to accept this reasoning: only a third of respondents to the Law Commission survey in the late 1980s thought divorce on unilateral demand

---

[244] Ellman (2000), 341. This was true as early as 1966: Law Com (1966), para 79.
[245] Cretney (1992), 474.
[246] Family Law (Scotland) Act 2006, s 10; also abolished desertion fact and the hardship bar, ss 11–12.
[247] Law Com (1988a), para 5.18.
[248] See Law Com (1990), para 2.15, above.
[249] Law Com (1988a), paras 4.6–4.7.
[250] Mortimer Commission (1966), para 48.
[251] Law Com (1988a), para 5.20.

would be acceptable. Like any other no-fault option, divorce on unilateral demand entails a very different conception of marriage and of the nature and extent of the public interest in divorce from a fault-based law. The state is entirely removed from adjudication on the end of the marriage, and can only protect the unwilling party via decisions relating to arrangements for children and finances.[252] Unlike divorce by mutual consent, no-fault unilateral divorce is criticized for undermining each spouse's ability to rely upon the marriage contract, and so damaging the quality of their partnership.[253]

If divorce on unilateral demand were acceptable, we would still need to consider whether divorce should be available immediately on that basis, or whether the parties should be required to separate (currently under English law for five years, under Louisiana's covenant law for two years or, for its standard marriage contract, just six months), or simply to wait for a period of time before divorce proceedings could be initiated, and if so, why and for how long. This brings us to consideration of divorce as a process over time.

5.7.4 DIVORCE AS A PROCESS OVER TIME

In these days of mass divorce, it has been suggested that the focus has shifted from delivering substantive justice to aggrieved parties to considerations related to 'consumer choice, efficiency and pragmatism'.[254] The values and interests at stake may now be reduced to 'easy and public access to divorce, the promotion of consensual divorce above unilateral divorce, the autonomy of the spouses and the protection of the weakest spouse'.[255] But the state may not be prepared to give up all attempts to regulate divorcing behaviour. The 'consumers' of divorce may not be left entirely free to divorce as and when they wish to. If the law can no longer be used to restrict the *substantive* grounds on which a divorce may be obtained, could the law be used to slow down and influence the decision-making *process*, either to guard against precipitate divorces, or to encourage those determined to divorce to do so in a particular way? At the very least, 'Would it not be ironic if a consumer were allowed to "back out" of an agreement to purchase life assurance or a timeshare after a "cooling-off" period, but would be bound with immediate effect to an agreement to divorce?'[256] Should couples be encouraged, to use the actor Gwyneth Paltrow's expression, to engage in a process of 'conscious uncoupling'?[257]

A period of separation

The law currently enforces a cooling-off on those who wish to divorce without proof of fault by requiring that they separate for two or five years. Separation affords the sole ground for divorce in Australia (one year) and New Zealand (two years).[258] The separation facts are criticized for discriminating against those who may find it difficult to satisfy the legal test

---

252 Ibid, para 4.14. Even if the divorce itself were not granted on the basis of fault, ancillary decisions still could be: see Ellman (1997), 218; Dnes (1998).

253 Rowthorn (1999); see also Scott (2002).

254 O'Donovan (1993), 112.

255 Boele-Woelki et al (2004), 48–9, discussing scrutiny of agreements on the consequences of divorce.

256 Schuz (1993), 581.

257 This is the expression deployed by Ms Paltrow, with much press and social media commentary, to describe her separation from her musician husband Chris Martin in 2014.

258 Family Law Act 1975 (Aus); Family Proceedings Act 1980 (NZ).

for separation.[259] But that could be avoided by reform enabling the court, as in Australia and New Zealand, to make financial orders to facilitate separation by would-be petitioners.[260] Indeed, it is because they seek immediate access to the courts' adjustive powers over the parties' assets that so many people rely on the immediate, fault-based facts instead.[261] But some commentators still doubt whether a separation ground would in practice operate satisfactorily and reduce conflict.[262]

A 'period of reflection and consideration': the FLA 1996

Another option is exemplified by Part II of the FLA 1996. This legislation was based on recommendations made by the Law Commission, subsequently revised by the government and further amended during its passage through Parliament.[263] The scheme received considerable support when originally proposed and would have revolutionized English divorce law. For reasons which we explore briefly below, the reform was never implemented and the legislation has been repealed.[264] But the scheme created by the FLA 1996 remains useful as an alternative model for divorce.

Under the FLA 1996 scheme, irretrievable breakdown would have remained the sole ground for divorce and the bar on divorce in the first year of marriage would still have applied, but there the similarity to the current law would have ended. The 'facts' would have been abolished, non-adversarial terminology adopted, and joint applications for divorce made possible. Separation prior to divorce would not have been required. Instead, the ground for divorce would have been established by a statement, made by the applicant(s) following the mandatory 'period of reflection and consideration', that the marriage had irretrievably broken down. During that period, parties would have been expected to consider whether their marriage could be saved and, if not, to resolve issues relating to the future care of their children and their property. The clock would only have started to run three months after the applicant(s) had attended a mandatory information meeting. Mediation came to be seen as a key way for parties to negotiate these issues on divorce. The only remaining significant element of *substantive* law requiring adjudication would have been provided by the hardship bar,[265] which was lowered during the passage of the Bill from 'grave' to 'substantial' hardship, and which (since divorces could no longer be categorized by reference to the fact relied on) would have been available in all cases. Divorce under this scheme would have taken much longer for parties who currently rely on the quick fault-based facts.[266]

A key feature of the FLA scheme was that the 'period of reflection and consideration' was not intended to operate neutrally, like a mere period of separation. Instead, a new role for the state on divorce and new obligations for divorcing spouses were envisaged.[267]

---

[259] See extract above p 345.

[260] Law Com (1990), para 3.25. See also Commission for European Family Law's proposals: Boele-Woelki et al (2004).

[261] Davis and Murch (1988), 141.

[262] Ibid, 142–5; cf Davies (1993) reporting the success of the separation ground in other jurisdictions; but that success may be partly attributable to greater availability of housing in those countries: Davis and Murch (1988), ibid.

[263] Law Com (1988a), (1990); LCD (1993), (1995).

[264] Albeit only after nearly 20 years by the Children and Families Act 2014, s 18.

[265] See 5.5.6.

[266] LCD (1995), para 2.7.

[267] See generally Reece (2003).

As Carol Smart has described, the radical nature of the proposed change generated fierce debate between two groups: those who advocated the retention of fault to provide clear, public 'rules of conduct' for marriage, the cornerstone of family and society; and those who viewed family in more fluid terms, where moral questions are negotiable matters for the parties themselves. The FLA 1996, a victory for the second group, would have transformed the state's role with regard to marriage and divorce but also made new demands on divorcing couples:

C. Smart, 'Divorce in England 1950–2000: A Moral Tale?', in S. Katz, J. Eekelaar, and M. Maclean (eds), *Cross Currents: Family Law and Policy in the US and England* (Oxford: OUP, 2000), 376–7

As with the debates some decades earlier, the main point of contention in the 1990s was over the best method(s) for the state to deploy in order to facilitate/ensure supportive, stable, and responsible family relationships...The core elements of the Bill, namely the information meetings, the period of reflection, and the preference for mediation over litigation, all constituted a prime example of the practice of governance as opposed to government. The theme of the legislation was based on the idea that people need knowledge about divorce and the financial problems it brings, the difficulties it creates for children, and the need to plan such things as resuming work and pension provision. The period of reflection was proposed as a form of 'time out' in which emotions could settle down in order to allow the divorcing couple to become more rational and more competent citizens, equipped either to manage the transition to divorce, or to change their minds and stay married. Mediation was intended as a way of helping to plan and to resolve any outstanding differences and problems mutually. The modern citizen envisaged by the Family Law Bill was the fact-gathering, rational, caring parent who would make decisions on the basis of knowledge. This citizen could be compared (unfavourably) with the divorced spouse of the former fault-based system who was encouraged to look backwards and cherish resentments and blame, who seized upon children as weapons in the battle, and who—in their emotional haze—failed to make proper provision either for themselves or for their former partners and children. The aim of governance would be to produce the former citizen. The aim of government in the latter scenario would be to adjudicate on who should be rewarded and who punished, while admonishing the most guilty for their failure.

Even amongst those who favour no-fault divorce, the new law was not universally supported. It was criticized for being unrealistic in hoping that couples would 'spend time reflecting on whether their marriage can be saved, and, if not to face up to the consequences of their actions and make arrangements to meet their responsibilities'.[268]

S. Cretney, 'Divorce Reform: Humbug and Hypocrisy or a Smooth Transition?', in M. Freeman (ed), *Divorce: Where Next* (Aldershot: Dartmouth, 1996a), 52–3

This is a very laudable aspiration. But how is this 'requirement' to be enforced? May not some of those concerned prefer to spend their time in the far more pleasurable activity of

---

[268] LCD (1995), para 4.16.

conceiving—necessarily illegitimate—babies? May not some spend the time seeking means of exploiting their emotional or financial advantage, or brooding on grievances and perhaps using the available legal procedures as a way of seeking satisfaction for the wrongs they have suffered? The way in which the Law Commission's proposals were presented seemed almost reminiscent of those earnest Victorian reformers who invented the so-called 'separate system'—prisoners deprived of all corrupting influences would be driven to reflect in their solitude on the evil of their ways and thereby be well prepared to receive the sympathy, advice and religious consolation provided for those truly humbled by their experience. It was, of course, all very well-intentioned; and yet succeeded in inflicting scarcely imaginable cruelty on hundreds of helpless human beings. We would all hope that the parties will indeed give anxious consideration to whether the marriage has broken down irretrievably and to the consequential arrangements. We must all hope that mediation and counselling will be successful in this respect. But the evidence for believing that these expectations will be fulfilled is not overwhelmingly convincing.

Cretney also accused the new law of hypocrisy: that the emphasis on reflection and consideration concealed what in fact amounted to divorce on unilateral demand:

It is true that the government's proposals will end the sometimes damaging ritual of filing a petition alleging—perhaps unjustly—that the other spouse has committed adultery or been guilty of behaviour such as to make it unreasonable for the spouses to go on living together. But a man who has behaved cruelly and unreasonably will still be able to insist on divorce against the wishes of his wife; and the wife's anger, grief and bitterness may reasonably not be assuaged by assurances that the new law promotes consideration and reflection—and that since her case is a simple one she is not to receive any public help to pay a lawyer who will defend her interests. There seems to be a serious risk that countless people will find themselves uncomprehendingly ensnared in a monstrous and costly legal/ social work/counselling nightmare. The Law Commission...identifies the 'incoherence' of the law and the confusion thereby caused to people caught up in the divorce process as one of the law's most significant weaknesses; and the Commission rightly attributes these defects to the compromise nature of the 1969 divorce reforms. But there is a serious risk that the incoherence and confusion will be perpetuated and even increased. We shall still have to pretend that the ground for divorce is the breakdown of the marriage; whereas the reality is that it is the wish of one party to divorce the other. The information and mediation sessions merely conceal that simple truth and, in so doing, they make matters worse.

The scheme could also be criticized for being patronizing and unduly restricting access to divorce for at least some couples. The decision to divorce is rarely taken lightly or quickly.[269] Many couples (especially, perhaps, those without children) may have separated and resolved all arrangements for the future long before initiating divorce proceedings. How might such couples feel if then required to reflect and consider for a further year? Might such a system encourage people to set that clock ticking early—perhaps enticing them into a divorcing mindset precipitately—to ensure that the option of immediate divorce would be there once the decision was reached? There should perhaps have been an alternative track for immediate divorce by mutual consent—or even unilaterally—for

---

[269] See Davis and Murch (1988).

parties who had been separated for a defined period and/or who had no minor children.[270] For example, immediate divorce is available in Sweden if both parties want it and they have no minor children. If only one party wishes to divorce or if the parties have children, they must ordinarily wait for a six-month period of reflection (during which they need not separate). But if they have been separated for two years, a divorce may be granted immediately.[271] John Eekelaar has observed that were childless marriages to be left effectively unregulated at divorce, there would be little to distinguish them from childless cohabitation; 'marriage will [to that extent] have become, in Clive's (1980) phrase, an "unnecessary legal concept"'.[272]

On the other hand, many couples are reported bitterly to regret having got divorced (though that may not mean that they would not still *want* a divorce, in the circumstances). The law might therefore be justified in imposing some waiting period on all cases. To deny immediate divorce to those who genuinely wish to have it may be a small price to pay for a system which does not risk propelling those undergoing emotional stress towards a divorce which they may later regret.

5.8 WHERE NEXT FOR ENGLISH DIVORCE LAW?

5.8.1 THE FATE OF THE FLA 1996 SCHEME

The fate of the FLA 1996 divorce scheme is instructive as it tells us a lot about current policy priorities in the family justice arena. The decision to abandon the FLA scheme was taken following pilot projects designed to explore the best format for the initial information meetings. The pilots (which were necessarily conducted in the context of the current law) had been devised simply to test the format for information delivery, but the government subsequently evaluated the results by reference to the likelihood, following receipt of the information, of parties electing to use mediation rather than seeking legal advice in relation to their divorce.[273] This reflected the way in which the Law Commission's original scheme had changed in emphasis as it developed in the hands of successive governments and in Parliament.[274] The Law Commission had conceived of the period for reflection and consideration principally as a way of proving irretrievable marital breakdown. Parties might well use mediation and other non-legal services during that period, but use of mediation was not central to the scheme at that stage. When the Conservative Government took over the project, divorce reform become inextricably linked with concerns to save marriages and to promote mediation in preference to legal services, and so the information meetings were inserted into the scheme. It then became clear under the Labour Government that these meetings would not be neutral conduits for the delivery of factual information. 'Information' here had a persuasive function, aimed at steering parties towards attempts to save their marriage or, if that were impossible, towards behaving

---

[270] For criticism of allowing children to affect the duration of any period, see LCD (1995), paras 4.17–4.18.
[271] Swedish Marriage Code, Chapter 5.
[272] Eekelaar (1991b), 171.
[273] Newcastle Centre for Family Studies (2001b), 21.
[274] See Eekelaar, Maclean, and Beinart (2000), ch 1.

'responsibly' in relation to their divorce; and 'responsibility' was synonymous with use of mediation.[275]

Given these ambitions, the Labour Government was 'disappointed'[276] by the results of the pilot projects. Only a small minority of couples were diverted to marriage counselling; counselling had limited success in preventing divorce, but did help individuals cope with the transition through divorce and improve the quality of their post-divorce relationship. The failure of the meetings to save more marriages was perhaps unsurprising: only one spouse had to attend the information meeting and that individual was often too far down the psychological road to divorce for the meeting to affect the decision to end the marriage. Nor were the meetings particularly successful in diverting couples into mediation: only 10 per cent of individuals attending the meetings went to mediation with their spouses within two years of the meeting, while 73 per cent went to lawyers in that time.[277] Interim results had found 39 per cent reporting that having attended the information meeting they were now *more likely* to seek legal advice.[278] This was not the ringing public endorsement of mediation for which the government had hoped, particularly bearing in mind that all those who participated in the pilot projects were volunteers, who might therefore have been expected to be more amenable to new options.

The pilot projects reported many positive findings—an overwhelming majority (90 per cent) of those who had attended meetings were glad to have done so; the information meetings succeeded in 'increasing knowledge and empowering citizens to take informed decisions'.[279] Yet despite these good outcomes, the FLA 1996 divorce scheme was abandoned.[280] The government's disappointment that parties still wished to use lawyers rather than mediators and so failed to match the image of 'responsible' divorce attracted strong criticism from John Eekelaar, worried by the implications of the government's position for the rule of law:

J. Eekelaar, 'Family Law: Keeping Us "On Message"', (1999) 11 *Child and Family Law Quarterly* **387, 395–6**

I do not wish to argue against the importance of people being under duties and having responsibilities. Indeed, to the extent that any individual has rights, others (individually or collectively) will have responsibilities to respect those rights. It is also the case that an individual's rights and duties are not exhausted by their statement in the law. This is obvious in the case of moral rights and duties. It is also true in relation to an individual's socially constructed rights and duties: so, while, for example, the law may not require an able, adult, child to give any assistance to his or her indigent parent, there may well be a socially accepted obligation to provide it. But in the examples discussed here, we have an apparent tension between what the state proclaims in its law and how it wants people actually to behave. The legal framework of marriage and divorce has, under the influence of liberal individualism, become a neutral edifice within which parties have worked out their lives according to a wide

---

275 See Reece (2003), Eekelaar (1999).
276 LCD (1999).
277 Newcastle Centre for Family Studies (2001a).
278 LCD (1999).
279 Walker (2000), 410.
280 LCD (2001).

> variety of beliefs and customs. Now the state is actively intervening, through institutions of its creation or to which individuals will be strongly steered, in an attempt to bring about certain forms of behaviour which are not legally required, and may not even be consistent with widely accepted social norms.

Eekelaar went on to note that the FLA 1996 allowed grants to be made for research into marital breakdown, its causes, and prevention methods, and funding for marriage counselling. He raised no objection to this expenditure, accepting that it might be thought right, even a matter of duty, for the state to seek through various means to promote 'good' behaviour. But are there limits to the appropriateness of such state intervention?

> Perhaps we would not feel uncomfortable if the state were to do this to modify behaviour to make people more racially tolerant, for example, or to discourage domestic violence. One might not even feel too uncomfortable with a scheme which attempts to motivate people to earn their income rather than rely on welfare benefits. Is it different when we are dealing with marriage and divorcing behaviour? It may be. The legal provisions themselves [i.e. the FLA 1996, and the substantive law governing children and property division on divorce] have largely moved away from a prescriptive role to a position of neutrality, although they do provide a range of options which are available to protect the vital interests of those who are harmed in their personal lives. This has emerged from gradual acceptance that the way people organise their personal lives evolves in response to changing moral, social and economic factors which are not easily controlled by governments. There can, I think, be no objection to the government playing a part, although by no means the sole part, in influencing those factors. We may, however, become uncomfortable when the government intervenes at key points in the institutional processes of marriage and divorce and attempts to impose its own vision of how people should be behaving at those times. At best, it risks being made to appear foolish and ineffectual. Worse, it can appear heavy handed, domineering and insensitive in an area of behaviour to which all citizens have a strong claim to privacy, provided that they do not threaten the clear interests of other individuals. But my main objection is *where it utilises the institutions of law itself to obstruct individuals from access to the rights conferred on them by law*. This could be deeply corrupting of the law itself. We should not forget that both marriage and divorce are *rights* and that post-divorce settlements *do* reflect legal entitlements (however imperfectly expressed in the discretionary system). Disenchantment with some of the excesses of the legal process should never obscure these facts. The role of the legal profession has perhaps never been more important in helping people to negotiate their way through some of the hazards which changing behaviour patterns and an increasingly complex material world visit on them.

Eekelaar's concerns have only been increased by subsequent policy developments in relation to the public funding of legal services and mediation in family cases, discussed at 1.2.7. These build on the notion that responsible action is synonymous with mediation and—by implication—inconsistent with hiring the services of lawyers instead, even as a means of achieving out of court settlement. We discuss those reforms and their broader implications on the Online Resource Centre.

5.8.2 RECENT DIVORCE REFORM PROPOSALS

Calls for reform of divorce law come regularly, not least from senior members of the judiciary. Shortly after the FLA 1996's tenth anniversary, Sir Nicholas Wall—the then President of the Family Division—founded his arguments for no-fault divorce on support for the institution of marriage:

> I do believe strongly in the institution of marriage as the best way to bring up children and that's one of the reasons why I would like to end the quick and easy divorces based on the fault system. I think that it actually undermines marriage.[281]

While some want fault to be reinstated in divorce law and beyond, for Sir Nicholas Wall fault simply promotes conflict and so makes it more difficult to maintain good relations post-divorce. The current President, Sir James Munby, has similarly asked recently whether fault should be removed, and consensual divorces granted without judicial supervision.[282] Asked in a press conference whether this would 'make divorce too easy and...undermine marriage', he said:[283]

> Well, it would make divorce no easier than it is at present. The reality is that we have and have had for quite some time in this country divorce by consent in the sense that if both parties wish there will be a divorce if they're able to establish the grounds for divorce which is very easy...The process...is an essentially bureaucratic administrative process...[284]

Resolution, the specialist family law solicitors' group, have proposed a straightforward no-fault divorce law. Under their scheme,[285] parties intending to divorce would attend information meetings regarding local legal and non-legal services (including counselling, mediation, help with parenting). One or both parties could then lodge a statement of marital breakdown that would start a six-month waiting period which could be shortened in exceptional circumstances or by reference to the length of any separation immediately preceding the lodging of the statement (thus potentially reducing the waiting period, apparently, to nothing). There would be no requirement for parties to separate during that period. On the conclusion of the waiting period, either party could apply for divorce by filing a declaration that the marriage had broken down. The s 5 hardship bar would be abolished, but the s 10(2) power to delay divorce retained.

The more modest proposals of the Centre for Social Justice would simply introduce a waiting period to the current MCA scheme.[286] Parties would have to give notice of intention to divorce and then wait three months before being entitled to apply for divorce. After three months (and within six months) of that notice, either or both parties together would be allowed to petition for divorce in the ordinary way. To ensure that the waiting period afforded parties space to reflect, no application for financial orders could be made during that time. The waiting period would be intended to help save marriages and allow time for information meetings, attempts at reconciliation, or for mediation or other out of court dispute resolution methods to be used.

---

[281] Verkaik (2006).

[282] Munby (2014a).

[283] Munby (2014b).

[284] All the more so now that legal advisers, rather than judges, normally discharge the task set by MCA 1973, s 1(3); see p 335 above.

[285] See Shepherd (2009).

[286] Centre for Social Justice (2009). See also Deech (2009a).

For the time being, however, the only response from Parliament has been to tinker with the process of divorce under the MCA 1973, rendering the procedure for undefended divorces even more bureaucratic and less judicial. Like previous dilutions of the procedure for divorce, this change was driven entirely by cost-saving rather than principled motives.[287] The Family Justice Review further recommended that the divorce paperwork be moved online and dealt with by a central court processing centre. Jonathan Herring queries whether online divorce is desirable:

J. Herring, 'Divorce, Internet Hubs and Stephen Cretney', in R. Probert and C. Barton (eds), *Fifty Years in Family Law* (Cambridge: Intersentia, 2012), 196–7

I am concerned that the completion of an internet form assessed by an administrator to complete a divorce lacks the solemnity that should mark the end of a marriage. We could, when a person dies, arrange for an economical and efficient way of disposing of the body. We do not. The death of the person is marked as a serious moment, respecting what has been lost and looking forward to the future. Allowing divorce by an internet form, appears to trivialise a loss for a couple. Of course the current law may be seen as little more than an administrative procedure by post. Is it any different that it is by the internet? Is it somehow undignified to obtain a divorce by a form which will presumably be slightly shorter than that required for a credit card? . . .

. . . [The demise of a marriage] is of public significance, which should be acknowledged by some kind of public act. The current judicial pronouncement is very limited, but is some kind of formal public acknowledgement. An administrator working through the internet does not play that kind of public role.

5.9 CONCLUSION

The British Social Attitudes survey shows that a large majority think it better to divorce than to continue in an unhappy marriage.[288] However, they would likely be less satisfied with the way in which English law currently handles divorce. As we have seen, English divorce law retains a large fault-based component which is relied upon by most divorcing spouses, not least to secure a quick divorce. It may be some years before the subject of divorce reform returns to the legislative agenda. Until then, spouses must continue to use the curious combination[289] of the MCA 1973 (experienced by most couples as fault-based) and its rather less than 'special' procedure, whilst being encouraged (despite the fault-based recriminations) to approach their situation in a forward-looking, constructive manner. The current law of divorce sits uncomfortably alongside other aspects of contemporary family law. Couples are now positively encouraged to make their own arrangements for children and child support and enabled to place more reliance on pre-nuptial agreements on divorce.[290]

---

287 MOJ/DFE (2012), 81.
288 Ross and Sacker (2010), table 6.3.
289 Cf LCD (1993), para 7.8.
290 See chapters 6, 7, and 11.

Why not also permit them to decide for themselves when their marriage is over by at least permitting divorce on the basis of mutual consent?

 ONLINE RESOURCE CENTRE

Questions, suggestions for further reading, and supplementary materials for this chapter (including updates on developments in this area of family law since this book was published) may be found on the Online Resource Centre at www.oxfordtextbooks.co.uk/orc/familytcm3e/.

6

FINANCIAL PROVISION
FOR CHILDREN

CENTRAL ISSUES

1. The principal responsibility for maintaining minor children lies with their legal parents, whatever the nature of their relationship.

2. Financial and property provision for children who live apart from one or both parents is dealt with by the Child Maintenance Service (CMS) and the courts.

3. CMS has principal jurisdiction to secure payment of regular child support from non-resident parents, calculated by reference to a rule-based, statutory formula under the Child Support Act 1991 (CSA 1991).

4. The courts have residual jurisdiction to order periodical payments for children in certain circumstances. They also have exclusive jurisdiction to make capital and property adjustment orders for the benefit of children. They make their decisions pursuant to wide statutory discretion.

5. Parents are now encouraged to make informal 'family-based arrangements' for child maintenance. This marks a significant change from the former policy of the state strictly enforcing non-resident parents' financial responsibility for their children in order to save public expenditure on welfare benefits. Parents with care may now retain any amount of child maintenance on top of any welfare benefits they receive. But the advent of family-based arrangements may reduce the proportion of parents with care receiving child support.

6. Non-resident parents continue to complain that child support and contact decisions are not more closely linked.

6.1 INTRODUCTION

This chapter examines financial support for children who live apart from one or both parents, whether in a single-parent family, step-family, or with other carers.[1] The law in

---

[1] We do not address the position of children looked after by the state.

this area is highly technical and so can appear rather dry. But beneath the dry technicality lie interesting and important policy questions, some of general importance throughout family law—including the use of private ordering, and the contrast between rule-based and discretionary decision-making. We tease out some of those issues in the last section of this chapter.

The development of the law has been driven by the rapid rise in single-parent families. In 1971, families headed by single parents accounted for only 7 per cent of families with dependent children. Now they make up nearly 30 per cent of such families in England and Wales,[2] and feature disproportionately amongst poorer households.[3] Single mothers generally have lower employment rates than other mothers, and are more likely than other parents to claim benefits or tax credits.[4] Since the vast majority of single parents are *mothers*, the poverty of these families has been regarded as a matter of gender equity.[5] But the issue has recently been conceptualized in terms of child poverty. Legislation has set governments an ambitious target to eliminate child poverty by 2020.[6]

There are three ways in which child poverty might be alleviated:

- by the state providing direct financial support to children's households, such as benefits and tax credits, and subsidized child-care facilities to enable parents to work;

- by parents (especially single mothers) boosting household income via paid employment; and

- where children do not live with both parents, by the parent with whom the child does not mostly live (the 'non-resident parent', usually the father) transferring resources to the child's household.

All three routes may be adopted to varying degrees: how they are balanced depends on current political preferences.[7]

The initial question is whether principal responsibility for children's maintenance, in single-parent families and otherwise, lies with the state or private individuals. Concerns about child poverty aside, the state has a direct interest in ensuring that parents maintain their children, because if parents fail to maintain their children the state may have to do so instead.[8] However, international human rights instruments do not require the state to assume the whole burden. The United Nations Convention on the Rights of the Child 1989 (UNCRC) places primary responsibility for supporting children on parents, and envisages only a 'safety net' function for the state,[9] requiring it to 'take all appropriate measures to secure the recovery of maintenance for the child from the parents or other persons having financial responsibility for the child'.[10]

---

[2] ONS (2014b), 5.

[3] DWP (2014a), 49.

[4] Maplethorpe et al (2010), chs 5 and 7; DWP (2014b), tables 2.4 and 2.10.

[5] Barnes, Day, and Cronin (1998), 71; see also Flaherty et al (2004), ch 6 on women and poverty; see also 3.2.2.

[6] Child Poverty Act 2010; Fortin (2009b), 337 et seq.

[7] See Lewis (1998) and (2000), 94–6. On possible roles for the state, see Eekelaar and Maclean (1986), 107–12.

[8] See 3.8.2 and chapter 12.

[9] See in particular Arts 18, 26, and 27 UNCRC; see Fortin (2009b), 334–5.

[10] Art 27(4) UNCRC, referred to in *Smith v Secretary of State for Work and Pensions* [2006] UKHL 35, [77]–[78]; Baroness Hale doubted whether Art 8 ECHR entailed the right to receive regular, reasonable maintenance; see also [65], Lord Walker.

The Labour Government increased child benefit, introduced child tax credit, and enhanced child-care facilities. But it also sought to reinforce private responsibility by getting more single parents (including parents of pre-school children) into paid employment, with changes to welfare benefits rules pushing single parents to seek work.[11] The Coalition Government continued that policy.[12] But while employment rates amongst single parents have increased, many of their jobs are low-skilled and low-paid. Many parents complain about continuing lack of affordable, flexible, good quality child-care, which acts as a barrier to employment or to better-paid employment.[13] The economic recession further hampered efforts to improve children's prospects via this route. Single parents' earnings may not be enough to lift these families out of poverty.[14] However, employment-based policies may be criticized for denying the social and economic value conferred on society by individuals caring for their own children, and the moral value of choosing to care rather than work.[15] Evidence about good outcomes for children suggests caution in choosing between full-time parental care and long hours in nursery or some other non-parental child-care.[16]

State obligation aside, the key question within the private sphere is how responsibility for supporting children should be allocated between separated parents. To what extent can 'non-resident parents' or other private individuals also be expected to contribute to a child's financial support? On whom should private obligations to maintain children be imposed: should the duty arise from legal or social parenthood? What if the legal parent[17] has had no social relationship with the child or no legal relationship with the other parent?[18] English law imposes principal private financial responsibility for children on their legal parents. That liability is enforced in various ways almost regardless of the parents' marital status. But the law provides remedies only for separated families. It generally does not permit children to obtain support from parents who are together—and, even when they are apart, strictly limits the right of children themselves to apply for support.

The provision made for children is often just part of a larger puzzle of financial remedies between separated parents. The importance of financial remedies for the children differs markedly depending on the nature of the parents' relationship. Where the parents were spouses or civil partners, provision for children is part of the package of financial remedies available on divorce/dissolution. We shall see in chapter 7 that the courts have substantial powers to order financial provision and property adjustment between such parents for their own benefit. In such cases, children will benefit indirectly from orders made for the benefit of their primary carers and so capital or property orders specifically for their benefit are less necessary (and may not be affordable). However, child support will be payable and, if there are surplus resources, additional provision for the children—such as payment of school fees—might also be made.

---

11 E.g. Welfare Reform Act 2009.
12 HM Government (2014).
13 DWP (2014c), Gingerbread (2012a).
14 Flaherty et al (2004), 168.
15 Fineman (2004), Family and Parenting Institute (2009).
16 See Fortin (2009b), 340–2.
17 See chapter 9.
18 See 6.7.3. On theories underlying parents' obligations, see Altman (2003); Eekelaar (1991a); Wikeley (2006a), ch 1.

By contrast, where the parents were not spouses or civil partners, there are far fewer, if any, remedies between the adults themselves. This leaves primary carers of children to shoulder alone the potential long-term economic effects of their role, such as reduced earning capacity owing to time taken out of the labour market.[19] Remedies for the benefit of children assume huge significance in this context, as substantial indirect benefit can accrue to primary carers from financial remedies for the child. However, that indirect benefit ends once the child becomes independent, potentially leaving these parents in a precarious economic position.

This area of the law has been in flux for some time, and so we begin this chapter with a brief history, before examining the law as it emerged following the latest statutory reforms of child support. The current legal and policy environment strongly encourage private ordering. So while we address the detail of the laws applied by the statutory child support agency and by the courts, later in the chapter we discuss parties' options for making their own arrangements for financial support of children. We use the terms 'child support' and 'child maintenance' interchangeably.

6.2 A BRIEF HISTORY OF FINANCIAL PROVISION FOR CHILDREN

6.2.1 PUBLIC AND PRIVATE LAW OBLIGATIONS TO MAINTAIN CHILDREN PRIOR TO 1993

The legal history of child maintenance is complex, related in Baroness Hale's account below. Nick Wikeley has doubted whether she is correct in asserting a right for the *child* to be maintained, rather than a right for the parent with care to receive maintenance for the child's support.[20] But her survey is nevertheless valuable. She began with Blackstone, who considered that parents were obliged to maintain their children as a matter of natural law;[21] but the common law offered no direct means of enforcing that duty:

R (Kehoe) v Secretary of State for Work and Pensions [2005] UKHL 48

BARONESS HALE:

51. Our law has always recognised the right of a child who is too young to fend for herself to be provided for by her parents. The problem has always been to find an effective method of enforcement. The child was too young to do so and the married mother had no separate right to sue her husband. Hence the machinery of enforcement was laid down in the Poor Laws...[22]

52. But the fact that the father's obligations were measured by the Poor Laws did not mean that the courts of law and equity would ignore them. The principles underlying the later statutory concept of 'wilful neglect to maintain' a wife or child, even the later liability to reimburse

---

[19] Maclean and Eekelaar (1993), 215.
[20] See Wikeley (2006b), extracted at p 399 below.
[21] Blackstone (1765), book 1, ch XVI.
[22] See extracts in 3.8.2.

the public purse for benefits expended, were those developed by the common law. Hence, just as the husband's common law duty to maintain his wife would normally be discharged by providing the home which they shared, the father's duty to maintain his children would be discharged by providing them with a home . . .

53. The common law courts would not intrude into the matrimonial relationship, or trespass upon the jurisdiction of the ecclesiastical courts over that relationship, by ordering the husband to make payments to his wife. But a wife who was living with the husband did have the apparent authority to contract as his agent for the expenses of the household. And if they were living apart, the common law recognised her agency of necessity . . .

54. . . . [O]nce it became possible for the wife to obtain custody of a child even against the father's will, the law recognised that her agency of necessity extended to necessaries for a child in her custody as well as for herself.

55. A further recognition by the common law of a duty to maintain was the opinion of the judges that it was an indictable misdemeanour at common law for a person under a duty to provide for an infant of tender years to neglect to do so and thereby injure his health . . . [See now s 1 of the Children and Young Persons Act 1933.] A parent or person 'legally liable to maintain' a child is deemed to have neglected him for this purpose if he has failed to provide adequate food, clothing, medical aid or lodging, even if he is not living with the child . . .

Baroness Hale then traced the history of the nineteenth-century statutes which first recognized the right in private law of one parent to obtain an order for periodical payments from the other for the child's benefit, both legitimate and illegitimate. These latter statutes were the forerunners of today's private law: the matrimonial and civil partnership legislation in which provision for children is considered alongside that for the adults, and Sch 1 to the Children Act 1989, which also provides for children of unmarried parents. Meanwhile, the successors of the Poor Laws retained the public law 'liable relative' procedure, enabling the state to recoup welfare benefits from relevant family members, here the non-resident parent of the child, whether or not the parents were married.[23] The operation of these laws in the 1970s and 1980s generated the political case for the child support legislation of 1991.

62. It was . . . intended that the receipt of national assistance, later to become supplementary benefit, and later still income support, should not carry a stigma. As Dr Stephen Cretney relates . . . in keeping with this new entitlement-based approach the benefit authorities changed their policy about seeking recovery from liable relatives. Instead of routinely seeking this, they would try to reach an agreement with the husband or father, and accept any offer which they considered reasonable. Rather than take proceedings themselves, they would encourage the mother to do so. The disadvantage for the mother was that she would then not know from week to week how much benefit she would get, because it all depended how much maintenance the husband or father had paid that week. The sensible solution eventually found was that she would assign or 'divert' any payment made into the magistrates' court to the benefit authorities. They could then issue her with an order book which she could safely cash each week. Although the benefit authorities retained their power to seek recovery from the liable relative, in practice this was rarely done even in cases where the mother had, for whatever reason, chosen not to bring proceedings.

23 See extracts in 3.8.2.

63. It was scarcely surprising that the courts would have this changed climate in mind when deciding what orders for financial provision should be made. They were not supposed to take means-tested benefits into account as a resource available to the wife and mother, but neither were they supposed to order a sum which would reduce the husband and father's income below that which he would receive for himself and his new family were he also on benefit: see *Barnes v Barnes* [1972] 1 WLR 1381....

64. It became common for divorcing parties to agree a 'clean break', in which the wife and children would retain the family home, where the mortgage interest would be met by the benefit authorities, while the husband was relieved of any further maintenance liabilities...The fact that there were still both private and public law liabilities to maintain the children receded into the background, especially as the risk that the benefit authorities would proceed against the absent parent were so slim...

6.2.2 THE BIRTH, DEVELOPMENT, AND DEMISE OF THE CHILD SUPPORT AGENCY

The creation of the Child Support Agency (CSA) and the statutory child maintenance regime which it administered was motivated by various economic and moral concerns. The first was that those formally liable to support children were not doing so, leaving the state to foot the resulting welfare benefits bill for the burgeoning population of single-parent families.[24] Non-resident parents were not significantly contributing to children's support either via private law maintenance orders or through the liable relative procedure for recouping welfare benefits. As Bradshaw and Millar recorded, there were good reasons for the decline in use of the liable relative procedure, not least the 1980s recession and the growth in births out of wedlock, which made it harder to identify the fathers; enforcement action was unlikely to prove cost-effective. Mothers claiming benefits were not penalized for failing to cooperate in any endeavours made by the state to obtain maintenance from the father.[25] But nor did mothers have any incentive to assist the benefit authorities or bring private law proceedings: where maintenance orders *were* made, they rarely exceeded mothers' benefits entitlements, so simply reduced their benefits, leaving them and their children no better off than they would have been without maintenance from the father.[26]

This fuelled political arguments about 'welfare dependency', underpinned by concerns—exploded by research, but tenacious nevertheless—that the situation was incentivizing lone-motherhood. It was time, it was thought, for single mothers' welfare benefits to be reduced by pursuing non-resident parents more vigorously for maintenance. These economic concerns coincided with moral concerns, also generated by the rises in divorce and single-parenthood,[27] as this extract from a speech given by Margaret Thatcher reveals. Indeed, it has been said that moral rather than economic factors were Thatcher's main concern:[28]

---

24 Bradshaw and Millar (1991), 64.
25 Ibid, 78–9.
26 Law Com (1982b), para 3.24.
27 Maclean and Eekelaar (1993), 210–11.
28 Maclean with Kurczewski (2011), 41–2.

Prime Minister Margaret Thatcher, National Children's Homes George Thomas Society Lecture, January 1990[29]

[W]hen one of the parents not only walks away from marriage but neither maintains nor shows any interest in the child, an enormous unfair burden is placed on the other. Nearly four out of five lone mothers claiming income support received no maintenance from the fathers. No father should be able to escape from his responsibility and that is why the Government is looking at ways of strengthening the system for tracing an absent father and making the arrangements for recovering maintenance more effective.

'Parenthood is for life' was the new soundbite; 'feckless fathers' were the new scapegoats.[30]

The response was the CSA 1991, quickly enacted with cross-party support. Despite the benefit authorities' apparent tolerance of single parents' past reliance on benefits, it was decided that a new administrative body—the CSA—should become responsible for extracting regular child maintenance from non-resident parents, instead of the courts.[31] The maintenance payable by 'absent parents' to 'parents with care' for their children would be calculated with a statutory formula, rather than on a discretionary, case-by-case basis. This would 'produce consistent and predictable results', with prompt collection, enforcement, and payment of maintenance to parents with care, organized by a single authority.[32] The courts would largely be confined to making capital orders.

A central part of the system was that the CSA took jurisdiction over cases in which single parents were claiming benefits, effectively replacing the liable relative procedure. This was intended to ensure that welfare payments made to parents with care were reimbursed by the liable non-resident parents. Parents with care receiving certain means-tested welfare benefits were compelled to cooperate with the CSA's efforts to secure maintenance from non-resident parents. Those who refused to cooperate risked a substantial cut in their benefits unless they could show 'good cause' for doing so; this was a particular issue for victims of domestic violence.[33] Under the original version of the scheme, support received reduced benefits paid to parents with care pound for pound—so they derived no benefit from the CSA's involvement. Latterly, a 'maintenance disregard' was introduced, permitting parents with care to retain the first £10 per week recovered from the non-resident parent; the balance (up to the value of their benefits) went to the state. Benefits cases constituted the vast bulk of the CSA's caseload, suggesting that the priority lay in cutting welfare benefit expenditure.[34]

The CSA was hampered throughout by chronic administrative problems[35] and the vociferous opposition[36] of 'absent parents' and, to a lesser extent, of parents with care.[37] 'Absent parents' had many complaints, not least the label 'absent' which implied that they played no role in their children's lives; the terminology was later changed to 'non-resident parent'.

---

[29] Extracted in Cretney (2003a), 474.

[30] Cf contemporaneous discussion of unmarried fathers and parental responsibility: 10.3.2.

[31] For a detailed history, see Wikeley (2006a), ch 5.

[32] DSS (1990), paras 5.1–5.2. Cf the courts' inability to cope with the increased caseload, resulting in delays: Maclean with Kurczewski (2011), 43.

[33] See CSA 1991, ss 6 and 46.

[34] Cf Wikeley (2006a), 129–30.

[35] Ibid, 126–33.

[36] See generally Diduck (2003), ch 7; Fortin (2009b), 346–7; and Davis et al (1998).

[37] See Glendinning et al (1994).

Many non-resident parents had second families or had made 'clean break' settlements on divorce,[38] and those who had previously been paying little or no maintenance claimed to be suffering hardship owing to the higher levels of maintenance now required.[39] The original Act's complex formula required large amounts of information and staff time to administer, was difficult to understand, and produced assessments which were frequently wrong and even more frequently challenged, or simply not paid. Legal aid not being available for legal representation in dealing with the CSA and appeal tribunals, many parents had to cope without a lawyer.[40] Many non-resident parents responded by simply resisting payment, but the investment of staff time on assessment left few resources for enforcement. The formula was simplified considerably and some limited discretion introduced—though not for cases already in the system. But having to operate different assessment systems for different cases depending on when they entered the system merely compounded the CSA's woes, as did diabolical IT systems.[41] Described as 'one of the greatest public administration disasters of recent times',[42] the CSA never met its creators' expectations. Reform was announced in 2006, following a review by Sir David Henshaw.[43]

6.2.3 THE NEW SCHEME AND THE CMS

D. Henshaw, *Recovering Child Support: Routes to Responsibility*
(London: TSO, 2006)

12. Improving enforcement of social norms and responsibilities was a key objective in the creation of the CSA. This was in response to the low levels of lone parents receiving maintenance. However, 16 years later the figures have barely improved. Although many non-resident parents do take financial responsibility for their children and pay regular maintenance, there is a widespread belief amongst others that it is possible and, in some cases, acceptable to avoid paying. This contributes to the fact that only around 30 per cent of parents with care are receiving any maintenance at all. Compliance with arrangements made through the CSA is lower than for arrangements made through other routes.

13. Cost-efficiency for the taxpayer has consistently been poor. In 2004/05, the CSA recovered £120 million in Income Support expenditure against costs of £425 million. In the region of £80 million was saved through other routes. Therefore, the system runs at a net cost to the taxpayer of around £200 million. There is also outstanding debt, in the form of unpaid maintenance, of over £3 billion.... One of the reasons for poor cost-efficiency is that...only a very small proportion of the Agency's caseload has the potential to recover funds for the state (that is a case with a positive liability where the parent with care is on benefits).

The Henshaw Report identified several policy and operational problems. Its recommendations were radical.

---

[38] See 7.6.2 and 6.7.2.
[39] Wallbank (1997), Collier (1994).
[40] Davis et al (1998), 126.
[41] On the operational problems, see Henshaw (2006), paras 18–20.
[42] Family Law Week (2007).
[43] Henshaw (2006); DWP (2006b).

D. Henshaw, *Recovering Child Support: Routes to Responsibility*
(London: TSO, 2006), 4–5

- At the moment, all parents with care claiming benefits are forced to use the Child Support Agency to agree maintenance. Around 70 per cent of new applicants are required to use the Agency. This requirement prevents parents from making private arrangements between themselves. As a result, it creates a large group of clients who do not wish to use the service.

- Reducing benefit entitlement pound for pound against maintenance collected means that neither parent has an incentive to co-operate with the Child Support Agency. Parents with care can see little or no increase in income and non-resident parents see money paid going to the state, not to their children.

- The complex nature of the cases makes it difficult for the system to keep up. Many of the clients have difficult situations with volatile income, regular movements in and out of work and complicated personal relationships....

Key recommendations

- The state should only get involved when parents cannot come to agreement themselves, or when one party tries to evade their responsibilities. Removing the barriers that currently prevent some parents from making their own arrangements would allow the state to focus on the more difficult cases and where effective enforcement is needed.

- Parents who are able to should be encouraged and supported to make their own arrangements. Such arrangements tend to result in higher satisfaction and compliance and allow individual circumstances to be reflected. We should end the policy of forcing all parents with care claiming certain benefits to use the Child Support Agency.

- Those who want a private arrangement to be legally enforceable would be able to obtain a consent order. This operation should be available to all parents. Those unable to use other routes would have access to the government back-up service.

- Allowing most parents with care to keep the maintenance paid would encourage both parents to co-operate, increasing the maintenance going to children.

- Safeguards can be introduced to prevent those parents with care in receipt of significant amounts of maintenance from also having full access to state benefits.

The government immediately accepted many of these recommendations and enacted them with cross-party support in the Child Maintenance and Other Payments Act 2008 (CMOPA 2008). The most radical reforms were the removal of all compulsion on parents with care to cooperate in attempts to obtain child support and the introduction of a *total* maintenance disregard, permitting them to keep all maintenance received on top of their benefits. For completeness, the liable relative rule was also abolished as it applied to the support of children.[44] These changes entailed a 'virtual abandonment' of the original CSA policy,[45]

---

[44] For criticism, see Wikeley (2008).
[45] Fehlberg and Maclean (2009).

profoundly altering the roles of non-resident parents and state in supporting children: the state now provides a basic level of support to parents with care via welfare benefits and/or tax credits; any contribution from non-resident parents, rather than reducing the state's burden, now supplements the child's household income. The Secretary of State promoted the reform on the basis that this policy could make an immediate and significant contribution to child poverty targets:[46]

Hansard, *Official Report*—Ministerial Statement on Child Support Redesign, Hansard HC Deb, vol 449, cols 597–9, 24 July 2006

The Secretary of State for Work and Pensions (Mr. John Hutton):

Both those changes will help more families to receive more maintenance and reduce the risk of child poverty. They reflect both the rights of children to be properly maintained by their parents and the right of society to ensure that parental responsibilities are properly discharged.

However, the success of the policy will depend on how many non-resident parents pay maintenance under a scheme in which parents are encouraged in various ways to make their own arrangements.

The White Paper preceding the CMOPA Bill set out 'four new principles' for a reformed child maintenance system. Compare these principles with the Secretary of State's remarks in the extract above: any reference to a right of the *child* is gone:

DWP, *A New System of Child Maintenance,* Cm 6979 (London: TSO, 2006b), paras 15–16

- **help tackle child poverty** by ensuring that more parents take responsibility for paying for their children and that more children benefit from this;

- **promote parental responsibility** by encouraging and empowering parents to make their own maintenance arrangements wherever possible, but taking firm action – through **a tough and effective enforcement regime** – to enforce payment where necessary;

- **provide a cost-effective and professional service** that gets money flowing between parents in the most efficient way for the taxpayer; and

- **be simple and transparent,** providing an accessible, reliable and responsive service that is understood and accepted by parents and their advisers and is capable of being administered by staff.

These four principles refocus the child maintenance system on meeting the needs of children. They make tackling child poverty the first and most critical test for reform, and they establish and enforce clear rights and responsibilities – the right of a person to make a claim and the resulting responsibility of the non-resident parent to pay.

---

[46] Henshaw (2006), para 24; and see Bryson et al (2013).

A new administrative body was created to replace the CSA, briefly the Child Maintenance and Enforcement Commission (C-MEC), now the Child Maintenance Service (CMS). CMS has begun to operate a different system of child support (described below) which it is hoped will be easier to operate. The transition from the CSA to CMS and its new scheme will, however, take some time. All new cases are now dealt with by CMS under the new scheme. Cases that were already in the system—administered by the CSA under (more than one[47]) previous versions of the CSA 1991 formula—are either being removed from the statutory system (where parents wish to make their own arrangements) or moved to the new CMS system.[48] It is expected that all remaining cases will be on the new CMS system by 2017.

In this chapter, we discuss child support law as it applies to all new cases, as contained in the heavily amended CSA 1991. One aspect of the latest reforms yet to be brought fully into force is the new armoury of enforcement powers for CMS, designed to enable it to deal more effectively with those cases that remain in the system. A major plank of the new policy is that more parents should make their own arrangements entirely outside the statutory scheme without CMS. However, since parties negotiating privately will often wish to bargain 'in the shadow of the law', we first examine the law that would apply were they not to reach agreement and apply instead to CMS. We address the legal framework for private ordering in this area and its practical implications at 6.6 and 6.7.2 below.

6.3 OVERVIEW OF THE CURRENT LAW

The law governing financial and property provision for children is contained in several statutes. In order to get an overview, it is helpful to divide the topic along two lines: (i) the identity of the children involved and their relationship with the potential payer; (ii) the type of remedy sought: see fig 6.1.

6.3.1 THE PARTIES' RELATIONSHIPS

Like most areas of contemporary child law, financial and property provision is almost blind to parents' marital status. What matters is the legal parent–child relationship. Parents' liability for their own children must be distinguished from the liability of step- and other social parents in relation to other 'children of the family'. Only spouses and civil partners may be liable to provide for children other than their own. Step-parental liability does not arise in cohabiting relationships,[49] or following a joint enterprise in creating a child by artificial insemination from which legal parenthood did not arise,[50] even if the non-parent has parental responsibility for the child via a child arrangements order.

---

[47] The original rules covered cases pre-1993—no such cases now exist as all affected children are now adult; the next set of rules governed cases arising before 2003, and the last those from 2003 until the new scheme came into force.

[48] See Child Support (Ending Liability in Existing Cases and Transition to New Calculation Rules) Regulations 2014, SI 2014/614.

[49] Children Act 1989 (CA 1989), s 105; Matrimonial Causes Act 1973 (MCA 1973), s 52; Civil Partnership Act 2004 (CPA 2004), s 72.

[50] *T v B* [2010] EWHC 1444; cf the new agreed parenthood provisions in the Human Fertilisation and Embryology Act 2008, discussed at 9.4.3.

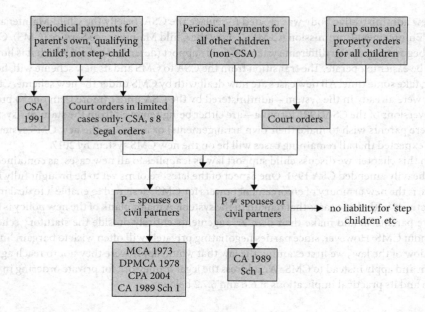

Figure 6.1 Financial and property provision for children

6.3.2 CMS OR COURT?

The law treats periodical payments and other forms of relief, such as lump sum and property adjustment orders, very differently. The courts have exclusive jurisdiction over the latter. CMS has principal jurisdiction over periodical payments for parents' *own* children under the CSA 1991. The court may only order periodical payments in limited circumstances: where CMS lacks jurisdiction in parent–child cases, in relation to step-children and others who are not the respondent's child, and where the CSA 1991 explicitly permits it. We examine the child support legislation at 6.4 and the courts' jurisdiction at 6.5.

6.4 CHILD SUPPORT: THE CURRENT LAW

Child support law is highly technical.[51] It is contained in primary legislation—the heavily amended CSA 1991—and secondary legislation, most importantly the Child Support Maintenance Calculation Regulations 2012,[52] referred to in the footnotes as the CSMCR 2012. Where statutory materials refer to the 'Secretary of State' acting, those actions are in practice taken by that agency, now CMS. Other materials extracted below refer variously to the CSA, C-MEC, and CMS, depending on which incarnation of the administrative body then existed.

[51] For detailed treatment, see CPAG (2014).
[52] SI 2012/2677.

6.4.1 THE RELEVANT PARTIES

Four categories of person are relevant to child support claims: the 'qualifying child'; the 'non-resident parent'; the 'person with care'; and 'relevant other children'. The Act ordinarily applies only where each of the first three is habitually resident in the UK.[53]

The 'qualifying child'

The Act only applies if the child for whom support is sought meets the definition in s 55; if not, the courts may instead have jurisdiction over child maintenance. In broad outline, a 'child' for these purposes is anyone under the age of 16; and anyone under the age of 20 who is either in full-time non-advanced education (i.e. below degree level), or is undertaking certain types of training.[54] If the individual is or has been a spouse or civil partner (including in a void union), he or she is not a 'child' in this context.[55] In order to be a 'qualifying' child, it must be shown that either one or both of his parents is in relation to him a 'non-resident parent'.[56] Child support is therefore not payable within intact families: the child must be living separately from at least one parent.

The 'non-resident parent'

The child's qualifying status turns on having at least one non-resident parent. 'Parent' is defined as 'any person who is in law the mother or father of the child'.[57] The CSA 1991 does not cover step-parents, from whom maintenance can only be obtained through the courts. No significance attaches to the relationship, if any, between the parents; they need never have married, cohabited, or had any substantial relationship. The bare fact of legal parentage suffices.

A parent is a 'non-resident' parent under s 3(2) if:

> (a) that parent is not living in the same household with the child; and
>
> (b) the child has his home with a person who is, in relation to him, a person with care.

'Not living in the same household' may include parents who live under the same roof as the child but maintain a separate household from the child and person with care.[58] Since the vast majority of non-resident parents are fathers, we refer to them in the text below as such, whilst acknowledging that there are cases where the roles are reversed.

The 'person with care'

> 3(3) A person is a "person with care", in relation to any child, if he is a person—
>
> (a) with whom the child has his home;

---

[53] CSA 1991, s 44.

[54] CSMCR 2012, reg 76: the definition is linked to eligibility for child benefit.

[55] CSA 1991, s 55(2), (3).

[56] Ibid, s 3.

[57] Ibid, s 54; see chapter 9. In case of dispute regarding parentage, see CSA 1991, s 26.

[58] See 5.5.5 for interpretation of the equivalent expression in divorce law.

> (b) who usually provides day to day care for the child (whether exclusively or in conjunction with any other person); and
>
> (c) who does not fall within a prescribed category of person.
>
> (4) The Secretary of State shall not, under subsection (3)(c), prescribe as a category—
>
>   (a) parents;
>
>   (b) guardians;
>
>   (c) persons named, in a child arrangements order under s 8 of the Children Act 1989, as persons with whom a child is to live...
>
> (5) For the purposes of this Act there may be more than one person with care in relation to the same qualifying child....

The regulations made under s 3(3)(c) exclude local authorities and their foster parents from the scope of 'person with care'.[59] 'Day to day care' is not defined, but has been held to turn not on the formal question of who holds parental responsibility for the child but on who undertakes the mundane, hands-on practicalities of looking after the child: 'it is about who puts food on the table, washes the child's clothes, deals with the letters from school and reads a bedtime story'.[60] We discuss below the designation of the parents who share the care of the child.

The 'relevant other child'

The existence of a 'relevant other child' may affect the amount of child support payable in respect of qualifying children. A child is 'relevant' if the non-resident parent or his partner with whom he shares a household (whether as spouses, civil partners, or cohabitants) receives child benefit in relation to that child.[61]

6.4.2 GENERAL PRINCIPLES

Child Support Act 1991, s 1

The duty to maintain

(1) For the purposes of this Act, each parent of a qualifying child is responsible for maintaining him.

(2) For the purposes of this Act, a non-resident parent shall be taken to have met his responsibility to maintain any qualifying child of his by making periodical payments of maintenance with respect to the child of such amount, and at such intervals, as may be determined in accordance with the provisions of this Act.

---

[59] CSMRC 2012, reg 78; but see regs 51 and 53 for other situations involving the local authority.
[60] *GR v CMEC (CSM)* [2011] UKUT 101 (AAC), [48].
[61] Sch 1, para 10C and CSMCR 2012, reg 77.

> (3) Where a maintenance calculation made under this Act requires the making of periodical payments, it shall be the duty of the non-resident parent with respect to whom the calculation is made to make those payments.

While the Act closely defines non-resident parents' duties, it says nothing about how parents with care discharge their maintenance responsibility. But it is implicit in the Act—and in the apparent rationale of the formula for calculating non-resident parents' liability (discussed below at 6.7.4)—that parents with care fulfil their duty by virtue of caring for the child.

Unlike the rest of child law, there is no general welfare principle in the CSA 1991. Given the rule-based rather than discretionary nature of the Act, that is perhaps unsurprising. Where CMS does have discretion, for example in making variations from the formula or in taking enforcement action, a welfare principle applies. The principle is relatively weak, requiring only that 'regard' be had to the child's welfare, not paramount or even first consideration. But it is wide ranging: the welfare of *any* child likely to be affected must be considered, not just that of the qualifying child and 'relevant other children'.[62]

6.4.3 APPLICATION TO CMS

Encouraging private agreement

A key policy of the new scheme is that, rather than apply to CMS, parents should wherever possible reach their own 'family-based arrangement' for child support:

Child Support Act 1991

9(2A) The Secretary of State may, with a view to reducing the need for applications [to the CMS]–

(a) take such steps as the Secretary of State considers appropriate to encourage the making and keeping of maintenance agreements, and

(b) in particular, before accepting an application [to the CMS under s 4], invite the applicant to consider with the Secretary of State whether it is possible to make such an agreement.

The potential CMS applicant is assisted by information provided by the Child Maintenance Options Service and its website, which provides an online calculator to help parents work out how much should be paid.

Application to CMS where agreement fails

If the non-resident parent and person with care cannot agree or one becomes dissatisfied with their agreement, either can apply to CMS for a maintenance calculation under the CSA 1991, s 4. However, consistently with the policy to encourage agreements, the law now disincentivizes applications by charging applicants a fee of £20 for making a formal maintenance calculation, and further fees for collecting maintenance for the person with care

---

[62] CSA 1991, s 2.

rather than have the non-resident parent pay directly ('Direct Pay').[63] Indeed, CMS will only make arrangements to collect child support on the person with care's behalf if:

(a) the non-resident parent agrees to the arrangements, or

(b) the Secretary of State is satisfied that without the arrangements child support maintenance is unlikely to be paid in accordance with the calculation.[64]

If CMS is used for collection, the non-resident parent is charged an additional 20 per cent on top of the child support payable and the person with care has 4 per cent deducted from the child support before it is handed over.[65] Applicants under the age of 19 and victims of domestic violence who have reported the abuse to an appropriate person[66] are exempt from the application fee, though not the collection fee.[67] We discuss at 6.7.2 the policy implications and potential practical effects of this change.

6.4.4 THE MAINTENANCE CALCULATION

The maintenance calculation under the CMS scheme is based on a formula that, in its simplest form, requires only two pieces of information: the gross income of the non-resident parent for the last tax year and the number of qualifying children. A fixed percentage of that income is usually payable, depending on the number of children. We discuss below add-ons to the formula used where there are relevant other children or the qualifying child stays overnight with the non-resident parent. Special rates apply to non-resident parents in particular circumstances.[68] Importantly, the income of the person with care is irrelevant, as is the income of any new partner of either party. So the non-resident parents' liability is not affected at all by the relative wealth of the person with care or her household. We discuss at 6.7.4 the rationale for the basic formula and the fairness of the assumptions on which it rests.

Basing the calculation on gross historic income

Until the new scheme came into force, the child support formula was based on the non-resident parent's current *net* earned income. But, adopting Henshaw's recommendation, for administrative ease, the formula is now based on the non-resident parent's *gross* earned income for the *last* year.[69] The gross historic income figure is in theory available from the tax authorities, and so using this as the basis for calculating child support should speed up assessment considerably.[70] The change to gross rather than net income makes almost no

---

[63] The Child Support Fees Regulations 2014, SI 2014/612.

[64] CSA 1991, s 4(2A).

[65] Fees Regulation, above.

[66] See the list of persons prescribed in the Guidance on reg 4(3) of the Child Support Fees Regulations 2014 (published 2 December 2013), which includes police, medical professionals, lawyers and courts, refuges, employers, and certain other professionals/support services.

[67] SI 2014/612, reg 4.

[68] For default rates and voluntary payments made pending a formal calculation, see CSMCR 2012, reg 49 and the Child Support (Voluntary Payments) Regulations 2000, SI 2000/3177.

[69] For the definition of 'gross income' see CSA 1991, Sch 1, para 10 and CSMCR 2012, regs 34–42. Periodic current income checks and regular annual reviews are carried out to update the calculation; see CSMCR 2012, regs 19–22.

[70] DWP (2006b), ch 4; cf the cautionary notes sounded by Wikeley (2007a), paras 19–21.

difference to the amounts of support payable—the formula has been adjusted to allow for the different basis of calculation.[71] Historic income being a known, fixed amount, the calculation is unaffected by fluctuations in income.[72] However, historic income is not necessarily a reliable guide to what non-resident parents can afford to pay now: the income for the last tax year may be very different—higher or lower—than current income. Where the difference in income is 25 per cent or greater, current income data may therefore be used instead.[73] CMS's administrative burden may be eased by such a high threshold having to be passed before calculations have to be revised. But it may pose significant trouble for non-resident parents caught by the legacy of past riches falling just below that threshold, who may find their payments unaffordable.[74]

The basic rate

The basic rate[75] applies to non-resident parents with gross weekly incomes of £200 and above. For the first £800 of gross income, non-resident parents must pay 12 per cent of income for one qualifying child, 16 per cent for two qualifying children, and 19 per cent for three or more. Additional income between £800 and £3,000 is subject to a 'basic plus' rate of 9 per cent for one, 12 per cent for two, and 15 per cent for three or more qualifying children.[76] Income over £3,000 per week is ignored entirely. As we shall see below, however, income above that threshold can be accessed via court-ordered periodical payments.[77]

Cases where the non-resident parent has 'relevant other children'

If the non-resident parent has one or more 'relevant other children', an extra step in the formula effectively permits the non-resident parent to reserve income for expenditure on children in his current household before the child support formula is used to calculate what he must pay to the qualifying child. The gross income is reduced by 11, 14, or 16 per cent, depending on the number of relevant other children, before the basic rate percentage is applied to the remainder.[78] The result is that the non-resident parent broadly ends up paying a similar percentage of his total gross income to the qualifying child(ren) as is reserved for the relevant other children, though in fact pays out slightly less to the qualifying child than he is permitted to reserve for the others. It had been suggested that the basic rate should instead be applied to all qualifying and relevant children of the non-resident parent, and for the resulting maintenance award to be apportioned equally between them.[79]

---

71 See CMEC (2012), DWP (2012), Appendix A; cf criticism by Gingerbread (2012b) of the definition of 'gross income' for these purposes.

72 DWP (2007a), para 16.3.

73 CSMCR 2012, reg 23; note the duty of employed non-resident parents to report increases in income: Child Support Information Regulations 2008, reg 9A.

74 See Work and Pensions Select Committee (2007), paras 125–34; DWP (2007a), para 16.

75 CSA 1991, Sch 1, para 2.

76 This second set of percentages for the second tranche of income is necessary to accommodate the different tax rates being applied at different levels of income. The resulting formula for the gross income scheme is considerably less tidy than the previous formula, which prescribed rates of 15, 20, and 25 per cent of net income for one, two, or three+ children respectively.

77 6.5.2 on 'top-up' orders.

78 CSA 1991, Sch 1, para 2(3).

79 DSS (1999), paras 2.9–2.15.

But the rule that has been adopted, whilst also aiming to provide roughly 'equal treatment' to the two sets of children,[80] gives the qualifying children much more than they would have received on the apportionment basis. For example, if one qualifying child and one relevant child were treated as two children under the basic rule, a father with gross income of £800 per month would notionally pay 16 per cent, £128; when apportioned equally between them, this would give the qualifying child just £64, rather than the £96 that he would had received on the basic rate of 12 per cent as one child. Under the rule adopted, that child will now receive £85.44, while a notional £88 is reserved for the relevant other child. This means that the father is notionally 'paying' over £173 for both children (though of course he keeps the money allocated for the relevant other child to spend himself), rather than just £128.

The reduced rate

The reduced rate[81] applies to non-resident parents on gross incomes of between £100 and £200 per week, to whom neither the flat nor the nil rate applies. They pay £7 for the first £100, and then a set percentage (different from the basic rate percentages) over the remaining amount, depending on the number of qualifying children and any relevant other children.

The flat rate

A flat rate[82] of £7 per week is payable by non-residents parents who earn less than £100 per week or who (or whose partners) receive one of several welfare benefits, pensions, or allowances. Where the non-resident parent's partner[83] is also a non-resident parent in respect of whom a maintenance calculation is in force and who receives one of the relevant benefits, each is required to pay half the flat rate. Even those living on benefits are required to accept some financial responsibility for their children.[84]

The nil rate

No support is payable by non-resident parents with gross weekly incomes below £7, and those who fall into one of several categories prescribed in regulations, including children,[85] prisoners, and parents aged 16–17 who receive certain means-tested benefits.[86]

---

[80] The rule adopted had originally been said to give a 'slight preference' to the first family (DSS (1999), ch 2, para 13), though in fact the amount allocated for the relevant other children was greater than that payable to the qualifying child as the deductions were originally made at the same percentages as the basic rate. In advocating the move to the current percentages, the government acknowledged that, and preferred the new percentages as providing 'more equal treatment' of both sets of children: C-MEC (2012), para 107.

[81] CSA 1991, Sch 1, para 3 and CSMCR 2012, reg 43.

[82] Ibid, Sch 1, para 4 and CSMCR 2012, reg 44.

[83] As defined in Sch 1, para 10(C)(4) and (5).

[84] Barnes et al (1998), 66 view this as an expensive public relations exercise: the costs of collection generally outweigh the income received.

[85] As defined in s 55(1), above.

[86] CSA 1991, Sch 1, para 5 and CSMCR 2012, reg 45.

Shared care

The terminology of 'non-resident parent' and 'person/parent with care' is a source of grievance where the child spends significant amounts of time, including overnight stays, with both parents. Both might regard themselves as 'persons with care', and neither as 'non-resident', even if a court order specifies that the child 'lives with' one parent only whilst merely 'spending time' with the other.[87] In these cases, whichever parent provides day-to-day care for the child to a 'lesser extent' than the other is classed as the non-resident parent; unless there is evidence to suggest otherwise, whichever parent receives the child benefit for the child is deemed to provide more care.[88]

In some cases—still rare—it is impossible to say that either parent provides less day-to-day care than the other. Such cases involve more than the child simply spending the same number of nights per year at each parent's house, and require closer analysis of the care actually provided, including expenditure on larger items such as clothing and equipment. Only where the parents are genuinely providing fully equal day-to-day care will neither be classed as non-resident, with the result that no child support will be payable by either parent, whatever their respective incomes.

Where, as is usual, one parent is clearly the primary carer, support remains payable but at a lower level, determined by the number of nights that the child spends with the 'non-resident' parent:

Child Support Act 1991, Sch 1, para 7[89]

(1) This paragraph applies where the rate of child support maintenance payable is the basic rate or a reduced rate [or is determined under special rules applicable to certain maintenance agreements, under para 5A].

(2) If the care of the qualifying child is, or is to be, shared between the non-resident parent and the person with care, so that the non-resident parent from time to time has care of the child overnight, the amount of child support maintenance which he would otherwise have been liable to pay the person with care [as calculated above] is to be decreased in accordance with this paragraph.

(3) First, there is to be a decrease according to the number of such nights which the Secretary of State determines there to have been, or expects there to be, or both during a prescribed twelve-month period.

(4) The amount of that decrease for one child is set out in the following Table—

Number of nights	Fraction to subtract
52 to 103	One-seventh
104 to 155	Two-sevenths
156 to 174	Three-sevenths
175 or more	One-half

---

87 See chapter 11.
88 CSMCR 2012, reg 50; *C v Secretary of State for Work and Pensions* [2002] EWCA Civ 1854.
89 Supplemented by CSMCR 2012, regs 46–7.

(5) If the person with care is caring for more than one qualifying child of the non-resident parent, the applicable decrease is the sum of the appropriate fractions in the Table divided by the number of such qualifying children.

(6) If the applicable fraction is one-half in relation to any qualifying child in the care of the person with care, the total amount payable to the person with care is then to be further decreased by £7 for each such child.[90]

(7) If the application of the preceding provisions of this paragraph would decrease the weekly amount of child support maintenance (or the aggregate of all such amounts) payable by the non-resident parent to the person with care (or all of them) to less than £7, he is instead liable to pay child maintenance at the rate of £7 per week, apportioned (if appropriate) in accordance with paragraph 6.

In flat rate cases, the fact of shared care for at least 52 nights over 12 months reduces the £7 assessment to nil.[91] We discuss the impact and fairness of the shared care rules further at 6.7.4 below.

Apportionment

What happens where non-resident parents have qualifying children by two or more partners, and each child lives with his or her other parent?

Child Support Act 1991, Sch 1, para 6

(1) If the non-resident parent has more than one qualifying child and in relation to them there is more than one person with care, the amount of child support maintenance payable is (subject to [rules regarding shared care]) to be determined by apportioning the rate between the persons with care.

(2) The rate of maintenance liability is to be divided by the number of qualifying children, and shared among the persons with care according to the number of qualifying children in relation to whom each is a person with care.[92]

Set-off

Sometimes, children are split between the parents—some living with one parent, while others live with the other. Technically, both parents are liable to pay support for the children in the other's care. CMS can treat child support liability as having been satisfied by setting off such counter-liabilities.[93] Similarly, CMS may also 'set-off' child support liability where

---

[90] See DSS (1999), para 7.17: this effectively shares the child benefit paid to the person with care.
[91] CSA 1991, Sch 1, para 8.
[92] See para 5A and CSMCR, reg 48 for the inclusion in the apportionment of children subject to family-based arrangements.
[93] CSA 1991, s 41C and Child Support (Management of Payments and Arrears) Regulations 2009, SI 2009/3151, reg 5.

the non-resident parent has made other payments which the person with care agrees may be treated as satisfying the liability, for example payments made under certain mortgages, rent, utility bills, council tax, and the cost of essential repairs to the child's home.[94]

6.4.5 VARIATIONS

The basic formula and add-ons discussed above operate strictly mathematically.[95] However, CMS has discretion to vary the amount payable in cases falling in one of the categories specified in the Act and accompanying regulations.[96] Variations—up or down—are designed to relieve specific injustices that might arise under the formula. Either party may apply for a variation at the outset or once a maintenance calculation is in force by applying for a revision.[97] It must first be shown that one of the 'cases' for a variation applies.

Special expenses

The first case concerns 'special expenses' of the non-resident parent which, it is argued, should reduce the maintenance payable.[98] Regulations deal exhaustively with the nature and level of expenses that may be claimed to justify the variation.[99] Broadly speaking, they include:

- average weekly travel and accommodation costs incurred regularly by the non-resident parent in maintaining contact with the qualifying child; in order to encourage regular contact, this includes costs connected with contact for which the non-resident parent receives a shared care deduction under the rules discussed above;[100]
- the maintenance element of boarding school fees, up to 50 per cent of the non-resident parent's income;[101]
- repayment of certain types of debts incurred when the non-resident parent and the person with care were still together for the benefit of specified family members (and not exclusively for the benefit of the non-resident parent). This includes mortgage payments over the home occupied by the parent with care and child, even if the non-resident parent retains an interest in that property, but not responsibility for other debts taken on by the non-resident parent as part of a financial settlement with the parent with care or court order;[102]
- repayment of limited other categories of mortgage, loan, and endowment insurance policies, but—by contrast with the previous case—not where the non-resident parent has any interest in the property over which the debt is secured;[103]

---

94 Ibid, reg 6.
95 *R v Secretary of State for Social Security, ex parte Biggin* [1995] 1 FLR 851.
96 See DSS (1995); CSA 1991, ss 28A–G, Schs 4A and 4B; CSMCR 2012, regs 47–75.
97 CSA 1991, s 16 and CSMCR 2012, regs 14–16.
98 CSA 1991, Sch 4B, para 2.
99 CSMCR 2012, regs 63–8.
100 Ibid, reg 63 and C-MEC (2012), Annex C, para 60; on the previous position, see Wikeley (2006a), 376.
101 Ibid, reg 66.
102 Ibid, reg 65.
103 Ibid, reg 67.

- additional costs necessarily incurred because of the long-term illness or disability of a relevant other child (less amounts received by way of relevant welfare benefits or other financial assistance received in respect of the illness or disability).[104]

In relation to the first four categories, a variation cannot be obtained if weekly expenses under any individual heading are below £10. But if they exceed £10, then the variation can reflect the full amount, not just the excess. If CMS considers any expenses to be unreasonably high or to have been unreasonably incurred, it may substitute such lower amount as it considers reasonable, which may be nil, though it must not put the non-resident in a position whereby he cannot continue to see the child as frequently as a court order permits.[105] There is evidence that some non-resident parents are unaware that liability can be varied for these contact-related expenses.[106]

Unearned and diverted income

The second remaining case[107] aims to prevent non-resident parents paying less than they should, given that the formula is based only on their earned income and does not view their financial circumstances in the round.[108] The following, in broad terms, may give grounds for a variation:[109]

- the non-resident parent has unearned income (e.g. from investments) exceeding £2,500 per annum;[110]
- the non-resident parent falls within the nil or flat rate category, but has an income exceeding £100 per week;[111]
- the non-resident parent has the ability to control the amount of his income,[112] and CMS believe that he has unreasonably reduced his income in order to reduce his child support liability by diverting it to other persons or for purposes other than providing his own income, for example by paying an unreasonably high salary to his partner for working in his business.[113]

Here, it has been said that parents with care are hampered in seeking variation on this ground, assuming that they even know it exists, if they have no access to the non-resident parent's financial details necessary to substantiate their case; CMS will not pass on to parents with care a breakdown of the non-resident parent's income.[114]

---

[104] Ibid, reg 64.

[105] Ibid, reg 68.

[106] Atkinson and McKay (2005), 113.

[107] CSA 1991, Sch 4B, para 4 and CSMCR 2012, regs 69–71. A third case had dealt with various issues unique to cases that arose pre-1993, all of which are now closed and so it is not discussed here.

[108] E.g. *Phillips v Peace* [1996] 2 FCR 237.

[109] See SI 2001/156, regs 18–20.

[110] CSMCR 2012, reg 69.

[111] Ibid, reg 70.

[112] Self-employed non-resident parents who can divert income from earned into unearned sources pose significant challenges: *Smith v Secretary of State for Work and Pensions* [2006] UKHL 35; Wikeley (2007a), paras 19–21.

[113] CSMCR 2012, reg 71.

[114] Gingerbread (2012b), paras 35–8.

The discretion

If one of the 'cases' applies, the CMS has a discretion whether to allow a variation. The CSA 1991 and regulations identify some specific factors to be considered in addition to the general welfare principle in s 2. These factors are instructive about the policies underpinning child support:

Child Support Act 1991

28E Matters to be taken into account

(1) In determining whether to agree to a variation, the Secretary of State shall have regard ... to the general principles set out in subsection (2) ...

(2) The general principles are that—

(a) parents should be responsible for maintaining their children whenever they can afford to do so;

(b) where a parent has more than one child, his obligation to maintain any one of them should be no less than his obligation to maintain any other of them.

(3) In determining whether to agree to a variation, the Secretary of State shall take into account any representation made to it—

(a) by the person with care or non-resident parent concerned; ...

(4) In determining whether to agree to a variation, no account shall be taken of the fact that—

(a) any part of the income of the person with care concerned is, or would be if the Secretary of State agreed to a variation, derived from any benefit; or

(b) some or all of any child support maintenance might be taken into account in some manner in relation to any entitlement to benefit. ...

28F Agreement to a variation

(1) The Secretary of State may agree to a variation if—

(a) it is satisfied that the case is one which falls within one or more of the cases set out in Part 1 of Schedule 4B or in regulations made under that Part [described above]; and

(b) it is its opinion that, in all the circumstances of the case, it would be just and equitable to agree to a variation.

(2) In considering whether it would be just and equitable in any case to agree to a variation, the Secretary of State—

(a) must have regard, in particular, to the welfare of any child likely to be affected if it did agree to a variation; and

(b) [to factors specified in regulations] ...

Child Support Maintenance Calculation Regulations 2012, SI 2012/2677, reg 60

Factors not taken into account for the purposes of section 28F

The following factors are not to be taken into account in determining whether it would be just and equitable to agree to a variation in any case—

(a) the fact that the conception of the qualifying child was not planned by one or both of the parents;

(b) whether the non-resident parent or the person with care of the qualifying child was responsible for the breakdown of the relationship between them;

(c) the fact that the non-resident parent or the person with care of the qualifying child has formed a new relationship with a person who is not a parent of that child;

(d) the existence of particular arrangements for contact with the qualifying child, including whether any arrangements are being adhered to;

(e) the income or assets of any person other than the non-resident parent;

(f) the failure by a non-resident parent to make payments of child support maintenance, or to make payments under a maintenance order or maintenance agreement; or

(g) representations made by persons other than the parties.

Once it has been decided to allow the variation, detailed regulations govern how the variation affects the maintenance calculation. In particular, where the variation involves augmenting the income to which the formula applies, any income above £3,000 per week is, as normal, ignored, and where the income is reduced, the non-resident parent is nevertheless required to pay at least the flat rate amount.[115]

6.4.6 TERMINATION OF THE CALCULATION

The maintenance calculation ceases to have effect if: (i) the non-resident parent or person with care dies; (ii) there is no longer any qualifying child;[116] or (iii) the non-resident parent ceases to be a parent of the qualifying child (e.g. following adoption).[117]

6.4.7 ENFORCEMENT OF CHILD MAINTENANCE

As we discussed at 6.4.3 above, the current law encourages parties not to rely on CMS. To this end, both parties must pay if CMS's collection service is used. Should non-resident parents need an additional incentive to comply, failure to pay may be met by a[ ] arsenal of enforcement tools.[118] That arsenal was recently augmented, despite critics' objection that the effectiveness of the existing enforcement powers had not been properly tested. But the government remains keen to send a strong signal about the importance of non-resident parents meeting their responsibility to pay child maintenance.

---

[115] CSMCR 2012, regs 72–5.
[116] *SL v CMEC (CSM)* [2010] AACR 24.
[117] CSA 1991, Sch 1, para 16(1).
[118] CSA 1991, ss 29–41A.

'Enforcement' via reliance on tax records

Whilst not an issue of enforcement as such, calculating maintenance by reference to historical gross income data obtained from the tax authorities itself provides early-stage 'enforcement'. Non-resident parents' ability to frustrate matters by withholding income information (particularly when self-employed) is hampered by this new approach.[119] However, the information available to CMS is only as good as that available to the tax authorities, who have not tended to investigate the affairs of low-earning taxpayers.[120]

Enforcement by CMS

Enforcement is entirely for CMS to instigate: the person with care cannot apply to the court to enforce maintenance, as we discuss below. Unlike any other financial liabilities (including court-ordered periodical payments), there is no limitation period during the child's minority on collection of child support arrears;[121] CMS can even chase defaulters beyond the grave.[122] Fees are payable by the non-resident parent for each type of enforcement action.[123] CMS may also impose penalty payments of up to 25 per cent of the sums due, which go to the state; the person with care gains no compensation or interest for late payment.[124]

The enhanced arsenal at CMS's disposal

Originally, the enforcement arsenal lay beyond the gateway of the 'liability order' (discussed below), which could only be obtained from the court. With a view to speeding up the process, the 2008 amendments put several of the enforcement powers in the hands of CMS itself. This means that an independent body will only be involved in the enforcement process if the non-resident parent appeals against CMS's proposed action. Many of these changes are not yet in force—in particular, the conferral on CMS, rather than the court, of the power to make liability orders and to order driving disqualifications/removal of passports—but we discuss the law as it will be once the reforms are implemented.[125] Since the courts' discretion *not* to make liability orders was limited—courts dealing with enforcement issues are barred from examining the correctness of the underlying maintenance calculation[126]—their removal from the process may not make much practical difference. However, serious concerns have been expressed about the implications of this move for citizens' right of access to court.

ONLINE RESOURCE CENTRE
Readers interested in those debates will find further materials on the Online Resources Centre page for chapter 6.

---

119 Note also the Child Support Information Regulations 2008, SI 2008/2551 and associated offences created by CSA 1991, s 14A.
120 Wikeley (2007a), para 20.
121 Cf Burrows (2010).
122 CSA 1991, s 43A.
123 The Child Support Fees Regulations 2014, SI 2014/612, Part 4.
124 CSA 1991, s 41A; SI 1992/1989, Part IIA, though it seems CMS is not yet using this power.
125 Footnotes identify provisions unimplemented at the time of writing.
126 See 6.4.8. *Farley v Child Support Agency and another* [2006] UKHL 31.

In taking any enforcement action, CMS is subject to its general duty under s 2 of the CSA 1991 to have regard to the welfare of any child likely to be affected by its decision.[127] CMS is free to implement its enforcement action before the deadline for appealing expires, provided that it thinks the liability would be unaffected by a successful appeal or—more surprisingly—if it nevertheless considers that it would be fair to proceed in all the circumstances.[128] Enforcement engages several rights of non-resident parents, in particular their right to respect for private life (Article 8), their right to a fair trial in the determination of civil rights and obligations (Article 6), and their right to peaceful enjoyment of possessions (Article 1 of Protocol 1).[129] As a public authority, CMS has a duty to act compatibly with Convention rights in its enforcement activities.[130]

Deduction from earnings orders

The first tool is the deduction from earnings order (DEO). In some jurisdictions, these are used as a convenient collection mechanism for all employed non-resident parents.[131] There had been plans to move to that standard collection model in the UK, but DEOs have returned to the enforcement rather than collection arena, with a fee payable by the non-resident parent for their use, though the legislation does not require that the non-resident parent be in default before the order is made.[132]

The DEO may be made by CMS without court involvement.[133] The order is addressed to the non-resident parent's employer, requiring them to deduct the sums due from the parent's pay and redirect them to CMS. A portion of non-resident parents' income is protected so DEOs cannot reduce their circumstances unreasonably.[134] A DEO should not be used where there is good reason not to, if specified adverse employment or family consequences might result.[135] Non-resident parents may appeal to the court against a DEO, but only on very limited grounds;[136] the order will not operate until the appeal deadline has passed. Parkinson has argued that in order to respect non-resident parents' dignity, CMS should offer the option of direct debit instead of a DEO wherever possible.[137] Where the non-resident parent is receiving welfare benefits, any child support due may be deducted from those.[138]

---

[127] *Brookes v Secretary of State for Work and Pensions and C-MEC* [2010] EWCA Civ 420.

[128] E.g. CSA 1991, s 32A(3).

[129] Cf *R (ota Denson) v Child Support Agency* [2002] EWHC 154: court-based liability order scheme held not to engage Art 8 or Art 1 of Protocol 1, but if engaged, readily justifiable; *Brookes v Secretary of State for Work and Pensions and C-MEC* [2010] EWCA Civ 420, [39]: doubted obiter whether, short of imprisonment, Art 8 engaged by enforcement action—but cf disqualification and curfew orders, discussed below. On Art 1 of Protocol 1, see *JM v United Kingdom* (App No 37090/06, ECHR) (11 October 2010).

[130] Human Rights Act 1998 (HRA 1998), s 6.

[131] They cannot be used against self-employed parents, the most problematic group.

[132] The non-resident parent may choose to have a DEO, but will have to pay the fee of £50.

[133] CSA 1991, ss 29 and 31; and see generally SI 1992/1989, reg 3 and Part III.

[134] Ibid, reg 11.

[135] SI 1992/1989, reg 3(3)–(5).

[136] CSA 1991, s 32(5)(6); SI 1992/1989, reg 22; *Secretary of State for Social Security v Shotton* [1996] 2 FLR 241.

[137] Parkinson (2007).

[138] CSA 1991, s 43.

Deduction orders: bank accounts

CMS can make regular[139] or lump sum[140] deduction orders (addressed to the institution holding the account) from various bank accounts in relation to both arrears and future payments where the non-resident parent is in default.[141] This tool is particularly useful against recalcitrant self-employed non-resident parents to whom DEOs cannot be applied. These powers are reinforced by CMS's right to apply to court for an anti-avoidance (or 'freezing') order, modelled on powers exercisable by the matrimonial courts. These orders are available on the ground that the non-resident parent has failed to pay and—intending to avoid payment—is about to make or has made a reviewable disposition, that is, a disposition other than one made for valuable consideration to a third party acting in good faith and with no notice of the intention to avoid paying maintenance.[142]

Liability orders and associated remedies

Under the 2008 reforms, CMS will itself be able to make the key gateway order[143]—the liability order[144]—which unlocks a number of further enforcement tools. Once it has made a liability order, CMS will be able to supply details of the child maintenance debt to credit reference agencies,[145] and enforce the liability order without court sanction by various means. First, it could take control of various items of the non-resident parent's property to sell in order to pay the outstanding debt;[146] regulations identify a wide range of property that is exempt from this process, broadly speaking those necessary for the non-resident parent's earning power or education (up to £1,350 worth), and basic domestic necessities.[147] Secondly, it could make a third party debt order: this would require third parties holding the liable person's funds to pay them to CMS. Finally, it could make a charging order: this would give CMS a security interest in any property subject to the order, so that in the event of sale (which may be expressly ordered for this purpose), a specified sum from the proceeds goes to CMS.[148]

'Wilful refusal or culpable neglect'

The last set of enforcement powers—the 'Exocet of enforcement'[149]—may be used only when the remedies discussed above have been tried but failed to yield up all or part of the debt,[150] and where CMS or (in some instances) the court[151] finds that the non-resident parent has

---

139 Attracting a fee of £50: Fees Regulation, SI 2014/612, reg 10.

140 For a fee of £200: ibid.

141 CSA 1991, ss 32A–K, SI 1992/1989, Part IIIA.

142 CSA 1991, s 32L, modelled on MCA 1973, s 37.

143 This change was not in force at the time of writing, so liability orders currently require an application to court.

144 CSA 1991, ss 32M–N.

145 Ibid, s 49D(3); cf concerns of Joint Committee for Human Rights under Art 8 (2007), 1.28; cf *R (ota Denson) v Child Support Agency* [2002] EWHC 154, [47].

146 CSA 1991, s 35(1); Tribunals, Courts and Enforcement Act 2007, Part 3; Taking Control of Goods (Fees) Regulation 2014, SI 2014/1.

147 Taking Control of Goods Regulations 2013, SI 2013/1894, reg 4.

148 CSA 1991, s 36.

149 *Karoonian v CMEC* [2012] EWCA Civ 1379, [7].

150 Ibid, [19].

151 The changes empowering CMS to act without court sanction in relation to driving licences and travel authorization are not in force at time of writing.

been guilty of 'wilful refusal or culpable neglect' to pay. These terms were explained in a different—but for our purposes similar—context as follows:

R (Sullivan) v Luton Magistrates' Court [1992] 2 FLR 196

Those are words which set the degree of blameworthiness necessary to attract an imprisonment order at a very high level. It is not just a matter of improvidence or dilatoriness. Something in the nature of a deliberate defiance or reckless disregard of the court's order is required.

Bird and Burrows note that outside the context of imprisonment—for example, curfew orders, driving disqualification—the threshold might be set a little less high, although the interference with liberty entailed in all of these measures mean the threshold cannot be lowered too far.[152]

Disqualification from holding driving licence or travel authorization

The most controversial new powers that will be exercisable by CMS are disqualification from driving and confiscation of passports, to be trialled for a two-year period. Magistrates have had the power to disqualify from driving for up to two years in cases of wilful refusal to pay or culpable neglect. The government was keen to move this power—and with it a new power to confiscate passports—to CMS. Its attempts to do so in CMOPA 2008 failed, following objections that it was unconstitutional for an administrative body to be empowered to remove passports. Unbowed, the government secured the passage of similar provisions in 2009, amending relevant sections of the CSA 1991.[153]

Under this reform, CMS will be able to make a 'disqualification order' in relation to a non-resident parent's driving licence, travel authorization (usually passport), or both for up to one year, where attempts to recover the debt by other means have failed entirely or partly, and there has been wilful refusal or culpable neglect to pay. Before exercising this power, CMS would have to consider 'whether the person needs the relevant document in order to earn a living'.[154] While CMS would be bound by s 2 to have regard to the welfare of any child likely to be affected by its decision and must act compatibly with Convention rights, there is no specific duty to consider whether the parent needs to drive or travel on a passport to spend time with the child. But CMS would have to be able to justify its action as necessary and proportionate under Article 8(2).[155] The government would doubtless say that these orders are intended not as punishment but encouragement, and that the non-resident parent can ensure contact takes place: he need only pay the bill.[156] But then, opponents counter, one might as well empower CMS

---

[152] (2009), 9.34.

[153] CSA 1991, ss 39B–E: not in force at time of writing.

[154] CSA 1991, s 39B(4).

[155] R (Plumb) v Secretary of State for Work and Pensions [2002] EWHC 1125, [19]; for unsuccessful argument in this vein in other contexts: Logan v United Kingdom (App No 24875/94, ECHR) (1996); Burrows v United Kingdom (App No 27558/95, ECHR) (1996).

[156] Cf Hansard HL Deb, col GC142, 2 July 2009, Lord McKenzie of Luton.

to impose curfews or imprison people without court sanction on the same basis—yet we have not taken that step.[157]

Court-based sanctions: curfew orders and committal to prison

The last resort remedies[158]—curfew orders or committal to prison for up to six weeks—may only be obtained from the magistrates' courts, again following a finding that the non-resident parent is guilty of wilful refusal to pay or culpable neglect to do so.[159] The courts are slow to exercise what is now an anomalous power to imprison debtors; the vast majority of sentences issued are suspended. Curfew orders—orders of up to six months' duration requiring the person to remain at specified places for specified periods of time of between two and 12 hours a day—were introduced in the 2008 reforms.[160] The court will have to ensure that any curfew avoids any conflict with the non-resident parent's religious beliefs, employment, or education. Conflict with arrangements for the non-resident parent to spend time with the child is again not expressly identified as a consideration, but courts considering curfews must act compatibly with Article 8 ECHR. Breach of a curfew will risk imprisonment for a specified period or until the debt is paid, if earlier.[161] For completeness, non-resident parents subjected to a curfew or committed to prison are searched for cash on the spot—no opportunity to recover arrears is to be missed.[162]

No enforcement of CMS calculations by person with care

Enforcement proceedings lie exclusively with CMS, which has full discretion as to whether and how to pursue cases; it can also accept part-payment or write off arrears in certain circumstances.[163] Persons with care cannot take enforcement proceedings, and have no party status in proceedings brought by CMS. They may only empower CMS to act for them and then only where a CMS calculation has been made.[164] We examine the position of those who opted for private ordering below at 6.6.

The exclusion of parents with care from enforcement was unsuccessfully challenged in *R (Kehoe) v Secretary of State for Work and Pensions*. The case raises fundamental questions about the nature of the child support obligation. The Kehoes had been married with four children. Following the divorce, Mrs Kehoe applied to the CSA. For ten years it extracted some maintenance from Mr Kehoe, but the process was painful and substantial arrears accumulated. Mrs Kehoe felt that she could have done better at enforcing her child support assessment than the CSA was apparently able to do. She argued that the system violated Article 6 ECHR by preventing her from judicially enforcing her civil right, as person with care, to receive child maintenance from the non-resident parent. The House of Lords, Baroness Hale dissenting, held that persons with care have no such civil right and that

---

[157] Ibid, Lord Pannick.
[158] *Karoonian v CMEC* [2012] EWCA Civ 1379, [29].
[159] CSA 1991, ss 39H–P and 40.
[160] Ibid, s 39I(1), (3); not in force at time of writing.
[161] Ibid, s 39N(4).
[162] Ibid, ss 39L and 40(10)–(10C); see also s 39D: not all in force at time of writing.
[163] Ibid, ss 41D–E.
[164] Ibid, s 4(2)(b). Nor may they apply for a court order: ibid, s 8—see p 401 below.

Article 6 was therefore not engaged. The majority view was based on its interpretation of the CSA 1991, in particular parts of s 4:

Child Support Act 1991, s 4

Child support maintenance

(1) A person who is, in relation to any qualifying child..., either the person with care or the non-resident parent may apply to the Secretary of State for a maintenance calculation to be made under this Act with respect to that child...

(2) Where a maintenance calculation has been made in response to an application under this section the Secretary of State may, if the person with care or non-resident parent with respect to whom the calculation was made applies to it under this section, arrange for—

  (a) the collection of the child support maintenance payable in accordance with the calculation;

  (b) the enforcement of the obligation to pay child support maintenance in accordance with the calculation....

(3) Where an application under subsection (2) for the enforcement of the obligation mentioned in subsection (2)(b) authorises the Secretary of State to take steps to enforce that obligation whenever it considers it necessary to do so, the Secretary of State may act accordingly....

R (Kehoe) v Secretary of State for Work and Pensions [2005] UKHL 48

LORD BINGHAM:

3. It is necessary first to examine whether Mrs Kehoe has a right to recover financial support for the maintenance of the children...from Mr Kehoe under the domestic law of England and Wales. Under the law as it stood before 1991 it was clear that she had such a right under the [MCA 1973, the Domestic Proceedings and Magistrates' Courts Act 1978 (DPMCA 1978)...and the CA 1989]. But these procedures were judged by the government of the day to be unsatisfactory...

Lord Bingham then examined the history and provisions of the CSA 1991 as it stood pre-CMOPA 2008 (including its treatment of benefits cases—see 6.2.2 above), and continued:

5....In *Huxley v Child Support Officer* [2000] 1 FLR 898, 908, Hale LJ...helpfully characterised the regime established by the 1991 Act:

"The child support system has elements of private and public law but fundamentally it is a nationalised system for assessing and enforcing an obligation which each parent owes primarily to the child. It replaces the powers of the courts, which can no longer make orders for periodical payments for children save in very limited circumstances. Unless she can secure a voluntary agreement at least as high as that which the CSA would assess, the PWC [parent with care] is expected to look to the Agency to assess her child support according to the formula, whether or not she is on benefit. The fact that it does her no direct good if she is on means-tested benefits, and that much CSA activity so far has been in relation to parents on benefit, does not alter the fundamental characteristics of the scheme."

> 6. That a caring parent in the position of Mrs Kehoe was given no right of recovering or enforcing a claim to child maintenance against a . . . non-resident parent was not a lacuna or inadvertent omission in the 1991 Act: it was the essence of the new scheme, a deliberate legislative departure from the regime which had previously obtained. The merits of that scheme are not for the House in its judicial capacity to evaluate. But plainly the scheme did not lack a coherent rationale. The state has an interest, most directly in cases where public funds are disbursed, but also more generally that children should be adequately supported. It might well be thought that a single professional agency, with the resources of the state behind it and an array of powers at its commend, would be more consistent in assessing and more effective and economical in enforcing payment than individual parents acting in a random and uncoordinated way. It might also be thought that the interposition of an independent, neutral, official body would reduce the acrimony which had all too frequently characterised applications for child maintenance by caring against absent or non-resident parents in the past which, however understandable in the aftermath of a fractured relationship, rarely enured to the benefit of the children. For better or worse, the process was deliberately changed.

That seriously undermined Mrs Kehoe's argument under Article 6, which guarantees access to an impartial tribunal for the determination of substantive civil rights and obligations but does not itself decide *what* substantive rights and obligations individuals should enjoy. Article 6, therefore, could not supply Mrs Kehoe with a right to recover child maintenance to which she had no right in English law.

> 10. Sympathetic though one must be with Mrs Kehoe, who appears to have suffered extreme frustration and a measure of loss, one cannot in my opinion ignore the wider principle raised by this case. This is that the deliberate decisions of representative assemblies should be respected and given effect so long as they do not infringe rights guaranteed by the Convention . . . Whether the scheme established by the 1991 Act is on balance beneficial to those whom it is intended to benefit may well be open to question, but it is a question for Parliament to resolve and not for the courts, since I do not consider that any article 6 right of Mrs Kehoe is engaged.

The majority took a narrow approach in interpreting the CSA 1991, Lord Hope, for example, concluding that because the Act did not expressly state that the parent with care had a right to receive maintenance or to require enforcement action, no such right existed to be protected under Article 6.[165] But while Lord Hope focused on the fact that the right had not been expressly *stated* in the Act, Baroness Hale considered that they had not been expressly *removed* and so survived the CSA scheme. She agreed that the scheme deprived parents of the right to *enforce* maintenance, but concluded that the underlying right (in her view, of the child) to *receive* maintenance was intact, raising an issue under Article 6. Her approach to the issues was distinctive:

BARONESS HALE (dissenting):

> 49. This is another case which has been presented to us largely as a case about adults' rights when in reality it is about children's rights. It concerns the obligation to maintain one's children and the corresponding right of those children to obtain the benefit of that obligation. The issue is whether the restrictions placed on direct access to the courts to enforce that obligation by section

---

[165] [2005] UKHL 48, [33]–[35].

8(1) and (3) of the [CSA 1991—see p 401 below] are compatible with article 6 of the [ECHR]. Article 6 is concerned only with the fair and impartial adjudication and enforcement of the rights recognised in domestic law. It does not guarantee any particular content to those rights. Put another way, the issue is whether the 1991 Act has defined the extent of the obligation and that right or whether it has merely altered the machinery for assessing and enforcing them. If it is the latter, then the underlying right still exists and the Act's provisions may be regarded as procedural only. If it is the former, then all that survive are the rights set out in the Act itself. In my view, it is not possible to answer that question by looking only at the rights contained in the 1991 Act itself. They have to be set in the context of the scope of the parents' obligations and the children's rights as a whole. The 1991 Act is only one of a number of ways in which the law recognises these.

She then set out the history of the public and private law in this area, extracted earlier in this chapter and in chapter 3, and the current position, noting public law's liable relative procedure (since abolished by CMOPA 2008 in relation to children), the common law duty of fathers to maintain their children, and the various court-based financial remedies for children considered at 6.5 below.

70. It is obvious, therefore, that the obligation of a parent to maintain his children, and the right of those children to have the benefit of that obligation, is not wholly contained in the 1991 Act. Far from it. The Act left all the previous law intact, merely precluding the courts from using their powers in cases where the Agency was supposed to do it for them...The 1991 Act contemplates that, as a minimum, children should have the benefit of the maintenance obligation as defined under the formula; but it does not contemplate that children should be limited to their rights under that Act; in appropriate circumstances, they may be supplemented or replaced in all the ways recounted earlier.

71. That being the case, it is clear to me that children have a civil right to be maintained by their parents which is such as to engage article 6...Their rights are not limited to the rights given to the parent with care under the [CSA 1991]. The provisions of that Act are simply a means of quantifying and enforcing part of their rights. I appreciate that the line between a procedural and a substantive bar is not always easy to draw...The formula is a substantive definition of the extent of the basic right. But in my view the continued existence of the wider rights, together with the wider objective of the 1991 Act to improve the provision made for children by their non-resident parents, places the collection and enforcement provisions of the Act on the procedural rather than substantive side of the line. A civil right to be maintained exists and *prima facie* children are entitled to the benefit of the article 6 rights in the determination and enforcement of that right.

72. The problem is that this is exactly what the system is trying to do. It is trying to enforce the children's rights. It is sometimes, as this case shows, lamentably inefficient in so doing. It is safe to assume that there are cases, of which this may be one, where the children's carer would be much more efficient in enforcing the children's rights. The children's carer has a direct and personal interest in enforcement which the Agency, however good its intentions, does not. Even [pre-CMOPA 2008] in benefit cases, where the state does have a direct interest in enforcement, it is not the sort of interest which stems from needing enough money to feed, clothe and house the children on a day-to-day basis. Only a parent who is worrying about where the money is to be found for the school dinners, the school trips, the school uniform, sports gear or musical instruments, or to visit the "absent" parent, not only this week but the next and the next for many years to come, has that sort of interest. A promise that the Agency is doing its best is not enough. Nor is the threat or reality of judicial review. Most people simply do not have access to the Administrative Court

in the way that they used to have access to their local magistrates' court. Judicial review may produce some action from the Agency, but what is needed is money from the absent parent. Action from the Agency will not replace the money which has been irretrievably lost as a result of its failure to act in time.

Having found that Article 6 was engaged, and that the Act's attempt to improve enforcement of the child's right to maintain was a legitimate aim, she then considered whether depriving the parent with care of the right to enforce maintenance assessed under the Act was proportionate:

> 74....I do not find that an easy question to answer...While the child support scheme was under review in the late 1990s, there was considerable debate about whether the courts should regain their power to make the basic award on the application of the parent with care. The formula would remain the same in all cases, but parents who were not receiving means-tested benefits would be able to apply to the courts rather than the Agency to award it. This was, however, rejected after careful consideration by the Government ([see DSS (1999), ch 8]). One can see why. The Government did not want to create 'one law for the rich and one for the poor'. It would be difficult to apply to the common case where the parent with care is sometimes in receipt of relevant benefits and sometimes is not...
>
> 75. This is just the sort of policy choice in a socio-economic field which the courts are usually prepared to leave to the judgment of Parliament....It would be difficult to hold that the scheme as a whole is incompatible with the children's rights to a speedy determination and enforcement of their claims.
>
> 76. But if I am right that the children's civil rights to be properly maintained by their parents are engaged, it follows that the public authority which is charged by Parliament with securing the determination and enforcement of their rights is under a duty to act compatibly with their article 6 right to the speedy determination and effective enforcement of those rights. Indeed [counsel for the Secretary of State] did not seek to argue that they were not. He accepted, for the sake of the issue before the House, that if article 6 was engaged in this case, the claim under section 7 of the [HRA 1998] for failing to act in compliance with those rights should proceed. It stands to reason that if the state is going to take over the enforcement of a person's civil rights it has a duty to act compatibly with article 6 in doing so....

The majority decision that there is no 'civil right' for the purposes of Article 6 to receive maintenance for one's children under the CSA 1991 has been branded 'disturbing'.[166] Nick Wikeley described the majority's reasoning as 'profoundly disappointing in their adoption of an unduly literalist and positivist approach to the question of statutory construction in *Kehoe*'. And there were further criticisms:

N. Wikeley, 'A Duty But Not a Right: Child Support after *R (Kehoe) v Secretary of State for Work and Pensions'*, (2006) 18 *Child and Family Law Quarterly* 287, 293–5

First, the two members of the majority who delivered short concurring speeches both relied in part on Mrs Kehoe's right to bring judicial review proceedings against the Secretary of State (in the guise of the Agency) as an indication that she was not without redress...[T]he

---

166 Douglas (2004b), discussing the same decision of the majority in the Court of Appeal.

proposition that judicial review is an adequate remedy will be greeted with at best some bemusement, and at worst hollow laughter, by those practitioners who have acted for parents with care in similar cases before the Administrative Court.

Secondly,...the majority placed considerable weight on the argument that the 1991 Act (which excluded the parent with care from the enforcement process) was an entirely new scheme which had 'replaced' the previous unsatisfactory private law remedies. This reading allowed the 1991 Act to be construed in isolation, so reinforcing the narrow perspective on the rights in issue.

Wikeley argued that the case law relied upon by the majority does not determine the point, and that other case law—not cited—is inconsistent with their conclusion that the Act altered the parties' substantive rights. He also doubted that the decision would pass muster before the European Court of Human Rights, which might regard a CSA maintenance calculation, certainly one endorsed by an appeal tribunal, as a judicial determination of a civil right:

Thus, the government's position in *Kehoe* may be difficult to sustain, not least as the outcome of the decision might well seem peculiar to a continental judiciary which will be more familiar with concepts of family solidarity. The Strasbourg bench will doubtless be even more puzzled once it is explained to them that, if the separating parents successfully negotiate a financial settlement and the parent with care is not on benefit, then a civil court may make a consent order embodying the terms of that agreement. It has never seriously been questioned that the parent with care enjoys a civil right to child maintenance in such circumstances....[The significance of this point] was simply ignored by the House of Lords. Moreover, if the Strasbourg court turns over this particular stone, they will find that the unfortunate paradoxes generated by the decision in *Kehoe* simply multiply...

Wikeley identifies four examples of this incoherence. First, a parent with care clearly has a right to *apply* for a maintenance assessment: if that assessment is delayed, Article 6 is engaged; but according to *Kehoe*, delays in *enforcing* an assessment once made fall outside Article 6. Secondly, a parent with care who has obtained a top-up order from the courts from a wealthy non-resident parent in addition to a CMS assessment (see 6.5.2 below) will have a civil right to enforce the former, but not the latter: 'it would seem that English law accords rather greater protection to the child's right to luxury rather than to mere subsistence'. Thirdly, whether the parent with care has a civil right for the purposes of Article 6 depends on whether the non-resident parent cooperates in obtaining a consent order for maintenance (see 6.5.2 below), which will engage Article 6. If not, the parent with care must proceed via the CSA, which will not: 'It hardly seems right that the whim of one party...should determine the legal rights of the other party in this way'. Finally, *non-resident* parents' Article 6 rights are clearly engaged by the process, allowing them to make arguments which, if successful, may prejudice the parent with care.[167]

---

[167] Wikeley (2006b), 294–5.

However, while it may reach the better result, Baroness Hale's judgment was not unproblematic in suggesting that English law recognizes maintenance as a right of the *child*, rather than of the parent with care:

N. Wikeley, 'A Duty But Not a Right: Child Support after *R (Kehoe) v Secretary of State for Work and Pensions*', (2006) 18 *Child and Family Law Quarterly* 287, 297–9, 301

If this is right, it requires a fundamental rethinking on the part of family law scholars. The traditional understanding was set out by J.C. Hall, writing in 1966: 'There was no civil obligation to maintain one's child at common law or in equity, but statute has imposed a duty'.

The common law cases provide scant support for the proposition that the common law clearly established a right of the child to maintenance, particularly where illegitimate.

What then of the legislative intervention prior to the 1991 Act? Baroness Hale...carefully explored the development of the various statutory codes for maintenance, both in public and private law. The public law mechanisms, dating back to the Poor Relief Act 1601, were always primarily concerned with indemnifying the public purse and discouraging immorality, and provide little support for the notion that children enjoy maintenance rights. Admittedly, the private law legislative measures have historically made a sharp distinction between spousal maintenance and child maintenance. However,...these statutes...all proceed on the assumption that it is the parent with care who will institute proceedings to enforce the maintenance obligation. In effect, the default position in English law is that children have no personal right to sue for maintenance. This might simply be seen as indicative of a mere lack of legal capacity, but the weight of authority [including that relating to tax and social security] would suggest that it points to the absence of any underlying legal right. We are thus some way from the position in the USA, where it seems to be accepted that 'the right to support lies exclusively with the child, and that a parent holds the child support payments in trust for the child's benefit'....

Wikeley will have been disappointed by the outcome of Mrs Kehoe's appeal to Strasbourg. The Court did not decide whether Article 6 was engaged (i.e. whether, contrary to the majority of the House of Lords, she had a civil right under domestic law to which Article 6 could attach). But even assuming that it was engaged, the Court found that Article 6 was not infringed. Mrs Kehoe had access to the remedy of judicial review. The Court considered (somewhat naïvely, given Wikeley's condemnation of this 'remedy') that it would not be unduly onerous to require her to use judicial review repeatedly, any more than she would probably have had to take enforcement action directly against Mr Kehoe repeatedly had she been entitled to do so. In conclusion, the Court made the following observations:

Kehoe v United Kingdom (App No 2010/06, ECHR) (2008)

49....The provision of a state enforcement scheme for maintenance payments *inter alia* benefits the many parents with care of children who do not have the time, energy, resources or inclination to be embroiled in ongoing litigation with the absent parent [sic] and allows the

State to pursue those absent parents who default on their obligations leaving their families on the charge of the social security system and the taxpayer. The mere fact that it is possible to envisage a different scheme which might also allow individual enforcement action by parents in the particular situation of the applicant is not sufficient to disclose a failure by the State in its obligations under Article 6.

Despite suggestions by Henshaw that the issue be reviewed, *Kehoe* survived CMOPA 2008 unscathed. Enforcement therefore remains a matter exclusively for CMS. This seems surprising now that the state's interest in the payment of child support is so attenuated: parents with care claiming benefits are no longer required to apply for child support and any maintenance they receive does not reduce their benefits entitlement. Allowing parents to enforce maintenance would also be consistent with encouraging parents to take responsibility for child support through private arrangements, relieving the state of the burden to act.[168] As Gillian Douglas has observed, the removal of compulsion in benefit cases could be said to reinstate the parent's right to seek child support by once more providing *all* parents with a choice of mechanisms for obtaining payment from the non-resident parent, and so clearly to engage Article 6.[169] But, given its reasoning in *Kehoe*, it is doubtful whether the Court's view of the compatibility of the English scheme with Article 6 would be altered by this. It is unlikely that a domestic court would find that *Kehoe* had been implicitly overruled, given the clear intention that *Kehoe* not be affected by the changes made to the child support scheme by CMOPA 2008 (apparently anxious that parents with care with difficult cases should not be burdened with the cost of enforcement),[170] and the style of statutory interpretation deployed by the House of Lords.[171]

6.4.8 CHALLENGING CMS DECISIONS

Absent any mechanism for enforcing a CMS maintenance calculation against the non-resident parents *directly*, persons with care (and non-resident parents wishing to challenge CMS decisions) are left to the various (quite limited) remedies exercisable against CMS where it fails to recover the maintenance due. Application may be made to CMS for a revision of its calculation in specified circumstances.[172] Applications for a supersession may be made if there has been a change of circumstances, error of law, or the original decision was made in ignorance of, or under a mistake as to, some material fact.[173] Thereafter, remedies lie outside CMS,[174] principally by way of appeals heard within the tribunal system[175] or judicial review, the adequacy of which as a remedy in this context has been doubted.[176] Disappointed parents with care and children cannot sue CMS where it fails to enforce a maintenance calculation effectively, either in negligence or under the HRA 1998.[177] The CSA 1991 scheme

---

[168] Henshaw (2006), para 67.

[169] Douglas (2009).

[170] DWP (2007a), para 28.

[171] Cf Burrows (2009b).

[172] CSA 1991, s 16 and CSMCR 2012, regs 14–16.

[173] Ibid, s 17 and regs 17–18.

[174] The Independent Case Examiner investigates claims of maladministration, but does not produce legally binding decisions; the DWP may offer ex gratia financial redress for any loss.

[175] CSA 1991, ss 20–4; CSMCR 2012, regs 28–33 and Sch. See CPAG (2014), ch 20.

[176] *Farley v Child Support Agency* [2006] UKHL 31, [20]; *R (Kehoe) v Secretary of State for Work and Pensions* [2005] UKHL 48, [72].

[177] *Rowley v Secretary of State for Work and Pensions* [2007] EWCA Civ 598.

overall has been found to be compliant with Article 8, so complaint must be taken within the statutory scheme or by judicial review.[178]

6.5 COURT-BASED PROVISION: THE CURRENT LAW

Where the courts have jurisdiction, they operate under various (broadly similar) statutes, depending on the nature of the proceedings and the parties' relationship. We must consider first whether the courts have jurisdiction at all. And for that purpose, we need to discuss periodical payments separately from other forms of order.

6.5.1 LUMP SUM AND PROPERTY-RELATED ORDERS

The courts have exclusive jurisdiction, unaffected by the CSA 1991, to make lump sum orders and orders in relation to property: property adjustment orders, property settlements, and orders for sale.[179] Where CMS has no jurisdiction to make a maintenance calculation, capital orders can be used to meet income requirements.[180]

6.5.2 PERIODICAL PAYMENTS

More complicated is the courts' jurisdiction to order periodical payments to or for the benefit of children. It is necessary to distinguish between cases where CMS has jurisdiction to make a maintenance calculation and cases where it does not.

Where CMS has jurisdiction

First, the general rule is that the courts have *no* power to order maintenance where CMS has potential or actual jurisdiction—that is, where there is a qualifying child in respect of whom a maintenance calculation could be or has been made.[181] The courts must not use capital orders (e.g. lump sums or property adjustment) as a means of evading this general rule; capital orders should be confined to meeting the child's capital rather than day-to-day income needs—such as home and furnishings, or a car for the primary carer's use.[182] A lump sum order will not be regarded as a maintenance order for these purposes unless specified to be for the purpose of maintenance.[183]

However, there are some exceptions to the general rule set out in CSA 1991, s 8, and the courts have identified one other.

---

178 *Treharne v Secretary of State for Work and Pensions* [2008] EWHC 3222, [15]–[18], [28].
179 MCA 1973, Part II; CPA 2004, Sch 5; CA 1989, Sch 1; DPMCA 1978, s 2(3); CPA 2004, Sch 6, para 2(2); CA 1989, Sch 1, para 5(2).
180 *V v V (Child Maintenance)* [2001] 2 FLR 799.
181 CSA 1991, s 8.
182 *Phillips v Peace* [1996] 2 FCR 237; *N v D* [2008] 1 FLR 1629.
183 *AMS v Child Support Officer* [1998] 1 FLR 955.

Consent orders

The most significant exception is that the courts can order periodical payments for the benefit of children with the consent of both parties.[184] Parties can thereby confer jurisdiction on the courts, and so avoid engaging with CMS. A standard practice has emerged to exploit this exception fully:

V v V (Child Maintenance) [2001] 2 FLR 799 (Fam Div)

WILSON J:

[18] My experience . . . has been that, even when parties require the court to determine other claims for [financial remedies on divorce], they have often reached agreement upon the level of periodical payments for the benefit of the children; and that they are keen for the court to make an order in that respect with a view . . . to excluding the possibility of [a maintenance calculation under the CSA] and to securing the facility for the court to resolve any future issue about the level of such payments in the exercise of its variation jurisdiction. In that event the court proceeds without difficulty to make the order under s 8(5).

[19] Even, however, when parties remain at odds as to the level of periodical payments for the children, they often wish the court to determine that issue as well as the other issues, thereby perhaps obviating the need for a return to court for a topping-up order[185] following [a maintenance calculation] and in any event securing the court's ongoing jurisdiction in the event of future such dispute. In my experience the court invariably wants to accommodate the parties in that regard. But, in the light of the general prohibition, how can it do so? Over the last 8 years the following mechanism, which I believe to be entirely legitimate, has evolved, namely that at the outset of the hearing the court makes an order by consent for periodical payments for the benefit of the children in the sum of five pence each and that at the end of the hearing it varies that order to the level of payments which it thinks fit.

[20] It may be argued that, technically, such a mechanism requires the preparation of three documents:

(a) a written agreement between the parties for the husband to pay five pence for the benefit of each of the children;[186]

(b) a nominal order, duly perfected, which reflects that agreement;[187] and

(c) a notice of application, duly issued, to vary that order.[188]

[21] My experience is that the written agreement at (a) and the notice of application at (c) rarely come into existence. I have no problem with that. My view is that, if the words 'by consent' appear above the nominal order, they satisfy the requirement of a written agreement and that any requirement for the issue of a notice of application can and should be waived.

However, we shall see at 6.6.1 below that consent orders cannot be relied on to exclude any possibility of an application to CMS long-term.

---

[184] CSA 1991, s 8(5); Child Maintenance (Written Agreements) Order 1993, SI 1993/620. On consent orders generally, see 7.7.1.

[185] Ibid, s 8(6).

[186] Ibid, s 8(5) and Child Maintenance (Written Agreements) Order 1993, SI 1993/620 require a written agreement which is then reflected in the court order.

[187] Thus complying with s 8(5) and SI 1993/620.

[188] CSA 1991, s 8(3A) allows the courts to vary validly made maintenance orders.

Top-up orders

The next exception concerns wealthy non-resident parents. CMS's maintenance calculation only covers gross income of up to £3,000 per week. The CSA 1991, s 8(6) preserves a power for the courts, where a maintenance calculation is in force in relation to the first £3,000,[189] to order top-up periodical payments in relation to the surplus. This does not automatically give the courts jurisdiction in 'big money' cases; parents with care must obtain a maintenance calculation before applying for this 'top-up' order.

Expenses connected with education and disability

The courts have jurisdiction to make orders designed to meet costs incurred in the child's education or training for a trade, profession, or vocation,[190] and to cover expenses attributable to the child's disability.[191] This power does not extend to nursery and child-minding fees.[192] Unlike 'top-up' orders, these orders may be made even if there is no maintenance calculation in force.

C v F (Disabled Child: Maintenance Orders) [1999] 1 FCR 39 (CA), 46

BUTLER-SLOSS LJ:

In general a court considering this difficult assessment should take into account in the broadest sense the expenses attributable to the child's disability. The additional help needed, the cost of feeding...additional help, a larger or better-appointed house, heating, clothing, car expenses, respite care are only some of the expenses which immediately spring to mind. The expenses attributable to the disability, broadly assessed, the income and allowances coming into the family housing the child under a disability have to be weighed in the balance against the income, assets, liabilities and outgoings of the person asked to meet some or all of those expenses.

'Segal' orders

The courts have carved out one further exception where it is making financial orders following the parents' divorce:

Dorney-Kingdom v Dorney-Kingdom [2000] 3 FCR 20 (CA), 24–5

THORPE LJ:

A practice has grown up, finding its origins before District Judge Segal in the Principal Registry, to make an order for spousal maintenance under s 23(1)(a) of the Matrimonial Causes Act 1973 that incorporates some of the costs of supporting the children as part of a

---

189 Note obiter suggestion in *CF v KM* [2010] EWHC 1754, [4]–[6] that the court can determine that the non-resident parent's income exceeds that threshold, even if any current CMS calculation assumes a lower income.

190 CSA 1991, s 8(7).

191 Ibid, s 8(8); 'disability' for these purposes is defined in s 8(9).

192 *Re L M (A Minor)* (CA), 9 July 1997, unreported.

global order. When a Segal order is made an important ingredient is that the overall sum will reduce pro tanto from the date upon which [CMS] brings in a [maintenance calculation]. The utility of the Segal order is obvious, since in many cases the determination of the [financial remedy] claims will come at a time when [CMS] has yet to complete its assessment of liability. It is therefore very convenient for a district judge to have a form of order which will carry the parent with primary care over that interim pending [CMS's] determination.

The proscription on the court making orders for child periodical payments other than by agreement, expressed in s 8(3) of the statute, could be said to be challenged, if not breached, by the mechanism of the Segal order. However, it seems to me to be just within the bounds of legitimacy, since it is no sort of ouster of or challenge to the jurisdiction of [CMS], but merely a holding until such time as [CMS] can carry out its proper function. But it seems to me absolutely crucial that if legitimacy is to be preserved, there must be a substantial ingredient of spousal support in the Segal order. If in any case there is a determination that the primary carer has no entitlement to periodical payments on her own account, any form of order that is not an agreed order plainly circumvents the statutory prohibition.

Variation of a court order duly made

The final exception is an adjunct of the previous four: the courts may vary maintenance orders that they have made, provided no maintenance calculation has subsequently been made by CMS.[193] While the extract above from *V v V (Child Maintenance)* demonstrates how this facility can be used to maximize the consent order exception,[194] commentators are divided on whether any variation of a consent order must itself be made by consent.[195]

Where CMS has no jurisdiction

Where CMS lacks jurisdiction to make a maintenance calculation, the courts have exclusive jurisdiction to order periodical payments for the benefit of a child. These situations are:

- where maintenance is sought from a step-parent or other person who is not a 'parent', and so in relation to whom the child in question is not a 'qualifying child' for the purposes of the CSA 1991;

- where the child is not a 'qualifying child' in relation to anyone—for example, if the child is older than the various age limits prescribed for the CSA 1991, or if there is no non-resident parent;

- where maintenance is sought from a person with care;[196]

- where any one or more of the person with care, non-resident parent, and qualifying child is not habitually resident in the UK;[197]

- where CMS's jurisdiction is ousted by binding private ordering: see 6.6.[198]

---

193 CSA 1991, s 8(3A).

194 [2001] 2 FLR 799.

195 See Wikeley (2006a), 209–10.

196 CSA 1991, s 8(10); see Wikeley (2006a), 198; this provision appears to have been overlooked in *N v C* [2013] EWHC 399 in concluding that there was no jurisdiction to make periodical payments in favour of the non-resident parent (though there were good reasons not to do so in that particular case).

197 CSA 1991, s 44.

198 Ibid, s 4(10).

It is important to distinguish between cases where CMS does not have jurisdiction, and those where it *does* have jurisdiction but has concluded or would conclude that the non-resident parent's situation warrants a nil calculation. The result produced by the CSA 1991 in such cases cannot be circumvented by resorting to the courts.[199]

6.5.3 THE STATUTORY SCHEMES

The courts' jurisdiction to make orders for the benefit of children arises from several statutes (see fig 6.1 above, p 376). Their powers under these Acts can be broadly divided into three categories, the first two applying only between spouses and civil partners.

- Cases of failure to maintain a child during marriage or civil partnership: DPMCA 1978/ CPA 2004, Sch 6; MCA 1973, s 27/CPA 2004, Sch 5, Part 9.

- Financial provision on or following divorce/dissolution, nullity, or judicial separation: MCA 1973, Part II and CPA 2004, Sch 5.

- A more widely available jurisdiction to order financial provision for the benefit of a child under CA 1989, Sch 1, regardless of the nature of the relationship between the parents.

For ease of exposition, we refer to each jurisdiction as proceedings or provisions relating to 'failure to maintain', 'divorce', and 'under the CA 1989, Sch 1', respectively. We refer collectively to provisions and proceedings within the first two jurisdictions as 'matrimonial'.

The extent of the courts' powers under each Act is slightly different.[200] The appropriate choice of statute turns on various factors. The parents' marital or civil partnership status is obviously significant. There is no need to show that one parent is 'non-resident' for the court to exercise its powers. But some of the statutes restrict the making and duration of orders where the parents are living together. The type of order sought and the identity of both parties are also relevant. In order to gain an overall impression of the nature and extent of the courts' powers, we approach the law thematically, rather than by statute, highlighting differences as they arise.

The orders available

On applications for failure to maintain, only periodical payment (secured and unsecured) and lump sum orders may be made. In all other cases, several remedies are available: periodical payments; lump sums; property settlements; and property transfers.[201] Periodical payments need not be payable from the respondent's income; maintenance can be paid from accumulated or borrowed capital.[202] In proceedings on divorce, periodical payment and lump sum orders can require payment to a third party, for example direct payment of school fees.[203] The divorce court can also vary ante- and post-nuptial settlements for the benefit of

---

199 Ibid, s 8(2).

200 We do not address issues regarding the parties' domicile, habitual residence, etc.

201 MCA 1973, ss 23 and 24; CPA 2004, Sch 5, Parts 1 and 2; CA 1989, Sch 1, para 1: see *Phillips v Peace* [2004] EWHC 3180; cf *B v B* [2007] EWHC 789.

202 *SW v RC* [2008] EWHC 73.

203 MCA 1973, s 23(1)(d)–(f); CPA 2004, Sch 5, para 2(d)–(f); the same applies in proceedings for failure to maintain, though not under the DPMCA/CPA Sch 6.

the child, and order sale of property as an adjunct to secured periodical payment, lump sum, and property adjustment orders.[204] None of these additional powers arises under the CA 1989, Sch 1. We examine what each type of order entails in chapter 7.[205]

Who can be made liable for whom?

Orders can be made not only against parents for the benefit of their own children, but also, where the parties are spouses or civil partners, against certain other adults for the benefit of 'children of the family':

> 'child of the family', . . . means—
>
> (a) a child of both of those parties; and
>
> (b) any other child, not being a child who is placed with those parties as foster parents by a local authority or voluntary organisation, who has been treated by both of those parties as a child of their family.[206]

When determining whether a child is a 'child of the family', it is irrelevant that a husband had so treated a child mistakenly believing that he was the father;[207] the court can consider those circumstances in deciding what, if any, order to make. But the definition of 'child of the family' depends on the relevant adults having formalized their relationship: cohabitants have no liability for each other's children.[208]

Who can apply?

In matrimonial proceedings, a current or former spouse or civil partner may apply against the other for an order in relation to a child of the family. Though they may not make an original application in proceedings for failure to maintain, children over 16 may apply for *variation* of existing orders.[209] If granted leave, children of the family may intervene in divorce proceedings to apply for financial relief. The child's guardian,[210] and a person who has (or is entitled to apply for) a child arrangements order naming that person as someone with whom the child is to live[211] may also apply.[212]

A broader range of persons may apply under the CA 1989, Sch 1, which applies whatever the nature of the parents' relationship. Since nearly half of births now involve unmarried parents,[213] this Act potentially has substantial practical importance.[214] It

---

[204] 'Property adjustment' here includes transfers, settlements, and variation of settlements: MCA 1973, s 24A, CPA 2004, Sch 5, Part 3.

[205] A series of cases have considered the use of CA 1989, Sch 1 orders to cover the applicant's legal costs: e.g. *PG v TW (No 1) (Child: Financial Provision: Legal Funding)* [2012] EWHC 1892.

[206] E.g. MCA 1973, s 52; CPA 2004, Sch 5, para 80(2); CA 1989, Sch 1, para 16(2): cognate definition of 'parent'.

[207] *W(RJ) v W(SJ)* [1972] Fam 152.

[208] *T v B* [2010] EWHC 1444.

[209] DPMCA 1978, s 20(12); MCA 1973, s 27(6A); CPA 2004, Sch 5, para 55, and Sch 6, para 39.

[210] CA 1989, s 5.

[211] Ibid, ss 8 and 10(4).

[212] FPR 2010, SI 2010/2955, r 9.10.

[213] ONS (2014c).

[214] *Re P (Child: Financial Provision)* [2003] EWCA Civ 837.

covers disputes arising between spouses, civil partners, cohabitants, or those connected only by shared parenthood; and between parents and other individuals who enjoy certain other legal relationships with the child. A parent, guardian,[215] special guardian,[216] or person with whom a child is to live under a child arrangements order[217] may apply for an order against a parent or, where the applicant is not a parent, from both parents. 'Parent' here includes those in relation to whom a child is a 'child of the family', so spouse or civil partner step-parents may be applicants and respondents.[218] An application may be brought against the primary carer by the non-resident parent in order to cover costs incurred for the child's benefit, such as costs to travel to see the child or to accommodate the child when in the care of the non-resident parent, but these will be unusual cases.[219] A spouse who has a 'clean break' financial settlement on divorce can apply under CA 1989, Sch 1 for the child's benefit, but awards in such cases will be exceptional.[220]

As we have seen, the CSA 1991 gives children no standing to apply for a maintenance calculation for themselves.[221] The opportunities for children to apply under the CA 1989, Sch 1 are limited, and reserved for older teenagers. Children over 18 may in certain circumstances apply for lump sum or periodical payments orders against their parents, but not against step-parents or others. No such application can be made where a periodical payments order was in force when the child attained 16. Children over 16 may, however, apply for variation of existing orders.[222] No children can apply for orders if their parents are living with each other in the same household.[223] They cannot apply for property adjustment orders at all.

The child's age and the duration of orders

Ordinarily, no order for financial provision or for the transfer or settlement of property may be made in favour of children aged 18 or above. The courts have held that while there is no rule against property orders extending into adulthood, they should be made only exceptionally. However, orders may be made to endure beyond 18 (and so beyond the age limit of the CSA 1991[224]) or be made after the child has reached that age if: (i) the child is receiving instruction at an educational establishment or is training for a trade, profession, or vocation; or (ii) there are special circumstances that justify the order.[225] Whilst it is commonplace for orders to last until the end of an undergraduate degree, including a gap year, they will not be made to last beyond that stage, notwithstanding the increasing trend for children to remain at home post-university.[226] *C v F (Disabled Child: Maintenance Orders)*

---

215 CA 1989, s 5.
216 Ibid, s 14A.
217 Ibid, s 8.
218 Ibid, Sch 1, para 16(2).
219 *N v C* [2013] EWHC 399; but see n 196 above regarding maintenance.
220 *PK v BC (Financial Remedies: Schedule 1)* [2012] EWHC 1382.
221 Cf the position in Scotland: CSA 1991, s 7.
222 CA 1989, Sch 1, para 6(4).
223 Ibid, Sch 1, para 2.
224 See discussion in *C v F (Disabled Child: Maintenance Orders)* [1999] 1 FCR 39.
225 DPMCA 1978, s 5; CPA 2004, Sch 6, para 27; MCA 1973, ss 27(6) and 29; CPA 2004, Sch 5, para 49; CA 1989, Sch 1, para 3.
226 *Re N (A Child)* [2009] EWHC 11; *Downing v Downing* [1976] Fam 288.

considered the 'special circumstances' exception in relation to disability, Butler-Sloss LJ observing that:

> It is part of the philosophy of the Children Act that a young person in [the child's] position with a total dependence upon others for the rest of his life should look for continuing financial support from his parents for whatever period may be necessary.[227]

Butler-Sloss and Thorpe LJJ concluded, obiter, that once the child ceased to be a 'qualifying child' for the purposes of the CSA 1991, the restriction on the courts' powers imposed by s 8(8) of that Act—that its periodical payments order could only cover expenses connected with the disability, and not with any other needs—would also cease, freeing the court to make orders for any purpose.

Periodical payments orders terminate on the payer's death.[228] If the parents are living together, payments may cease to be payable or not be ordered at all. While an order may be made for the child's benefit while the parents are living together under some of the 'failure to maintain' jurisdiction and the CA 1989, Sch 1, it will terminate after the parties have lived together, or resumed cohabitation, for over six months.[229]

6.5.4 THE GROUNDS FOR ORDERS AND THE COURTS' DISCRETION

The 'failure to maintain' provisions specify the ground on which orders under those Acts may be made for the child's benefit: that the respondent has failed to provide, or make a proper contribution towards, reasonable maintenance for the child in question.[230] The other legislation does not specify any ground for the exercise of the courts' powers. Nevertheless, the courts tend to confine themselves to providing for the child's 'maintenance', however broadly that term is construed.[231] Each statute sets out a checklist of factors for the courts to consider in exercising their discretion very similar to those applying to financial remedies between spouses on divorce. The checklists are broadly identical, but we highlight differences.[232]

Only in proceedings on divorce is it expressly stated that 'first consideration' must be given to the welfare while a minor of any child of the family.[233] The welfare principle in the CA 1989 does not apply to decisions about children's maintenance,[234] but it has nevertheless been held that the child's welfare is at least a relevant consideration.[235]

---

[227] [1998] 2 FLR 1, 3.

[228] DPMCA 1978, s 5(4); CPA 2004, Sch 6, para 27(6); CA 1989, Sch 1, para 3(3); MCA 1973, s 29(4); and CPA 2004, Sch 5, para 49: save for arrears due.

[229] DPMCA 1978, s 25(1); CPA 2004, Sch 6, para 29; CA 1989, Sch 1, para 3(4).

[230] DPMCA 1978, s 1(b); CPA 2004, Sch 6, para 1; MCA 1973, s 27(1); CPA 2004, Sch 5, para 39(1).

[231] *A v A (Financial Provision for Child)* [1995] 1 FCR 309. CA 1989, Sch 1, para 5 expressly permits lump sums to cover expenses incurred in connection with the child's birth.

[232] DPMCA 1978, s 3; CPA 2004, Sch 6, para 6; MCA 1973, ss 25(1), (3)–(4), and 27(3A); CPA 2004, Sch 5, paras 20 and 22; CA 1989, Sch 1, para 4.

[233] MCA 1973, s 25(1) and CPA 2004, Sch 5, para 20.

[234] See ss 1 and 105, definition of 'upbringing'.

[235] *J v C (Child: Financial Provision)* [1998] 3 FCR 79.

Re P (A Child: Financial Provision) [2003] EWCA Civ 837

THORPE LJ:

44. . . . I would only wish to amplify [that] by saying that welfare must be not just 'one of the relevant circumstances' but, in the generality of cases, a constant influence on the discretionary outcome. I say that because the purpose of the statutory exercise is to ensure for the child of parents who have never married and who have become alienated and combative, support and also protection against adult irresponsibility and selfishness, at least insofar as money and property can achieve those ends.

In deciding whether and, if so, how to exercise their powers under the Acts, the courts must consider all the circumstances,[236] particularly:[237]

- the child's financial needs;
- the child's income, earning capacity (if any), property, and other financial resources;
- in matrimonial proceedings: the current or former spouses/civil partners' income, earning capacity (including that earning capacity which it would be reasonable to expect each party to take steps to acquire), property and other financial resources; their financial needs, obligations, and responsibilities, both now and likely in the foreseeable future;
- under the CA 1989, Sch 1: those same aspects of the parents' financial situation; and, where the applicant is not a parent of the child, the financial situation of that person. But the court is not directed to consider any earning capacity that it would be reasonable to expect a party to take steps to acquire;
- any physical or mental disability of the child (and in matrimonial proceedings of either spouse/civil partner);
- the standard of living enjoyed by the family before: (i) the failure to make reasonable provision for the child (failure to maintain cases); (ii) the breakdown of the marriage/civil partnership (divorce cases). This factor is not listed in the CA 1989, Sch 1, where the parents may never have lived together or with the child;[238]
- the manner in which the child was being, or was expected to be, educated or trained.

Where orders are sought for the benefit of a 'child of the family' who is not in law the respondent's child, the court must also consider:

- whether the respondent assumed any responsibility for the child's maintenance; and, if he did, the extent to and the basis on which he assumed that responsibility; and the length of time during which he discharged that responsibility;
- whether in assuming and discharging that responsibility the respondent did so knowing that the child was not his own;
- the liability of any other person to maintain the child: for example, the child's legal parent, who may be liable to make child support payments.

---

[236] Including egregious conduct: *O v P* [2014] EWHC 2225, [128].
[237] See n 232.
[238] But see *N v D* [2008] 1 FLR 1629.

6.5.5 PRINCIPLES FROM THE CASE LAW

Most reported cases involve extremely wealthy respondents (so-called 'big money' cases) and unmarried parents. In 'ordinary wealth' divorce cases, child support liability generally consumes respondents' free income, and the parties cannot afford to litigate, so very few reported cases address their situation. Capital and property orders, particularly regarding the former matrimonial home, are more likely to be made for the benefit of primary carers than for children, but the children obtain substantial indirect benefit from such orders. By contrast, where the respondent is wealthy and/or the parties were not spouses or civil partners so there is no jurisdiction to adjust capital or make income orders between the adults, orders for the child may be financially feasible and important for the welfare of the child's household.[239] As it does when granting financial remedies on divorce, the court must ensure that the orders made achieve overall fairness for both parties and, where funds are limited, finances may be quite tight for both:[240]

DE v AB [2011] EWHC 3792

BARON J:

46. Neither of these parties seems sufficiently to have considered or expected that a sexual relationship would lead to the birth of a child. However, that is a known consequence. If a child arrives, then parenthood brings with it significant financial and other responsibilities. Both these parties have to make a continuing contribution in that regard for the good of their son. Both will suffer financially because the new circumstances mean that they do not have the freedom and the financial flexibility that they once had. But that is a consequence of their own actions. As adults, they have to bear responsibility for such.

Unwanted births and births to unmarried parents

As the opening of that extract from *DE v AB* suggests, applications for financial provision sometimes prompt respondents to claim that the conception was accidental, the birth unwanted, and the relationship between the parents, and between respondent parent and child, insubstantial.

J v C (Child: Financial Provision) [1998] 3 FCR 79 (Fam Div), 81–3

HALE J:

...[A]lthough para 4(1) of Sch 1 to the 1989 Act tells me to consider all the circumstances, I do not consider that any great weight should be attached either to the circumstances of T's birth or to the length or quality of her [parents'] relationship. There is nothing in the private law provisions to distinguish between different children on such grounds. The policy of the Child Support Act 1991 was that people who had children should support them, whether or

---

[239] Cf Law Com (2006), paras 4.34–4.46 on the under-use of the CA 1989, Sch 1.
[240] *DE v AB* [2011] EWHC 3792, [41].

> not those were wanted children. As a general proposition children should not suffer because their parents are irresponsible or uncaring towards them. I note that there is an example of an order being made against a father who had wanted the mother to have a termination in the case of *Phillips v Peace* [1996] 2 FCR 237....
>
> ...The underlying principle [is] that children should not suffer just because their parents had, for whatever reason, not been married to one another.
>
> Equally of course they should not get more...

The basic objective: meeting the child's needs

The courts view their objective as being simply to cater for the child's needs, however wealthy the respondent parent. By contrast with spouses and civil partners, who can generally claim a form of entitlement to share family assets on divorce,[241] children are merely dependants to be maintained until adulthood.[242] However, in assessing the extent of the child's needs, the courts have regard to the resources and standard of living of the respondent parent (and, where applicable, the standard of living enjoyed by the family during the parents' relationship[243]), taking the view that the child's situation should bear some reasonable resemblance to that of the parent.[244] Determining the extent of the child's 'needs' is an uncertain art.[245] Whilst orders must be 'for the benefit of the child', it is enough for a 'welfare' benefit, rather than a financial benefit, to accrue to the child.[246] So orders may be made transferring property from one parent to the other in order to make it available for the child's occupation with that parent.[247]

Orders are ordinarily intended only to benefit the child during minority or until completion of education, not for life.[248] It would therefore be improper to order an outright transfer of property (e.g. a home), rather than a settlement of that property during the child's dependence. It would similarly be inappropriate to order periodical payments that would not be exhausted in meeting the child's needs during the term of the order.[249]

Indirect benefit for others

These orders may only be made 'for the benefit of the child'. Applicants who were not the respondent's spouse or civil partner cannot obtain financial remedies for their own benefit. However, orders made for the benefit of the child can provide such individuals (and any other children living with them for whom the respondent is not liable[250]) with

---

[241] See 7.5.4.

[242] *A v A (Financial Provision for Child)* [1995] 1 FCR 309; *Kiely v Kiely* [1988] 1 FLR 248; *Re A (A Child)* [2014] EWCA Civ 1577.

[243] *N v D* [2008] 1 FLR 1629, [23].

[244] *J v C (Child: Financial Provision)* [1998] 3 FCR 79, 87.

[245] Gilmore (2004b), 112; compare 'needs' on divorce: see 7.5.2.

[246] This includes legal costs of proceedings taken for the child's benefit: e.g. *PG v TW (Child: Financial Provision: Legal Funding) (No 1)* [2012] EWHC 1892.

[247] *K v K (Minors: Property Transfer)* [1992] 1 WLR 530.

[248] *A v A (Financial Provision for Child)* [1995] 1 FCR 309. Cf *Tavoulareas v Tavoulareas* [1998] 2 FLR 418; criticized by Gilmore (2004b).

[249] *Re P (A Child: Financial Provision)* [2003] EWCA Civ 837, [49], in relation to the carer's allowance.

[250] *Morgan v Hill* [2006] EWCA Civ 1602; cf the child born later in *Phillips v Peace* [2004] EWHC 3180, [11].

substantial indirect benefit. The courts have generally been happy to contemplate such indirect benefit, considering it to be in children's best interests that those living with them enjoy standards of living similar to their own.[251] In particular, the child's need for a carer requires that that carer's needs, particularly regarding accommodation, be considered, but only whilst the child is dependent.[252] Indeed, the non-resident parent may also need accommodation adequate for the child to stay overnight regularly. However, the courts are alert to claims that are, in substance, for the benefit of the adult applicant or her other children rather than the respondent's child.[253] In *Morgan v Hill*, the Court of Appeal emphasized that whilst it was difficult to disentangle the indirect costs (e.g. of housing, running a car, and so on) pertaining to each individual in the household (contrast the identifiable direct costs of food and clothing for each person), it was important in principle not to lose sight of the extent of the respondent's liability. We explore this issue insofar as it relates to the 'carer element' of periodical payments below. It is suggested that where the primary carer has children with different parents, it might be fairest to bring consolidated actions against all respondents and apportion the liability for the children between them.[254]

Property orders

The following extract exemplifies the courts' approach to capital orders, here regarding a child's housing under the CA 1989, Sch 1. As is typical of the reported cases, the respondent was wealthy. Ward J considers the factors in para 4:

A v A (Financial Provision for Child) [1995] 1 FCR 309 (Fam Div), 315–16

WARD J:

The father is so rich he could transfer this property and not even be aware that he had done so. His obligations and responsibilities are to provide for the maintenance and education of his child until she has completed that education, including her tertiary education, and reached independence. There is no special circumstance which imposes on him any moral duty to advance capital or income to her once he has fulfilled that duty. Her financial needs are to be considered, and it is noticeable that they are the "financial needs of the child", which again suggests that adult needs are not ordinarily relevant. The child has no income. She has no physical or mental disability. I must have regard to the manner in which she was being or was expected to be educated or trained, and the implication in those words is once more that the obligation to maintain ceases when that educational training ceases.... There is no special circumstance I can find which would require this father to do more than maintain his daughter until she is independent. I therefore reject her claim for the transfer of the property to her absolutely.

---

[251] *A v A (Financial Provision for Child)* [1995] 1 FCR 309; *J v C (Child: Financial Provision)* [1998] 3 FCR 79.

[252] *Haroutunian v Jennings* (1980) 1 FCR 62; *Re A (A Child)* [2014] EWCA Civ 1577.

[253] *J v C (Child: Financial Provision)* [1998] 3 FCR 79; *Re S (Unmarried Parents: Financial Provision)* [2006] EWCA Civ 479; and in the case of application by non-resident parent: *N v C* [2013] EWHC 399.

[254] [2006] EWCA Civ 1602, [38]–[39].

The judge refused simply to accept an undertaking from the father that he would allow the child to occupy the property: the child needed the security of a beneficial interest in the home, and so made a property settlement order for the child:[255]

> The terms of the trust... should be that the property be conveyed to trustees... to hold the same for A for a term which shall terminate six months after A has attained the age of 18, or six months after she has completed her full-time education, which will include her tertiary education, whichever is latest. I give her that period of six months to find her feet and arrange her affairs. The trustees shall permit her to enjoy a reasonable gap between completing her school education and embarking upon her further education.
>
> I have regard to para. 4(1)(b) which requires me to consider the financial needs, obligations and responsibilities of each parent and also subpara. (c) which requires me to have regard to the financial needs of the child. The mother's obligation is to look after A, and A's financial need is to provide a roof over the head of her caretaker. It is, indeed, [the] father's obligation to provide the accommodation for the living-in help which A needs. Consequently, it must be a term of the settlement that while A is under the control of her mother and thereafter for so long as A does not object, the mother shall have the right to occupy the property to the exclusion of the father and without paying rent therefor, and for the purpose of providing a home and care and support for A.

Periodical payments: the carer's allowance

Where the courts have jurisdiction in relation to periodical payments, for example in 'top-up' cases under s 8(6) of the CSA 1991, and where the available funds are extensive, they include an allowance to cover the needs of the child's carer. This practice was affirmed in the Court of Appeal's first decision under the CA 1989, Sch 1. This extract describes the approach that should be taken in 'big money' cases to capital provision, before turning to the question of maintenance and the carer's allowance. The parents had not married, so the non-resident parent had no responsibility to support the parent with care in her own right. Thorpe LJ first determined what housing and associated lump sum orders were required for furnishings, a car, and so on:

Re P (A Child: Financial Provision) [2003] EWCA Civ 837

THORPE LJ:

47. Those issues settled the judge can proceed to determine what budget the mother reasonably requires to fund her expenditure in maintaining the home and its contents and in meeting her other expenditure external to the home, such as school fees, holidays, routine travel expenses, entertainments, presents, etc. In approaching this last decision, the judge is likely to be assailed by rival budgets... Invariably the applicant's budget hovers somewhere between the generous and the extravagant. Invariably the respondent's budget expresses parsimony.... But it is worth emphasising the trite point that... an order for periodical payments is always variable and will generally have to be revisited to reflect both relevant

---

255 See also *Re P (A Child: Financial Provision)* [2003] EWCA Civ 837, [45].

changes of circumstance and also the factor of inflation. Therefore...the court should discourage undue bickering over budgets. What is required is a broad commonsense assessment. What the court first ordains may have a comparatively brief life before a review is claimed by one or other party.

48. In making this broad assessment how should the judge approach the mother's allowance, perhaps the most emotive element in the periodical payments assessment? The respondent will often accept with equanimity elements within the claim that are incapable of benefiting the applicant (for instance school fees or children's clothing) but payments which the respondent may see as more for the benefit of the applicant than the child are likely to be bitterly resisted. Thus there is an inevitable tension between the two propositions, both correct in law, first that the applicant has no personal entitlement, second that she is entitled to an allowance as the child's primary carer. Balancing this tension may be difficult in individual cases. In my judgment, the mother's entitlement to an allowance as the primary carer (an expression which I stress) may be checked but not diminished by the absence of any direct claim in law.

49. Thus...the court must recognise the responsibility, and often the sacrifice, of the unmarried parent (generally the mother) who is to be the primary carer for the child, perhaps the exclusive carer if the absent parent disassociates from the child. In order to discharge this responsibility the carer must have control of a budget that reflects her position and the position of the father, both social and financial. On the one hand she should not be burdened with unnecessary financial anxiety or have to resort to parsimony when the other parent chooses to live lavishly. On the other hand whatever is provided is there to be spent at the expiration of the year for which it is provided. There can be no slack to enable the recipient to fund a pension or an endowment policy or otherwise to put money away for a rainy day. In some cases it may be appropriate for the court to expect the mother to keep relatively detailed accounts of her outgoings and expenditure in the first and then in succeeding years of receipt. Such evidence would obviously be highly relevant to the determination of any application for either upward or downward variation.

Whilst keeping accounts may be sensible, these observations have been questioned: requiring that accounts be regularly reported to the respondent may be unhelpful, intrusive, a cause of friction, and so counterproductive.[256] As to the question of making savings, it was noted in *Re C (Financial Provision)* that the primary carer should be allowed to save up for recurrent expenditure which arises less frequently than annually: it is *personal* saving which is barred.[257]

Thorpe LJ made the following observations in quantifying the carer element (note that the father had 'unlimited means' and the court had approved budgets of £1 million to acquire central London accommodation for the child and mother and £100,000 for its furnishing):

42.... [In] *A v A* [above, decided in 1995], in explaining his quantification of an allowance for the mother's care Ward J said:

"I bear in mind a broad range of imprecise information from the extortionate demands (but excellent service) of Norland nannies, to au pair girls and mother's helps, from calculations in

---

[256] *Re P* [2003] EWCA Civ 837, [75] per May LJ; *Re C (Financial Provision)* [2007] 2 FLR 13; cf accounting for the expenditure of a lump sum paid for a specific purpose: *Re N (A Child)* [2009] EWHC 11, [32]–[33].
[257] [2007] 2 FLR 13.

personal injury and fatal accident claims and from the notice-boards in the employment agencies I pass daily. I allow £8,000 under this head. It is almost certainly much less than the father would have to pay were he to be employing staff, but to allow more would be—or would be seen to be—paying maintenance to the former mistress who has no claim in her own right to be maintained."

43. I cannot agree with that reservation. I believe that a more generous approach to the calculation of the mother's allowance is not only permissible but also realistic. Nor would I have regard to calculations in either personal injury or fatal accident claims. It seems to me that such cross-references only risk to complicate what is an essentially broad-brush assessment to be taken by family judges with much expertise and experience in the specialist field of ancillary relief....

54. In making an independent assessment [of the periodical payments order] in the exercise of my own discretion, I have regard to the likely cost of running the home that the trustees will buy for the mother and L [the child]. I have regard to the fact that the mother is to be L's primary carer. I would not relate that to the cost of a Norland nanny. That would be to demean the mother's role. Mothers provide 24-hour care for children. That level of care would be difficult to buy in, even for a father as rich and resourceful as this. In the real world nannies are entitled to days off, weekends off and holidays.... I would take a broad-brush figure of £70,000 per annum from which the father is entitled to deduct the amount of state benefits that the mother receives for L. Of course it is easy to say that that represents a liability of approximately £1,500 a week for a two-year-old child. But that is a distortion of the reality that £70,000 is a budget to enable the mother to run the home for [the child] and to provide her additional needs....

As May LJ noted in *Re P*, cases involving sums such as these are atypical and so should not be used as a benchmark for future cases.[258]

In *F v G (Child: Financial Provision)*, a full carer's allowance was made even though the mother was working full-time. The court considered that she should be able to choose whether to spend that allowance on hiring child-care and continue to work, securing her own financial future, or alternatively to work part-time and care for the child herself.[259] This was not considered to offend *Re P*'s prohibition on any 'slack' being made available to the parent with care: any savings would derive from her own earnings, should she choose to work.

A carer's allowance can also be justified in relation to teenage children, even when at university: they still need someone to provide a home for them, and can be as demanding in terms of a carer's time and attention, albeit very differently, as younger children.[260]

GW v RW (Financial Provision: Departure from Equality) exemplifies a different approach to fixing periodical payments.[261] This was a big money case where the court had full jurisdiction over child maintenance because the parent with care and children were not habitually resident in the UK. The parents were divorcing, so their financial and property disputes had been dealt with under the MCA 1973; the wife, broadly speaking, was awarded 40

---

258 See also *Re S* [2006] EWCA Civ 479.
259 [2004] EWHC 1848, [44]–[54].
260 *N v D* [2008] 1 FLR 1629, [24]–[25]; *H v C* [2009] EWHC 1527.
261 See also *E v C (Calculation of Child Maintenance)* [1996] 1 FLR 472; *A v M* [2005] EWHC 1721; *Re M-M (Schedule 1 Provision)* [2014] EWCA Civ 276.

per cent of the substantial assets. We examine s 4(10) of the CSA 1991, referred to in this extract, below at 6.6.1. The judge identified two main principles:

GW v RW [2003] EWHC 611

NICHOLAS MOSTYN QC (sitting as a deputy High Court judge):

74. ...First, I am of the view that the appropriate starting point for a child maintenance award should almost invariably be the figure thrown up by the...child support rules. The Government's express policy in making awards of child maintenance susceptible to abrogation and replacement by a maintenance calculation by the CSA (see 4(10)(aa) Child Support Act 1991) was that child maintenance orders should be negotiated:

'...in the shadow of the CSA. All parties will know that either parent can turn to the CSA in future, and that it will therefore be sensible to determine child maintenance broadly in line with CSA assessment rates.' [See DSS (1999), ch 8]

If a child maintenance order, whether made by consent or after a contest, is markedly at variance with the calculation under the [child support] regime then there will be a high temptation for one or other party after the order has been in force for a year, and after giving two months' notice, to approach the CSA [as it then was] for a calculation. Quite apart from the obvious acrimony that this would engender, a calculation in a different amount to the figure originally negotiated or awarded may cast doubt on the fairness of the original ancillary relief settlement between the parties, leading to further litigation. These spectres should be avoided at all costs.

75. The second principle is that notwithstanding that the income of the parent with care is disregarded in the calculation of child support...it is reasonable to expect the parent with care who has received a substantial share of the parties' assets to contribute to the support of the children.... It should be noted that the Government justified the omission of the parent with care's income in the new formula on the ground that she would from her own resources be making a substantial contribution to the support of the children....

77. Having regard to these principles my decision is as follows:

77.1. I am satisfied that there should be some increase on the starting point of the maximum CSA calculation that would be applicable here. The husband has an income well in excess of the capped amount of [£2,000 per week—the then ceiling for the CSA]. I am also of the view that where a proportionate division of the main assets has been effected [60% to H, 40% to W] then that proportion should inform the division of the child maintenance costs....I therefore award general maintenance of [60% of those costs] per child per annum payable quarterly in advance...to continue until each respective child attains 18 years of age or completes full time tertiary education if later....Once a child enters tertiary education the payments will be made, as H has suggested, as to two-thirds to the child direct and one-third to W.

77.2. In addition H will pay all the educational costs of the children, to include reasonable extras until the conclusion of full-time tertiary education.

77.3. H will also pay all the costs of travel for contact, to include the cost of an accompanying nanny until the younger child's seventh birthday.

The child support formula can legitimately and sensibly provide a *starting point* for determining the level of court-ordered periodical payments, not least as a guide to determining the extent of the child's needs, as measured by reference to the non-resident parent's living standard (insofar as that is roughly reflected in his income level). However, the courts are required to have regard to a wider range of circumstances than that, and so must be free to depart from the formula where fairness requires it.

6.5.6 ENFORCEMENT OF COURT ORDERS

The courts have broad powers to enforce their own orders, corresponding with those available in matrimonial and civil partnership cases.[262]

6.6 'FAMILY-BASED ARRANGEMENTS' AND OTHER PRIVATE ORDERING

A key recommendation of Henshaw was that all parents should be free and encouraged to make their own arrangements for child support, without the intervention of a public authority. Various provisions in the CSA 1991 and regulations outlined above support this policy:

- s 9(2A) specifically empowers the state to encourage private maintenance agreements, and to explore that possibility with a person with care before she makes any application to CMS;
- s 4(2A) allows the state to collect maintenance for the person with care only if either the non-resident parent agrees or it is satisfied that payment will otherwise not be made;
- the application fee for a formal CMS maintenance calculation; and further charges for collection of child support, levied against both parties.

In this section, we consider the legal framework within which such private arrangements are made. We consider the policy implications of the new emphasis on private ordering at 6.7.2.

6.6.1 PRIVATE ORDERING OF MAINTENANCE

The statutory provisions governing the legal effect of private ordering undertaken in relation to child maintenance (i.e. matters falling within the jurisdiction of CMS) are quite difficult to follow, but their overall effect—which we explain below—is clear:

Child Support Act 1991

4...

(10) No application [to CMS] may be made at any time under this section with respect to a qualifying child or any qualifying children if—

    (a) there is in force a written maintenance agreement made before 5th April 1993, or a maintenance order made before [6th April 2002], in respect of that child or those children and the person who is, at that time, the non-resident parent; or

---

262 See 7.3.6.

(aa) a maintenance order made on or after [6th April 2002] is in force in respect of them, but has been so for less than the period of one year beginning with the date on which it was made;...

8...

(11) In this Act "maintenance order", in relation to any child, means an order which requires the making or securing of periodical payments to or for the benefit of the child and which is made under—

(a) Part II of the Matrimonial Causes Act 1973;

(b) the Domestic Proceedings and Magistrates' Courts Act 1978;...

(e) Schedule 1 to the Children Act 1989;

(ea)Schedule 5, 6 or 7 to the Civil Partnership Act 2004; or

(f) any other prescribed enactment,[263] and includes any order varying or reviving such an order.

9 Agreements about maintenance

(1) In this section "maintenance agreement" means any agreement for the making, or for securing the making, of periodical payments by way of maintenance...to or for the benefit of any child.

(2) Nothing in this Act shall be taken to prevent any person from entering into a maintenance agreement....

(3) Subject to section 4(10)(a)..., the existence of a maintenance agreement shall not prevent any party to the agreement, or any other person, from applying for a maintenance calculation with respect to any child to or for whose benefit periodical payments are to be made or secured under the agreement.

(4) Where any agreement contains a provision which purports to restrict the right of any person to apply for a maintenance calculation, that provision shall be void...[264]

Parents are free to make 'family-based arrangements' (as the government calls them), which may be theoretically enforceable as contracts.[265] However, like separation agreements made between spouses on divorce,[266] the existence of such agreements cannot prevent either party at any time applying to CMS for a maintenance calculation. That calculation then replaces the agreement, which is no longer enforceable.[267]

Parties who want greater certainty should enshrine their agreement in a consent order. Consent orders made before 6 April 2002 are binding for their duration; neither party can undermine the order by applying to CMS. But the status of consent orders made since then is more complicated. Whilst theoretically capable of variation and enforcement for their duration, once the order has been in place for one year, either party is free to apply to CMS

---

[263] Child Support (Maintenance Arrangements and Jurisdiction) Regulations 1992, SI 1992/2645, reg 2.
[264] Further subsections relate to courts' powers to vary certain maintenance agreements.
[265] *Darke v Strout* [2003] EWCA Civ 176.
[266] See 7.7.2.
[267] CSA 1991, s 10(2); SI 1992/2645, reg 4.

for a maintenance calculation which will supplant what the parties agreed and deprive the court of jurisdiction.[268] So, for their first year of operation, consent orders offer more security than mere agreements; but after that year, they are as vulnerable as agreements to CMS's intervention.[269] The bar in s 4(10)(aa) on applying for child support during the first year of a consent order for maintenance does not apply to orders made for either educational fees or special expenses associated with the child's disability: such orders are designed to deal with matters other than the child's basic maintenance.[270]

It follows that parties' ability to avoid using CMS through private ordering requires ongoing, mutual consent. As was observed in *GW v RW (Financial Provision: Departure from Equality)*,[271] parties seeking to avoid CMS's involvement should consider what the CSA 1991 formula would provide if it were applied to their case. Then neither party will have any incentive to apply to CMS. A court invited to enshrine in a consent order a maintenance agreement which departed substantially from the calculation that CMS might be expected to make is likely to ask careful questions before making the order.

The government rejected Henshaw's recommendation that the 12-month rule rendering consent orders vulnerable to attack via CMS be dropped, leaving such cases entirely within the court system. Others argued for a return to an entirely court-based system, in which child maintenance would be addressed alongside all the other issues over which the courts have jurisdiction on relationship breakdown.[272] But others were concerned that the emphasis on court-based private ordering may be detrimental to children and primary carers where there was an imbalance of power, and costly to those who cannot readily access the courts.[273] The government firmly opposed both ideas:

DWP, *Report on the Child Maintenance White Paper: Reply by the Government,* **Cm 7062** (London: TSO, 2007b)

7.1 ...The Government wants to give parents the choice of resolving child maintenance either by private agreement, or by recourse to a straightforward and transparent administrative process. It is the Government's view that providing a further parallel State child maintenance system operating on very different principles and with the ability to set very different levels of child maintenance would add a further level of complexity that would not, for the vast majority of clients, lead to a better service.

8.1 ....The 12-month rule ensures that Consent Orders contain fair and consistent levels of child maintenance and provides parents with a route back into the assessment, collection and enforcement services of C-MEC if their order breaks down. Removal of the 12-month rule would keep parents locked into the court system and would enable the courts to make awards that were not consistent with the formula.

8.2 We want parents to agree fair and sustainable child maintenance arrangements, and to ensure that, if agreements do break down or circumstances change, children can continue

---

[268] Ibid, s 10(1) and reg 3.

[269] Practitioners seek to avoid this rule by use of 'Christmas orders': periodical payments orders for the benefit of children expressed to start and end on Christmas Day each year, only to be automatically replaced by a new such order: Resolution (2009), 138. No reported decision has yet adjudicated on their effectiveness.

[270] Child Support Act 1995, s 18(6).

[271] [2003] EWHC 611, [74].

[272] Pirrie (2006).

[273] CPAG (2006).

to receive maintenance because their parents will still have the opportunity to access the services provided by C-MEC.

One of the faults of the past was that courts authorised clean-break settlements leaving children stranded in poverty without any ongoing child maintenance. The Government does not want to return to this past scenario and the 12-month rule appears to be effectively discouraging this type of settlement.

The government promised to explore with stakeholders ways of improving the interface between family court and CMS to help families resolve all issues smoothly.

6.6.2 PRIVATE ORDERING OF OTHER FINANCIAL ISSUES FOR CHILDREN

Parents are free to reach private agreements regarding financial and property provision falling outside CMS's jurisdiction for the benefit of children: for example, an agreement to hold a house on trust for the child and primary carer to occupy, or regarding school fees. Again, parents may simply conclude an agreement or—for greater certainty—obtain a consent order. The latter option is fully binding—and variable—like any other order.[274] An agreement not so formalized may be binding as a contract, save that the courts' powers over the matters for which they have jurisdiction cannot be ousted by agreement. Either party may therefore apply to court for provision different from that agreed, or ask the court to vary the agreement either because of a change of circumstances or because the agreement 'does not contain proper financial arrangements with respect to the child'.[275] The Court of Appeal held in *Morgan v Hill* that the same principles apply whichever route is taken.[276] The applicant need only show lack of proper financial arrangements; no higher threshold of inadequacy need be crossed. But any court order varying or departing from what had been agreed must be just having regard to all the circumstances, and the existence and terms of the agreement are a 'very important circumstance'.[277] This approach, similar to that taken to agreements made between spouses on divorce, discourages applications made merely because parties become dissatisfied with their bargain.

6.7 POLICY QUESTIONS RELATING TO FINANCIAL SUPPORT OF CHILDREN

The law relating to financial provision for children raises several important policy questions. In this section, we explore five issues: child support as a matter of children's rights or parents' responsibilities; public intervention, family privacy, and private ordering; the relevance of legal and social parenthood to child support liability; the theoretical basis of child support formulae; and the contrast between rules and discretion as tools for determining the extent of financial responsibility for children.

---

[274] See 7.7.1.
[275] CA 1989, Sch 1, para 10; MCA 1973, s 35.
[276] [2006] EWCA Civ 1602, [34].
[277] Ibid, [28]; cf *Edgar v Edgar* [1980] 1 WLR 1410, discussed at 7.7.2.

6.7.1 CHILDREN'S RIGHTS OR PARENTS' RESPONSIBILITIES?

Key government papers on child support have had child-centred titles: 'Children Come First', 'Children First: a new approach to child support', 'Children's Rights and Parents' Responsibilities'. The Henshaw Report asserted that 'children have a right to appropriate support', though also used the language of 'welfare'.[278] Various questions arise when attempting to formulate a rights-based approach to financial provision for children, not least: what is the content of the right and against whom is it exercisable? Readers may wish to refer to the extracts at 8.5.2 from the theoretical work of Eekelaar and others on whom Nick Wikeley relies in developing his rights-based approach:

N. Wikeley, *Child Support: Law and Policy* (Oxford: Hart Publishing, 2006a), 8–10

[C]hildren's basic interests mean that children have a right that their essential needs for food, shelter and clothing are satisfied. This right may be conceptualised in two parallel and complementary ways. First, it might be characterised as a fundamental human right, which is vested in children by virtue of their membership of the wider community and irrespective of their own parents' particular circumstances. In the United Kingdom, the availability of child benefit as a universal[279] social security benefit may be seen as a tangible manifestation of this principle, in that it reflects a (modest) contribution by society at large to assist all parents (for the most part) in meeting the costs of raising their children. The resource implications for the state of the child's fundamental human right to support may be more extensive in some circumstances: [e.g. orphans]. Secondly, the child's right to support might be construed as a correlative claim-right, in the sense that failure to satisfy those needs would amount to a breach of duty by an individual subject to corresponding obligations. The decision to impose such a duty on a particular individual – for example, the child's parent(s) – will be the outcome of a process of weighing up a range of considerations drawn from the realms of moral insight and social policy. These factors will also influence the priority which is accorded within society to the child's correlative right to (private) child support, as against the contribution made by (public) child support.

One undoubted benefit of such a twin-track approach to understanding the child's right to support is that it would appear to command widespread popular support. A further advantage of this framework is its universality in that it is not predicated on family breakdown; in principle it applies just as much to children who live in intact families as to those whose parents have separated (or indeed whose parents have never lived together at all). Yet in practice...the state is inhibited from seeking to regulate the distribution of resources within the private domain of the intact family. For this reason, the problems of identifying and quantifying a child's basic needs remain largely hidden from view. It is the public fact of separation that throws these questions into sharp relief: even if we assume that child support is first and foremost a call on parental income, how do we define a child's basic needs?

The options range from securing a minimum, uniform subsistence level of support for all children, or relating maintenance to the standard of living of the particular family, an

278 Henshaw (2006), 2; see also Hutton (2006).
279 Higher rate taxpayers no longer enjoy this benefit.

approach which gets further from the needs-based paradigm and so from a fundamental human right:

[I]t may be possible to resolve this dilemma by returning to Eekelaar's analysis of children's rights in terms of basic, developmental and autonomy interests. Applying this taxonomy, we might argue that children enjoy a fundamental human right to child support in terms of having their basic living needs met, and that these are to be satisfied by a combination of public and private resource (the precise balance between those two sources to be determined by both value judgments and social policy considerations). On top of this, we might also contend that children have at the very least a legitimate expectation that they will benefit from the standard of living enjoyed by both their parents, irrespective of with which parent they actually happen to reside. This is, admittedly, a question of values and political choices rather than fundamental human rights. Obviously, the state itself cannot fund such expectations... One may, however, suggest that it is not unreasonable for the state to create the legal structures within which such expectations may be realised. The nomenclature of legitimate expectations, rather than rights, is deliberate, in that it implies that such expectations may be subject to compromise where there are other compelling interests to take into account. Its importance, however, lies in the message that child support is not simply a question of ensuring that food is put on the table and clothes on the child's back. Rather, child support is about improving the child's overall life chances – a matter in which society at large has a considerable interest and investment.

Current English law cannot readily be explained in rights-based terms, notwithstanding Baroness Hale's speech in the *Kehoe* case[280] and the radical change in the state's interest in recovery of child support post-CMOPA 2008. Pre-CMOPA, when the state was the principal beneficiary of child support in public law cases, the notion that this was a child's rights measure was problematic.[281] But even now that child support fully supplements children's household income, the matter remains doubtful. There is no reference in governmental policy documents to the UNCRC's guarantees.[282] The legislation does not conceptualize financial provision as a children's rights issue: attempts to affirm the child's right to maintenance on the face of CMOPA 2008 failed.[283] As we have seen, children have no right to apply to CMS and limited opportunities to apply to court for financial provision. It was held in *Treharne v Secretary of State for Work and Pensions* that Article 8 created no economic right to receive regular, reasonable maintenance:[284] the right to respect for family life is concerned to guard against impairment of the 'love, trust, confidence, mutual dependence and unrestrained social intercourse which are the essence of family life',[285] and the right to respect for private life to protect 'the sphere of personal and sexual autonomy'. While family and private life may be tougher as a result (in that case) of the state's failure to recover unpaid maintenance, that 'cannot be said to affect the core values attached to those concepts'.[286]

---

[280] *R (Kehoe) v Secretary of State for Work and Pensions* [2005] UKHL 48: see Wikeley (2006b), p 399 above.

[281] Parker (1991).

[282] Henricson and Bainham (2005), 44.

[283] E.g. Hansard HL Deb, vol 698, cols GC275–80, 29 January 2008.

[284] [2008] EWHC 3222, [19]–[20], [29], [30].

[285] Ibid, [24], quoting from *M v Secretary of State for Work and Pensions* [2006] UKHL 11, [5] per Lord Bingham.

[286] Ibid, [31].

The new focus on private ordering leaves children dependent on parents' actions: whether maintenance is paid at all, in what form and amount, depends on adults' agreement or on the person with care applying to CMS or court. CMOPA 2008's reinstatement of family privacy in this sphere, discussed at 6.7.2, detracts from any notion that the child has an independent right to be maintained. As Stephen Parker has observed, if anyone has a right here it is the person with care[287]—but even that right is doubtful after *Kehoe*. Moreover, it is perhaps an odd fundamental human right which applies only to the children of parents who are living apart:

S. Parker, 'Child Support in Australia: Children's Rights or Public Interest?', (1991) 5 *International Journal of Law and the Family* 24, 55

What particular class of children is intended as the class of right-holder? It cannot be children in one-parent families because, for example, a child whose father has died or disappeared is not covered by the Scheme. The obvious counter to this is that the putative right is to share in *parental* income and that the establishment of a guaranteed maintenance scheme for *all* children (which would belong to the more contestable class of welfare rights) was never intended. Whilst this might be true, it is difficult to see what exactly the child gains in insisting that the *parent* provides the money,[288] when set alongside the advantage of simply having the benefit of that amount of money from somewhere. A Scheme more obviously in line with this theory of children's rights would guarantee to all children the same sort of income as in the normal case [of children living with two parents] but quite separately institute a reimbursement mechanism for those absent parents who can be tracked down.[289]

It may be more appropriate to focus on the second part of the title of the government's 1999 paper: 'Parents' Responsibilities'. Indeed, more recent titles place the emphasis here—for example, 'Strengthening families, promoting parental responsibility'.[290] Rebecca Bailey-Harris's comments on the Australian system are apposite to the UK context:

R. Bailey-Harris, 'Child Support: Is the Right the Wrong One?', (1992) 6 *International Journal of Law and the Family* 169, 171

[A]rguably *any* rights analysis is inappropriate: the scheme is more properly viewed as being based on obligation ie the enforcement of parental *obligations* to support their children. The language employed in the [Australian legislation—compare CSA 1991, s 1] is of symbolic significance: it is framed entirely in terms of parental duty. It is not suggested that an obligations analysis is necessarily less capable of promoting the child's interests than a rights analysis;[291] nevertheless the two approaches must be recognized as conceptually distinct.

---

287 Parker (1991), 53–5.
288 Cf Altman (2003), Eekelaar (1991a).
289 Compare the Finer Committee proposals (DHSS (1974)) for a guaranteed maintenance allowance for all lone-parent families: Lewis (1998) and Douglas (2000a).
290 DWP (2011).
291 See O'Neill (1992).

> If the Child Support Scheme is to be analyzed in obligation terms, the nature of the parental obligation it creates merits analysis. It arises from procreation and not from nurturing; it is not necessary for a liable parent to have lived with the custodian. It is an obligation which may exist without any correlative benefit..., the legislation having set its face squarely against any necessary link between access [i.e. time spent by the non-resident parent with the child] and financial support.

But while 'parental responsibility' has been in the foreground of child support debates, its meaning has changed over time. Margaret Thatcher was concerned about the irresponsibility of feckless fathers who paid nothing towards their children's upbringing, but the latest reforms adopt a rather different approach. The meaning of 'parental responsibility' here does not correspond with the term as used in s 3 of the CA 1989, discussed in chapter 10, not least because child support is payable by 'parents' whether or not they have 'parental responsibility' (as defined by s 3) for the child. The concept is being deployed here in a wider sense[292] which contains echoes of the sort of 'responsibility' which features in divorce law and policy debates.[293] Just as government wishes spouses to 'divorce responsibly', so it is desirous that parents make 'responsible' arrangements for child maintenance and act 'responsibly' by endeavouring to make private agreements rather than by relying on the state to do it for them.[294] And so we see a shift also in the nature of the state's role here: not 'government'—strictly enforcing legal duties in all cases—but 'governance'—seeking to nudge[295] private individuals' behaviour to conform to a desirable norm.[296]

However, just as it is questionable whether divorcing couples would use a 'period of reflection and consideration' in the responsible manner intended by divorce policy-makers, so it is doubtful to what extent parents will (be able to) reach private arrangements for child maintenance that provide a proper level of financial support— and so contribute to child poverty targets—without a more assertive role for the state. The rhetoric of 'parental responsibility' may be rather empty. But if the child support regime is as weak on parental responsibility as it is on children's rights, then what is it about? Some might argue that it is driven by pragmatic, operational efficiency concerns of the state, and not by rights, interests, or concerns of the individuals involved, least of all the child.[297]

6.7.2 PUBLIC AND PRIVATE

The dichotomy between public and private spheres, and the justification for state (public) intervention in family (private) life, is a prevalent theme in family law.[298] Several issues pertaining to that theme arise in relation to financial provision for children: the state's roles in intact and separated families; the nature of the privacy afforded to families; and the impact of family privacy and private ordering on vulnerable family members.

---

[292] Cf Fox Harding (1991a), (1991b), and Eekelaar (1991c).
[293] See chapter 5.
[294] Cf discussion of this theme at 5.8.1.
[295] See the government's so-called 'Nudge Unit', the Behavioural Insights Team, applying theories from behavioural economics and psychology to public policy and services: <www.gov.uk/government/organisations/behavioural-insights-team>.
[296] Compare Smart's analysis of divorce reforms at p 357 above.
[297] Fortin (2009b), 354; Wikeley (2007b).
[298] See 1.2.7.

Protecting the private sphere

Financial provision cannot be sought for or by children living with both parents. Only where one or both parents live apart from the child or are severing their legal relationship does the law offer any remedy. The private realm of the nuclear family is immune from state interference. But we must beware of viewing family law in purely negative terms: in *defining* what is 'dysfunctional' and therefore warrants legal intervention, the law implicitly promotes 'accepted', and so private, family forms and behaviours.[299] The non-intervention of law in intact families has implications for the status and rights of children.

A. Diduck, *Law's Families* (London: Butterworths, 2003), 166

When children and parents live in the same household, the law says very little about how they carry out their financial obligations to each other. It is clear, however, that children have no right to share in the overall family wealth, but simply the right to be supported during their dependence....Law thus does not assume democracy or children's economic 'citizenship' within the family, but rather relies upon an idea of children's status to endorse their (economic) dependency.

This can produce strange inequalities. For example, the restrictions on children's right to apply against their own parents may place the children of separated parents in a stronger position than those living with both parents. While children of divorced parents may apply for support during university, children from intact families may not, even if their parents are not supporting them adequately, and even though their eligibility for student loans and grants is generally determined by reference to parental resources.[300]

Pre-CMOPA 2008, the public/private line was drawn very differently where the parent with care was on benefits. The state actively intervened in family life to recoup welfare benefits paid out from child support received, requiring parents with care to cooperate in this exercise despite the very limited personal benefit (up to £10 per week) that would accrue to them in consequence. Meanwhile, the privacy of 'middle class' families not reliant on state support was preserved, not required to engage with the CSA regime unless one party wished to do so. The radical reforms effected by CMOPA 2008, not only removing compulsion in benefit cases and creating a full maintenance disregard, but also abolishing the liable relative rule as it applied to children, considerably reinforce the privacy of all families.

A limited form of privacy?

However, the privacy available is somewhat limited. As we saw at 6.6.1, on the face of it, the law gives parents good reason both to fix periodical payments at levels prescribed by the CSA formula and also to view periodical payment, so calculated, as the only—or at least the primary—means of discharging the child support obligation. Some parents might have preferred to do this some other way in order to achieve a clean break:[301] that is, to make capital transfers now in lieu of maintenance and so terminate the parties' financial

---

299 O'Donovan (1985).
300 Education (Student Support) Regulations 2011, SI 2011/1986, Sch 4; Maclean and Eekelaar (1997), 43.
301 See 7.6.

relationship.[302] But because private ordering over maintenance cannot be guaranteed to stick beyond the first year of any consent order enshrining such an agreement, non-resident parents may be unwilling to make such settlements. On this view, parents should take full account of potential CMS support obligations when negotiating other aspects of their financial settlement on divorce. 'Private ordering' so understood seems to have (limited) procedural rather than substantive content: the parties' freedom is to behave amicably within the substantive framework set down by the law, not to agree their own terms.

But in promoting 'family-based arrangements', the state is sending parents mixed signals. The CM Options website encourages such arrangements in the following terms:[303]

> The most important thing about family-based arrangements . . . is that you and the other parent can decide between yourselves what, when and how you will both support your child. This can mean fewer arguments about money, and may also help you work together in other ways, which is usually in children's best interests.

The site goes on to suggest various ways in which the non-resident parent might pay, including 'a larger "lump sum" at various points in the child's life'.[304] While it is suggested that some parents find it easiest to base their agreement on the CSA formula, no mention is made of the fact that arrangements taking a different approach are vulnerable to being upset by an application to CMS for a formal calculation by either party. The freedom of family-based arrangements may prove to be something of a trap for the unwary (and uninformed) in such cases.[305]

As we saw earlier, if parents do apply to CMS, they cede even procedural privacy: enforcement falls entirely into the hands of the state.[306] Once the state has been engaged, the family moves itself into the public sphere and so loses control. But CMS has no power to enforce privately negotiated maintenance arrangements. Parents with an agreement (whether a mere contract or one enshrined in a consent order) must therefore use the courts' more limited enforcement powers, while remaining vulnerable to the possibility that the other party may unilaterally shift the case into the public sphere by applying to CMS for a maintenance calculation.[307] The lack of reliable enforcement mechanism for family-based agreements may discourage parents with care from trying to reach agreement instead of applying to CMS (though see the discussion in the next section regarding the impact of fees).[308] The government justified its policy on the basis that parents whose private arrangement fails should—on payment of an application fee—have easy access to CMS, which, it is said, will provide 'swift intervention'. In echoes of past child support debates, the new administrative body was repeatedly portrayed in the parliamentary debates as hyper-efficient, by contrast (at least implicitly) with the courts to which parties might otherwise have to turn (and get

---

[302] This had been common pre-CSA 1991: *R (Kehoe) v Secretary of State for Work and Pensions* [2005] UKHL 48, [64] extracted above, p 370. For the problems encountered when the CSA 1991 was implemented, see *Crozier v Crozier* [1994] Fam 114; *Smith v McInerney* [1994] 2 FLR 1077, and the introduction of a special variation ground for such cases in 1995.

[303] <www.cmoptions.org/en/family/>.

[304] <www.cmoptions.org/en/family/what-to-include.asp>.

[305] No variation ground exists to accommodate such cases, cf the old variation ground to achieve fair outcomes for clean break settlements made pre-CSA 1991.

[306] *R (Kehoe) v Secretary of State for Work and Pensions* [2005] UKHL 48.

[307] See 6.6.1.

[308] Wikeley (2007b), 446–7.

'stuck') if the 12-month rule relating to enforcement of consent orders were abolished.[309] It remains to be seen whether CMS will perform any better than its ill-fated predecessors: much will depend on the size and nature of its caseload, the transition of existing cases to the new scheme, and the effectiveness of its IT systems.

So, child support is privatized insofar as liability rests with private individuals and family-based arrangements are strongly encouraged (despite their legally insecure foundations), but 'publicized' insofar as the state, in theory, ultimately controls nearly all aspects of that liability. This undermines what one commentator describes as the 'important principle of autonomy for parents in whom the state has no direct financial interest (other than the raising of taxes)'.[310]

Whose privacy? The dangers of private ordering

Private ordering does not come without dangers. Most fundamentally, it has been argued that privatizing child support—making child maintenance the primary responsibility of private individuals rather than the state—ensures women's dependence on men.[311] When parents with care on benefit were obliged to participate in recovery of child support, the dysfunctional, fatherless family was forced by the state to 'reconnect' via the enforcement of financial obligations.[312] However, a greater danger may arise now that private ordering is the preferred route and application to CMS depends entirely on private action and ability to pay the fee.

Freeing parents to make their own arrangements does not necessarily mean that satisfactory—or any—child support will be paid. Private ordering brings the danger that outcomes will be dictated by the preferences of the more powerful party,[313] particularly where there is an imbalance of power or information[314] between them. It is striking that a survey of separated parents just before the policy changes found that parents with care who were using the CSA to obtain maintenance were much less enthusiastic than non-resident parents about the move to private agreements.[315] If a non-resident parent does not want to pay, or to pay at the level requested by the parent with care, he may just refuse to reach any such agreement. The onus will then be on the parent with care to remove the dispute from the private sphere by applying to CMS.

The government was confident that offering full information and support to parents with care would empower them to seek the child maintenance to which they are entitled, if not by agreement then via CMS. But there is an important distinction between simply providing information and support, and providing *independent advice* tailored to the circumstances of each family. The controversial introduction of the £20 application fee[316] only increases the

---

309 E.g. Hansard HL Deb, col GC525, 5 February 2008; HC Public Bill Committee, cols 246–7, 9 October 2007; and see extract above at p 419 from DWP (2007b).

310 Mostyn (1999), 97.

311 Lewis (1998), 275.

312 Diduck (1995), 539.

313 Work and Pensions Select Committee (2007), para 179; see also Hansard, Public Bill Committee, col 49 (Nick Wikeley) and cols 70, 72 (Janet Allbeson) 17 July 2007; Hansard HL Deb, cols GC382–3. On factors impacting on behaviour around child support, see Andrews et al (2011).

314 Parents negotiating privately do not have the benefit of courts' powers to require disclosure.

315 Wikeley et al (2008).

316 The original proposal of a £100 fee suffered a spectacular parliamentary defeat, led by former Conservative Lord Chancellor, Lord Mackay during the Report stage on the Welfare Reform Bill 2012.

difficulties. In this extract, Gingerbread—an NGO providing expert advice, practical support, and campaigning for single parents—outlines the problems.

Gingerbread, *Government Plans for Child Maintenance:* Gingerbread *Briefing* (2011)

8.... Voluntary agreements can work well. For example, families with a voluntary agreement are more likely to receive the full amount of child maintenance on time than those receiving maintenance through the CSA (69 per cent compared to 57 per cent). But a moment's reflection reveals the obvious: that if parents are in agreement, by definition the money is more likely to be paid. The success figures for those with voluntary arrangements are always likely to be good, because where an agreement breaks down, the parent with care is likely to move from a voluntary arrangement to using the CSA instead. It is not the fact that an arrangement is voluntary which makes it work; rather this is down to the circumstances of the parents who entered into the agreement.

9. Research indicates that only some parents are likely to be able to make successful voluntary arrangements for maintenance, and that their success is associated with certain characteristics. Analysis shows, for example, that private agreements are less likely where the mother and father have never lived together, or they separated some time ago. Factors shown to facilitate successful private agreements include:

- Amicable relations between the parents...
- Higher household incomes...
- The parent with care being in work...
- A continuing engagement of the non-resident parent with the children...

10. The profile of parents who use the Child Support Agency is considerably different. Their circumstances are likely to make achieving private voluntary arrangements less likely.

- Only 28 per cent of parents with care using the CSA reported friendly relations with the other parent, compared to 41 per cent of parents not using the CSA.
- Parents with care using the CSA were more likely than those not using the CSA to say that their relationship had ended because they argued all the time (36 per cent compared to 24 per cent).
- More parents with care using the CSA said violence towards them from an ex-partner was the cause of their break-up (24 per cent), compared to those not using the CSA (18 per cent).
- 39 per cent of parents with care using the CSA had an income under £10,000 compared to 30 per cent of parents with care not using the CSA.
- Only 23 per cent of the former were working full-time, compared to 38 per cent of the latter.

11. There is an over-simplistic view in the government's Green Paper [DWP (2011)] that, somehow, if parents were pushed down the road of voluntary arrangements, all the characteristics associated with voluntary arrangements would happen as well. The paper says, for example, that "parents report higher levels of contact between non-resident parents and their children when they have made their own maintenance arrangements". In reality, all experts agree that the associated link between contact and maintenance or vice versa, or between parental relations and the engagement of the non-resident parent with the

children – is a complex one, where what is cause and what effect is difficult to discern. For example, on the one hand, up to a quarter of non-resident parents within the CSA reported they were paying maintenance but not having contact. On the other hand, 70 per cent of parents with care not using the CSA said their child was having contact with the non-resident parent, but only 38 per cent of such parents were receiving any maintenance. Using financial and procedural pressure to push parents into making their own child maintenance arrangements will not necessarily result in reduced conflict and more engaged non-resident parents as the Green Paper hopes; but it will certainly make many children poorer....

13. The key feature of a purely private agreement is that it is one voluntarily entered into by both parties, which cannot be enforced by the courts or the CSA. The government fails to acknowledge that what may seem advantageous to the paying parent about private arrangements – that they are flexible as to amount and timing and do not involve interference from the state – may be seen as potential disadvantages to the recipient parent, with day-to-day care of the child: payments are not regular, may be for lower amounts than the statutory formula, and if not paid, there is no redress. Much therefore depends on the degree of trust between the parents in question when reaching an agreement, and their mutual commitment to the best interests of their children.

14. DWP research looking at private arrangements between separated parents prior to the involvement of the CSA noted that "overall, non-resident parents appear to wield a disproportionate amount of power over establishing financial arrangements following separation, regardless of the type of arrangement adopted"...

17. The proposed procedural and financial barriers to use of the statutory system would bite first on parents with care wishing to use the statutory child maintenance system. The explicit aim is to turn them towards attempting to negotiate a voluntary child maintenance arrangement with the other parent instead. At this point, this is no equivalent mechanism pushing the non-resident parent to actively engage in reaching a mutually agreeable arrangement. It is only after a parent with care has paid [an] application fee[317] that financial 'encouragement' to the non-resident parent to reach a private agreement kicks in. In effect, the charging regime proposed weakens the negotiating position of the parent with care still further; knowing of the charges a parent with care would have to pay, an unwilling non-resident parent may use them as an excuse to offer less....

19. Paradoxically, even for many of those who don't use the statutory system, its existence is important. It is precisely because a parent with care can easily access the state child support service that non-resident parents are more likely to agree good private arrangements in its shadow....

Parents with care may be unable or unwilling, for all sorts of reasons, to secure child maintenance. A quarter of parents with care on benefits who were CSA clients in one study indicated that they would probably not make any arrangement for maintenance once free to do so.[318] A survey of parents using the government's telephone advice service found that well over a third of children in principle entitled to receive child support receive no maintenance from their non-resident parent.[319] A study of single parents on benefits found only a third of them received any maintenance at all, and many of those did not receive regular payment in full.[320] The government's own impact assessment of

---

317 At the time Gingerbread were writing, the proposed fee for applicants not on benefits was £100; the fee as introduced is £20, still a lot for many single parents.

318 Wikeley et al (2008).

319 Allen and Goldstein (2012).

320 Bryson et al (2013).

the reforms forecast that around 100,000 of the CSA caseload with a calculation requiring payment would leave the statutory system but not make alternative arrangements, 'at least not initially'.[321] Where no (or no effective) family-based arrangement is reached and, for whatever reason, no application to CMS is made, the child's household income will receive no boost from child support. In some cases—for example, where payment would be at the flat rate—any contribution from the non-resident parent may seem small in raw terms. Some parents with care may decide it is not worth the potential aggravation or cost to pursue that payment. But others may be left below the poverty line without it.[322] It is laudable to encourage agreement where agreement is attainable, but one cannot legislate with only easy cases in mind. A policy aimed to increase 'parental responsibility' and promote family autonomy may ironically mark increased abdication from that responsibility and allow imbalances of power within families to damage children's economic well-being.

6.7.3 LEGAL AND SOCIAL PARENTHOOD

Parents have differing views about the link between child support payments and the social relationship between the liable party and the child. Should child support liability inexorably flow from legal, rather than social parenthood? And what links should exist between financial support and the time the child spends with each parent?

Who should pay for whom?

Much opposition to the CSA 1991 has arisen from differing perceptions about who should be liable for whom, and which children should have priority call on adults' income. This issue particularly affects step-families. Establishing such new family bonds has long been recognized as an optimum way for mothers and children to improve their economic lot after breakdown of the parents' relationship.[323] Because the law places primary responsibility for children's maintenance on legal parents, some families are in a chain of households along which money is passed: the father of children in one household pays child support to children from his first relationship, while the step-father of his children in turn sends money to yet another household for children from his earlier relationship, and so on.[324] Inevitable breaks in the chain leave some individuals supporting two sets of children.[325] As Jane Millar astutely observes, 'people's lives are far messier in reality than [the Child Support Act] policy can easily allow for'.[326] Few can afford to sustain two households.[327] Mavis Maclean even asks, 'If society accepts serial partnering, should it bite the bullet and pay for the children out of public funds?'[328]

---

[321] DWP (2013), para 122.

[322] See Bryson et al (2013).

[323] Marsh and Vegeris (2004).

[324] Barton (1999), 705 advises non-resident parents to join such households in order to reduce their own liability whilst their new household also enjoys that income from the other non-resident parent.

[325] Davis et al (1998), 229.

[326] Millar (1996), 189.

[327] Gibson (1991), 343.

[328] Maclean with Kurczewski (2011), 54.

In the early days of the CSA 1991, commentators considered the likely impact of its reinforcement of obligations deriving from legal parenthood:

M. Maclean and J. Eekelaar, 'Child Support: The British Solution', (1993) 7
International Journal of Law and the Family 205, 226

The creation of children is now more likely to have lasting effect on the lives of men, as it always has for women. We are less certain, however, about the extent to which the scheme subordinates the social family to the biological principle. Whether this will enhance individual responsibility as is hoped is unpredictable and, in a society where so many family relationships cross households, it may not make good economic sense to shift resources across families to such an extent and with such cost.

R. Boden and M. Childs, 'Paying for Procreation: Child Support Arrangements in the UK', (1996) 4 *Feminist Legal Studies* 131, 156

This biological determinism as the basis for financial obligations indicates how heavily involved the state is in defining the private realm of the family and family obligations. In their real lives people may have assumed kinship responsibilities with regard to step-children and new partners. Yet here the state is retrospectively redetermining obligations based on biological parentage, refusing to recognise the private realm social relationships which may exist. One type of kinship, that based on biology, is privileged over that based on social or cultural foundations. The state is not reasserting the rightful role of the private realm of the family, it is imposing its own definition of that role in an attempt to relieve itself of a public expenditure commitment [pre-CMOPA 2008]. One result may be an adverse effect on women whose partners are deemed to have more important financial commitments to previous children.

Research confirmed that emphasis on biological (legal) parenthood clashes with some social perceptions. As with private ordering, parents with care and non-resident parents held different views:

M. Maclean and J. Eekelaar, *The Parental Obligation: A Study of Parenthood Across Households* (Oxford: Hart Publishing, 1997), 149–50

[T]he "social" dimension of parenthood plays a far more important part in the performance of the parental role (and therefore probably in the perception of parental obligations) than the policy underscoring the Child Support Act allowed. This is seen in the following major findings: *first*, a strong association between the maintenance of contact with and support by the "outside" parent and the age of the child at separation; *secondly*, the strong negative effect which the presence or subsequent acquisition of a partner by either parent had on the maintenance of contact with and support by the "outside" parent of children with whom they had not lived, or with whom they had lived only for a relatively short time; and *thirdly*, the strong association between payment of support and the exercise of contact.

However, the attitudinal survey showed that there was a strong gender factor lying behind people's perceptions of their cross-household support obligations. The fathers [non-resident parents] related their obligations much more closely to the exercise of social parenthood both by themselves and by another man who may have joined the mother's household than the mothers would have allowed. In view of such a division, we should perhaps not speak of *a* social rule, but of *two conflicting* social rules. The empirical data strongly showed the fathers acting consistently with the viewpoints they expressed in the attitudinal survey. They can be said to assume a social rule which can be formulated in three stages: (i) a prior social parenthood developed in a household can be extended beyond that household after parental separation; (ii) social parenthood so extended can create a social obligation to provide support; and (iii) such social obligations can co-exist with the social obligations associated with subsequently acquired social parenthood. Since each stage is dependent on the preceding stage for its existence, *if an initial social parenthood had not existed, or, if it had existed, if it was not extended after separation*, the men will be reluctant to view any support obligation based solely on their natural fatherhood as co-existing with subsequent social parenthood and will be inclined to assume that the obligation attaches to a man who later takes on social parenthood with respect to their child.

The researchers concluded that the implications of their findings for the scope of child support obligations were complicated:

It could not be right to conclude that fathers...should have no support obligations towards the children they have procreated simply because they have not lived with them. It also seems dangerous to say that only those fathers who have looked after their children should have continuing obligations towards them, for this seems to punish virtue. Furthermore, the mothers saw that natural fatherhood, at least when initiated in marriage, created in itself a strong support obligation and were less likely than fathers to see this as lapsing if the child acquired a stepfather. It is not surprising that mothers should place more weight on natural parenthood and fathers more weight on social parenthood because, for almost all mothers, but by no means all fathers, natural parenthood and social parenthood coincide.

...A support obligation which accompanies or arises from social parenthood is embedded in that social parenthood; thus the payment of support can be seen as part of the relationship maintained by continued contact. But an obligation based on natural parenthood rests on the policy of instilling a sense of responsibility for individual action and equity between fathers who do and fathers who do not exercise social parenthood.

This re-emphasis of the obligations of legal parenthood reversed the courts' previous 'pragmatic policy' of allowing men to move on, economically, to new families, and attracted huge opposition.[329] Some fathers claimed (unsuccessfully on the facts) that their Article 8 ECHR rights were being interfered with insofar as child support obligations contributed to the break-up of second families.[330] As we saw when examining the significance of 'relevant other children' to the basic rate formula at 6.4.4, the CSA 1991 scheme now makes quite significant allowance for children in the non-resident parent's new family. Indeed, it may be argued that the formula goes too far to accommodate them by giving insufficient weight to the substantial material benefits that accrue to those children from living with the non-resident parent, for example sharing the fruits of his expenditure on the fixed costs of

---

[329] Diduck (2003), 181.
[330] *Burrows v United Kingdom* (App No 27558/95, ECHR) (1996).

providing a home which are not increased by their presence in the household. We explore these issues further below at 6.7.4 when we examine the basis of the formula.

The relationship between the child's living arrangements and child support

A perennial issue in child support policy has been the link—or lack of it—made between child support liability and whether the non-resident parent spends any time with—and how much time he spends with—the child for whom he is paying.

How to deal with shared care

As we have seen, overnight stays reduce child support liability and a variation can be made to reflect contact costs.

J. Wallbank, 'The Campaign for Change of the Child Support Act 1991: Reconstituting the "Absent" Father', (1997) 6 *Social and Legal Studies* 191, 197

This . . . can be interpreted in a number of ways: it might be viewed as consolidating the government's commitment to ensuring that parental contact with children is maintained; alternatively [it] might be considered as part of a package of changes which attempted to appease the mass of middle-class fathers who voiced their grievances about the Act in a vociferous manner; less cynically perhaps it could have been a very real attempt to respond to the problems caused by the inflexibility of the formula. Whatever the motivation . . . the change has the effect of highlighting the desirability of maintaining links between a father and his child(ren). . . .

One feared disadvantage of allowing reductions in child support to reflect overnight stays is an increase in disputes over child arrangements under the CA 1989, s 8. Non-resident parents have clear financial (as well as emotional) incentives to maximize time spent with the child overnight; parents with care conversely have financial incentives to try to minimize such arrangements.

However, as Wikeley has explained, the shared care rules—aimed to encourage contact and improve compliance in payment of child support—do not match the expectations of non-resident parents, who tend to view shared care rules as a way of reflecting their direct expenditure on the child by discounting their maintenance liability more fully than the rules permit.[331] It is unusual for care to be so fully shared that no child support liability arises at all. More commonly, even if the child stays overnight with the non-resident parent for half the nights in the year, the liability will be halved at most.

But the rules can also appear unfair to parents who provide substantial day-time care without providing extensive overnight care. When *R (Plumb) v Secretary of State for Work and Pensions*[332] was decided, the then rules only permitted a deduction if the child spent at least 104 nights per annum with the non-resident parent.[333] The child's mother—the parent with care—had a new partner and was earning £15,000 full-time, with accommodation provided. Mr Plumb was less well-off than the mother, but provided substantial amounts of

---

331 Wikeley (2006a), 313–14.
332 [2002] EWHC 1125.
333 No breach of the ECHR was found.

care for the child as non-resident parent: there were frequent overnight stays (but fewer than 104 nights) and considerable after-school and weekend day-care and meals—an estimated 1,600 hours and 260 meals per annum. Despite all this, his liability could not be reduced. Even now, his deduction would be based exclusively on the fact of overnight stays: save in those cases where it can be argued that the parents provide equal care, no account is taken of the actual level of care or expenditure on the child made by each parent, including on costly items such as clothing. So a non-resident parent whose child stayed overnight as often as Mr Plumb's but who provided no day-care or evening meals would receive the same deduction as Mr Plumb.

It is clearly questionable whether this rough-and-ready mechanism produces just results for either parent, even putting aside Mr Plumb's complaint. The marginal costs (e.g. on meals) saved by parents with care on those nights when the child is with the non-resident parent may be dwarfed by the reduction in the maintenance they receive as a result of the shared care rules. But similarly, the additional fixed costs to the non-resident parent of having to provide accommodation adequate to have the child stay overnight may far exceed the deduction he is granted. A daytime-hours rule was rejected on the basis that hours could not be reliably counted.[334] But it may not be possible to count nights much more reliably, particularly on the boundaries between bands, where one night more or fewer makes a big difference.

The issue of shared care was considered during the recent reform debates. One group in particular, Families Need Fathers, have argued that the shared care rules should be abolished in order better to recognize and promote shared parenting and the costs incurred by the 'non-resident' parent,[335] and both Henshaw and the Work and Pensions Select Committee advocated no liability in cases where care is shared 50:50.[336] That is only the case, as discussed above, where the parents really are providing qualitatively equal care—not based just on the number of nights—such that there is no non-resident parent at all.[337] But otherwise, the rules were tweaked only slightly to allow maintenance to be determined on the basis of the *expected* level of shared care. And where parents agree that care is shared to some extent but cannot agree how much shared care is provided, CMS will assume that the non-resident parent has the child for one night a week—thus attracting the one-seventh reduction.[338]

But it is doubtful whether extinguishing liability entirely in equally shared care cases is right. Where the parents have more or less equal financial resources, such that both are able to provide similar standards of living for the child, that outcome makes sense. However, more commonly one parent has greater resources than the other, in which case—even where care is fully shared—there is a strong case for some resource-transfer between the two households, in order to share the economic burden of child-care more equitably between the parents. Indeed, as we discuss at 6.7.4 below, where (unusually) the person with care has greater resources than the non-resident parent with whom the child spends time, there is a case for requiring maintenance to be paid to the non-resident parent.

---

[334] DSS (1999), para 7.20.

[335] Families Need Fathers (2007). Note also that child benefit and child tax credit cannot be shared. See also Gilmore (2007).

[336] Henshaw (2006), Work and Pensions Select Committee (2007).

[337] In theory, the court would have full jurisdiction here, there being no 'qualifying child', but it is doubtful—given the high levels of cooperation required to operate a fully shared care system—that parents in such a case would be in dispute and so go to court; they might, of course, transfer resources between households voluntarily.

[338] CSMCR 2012, reg 47.

The irrelevance of contact

The shared care rules and contact-cost variation aside, the law makes no link between contact and child support. The non-resident parent must in principle pay child support at the prescribed rate whether or not he has any sort of contact with the child (for whatever reason). No discount is applied where the parent with care refuses to allow the non-resident parent to spend time, or otherwise have contact, with the child, even if she is breaching a court order in doing so.[339] Whether the non-resident parent has contact is a factor expressly not to be taken into account when CMS decides whether the grant a variation. A father's *failure* to pay maintenance is not given substantial weight in courts' decisions to grant parental responsibility (in the strict sense), at least where he has otherwise demonstrated devotion to the child.[340] And it was held in *Re B (Contact: Child Support)*[341] that it would be inappropriate when making orders for *contact* to consider the impact of different arrangements on child support liability, in particular under the shared care rules:[342] that would introduce a factor unrelated to the child's welfare into the CA 1989 decision-making process. Stephen Gilmore has strongly criticized that decision, arguing that—reflecting a wider trend[343]—it neglects parents' rights to respect for family life with their children under Article 8 ECHR. While those rights may frequently be outweighed by the child's interests, they cannot be simply ignored. If a decision about contact so increases the non-resident parents' child support liability that exercising contact becomes problematic, an Article 8 issue arises and cannot be sidelined as 'irrelevant'.[344]

The lack of link has been debated several times, most recently by the Family Justice Review, owing to non-resident fathers' frustration with cases where mothers to their eyes unreasonably refuse contact. The Review initially considered that the court should have the option, if in the child's best interests, to alter or suspend child support payments as a way of enforcing contact orders. But following its consultation exercise, the Review decided against any change, concluding that it

> would be wrong to risk strengthening the view that it is acceptable not to pay maintenance when there are contact difficulties or for that matter, that contact can be withheld when maintenance is not being paid.[345]

The Review felt any other approach could encourage litigation and undermine private arrangements. Douglas et al expand on that concern:

G. Douglas et al, 'Contact is not a Commodity to be Bartered for Money', (2011) 41 *Family Law* 491, 495

Far from promoting private resolution the result would be to trigger recourse either to the child support system, or to the courts. Issues of 'fault' as well as 'mere' matters

---

[339] See chapter 11 on enforcement powers for child arrangements orders.

[340] *Re H (Parental Responsibility: Maintenance)* [1996] 1 FLR 867.

[341] [2006] EWCA Civ 1574.

[342] 6.4.4.

[343] See 8.4.4.

[344] Gilmore (2007). The argument in *Logan v United Kingdom* (App No 24875/94, ECHR) (1996) that this violated Art 8 failed the facts.

[345] Norgrove (2011), 171.

of whether contact did or did not take place, and why, would have to be examined. The law would have to prescribe what kinds of contact arrangements would 'count' for the purposes of a reduction (direct only or to include indirect forms?); it would have to determine how much contact would be required to trigger a reduction (would the loss of one day per month suffice to do so, or would the contact have to be more than de minimis?); it would have to set out whether a single breach of contact would trigger a reduction or whether repeat breaches of the arrangement would be required; and it would have to decide what to do if the evidence showed that the refusal of contact was the child's decision rather than that of the parent. It can be seen that the issue raises precisely the kinds of emotionally-charged and highly conflictual matters that the courts and government have sought to hard to remove from the arena of post-separation parenting.

But not all parents agree with the formal legal position. A large-scale survey of CSA clients made the following findings:

N. Wikeley et al, *National Survey of Child Support Agency Clients*, DWP Research Report No 152 (Leeds: Corporate Document Service, 2001), 153

A question which underpins much of the discussion concerning the expectation that NRPs [non-resident parents] pay significant sums in child support concerns the appropriateness of requiring such payments in circumstances where the father (as it usually is) has little, if any, contact with his children and so does not derive any benefit from his 'investment'....[It] is important to acknowledge that a survey methodology cannot possibly do justice to the complexities of this issue.

As one might have expected, NRPs were more likely to assert as an absolute principle that payment of 'full' maintenance should entitle the NRP to have regular contact with his children. Only 16 per cent dissented. A majority of PWCs likewise seemed willing to sign up to this as an absolute principle, although 25 per cent equivocated, suggesting (wisely) that the answer to this question would depend on the particular circumstances of the case.

We gave this theme a somewhat sharper edge by asking whether, in circumstances where the NRP is denied contact with his children, he should pay less maintenance. (This, needless to say, is to oversimplify the 'contact' issue, certainly as it would be perceived by many parents with care.) The question nonetheless exposed sharp differences between the attitudes of NRPs and PWCs...NRPs were much more likely to assert that a denial of contact should lead to a reduced maintenance obligation. Over 50 per cent supported this proposition without any qualification. Less than 20 per cent of PWCs took the same view.

Researchers have found correlations between frequency of contact and both payment rates and parents' perception of the child support system as fair.[346] However, Maclean and Eekelaar concluded that fathers do not exercise contact *because* they are paying support—the status of the previous relationship between the parents was more important both to contact

---

[346] Wikeley at al (2001); Davis and Wikeley (2002).

being exercised and child support being paid.[347] The general population also appears to link contact and child support in determining how much child support should be paid, particularly where the parent with care is unreasonably refusing contact and, interestingly, where the non-resident parent is unreasonably refusing to see the child.[348] Moreover, survey data indicate contact and child support are in fact linked in many families, whatever the law may say, with very high levels of non-payment amongst fathers who have no contact with their children.[349] As ever, what happens on the ground does not necessarily correspond with what the law says ought to happen. The move to 'family-based arrangements' may see an increase in non-payment amongst this group, as well as other contact-related variations from what the CMS scheme would prescribe, particularly for shared care cases. Indeed, the fact that the CM Options website encourages parents to include arrangements for contact in the same agreement as child support payments may only encourage this linkage in practice.[350]

6.7.4 THE POLICY CHOICES BEHIND THE FORMULA

One of the most complex but important issues in child support is the formula for calculating liability. It is easy to lose sight of the fact that there are policy questions behind all the maths, as Ellman et al have observed:

> The mechanical and precise nature of the support calculation creates the illusion that the numbers reflect some objective, scientific fact, when they actually reflect important policy choices about which people may differ.[351]

The formula design partly depends on whether the aim is to achieve 'collective justice' between the parents (and child) or 'distributive justice' between parents and state, the parents compensating the state for benefits paid for the child.[352] The latter type of scheme might not be responsive to facts which might be relevant to achieving justice between the private individuals involved: for example, capital settlements already made for benefit of children, contact costs, obligations to new families, and resources of the parent with care's new partner.[353] The level of support would evidently also be fixed by reference to the costs the state was trying to recoup. The child support scheme is clearly no longer concerned with the state's expenditure, so the focus is on justice as between the private parties. But what conception of justice? What is it fair to require a non-resident parent to pay, and how should that be measured? Commentators identify two principal types of formula.[354]

- Cost-sharing: the cost of raising the child should be shared between the parents. This type of formula requires answers to two basic questions: (i) what are those costs—are we concerned only with basic necessities, or is a more subjective assessment of the child's needs to be used, having regard to the parties' standard of living? and (ii) how should

347 (1997), 128; cf Bradshaw et al (1999) and Wilson (2006) on the complex social inter-relationship of contact and maintenance.
348 Bryson et al (2015).
349 Poole et al (2013), table 20.
350 <www.cmoptions.org/en/family/what-to-include.asp>.
351 Ellman et al (2014), 295.
352 Maclean and Eekelaar (1997), 42.
353 Ibid, 39 and 42; Davis et al (1998), 217.
354 Eekelaar and Maclean (1986), ch 7; Parker (1991); Wikeley (2006a), ch 1.

they be shared—equally between the parents, or on some other basis, for example in proportions reflecting their respective incomes? As we discuss below, a cost-sharing model must be careful not to underestimate the 'true' costs of child-rearing or to over-estimate either parent's ability to contribute towards those costs.

- Resource-sharing: the child should share a given proportion of the non-resident parent's resources. Most generously, this might aim to achieve equivalent household standards of living for non-resident parent and child, regardless of whether that involves support being paid at a level which exceeds the needs-related costs of raising the child, however measured. Less generously, it might be capped at some level of parental income so as not to extend too far beyond a needs-based measure.

The rationale of the current statutory formula, calculated as 'fraction of gross income per child', is less than clear and certainly open to criticism.[355] The percentages of non-resident parental income that are payable were apparently based on evidence not about the cost of raising children (as such), but rather on evidence about *expenditure* on children by intact families. It was suggested that intact families on average spend around 30 per cent of their joint net income on a child; and that therefore the non-resident parent should pay half of that now the family is separated—15 per cent under the net scheme rules, 12 per cent in the new gross scheme.[356] Ellman et al have identified an immediate problem: if 30 per cent of *joint* income was spent directly on the child while the family was intact, should that not mean each parent continuing to contribute 30 per cent of their own income post-separation to ensure the equivalent level of expenditure now?[357] However, there is a more profound difficulty with this sort of approach, as those authors, who conducted a large-scale public attitudinal survey on child support, describe:

I. Ellman, S. McKay, J. Miles, and C. Bryson, 'Child Support Judgments: Comparing Public Policy to the Public's Policy', (2014) 28 *International Journal of Law, Policy and the Family* 274, 295–6

[T]ranslating estimates of parental expenditures on children in *intact* families, into required support amounts in a child support guideline applied to *separated* families, is a tricky business involving many policy choices...

The most basic policy choice is deciding what counts as an 'expenditure on children'. The standard method...imagines a hypothetical childless couple at some income level, and then asks how much *more* they would need to spend to maintain their living standard when a child or children are added to their household. But additional expenditures occasioned by the new child do not, of course, include things the parents also spent money on when childless, even though many of these continuing expenditures benefit the newly added children. So the cost of any changes in housing required to maintain the same living standard—perhaps, for example, the additional cost of a larger home—counts as an expenditure on children, but the base cost of having a home in the first place does not. Such a system thus assumes the father should share, for example, in the additional cost of the extra bedroom, but not in the cost of the kitchen, bathroom, or living room, since the childless couples already had those. Additions to the food or clothing budget are counted, but not the cost of a car (except to the extent it is greater after children than before, which is not especially likely).

---

[355] Fortin (2009), 347–8.
[356] DSS (1999), para 2.5, citing Middleton et al (1997), para 16.
[357] Ellman et al (2014), n 28.

In short, the intact family makes many expenditures that confer benefits on children that are not included in the standard child expenditure estimates upon which most support guidelines are based, because they are 'joint expenditures' that benefit *everyone* in the household. The necessary premise of such a calculation is that the parents are equally capable, after separation, of providing the foundational living standard that the intact family enjoyed before separation, so that the child support system need only address how parents should share the *additional* expenditures the couple incurs by having a child. But where the mother earns less than the father, this premise is wrong. Providing her with the father's share of the cost of an extra bedroom does not help much if, now on her own, she cannot afford the rest of the home to which it is attached. A spousal maintenance order, if there were one, could deal with that discrepancy; a child support schedule based on estimates of 'child-only' expenditures, excluding joint expenditures that benefit children along with other household members, cannot.

When the two parents have relatively similar incomes, basing support amounts on child-only expenditures is not very problematic: in that case the parents face similar financial challenges from the separation, children aside. If they are in the same situation with respect to paying for the foundational household expenditures, it may make sense to focus exclusively on the additional expenditures occasioned by the children. But as the two parents' incomes become more disparate, the situation changes. The lower-income parent suffers a more precipitous drop in living standard from the separation than does the higher-income parent. And as the lower-income parent is most often also the mother with whom the child primarily lives, that steeper fall becomes a matter that the child support law should reasonably be expected to address. Of course, income transfers between parents through the child support system are not the only potential source of assistance for the low-income mother, and can in any event provide little real help in the common case in which the father is also low-income. Benefits provided through public programmes necessarily play a critical role. But they are alone often inadequate, and are not intended to and in fact cannot provide children of higher-income fathers with the amenities these children were accustomed to and some of which, at least, their fathers are still able to provide after separation.

A system requiring the father to pay his share of just the child-only expenditures might be explained as maintaining the status quo: he is then contributing, after separation, precisely the same amount toward his children that he did before separation. But it is the same amount of only the additional 'child-only' expenditures. He retains all he contributed to the foundational joint expenditures, even though these must be duplicated after separation when the parents need two kitchens rather than one. In effect, this system shields the higher-income father from contributing his share to the duplicated costs that are the inevitable consequence of separation, leaving the lower-income mother to bear them on her own.

It is worth contrasting the basis of the child support formula—which makes no provision for these sort of 'fixed' costs incurred by the parent with care in providing the child's principal home—with the discretion under the CA 1989, Sch 1 (in particular), under which courts regularly make orders providing a home for the primary carer and child, together with a carer's allowance. Such orders can help primary carers to meet their fixed costs,[358] though only of course if there is capital available to do so.

Meanwhile, under the child support formula 'relevant other children' living with the father are amply catered for by sharing the benefit of his expenditure on his own home, as well as being protected by the reduction in the formula applied in such cases. It may be asked whether they are over-provided for—certainly, their situation may be more comfortable than that of the qualifying child where the non-resident father has a higher income than the parent with care.

---

358 On concerns regarding the 'hidden alimony' effect of this, see Ellman and Braver (2011).

Equally, however, in other cases, the current formula's failure to take into account the income of the parent with care or any new partner she has may mean some non-resident parents are paying more than is fair. Currently, non-resident parents must pay regardless of their economic standing relative to the parent with care, and so regardless of whether the parent with care needs any payment to help cover her household expenditure.[359] Such cases may be few: in 2000, 96 per cent of earning non-resident parents' former partners were on weekly incomes below £100.[360] And disregarding the income of parents with care may act as a work incentive, increasing the income of the child's household. But many non-resident parents may regard this failure to consider the parent with care's household income as unfair, and the attitude survey indicates that the British public shares those misgivings. The survey team concluded from their data that:

> the public believes the amount of support that the law should require the father to pay:
> 1. Should depend on both the father's income and the mother's income . . .
> 2. Should increase with the father's income, all else being equal . . .
> 3. Should decline as the mother's income increases, all else being equal, not only in pounds but also as a percentage of the father's income . . .
> 4. Should continue to rise with the father's income beyond the point needed to ensure the child is not in poverty, thus permitting the child access to amenities as well. . . . One expects there is some level of affluence beyond which the public believes the support amount need not rise, but if so, that level was not reached in any of the [questions respondents to the survey were asked].[361]

A formula based on these criteria would look very different from that currently used in English law.

6.7.5 RULES OR DISCRETION?

Child support law provides a powerful example of family law operated on the basis of rules, in preference to discretionary decision-making. This is a theme that we introduced at 1.2.2 and on which readers will find further materials on the Online Resource Centre.[362] Many jurisdictions have adopted more rule-based child support laws, some applied by courts rather than by an administrative body.[363] There are arguments both ways.

Discretion claims some advantages over rule-based systems, certainly as manifested by the original, highly complex CSA 1991 formula before variations were introduced:

Phillips v Peace [1996] 2 FCR 237 (Fam Div), 239

JOHNSON J:

It is of the essence of the policy underlying the Child Support Act 1991 that child support is to be assessed according to a mathematical formula which is to be applied rigorously, seemingly without any significant element of discretion to cater for the needs of a child in

---

359 Douglas (2004a), 206.
360 Wikeley (2000), 822.
361 Ellman et al (2014), 292.
362 Supplementary materials to chapter 1.
363 E.g. in Canada and the United States, where judges use the formulae/guidelines: see Rogerson (2014).

the circumstances of the child with whom I am concerned....This is quite contrary to the practice of the court which for generations, in seeking to assess entitlements to financial support for former spouses or children, has sought to achieve a result which is fair, just and reasonable, based on the realities and the practicalities.

But court-based discretion carries disadvantages too:

G. Davis, S. Cretney, and J. Collins, *Simple Quarrels* (Oxford: OUP, 1994), 256

...along with discretion goes *uncertainty: the elevation of professional judgment* (because only lawyers, who deal with these matters all the time, have the necessary knowledge and skill to weigh up the competing factors); *an almost limitless need for information about family finances* (because discretion, if it is to be justified at all, has to be based on a minute examination of differing circumstances); and *the demand for large amount of professional time* (because the discretion, if it is not to be exercised arbitrarily, takes time). In practice, of course, there is a limit to the amount of lawyer-time which divorcing couples can purchase, and also a limit to the amount which the State is prepared to support. Court-time is likewise expensive and has, somehow, to be rationed.

As we shall see in chapter 7, similar arguments play out in relation to financial remedies between spouses on divorce, where child support is one part of the wider economic package:

E. Jackson et al, 'Financial Support on Divorce: The Right Mixture of Rules and Discretion?', (1993) 7 *International Journal of Law and the Family* 230, 231–2

In any child support system which depends on discretion, there will tend to be public dissatisfaction if one father finds out that he pays twice as much as his neighbour, or one mother discovers that she receives half as much as hers. In a situation where dissatisfied payers can and do just cease payments without much fear of recourse, it is important to minimize public mistrust. In addition to the problems of inconsistency, a system of discretion will make it very difficult for lawyers to predict the outcome of an adjudication. This may mean that more couples will fight full adversarial battles, and have to bear increasing legal costs and the strain of protracted litigation. Alternatively they may accept unsatisfactory settlements in preference to the high-cost, high-risk strategy of litigation....

On the other hand, taking decisions more formulaically creates problems too:

It might be thought that, in making the 'ancillary' matters part of an administrative process, divorce can cease to be a time for conflict and instead simply be the civilized ordering of a couple's affairs. Nonetheless, the rush to simplicity and certainty may underestimate the complexity of the issues to be resolved and fail to do justice to them. The divorce represents a substantial upheaval for the spouses and their children, and it takes a great deal of time to work out how their domestic arrangements should be restructured. Indeed, there are so many complex issues that it is difficult to envisage a formula that could encompass them all. Most couples just want to sort out a workable solution and not become embroiled in protracted legal battles. If thoroughness is sacrificed in the interests of administrative effi-ciency, simplicity and cost-cutting, problems may not be addressed adequately at the time of the divorce and may re-emerge later with extra complications.

...As family law continues to move towards interlocking systems, rules, and formulae, it might be timely to question if there should be limits to these trends. What, if anything, is worth retaining from a discretion-based system? Can the trend towards rules go too far? To what extent does discretion...allow divorcing people to be flexible, responsive to need, and open to compromise? Will formula-based approaches to maintenance gain in predictability, generosity, and consistency but at a cost of greater rigidity and an inability to make adjust-ments to the overall financial package?

Even though discretion may not facilitate the resolution of disputes without the need for legal representation and may lead to inconsistencies, it might nevertheless be fairer for the decision-maker to examine each case individually before deciding how much this father should pay.

Rule-based systems are not a panacea, and discretion is not perfect. But we do not have to choose between them. Rule-based systems can be more or less complex, demanding more or less infor-mation for their operation.[364] There are some (limited) discretionary components to the current CMS scheme, and the emphasis on family-based arrangements now affords increased scope for 'discretion', albeit exercised by the parties and not necessarily in accordance with legal criteria. Yet there is also growing interest in England and Wales in moving financial remedies on divorce towards a more formulaic model, as we shall discuss at 7.5.5. Getting the balance between 'individualized justice' and 'average justice'[365] right is a difficult exercise.

6.8 CONCLUSION

Child support provides a valuable case study for several key debates in contemporary family law. The nature of family obligations—should responsibility attach to legal status, or to the actual performance of social family roles? The relationship between family and state—should financial obligations be for families to agree wherever possible, or should the state ever inter-vene? Family law techniques—are family disputes better dealt with by way of wide discretion or more certain rules, and by courts or administrative agencies? Ironically, the figure who often fades into the background is the child. What combination of private law obligations and state-based provision would best meet children's needs, and what *rights* of children should we recognize here?

ONLINE RESOURCE CENTRE

Questions, suggestions for further reading, and supplementary materials for this chapter (including updates on developments in this area of family law since this book was published) may be found on the Online Resource Centre at **www.oxfordtextbooks.co.uk/orc/familytcm3e/**.

---

[364] For criticism of the original CSA scheme, see Horton (1995); for discussion of the influential Canadian support guidelines, see Rogerson (2014).
[365] Rogerson (2002), 6.

7

PROPERTY AND FINANCES WHEN RELATIONSHIPS END

CENTRAL ISSUES

1. English law has no special regime of property ownership *during* marriage and civil partnership. However, on relationship breakdown, it treats different types of family distinctly.

2. On divorce/dissolution, the courts have wide discretionary powers under the Matrimonial Causes Act 1973 (MCA 1973) and Civil Partnership Act 2004 (CPA 2004) to make financial orders (formerly known as 'ancillary relief') adjusting the parties' property rights and requiring ongoing financial provision between them in order to achieve a 'fair' result.

3. The House of Lords in *Miller; McFarlane* [2006] UKHL 24 identified three elements of a 'fair' outcome: meeting need; compensating for 'relationship-generated disadvantage'; and equal sharing. The statute requires that first consideration be given to the welfare of minor children of the family. It is usually possible only to meet the parties' needs, insofar as limited resources allow.

4. The 'clean break' principle encourages the courts where appropriate to terminate ongoing financial ties between the parties, for example by ordering one-off capital transfers and no periodical payments.

5. The law is ambivalent about private ordering in this sphere. Parties can make agreements binding on divorce only by converting them into an order by consent and cannot by agreement deprive each other of the right to apply to court. But a court invited to grant orders inconsistent with an agreement will have regard to the agreement's terms and may determine that fairness requires that its order should reflect what the agreement provides.

6. On the breakdown of other family relationships, laws considered in previous chapters determine the outcome of property disputes: those governing parties' property ownership; occupation of the shared home; and financial and property provision for the benefit of children. These parties can regulate their affairs by contract.

7.1 INTRODUCTION

Media coverage of financial settlements on divorce provides a seriously distorted impression of the real world. The media relate stories about the wives of premiership footballers, entrepreneurs, and rock stars seeking multi-million pound 'pay-outs'. The reality for thousands of families affected by divorce each year is 'just about keeping heads above water'. Divorcing couples, with the aid of solicitors and/or mediators, and in the last resort the courts, must conjure as beneficial (or as least detrimental) an outcome as possible for all parties from limited assets. We discussed in chapter 6 the various financial remedies for children whose parents live apart, whatever the legal status of the parents' relationship. Our focus here is on remedies for the benefit of the adults. In that context, the law distinguishes sharply between marriage/civil partnership[1] and other relationships.

Spouses and civil partners have access to powerful financial remedies on divorce/dissolution, enabling the courts to adjust property rights and order ongoing financial provision, regardless of the parties' property rights.[2] These financial orders[3] are still sometimes referred to as 'ancillary relief', reflecting a time when the main issue would be whether the marriage should be dissolved at all, and the grant of financial orders was a subsidiary consequence.[4] The main dispute is now more likely to concern the financial settlement, the vast majority of divorces themselves being undefended. One key issue is the basis on which financial orders are made.

The picture is very different on breakdown of other family relationships. The general law provides almost the only basis for resolving property disputes. There is little scope for adjusting property rights, and no periodical financial support. As we saw in chapter 3, outcomes produced by the general law are heavily criticized, fuelling calls for reform.

7.2 THE SOCIAL CONTEXT

Economic problems on relationship breakdown, marital or not, are most acutely felt where the parties are parents.[5] Many couples adopt specialized roles within the family economy, at least for some periods of their relationship, one party concentrating on breadwinning and paying the mortgage, while the other gives up or limits paid employment to look after home and family.[6] While they are together, all will usually appear to be well: they have a home, an income, and may be accumulating savings and a pension for later life which will support both spouses. The fact that technically each party owns his or her 'separate property' and has no claim over the other's assets may not seem to matter. But relationship breakdown exposes the vulnerabilities created by role-specialization in a separate property system, particularly for those who worked unpaid in the home.

---

[1] Identical legislation applies to spouses and civil partners; for ease of exposition, we generally refer to 'divorce' and 'spouses', and refer only to MCA 1973 provisions: identical provisions for civil partners are in CPA 2004, Sch 5.

[2] Cf *Tee v Hillman* [1999] 2 FLR 613; *Miller Smith v Miller Smith* [2009] EWCA 1297.

[3] Family Procedure Rules 2010 (FPR 2010), r 2.3.

[4] Cretney (2003a), 396, 402.

[5] E.g. Eekelaar and Maclean (1986), Eekelaar (1998a), Hale (2004).

[6] Diduck (2003), 149–52; see 3.2.2.

Without the wealth-transfer informally enjoyed during marriage, such individuals are economically vulnerable on separation.[7] With reduced earning capacity, reduced pension and other personal savings,[8] and often with continuing child-care obligations that limit opportunities to maximize earning capacity, many primary carers (and the children living with them) experience substantial drops in their standard of living.[9] Financial settlements on divorce therefore relate to a wider discussion of gender and social policy on issues such as child-care and employment rights.[10] Even with the benefit of special statutory remedies, the negative economic impact of divorce is often great, particularly during a time of recession. At least one party may often have to rely on state support to some extent, whether welfare benefits or social housing.[11] Questions arise about the respective responsibility of private individuals and the state to support the family after divorce.[12]

Feminist scholars disagree about the appropriate response:

J. Carbone, 'Feminism, Gender and the Consequences of Divorce', in M. Freeman (ed), *Divorce: Where Next?* (Ashgate: Dartmouth, 1996), 181–2

As a descriptive undertaking, there is near unanimity, both within feminist circles and without, as to the role of gender in accounting for the economic consequences of divorce. Women generally, for reasons attributable to gender, earn less than men. Marriage increases the gap as married women, who bear the overwhelming responsibility for child-rearing, earn less than single women, while married men increase their earnings over single men. At divorce, mothers overwhelmingly retain physical custody of their children, and the pressures of single parenthood interfere with labour force participation... Accordingly, divorce almost inevitably lowers the standard of living of the custodial family and, for systemic reasons related to gender, leaves the vast majority of divorced women in a financially more precarious position than their former husbands.

Despite the near unanimous embrace of this picture of divorce, there is considerable disagreement, both within feminist circles and without, as to the implications. The disagreement starts with the central feature of the gendered division of family responsibilities: what Mary Becker describes as mothers' greater, and qualitatively different, attachment to their children...

Nonetheless, feminists have been slow to call attention to this central difference in men and women's approach to family. When feminist scholarship does acknowledge it, it is without agreement on cause and effect. And although the source of women's greater attachment to children may well be irrelevant to the determination of public policy, feminists are no closer to agreement on possible solutions. 'Liberal' feminists believe that it is the gendered division of labour itself that ensures women's subordination to men and that, unless there is genuinely shared responsibility for childbearing, equality is impossible. 'Cultural feminists' or 'feminists of difference' believe that the principal problem is not that women disproportionately care for

---

7 Rake (2000), ch 4.

8 Ibid, ch 6; Price (2009).

9 Eekelaar and Maclean (1997), esp tables 7.8–7.10; Fisher and Low (2009).

10 See Herring (2005a).

11 34 per cent entrants to the social rented sector in 2007/8 who had previously been owners cited divorce or separation as their reason for moving: DCLG (2009), 108, table 4.5.

12 Ferguson (2008), Miles (2011a).

children, but that society so undervalues child-rearing. In between are many feminists who believe that equality requires both greater sharing of the responsibility for child-rearing *and* greater support for the child-rearing role.

If the other spouse wants to 'move on', an aspiration apparently legitimized by no-fault divorce,[13] it may be difficult for (usually) him to support the first family. His income is less likely to have been damaged by separation,[14] but being required to support the first family will increase his financial *obligations* and he may take some time to find accommodation.[15] The family economy that supported one household struggles to support two, and the interests of women and children in second families conflict with those in the first. The increasing trend for children to spend substantial amounts of time with both parents post-divorce further increases the pressure on the limited resources, if both parents want accommodation large enough for themselves and the children.[16]

7.3 REMEDIES ON DIVORCE: THE ORDERS AVAILABLE

The courts' powers on divorce provide a flexible toolkit for transferring resources. The choice of tools and the amounts transferred in each case depend on the *basis* for exercising the powers—in what circumstances and for what purpose should orders be made? We address that in the next section. Here, we ask the mechanical question—what can the court do?

The aim is produce a financial 'package' achieving the optimum outcome for the parties and their children, using whatever powers are available.[17] Child maintenance is often an important component, dealt with either via a consent order, informally in a private agreement, or via the statutory agency.[18] Given the extensive powers to make orders for the benefit of the primary carer on divorce, capital orders for the children may seldom be required.[19] Our focus here is on orders for the benefit of the spouses.

The first step is always to identify and value the assets available for distribution.[20] This is usually straightforward, but in high-value cases, in particular, this can involve complex legal questions that are beyond the scope of this book. In short, the courts' powers are exercisable only in relation to resources belonging to one or both spouses. They cannot make orders over property owned beneficially by third parties, whether family members,[21] companies,[22] or trusts[23] (other than 'nuptial settlements', which the matrimonial court can vary[24]).

---

[13] Symes (1985), 52–3.

[14] Eekelaar and Maclean (1997), table 7.11; Fisher and Low (2009).

[15] Perry et al (2000).

[16] See chapter 11.

[17] Jackson et al (1993), 244–5.

[18] See chapter 6, and 6.5.2 on consent orders.

[19] Cf cases involving unmarried parents, discussed at 7.8.2.

[20] *Charman v Charman* [2007] EWCA Civ 503, [67].

[21] *TL v ML and others (Ancillary Relief: Claim Against Assets of Extended Family)* [2005] EWHC 2860.

[22] *Prest v Petrodel Resources Ltd and others* [2013] UKSC 34; George (2013b).

[23] *Charman v Charman* [2007] EWCA Civ 503.

[24] MCA 1973, s 24(1)(c): *Ben Hashem v Ali Shayif* [2008] EWHC 2380.

Nor will the courts assume that a third party will make resources available to satisfy an order that the respondent cannot otherwise meet or to support the respondent by replenishing his coffers, though it may make findings about the likelihood of that occurring and take such resources into account.[25] It is essential to this process that the parties provide the court with full and frank disclosure regarding their assets. The court can draw adverse inferences about the resources of parties who are failing to disclose their assets,[26] but doing even that depends on the court knowing that something is not being disclosed.[27]

7.3.1 FINANCIAL PROVISION

Periodical payments

Periodical payments are often referred to as 'maintenance', but may be used for any purpose.[28] Commonly paid from income to help meet the recipient's day-to-day needs, they are simply a mechanism for transferring resources, weekly, monthly, or on some other timetable, between the parties. They may be expressed as a fixed sum (perhaps index-linked, to increase automatically with costs of living) or as a percentage of some resource of the payer's, such as a bonus; where a percentage payment from a bonus is used to meet income needs, it should be subject to a cap to ensure payment does not exceed those needs.[29] We address the potential duration of periodical payments orders in discussing the 'clean break' principle at 7.6.1 below. The order may require that payments be 'secured':[30] a capital sum is set aside from which payments can continue should the payer default or die, avoiding the need for enforcement proceedings or to seek continued support from the deceased's estate.[31] Periodical payments orders can be varied at any point, as to the amount payable, the timetable for payment, and the duration of the liability.[32] They terminate automatically if the recipients marries or forms a civil partnership.[33]

Lump sums

The court can order one party to pay the other a capital sum or sums, either in full or by instalments.[34] An order for a discrete lump sum or sums cannot be varied. However, a lump sum payable by instalments can be varied both as to the timetable for instalments and quantum.[35] Lump sums remain payable despite the recipient's subsequent marriage or civil partnership.

---

[25] *Thomas v Thomas* [1995] 2 FLR 668, *Charman v Charman* [2007] EWCA Civ 503.
[26] *Prest v Petrodel Resources Ltd and others* [2013] UKSC 34, [45]; *NG v SG (Appeal: Non-Disclosure)* [2011] EWHC 3270; *Young v Young* [2013] EWHC 3637.
[27] Cf *Tchenguiz v Imerman* [2010] EWCA Civ 908; Probert (2011c).
[28] *Miller; McFarlane* [2006] UKHL 24, [31]–[34].
[29] *Parr v Parr* [2013] EWHC 4105.
[30] MCA 1973, s 23(1)(b).
[31] Inheritance (Provision for Family and Dependants) Act 1975.
[32] MCA 1973, s 31.
[33] Ibid, s 28(3).
[34] Ibid, s 23(1)(c).
[35] Ibid, s 31(2)(d); *Hamilton v Hamilton* [2013] EWCA Civ 13.

7.3.2 PROPERTY ADJUSTMENT AND ORDERS FOR SALE

The courts have various powers to adjust the parties' rights over capital assets: transfer of property from one to the other; settlement of property for the benefit of one or both parties; varying or extinguishing the parties' interests under existing nuptial settlements.[36] These one-off orders cannot be varied, though there is limited scope for them to be set aside and appealed against outside the normal time limits.[37] The courts can order the sale of property to facilitate the performance of property adjustment orders, orders for lump sums, and secured periodical payments.[38]

Orders relating to the owner-occupied home

The family home is commonly the most valuable asset at stake, subject to any mortgage debt. There are various ways in which it can be used on divorce. Pending a final determination of the home's fate, it may be appropriate to make occupation orders under the Family Law Act 1996 (FLA 1996).[39]

The house could be sold immediately and the proceeds (after any mortgage debt has been paid) divided in defined shares, providing each party with resources to fund new accommodation. However, the net equity in the home (even combined with each party's ability to raise fresh mortgage finance) may not be enough to enable both to rehouse. Alternatively, the house could be transferred outright to one spouse, perhaps in return for a lump sum payment or for that spouse forgoing other claims. Or the house might be made the subject of a settlement allowing one spouse and the children to occupy it until a specified date or event following which it will be sold and the proceeds split; a similar effect can be achieved by an outright transfer subject to a charge in the other party's favour to be realized on sale. Various events can be used as the trigger for sale, as illustrated by 'Mesher' and 'Martin' orders. The operation of these types of orders can generate conflict, which may be a factor that weighs against using them if a fair result can be achieved some other way.[40]

A *Mesher* order[41] settles the property on the parties in defined shares to be realized on sale once the youngest child reaches a particular age, or finishes a specified level of education, or (earlier) on further order; until then, the children and primary carer occupy the property. This may be feasible only if: (i) the other parent can obtain alternative accommodation without immediate access to his or her share of the capital; (ii) the primary carer will be able to fund new accommodation following the sale, bearing in mind the continuing impact on earning capacity of ongoing child-care responsibility until sale;[42] and (iii) the parties can maintain mortgage or other outgoings on the former matrimonial home whilst also funding the other party's new home. A *Mesher* order may be an unattractive option, simply 'postpon[ing] the evil day' for the party left in occupation.[43]

---

[36] Ibid, s 24; e.g. *AB v CD* [2014] EWHC 2998.
[37] See 7.6.3.
[38] MCA 1973, s 24A.
[39] See 4.5.3.
[40] *S v B* [2004] EWHC 2089.
[41] [1980] 1 All ER 126.
[42] *S v B* [2004] EWHC 2089.
[43] *Harvey v Harvey* [1982] Fam 83, 89.

A *Martin* order[44] triggers sale on the occurrence of some event in the life of the spouse who will occupy the property, such as remarriage, cohabitation, death, or that spouse electing to leave the property. This potentially further delays the other party's access to his or her capital share, but provides greater protection for the occupying spouse, who may otherwise struggle to find alternative accommodation without public assistance. However, that 'protection' may seriously restrict the occupying party's freedom: that spouse might wish to move, for example to take up a new job or to be near family, but that spouse's share following the required sale might be insufficient to acquire a home in the new location.[45]

The court's powers are not unlimited. For example, it cannot order one party to pay sums to a third party (e.g. a mortgage lender) or adjust the parties' liabilities under the mortgage. Any mortgagee must receive notice of the proceedings and an opportunity to be heard;[46] their consent may be required to any transfer, and, even if the property is transferred, the original mortgagor(s) remain liable to repay the loan unless the mortgagee consents to transfer the liability.[47] There are various ways of coping with these restrictions. Parties commonly 'undertake' to do something, or to use best endeavours to achieve something (e.g. to secure the lender's agreement to transfer the mortgage), which the court cannot order.[48] Such undertakings can be enforced like court orders, though the court cannot order specific performance;[49] where aspects of the orders are premised on the undertakings, the orders could be set aside or varied if the undertakings are breached. An undertaking by one spouse to pay the mortgage can be supported by a nominal order for periodical payments; if that spouse fails to pay, that order can be varied to give the recipient funds with which to pay directly. The party who is not mortgagor can also undertake to indemnify the other for mortgage payments, or (if occupying) to pay an occupation rent.[50]

Orders relating to rented homes

The courts can transfer various types of tenancy to one party, whether the property was previously rented by one or both parties. Many types of tenancy can be transferred under MCA 1973, s 24, but there are also relevant powers under the FLA 1996.[51] The FLA 1996 sets out a checklist of factors which the court must consider in exercising its discretion.[52] The landlord is entitled to be heard before an order is made.[53] Where the landlord is a housing authority, it may allocate new housing to one or both parties without a court order, at least where they are in agreement.[54] Access to social housing is a matter for the local authority,

---

[44] [1978] Fam 12.

[45] Deech (1982), 633.

[46] FPR 2010, r 9.13.

[47] *Livesey v Jenkins* [1985] AC 424, 444.

[48] See Black et al (2012), 30.135 et seq.

[49] See *N v N (Divorce: Ante-Nuptial Agreement)* [1999] 2 FCR 583, 596; *Livesey v Jenkins* [1985] AC 424, 444; *L v L* [2006] EWHC 956, [61]; cf Law Society (2003), para 293, doubting the enforceability of undertakings.

[50] *Harvey v Harvey* [1982] Fam 83.

[51] Sch 7.

[52] Ibid, para 5.

[53] Ibid, para 14(1).

[54] Law Com (2006), para 3.58.

whose hands cannot be tied by court orders, for example arranging for children to live with both parties.[55]

7.3.3 ORDERS RELATING TO PENSIONS

Pensions are important forms of saving to provide income in retirement.[56] The courts have two main powers over pension funds: pension attachment and pension sharing. Pension attachment is a type of financial provision order,[57] directed not at the pension-holder but at that spouse's pension trustees. When the pension or relevant death-in-service benefit falls due, some defined portion of the pension or benefit is paid to the other spouse. Neither the court nor the other spouse can control whether and when the pension will fall due, or how valuable it will be. Partly for that reason, pension attachment is little used. The preferred option is pension sharing, available in relation to almost all except the basic state pension.[58] The court orders that part of one party's pension fund be debited and immediately transferred to establish an independent fund for the other spouse. This avoids the difficulties associated with pension attachment and helps achieve a clean break. If the pension share will generate sufficient income in later life for the recipient, there may be no need for periodical payments beyond retirement. Alternatively, the value of the pension might be 'offset' against other assets, for example giving a greater share in the value, or all, of the house to one spouse in return for lower or no share of the pension.[59] But this is a problematic exercise, given the difficulties of comparing pension and other assets.[60]

7.3.4 WHEN MAY ORDERS BE MADE?

All orders are available on divorce and nullity, and all bar pension sharing on judicial separation. Orders may be made at any time following the grant of decree nisi,[61] but will not take effect until after decree absolute.[62] The intervening period can be covered by orders for maintenance pending suit and interim maintenance,[63] and legal services payment orders to enable the economically weaker party to pay for legal advice and assistance related to the divorce and related financial proceedings.[64] Orders may also be made after decree absolute; there is no formal limitation period, though applications brought years after divorce may be difficult to sustain.[65] A party who has remarried or formed a new civil partnership cannot make an application, but can pursue an application made in the original divorce petition.[66]

---

[55] *Holmes-Moorhouse v Richmond LBC* [2009] UKHL 7: see p 767.
[56] See generally Woodward with Sefton (2014), Woodward and Sefton (2014).
[57] MCA 1973, ss 25B–D.
[58] Ibid, ss 21A, 24B–D.
[59] *Martin-Dye v Martin-Dye* [2006] EWCA Civ 681, [85].
[60] *Maskell v Maskell* [2003] 1 FLR 1138; Woodward with Sefton (2014), 4 and ch 8.
[61] Cf *JP v NP (Financial Remedies: Costs)* [2014] EWHC 1101.
[62] MCA 1973, ss 23(5) and 24(3); see p 337 above.
[63] Ibid, s 22.
[64] Ibid, ss 22ZA–B; *Rubin v Rubin* [2014] EWHC 611.
[65] *Wyatt v Vince* [2015] UKSC 14, reversing a decision to strike out an application made nearly 20 years after the decree absolute; cf *Hill v Hill* [1998] 1 FLR 198.
[66] MCA 1973, s 28(3); *Whitehouse-Piper v Stokes* [2008] EWCA Civ 1049.

7.3.5 AFTER THE ORDER

Dealing with changing circumstances

Evidently, the parties' circumstances may change following the divorce—the fortunes of either spouse might improve or deteriorate in a way that makes the orders made on divorce appear unfair. At 7.6.1 below, we discuss the desirability of orders being made in such a way that the parties' financial, as well as legal, relationship terminates on divorce. However, often that cannot be achieved and, in particular, periodical payments may be ordered. As noted above, the courts can vary particular types of orders under MCA 1973, s 31, including periodical payments; so, for example, if it becomes difficult for the payer to afford the required payments or if the payee becomes self-sufficient sooner than expected, the order may be varied or discharged. Capital orders generally cannot be varied—they are intended to achieve finality. But we consider at 7.6.3 the limited grounds on which an appeal may be launched (later than the normal 21-day window after the order was made) where circumstances have changed.

Enforcement

The courts have wide-ranging powers to enforce financial orders against defaulters. But the law in this area is notoriously labyrinthine and procedurally complex,[67] and a Law Commission project began in 2014 aimed to recommend a 'simpler and more intuitive enforcement process'.[68] Key powers currently include attachment of earnings; warrants of control: the seizure and sale of goods to pay the debt; orders requiring a third party holding funds belonging to the liable party (e.g. a bank) to pay them to the applicant; charging orders, giving the applicant a security interest in property belonging to the payer realizable on sale; and committal to prison for up to six weeks: the last resort to be used where the defaulting payer can pay but is wilfully refusing or culpably neglecting to do so. Failure to execute relevant documentation for property adjustment or to give up vacant possession prior to sale can be rectified by the court executing the documents or making an order for possession.[69]

7.4 THE PRINCIPLES GOVERNING THE GRANT OF RELIEF: AN INTRODUCTION

Having identified the tools, we now examine the basis on which they may be used. English law allocates resources on divorce not in accordance with statutory rules but on the basis of a wide judicial discretion. The basic principles are uniform, whether the case involves opposite-sex or same-sex spouses, or civil partners.[70] However, features of at least some same-sex relationships (such as a more equal division of labour during the relationship) may mean that one tends to see different *outcomes* from those typical of many opposite-sex

---

67 *Constantinides v Constantinides* [2013] EWHC 3688.
68 Law Com (2015).
69 For detailed discussion, see Black et al (2012), ch 33 and Law Com (2015).
70 *Lawrence v Gallagher* [2012] EWCA Civ 394. Cf Leckey (2013) questioning the aptness of this.

divorces. But like cases should be treated alike, regardless of their form and gender pattern. Application of the principles between same-sex couples may provide a valuable, gender-neutral, and ahistorical context in which to re-evaluate the principles as they apply in the ideologically loaded, traditionally gendered context of marriage.[71] So too may contemplating the principles' used in opposite-sex marriages where the 'traditional' roles have been reversed.[72]

7.4.1 A BRIEF HISTORY

The history of financial relief on divorce is closely related to the history of divorce itself. Fault-based divorce law pre-1969 was accompanied by fault-based financial provision:

Law Commission, *The Financial Consequences of Divorce: The Basic Policy*, Law Com No 103 (London: HMSO, 1980)

13. Prior to 1971...the main features of the law governing the financial consequences of divorce were based on the assumption that (subject perhaps to the exception that a wife who was technically "guilty" might nevertheless expect some financial provision) the function of divorce was to give relief where a wrong had been done. The right and duty of maintenance was related to the performance of reciprocal maintenance obligations; a husband who was at fault should continue to support his wife, but conversely it would be unjust to require a husband who had "performed substantially all his matrimonial obligations to continue to provide maintenance for a wife who had substantially repudiated hers." The concept of a life-long right to and duty of support was thus inextricably linked with the concept of divorce as a relief for wrongdoing.

The Divorce Reform Act 1969 replaced the concept of matrimonial offence with irretrievable breakdown of marriage as the sole ground for divorce. This might have been expected to affect the basis on which financial relief should be granted. However, the Law Commission report underpinning the financial relief legislation of 1970 did not examine basic principles.[73] The abandonment of the contractual, fault-based model left a 'normative vacuum'.[74] The legislation required courts to consider a checklist of factors, of which the parties' conduct was just one. Orders could now be made in favour of *either* party, whoever had petitioned for divorce. Following pre-1969 case law, the court was ultimately directed:

...so to exercise [its] powers as to place the parties, so far as it is practicable and, having regard to their conduct, just to do so, in the financial position in which they would have been if the marriage had not broken down and each had properly discharged his or her financial obligations and responsibilities towards the other.[75]

---

[71] Wilson (2007), 37; see also Lind (2004), extracted at 2.3.2 above.
[72] Parkinson (2011), 256; Diduck (2011b), 313–14; Bendall (2014), 269–70.
[73] Law Com (1969).
[74] Dewar (2003), 426.
[75] Matrimonial Proceedings and Property Act 1970, s 5(1).

The practical problems with this 'minimal loss' principle quickly became apparent.[76] The objective was usually unattainable as resources were insufficient to meet the parties' basic needs: the principle was more aptly described as 'equal misery' than 'minimal loss'.[77] There were concerns that continuing obligations caused financial hardship to husbands and their new families, but equally that wives were receiving inadequate provision and relying on welfare benefits.[78] Fundamentally, the minimal loss objective seemed incompatible with no-fault divorce.

Law Commission, *The Financial Consequences of Divorce: The Basic Policy*, Law Com No 103 (London: HMSO, 1980)

> 30. We think that the arguments against the retention of a principle of life-long support at the standard enjoyed during the marriage can most easily be analysed and considered under four heads:
>
> (i) A duty of life-long support is now out of date because it is rooted in the concept of marriage as a life-time union. If marriage were indeed still a life-long institution, it might perhaps be reasonable that the parties should expect that the benefits and burdens incident to the status of marriage would not be affected by divorce; but (it is said) in modern conditions it is unrealistic for married couples not to accept that there is a very real possibility that their marriage will break down. It is thus correspondingly unrealistic for them to suppose that if this should happen their financial position would remain unaffected.
>
> (ii) The change in the juristic basis of divorce from matrimonial offence to irretrievable breakdown has fundamentally altered the validity of the law's approach to support obligations. On this argument the obligation to provide life-long support is based on the analogy between marriage and contract, under which compensation would be available for its breach. Consequently, it is argued that now that divorce is available whenever the marriage has broken down, irrespective of whether one or other of the parties is in breach of his or her matrimonial obligations, it is inappropriate for the law to continue to found the parties' respective financial obligations after divorce on the now largely irrelevant notion of breach of duty; and it is unjust to do so since the present law may require a man to maintain his wife when she has herself been entirely responsible for the breakdown.
>
> (iii) The objective of life-long support is almost invariably impossible to attain because in most cases one man's resources are insufficient to support two households.
>
> (iv) The concept of a life-long support obligation is based on wholly out of date views of the division of function between husband and wife as well as of the economic status of women.

The first and fourth of these arguments could be overstated. While divorce was no longer rare, many wedding couples might still expect or intend a lifelong union.[79] While wives were more economically active, large differences in spouses' employment patterns, particularly following the birth of children, meant that men and women were far from being on

---

76 See Cretney (2003a), 427–8.
77 *Miller; McFarlane* [2006] UKHL 24, [126].
78 Law Com (1980), paras 25–8.
79 Ibid, paras 31–4.

an equal economic footing and many wives could not be self-sufficient on divorce.[80] The second argument had more weight, the courts having decided that detailed investigation of conduct other than in extreme cases would subvert the aims of no-fault divorce.[81] As the Law Commission asked, 'If...the essence of the obligation of life-long support on divorce is that it represents compensation for a wrong done to the financially weaker party, yet the courts no longer investigate the question of blame, how (it is asked) can the obligation to support still be justified?'[82] The policy represented by the minimal loss principle no longer commanded support.[83] The MCA 1973, Part II was accordingly amended in 1984,[84] giving us the law in force today.[85]

7.4.2 THE CURRENT LAW: THE STATUTORY DISCRETION

Any examination of the current law must begin with the statute. In this extract, we have italicized key wording added, along with the clean break provision s 25A, in 1984:

Matrimonial Causes Act 1973

25 Matters to which the court is to have regard in deciding how to exercise its powers [to order financial provision, property adjustment, sale, and pension sharing]

(1) It shall be the duty of the court in deciding whether to exercise its powers [to order financial provision, property adjustment, sale, or pension sharing] and, if so, in what manner, to have regard to all the circumstances of the case, *first consideration being given to the welfare while a minor of any child of the family who has not attained the age of eighteen.*

(2) As regards the exercise of the powers of the court [to make such orders] in relation to a party to the marriage, the court shall in particular have regard to the following matters—

   (a) the income, earning capacity, property and other financial resources which each of the parties to the marriage has or is likely to have in the foreseeable future, *including in the case of earning capacity any increase in that capacity which it would in the opinion of the court be reasonable to expect a party to the marriage to take steps to acquire;*

   (b) the financial needs, obligations and responsibilities which each of the parties to the marriage has or is likely to have in the foreseeable future;

   (c) the standard of living enjoyed by the family before the breakdown of the marriage;

   (d) the age of each party to the marriage and the duration of the marriage;

   (e) any physical and mental disability of either of the parties to the marriage;

   (f) the contributions which each of the parties has made or is likely in the foreseeable future to make to the welfare of the family, including any contribution by looking after the home or caring for the family;

---

[80] Ibid, paras 45–57.
[81] *Wachtel v Wachtel* [1973] Fam 72; see 7.5.6 below.
[82] Law Com (1980), para 41.
[83] Law Com (1981), para 17.
[84] Matrimonial and Family Proceedings Act 1984.
[85] For more recent history, see Law Com (2011), Part 3.

(g) the conduct of each of the parties, *if that conduct is such that it would in the opinion of the court be inequitable to disregard it;*

(h) in the case of proceedings for divorce or nullity of marriage, the value to each of the parties to the marriage of any benefit which, by reason of the dissolution or annulment of the marriage, that party will lose the chance of acquiring.[86] ...

25A Exercise of the court's powers in favour of party to marriage on decree of divorce or nullity of marriage

(1) Where on or after the grant of a decree of divorce or nullity of marriage the court decides to exercise its powers [to make such orders] in favour of a party to the marriage, it shall be the duty of the court to consider whether it would be appropriate so to exercise those powers that the financial obligations of each party towards the other will be terminated as soon after the grant of the decree as the court considers just and reasonable ....

52 Interpretation

(1) In this Act—

"child" in relation to one or both of the parties to a marriage, includes an illegitimate child of that party or, as the case may be, of both parties;

"child of the family", in relation to the parties to a marriage, means—

(a) a child of both of those parties; and

(b) any other child, not being a child who is placed with those parties as foster parents by a local authority or voluntary organisation, who has been treated by both of those parties as a child of their family.

Similarly, on applications to vary orders, the court must give first consideration to the welfare of minor children of the family, and have regard to all the circumstances, including any relevant change of circumstance and the clean break principle.[87] We discuss that principle at 7.6 below.

The most striking feature of these provisions is that no ultimate objective is identified. The 1984 legislation removed the minimal loss principle, but the 'replacements'—first consideration to the welfare of minor children, and the clean break principle—do not perform an equivalent function.[88] If anything, they clash: the individualism implicit in the clean break principle jars with the idea of continuing obligations and constraints where there are dependent children.[89] But they perhaps signal a new focus on the parties' ongoing relationship as parents, distinctly from their concluded relationship as spouses.[90] The factors in the statutory checklist point in different directions, some suggesting forward-looking, needs-based awards, others encouraging a retrospective evaluation of parties' contributions. Since English law operates separate property during marriage, there must be some

---

86 I.e. benefits that would have been enjoyed had the party remained married, e.g. a widow's pension.
87 MCA 1973, s 31(7).
88 Cf Family Law (Scotland) Act 1985; Scot Law Com (1981); Deech (1982).
89 Diduck (2003), 142.
90 Douglas (2012), 223.

rationale for redistributing the parties' resources on divorce.[91] But the legislation provides none. As one Australian judge has described it, the family judge's situation is like that of:

> …a bus driver who is given a large number of instructions about how to drive the bus, and the authority to do various actions such as turning left or right. There is also the occasional advice or correction offered by three senior drivers. The one piece of information which he or she is not given is where to take the bus. All he or she is told is that the driver is required to drive to a reasonable destination.[92]

The courts have been left to decide for themselves where to go, and their direction has changed over time, generating a vast academic literature seeking both to explain what the law is (which is less than straightforward) and to debate the principles which *should* govern financial orders.[93] As one practitioner put it:

> There is something in the work of archaeologists that reflects the current difficulties faced by family lawyers. The excavation requires a large group of people to pick through the rubble to find a few nuggets, which are delivered to a learned few, who develop a theory to unlock the mysteries of the investigation.[94]

7.5 EXERCISING THE STATUTORY DISCRETION: PRINCIPLES FROM THE CASE LAW

The basic principle identified by the judges is 'fairness'. But as Lord Nicholls remarked in *White v White*, 'fairness, like beauty, lies in the eye of the beholder'.[95] He went further in *Miller; McFarlane*:

Miller v Miller; McFarlane v McFarlane [2006] UKHL 24

LORD NICHOLLS:

4. Fairness is an elusive concept. It is an instinctive response to a given set of facts. Ultimately it is grounded in social and moral values. These values, or attitudes, can be stated. But they cannot be justified, or refuted, by any objective process of logical reasoning. Moreover, they change from one generation to the next. It is not surprising therefore that in the present context there can be different views on the requirements of fairness in any particular case…

6. …Implicitly the courts must exercise their powers so as to achieve an outcome which is fair between the parties. But an important aspect of fairness is that like cases should be treated alike. So, perforce, if there is to be an acceptable degree of consistency of decision

---

[91] *Miller; McFarlane* [2006] UKHL 24, [137], citing a lecture by Ward LJ (2004).
[92] Chisolm J, quoted in Parkinson (1999), 53 and Law Com (2012), para 3.3.
[93] E.g. Eekelaar (1991a), ch 4; Diduck and Orton (1994); Eekelaar and Maclean (1997); Eekelaar (1998a); Diduck (2003), ch 6, (2011a), (2011b); Bailey-Harris (2005); Miles (2005), (2008), (2011a); Cooke (2007).
[94] Pirrie (2007).
[95] [2001] 1 AC 596, 599.

from one case to the next, the courts must themselves articulate, if only in the broadest fashion, what are the applicable if unspoken principles guiding the court's approach...

9. The starting point is surely not controversial. In the search for a fair outcome it is pertinent to have in mind that fairness generates obligations as well as rights. The financial provision made on divorce by one party for the other, still typically the wife, is not in the nature of largesse. It is not a case of 'taking away' from one party and 'giving' to the other property which 'belongs' to the former. The claimant is not a suppliant. Each party to a marriage is *entitled* to a *fair* share of the available property. The search is always for what are the *requirements* of fairness in the particular case.

Miller; McFarlane identified three broad principles, rationales, or 'strands' underpinning the 'fair' result: need, compensation, and (equal) sharing. The outcomes generated by these principles in individual cases vary substantially, depending on factors such as the scale of the parties' resources, whether they have children, the degree of financial interdependence, and the length of the marriage. All three principles have something important to tell us about the law's understanding of the economic relationship created by marriage and civil partnership.

Miller and *McFarlane* were both 'big money' cases, but otherwise very different. The Millers had been married less than three years and had no children; the McFarlanes were married for over 16 years, with three children. Mrs Miller had worked in public relations until the first year of the marriage; Mrs McFarlane had given up a successful professional career in order to raise the family and support her husband, whose career prospered. Mr Miller had amassed a fortune before the marriage; the McFarlanes had started out in life together. What did 'fairness' demand in these very different cases?

Our discussion is chiefly organized around the three principles identified by the House of Lords. However, some judges are clearly more comfortable than others with the principled approach.[96] The courts regularly reiterate that the exercise remains discretionary, guided by the s 25 factors and focused on obtaining a 'fair' result. The three principles are not 'separate heads of claim', and should not be routinely argued in straightforward cases which (as we discuss below) focus on needs.[97] It is often said that the court is engaged in a holistic, 'intuitive' pursuit of fairness,[98] informed but not constrained by the principles, or whichever of them is deemed most relevant.[99] But while these cases are 'fact specific', in the sense that many different circumstances might have to be examined, 'fairness' cannot be the sole criterion. Fairness itself requires consistency in decision-making, so 'fairness' (even alongside 'non-discrimination'[100]) cannot be left to the judgement of individual courts. It requires principled shape and content so that some measure of predictability is achieved.[101] While any given set of facts will generate a range of reasonable outcomes, the courts' basic approach should be broadly similar, whichever judge (if any) the parties find themselves

---

[96] Compare the emphasis of strong discretion in *B v B* [2008] EWCA Civ 543 and *Robson v Robson* [2010] EWCA Civ 1171; and the exercise of the discretion within guidelines provided by the principles in *Jones v Jones* [2011] EWCA Civ 11, *K v L* [2011] EWCA Civ 550.

[97] *R v R* [2011] EWHC 3093, [9], [55]–[56].

[98] E.g. *RP v RP* [2006] EWHC 3409, [58]; *VB v JP* [2008] EWHC 112, [45], [52]; *McFarlane v McFarlane (No 2)* [2009] EWHC 891, [112], [118].

[99] *B v B* [2008] EWCA Civ 543, [50]–[51].

[100] Ibid, asserting that only two principles have universal application: fairness and non-discrimination.

[101] *N v F* [2011] EWHC 586, [7]–[8].

before. Otherwise, the exercise becomes unacceptably arbitrary and settlement hard to achieve. So we must try to develop a coherent view of the case law, analysing the principles and their inter-relationship, and consider when one principle or feature of the case might assume 'magnetic importance',[102] to try to ascertain where the courts' sense of 'fairness' takes them. However, 'It is prudent to remember that [the House of Lords' speeches] are explanations of and expansions upon the statute, not the statute itself'.[103] So we begin with the factor that statute requires be given first consideration.

7.5.1 FIRST CONSIDERATION: THE WELFARE OF THE CHILDREN

Children's maintenance requirements are dealt with primarily via child support, but their interests may influence provision between the adults in various ways:

Miller v Miller; McFarlane v McFarlane [2006] UKHL 24

BARONESS HALE:

128. . . . [S]ection 25(1) . . . is a clear recognition of the reality that, although the couple may seek to go their separate ways, they are still jointly responsible for the welfare of their children. The invariable practice in English law is to try to maintain a stable home for the children after their parents' divorce. Research indicates that it is more successful in doing this than in securing a comparable income for them in future (see, eg [Arthur et al (2002)]). Giving priority to the children's welfare should also involve ensuring that their primary carer is properly provided for, because it is well known that the security and stability of children depends in large part upon the security and stability of their primary carers (see eg [Lewis (2001a)] p 178).

Children's welfare in this context is only the first, not paramount, consideration,[104] and only during the children's minority. However, the courts acknowledge that children remain financially dependent and live at home long after reaching 18.[105] Other children's interests (such those from a previous or subsequent relationship) may be relevant insofar as they affect parties' needs and obligations.[106] Children's interests frequently affect decisions about housing, and may also impact on whether and when it is reasonable to expect the primary carer to undertake paid employment.

7.5.2 THE 'EVERYDAY CASE': MEETING THE PARTIES' MATERIAL NEEDS

The first of the House of Lords' three principles derives from the second factor in s 25(2): financial needs.

---

[102] E.g. *McCartney v Mills McCartney* [2008] EWHC 401, [301].
[103] *Charman v Charman* [2006] EWHC 1879, [114] per Coleridge J.
[104] *Suter v Suter* [1987] Fam 111, 123–4.
[105] *Richardson v Richardson (No 2)* [1994] 2 FLR 1051.
[106] *Roberts v Roberts* [1970] P 1.

Miller v Miller; McFarlane v McFarlane [2006] UKHL 24

LORD NICHOLLS:

11. This element of fairness reflects the fact that to a greater or lesser extent every relationship of marriage gives rise to a relationship of interdependence. The parties share the roles of money-earner, home-maker and child-carer. Mutual dependence begets mutual obligations of support. When the marriage ends fairness requires that the assets of the parties should be divided primarily so as to make provision for the parties' housing and financial needs, taking into account a wide range of matters such as the parties' ages, their future earning capacity, the family's standard of living, and any disability of either party. Most of these needs will have been generated by the marriage, but not all of them. Needs arising from age or disability are instances of the latter.

Need assumes 'magnetic importance' in high-value cases where all or most of the assets are classed as non-matrimonial,[107] for example where the wealth was acquired by one party prior to the marriage.[108] As is lavishly exemplified by *McCartney v Mills McCartney*,[109] the courts interpret 'need' by reference to the marital standard of living;[110] the 'needs' of the rich are more substantial than the needs of the rest; they might even extend to a 'need' to keep horses.[111] But the ex-spouse cannot expect to be maintained indefinitely at that level by the other party after a short marriage;[112] the court will seek instead to enable that party to transition back to a standard of living that he or she can sustain.[113]

In what Emma Hitchings has dubbed the 'everyday' cases[114]—where the resources do not exceed the parties' needs—the needs of both parties (and associated pragmatic issues) are the only real consideration, to the exclusion of compensation and equal sharing. In many cases, it is impossible, given the limited resources and debts, even to cover both parties' needs fully—life after divorce is often unavoidably tough for both.[115] 'Creativity and common sense'[116] are required to stretch the resources as far as possible. This dominance of needs in the everyday case is easily overlooked, given the focus of most reported cases:

Jones v Jones [2011] EWCA Civ 41

WALL P:

69. . . . [I]t seems to me unfortunate that our law of [financial] relief should be largely dictated by cases which bear no resemblance to the ordinary lives of most divorcing couples and to the average case heard, day in and day out, by district judges up and down the country. The

---

107 See 7.5.4.
108 *McCartney v Mills McCartney* [2008] EWHC 401; *Y v Y* [2012] EWHC 2063; *J v J* [2011] EWHC 1010.
109 Ibid.
110 *Miller; McFarlane* [2006] UKHL 24, [138]; s 25(2)(c).
111 *S v S* [2008] EWHC 519.
112 Duration of marriage for these purposes includes any immediately preceding period of stable cohabitation: *GW v RW* [2003] EWHC 611.
113 *G v G* [2012] EWHC 167, [136].
114 Hitchings (2009a), (2010).
115 *AL v AL* [2011] EWHC 3150, [50].
116 *R v R* [2011] EWHC 3093, [9].

> sums of money – including the costs – involved in this case are well beyond the experience and even the contemplation of most people. Whether the wife has £5 [million] or £8 million, she will still be a very rich woman and the application of the so called "sharing" and "needs" principles may look very different in cases where the latter predominates and the parties' assets are a tiny percentage of those encountered here.

In the absence of much illustrative case law, the Law Commission's work offers valuable insight into how such cases are dealt with. Surprisingly, perhaps, the law on needs is rather unclear: '[M]ost family lawyers are confident that needs is something they know when they see it; none can offer a definition, although all can offer explanations and descriptions of what "needs" can include.'[117]

Law Commission, *Marital Property Agreements*, Law Com CP 198 (London: TSO, 2011)

> 2.28...We can identify a number of distinctive features of the courts' interpretation:
>
> (1) In looking at the parties' income needs the courts are aware of the difficulties experienced by those who have given up work, wholly or in part, to look after children. It is not assumed that people can readily return to work in later years, nor that they can recover economically from years out of employment. Orders for periodical payments reflect this. [See 7.6 below]
>
> (2) Needs encompasses the value of a home. We live in a society where owner-occupation is highly valued, and where the market for private rented accommodation is nowhere near so plentiful or so acceptable as it is, for the most part, in continental Europe. Considerable emphasis is therefore placed on the division of the capital value of the family home, whether immediately or at a later stage when the children leave home.
>
> (3) In assessing the parties' housing needs the courts are mindful of the ability of each party to obtain and support a mortgage loan. Someone who has given up work to care for children will often receive a larger share in the capital value of the family home when it is sold than will a parent who has not given up work and has therefore had a continuing (and perhaps growing) mortgage capacity.
>
> (4) So far as possible, the courts try to avoid allowing either party to leave the other dependent on state benefits, on the basis that it is not acceptable to pass on one's individual responsibilities to the state. However, on occasions that is not possible,[118] and the courts will avoid making an order that leaves someone in a position where he or she would be better off not working.[119]
>
> (5) The concept of needs is sufficiently long-term to encompass provision for retirement.... [T]he courts...have the power to make [pension sharing] orders and so can share an asset that was intended by the spouses originally as a joint provision for their old age.

Against that backdrop, we now examine some specific issues related to need.

---

[117] Law Com (2012), para 3.25.
[118] *Delaney v Delaney* [1990] 2 FLR 457.
[119] *Furniss v Furniss* (1982) 3 FLR 46.

Housing first

Wherever there are minor children, the court's priority is securing accommodation for them, their primary carer, and (if possible)[120] the other parent:

M v B (Ancillary Proceedings: Lump Sum) [1998] 1 FCR 213 (CA), 220

THORPE LJ:

In all these cases it is one of the paramount considerations, in applying the s 25 criteria, to endeavour to stretch what is available to cover the need of each for a home, particularly where there are young children involved. Obviously the primary carer needs whatever is available to make the main home for the children, but it is of importance, albeit it is of lesser importance, that the other parent should have a home of his own where the children can enjoy their contact time with him. Of course, there are cases where there is not enough to provide a home for either. Of course, there are cases where there is only enough to provide one. But in any case where there is, by stretch and a degree of risk-taking, the possibility of a division to enable both to rehouse themselves, that is an exceptionally important considera-tion and one which will almost invariably have a decisive impact on outcome.

Here the judge had the opportunity to make a division which would just about enable each to rehouse. True, if the wife was to go for [the house she preferred] it would require some sacrifice on the part of her family and some burden of future mortgage. True, on the husband's side it would entail taking advantage of his ability to defer the [legal aid authority's] charge in respect of his costs.[121] But those are the sort of methods to which the court regu-larly has to have recourse in cases where the money is only just enough . . . [122]

Even if the home is retained for occupation by the children and primary carer during the chil-dren's minority, it may be appropriate for the other spouse to retain a share in its capital value under a *Mesher* order.[123] But the parties' respective needs and resources may indicate that the primary carer should retain the property either on a *Martin* basis or outright.[124] Some primary carers place such weight on securing immediate housing that they forgo periodical payments or the long-term security offered by a share of the other spouse's pension fund in order to secure the home.[125] This sort of trade-off may be economically unwise, viewed in the longer term.[126]

The source of available resources

The court must have regard to all available financial resources of the parties. All assets may in principle be used to meet the parties' needs, including wealth accumulated prior to the marriage; acquired by gift or inheritance during it;[127] years after separation;[128] or from a

---

120 E.g. *B v B (Financial Provision: Welfare of Child and Conduct)* [2002] 1 FLR 555.
121 The statutory charge recovering public funding for legal services: Black et al (2012), ch 2.
122 See also *Fisher-Aziz v Aziz* [2010] EWCA Civ 673.
123 *Elliott v Elliott* [2001] 1 FCR 477; see p 448 above.
124 *B v B (Mesher Order)* [2002] EWHC 3106.
125 Perry et al (2000).
126 See Woodward with Sefton (2014).
127 *White v White* [2001] 1 AC 596, at 610.
128 *Schuller v Schuller* [1990] 2 FLR 193; *Vaughan v Vaughan* [2010] EWCA Civ 349, [42].

personal injury claim.[129] The parties' ability to borrow is also relevant, whether to release the value of otherwise illiquid assets or to acquire new property. But if all or most of the property available for division is 'non-matrimonial' for the purposes of the sharing principle, discussed below, it may be appropriate to moderate the level of need to be catered for,[130] unless the marriage was long.[131]

Public benefits and housing inevitably have an important role in resolving low-value cases.[132] Tax credits are especially important, as their means-testing rules take no account of maintenance payments received on divorce; by contrast, entitlement to key means-tested welfare benefits is reduced pound for pound by receipt of spousal maintenance.[133] The mere fact that one party is likely to become reliant on state support following divorce may not itself justify a financial order, particularly if the marriage was short or childless.[134] But, although a former spouse is not a 'liable relative' from whom benefits payments may be recouped by the state, it is generally considered undesirable that the state should pick up the bill if the ex-spouse can and should reasonably be expected to provide support.[135] The law must therefore determine when, on what basis, and for how long[136] an ex-spouse, rather than the state, should have to provide support.

The source of the parties' needs

This brings us to a key question: the particular needs for which an ex-spouse can be made responsible.[137]

North v North [2007] EWCA Civ 760

THORPE LJ:

32. . . . There are of course two faces to fairness. The order must be fair both to the applicant in need and to the respondent who must pay. In any application under Section 31 [for variation of a periodical payment order] the applicant's needs are likely to be the dominant or magnetic factor. But it does not follow that the respondent is inevitably responsible financially for any established needs. He is not an insurer against all hazards nor, when fairness is the measure, is he necessarily liable for needs created by the applicant's financial mismanagement, extravagance or irresponsibility. The prodigal former wife cannot hope to turn to a former husband in pursuit of a legal remedy, whatever may be her hope that he might out of charity come to her rescue.

An ex-spouse may clearly be required to help meet needs generated by the relationship itself: for example, where one spouse gave up paid employment to raise the children and so is not self-sufficient; or where domestic violence caused some disability impairing the

---

[129] *Mansfield v Mansfield* [2011] EWCA Civ 1056.

[130] *N v F* [2011] EWHC 586, [16]–[19]; *B v B* [2012] EWHC 314, [89]; *G v B* [2013] EWHC 3414, [81]–[82].

[131] *Robson v Robson* [2010] EWCA Civ 1171, [8].

[132] See 3.8.2 above; Black et al (2012), ch 24.

[133] Contrast the full maintenance disregard in relation to child support payments: see p 373 above.

[134] *SRJ v DWJ (Financial Provision)* [1999] 3 FCR 153, 160 per Hale J.

[135] *Peacock v Peacock* [1984] 1 All ER 1069; cf *Delaney v Delaney* [1991] FCR 161.

[136] See 7.6 below.

[137] See Eekelaar and Maclean (1986), 39–41.

victim's earning capacity.[138] It is less clear whether and when responsibility may extend to needs which have not been produced by the marriage: for example, arising from long-term unemployment, illness, disability, or old age, particularly where those problems arise following separation.[139] Although not necessary for their decision, both Lord Nicholls and Baroness Hale considered this issue. While Lord Nicholls referred generally to needs arising from disability,[140] Baroness Hale's view was qualified:[141]

Miller v Miller; McFarlane v McFarlane [2006] UKHL 24

BARONESS HALE:

137. . . . The cardinal feature is that each [of the three principles: need, sharing, and compensation] is looking at factors which are linked to the parties' relationship, either causally or temporally, and not to extrinsic, unrelated factors, such as a disability arising after the marriage has ended.

138. . . . The most common rationale is that *the relationship has generated needs* which it is right that the other party should meet . . . This is a perfectly sound rationale where the needs are the consequence of the parties' relationship, as they usually are. The most common source of need is the presence of children, whose welfare is always the first consideration, or of other dependent relatives, such as elderly parents. But another source of need is having had to look after children or other family members in the past. Many parents have seriously compromised their ability to attain self-sufficiency as a result of past family responsibilities. Even if they do their best to re-enter the employment market, it will often be at a lesser level than before, and they will hardly ever be able to make up what they have lost in pension entitlements. A further source of need may be the way in which the parties chose to run their life together. Even dual career families are difficult to manage with completely equal opportunity for both. Compromises often have to be made by one so that the other can get ahead. All couples throughout their lives together have to make choices about who will do what, sometimes forced upon them by circumstances such as redundancy or low pay, sometimes freely made in the interests of them both. The needs generated by such choices are a perfectly sound rationale for adjusting the parties' respective resources in compensation.

The Scottish Law Commission examined this area when recommending that awards should be possible on the grounds of 'grave financial hardship', one of five principles on which relief can be based under the Family Law (Scotland) Act 1985. But they felt that the principle should have limited operation:[142]

Scottish Law Commission, *Report on Aliment and Financial Provision*, Scot Law Com No 67 (Edinburgh: HMSO, 1981)

3.110 . . . We do not think, for example, that a man who suffers hardship on being made redundant at the age of 52 should have a claim for financial provision against a former wife

---

[138] *Jones v Jones* [1976] Fam 8.

[139] E.g. *Ashley v Blackman* [1988] Fam 85; *Re G (Financial Provision: Liberty to Restore Application for Lump Sum)* [2004] EWHC 88. See Law Com (2012), case study 3 and para 4.42.

[140] See [11], in extract above.

[141] See also *Radmacher v Granatino* [2010] UKSC 42, [187].

[142] See also Law Com (1980), para 72.

> whom he divorced thirty years before. We think that the general principle should be that after the divorce each party bears the risk of *supervening* hardship without recourse against the other. It should therefore be made clear in the legislation that it is only where the likelihood of grave financial hardship is established at the time of the divorce that a claim will arise [on that basis]. We recognise that if the principle is framed in this way there will be cases falling narrowly on the "wrong" side of the line. The man or woman paralysed as a result of a road accident six months before the divorce would have a claim for financial provision. The man or woman who suffered a similar injury six months after the divorce would not. We consider, however, that a line has to be drawn somewhere and that the right place to draw the line is the date when the legal relationship between the parties comes to an end. After that each should be free to make a new life without liability for future misfortunes which may befall the other.

On this view, a former spouse cannot be expected to meet all needs, howsoever arising, however short the marriage, and however long ago the divorce.[143]

By contrast, with the clarity of the Scottish position, the English cases do not clearly delineate the extent of responsibility for need. In *Seaton v Seaton*,[144] the husband had become dependent on the wife after being sacked, failed to hold down a job because of drink, and suffered a debilitating stroke shortly before the divorce which left him wholly dependent with no prospect of recovery. The wife was relieved of ongoing liability to support him, though it is unclear whether because of the long-term nature of the husband's dependency or his prior delinquency. By contrast, in *Fisher v Fisher*, the ex-husband was required to continue paying periodical payments to his ex-wife (who was caring for their child) when she was unable to support herself through employment owing to the birth of another child fathered by a third party.[145]

It may sometimes be proper to require an ex-spouse to provide support following redundancy, illness, or disability, even where that occurs long after divorce. While the unmet need may be triggered by an event unrelated to the marriage, the applicant's inability to support herself at that point may be because she lacks any financial cushion having given up paid employment in order to care for the family during (and following) the marriage.[146] But in *North v North*, the prospering ex-husband was required to make modest annual payments to his ex-wife of 14 years, some 20 years after the divorce, when, having been financially secure in England, the wife's position became precarious following her emigration and unwise investment decisions.[147] Importantly, the Court of Appeal rejected the husband's argument that an applicant in the wife's position should be required, as a matter of principle, to prove that 'despite her best efforts, her attempts at self-help had failed' before being able to proceed with an application to vary a periodical payments order. The circumstances relating to her present need were to be examined in the exercise of the court's broad discretion, in pursuit of the overarching objective to attain a fair result. On the facts, and given Thorpe LJ's statement of principle extracted above, the award of any periodical payment was rather surprising.

---

[143] Cf Diduck (2011a), (2011b), Miles (2011a).
[144] [1986] 2 FLR 398.
[145] [1989] 1 FLR 432.
[146] E.g. *Whiting v Whiting* [1988] 1 WLR 565, 580.
[147] Cf *Yates v Yates* [2012] EWCA Civ 532.

The needs and resources of second families

The court must also consider the needs and obligations of the respondent and any new dependants, whether the respondent is legally or, as in the case of step-children or a cohabiting partner, only morally obliged to maintain them.[148] In *Vaughan v Vaughan (No 2)*, it was said that 'although [the court] should not go so far as to give priority to the claims of the first wife, it should certainly not give priority to the claims of the second wife'.[149] In *Delaney v Delaney*, the wife was renting the former matrimonial home with the two children; the husband had bought a new three-bedroomed property with his girlfriend on a shared equity basis, wishing to start a family. Any obligation to the first family would leave the husband's household with an amount 'barely adequate to sustain any reasonable way of life'.[150] The Court of Appeal balanced support for the primary carer, who may have benefits entitlements, against the husband's new family.

Delaney v Delaney [1991] FCR 161 (CA), 165–6

WARD J:

[T]he approach of this court in this case must be, first, to have regard to the need of the wife and the children for proper support. Having assessed that need, the court should then consider the ability of the husband to meet it. Whilst this court deprecates any notion that a former husband and extant father may slough off the tight skin of familial responsibility and may slither into and lose himself in the greener grass on the other side, nonetheless this court has proclaimed and will proclaim that it looks to the realities of the real world in which we live, and that among the realities of life is that there is a life after divorce. The ... husband is entitled to order his life in such a way as will hold in reasonable balance the responsibilities to his existing family which he carries into his new life, as well as his proper aspirations for that new future. In all life, for those who are divorced as well as for those who are not divorced, indulging one's whims or even one's reasonable desires must be held in check by the constraints imposed by limited resources and compelling obligations. But this husband's resources, even when one adds to them the contribution made by his girl friend, are very limited indeed.

In the circumstances, this was a proper case to bring the wife's welfare benefit entitlements into account.

Can the resources of a respondent's new partner be considered in deciding what, if any, order to make against the respondent? If working, the partner can be expected to contribute to the respondent's household costs, thereby reducing his expenditure and freeing up resources for the first family. But the court will not ordinarily make orders against respondents which can only be satisfied by using the resources of their new partner, or other third party, or by making orders that leave respondents dependent on a third party.[151]

---

[148] *Roberts v Roberts* [1970] P 1.
[149] [2010] EWCA Civ 349.
[150] Note that the husband would now remain technically liable to pay child support at the relevant rate: see chapter 6.
[151] *Macey v Macey* (1982) 3 FLR 7; and n 25 above.

Elsewhere, the question is whether and how a new partner of the (would-be) *recipient* of periodical payments is relevant.[152] Either the recipient has a new partner when the court is first invited to make the order, or a new partner arrives later, prompting an application to vary the order. Where the recipient marries or forms a civil partnership before any order has been made, any application is now barred by statute and any existing order for periodical payments automatically terminates.[153] But cohabitation does not have the same effect. Orders commonly provide that periodical payments will cease if the recipient cohabits with a third party for six months. But if no such term was included, the payer wishing to cease or reduce payment must seek a variation. A cohabitant or other committed life partner[154] who can afford to contribute to the recipient's household should do so to the extent that he or she has capacity to pay;[155] orders have been reduced, discharged, or rendered nominal accordingly.[156]

But there is disagreement about the weight which should, in principle, be attached to cohabitation. In *Atkinson v Atkinson*,[157] the Court of Appeal held that cohabitation should not be equated with marriage, a position affirmed in *Grey v Grey*,[158] despite the 'heretical' reservations of Coleridge J in *K v K*.[159] Coleridge J had argued that given the rise in cohabitation and births outside marriage, and the functional and social equivalence to marriage of lengthy, settled cohabitation, it was too easy for an ex-spouse to avoid periodical payments being automatically terminated by cynically not marrying the new partner, thus putting the onus on the payer to seek a variation of the order.[160] But the Court of Appeal is clear that the matter must be left to Parliament to determine. In the meantime, cohabitation is just another factor to weigh in the balance of fairness, albeit one that can attract considerable weight. This clash between law and social practice is difficult to reconcile. While many cohabiting relationships are akin to marriage, others are less stable. Moreover, as the wife in *K v K* argued, cohabitants—unlike spouses—have no legal obligations of mutual support, whether during their relationship or following separation.[161]

Criticism of the law relating to needs

The Law Commission has made several criticisms of the current law relating to 'need': it lacks principle, offering no consistent explanation for when and why one ex-spouse should have to meet the other's needs; it is inaccessible to the lay person, being ascertainable only from close scrutiny of the case law; it is crucially unclear, both as to how much should be paid and for how long;[162] and there is dissatisfaction with the level of awards,

---

[152] See also *Chadwick v Chadwick* [1985] FLR 606: whether *Martin* order more appropriate than outright transfer.

[153] MCA 1973, s 28(1)(a), (3).

[154] *Grey v Grey (No 3)* [2010] EWHC 1055.

[155] *Grey v Grey* [2009] EWCA Civ 1424, [28].

[156] E.g. *Suter v Suter* [1987] Fam 111.

[157] [1988] Fam 93.

[158] [2009] EWCA Civ 1424.

[159] [2005] EWHC 2886.

[160] Cf Diduck (2011b), 307–8.

[161] See 3.8.1 and 7.8.

[162] See 7.6.1 below.

some being regarded as too high, others far too low.[163] Of most concern are apparent geographical inconsistency and lack of transparency:

Law Commission, *Matrimonial Property, Needs and Agreements*, Law Com No 343 (London: TSO, 2014)

2.45 First, there is evidence of significant regional differences in the levels of support likely to be awarded in different courts. This is not so much about amounts as about duration....

2.50 In 2010, the Law Reform Committee of the General Council of the Bar said to us:

There exists an almost "policy based" approach by the courts as to whether they provide for joint lives, or term orders [i.e. periodical payments for an indefinite period or fixed duration – see 7.6 below]. For example, the Principal Registry of the Family Division [now the Central Family Court] and High Court tend to make joint lives orders, other major court centres do not. The impact is that clients and solicitors openly forum shop and an element of geographical lottery is introduced to these orders....

2.52 One of the questions asked in the Resolution survey, conducted specifically to support this project, was whether practitioners had ever issued proceedings in a particular court, or area of the country, because of a belief that the outcome to their client would be more favourable than issuing elsewhere. The majority of the 234 practitioners who responded (57%) indicated that they had issued proceedings in particular location or court because they thought that it would yield a more favourable outcome for their client.

2.53 There is sufficient evidence of regional inconsistency, and of its being used strategically by legal advisers, for us to regard it as problematic....

2.54 Second, there is a lack of transparency. Certainly, family lawyers are familiar both with the law and with the practice of their local courts, and they can advise on the most likely outcome of litigation and so enable their clients to settle. But most people cannot afford lawyers. Many who previously had access to legal advice are no longer entitled to legal aid. They are able to access the courts, of course; but the process is more difficult without lawyers (for both the parties and the judiciary) and there is great concern that the court system will not be able to cope. In any event, at present most divorces are not accompanied by litigation about financial orders, and the court system does not have the capacity to accommodate the adjudication of a greater proportion of disputes; so it is no answer to the problem of the withdrawal of legal aid to say that the parties always have access to judicial discretion. This is not a reality.

Rather than recommend any statutory reform to remedy these problems, the Commission instead recommended that the Family Justice Council provide plain English guidance for lay people to help them understand how the law in this area works, and draft guidance addressed to judges and practitioners regarding the meaning of financial needs:

encouraging the courts to make orders that will enable the parties to make a transition to independence, to the extent that that is possible in the light of choices made within the marriage, the length of the marriage, the marital standard of living, the parties' expectation of a home, and their continuing shared responsibilities [importantly, childcare].[164]

---

163 Law Com (2012), from para 3.30.
164 Law Com (2014), para 3.88.

7.5.3 COMPENSATION: RELATIONSHIP-GENERATED ECONOMIC DISADVANTAGE

Miller v Miller; McFarlane v McFarlane [2006] UKHL 24

LORD NICHOLLS:

13. Another strand, recognised more explicitly now than formerly, is compensation. This is aimed at redressing any significant prospective economic disparity between the parties arising from the way they conducted their marriage. For instance, the parties may have arranged their affairs in a way which has greatly advantaged the husband in terms of his earning capacity but left the wife severely handicapped so far as her own earning capacity is concerned. Then the wife suffers a double loss: a diminution in her earning capacity and the loss of a share in her husband's enhanced income. This is often the case. Although less marked than in the past, women may still suffer a disproportionate financial loss on the breakdown of a marriage because of their traditional role as home-maker and child-carer...

15. Compensation and financial needs often overlap in practice, so double-counting has to be avoided. But they are distinct concepts, and they are far from co-terminous. A claimant wife may be able to earn her own living but she may still be entitled to a measure of compensation.

With occasional exceptions,[165] the compensation strand received a cool reception from practitioners and lower courts, perceived (rightly or wrongly) to lack statutory foundation,[166] to be impractical, speculative, and potential costly to operate, unless very tightly circumscribed,[167] and to be unprincipled.[168] Like arguments about conduct and 'stellar contributions', discussed below, the argument seems to be one that the courts only rarely entertain,[169] and there is considerable overlap between compensation and the other two principles. In any case, since the available resources are often insufficient even cover the parties' needs, there is no room for any distinct element of 'compensation'.

The speeches of Lord Nicholls and Baroness Hale identify two distinct potential issues: (i) loss of earning capacity sustained by a spouse who reduced or gave up paid employment in order to care for the family; (ii) enhancement of one spouse's income and earning capacity which is partly attributable to the other's support. They touched only briefly on the latter issue. Some earlier big money cases had seen awards of periodical payments exceeding needs, ostensibly made as part of a 'bridging period' prior to a clean break,[170] but perhaps better understood as recognizing the applicant's contribution to the respondent's earning capacity.[171] Notably, in *Parlour v Parlour*,[172] the wife had contributed to the

---

[165] Notably *Lauder v Lauder* [2007] EWHC 1227.

[166] But see *Charman v Charman* [2007] EWCA Civ 503, [71]; Miles (2005).

[167] E.g. *RP v RP* [2006] EWHC 3409, [59]–[64]; *SA v PA* [2014] EWHC 392, [36].

[168] E.g. *CR v CR* [2007] EWHC 3334, [79]; Deech (2009c); Parkinson (2011), 257–8; cf Miles (2008), esp 391–2.

[169] Viney and Brunsdon-Tully (2014).

[170] E.g. *Q v Q (Ancillary Relief: Periodical Payments)* [2005] EWHC 402.

[171] Cf *M v M* [2004] EWHC 688: award based on the wife's future contributions to caring for their special needs child.

[172] [2004] EWCA Civ 872, [39]–[40], [46].

acquisition and retention of the husband's earning capacity, having rescued the Arsenal footballer from a 'laddish' culture, enabling him to flourish under the subsequent management of Arsène Wenger. Subsequent case law has explored this issue both as an aspect of compensation—for the applicant's inability now to share in those future earnings—and of equal sharing. However argued, many of the underlying concerns are similar, so we address this issue at 7.5.4 with the sharing principle, and focus here on the first idea: compensation for 'relationship-generated disadvantage'.[173]

Compensation: a distinct principle?

In principle, where resources permit, the compensation principle could justify an award exceeding need or an equal share of the assets in an appropriate case: the scale of Mrs McFarlane's career disadvantage 'went well beyond the compensation afforded by a generous interpretation of her needs'.[174] Paradigm cases of relationship-generated disadvantage, such as Mrs McFarlane's, involve applicants whose earning capacity has been impaired by past and/or future child-care responsibility.[175] But the idea of compensation for loss of earning capacity predates *Miller; McFarlane*:

SRJ v DWJ (Financial Provision) [1999] 3 FCR 153 (CA), 160

HALE LJ:

This was a long marriage. The couple had 27 years together. There were four children. It was a classic example of the sort of case where the wife could have continued to work as a teacher; indeed, she did for some of the time. But she gave up her place in the world of work to concentrate upon her husband, her home and her family. That must have been a mutual decision from which they both benefited. It means that the marriage has deprived her of what otherwise she might have had. Over the many years of that marriage she must have built up an entitlement to some compensation for that. It is not only in her interests but in the community's interests that parents, whether mothers or fathers, and spouses, whether wives or husbands, should have a real choice between concentrating on breadwinning and concentrating on home-making and child rearing, and do not feel forced, for fear of what might happen should their marriage break down much later in life, to abandon looking after the home and the family to other people for the sake of maintaining a career.

Short marriages which produce children may also generate compensation-based arguments, as may childless marriages in which one spouse gives up a lucrative career so that the parties can relocate for the sake of the other's career.[176] In *B v B (Mesher Order)*, the parties had been married for only one year, but had a child, Will. A lump sum was ordered to allow the wife to buy a house for herself and Will. Should this be done on a *Mesher* basis, reserving a portion of the capital for the husband on Will's independence, or transferred outright?

---

173 *Miller; McFarlane* [2006] UKHL 24, [140].
174 *VB v JP* [2008] EWHC 112, [60]; see also *Miller; McFarlane* [2006] UKHL 24, [15].
175 See also *H v H* [2014] EWCA Civ 1523.
176 *Murphy v Murphy* [2009] EWCA Civ 1258.

Munby J agreed with the 'common sense view of the future realities', depicted by counsel for the wife, that:

B v B (Mesher Order) [2002] EWHC 3106

MUNBY J:

...the wife's major contribution to this marriage...is the fact that she, for the next 16 years or so (and I put it that way because Will is now approximately two years old), will have the very considerable burden of looking after him and bringing him up...

Furthermore...in the nature of things the performance by the wife of her obligations... will inevitably impact adversely upon her earning capacity. Not merely her capacity to earn an income during that part of her life, during Will's early years when she will not be able to work at all; not merely during that part of Will's later childhood during which she will be able to work part-time perhaps on an increasing scale. But even after Will is off her hands, her continuing earning capacity, even when she is free to work full-time, will be significantly reduced...by the fact that for a number of years she will have been out of the job market. She will therefore find herself, when Will is 18, in her mid-40s, even if free to work full-time, not able to get the kind of job which will generate the kind of income which by then she could realistically have hoped to obtain had she not had the interruption of looking after Will.

Moreover...that impacts not merely upon her earning ability in the sense of her income, it impacts seriously (and he suggests decisively) upon her ability...ever to generate capital, whether by way of acquiring a property on a mortgage, or more particularly by way of building up a pension fund.

Meanwhile, the husband would readily make back the capital and had substantial pension funds which were untouched by the order. The outright transfer of the house to the wife was therefore upheld.

Failing to recognize career sacrifice such as Mrs McFarlane's would often leave an imbalance between the parties. In theory, such cases call for close examination of the quantum of appropriate compensation,[177] especially where the full and final settlement of a clean break is contemplated.[178] But the order should not create a new imbalance which operates unfairly against the respondent. There are only limited assets available for distribution and these are not tort claims: the respondent is not paying damages for injury sustained owing to his blameworthy conduct, regardless of his own needs and legitimate claims. The sacrifice of curtailing paid employment should ordinarily be viewed as the product of a joint decision made as part of spouses' lifestyle choices for their relationship. The economic consequences of that choice should be fairly shared, given the finite resources that their partnership has generated and both parties' interests; there should be no question of the applicant emerging with a superior standard of living.[179]

---

[177] [2008] EWHC 112, [60]; see criticism of the judge's reasoning in H v H [2014] EWCA Civ 1523.

[178] Ibid, [61], [66]. Since periodical payments terminate on remarriage, only a capital award will guarantee full compensation unaffected by that possibility.

[179] See McFarlane v McFarlane (No 2) [2009] EWHC 891, [44]–[45], [113]–[114]; Miles (2008).

However the award is measured, fairness to respondents also dictates that applicants should be expected to 'mitigate' their disadvantage, for example by returning to paid employment once child-care obligations permit. In assessing what earning capacity it would be reasonable to expect such parties to acquire,[180] courts consider their ages and the duration of their absence from the labour market.[181] But, as *SRJ v DWJ* indicates,[182] there are important social questions about what can reasonably be expected of parents: some parents wish to work, or feel they have to do so; others prefer to undertake child-care personally as far as possible and limit work commitments accordingly. Hale LJ assumed that the parties' decisions in *SRJ v DWJ* about employment and child-care were mutual—but what if one party contends otherwise? Respondents may also wish to make lifestyle choices after divorce that reduce their income and so limit their ability to make periodical payments.[183]

Career sacrifice or downscaling has sometimes been characterized not as a 'relationship-generated disadvantage', but rather a lifestyle choice by that spouse for which they alone should bear responsibility.[184] There was a stark divergence of view in *Radmacher v Granatino* between the majority and Baroness Hale, dissenting, regarding the husband's decision in that case to move from merchant banking to a less lucrative academic career.[185] While the majority put this decision in the personal lifestyle choice bracket, Baroness Hale viewed his decision as one made in the context of his marriage with his wife's support. As Alison Diduck has argued, the difference here lies between viewing parties as exercising 'abstract agency' as autonomous individuals, or viewing their decisions contextually, within a mutually supportive relationship.[186]

Radmacher v Granatino [2010] UKSC 42

BARONESS HALE:

188....Most spouses want their partners to be happy—partly, of course, because they love them and partly because it is not much fun living with a miserable person. So, choices are often made for the sake of the overall happiness of the family. The couple may move from the city to the country; they may move to another country; they may adopt a completely different lifestyle; one of them may give up a well-paid job that she hates for the sake of a less lucrative job that she loves; one may give up a dead-end job to embark upon a new course of study. These sorts of things happen all the time in a relationship. The couple will support one another while they are together. And it may generate a continued need for support once they are apart. Whether this is seen as needs or compensation may not matter very much. It can only be for this reason that the husband in this case had any real claim upon his wife apart from his claims as the father of her children.

---

180 Cf the reference to future earning capacity in MCA 1973, s 25(2)(a).
181 *Leadbeater v Leadbeater* [1985] FLR 789.
182 [1999] 2 FLR 176, 182.
183 Moor and Le Grice (2006).
184 E.g. Mostyn J's analysis of Mrs McFarlane's decision: *SA v PA* [2014] EWHC 392, [28]; *S v S* [2006] EWHC 2793, [59].
185 *Radmacher v Granatino* [2010] UKSC 42, [121], cf [186]–[188].
186 (2011b), from 306. See also Bendall (2014), 269.

Compensation: need in disguise?

However, for all the theoretical discussion, these cases may in fact best be understood not as introducing an entirely separate rationale for the financial order, but rather as underscoring the justification for generous needs-based awards:[187]

Law Commission, *Marital Property Agreements*, Law Com CP 198
(London: TSO, 2011)

> 2.56 The introduction of compensation as a distinct concept has made no difference in the level or the nature of the awards made. We think that it may be best regarded as a way of spelling out something that has always been regarded as an element of needs.... Having compensation articulated separately is useful because it draws attention to financial consequences that may not be obvious...
>
> 2.58. The recognition that an award focused on this type of disadvantage is a form of compensation may help the courts to focus their attention upon the real value of what has been lost. It is arguable that the introduction of compensation as a separate concept is simply a teasing out of the complex notion of "needs generously interpreted", at least in the way that the courts have applied it so far.

This view is supported by various judicial remarks: the concept of 'relationship-generated disadvantage... is intended principally to ensure that the court does not overlook the effect on a spouse of a loss of career';[188] the point merits separate attention from the other principles 'to ensure that the courts adopt a non discriminatory approach in the exercise of the discretion',[189] achieving overall equality of outcome between the parties.[190]

Close examination of *McFarlane*—the supposedly paradigm case—also supports this view. Both spouses had successful professional careers, but they decided the wife should stop to look after the home and family. By the divorce, the husband was earning over £750,000 net annually, a sum far exceeding the family's needs. The House of Lords held that annual periodical payments of £250,000 should be paid both to meet the wife's needs and to compensate her for forgone earning capacity. There was no explanation of how that figure was reached, or to what extent it compensated rather than met need. When *McFarlane* returned to court on a variation application,[191] Charles J considered that, given the parties' long marriage and its character as a joint enterprise, fairness required that the wife should maintain her current standard of living for life, with no drop on retirement, as might otherwise have been expected. It could at least be said that, had she not given up her career, she would have been able to maintain that standard herself, but instead, the parties had so conducted themselves that they would depend on the husband's income. However, rather than try to estimate the wife's earnings losses the order effectively provided a *very* generous assessment of need.[192]

---

[187] E.g. *Lauder v Lauder* [2007] EWHC 1227, *VB v JP* [2008] EWHC 112, [59], [82].
[188] *W v W* [2009] EWHC 3076, [97].
[189] *H v H* [2014] EWCA Civ 1523, [41]; see also *SA v PA* [2014] EWHC 392, [36(iv)].
[190] *Vaughan v Vaughan* [2007] EWCA Civ 1085, [50]; *CR v CR* [2007] EWHC 3334, [95].
[191] [2009] EWHC 891.
[192] See also *H v H* [2014] EWCA Civ 1523.

Compensating for what?

John Eekelaar argues that the *McFarlane* formulation of compensation is misguided:[193]

J. Eekelaar, 'Property and Financial Settlements on Divorce—Sharing and Compensating', (2006a) 36 *Family Law* **754, 756**

Baroness Hale described the compensation as being for 'relationship-generated disadvantage'...Does this mean that *any* loss, or opportunity foregone, as a result of entering the relationship should be (fully?) compensated? Lord Hope remarked that it would be unfair if 'a woman who has chosen motherhood over her career in the interests of her family' were to be 'denied a fair share of the wealth that her husband has been able to build up...out of the earnings that he is able to generate when she cannot be compensated for this out of capital'...Yet there are strong arguments against approaching the compensation issue in this way. Some are practical. In many cases the financial benefits of an 'alternative life' are too speculative to provide an appropriate measure. But also, there must be a high possibility that, had the applicant not had the relationship with the respondent, he or she will have had one with another person. The 'alternative life' may never have happened anyway. As the [American Law Institute] put it:

'[The wife] has not lost a career, for that is not what she had sought. She instead lost the opportunity to have her children with someone with whom she would enjoy an enduring relationship. The most direct measure of her financial loss would compare her situation at divorce to the hypothetical situation had she married a different man'....

The compensation is, therefore, for the consequences of the differential risk between the parties of the consequences of the separation. As Lord Nicholls said, the compensation element would be 'aimed at redressing any significant prospective economic disparity between the parties arising from the way they conducted their marriage' (at para [13]). This must refer to the disparity after the separation, not before it. Suppose the respondent earns less than the applicant after separation, but the applicant would nevertheless have earned more were it not for the relationship. Surely there should be no claim against the respondent. If there is no disparity, so the risk has turned out even, there again seems no case for compensation...

7.5.4   ENTITLEMENT: EQUAL SHARING

The equal sharing principle originates in *White v White*. The Whites had been married for over 30 years and had three children, all adult by the time of the divorce. They had built a successful farming business, the wife working as an active business partner and raising the family. The assets exceeded the parties' financial needs:

---

193 See also Ellman (2007).

White v White [2001] 1 AC 596, 605–6, 608

LORD NICHOLLS:

In seeking to achieve a fair outcome, there is no place for discrimination between husband and wife and their respective roles. Typically, a husband and wife share the activities of earning money, running their home and caring for their children. Traditionally, the husband earned the money, and the wife looked after the home and the children. This traditional division of function is no longer the order of the day. Frequently both parents work. Sometimes it is the wife who is the money-earner, and the husband runs the home and cares for the children during the day. But whatever the division of labour chosen by the husband and wife, or forced upon them by circumstances, fairness requires that this should not prejudice or advantage either party when considering paragraph (f), relating to the parties' contributions. This is implicit in the very language of paragraph (f): "...the contribution which *each*...has made or is likely...to make to the *welfare of the family*, including any contribution by looking after the home or caring for the family". (Emphasis added.) If, in their different spheres, each contributed equally to the family, then in principle it matters not which of them earned the money and built up the assets. There should be no bias in favour of the money-earner and against the home-maker and the child-carer...

A practical consideration follows from this. Sometimes, having carried out the statutory exercise, the judge's conclusion involves a more or less equal division of the available assets. More often, this is not so. More often, having looked at all the circumstances, the judge's decision means that one party will receive a bigger share than the other. Before reaching a firm conclusion and making an order along these lines, a judge would always be well advised to check his tentative views against the yardstick of equality of division. As a general guide, equality should be departed from only if, and to the extent that, there is good reason for doing so. The need to consider and articulate reasons for departing from equality would help the parties and the court to focus on the need to ensure the absence of discrimination.

He found that the established case law, which confined wives in big money cases to awards satisfying their 'reasonable requirements', leaving the surplus to the money-making husband, was not supported by the statute or the objective of fairness:

If a husband and wife by their joint efforts over many years, his directly in his business and hers indirectly at home, have built up a valuable business from scratch, why should the claimant wife be confined to the court's assessment of her reasonable requirements, and the husband left with a much larger share? Or, to put the question differently, in such a case, where the assets exceed the financial needs of both parties, why should the surplus belong solely to the husband? On the facts of a particular case there may be a good reason why the wife should be confined to her needs and the husband left with the much larger balance. But the mere absence of financial need cannot, by itself, be a sufficient reason. If it were, discrimination would be creeping in by the back door. In these cases, it should be remembered, the claimant is usually the wife. Hence the importance of the check against the yardstick of equal division.

The facts of *White* fell squarely within the premise for Lord Nicholls' equality yardstick. But there was held to be good reason to depart from equality in recognition of financial help given by Mr White's father.[194]

---

[194] See Cooke (2011b).

White had particular significance for older spouses. The needs associated with old age may be substantial but are time-limited. Pre-*White*, an elderly wife who needed only a small capital sum to generate income for the rest of her life might receive less following a decades-long marriage than a younger applicant after a shorter marriage. *White* offered such applicants a substantial award reflecting their contributions over a long marriage.[195]

However, *White* left many questions unanswered. Did the 'yardstick' of equal division apply only where assets exceeded the parties' needs? Did it apply only to long marriages? What if one party had arrived in the marriage with substantial wealth already? What if one party inherited a large sum of money during the marriage? Could it be argued that the parties had not 'contributed equally' to the family's welfare, so that the party who had made a 'stellar contribution' could take a larger share? And how, for these purposes, should the ostensibly incommensurable contributions of homemaker and breadwinner be compared?

Miller returned the question to the House of Lords on facts very different from *White*'s: a short, childless marriage to which the husband brought considerable wealth. How, if at all, should the equality yardstick apply here? And to what property should it apply? Their Lordships parted company on the latter point, albeit reaching the same outcome on the facts: £5 million to Mrs Miller (the matrimonial home and capital to generate nearly £100,000 per annum). This award, under a third of the value of the wealth acquired during the marriage, less than one-sixth of Mr Miller's total estimated wealth, recognized that the gains made during the marriage derived largely from pre-marital business endeavours. The main speeches were delivered by Lord Nicholls and Baroness Hale. Lord Hoffmann agreed with Baroness Hale; Lord Hope agreed with both on all points relevant to the disposal of the case; Lord Mance did likewise, but preferred Baroness Hale's analysis on some points. Regrettably, *Miller; McFarlane* left several questions unanswered, and posed new problems, to which subsequent Court of Appeal authorities unfortunately give mixed answers.

The basic principle applies equally to all marriages, whatever their duration:

Miller v Miller; McFarlane v McFarlane [2006] UKHL 24

LORD NICHOLLS:

16. A third strand [after need and compensation] is sharing. This 'equal sharing' principle derives from the basic concept of equality permeating a marriage as understood today. Marriage, it is often said, is a partnership of equals. In 1992 Lord Keith of Kinkel approved [the] observation that 'husband and wife are now for all practical purposes equal partners in marriage': *R v R* [1992] 1 AC 599 [the marital rape exemption case]. This is now recognised widely, if not universally. The parties commit themselves to sharing their lives. They live and work together. When their partnership ends each is entitled to an equal share of the assets of the partnership, unless there is a good reason to the contrary. Fairness requires no less. But I emphasise the qualifying phrase: 'unless there is good reason to the contrary'. The yardstick of equality is to be applied as an aid, not a rule.

17. This principle is applicable as much to short marriages as to long marriages: see *Foster v Foster* [2003] EWCA Civ 565...A short marriage is no less a partnership of equals than a long marriage. The difference is that a short marriage has been less enduring. In the nature of things this will affect the quantum of the financial fruits of the partnership.

---

195 *White v White* [2001] 1 AC 596, 609, criticizing the '*Duxbury* paradox'.

18. A different approach was suggested in *GW v RW (Financial Provision: Departure from Equality)* [2003] 2 FLR 108...There the court accepted the proposition that entitlement to an equal division must reflect not only the parties' respective contributions 'but also an accrual over time'...It would be 'fundamentally unfair' that a party who has made domestic contributions during a marriage of 12 years should be awarded the same proportion of the assets as a party who has made the domestic contributions for more than 20 years....

19. I am unable to agree with this approach. This approach would mean that on the breakdown of a short marriage the money-earner would have a head start over the home-maker and child-carer. To confine the *White* approach to the 'fruits of a long marital partnership' would be to re-introduce precisely the sort of discrimination the *White* case...was intended to negate.

BARONESS HALE:

141. A third rationale [after needs and compensation] is *the sharing of the fruits of the matrimonial partnership*. One reason given by the Law Commission for not adopting any one single model was that the flexibility of section 25 allowed practice to develop in response to changing perceptions of what might be fair. There is now a widespread perception that marriage is a partnership of equals. The Scottish Law Commission found that this translated into widespread support for a norm of equal sharing of the partnership assets when the marriage ended, whatever the source or legal ownership of those assets...A decade earlier, the English Law Commission had found widespread support for the automatic joint ownership of the matrimonial home, even during marriage...[T]he authors of *Settling Up* [Arthur et al (2002)] p 56, found that "there appeared to be a relatively widespread assumption that an 'equal' or 50/50 division was the normal or appropriate thing to do", alongside a recognition of needs and entitlements (but their respondents' views on entitlements might not be quite the same as the lawyers', a point to which I shall return)...

143....[T]here are many cases in which the approach of roughly equal sharing of partnership assets with no continuing claims one against the other is nowadays entirely feasible and fair. One example is *Foster v Foster* [2003] EWCA Civ 565..., a comparatively short childless marriage, where each could earn their own living after divorce, but where capital assets had been built up by their joint efforts during the marriage. Although one party had earned more and thus contributed more in purely financial terms to the acquisition of those assets, both contributed what they could, and the fair result was to divide the product of their joint endeavours equally. Another example is *Burgess v Burgess* [1996] 2 FLR 34, a long marriage between a solicitor and a doctor, which had produced three children. Each party could earn their own living after divorce, but the home, contents and collections which they had accumulated during the marriage could be equally shared. Although one party might have better prospects than the other in future, once the marriage was at an end there was no reason for one to make further claims upon the other.

So the principle of equal sharing is available whatever the duration of the marriage. But beyond that the scope and application of the principle is unclear. Several related questions arise.

- Does the principle operate as a presumption or starting point?
- What is its relationship with the other principles?

- To what property does the principle apply?
- What constitutes 'good reason' to divide the assets other than equally?

Does the equal sharing principle provide a starting point?

Lord Nicholls in *White* was adamant that judges must not curtail the wide discretion conferred by the MCA 1973 by treating equal sharing as a presumption or starting point. He deployed it instead as a final 'check', having provisionally decided what outcome would be fair given the s 25 checklist. However, in *Charman v Charman*, the Court of Appeal interpreted *Miller; McFarlane* as treating equal sharing as an appropriate—though not mandatory—starting point. In their view, the equal sharing principle means that 'property should be shared in equal proportions unless there is good reason to depart from such proportions'.[196] By contrast, in the subsequent Court of Appeal case *B v B*, Hughes LJ treated equal sharing as a retrospective yardstick and Wall LJ emphasized the width of the discretion to reach a 'fair' outcome.[197] This difference of view is regrettable, though it is worth noting that *B v B* was not a 'big money' case and that the wife had brought all the assets to the marriage: these are both reasons for quickly departing from a starting point of equal sharing to make some other award, as we discuss below. This difference in approach to the equal sharing principle reflects the deeper difference in approach to the s 25 exercise that we noted at 7.5 above, in which certain judges continue to emphasize the strongly discretionary nature of the exercise whilst other judges seek increasingly to contain the exercise within principled bounds. We explore various examples of that below, and the uncertainty to which the difference of view gives rise.

What is the relationship of equal sharing to the other principles?

In most cases, as Lord Nicholls indicates, equal sharing will not be determinative of the outcome, or even carry much weight. Other concerns—whether need, compensation, conduct (see 7.5.6), or the desirability of a clean break (7.6.1)—may dictate unequal sharing of the available capital.

Departing from equal sharing in favour of need in 'everyday' cases

It is important to emphasize that in 'everyday' cases, that is, those where the assets do not exceed the parties' needs (construed liberally by reference to the parties' standard of living), the equal sharing principle is largely irrelevant. In many such cases, the applicant, typically a wife who reduced her paid employment to raise the children, may receive rather *more* than half of the assets in order to protect the children's welfare and to cater for her needs as their primary carer, in both the short and longer term. If the objective is to give the parties an 'equal start on the road to independent living', unequal division may be necessary:[198]

---

196 [2007] EWCA Civ 503, [65].
197 [2008] EWCA Civ 543, [24], [50]–[60]. See also *Robson v Robson* [2010] EWCA Civ 1171.
198 *Miller; McFarlane* [2006] UKHL 24, [144].

Miller v Miller; McFarlane v McFarlane [2006] UKHL 24

BARONESS HALE:

136. ...Giving half the present assets to the breadwinner achieves a very different outcome from giving half the assets to the homemaker with children...

142. ...[A]n equal partnership does not necessarily dictate an equal sharing of the assets. In particular, it may have to give way to the needs of one party or the children. Too strict an adherence to equal sharing and the clean break can lead to a rapid decrease in the primary carer's standard of living and a rapid increase in the breadwinner's. The breadwinner's unimpaired and unimpeded earning capacity is a powerful resource which can frequently repair any loss of capital after an unequal distribution... Recognising this is one reason why English law has been so successful in retaining a home for the children.

However, it might be argued that the fact that the conclusion is likely to be unequal sharing does not mean that there is no point taking equal shares as a starting point in these cases, even if one will quickly depart from that position to provide fuller financial relief in order to ensure that the applicant's needs are met. There may be something vital to be gained from acknowledging that the applicant is *entitled* to at least half of the assets, and not merely a 'needy supplicant'. This may be particularly important where parties are negotiating privately, where the concept of entitlement may help reduce any imbalance in power where most of the assets are owned by the respondent.[199]

The relationship between equal sharing and the other principles in high-value cases

It is only where the assets exceed the parties' needs that equal sharing assumes potentially determinative significance, and the interaction between all three principles becomes important.[200]

The relationship between equal sharing and need is straightforwardly explained in *Charman*.[201] Equal sharing may be departed from where need in fairness requires it. But an applicant is not to be denied an equal share on the basis that it exceeds his or her needs.[202] Equal sharing is not to be applied only to any surplus remaining after the parties' needs have been met: that approach would encourage each party to inflate their budgets in order to secure a larger overall share. But the equal sharing principle may subsume any claim based on need where the share awarded is sufficient to cover those needs.[203]

The place of compensation is more difficult. There are concerns about the risk of double-counting:[204] that is, of 'compensating' the applicant several times over for the same disadvantage under more than one of the principles. Just as equal sharing may subsume 'need', so need will generally subsume compensation: as we have seen, the courts essentially use compensation as a justification for generously assessed needs-based awards. The adequacy of an equal share to meet compensation has been acknowledged in relation to wives with 'ordinary career prospects' where that equal share will leave them with a very

---

199 Diduck (1999).
200 See Miles (2008).
201 Cf Law Com (2012), from para 4.96.
202 [2007] EWCA Civ 503, [73].
203 Ibid, [73], [77(c)].
204 *RP v RP* [2006] EWHC 3409, [64].

comfortable standard of living.[205] If the capital is insufficient for an equal share to achieve that outcome, fairness may then require either that the wife receive more capital on a clean break,[206] or that she receive periodical payments. But the trend of the cases, discussed above, clearly indicates that even in the case of a high-flying wife with an apparent case for compensation, any 'extra' beyond equal sharing will be calculated on a generous needs basis. In short: if needs (generously assessed) subsume the compensation principle, and equal sharing subsumes needs in high-value cases, compensation seems to drop out of the picture as a truly independent principle.

To what property does equal sharing apply?

The views in the House of Lords

Where the equal sharing principle is applicable, a key question is what property falls within the equal sharing pool. Lord Nicholls took a broad view:

Miller v Miller; McFarlane v McFarlane [2006] UKHL 24

LORD NICHOLLS:

20.... The rationale underlying the sharing principle is as much applicable to 'business and investment' assets as to 'family' assets...

Matrimonial property and non-matrimonial property

22.... The statute requires the court to have regard to all the circumstances of the case. One of the circumstances is that there is a real difference, a difference of source, between (1) property acquired during the marriage otherwise than by inheritance or gift, sometimes called the marital acquest but more usually the matrimonial property, and (2) other property. The former is the financial product of the parties' common endeavour, the latter is not. The parties' matrimonial home, even if this was brought into the marriage at the outset by one of the parties, usually has a central place in any marriage. So it should normally be treated as matrimonial property for this purpose. As already noted, in principle the entitlement of each party to a share of the matrimonial property is the same however long or short the marriage may have been.

23. The matter stands differently regarding property ('non-matrimonial property') the parties bring with them into the marriage or acquire by inheritance or gift during the marriage. Then the duration of the marriage will be highly relevant. The position regarding non-matrimonial property was summarised in the *White* case [2001] 1 AC 596, 610:

'Plainly, when present, this factor is one of the circumstances of the case. It represents a contribution made to the welfare of the family by one of the parties to the marriage. The judge should take it into account. He should decide how important it is in the particular case. The nature and value of the property, and the time when and circumstances in which the property was acquired, are among the relevant matters to be considered....'...

---

205 E.g. *CR v CR* [2007] EWHC 3334, [92]; endorsed in *VB v JP* [2008] EWHC 112, [59]; *B v B* [2010] EWHC 193; see also [2006] UKHL 24, [154]; *Charman v Charman* [2007] EWCA Civ 503, [76(b)].

206 E.g. *CR v CR* [2007] EWHC 3334.

Flexibility

26. This difference in treatment of matrimonial property and non-matrimonial property might suggest that in every case a clear and precise boundary should be drawn between these two categories of property. This is not so. Fairness has a broad horizon. Sometimes, in the case of a business, it can be artificial to attempt to draw a sharp dividing line as at the parties' wedding day. Similarly the "equal sharing" principle might suggest that each of the party's assets should be separately and exactly valued. But . . . [the] costs involved can quickly become disproportionate . . .

27. Accordingly, where it becomes necessary to distinguish matrimonial property from non-matrimonial property the court may do so with the degree of particularity or generality appropriate in the case. The judge will then give to the contribution made by one party's non-matrimonial property the weight he considers just. He will do so with such generality or particularity as he considers appropriate in the circumstances of the case.

By contrast, Baroness Hale contemplated a potentially smaller sharing pool:

BARONESS HALE:

149. The question . . . is whether in the very big money cases, it is fair to take some account of the source and nature of the assets, in the same way that some account is taken of the source of those assets in inherited or family wealth. Is the 'matrimonial property' to consist of everything acquired during the marriage (which should probably include periods of pre-marital cohabitation and engagement) or might a distinction be drawn between "family" and other assets? Family assets were described by Lord Denning MR in the landmark case of *Wachtel v Wachtel* [1973] Fam 72, at 90:

"It refers to those things which are acquired by one or other or both of the parties, with the intention that there should be continuing provision for them and their children during their joint lives, and used for the benefit of the family as a whole".

Prime examples of family assets of a capital nature were the family home and its contents, while the parties' earning capacities were assets of a revenue nature. But also included are other assets which were obviously acquired for the use and benefit of the whole family, such as holiday homes, caravans, furniture, insurance policies and other family savings. To this list should clearly be added family businesses or joint ventures in which they both work. It is easy to see such assets as the fruits of the marital partnership. It is also easy to see each party's efforts as making a real contribution to the acquisition of such assets. Hence it is not at all surprising that Mr and Mrs McFarlane agreed upon the division of their capital assets, which were mostly of this nature, without prejudice to how Mrs McFarlane's future income provision would be quantified.

150. More difficult are business or investment assets which have been generated solely or mainly by the efforts of one party. The other party has often made some contribution to the business, at least in its early days, and has continued with her agreed contribution to the welfare of the family (as did Mrs Cowan [*Cowan v Cowan* [2001] EWCA Civ 679]). But in these non-business-partnership, non-family asset cases, the bulk of the property has been generated by one party. Does this provide a reason for departing from the yardstick of equality? On the one hand is the view, already expressed, that commercial and domestic contributions are intrinsically incommensurable. It is easy to count the money or property which one has acquired. It is impossible to count the value which the other has added to their lives together. One is counted in money or money's worth. The other is counted in domestic comfort and happiness. If the law is to avoid discrimination between the gender

roles, it should regard all the assets generated in either way during the marriage as family assets to be divided equally between them unless some other good reason is shown to do otherwise.

151. On the other hand is the view that this is unrealistic. We do not yet have a system of community of property, whether full or deferred. Even modest legislative steps towards this have been strenuously resisted. Ownership and contributions still feature in divorcing couples' own perceptions of a fair result, some drawing a distinction between the home and joint savings accounts, on the one hand, and pensions, individual savings and debts, on the other (*Settling Up*, [Arthur et al (2002)] chapter 5). Some of these are not family assets in the way that the home, its contents and the family savings are family assets. Their value may well be speculative or their possession risky. It is not suggested that the domestic partner should share in the risks or potential liabilities, a problem which bedevils many community of property regimes and can give domestic contributions a negative value. It simply cannot be demonstrated that the domestic contribution, important though it has been to the welfare and happiness of the family as a whole, has contributed to their acquisition. If the money maker had not had a wife to look after him, no doubt he would have found others to do it for him. Further, great wealth can be generated in a very short time, as the *Miller* case shows; but domestic contributions by their very nature take time to mature into contributions to the welfare of the family.

Equal sharing may never be appropriate in relation to so-called 'unilateral' assets', that is, the fruits of a business in which only one spouse had worked and which were not used for the family's benefit[207] in two cases: (i) short marriages, such as *Miller*; and (ii) dual-career marriages where the parties kept part of their assets separate:[208]

Miller v Miller; McFarlane v McFarlane [2006] UKHL 24

BARONESS HALE:

153.... [I]n a matrimonial property regime which still starts with the premise of separate property, there is still some scope for one party to acquire and retain separate property which is not automatically to be shared equally between them. The nature and the source of the property and the way the couple have run their lives may be taken into account in deciding how it should be shared. There may be other examples. Take, for example, a genuine dual career family where each party has worked throughout the marriage and certain assets have been pooled for the benefit of the family but others have not. There may be no relationship-generated needs or other disadvantages for which compensation is warranted. We can assume that the family assets, in the sense discussed earlier, should be divided equally. But it might well be fair to leave undisturbed whatever additional surplus each has accumulated during his or her working life. However, one should be careful not to take this approach too far. What seems fair and sensible at the outset of a relationship may seem much less fair and sensible when it ends. And there could well be a sense of injustice if a dual career spouse who had worked outside as well as inside the home throughout the marriage ended up less well off than one who had only or mainly worked inside the home.

---

207 *S v S* [2006] EWHC 2793, [30].
208 Cf *Charman v Charman* [2007] EWCA Civ 503, [82]–[86].

LORD MANCE:

170.... [T]here can be marriages, long as well as short, where both partners are and remain financially active, and independently so. They may contribute to a house and joint expenses, but it does not necessarily follow that they are or regard themselves in other respects as engaged in a joint financial enterprise for all purposes. Intrusive inquiries into the other's financial affairs might, during the marriage, be viewed as inconsistent with a proper respect for the other's personal autonomy and development, and even more so if the other were to claim a share of any profit made from them. In such a case the wife might still have the particular additional burden of combining the bearing of and caring for children with work outside the home. If one partner (and it might, with increasing likelihood I hope, be the wife) were more successful financially than the other, and questions of needs and compensation had been addressed, one might ask why a court should impose at the end of their marriage a sharing of all assets acquired during matrimony which the parties had never envisaged during matrimony. Once needs and compensation had been addressed, the misfortune of divorce would not of itself, as it seems to me, be justification for the court to disturb principles by which the parties had chosen to live their lives while married.

Lord Mance's last remarks presage the Supreme Court decision in *Radmacher v Granatino* regarding the impact on the sharing principle of marital agreements, discussed at 7.7 below.[209] If parties kept their assets separate during marriage, equal sharing on divorce seems discordant with their view of their own marriage. Rather than relying on judges' characterization of individual marriages, attempting to infer parties' intentions from their conduct, it may be rather safer to rely on the parties' express agreement on the matter.[210]

The views in the Court of Appeal

Since *Miller; McFarlane*, two rather different approaches to equal sharing have emerged from Court of Appeal judges. The key issue is the place of 'non-matrimonial property' in the equal sharing exercise. Property may be 'non-matrimonial' for various reasons, for example having been accumulated by one spouse before the marriage,[211] inherited by one of them,[212] or generated post-separation.[213]

In *Charman v Charman*,[214] the court preferred the view that, subject to narrow exceptions, the principle applies to *all* of the parties' property, whether designated 'matrimonial' or not. It felt that any alternative risked being discriminatory and undermining the sharing principle. But this approach would not make it unnecessary to identify different categories of property: the fact that certain property can be described as 'non-matrimonial' would be likely to provide a 'good reason' for unequal sharing, particularly after shorter marriages, as we discuss below.[215]

---

[209] Cf *Parra v Parra* [2002] EWCA Civ 1886, where parties had deliberately arranged to share assets equally.

[210] Cf the problems with intention in the trusts context, discussed at 3.4.7.

[211] E.g. *McCartney v Mills McCartney* [2008] EWHC 401, *Jones v Jones* [2011] EWCA Civ 41, *N v F* [2011] EWHC 586.

[212] E.g. *B v B* [2008] EWCA Civ 543; *L v L* [2008] EWHC 3328; *K v L* [2011] EWCA Civ 550.

[213] See p 485 below.

[214] [2007] EWCA Civ 503.

[215] Ibid, [66].

By contrast, the court in *Jones v Jones*,[216] preferred to separate 'non-matrimonial' assets from 'matrimonial' assets: the latter would ordinarily be shared equally, but the former would ordinarily not be shared at all (save as required by reference to the needs/compensation principle). On this approach, equal sharing would apply only to property generated during marriage other than by gift or inheritance, corresponding with the idea that sharing the 'fruits of the partnership' flows from the parties' contributions during the marriage. Wilson LJ compared the merits of the two approaches:

Jones v Jones [2011] EWCA Civ 41

WILSON LJ:

35. Criticism can easily be levelled at both approaches. In different ways they are both highly arbitrary. Application of the sharing principle is inherently arbitrary; such is, I suggest, a fact which we should accept and by which we should cease to be disconcerted...The exercises, on the one hand, of adopting A and of testing against B and, on the other, of adopting B and testing against A may indeed have subtly different consequences. At all events in this case, particularly in circumstances in which a central valuation mandated by it has been crystallised by sale, I prefer in the first instance to adopt [the approach which deals separately with matrimonial and non-matrimonial assets].

That Wilson LJ specified that this was the right approach 'in this case' makes clear that he is not propounding this approach as a rule. The *Jones* approach depends on the court being able to ascribe a clear value to each pool of property, though the onus is surely on the party wishing to establish the existence and value of non-matrimonial assets to do so.[217] Where the existence of non-matrimonial property is clear but its valuation more problematic, the alternative 'broad-brush' approach[218] may be preferable. But it is perhaps no coincidence that there is no reported case in which non-matrimonial property has been shared under this principle (rather than to meet need), and the Law Commission, along with some High Court judges,[219] prefer the *Jones* approach for its clarity and predictability, both useful aids to settlement.[220]

When will there be good reason to divide the assets other than equally?

Aside from cases where another principle—such as need—dictates unequal shares, unequal shares may be ordered as a result of departures made 'within' the sharing principle itself.[221] As Elizabeth Cooke has argued, these departures betray an ambiguity in the sharing principle's rationale: is it based on the idea of marriage as a partnership which of itself justifies equal sharing of property; or is it based more or less precisely on the notion that the parties have actually made contributions of equal value and that it is these contributions which

---

216 [2011] EWCA Civ 41; see also *K v L* [2011] EWCA Civ 550.
217 *N v F* [2011] EWHC 586, [14].
218 *K v L* [2011] EWCA Civ 550, [22].
219 Notably Mostyn J: *S v AG* [2011] EWHC 2637, *N v F* [2011] EWHC 586; cf Moylan J: *AR v AR* [2011] EWHC 2717, *SK v WL* [2011] 1 FLR 1471.
220 Law Com (2014), para 8.81.
221 *Charman v Charman* [2007] EWCA Civ 503, [65].

justify the equal share? If the 'partnership' approach is taken, it is harder to argue against equal sharing than under the 'valuation' approach, which invites dispute about what each party contributed (financially or otherwise) to the marriage and over what period. In the following sections, we consider further the treatment of non-matrimonial property, and the specific issues of resources acquired post-separation, 'stellar' contributions, and risky or illiquid assets.

The treatment of 'non-matrimonial' property: passage of time or changed circumstances?

Reflecting the two different approaches to non-matrimonial property outlined above, there are two different views about when originally non-matrimonial assets may become available for sharing.

Under s 25(2)(d), the court must consider 'the duration of the marriage', now measured to include cohabitation seamlessly preceding the marriage.[222] Courts that treat the equal sharing principle as applicable to the entire asset pool are more inclined to depart from equal sharing after short marriages in recognition of the 'non-matrimonial' character of some of the assets. After long marriages, by contrast, the case for crediting the owner of non-matrimonial property wanes, especially if the property has been used to the family's benefit, such as to buy the family home:[223]

Miller v Miller; McFarlane v McFarlane [2006] UKHL 24

LORD NICHOLLS:

24. In the case of a short marriage fairness may well require that the claimant should not be entitled to a share of the other's non-matrimonial property. The source of the asset may be a good reason for departing from equality. This reflects the instinctive feeling that parties will generally have less call upon each other on the breakdown of a short marriage.

25. With longer marriages the position is not so straightforward. Non-matrimonial property represents a contribution made to the marriage by one of the parties. Sometimes, as the years pass, the weight fairly to be attributed to this contribution will diminish, sometimes it will not. After many years of marriage the continuing weight to be attributed to modest savings introduced by one party at the outset of the marriage may well be different from the weight attributable to a valuable heirloom intended to be retained in specie. . . . To this non-exhaustive list should be added, as a relevant matter, the way the parties organised their financial affairs.[224]

Where the marriage is long, courts adopting this view have tended to take a broad-brush approach to the treatment of non-matrimonial property in their awards.[225]

---

[222] *GW v RW* [2003] EWHC 661; cf Gilmore (2004a).
[223] *L v L* [2008] EWHC 3328.
[224] See also Baroness Hale, [147], [152].
[225] E.g. *C v C* [2007] EWHC 2033; *H v H* [2008] EWHC 935.

By contrast, those courts that view non-matrimonial property as prima facie excluded from any equal sharing contemplate that such property may move into the sharing pool, though not merely by virtue of the passage of time:

K v L [2011] EWCA Civ 550

WILSON LJ:

18.... I believe that the true proposition is that the importance of the source of the assets *may* diminish over time. Three situations come to mind:

(a) Over time matrimonial property of such value has been acquired as to diminish the significance of the initial contribution by one spouse of non-matrimonial property.

(b) Over time the non-matrimonial property initially contributed has been mixed with matrimonial property in circumstances in which the contributor may be said to have accepted that it should be treated as matrimonial property or in which, at any rate, the task of identifying its current value is too difficult.[226]

(c) The contributor of non-matrimonial property has chosen to invest it in the purchase of a matrimonial home which, although vested in his or her sole name, has – as in most cases one would expect – come over time to be treated by the parties as a central item of matrimonial property.

The situations described in (a) and (b) above were both present in *White*. By contrast, there is nothing in the facts of the present case which logically justifies a conclusion that, as the long marriage proceeded, there was a diminution in the importance of the source of the parties' entire wealth, at all times ring-fenced by share certificates in the wife's sole name which to a large extent were just kept safely and left to reproduce themselves and to grow in value.

Those last observations leave room for a different conclusion to be reached, for example where the non-matrimonial property has increased in value thanks to the parties' joint endeavours.[227]

Resources acquired post-separation

Some cases have addressed the proper treatment of resources acquired post-separation, particularly bonuses, both in terms of equal sharing and compensation for the applicant's lost opportunity to share in that future wealth. The basic argument is that the respondent would not have been able to acquire that earning capacity without the applicant's contributions and so it would be unfair for him to retain that surplus alone, leaving a large disparity between the parties' living standards post-divorce. The courts have ruled out the notion that earning capacity itself can be treated as an asset to be shared (or to be excluded from sharing on the basis that it was acquired before the marriage).[228] But can the applicant nevertheless benefit from post-separation bonus payments?

---

226 E.g. *AC v DC (No 2)* [2012] EWHC 2420.
227 Cf Law Com (2012), para 6.10(4); *AR v AR* [2011] EWHC 2717, [77].
228 *Jones v Jones* [2011] EWCA Civ 41, [23]–[28].

In *H v H*, the wife had agreed to relocate to Japan with the children for the sake of the husband's career.[229] Charles J took a restrictive approach to the wife's claim related to the husband's post-separation bonuses, feeling it necessary to ensure that the 'pendulum does not swing too far' in favour of wives.[230] To succeed, she would have to satisfy a 'but for' test demonstrating the continuing influence of her input to the family's welfare as a factor contributing to an *enhancement* in the husband's future earnings, that is, over and above what he could have earned alone. That would show that the future earnings were a fruit of the marital partnership, albeit now ended. That will be very difficult to prove, especially from purely domestic contributions:

H v H [2007] EWHC 459

CHARLES J:

82. . . . [T]he wife's role and contribution to the marital partnership [which] was of great assistance to the husband in furthering his career is a consequence of the choices made by the parties to the marriage. Such a contribution as a supporter of the husband's career, as a home maker and as a caretaker of the children by a wife is substantial. In general, depending on, and subject to, factors such as the position at the start of the marital partnership and its length, on a non-discriminatory, equal and fair approach it founds the conclusion that pursuant to the yardstick there should be an equal division of the product of the husband's income earned *during* the marital partnership.

83. In my view the position changes when the marital partnership ends. This is because the joint venture and participation of the parties as equal partners in that marital partnership . . . ends. After that termination the focus is no longer on the effects of the contributions of the parties as equal partners in assessing the product of their partnership but with the *effects* of their separate contributions as the source of the husband's income in the future.

84. In considering the position after the termination of the marital partnership . . . it is the role and contribution of a wife during the marital partnership that forms the basis of the element of the husband's earning capacity and future income (i.e. his *enhanced* income or earning capacity) that can be said to be a fruit of that partnership. As Lord Nicholls points out . . . in *Miller & McFarlane* the spadework for rewards received towards the end, and after the end, of the marital partnership has been done during it. The wife's role and contributions have enabled the husband to create a working environment which has produced greater (enhanced) rewards of which she should have a fair share.

85. However, in my view the balance of his future income and earning capacity is the product of the husband's talents, energy and good fortune, notwithstanding that he has been supported by the wife, and they have been applied, expended and enjoyed during the marital partnership.

86. [A] wife who continues to act as the primary caretaker of the children of a marriage in a separate household continues to make a contribution to the welfare of the <u>family</u> (my emphasis), or the marriage, after the end of the marriage . . . In my view so does the husband who continues to meet their financial needs. But as this is looking at the position after the marriage is over these contributions whether described as being to the family or the marriage are not, in my view, contributions to the marital partnership because that is over.

---

[229] [2007] EWHC 459.
[230] Ibid, [96].

87. I do not accept that such contributions by a wife to the family after the end of the marital partnership can generally be said to warrant a conclusion that a proportion of the husband's future income continues to be attributable to the wife's domestic contribution and thus a fruit of the marital partnership. [emphasis added]

Despite these conclusions, Charles J held that given the marriage's length, the wife's contributions, and the expected increase in the husband's income to which she could be said to have made some small (if incalculable) contribution, her award should include a 'run-off' component to help smooth the transition towards independent living.[231]

This reasoning may be compared with *CR v CR*,[232] where Bodey J appeared to be more sympathetic to a wife's claim relating to her husband's future earnings where there was a 'financial continuum'—that is, he continued to work as he had during the marriage when the seeds of his post-separation success were sown—rather than 'any new source of risk, endeavour, or luck'. Bodey J considered that assets acquired by the husband following separation (indeed, for the rest of his life[233]) were a product of the wife's support of his career during the marriage. He accommodated that factor in what he regarded as 'the most straightforward and least controversial way': a generous assessment of the wife's needs.[234]

Stellar contributions

The equal sharing principle is grounded in part on the assumption that the parties' contributions are equal: 'Absent reliance on exceptional contribution and/or on conduct, evidence is not required about the nature of each party's contribution during the marriage beyond a broad history of the marriage.'[235] But 'stellar' contributions warranting departure from equal sharing are exceptional:

Miller v Miller; McFarlane v McFarlane [2006] UKHL 24

BARONESS HALE:

146....Following *White v White*..., the search was on for some reason to stop short of equal sharing, especially in 'big money' cases where the capital had largely been generated by the breadwinner's efforts and enterprise. There were references to exceptional or 'stellar' contributions...These, in the words of Coleridge J in *G v G (financial provision: equal division)* [2002] EWHC 1339 (Fam) ..., opened a 'forensic Pandora's box'. As he pointed out ...:

"[W]hat is 'contribution' but a species of conduct?...Both concepts are compendious descriptions of the way in which one party conducted him/herself towards the other and/or the family during the marriage. And both carry with them precisely the same undesirable consequences. First, they call for a detailed retrospective at the end of a broken marriage just at a time when parties should be looking forward, not back...But then, the facts having been established, they each call for a value judgment of the worth of each side's behaviour and translation of that worth into actual money. But by what measure and using what criteria?...Is there such a concept as

---

231 Ibid, [90].
232 [2007] EWHC 3334, [40]–[41].
233 Ibid, [104].
234 Ibid, [95]–[96].
235 *AR v AR* [2011] EWHC 2717, [75].

an exceptional/special domestic contribution or can only the wealth creator earn the bonus?...It is much the same as comparing apples with pears and the debate is about as sterile or useful."

A domestic goddess self-evidently makes a 'stellar' contribution, but that was not what these debates were about. Coleridge J's words were rightly influential in the later retreat from the concept of special contribution in *Lambert v Lambert* [2002] EWCA Civ 1685 ...It had already been made clear in *White v White*...that domestic and financial contributions should be treated equally. Section 25(2)(f) of the 1973 Act does *not* refer to the contributions which each has made to the parties' *accumulated wealth*, but to the contributions they have made (and will continue to make) to the *welfare of the family*. Each should be seen as doing their best in their own sphere. Only if there is such a disparity in their respective contributions to the *welfare of the family* that it would be inequitable to disregard it should this be taken into account in determining their shares.

Or as Lord Nicholls put it:

68....The wholly exceptional nature of the earnings must be, to borrow a phrase more familiar in a different context [conduct—see 7.5.6], obvious and gross.

Shortly after *Miller; McFarlane*, Mrs Charman received £48 million, a 37 per cent share of the fortune accumulated from scratch by the husband's business activities over the parties' nearly 30-year marriage. However, that award was reduced from what it might have been in recognition of his stellar contribution. The first instance judge considered how to recognize a successful stellar contribution argument in the award:

Charman v Charman [2006] EWHC 1879

COLERIDGE J:

125. If adjustment is appropriate, especially in these huge money cases, I think, it should be meaningful and significant and not a token one. It either means something and the court should so mark it or it does not...The sharp carving knife rather than the salami slicer is the appropriate tool. Having said that any adjustment should not be so great as to actually impact on the wife's standard of living where, as here, no conduct of the wife's is relevant other than it being conceded that she was a fully attentive wife and mother. But reduction in living standard is highly unlikely in this class of case, given that what is being divided up is the surplus fat in the case, way over and above any amount required to meet the payee spouse's needs

On appeal, the Court of Appeal provided admittedly arbitrary guidance on the thickness of slice which the knife should carve: somewhere between 55:45 and 66.6:33.3 in favour of the contributor.[236]

Accumulation of wealth does not of itself make a financial contribution 'stellar'; some spark of genius is required,[237] which has 'a striking evidential foundation which so clearly stands out that the question almost answers itself'.[238] There is no specific monetary threshold

---

[236] [2007] EWCA Civ 503, [90]–[91].
[237] Ibid, [80].
[238] *Evans v Evans* [2013] EWHC 506, [132].

which must be exceeded before wealth-creation becomes 'special': that would encourage a presumption that a special contribution had been made wherever the threshold was exceeded.[239] When a court is considering financial remedies, contributions which have directly led to the acquisition of the assets being divided are perhaps easier to recognize and respond to in financial terms than more intangible domestic contributions; and the argument tends only to arise where there is considerable wealth available with which to acknowledge it.

Indeed, it is hard to envisage a stellar 'domestic' contribution, even (as is common) where one spouse is both engaging in paid employment and doing the larger share of the housework.[240] Thorpe LJ in *Lambert v Lambert* regarded as 'distasteful' the example of a mother caring for a handicapped child.[241] It is not obvious that these contributions are sufficiently rewarded by their equal share: the spouse who makes efforts way beyond the call of 'wifely' duty receives the same as one who made considerably less effort, whether because slapdash with the housework, or because blessed by healthy children or the assistance of domestic staff. However, arguing 'stellar' domestic contributions may tend to denigrate the other spouse's efforts at home, so may be ruled out as an attempt to impugn the respondent's 'conduct'.[242]

Risky and illiquid assets

Even if they fall within the equal sharing pool, the nature of particular assets may nevertheless justify unequal sharing. Where assets are 'illiquid', for example because tied up in a family farm or private company, the courts do not insist on an equal division immediately, if at all: such assets cannot be divided like cash. To facilitate an 'orderly redistribution of wealth',[243] courts may effect equal sharing over time via periodical payments pending the release of the capital.[244] A fair distribution of 'copper-bottomed' and 'risk-laden' assets is generally also necessary.[245] The former, such as land and cash, have a reliable value, are readily saleable, but may yield a more modest income. The latter, such as shares, may yield a higher income but be less readily saleable, more susceptible to loss of capital value or income potential, or be difficult to value as capital at all and better treated as a source of income.[246] If one party is to have a larger share of the risk-laden assets (e.g. a shareholding in a private company), it may be appropriate, given the extra risk thereby taken on, for that party to retain what may appear to be a larger share of the overall assets.[247]

The indeterminacy of the equal sharing principle

Having reviewed some of the key questions arising under the equal sharing principle, it is worth reverting to Cooke's question about its underlying rationale:[248] do we have

---

239 *Charman v Charman* [2007] EWCA Civ 503, [87]–[88].
240 See Scully (2003).
241 [2002] EWCA Civ 1685, [45].
242 *Sorrell v Sorrell* [2005] EWHC 1717; see 7.5.6.
243 *N v N (Financial Provision: Sale of Company)* [2001] 2 FLR 69, 71.
244 *F v F (Clean Break: Balance of Fairness)* [2003] 1 FLR 847.
245 *Wells v Wells* [2002] EWCA Civ 476; cf *Myerson v Myerson* [2009] EWCA Civ 282, discussed below at p 504.
246 *A v A* [2004] EWHC 2818.
247 *N v N (Financial Provision: Sale of Company)* [2001] 2 FLR 69.
248 Cooke (2007).

a partnership approach or a valuation approach? Somewhat incoherently, it seems we have both:

J. Miles, *'Charman v Charman (No 4)*: Making Sense of Need, Compensation and Equal Sharing after *Miller/McFarlane*', (2008) 20 *Child and Family Law Quarterly* 378, 385–6

For example, a starting point of equal sharing in relation to (almost) the entire asset pool implies a deep, universal partnership. Yet the grounds on which equal sharing might be denied 'within' that principle suggest alternative rationales. Either a rough valuation approach, which responds to the claim that one party has made an 'unmatched' contribution, whether a stellar contribution or some form of non-matrimonial wealth. Or a more sophisticated form of partnership, whereby the increasing duration of the marriage reduces scope for arguing that the partnership should take a shallower form....

Again, the partnership view is supported by the possible exceptions to equal sharing in relation to 'unilateral' assets: the short duration (how short?) or the spouses' financial independence makes universal partnership too intense. (Though...the shallower partnership entailed in the sharing of core 'matrimonial' assets is countenanced even in those cases). Equally, however, these cases could be presented as illustrations of the need for non-owner spouses to make some plausible claim that they have indirectly contributed to the acquisition of those assets: a valuation approach.

Other cases seem firmly to adopt valuation, for example, where applicants seek to share in post-separation earning capacity. Here the question has been framed in terms of whether the applicant can demonstrate the continuing influence of her contribution to the welfare of the family as a factor contributing to an enhancement in the respondent's earnings post-separation. At the very least, the termination of the marital partnership on separation excludes a partnership model, and requires that a valuation approach be taken to claims in relation to property acquired after that point. The court's remarks in *Charman* about the rare cases where one would permit a stellar contribution argument also lie with the 'valuation of contributions' rather than 'partnership' rationale:

'the statutory requirement in every case to consider the contributions which each party has made to the welfare of the family...would be inconsistent with a blanket rule that their past contributions to its welfare must be afforded equal weight.'

Unsurprisingly, it is in cases perceived to lie further from the paradigm of marital partnership – for example, short marriages or where property is acquired post-separation – that we apparently no longer feel comfortable with the implications of a partnership-based sharing principle, and so fall back on a valuation approach, insisting on concrete demonstration of actual contribution to rebut the unmatched contribution argument.

If so, perhaps we should simply adopt Baroness Hale's narrower approach to the scope of marital partnership. The *Jones* approach to non-matrimonial assets helps to reinforce the partnership approach for the other assets. Indeed, it points us towards potential statutory reform.

7.5.5 REFORM?

Reform of financial remedies on divorce was under consideration before *White* and *Miller; MacFarlane* but not pursued.[249] *Miller; McFarlane* prompted renewed calls for legislative

---

[249] Ancillary Relief Advisory Group (1998): see (1998) FL 380; HO (1998), (1999).

reform, not least because of lack of predictability and the size of awards generated in 'big money' cases.[250] The Law Commission's recent work has dealt only with some aspects of the current law, rather than a wholesale review.[251] Any such review would have to consider not only what the principles underpinning financial relief on divorce should be, but also whether a system based on judicial discretion is too unpredictable and uncertain, particularly for parties acting without legal advice.[252] That has certainly been a motivating factor for the Law Commission, as we noted from its conclusions on the current law relating to needs at 7.5.2 above. Should statute therefore set out clear objectives, principles, or guidelines for the courts, or even prescribe rules determining how resources should be divided on divorce?[253]

English law could take the trend of the more hard-edged sharing case law to its logical conclusion and adopt a rule-based deferred community of property on divorce: 'matrimonial property' (as defined by the rules of the scheme) would be shared, 'non-matrimonial property' would not be.[254] Any such system would have to be accompanied by maintenance or spousal support, which could take the form of capital transfers as well as periodical payments, but the calculation of that component of financial relief might also be subjected to more constraint in order to achieve more predictability. In criticizing the compensation principle, John Eekelaar suggested that awards might better be determined by reference to some sort of formula based on the disparity in the parties' incomes and the duration of the marriage.[255] The Law Commission too has sympathy for moving to a formulaic approach,[256] which might be used to achieve outcomes underpinned by a theory of financial provision on divorce aimed to 'unravel the merger over time', rather than either 'need' or 'compensation' as currently understood:

Law Commission, *Matrimonial Property, Needs and Agreements*, Law Com CP 208 (London: TSO, 2012)

4.52 A compensatory theory, based on the idea of reversing losses generated by the marriage or civil partnership, has some very hard edges; as well as generating evidential difficulties it can be said to be individualistic and unduly financial in its focus. A very different approach is to be found in the group of theories which build on the idea of "merger over time" and make proposals that focus on the unravelling of that merger without an assessment of individual economic contributions to the marriage. These theories are also known as "income-sharing theories" because that is the mechanism they advocate for the calculation of spousal support.

4.53 "Merger over time" is a description of what happens within a marriage:

[An approach to spousal support] is to see the spouses as merging into each other over time. In this model, the longer they are married, the more their human capital should be seen as intertwined

---

250 E.g. *Charman v Charman* [2007] EWCA Civ 503, [106]–[126].

251 Law Com (2008), from para 5.4; (2011), (2012), (2014).

252 Cf findings of Hitchings (2009a) for represented parties.

253 See Eekelaar (2006a), (2010); Law Society (2003); Douglas and Perry (2001). There are several international examples on which to draw: e.g. Rogerson (2002), Department of Justice (2008), Ellman (2005), (2007).

254 See Scherpe (2012); Cooke (2009), Cretney (2003b); Cooke, Barlow, and Callus (2006).

255 (2006a), extracted above at p 473.

256 Law Com (2014), from para 3.121.

> rather than affixed to the individual spouse in whose body it resides. This idea is consistent with the notion that human capital needs constant renewal – a regular tune-up, repair, and parts replacement model, if you like. After a while, one can less and less distinguish between what was brought into the marriage and what was produced by the marriage. Moreover, the longer the marriage, the longer the spouse in a dependent role has likely submerged her or his identity and earning capacity into the marital collective.
>
> One way to implement such a concept would be to give each spouse a percentage interest in the other's human capital/future earnings based upon the duration of the marriage. [257]

The Canadian spousal support advisory guidelines, which received close attention from the Law Commission, offer an example of how such a 'formula' can—quite unlike the child support formula that we examined in chapter 6—provide a flexible range of figures within which the award in an individual case may be fixed.[258]

The challenges are significant, not least given the strong attachment of many family lawyers to the broad discretion afforded by s 25:

E. Jackson et al, 'Financial Support on Divorce: The Right Mixture of Rules and Discretion?', (1993) 7 *International Journal of Law and the Family* 230, 252–3

> Ultimately it is the outcome of negotiations regarding financial arrangements on divorce which is important for the parties. Nonetheless, concentration on the final settlement disguises the importance of the reasoning process. The theoretical framework on which the issues are pinned is of great significance. If the legal regulation of economic distribution is underpinned by a belief in the importance of the satisfaction of rights-based claims, then clear rules are essential so that those rights may be prospectively evaluated. If, on the other hand, the law attempts to fulfil needs and expectations, discretion must be used to assess their relative importance in the light of competing claims and available resources.
>
> One approach is not necessarily better than the other. The issues raised by the economics of divorce are many and diverse. . . . [T]he most complex decision which must be made involves the family home. Here a settlement must deal with the settling-up of property rights in a substantial capital sum, while being sensitive to the importance of the continuing use-value of the home. The matter is further complicated by the fact that a decision concerning the property rights of two adults must also take account of the needs of the children for a stable and satisfactory home environment. If rights are best served by clear rules and needs best served by the sensitive exercise of discretion, we appear to have reached an impasse. Perhaps it is best to acknowledge that the process is not susceptible to a clear and elegant exegesis. We should gain reassurance from the obvious care taken by solicitors in trying, as nearly as possible, to resolve the irresolvable.

However, as the Law Commission observe in the extract at p 467 above, in the current setting of family justice, that 'reassurance' may be absent from most cases. It has recommended that the government support the formation of an inter-disciplinary working group to pursue the matter further.[259]

---

[257] Sugarman (1990), 159–60.

[258] Law Com (2012), from para 4.69; Law Com (2014), from para 3.121,

[259] Law Com (2014), para 3.159.

7.5.6 THE PARTIES' CONDUCT

Conduct provides a distinctive reason for departing from equal sharing, or for curtailing or increasing[260] awards based on need or compensation. Conduct was central to financial relief under fault-based divorce, but under no-fault divorce is rarely relevant.

Wachtel v Wachtel [1973] Fam 72 (CA), 89–90

LORD DENNING MR:

Parliament has decreed: "If the marriage has broken down irretrievably, let there be a divorce." It carries no stigma, but only sympathy. It is a misfortune which befalls both. No longer is one guilty and the other innocent. No longer are there long contested divorce suits. Nearly every case goes uncontested. The parties come to an agreement, if they can, on the things that matter so much to them. They divide up the furniture. They [make arrangements for] the children, the financial provision for the wife, and the future of the matrimonial home. If they cannot agree, the matters are referred to a judge in chambers.

When the judge comes to decide these questions, what place has conduct in it? Parliament still says that the court has to have "regard to their conduct" . . . Does this mean that the judge in chambers is to hear their mutual recriminations and to go into their petty squabbles for days on end, as he used to do in the old days? Does it mean that, after a marriage has been dissolved, there is to be a post mortem to find out what killed it? We do not think so. In most cases both parties are to blame—or, as we would prefer to say—both parties have contributed to the breakdown.

It has been suggested that there should be a "discount" or "reduction" in what the wife is to receive because of her supposed misconduct, guilt or blame (whatever word is used). We cannot accept this argument. In the vast majority of cases it is repugnant to the principles underlying the new legislation, and in particular the [Divorce Reform] Act of 1969. There will be many cases in which a wife (though once considered guilty or blameworthy) will have cared for the home and looked after the family for very many years. Is she to be deprived of the benefit otherwise to be accorded to her by section [25(2)(f)] because she may share responsibility for the breakdown with her husband? There will no doubt be a residue of cases where the conduct of one of the parties is in the judge's words . . . "both obvious and gross," so much so that to order one party to support another whose conduct falls into this category is repugnant to anyone's sense of justice. In such a case the court remains free to decline to afford financial support or to reduce the support which it would otherwise have ordered. But, short of cases falling into this category, the court should not reduce its order for financial provision merely because of what was formerly regarded as guilt or blame. To do so would be to impose a fine for supposed misbehaviour in the course of an unhappy married life. [Counsel for the husband] disputed this and claimed that it was but justice that a wife should suffer for her supposed misbehaviour. [The parties had been found equally responsible for the marital breakdown]. We do not agree. Criminal justice often requires the imposition of financial and indeed custodial penalties. But in the financial adjustments consequent upon the dissolution of a marriage which has irretrievably broken down, the imposition of financial penalties ought seldom to find a place.

[260] *Jones v Jones* [1976] Fam 8, 15.

The House of Lords affirmed this restrictive approach in *Miller; McFarlane*. Mrs Miller argued that the shortness of the marriage should not reduce her award because its shortness was caused by Mr Miller's affair. Her argument found favour with the lower courts, but was unanimously dismissed by the House of Lords.[261] They also dismissed the associated argument that a spouse should have his or her 'expectation' loss remedied on divorce, as if it were an action for breach of contract:[262]

Miller v Miller; McFarlane v McFarlane [2006] UKHL 24

LORD NICHOLLS:

'Legitimate expectation'

56....The judge [in *Miller*]said the key feature was that the husband gave the wife a legitimate expectation that in future she would be living on a higher economic plane.

57. By this statement I doubt whether the judge was doing more than emphasise the importance...of the standard of living enjoyed by Mr and Mrs Miller before the breakdown of their short marriage. This is one of the matters included on the statutory check list. The standard of living enjoyed by the Millers during their marriage was much higher than the wife's accustomed standard and much higher than the standard she herself could afford.

58. If the judge meant to go further than this I consider he went too far. No doubt both parties had high hopes for their future when they married. But hopes and expectations, as such, are not an appropriate basis on which to assess financial needs. Claims for expectation losses do not fit altogether comfortably with the notion that each party is free to end the marriage. Indeed, to make an award by reference to the parties' future expectations would come close to restoring the 'tailpiece' which was originally part of section 25. By that tailpiece the court was required to place the parties, so far as practical and, having regard to their conduct, just to do so, in the same financial position as they would have been had the marriage not broken down. It would be a mistake indirectly to re-introduce the effect of that discredited provision.

While surveys of the legal profession find strong support for the exclusion of conduct arguments in this context,[263] it is not popular with the divorcing public[264] and some parliamentarians.[265] Even some judges have expressed disquiet about the amorality implied by the exclusion of fault.[266] Recognizing fault, or responsibility for deciding to end marriage without good cause, is regarded by some commentators as a basic aspect of justice on divorce.[267] Nevertheless, fault seems destined to play only a peripheral role.

Where it is taken into account, like the parties' contributions, 'conduct' poses a challenge—how is the financial significance of conduct to be measured? In one case, the

---

[261] [2006] UKHL 24, [59]–[63], [145], [164].
[262] Cf the history of fault-based divorce and the minimum loss principle: Law Com (1980), paras 10–12.
[263] Solicitors Journal (2006).
[264] Law Com (1981), para 36; media reaction to *Miller*.
[265] An amendment to the FLA 1996 designed to give conduct greater prominence was never implemented.
[266] Davis and Murch (1988), 16–17.
[267] E.g. economists such as Rowthorn (1999); Dnes (1998); cf Eekelaar (2006b) and Ellman (1997): see 5.7.1.

husband was convicted for attempted murder of the wife in front of the children. This was at the top end of the scale of conduct that should be taken into account:[268]

H v H (Financial Relief: Attempted Murder as Conduct) [2005] EWHC 2911

COLERIDGE J:

44. How is the court to have regard to his conduct in a meaningful way? I agree with [counsel for the husband] that the court should not be punitive or confiscatory for its own sake. I therefore consider that the proper way to have regard to the conduct is as a potentially magnifying factor when considering the wife's position under the other subsections and criteria. It is the glass through which the other factors are considered. It places her needs, as I judge them, as a much higher priority to those of the husband because the situation the wife now finds herself in is, in a very real way, his fault. It is not just that she is in a precarious position, which she might be for a variety of medical reasons, but that he has created this position by his reprehensible conduct. So she must, in my judgment and in fairness, be given a greater priority in the share-out.

The offence had impacted directly on the wife's mental health and destroyed her career and earning capacity; she had had to move away from the area and would obviously receive no financial or other support from the husband in raising the children.

46. Those are the ways, in my judgment, in which this conduct has impacted directly on the wife's life and it is against that that I turn now to consider the needs of the parties, and first the needs of the wife and the children. It seems to me that so far as practical she should be free from financial worry or pressure. So far as housing is concerned, by far the most important aspect of her security is a decent and secure home for herself and the children. If she feels she is in a nice, new home of her choosing that will be beneficial therapeutically to her . . . .

48. The husband too would like a home when he is released from prison. He would like a home, he says, similar to that of the wife's . . . . If it is possible to achieve that, then of course it is reasonable as well. But as I have indicated, because of his conduct, he has to come very much second place in the queue.

49. So far as incomes are concerned, again the wife should, in my judgment, be as secure as possible and not be under pressure to have to work more than she can really cope with. She wants no recourse to the husband so this will be on a clean break basis . . . .

The judge awarded the wife three-quarters of the assets.

It is not necessary to show that the 'victim' was entirely blameless before it will be equitable to take account of the other spouse's conduct.[269] Conduct after marital breakdown is relevant, even if several years after the divorce.[270] Relevant conduct is 'the elephant in the room; incapable of definition but easy to recognise'.[271] It induces not a 'gulp' but a

---

[268] See also *K v L* [2010] EWCA Civ 125.
[269] *Kyte v Kyte* [1988] Fam 145, 155.
[270] *Evans v Evans* [1989] 1 FLR 351.
[271] *Charman v Charman* [2006] EWHC 1879, [115] per Coleridge J.

'gasp'.[272] 'Ordinary' instances of 'behaviour' and adultery on which many divorce petitions are based are insufficient.[273] Cases in which conduct has been taken into account have been extreme. They include inciting third parties to murder the other spouse,[274] assisting the other spouse's attempted suicide for personal gain,[275] other serious domestic violence,[276] and abduction of the parties' child.[277] In *K v K (Conduct)*, the court took into account the husband's serious drinking problem, his unreasonable failure to seek employment follow-ing redundancy, and his neglect of the house which forced its sale; meanwhile, the wife supported the household and endeavoured to pay the mortgage from her earnings. Since the separation, the wife had made considerable efforts to improve her financial situation, and the husband's application for financial relief was largely rejected.[278] In *Clark v Clark*, a younger woman heavily in debt married a millionaire approaching his 80s; exercised undue influence over him to persuade him to pay her debts, spend vast sums of money, and transfer substantial assets to her; refused to consummate the marriage or cohabit; and confined him at times to a caravan in the grounds or an annexe in the property, while she resided in the main house with her boyfriend. Six years on, the old man, by then reduced to a 'pitiful' state, was rescued by relatives. The wife was perhaps lucky to receive the £175,000 that she did.[279]

Financial misconduct and anti-avoidance powers

The courts also take into account financial misconduct in dissipating the assets available for division,[280] for example by gambling the family assets and diverting funds from payment of the mortgage on the matrimonial home to a mistress;[281] or fraudulently remortgaging the family home.[282] Unlike other forms of misconduct, this behaviour is more readily measur-able in financial terms.

Special rules deal with conduct where a purpose[283] of the respondent was to 'defeat' the other party's claim, whether by preventing it from being made, reducing its amount, or frustrating or impeding its enforcement.[284] The court has statutory 'anti-avoidance' powers to recover assets disposed of by the respondent,[285] restrain such transactions before they go ahead, and prevent the transfer of assets out of the jurisdiction.[286] It is not possible to chal-lenge a completed disposition if it was made for valuable consideration (other than marriage

---

[272] *S v S* [2006] EWHC 2793, [57].

[273] MCA 1973, s 1.

[274] *Evans v Evans* [1989] 1 FLR 351.

[275] *Kyte v Kyte* [1988] Fam 145.

[276] *H v H (Financial Provision: Conduct)* [1994] 2 FLR 801; cf *S v S* [2006] EWHC 2793, criticized by Choudhry and Herring (2010), 410.

[277] *B v B (Financial Provision: Welfare of Child and Conduct)* [2002] 1 FLR 555.

[278] [1990] 2 FLR 225.

[279] [1999] 2 FLR 498, 509.

[280] E.g. *Clark v Clark* [1999] 2 FLR 498.

[281] Suspected in *M v M (Third Party Subpoena: Financial Conduct)* [2006] 2 FCR 555.

[282] *Le Foe v Le Foe and Woolwich plc* [2001] 2 FLR 970.

[283] It need not be the sole or main intention: *Kemmis v Kemmis* [1988] 1 WLR 1307.

[284] On the preservation of joint periodic tenancies in anticipation of tenancy transfer see: *Newlon Housing Trust v Al-Sulaimen* [1999] 1 AC 313; *Muema v Muema* [2013] EWHC 3864; Conway (2001), Bridge (1998).

[285] Cf *Ansari v Ansari* [2008] EWCA Civ 1456.

[286] MCA 1973, s 37. See generally *AC v DC (Financial Remedies: Effect of s 37 Avoidance Orders)* [2012] EWHC 2032; *UL v BK (Freezing Orders: Safeguards: Standard Examples)* [2013] EWHC 1735. Injunctive relief may be available against other financially prejudicial behaviour: *R v R* [2013] EWHC 4244.

or civil partnership[287]) to a person acting in good faith and without actual or constructive notice[288] of any intention on the part of the transferor to defeat his or her spouse's claim for financial relief. But any other past or proposed disposition[289] by a spouse while the case is ongoing[290] is 'reviewable'. If made with the intention to defeat a claim, a reviewable disposition may be set aside. If made less than three years before the claim for financial relief, and it would defeat the claim, it will be presumed (and so for the respondent to prove otherwise) that the disposition was made with that intention.[291] Where a transfer (e.g. movement of funds between bank accounts) leaves a third party holding the asset on bare trust for the spouse, the asset will still be regarded as belonging to the spouse in any event.[292]

Where these powers cannot be relied upon to recover property and so return it to the pool of assets awaiting distribution (e.g. because the third party to whom the assets were transferred acted in good faith and without notice), the court can instead take the relevant conduct into account when deciding how to divide the assets. The spouse who disposed of the assets is likely to be penalized to some extent in that division.[293]

Litigation misconduct

One spouse's conduct of the financial remedy litigation may require the other to incur unnecessary legal costs, for example by failing to make full and prompt disclosure, concealing or disposing of assets, making groundless allegations or exaggerated claims, pursuing clearly futile legal points, or failing to accept a reasonable offer. Litigation misconduct can be taken into account either by reducing the offending party's share of the assets,[294] or more usually by making a costs order.[295] The costs rules encourage reasonable and proportionate conduct of litigation.[296] But costs orders are not always the better option. In *Clark v Clark*, since the husband had effectively been funding both sides' legal costs, a costs order would have imposed no real penalty on the wife, and so her litigation misconduct was properly reflected in the quantification of her award.[297] Proceedings for contempt of court may also be brought to deal with litigation misconduct.[298]

Nullity cases: criminal offences relating to the marriage or civil partnership

Special issues arise in relation to marriages or civil partnerships that are void in circumstances involving commission of a criminal offence by one or both parties,[299] whether

---

287 Curiously, the MCA and CPA refer respectively to 'marriage' and 'civil partnership', and neither to both; it might have been expected that each statute would encompass both possibilities, which are of equivalent significance.

288 *Kemmis v Kemmis* [1988] 1 WLR 1307.

289 Except provision in a will or codicil: MCA 1973, s 37(6).

290 *Nightingale v Nightingale* [2014] EWHC 77, including where the order is made but not yet performed; cf *Ahmed v Mustafa* [2014] EWCA Civ 277.

291 Equivalent tests apply to planned dispositions.

292 *Purba v Purba* [2000] 1 FLR 444.

293 *Le Foe v Le Foe and Woolwich plc* [2001] 2 FLR 970. On 'add-backs', e.g. *US v SR (No 3)* [2014] EWFC 24.

294 *F v F* (2008) 38 FL 183.

295 *Young v Young* [1998] 2 FLR 1131, 1140.

296 FPR 2010, Part 28.

297 [1999] 2 FLR 498.

298 E.g. *Young v Young* [2012] EWHC 38, [2013] EWHC 34.

299 Cf where the marriage was merely void: *Mendal v Mendal* [2007] EWCA Civ 437.

bigamy[300] or perjury on some issue material to the validity of the union. There is clearly no obstacle to the innocent spouse applying for financial relief on the nullity application. But should the 'guilty' spouse effectively be able to profit from his or her crime by making an application?

In *Whiston v Whiston*, it was held that a bigamist could be barred as a matter of public policy from seeking financial relief from the innocent spouse.[301] But it has since been held in relation both to bigamy[302] and perjury (regarding the spouse's gender)[303] that such criminal behaviour does not necessarily bar an application by the guilty party. Instead, it should be one factor for the court to consider in exercising its wide discretion, albeit one that may yield a nil award in appropriate circumstances. In cases such as *Whiston* and *S-T (formerly J) v J*, the respondent is entirely innocent and so should not be required to satisfy any claims by the bigamist/perjurer. But where, as in *Rampal*, the respondent knew of the impediment to the marriage, and engineered the marriage despite it, orders against him or her are less obviously unjust. While acknowledging that *Whiston* would permit a claim by bigamists as culpable as the applicant in *Whiston* to be struck out, the court in *Rampal v Rampal (No 2)* preferred the discretionary route, which allows all the circumstances to be considered.[304]

'Positive' conduct

Relevant conduct may also be positive: for example, an argument that one party has made exceptional contributions to the family. We have addressed this issue in relation to equal sharing, where contributions and conduct are regarded as two sides of the same coin.[305] The relevance of parties' agreements is considered below at 7.7.

7.6 ACHIEVING FINALITY ON DIVORCE

In this section we explore two issues related to finality on divorce: the clean break principle; and the grounds on which an order designed to provide a once-and-for-all settlement of the parties' claims may be undone.

7.6.1 TERMINATING ONGOING FINANCIAL RELATIONS BETWEEN THE PARTIES

The clean break principle was introduced on repeal of the minimum loss principle following heated debate about what maintenance obligations, if any, should survive divorce. Some complained that ex-wives were becoming 'alimony drones', permitted to live a life of 'parasitic'[306] idleness at the expense of their former husbands and their second families.[307]

---

300 There is no offence of bigamy in the case of civil partnership, though the 'bigamist' may be guilty of perjury.
301 [1995] Fam 198.
302 *Rampal v Rampal* [2001] EWCA Civ 989, [2002] Fam 85.
303 *S-T (formerly J) v J* [1998] Fam 103.
304 [2001] EWCA Civ 989; applied in *Hashem v Shayif* [2008] EWHC 2380.
305 *Miller; McFarlane* [2006] UKHL 24, [164] per Lord Mance.
306 Deech (1977), 232; cf O'Donovan (1982).
307 For accounts of the Campaign for Justice on Divorce, see Eekelaar (1991b), 34–6.

Women's groups and others strongly opposed the introduction of the clean break.[308] Subsequent research demonstrated that the concept of the alimony drone was unreal: most ex-wives received such low maintenance that, unless they were employed, it would simply be diverted to the state to recoup welfare benefit payments; ex-wives therefore had a clear incentive to work in order for maintenance payments to augment their income.[309]

The clean break principle is manifest in several statutory provisions. Section 25(2)(a) requires the court to have regard not only to current resources but also resources available to each party in the foreseeable future, including any increase in earning capacity which it would be reasonable to expect them to acquire. Section 25A requires the court to consider whether it would be appropriate to exercise its powers in such a way as to terminate the parties' financial obligations to each other as soon as is just and reasonable after the divorce. Essentially, the court should ask itself whether it can produce a package of orders which achieves fairness without periodical payments or other ongoing ties. If assets are very extensive, a large lump sum can be used to generate investment income to meet living costs.[310] In lower value cases, a larger share of capital to the economically weaker party may offset the need for periodical payments, for example if that party can then service alone the smaller mortgage required given the larger deposit on a new home. Or more capital may compensate for no periodical payments if the other party, despite having higher income, simply cannot afford to pay,[311] or may be an unreliable payer.[312]

If the court decides to effect an immediate clean break, it will dismiss any periodical payment application under s 25A(3). If it decides that no payments are needed currently but wants to leave the door open, it can make a nominal order that can be varied in future if circumstances change.[313] Section 25A(2) requires the court to consider whether it would be appropriate to make the order only for a term long enough for the recipient 'to adjust without undue hardship to the termination of his or her financial dependence on the other party'.[314] Periodical payments orders always cease if the recipient marries or forms a civil partnership,[315] but may otherwise be made to last for the parties' joint lives,[316] until further order, until some specified event, or for a fixed period (a 'term order').[317] The order can be structured so that the payments reduce year by year in line with anticipated increases in the recipient's earnings.[318] Where pension sharing has been ordered, any periodical payment order may be structured so as to end (or reduce) when the recipient's pension becomes payable. The clean break can even extend beyond the grave by barring any application by the ex-spouse under the Inheritance (Provision for Family and Dependants) Act 1975, s 15.

If the order has no fixed end point, the onus will be on the payer to seek a variation under s 31 reducing or extinguishing the order in light of changed circumstances. If a fixed term is imposed, the onus will be on the recipient to seek an extension of that term before the

---

308 Including the Law Society: Symes (1985), n 10.
309 Eekelaar and Maclean (1986).
310 A 'Duxbury fund': Duxbury v Duxbury [1990] 2 All ER 77.
311 A v L [2011] EWHC 3150
312 Robson v Robson [2010] EWCA Civ 1171, [86].
313 E.g. Whiting v Whiting [1988] 1 WLR 565.
314 Cf if periodical payments ordered for compensatory purposes rather than need, as in McFarlane [2006] UKHL 24, [38]–[39], [97]: order made for joint lives.
315 MCA 1973, s 28(3).
316 The order may survive the payer's death if secured: ibid, s 28(1)(b).
317 Ibid, s 28(1).
318 Murphy v Murphy [2014] EWHC 2263, [22]; G v G [2012] EWHC 167.

order expires under s 31; the courts approach such applications strictly.[319] If the court is confident that no extension should be permissible, the order can bar that option upfront.[320] On addressing an application to vary a periodical payments order, s 31(7) requires the court to revisit its original decision under s 25A(2) in light of the current circumstances. So if the resources available did not permit a clean break at the point of divorce but there are now sufficient assets, a clean break can be effected later (e.g. on the payer's retirement) facilitated by fresh capital orders.[321]

The legal relevance and weight of the clean break principle has been controversial. The Court of Appeal had interpreted the Act as imposing a duty to achieve a clean break wherever possible.[322] But the House of Lords rejected this approach in *Miller; McFarlane*: the 'principle' is not a prima facie universal requirement,[323] but a practical consideration to be borne in mind when structuring the settlement which fairness—identified by reference to the three strands and s 25 checklist—demands in the individual case.

Miller v Miller; McFarlane v McFarlane [2006] UKHL 24

BARONESS HALE:

133. Section 25A is a powerful encouragement towards securing the court's objective by way of lump sum and capital adjustment (which now includes pension sharing) rather than by continuing periodical payments. This is good practical sense. Periodical payments are a continuing source of stress for both parties. They are also insecure. With the best will in the world, the paying party may fall on hard times and be unable to keep them up. Nor is the best will in the world always evident between formerly married people. It is also the logical consequence of the retreat from the principle of the life-long obligation. Independent finances and self-sufficiency are the aims. Nevertheless, section 25A does not tell us what the outcome of the exercise required by section 25 should be. It is mainly directed at how that outcome should be put into effect.

134. Hence, these . . . pointers [including the requirement that first consideration be given to the welfare of the children] do make it clear that a clean break is not to be achieved at the expense of a fair result . . .

While a clean break must always be considered, the courts have been cautious about imposing it where dependent children's needs continue to inhibit the primary carer's ability to undertake paid employment, or might do so in future, even after a short marriage.[324] A clean break may also be inappropriate where the children are independent but one spouse's earning capacity has been impaired by past child-care responsibilities,[325] or where children of the marriage have special needs demanding long-term care well into adulthood.[326]

---

[319] *Fleming v Fleming* [2003] EWCA Civ 1841; but see n 323 below.
[320] MCA 1973, s 28(1A).
[321] MCA 1973, s 31(7B); *Miller; McFarlane* [2006] UKHL 24, [131].
[322] *Fleming v Fleming* [2003] EWCA Civ 1841; *McFarlane; Parlour* [2004] EWCA Civ 872.
[323] Their Lordships appear to accept *Fleming v Fleming* [2003] EWCA Civ 1841 (despite its incompatibility with *Flavell v Flavell* [1997] 1 FLR 353) on the application of the clean break principle to attempts to extend fixed-term orders: *Miller; McFarlane* [2006] UKHL 24, [97], [155]; cf *SS v NS* [2014] EWHC 4183, [44].
[324] E.g. *B v B (Mesher Order)* [2002] EWHC 3106; cf *Chiva v Chiva* [2014] EWCA Civ 1558.
[325] *Flavell v Flavell* [1997] 1 FLR 353.
[326] *V v C* [2004] EWHC 1739.

Deciding whether and when a clean break can be achieved requires that some view be reached about applicants' prospects for improving their earning capacity, at least (where any award would be based on need) to the point of becoming self-sufficient, bearing in mind child-care costs required to enable applicants to work.[327] Applicants must take reasonable steps to become self-sufficient and, we may suppose, to mitigate any loss of earning capacity that underpins a compensation argument.[328] Ex-wives cannot 'freeload' on former husbands, but nor can respondents offload their responsibility on the state by simply relying on the applicant's benefit and tax credit entitlements (although those will commonly form an important part of the package). But the courts warn against unduly optimistic or speculative forecasts, particularly where the applicant is middle-aged and would have to retrain: orders should not be made 'more in hope than in serious expectation'.[329] Ultimately, the question is whether the applicant *can* adjust and become self-sufficient, not whether she *should* do so:[330]

Murphy v Murphy [2014] EWHC 2263

HOLMAN J:

36. I do not know, nor do the parties know, what the future will bring. It may be that this wife will find another partner with whom she chooses to share her life and the maintenance will all end. It may be that she will be able later, if not sooner, to obtain well remunerated employment, carrying with it a good pension, and any dependence will end. But at the moment this lady [who had twins aged 3] is in a precarious position. She is very largely dependent on her husband, and it is frankly impossible for me to form the opinion that section 25A(2) requires as the trigger to then making a term order.

But if she *can* become self-sufficient, she *should*—she cannot choose not to work and just seek periodical payments instead.[331]

7.6.2 THE CLEAN BREAK IN PRACTICE

In high-value cases, the available capital will usually make a clean break readily achievable. The difficulties arise in normal cases, where the capital is insufficient to cover the parties' needs, including their income needs. However, as the Law Commission noted in its criticism of the law relating to needs,[332] there appears to be substantial geographical inconsistency in the operation of the law, particularly in the likelihood of a clean break, immediate or deferred, being ordered. In many regions, it appears that orders for periodical payments for the spouse are relatively uncommon, even between couples with dependent children.[333] One survey of cases in four courts around the country found spousal periodical payments in only 12.5 per cent of cases and 'joint lives' orders in only

---

327 *Murphy v Murphy* [2014] EWHC 2263, [26].
328 See Eekelaar (1991b), 86–7.
329 *Flavell v Flavell* [1997] 1 FLR 353, 358.
330 *C v C* [1997] 2 FLR 26, adopted in *Murphy v Murphy* [2014] EWHC 2263, [32].
331 *G v G* [2012] EWHC 167, [139].
332 See extract at p 467 above.
333 MOJ (2012), tables 2.6–2.7; Perry et al (2000); Davis et al (2000).

4 per cent.[334] Bear in mind too that there are no financial orders at all in around two-thirds of divorces. It cannot safely be assumed from this that wives (the principal recipients of such orders) are self-sufficient on divorce; one study of survey data found that women's household income drops substantially following divorce whereas men's rises, and that while wives partially recover their position this is driven by their re-partnering rather than through the labour market.[335]

However, it is important to bear in mind that a clean break can only ever be effected between the spouses themselves: where there are dependent children, the theoretical ongoing requirement to pay child support precludes a full economic break between the parties' households. Where money is tight, paying child support may exhaust respondents' disposable income and/or primary carers may be satisfied topping up their income with benefits and tax credits, preferring not to seek spousal maintenance as well.[336] Before the Child Support Act 1991 (CSA 1991), divorcing parents often reached settlements in which primary carers gave up maintenance for themselves and the children in return for an outright transfer of the home. The CSA 1991 required non-resident parents to pay child support whatever capital settlement had been reached on divorce,[337] removing non-resident parents' incentive to abandon any stake in the capital.[338] However, one study suggested that many parents continued to reach informal agreements outside the child support system which achieved a clean break.[339] Now that policy favours 'family-based arrangements' for child support, such settlements may become more common—but it is a dangerous path for a non-resident parent to take, bearing in mind that the primary carer remains free to apply for child support at any point, and that any earlier capital settlement will be irrelevant in calculating the required maintenance.[340]

7.6.3 APPLICATIONS TO SET ASIDE AND FOR LEAVE TO APPEAL FINAL ORDERS

Periodical payment and a limited range of other orders can be varied at any point.[341] By contrast, one-off orders such as property transfers and lump sums seek to dispose of the parties' affairs once and for all. These orders cannot be varied and the court's jurisdiction ordinarily ceases once an order is made and executed.[342] They can only be altered later if there are grounds either: (i) for the order to be 'set aside' because it is tainted at the outset by some underlying flaw;[343] or (ii) for one party to be granted leave to appeal outside the usual time limit in the light of changed circumstances (akin to frustration).[344]

---

[334] Woodward with Sefton (2014), 20–2; see earlier Barton and Bissett-Johnson (2000).
[335] Fisher and Low (2009).
[336] Barton (1998).
[337] See generally 6.7.2.
[338] Deech (1996), 95.
[339] Perry et al (2000), even in some cases (pre-Child Maintenance and Other Payments Act 2008) where the parent with care was on benefits.
[340] Cf the potential for set-off of certain expenditure: p 384 above.
[341] MCA 1973, s 31.
[342] Cf *Thwaite v Thwaite* (1981) 2 FLR 280; *L v L* [2006] EWHC 956, [63]–[67].
[343] FPR 2010, r 4.1(6).
[344] *Cornick v Cornick* [1994] 2 FLR 530; for full review of these mechanisms, see *L v L* [2006] EWHC 956.

Setting orders aside

Orders can be set aside on limited grounds, including fraud, mistake, and non-disclosure or misrepresentation of facts, but only where knowledge of the truth would have made a substantial difference to the order made.[345] This reflects the parties' 'duty of full and frank' disclosure owed to each other and the court.[346] Examples include the concealment of an impending remarriage[347] or lucrative new job,[348] or of the existence, value, and marketability of key assets.[349] Where the order is based on the parties' agreement, issues may arise regarding the validity of that agreement. But it has been held that undue influence will not provide grounds for setting aside a consent order.[350] Nor will bad legal advice.[351] But lack of capacity to agree to a consent order will.[352]

Appealing out of time

Late appeals brought in light of new events are only exceptionally permitted: the clean break achieved by capital orders would be undermined if parties were free to seek some alteration given changes in their fortunes. If leave is granted, the case is reconsidered in light of all the circumstances at the time of the appeal.[353] The leading authority involved the most dramatic change of circumstance conceivable: shortly after the court had ordered a clean break settlement, transferring the matrimonial home to the wife for her to occupy with the children, she killed the children and committed suicide. On what grounds could leave be granted to appeal against the order?

Barder v Calouri [1988] AC 20, 41, 43

LORD BRANDON:

My Lords, the question whether leave to appeal out of time should be given on the ground that assumptions or estimates made at the time of the hearing of a cause or matter have been invalidated or falsified by subsequent events is a difficult one. The reason why the question is difficult is that it involves a conflict between two important legal principles and a decision as to which of them is to prevail over the other. The first principle is that it is in the public interest that there should be finality in litigation. The second principle is that justice requires cases to be decided, so far as practicable, on the true facts relating to them, and not on assumptions or estimates with regard to those facts which are conclusively shown by later events to have been erroneous...

A court may properly exercise its discretion to grant leave to appeal out of time from an order for financial provision or property transfer made after a divorce on the ground of new

---

345 *Livesey v Jenkins* [1985] AC 424; *Sharland v Sharland* [2014] EWCA Civ 95, currently on appeal to the Supreme Court.

346 Ibid.

347 Ibid.

348 *Bokor-Ingram v Bokor-Ingram* [2009] EWCA Civ 412.

349 *Vicary v Vicary* [1992] 2 FLR 271.

350 *Tommey v Tommey* [1983] Fam 15, doubted in *Livesey v Jenkins* [1985] AC 424, 440.

351 *L v L* [2006] EWHC 956, [47]–[53].

352 *MAP v RAP* [2013] EWHC 4784.

353 *Smith v Smith (Smith and others Intervening)* [1992] Fam 69.

events, provided that certain conditions are satisfied. The first condition is that new events have occurred since the making of the order which invalidate the basis, or fundamental assumption, upon which the order was made, so that, if leave to appeal out of time were to be given, the appeal would be certain, or very likely, to succeed.[354] The second condition is that the new events should have occurred within a relatively short time of the order having been made. While the length of time cannot be laid down precisely, I should regard it as extremely unlikely that it could be as much as a year, and that in most cases it will be no more than a few months. The third condition is that the application for leave to appeal out of time should be made reasonably promptly in the circumstances of the case. To these three conditions...I would add a fourth, which it does not appear has needed to be considered so far, but which it may be necessary to consider in future cases. That fourth condition is that the grant of leave to appeal out of time should not prejudice third parties who have acquired, in good faith and for valuable consideration, interests in property which is the subject matter of the relevant order.

It was clear that a fundamental assumption of the order, shared by the parties and the court,[355] was that the wife and children would indefinitely require a suitable home. That was invalidated by their sudden deaths, and the order was set aside. By contrast, the wife's death in *Richardson v Richardson* did not undermine the basis of an order based on the sharing principle, rather than on her needs.[356]

Subsequent cases in which these criteria have been applied include: the death[357] or remarriage of one party, at least insofar as it affects that spouse's need for housing;[358] misvaluation of key assets; significant changes in value generated by subsequent events (not mere market conditions or natural price fluctuations, however unforeseeable);[359] changes in the law of financial relief.[360] The parties' reconciling after the divorce and cohabiting long-term seems not to constitute a *Barder* event.[361] Nor, at a time when few jobs are wholly secure, does redundancy.[362] The uncertain times of global recession generated several attempts to appeal out of time by respondents who had elected to take the risky assets and lost out,[363] and by applicants who regretted having deliberately forgone a stake in speculative assets which then grew in value.[364] The courts rejected these applications on *Barder* principles: if you deliberately choose risk over certainty, or certainty over risk, you cannot later complain that you struck the wrong deal.

---

[354] On the basis that had the event been foreseen *at the time of the original order*, a different order would have been made: *Williams v Lindley* [2005] EWCA Civ 103.

[355] *Dixon v Marchant* [2008] EWCA Civ 11, [25].

[356] [2011] EWHC 79.

[357] E.g. *Smith v Smith (Smith and other Intervening)* [1992] Fam 69.

[358] *Dixon v Marchant* [2008] EWCA Civ 11; cf *B v B (Financial Provision: Leave to Appeal)* [1994] 1 FLR 219; *Chaudhuri v Chaudhuri* [1992] 2 FLR 73. Cohabitation would probably also be relevant: cf *Cook v Cook* [1988] 1 FLR 521.

[359] See *Cornick v Cornick* [1994] 2 FLR 530, and cases reviewed therein; *Middleton v Middleton* [1998] 2 FLR 821.

[360] *S v S (Ancillary Relief: Consent Order)* [2002] EWHC 223: *White v White* [2001] 1 AC 596 not a *Barder* event because foreseeable at the relevant time.

[361] *Hill v Hill* [1997] 1 FLR 730 (FD), rvsd on different grounds in [1998] 1 FLR 198 (CA).

[362] *Maskell v Maskell* [2001] EWCA Civ 858, [4].

[363] *Myerson v Myerson* [2009] EWCA Civ 282.

[364] *Walkden v Walkden* [2009] EWCA Civ 627.

7.7 PRIVATE ORDERING: MARITAL AGREEMENTS

Financial disputes on divorce are rarely resolved by contested litigation.[365] Agreement is the norm, whether reached by lawyer-led negotiation,[366] mediation, or privately.[367] A small number of couples are now also agreeing to use arbitration; as we noted at 1.2.7, this is a rather different sort of agreement—not to specific terms, but rather to a non-court-based process that will decide those terms for them. If the case is contested, the court process provides incentives and opportunities for settlement, in particular: the requirement to attend a mediation information and assessment meeting before starting proceedings;[368] the requirement of full and frank disclosure;[369] 'first directions appointments' to define the issues in dispute;[370] settlement-oriented 'financial dispute resolution' appointments;[371] costs rules;[372] and various codes of conduct and protocols.[373] Only around 5 per cent of all financial orders are made following adjudication of contested proceedings; and only around a third of all divorces have any sort of financial order made at all.[374]

However, two basic questions arise. (1) Are financial agreements made on separation legally enforceable? (2) Can parties reach a binding agreement in advance, whether before or during marriage, about how their assets and income will be shared (or not shared) in the event of any future divorce? Currently, no form of purely private ordering is straightforwardly enforceable.

The key underlying principle emanates from *Hyman v Hyman*:[375] parties cannot oust the jurisdiction of the matrimonial court by agreement, including an agreement to go to arbitration. So no agreement can prevent the court from considering what provision would be fair; and the court is not bound to determine that the parties' agreement produces a fair outcome—it can impose its own, different order. With that principle in mind, we shall work backwards from the point of divorce, starting with the only really secure form of private ordering—consent orders—and ending with the most controversial—pre-nuptial agreements.

7.7.1 CONSENT ORDERS

Most parties agree how to divide their property and finances. However, to achieve certainty and finality they should enshrine that agreement in a court order: a 'consent

---

365 See generally, Hitchings, Miles, and Woodward (2013).

366 Including collaborative law, see *S v P (Settlement by Collaborative Law Process)* [2008] 2 FLR 2040.

367 On problematic aspects of settlement, see Diduck (2003), 153–8; and 1.2.3 and 5.8.

368 See p 25 above.

369 *Livesey v Jenkins* [1985] AC 424.

370 FPR 2010, r 9.15.

371 Ibid, r 2.61D–E; *Rose v Rose* [2002] EWCA Civ 208; see generally Black et al (2012), ch 30.

372 See n 296; including Ungley orders, potentially imposing a costs sanction on a party who unreasonably refuses to engage in mediation.

373 E.g. Law Society (2010); Resolution (2012).

374 MOJ (2014a), tables 2.5 and 2.6.

375 [1929] AC 601.

order'.[376] Most financial orders are made by consent, rather than contested, around 70 per cent following simple consent order applications and around a quarter following settlement of contested proceedings.[377] To obtain the order, parties present prescribed information to the court, essentially an overview of key financial and other data relevant to s 25, including a summary of their income and capital positions, the parties' and children's accommodation, their ages, the duration of the marriage, and any re-partnering plans. The court then determines whether their draft order should be made, or whether further inquiry is necessary.[378] Once the agreement is transposed into an order, the parties' rights and obligations flow directly from the order itself.[379] A consent order is as binding as one made following contested litigation, so can only be varied, appealed against, or set aside on the grounds discussed above.[380] Some decisions indicate that because a consent order is based on agreement, the court considering an application for variation or appeal out of time should be particularly slow to intervene.[381] Consent orders cannot include provisions that the court could not have ordered in contested litigation, except as undertakings.[382]

The court's role in making a consent order in financial remedy cases is distinctive, lying somewhere between 'rudimentary rubber stamp' and 'forensic ferret', 'a watchdog, but not a bloodhound', 'entitled but not obliged to play the detective'.[383]

Pounds v Pounds [1994] 1 WLR 1535 (CA), 1537–41

WAITE LJ:

In most areas of our law, parties to litigation who are sui juris and independently advised can settle their differences on terms which are included by agreement in an order or rule of court... with the authority of a judge who may not be aware of the terms of the deal at all..., still less be concerned with any question as to their suitability or fairness. That is not so in financial proceedings between husband and wife, where the court does not act, it has been said, as a rubber-stamp: the judge will be concerned, whether the order be made by consent or imposed after argument, to be satisfied that the criteria of sections 25 and 25A of the Matrimonial Causes Act 1973 have been duly applied...

When the House of Lords ruled in *Livesey (formerly Jenkins) v Jenkins* [1985] A.C. 424... that the duty of disclosure of assets was owed by spouses not only to each other but to the court, it did so upon the basis that it was the function of the court in every case, whether it was proceeding by consent of the parties or after a contested hearing, to be satisfied that the provision made by the order fulfilled the criteria laid down by section 25... It is clear, however, that this was intended to be an assertion of general principle only, and not to impose on the court the need to scrutinise in detail the financial affairs of

---

[376] On the process, see Hitchings et al (2013), ch 1. On whether agreement has been reached, see *Xydhias v Xydhias* [1999] 1 FLR 683; *Radmacher v Granatino* [2010] UKSC 42, [148]–[149] per Baroness Hale.

[377] MOJ (2014a), table 2.6.

[378] MCA 1973, s 33A; FPR 2010, r 9.26: see *Pounds* extract, below.

[379] *De Lasala v De Lasala* [1980] AC 546, 560.

[380] See 7.3.5 and 7.6.3.

[381] *Richardson v Richardson (No 2)* [1996] 2 FLR 617.

[382] *Livesey v Jenkins* [1985] AC 424, 444.

[383] *B-T v B-T (Divorce: Procedure)* [1990] 2 FLR 1, 17; *L v L* [2006] EWHC 956, [73].

the parties who came to it for approval of an independently negotiated bargain. It could not be otherwise, for earlier that year Parliament had specifically enacted a more cursory regime for the scrutiny of consent orders [in MCA 1973, s 33A] of which subsection (1) reads as follows:

"Notwithstanding anything in the preceding provisions of this Part of this Act, on an application for a consent order for financial relief the court may, unless it has reason to think that there are other circumstances into which it ought to inquire, make an order in the terms agreed on the basis only of the prescribed information furnished with the application."

The "prescribed information" is that required by [FPR 2010, r 9.26 – see text above].

Forms for use in supplying those particulars...run to no more than two pages, and the space allowed in the boxes for financial information is very restrictive indeed [see currently Form D81[384]].

The effect of section 33A and the Rules and Directions made under it is thus to confine the paternal function of the court when approving financial consent orders to a broad appraisal of the parties' financial circumstances as disclosed to it in summary form, without descent into the valley of detail. It is only if that survey puts the court on inquiry as to whether there are other circumstances into which it ought to probe more deeply that any further investigation is required of the judge before approving the bargain that the spouses have made for themselves.

In the case of applications based on arbitrated outcomes, it has been said that the court should approve the order based on that decision 'unless something leaps off the page to indicate that something has gone seriously wrong in the arbitral process as fundamentally to vitiate the arbitral award'.[385]

It has been doubted whether the paternalism underpinning the rule in *Hyman v Hyman*, requiring parties to submit to the authority of the court in order to secure a binding settlement, is exercised in practice:

S. Cretney, 'From Status to Contract?', in F. Rose (ed), *Consensus ad Idem* (London: Sweet & Maxwell, 1996b), 277

[T]he question of whether a court can sensibly discharge [the function described by Waite LJ]...is self-evidently difficult; and it may well be that different judges approach their tasks in different ways... [I]t is difficult to be confident that the investigation which the court is able to carry out is sufficient to ensure that the terms embodied in its order do not take advantage of the vulnerability of one of the parties.... [Given the limited information available to it,] it seems questionable how far the court is really in a position to make any informed judgment about the fairness of the agreement to which it is asked to give effect.[386]

On the other hand, significant investigation by the court may be undesirable: 'Officious inquiry may uncover an injustice, but it is more likely to disturb a delicate negotiation and

---

384 <www.hmcourtsservice.gov.uk/courtfinder/forms/d81_e1205.pdf>.
385 *S v S (Financial Remedies: Arbitral Award)* [2014] EWHC 7, [21].
386 See also Davis et al (2000), 48 and 63–4.

produce the very costly litigation and the recrimination which conciliation is designed to avoid'.[387]

Recent empirical research found a mixed picture, with some judges (at least) prepared to intervene quite frequently to query the substantive fairness of proposed orders in correspondence, sometimes requiring the parties to appear in person to explain the agreement (or to check that parties acting without a lawyer understood what they were agreeing to), and even very occasionally refusing to make orders in the terms proposed where dissatisfied with the agreement's fairness.[388]

E. Hitchings, J. Miles, and H.Woodward, *Assembling the Jigsaw Puzzle: Understanding Financial Settlement on Divorce* (University of Bristol, 2013), 54, 57–8

Many applications pass through the court straightforwardly with no query. Most obviously, where the proposed order is within the expected parameters for a case of that nature (given type and size of assets / length of marriage / presence of children) the judge will perceive no need to query the application, at least not on substantive grounds. By contrast, where the agreement appeared to be outside the normal range of settlement options, [solicitor] interviewees anticipated judicial intervention. [One solicitor's] most recent case involved an uneven split – 20:80 [wife:husband]: *"I guess, on the face of it, you may say that this was outside the parameters because that's exactly what the judge is saying. But one person's interpretation of what's outside the parameters compared to another – it's grey, isn't it?"* The judge queried whether the settlement was fair, particularly in relation to the wife and children's housing needs, and her income position and needs. Both parties' solicitors wrote to explain why the agreement was structured as it was (parties wanting a clean break, wife made limited contributions and now living with a new partner earning a decent salary sufficient to meet her needs, former matrimonial home pre-acquired with work done on it before the marriage). They were waiting to hear whether it had been approved....

But it seems that not all judges would view the same order in the same way:

Interviewees suggested that particular expectations about the paperwork depend[ed] on the court or the particular judge. To some extent, this was something that practitioners could anticipate in order to try to ensure the smooth passage of their application....[One] solicitor suggested that knowledge of the local court and of the local judge enabled their more recent consensual case to go through without a hitch: *"(W)hat he likes is a lovely long letter to go with the Statement of Information that says what's the logic behind this order."* ...This practitioner also raised the issue of variation in the level of judicial scrutiny at different courts: *"You might as well toss a coin ...I'm quite disillusioned at the inconsistency. That's a nice way of saying it."* ...

When explaining possible inconsistencies in approach to clients, [another solicitor] suggested that they explain to clients that, on one day, one judge will look at the consent application and give you a tick, and another judge will say that *"there's absolutely no way I'm agreeing to this"*. This solicitor suggested that this disparity in approach reflected differing levels of experience amongst the judiciary in family law (without elaborating on what level of experience yielded a more inquisitive and challenging approach).

---

[387] *Harris v Manahan* [1997] 1 FLR 205, 213.
[388] Hitchings et al (2013), 60–1.

Given the inherent limitations on the court's ability to review applications, it has been said that the parties' lawyers (if any[389]) have a corresponding responsibility to secure fair outcomes and to minimize scope for subsequent challenge.[390] But the interests of securing finality in emotionally fraught financial litigation following divorce dictate that orders cannot be set aside because of bad legal advice.[391]

7.7.2 SEPARATION AND MAINTENANCE AGREEMENTS

What about agreements made at the point of divorce which have not been enshrined in a consent order? Separation agreements do not offer certainty and finality because, unless and until a consent order is obtained, *Hyman* leaves both parties free to apply for financial orders inconsistent with the agreement. However, even if the parties intend to obtain a consent order, there is often a delay between agreement and order.[392] Moreover, since the court cannot make any orders[393] until the decree nisi is granted, the parties may need to rely on their agreement for some time in divorces proceeding on either of the 'separation' facts.[394]

Insofar as separation agreements deal with an actually impending separation or divorce, they may be contractually valid.[395] Specifically, written agreements 'between the parties to a marriage' before or after divorce making financial arrangements are binding (save insofar as they purport to oust the court's jurisdiction) under s 34 of the MCA 1973. The ordinary requirement of consideration from the payee may be dealt with by the use of a deed.[396] The need to prove an intention to create legal relations, problematic if the parties are apparently in domestic harmony,[397] will not be difficult where the agreement is in writing and made with legal advice, particularly where a divorce is pending.[398] However, although binding to that extent in contract, maintenance agreements falling within s 34 and other separation agreements may be challenged via two routes.

First, s 35 empowers the court to alter s 34 agreements where:

> by reason of a change in the circumstances in the light of which any financial arrangements contained in the agreement were made or, as the case may be, financial arrangements were omitted from it (including a change foreseen by the parties when making the agreement), the agreement should be altered so as to make different, or, as the case may be, so as to contain, financial arrangements.[399]

---

[389] On the issue of litigants in person in financial cases, see Hitchings et al (2013), ch 5.

[390] *Dinch v Dinch* [1987] 1 WLR 252, 255.

[391] *L v L* [2006] EWHC 956. Contrast the position applying to separation agreements, nn 404–5 below. The lawyers might be liable in negligence: *Arthur JS Hall and Co (A Firm) v Simons et al* [2002] 1 AC 615.

[392] Cf the circumstances in *Rose v Rose* [2002] EWCA Civ 208.

[393] Save maintenance pending suit, s 22, legal services orders, s 22ZA, and financial provision: s 27, MCA 1973.

[394] Cretney (1996b), 278; cf the huge (accidental) delay in *T v T (Agreement not Embodied in Consent Order)* [2013] EWHC B3.

[395] *Hyman v Hyman* [1929] AC 601; compare pre-nuptial agreements, below.

[396] Cf *Bennett v Bennett* [1952] 1 KB 249, which prompted enactment of the precursor of s 34. Cf *Xydhias v Xydhias* [1999] 1 FLR 683 on the compromise of a financial remedy claim not concluded in a deed: *MacLeod v MacLeod* [2008] UKPC 64, [26].

[397] *Balfour v Balfour* [1919] 2 KB 571.

[398] *Merritt v Merritt* [1970] 1 WLR 1211.

[399] MCA 1973, s 35(2)(a). Following death of one party, see MCA 1973, s 36. The court may also alter agreements insofar as they '[do] not contain proper financial arrangements with respect to any child of the family': s 35(2)(b): see 6.6.

The court has the discretion, to be exercised as appears 'just having regard to all the circumstances', to vary existing terms or insert wholly new terms into the agreement (e.g. by making provision for the making of periodical payments where none had originally been agreed). However, s 35 is rarely if ever used.[400]

Far more important in practice is the second route. The MCA preserves the *Hyman* principle that maintenance agreements cannot prevent an application to court for alternative provision.[401] So parties seeking greater provision—or those no longer wishing to pay what they agreed—can apply for financial orders in the ordinary way. However, the court hearing that application will take account of the agreement's existence[402] and circumstances surrounding it when deciding under s 25 what financial orders would be 'fair'.[403]

The leading case on the court's approach to financial applications made despite a separation agreement is *Edgar v Edgar*. Contrary to her lawyers' advice that she was entitled to substantially more, the wife had agreed by deed to a capital sum and periodical payments and covenanted not to apply for further capital provision. She applied to the court, claiming that she had made the agreement because she was desperate to leave the husband, by whose wealth and position she felt overpowered:

Edgar v Edgar [1980] 1 WLR 1410 (CA), 1417–18

ORMROD LJ:

To decide what weight should be given, in order to reach a just result, to a prior agreement not to claim a lump sum, regard must be had to the conduct of both parties, leading up to the prior agreement, and to their subsequent conduct, in consequence of it. It is not necessary in this connection to think in formal legal terms, such as misrepresentation or estoppel; *all* the circumstances as they affect each of two human beings must be considered in the complex relationship of marriage. So, the circumstances surrounding the making of the agreement are relevant. Und[ue] pressure by one side, exploitation of a dominant position to secure an unreasonable advantage, inadequate knowledge, possibly bad legal advice,[404] an important change of circumstances, unforeseen or overlooked at the time of making the agreement, are all relevant to the question of justice between the parties. *Important too is the general proposition that formal agreements, properly and fairly arrived at with competent legal advice, should not be displaced unless there are good and substantial grounds for concluding that an injustice will be done by holding the parties to the terms of their agreement.* [emphasis added] There may well be other considerations which affect the justice of this case; the above list is not intended to be an exclusive catalogue...

Eastham J. in the present case, approached the problem on these lines. He summarised the law in five propositions:

"(1)...(and this is not contested) notwithstanding the deed..., the wife is entitled to pursue a claim under section 23 of the Act. (2) If she does pursue such a claim, the court not only has jurisdiction to entertain it but is bound to take into account all the considerations listed in section

---

[400] *Radmacher v Granatino* [2009] EWCA Civ 649, [134].

[401] MCA 1973, ss 34(1), 35(1), (6).

[402] Decided not by reference to contractual principles, but in the exercise of the court's discretion: *Xydhias v Xydhias* [1999] 1 FLR 683; see Cretney (1999).

[403] *Hyman v Hyman* [1929] AC 601, 609, and 629.

[404] *Camm v Camm* (1983) 4 FLR 577: 'bad' does not connote 'negligent', 580.

25 of the Act. (3) The existence of an agreement is a very relevant circumstance under section 25 and in the case of an arm's length agreement, based on legal advice between parties of equal bargaining power, is a most important piece of conduct to be considered under section 25. (4) Providing that there is equality above, the mere fact that the wife would have done better by going to the court, would not generally be a ground, for giving her more as, in addition to its duty under section 25, the court had a duty also to uphold agreements which do not offend public policy. (5) If the court, on the evidence, takes the view that having regard to the disparity of bargaining power, it would be unjust not to exercise its powers under section 23 (having regard to the considerations under section 25), it should exercise such powers even if no fraud, misrepresentation or duress is established which, at common law, would entitle a wife to avoid the deed."

I agree with these propositions, subject to two reservations. First, as to proposition (4), I am not sure that it is helpful to speak of the court having "a duty" to uphold agreements, although I understand the sense in which the word was used. Secondly, the reference to "disparity of bargaining power" in proposition (5) is incomplete.... [What is required is a situation] where one spouse takes an unfair advantage of the other in the throes of marital breakdown, a time when emotional pressures are high, and judgment apt to be clouded.... There can be no doubt in that in this case, as in so many, there is a disparity of bargaining power. The crucial question, however, for present purposes, is not whether the husband had a superior bargaining power, but whether he exploited it in a way which was unfair to the wife, so as to induce her to act to her disadvantage.

The court found that it was fair to hold her to the agreement: the husband had not abused his position and the wife was driven by her desire to achieve independence.[405]

Cases vary in their description of the approach to be taken to separation agreements and the *Edgar* criteria, though differences of emphasis may simply reflect the facts of the individual cases. Sometimes, the approach seems to be that, unless the party seeking to depart from the agreement can show that the case satisfies one of the *Edgar* criteria, the court will give effect to the agreement without reviewing the parties' current circumstances.[406] At other times, the courts have emphasized that agreements are just one factor in the global s 25 analysis.[407] Amendments to the 1973 Act since *Edgar* requiring that first consideration be given to the welfare of minor children of the family deprive agreements of primary status in such cases.[408] Clearly, more weight will generally be given to agreements concluded with independent, good quality legal advice, and full disclosure.[409] But as *Radmacher v Granatino* (discussed below) shows, neither is a necessary precondition for a court to attach decisive weight to an agreement.

The Privy Council held in *MacLeod v MacLeod* that the same approach should be taken, whether the agreement is challenged via s 35 or by a straightforward application for financial orders.[410] So the court hearing the latter application may decide in the exercise of its

---

[405] Cf *Camm v Camm*, ibid, in which the wife was also found to have received bad legal advice.

[406] *Smith v McInerney* [1994] 2 FLR 1077; *X v X (Y and Z Intervening)* [2002] 1 FLR 508; *T v T* [2013] EWHC B3.

[407] *Smith v Smith* [2000] 3 FCR 374: Black J held that *Smith* did not indicate a different approach: *A v B (Financial Relief: Agreements)* [2005] EWHC 314.

[408] *Richardson v Richardson (No 2)* [1994] 2 FLR 1051.

[409] See generally *X v X (Y and Z Intervening)* [2002] 1 FLR 508, [103].

[410] [2008] UKPC 64, [41]; cf *Simister (No 1)* [1987] 1 FLR 194.

s 25 discretion to depart from the agreement given a change of circumstance. Baroness Hale suggested that what was needed was 'the sort of change which would make those arrangements manifestly unjust', though in *Radmacher* she retracted the word 'manifestly' as imposing too strict a test.[411] Crucially, going beyond what s 35 allows, the court under *Edgar* principles may also depart from the agreement because of the circumstances in which the agreement was made. However, the mere fact that a court would have made different provision will not of itself justify departure from the agreement.[412] Baroness Hale also noted the general point of public policy that, regardless of any change of circumstance, an obligation that ought to be met by a family member should not be cast onto the public purse.[413]

The 'limbo' status of separation agreements—neither straightforwardly binding nor irrelevant—has attracted judicial criticism:

Pounds v Pounds [1994] 1 WLR 1535 (CA), 1550–1

HOFFMANN LJ:

[I]t does seem to me that the law is in an unsatisfactory state. There are in theory various possible answers to the problem. One might be that an agreement between the parties, at least where each has independent legal advice, is binding upon them subject only to the normal contractual remedies based on fraud, misrepresentation, undue influence, etc. At present, the policy of the law as expressed in *Hyman v Hyman*...is against such a solution. The court retains its supervisory role and only its order gives finality. Another answer might be that when parties are negotiating with a view to an agreement which will be embodied in a consent order, everything should be treated as without prejudice negotiation until the order is actually made. In the latter case, the parties would know that until the court had given its imprimatur, nothing which they had negotiated was legally binding or even admissible. If one of them changed his or her mind, they would have either to go back to the negotiating table or litigate the matter de novo. This may be tiresome, as in the case of a house purchase where one party changes his or her mind before contracts are exchanged. But the parties would at least know where they stood. The result of the decision of this court in *Edgar v Edgar*...and the cases which have followed is that we have, as it seems to me, the worst of both worlds. The agreement may be held to be binding, but whether it will be can be determined only after litigation and may involve...examining the quality of the advice which was given to the party who wishes to resile. It is then understandably a matter for surprise and resentment on the part of the other party that one should be able to repudiate an agreement on account of the inadequacy of one's own legal advisers, over whom the other party had no control and of whose advice he had no knowledge. The husband's counsel, who has considerable experience of these matters, told us that he reckoned that in Northampton an agreement has an 80 per cent chance of being upheld but that attitudes varied from district judge to district judge. In our attempt to achieve finely ground justice by attributing weight but not too much weight to the agreement of the parties, we have created uncertainty and...added to the cost and pain of litigation.

---

411 [2010] UKSC 42, [168].
412 Ibid, [42].
413 Ibid, [41].

7.7.3 POST-NUPTIAL AGREEMENTS

We turn now to agreements not made at the point of divorce, but earlier in the marriage—possibly during a 'rocky' patch[414] and/or varying an earlier pre-nuptial agreement[415]—setting out what would happen in the (hypothetical) eventuality of a future divorce.

Until the Privy Council decision in *MacLeod v MacLeod*, there were question marks over the validity of such 'post-nuptial' agreements: were they void on grounds of public policy for improperly contemplating and so potentially encouraging divorce? The Privy Council held that any such public policy objection no longer applies, concluding from the fact that s 34 applies to agreements made 'between the parties to a marriage' that post-nuptial agreements fall within s 34's regulation of 'maintenance agreements'. On that view, provided they were made in writing with intention to create legal relations and consideration (or by a deed), such agreements would be valid and binding by statute.[416] It would further follow from this that post-nuptial agreements could be challenged in the same way as separation agreements: via s 35 or, more likely, an application for financial orders subject to *Edgar* principles.

However, the majority of the Supreme Court in *Radmacher* took the view (only obiter, as that case concerned a *pre*-nuptial agreement) that this interpretation of s 34 is erroneous: that Parliament in 1973 cannot have intended to include within s 34 agreements understood at that time still to be void on grounds of public policy.[417] Rather than align post-nuptial agreements with separation agreements, the majority of the Supreme Court therefore preferred to align them with pre-nuptial agreements. We discuss the court's approach to those agreements in the next section: in short, neither type of agreement is now void on grounds of public policy, the *Hyman* principle entitles the matrimonial court to order provision different from that agreed, but that court will give the agreement decisive weight where freely entered into with full appreciation of its implications unless it would not be fair to hold the parties to it.[418]

Given the law as it emerges from *Radmacher*, little may turn on the particular type of agreement involved: all are subject to the *Hyman* principle, all are examined in a fact-sensitive way in pursuit of a fair outcome, and all agreements reached as a true exercise of the parties' autonomy will be upheld unless it would be unfair to do so.[419] But it is clear that a substantial change of circumstances of the sort that will in fairness demand provision different from that agreed is more likely to occur between the conclusion of a post-nuptial agreement and subsequent divorce than following a separation agreement, which generally deals with known circumstances prevailing at the time of the impending divorce.[420] Like a pre-nuptial agreement, a post-nuptial agreement concluded early in the marriage will often try to cater for what will happen 'in an uncertain and unhoped for future'.[421]

[414] E.g. *NA v MA* [2006] EWHC 2900.
[415] E.g. *MacLeod v MacLeod* [2008] UKPC 64.
[416] Ibid, [35]–[39].
[417] [2010] UKSC 42, [54]–[55].
[418] Ibid, [75].
[419] Compare the italicised words in the extract from *Edgar* above with para 75 of *Radmacher v Granatino* [2010] UKSC 42 below.
[420] Ibid, [65].
[421] Ibid, [59]; cf if the marriage is very short: *BN v MA* [2013] EWHC 4250, [25].

7.7.4 PRE-NUPTIAL AGREEMENTS

Pre-nuptial agreements, sometimes called 'ante-nuptial' agreements, until recently had the most tenuous status of all types of marital agreement. As just noted, they and post-nuptial agreements are regarded by the Supreme Court as appropriately subject to the same legal principles.

The public policy objection removed

Like any other marital agreement, pre-nuptial agreements are subject to the *Hyman* principle, but until recently their status (and that of post-nuptial agreements) was further weakened by the fact that they were regarded as entirely *void* as a matter of contract law on grounds of public policy.[422] This public policy objection had been stated in various ways over the years, but essentially it was considered objectionable that couples should reach agreements which potentially encouraged one or other party to instigate divorce. Baroness Hale described the argument in the following terms:

Radmacher v Granatino [2010] UKSC 42

143.... This rule was developed in the context of agreements or settlements which made some or better financial provision for the wife if she were to live separately from her husband. Such an agreement could be seen as encouraging them to live apart – for example, by encouraging her to leave him, if it was sufficiently generous or more than she would get if she stayed with him, or encouraging him to leave her, or to agree to her going, if it were not so generous. Such encouragement was seen as inconsistent with the fundamental, life-long and enforceable obligation of husband and wife to live with one another.

Such agreements were therefore simply unenforceable as contracts. However, somewhat confusingly,[423] despite being contractually void pre-nuptial agreements were not ignored and, in certain circumstances, came to be given substantial—even decisive—weight.[424]

The current law was definitively stated by the Supreme Court in *Radmacher v Granatino*, though it may be argued that the decision in that case did not mark a radical departure from what was already a trend to give determinative weight to pre-nuptial agreements in appropriate circumstances.[425] The court, by majority (Baroness Hale dissenting in certain key respects), held first—and obiter—that the public policy objections to pre-nuptial agreements are now obsolete and so no longer apply.[426] The Privy Council in *MacLeod*, led by Baroness Hale, had reached the same conclusion (again arguably obiter) in relation to *post*-nuptial agreements but declined (clearly obiter) to extend its reasoning to *pre*-nuptial agreements. This purported distinction between pre- and post-nuptial agreements was heavily

---

[422] *MacLeod v MacLeod* [2008] UKPC 64, [31]–[33].

[423] *Radmacher v Granatino* [2009] EWCA Civ 649, [64].

[424] Ibid; *Crossley v Crossley* [2007] EWCA Civ 1491; *M v M (Pre-Nuptial Agreement)* [2002] 1 FLR 654; *K v K* [2003] 1 FLR 120.

[425] E.g. *Crossley v Crossley*, ibid; cf the needs-based provision made in *M v M (Prenuptial Agreement)* and *K v K (Ancillary Relief: Prenuptial Agreement)*, ibid.

[426] [2010] UKSC 42, [52].

criticized by commentators and its coherence respectfully doubted by the Court of Appeal in *Radmacher*.[427] Since the duty of spouses to cohabit is no longer legally enforceable[428] (save insofar as desertion provides grounds for divorce), the basis for the public policy argument against both types of agreement has disintegrated.

The Privy Council had also suggested in *MacLeod* that parties to pre-nuptial agreements need protection from pressures to which parties to 'post-nups' are not subject: the agreement might be 'the price which one party may extract for his or her willingness to marry' at all.[429] But parties to post-nuptial agreements might be susceptible to equally powerful if different pressure, as *NA v MA* illustrates. Here the wife, who was entirely dependent on the husband and his family, was bullied into signing the agreement following the discovery of her adultery. The agreement was a non-negotiable condition of the marriage continuing (and of her returning home). He knew that she felt overwhelmingly guilty about the adultery and was desperate to save the marriage for the sake of the children. Baron J had no difficulty in departing from this agreement on *Edgar* grounds given the wife's evident subjection to undue influence.[430]

In view of these similarities between the pre- and post-nuptial context, the Supreme Court in *Radmacher* therefore rejected a sharp distinction between pre- and post-nuptial agreements, preferring to treat them on the same footing.

The *Hyman* principle: the treatment of agreements in the matrimonial court

However, whilst all forms of nuptial agreements are now understood to be contractually valid, a majority regarded their contractual enforceability to be a 'red herring':[431] because they are all subject to the *Hyman* principle, and so can all be departed from in the exercise of the matrimonial court's discretion under the MCA 1973 following divorce.[432] The key question is what approach that court will take when faced with an application for financial orders where the parties had reached a pre- or post-nuptial agreement. From this point, Baroness Hale largely agreed with the substance of the majority's position, though she adopted a different emphasis (regarded by Lord Mance as unlikely to make any difference in practice). The majority described their approach in the following terms, essentially providing a new starting point for cases where there is an agreement:

Radmacher v Granatino [2010] UKSC 42

75. *White v White* and *Miller v Miller* establish that the overriding criterion to be applied to ancillary relief proceedings is that of fairness and identify the three strands of need, compensation and sharing that are relevant to the question of what is fair. If an ante-nuptial agreement deals with those matters in a way that the court might adopt absent such an

---

427 See Miles (2009).

428 Since, in particular, the abolition of decree for restitution of conjugal rights: Matrimonial Proceedings and Property Act 1970, s 20.

429 *MacLeod v MacLeod* [2008] UKPC 64, [36].

430 [2006] EWHC 2900; see also the bizarre circumstances in *Kremen v Agrest (No 11)* [2012] EWHC 45.

431 Cf Miles (2011c), 439–40 on contexts in which contractual validity matters.

432 *Radmacher* [2010] UKSC 42, [62]–[63]; cf Lord Mance [128] and Baroness Hale [159].

agreement, there is no problem about giving effect to the agreement. The problem arises where the agreement makes provisions that conflict with what the court would otherwise consider to be the requirements of fairness. The fact of the agreement is capable of altering what is fair. It is an important factor to be weighed in the balance. We would advance the following proposition, to be applied in the case of both ante- and post-nuptial agreements . . . :

"The court should give effect to a nuptial agreement that is freely entered into by each party with a full appreciation of its implications unless in the circumstances prevailing it *would not* be *fair* to hold the parties to their agreement." [italics added]

Baroness Hale preferred to formulate the test the other way around,[433] asking 'Did each party freely enter into an agreement, intending it to have legal effect and with full appreciation of its implications. If so, in the circumstances as they now are, *would it be fair* to hold them to their agreement?'.[434] But whether expressed negatively or positively, what does 'fairness' consist of in this context? The majority went on:

76. That leaves outstanding the difficult question of the circumstances in which it will not be fair to hold the parties to their agreement. This will necessarily depend upon the facts of the particular case, and it would not be desirable to lay down rules that would fetter the flexibility that the court requires to reach a fair result. There is, however, some guidance that we believe that it is safe to give directed to the situation where there are no tainting circumstances attending the conclusion of the agreement.

There are therefore two stages to the inquiry, though the court may in practice examine their combined effect in its pursuit of fairness.[435] The first stage achieves what Jens Scherpe calls 'protection of autonomy', seeking to ensure that both parties really did agree: are there any 'tainting circumstances' present at the outset that detract from the weight to be accorded to the agreement? Even if not, the court then moves to the second stage in which the parties—or one of them—is 'protected from' the consequences of that exercise of their autonomy: would it nevertheless now be unfair to hold the parties to the agreement?[436]

BN v MA [2013] EWHC 4250

MOSTYN J:

17. . . . [G]iven the important notice in its prominent font at the beginning of the [pre-nuptial agreement] stating that it is intended to confirm separate property interests and to be determinative of the division of their assets, it must be obvious that the principal object of the exercise in this case (as indeed in every case where a nuptial agreement is signed) is to avoid subsequent expensive and stressful litigation; and it is for this reason . . . that the law adopts a strict policy of requiring demonstration of something unfair before it will open the Pandora's Box of litigation . . .

---

[433] See Scherpe (2011b), 526 on the impact on the burden of proof.
[434] Ibid, [169]. Cf Lord Mance [129].
[435] Ibid, [73].
[436] Scherpe (2011a), (2011b).

Step 1: factors tainting the agreement from the outset

The court in *Radmacher* identified several issues that might undermine an agreement from the outset, going beyond what contract law would regard as a vitiating factor (e.g. fraud, duress, and so on),[437] and subsequent cases explore these issues in different fact situations. Both parties must have entered into the agreement 'of their own free will, without undue influence and pressure, and informed of its implications'. The absence of independent legal advice or full disclosure of each party's assets will not necessarily undermine the agreement: while both might be 'obviously desirable', what matters is that 'each party should have all the information that is *material* to his or her decision, and that each party should intend that the agreement should govern the financial consequences of the marriage coming to an end'.[438] M. Granatino had received no disclosure and foregone the opportunity to take independent legal advice, but, as a highly financially literate man, he clearly understood the German pre-nuptial agreement, insisted on by his fabulously wealthy wife, that neither spouse would have any sort of claim against each other on divorce; the lack of advice and disclosure had no impact on his decision.[439] Many cases involve parties who made their agreement under a foreign law which allows for agreements to be binding despite lack of advice or disclosure.[440] Here the judge might be concerned to establish whether the parties contemplated that the agreement might be invoked on divorce to displace a discretionary regime of financial remedies, such as English law's, as well as to operate under the foreign law, particularly perhaps if the agreement purports to exclude all claims (including maintenance/needs-based claims),[441] and not just govern property division.[442]

In considering whether the parties were under undue pressure, the court will have regard to their 'emotional state' and their circumstances at the time of the agreement, such as their 'age and maturity' and their relationship history; we might also add to the list whether the woman is pregnant:

Radmacher v Granatino [2010] UKSC 42

72....[For couples where either or both have been married or in long-term relationships before] their experience of previous relationships may explain the terms of the agreement, and may also show what they foresaw when they entered into the agreement. What may not be easily foreseeable for less mature couples may well be in contemplation of more mature couples. Another important factor may be whether the marriage would have gone ahead without an agreement, or without the terms which had been agreed. This may cut either way.

---

[437] *Radmacher v Granatino* [2010] UKSC 42, [71]–[72].

[438] Ibid, [68]–[69]. In purely English cases, such intention will more readily be found for agreements concluded post-*Radmacher*: [70].

[439] Ibid, [114]–[117], upholding the Court of Appeal decision; see Miles (2009). See subsequently *Z v Z (No 2)* [2011] EWHC 2878, *V v V* [2011] EWHC 3230; cf the lack of understanding in *GS v L* [2011] EWHC 1759.

[440] Ibid, [74].

[441] *Kremen v Agrest (No 11)* [2012] EWHC 45, [73]; *B v S* [2012] EWHC 265, [20], *AH v PH* [2013] EWHC 3873, [53].

[442] *Z v Z (No 2)* [2011] EWHC 2878, *V v V* [2011] EWHC 3230, *SA v PA* [2014] EWHC 392.

If the agreement fails at step 1, it will not attract the benefit of the paragraph 75 presumption, but may nevertheless (depending on the nature and strength of the 'tainting' factor) attract some weight in the exercise of the court's discretion.[443]

Step 2: the 'fairness' of upholding the agreement at the point of divorce

The next step is to examine the 'fairness' of giving effect to the agreement at the point of divorce. In addition to the remarks made at paragraphs 75 and 76 (extracted above) the court identified several relevant factors. The agreement cannot 'prejudice the reasonable requirements of any children of the family', whose welfare are by statute the 'first consideration' on granting financial relief.[444] Beyond that, however, the court should respect the parties' autonomy and their choice about how to regulate their financial affairs: 'It would be paternalistic and patronising to override their agreement simply on the basis that the court knows best'. This will especially be the case where the agreement dealt with known circumstances, unlikely in the case of a pre-nuptial agreement preceding a long marriage. Agreements that simply preserve a particular item of 'non-matrimonial property', such as an inheritance, may also attract more weight.[445] Contrast an agreement dealing with 'the contingencies of an uncertain future',[446] where changed circumstances over the course of decades may have rendered the agreement unfair.[447] Baroness Hale was particularly eloquent in her treatment of the last point:

Radmacher v Granatino [2010] UKSC 42

BARONESS HALE:

175. The focus both of my test and that of the majority is upon whether it is now fair to give effect to the agreement. The longer it is since the agreement was made, the more likely it is that later events will have overtaken it. Marriage is not only different from a commercial relationship in law, it is also different in fact. It is capable of influencing and changing every aspect of a couple's lives: where they live, how they live, who goes to work outside the home and what work they do, who works inside the home and how, their social lives and leisure pursuits, and how they manage their property and finances. A couple may think that their futures are all mapped out ahead of them when they get married but many things may happen to push them off course – misfortunes such as redundancy, bankruptcy, illness, disability, obligations to other family members and especially to children, but also unexpected opportunities and unexplored avenues. The couple are bound together in more than a business relationship, so of course they modify their plans and often compromise their individual best interests to accommodate these new events. They may have no choice if their marriage is to survive. There may be people who enter marriage in the belief that it will not endure, but for most people the hope and the belief is that it will. There is also a public interest in the stability of marriage. Marriage and relationship breakdown can have many damaging effects for the parties, their children and other members of their families, and also for society as a whole. So there is also a public interest in encouraging the parties to make adjustments to their roles and life-styles for the sake of their relationship and the welfare of their families.

---

[443] *AH v PH* [2013] EWHC 3873, [50].
[444] *Radmacher*, [77].
[445] Ibid, [78]–[79].
[446] Ibid, [78].
[447] Ibid, [80].

176. All of this means that it is difficult, if not impossible, to predict at the outset what the circumstances will be when the marriage ends. It is even more difficult to predict what the fair outcome of the couple's financial relationship will be...

The most significant part of the court's decision, following on from these concerns, is that if one party is left in a 'predicament of real need', while the other enjoys a sufficiency or more' at the end of the marriage, a court may readily find an agreement making no provision for that party to be unfair; likewise where one spouse's devotion to the domestic sphere freed the other to accumulate wealth: there too, allowing the breadwinner to keep all is likely to be considered unfair. In those circumstances, provision based on need and/or compensation is likely to be ordered, notwithstanding any agreement. But provision based on equal sharing is unlikely to be ordered. Indeed, where neither party is in need on divorce (so that needs-based provision would not be warranted anyway), it may be fair to make no provision at all.[448] In short: while a nuptial agreement may readily displace the equal sharing principle, provision for needs (and compensation) on divorce appears to constitute an irreducible core obligation of marriage, such that agreements should provide for each party's needs in order to be upheld.

Radmacher could therefore be viewed as a coda to the sharing principle, the agreement providing another 'good reason' to 'depart from' equal sharing on the basis that the parties clearly signal that their marriage is not one to which the premise of the equal sharing principle applies at all or with full force,[449] or simply on the basis that the parties are themselves clearly defining what property counts as 'non-matrimonial' and so beyond the reach of that principle. But this differential treatment of sharing and needs/compensation also places significant weight on an issue which, as we discussed at 7.5.2 above, English law has yet satisfactorily to address: when does a former spouse come under an obligation to meet the other's needs, and how extensive (in terms of quantum and duration) is that obligation? And how, if at all, is the concept of 'real need' more limited than our ordinary understanding of 'needs' in these cases?

Radmacher and subsequent cases suggest that agreements purporting to exclude all provision may have more emphatic impact on the outcome than agreements purporting only to govern property division, displacing only the equal sharing principle. In the latter circumstances, courts have disapplied the sharing principle but the extent of needs-based provision has varied. The wife in *Z v Z (No 2)*,[450] whose French pre-nuptial agreement created separate property (excluding equal sharing) but did not exclude maintenance, received full, 'generously assessed' needs-based provision from Moor J following a long marriage and three children, the husband having conceded that such provision should be made. However, in *V v V*,[451] Charles J was prepared to allow a Swedish agreement precluding sharing of pre-acquired and gifted/inherited property to limit the extent of the wife's needs-based provision. Compared with *Z v Z (No 2)*, this marriage was shorter, the wife younger, and much of the property pre-acquired, but Charles J's approach, curtailing the extent of outright provision to the wife, indicates that an agreement dealing only with property may nevertheless affect the court's approach to needs.[452] This might be explicable on the basis that 'generous

---

448 Ibid, [81]–[82], and [178].
449 See Miles (2012), 101; cf the potential for ex post facto judicial determination of this in *Miller; McFarlane* [2006] UKHL 24, discussed at p 482 above.
450 [2011] EWHC 2878.
451 [2011] EWHC 3230.
452 Ibid, [95].

assessment' of needs is itself a manifestation of the sharing/partnership ideology of marriage, to be disapplied where the parties have excluded or significantly modified the application of sharing in their case.[453]

Where the agreement purports to exclude all claims, by contrast, the courts have been more restrictive, deploying the 'predicament of real need' concept strictly. In *Radmacher* itself, where the parties would be sharing child-care, the majority considered it fair to hold the parties to the agreement to the extent that no provision should be made for the husband in his own right once the children reached independence. The wife had discharged the husband's substantial debts and the Court of Appeal had ordered ample provision for the children from which the husband would indirectly benefit throughout the children's minority (e.g. the provision of accommodation and substantial maintenance, including a carer allowance). But the husband had earning capacity, there was no evidence that he would at any point struggle to meet his own needs, and he had no claim for 'compensation'.[454] It would therefore be fair to hold him to his agreement to have no share in his wife's property—indeed, it would be unfair to depart from that agreement.[455] By contrast, the husband in *Luckwell v Limata* was found to be in such a predicament, with no home, no capital, substantial debts, no real income or substantial earning capacity, no borrowing capacity and less time (given his age) to rebuild his position, that *lifetime* provision was fair—but, crucially, not *outright* provision (save again to discharge his debts). A home would therefore be made available for his occupation, initially sufficient to accommodate the children too, but once they attained independence, in a more modest property, again with only the right to occupy.[456]

7.7.5 REFORM?

The Law Commission had begun a project on marital property agreements before the Supreme Court decision in *Radmacher*. Despite that decision, reform remains a live issue because the *Hyman* principle (which only Parliament could remove) means that in theory the court retains full jurisdiction despite the existence of an agreement. Should couples be able to exclude that jurisdiction entirely by agreement in any circumstances? Even the current position is controversial. One commentator described *Radmacher* as marking the 'death knell' of marriage.[457] Others argued that by permitting parties to exclude the equal sharing principle, *Radmacher* undermined key advances effected by *White* and *Miller; McFarlane*:[458]

J. Herring, P. Harris, and R. George, 'Ante-Nuptial Agreements: Fairness, Equality and Presumptions', (2011) 127 *Law Quarterly Review* 335, 338

Does it really matter if marriage is now a contract? It does. Intimate relationships, especially those involving children, create inequalities in the parties' economic position. Through the

---

[453] Miles (2011c), 443; see also cases suggesting narrower needs-based provision from non-matrimonial property, p 462 above.
[454] See p 471 above.
[455] *Radmacher*, [123].
[456] [2014] EWHC 502.
[457] Herring (2010).
[458] See also Diduck (2011).

obligations of support which marriage creates, the state has sought to provide some protection from the risks faced by those entering intimate relationships. In *White v White* ...and *Miller; McFarlane* ...the House of Lords developed the law on ancillary relief to ensure that orders met the needs of the parties; provided compensation for any losses caused by the marriage; and shared, at least, the fruits of the partnership. These were important principles needed to combat gender discrimination and prevent exploitation of the wife's labour. Yet in *Radmacher*, the Supreme Court tells us that the couple can agree to bypass this protection. This is remarkable. There are few, if any, other areas of law where a person can engage in gender discrimination because the other person has consented to the treatment. For so long, marriage has been a vehicle for oppression and disadvantage for women, and it is unfortunate that, so soon after having amended the law on ancillary relief so that marriage can be a tool for protecting women's interests, the court should allow men to create agreements which remove that protection...

To this, it might be said that at least those men may now be offering to marry. Before *Radmacher*, some legal advisers of the wealthy advised them not to marry at all—now, they are advised to marry with a pre-nup.[459] If a wealthy individual refuses to marry their partner, the parties might nevertheless continue to cohabit and have children, all with very little legal protection in case of separation.[460] Jurisdictions which operate systems of community of property or other sharing systems on divorce permit couples to opt out, but few permit opting out of maintenance.[461] So *Radmacher* may simply have brought English law closer to that position—are all of those other jurisdictions wrong to permit couples to opt out of sharing?

On another level, there are concerns about the impact of negotiating pre-nups on relationships. Some supporters of pre-nups consider that negotiating one's own marriage contract could, at best, 'foster the norms of commitment, reciprocity and openness in personal relationships, norms which are integral to egalitarian and democratic relationships'.[462] But the experience could, at first sight at least, be less beneficial:[463]

B. Fehlberg and B. Smyth, 'Binding Pre-Nuptial Agreements in Australia: The First Year', (2002) 16 *International Journal of Law, Policy and the Family* 127, 135

According to family lawyers, one of the major factors inhibiting entry into agreement is difficulty experienced at a personal level between couples during the process of negotiating agreements. Relationship tension reportedly increased when the parties and their legal representatives began formal negotiations regarding the terms of the agreement. Family lawyers, mindful of the agreement's central purpose of offering certainty for the future, were evidently keen to sort out the fine details and to 'reality test' agreements (by asking 'what if?' questions). Yet this process was often confronting for clients as they sat with their beloved and their respective legal representatives around the negotiating table. One practitioner, for example, said that the three clients who had contacted her regarding

---

459 Vardag and Miles (2015).
460 See 7.8 below.
461 See generally Scherpe (ed) (2012).
462 Kingdom (2000), 24; see also Vardag and Miles (2015).
463 See also Reece (2014).

entry into a pre-nuptial agreement had not gone ahead and entered an agreement due to 'difficulties in negotiation leading to abandonment of the agreement, and sometimes of the relationship'.

But might parties driven to separate by that experience in fact have had short-lived marriages in any event, owing to fundamental disagreements about financial issues?[464]

The difficulty of adjudicating on these and other concerns is reflected in a public survey on pre-nuptial agreements, which yielded the ostensibly contradictory findings that 58 per cent of respondents agreed that 'binding pre-nuptial agreements are a good way of allowing couples to decide privately what should happen in the event of divorce', while 65 per cent agreed with the statement that 'binding pre-nuptial agreements are a bad idea because it is too difficult to predict what will be fair at the end of a marriage'.[465] Following extensive consultation, the Law Commission recommended reform:

Law Commission, *Matrimonial Property, Needs and Agreements*, Law Com No 343 (London: TSO, 2014)

Autonomy

5.28 Why should it not be possible for a couple to choose the financial consequences of the ending of their relationship, rather than having those consequences imposed upon them? Those who enter into marital property agreements have the capacity for marriage or civil partnership, and indeed to enter into other contracts between themselves; why should they not have capacity to enter into an agreement about their future financial status? It has been suggested that the paternalism of the law of financial orders is inappropriate in a modern world. In 2009 the Court of Appeal [in *Radmacher*] said that to assume one party is "unduly susceptible to . . . demands . . . is patronising, in particular to women". Lord Justice Wilson suggested that it would be preferable for the "*starting point* to be for both parties to be required to accept the consequences of whatever they have freely and knowingly agreed" . . .

5.30 However, we accept . . . that the argument for autonomy has to be regarded with caution: those who marry or form civil partnerships are adults and can take their own decisions, but it is a matter of experience that people are willing to agree, when they are in love, to things that they would not otherwise contemplate. . . . [W]e know that people tend to be unrealistically optimistic about both the likelihood that they will divorce and their future fortunes. A fiancé(e) may enter into an agreement at the other's request in the firm belief that the relationship will never end. He or she may not really want the agreement to take effect, or may not have thought through the consequences of entering into it.

5.31 Furthermore there may be pressure. Practitioners in a study by Dr Emma Hitchings talked of the pressures their clients may face when being encouraged to sign a pre-nuptial agreement. Dr Hitchings reported that:

Time and again practitioners raised the "typical scenario" of the financially stronger party exerting emotional pressure upon their client (normally the financially weaker party), through the "I won't marry you if you don't sign the agreement" argument.

---

[464] Vardag and Miles (2015), cf Hitchings (2011), 28.
[465] Barlow and Smithson (2012), 307–8.

Indeed, the law already recognises the possibility of pressure within a close relationship, in the context of the law relating to undue influence in contracts . . .

5.32 We think that it is possible, to some extent, for the law to counteract pressure by imposing certain pre-conditions for the validity of a qualifying nuptial agreement and we have attempted to ensure that our suggested reform would do so. For example, . . . we recommend that the parties to a qualifying nuptial agreement must take legal advice and receive disclosure, and that qualifying nuptial agreements should not be concluded within the 28 day period leading up to the day of the wedding. We accept, however, that legal pre-conditions cannot entirely eliminate the probability that some people may agree qualifying nuptial agreements that they would later regret.

5.33 The other reason for caution is that we have to be very clear about what the autonomy, or freedom, in question is. All couples, under the current law, have the freedom to agree whatever they like by way of financial settlement when their relationship comes to an end. The autonomy that is prayed in aid of binding marital property agreements is not simply the freedom to make an agreement, nor simply the freedom to do as one wishes. It is the freedom to force one's partner to abide by an agreement when he or she no longer wishes to do so. It is freedom of contract, but it is therefore freedom to use a contract to restrict one's partner's choices.

5.34 So the autonomy argument is a strong one but it raises concerns as well. These concerns . . . have led to our decision . . . to limit the scope of qualifying nuptial agreements. We recognise that there may be pressure on one party to sign an agreement, and that that party may enter the agreement unwillingly or with unrealistic optimism. Thus, whilst a party may regret the agreement, or have his or her choices restricted, we have decided that the court's jurisdiction to make provision for needs should not be ousted by a qualifying nuptial agreement and so no party will be left without resources following separation.

Certainty and the cost of discretion

5.35 Much stronger, we feel, than the argument for autonomy is the argument for certainty. As one member of the public put it [in their consultation response]:

Surely the most important point of a pre-nuptial agreement is to provide both parties with a high degree of certainty as to the outcome in the event of a breakdown of their forthcoming marriage and to reduce the need to resort to expensive legal redress in the event of the breakdown.

5.36 Again, of course, that freedom exists under the current law, provided there is agreement at the point when the relationship ends. What is being argued is that it is important for the parties to have certainty in advance that a partner will not be able to re-open the financial agreement by resorting to the court, and that that limitation upon one partner's freedom is justified in the interests of both by ensuring that neither will be involved in the uncertainty, stress and cost of litigation. The fact that the terms of a marital property agreement are always subject to the court's review means that it is currently never possible to be certain, in advance, that an agreement will determine the outcome of the financial relief process.

5.37 Certainty may be particularly important for those who are remarrying and have children from a previous marriage, and for those who wish to protect inherited or "family" wealth from division upon divorce. Under the current law there is no guarantee that a party who has children from a previous relationship will be able to preserve assets to pass on to those children, whilst a binding qualifying nuptial agreement would allow a party to do just that....[T]he law on non-matrimonial property is unclear, both in terms of what property can be considered "non-matrimonial" and in terms of the effect that the existence of non-matrimonial property will have on the eventual division of assets by the court. A qualifying nuptial agreement would allow the parties to define, from the outset of the relationship, what property should be split between them and the way in which it should be split.... [T]hese two situation are ones in which the public feel that a pre-nuptial agreement may be sensible and pragmatic [see Barlow and Smithson (2012)].

5.38 It may be argued that couples can, following *Radmacher v Granatino*, already be reasonably sure that pre-nuptial agreements will be upheld. However, the fact that the terms of marital property agreement are always subject to the court's review means that it is currently never possible to be certain, in advance, that an agreement will determine the outcome of the financial relief process.

The international perspective

5.39...[A] great number of other jurisdictions allow binding marital property agreements. The introduction of qualifying nuptial agreements would bring our laws into step with those jurisdictions, allowing couples who had made their agreements in another country to rely on the binding nature of the agreement if they subsequently moved to England or Wales. One consultee, a member of the public, told us of his unhappy experience of moving here with his wife, only to find that it was no longer guaranteed that their pre-nuptial agreement would be upheld by the courts. The introduction of qualifying nuptial agreements could encourage the movement of wealthy foreign nationals to this jurisdiction by offering them the opportunity to replicate, or come close to replicating, the certainty of outcome on divorce and preservation of wealth which they may enjoy in their jurisdiction of origin. This could benefit England and Wales economically. Qualifying nuptial agreements could also reduce disputes between foreign national couples who seek to litigate, on an English divorce, over the status of their foreign agreement, since such couples could simply reproduce the terms of their foreign pre-nuptial agreement as a qualifying post-nuptial agreement upon moving to England and Wales. This could save time, money and stress for those involved, and potentially reduce the burden on our courts.

The Commission therefore recommended legislation to create a universal regime for all categories of marital agreement—pre-nups, post-nups, and separation agreements. They would be binding provided the preconditions for 'qualifying' status were satisfied. Those preconditions are much tougher than step 1 of the *Radmacher* regime. Such an agreement would have to be valid in contract law; made by deed more than 28 days before the wedding or civil partnership; and contain a statement signed by both parties that each understood the agreement's nature and its effect in removing the court's discretion to make financial orders on divorce, save in so far as the agreement left either party without provision for their financial needs. Each party at the time of making the agreement would have had to receive disclosure of material information about the other's financial situation and independent legal advice explaining the nature of the agreement and its effect on that party's rights.[466] The scheme's preservation of the court's right to provide for the parties' needs (understood in the normal sense, rather than a narrower, 'real need' sense[467]) is intended to provide an appropriate balance between autonomy and protection against the dangers

---

[466] See Law Com (2014), ch 6.
[467] Ibid, para 5.82.

of pressure, imbalance of power, and optimism bias.[468] Parties would therefore be able to protect their financial interests but not at the expense of disturbing the core obligation to provide for a spouse's needs. The 'primary function of family law' to protect the vulnerable would thus continue to be met.[469]

7.8 REMEDIES ON OTHER TYPES OF FAMILY RELATIONSHIP BREAKDOWN

While spouses and civil partners have access to special statutory financial remedies on divorce, where other family relationships break down—for example, cohabitants, blood relatives, platonic home-sharers—the parties must use a patchwork of common law and statutory rights and remedies. These do not provide a coherent substantive or procedural response to the financial and property-related problems associated with family breakdown.[470]

7.8.1 THE GENERAL LAW APPLIES

The starting point is that the general law determines ownership and other rights in relation to property: the parties' shared home, its contents, other chattels, bank accounts, and so on. The courts have no powers to adjust the parties' property rights, and neither party can be ordered to make periodical payments to the other.[471] Each party will leave with what the general law says he or she owns, and nothing more. It is in this context that criticisms made of that law have most urgency.[472] Readers should refer to the discussion and criticism of *Stack v Dowden* and related cases in chapter 3.

7.8.2 REMEDIES FOR THE BENEFIT OF CHILDREN

The most substantial statutory remedies exist for the benefit of any children of the parties under the CSA 1991 and the Children Act 1989 (CA 1989), Sch 1.[473] These remedies potentially offer the primary carer of the children indirect benefit: that party's household income may be increased by receipt of child support; the provision of accommodation for the benefit of such children clearly benefits the primary carers. However, orders under the CA 1989 are relatively unusual outside the big money context, and various limitations on the court's powers, not least its inability to adjust the capital entitlements of the adult parties or to order sale, inhibit their usefulness. Moreover, since these remedies offer protection ordinarily only during the children's minority, any indirect benefit obtained by the primary carer ceases with the order. The CA 1989 does not apply where the children

---

[468] Ibid, from para 5.42.
[469] Ibid, para 5.81.
[470] For detailed examination and criticisms of the law in the context of cohabitation, see Law Com (2006), Parts 3 and 4.
[471] *Windeler v Whitehall* [1990] 2 FLR 505. Cf equitable accounting discussed on the Online Resource Centre.
[472] See 3.4.7.
[473] See chapter 6.

have left home, leaving the former primary carer, who may have been out of paid employment for years, with no remedy (direct or indirect) to address any ongoing economic vulnerability.[474]

7.8.3 DISPUTES REGARDING THE FORMER FAMILY HOME

Where the parties shared a home, the most important issue on relationship breakdown is future occupation or sale of that property. The solution to this problem depends on: who owns or rents the property and whether it is solely or co-owned; the nature of the parties' relationship; and whether there are any children in whose favour an order might be made under the CA 1989, Sch 1. We address two categories of case:

(1) disputes between co-owners under the general law of trusts: Trusts of Land and Appointment of Trustees Act 1996 (TOLATA 1996); and

(2) disputes between an owner and non-entitled applicant under the FLA 1996.

We consider the interaction between the TOLATA 1996 and applications under the CA 1989, Sch 1 in relation to case (1). But case (2) must also be read subject to the important qualification that wherever the applicant has a dependent child of the respondent living with him or her, the CA 1989, Sch 1 may apply, providing greater indirect protection (if only for the duration of that child's minority) than any FLA 1996 order would allow. We also consider tenancy transfers.

Disputes between co-owners

Suppose two or more family members who co-own the home are in dispute about its continued occupation. One wishes to remain in the property while the other wishes to sell it and release his or her capital share.[475] Whether the parties are co-trustees, or sole-trustee and beneficial co-owner, various court applications are possible.

First, disputes regarding both the occupation and sale of the property may be heard under TOLATA 1996, s 14. Under s 15(1), the court must have regard to the following factors in determining such disputes:

(a) the intentions of the person or persons (if any) who created the trust,

(b) the purposes for which the property subject to the trust is held,

(c) the welfare of any minor who occupies or might reasonably be expected to occupy any land subject to the trust as his home, and

(d) the interests of any secured creditor of any beneficiary.

In considering disputes regarding occupation, the court must also have regard to the circumstances and wishes of each of the beneficiaries who is in principle entitled to occupy,[476] and in disputes regarding sale, the circumstances and wishes of all adult beneficiaries entitled to an interest in possession.[477]

---

[474] See Law Com (2006), paras 4.34–4.46.
[475] See generally Hopkins (2009).
[476] TOLATA 1996, s 15(2).
[477] Ibid, s 15(3).

Secondly, if the co-owners are 'associated persons',[478] disputes regarding *occupation* can be dealt with by an order under the FLA 1996, s 33, discussed in chapter 4.

Finally, if the parties have dependent children, an application may be made under CA 1989, Sch 1 for orders relating to the occupation of the parties' home and transfer or settlement of other assets for the benefit of the children,[479] discussed in chapter 6.

Competing claims under these three Acts should be heard together,[480] but combining them is not straightforward, either procedurally (the first is a civil matter, the other two family proceedings)[481] or substantively (each confers different powers to be exercised on different criteria). As such, they compare unfavourably with the 'one-stop-shop' of the MCA 1973. The CA 1989 gives particular prominence to the needs of the children, and should be considered first in any combined TOLATA/CA case. Applications concerning the children's future living arrangements should ideally be determined by the same judge.[482] Where there are no children, the FLA 1996, tailored specifically for the family context, is the preferred framework for dealing with the question of occupation, rather than TOLATA 1996. However, TOLATA 1996 must be used to resolve the timing of any sale.[483]

Despite the procedural maze, this legislation can provide outcomes regarding the family home not dissimilar to those achievable under the MCA 1973. In many cases, the main purpose of the trust will have been to provide a family home for the children. Even after the adults have separated, the trust's purpose may still be fulfilled by providing a home for the children. However, trusts law may produce outcomes unsuited to the realities of family life.[484] Arden LJ's approach to TOLATA 1996, s 15 in a family case has been criticized for making unrealistic expectations about whether and how parties articulate their intentions about co-owned family homes.[485] In *W v W*, an unmarried couple had purchased a home in joint names. They started a family and so extended the house to provide an extra bedroom. The relationship broke down. The father, with whom the two children were to live, wished to retain the home. The mother wanted an immediate sale.

W v W (Joinder of Trusts of Land Act and Children Act Applications) [2003] EWCA Civ 924

ARDEN LJ:

22. . . . The [father] submits that the judge was entitled to have regard to the intention of the parents formed after the trusts of land was created. [Arden LJ set out TOLATA 1996, s 15(1), and decided that the intention referred to in para (a) must be held in common by all parties creating the trust.]

23. The question then remains whether the intention could include intention subsequently come to . . . I do not myself consider that this is the correct construction. Parliament has used the word "intention" which speaks naturally to the intentions of persons prior to the creation

---

478 FLA 1996, s 62(3): see 4.5.1.
479 The courts only have limited jurisdiction to make periodical payments orders: see 6.5.2.
480 *W v W (Joinder of Trusts of Land Act and Children Act Applications)* [2003] EWCA Civ 924, [5].
481 Cf *Seabrook v Sullivan* [2014] EWHC 4110, [24].
482 Ibid, [15] and [17].
483 *Chan v Leung* [2002] EWCA Civ 1075, [46]–[48].
484 See 3.4.7 for similar criticism of implied trusts and proprietary estoppel.
485 Gray and Gray (2009), at 7.5.98, n 1; Probert (2007a).

of the trust. If that were not its meaning, then it is not clear whether the court should be looking at the parties' intentions at the date of the hearing or at some other antecedent point in time and, if so, what date. If Parliament meant the present intention, it would have used some such word as "wishes" rather than the word "intention" which implies some statement or opinion as to the future. In all the circumstances, I consider that the [father's] submissions on the point of law on this point are not correct.

24. I turn now to the...point...that the judge had failed to deal with a submission by the father that there was an additional purpose come to after the property was purchased and the parties had been living there...namely to provide a home for the children. I would accept that, for the purposes of section 15(1)(b), purposes could have been formulated informally, but they must be the purposes subject to which the property is held. The purpose established at the outset of the trust which, on the judge's finding, did not include the provision of a home for children, could only change if both parties agreed. There was no evidence from which the judge could find that the mother agreed to the additional purpose spoken to by the father...

Such a narrow reading of the mother's probable intentions following the birth of her two children, and the suggestion that it may be impossible to form intentions after the creation of the trust, pose difficulties for applications to postpone sale for the sake of children of the family under TOLATA 1996, and neglect the independent status afforded to children's interests by s 15(1)(c). In the event, the property was sold as the father could afford alternative accommodation with his share of the proceeds.

Section 15(1)(c) aside, the children's needs may support a claim under the CA 1989, Sch 1. In *Re Evers' Trust*, the court applauded the fact that it could make orders under the trusts legislation, and now under the CA 1989, Sch 1, very similar in effect to matrimonial *Mesher* and *Martin* orders.[486] Sale can be postponed and one party permitted to occupy to the exclusion of the other, for example until the children leave home or reach a prescribed age,[487] or until the occupying party marries or cohabits with a third party, dies, or no longer requires the property.[488] The court can require the occupant to pay 'rent' to the excluded party.[489] But where the property is to be occupied by one party with the children, the parties' obligations to those children may make it inappropriate to make such an order.[490] The crucial *difference* between these cases and the matrimonial/civil partnership context is that here the court cannot adjust the parties' beneficial shares in the property. Those are fixed by the law of trusts. Any capital award made under CA 1989, Sch 1 will revert to the payer once the children are independent.[491]

Occupation orders under the FLA 1996

What if the party wishing to remain in occupation has no beneficial interest in the property or other relevant entitlement under the general law? That person is likely to be a bare licensee, whose occupation can be terminated with reasonable notice.[492] But even an individual

---

[486] [1980] 1 WLR 1327, 1333.
[487] *Parkes v Legal Aid Board* [1997] 1 WLR 1547.
[488] Cf *Holman v Howes* [2007] EWCA Civ 877 where an estoppel had arisen in the occupant's favour.
[489] TOLATA 1996, s 13, subject to s 15 factors.
[490] *Stack v Dowden* [2005] EWCA Civ 857, [61]–[63]; cf [2007] UKHL 17, [94] and [155].
[491] See p 412 above; *Norris v Hudson* [2005] EWHC 2934.
[492] E.g. *Hannaford v Selby* (1976) 238 EG 811.

with no right to occupy (a 'non-entitled' person) may be able to obtain an occupation order under the FLA 1996.[493] However, 'non-entitled' applications can only be brought by current and former spouses, civil partners, and cohabitants. Other family members, such as relatives and unrelated home-sharers, are left to the general law governing licences. Moreover, the protection offered by the FLA 1996 to non-entitled cohabitants and former cohabitants is limited, in terms both of the basis on which the court makes its decision and the duration of any potential order.[494] It can at best provide a short-term solution to the accommodation needs of non-entitled applicants. Moreover, while the court can make ancillary orders for the payment of various outgoings in relation to property subject to an occupation order, it cannot use that power to provide maintenance for either party.[495] If there are dependent children, the CA 1989 may provide much longer term protection of occupation for the children (and their primary carer), as well as other financial provision, but no capital or income payment for the primary carer in her own right.

Rented homes

There is one exception to the basic proposition that the courts have no adjustive powers outside the MCA 1973 and the CPA 2004. Where cohabitants rented their home, the courts have the same powers under the FLA 1996 to order a transfer of that tenancy as they do between spouses and civil partners.[496] The power applies only between former cohabitants and not between other home-sharers. Jurisdiction arises when the parties 'cease to cohabit'.[497] The criteria to which the court must have regard in exercising its discretion are set out in the Act.[498] The party to whom the transfer is made may be required to compensate the other.[499] The landlord of the property has a right to be heard before any such order is made.[500] Since many private sector tenancies now offer limited security of tenure in any event, the practical benefit offered by Sch 7 may be limited.[501]

The occupation order regime of the FLA 1996 applies to rented property as it does to owner-occupied property,[502] so a sole or joint tenant may apply for an occupation order under s 33 and a non-entitled cohabitant under s 36. The general law of licences also applies.

7.8.4 PRIVATE ORDERING

Parties can try to avoid the problems that might be encountered in trying to use the general law to determine disputes following separation by creating their own solution by agreement in advance or on separation. Any two or more people can regulate the ownership of property via express declarations of trust.[503] However, question marks have dogged the legal

---

[493] Note also FLA 1996, ss 35(11)–(12), 36(11)–(12): can apply as a non-entitled applicant without prejudice to subsequently claiming a beneficial interest.

[494] FLA 1996, ss 36 and 38.

[495] Ibid, s 40; Law Com (1992), para 4.41.

[496] Ibid, Sch 7.

[497] Cf *Gully v Dix* [2004] EWCA Civ 139.

[498] FLA 1996, Sch 7, para 5.

[499] Ibid, para 10.

[500] Ibid, para 14(1).

[501] Note also problems regarding notice to quit joint periodic tenancies: Law Com (2006), para 3.61; *Sims v Dacorum BC* [2014] UKSC 63.

[502] E.g. *Chalmers v Johns* [1999] 2 FCR 110.

[503] See 3.4.1.

enforceability of *contracts* making financial arrangements between cohabitants. The courts may hesitate to find an intention to create legal relations between parties to an ongoing relationship, unlike parties clearly dealing at arm's length following relationship breakdown.[504] Just as domestic contributions struggle to count as detrimental reliance for the purpose of the laws of implied trusts and estoppel, it may be hard to establish consideration by promising to undertake such tasks.[505] However, these problems can be overcome with an appropriately drafted deed.

But another factor has bedevilled contracts between cohabitants: a contract for which the performance of extra-marital sexual relations appears to form part of the consideration is void on public policy grounds. While that is not a problem for contracts made following separation (where the provision being agreed is clearly a consequence of the relationship, rather than a condition of it), it is potentially problematic for contracts made earlier.[506] However, it is widely accepted that a contract made between cohabitants governing their property and financial entitlements, whether during the relationship or following its future demise, will be upheld.[507] This view was reinforced from the unlikely source of a case involving a 'Swedish sex slave'. A negligence action was brought against solicitors in connection with the drafting of an agreement for a 'master/slave' relationship between two men which provided, inter alia, that the property of the 'slave' would be transferred absolutely to the 'master'. In the course of striking out the claim on the merits, the judge considered the agreement's validity. Was it void because 'meretricious'? This agreement was, but others—simply governing cohabitants' property rights—could be valid. In considering the 'unlawfulness' of cohabitants' sexual relationship, the judge referred to Tony Honoré's book, *Sex Law*:

Sutton v Mischon de Reya and another [2003] EWHC 3166, [2004] 3 FCR 142

HART J:

22. . . . 'Whatever the reason, and however stable the relation, sexual intercourse between an unmarried couple is "unlawful" though it is not in general a crime . . . A contract for which the whole or part of the consideration is sexual intercourse (or any other sexual relation) outside marriage is void, as is a contract which tends to promote unlawful sexual intercourse. So, if Jack agrees to support Jill to whom he is not married on condition that she keeps house for him and that they have sexual intercourse, the whole agreement is void even if they mean it to be a legally binding one. It makes no difference that the agreement to have sex is understood rather than expressed.'

But, as [Honoré] went on to point out, that analysis does not prevent the cohabitors from entering into perfectly valid legal relations concerning their mutual property rights, or even (he suggests) as to other ancillary matters such as how they will divide up the work. Such a contract will not be a contract of cohabitation but a contract between cohabitors. He suggested that there was no reason why such a contract should not be upheld even though its tendency in fact might be to encourage the continuation of the "unlawful" sexual relationship.

---

[504] E.g. *Jones v Padavattan* [1969] 1 WLR 328, 332.
[505] *Horrocks v Foray* [1976] 1 WLR 230, 239.
[506] Probert (2004d), 459 and generally, for analysis of the old cases.
[507] E.g. Masson, Bailey-Harris, and Probert (2008), 5-007.

23. If that is the right distinction to draw (ie a distinction between a contract *for* sexual relations outside marriage and a contract *between* persons who are cohabiting in a relationship which involves such sexual relations), it is not, in my judgment, difficult even for a moron in a hurry... to see on which side of the line the cohabitation deed in this case falls. It was not a property contract between two people whose sexual relationship involved them in cohabitation. It was itself an attempt to express the sexual relationship in the property relations contained in the contract (or, as [counsel for the claimant] himself put it, the property relation "sprang from" the desire to give the sexual role-play verisimilitude). It was an attempt to reify an unlawful ideal.

While the remarks of Hart J are welcome, there is still no contemporary decision upholding a contract between cohabitants.[508] The Law Commission recommended that clarifying legislation would be welcome, for the avoidance of doubt.[509] Since these contracts do not displace any special statutory remedies akin to the MCA 1973, no *Hyman* point arises.[510]

However, it is questionable how many couples do or, if the law were clarified, would regulate their affairs by contract:[511]

R. Probert, '*Sutton v Mishcon de Reya and Gawor & Co*—Cohabitation Contracts and Swedish Sex Slaves', (2004d) 16 *Child and Family Law Quarterly* 453, 461–2

In a study by Lewis [(1999)], only one-quarter of respondents agreed with the statement that 'people who are going to live together or get married should write down beforehand how they will divide their finances in case they split up'. In the accompanying qualitative study, 20 of the 73 respondents were in favour of contracts: those opposed suggested that contracts were 'too cold', 'defeatist', and inappropriate in view of the way that relationships change over time and demand flexibility. Barlow and James [(2004)] have suggested that their more recent research suggests greater enthusiasm for a contractual solution. Certainly, their respondents were positive about the idea of a partnership register... but such a scheme confers status as well as regulating the rights of the parties, and may be more attractive for that reason. In any case, their enthusiasm was not matched by formal arrangements. The number who actually enter into a contract is likely to be considerably smaller than those who are willing to contemplate one in theory: first, both parties must agree in theory that a contract is a good idea, secondly, they must agree on what the terms of the contract are to be, and thirdly, they must actually get round to entering into such a contract. The failure of couples thus to regulate their lives is well documented.

But from a psychological perspective, it may be undesirable to encourage contracting between couples whose relationship is good. Couples are commonly accused of suffering from 'optimism bias'—assuming that *their* relationship will not founder despite statistical evidence indicating that many relationships do end, and so failing to protect their position against that risk in advance. But should we burst the bubble by encouraging couples to sit

---

508 Though note contractual licence cases such as *Tanner v Tanner* [1975] 1 WLR 1346, *Chandler v Kerley* [1978] 1 WLR 693 involving 'mistresses' set up in a home by their partners.

509 Law Com (2007), para 8.25.

510 Cf 7.7 above.

511 See also Reece (2014).

down and contract for that possibility? These arguments might apply equally, or with even more force, to couples negotiating pre-nuptial agreements:[512]

H. Reece, 'Leaping without Looking', in R. Leckey (ed), *After Equality*
(Abingdon: Routledge, 2014), 123–4[513]

Although diverse roots of the optimism bias have been suggested it is commonly accepted that at least part of the explanation is that we base our predictions on a mental simulation of ourselves engaging in the actions necessary for the outcome, and our simulation tends to dwell on the positive, not negative, possibilities. Once we have conjured up a positive mental picture of the future event, we see that picture as more likely, especially because imagining that picture crowds out any other...Moreover, our mental picture of a positive future event is rich and vivid, this clear picture reinforcing our belief that the positive event is probable. In contrast, when Sharot [a researcher]...asked people to visualize separation from their partner, their mental picture was blurry. We make a close connection between clarity and probability and between fuzziness and improbability; we have a fuzzy picture of an event that we believe is unlikely, and, if our picture is fuzzy, then we believe that the event is unlikely.

Crucially, if we make ourselves conjure up clearer pictures of negative events, then we regard those negative events as more likely. Explaining a negative event makes for a clearer picture, to such an extent that explaining the negative event may affect us similarly to experiencing the negative event, altering our behaviour....Moreover, just like a positive picture, generating a negative picture also crowds out alternative, positive scenarios. Once cohabitants focus in on the potential failure of their relationship, they may believe their relationship is more likely to fail, which may, in turn, cause them to act as if the relationship is failing, causing the relationship to fail.

Those who wish to persuade cohabitants to reach agreement may find it necessary to dent unrealistic optimism, with negative impact on cohabiting relationships. Moreover, the process of reaching cohabitation agreements may dent unrealistic optimism, with negative impact on cohabiting relationships. The more seriously cohabitants take the process, the more their optimism may be damaged. The less seriously cohabitants take the process, the less their optimism will be dented, and the worse an agreement they may make.

7.8.5 NEW STATUTORY REMEDIES FOR COHABITANTS?

If couples cannot or should not protect their own positions through contract, should the law ensure better protection of vulnerable parties by providing financial remedies on separation? If a cohabiting relationship ends on the death of one of the parties, the survivor can seek reasonable financial provision under the Inheritance (Provision for Family and Dependants) Act 1975, even if the deceased made no will. But there is no equivalent statutory scheme on separation. Several other jurisdictions, including Scotland[514] and Ireland,[515] now have such remedies.[516]

The Law Commission was asked to examine this issue, prompted by concerns that the current law produces what many regard as unfair results, particularly at the end of long-term relationships and those in which the couple had a child.[517] Discussion of reform in this area

---

[512] Reece (2014), 120.
[513] References omitted.
[514] Family Law (Scotland) Act 2006.
[515] Civil Partnership and Certain Rights and Obligations of Cohabitants Act 2010.
[516] See Law Com (2006), Appendix C.
[517] See Arthur et al (2002).

provokes strong responses.[518] The first question is whether the law should be reformed at all, and if so, in which cases. This is a large question of social policy. For many, the idea that cohabitants should have statutory remedies on relationship breakdown is unacceptable. Rather than giving cohabitants the remedies that many mistakenly believe they already have,[519] the state should endeavour to educate them about the substantial legal differences between marriage/civil partnership and cohabitation.[520] Then, it is argued, those who continue to cohabit can confidently be said to have rejected marriage, and it would therefore be unjustifiable to impose on them legal regulation that they have consciously rejected and not created by contract.[521] Other opponents of reform fear that any legal recognition of cohabitation would undermine the institution of marriage, arguing that provision of legal recognition outside marriage would remove an incentive to marry.[522]

At the opposite end of the debate are those who argue that cohabitants should be brought fully within the MCA 1973. The economic vulnerability experienced by many cohabitants and their children on separation is no different from that encountered on divorce. These commentators regard the flexible MCA regime as the best tool to deal with these practical problems, enabling the courts to differentiate those short-term, childless relationships at the end of which no remedy is called for, from longer term, more economically interdependent partnerships which merit relief. It is argued that this would bring the law into line with people's expectations and social practices.[523]

The Law Commission recommended a middle path, seeking to respect the autonomy of those couples who wish to keep the law out of their relationships, whilst providing some level of protection to those left economically vulnerable on separation because of their contributions to the relationship.[524] The key aspects of the recommendations for remedies on separation were as follows.

- A new statutory scheme should provide financial relief between 'eligible' cohabitants, without requiring the parties to have 'opted in' by prior registration or agreement.

- Cohabitants would be 'eligible' to apply for financial relief under a new scheme if they had:
  - been living as a couple in a joint household; and had either
  - had a child together (born during, before, or following their cohabitation), or
  - had lived together for a minimum duration, which should be set by statute somewhere within a range between two and five years.[525]

- Couples should be able to 'opt out' of the scheme and make their own binding arrangements at any time.
  - Such agreements would be enforceable if they were in writing, signed by the parties, and made clear the parties' intention to disapply the statute; independent legal advice would not be a precondition of enforceability.

[518] Cf the history of the Family Violence and Domestic Homes Bill 1995, which preceded the FLA 1996: Hale (2004), 419 and see 2.8.2.

[519] See the common law marriage myth: 2.8.2.

[520] See the Living Together Campaign. Cf Reece (2014).

[521] E.g. Deech (1980b).

[522] E.g. generally, Morgan (2000). For evaluation of these arguments, see Law Com (2006), Part 5.

[523] E.g. Barlow et al (2005), Bailey-Harris (1996).

[524] Law Com (2007).

[525] Separate recommendations were made regarding eligibility where a couple have a child living with them who is not in law the child of both of them.

- But the court should be entitled to set aside an otherwise binding opt-out agreement if enforcement would cause manifest unfairness given circumstances at the time the agreement was made or a later change of circumstances that had not been foreseen when the agreement was made.

- Where a couple were 'eligible' and there was no binding opt-out agreement, the courts should have a discretion to grant the same types of orders as under the MCA 1973, save that periodical payments orders should only be available in respect of future child-care costs.

- But those orders should be granted on a basis different from that applying between spouses on divorce,[526] which appears to correspond most closely with the 'compensation' strand from *Miller; McFarlane*.[527] The exercise of the court's discretion should be focused on addressing the economic impact of contributions arising from the parties' relationship and made by the applicant to the parties' shared lives or to the welfare of members of their families.

- Specifically, an applicant would have to prove that following separation:

  - the respondent retained an economic benefit (whether in the form of capital, income, or earning capacity) arising from contributions made by the applicant during the relationship (e.g. financial contributions to the acquisition of property held in the respondent's name or physical labour increasing the value of the respondent's property), and/or

  - the applicant sustained an economic disadvantage (in the form of lost future earnings or earning capacity, or reduced savings, including pension savings) flowing from economic sacrifices made because of that party's contribution to the relationship (typically, giving up paid employment to care for dependants), or as a result of continuing child-care responsibilities following separation.[528]

The Law Commission's recommendations were met with various criticisms. Some disagreed with the basic policy, either wanting cohabitants to be subject to the same law as spouses; opposing *any* reform; or promoting alternative schemes. Others criticized the complexity of the scheme and problems that might be encountered attempting to prove and quantify claims under it.[529] The Labour Government deferred any final decision pending research into the costs and efficacy of recent reform in Scotland introducing similar remedies between cohabitants in the Family Law (Scotland) Act 2006. Research into the first three years' operation of the Scottish provisions was duly published,[530] but the Coalition Government decided against legislative action on the basis that the findings did 'not provide... a sufficient basis for change in the law'.[531] Meanwhile, public attitudes appear strongly to support financial remedies between

---

[526] Appendix C to the Report explains the Commission's reasons for rejecting alternative schemes, including the MCA 1973.

[527] See *Gow v Grant* [2012] UKSC 29, [45].

[528] Appendix B to the Report illustrates the operation of the recommended scheme with examples.

[529] Probert (2007b), (2009d); Douglas, Pearce, and Woodward (2008).

[530] Wasoff, Miles, and Mordaunt (2010).

[531] Hansard HC Deb, cols 15–16WS, 6 September 2011; see also Hansard HL Deb, vol 730, cols 118–20, 6 September 2011, Lord McNally. Cf Lord Marks' Private Member's Bill, the Cohabitation Rights Bill [HL] 2014–15.

cohabitants in certain circumstances,[532] and calls for reform—from the highest levels—continue:

Gow v Grant [2012] UKSC 29

LADY HALE:

50. Responding to the Government's announcement...Professor Elizabeth Cooke, the Law Commissioner who leads the Commission's work in family and property law, said this:

"We hope that implementation [of the Commission's recommendations] will not be delayed beyond the early days of the next Parliament, in view of the hardship and injustice caused by the current law. The prevalence of cohabitation, and the birth of children to couples who live together, means that the need for reform of the law can only become more pressing over time."

As Professor Cooke also pointed out, the "existing law is uncertain and expensive to apply and, because it was not designed for cohabitants, often gives rise to results that are unjust". The reality is that the "sufficient basis for changing the law" had already been amply provided by the long-standing judicial calls for reform (dating back at least as far as *Burns v Burns* [1984] Ch 317, at 332); by the Law Commission's analysis of the deficiencies in the present law and the injustices which can result; by the demographic trends towards cohabitation and births to cohabiting couples...; and by the widespread belief that cohabiting couples are already protected by something called "common law marriage"...There was no need to wait for experience north of the border to make the case for reform.

Several commentators have argued that debates about remedies for cohabitants have been distorted by a focus on the formal status rather than functions of relationships, and so on the perceived need to give cohabitant-applicants 'less' than an equivalent divorce-applicant. This, combined with the equal sharing principle's emphasis of the marriage partnership (largely regardless of the parties' actual contributions), leaves individuals in functionally similar circumstances being treated very differently:[533]

L. Glennon, 'The Limitations of Equality Discourses on the Contours of Intimate Obligations', in J. Wallbank, S. Choudhry, and J. Herring (eds), *Rights, Gender and Family Law* (Abingdon: Routledge, 2010), 197–8

The result is that familial caregiving is not considered as a valued activity in its own right, but is conceptualised through the lens of the relationship form in which it takes place. As such, it can be said that these mutually informing equality discourses [about the recognition of non-traditional family forms and about non-discrimination between breadwinner and home-maker], whilst having transformative potential, have failed to generate a root and branch approach to family law development which would strip back the assumptions upon which current norms are based and encourage a deeper connection between the functions which a family (family members) perform(s) and the obligations to which it (they) are subjected.

---

[532] Barlow et al (2008).
[533] See also Wong (2009), Bottomley and Wong (2006). But compare Probert's reservations (2009c) about such arguments, noted at p 111 above.

> By contrast, a preferable approach to the construction of legal obligations between adults would de-emphasise relationship form and encourage a more direct consideration of relationship functions. In this way, the focus on actual interdependencies, such as those arising through shared parenthood, would encourage a more direct and positive value to be placed on familial caregiving. It would also allow more accurate demarcations to replace the current bright line distinctions drawn between the married and unmarried which prevents a proper evaluation of the mutual dependencies which can arise in couple-based relationships of varying forms. Such an approach...would help to bring legal ideology into line with the emerging social view, revealed in the recent British Social Attitudes Report, that 'most people seem to place the emphasis on successfully 'doing' family in practice, whatever situation people find themselves in, rather than on the supposed functionality of different family forms'.

Indeed, viewed in these terms, cohabitants are not the only candidates for remedies on relationship breakdown. Australian states have extended financial relief in this area to other 'domestic' or 'personal' relationships, in some instances even without requiring that the parties shared a household.[534] English law recognizes some such relationships in the event of death: 'dependants' of the deceased—those who were being maintained, wholly or partially, by the deceased immediately before his or her death—may apply for provision under the Inheritance (Provision for Family and Dependants) Act 1975. But for the time being, should their relationship founder during the parties' joint lives, these families, like cohabitants, remain reliant for their protection on the general law and limited statutory remedies.

7.9 CONCLUSION

The law relating to family finances and property on relationship breakdown is highly technical in practice and conceptually sophisticated. However, beneath that complexity lie fundamental questions about the nature of marriage, civil partnership, and other family relationships. Are they relationships of dependency and support, joint ventures between equal partners, or associations between economically independent individuals? And what is the role of the state in all this: to intervene to protect the economically vulnerable, to stand back and allow parties freedom to make their own arrangements, or to make structural changes in the workplace and elsewhere in the public sphere to help improve women's economic position generally and so reduce the economic disparities experienced on relationship breakdown?

ONLINE RESOURCE CENTRE
Questions, suggestions for further reading, and supplementary materials for this chapter (including updates on developments in this area of family law since this book was published) may be found on the Online Resource Centre at **www.oxfordtextbooks.co.uk/orc/familytcm3e/**.

---

[534] Property (Relationships) Act 1984 (NSW); Domestic Relationships Act 1994 (ACT); Relationships Act 2003 (Tas); see Mee (2004), 427–9.

8

FUNDAMENTAL PRINCIPLES
IN THE LAW RELATING
TO CHILDREN

CENTRAL ISSUES

1. The welfare of the child is the paramount consideration in most court-adjudicated disputes about children's upbringing. This means the rights and interests of others are relevant only insofar as they bear upon the child's interests. This has led to debate about the compatibility of the paramountcy principle with Article 8 of the European Convention on Human Rights (ECHR).

2. The paramountcy principle only applies where the 'upbringing' of a child is *directly* in issue before a *court*. In cases which affect children less directly, or where a state body other than a court is determining the issue, the child's welfare is 'a primary consideration' under the United Nations Convention on the Rights of the Child.

3. The welfare principle is criticized for its indeterminacy and lack of transparency. Measures to curtail judicial discretion, such as statutory checklists and scientific evidence, only partially address these problems.

4. Alternatives to the welfare principle remain closely wedded to its basic premises: that children should be afforded special consideration in the decision-making process.

5. Children's rights play an increasingly important role in English family law. Although difficult to uphold when children seek to act in ways considered inimical to their welfare, the rights of children are now widely recognized and respected.

6. The Children Act 1989 (CA 1989) enshrines a policy of non-intervention in private family life. The relationship between this policy and the paramountcy principle is debatable.

8.1 INTRODUCTION

The law relating to children covers a great many issues. Who, as a matter of law, should be recognized as being a parent, and what does it mean to be a parent? In what ways, if any, should the rules be different for mothers and for fathers, for married and for unmarried parents, for opposite-sex and for same-sex parents? Can a child have only two parents? What about cases involving artificial insemination, surrogacy, or adoption?

Separately, we need to ask questions about who should have the responsibilities and powers associated with raising a child, which English law terms 'parental responsibility' (PR). Often the answer will be 'the child's parents' (once we work out what the law means by that), but not always. The questions of who should have PR, how they should get it, and whether they can have it removed from them, are all important and difficult. At the same time, we need to grapple with children's own autonomy and rights, particularly when important decisions have to be made about their lives. What if a child disagrees with the view of those with PR? Should we answer that question differently in the case of a five-year-old child and a 15-year-old child?

Two particular factual contexts in family law provide a focus for examining the legal approach to children. One is the situation when parents have separated or divorced, and they are unable to agree about the arrangements that should be put in place for their children. These disputes involve questions about which parent the child should live with (which may be both, of course), and what time he or she should spend with the other parent. We also address more specific questions, such as disputes about a proposed change of the child's surname, about schooling, or about where, geographically, the child should live.

The second factual issue that we address in detail is the situation when children are being abused or neglected. When should the state take action to protect children from harm, and from what sorts of harm should children be protected? When, if ever, should children be removed from their birth families, and in what circumstances should this take place? Moreover, once children are removed, what should happen next?

These are all difficult and important questions, and we address them (and many more) over the course of the following chapters. There are many different approaches to these issues, and the topics which we discuss are controversial, giving rise to strong feelings on all sides of the debate. The purpose of this chapter is to introduce some of the core ideas and legal approaches which underpin the later chapters, and to examine the ways in which different perspectives can be seen to have influenced the development of English law.

We begin by exploring the welfare principle and its central role in child law today. The problems and limitations of the principle are addressed, before the chapter considers the alternatives to a welfare-orientated approach. Contemporary challenges to the welfare principle are explored, particularly the pressure from advocates of parental rights who now find vital support for their approach in the Human Rights Act 1998 (HRA 1998). We then consider children's rights as an alternative to a welfare-orientated approach. The different theoretical perspectives on the concept of children's rights are explored, before looking at the extent to which this approach has gained acceptance within domestic family law. Finally, the chapter considers the importance of the 'non-intervention' principle and the possible tension between a commitment to maximizing children's welfare whilst supporting only a minimalist role for the state, including promoting family dispute resolution in the private realm.

8.2 THE WELFARE PRINCIPLE

8.2.1 THE PARAMOUNTCY OF THE CHILD'S WELFARE

The welfare principle is central to the resolution of child-related disputes under English law. It is enshrined in s 1 of the CA 1989:

Children Act 1989, s 1

(1) When a court determines any question with respect to—

(a) the upbringing of a child; or

(b) the administration of a child's property or the application of any income arising from it,

the child's welfare shall be the court's paramount consideration.

The same principle is enshrined in s 1 of the Adoption and Children Act 2002 (ACA 2002):

Adoption and Children Act 2002, s 1

(1) This section applies whenever a court or adoption agency is coming to a decision relating to the adoption of a child.

(2) The paramount consideration of the court or adoption agency must be the child's welfare, throughout his life.

This means that whenever a court determines any question relating to the upbringing of a child, whether concerning adoption, living arrangements after parental separation, medical treatment, or taking a child into state care, the child's welfare must be the paramount consideration.

The meaning of 'paramount'

In *J v C*, the House of Lords had to interpret the word 'paramount' as then found in s 1 of the Guardianship of Infants Act 1925.[1] Lord MacDermott gave the clearest judgment as to the meaning to be attributed to the term:

J v C [1970] AC 668, 710–11

LORD MacDERMOTT:

The second question of construction is as to the scope and meaning of the words "shall regard the welfare of the infant as the first and paramount consideration." Reading these words in their ordinary significance...it seems to me that they must mean more than that

---

[1] For commentary on the history of, and subsequent reaction to, *J v C*, see Lowe (2011).

the child's welfare is to be treated as the top item in a list of items relevant to the matter in question. I think they connote a process whereby, when all the relevant facts, relationships, claims and wishes of parents, risks, choices and other circumstances are taken into account and weighed, the course to be followed will be that which is most in the interests of the child's welfare as that term has now to be understood. That is the first consideration because it is of first importance and the paramount consideration because it rules upon or determines the course to be followed.

It is widely accepted that 'paramount' means that factors are relevant to the court when determining any aspect of the child's upbringing only if and insofar as they affect the child's welfare in some way. The child's welfare is thus determinative, with other potentially relevant factors, such as the wishes and feelings of the child's parents, taken into account only insofar as they have a bearing upon the best interests of the child. It is sometimes said that this approach means that the child is being viewed in isolation from his or her family,[2] and that welfare is the 'single deciding factor'.[3] However, it can also be said that 'welfare' is not in itself a factor: deciding what is in the child's best interests requires an analysis of many factors. Consequently, saying that certain factors, such as parents' rights or wishes, are relevant only in their bearing on the child's welfare does not necessarily undermine their importance. Whenever a decision requires that many considerations be taken into account, each one of those factors may appear to be subordinate to the final decision—that does not necessarily mean that they are unimportant or given inadequate weight in the process.[4]

The meaning of 'welfare'

In order to give some substantive content to the welfare principle, both the CA 1989 and the ACA 2002 contain a 'checklist' of factors that the judge should take into account when trying to determine the welfare of any particular child. The checklists provide valuable guidance as to the most important matters to be considered. The checklist applied in child-related disputes falling under the CA 1989 is contained in s 1(3):

Children Act 1989, s 1

(3) In the circumstances mentioned in subsection (4), a court shall have regard in particular to—

  (a) the ascertainable wishes and feelings of the child concerned (considered in the light of his age and understanding);

  (b) his physical, emotional and educational needs;

  (c) the likely effect on him of any change in his circumstances;

  (d) his age, sex, background and any characteristics of his which the court considers relevant;

---

[2] Herring (1999a), 225.

[3] Choudhry and Fenwick (2005), 456.

[4] George (2015). For consideration of a similar issue from a children's rights perspective, see Ferguson (2013b), 197–9.

> (e) any harm which he has suffered or is at risk of suffering;
>
> (f) how capable each of his parents, and any other person in relation to whom the court considers the question to be relevant, is of meeting his needs;
>
> (g) the range of powers available to the court under this Act in the proceedings in question.

The application of the welfare checklist is mandatory only in the circumstances specified in s 1(4):

- a *contested* application to make, vary, or discharge a s 8 order (i.e. a child arrangements, specific issue, or prohibited steps order);
- an application to make, vary, or discharge a special guardianship order or an order under Part IV of the Act (i.e. care and supervision orders), whether contested or not.

A similar checklist to be applied in the context of adoption is set down in s 1(4) of the ACA 2002.[5]

The Children and Families Act 2014 (CFA 2014) also added an important (but linguistically complicated) provision to the CA 1989 about the importance of parents being involved in their children's lives after parental separation. The following provision applies in contested private law disputes when the court is considering making or discharging a s 8 order or a parental responsibility order:

Children Act 1989, s 1

> (2A) A court...is as respects each parent within subsection (6)(a) to presume, unless the contrary is shown, that involvement of that parent in the life of the child concerned will further the child's welfare.
>
> (2B) In subsection (2A) "involvement" means involvement of some kind, either direct or indirect, but not any particular division of a child's time.
>
> (6) In subsection (2A) "parent" means parent of the child concerned; and, for the purposes of that subsection, a parent of the child concerned—
>
> (a) is within this paragraph if that parent can be involved in the child's life in a way that does not put the child at risk of suffering harm; and
>
> (b) is to be treated as being within paragraph (a) unless there is some evidence before the court in the particular proceedings to suggest that involvement of that parent in the child's life would put the child at risk of suffering harm whatever the form of the involvement.

The welfare checklist sets out relevant factors in a value-neutral way, telling the court what to think about, but giving no guidance about the relevance that each factor will have to the decision. The parental involvement provision, on the other hand, directs the court to presume that it will be in the child's interests for each parent to be involved in the child's life (though the form of the involvement is left open) unless there is evidence to show that the parent cannot be involved without putting the child at risk.

---

[5] See 13.4.1.

The courts have interpreted the concept of the child's 'welfare' or 'best interests' broadly, as illustrated by Munby LJ's judgment in *Re G (Education: Religious Upbringing).*[6]

Re G (Education: Religious Upbringing) [2012] EWCA Civ 1233

MUNBY LJ:

26. 'Welfare', which in this context is synonymous with 'well-being' and 'interests'... extends to and embraces everything that relates to the child's development as a human being and to the child's present and future life as a human being. The judge must consider the child's welfare now, throughout the remainder of the child's minority and into and through adulthood.... How far into the future the judge must peer – and with modern life expectancy a judge dealing with a young child today may be looking to the 22nd century – will depend upon the context and the nature of the issue.

27.... Evaluating a child's best interests involves a welfare appraisal in the widest sense, taking into account, where appropriate, a wide range of ethical, social, moral, religious, cultural, emotional and welfare considerations. Everything that conduces to a child's welfare and happiness or relates to the child's development and present and future life as a human being, including the child's familial, educational and social environment, and the child's social, cultural, ethnic and religious community, is potentially relevant and has, where appropriate, to be taken into account. The judge must adopt a holistic approach.

Re G is also important for the Court of Appeal's discussion of other elements relating to the understanding of welfare. For example, it is clear from Munby LJ's judgment that our understanding of welfare has to keep pace with changing ideas in society, whether informed by new understanding of science or technology, or whether simply based on changes to social attitudes.[7] Munby LJ linked his reference to the child's happiness to the Aristotelian notion of 'the good life': it is not about hedonistic pleasure, but rather 'such things as the cultivation of virtues and the achievement of worthwhile goals'.[8] The judge also emphasized that children's welfare cannot be assessed in isolation, because the child's relationships with others are crucial: 'a child's relationships, both within and without the family, are always relevant to the child's interests; often they will be determinative'.[9]

ONLINE RESOURCE CENTRE
We examine more of the literature about *Re G* on the Online Resource Centre.

---

[6] Further extracts from *Re G* can be found at 11.6.4. See also *An NHS Trust v MB* [2006] EWHC 507.

[7] *Re G (Education: Religious Upbringing)* [2012] EWCA Civ 1233, [33]. For discussion and criticism, see Taylor (2013).

[8] Ibid, [29].

[9] Ibid, [30]. In *Re Y (Removal from Jurisdiction: Failure to Consider Family Segmentation)* [2014] EWCA Civ 1287, [39], Ryder LJ reiterated that '[t]he impact of the decision on [a] non subject child [i.e. a child not the subject of an application before the court], like the impact of the decision on the family unit, is a fact and/or a value judgment of considerable importance.'

When will the welfare principle apply?

Although the welfare principle is of central importance in most legal disputes concerning children, there are some important limitations on when it applies.

'When a court determines any question'

The mandate in s 1 of the CA 1989 is only directed at the *courts*. It does not apply to any other decision-making body, public or private, exercising power and responsibility over children. Parents' liberty to prioritize other needs and interests, including their own or those of siblings, when making decisions in the ordinary course of family life is unaffected. Similarly, local authorities taking decisions with respect to 'looked after' children do not have to prioritize the best interests of any individual child: they can take into account wider considerations, such as their own limited financial resources. This makes the welfare principle of much narrower application than is envisaged by Article 3(1) of the UN Convention on the Rights of the Child (UNCRC):

United Nations Convention on the Rights of the Child, Article 3

(1) In all actions concerning children, whether undertaken by public or private social welfare institutions, courts of law, administrative authorities or legislative bodies, the best interests of the child shall be a primary consideration.

However, the UNCRC's 'trade-off' for such broad application of the welfare principle, extending even to private institutions, is that the obligation imposed on state authorities is significantly weakened: the welfare of the child is only *a primary* as opposed to *the paramount* consideration. Making the child's welfare 'a primary consideration' allows considerable scope for the decision-maker to take into account a wide range of factors other than the particular interests of the child.

The importance of Article 3 was discussed by Lady Hale in *ZH (Tanzania) v Secretary of State for the Home Department*, an immigration case to which the paramountcy principle in the CA 1989 did not apply.

ZH (Tanzania) v Secretary of State for the Home Department [2011] UKSC 4

LADY HALE:

The UNCRC and the best interests of the child

21. It is not difficult to understand why the Strasbourg Court has become more sensitive to the welfare of the children who are innocent victims of their parents' choices. For example, in *Neulinger v Switzerland* (application no 41615/07, ECHR) (2010), para 131, the Court observed that "the Convention cannot be interpreted in a vacuum but must be interpreted in harmony with the general principles of international law. Account should be taken...of 'any relevant rules of international law applicable in the relations between the parties' and in particular the rules concerning the international protection of human rights". The Court went on to note, at para 135, that "there is currently a broad consensus—including in international

law—in support of the idea that in all decisions concerning children, their best interests must be paramount".

22. The Court had earlier, in paras 49 to 56, collected references in support of this proposition from several international human rights instruments...All of these refer to the best interests of the child, variously describing these as "paramount", or "primordial", or "a primary consideration". To a United Kingdom lawyer, however, these do not mean the same thing.

23. For our purposes the most relevant national and international obligation of the United Kingdom is contained in article 3(1) of the UNCRC:

"In all actions concerning children, whether undertaken by public or private social welfare institutions, courts of law, administrative authorities or legislative bodies, the best interests of the child shall be a primary consideration."

This is a binding obligation in international law, and the spirit, if not the precise language, has also been translated into our national law....

25....[I]t is clear from the recent jurisprudence that the Strasbourg Court will expect national authorities to apply article 3(1) of UNCRC and treat the best interests of a child as "a primary consideration". Of course, despite the looseness with which these terms are sometimes used, "a primary consideration" is not the same as "the primary consideration", still less as "the paramount consideration". [Counsel], to whom we are grateful for representing the separate interests of the children in this case, boldly argued that immigration and removal decisions might be covered by section 1(1) of the Children Act 1989.... However, questions with respect to the upbringing of a child must be distinguished from other decisions which may affect them. The UNHCR, in its Guidelines on Determining the Best Interests of the Child (May 2008), explains the matter neatly, at para 1.1:

"The term 'best interests' broadly describes the well-being of a child....The CRC neither offers a precise definition, nor explicitly outlines common factors of the best interests of the child, but stipulates that:

- the best interests must be the determining factor for specific actions, notably adoption (Article 21) and separation of a child from parents against their will (Article 9);
- the best interests must be a primary (but not the sole) consideration for all other actions affecting children, whether undertaken by public or private social welfare institutions, courts of law, administrative authorities or legislative bodies (Article 3)."

This seems to me accurately to distinguish between decisions which directly affect the child's upbringing, such as the parent or other person with whom she is to live, and decisions which may affect her more indirectly, such as decisions about where one or both of her parents are to live. Article 9 of UNCRC, for example, draws a distinction between the compulsory separation of a child from her parents, which must be necessary in her best interests, and the separation of a parent from his child, for example, by detention, imprisonment, exile, deportation or even death.

26. Nevertheless, even in those decisions, the best interests of the child must be a primary consideration.

ONLINE RESOURCE CENTRE

The subsequent consideration of the UNCRC in *R (SG) v Secretary of State for Work and Pensions* [2015] UKSC 16 is considered in detail on the Online Resource Centre.

'Upbringing of the child'

One of the most significant limitations on the application of the welfare principle under the CA 1989 is that it only applies to questions where the 'upbringing of the child' is *directly* in issue. This is important because several questions which clearly affect a child's interests have been held to be only *indirectly* concerned with upbringing, including:

- applications for an occupation or non-molestation order under Part IV of the Family Law Act 1996;[10]

- applications for the use of scientific tests to determine the parentage of a child under s 20 of the Family Law Reform Act 1969;[11]

- applications for leave to apply for a s 8 order (e.g. child arrangements orders) under s 10 of the CA 1989;[12]

- disputes concerning publication of potentially damaging details about a child's background where the publicity does not relate directly to some aspect of the child's upbringing.[13]

Best interests of more than one child relevant

A third important limitation on the application of the welfare principle is where the upbringing of two or more children is in question in court proceedings. While the court may consider the effect of imposing different solutions on a sibling group, it is essential that the welfare of each child be considered separately.[14] In situations where the best interests of each child, when taken individually, point to a different and irreconcilable outcome, it can be impossible for the court to fulfil its duty to give effect to the best interests of each child. Whichever approach the court adopts, the paramountcy principle will be compromised.

It is important to note that the problem only arises where *both children* are to be the subject of the proposed orders and all the proposed orders are to be determined in accordance with the paramountcy principle. Even though two or more minors are involved, if only one child is the *subject* of the proceedings before the court then the issue will not arise.[15] The correct approach where two children are the subject of proposed orders was confirmed by the Court of Appeal in *Re A (Children) (Conjoined Twins: Surgical Separation)*.[16] The court held that should a conflict develop between the paramount interests of two children, a balancing exercise weighing up the potential benefits and detriments of the possible outcomes to each of the two children must be undertaken and whichever course of action believed to cause the least overall harm adopted.[17] The case concerned an application for a declaration that it would be lawful

---

10 See chapter 4.

11 *Re H (A Minor) (Blood Tests: Parental Rights)* [1997] Fam 89, 104. See pp 615–18.

12 *Re A (Minors: Residence Order)* [1992] Fam 182. See 11.3.2.

13 *Re Z (A Minor) (Freedom of Publication)* [1997] Fam 1. For the correct approach to such disputes post-implementation of the HRA 1998, see *Re S (A Child) (Identification: Restrictions on Publication)* [2004] UKHL 47.

14 *Re LC (Children) (Abduction: Habitual Residence: State of Mind of Child)* [2014] UKSC 1; *Re S (Relocation: Interests of Siblings)* [2011] EWCA Civ 454.

15 *Birmingham City Council v H (A Minor)* [1994] 2 AC 212, 218–23. Note that the rights and interests of a non-subject child who is potentially affected by a decision must still be respected and given due weight by the court: see *Re Y (Removal from Jurisdiction: Failure to Consider Family Segmentation)* [2014] EWCA Civ 1287, [40].

16 [2001] Fam 147.

17 Ibid, 181–97. This approach was suggested, obiter, by Wall J in *Re T and E (Proceedings: Conflicting Interests)* [1995] 1 FLR 581, 582–9. *Re A* is discussed in further detail below at pp 709 and 713–15.

for doctors to undertake surgical separation of conjoined twins, Jodie and Mary, against the wishes of the twins' parents and with the inevitable consequence that Mary, the weaker twin, would die. Without the separation both twins would die within a few months.

Re A (Children) (Conjoined Twins: Surgical Separation) [2001] Fam 147 (CA), 181–97

WARD LJ:

[T]he operation will be in Jodie's interests [it would give her the chance of a normal life] but not in Mary's [the operation would hasten her certain death]. Can that conflict be resolved and if so how?

...[T]he question arises directly in this case and because it is the right to life of each child that is in issue, the conflict between the children could not be more acute. If the duty of the court is to make a decision which puts Jodie's interests paramount and that decision would be contrary to the paramount interests of Mary, then, for my part, I do not see how the court can reconcile the impossibility of properly fulfilling each duty by simply declining to decide the very matter before it. That would be a total abdication of the duty which is imposed upon us. Given the conflict of duty, I can see no other way of dealing with it than by choosing the lesser of the two evils and so finding the least detrimental alternative. A balance has to be struck somehow and I cannot flinch from undertaking that evaluation, horrendously difficult though it is...

Having conducted the required balancing exercise, Ward LJ concluded that the scales came down heavily in favour of giving Jodie the chance of a normal life. Permission was thus granted for the operation to be carried out.[18]

8.2.2 CRITICISMS OF THE WELFARE PRINCIPLE

Indeterminacy

The concept of the child's welfare is notoriously vague, leaving considerable discretion in the hands of individual judges as to what they consider to be in a child's best interests. This indeterminacy has been the subject of considerable criticism. In particular, it is argued that the nebulous nature of the principle allows cases to be determined in accordance with nothing more principled than the personal prejudices and untested assumptions of individual judges.

---

[18] Brooke LJ agreed with Ward LJ on the issue of the children's best interests and how the conflict between them should be resolved. Robert Walker LJ disagreed, finding that the operation would be in Mary's best interests as well as Jodie's, because it would give them both back their bodily integrity. On his analysis no conflict therefore arose between the best interests of the two children. For an alternative way in which the case might have been decided, giving greater weight to the views of the twins' parents, see Hastings (2010).

R. Mnookin, 'Child-Custody Adjudication: Judicial Functions in the Face of Indeterminacy', (1975) 39 *Law and Contemporary Problems* **226, 229–61**

[T]he determination of what is "best" or "least detrimental" for a particular child is usually indeterminate and speculative. For most custody cases [i.e. disputes about children's living arrangements], existing psychological theories simply do not yield confident predictions of the effects of alternative custody dispositions. Moreover, even if accurate predictions were possible in more cases, our society today lacks any clear-cut consensus about the values to be used in determining what is "best" or "least detrimental."

B. The Indeterminacy of Present-Day Standards

…When a judge must resolve a custody dispute, he is committed to making a choice among alternatives. The very words of the best-interests-of-the-child principle suggest that the judge should decide by choosing the alternative that "maximizes" what is best for a particular child. Conceived this way, the judge's decision can be framed in a manner consistent with an intellectual tradition that views the decision process as a problem of rational choice. In analyzing the custody decision from this perspective, my purpose is not to describe how judges in fact decide custody disputes nor to propose a method of how they should. Instead, it is to expose the inherent indeterminacy of the best interests standard.

1. Rational Choice

Decision theorists have laid out the logic of rational choice with clarity and mathematical rigor for prototype decision problems. The decision-maker specifies alternative outcomes associated with different courses of action and then chooses that alternative that "maximizes" his values, subject to whatever constraints the decision-maker faces. This involves two critical assumptions: first, that the decision-maker can specify alternative outcomes for each course of action; the second, that the decision-maker can assign to each outcome a "utility" measure that integrates his values and allows comparisons among alternative outcomes. Choice does not require certainty about the single outcome that will in fact flow from a particular action. Treating uncertainty as a statistical problem, models have been developed that allow decisions to be made on the basis of "expected" utility…

2. A Custody Determination under the Best-Interests-of-the-Child Principle

Assume that a judge must decide whether a child should live with his mother or his father when the parents are in the process of obtaining a divorce. From the perspective of rational choice, the judge would wish to compare the expected utility for the child of living with his mother with that of living with his father. The judge would need considerable information and predictive ability to do this. The judge would also need some source for the values to measure utility for the child. All three are problematic.

a. The Need for Information: Specifying Possible Outcomes

In the example chosen, the judge would require information about how each parent had behaved in the past, how this behavior had affected the child and the child's present condition. Then the judge would need to predict the future behavior and circumstances of each parent if the child were to remain with that parent and to gauge the effects of this behavior and these circumstances on the child. He would also have to consider the behavior of each parent if the child were to live with the other parent and how this might affect the child . . .

One can question how often, if ever, any judge will have the necessary information. In many instances, a judge lacks adequate information about even the most rudimentary aspects of a child's life with his parents and has still less information available about what either parent plans in the future . . .

b. Predictions Assessing the Probability of Alternative Outcomes

Obviously, more than one outcome is possible for each course of judicial action, so the judge must assess the probability of various outcomes and evaluate the seriousness of possible benefits and harms associated with each. But even where a judge has substantial information about the child's past home life and the present alternatives, present-day knowledge about human behavior provides no basis for the kind of individualized predictions required by the best-interests standard. There are numerous competing theories of human behavior, based on radically different conceptions of the nature of man, and no consensus exists that any one is correct. No theory at all is considered widely capable of generating reliable predictions about the psychological and behavioral consequences of alternative dispositions for a particular child . . .

c. Values to Inform Choice: Assigning Utilities to Various Outcomes

Even if the various outcomes could be specified and their probability estimated, a fundamental problem would remain unsolved. What set of values should a judge use to determine what is in a child's best interests? If a decision-maker must assign some measure of utility to each possible outcome, how is utility to be determined?

For many decisions in an individualistic society, one asks the person affected what he wants. Applying this notion to custody cases, the child could be asked to specify those values or even to choose. In some cases, especially those involving divorce, the child's preference is sought and given weight. But to make the child responsible for the choice may jeopardize his future relationship with the other parent. And we often lack confidence that the child has the capacity and the maturity appropriately to determine his own utility.

Moreover, whether or not the judge looks to the child for some guidance, there remains the question whether best interests should be viewed from a long-term or short-term perspective. The conditions that make a person happy at age seven to ten may have adverse consequences at age thirty. Should the judge ask himself what decision will make the child happiest in the next year? Or at thirty? Or at seventy? Should the judge decide by thinking about what decision the child as an adult looking back would have wanted made? In this case, the preference problem is formidable, for how is the judge to compare "happiness" at one age with "happiness" at another age?

Deciding what is best for a child poses a question no less ultimate than the purposes and values of life itself. Should the judge be primarily concerned with the child's happiness? Or with the child's spiritual and religious training? Should the judge be concerned with the economic "productivity" of the child when he grows up? Are the primary values of life in warm, interpersonal relationships, or in discipline and self-sacrifice? Is stability and security for a child more desirable than intellectual stimulation? These questions could be elaborated endlessly. And yet, where is the judge to look for the set of values that should inform the choice of what is best for the child? Normally, the custody statutes do not themselves give content or relative weights to the pertinent values. And if the judge looks to society at large, he finds neither a clear consensus as to the best child rearing strategies nor an appropriate hierarchy of ultimate values.

Lack of transparency and irrelevant considerations

Helen Reece has made a similarly strong attack on the welfare principle. Her concern focuses not on indeterminacy, but the way in which untested policies and principles which have little or nothing to do with the best interests of the child (some based on little more than ignorance or prejudice), are able to find their way into child-related disputes through the medium of the welfare principle.

H. Reece, 'The Paramountcy Principle: Consensus or Construct?', (1996)
49 *Current Legal Problems* 267, 273, and 293–8

The indeterminacy and value-laden nature of custody decisions lead critics to characterise the ultimate results as subjective, individualistic, and idiosyncratic, arbitrary, and capricious. A more extreme version of this criticism is that adjudication under the paramountcy principle yields something close to a random pattern of outcomes. Slightly more radical variants of this argument suggest that judges' decisions may be informed by their middle and upper-class backgrounds, by their patriarchal values, or simply by their personal prejudices...

[These criticisms of the welfare principle] miss the mark. It is true that the paramountcy principle itself is indeterminate, but this indeterminacy has enabled a determinate policy to take over; where one parent does not fit into the traditional mould, the results of residence disputes can be predicted with as much accuracy as can legal cases generally. It is true that these decisions are value-dependent, but they depend on a value rather than on values. It follows that the claim that results in children's cases are subjective and depend on the views of the individual judge is false...

It emerges that the indeterminacy of children's welfare has allowed other principles and policies to exert an influence from behind the smokescreen of the paramountcy principle. I am referring here to principles and policies which are extraneous to children's welfare...[such as the principle that a child should live with the parent who is best able to create a 'normal' family environment].

[O]nce we have recognised that children's welfare does not really determine the course to be followed, the paramountcy principle becomes even less sacred: not only is the principle impossible to justify when taken at face value, the reality is that it is not even applied. We are now in a position to challenge the argument that the paramountcy principle is a harmless statement of intent....Its danger lies in impeding open debate, open debate about which principles and which policies other than children's welfare should be given what weight in children's cases...

Indeed, this smothering of debate may not be so much the danger of, but rather the very purpose of, the paramountcy principle. King has argued that the paramountcy principle has an important symbolic function in legitimating the resolution of disputes. Whatever the contestants' view of the eventual decision, they unite with the judge in accepting the principle that the child's interests are paramount.

Not everyone agrees that the discretionary nature of the welfare principle with its attendant uncertainty and unpredictability is a problem. In fact, Herring perceives it as a positive strength.[19] However, there are various ways in which the law could try

[19] Herring (2005b), 161; see also George (2012a), ch 7.

to address the concerns raised by Mnookin and Reece. One option would be to take a more 'scientific' approach to determining what will maximize the child's welfare, relying on 'objective' scientific evidence, drawn from a range of disciplines such as paediatrics, psychology, and sociology. The ready justification expert scientific evidence can provide for difficult and often controversial decisions has obvious attractions for the courts. Greater reliance on scientific evidence is not, however, without its problems. Mnookin doubts the value of this type of evidence in trying to predict future outcomes for an individual child.

R. Mnookin, 'Child-Custody Adjudication: Judicial Functions in the Face of Indeterminacy', (1975) 39 *Law and Contemporary Problems* 226, 258–60 and 287

While psychiatrists and psychoanalysts have at times been enthusiastic in claiming for themselves the largest possible role in custody proceedings, many have conceded that their theories provide no reliable guide for predictions about what is likely to happen to a particular child. Anna Freud, who has devoted her life to the study of the child and who plainly believes that theory can be a useful guide to treatment has warned: "In spite of . . . advances there remain factors which make clinical foresight, i.e. prediction, difficult and hazardous," not the least of which is that "environmental happenings in a child's life will always remain unpredictable since they are not governed by any known laws . . . "

Various studies have attempted to trace personality development to specific anteced-ent variables to show that these variables have the same effects on different children. This connection is now widely questioned by experimental psychologists . . . who think that infants experience external events in individual ways. The implication of this for pre-diction is described very well by Skolnick: "[I]f the child selectively interprets situations and events, we cannot confidently predict behaviour from knowledge of the situation alone" . . .

Having custody disputes determined by embracing more and more of the niceties of psy-chological and psychiatric theories requires careful analysis of the limits of these theories, their empirical bases, and the capacity of our legal system to absorb this new doctrine. In cases where, from the child's perspective, each claimant has a psychological relation-ship with the child, I doubt whether there would often be widespread consensus among experts about which parent would prove psychologically better (or less detrimental) to the child. Often each parent will have a different sort of relationship with the child, with the child attached to each. One may be warm, easy-going, but incapable of discipline. The other may be fair, able to set limits, but unable to express affection. By what criteria is an expert to decide which is less detrimental? Moreover, even the proponents of psychologi-cal standards have acknowledged how problematic it is to evaluate relationships from a psychological perspective unless a highly trained person spends a considerable amount of time observing the parent and child interact or talking to the child. Superficial examinations by those without substantial training may be worse than nothing. And yet, that is surely a high risk.

Even with the best trained experts, the choice would be based on predictions that are beyond the demonstrated capacity of any existing theory. While the psychologists and psychiatrists have made substantial therapeutic contributions, they are not soothsayers capable of predict-ing with any degree of confidence how a child is likely to benefit from alternative placements. When the expert does express a preference, it too often is based on an unexpressed value preference. What is psychologically least detrimental will usually be no more determinate for expert and nonexpert alike than what is in a child's best interests; and to reframe the question in a way that invites predictions based on the use of labels and terminology developed for treatment is both demeaning to the expert and corrupting for the judicial process.

The current limitations of scientific disciplines in trying to predict future outcomes is not the only concern. Commentators writing from a feminist perspective have noted how the legal process makes selective use of scientific evidence, often to provide apparently unqualified support for a particular ideological position or policy. Writing about the law's regulation of children's relationships with a parent with whom they do not live (then termed 'contact'), Felicity Kaganas is highly critical of the use of 'child welfare science' to reinforce an ideology on post-divorce parenting which prioritizes the importance of contact with non-resident fathers at the expense of the legitimate concerns and interests of mothers. As she points out, the scientific research on this issue is not straightforward.

F. Kaganas, 'Contact, Conflict and Risk', in S. Day Sclater and C. Piper (eds), *Undercurrents of Divorce* (Aldershot: Ashgate, 1999b), 99, 105–10

[The] elevation [of contact] into a priority for law, along with the goal of reducing conflict, has been coterminous with the growth of child welfare knowledge focusing on these matters and courts have turned to this body of knowledge in justifying their decisions. Even in 1973, Latey J in *M v M* invoked not only 'common sense' and 'human experience', but also referred to 'medical and other expert discovery' favouring contact...

The version of the research studies that has shaped the dominant discourse about divorce and contact is clearly a simplified one. In this version, divorce damages children and, in order to limit that damage it is essential to ensure that conflict is reduced or eliminated and that contact is maintained. The more nuanced and complex features of the research are absent...A recent review of research in the field confirms that it is characterised by greater complexity and greater uncertainty than the law allows. Rodgers and Pryor observe that, 'there is no simple or direct relationship between parental separation and children's adjustment, and poor outcomes are far from inevitable.' Nor can it be assumed, they say, that the disadvantages to children identified by researchers are attributable to the separation. And although they ultimately favour contact, they note that the loss or absence of a parent does not appear to have a very significant effect on children and that it is the quality and not the frequency of contact that matters. Furthermore, they identify factors such as the ability of parents to recover from the psychological distress as being important for children's ability to adjust.

Moreover, there is conflicting research in this field. Yet little credence is attached to studies that contradict what Maclean and Eekelaar term the 'new orthodoxy'...

Whilst Kaganas recognizes that to some extent the law needs to simplify and reduce the complexity of the research evidence for its own purposes, she criticizes the way the child welfare science has been 'interpreted' to serve certain pre-defined ends.

King and Piper argue that reductionism and the simplification of child welfare knowledge is an inevitable consequence of law's autopoetic nature. Law cannot incorporate external discourses, they say, without reconstructing them in a way that 'makes sense' within law, enabling it to codify events as lawful or unlawful. These legal reconstructions of the complex discourse of child welfare are 'necessarily simplistic because law by its very nature needs clear normative principles'.

The process of reconstruction is unavoidable; the law cannot ignore child welfare science and still purport to be applying principles and making decisions that serve the best interests of children. Law as a system of communication has nothing to say about what is good or bad for children. In contemporary society this is the preserve of experts within child welfare science, whose expertise confers on their work a claim to truth. Child welfare science alone can claim authoritatively to tell us what will best serve children's interests and which events or choices will lead to which outcomes for children.

Yet the need for clear normative principles legitimated by science does not of itself explain the way in which the law has reconstructed child welfare science in the context of contact. It has had to make choices from a range of available principles. It could, for example, have chosen to adopt the principle that contact should not be ordered against the wishes of the resident parent but chose, instead, the opposite. The reason for this must be that a decision to give the resident parent a veto would run counter to a dominant discourse surrounding contact which has been informed by political as well as child welfare imperatives. Currently, government and professional groupings, as well as popular culture reflected in the media, all espouse a particular understanding of the consequences of separation and divorce for children. This understanding has been accorded the status of taken-for-granted truth and cannot fail to impact on the legal system if it is to retain credibility. And the law, in making pronouncements consistent with the dominant discourse, confirms its 'rightness'.

Thus, whilst the scientific disciplines have an important contribution to make in improving understanding about how best to maximize children's welfare, the use of scientific evidence in the judicial process is not without significant difficulties.[20]

An alternative way in which the judge's discretion could be curtailed is to move towards a more transparent, rule-based system in which the guiding principles and values to be applied in determining a child's interests are more clearly articulated. However, to develop such rules or principles is a value-laden exercise fraught with just the same difficulties as more individualized decision-making. Whilst recognizing the problem of indeterminacy, Mnookin doubts whether a rule-based system would prove any more successful than the current discretionary model.

R. Mnookin, 'Child-Custody Adjudication: Judicial Functions in the Face of Indeterminacy', (1975) 39 *Law and Contemporary Problems* 226, 262–4

[A]djudication by a more determinate rule would confront the fundamental problems posed by an indeterminate principle. But the choice between indeterminate standards and more precise rules poses a profound dilemma. The absence of rules removes the special burdens of justification and formulation of standards characteristic of adjudication. Unfairness and adverse consequences can result. And yet, rules that relate past events or conduct to legal consequences may themselves create substantial difficulties in the custody area. Our inadequate knowledge about human behavior and our inability to generalise confidently about the relationship between past events or conduct and future behavior make the formulation of

---

[20] See also Barnett (2000), 137–40.

rules especially problematic. Moreover, the very lack of consensus about values that make the best-interests standard indeterminate may also make the formulation of rules inappropriate: a legal rule must, after all, reflect some social value or values. An overly ambitious and indeterminate principle may result in fewer decisions that reflect what is known to be desirable. But rules may result in some conspicuously bad decisions that could be avoided by a more discretionary standard...

As we have seen, qualified steps towards the adoption of a more rule-based system are evident in the CA 1989 and the ACA 2002 in the form of the welfare checklists and the parental involvement provision added by the CFA 2014. However, whilst these provisions provide some substantive content to the welfare principle, they do not provide a complete answer to concerns about its vagueness and indeterminacy. No particular weight or order of priority is attributed to the various factors on the checklists and there is no guidance as to whether, in certain situations, one or more of them will have particular importance. The judge is thus still afforded considerable discretion as to the weight to be attributed to each factor in any particular case. In some cases, the judge may simply disregard certain factors as irrelevant, though that issue is less likely to arise in respect of the parental involvement provision.

Why should the child's welfare be paramount?

As Reece remarks, 'the paramountcy principle rests on an astonishingly solid consensus, both inside and outside the discipline of Family Law'.[21] It may be thought that given the strong support for the welfare principle, the justification for prioritizing the interests of one child over all other interests would be self-evident. However, articulating a convincing reason why children should always take priority is not necessarily straightforward. Reece outlines the most common arguments, none of which she finds convincing.

H. Reece, 'The Paramountcy Principle: Consensus or Construct?', (1996) 49 *Current Legal Problems* 267, 276–81

Children are more vulnerable

This is the most common justification for the paramountcy principle. For example, Cretney writes that the 'welfare principle is widely supported because...children who are necessarily vulnerable and dependent must be protected from harm'. A variation of this argument is that children's welfare should be paramount as a way of 'bending the stick', that in a world run by adults, there would otherwise be a danger that children's interests would be completely overlooked.

This argument holds the key to the consensus behind the paramountcy principle. Resting as it does on vulnerability, it has great resonance in the current political climate, in which vulnerability generally attracts priority...Even on its own terms this argument is flawed: in a case under the Children Act, the child will not necessarily be the most vulnerable individual...

Since the argument explains the consensus behind the paramountcy principle, it could not be more crucial to recognise the fallacy contained at the heart of the argument. The fallacy lies in the equation of priority with protection. It is self-evident that, as a general rule, children

---

[21] Reece (1996), 268.

need more protection than adults. From this statement it does not follow that children should be prioritized over adults...

Children must be given the opportunity to become successful adults

'[T]he care of our children must be a prime priority. Within each child is the person he will one day become. Inside each of us is the child we once were' [Baroness Strange]. According to this argument, childhood is important because of its psychological significance; unless we do what is best for children, they will not be able to flourish into adults. The argument is self-defeating because it makes the importance of childhood contingent on, and subordinate to, the importance of adulthood: if decisions are made which sacrifice adults' interests to children's interests, there is little point becoming a successful adult.

More broadly, this argument is self-defeating because it promotes the future at the expense of the present, and indeed Leach argues explicitly that children are important because they are our future. The resonance of this yearning for the future reflects a social malaise. Although a preoccupation with the future is often favourably contrasted with a preoccupation with the past, the reality is that both represent an attempt to escape the present. A society which puts its hope in simply reproducing itself is a society which has lost its sense of purpose. It reduces the destiny of humans to ensuring that others take their place.

Adults create children

'Grown-ups...make free decisions, pooled their genes, created a baby and have to take the consequences...Children come first. We invited them to life's party' [Libby Purves]. It is not self-evident that the creation is more important than the creator; the opposite argument is equally plausible and indeed forms the basis of most religions. Moreover, the argument only achieves coherence in relation to parents; when the paramountcy principle ignores the interests of anyone other than a natural parent, it ignores the interests of someone who had no control over whether the child was born.

Argument from Solomon

This argument, which again could only conceivably justify the paramountcy principle in its application to parents, is that the desire to sacrifice one's own interests to those of one's child is the very mark of being a parent. If the argument is that this is how things are, then it stands defeated by legal disputes between parents and children. If the argument is that this is what it means to be a good parent, first, this is not self-evident, and secondly...there are more important values than being a good parent.

Utilitarian arguments

...All the previous arguments have justified the importance attached to children's welfare as a primary good. Two final arguments return to the utilitarian premises which initiated the discussion, but cast the net more broadly to include effect on society. More specifically, Barton and Douglas argue that children are important for the continuity of order in society and Parker suggests that giving greater weight to children's welfare maximises the welfare of society. However,...when we raise the discussion to the social level, as indeed we should, the reasons to reject the paramountcy principle are far stronger than any reasons to retain it.

Reece argues that prioritizing the interests of children over all other relevant parties simply cannot be justified.[22]

Not everyone agrees, though. It can be said, for example, that the paramountcy principle applies only to questions about the *upbringing* of a child, where the child is at the very heart of the case. In other areas, where the child is merely *part* of the case, his or her welfare is not paramount.[23] Does the fact that the dispute is about the child offer a justification for focusing attention on the child's interests, even though that approach might not be acceptable in other contexts?

8.3 ALTERNATIVES TO THE WELFARE PRINCIPLE

For those who are critical of the welfare principle, the question inevitably arises as to whether there is a better approach to decision-making about children. There are several alternatives, reflecting Reece's view that decision-making in family law needs to be more transparent and disciplined and that automatically prioritizing the child's interests is wrong. The alternatives thus seek to find a way to identify the legitimate rights and interests of all affected parties and to bring those interests fairly into the decision-making process.

8.3.1 RE-CONCEPTUALIZING THE WELFARE PRINCIPLE

Reece's concerns regarding the 'unduly individualistic' nature of the welfare principle are shared by Herring.[24] In light of these concerns, he has developed an alternative theory which he terms 'relationship-based welfare'.[25] This approach is based on the principle that a child should not be seen as an isolated individual but as an integral part of a wider family network. In his view, the interdependence of the child on this wider family network should constitute a core consideration in the decision-making process: not least because teaching the child the importance of respecting the needs and interests of others is core to the child's welfare.[26]

J. Herring, 'The Welfare Principle and the Rights of Parents', in A. Bainham, S. Day Sclater, and M. Richards (eds), *What is a Parent? A Socio-Legal Analysis* (Oxford: Hart Publishing, 1999b), 89, 101–3

The conception of the welfare principle adopted by the courts is often too narrowly individualist and focuses on a self-centred approach to welfare. A broader version of the welfare principle could allow consideration of the parent's interests. There are two elements to the argument for pursuing a wider understanding of the welfare principle. The first is that it is part of growing up for a child to learn to sacrifice as well as claim benefits. Families, and society in general, are based on mutual co-operation and support. So it is important to encourage a

---

[22] Ibid, 275. It may be noted that children are the 'subjects' of proceedings about their upbringing, but are rarely participants in those disputes: see 11.3.3.

[23] George (2015).

[24] Herring (1999a), 233.

[25] Herring (1999a) and (1999b).

[26] See also Herring and Taylor (2006), 533.

child to adopt, to a limited extent, the virtue of altruism and an awareness of social obligation. It needs to be stressed that it is a very limited altruism that is being sought. Children should only be expected to be altruistic to the extent of not demanding from parents excessive sacrifices in return for minor benefits.

The second element of this approach is that the child's welfare involves ensuring that the child's relationships with the other family members are fair and just. A relationship based on unacceptable demands on a parent is not furthering a child's welfare...

It is in the child's welfare to be brought up in a family whose members respect each other and so, on occasion, sacrifices may be required from the child...

The effect of this approach is to move away from conceiving the problem as a clash between children and parents and in terms of weighing two conflicting interests, and towards seeing it rather as deciding what is a proper parent-child relationship. The child's welfare is promoted when he or she lives in a fair and just relationship with each parent. Understood in this way, the welfare principle can protect children while properly taking into account parent's rights.

The argument can also operate where a child's welfare may require a sacrifice for the obtaining of some greater social good...

As Herring notes, one advantage of his approach is that it does not entail abandoning the centrality of the paramountcy principle. Herring has the more limited objective of 're-conceptualizing' what we mean by welfare. However, it could be argued that this is not a marked departure, if a departure at all, from the approach that the courts take in practice already.

R. George, *Ideas and Debates in Family Law* (Oxford: Hart Publishing, 2012), 118

[W]hile the welfare principle might, on occasion, require an outcome which did indeed "cause a huge level of harm to others", such a solution will be exceptional, because the harm to others – particularly a parent or other family member – will in itself impact adversely on the child, which will be a significant factor to take into account when deciding what is in the child's best interests in the first place.

In *J v C* itself, the House of Lords explained that the welfare principle involved

"a process whereby, when all the relevant facts, relationships, claims and wishes of the parents, risks, choices and other circumstances *are taken into account and weighed*, the course to be followed will be that which is most in the interests of the child's welfare as that term has now to be understood. That is the first consideration because it is of first importance and the paramount consideration because it rules upon or determines the course to be followed."

The suggestion that the welfare principle requires the child to be viewed in isolation from his or her family and community would seem to ignore the first part of this explanation of the process....

J v C remains the leading explanation of the process involved in the welfare principle, and shows that only factors which have *no bearing whatever* on the child's welfare need be discounted. This approach is somehow morphed in some critics' analysis to suggest that welfare is a stand-alone factor, as if the child's welfare were unaffected by those around him or her. Of course some factors will be more important to the child's welfare than others, and part of the court's job is to assess the relevance of each factor—but factors which are of indirect relevance to welfare may still be important in the overall assessment of an individual case.

Herring's approach may also prove problematic from the child's perspective, in that once it is conceded that the rights and interests of the parents are relevant to the child's welfare, the child's welfare may be subsumed within the parents' interests. Eekelaar is critical of Herring's approach for this reason, pointing out that it was not so long ago that the view was taken that 'recognition of the pre-eminence of the father was in the child's interests'.[27] Arguably this problem continues today, but with the child's interests now being more commonly identified with the interests of the mother.

Eekelaar proposes a more radical alternative which, in seeking to ensure that proper regard is paid to the interests of others, abandons the paramountcy principle.

J. Eekelaar, 'Beyond the Welfare Principle', (2002a) 14 *Child and Family Law Quarterly* 237, 242–5

It might appear that many dilemmas in family law involve resolving issues at which the future well-being...of various people are at stake. How are these issues best resolved? A crude utilitarian attempt at maximising the well-being of the greatest number could not be accepted, since this would pay insufficient regard to extreme adverse affects of certain outcomes on the well-being of particular individuals. The best solution is surely to adopt the course that avoids inflicting the most damage on the well-being of any interested individual. The methodology can be illustrated in this way. Suppose one could assign a value to the degree of benefit and detriment to the well-being of all interested parties under various possible solutions. The following would be a simple case. C is the child. X and Y are adult participants. Minus values indicate an outcome that has more detriment than benefit for the party:

- Solution 1: C (+15); X (+10); Y (–30).
- Solution 2: C (+10); X (+10); Y (–20).
- Solution 3: C (+5); X (–5); Y (–10).

Solution 1 would be chosen under the best interests test. Solution 2 would be chosen under general utilitarianism (since the overall benefit/detriment scores are: –5 (solution 1); 0 (solution 2); and –10 (solution 3)). Under the suggested methodology, solution 3 should be chosen, for although it reduces the benefit to C (and to X), the detriment to Y is far less...

It seems very difficult to advocate a solution that is, on these assumptions, the least beneficial to the child of all three solutions. But on closer examination, some merits appear. It *considerably* reduces the detriment for Y. It may be that the disadvantage to the child is a price worth paying...Of course, the evaluation of the benefits and detriments on various parties is a matter of judgment in each case, but this is true in all matters of adjudication, including, of course, the welfare test. It is a delusion to believe that such matters can be evaluated with scientific objectivity. Nevertheless, it is safe to say that special care must be taken in evaluating the impact or potential impact, of a solution on the well-being of children, for it is always necessary to remember children's vulnerability and the potential longer term effects on them, than on adults, of many decisions...

---

[27] Eekelaar (2002), 238.

Although Eekelaar rejects the paramountcy principle, he still affords the child a privileged position within the decision-making process:

Qualifications—privileges and appropriateness

Unfortunately, this does not conclude the matter. It might be difficult (but not impossible) to envisage solutions that hold *nothing but* detriment to the child. It is easier to imagine this for an adult. Yet it is possible to imagine an outcome for a child where detriments *exceed* benefits. How, then, would a decision be made between the following two solutions?

- Solution 1: C (+10); X (+10); Y (–30).
- Solution 2: C (–10); X (–15); Y (–15).

Here the price paid in solution 2 for reducing Y's detriment is to spread the hardship around relatively equally. It certainly would not satisfy general utilitarianism. Should it satisfy anyone? I think the answer must be to hold that no solution should be adopted where the detriments outweigh the benefits for the child unless that would be the result of *any* available solution, so that it is unavoidable. There should be no negative quantity for C. In this way, the interests of children would be *privileged* in the calculus, but not given priority. This could be justified on the basis that, whatever we might say about future generations, they at least have no control whatsoever over our actions. It behoves us, therefore, when considering the consequences of our actions, to treat our successors as always innocent and to allow them to start their lives, as far as possible, without deficits from what we have done. For the same reason, the privilege should allow resolution in favour of children where the value of benefits and detriments between them and other parties is minimal or very speculative.

Eekelaar's approach has the advantage that, by separating out the individual rights and interests of all affected parties, it brings much greater transparency to the decision-making process. This is preferable to concealing those interests behind the obscurity of the welfare principle. Eekelaar also provides some comfort for strong adherents to a welfare-centred approach by continuing to privilege the children's interests in the form of a long-stop guarantee that no solution will ever be adopted which results in a net detriment to the child. The child's basic interests are thus safeguarded, whilst creating a better balance between the rights and interests of all parties. However, as Eekelaar acknowledges, the downside of his approach is its complexity, making it difficult to apply in practice.[28] This is perhaps inevitable. Family life is complex and disputes about a child are rarely easy to resolve. It is perhaps better to face this complexity than to hide behind the apparent safety of the welfare principle.

Whether one finds these alternatives to the welfare principle convincing, the question is no longer merely a matter for academic speculation. Following the implementation of the HRA 1998, there is a very real question whether the welfare-orientated approach of the CA 1989 and the ACA 2002 can be sustained in the face of the rights-based approach of the ECHR.

---

[28] Eekelaar (2002), 248.

8.4 A RIGHTS-BASED APPROACH TO CHILD-RELATED DISPUTES

Before considering whether the paramountcy principle can be reconciled with the rights-based approach of the ECHR, the potential relevance of the Convention to disputes concerning children must first be explored. Anyone seeking to take advantage of the ECHR and its rights-based approach in a family dispute must first establish that they fall within the scope of the ECHR's protection. The most important provision of the ECHR here is the right to respect for family life, guaranteed under Article 8.

8.4.1 ESTABLISHING A 'RIGHT' UNDER ARTICLE 8(1)

In order to fall within the scope of Article 8(1), the applicant must first establish the existence of 'family life'. A well-established line of authority makes it clear that Article 8 affords respect only to existing family relationships: it does not safeguard the 'mere desire' to found a family or create new familial relationships.[29] Establishing the existence of family life is not always straightforward. The European Court has generally favoured the traditional, heterosexual, married unit where the existence of family life between both the parents and the child is established automatically by virtue of the marital tie.[30] Establishing family life between parent and child where the parents are not married is more difficult. The relationship between unmarried mothers and their children was dealt with in the seminal case of *Marckx v Belgium*.[31] At the time of the application, illegitimate children suffered a number of disadvantages under Belgian law when compared with legitimate children, including the fact that no legal bond was automatically created between illegitimate children and their mothers by the mere fact of birth. The European Court held that Article 8 protects the family life of both the 'legitimate' and the 'illegitimate' family, thereby bringing the position of an 'illegitimate' child into line with that of a 'legitimate' child as regards the mother–child relationship.

The European Court has not, however, taken the same step with respect to the relationship between an unmarried father and his children. Although *Marckx* states unequivocally that Article 8 'makes no distinction between the "legitimate" and the "illegitimate" family', the European Court has resisted assuming the existence of family life between an unmarried father and his children on the basis of a mere biological bond. The Court therefore has tended to require unmarried fathers to demonstrate the existence in practice of 'close personal ties' between himself and the child, or at least between himself and the child's mother, before he can claim the protection of Article 8. The Court has held that factors relevant to determining whether de facto family life has been established include cohabitation (usual but not essential), the nature of the relationship between the parents, and the father's demonstrable commitment to the child both before and after the birth.[32] However, in *Anayo v Germany*,[33] the European Court held that 'family life'

---

[29] See, e.g., *Fretté v France* (App No 36515/97, ECHR) (2003), [32].
[30] *Al Nashif v Bulgaria* (App No 50963/99, ECHR) (2003); see also *Kosmopoulou v Greece* (App No 60457/00, ECHR) (2004), [42].
[31] (A/31, ECHR) (1979–80), [31].
[32] *Lebbink v Netherlands* (App No 45582/99, ECHR) (2004).
[33] (App No 20578/07, ECHR) (2010).

may extend to the '*potential*' relationship between an unmarried father and his child where the absence of an established relationship cannot be attributed to the father. While reiterating that '[a]s a rule, cohabitation is a requirement for a relationship amounting to family life', the Court acknowledged that there may be exceptional cases in which family life is established without this element.[34] The Court suggested that 'relevant factors' in making this assessment would include the nature of the relationship between the natural parents and a demonstrable interest in and commitment by the father to the child before and after the birth'.[35]

Although the European Court has treated the traditional married unit more favourably than the unmarried family, its willingness to embrace de facto as well as de jure family life has enabled unconventional family relationships to benefit from the protection of the ECHR. Importantly, this has included the relationship between transsexual parents and their children, and gay and lesbian parents and their children.[36]

Outside the immediate family unit of parents and child, the Court has suggested that the protection of 'family life' under Article 8 extends to include near relatives such as grandparents, siblings, aunts, uncles, and cousins.[37] Rather oddly, the Strasbourg jurisprudence suggests that it may be easier for grandparents to establish 'family life' for the purposes of Article 8 than the child's father.[38]

8.4.2 ESTABLISHING A BREACH OF ARTICLE 8(1)

Once the existence of family life has been established, the enquiry moves on to consider whether the state is, prima facie, in breach of any of its obligations under Article 8. The specific obligations imposed on the state by Article 8 are many and varied. We give just a flavour here.

Perhaps the most fundamental obligation imposed on the state under Article 8 is to respect the 'mutual enjoyment by parent and child of each other's company', what the European Court describes as a 'fundamental element of family life'.[39] Any state action in the public or private sphere which prevents or hinders the parent and child from exercising this right, such as refusing an order for a parent to spend time or have contact with their child, or taking a child into state care, constitutes a prima facie violation of Article 8(1).[40]

The primary object of Article 8 is thus to protect individuals against arbitrary intervention by public authorities. However, as held in *Marckx v Belgium*, Article 8 also imposes positive obligations on the state, one of the most important of which is to ensure the integration of a child into his or her family.[41] A second positive obligation imposed on

---

[34] Ibid, [56].

[35] Ibid, [57]. Note the similarity between these factors and those used by the domestic courts when determining application for parental responsibility orders from unmarried fathers: see 10.3.2.

[36] *X, Y and Z v United Kingdom* (App No 21830/93, ECHR) (1997); *da Silva Mouta v Portugal* (App No 33290/96, ECHR) (1999).

[37] *Marckx v Belgium* (A/31, ECHR) (1979–80), [45].

[38] *C v X,Y,Z County Council* [2007] EWCA Civ 1206, [31] and [39].

[39] *KA v Finland* (App No 27751/95, ECHR) (2003), [92]. See also *Venema v Netherlands* (App No 35731/97, ECHR) (2003), [71].

[40] *KA v Finland* (App No 27751/95, ECHR) (2003), [45]. *Hoffman v Austria* (A/255-C, ECHR) (1994).

[41] (A/31, ECHR) (1979–80), [31].

the state is to take all reasonable measures to reconcile parent and child where family life, for whatever reason, has broken down. This is now well established in both the public and private law context.[42]

Finally, Article 8 offers procedural as well as substantive protection, requiring that the decision-making process is both transparent and fair. In particular, the public authority (whether a local authority, an adoption agency, or the court) must ensure that 'the parents have been involved in the decision-making process, seen as a whole, to a degree sufficient to provide them with the requisite protection of their interests'.[43]

8.4.3 JUSTIFYING A BREACH UNDER ARTICLE 8(2)

If the applicant is able to establish a prima facie breach of Article 8(1), the next question is whether the breach can be justified in accordance with Article 8(2): (i) that the act in question was 'in accordance with the law'; (ii) that it pursued a legitimate aim; and (iii) was 'necessary in a democratic society'.[44] This last requirement gives rise to the most difficult questions, requiring a careful balancing exercise between the various rights and interests at stake. It is at this stage of the decision-making process that we reach the crux of the issue: in carrying out this balancing exercise, what weight is to be attributed to the child's interests? In particular, are the child's interests to be regarded as the paramount or determining factor, such that any interference with the adult applicant's rights will be deemed 'necessary in a democratic society' provided the measure in question was taken with the aim of protecting the child? It is the answer to this question which determines whether the welfare-orientated approach of English law can survive implementation of the HRA 1998.

8.4.4 CAN THE PARAMOUNTCY PRINCIPLE BE RECONCILED WITH ARTICLE 8?

Academic commentators were divided on whether the implementation of the HRA 1998 in 2000 would necessitate change to the paramountcy principle. It was certainly arguable that pursuant to s 3 of the HRA 1998 the welfare principle, as traditionally understood under English law, would have to be 're-interpreted' in order to give greater recognition to the independent rights and interests of the child's parents, perhaps along the lines suggested by Herring[45] or by 'downgrading' the interests of the child from the paramount to perhaps the primary or principal consideration. It was equally arguable that if such re-interpretation of the word 'paramount' was considered impossible, the paramountcy principle under the CA 1989 and ACA 2002 would find itself subject to a declaration of incompatibility under s 4 of the HRA 1998.

---

[42] *Haase v Germany* (App No 11057/02, ECHR) (2005), [93]; *Glaser v United Kingdom* (App No 32346/96, ECHR) (2000).

[43] *W v United Kingdom* (App No 9749/82, ECHR) (1988), [62]–[64].

[44] These requirements are discussed more generally at 1.2.1.

[45] See 8.3.1.

Pre-implementation of the HRA 1998

Immediately preceding implementation, there were clear signs of judicial opposition to any attempt to 're-interpret' or 'downgrade' the welfare principle in light of the ECHR. The family judiciary's approach towards the ECHR, which some regard as 'dismissive',[46] was presaged by the House of Lords' decision in *Re KD (A Minor) (Ward: Termination of Access)*, a case concerning an application for contact with a child in local authority care. In addressing the possible implications of the ECHR for domestic family law, Lord Oliver held that the difference between the welfare-orientated approach as interpreted and approved by the House of Lords in *J v C* and the rights-based approach of the ECHR was 'semantic only'.

Re KD (A Minor) (Ward: Termination of Access) [1988] 1 AC 806, 820 and 824–7

LORD OLIVER:

Such conflict as exists...lies only in differing ways of giving expression to the single common concept that the natural bond and relationship between parent and child gives rise to universally recognised norms which ought not to be gratuitously interfered with and which, if interfered with at all, ought to be so only if the welfare of the child dictates it...

When the jurisdiction of the court is invoked for the protection of the child the parental privileges do not terminate. They do, however, become immediately subservient to the paramount consideration which the court has always in mind, that is to say the welfare of the child. That is the basis of the decision of your Lordships House in *J v C*...and I see nothing in [the Strasbourg case law] which contradicts or casts doubt upon that decision or which calls now for any reappraisal of it by your Lordships....

Whatever the position of the parent may be as a matter of law—and it matters not whether he or she is described as having a "right" in law or a "claim" by the law of nature or as a matter of common sense—it is perfectly clear that any "right" vested in him or her must yield to the dictates of the welfare of the child. ...As a general proposition a natural parent has a claim to access to his or her child to which the court will pay regard and it would not I think be inappropriate to describe such a claim as a "right". Equally, a normal assumption is...that a child will benefit from continued contact with his natural parent. But both the "right" and the assumption will always be displaced if the interests of the child indicate otherwise and I find nothing in the [Strasbourg case law] which suggests otherwise.

Lord Oliver's judgment in *Re KD* provides the courts with an easy answer to the dilemma of whether the welfare principle can be reconciled with the ECHR.[47] However, some scholars question whether the ECHR arguments can be so easily dismissed as no more than 'semantic'.

---

[46] Harris-Short (2005), 354.
[47] Fortin (1999a).

J. Herring, 'The Human Rights Act and the Welfare Principle in Family Law—Conflicting or Complementary?', (1999a) 11 *Child and Family Law Quarterly* 223, 231

In a case based on the Convention, concerning, say, denying a parent access to a child, the starting point is the parent's right to contact. In order to justify a breach there must be clear and convincing evidence that the contact would infringe the rights and interests of the child to such an extent as to make the infringement necessary and proportionate. However, an approach based on the Children Act's welfare principle might start with a factual presumption that the welfare of the child is promoted by contact with parents, but this could be rebutted by evidence that the welfare is not thus enhanced in the particular case.

The difference is twofold. First, less evidence is required to rebut the factual presumption of welfare than to demonstrate that the breach of a right is *necessary* in a democratic society. Secondly, the nature of the question is different. It is essentially an evidential question in the welfare approach. The law is clear—the order which should be made is that which best promotes the child's welfare. The question is then a factual one—which order will actually promote the child's welfare? Whereas in the European Convention approach, it is a question of judgment—whether the harm to the child is sufficient to make the breach 'necessary' as understood by the law.

Post-implementation case law

Following implementation of the HRA 1998 in 2000, judges have continued their defence of the welfare principle against incursion by the rights-based reasoning of the ECHR. In general, the courts have taken the view that a decision in accordance with the child's best interests will *automatically* comply with Article 8. The judgment of Wall J in *Re H (Children) (Contact Order) (No 2)* typifies this approach. The case concerned an application by the child's father to spend time with the child (or to 'have direct contact', as it was then termed) against the mother's wishes. The mother opposed contact because the father was suffering from Huntington's disease and posed a potential risk to the child.

Re H (Children) (Contact Order) (No 2) [2001] 3 FCR 385 (Fam Div)

WALL J:

[59] Finally, it will be apparent that I have made no mention of the European Convention for the Protection of Human Rights and Fundamental Freedoms in this judgment. Inevitably, however, every order made under s 8 of the 1989 Act represents in some measure an interference by a public authority (the court) in the right to respect for family life contained in art 8. The court's interference must, of course, be in accordance with the powers given to the court under the 1989 Act, and proportionate. Every application involves the court balancing the rights of the participants to the application (including the children who are the subjects of it) and arriving at a result which is in the interests of those children (or least detrimental to those interests) and proportionate to the legitimate aims being pursued. However, it seems to me that a proper application of the checklist in s 1(3) of the 1989 Act is equivalent to the balancing exercise required in the application of art 8, which is then a useful cross-check to

> ensure that the order proposed is in accordance with the law, necessary for the protection of the rights and freedoms of others and proportionate. In my judgment, and for all the reasons I have given, the order I am making in this case fulfils those criteria.

The same approach was adopted by the Court of Appeal in *Payne v Payne*[48] and confirmed by the House of Lords in *Re B (A Minor) (Adoption: Natural Parent)*.[49] The clear message from these cases was that post-implementation of the HRA it was 'business as usual'.

More recently, the Supreme Court has given further thought to the way in which Article 8 interacts with domestic law. *Re B (Care Order: Proportionality: Criterion for Review)* was a child protection case in which the child—whom the Justices named Amelia—was removed from her parents at birth because of concerns about the standard of care which she would receive if left with her mother. The trial judge, HHJ Cryan, found the threshold test in s 31 of the CA 1989 to be crossed (Amelia was at risk of suffering significant harm) and determined that her welfare demanded that she be freed for adoption. While the Supreme Court reiterated the earlier view that there is no incompatibility between the welfare principle and Article 8, the reasons which the Justices identified as supporting this view may be more developed than in some of the earlier case law.[50]

Re B (Care Order: Proportionality: Criterion for Review) [2013] UKSC 33

LORD WILSON:

32. Judge Cryan's care order in relation to Amelia with a view to her adoption represented an interference with the exercise by Amelia, by M and by F of their rights to respect for their family life. It was therefore lawful only if, within the meaning of article 8(2) of the Convention, it was not only in accordance with the law but also "necessary" in a democratic society for the protection of the right of A to grow up free from harm. In *Johansen v Norway* (1997) the European Commission of Human Rights observed, at para 83, that "the notion of necessity implies that the interference corresponds to a pressing social need and, in particular, that it is proportional to the legitimate aim pursued".

33. In a number of its judgments the European Court of Human Rights, "the ECtHR", has spelt out the stark effects of the proportionality requirement in its application to a determination that a child should be adopted. Only a year ago, in *YC v United Kingdom* (2012), it said:

"134 The Court reiterates that in cases concerning the placing of a child for adoption, which entails the permanent severance of family ties, the best interests of the child are paramount. In identifying the child's best interests in a particular case, two considerations must be borne in mind: first, it is in the child's best interests that his ties with his family be maintained except in cases where the family has proved particularly unfit; and secondly, it is in the child's best interests to ensure his development in a safe and secure environment. It is clear from the foregoing that family ties may only be severed in very exceptional circumstances and that everything must be done to preserve personal relations and, where appropriate, to 'rebuild' the family. It is not enough to show that a child could be placed in a more beneficial environment for his upbringing. However, where the maintenance of family ties would harm the

---

[48] [2001] EWCA Civ 166.
[49] [2001] UKHL 70; see Harris-Short (2002); extracts from *Re B* can be found at 13.5.5 and 13.6.4.
[50] Further extracts from *Re B* are found at 11.6.7, 12.5.3, and 13.4.3.

child's health and development, a parent is not entitled under article 8 to insist that such ties be maintained."

Although in that paragraph it did not in terms refer to proportionality, the court had prefaced it with a reference to the need to examine whether the reasons adduced to justify the measures were relevant and sufficient, in other words whether they were proportionate to them.

34. In my view it is important not to take any one particular sentence out of its context in the whole of para 134 of the *YC* case: for each of its propositions is interwoven with the others. But the paragraph well demonstrates the high degree of justification which article 8 demands of a determination that a child should be adopted or placed in care with a view to adoption. Yet, while in every such case the trial judge should, as Judge Cryan expressly did, consider the proportionality of adoption to the identified risks, he is likely to find that domestic law runs broadly in parallel with the demands of article 8. Thus domestic law makes clear that:

(a) it is not enough that it would be *better* for the child to be adopted than to live with his natural family *(Re S-B (Children) (Care Proceedings: Standard of Proof)* [2009] UKSC 17); and

(b) a parent's consent to the making of an adoption order can be dispensed with only if the child's welfare so *requires* (section 52(1)(b) of the Adoption and Children Act 2002); there is therefore no point in making a care order with a view to adoption unless there are good grounds for considering that this statutory test will be satisfied.

LORD NEUBERGER P:

73....As Lady Hale (who knows more about this than anybody) says in para 194, the 1989 Act was drafted with the Convention in mind; in any event, with the coming into force of the Human Rights Act 1998 ("the 1998 Act"), the 1989 Act must now, if possible, be construed and applied so as to comply with the Convention. So too the Adoption and Children Act 2002 ("the 2002 Act") must, if possible, be construed and applied so as to comply with the Convention. It also appears to me that the 2002 Act must be construed and applied bearing in mind the provisions of the UN Convention on the Rights of the Child 1989 ("UNCRC").

75. As already mentioned, it is clear that a judge cannot properly decide that a care order should be made in such circumstances, unless the order is proportionate bearing in mind the requirements of article 8.

76. It appears to me that, given that the Judge concluded that the section 31(2) threshold was crossed, he should only have made a care order if he had been satisfied that it was necessary to do so in order to protect the interests of the child. By "necessary", I mean, to use Lady Hale's phrase in para 198, "where nothing else will do". I consider that this conclusion is clear under the 1989 Act, interpreted in the absence of the Convention, but it is put beyond doubt by article 8. The conclusion is also consistent with UNCRC.

Put another way, the judges appear to be saying that not only was the CA 1989 drafted so as to be compatible with the ECHR, but that its application in practice is informed by developments in the Strasbourg jurisprudence. The same result is reached whether under the CA 1989 or under Article 8, not because the two approaches are necessarily identical in theory, but because the welfare principle is applied in such a way as to make them identical in practice.

The Strasbourg jurisprudence

Is the approach of the English judiciary to the paramountcy principle well founded in the Strasbourg jurisprudence? At one time, commentators were fairly clear that the answer was 'no',[51] but the situation is now less clear. At the heart of Article 8(2) and the balancing exercise it requires is the concept of proportionality. 'Proportionality' demands that there exist a 'fair balance' or 'reasonable relationship' between the legitimate aim pursued and the means used to achieve it. Consequently, whilst an act carried out to protect the legitimate rights and interests of the child will have the *potential* to justify a prima facie breach of the rights of the child's parents, it will not *automatically* do so. In some cases, such will be the gravity of the interference with the birth parents' rights that only very weighty welfare considerations will satisfy the ECHR need for proportionality.[52]

For many years, the approach of the European Court to child welfare and Article 8 was set down by *Johansen v Norway*, which concerned a mother's challenge to the Norwegian authorities' decision to take her child into care and terminate her parental rights and responsibilities with a view to placing the child for adoption. The Norwegian government expressly argued that in a case of this nature 'rather than attempting to strike a "fair balance" between the interests of the natural parent and the child', the best interests of the child should be paramount. The European Court clearly rejected this interpretation of the required balancing exercise.

Johansen v Norway (App No 17383/90, ECHR) (1997)

78. The Court considers that taking a child into care should normally be regarded as a temporary measure to be discontinued as soon as circumstances permit and that any measures of implementation of temporary care should be consistent with the ultimate aim of reuniting the natural parent and the child...In this regard, a fair balance has to be struck between the interests of the child in remaining in public care and those of the parent in being reunited with the child...In carrying out this balancing exercise, the Court will attach particular importance to the best interests of the child, which, depending on their nature and seriousness, may override those of the parent. In particular, as suggested by the Government, the parent cannot be entitled under Article 8 of the Convention...to have such measures taken as would harm the child's health and development.

In the present case the applicant had been deprived of her parental rights and access in the context of a permanent placement of her daughter in a foster home with a view to adoption by the foster parents...These measures were particularly far-reaching in that they totally deprived the applicant of her family life with the child and were inconsistent with the aim of reuniting them. Such measures should only be applied in exceptional circumstances and could only be justified if they were motivated by an overriding requirement pertaining to the child's best interests...

Much of the subsequent case law faithfully followed the *Johansen* approach, often quoting directly from the judgment and emphasizing the need to strike a 'fair balance' between, on the one hand, the rights and interests of the child's parents and, on the other, the rights

---

[51] Bonner, Fenwick, and Harris-Short (2003), 580–1.
[52] Ibid. See also Herring and Taylor (2006), 527–9.

and interests of the child. This approach was adopted in both the public and private law contexts,[53] and some commentators argued strongly that it was difficult to reconcile the *Johansen* approach with the welfare principle as understood in English law.[54]

However, a number of recent authorities have departed from the *Johansen* approach and provide some scope for defending the paramountcy principle.[55] The most significant is the Grand Chamber decision in *Neulinger and Shuruk v Switzerland*,[56] which arose out of international child abduction proceedings in relation to children taken to Switzerland.

Neulinger and Shuruk v Switzerland (App No 41615/07, ECHR) (2010)

134. In this area the decisive issue is whether a fair balance between the competing interests at stake – those of the child, of the two parents, and of public order – has been struck, within the margin of appreciation afforded to States in such matters...bearing in mind, however, that the child's best interests must be the primary consideration...The child's best interests may, depending on their nature and seriousness, override those of the parents...The parents' interests, especially in having regular contact with their child, nevertheless remain a factor when balancing the various interests at stake...

135. The Court notes that there is currently a broad consensus – including in international law – in support of the idea that in all decisions concerning children, their best interests must be paramount (see the numerous references in paragraphs 49–56 above, and in particular Article 24 § 2 of the European Union's Charter of Fundamental Rights). As indicated, for example, in the Charter, "[e]very child shall have the right to maintain on a regular basis a personal relationship and direct contact with both his or her parents, unless that is contrary to his or her interests".

136. The child's interest comprises two limbs. On the one hand, it dictates that the child's ties with its family must be maintained, except in cases where the family has proved particularly unfit. It follows that family ties may only be severed in very exceptional circumstances and that everything must be done to preserve personal relations and, if and when appropriate, to "rebuild" the family (see *Gnahoré* [*v France* (App No 40031/98) (2000)]). On the other hand, it is clearly also in the child's interest to ensure its development in a sound environment, and a parent cannot be entitled under Article 8 to have such measures taken as would harm the child's health and development...

139. In addition, the Court must ensure that the decision-making process leading to the adoption of the impugned measures by the domestic court was fair and allowed those concerned to present their case fully...To that end the Court must ascertain whether the domestic courts conducted an in-depth examination of the entire family situation and of a whole series of factors, in particular of a factual, emotional, psychological, material and medical nature, and made a balanced and reasonable assessment of the respective interests of each person, with a constant concern for determining what the best solution would be for the abducted child in the context of an application for his return to his country of origin.

---

53 See, e.g., *Buchberger v Austria* (App No 32899/96, ECHR) (2003), [40]; *Sahin v Germany; Sommerfeld v Germany* (App No 30943/96, ECHR) (2003), [66]; and *Gorgula v Germany* (App No 74969/01, ECHR) (2004), [43].

54 See, e.g., Bonner, Fenwick, and Harris-Short (2003), 582–3.

55 The first of these cases was *Yousef v Netherlands* (App No 33711/96, ECHR) (2002), though at the time it appeared to be an outlier from the general approach.

56 (App No 41615/07, ECHR) (2010).

Of particular relevance to the English debates is the subsequent decision of *YC v United Kingdom*,[57] which applied this approach to a review of an adoption order following care proceedings in the English courts, governed by the ACA 2002. The Strasbourg Court observed that 'the considerations listed in s 1 of the 2002 Act...broadly reflect the various elements inherent in assessing the necessity under Art 8 of a measure placing a child for adoption. In particular, it considers that in seeking to identify the best interests of a child and in assessing the necessity of any proposed measure in the context of placement proceedings, the domestic court must demonstrate that it has had regard to, inter alia, the age, maturity and ascertained wishes of the child, the likely effect on the child of ceasing to be a member of his original family and the relationship the child has with relatives.'[58] The Court went on to say that the fact that the English judgment made no explicit reference either to Article 8 or to the detail of the checklist factors did not mean that the decision was not compatible with the ECHR.

YC v United Kingdom (Application No 4547/10, ECHR) (2012)

> 147....[I]t is clear that [the judge] directed his mind, as required under Art 8 of the European Convention, to [the child's] best interests and that, in reviewing the applicant's application for a further assessment, considered whether in the circumstances rehabilitation of [the child] to his biological family was possible. He concluded that it was not. In reaching that decision he had regard to various relevant factors and made detailed reference to the reports and oral evidence of the social worker, the guardian (whose report was based on full consideration of the welfare checklist) and [a psychologist], all of whom identified the various issues at stake.

In the light of these developments in the thinking of both the domestic courts and the Strasbourg Court, it is questionable whether the incompatibility which commentators once saw between the two approaches is now so pronounced.[59]

8.5 CHILDREN'S RIGHTS

In contrast to the notion of parents' rights, one area of rights-based discourse which has not received a great deal of attention following implementation of the HRA 1998 is children's rights.[60] The explanation for this lies not only in the inadequacies of the ECHR as a vehicle for the protection of children's rights, but deep ambivalence about the concept of children's rights within contemporary legal, political, and social thinking.[61] However, despite struggling to gain a secure foothold in mainstream family law, the idea of children's rights provides a potentially important challenge to the centrality of the welfare principle. Many children's rights are based on a very different understanding of childhood from that of a welfare-orientated approach. Whereas the latter tends to emphasize the incapacity

---

[57] (App No 4547/10, ECHR) (2012).

[58] Ibid, [135].

[59] Simmonds (2012), George (2015).

[60] For a review of progress in advancing children's rights post-implementation of the HRA 1998, see Fortin (2004) and (2006).

[61] Fortin (2014).

and vulnerability of children, much of children's rights discourse tends to emphasize the autonomy of children and their capacity for independent thought and action. The paternalism of the welfare principle and the 'liberationist' tendencies of a children's rights approach are not, however, mutually exclusive: indeed, there is considerable overlap between the concept of welfare and rights.[62] Adherents to the welfare approach will readily concede that for children entering their teenage years it is often in their best interests that they should begin to take responsibility for their own futures, to become self-determining beings.[63] Similarly, proponents of children's rights would agree that children, particularly young children, have a right to special protection and care thereby ensuring their future welfare is maximized. As is evident from the case law, difficulties tend to arise when teenagers begin to struggle for independence from those in authority, wanting to determine for themselves how their future welfare will be secured.

We begin this section by looking at the theoretical foundations of children's rights and why the protection of children's rights, as opposed to children's welfare, may be important. We then move on to consider the extent to which children's rights have gained acceptance in English law.

8.5.1 ARE CHILDREN'S RIGHTS IMPORTANT?

Since the implementation of the HRA 1998, a strong 'culture of rights' has developed within the UK. However, children, unlike adults, are still not widely perceived as natural beneficiaries of rights. There remains deep ambivalence about the value of trying to attribute rights to children, with the result that children, as a group, are often excluded from contemporary rights-based discourse.[64] The reasons for such scepticism are varied. For some commentators, such as Onora O'Neill, rights can only ever offer a partial understanding of the obligations and duties owed by society to children.[65] Believing children's situation to be fundamentally different from other oppressed groups, she argues that rights-based discourse is an inappropriate legal and political tool to empower and protect this particularly vulnerable and often disadvantaged group.

O. O'Neill, 'Children's Rights and Children's Lives', (1992) 6 *International Journal of Law and the Family* 24, 36–9

Appeals to children's rights might have political and rhetorical importance if children's dependence on others is like that of oppressed social groups whom the rhetoric of rights has served well. However, the analogy between children's dependence and that of oppressed groups is suspect. When colonial peoples, or the working classes or religious and racial minorities or women have demanded their rights, they have sought recognition and respect for capacities for rational and independent life and action that are demonstrably there and thwarted by the denial of rights... But the dependence of children is very different from the dependence of oppressed social groups on those who exercise power over them.

---

[62] For more detailed discussion, see Fortin (2006), 311–12 and 317–18.
[63] Ibid, 317–18.
[64] See generally, ibid.
[65] O'Neill (1992), 25–9.

Younger children are completely and unavoidably dependent on those who have power over their lives. Theirs is not a dependence which has been artificially produced (although it can be artificially prolonged); nor can it be ended merely by social or political changes, nor are others reciprocally dependent on children...It is not surprising that oppressors often try to suggest that they stand in a paternal relation to those whom they oppress: in that way they suggest that the latter's dependence is natural and irremediable and their own exercise of power a burden which they bear with benevolent fortitude. The vocabulary and trappings of paternalism are often misused to mask the unacceptable faces of power. It is not mere metaphor but highly political rhetoric, when oppressors describe what they do as paternalistic...

The crucial difference between (early) childhood dependence and the dependence of oppressed social groups is that childhood is a stage of life, from which children normally emerge and are helped and urged to emerge by those who have most power over them. Those with power over children's lives usually have some interest in ending childish dependence. Oppressors usually have an interest in maintaining the oppression of social groups...

Children are more fundamentally but less permanently powerless; their main remedy is to grow up.

O'Neill can be criticized for underestimating the similarity of children's oppression at the hands of patriarchal and/or matriarchal authority to that of other oppressed groups. O'Neill portrays the incapacity, dependence, and vulnerability of children as a natural and inevitable state, a state from which a child will 'naturally' emerge upon reaching majority. It is questionable, however, whether the perceived incapacity and dependence of children is any more 'natural' than the 'natural' dependence of slaves and women was once thought to be. It can be argued that rather than a natural state, childhood as currently depicted in western societies is socially constructed, created to serve some wider societal interest.[66] Smith suggests that one such interest is that of the state in ensuring that children grow up to be responsible citizens.[67] The interests of individual adults, and in particular parents, are also served by a conception of childhood dominated by ideas of dependency and vulnerability, in which a protective role for the adult is guaranteed.

C. Smith, 'Children's Rights: Judicial Ambivalence and Social Resistance', (1997)
11 *International Journal of Law, Policy and the Family* 103, 134–5

In contradistinction to the progress and order of modernity, post-modernity heralds a scepticism about the relationship between 'scientific investigation' and universal knowledge. In so doing it introduces a sense of uncertainty about what, if anything, may be construed as truth, and how, in the absence of shared values, understandings and knowledge, order and progress can be maintained...As individuals, we have come to lack an economic identity which was previously determined by secure and progressive employment opportunities, and we have lost a familial identity which was traditionally confirmed by the continuity of stable community and family relationships. Our sense of society has similarly been eroded by increasing 'globalization' externally, and the fragmentation of social structure internally. In these circumstances which characterise post-modernity, Jenks argues that adult-child relationships

---

[66] Smith (1997), 109, 133.
[67] Ibid, 132.

have come to provide the sense of closeness, affection and stability which it is hard to find elsewhere. He summarises the nature of this bond between adults and children thus:

Oddly enough children are seen as dependable and permanent, in a manner to which no other person or persons can possibly aspire. The vortex created by the quickening of social change and the cultivation of our perceptions of such change means that whereas children used to cling to us, through modernity, for guidance into their/our 'futures', now we, through late modernity, cling to them for nostalgic groundings, because such change is both intolerable and disorientating for us.

If we are prepared to take Jenks' analysis seriously then it may go some way towards explaining why we so stubbornly resist accepting that a child's right to decide should take precedence over an adult's protective interpretation of their best interests. We can talk all we like about respecting children's wishes, listening to their views and responding to them as intentional subjects rather than objects of concern, but we are not prepared to withdraw our protection or to abandon the legal distinction between children and adults. To do so would strike at the very heart of the adult-child relationship which enables adults to locate themselves emotionally, as being affectionate, caring, protective, and socially, as being responsible for moulding the next generation of citizens.

For some, the argument that our current understanding of childhood is fuelled by post-modern angst and uncertainty may seem a little far-fetched. However, Jenks' analysis does serve to highlight O'Neill's somewhat idealistic view of the parent–child relationship. O'Neill perhaps underestimates the extent to which adults, and particularly parents, do have a clear self-interest in maintaining control over their children's lives. Many parents have strong aspirations about the type of people they want their children to be. Very often they have invested heavily, emotionally and financially, in their futures. Recognizing children's capacity for autonomous decision-making, giving them the freedom to determine their own path in life, can jeopardize strongly held parental hopes and dreams.

In seeking to convince a sceptical public of the importance of children's rights, children's rights advocates have tried to focus on the realities of children's lives, challenging some of the more idealistic assumptions about childhood, including the parent–child relationship.

M. Freeman, 'Taking Children's Rights More Seriously', (1992) 6 *International Journal of Law and the Family* 52, 55–6

The arguments put [against children's rights] tend to take one or more of three forms.

First, there is the argument that the importance of rights and rights-language themselves can be exaggerated. That there are other morally significant values, love, friendship, compassion, altruism, and that these raise relationships to a higher plain than one based on the observance of duties cannot be gainsaid. This argument may be thought particularly apposite to children's rights, particularly in the context of family relationships. Perhaps in an ideal moral world this is true. Rights may be used to resolve conflicts of interest and in an ideal world there would be harmony and these would not exist. But it is not an ideal world—certainly not for children. Children are particularly vulnerable and need rights to protect their integrity and dignity. 'Solitary, poor, nasty, brutish and short' (Hobbes, 1651) may not be a description of a state of nature . . . but it may come close to describing what a world without rights would look like for many children . . .

The second argument is in one sense related to the first. It assumes that adults already relate to children in terms of love, care and altruism, so that the case for children's rights becomes otiose. This idealizes adult-child relations: it emphasises that adults (and parents in particular) have the best interests of children at heart. There is a tendency for those who postulate such an argument to adopt a *laissez-faire* attitude towards the family. Thus, the only right for children...is the child's right to autonomous parents...

The third argument equally rests on a myth. It sees childhood as a golden age, as the best years of our life. Childhood is synonymous with innocence. It is the time when, spared the rigours of adult life, we enjoy freedom, experience play and joy. The argument runs: just as we avoid the responsibilities and adversities of adult life in childhood, so there should be no necessity to think in terms of rights, a concept which we must assume is reserved for adults. Whether or not the premise underlying this were correct or not, it would represent an ideal state of affairs, and one which ill-reflects the lives of many of today's children and adolescents...

For children's rights advocates, children's rights are important because of their potential to protect children from suffering and exploitation at the hands of others. Rights give children's interests, regardless of age, a status equal to the interests of adults, meaning they cannot be easily disregarded: the child, as person, as individual, has to be respected. Freeman continues:

Rights are important because those who lack rights are like slaves, means to the ends of others, and never sovereigns in their own right. Those who may claim rights, or for whom rights may be claimed, have a necessary pre-condition to the constitution of humanity, of integrity, of individuality, of personality.

8.5.2 THE THEORETICAL FOUNDATIONS OF CHILDREN'S RIGHTS

There are two main competing approaches to children's rights: (i) the 'will' or 'power' theory; and (ii) the 'interest' theory. These two theories have very different implications for the law's approach to childhood and, in particular, differ in the extent to which they challenge the paternalism of the welfare principle. Tom Campbell provides a detailed explanation of both theories, beginning with the will or power theory of rights.

The will or power theory of rights

T. Campbell, 'The Rights of the Minor: As Person, as Child, as Juvenile, as Future Adult', (1992) 6 *International Journal of Law and the Family* 1, 4–5

On the power theory, a right is a normative capacity that the bearer may choose to use for the furtherance of his or her own interests or projects, a sanctioned exercise of legitimate control over others...In its limited forms, the power theory is that the formal analysis of the structure of rights must be carried out in terms of the mechanisms available for invoking, waiving and enforcing rights, all of which are said to depend on the exercise of will by the right-bearer. Thus a right may give a normative control over others which may be used at the discretion of the right-holder to activate those obligations the performance of which she judges to be advantageous to herself or her projects. It follows that only those capable of claiming, demanding or waiving a right can be the bearers of rights. Hence, for instance, small children, being in no position to exercise this sort of control over the obligations of others, have no rights.

The embarrassment for the power theorists of denying rights to children may seem to be avoided by allowing that a proxy, such as a parent, may exercise, on behalf of a child, the discretionary powers which constitute the rights in question. However, on the power theory, this must be less than a full possession of a right since the bearer's will, the exercise of which is definitive for the existence of the right, is not involved. Indeed, it would appear, on the assumptions of the theory, that the proxy is the right-holder. After all, it is she who possesses the power which is said to constitute the right. In other words, children's rights exercised by proxies are certainly less than full rights as defined by the power theory. Moreover, at least for some theorists, the process of choosing to exercise one's rights is part of what gives importance to rights, for it is the exercise of choice in matters of importance to the individual that enhances the dignity and exhibits the autonomy of the right-holder. On this view, while the natural capacity to make choices of this sort comes to minors in the course of their normal development, it is only in so far as the individual minor has come to possess these capacities, and hence to resemble an adult, that he or she can have rights. For young children there can be no such choices, and hence, no genuine rights.

In the fuller version of the power theory, rights are related substantively to capacities for choice and rational action in that, at least as far as fundamental rights are concerned, all rights relate to the exercise of practical rationality and self-determination, in that rights have the function of protecting and furthering these capacities. In its purest form, the fuller version of the power theory is that all rights are materially based in the presupposition of the value pre-eminence of the distinctively rational elements of human nature. It is because human beings have the power of reasoned self-determination that they can have rights, these rights being for the protection of the exercise of these capacities or related to the prerequisites of rational action, such as life itself. In this way, the whole rights viewpoint is a working out of some ideal of Kantian rationalism as the distinctive value-basis of human existence.

Clearly, on the fuller version of the power theory, minors can have rights only to the extent that they have acquired adult-like capacities for reasoned decision-making and willed conduct under the control of rational moral agency. To some people this is an outrageous denial of the value significance of young children which exposes the intellectual and moral limitations of the power theory. Children are no less precious on account of the immaturity of their characteristically adult capacities.

As Campbell argues, the will or power theory of rights can lead to a complete denial that children, particularly young children, can be sensibly regarded as rights-holders. However, there is scope within this particular theory of rights for a more radical interpretation. The will or power theory does not necessarily exclude children as rights-holders. What it requires from children is the capacity for reasoned, rational thought. Once a child has that capacity, there can no longer be any objection to that child being accorded the same rights as others. The crux of the issue thus becomes at what point it can be said that a child acquires the necessary skills and maturity to hold and exercise rights. In response, the so-called 'child liberationists' argue that children have the capacity for rational, reasoned, decision-making from a much earlier age than western society has generally been willing to acknowledge, a fact attributable to adults' self-interest in retaining control over children.[68] They thus contend that children, even very young children, have the capacity to be self-determining, autonomous beings capable of holding and exercising rights.

However, whilst this theory does not entirely exclude children as rights-holders, it does have important limitations. Attributing rights to children on the basis of their adult-like capacities tends to conceptualize children as 'little adults', making their respective rights and interests virtually indistinguishable. Children's rights to various forms of autonomy and freedom, such as the right to freedom of expression or the right to determine their own health care, are emphasized at the potential expense of other core interests, particularly of young children. This, according to Campbell, is to adopt only a partial view of childhood. It attributes no value to the distinctive interests of children, 'as children'. This leads him to prefer the much broader, interest theory of rights.

The interest theory of rights

T. Campbell, 'The Rights of the Minor: As Person, as Child, as Juvenile, as Future Adult', (1992) 6 *International Journal of Law and the Family* 1, 5–6

According to this—the interest—theory of rights, children have rights if their interests are the basis for having rules which require others to behave in certain ways with respect to these interests. It is enough that there are ways of identifying these interests and arranging and enforcing duties which meet the requirements that they set. There is no presupposition that these interests are expressions of rational capacities, although some of them may be. Nor is there any assumption that the performance of the correlative interest-saving duties must be triggered or set aside by the choice of the right-bearer, although this may often be the preferred way to protect the interests concerned....

Taking the offensive, interest theorists claim to be able to explain a wider range of rights than the power theorists who have to resort to subtle reconstructions of those specific rights where there is no evident link to capacities of choice. Thus, the right not to be tortured has to be interpreted by a full power theorist as being grounded in something like the fact that torture interferes with the processes of rational decision-making. The interest theorist may retort that it also hurts. Similarly, the interest theorist can persuasively argue that there is nothing particularly indirect about the ascription of rights to mentally handicapped adults and small children, whereas the power theorist...has difficulty with these classes of persons.

The concept of childhood embraced by the interest theory of rights is much broader and allows for the core interests of even very young children to be elevated to the status of rights. Campbell argues that children's interests change throughout childhood, with different rights being particularly important at different stages of children's development. During the latter stages of childhood, as the child develops the capacity for independent decision-making, the

---

[68] Ibid, 106. See also Fortin (2009b), 4–5.

autonomy or freedom interests identified with the will or power theory become of increasing importance. However, during very young childhood, needs-based rights, more closely identified with a traditional welfare approach, predominate.

It can be difficult to identify the core interests of children which are of such fundamental importance that they should be elevated to the status of rights. Identifying those rights that children, as children, would value raises particular difficulties. Eekelaar has developed one possible solution to this dilemma.

J. Eekelaar, 'The Emergence of Children's Rights', (1986) 6 *Oxford Journal of Legal Studies* 161, 169–71

We here meet the problem that children often lack the information or ability to appreciate what will serve them best. It is necessary therefore to make some kind of imaginative leap and guess what a child might retrospectively have wanted once it reaches a position of maturity. In doing this, values of the adult world and of individual adults will inevitably enter. This is not to be deplored, but openly accepted. It encourages debate about these values. There are, however, some broad propositions which might reasonably be advanced as forming the foundation of any child's (retrospective) claims. General physical, emotional and intellectual care within the social capabilities of his or her immediate caregivers would seem a minimal expectation. We may call this the 'basic' interest. What a child should expect from the wider community must be stated more tentatively. I have elsewhere suggested the formulation that, within certain overriding constraints created by the economic and social structure of society (whose extent must be open to debate), all children should have an equal opportunity to maximize the resources available to them during their childhood (including their own inherent abilities) so as to minimize the degree to which they enter adult life affected by avoidable prejudices incurred during childhood. In short, their capacities are to be developed to their best advantage. We may call this the 'developmental' interest...

There is a third type of interest which children may, retrospectively, claim. A child may argue for the freedom to choose his own lifestyle and to enter social relations according to his own inclinations uncontrolled by the authority of the adult world, whether parents or institutions...We may call them the 'autonomy' interest.

Campbell criticizes this reliance on 'retrospective judgment', arguing that such an approach is inevitably adult-centred.[69] He points out that Eekelaar relies exclusively on an adult perspective and that adults considering childhood with hindsight tend to minimize the sufferings and sacrifices made, dismissing such misery as unimportant in light of the benefits and advantages they now enjoy.[70] This is a clear problem with any 'substituted judgment' approach. Giving children a much more direct voice in defining their own interests would help achieve a better balance.

Children's rights and paternalism

The interest theory of rights is not unproblematic. On the positive side, the strong correlation between interests and rights means that children's rights are more easily reconciled with the

[69] Campbell (1992), 20–1.
[70] Ibid.

welfare principle, which in turn renders children's rights less challenging for policy-makers and more easily integrated into mainstream family law. Indeed, Fortin argues that there is no conflict between children's rights and children's welfare.[71] However, on the negative side, tying children's rights so closely to children's interests makes children's rights vulnerable to the paternalism of a welfare-centred approach. As noted above, there is a danger that children will only be accorded such rights as adults deem to be consistent with welfare. Thus, whilst children will readily be accorded the right to special protection and care, they may be denied the right to refuse life-saving medical treatment, such a right being regarded as inimical to their best interests.

The danger of slipping back into adult paternalism is not just a problem for the interest theory of rights. In fact, faced with the stark realities of allowing even older children to determine their own path in life, Campbell emphasizes that both the interest theory and the power/will theory of rights can be appropriately qualified with paternalistic interventions where necessary.[72]

Freeman, a strong proponent of children's rights, agrees that an element of paternalism is often necessary in order to protect children from themselves.[73]

M. Freeman, 'Taking Children's Rights More Seriously', (1992) 6 *International Journal of Law and the Family* 52, 65–6

To respect a child's autonomy is to treat that child as a person and as a rights-holder. It is clear that we can do so to a much greater extent than we have assumed hitherto. But it is also clear that the exercising of autonomy by a child can have a deleterious impact on that child's life chances. It is true that adults make mistakes too (and also make mistakes when interfering with a child's autonomy). Having rights means being allowed to take risks and make choices. There is a reluctance to interfere with an adult's project. This reluctance is tempered when the project pursuer is a child by the sense that choice now may harm choice later . . .

  If we are to make progress we have to recognize the moral integrity of children. We have to treat them as persons entitled to equal concern and respect and entitled to have both their present autonomy recognized and their capacity for future autonomy safeguarded. And this is to recognize that children, particularly younger children, need nurture, care and protection. Children must not, as Hafen (1977) put it, be 'abandoned' to their rights.

The difficult question in seeking to reconcile the competing demands of autonomy and protection is where the line justifying adult intervention should be drawn. Freeman suggests that intervention will be justified to protect children against irrational actions. Which simply begs the question: what will constitute an irrational action? In particular, will any action with which an adult disagrees be labelled irrational?

---

[71] Fortin (2006), 311–12.
[72] Campbell (1992).
[73] See also Fortin (2004), 259–60.

M. Freeman, 'Taking Children's Rights More Seriously', (1992) 6 *International Journal of Law and the Family* **52, 67–9**

[W]hat is to be regarded as 'irrational' must be strictly confined. The subjective values of the would-be protector cannot be allowed to intrude...Nor should we see an action as irrational unless it is manifestly so in the sense that it would undermine future life choices, impair interests in an irreversible way. Furthermore, we must tolerate mistakes...But we also would be failing to recognize a child's integrity if we allowed him to choose an action, such as using heroin or choosing not to attend school, which could seriously and systematically impair the attainment of full personality and development subsequently. The test of 'irrationality' must also be confined so that it justifies intervention only to the extent necessary to obviate the immediate harm, or to develop the capacities of rational choice by which the individual may have a reasonable chance of avoiding such harms.

The question we should ask ourselves is: what sort of action or conduct would we wish, as children, to be shielded against on the assumption that we would want to mature to a rationally autonomous adulthood and be capable of deciding on our own system of ends as free and rational beings? We would, I believe, choose principles that would enable children to mature to independent adulthood. One definition of irrationality would be such as to preclude action and conduct which would frustrate such a goal. Within the constraints of such a definition we would defend a version of paternalism: not paternalism in its classical sense for, so conceived, there would be no children's rights at all...

To take children's rights more seriously requires us to take seriously nurturance and self-determination. It demands of us that we adopt policies, practices, structures and laws which both protect children and their rights. Hence the *via media* of 'liberal paternalism'.

Whichever theory of rights is preferred, it is difficult to escape the attractions of adult paternalism. And, perhaps not surprisingly, this will emerge as a dominant theme as we explore the current approach to children's rights in English law.

8.5.3 THE DEVELOPMENT OF CHILDREN'S RIGHTS IN ENGLISH LAW

The emancipation of children from the control of their fathers

The twentieth century witnessed a fundamental shift in understanding about the parent–child relationship. At the turn of the nineteenth century, this relationship was governed by the historic concept of 'guardianship', which conferred on the father of his legitimate children complete authority over their person and property.[74] By the early part of the twentieth century, 'paternal authority' had been transformed into 'parental authority', but the nature of the parent–child relationship had not undergone significant change.[75] Parents were understood to possess all the necessary power and authority over a child that would enable them to control every aspect of the child's upbringing. This power and authority

---

[74] *In re Agar-Ellis* (1883) 24 Ch D 317.

[75] The statutory process of placing mothers in a position of equality with fathers began with the Guardianship of Infants Act 1886, s 5.

was enshrined in the parental right or bundle of rights often simply referred to as the 'right to custody and control'. The primary concern of the law was to protect this right from any outside interference.

During the twentieth century, attitudes towards children began to change with important consequences for the parent–child relationship. Growing concern with the welfare of children initiated the gradual liberation of children from their parents, with the result that children were no longer regarded as their parents' possessions. The control and authority that parents enjoyed over their children was gradually replaced with the embryonic idea that children were also autonomous individuals with enforceable rights of their own. The emerging concept of children's rights had far-reaching significance for the concept of parenthood. If children possess rights then somebody must hold the corresponding duty or responsibility to protect them. That person is the parent. It is these duties and responsibilities that now dominate the concept of parenthood in English law.[76]

Whilst the general concept of parental rights is currently undergoing a certain renaissance, the parental right to custody and control has been fundamentally transformed. This right is now understood as a *conditional* right. It inheres for the benefit of the child and not the parent.[77] Thus, the right to custody and control is of only instrumental value: that is, it exists only insofar as necessary for the fulfilment of parental duties. This understanding of the relationship between children's rights and parental rights and duties was usefully summarized by L'Heureux-Dubé J in the Canadian Supreme Court.

Young v Young [1993] 4 SCR 3

L'HEUREUX-DUBÉ J:

The power of the custodial parent is not a "right" with independent value which is granted by the courts for the benefit of the parent, but is designed to enable that parent to discharge his or her responsibilities and obligations to the child. It is, in fact, the child's right to a parent who will look after his or her best interests...It has long been recognized that the custodial parent has a duty to ensure, protect and promote the best interests of the child. That duty includes the sole and primary responsibility to oversee all aspects of day to day life and long-term well-being, as well as major decisions with respect to education, religion, health and well-being.

It is this view of parenthood which underpins the House of Lords' decision in *Gillick v West Norfolk and Wisbech Area Health Authority*,[78] discussed below. As will be seen, it has important implications as to the scope of the parents' decision-making authority within the parent–child relationship.

---

[76] See chapter 10.

[77] This contrasts with parental rights as enshrined in Art 8 ECHR which are properly conceptualized as autonomous rights which inhere for the benefit of the parent.

[78] [1986] AC 112.

8.5.4 CHILDREN'S RIGHTS IN THE COURTS

Children's welfare-based rights to care and protection

The courts have had less difficulty embracing children's rights where there is no inconsistency between the child's rights and the child's welfare. To talk of a child's right to be protected from parental abuse or neglect, or to be provided with the basic necessities of life, is uncontentious and raises no challenge to a welfare-orientated approach. Thus, where the issue relates to a young child's health and safety, such as whether a child should be tested for HIV, the judiciary have comfortably employed the language of welfare and rights interchangeably.[79]

Children's autonomy rights

The Gillick decision

As expected, the real test of judicial commitment to children's rights came in a case which raised the more challenging issue of a child's right to self-determination.[80] *Gillick* concerned a challenge to a memorandum of guidance issued by central government to local health authorities containing a section on the provision of contraceptive advice and treatment to children under the age of 16. In essence, the guidance suggested that contraceptive advice and treatment could be provided without informing the child's parents or obtaining parental consent. Mrs Gillick, a mother of five girls, wrote to her local health authority requesting assurance that no contraceptive advice or treatment would be given to any of her daughters whilst under the age of 16 without her knowledge and consent. The health authority refused to give such assurance arguing that in accordance with the central guidance, such a decision would be a matter of clinical judgement for the individual doctor. Mrs Gillick consequently sought a declaration that the guidance was unlawful, in particular, that it unlawfully interfered with her parental rights and duties. The House of Lords, by a majority, dismissed her complaint:

Gillick v West Norfolk and Wisbech Area Health Authority [1986] AC 112, 166–75, 181–90

LORD FRASER:

[P]arental rights to control a child do not exist for the benefit of the parent. They exist for the benefit of the child and they are justified only in so far as they enable the parent to perform his duties towards the child, and towards other children in the family . . .

From the parents' right and duty of custody flows their right and duty of control of the child, but the fact that custody is its origin throws but little light on the question of the legal extent of control at any particular age . . .

---

[79] See, e.g., *Re C (HIV Test)* [1999] 2 FLR 1004, 1016 and 1021 and *R v Secretary of State for Education and Employment and others, ex parte Williamson* [2005] UKHL 15. Fortin provides a somewhat more pessimistic analysis. See Fortin (2006), 300–3.

[80] See generally, Fortin (2009b), ch 5.

It is, in my view, contrary to the ordinary experience of mankind, at least in Western Europe in the present century, to say that a child or a young person remains in fact under the complete control of his parents until he attains the definite age of majority, now 18 in the United Kingdom, and that on attaining that age he suddenly acquires independence. In practice most wise parents relax their control gradually as the child develops and encourage him or her to become increasingly independent. Moreover, the degree of parental control actually exercised over a particular child does in practice vary considerably according to his understanding and intelligence and it would, in my opinion, be unrealistic for the courts not to recognise these facts. Social customs change, and the law ought to, and does in fact, have regard to such changes when they are of major importance...

[T]he view that the child's intellectual ability is irrelevant cannot, in my opinion, now be accepted. It is a question of fact for the judge (or jury) to decide whether a particular child can give effective consent to contraceptive treatment.

In times gone by the father had almost absolute authority over his children until they attained majority....

Once the rule of the parents' absolute authority over minor children is abandoned, the solution to the problem in this appeal can no longer be found by referring to rigid parental rights at any particular age. The solution depends upon a judgment of what is best for the welfare of the particular child. Nobody doubts, certainly I do not doubt, that in the overwhelming majority of cases the best judges of a child's welfare are his or her parents. Nor do I doubt that any important medical treatment of a child under 16 would normally only be carried out with the parents' approval. That is why it would and should be "most unusual" for a doctor to advise a child without the knowledge and consent of the parents on contraceptive matters. But, as I have already pointed out, Mrs. Gillick has to go further if she is to obtain the first declaration that she seeks. She has to justify the absolute right of veto in a parent. But there may be circumstances in which a doctor is a better judge of the medical advice and treatment which will conduce to a girl's welfare than her parents...

The only practicable course is to entrust the doctor with a discretion to act in accordance with his view of what is best in the interests of the girl who is his patient. He should, of course, always seek to persuade her to tell her parents that she is seeking contraceptive advice, and the nature of the advice that she receives. At least he should seek to persuade her to agree to the doctor's informing the parents. But there may well be cases, and I think there will be some cases, where the girl refuses either to tell the parents herself or to permit the doctor to do so and in such cases, the doctor will, in my opinion, be justified in proceeding without the parents' consent or even knowledge provided he is satisfied on the following matters: (1) that the girl (although under 16 years of age) will understand his advice; (2) that he cannot persuade her to inform her parents or to allow him to inform the parents that she is seeking contraceptive advice; (3) that she is very likely to begin or to continue having sexual intercourse with or without contraceptive treatment; (4) that unless she receives contraceptive advice or treatment her physical or mental health or both are likely to suffer; (5) that her best interests require him to give her contraceptive advice, treatment or both without the parental consent...For those reasons I do not consider that the guidance interferes with the parents' rights.

LORD SCARMAN:

Parental right and the age of consent...

Parental rights clearly do exist, and they do not wholly disappear until the age of majority. Parental rights relate to both the person and the property of the child...But the common law has never treated such rights as sovereign or beyond review and control. Nor has our law ever treated the child as other than a person with capacities and rights recognised by law. The principle of the law, as I shall endeavour to show, is that parental rights are derived from parental duty and exist only so long as they are needed for the protection of the person and property of the child. The principle has been subjected to certain age limits set by statute for certain purposes: and in some cases the courts have declared an age of discretion at which a child acquires before the age of majority the right to make his (or her) own decision. But these limitations in no way undermine the principle of the law, and should not be allowed to obscure it.

Let me make good, quite shortly, the proposition of principle.

First... when a court has before it a question as to the care and upbringing of a child it must treat the welfare of the child as the paramount consideration in determining the order to be made. There is here a principle which limits and governs the exercise of parental rights of custody, care and control. It is a principle perfectly consistent with the law's recognition of the parent as the natural guardian of the child; but it is also a warning that parental right must be exercised in accordance with the welfare principle and can be challenged, even overridden, if it be not.

Secondly, there is the common law's understanding of the nature of parental right... It is abundantly plain that the law recognizes that there is a right and a duty of parents to determine whether or not to seek medical advice in respect of their child, and, having received advice, to give or withhold consent to medical treatment. The question in the appeal is as to the extent, and duration, of the right and the circumstances in which... it can be overridden by the exercise of medical judgment...

The principle is that parental right or power of control of the person and property of his child exists primarily to enable the parent to discharge his duty of maintenance, protection and education until he reaches such an age as to be able to look after himself and make his own decisions.... Although statute has intervened in respect of a child's capacity to consent to medical treatment from the age of 16 onwards, neither statute nor the case law has ruled on the extent and duration of parental right in respect of children under the age of 16. More specifically, there is no rule yet applied to contraceptive treatment... It is open, therefore, to the House to formulate a rule. The Court of Appeal favoured a fixed age limit of 16... They sought to justify the limit by the public interest in the law being certain. Certainty is always an advantage in the law, and in some branches of the law it is a necessity. But it brings with it an inflexibility and a rigidity which in some branches of the law can obstruct justice, impede the law's development, and stamp upon the law the mark of obsolescence where what is needed is the capacity for development. The law relating to parent and child is concerned with the problems of the growth and maturity of the human personality. If the law should impose upon the process of "growing up" fixed limits where nature knows only a continuous process, the price would be artificiality and a lack of realism in an area where the law must be sensitive to human development and social change. If certainty be thought desirable, it is better that the rigid demarcations necessary to achieve it should be laid down by legislation after a full consideration of all the relevant factors than by the courts confined as they are by the forensic process to the evidence adduced by the parties and to whatever may properly fall within the judicial notice of judges. Unless and until Parliament should think fit to intervene, the courts should establish a principle flexible enough to enable justice to be achieved by its application to the particular circumstances proved by the evidence placed before them.

The underlying principle of the law was exposed by Blackstone and can be seen to have been acknowledged in the case law. It is that parental right yields to the child's right to make his own decisions when he reaches a sufficient understanding and intelligence to be capable of making up his own mind on the matter requiring decision...

In the light of the foregoing I would hold that as a matter of law the parental right to determine whether or not their minor child below the age of 16 will have medical treatment terminates if and when the child achieves a sufficient understanding and intelligence to enable him or her to understand fully what is proposed. It will be a question of fact whether a child seeking advice has sufficient understanding of what is involved to give a consent valid in law. Until the child achieves the capacity to consent, the parental right to make the decision continues save only in exceptional circumstances...

I am, therefore, satisfied that the department's guidance can be followed without involving the doctor in any infringement of parental right.

[On the issue of consent and the purported interference with parental rights and duties, **Lord Bridge** agreed with both **Lord Fraser** and **Lord Scarman**.]

It is difficult to discern the ratio of *Gillick* on the question of the existence and scope of children's rights vis-à-vis the rights of the parents. The issue has sparked considerable academic debate. However, both Lord Fraser and Lord Scarman appear to confirm that the parental right to custody and control is wholly derived from the parents' duties and responsibilities to the child and thus depends on the continuing existence of those duties. Furthermore, they hold that the parental right to custody and control is forever dwindling and diminishing in importance as the child grows older because, as children mature, they become increasingly capable of exercising their own rights and decision-making powers. It follows logically from this that parents' rights cannot be ascertained by reference to any particular fixed age, but depend on the degree of intelligence and understanding of the child in question. Essentially, the question is whether the child has sufficient maturity to make his or her own decisions. Lord Scarman also appears to go one step further than Lord Fraser in holding in unequivocal terms that the child's right and the corresponding parental right cannot coexist. He thus suggests that parents' and children's rights exist on a continuum such that once a child reaches the required level of 'Gillick competency', the purpose behind the parental right is exhausted and must yield to the right of the child.

For children's rights advocates, Lord Scarman's judgment seemed to hold enormous promise. An interpretation of the *Gillick* decision in line with his judgment would significantly erode parental authority and control over children, particularly as they enter their teenage years. For this reason, many commentators hailed *Gillick* as a landmark decision in securing children's basic autonomy rights. In line with the power or will theory, Lord Scarman's approach suggested that as soon as children were deemed to have the necessary rational will, they would be regarded as autonomous rights-holders, able to make decisions free from parental control.

However, to champion children's autonomy when it enables the child to make decisions many would deem in the child's best interests, such as receiving confidential contraceptive advice and treatment before embarking on a sexual relationship, is one thing. To continue to champion that right when the child is refusing life-saving treatment is more difficult, even for the most ardent 'child liberationist'.

It is perhaps for this reason that the more radical interpretation of *Gillick* and its promise of delivering real autonomy for older children has not been realized. In what many regard as a retreat from *Gillick*, children's autonomy rights have been consistently qualified by a return to a more paternalistic approach, swinging the scales heavily back in favour of protecting parental authority.

The retreat from Gillick

The first sign that *Gillick* would be subjected to a conservative application came in *Re E (A Minor) (Wardship: Medical Treatment)*.[81] *Re E* concerned a 15-year-old boy ['A'] with leukaemia who urgently required a blood transfusion. Both the boy and his parents were devout Jehovah's Witnesses and therefore refused to consent to treatment, blood transfusions being contrary to the tenets of their faith. Ward J accepted that a *Gillick* competent child could validly withhold consent to treatment. However, he avoided the difficult consequences of such a conclusion by refusing to find that the child had sufficient understanding and maturity to be regarded as *Gillick* competent, despite his 'obvious intelligence'. The child was thus deemed incapable of refusing treatment.

Re E (A Minor) (Wardship: Medical Treatment) [1992] 2 FCR 219, 224–7

WARD J:

I am quite satisfied that A does not have any sufficient comprehension of the pain he has yet to suffer, of the fear that he will be undergoing, of the distress not only occasioned by that fear but also—and importantly—the distress he will inevitably suffer as he, a loving son, helplessly watches his parents' and his family's distress. They are a close family, and they are a brave family, but I find that he has no realization of the full implications which lie before him as to the process of dying. He may have some concept of the fact that he will die, but as to the manner of his death and to the extent of his and his family's suffering I find he has not the ability to turn his mind to it nor the will to do so. Who can blame him for that?

If, therefore, this case depended upon my finding of whether or not A is of sufficient understanding and intelligence and maturity to give full and informed consent, I find that he is not.

The boy who was the subject of the application in *Re E* refused to give his consent to continuing treatment upon reaching the age of 18 and died shortly thereafter.[82]

The next important 'blow' to *Gillick*'s effectiveness as a vehicle for protecting children's autonomy rights came in *Re R (A Minor) (Wardship: Consent to Treatment)*. The *Gillick* decision concerned the right of a minor to *consent* to medical treatment and the relationship between the child's right of consent and that of the parents. It did not specifically address two further questions: (i) the right of a minor to *refuse* medical treatment and the relationship between the child's and the parents' right of refusal; and (ii) the child's rights vis-à-vis the power of the court under its inherent jurisdiction.[83] Both of these questions were addressed by Lord Donaldson MR in the Court of Appeal in *Re R* and on both questions Lord Donaldson MR, giving the lead judgment, sanctioned strong paternalistic intervention where necessary.[84] *Re R* concerned a disturbed 15-year-old girl who was suffering from a psychotic illness manifesting itself from time to time in periods of violence, paranoia, hallucinations, and suicidal tendencies. When rational and stable she refused to consent to anti-psychotic drugs being administered to her. On the question of whether

---

[81] [1992] 2 FCR 219.

[82] Fortin (2009b), 154.

[83] We discuss the inherent jurisdiction of the High Court at 8.7.

[84] For excellent discussion of this decision, see Fortin (2009b), 155–8.

her refusal to consent to treatment should be treated as determinative of the matter, Lord Donaldson held that it could not be.

Re R (A Minor) (Wardship: Consent to Treatment) [1992] Fam 11 (CA), 22–6

LORD DONALDSON MR:

It is trite law that in general a doctor is not entitled to treat a patient without the consent of someone who is authorised to give that consent. If he does so, he will be liable in damages for trespass to the person and may be guilty of a criminal assault. This is subject to the necessary exception that in cases of emergency a doctor may treat the patient notwith-standing the absence of consent, if the patient is unconscious or otherwise incapable of giving or refusing consent and there is no one else sufficiently immediately available with authority to consent on behalf of the patient. However consent by itself creates no obliga-tion to treat. It is merely a key which unlocks a door. Furthermore, whilst in the case of an adult of full capacity there will usually only be one keyholder, namely the patient, in the ordinary family unit where a young child is the patient there will be two keyholders, namely the parents, with a several as well as a joint right to turn the key and unlock the door. If the parents disagree, one consenting and the other refusing, the doctor will be presented with a professional and ethical, but not with a legal, problem because, if he has consent of one authorised person, treatment will not without more constitute a trespass or a criminal assault...

In the instant appeal [counsel], appearing for the Official Solicitor, submits that (a) if the child has the right to give consent to medical treatment, the parents' right to give or refuse consent is terminated and (b) the court in the exercise of its wardship jurisdiction is only entitled to step into the shoes of the parents and thus itself has no right to give or refuse consent....

The key passages upon which counsel relies are to be found in the speech of Lord Scarman...

What [counsel's] argument overlooks is that Lord Scarman was discussing the parent's right "to *determine* whether or not their minor child below the age of 16 will have medi-cal treatment"...A right of determination is wider than a right to consent. The parents can only have a right of determination if *either* the child has no right to consent, that is, is not a keyholder, *or* the parents hold a master key which could nullify the child's consent. I do not understand Lord Scarman to be saying that, if a child was "*Gillick* competent", to adopt the convenient phrase used in argument, the parents ceased to have an independent right of con-sent as contrasted with ceasing to have a right of determination, that is, a veto. In a case in which the "*Gillick* competent" child refuses treatment, but the parents consent, that consent *enables* treatment to be undertaken lawfully, but in no way determines that the child shall be so treated. In a case in which the positions are reversed, it is the child's consent which is the enabling factor and again the parents' refusal of consent is not determinative. If Lord Scarman intended to go further than this and to say that in the case of a "*Gillick* competent" child, a parent has no right either to consent or to refuse consent, his remarks were obiter, because the only question in issue was Mrs. Gillick's alleged right of veto. Furthermore I con-sider that they would have been wrong.

One glance at the consequences suffices to show that Lord Scarman cannot have been intending to say that the parental right to consent terminates with the achievement by the child of "*Gillick* competence". It is fundamental to the speeches of the majority that the capacity to consent will vary from child to child and according to the treatment under consideration, depending upon the sufficiency of his or her intelligence and understanding of that treatment. If the position in law is that upon the achievement of "*Gillick* competence" there is a transfer of the right of consent from parents to child and there can never be a concurrent right in both, doctors would be faced with an intolerable dilemma, particularly when the child was nearing the age of 16, if the parents consented, but the child did not....I do not believe that that is the law...

Both in this case and in *In Re E*, the judges treated *Gillick*...as deciding that a "*Gillick* competent" child has a right to refuse treatment. In this I consider that they were in error. Such a child can consent, but if he or she declines to do so or refuses, consent can be given by someone else who has parental rights or responsibilities. The failure or refusal of the "*Gillick* competent" child is a very important factor in the doctor's decision whether or not to treat, but does not prevent the necessary consent being obtained from another competent source.

The wardship jurisdiction

In considering the wardship jurisdiction of the court, no assistance is to be derived from *Gillick*'s case, where this simply was not in issue...It is, however, clear that the practical jurisdiction of the court is wider than that of parents...It is also clear that this jurisdiction is not derivative from the parents' rights and responsibilities, but derives from, or is, the delegated performance of the duties of the Crown to protect its subjects and particularly children who are the generations of the future.

...I see no reason whatsoever why [the court exercising its wardship powers] should not be able, and in an appropriate case willing, to override decisions by "*Gillick* competent" children who are its wards or in respect of whom applications are made...

Conclusion

1. No doctor can be required to treat a child, whether by the court in the exercise of its wardship jurisdiction, by the parents, by the child or anyone else. The decision whether to treat is dependent upon an exercise of his own professional judgment, subject only to the threshold requirement that, save in exceptional cases usually of emergency, he has the consent of someone who has authority to give that consent. In forming that judgment the views and wishes of the child are a factor whose importance increases with the increase in the child's intelligence and understanding.

2. There can be concurrent powers to consent. If more than one body or person has a power to consent, only a failure to, or refusal of, consent by all having that power will create a veto.

3. A "*Gillick* competent" child or one over the age of 16 will have a power to consent, but this will be concurrent with that of a parent or guardian.

4. "*Gillick* competence" is a developmental concept and will not be lost or acquired on a day to day or week to week basis....

5. The court in the exercise of its wardship or statutory jurisdiction has power to override the decisions of a "*Gillick* competent" child as much as those of parents or guardians....

[**Staughton LJ** expressed no opinion on the question of whether the parent's right to consent to treatment continued to exist alongside that of the competent child but agreed with **Donaldson MR** as to the scope of the court's inherent jurisdiction. **Farquharson LJ** decided the case on the basis that the child lacked *Gillick* competency.]

Lord Donaldson's judgment in *Re R* makes two points clear. First, a *Gillick* competent child has no right to veto treatment: parents do not lose their independent right to consent upon the child becoming *Gillick* competent—the two rights coexist. This means that provided the doctor obtains the consent of either the child or the parent, the treatment can proceed.[85] Secondly, the court exercising its inherent jurisdiction can override both the child and the parents. Consequently, even if both a *Gillick* competent child and the parents refuse treatment, the court acting in the child's best interests can grant permission for the treatment to proceed.

The strong swing back in favour of paternalism, even in the case of *Gillick* competent children or children over the age of 16, was taken a step further by Lord Donaldson in *Re W (A Minor) (Medical Treatment: Court's Jurisdiction)*.[86] In this case, Lord Donaldson held that, despite a 16-year-old having a clear statutory right to consent to treatment under s 8 of the Family Law Reform Act 1969 (FLRA 1969), a 16-year-old's *refusal* to consent could be overridden by anyone holding parental responsibility or the court.

More recent judgments appear to have adopted something of a middle ground. The Court of Appeal in *Wyatt v Portsmouth NHS Trust*[87] suggested that the 'intellectual milestones' in a case involving potential medical treatment were simple, even though the decision itself would often be very difficult.[88] Wall LJ, giving the judgment of the court, noted the paramountcy of the child's welfare and suggested a number of considerations.[89] First, the issue should be addressed from the perspective of the patient. Secondly, there is a 'strong presumption' in favour of treatment which prolongs the child's life, but that presumption is not irrebuttable. Thirdly, best interests must be holistic, including both medical and emotional issues. All these factors would need to be balanced by the judge in determining the best outcome. It may be noted that this list of considerations gives little, if any, attention to the child's own views, other than that the process is conducted 'from the assumed point of view of the patient'. Moreover, the cases applying this approach appear to continue to favour treatment even when it is strongly opposed by the adolescent patient.[90]

The wider significance of *Gillick*

In many ways, the post-*Gillick* era was disappointing for children's rights advocates, particularly regarding control over medical treatment. However, the conservatism shown in these difficult 'life and death' cases should not obscure the wider significance of *Gillick*. Freed from the acute circumstances of the medical cases, *Gillick* fundamentally transformed the way the law thought about children and parenthood, with the concept of '*Gillick* competency' providing a touchstone for children's rights to self-determination. Two decisions in the mid-2000s exemplify the extent to which the concept of children's autonomy rights have now taken hold in the law.

The first case concerned an application by three teenage children to be separately represented in private law proceedings between their parents.[91] The judge dismissed the

---

[85] Applied in *Re K, W and H (Minors) (Medical Treatment)* [1993] 1 FLR 854.

[86] [1993] Fam 64. For a partial defence of *Re W* and *Re R*, see Gilmore and Herring (2011), where the authors draw a distinction between a refusal to consent and a refusal of treatment. For a response, suggesting that this approach is unworkable in practice, see Cave and Wallbank (2012).

[87] [2005] EWCA Civ 1181.

[88] Compare the list of considerations set out by Abella J in the Supreme Court of Canada: *AC v Manitoba (Director of Child and Family Services)* [2009] SCC 30.

[89] Ibid, [87].

[90] Ibid; see also *Re A (A Child)* [2014] EWHC 920.

[91] See further 11.3.3.

application. The Court of Appeal overturned the decision, Thorpe LJ placing significant emphasis on the children's right to freedom of expression and participation, even if such participation was contrary to the court's judgment on welfare.[92]

Mabon v Mabon [2005] EWCA Civ 634

THORPE LJ:

25.... In our system we have traditionally adopted the tandem model for the representation of children who are parties to family proceedings, whether public or private. First the court appoints a guardian ad litem who will almost invariably have a social work qualification and very wide experience of family proceedings. He then instructs a specialist family solicitor who, in turn, usually instructs a specialist family barrister. This is a Rolls Royce model and is the envy of many other jurisdictions. However its overall approach is essentially paternalistic. The guardian's first priority is to advocate the welfare of the child he represents. His second priority is to put before the court the child's wishes and feelings. Those priorities can in some cases conflict. In extreme cases the conflict is unmanageable. That reality is recognised by the terms of rule 9.2A.[93] The direction set by rule 9.2A(6) is a mandatory grant of the application provided that the court considers "that the minor concerned has sufficient understanding to participate as a party in the proceedings concerned." Thus the focus is upon the sufficiency of the child's understanding in the context of the remaining proceedings....

29. In testing the sufficiency of a child's understanding I would not say that welfare has no place. If direct participation would pose an obvious risk of harm to the child arising out of the nature of the continuing proceedings and, if the child is incapable of comprehending that risk, then the judge is entitled to find that sufficient understanding has not been demonstrated. But judges have to be equally alive to the risk of emotional harm that might arise from denying the child knowledge of and participation in the continuing proceedings...

32. In conclusion this case provides a timely opportunity to recognise the growing acknowledgement of the autonomy and consequential rights of children, both nationally and internationally.... [94]

The second case posed a direct threat to the *Gillick* decision. The case concerned DOH guidance published in 2004 regarding confidentiality attaching to advice and treatment given to a child under 16 on sexual matters, including contraception, sexually transmitted infections, and abortion. The guidance stated that in certain circumstances a doctor could provide advice and treatment to a child under 16 without first notifying the parents. The applicant challenged the legality of the guidance, arguing that it undermined the right and responsibility of parents to provide guidance, help, and support to their teenage children, as guaranteed by Article 8 ECHR. The applicant did not challenge the child's right to consent to treatment (the issue in *Gillick*). Her challenge was limited to her right as a parent to be notified should her daughter approach a doctor for advice and/or treatment, particularly on matters relating to abortion. Silber J dismissed the application, finding that he was bound by the decision of the House of Lords in *Gillick*. The importance of recognizing the child's

---

92 For a critique of the way in which the Court of Appeal draws a distinction between the children's rights and the children's welfare, see Fortin (2006), 310–12. Fuller extracts from *Mabon* are found below, pp 742.

93 Now Practice Direction 16A (2014), which is extracted at pp 741.

94 See also *Cambra v Jones and Jones* [2014] EWHC 913.

autonomy rights was again a prominent theme, with the provisions of the UNCRC given particular weight.

R (Axon) v Secretary of State for Health (Family Planning Association Intervening) [2006] EWHC 37

SILBER J:

64. It is appropriate to bear in mind that the ECHR attaches great value to the rights of children... Furthermore the ratification by the United Kingdom of the United Nations Convention on the Rights of the Child ("UNC") in November 1989 was significant as showing a desire to give children greater rights. The ECHR and the UNC show why the duty of confidence owed by a medical professional to a competent young person is a high one and which therefore should not be overridden except for a very powerful reason. In my view, although family factors are significant and cogent, they should not override the duty of confidentiality owed to the child...

76. ... It is appropriate at this stage to set out some of the relevant provisions of the UNC which was adopted in November 1989 and so post-dated *Gillick*. It has now been ratified by the United Kingdom...

Silber J then set out Articles 5, 12, and 16 of the UNCRC and referred to the decision of Thorpe LJ in *Mabon v Mabon* before continuing:

79. Although the facts in *Mabon* were very different from those in the present case, [Thorpe LJ's comments] do illustrate that the right of young people to make decisions about their own lives by themselves at the expense of the views of their parents has now become an increasingly important and accepted feature of family life...

80. In the light of this change in the landscape of family matters, in which rights of children are becoming increasingly important, it would be ironic and indeed not acceptable now to retreat from the approach adopted in *Gillick* and to impose additional new duties on medical professionals to disclose information to parents of their younger patients.

On the question of whether the DOH guidance violated the rights of the parent under Article 8 ECHR, Silber J applied the 'dwindling right' analysis to conclude that the parent's Article 8 rights would yield upon the child acquiring sufficient maturity and understanding to make his or her own decisions on such matters:

127. I am unable to accept [counsel's] contention that by permitting a medical professional to withhold information relating to advice or treatment of a young person on sexual matters, the article 8 rights of the parents of the young person were thereby infringed...

128. In order to decide whether parents have what [counsel] describes as "the right to parental authority over a child" having regard to their having parental duties, the age and maturity of the young person is of critical importance. ...[A]ny right to family life on the part of a parent dwindles as their child gets older and is able to understand the consequence of different choices and then to make decisions relating to them.

130. As a matter of principle, it is difficult to see why a parent should still retain an article 8 right to parental authority relating to a medical decision where the young person concerned understands the advice provided by the medical professional and its implications. Indeed,

any right under article 8 of a parent to be notified of advice or treatment of a sexual matter as part of the right claimed by [counsel] must depend on a number of factors, such as the age and understanding of their offspring. The parent would not be able to claim such an article 8 right to be notified if their son or daughter was, say, 18 years of age and had sought medical advice on sexual matters because in that case the young person was able to consent without parental knowledge or consent... The reason why the parent could not claim such a right is that their right to participate in decision-making as part of the right claimed by [counsel] would only exist while the child was so immature that his parent had the right of control... Lord Fraser and Lord Scarman in *Gillick*... both adopted the statement of Lord Denning MR *in Hewer v Bryant* [1970]... that the parent's right as against a child is "a dwindling right". As Lord Scarman explained, a parental right yields to the young person's right to make his own decisions when the young person reaches a sufficient understanding and intelligence to be capable of making up his or her own mind in relation to a matter requiring decision... and this autonomy of a young person must undermine any article 8 rights of a parent to family life. In my view, any article 8 right of the kind advocated by [counsel] must be seen in that light so that once the child is sufficiently mature in this way, the parent only retains such rights to family life and to be notified about medical treatment if but only if the young person so wishes....

132. There is nothing in the Strasbourg jurisprudence, which persuades me that any parental right or power of control under article 8 is wider than in domestic law, which is that the right of parents in the words of Lord Scarman "exists primarily to enable the parent to discharge his duty of maintenance, protection and education until he reaches such an age as to be able to look after himself and make his own decisions"... The parental right to family life does not continue after that time and so parents do not have article 8 rights to be notified of any advice of a medical professional after the young person is able to look after himself or herself and make his or her own decisions.

Children's rights are thus gradually becoming an accepted part of everyday discourse in the family courts. However, of crucial importance to the development of this discourse is the way in which children's rights are perceived and implemented under the HRA 1998.

8.5.5 CHILDREN'S RIGHTS AND THE ECHR

Children have rights under the ECHR in the same way as adults. Of the greatest potential significance in protecting the welfare and autonomy rights of children are Articles 3 (the right not to be subjected to torture or to inhuman or degrading treatment), 5 (the right to liberty and security of the person), and 8 (the right to respect for private and family life).[95] Despite the judiciary remaining firmly wedded to the paramountcy principle as the best way of protecting children's interests against adult-centred concerns, talking in terms of children's rights rather than welfare is particularly important in an era of growing rights consciousness.[96] As understood under English law, rights are qualitatively different from other legal interests. In the words of Gavin Phillipson, 'rights have a special status'.[97] They have an assumed weight and importance. To talk of children's *rights* thus underlines

[95] For a detailed discussion of how rights protected under the HRA 1998 could strengthen the claims of autonomous teenagers, see Fortin (2006), 314–17, 320–1.
[96] For detailed discussion, see Fortin (2006).
[97] Phillipson (2003), 750.

their significance. This is essential given the current preoccupation with parents' rights under the ECHR. If parents' interests are to be routinely articulated in terms of rights, it is important that children's interests are similarly conceptualized. Otherwise, there is a danger that should the parents' and child's interests conflict (e.g. should parents claim the right to discipline their children using physical force in accordance with their religious beliefs), the child's interests (to physical and mental integrity) will be treated as somehow less weighty and important than those of the parents—as simply welfare-based exceptions to the parents' rights as opposed to rights with equal standing.[98] Children's rights, even in areas where the welfare approach would also apply, are thus important. They ensure that children's interests are taken equally seriously in the decision-making process.

One of the potential drawbacks in routinely articulating children's interests as rights is the potential complexity it introduces into the decision-making process. Most child-related disputes involve many potentially conflicting rights, both between the rights of the parents and child and between the child's own rights. Such conflicts should not, however, deter the courts from fully engaging with rights-based reasoning. Building on House of Lords authority in the sphere of media freedom,[99] academics have developed a 'discipline'—termed a 'parallel analysis'—to resolve such conflicts while seeking to give proper weight and value to all the rights engaged.[100]

As Fortin notes, 'the domestic courts have responded to the demands of the HRA in an extraordinarily haphazard manner when dealing with children's cases'.[101] However, it is not in children's interests for the courts to prevaricate on the question of children's rights. A rights-based approach has the potential to strengthen rather than weaken the court's focus on the child.[102] A principled, transparent, and fair approach to resolving inevitable conflicts of rights can be utilized. It is thus to be hoped that the limited and 'patchy' progress made by the courts in advancing children's interests through the discourse of rights in certain child-related disputes can be developed and extended into areas of child law that currently remain dominated by adult-centred concerns and perspectives on 'welfare'.[103]

8.6 NON-INTERVENTION IN PRIVATE FAMILY LIFE

The 'non-intervention' or 'no order' principle is central to the legislative scheme set out in the CA 1989.

Children Act 1989, s 1

(5) Where a court is considering whether or not to make one or more orders under this Act with respect to a child, it shall not make the order or any of the orders unless it considers that doing so would be better for the child than making no order at all.

---

[98] Fortin (2006), 310.
[99] Re S (A Child) (Identification: Restrictions on Publication) [2003] EWCA Civ 963; Campbell v MGN Ltd [2004] UKHL 47.
[100] See Choudhry and Fenwick (2005) and Fortin (2006).
[101] Fortin (2006), 300.
[102] Ibid, 313–14.
[103] Fortin (2004), 271; Fortin (2006).

While the application and interpretation of this provision in the courts has been some-what haphazard,[104] s 1(5) has commonly been interpreted to constitute a *presumption* against making formal orders in matters relating to the upbringing of children unless it can be positively shown that such an order is in the child's best interests. This inter-pretation could be a fundamentally important philosophical commitment to a particu-lar relationship between the family and the state.[105] Arguably inspired by the policies of the Thatcher era, in which a minimalist state and the self-sufficiency and auton-omy of the family unit were core ideals, it is argued that s 1(5) represents a policy of non-intervention in family life whereby parents are to be left to the task of raising their children free from scrutiny and intervention by the state. These aims are reflected in an article written by the Law Commissioner responsible for the reports which led to the Children Act.

B. Hoggett, 'The Children Bill: The Aim', (1989) 19 *Family Law* 217, 217–18

The Bill assumes that bringing up children is the responsibility of their parents and that the State's principal role is to help rather than to interfere. To emphasize the practical reality that bringing up children is a serious responsibility, rather than a matter of legal rights, the concep-tual building block used throughout the Bill is 'parental responsibility' . . . .

Non-intervention

In keeping with reinforcing rather than undermining parental responsibility, the Bill seeks to keep compulsory intervention to a minimum. Courts, therefore, should not make any order at all unless doing so would be better for the child than making none. In the public law sphere, this means that even if the required conditions for making a care order or a supervision order exist, the court has to ask itself what such an order will do to improve the child's overall welfare . . . .

In the private law sphere, it is intended to remove any assumption that the court should make an order simply because the parents are separated or divorced. Often, a custody order under the [pre-1989] law is seen as 'part of the package'.

While it is not without its critics,[106] a 'non-interventionist' approach to the family has deep foundations in legal and political thought. The principle is grounded in a certain belief about the family and its role in society, in particular, that parents are better placed than the state to know what is best for their children and therefore should be trusted to raise them as they see fit.[107] Allied to this strong faith in the institution of the family, those in favour of a non-interventionist approach (or what Lorraine Fox Harding terms a laissez-faire approach) often harbour a deep mistrust of the state and question the legitimacy of any purported interference into the privacy of family life.

---

[104] Bailey-Harris, Barron, and Pearce (1999); Harris and George (2010).
[105] Harris and George (2010), 154–5.
[106] See, e.g., Bainham (1998).
[107] *B(R) v Children's Aid Society of Metropolitan Toronto* [1995] 1 SCR 315.

L. Fox Harding, 'The Children Act 1989 in Context: Four Perspectives in Child Care Law and Policy (I)', (1991a) 13 *Journal of Social Welfare and Family Law* 179, 182–6

(1) Laissez-faire and patriarchy

Underlying the *laissez-faire* perspective lies a mistrust of the state and its powers. There is a strong undercurrent of feeling in this view that the state should in general keep out of certain "private" areas of citizens' lives, with restricted exceptions. In particular, domestic and family life are seen as a relatively private arena which should not be invaded by the agents of the state except with due cause, such cause usually being associated with criminality . . .

The most notable child care authors associated with the *laissez-faire* position are Goldstein *et. al.*, who set out their views in two works, *Beyond the Best Interests of the Child* and *Before the Best Interests of the Child*. In the earlier work, the authors used psychoanalytical theory to develop child placement guidelines which would safeguard the child's psychological needs. Of importance were two "value preferences": that the law must make the child's needs paramount, and a value preference for privacy and minimum state intervention. This stems from the need to safeguard the child's need for continuity, and therefore to safeguard the right of parents to raise their children as they see fit, free of state intrusion, except in cases of neglect and abandonment. The value preference is reinforced by the view that the law is a crude instrument, incapable of effectively managing complex parent-child relationships.

. . . In their later work, *Before the Best Interests of the Child*, they developed further their theme of parental control undisturbed by state intervention except in extreme cases. The question posed in their book is essentially when the state *is* justified in overriding the autonomy of families. They consider that: "the child's need for safety within the confines of the family must be met by law through its recognition of family privacy as the barrier to state intrusion upon parental autonomy in child rearing". The authors' position is that "A policy of minimum coercive intervention by the state thus accords not only with our firm belief as citizens in individual freedom and human dignity, but also with our professional understanding of the intricate developmental processes of childhood". In every case the law should ask "whether removal from an unsatisfactory home is the beneficial measure it purports to be" . . .

The main elements of this perspective therefore appear to be a belief in the benefits for society of a minimum state which engages in only minimal intervention in families; and a complementary belief in the value to all, including children, of undisturbed family life where adults can get on with bringing up their children in their chosen way. It is argued that adults have a right to do this, and it is better for the children too. The bearing and rearing of a child produces a special bond between parents and child and it is damaging to disrupt it, though it is accepted that it may be necessary to do so *in extreme cases* to avert a greater evil . . .

It may be hypothesised that the thinking of the "new right" on autonomous (and probably patriarchal) families, and on the drawbacks of state intervention in general, had some influence, if only indirectly, on the non-intervention aspect of the [Children] Act. As already noted, it is consonant with other aspects of Conservative policy in the 1980s, and with new right ideology on the issues of family and state.

A non-interventionist approach to family life as enshrined in s 1(5) has important implications in both the public and private law context. A 'hands-off' approach to the family has perhaps the most obvious impact in public law proceedings aimed at protecting the child from parental neglect and abuse. The CA 1989 thus demands that a threshold of significant harm is crossed before state intervention can be justified.[108] In private law proceedings, a

---

[108] See chapter 12, esp 12.5.3.

non-interventionist approach is particularly important in the context of family breakdown. One manifestation of the 'privatizing' trend in family law has been the emphasis on promoting 'privately' negotiated agreements rather than relying on state-adjudicated outcomes.[109] However, the question is whether the state should intervene to regulate disputes over essentially 'private' matters where the parties have been able to reach their own agreement. If the state respects the privacy of the family when it is intact, can state intervention on the sole basis of the parent's separation be justified? In attempting to provide such justification, some commentators simply question whether parents can be trusted to promote the child's, as opposed to their own, best interests when the family is in crisis. It is argued that there is a legitimate public interest and even duty to protect the interests of children subject to the risks of family breakdown. Adopting this approach, the non-intervention principle not only compromises commitment to the welfare principle, particularly if the issue has been brought before the court, but is an irresponsible abdication of responsibility. Intervention to protect the child, even in the sphere of private family matters, is thus regarded as legitimate.

G. Douglas et al, 'Safeguarding Children's Welfare in Non-Contentious Divorce: Towards a New Conception of the Legal Process', (2000) 63 *Modern Law Review* 177, 179–80

As divorce has become increasingly common and the concept of 'parental responsibility' has come to underpin modern child law, the question of whether it is appropriate for the state, through the court, to scrutinise parents' decisions for their children in the absence of any dispute has been raised. One argument in favour of some sort of 'welfare check' is that given by Gerald Caplan:

By voluntarily approaching the courts to dissolve their marriage, parents explicitly open up their private domain to public scrutiny and intervention. Their request for divorce is a formal statement that their marriage has broken down and constitutes an invitation to the representatives of society to assess the consequences for themselves and their children . . .

But this view begs several questions. First, it by no means follows that, just because a couple seeks a divorce, they thereby willingly lay themselves open to state scrutiny. After all, there is no alternative to engaging with whatever is required of them by the legal system if they wish to obtain a licence to remarry. Secondly, no 'marker' is flagged up if parents merely separate and do not take divorce proceedings (or if the parents are unmarried), but the needs of the child may be no different. Thirdly, the form and efficacy of intervention must be assessed. 'Intervention' for its own sake may be at best, irrelevant and at worst, iatrogenic. Further, one must query whether, in the age of mass divorce, there are the resources to permit any meaningful and beneficial legal 'intervention' to occur. Indeed, one can trace over the last half century, a progressive withdrawal from any attempt to scrutinise divorces . . .

Nonetheless, there is very good reason for the state to be concerned about the interests of children when their parents' relationship breaks down and to use the legal system as well as other mechanisms and services, to try to address these. There is a considerable body of research evidence suggesting that children may face detrimental outcomes from parental separation and divorce . . . Given the level of divorce and separation in this country and the numbers of children affected, there is a strong justification in ensuring that social—and legal—policies and practices are designed to tackle and reduce this risk.

---

[109] See generally 1.2.7.

Bainham has expressed similar concern about the trend towards private ordering on divorce. He suggests a normative framework reflecting accepted societal standards should be enshrined within the law to guide the family in post-separation decision-making. In his view, the absence of such normative standards from the CA 1989 is a serious omission.

A. Bainham, 'The Privatisation of the Public Interest in Children', (1990) 53 *Modern Law Review* 206, 207 and 210–14

A basic philosophy enshrined in the 1989 Act is that the state's role in the family is a primarily supportive one and that it should not intervene at all unless it is necessary to do so. There is nothing in the reformed legislation which contradicts (and a great deal which supports) the notion that the family, and specifically child care, is an area which ought to remain unregulated by law unless the need for regulation can be positively demonstrated...

...I have no quarrel with either the intended marginalisation of the judicial role or with the view that child care arrangements brought about by agreement are more likely to work than those which result from attempts at compulsion. But I want to suggest that this scheme, by regarding private agreements as sacrosanct, fails to give adequate recognition to the *public* interest in children. In developing this argument it must be conceded that, on one interpretation, the Act has simply re-defined the public interest and has not diluted it. On this view, the public interest is seen as best served by facilitating parental agreements. In other words, the theory would be that it is in children's best interests (and consequently the public interest) that parents should agree on their future care. But...whichever way the policy shift is described there can be little doubt that an area which hitherto was thought appropriate for legal regulation will in future be substantially de-regulated.

The crucial point is that there has been no attempt in the legislation to influence the nature or content of parental agreements following divorce other than through the somewhat nebulous and indirect notion of continuing parental responsibility. Parental agreement would arguably have been a more acceptable means of meeting the public interest if the legislation had also established some normative standards for child rearing, both in the context of united families and on divorce, to act as a benchmark or basis for private ordering. Yet the legislation tells us nothing about what is involved in the discharge of parental responsibility...

It is disconcerting that the model apparently believed to be representative of what society considers desirable should be one in which private ordering is seen as an end in itself whatever the quality or nature of the agreements reached.

In practice, research carried out by Bailey-Harris, Barron, and Pearce suggests s 1(5) has received a mixed response from the judiciary.

R. Bailey-Harris, J. Barron, and J. Pearce, 'Settlement Culture and the Use of the "No Order" Principle under the Children Act 1989', (1999a) 11 *Child and Family Law Quarterly* 53, 59–61

[S]ection 1(5) receives a very mixed response in practice at county court level...[T]he evidence from our study could be interpreted as suggesting two themes. First, the 'no order principle' is invoked by judges to reinforce the concept of parental autonomy and the vigorous promotion of agreement, this results in the court declining or refusing to make an order even when parties have sought one. It is highly questionable whether this use of the principle accords with the original intention of the legislature, and we found that it could be productive of acute dissatisfaction on the part of parents who were expecting an adjudicated outcome. Secondly, and in complete contrast, the principle is very commonly breached or not observed by judges, particularly when legal practitioners press for resolution by consent order... Our file survey showed that, overall, a substantive order was made in 67 per cent of cases, no substantive order in 27 per cent, and an order of 'no order' in 5 per cent. The extent of non-observance of the principle by the courts we sampled is thus immediately apparent.

To pursue the first theme: it is possible to argue from the evidence of our study that in practice the courts are using the 'no order principle' in cases to which it was never intended to apply. In many cases where there is originally real conflict between parents who have invoked the court's jurisdiction specifically to resolve their dispute, the principle is invoked by judges to reinforce the promotion of parental autonomy and agreement as the preferred mode of resolution: the court asserts that no order is needed where parents can eventually agree, even though their preferred original intention was to obtain an order.

Our study reveals many examples of judges using the rhetoric of parental autonomy to justify the refusal to make an order, even in proceedings where there is real dispute and where proceedings are protracted...

There is considerable evidence of the dissatisfaction of parents with the outcome of 'no order' when they consider that they have invoked the court's jurisdiction precisely for the exercise of its authority in a matter which they find difficult to resolve themselves. In other words, the use of the 'no order' approach by the court to reinforce its promotion of parental autonomy is often at odds with parental expectations of the process...

8.7 THE INHERENT JURISDICTION OF THE HIGH COURT

In a very small minority of cases, the courts find that the statutory remedies that they have do not provide any way to deal with a problem that has arisen with regard to a child. One solution in exceptional cases is for a High Court judge to invoke what is called the inherent jurisdiction of the High Court. The inherent jurisdiction stems from the Crown's innate power and responsibility to protect its subjects, that power having been vested in the court. It is said that the power of the court under the inherent jurisdiction is theoretically limitless except where Parliament has imposed specific restrictions.[110] Now most commonly used in certain types of international case, the inherent jurisdiction can be invoked in many situations where no statutory remedy is available, and wide-ranging injunctions and other remedies are available.[111]

One common tool within the inherent jurisdiction is *wardship*. When a child becomes a ward of the court,[112] a number of immediate and important things happen. The child comes

---

[110] See, e.g., *Re E (SA) (A Minor) (Wardship)* [1984] 1 WLR 156.

[111] See, e.g., *JP v LP* [2014] EWHC 595 (orders regulating a surrogacy arrangement which fell outside the statutory scheme); *Birmingham City Council v Sarfraz Riaz* [2014] EWHC 4247 (injunctions to protect a 17-year-old girl from sexual exploitation).

[112] In fact, it is when someone makes an *application* for a child to be made a ward, since the court's protection applies even before a formal order is made.

under the jurisdiction of the court, and can be protected by all the powers that the court has. No significant decision about the child's upbringing can be made without the court's permission, and parental rights over the child are effectively superseded by the court's own powers. In exercising these powers, the child's welfare is the court's paramount concern, and the court must 'act in the way best suited in its judgment to serve the true interest and welfare of the ward', as Lord Scarman put it in *Re E (SA).*[113]

The CA 1989 cut the use of wardship very substantially. Prior to the Act, it had been common for local authorities to use wardship in child protection proceedings; s 100 of the CA 1989 radically limits this approach.[114] The creation of *prohibited steps orders* and *specific issue orders* under s 8 of the Act also created a statutory route which could often achieve the same practical outcome as wardship. Nonetheless, the court's inherent jurisdiction remains important in a number of circumstances.

 ONLINE RESOURCE CENTRE

We discuss the inherent jurisdiction of the High Court in more detail on the Online Resource Centre.

8.8 CONCLUSION

The various approaches to child-related disputes are not, of course, mutually exclusive. Finding an acceptable balance or compromise between them is one of the greatest challenges for family lawyers. From the following chapters it will be clear that, despite the recent trend towards a more rights-based culture in family law, the welfare principle predominates. However, despite this, parents' rights, children's rights, and a non-interventionist ethos are all important and will be evident, to varying degrees, in the discussion to follow. So, with these underlying principles in mind, we turn to our first substantive question: who are a child's legal parents?

 ONLINE RESOURCE CENTRE

Questions, suggestions for further reading, and supplementary materials for this chapter (including updates on developments in this area of family law since this book was published) may be found on the Online Resource Centre at **www.oxfordtextbooks.co.uk/orc/familytcm3e/.**

---

[113] [1984] 1 WLR 156.

[114] If a child who is already a ward is made the subject of a care order, the wardship immediately ceases: CA 1989, s 91(4).

9

BECOMING A LEGAL PARENT AND THE CONSEQUENCES OF LEGAL PARENTHOOD

CENTRAL ISSUES

1. There are many possible answers to the question 'who are a child's parents?' Genetic, gestational, and social parents may all have convincing claims to the status of 'legal parenthood'.

2. Legal parenthood confers a fundamentally important status on both parent and child, making the child a member of the parent's family and bringing with it a core bundle of rights and responsibilities.

3. In the context of natural procreation, the crucial factor in determining a child's legal parents is the genetic tie between parent and child. This is easily established in the case of the mother. Determining the identity of a child's genetic father is more difficult. Disputes focus today on whether scientific tests should be ordered to put the parentage of a child beyond doubt. Adopting both a rights-based and welfare approach, establishing genetic truth is now regarded as a centrally important consideration.

4. In the context of assisted reproduction, the intended social parents are generally accorded legal parenthood. Freed from biological constraints, this opens up a much more flexible concept of parenthood. For a long time, English law remained faithful to the heterosexual norm that a child should have one legal father and one legal mother. However, the Human Fertilisation and Embryology Act 2008 (HFEA 2008) revolutionized this position by allowing a child, from birth, to have two legal parents of the same sex.

5. Where genetic parentage does not coincide with legal parenthood, the continuing role of the genetic progenitors must be addressed. The right of donor-conceived children to information about their genetic background has been a particularly contentious issue.

6. Surrogacy remains a 'grey' area, neither condemned nor approved by law. Although the HFEA 2008 now facilitates surrogacy in a much wider range of circumstances, considerable uncertainty remains where the surrogacy arrangement breaks down.

9.1 INTRODUCTION

One might have thought becoming a parent was a relatively straightforward matter. Man meets woman, they embark upon a sexual relationship, woman becomes pregnant, and nine months later they become parents. However, even with the assistance of new fertility treatments, becoming a parent can be anything but straightforward and, whether or not one conceives through natural means, gaining legal recognition of one's status as a parent can prove an even more difficult and complicated process.

Who are a child's parents? If you posed this question to a group of passengers on the Clapham omnibus, you would probably elicit a wide variety of responses. One passenger might respond that it is the man and woman who are linked by blood to the child: the genetic parents. Another passenger might respond that it is the woman who gives birth to the child: the gestational mother, and perhaps her husband or partner.[1] Yet another passenger might respond that it is the people who intend to be the parents: the intentional parents. Another might suggest it is those who actually love, nurture, and care for the child: the social parents. The concept of parenthood and who should be regarded as a child's parents is thus a strongly contested question. Disagreement as to the identity of a child's parents may be further intensified when the question of assisted reproduction is raised. The passengers who confidently asserted that the blood tie should form the basis for determining parenthood may feel less sure of their position when the scenario of a married couple receiving fertility treatment using donated sperm (termed 'artificial insemination by donor', or AID) is put to them. Would our passengers still consider that the sperm donor, the person with the genetic link to the child, and not the husband receiving fertility treatment with his wife, should be regarded as the father? How would they respond to the challenges raised by surrogacy? Would they consider that the man and woman who can claim a genetic link to the child (who may or may not be the commissioning couple)[2] should be regarded as the parents? Would they remain of that view when faced with the possibility that the genetic and gestational mothers may be different? Would they now consider that the gestational, not the genetic, mother should prevail? Alternatively, could they both be recognized as the child's mother? Does the child have to be limited to just two legal parents? And do those legal parents have to be based on the heterosexual norm of one mother and one father?

And what are the legal consequences of all this? Passengers who think that the genetic tie should determine the identity of a child's parents may not agree that any legal rights and responsibilities should flow from that status. They may, for example, baulk at the idea that a man who raped a married woman, whilst correctly described as the father of any resulting child, should have any *legal* status in relation to the child. When pushed further, our passengers may again begin to waiver in their original conviction that it should be the person with the genetic tie, rather than the person who loves, nurtures, and cares for the child, who should be regarded in law as the parent. If, for example, the husband of the raped woman has accepted the child as his own and intends to raise the child, with his wife, as part of their family unit, should he not be accorded the legal rights and responsibilities of parenthood? One response to this dilemma would be to separate the status

---

[1] The genetic and/or gestational parents are often referred to as the 'natural' parents. Cf Baroness Hale's judgment in *Re G (Residence: Same-Sex Partner)* [2006] UKHL 43, [32]–[37] below where she includes social or intentional parents within this term.

[2] The couple for whom the surrogate carries the child.

of being a 'parent' from holding any legal rights and responsibilities with respect to the child. Could the law not recognize that several people may play different but complementary 'parenting' roles in relation to a child, with different legal rights and responsibilities attaching to each?

Our passengers may by now be feeling somewhat bewildered. These are complex and difficult questions. And they are questions that become increasingly difficult to answer as the diversity and fluidity in modern family life intensifies and innovations in assisted reproduction continue to stretch the boundaries of possibility. Asexual reproduction using only one genetic source is now within scientific reach. How long before we are pondering the identity of the parents of a cloned human embryo grown to term outside a woman's uterus? The fluidity of modern family life and the relentless march of 'scientific progress' will require us to find increasingly nuanced answers to the deceivingly simple question, who are a child's parents?

The principal aim of this chapter is to examine how one acquires the status of 'being a parent' under English law, what we shall refer to as 'legal parenthood'. We begin by examining differing concepts of 'parenthood' and possible approaches to determining legal parenthood. We then move on to consider the current legal framework for identifying a child's legal parents where a child is conceived through natural procreation, before examining the problems and challenges raised by use of assisted reproduction techniques, including surrogacy. Finally, we briefly consider adoption, a unique means of acquiring the legal status of parenthood under English law.[3]

9.2 CONCEPTS OF PARENTHOOD AND POSSIBLE APPROACHES TO DETERMINING LEGAL PARENTHOOD

9.2.1 WHAT IS A 'PARENT'?

Martin Johnson has identified four possible components to parenthood:

M. Johnson, 'A Biomedical Perspective on Parenthood', in A. Bainham, S. Day Sclater, and M. Richards (eds), *What Is a Parent? A Socio-Legal Analysis* (Oxford: Hart Publishing, 1999), 47–8

First there is a genetic component to parenthood. We now know that biologically the production of a viable human conceptus *requires* two distinctive subsets of chromosomes, one of which *must* be derived from a woman and the other from a man. The mother's egg alone also contributes a much smaller additional and essential chromosome (<1 per cent of total genetic material) in a non-nuclear structure called a mitochondrion, whilst the father's sperm contributes a non-chromosomal structure which is, however, essential for cell survival and proliferation in the embryo. Thus, genetic parents of both sexes are required and make non-equivalent contributions to their off-spring.

Secondly, there is a coital component to parenthood. Since fertilisation occurs inside the body, an act of coitus or mating is required between male and female...

---

[3] Adoption is considered in detail in chapter 13.

Thirdly, there is a gestational or uterine component to parenthood, which is exclusively the province of the female. The mother provides a uterus and there is accumulating evidence that her behaviour, mental state, diet and health during pregnancy may affect enduringly the health, traits and well-being of the child that is subsequently born. The tendency to overlook this important parental contribution to the child may have over-emphasised the significance of the genetic component to parenthood.

Finally, there is a post-natal component to parenthood. Higher primates such as humans transmit not just their genes, but also their culture from one generation to another. Post-natal parenthood is sometimes called "social parenthood", but since this component of parenthood has evolved it does have an important biological component to it.

These four aspects of parenthood—genetic, coital, gestational, and social—may be performed by various people. Leaving aside possible future developments in assisted reproduction, a child must currently have two genetic parents: one male and one female. In most cases, the child's genetic parents will have engaged in an act of coitus to achieve fertilization. However, the development of assisted reproduction techniques means that coitus is no longer an essential element of parenthood and may be absent in a significant minority of cases. In addition to two genetic parents, all children must have a gestational mother. Although the gestational mother will generally also be the genetic mother, the advent of in vitro fertilization (IVF) means that again this will not necessarily be the case. The possibility of using donated eggs (whether in the context of fertility treatment or for the purposes of surrogacy) means that genetic and gestational motherhood can now be located in two different women. Post-natal or social parenthood is the most open component of parenthood. It is often equated with intentional parenthood because it results from an act of will on the part of the parent. Social parents can be identified as those individuals who care for and nurture a child day-to-day. The crucial post-natal or social aspect of parenthood is usually performed by the genetic (and gestational) parents. Social parenthood can, however, be divorced from both genetic and gestational parenthood. Typical situations where this will occur include assisted reproduction using AID, surrogacy, adoption, and cohabitation between a genetic and non-genetic parent, such as step-parents. Once parenthood is freed from its genetic roots, it opens up endless possibilities. Social parenthood can be performed by an infinite number of people, at different times in the child's life, and with no limitation as to gender or status. Thus a child's social parents may range from the child's genetic and gestational mother and her husband to a gay couple who have neither a genetic nor gestational link to the child.

Baroness Hale tried to unpack the complexity and potential significance of these various components of parenthood in *Re G (Children) (Residence: Same-Sex Partner)*.[4]

Re G (Children) (Residence: Same-Sex Partner) [2006] UKHL 43

BARONESS HALE:

33. There are at least three ways in which a person may be or become a natural parent of a child, each of which may be a very significant factor in the child's welfare, depending upon the circumstances of the particular case. The first is genetic parenthood: the

---

[4] [2006] UKHL 43, [32]–[37]. For the facts and further extracts from *Re G*, see 11.6.7.

provision of the gametes which produce the child. This can be of deep significance on many levels. For the parent, perhaps particularly for a father, the knowledge that this is "his" child can bring a very special sense of love for and commitment to that child which will be of great benefit to the child...For the child, he reaps the benefit not only of that love and commitment, but also of knowing his own origins and lineage, which is an important component in finding an individual sense of self as one grows up. The knowledge of that genetic link may also be an important (although certainly not an essential) component in the love and commitment felt by the wider family, perhaps especially grandparents, from which the child has so much to gain.

34. The second is gestational parenthood: the conceiving and bearing of the child. The mother who bears the child is legally the child's mother, whereas the mother who provided the egg is not...While this may be partly for reasons of certainty and convenience, it also recognises a deeper truth: that the process of carrying a child and giving him birth (which may well be followed by breast-feeding for some months) brings with it, in the vast majority of cases, a very special relationship between mother and child, a relationship which is different from any other.

35. The third is social and psychological parenthood: the relationship which develops through the child demanding and the parent providing for the child's needs, initially at the most basic level of feeding, nurturing, comforting and loving, and later at the more sophisticated level of guiding, socialising, educating and protecting...

36. Of course, in the great majority of cases, the natural mother combines all three. She is the genetic, gestational and psychological parent. Her contribution to the welfare of the child is unique. The natural father combines genetic and psychological parenthood. His contribution is also unique...

37. But there are also parents who are neither genetic nor gestational, but who have become the psychological parents of the child and thus have an important contribution to make to their welfare. Adoptive parents are the most obvious example, but there are many others.

Whilst some commentators have welcomed Baroness Hale's apparent inclusion of psychological/social parenthood within her understanding of 'natural' parenthood, her suggestion that genetic parenthood, and genetic/gestational motherhood in particular, should be regarded as of unique importance has proved considerably more contentious.[5] Indeed, Lady Hale herself has acknowledged that it is 'a fair criticism of my opinion that it appeared to attach too much weight to the carrying mother's role'.[6]

9.2.2 THE IMPORTANCE OF LEGAL PARENTHOOD

Legal parenthood confers an important legal status on both parent and child. Andrew Bainham argues that it represents the most fundamental relationship between parent and child.[7] Unlike parental responsibility (the legal authority to make decisions with respect to a child's upbringing),[8] which can be conferred on a succession of different social carers

---

[5] For an excellent critique, see Diduck (2007), and for an alternative way in which the case could have been decided, Diduck (2010); but cf Bainham (2007b). For further discussion, see below at pp 779–82.

[6] Hale (2014), 30.

[7] Bainham (1999), 32–3.

[8] See chapter 10.

during the child's minority, legal parenthood can be held by only two individuals at any one time—usually, but no longer necessarily, the child's 'mother' and the child's 'father'. Legal parenthood is also permanent, non-alienable, and has legal consequences for an individual throughout life, not just during childhood.[9] As Bainham argues, legal parenthood makes the child a member of a family. The legal consequences that attach to legal parenthood therefore represent a core body of rights and responsibilities that flow from the fact that X is Y's child and belongs to Y's family. Although for many parents, particularly those deprived of parental responsibility, the authority to make decisions about a child's upbringing may seem more important and meaningful, the rights and responsibilities attaching to legal parenthood are also significant. For example, a child's core familial relationships for the purposes of determining restrictions on marriage and criminal prohibitions relating to incest are determined in accordance with the child's legal parenthood.[10] Entitlements on intestacy are determined by reference to legal parenthood, as are citizenship rights under the British Nationality Act 1981. Perhaps of greatest importance to many, particularly fathers, is that the duty to maintain a child financially rests with the legal parents.[11]

9.2.3 COMPETING APPROACHES TO DETERMINING A CHILD'S LEGAL PARENTS

In determining legal parenthood, the law has to make a choice, as a matter of policy, which of these aspects of parenthood should be given priority: genetic, gestational, or social.[12] The law has not always taken a consistent approach. There is nothing, in principle, to prevent the law according legal parenthood to more than two people, and nothing, in principle, which dictates that a child's parents must consist exclusively of one man and one woman. However, historically, legal parenthood under English law has been strictly gendered, the law insisting on the heterosexual norm that every child at birth should have two legal parents: one legal mother and one legal father.[13] This was made clear in *X, Y and Z v United Kingdom*,[14] where the Registrar General refused to register a female-to-male transsexual as the father of a child born to his long-term partner by means of assisted insemination using donated sperm. In refusing his application, the Registrar General took the view that only a biological male could be regarded as the father of a child for the purposes of registration.[15] The applicant challenged that decision in the European Court of Human Rights. The Court, by majority, found in favour of the UK government, holding that there had been no violation of Article 8 or Article 8 in conjunction with Article 14. It was emphasized that the applicant's inability to be recognized as the legal father by being entered as such on the child's birth certificate did not in any way affect his capacity to act as the child's social father, particularly as

---

[9] Legal parenthood can only be terminated by adoption or the making of a parental order under s 54 of the HFEA 2008.

[10] See Marriage Act 1949, Sch 1 and Sexual Offences Act 2003, ss 64–5.

[11] Child Support Act 1991, s 1(1); Children Act 1989 (CA 1989), Sch 1. See chapter 6.

[12] As the coital aspect of parenthood is no longer present in all cases it is excluded as an appropriate basis for determining legal parenthood.

[13] The possibility of adoption by a sole applicant means that a child post-adoption may have only one legal parent.

[14] (App No 21830/93, ECHR) (1997).

[15] Ibid, [17].

he could apply for parental responsibility by means of a shared residence order (which would now be expressed as a child arrangements order under which the child lives with two people in different households).[16]

This approach to parenthood is strongly rooted in the heterosexual biological imperative of natural procreation that a child must have one genetic/gestational mother and one genetic father. Day Sclater, Bainham, and Richards argue that in the wake of scientific advances in DNA testing, this genetic model of parenthood has become even more firmly entrenched.[17]

S. Day Sclater, A. Bainham, and M. Richards, 'Introduction', in A. Bainham, S. Day Sclater, and M. Richards (eds), *What Is a Parent? A Socio-Legal Analysis* (Oxford: Hart Publishing, 1999), 15

Developments in the technologies and procedures for DNA testing, used to establish paternity, have undoubtedly contributed to the new constructions of fathers in biological rather than social terms. As Neale and Smart argue, the newly emerging model of family life . . . is one which venerates biological kin ties and has entailed a refashioning of the legal status of biological parenthood; parenthood has begun to supersede marriage as the bedrock of "the family" and as the central mechanism for the legal regulation of domestic life. If marriage is no longer for life, then (biological) parenthood is. Biology now provides the main basis upon which claims to parental status rest. The increasing availability of genetic testing for a range of inherited conditions, as well as for paternity, and the increasing visibility of the micro-structures which make up our bodies, have given added impetus to the salience of "biology" and "genetics" in relation to the question of "what is a parent?"

Whilst arguing that the law must afford appropriate recognition to the importance of social parenthood by conferring on social parents the legal rights and duties required to raise a child (parental responsibility), Bainham supports the approach whereby legal parenthood is based exclusively on the genetic tie. His reasons focus on the unique significance of genetic parentage.

---

[16] Ibid, [50]. It has subsequently been confirmed that the 'fatherhood' provisions in the Family Law Reform Act 1987 and the Human Fertilisation and Embryology Act 1990 (HFEA 1990) are specifically gendered, restricting the acquisition of 'fatherhood' to a man. See: *J v C (Void Marriage: Status of Children)* [2006] EWCA Civ 551. Although the legal parenthood of transsexual parents would now be dealt with in accordance with the terms of the Gender Recognition Act 2004, *J v C* also confirmed that the legal acquisition of male gender by means of a Gender Recognition Certificate has no retrospective effect. If the purported father was thus legally a woman at the time of the child's birth, he cannot acquire the status of 'fatherhood' under English law. Note that the new s 12(2A) of the CA 1989 would allow the court to make a parental responsibility order for the father if he had the benefit of *any* child arrangements order—it is no longer necessary to have the equivalent of a residence order, though that form of order has the advantage of bringing parental responsibility *automatically*, whereas a child arrangements order which involves spending time or having contact merely creates the *possibility* of conferring parental responsibility.

[17] Other commentators have also noted the increasing trend towards the 'geneticization' of parenthood (particularly fatherhood), albeit they are considerably more critical of this approach. See, especially, Sheldon (2009).

A. Bainham, 'Parentage, Parenthood and Parental Responsibility', in A. Bainham, S. Day Sclater, and M. Richards (eds), *What Is a Parent? A Socio-Legal Analysis* (Oxford: Hart Publishing, 1999), 27

In allocating parental responsibility to more and more social parents, is it necessary or desirable to go the extra mile and confer on them legal parenthood? It will be my strong contention that this is neither necessary nor desirable and that legal parenthood, with some exceptions, ought to be confined to genetic parents. This is because those legal effects, which are peculiar to parenthood, are fundamental to the genetic link...

What are these fundamental effects of legal parenthood which do not pass with parental responsibility? The first is arguably the most important and is also the most frequently neglected. This is that legal parenthood, but not parental responsibility, makes the child a member of a family, generating for that child a legal relationship with wider kin going well beyond the parental relationship...[T]he social or psychological value of belonging to a particular family is a nebulous subject for lawyers and is more the terrain of the anthropologist or psychologist. What the lawyer *can* point out is that the loss of the legal status of parent will entail the loss, at least in law, of these wider relationships...

Other effects which arise specifically from legal parenthood are financial liability for child support, the right to object or consent to adoption (though this also depends on possessing parental responsibility), and the right to object to a change of the child's surname and to removal of the child from the jurisdiction, the right to appoint a guardian (although...the parent must possess parental responsibility), a presumption of contact where a child is in care and an automatic right to go to court...

Are these distinctive legal effects just anomalies, historical accidents of the piecemeal development of the law?...It is my contention that on the contrary, they continue to serve a vital purpose in that they give expression to the continuing importance of the genetic link. What they all have in common is that they relate to fundamentals which go beyond the everyday decisions involved in upbringing...If we are to move in the direction of giving effect to a child's right to knowledge of genetic origins we are going to need some legal means of preserving the genetic connection and it is the concept of legal parenthood which currently achieves this...

Bainham suggests that three key principles should guide the law's approach to determining legal parenthood: (i) a commitment to truth; (ii) individual autonomy; and (iii) priority for the rights and interests of those primarily affected—the individuals who result from reproduction.[18] In his view, conferring legal parenthood on the basis of biological truth, rather than the 'fiction' of social parenthood, best protects these core values.[19]

Barton and Douglas are more cautious about a genetic approach. They argue that there has been a perceptible swing in the law towards according precedence to intentional or social parenthood, particularly in the wake of the statutory regime introduced by the HFEA 1990 (now further entrenched by the HFEA 2008) for determining legal parenthood in the context of assisted reproduction. Indeed, they suggest 'it is now the primary test of legal parentage'.[20]

A model of legal parenthood which is based on the intention to parent or the 'function' or 'doing' of parenting has always had the potential to revolutionize English law's historical approach to determining a child's legal parents. Freed from the biological imperative, legal

---

[18] Bainham (2008a), 323–4.

[19] Ibid. It is not clear from Bainham's argument why genetic truth can only be adequately protected through the attribution of legal parenthood to the genetic parents.

[20] Barton and Douglas (1995), 51.

parenthood need not be restricted to two people of the opposite sex, or indeed to only two people. The HFEA 1990 and HFEA 2008 have seen this revolutionary potential at least partially realized. The first inroad into the gendered heterosexual model of legal parenthood was made by the Adoption and Children Act 2002 (ACA 2002) which, for the first time, enabled a same-sex couple to adopt. Thus, since 2002, the law has not demanded that a child have one legal mother and one legal father. The HFEA 2008 took this considerably further by permitting the deliberate creation of a child who will be born into a family consisting of two parents of the same sex. A child with two legal mothers but no legal father (strictly, in accordance with the Act, the child will have one 'mother' and a second female 'parent') is thus possible, as is a child with no legal mother but two legal fathers following a successful surrogacy arrangement (strictly two male 'parents'). By removing any continuing discrimination against same-sex couples in the regulation of access to, and the legal consequences of, assisted reproduction, same-sex couples can become legal parents on the same basis as a heterosexual couple. The legitimacy of same-sex parenting has been accepted—at least by the legislature. This considerable liberalization of the law on parenthood in the context of assisted reproduction clearly embraces intentional (rather than genetic) parenthood and accepts the equal worth of a diverse range of family relationships. Parenthood has moved a step closer to being a gender-neutral activity.

So do these radical changes fundamentally undermine the genetic or biological basis of legal parenthood in English law? As we examine the current legal framework for determining legal parenthood, it will become apparent that there is no clear answer to this question, English law drawing upon both the genetic and social models of parenthood depending on the particular social need. Those searching for a coherent policy underlying the law's approach will be disappointed. Indeed, Jackson describes the current law as 'spectacularly confused and confusing'.[21] The choice as to which model should predominate in any particular context has been driven by pragmatic considerations as much as by matters of policy and principle. In the context of natural procreation and until the recent advances in DNA testing, difficulties in establishing genetic parentage with any certainty influenced legal policy, as did social and legal considerations concerning the vulnerable status of illegitimate children. However, as the accuracy of genetic testing has improved, and the legal category of illegitimacy has been purged from English law, genetic parentage has become increasingly important in the determination of legal parenthood for children conceived through natural reproduction. In stark contrast, in the context of assisted reproduction different pragmatic considerations, such as the desire to avoid the seemingly nonsensical result of a sperm donor acquiring legal responsibility for financially maintaining his genetic offspring, have driven legal policy, with the result that social or intentional parenthood, with some notable exceptions, has become the central determining principle.

9.3 DETERMINING PARENTHOOD IN THE CONTEXT OF NATURAL REPRODUCTION

9.3.1 ESTABLISHING MATERNITY

In the context of *natural reproduction*, English law has traditionally placed the greatest emphasis on the genetic link between parent and child.[22] Establishing legal parenthood,

---

[21] Jackson (2006), 60.

[22] As exemplified by the cases of *B v B and F (No 1)* [1969] P 37 and *Re M (Child Support Act: Parentage)* [1997] 2 FLR 90.

at least as far as motherhood is concerned, is therefore relatively straightforward. As Lord Simon famously pointed out in the *Ampthill Peerage Case*,[23] in the case of the child's mother this genetic link can be incontrovertibly proved, as a matter of fact, by parturition.[24] The woman who gives birth to the child is the child's genetic mother and thus the legal parent.[25]

9.3.2 ESTABLISHING PATERNITY

Married fathers and the presumption of legitimacy

Determining a child's father is potentially more complicated. Establishing the genetic link between father and child has, in the past, proved difficult. Without the incontrovertible proof of parturition and, in the absence of accurate genetic testing, the law has had to rely on certain presumptions in order to establish paternity. In the case of children born to married parents, the common law has *presumed* that the mother's husband is the child's genetic father and thus the legal parent. This presumption applies if the man was legally married to the mother either at the date of conception or at the date of birth. Where the mother manages to be married to two different men at the date of birth and the date of conception, Bainham argues that she will be able to register her second husband as the father unless challenged by the first.[26]

Where the parents of a child are married, both parents are obliged to register the child within 42 days of the birth.[27] Either the child's mother or her husband can attend at the registrar's office and enter the husband's name as the child's father without producing any further evidence of his paternity. As Bainham points out, despite the operation of the *pater est* presumption, the birth register is supposed to reflect biological truth, it simply being assumed the mother's husband is indeed the biological father.[28] Moreover, the mother and her husband are under a duty to tell the truth, it being a criminal offence to register the husband as the child's father when they know that he is not in fact the biological father.[29] However, it is estimated that in 2–10 per cent of cases the mother's husband is wrongly named as the child's genetic father on the birth certificate.[30]

The common law presumption that the mother's husband is the father has, in the past, been difficult to displace. Until the law was amended by the Family Law Reform Act 1969 (FLRA 1969), s 26, the presumption could only be rebutted by evidence establishing beyond reasonable doubt that the husband could not be the father.[31] Although the civil standard of proof now applies, it was held in *W v K (Proof of Paternity)* that this would be harder to discharge than is ordinarily the case.[32] In addition to this high standard of proof, severe restrictions were historically imposed on the evidence that could be adduced at trial. For example,

---

[23] [1977] AC 547.

[24] Ibid, 577.

[25] With the advent of IVF this is no longer necessarily the case outside natural reproduction.

[26] Bainham (2008b), 454. Cf Lowe and Douglas who argue that the wife should be afforded the presumption of fidelity during marriage and thus her husband at the date of conception should be deemed the legal father. Lowe and Douglas (2015), 261.

[27] Births and Death Registration Act 1953, s 2.

[28] Bainham (2008b), 452–3.

[29] Ibid.

[30] Ibid, fn 108.

[31] Cretney (2003a), 534.

[32] [1988] 1 FLR 86.

out of concern for public decency, the law refused to hear evidence that the parties were not actively engaging in sexual intercourse at the relevant time.[33] This restrictive approach was explained by the fact that the child's legitimate status depended on the presumption that the mother's husband was the legal father. Given the significance of legitimacy, the courts were extremely reluctant to 'bastardize' a child without the strongest possible proof.[34]

In light of recent scientific, social, and legal changes, the courts' reluctance to disturb the common law presumption in favour of the husband has changed. For most of the twentieth century, although priority was *purportedly* accorded to the genetic link between parent and child, the law was more concerned with protecting the *appearance* of legitimacy than with establishing the *truth* about a child's genetic parentage.[35] Thus, as Barton and Douglas point out, legal fatherhood really turned not upon the man's relationship with the child, but on the status of his relationship with the mother.[36] In recent years this has changed, with the law now firmly committed to upholding the importance of biological truth.

Unmarried fathers and the presumption based on registration of the birth

Increasing numbers of children are now born to parents outside marriage. For the 47 per cent of children born to unmarried parents in England and Wales,[37] there is no automatic presumption as to their paternity. However, registration on the birth certificate is regarded as good prima facie evidence that the man named is the child's father.[38] In 2012, 88 per cent of children born outside marriage were registered jointly by both parents, and in 70 per cent of those cases the parents were registered as resident at the same address.[39] In most cases, birth registration is therefore an extremely important tool in helping to establish the child's paternity.

There remains, however, a small minority of cases (5.7 per cent of all births in 2012) in which the birth of a child is registered solely by the child's mother.[40] In these cases there is no presumption as to the child's paternity.

As a matter of law, only the child's mother, where she is unmarried, has a duty to register the child.[41] Registration of the child's father requires the active agreement of both parents or the production of an appropriate court order.[42] This means that where the child's mother does not want the child's father registered on the birth certificate she can simply withhold her consent to joint registration. In order to try to reduce the number of sole registrations, part of the Welfare Reform Act 2009 aimed to make joint registration in effect compulsory.

---

[33] Cretney (2003a), 534.

[34] Ibid, 533.

[35] See Bainham (2008b), 451.

[36] Barton and Douglas (1995), 53.

[37] ONS (2013a).

[38] In the absence of an entry in favour of the putative father on the birth register, the making of a parental responsibility order may also constitute good prima facie evidence as to the child's paternity. It was held in *R v Secretary of State for Social Security, ex parte W* [1999] 2 FLR 604, that because the court can only make a parental responsibility order under s 4 of the CA 1989 in favour of the child's father, it must be implicit in making the order that the man is 'found or adjudged' to be the child's father. The same reasoning would presumably apply to the existence of a parental responsibility agreement between the child's parents.

[39] ONS (2013a).

[40] Ibid.

[41] Births and Deaths Registration Act 1953, s 10.

[42] Ibid. See Barton and Douglas (1995), 56–7.

However, the relevant sections have never been implemented and there is no indication at the time of writing that the government has any plans to bring them into force.[43]

ONLINE RESOURCE CENTRE

We discuss the unimplemented reforms of the Welfare Reform Act 2009, along with the academic debates around it, on the Online Resource Centre.

The debate over the joint registration reforms brings into sharp relief some of the most contentious issues currently dominating the law relating to parents and children. At the heart of the strongly opposing views are fundamentally competing visions as to the importance of genetic, as opposed to functional or social, parenthood. As mothers typically fulfil the requirements of both genetic and social parenthood, this debate inevitably focuses on the 'problem' of genetic fathers. As Sheldon notes, the reforms are interesting for what they reveal about the previous Labour Government's wider policy agenda on fatherhood.

S. Sheldon, 'From "Absent Objects of Blame" to "Fathers Who Want to Take Responsibility": Reforming Birth Registration Law', (2009) 31 *Journal of Social Welfare and Family Law* 373, 374–5

[T]he proposed changes rely on a number of important assumptions about fatherhood and how it should be regulated. Notably, within this reform process, the term 'father' is assumed to mean the genetic father with no seeming awareness that the word is also often used in other ways...Neither is there any evidence of a concern which was highly significant in early family law and policy: the potential adverse impact of recognising the genetic father on the social family unit in which a child may live with his or her new partner. Further...the reform process reflects a commitment to equality between mothers and fathers and a particular vision of what this entails; an emphasis on independent, unmediated relationships between men and their children; a conflation of men's and children's interests, expressed in appeals to child welfare; an understanding of fatherhood as implying active engagement with children rather than a (merely) disciplinary or breadwinner role; and significant 'policy optimism' both about the desire of fathers to be more involved with their offspring and the likely success of initiatives in parenting as a means of addressing broader social problems....

This raises key questions for family lawyers: should the fact of genetic fatherhood itself be sufficient to confer legal rights and responsibilities on the father? Does a children's rights perspective demand legal recognition of the genetic father? Does equality demand that genetic fathers are accorded exactly the same legal rights as genetic (and social) mothers regardless of whether the father intends to meet the responsibilities of social fatherhood—or does 'real equality' demand something more nuanced? Is active and involved fathering by the biological father of such central importance to securing better outcomes for children that it should be promoted and supported by the law even if the welfare of the mother, and

---

[43] The plan to make joint birth registration mandatory divided academic opinion. Compare Bainham (2008b), who largely welcomed the reforms, and Wallbank (2009), who challenged the government's unquestioning acceptance of the perceived welfare gains from promoting and supporting genetic fatherhood through birth registration.

possibly the immediate welfare of the child, will be compromised? We will meet these questions repeatedly throughout the following chapters.

Court proceedings to determine the paternity of a child

Where the paternity of a child is disputed, s 55A of the Family Law Act 1986 (FLA 1986) provides that the child, the child's mother, the putative father, the Child Maintenance and Enforcement Commission, or any other sufficiently interested person (including the person with care of the child for the purposes of the Child Support Act 1991 (CSA 1991)) can make a free-standing application to the court for parentage to be determined.

Family Law Act 1986, s 55A

(1) Subject to the following provisions of this section, any person may apply to the High Court or the family court for a declaration as to whether or not a person named in the application is or was the parent of another person so named.

(2) ...

(3) Except in a case falling within subsection (4) below, the court shall refuse to hear an application under subsection (1) above unless it considers that the applicant has a sufficient personal interest in the determination of the application (but this is subject to section 27 of the Child Support Act 1991) [which provides that the person with care of the child will be deemed to have sufficient personal interest and exempts the Child Maintenance and Enforcement Commission from this requirement].

(4) The excepted cases are where the declaration sought is as to whether or not—

　(a) the applicant is the parent of a named person;

　(b) a named person is the parent of the applicant; or

　(c) a named person is the other parent of a named child of the applicant.

(5) Where an application under subsection (1) above is made and one of the persons named in it for the purposes of that subsection is a child, the court may refuse to hear the application if it considers that the determination of the application would not be in the best interests of the child.

A declaration made pursuant to s 55A is binding on all persons and for all purposes, including the CSA 1991.[44]

A child may also apply under s 56 of the FLA 1986 for a declaration as to his or her legitimacy. A dispute over parentage may also be determined when raised in existing civil proceedings, such as an application for parental responsibility under s 4 of the CA 1989.

Proving paternity: rebutting the presumptions and the advent of DNA testing

If a child has been born to unmarried parents and the birth register is silent as to paternity, the applicant will simply have to prove their case on the balance of probabilities.[45] Where

---

[44] FLA 1986, s 58(2).
[45] FLA 1986, s 58(1).

a presumption applies, the person seeking to challenge the presumption must adduce sufficient evidence to rebut the presumption on the usual civil standard of proof.

Family Law Reform Act 1969, s 26

Any presumption of law as to the legitimacy or illegitimacy of any person may in any civil proceedings be rebutted by evidence which shows that it is more probable than not that that person is illegitimate or legitimate, as the case may be, and it shall not be necessary to prove that fact beyond reasonable doubt in order to rebut the presumption.

The effect of this provision has been explained by Lord Reid.

S v McC and M; W v W [1972] AC 24 (HL), 41

LORD REID:

That means that the presumption of legitimacy now merely determines the onus of proof. Once evidence has been led it must be weighed without using the presumption as a make-weight in the scale for legitimacy. So even weak evidence against legitimacy must prevail if there is not other evidence to counterbalance it. The presumption will only come in at that stage in the very rare case of the evidence being so evenly balanced that the court is unable to reach a decision on it. I cannot recollect ever having seen or heard of a case of any kind where the court could not reach a decision on the evidence before it.

Presumptions about a child's paternity and the standard of proof required to rebut them remain technically relevant to determining disputes over parentage. However, the advent of widely accessible, accurate DNA testing means that paternity can now be established with virtual certainty. Where the court makes a direction for DNA tests to be taken, legal niceties about the onus and standard of proof required to rebut a presumption are therefore of little, if any, continuing significance: the DNA tests will be determinative. Indeed, the continuing relevance of the presumption of legitimacy has been explicitly questioned by Thorpe LJ.

Re H and A (Children) (Paternity: Blood Test) [2002] EWCA Civ 383

THORPE LJ:

30. The judge made it plain that in the absence of scientific evidence then the issue was to be decided on the application of 'a very important, well established principle…that is, the presumption of the legitimacy of children born during the currency of the marriage'…Twenty years on I question the relevance of the presumption or the justification for its application. In the nineteenth century, when science had nothing to offer and illegitimacy was a social stigma as well as a depriver of rights, the presumption was a necessary tool, the use of which required no justification. That common law presumption, only rebuttable by proof beyond reasonable doubt, was modified by section 26 of the Family Law Reform Act 1969

by enabling the presumption to be rebutted on the balance of probabilities. But as science has hastened on and as more and more children are born out of marriage it seems to me that the paternity of any child is to be established by science and not by legal presumption or inference.

The key question in present-day paternity disputes is thus whether the court should make the direction for tests so that the truth about a child's genetic parentage can be established with the certainty science now offers.

Directing tests under the FLRA 1969, s 20

Possible approaches

The relevant statutory provisions governing the use of scientific tests in disputes over parentage are found in ss 20–25 of the FLRA 1969.

Family Law Reform Act 1969, s 20

(1) In any civil proceedings in which the parentage of any person falls to be determined, the court may, either of its own motion or on an application by any party to the proceedings, give a direction—

   (a) for the use of scientific tests to ascertain whether such tests show that a party to the proceedings is or is not the father or mother of that person; and

   (b) for the taking, within a period specified in the direction, of bodily samples from all or any of the following, namely, that person, any party who is alleged to be the father or mother of that person and any other party to the proceedings;

and the court may at any time revoke or vary a direction previously given by it under this subsection.

Section 20 confers discretion on the court as to whether a direction for tests should be made. In exercising that discretion, several factors could influence the court's decision:

The rights of the child

First, it could be argued that children have a fundamental right to know the truth about their parentage.

United Nations Convention on the Rights of the Child, 1989

7. The child shall be registered immediately after birth and shall have the right from birth to a name, the right to acquire a nationality and, as far as possible, the right to know and be cared for by his or her parents…

8. State Parties undertake to respect the right of the child to preserve his or her identity, including nationality, name and family relations as recognised by law without unlawful interference.

Although the word 'parent' in Article 7 is open to differing interpretations, Bainham puts forward a convincing case that it should be taken to refer to genetic, as opposed to social, parentage.

A. Bainham, 'Parentage, Parenthood and Parental Responsibility', in A. Bainham, S. Day Sclater, and M. Richards (eds), *What Is a Parent? A Socio-Legal Analysis* (Oxford: Hart Publishing, 1999), 37–8

[T]he Convention contains no definition of "parents" and its meaning is therefore legitimately a matter of interpretation upon which opinions may differ. It is argued here, for a number of reasons, that the expression should be interpreted in the conventional sense of genetic parents. First, the history of Articles 7 and 8 reveals that the concern of the international community was with the rights of children from the moment of birth and in relation to their birth parents. It was precisely the threat of removal of the child from the birth parents by others which was the *raison d'etre* of Article 8. Secondly, we must remember that the Convention is a *legal* document. In 1989, when it was adopted, there was, for example, no legislation anywhere in the world regulating assisted reproduction which has been the engine for the re-evaluation of traditional definitions of parenthood. Leaving aside adoption, legislation worldwide has traditionally defined parenthood as genetic parenthood. The legal tie has closely followed the genetic connection. Thirdly...the jurisprudence generated under another international Convention, the European Convention on Human Rights, again supports the notion of "family life" from birth and has confirmed that this includes the potential relationship of a child with his or her genetic father even where unmarried. Finally...the conventional interpretation was adopted by the Court of Appeal in the one reported decision which directly invokes Article 7. For all these reasons it is submitted that "parents" in the Convention was intended to mean genetic parents and thus the onus is very firmly on those who would argue for an unconventional interpretation.

The principle that children have a fundamental right to know the truth about their genetic parentage has found favour amongst some English judges. In *Re R (A Minor) (Contact: Biological Father)*, which concerned a dispute between the child's mother and her former husband in relation to a child who had been raised to believe, incorrectly, that the man with whom the mother was now cohabiting was her father, Butler-Sloss LJ held in unequivocal terms that the child 'has a right in this case to know the truth'.[46]

Further support for a children's rights approach can be found in Article 8 of the European Convention on Human Rights (ECHR).[47] It has been held that individuals have a 'private life' interest in ascertaining, through paternity proceedings, the identity of their genetic parents.

Mikulić v Croatia (App No 53176/99, ECHR) (2002)

51. As regards paternity proceedings, the Court has held on numerous occasions that such proceedings do fall within the scope of Article 8...

52. The present case differs...in so far as no family tie has been established between the applicant and her alleged father. The Court reiterates, however, that Article 8, for its part, protects not only "family" but also "private" life.

---

[46] [1993] 2 FLR 762, 768.
[47] For commentary, see Fortin (2009a), 345–7.

53. Private life, in the Court's view, includes a person's physical and psychological integrity and can sometimes embrace aspects of an individual's physical and social identity. Respect for "private life" must also comprise to a certain degree the right to establish relationships with other human beings . . .

There appears, furthermore, to be no reason of principle why the notion of "private life" should be taken to exclude the determination of the legal relationship between a child born out of wedlock and her natural father.

54. The Court has held that respect for private life requires that everyone should be able to establish details of their identity as individual human beings and that an individual's entitlement to such information is of importance because of its formative implications for his or her personality . . .

55. In the instant case the applicant is a child born out of wedlock who is seeking, by means of judicial proceedings, to establish who her natural father is. The paternity proceedings which she has instituted are intended to determine her legal relationship with H.P. [the putative father] through the establishment of the biological truth. Consequently, there is a direct link between the establishment of paternity and the applicant's private life.

The facts of the case accordingly fall within the ambit of Article 8.

The rights of the putative father

A second factor that may incline the court to make a direction for tests is again rights-based but broadens the scope of the enquiry to include other family members. The European Court of Human Rights has held that under Article 8 ECHR the putative father's right to respect for his private and family life includes the right to have his paternal status and any potential relationship with his child recognized and protected under domestic law or, indeed, to have his paternity excluded.[48] This may require the state to have some mechanism in place whereby the putative father can establish or challenge his legal paternity by, for example, DNA testing and registration/de-registration on the birth register. In *Kroon v Netherlands* it was held that the applicant's inability to obtain recognition of his paternity because the child had been born whilst the mother was still married and was therefore presumed to be the legitimate child of her former husband, constituted a breach of the genetic father's right to respect for family life under Article 8. Under Dutch law, only the husband could challenge the presumption of paternity in his favour.

Kroon v Netherlands (App No 18535/91, ECHR) (1994)

32. According to the principles set out by the Court in its case-law, where the existence of a family tie with a child has been established, the State must act in a manner calculated to enable that tie to be developed and legal safeguards must be established that render possible as from the moment of birth or as soon as practicable thereafter the child's integration in his family . . .

---

[48] On the 'family life' aspect of Art 8 where de jure or de facto family ties can be established between the child and the putative father, see *Kroon v Netherlands* (App No 18535/91, ECHR) (1994), [30] and *Rozanski v Poland* (App No 55339/00, ECHR) (2006), [63]–[64]. As to the 'private life' right engaged in issues regarding the determination of a putative father's legal relations with his child, see *Shofman v Russia* (App No 74826/01, ECHR) (2005), [30] and *Tavli v Turkey* (App No 11449/02, ECHR) (2006), [25].

> 40. In the Court's opinion, "respect" for "family life" requires that biological and social reality prevail over a legal presumption which, as in the present case, flies in the face of both established fact and the wishes of those concerned without actually benefiting anyone.... There has accordingly been a violation of Article 8.

The guiding principle to emerge from *Kroon* (that 'biological and social reality' should prevail over legal presumptions) is consistent with the child's right to know the truth of genetic paternity as established in *Mikulić*.[49] It has, however, subsequently been held in *Rozanski v Poland* that this principle will be accorded less weight where the parents do not agree about the desirability of establishing the putative father's status.[50] It is, moreover, clear that the right to biological certainty suggested by *Kroon* is not absolute but must be balanced against other competing interests.[51] Thus the interests of the child and, in particular, the importance of preserving stability and certainty in the child's legal relationships, along with a focus on the importance of the functioning and quality of actual relationships already formed, have been found by the Court to constitute a *potential* justification for imposing various restraints, such as time limits, on challenging the child's paternity.[52] The competing Article 8 right of the child's mother not to be subjected to unwanted and potentially destabilizing interference with her existing family life is also a relevant consideration.

The child's best interests

A third approach that may influence the court's determination of the question of DNA tests rejects rights-based arguments in favour of prioritizing the child's welfare. Adopting this approach, it is argued that the question should simply be determined by asking what is in the child's best interests. If making a direction for DNA testing will secure the child's future welfare, tests should be ordered. If the tests may jeopardize the child's future security and happiness, they should be refused.

The problem is that disputes inevitably arise as to whether tests are in the child's best interests. As discussed in chapter 8, the indeterminacy of the welfare principle renders it subject to differing interpretations depending on prevailing social attitudes and trends, and the individual preferences of the decision-maker. Consequently, whilst at one time protecting the child against the detrimental consequences of illegitimacy may have been the court's overriding consideration, the declining social stigma surrounding illegitimacy and the final abolition of any legal distinction between a legitimate and illegitimate child[53] opened the way for competing discourses concerning the child's welfare to enter the field. Thus today's debates tend to centre on issues such as whether determining the truth about parentage risks destabilizing the child's existing family unit, how likely it is

---

[49] See also *Tavli v Turkey* (App No 11449/02, ECHR) (2006), [34]–[36].

[50] (App No 55339/00, ECHR) (2006), [67].

[51] For a short commentary, see Bainham (2007), esp at 280–1.

[52] See most recently *Kautzor v Germany* (App No 23338/09, ECHR) (2012). Although violations of Art 8 were found in the cases of *Shofman* (inflexible time limit for challenging paternity), *Rozanski* (unable to personally bring direct proceedings to establish his paternity), and *Tavli* (unable to reopen paternity proceedings in light of new DNA evidence), in each case the European Court undertook this careful balancing of interests. See *Shofman v Russia* (App No 74826/01, ECHR) (2005), [43]–[46]; *Rozanski v Poland* (App No 55339/00, ECHR) (2006), [73]–[80]; *Tavli v Turkey* (App No 11449/02, ECHR) (2006), [32]–[38].

[53] FLRA 1987, s 1.

that the mother's partner is the father, the stability of the mother's existing relationship, the likelihood of the child being able to develop a meaningful relationship with the putative father, and whether doubts concerning the child's parentage have already entered the public arena.[54]

The public interest in the smooth administration of justice

Finally, the issue of whether the court should make a direction for DNA tests can be looked at from a completely different perspective. This fourth approach does not focus on the rights and interests of the parties to the dispute but on the wider public interest. It is argued that once court proceedings have been initiated there is a legitimate public interest in establishing the truth. Consequently, in order to ensure the fair and just administration of justice, the best available evidence should be brought before the court, even if it prejudices the particular rights and interests of the individuals concerned.

Case law under the FLRA 1969, s 20

There is evidence of all the arguments considered above being considered in the case law. In seeking to resolve the conflicts created, the courts have not always adopted a consistent approach. In recent years the preferred approach has been to make a direction for tests, the rationale tending to focus on the child's right to know the truth about his or her genetic parentage, an approach which is considered entirely consistent with the child's best interests.

In *S v McC and M; W v W*,[55] the House of Lords attempted to lay down authoritative guidance as to when a direction for tests should be made under s 20(1) of the FLRA 1969. The conjoined cases both concerned an attempt by the wife's husband to rebut the presumption of legitimacy following the wife's adultery. In making a direction for tests, the House of Lords made clear the declining importance being placed on the child's legitimacy and the court's primary concern, not with the child's welfare, but with the wider public interest in establishing the truth. The principles derived from the House of Lords' judgments have been effectively summarized by Balcombe LJ:

Re F (A Minor) (Blood Tests: Parental Rights) [1993] Fam 314 (CA), 318

BALCOMBE LJ:

From the speeches in the House of Lords the following principles can be derived: (1) The presumption of legitimacy merely determines the onus of proof...(2) Public policy no longer requires that special protection should be given by the law to the status of legitimacy...(3) The interests of justice will normally require that available evidence be not suppressed and that the truth be ascertained whenever possible...In many cases the interests of the child are also best served if the truth is ascertained...(4) However, the interests of justice may conflict with the interests of the child. In general the court ought to permit a blood test of

---

[54] But see *L v P (Paternity Test: Child's Objections)* [2011] EWHC 3399, where a '*Gillick* competent' 15-year-old child objected to having a DNA test. While emphasizing that a child's objections would not be determinative, Hedley J considered the child to have a reasonable basis for objecting and refused to order testing.

[55] [1972] AC 24.

a young child to be taken unless satisfied that that would be against the child's interests; it does not need first to be satisfied that the outcome of the test will be for the benefit of the child...(5) "It is not really protecting the child to ban a blood test on some vague and shadowy conjecture that it may turn out to be to its disadvantage: it may equally well turn out to be for its advantage or at least do it no harm".

Given the House of Lords' strong guidance that a direction for blood tests should ordinarily be made, it is somewhat surprising that the Court of Appeal in *Re F* managed to reach the opposite conclusion. *Re F* concerned a typical paternity dispute. The child was conceived whilst the wife was having sexual relations with both her husband and the putative father. The mother's relationship with the putative father ended before the child was born and the child was being raised as the child of the husband within the existing family unit. The putative father applied for parental responsibility and contact under the CA 1989. Paternity was disputed. Although paying lip-service to the requirement that blood tests must be shown to positively harm the child's interests (the approach adopted in *S v McC and M*),[56] in determining whether a direction for blood tests should be made, the Court of Appeal appeared to apply the different test of whether the tests would promote the child's interests. In determining this question, the Court of Appeal held that the child's interests lay not in ascertaining the 'abstract' truth about her true genetic parentage, but in providing support and protection to the existing family unit.

Re F (A Minor) (Blood Tests: Parental Rights) [1993] Fam 314 (CA), 319–22

BALCOMBE LJ:

B [the putative father] criticised the judge's decision on a number of grounds. He submitted that the judge was wrong to base his decision, at least in part, on the probable outcome of B's applications for parental responsibility and contact; that in any event the interests of justice and E's [the child's] own welfare required that her true paternity be established. In our judgment that submission is fundamentally misconceived. As is apparent from the provisions of section 20(1) of the Family Law Reform Act 1969, the power to direct the use of blood tests to determine parentage only arises "in civil proceedings in which the paternity of any person falls to be determined." If the probable outcome of these proceedings will be the same whoever may be the natural father of E, then there can be no point in exposing E to the possible disadvantages of a blood test. We agree with the judge that in the circumstances of this case there is no realistic prospect of B succeeding at the present time in his applications for parental responsibility and contact since we do not see how such orders could benefit E...

On the issue whether it was in E's interests to have the identity of her natural father determined with such degree of certainty as scientific tests can provide, B submitted that it must inevitably be in E's interests to know the truth about her parentage; her interests should not be subordinated to those of Mr and Mrs F [the mother and her husband]. This may well be true, but now and for the first few years of her life E.'s physical and emotional welfare are inextricably bound up with the welfare of the family unit of which she forms part: any harm to the welfare of that unit, as might be caused by an order for the taking of blood tests, would inevitably be damaging to E.

[56] See also *Re L* [2009] EWCA Civ 1239, [11]–[14].

The child's right to knowledge of her genetic parentage, as well as the wider public interest in ascertaining the truth, were raised but cursorily dismissed.

B also referred us to the United Nations Convention on the Rights of the Child...which has been ratified by the United Kingdom, and in particular to article 7 which provides that a child shall have, "as far as possible, the right to know and be cared for by his or her parents." B submitted that E's welfare included her rights under this article. Whether or not B is included in this definition of a parent within the meaning of this article, it is not in fact possible for E to be cared for by both her parents (if B is such). No family unit exists or has ever existed, between B and Mrs F, and if B were able to assert his claims to have a share in E's upbringing it would inevitably risk damaging her right to be cared for by her mother, Mrs F...

E's welfare depends for the foreseeable future primarily upon her relationship with her mother. B expressly conceded that he did not dispute the right of Mrs F to have E living with her. Anything that may disturb that relationship or the stability of the family unit within which E has lived since her birth is likely to be detrimental to E's welfare, and unless that detriment is shown to be counter-balanced by other positive advantages to her which an order for the taking of blood tests could confer, then the judge's refusal to order blood tests was not merely an exercise of his discretion with which we cannot interfere, but one with which in the circumstances of this case we agree.

B made a number of other points by way of criticism of the judgment below, including the point that the public interest, as well as E's own personal interest, requires that the truth about her paternity be ascertained if possible. However, in the last resort it is clear that E's interests must be the decisive factor; where, as here, the judge was satisfied that it would be against E's interests to order blood tests to be taken—a decision with which we agree—then it was both his duty and his right to refuse the application. It was for these reasons that we dismissed this appeal.

[The first instance judge's refusal to make a direction for blood tests was upheld.]

The Court of Appeal's judgment met with a mixed academic reaction. Barton and Douglas welcomed the court's preference for the presumed legal parenthood of the mother's husband, as evidence of the 'growing importance of the social, as opposed to genetic aspect of parenthood'.[57] Fortin was, however, more critical, arguing, on the basis of evidence from the field of adoption, that the court 'should have given far greater weight to the psychological value to E of knowing the truth about her origins'.[58] She also criticized the court for failing to keep the issue of the child's genetic parentage separate from that of the putative father's prospects of establishing a meaningful social relationship with the child.[59] However, as discussed below, recent case law has prompted Fortin to reconsider these views.[60]

The Court of Appeal's apparent departure from the House of Lords' preference for determining the truth of parentage was, in any event, short-lived. The issue returned to the Court of Appeal in *Re H (A Minor) (Blood Tests: Parental Rights)*. The case was very similar on its facts to *Re F* although it was very unlikely the mother's husband could be the child's genetic father as he had had a vasectomy and sexual relations between them were very poor at the time of conception. The mother, nevertheless, disputed the putative father's paternity. In making a direction for scientific tests, Ward LJ reasserted and refined the House of Lords'

---

[57] Barton and Douglas (1995), 61.
[58] Fortin (1994), 298.
[59] Ibid.
[60] Fortin (2009a). See below at pp 621–2.

principles from *S v McC and M*. On the question of welfare, the Court of Appeal confirmed that 'welfare does not dominate this decision', although most of the judgment is devoted to whether blood tests would be in the child's best interests. The decision is also distinctive for the emphasis placed on the child's right to know the truth about his or her genetic parentage, an approach Ward LJ clearly considered entirely consistent with the child's welfare.

Re H (A Minor) (Blood Tests: Parental Rights) [1997] Fam 89 (CA)

WARD LJ:

(5) In my judgment every child has the right to know the truth unless his welfare clearly justifies the cover up. The right to know is acknowledged in the United Nations Convention on the Rights of the Child... there are two separate rights, the one to know, and the other to be cared for by, one's parents...

(9) Given the real risk bordering on inevitability that [the child] will at some time question his paternity, then I do not see how this case is not concluded by the unassailable wisdom expressed by Lord Hodson [in *S v McC and M*]...:

"The interests of justice in the abstract are best served by the ascertainment of the truth and there must be few cases where the interests of children can be shown to be best served by the suppression of truth."

If, as she should, this mother is to bring up her children to believe in and to act by the maxim, which is her duty to teach them at her knee, that honesty is the best policy, then she should not sabotage that lesson by living a lie.

(10) If the child has the right to know, then the sooner it is told the better. The issue of biological parentage should be divorced from psychological parentage. Acknowledging the applicant's parental responsibility should not dent the husband's social responsibility for a child whom he is so admirably prepared to care for and love irrespective of whether or not he is the father....

(11) If [the child] grows up knowing the truth, that will not undermine his attachment to his father figure and he will cope with knowing he has two fathers. Better that than a time-bomb ticking away.

The wider public interest in the smooth administration of justice does not feature in the Court of Appeal's reasoning.

The judgment in *Re H* is also significant for the clear distinction drawn between the child's genetic and social parents. It is thus emphasized that it is perfectly possible for a child to have two 'fathers'—one genetic and one social—and that the two parental roles are not necessarily mutually exclusive. Ward LJ does, however, make it clear that the two parents may serve quite different functions in relation to the child, and whilst the child has a right to know his or her genetic parentage, this does not necessarily involve trying to foster a personal relationship between them. The child's right to know should therefore not be seen as threatening or detracting from the parenting role of the social or psychological parent.

The impact of the Human Rights Act 1998

Re H is now regarded as the leading authority on when it is appropriate to make a direction for DNA tests.[61] Although the child's welfare is not the paramount consideration,

---

[61] *Re T (A Child) (DNA Tests: Paternity)* [2001] 3 FCR 577, 583.

the child's rights and interests are very much the focus of concern. However, one argument which was not dealt with by the Court of Appeal in *Re H*, but could not be avoided following the implementation of the Human Rights Act 1998 (HRA 1998), was whether the putative father could rely on any rights under Article 8 to disturb what was now, essentially, an exclusively child-centred approach. Until this point, arguments focusing on the Article 8 rights of the putative father had been absent from the case law. However, the issue was tackled in *Re T (A Child) (DNA Tests: Paternity)*, Bodey J's judgment making it clear that, following implementation of the HRA 1998, it was business as usual. The facts of *Re T* were somewhat unusual. The mother, who was married but unable to conceive a child with her husband, had engaged in sexual intercourse with several men, including the putative father, at around the same time, in the hope of becoming pregnant. It was always intended that the resulting child would be raised within the existing family unit. However, the putative father, who had had some contact with the child, applied for parental responsibility and to spend time with the child. The husband responded by asserting his paternity. The putative father's application was specifically triggered by the implementation of the HRA 1998. Having confirmed that the child's welfare was not paramount and that the child's interests had to be balanced against the competing interests of the adults, Bodey J went on to address the rights-based arguments.

Re T (A Child) (DNA Tests: Paternity) [2001] 3 FCR 577 (Fam Div), 583–6

BODEY J:

There is no significant dispute that T [the child] has a right to respect for his private life (in the sense of having knowledge of his identity, which encompasses his true paternity) and a right to respect for his family life with each of his natural parents, all things being equal.

T also has what may (as here) be mutually 'competing' rights to respect for his private and family life, in the *other* sense that the stability of his present de facto family life should not be put at risk, except as may otherwise be held to be in his interests, and pursuant to art 8(2).

It is further common ground that the mother and her husband have a right to respect for their private and family life, comprising a right that the same should not be intruded upon, or interfered with, except as may be necessary to give effect to T's and (if he has them) the applicant's rights.

So far as the applicant is concerned, he may or may not (depending on the facts and on whether he is in truth the biological father) have a right to respect for a family life encompassing—all things being equal—the society of, and a relationship with T, and/or a knowledge of T's progress.

It is accepted between the parties that if and when these various Convention rights pull in opposite directions, then the crucial importance of the rights and best interests of the child fall particularly to be considered...

I am entirely satisfied that in evaluating and balancing the various rights of the adult parties and of T under art 8, the weightiest emerges clearly as being that of T, namely that he should have the possibility of knowing, perhaps with certainty, his true roots and identity.

I find any such interference as would occur to the right to respect for the family/private life of the mother and her husband, to be proportionate to the legitimate aim of providing T with the possibility of certainty as to his real paternity, a knowledge which would accompany him throughout his life.

Applying art 8 in this way (regardless of whether or not the applicant has established what, if he is the father, would constitute family life with T) confirms my previous view that I should grant the applicant's application.

[Bodey J went on to consider, obiter, whether the applicant would be able to establish a right to respect for family life for the purposes of Article 8. He concluded that the applicant's relationship with the child and the child's mother lacked sufficient constancy and commitment to create the necessary de facto family ties to establish the family life right under Article 8. The alternative private life limb of Article 8 was not considered.]

Consent requirements for the taking of samples

On the basis of the most recent authorities, it is now tolerably clear that when paternity is disputed the court will make a direction for scientific tests to determine the issue. There is, however, a further hurdle to be negotiated. Regardless of any direction the court might make, a bodily sample cannot be taken from any party to the litigation for the purpose of carrying out the tests without that person's consent.[62]

The child's consent to the taking of samples

In the case of a minor who is 16 years or over, s 21(2) of the FLRA 1969 provides that the minor can give an effective consent to the taking of bodily samples in the same way as a person of full age and capacity. For minors who are under 16, the consent of the person with 'care and control' is required. If consent is withheld, the court can override the refusal if satisfied that taking the sample would be in the child's best interests.

Family Law Reform Act 1969, s 21

(3) A bodily sample may be taken from a person under the age of sixteen years, not being a person as is referred to in subsection (4) of this section,

    (a) if the person who has the care and control of him consents; or

    (b) where that person does not consent, if the court considers that it would be in his best interests for the sample to be taken.

This appears to set down a straightforward welfare test for determining whether samples should be taken if the person with care and control does not consent. This is different from the qualified welfare test set down in *S v McC and M* and *Re H* for determining whether a direction for tests should be made under s 20(1). It is not yet clear how the courts will deal with the slightly differing demands of the two provisions. Although the child's welfare is not the only consideration in determining whether a direction for tests should be made, before making a direction under s 20(1) the court will have given detailed consideration to the issue and reached a firm conclusion as to whether or not DNA tests are in the child's

---

[62] FLRA 1969, s 21(1).

best interests or at least not adverse to them. Section 21 may therefore be rendered a mere formality, the court invariably ordering that samples be taken once the direction for testing is made. Indeed, there is a clear trend in the current case law, at least where consent to the taking of samples is in issue, to conflate the requirements of ss 20 and 21 of the FLRA 1969 and decide the case by means of an unqualified application of the welfare principle.[63] This will invariably lead both to a direction for DNA tests to be carried out and an order for the taking of samples. This was the approach adopted in the case of *Re D (Paternity)* which unusually involved the vehement opposition of an 11-year-old child to the taking of samples.[64] Hedley J's analysis focused exclusively on the child's best interests with no distinction drawn between the requirements of ss 20 and 21 of the FLRA 1969. Despite the child's clear and determined opposition, Hedley J ordered that a sample be taken for the purposes of testing, albeit he stayed the order to remove the immediate pressure on the child.[65]

The decision in *Re D* has generated concern that the emphasis on genetic truth is such that it is being dogmatically pursued even where, on the particular facts, it is strongly arguable that it may be better for the child to preserve stability and security in his or her current relationships. Fortin, who previously supported the child's right to know, has voiced concerns about this trend. She argues that the preoccupation with biological truth has more to do with serving the rights and interests of the adults than those of the child, particularly where paternity disputes are being driven, not by the child's right to information about his or her genetic origins, but by the putative father's desire to establish a social relationship with the child based on nothing more than the genetic tie.

J. Fortin, 'Children's Right to Know Their Origins: Too Far, Too Fast?', (2009a) 21 *Child and Family Law Quarterly* 336, 338–54

When writing my critique of *Re F* [see above], I had perhaps overlooked the dangers for children of the assumption that they all have a right to knowledge of their origins...The decision in *Re D* provokes a feeling of unease...Surely a child has a right *not* to know the identity of his father if he himself believes, with some grounds, that his entire life would be disrupted by such knowledge? Indeed, the view that *all* children have a right to know their parents' identity may sometimes achieve more harm than good, given the danger of the two issues being confused—the child's need to know about his origins and his possible need for a social relationship with his biological parent...When dealing with applications from putative fathers, it is arguable that the domestic courts are extending a child's right to know beyond its appropriate boundaries...[T]he disputes being litigated have little to do with children's right to knowledge of their origins. The DNA testing applications brought by putative fathers are not brought to provide the child with information alone, they are the initial stages of attempts to establish a social relationship between father and child based on assumptions about biological connectedness. The putative fathers' assumption that once the biological ties between father and child have been clearly identified, they should be fulfilled by a social relationship produces an elision of the right to know the parent's identity, with the right to know and have a relationship with that parent. Whether or not claims can be justified by reference to the child's own rights, such an elision concentrates the court's attention on the putative father's

---

[63] *Re T (A Child) (DNA Tests: Paternity)* [2001] 3 FCR 577; *Re H and A* [2002] 1 FLR 1145.
[64] [2006] EWHC 3545.
[65] Ibid, [29]–[30].

position and his own interests—countered by those of the mother . . . These are adult-centred arguments which spring from adult-centred disputes over children who are treated as the property of those who can establish biological connectedness. There are dangers that such an approach, unsupported by research will not benefit some children. Indeed, in some cases like *Re D (Paternity)* where the child himself rejects the need to know the identity of his father, it may psychologically damage him. That case reinforces Smart's warning . . . about the dangers of allowing the law to insist on only one kind of truth—'the truth of science' above those other claims concerned with 'caring, relationality and the preserve of kinship bonds'.

The consent of adult parties and the drawing of adverse inferences

Under s 21(3), the problem of a lack of consent with respect to the child can now usually be avoided. The need for consent is more difficult where one of the adults refuses to cooperate. This is most likely to arise where the putative father is denying paternity to avoid paying child support. There is no statutory equivalent to s 21(3) giving the court the authority to override the putative father's refusal. The courts have, however, made it clear that they will not allow themselves to be dictated to by intransigent parties and the stated intention of one party to withhold consent will not preclude them from making a direction for tests.[66] A refusal to submit to the tests does not amount to contempt of court and cannot be met by the court's punitive powers.[67] To withhold consent is, however, to play a dangerous game. The court can draw whatever inferences it feels appropriate from a party's refusal to cooperate,[68] including an inference as to the actual paternity of the child.[69] As was made clear in *Re A (A Minor) (Paternity: Refusal of Blood Test)*, this is an effective weapon against an intransigent party. The facts of *Re A* are fairly typical of paternity disputes where liability to provide financial support for the child is at stake. At the time of the child's conception, the mother was having sexual relations with three different men. She claimed maintenance against just one, a man the Court of Appeal described as being 'of some substance'.[70] The man refused to comply with a direction for blood tests, arguing that it would be unjust to compel him to submit to a test and risk paternity being conclusively established against him when two other men who were equally likely to be the child's father were not being exposed to the same risk. The argument was dismissed.

Re A (A Minor) (Paternity: Refusal of Blood Test) [1994] 2 FLR 463 (CA), 472–3

WAITE LJ:

The starting-point must be that the old uncertainties which formerly surrounded issues of disputed paternity when a mother had been sexually involved with two or more men at the time of conception are now banished altogether. Genetic testing, already advanced to a high degree of probability through the negative techniques of exclusion, has now moved on to the point where it has become possible to achieved [sic] positive certainty. That has had a

---

[66] *Re H (A Minor) (Blood Tests: Parental Rights)* [1997] Fam 89, 101.
[67] *Re G (A Minor) (Blood Test)* [1994] 1 FLR 495, 499–500.
[68] FLRA 1969, s 23.
[69] *Re A (A Minor) (Paternity: Refusal of Blood Test)* [1994] 2 FLR 463, 472.
[70] Ibid, 464.

profound effect on cases like the present, where a mother has been having relations with different men at the time of conception. Any man who is unsure of his own paternity and harbours the least doubt as to whether the child he is alleged to have fathered may be that of another man now has it within his power to set all doubt at rest by submitting to a test. It has ceased, therefore, to be possible for any man in such circumstances to be forced against his will to accept paternity of a child whom he does not believe to be his.

Against that background of law and scientific advance, it seems to me to follow, both in justice and in common sense, that if a mother makes a claim against one of the possible fathers, and he chooses to exercise his right not to submit to be tested, the inference that he is the father of the child should be virtually inescapable. He would certainly have to advance very clear and cogent reasons for this refusal to be tested—reasons which it would be just and fair and reasonable for him to be allowed to maintain.

It is open to the party withholding consent to show good cause why his refusal to cooperate is justified. Absent such justification, however, the drawing of an adverse inference against the party disputing paternity seems virtually inevitable, even if, as was made clear in the case of *F v Child Support Agency*,[71] one of the other putative fathers is married to the child's mother and a presumption of legitimacy therefore applies.

Telling the child the truth about paternity

If scientific tests are ordered and the truth about paternity established, the next question is whether, and if so how, the child should be told. Not surprisingly, many mothers who oppose DNA testing are equally resistant to telling the child the result, particularly where it threatens the child's security within the existing family unit. It is, however, clear that the court can compel a parent to tell the child the truth about his or her paternity. In *Re F (Paternity Jurisdiction)*,[72] Thorpe LJ held that the question of whether a child should be told the truth is a question relating to the exercise of an aspect of parental responsibility which can be controlled by a specific issue order or under the court's wardship jurisdiction.[73] Moreover, he made it clear that concerns over the enforceability of such orders were unfounded: if the parent refuses to cooperate, the court can put in place alternative mechanisms for ensuring the children are told, possibly involving mental health professionals.[74]

9.4 DETERMINING PARENTHOOD IN THE CONTEXT OF ASSISTED REPRODUCTION

9.4.1 THE BRAVE NEW WORLD OF ASSISTED REPRODUCTION

For family lawyers, post-war developments in assisted reproduction raised a number of challenging new questions. One of the key difficulties for policy-makers is the number of

---

71 [1999] 2 FLR 244.
72 [2007] EWCA Civ 873.
73 Ibid, [8], [14].
74 Ibid, [17]–[18].

different treatments available and the vast range of circumstances in which people may seek to take advantage of them. Nearly 50,000 women had IVF treatment in 2011, and over 17,000 children were born that year, amounting to 2.2 per cent of all children born in the UK.[75]

Whilst scientific advances in reproductive medicine have generally been welcomed for giving much needed hope to infertile couples, there have also been strong voices of dissent. Concern tends to focus on what is perceived as the potential use of these treatments for social, as opposed to medical reasons. Single women and same-sex couples are typically targeted as the most likely 'deviants' to seek to exploit the developments.[76] A married couple unable to conceive for medical reasons are likely to engender considerable sympathy. IVF using their own gametes to assist in conception raises relatively few problems for our traditional concepts of 'family' and 'parenthood'. At the other extreme is the story of same-sex couple, Tony Barlow and Barrie Drewitt. The couple entered into a surrogacy agreement in the United States, as a result of which twins, Aspen and Saffron, were born. The embryos were created using the eggs of one woman, Tracie McCune, making her the twins' genetic mother.[77] The eggs were fertilized in vitro, that is outside the woman's uterus, using the sperm of both Tony and Barrie. It is thus unclear which of the two men is the twins' genetic father.[78] The embryos were then transferred into a second woman, Rosalind Bellamy, the surrogate, who carried the twins to term. Rosalind is thus the twins' gestational mother. This case raises much greater challenges for English law's traditional concepts of 'family' and 'parenthood'.

As the story of Barrie and Tony graphically illustrates, the act of reproduction is no longer tied to the need for heterosexual intercourse. Although artificial insemination using donor sperm has probably been practised on an informal 'DIY' basis for years, the ability to create an embryo in vitro raises the spectre of a previously unknown fragmentation of parenthood. There are now several individuals who can contribute to the creation of a single embryo and who are able to point to equally credible but competing claims to parenthood of the resulting child. Out of the complicated arrangement entered into by Barrie and Tony there is no easy answer to the question of who the law should regard as the twins' legal parents. Should the twins' genetic parentage (the genetic father and Tracie) or social parentage (Barrie and Tony) be accorded legal priority? The decision to use two different women to act as egg donor and surrogate also raises the question of whether the genetic mother (Tracie) or the gestational mother (Rosalind) should be accorded legal priority. A Californian Supreme Court judge seeking to resolve this dilemma decided that Barrie and Tony should be entered as 'parent one' and 'parent two' on the twins' birth certificates.[79] In the eyes of Californian law, Saffron and Aspen thus have no legal mother and two legal fathers. Such an approach fundamentally challenges our traditional concepts of the heterosexual family. The possibilities created by assisted reproduction dramatically expose the extent to which English family law is willing to embrace unconventional family forms.[80]

However, before turning to consider how the law on parenthood has responded to these developments in assisted reproduction, we will briefly consider an increasingly important and closely related question: the right of an individual to access fertility treatment.

---

[75] HFEA (2012).

[76] As to the concerns expressed in the parliamentary debates preceding the HFEA 1990, see: Jackson (2002), 195; Douglas (1993), 57–8; and Roberts (2000), 49.

[77] Hibbs (2001), 736.

[78] Ibid, 737.

[79] Ibid, 736–7.

[80] For an argument concerning the need for English law to embrace post-modern difference and 'otherness' in the context of assisted reproduction, see Langridge and Blyth (2001).

9.4.2 ACCESS TO TREATMENT: IS PARENTHOOD A RIGHT OR A PRIVILEGE?

Infertility can be devastating for those affected but developments in assisted reproduction mean that there are now several ways in which couples can be helped. However, whilst one may feel considerable sympathy for these couples, it does not necessarily follow that they have a right to demand access to treatment, and that argument may be even stronger for individuals and couples who are not infertile but seek access to assisted reproductive techniques for other, perhaps social, reasons. There are several arguments against allowing individuals to access fertility treatment.

DHSS, *Report of the Committee of Inquiry into Human Fertilisation and Embryology*, Cm 9314 (London: HMSO, 1984)

2.3 Arguments have been put to us both for and against the treatment of infertility. First, we have encountered the view that in an over-populated world it is wrong to take active steps to create more human beings who will consume finite resources. However strongly a couple may wish to have children, such a wish is ultimately selfish. It has been said that if they cannot have children without intervention, they should not be helped to do so. Secondly, there is a body of opinion which holds that it is wrong to interfere with nature, or with what is perceived to be the will of God. Thirdly, it has been argued that the desire to have children is no more than a wish; it cannot be said to constitute a need. Other people have genuine needs which must be satisfied if they are to survive. Thus services designed to meet those needs must have priority for scarce resources.

The Warnock Committee was unpersuaded by these arguments,[81] and following its recommendations, the UK has taken a fairly liberal approach to the provision of fertility treatment. Clinics specializing in assisted reproduction have been established in both the private and the public sector, albeit subject to the strict licensing conditions set down in the HFEA 1990 and closely regulated by the Human Fertilisation and Embryology Authority (HFEA). The wide availability of fertility treatment does not, however, translate into a right to treatment.

The right to access fertility treatment can be conceptualized as a right to found a family or, more broadly, as a right to reproductive freedom. Emily Jackson makes a strong case as to why those who wish to have children should be afforded the freedom to do so, focusing her arguments on the right of individuals to a protected 'zone of privacy' in which decisions concerning reproduction can be made.[82]

E. Jackson, 'Conception and the Irrelevance of the Welfare Principle', (2002) 65 *Modern Law Review* 176, 177–8

Of course for the vast majority of people, deciding whether or not to conceive is not susceptible to legal control. People who conceive through heterosexual sexual intercourse do so without any external scrutiny of the merit or otherwise of their decision. Monitoring these

---

[81] DHSS (1984), para 2.4.
[82] See also Alghrani and Harris (2006), 192 and 195–6.

exceptionally personal choices in order to identify ill-judged or improper conception decisions would be unreservedly condemned as an unacceptably intrusive abuse of state power...I would suggest that there are broadly two different justifications for the presumption that normally exists in favour of privacy in procreative decision-making. First, interfering with a particular individual's decision to conceive a child would usually involve violating their bodily integrity and sexual privacy...The second and I would argue equally important reason for respecting people's conception choices is that the freedom to decide for oneself whether or not to reproduce is integral to a person's sense of being, in some important sense, the author of their own life plan. For most people, these two justifications for reproductive privacy mesh together in the requirement that we treat both their body and their life plan with respect. We should, however, remember that those individuals whose procreative preferences can be disregarded without simultaneously violating their bodily integrity and sexual privacy nevertheless retain their interest in being able to make exceptionally personal and important decisions according to their own conception of the good.

In considering the right to reproductive freedom, a distinction needs to be made between what Jackson terms 'positive and negative liberty'.[83] There is an important difference between, on the one hand, the state interfering with the decision of an individual to seek fertility treatment in the private sphere and, on the other, the state refusing to provide unfettered access to state-funded treatment. The former seeks to impose a negative obligation of non-interference on the state, whilst the latter seeks to impose a positive obligation on the state to guarantee access to treatment for all. The argument in favour of recognizing the former right is considerably stronger than the latter, where other considerations such as the rationing of resources and prioritization of medical treatment within the NHS are legitimate considerations.[84] Where, however, there are no resource issues at stake, the legitimacy of the state seeking to scrutinize and restrict an individual's procreative freedom is harder to sustain.

E. Jackson, 'Conception and the Irrelevance of the Welfare Principle', (2002) 65 *Modern Law Review* 176, 177–8

My claim is that we should refrain from scrutinising the pre-conception decisions of adults who intend to bring about a child's creation just as we would if they had happened to be able to conceive naturally. Notice that this is not the same as saying that people have a *right* to be provided with fertility treatment. On the contrary, my argument here is much more modest. It is simply that we should each have the liberty to shield certain personal decisions from public scrutiny. The decision to conceive a child goes to the heart of an individual's identity and is precisely the sort of choice that we all ought to be able to make within the privacy of our most intimate relationship. I argue that it is therefore unfair to take advantage of the opportunity afforded by their biological incapacity in order to assess the wisdom of an infertile couple's decision to start a family. We may not be able to fund their treatment, or there might be no treatment that is clinically appropriate for them. But evaluating an infertile couple's fitness to parent deprives them of the decisional privacy that the majority of people are rightly able to take for granted.

---

[83] Jackson (2002), 184.
[84] Ibid, 184–5.

The right to reproductive freedom under Article 8 ECHR

In order to assist an individual seeking access to fertility treatment, the right to reproductive freedom must first be recognized under English law. The prevailing approach, prior to the implementation of the HRA 1998, was that an individual had the right to seek investigation and advice concerning their infertility and a right to be considered for treatment. There was, however, no unfettered right to treatment in either the public or private sector. This general approach, recommended by the Warnock Committee,[85] was endorsed in *R v Ethical Committee of St Mary's Hospital (Manchester), ex parte H*.[86] The implementation of the HRA 1998 has not changed this basic position. The issue of whether there is a Convention right to access fertility treatment arose in *Evans v United Kingdom*.[87] *Evans* did not concern a straightforward claim to treatment. Ms Evans was attending a clinic for fertility treatment with her partner, Mr Johnston, when it was discovered she had cancerous tumours in both ovaries. As a result, she underwent the first stage of IVF treatment to remove as many eggs as possible for use in future treatment. The eggs were fertilized using Mr Johnston's sperm and the resulting embryos frozen whilst Ms Evans underwent treatment for cancer. Before she recovered sufficiently for an embryo transfer to be carried out, the couple separated and Mr Johnston withdrew his consent to the further storage and use of the embryos. This meant that under the terms of the HFEA 1990, Sch 3, the embryos had to be removed from storage and destroyed. Ms Evans claimed that Mr Johnston's right to withdraw his consent violated her Article 8 right to respect for private and family life. In line with the approach adopted by the Court of Appeal hearing the case at the domestic level,[88] the Grand Chamber of the European Court held that the right to decide whether to become a genetic parent (and to realize that right by accessing fertility treatment) fell within the ambit of the Article 8 right to respect for private life, this right being broadly interpreted to incorporate any aspect of one's personal liberty and freedom.

Evans v United Kingdom (App No 6339/05, ECHR) (2007)

71. It is not disputed between the parties that Article 8 is applicable and that the case concerns the applicant's right to respect for her private life. The Grand Chamber agrees with the Chamber that "private life", which is a broad term encompassing, *inter alia*, aspects of an individual's physical and social identity including the right to personal autonomy, personal development and to establish and develop relationships with other human beings and the outside world...incorporates the right to respect for both the decisions to become and not to become a parent.

72. It must be noted, however, that the applicant does not complain that she is in any way prevented from becoming a mother in a social, legal, or even physical sense, since there is no rule of domestic law or practice to stop her from adopting a child or even giving birth to a child originally created *in vitro* from donated gametes. The applicant's complaint is, more precisely, that the consent provisions of the 1990 Act prevent her from using the embryos

---

85 DHSS (1984), para 2.12.
86 [1988] 1 FLR 512.
87 (App No 6339/05, ECHR) (2007).
88 *Evans v Amicus Healthcare Ltd* [2004] EWCA Civ 727, [108].

she and J [her former partner] created together, and thus, given her particular circumstances, from ever having a child to whom she is genetically related. The Grand Chamber considers that this more limited issue, concerning the right to respect for the decision to become a parent in the genetic sense, also falls within the scope of Article 8.

It was subsequently confirmed in *Dickson v United Kingdom* that state-imposed restrictions on accessing assisted reproduction engages Article 8 and the right to respect for the decision to become a genetic parent.[89] It is, however, equally clear from *Evans* and *Dickson* that Article 8 is a qualified right: it does not confer an absolute right to become a parent using any technological means possible.

Legitimate restrictions on the right to reproductive freedom: Article 8(2)

Procreative liberty and the need for unequivocal consent

The state can legitimately regulate and restrict the right to fertility treatment in order to safeguard the rights and interests of others. In *Evans*, the Court of Appeal held that the interference with Ms Evans' Article 8 rights was justified to protect the competing Article 8 rights of Mr Johnston, in particular, his *equal* right to procreative liberty including his right to choose not to become a father.

Evans v Amicus Healthcare Ltd [2004] EWCA Civ 727

ARDEN LJ:

109. The next question is whether the interference is justified under article 8(2). In the 1990 Act Parliament has taken the view that each genetic parent should have the right to withdraw their consent for as long as possible. It was not inevitable that Parliament should take that view. Subject to the possible effect of the Convention, Parliament could have taken the view that, as in sexual intercourse, a man's procreative liberty should end with the donation of sperm but that, in the light of the woman's unique role in making the embryo a child, she should have the right to determine the fate of the embryo. But Parliament did not take that view. Nor did Parliament take the view that the court should have any power to dispense with the requirement for consent of both parties, even when circumstances occur which were not envisaged when the original arrangements were made.

110...I consider that the imposition of an invariable and ongoing requirement for consent in the 1990 Act in the present type of situation satisfies article 8(2) of the Convention.... As this is a sensitive area of ethical judgment, the balance to be struck between the parties must primarily be a matter for Parliament...Parliament has taken the view that no one should have power to override the need for a genetic parent's consent. The wisdom of not having such a power is, in my judgment, illustrated by the facts of this case. The personal circumstances of the parties are different from what they were at the outset of treatment, and it would be difficult for a court to judge whether the effect of Mr Johnston's withdrawal of his consent on Ms Evans is greater than the effect that the invalidation of that withdrawal of consent would have on Mr Johnston. The court has no point of reference by which to make that sort of evaluation. The fact is that each person has a right to be protected against interference with their

---

[89] *Dickson v United Kingdom* (App No 44362/04, ECHR) (2007).

private life. That is an aspect of the principle of self-determination or personal autonomy. It cannot be said that the interference with Mr Johnston's right is justified on the ground that interference is necessary to protect Ms Evans's right, because her right is likewise qualified in the same way by his right. They must have equivalent rights, even though the exact extent of their rights under article 8 has not been identified.

111. The interference with Ms Evans's private life is also justified under article 8(2) because, if Ms Evans's argument succeeded, it would amount to interference with the genetic father's right to decide not to become a parent. Motherhood could surely not be forced on Ms Evans and likewise fatherhood cannot be forced on Mr Johnston, especially as in the present case it will probably involve financial responsibility in law for the child as well.

The Grand Chamber of the European Court agreed that the HFEA's strict provisions on consent were a proportionate response to the legitimate need to protect the procreative liberty of *both* parties embarking upon fertility treatment.[90]

This strict approach to consent was retained when the legislative framework governing assisted reproduction was reformed in 2008. The HFEA 2008 amends Sch 3 to the HFEA 1990 to introduce a 12-month 'cooling off' period.[91] This allows the embryos to continue to be stored for 12 months following the withdrawal of consent by one party in the hope that an amicable agreement about their future use and storage can be reached. However, if the parties cannot reach agreement the embryos must still be destroyed on the expiration of the 12-month period.

The best interests of the child

The most important way in which the state regulates access to fertility treatment is through the welfare principle, the mechanism by which the rights and interests of any future child can be protected.

Human Fertilisation and Embryology Act 1990, s 13

(5) A woman shall not be provided with treatment services unless account has been taken of the welfare of any child who may be born as a result of the treatment (including the need of that child for supportive parenting), and of any other child who may be affected by the birth.

The child's welfare constitutes a legitimate qualification on the right of the prospective parents to procreative liberty under Article 8(2).[92] However, restricting access to fertility treatment on the basis of the child's welfare has been fiercely criticized. In practice, it is intrinsically difficult to apply the best interests principle to such an abstract question as the welfare of a child who does not yet exist. Indeed, Emily Jackson, one of the strongest critics, argues that to attempt to do so is 'disingenuous and essentially meaningless'.

---

90 *Evans v United Kingdom* (App No 6339/05, ECHR) (2007), [89]–[92].
91 HFEA 1990, Sch 3, para 4A.
92 *Dickson v United Kingdom* (App No 44362/04, ECHR) (2007), [76].

E. Jackson, 'Conception and the Irrelevance of the Welfare Principle', (2002) 65
Modern Law Review 176, 193

Unlike factors that go to the heart of whether infertility treatment is, for example, clinically advisable or publicly affordable, the pre-conception welfare principle represents an invidious and opportunistic invasion of infertile people's privacy. Deciding to try to conceive a child through sexual intercourse is usually assumed to be a *self-regarding* decision that takes place within the privacy of a couple's intimate relationship. Yet biological infertility somehow serves to convert this choice into an *other-regarding* decision that must be judged according to its likely impact upon this 'other', namely the child that might be born... [R]egardless of whether the child's welfare is described as a medical or social outcome, for several interconnected reasons I believe that attempting to ration treatment using section 13(5) is both tautologous and unjust. First if the alternative is non-existence, it will in fact invariably be in the particular future child's best interests to be conceived. It is therefore simply illogical for the HFEA to insist that treatment should... be refused if the centre believes that it would not be in the interests of any resulting child, because, as John Robertson has explained, from the child's perspective, the risk-creating activity is welcome, since there is no alternative way for this child to be born.

The HFEA is responsible for issuing guidance on how fertility clinics are to apply s 13(5). The HFEA has recently taken a much more permissive approach, effectively enshrining a presumption in favour of treatment unless there is evidence that any resulting child would be at risk of significant harm.[93] Indeed, Smith argues that this 'light touch' approach has rendered s 13(5) almost redundant.[94] The European Court added its voice to the debate in *Dickson v United Kingdom*.[95] *Dickson* concerned the right of a prisoner serving life imprisonment to access assisted insemination services so that he and his partner, who would be too old to conceive naturally by the time of his anticipated release, could attempt to begin a family. The Home Secretary, applying the policy then in force, refused permission for Mr Dickson to access such services. Although it was accepted by the court that the child's welfare was, in principle, a legitimate restriction on the applicants' rights to access artificial insemination facilities, it was clear that such is the importance of the procreative right at stake under Article 8 that significant welfare concerns, going beyond those which were evident on the facts of this particular case, would be needed in order for the state to successfully justify its interference.

Dickson v United Kingdom (App No 44362/04, ECHR) (2007)

76. [T]he Government argued that the absence of a parent for a long period would have a negative impact on any child conceived and, consequently, on society as a whole.

The Court is prepared to accept as legitimate, for the purposes of the second paragraph of Article 8, that the authorities, when developing and applying the Policy, should concern

---

[93] HFEA (2005), foreword. For detailed discussion, see Alghrani and Harris (2006), 196–201.
[94] Smith (2010), 51.
[95] (App No 44362/04, ECHR) (2007).

themselves, as a matter of principle, with the welfare of any child: conception of a child was the very object of the exercise. Moreover, the State has a positive obligation to ensure the effective protection of children...However, that cannot go so far as to prevent parents who so wish from attempting to conceive a child in circumstances like those of the present case, especially as the second applicant was at liberty and could have taken care of any child conceived until such time as her husband was released.

In balancing the private and public interests engaged under Article 8, the Court seemed to place a much more onerous obligation on the state when seeking to justify restrictions imposed on access to reproductive treatment, particularly if the sole ground on which it purported to do so was the welfare of the child.

The question of whether access to treatment should continue to be regulated on the basis of a welfare test was thoroughly reviewed prior to the reforms enshrined in the HFEA 2008. In the preceding White Paper, the government concluded that given recent changes in HFEA guidance, s 13(5) constituted a legitimate and proportionate restriction on an individual's reproductive liberty.[96] Controversially, however, the government decided to amend s 13(5) in one important respect. As originally enacted in the HFEA 1990, s 13(5) required clinics to have particular regard not to the need of the child for *supportive parenting* but to the need of the child for a *father*. Commentators were extremely critical of the way in which this requirement had been applied in practice. Research by Gillian Douglas, for example, suggested that s 13(5) was being used, at least in the early 1990s, to screen out individuals presumed to be socially 'undesirable' parents, such as single mothers and same-sex couples, without any substantive consideration of their actual parenting ability or the likely welfare of any future child.[97] According to her findings, clinics were routinely making ill-informed judgements based on inadequate information and prejudice. In reviewing s 13(5), the government was clearly sensitive to these concerns and expressed some disquiet about the state's role in determining what constitutes an 'acceptable' family form through the imposition of controls on fertility treatment. This concern was reinforced by the government's heightened commitment to the equal treatment of same-sex couples following implementation of the Civil Partnership Act.

DH, *Review of the Human Fertilisation and Embryology Act. Proposals for Revised Legislation (Including Establishment of the Regulatory Authority for Tissue and Embryos),* Cm 6989 (London: HMSO, 2006)

2.25 Responses to the Government's consultation from individual members of the public generally favoured retention of a reference to the child's need for a father, as part of the consideration of the welfare of the child. Many thought that the legislation should be revised to refer to a need for both a mother and a father. The Government has carefully considered this matter, and in particular has taken into account considerations of the proper role of the State, and of clinicians, in seeking to determine family forms via controls on access to

---

[96] DH (2006), paras 2.22–2.24.
[97] Douglas (1993), 62–9. In more recent years, Smith argues that s 13(5) has posed no real obstacle to single women and lesbians seeking treatment. See Smith (2010), 51.

medically-assisted conception, particularly in the light of more recent enactments such as the law relating to civil partnerships.

2.26 **On balance, the Government has decided to propose that the reference to the need for a father (in consideration of the welfare of the child) should be removed from the Act.** The Government is not convinced that the retention of this provision could be justified in terms of evidence of harm, particularly when weighed against the potential harms arising from the consequences of encouraging some women who wish to conceive to make private arrangements for insemination rather than use licensed treatment services.

The Joint Parliamentary Committee charged with scrutinizing the draft legislation was unhappy with this proposal, the majority thinking that it would be detrimental to remove the requirement to take into account the 'need for a father'.[98] They therefore proposed retaining the current provision in s 13(5) but making it clear that it could be interpreted to mean 'second parent' rather than 'father'. The Committee's principal concern appeared to be the spectre of a growth in single parents rather than an increase in the number of same-sex couples accessing treatment. In its response, the government reiterated that the research tends to show that 'the factor of prime importance is quality of parenting rather than parental gender per se',[99] and referred to the view of the House of Commons Science and Technology Committee that s 13(5) could be wrongly interpreted to 'imply that unjustified discrimination against "unconventional families" is acceptable'.[100]

Opposition to the proposed amendment in Parliament was more clearly concerned with the apparent endorsement of fatherless families and the negative message this would send out about the importance of fathers and their role in the upbringing of children. For some, the proposed amendment constituted an unacceptable attack on the normative heterosexual foundations of family life.

L. Smith, 'Clashing Symbols? Reconciling Support for Fathers and Fatherless Families after the Human Fertilisation and Embryology Act 2008', (2010) 22 *Child and Family Law Quarterly* 46, 51–2

[S]ome of the opposition to amendment of s 13(5) represents displaced discomfort with the amendments relating to same-sex parenting, and an attempt legally to fetter same-sex parenting 'through the back door'... [I]t is not the importance of fatherhood per se which concerns opponents. Rather it is fatherhood as an anchor for the traditional, heterosexual parenting paradigm which loses some of its primacy as non-traditional family types become acceptable....

Broadly speaking, the opposition arguments that were presented during the Parliamentary debates can be separated into three strands. First, it was claimed that removal of the reference to the child's need for a father from section 13(5) HFE Act 1990 would send out a powerful and harmful symbolic message that fathers are not needed. Secondly, it was suggested that the move runs counter to recent government backed efforts to promote involved fatherhood and to encourage contact between children and genetic fathers. Finally, it was

---

[98] Recommendation 22. DH (2007), 15.

[99] For a brief discussion of this research, see Smith (2010), 59–62.

[100] DH (2007), paras 55–6.

asserted that it is unacceptable to dismiss the child's need for a father when a weight of evidence indicates that the presence or absence of a father has a vital impact on levels of child well-being...

The government was sympathetic to many of these arguments concerning the importance of 'father presence'. However, at least in this context, its commitment to ensuring the equal treatment of same-sex couples seeking fertility treatment prevailed.

It is unsurprising that the amendments to s 13(5) proved so contentious. As amended, it not only sanctions the deliberate creation of fatherless children but confers legal approval on non-conventional family forms that present a direct challenge to the normative heterosexual foundations of family life.[101] And whilst this was welcomed by many, s 13(5) did not sit well with the previous Labour Government's strong commitment to promoting and supporting genetic fatherhood in other key areas of family law.[102] These contradictions and tensions at the heart of contemporary family policy are carefully drawn out by Smith.

L. Smith, 'Clashing Symbols? Reconciling Support for Fathers and Fatherless Families after the Human Fertilisation and Embryology Act 2008', (2010) 22 *Child and Family Law Quarterly* 46, 54–5, 56–7

In recent years the government has placed its support behind same-sex parenting by initiating various pieces of legislation...The provisions contained in the HFE Act represent a further attempt to remove legal obstacles to the recognition of same-sex parenting arrangements. Each of these developments marks a departure from law's historical support for the heterosexual family unit. As such each also implicitly endorses both existing and prospective fatherless families. Moreover, these legislative developments have been bolstered by policy level rhetoric indicating an intention to support diversity rather than conventionality in family life...

In parallel with these developments, however, the government has repeatedly emphasised its commitment to the idea that the traditional married family is the best environment in which to bring up children...These and other, similar, tributes to the hetero-normative family have given opponents of the Act ample opportunity to criticise countervailing efforts to facilitate the establishment of families by same-sex couples. Given that the government has intimated on multiple occasions that being brought up in a traditional heterosexual family unit is inherently advantageous to children, it is no small wonder that its attempts to support same-sex parenting in the present context have been the subject of criticism. Furthermore, the force of the message in support of the marital, necessarily heterosexual family is repeatedly reinforced by more specific and widespread promotion of the importance of fathers in children's lives....

[W]hile lobbyists and judges eulogise the contributions made by fathers to their children's welfare and invoke the powerful language of rights, policy makers have referred to 'the *vital* role played by fathers'. Such statements present the connection between child well-being and father presence as absolute and this gives the government's suggestion that lesbian parents – who by definition will normally form fatherless families – can bring up

---

[101] Smith (2010), 51–2.
[102] See, especially, disputes about children's upbringing, discussed in chapter 11.

children satisfactorily a hollow ring. It begins to look as if the government is indeed clashing its own symbols in terms of its various expressions of support for fathers and support for fatherless families.

The right to reproductive freedom under Article 12 ECHR

At least on the face of the ECHR, Article 12 may seem a more promising route to establishing a right to reproductive treatment because, unlike Article 8, Article 12 appears to establish an unqualified right. The 'right to found a family' under Article 12 has, however, been subjected to a conservative interpretation by the European Court.[103] There is no clear authority bringing assisted reproduction within the scope of Article 12.[104] However, the argument that the right to utilize assisted reproductive techniques, such as IVF, *should* fall within the right to 'found a family' is convincing, particularly as it has been held that adoption, which is arguably not as close to natural reproduction as IVF, has been found to fall within the scope of the provision.[105] That said, even if the right to artificial reproduction is found, in principle, to fall within the scope of Article 12, the right remains expressly subject to 'national laws governing the exercise of the right'. The state is thus afforded wide discretion as to who should be allowed to take advantage of the right and under what conditions.[106] A state could thus legitimately restrict its treatment to married couples suffering from infertility on medical grounds, particularly as the right to marry and the right to found a family under Article 12 are closely linked in the Strasbourg case law.[107]

Legitimate restrictions on the right to found a family

The right to 'found a family', despite the unqualified nature of the wording of Article 12, has been held to be less than absolute. In *R (Mellor) v Secretary of State for the Home Department*, it was held that the limitations applicable to Article 8 also apply to Article 12. The state can therefore regulate and restrict the 'right to found a family' under Article 12 in order to protect the public interest or the rights and interests of others, including the future child. This was confirmed in *Dickson v United Kingdom*, the Chamber holding that, 'an interference with family life which is justified under paragraph 2 of Article 8 of the ECHR cannot at the same time constitute a violation of Article 12'.[108] This qualification on the right to found a family would appear to have survived the House of Lords' judgment in *R (Baiai) v Secretary of State for the Home Department*, in which the House of Lords held that the right to marry could not be qualified by reading into Article 12 the restrictions of Article 8(2).[109] Both Lord Bingham and Baroness Hale appeared to draw a distinction between the two rights protected under Article 12, the right to marry being regarded as particularly 'strong' and 'fundamental' in contrast to the right to found a

---

[103] Harris, O'Boyle, and Warbrick (1995), 434.

[104] See Harris (1995), 69.

[105] *X and Y v United Kingdom* 12 DR 32, 34 and *X v Netherlands* 24 DR 176, 177–8. For commentary, see Harris, O'Boyle, and Warbrick (1995), 441.

[106] Ibid. With respect to adoption see: *Fretté v France* (App No 36515/97, ECHR) (2003).

[107] Harris, O'Boyle, and Warbrick (1995), 442.

[108] *Dickson v United Kingdom* (App No 44362/04, ECHR) (2006), [41].

[109] [2008] UKHL 53, [15] (Lord Bingham), [46] (Baroness Hale).

family which 'the Strasbourg authorities have not in practice upheld...with the same firmness'.[110]

9.4.3 DETERMINING PARENTHOOD UNDER THE HFEA 2008

The common law's traditional emphasis on genetic parenthood can look inappropriate when applied in the context of assisted reproduction. For example, when determining the paternity of a child born through the use of AID, it does not seem right for a sperm donor who is unaware of the child's existence to be regarded as the child's legal father, particularly if that status involves a duty to maintain the child. It seems equally illogical for the husband of a woman receiving AID treatment to be regarded in law as a stranger to the child he intends to raise as his own. In the case of disputes over maternity, the law has to contend not only with a potential split between genetic and social motherhood but the further complication of a split between genetic and gestational motherhood. As assisted reproduction became more widely available, it became clear that the common law's emphasis on genetic parenthood could not be sustained in this particular context. The HFEA 1990 was intended to provide a comprehensive scheme for determining the legal parenthood of children conceived via assisted reproductive techniques. This scheme was comprehensively revised by the HFEA 2008, which introduced quite radical changes to the way in which legal parenthood is determined in this context. Most notably, Parliament made it much easier for same-sex couples to acquire legal parenthood following fertility treatment by introducing provisions comparable to those in place for heterosexual married and unmarried couples. Respect for a diverse range of family forms and the need for the HFEA to keep pace with other developments in family law underpinned the government's approach.

DH, *Review of the Human Fertilisation and Embryology Act. Proposals for Revised Legislation (Including Establishment of the Regulatory Authority for Tissue and Embryos),* **Cm 6989** (London: HMSO, 2006)

2.67 In undertaking its review of the HFE Act, the Government aimed to consider the extent to which changes may be needed to better recognise the wider range of people who seek and receive assisted reproduction treatment in the early 21st Century. The Government has also considered the impact of other legal changes that have occurred since the HFE Act came into force in 1991. For example, the coming into force of the Civil Partnership Act 2004 created a new legal relationship which two people of the same sex can form by registering as civil partners of each other. Important rights and responsibilities flow from forming a civil partnership including for civil partners to be assessed in the same way as spouses for child support.

2.68 Also, whereas it has for many years been possible for a single person to adopt a child, recent changes have enabled unmarried and same-sex couples jointly to adopt children. Other relevant changes include the fact that an unmarried man can acquire parental responsibility for a child through jointly registering the birth together with the child's mother.

---

[110] Ibid.

> 2.69 Given other legal changes since the HFE Act was enacted, and in particular, existing policy to create parity between civil partners and married couples, **the Government proposes to revise the status and legal parenthood provisions of the HFE Act to enable a greater range of persons to be recognised as parents following assisted reproduction.** This will involve introducing parenthood provisions for civil partners and other same-sex couples in line with those for married and unmarried couples respectively. Changes will apply both to the recognition of parental status following the use of donor gametes, and the acquisition of parental orders following surrogacy. In the latter case, this means that as well as married couples, civil partners and other couples in a stable relationship will be able to apply for a parental order.

These proposals were given effect in Part 2 of the HFEA 2008.

Mothers: s 33

Genetic, gestational, and social motherhood may now be located in three different women. The Warnock Committee considered that in the interests of certainty the gestational mother should, for all legal purposes, be accorded the legal status of motherhood.[111] This recommendation was enshrined in s 27(1) of the HFEA 1990 and retained without being reconsidered in s 33(1) of the HFEA 2008.

Human Fertilisation and Embryology Act 2008, s 33

(1) The woman who is carrying or has carried a child as a result of the placing in her of an embryo or of sperm and eggs, and no other woman, is to be treated as the mother of the child.

Determining maternity is thus straightforward: the woman who gives birth to the child is always regarded as the legal mother. Egg donation, in accordance with the Warnock Committee's recommendations, is regarded as absolute, with the genetic mother/egg donor being treated in exactly the same way as a sperm donor: no legal rights or duties attach by virtue only of her genetic parentage.[112] In most cases of egg/embryo donation, this approach best meets the needs and interests of the child, the intended parents, and the donor. The only context where it may be problematic is surrogacy.[113] In such cases, the genetic/social mother may have an equally compelling case for recognition of her maternal status. The particular problems to which surrogacy arrangements give rise will be discussed below.

Fathers and second female parents: ss 34–40

The following provisions on legal parenthood only apply where the condition set down in s 34 of the HFEA 2008 is satisfied: that the child 'is being or has been carried by a woman as a

---

[111] DHSS (1984), para 6.8.
[112] Ibid.
[113] Douglas (1991), 129.

result of the placing in her of an embryo or of sperm and eggs or her artificial insemination'. In other words, conception by means of natural sexual intercourse is explicitly excluded from the scope of the legislation.

Married fathers: s 35

Determining paternity is considerably more complicated than determining maternity. In making its recommendations, the Warnock Committee was strongly influenced by the importance of maintaining the child's legitimacy and at least the appearance of a traditional family unit. Where the husband's own sperm is used in his wife's treatment, the common law will apply and, as the genetic father, he will be the legal father. Section 38(2) provides that even where donor sperm is used, the husband is still entitled to rely on the common law presumption of legitimacy until that presumption is rebutted by means of DNA tests. Where it is clear that the husband is not the genetic father, s 35(1) provides that he will still be regarded as the child's legal father unless he did not consent to the treatment.

Human Fertilisation and Embryology Act 2008, s 35

35 Woman married to a man at time of treatment

(1) If—

    (a) at the time of the placing in her of the embryo or of the sperm and eggs or of her artificial insemination, W [the woman] was a party to a marriage with a man, and

    (b) the creation of the embryo carried by her was not brought about with the sperm of the other party to the marriage,

then, subject to section 38(2) to (4) [the common law presumption of legitimacy], the other party to the marriage is to be treated as the father of the child unless it is shown that he did not consent to the placing in her of the embryo or the sperm and eggs or to her artificial insemination (as the case may be).

The onus to prove the absence of consent is on the husband. It has been suggested, obiter, that the fact the husband has not given written consent will not be sufficient by itself to show he did not consent.[114] However, in determining whether the husband has given his consent, the question of what the husband must have consented to in order for legal parenthood to be conferred, has, under the identical provision in the previous legislation, been strictly construed. The issue was dealt with in the difficult case of *Leeds Teaching Hospital NHS Trust v A*. Two couples, Mr and Mrs A (a white couple) and Mr and Mrs B (a black couple), were receiving fertility treatment at the same clinic. Neither couple consented to treatment using donated gametes. By mistake, Mr B's sperm was used to fertilize Mrs A's eggs. The embryos were implanted in Mrs A, resulting in the birth of mixed-race twins. The mistake was immediately apparent and DNA tests confirmed Mr B was the twins' genetic father. Mr B applied for a declaration of parentage under s 55A of the FLA 1986. The legal position was relatively clear. Mrs A was the twins' mother and if Mr A could bring himself within the terms of s 28(2) (the precursor to s 35(1) of the HFEA 2008) he would be deemed

---

114 *Re G (Surrogacy: Foreign Domicile)* [2007] EWHC 2814, [39].

the twins' legal father. If, however, he fell outside the scope of the HFEA 1990, the common law position would prevail and Mr B, as the twins' genetic father, would be regarded as the legal father. The application of s 28(2) turned on whether, given the mistake, Mr A could be said to have consented to his wife's treatment. Mr and Mrs A argued that a valid consent had been given.

Leeds Teaching Hospital NHS Trust v A and others [2003] EWHC 259

DAME ELIZABETH BUTLER-SLOSS P:

25. . . . Subsection (2) applies unless it is shown that Mr A 'did not consent to . . . her insemination'. It is obvious that s 28 is not relevant if the sperm given by Mr A was used since he is then the biological father and the twins are the legitimate children of Mr and Mrs A. The question is whether Mr A consented to the insemination of Mrs A by a third person (for the purposes of this argument, 'a donor').

26. . . . [Counsel] argued that Mr A gave a broad consent to the placing of an embryo sufficient to treat him as the father unless it could be shown that Mr A had not consented. He did not raise the issue nor seek to set aside the presumption.

27. The insurmountable problem, in my view, to that approach, is the question—to what did he consent? . . . The 'course of treatment' to which he consented was that outlined in Mrs A's consent form. . . . Mrs A consented to her eggs being used and mixed with her husband's sperm. She did not consent to her eggs being mixed with named or anonymous donated sperm. She consented to the placing of not more than two resulting embryos in her uterus.

28. Mr A certainly gave his consent to the placing in his wife of 'an embryo'. The embryo actually placed in Mrs A was a fundamentally different embryo from one that might have been created by the use of Mr A's sperm . . . The question whether the husband consented is a matter of fact which may be ascertained independently of the views of those involved in the process. On the clear evidence provided in the consent forms Mr A plainly did not consent to the sperm of a named or anonymous donor being mixed with his wife's eggs. This was clearly an embryo created without the consent of Mr and Mrs A.

[**Butler-Sloss P** refused to make a declaration of parentage in favour of Mr A and adjourned the application of Mr B. It was agreed by the parties that the twins should remain living with Mr and Mrs A.]

It is thus clear that in order for a husband's consent under s 28(2) (now s 35(1) of the HFEA 2008) to be valid, he must consent to the actual treatment received. If no such consent was given, he cannot be regarded as the legal father.

Assuming consent, s 35(1) prioritizes the intended social father over the genetic father. This again reflects the intentions of all the parties and will usually best serve the child's interests, the intended parents, and the donor.[115] Section 35(1) is, however, far from revolutionary in negating the importance of the genetic tie. As seen above, attaching children to their fathers through the fact of marriage to the mother, is in many ways nothing more than what the common law has been doing for centuries through the presumption of legitimacy.

---

[115] For a straightforward example of the application of the identical provision on married fathers as contained within the HFEA 1990, see *Re CH (Contact Parentage)* [1996] 1 FLR 569.

Unmarried fathers: ss 36–8

Unmarried fathers are dealt with under ss 36–8. Although overshadowed by the more radical provisions on same-sex parents, s 36 remains in many ways a remarkable provision. It confers the status of legal parenthood on a man who is neither related to the child by blood or by marriage to the child's mother provided the fatherhood conditions set down in s 36 are satisfied.

Human Fertilisation and Embryology Act 2008, ss 36–7

36 Treatment provided to woman where agreed fatherhood conditions apply

If no man is treated by virtue of section 35 [mother's husband] as the father of the child and no woman is treated by virtue of section 42 [mother's civil partner—see below] as a parent of the child but—

(a) the embryo or the sperm and eggs were placed in W [the woman], or W was artificially inseminated, in the course of treatment services provided in the United Kingdom by a person to whom a licence applies,

(b) at the time when the embryo or the sperm and eggs were placed in W, or W was artificially inseminated, the agreed fatherhood conditions (as set out in section 37) were satisfied in relation to a man, in relation to treatment provided to W under the licence,

(c) the man remained alive at that time, and

(d) the creation of the embryo carried by W was not brought about with the man's sperm,

then, subject to section 38(2) to (4) [presumption of legitimacy], the man is to be treated as the father of the child.

37 The agreed fatherhood conditions

(1) The agreed fatherhood conditions referred to in section 36(b) are met in relation to a man ("M") in relation to treatment provided to W under a licence if, but only if,—

(a) M has given the person responsible a notice stating that he consents to being treated as the father of any child resulting from treatment provided to W under the licence,

(b) W has given the person responsible a notice stating that she consents to M being so treated,

(c) neither M nor W has, since giving notice under paragraph (a) or (b), given the person responsible notice of the withdrawal of M's or W's consent to M being so treated,

(d) W has not, since the giving of the notice under paragraph (b), given the person responsible—

(i) a further notice under that paragraph stating that she consents to another man being treated as the father of any resulting child, or

(ii) a notice under section 44(1)(b) stating that she consents to a woman being treated as a parent of any resulting child, and

(iii) W and M are not within prohibited degrees of relationship in relation to each other.

(2) A notice under subsection 1(a),(b) or (c) must be in writing and must be signed by the person giving it.

Several conditions must be satisfied in order for s 36 to confer legal parenthood on the putative father.

(i) The putative father's sperm must not have been used.

(ii) The mother must have no husband who falls within the terms of s 35 and no wife or civil partner who falls within the terms of s 42. Priority in determining legal parenthood therefore continues to be accorded to these formal legal relationships.

(iii) Treatment must have been provided by a licensed clinic in the UK. This means that unlike married couples falling within the terms of s 35, an unmarried couple making a 'DIY' attempt at AID at home will not be able to rely on the determination of parenthood under s 36. If a couple does embark upon DIY treatment, the common law will apply and the donor, as the genetic father, will be regarded as the child's legal father.[116] This requirement to attend at a licensed clinic allows the state, in the absence of marriage, to exercise greater control over access to treatment.

(iv) The agreed fatherhood conditions must be satisfied at the point at which the embryo or the sperm and eggs were placed in the mother or the mother was artificially inseminated.[117] The putative father must also have been alive at this point.

The agreed fatherhood conditions are set down in s 37, which establishes a straightforward process of notification: the mother and the putative father must both have notified the licensed provider in writing that they consent to the man being treated as the legal father of any resulting child. That notification can be withdrawn by either the mother or the putative father at any point up to the point of embryo transfer or insemination of the woman with the eggs and/or sperm. If consent is withdrawn by either party then legal fatherhood cannot be conferred on that man. The putative father is also prevented from being accorded legal fatherhood if, before the point of embryo transfer or insemination, the mother provides a further notice to the clinic, in writing, that she consents to another man or woman being treated as the legal father or second parent of the child. Provided this second man or woman is able to satisfy the agreed fatherhood or agreed female parenthood conditions, then he or she will be deemed the legal parent.

Although s 37(1)(e) prevents legal parenthood from being conferred on a man and woman falling within the prohibited degrees of relationship, legal fatherhood is otherwise conferred on the putative father by a simple process of agreement. There is no requirement for the mother and father to be cohabiting or indeed involved in any kind of intimate relationship. It is perfectly possible for two friends to decide to parent a child together—subject to being able to satisfy the licensed provider that the arrangement gives rise to no welfare concerns under s 13(5).

Where these conditions are satisfied, the man will be treated for all legal purposes as the father of the child.[118]

Deceased fathers: ss 39–40

Under the HFEA 1990, Sch 3, para 8(1), it is clear that gametes cannot be preserved and stored, save in tightly defined circumstances, without the gamete provider's written

---

[116] As to the jurisdictional requirement, see *U v W (Attorney General Intervening)* [1998] Fam 29, 44–5.
[117] HFEA 2008, s 36(b).
[118] Ibid, s 48(1).

consent.[119] It is, however, possible for a woman to use the frozen sperm or an embryo created using the gametes of her deceased husband/partner provided he specifically consented to their continued storage and use after his death.[120] It is also possible, if the man agreed to being treated as the father of any resulting child,[121] for the mother to enter that man as the child's father in the birth register.[122] Similar provisions apply where an embryo is created using donated sperm but is only transferred to the woman after her husband or partner's death.[123] Again, provided her husband or partner gave written consent to the use of the embryo after his death and to being treated as the child's father, he can be registered posthumously on the birth register. Registration on the birth register does not, however, in these circumstances confer legal fatherhood on the deceased man as the legislation specifically provides that he will not be treated in law as the father of the child for any other purposes.[124]

Second female parent: ss 42–7

Sections 42–7 of the Act contain the new and clearly more controversial provisions on determining parenthood where a woman receives fertility treatment together with her female partner. The provisions for determining the legal status of the second female parent are identical to those for determining fatherhood but 'father' is replaced with 'second parent'.

Human Fertilisation and Embryology Act 2008, ss 42–4

42 Woman in civil partnership or marriage to a woman at time of treatment

(1) If at the time of the placing in her of the embryo or the sperm and eggs or of her artificial insemination, W [the mother] was a party to a civil partnership or a marriage with another woman, then subject to section 45(2) to (4) [presumption of legitimacy], the other party to the civil partnership or marriage is to be treated as a parent of the child unless it is shown that she did not consent to the placing in W of the embryo or the sperm and eggs or her artificial insemination (as the case may be)....

43 Treatment provided to woman who agrees that second woman to be parent

(1) If no man is treated by virtue of section 35 [mother's husband] as the father of the child and no woman is treated by virtue of section 42 [mother's civil partner] as a parent of the child, but—

(a) the embryo or the sperm and eggs were placed in W, or W was artificially inseminated, in the course of treatment services provided in the United Kingdom by a person to whom a licence applies,

---

[119] See *R v HFEA, ex parte Blood* [1999] Fam 151 and *L v Human Fertilisation and Embryology Authority* [2008] EWHC 2149.

[120] HFEA 1990, Sch 3, para 2(2).

[121] HFEA 2008, ss 39(1)(c), 40(1)(e), and 40(2)(c).

[122] Ibid, ss 39(1)(d), 39(3), 40(1)(f), 40(2)(g), and 40(4).

[123] Ibid, s 40.

[124] Ibid, s 48(3).

(b) at the time when the embryo or the sperm and eggs were placed in W, or W was artificially inseminated, the agreed female parenthood conditions (as set out in section 44) were met in relation to another woman, in relation to treatment provided to W under that licence, and

(c) the other woman remained alive at that time,

then, subject to section 45(2) to (4), the other woman is to be treated as a parent of the child.

44 The agreed female parenthood conditions

(1) The agreed female parenthood conditions referred to in section 43(b) are met in relation to another woman ("P") in relation to treatment provided to W under a licence if, but only if,—

(a) P has given the person responsible a notice stating that P consents to P being treated as a parent of any child resulting from treatment provided to W under the licence,

(b) W has given the person responsible a notice stating that W agrees to P being so treated,

(c) neither W nor P has, since giving notice under paragraph (a) or (b), given the person responsible notice of the withdrawal of P's or W's consent to P being so treated,

(d) W has not, since the giving of the notice under paragraph (b), given the person responsible—

(i) a further notice under that paragraph stating that W consents to a woman other than P being treated as a parent of any resulting child, or

(ii) a notice under section 37(1)(b) stating that W consents to a man being treated as the father of any resulting child, and

(e) W and P are not within prohibited degrees of relationship in relation to each other.

(2) A notice under subsection (1)(a), (b) or (c) must be in writing and must be signed by the person giving it.

Section 46 reproduces s 40 to permit parenthood to be conferred on a deceased second female parent for the purposes of birth registration where the consent requirements are met.

Where either s 42 or s 43 applies, the woman is treated as the second parent of the child for all legal purposes.[125] The Act further provides that where there is a second female parent, no man is treated as the child's father.[126] Thus, a child can be born into a family consisting of two female parents and no legal father.

Sperm and egg donors

Where either s 35, 36, 42, or 43 applies, no other person is to be treated as the father of the child.[127] In most cases, this will be sufficient to protect a sperm donor from legal parenthood. However, further protection is provided by s 41 which stipulates that provided a donor has given the requisite consent and his sperm was used in accordance with that consent, the man is not to be treated as the child's father. Where s 41 applies and there

[125] Ibid, s 48(1).
[126] Ibid, s 45(1).
[127] Ibid, s 48(1).

is no man who qualifies for legal fatherhood under s 35 or 36, the child will be legally fatherless.[128] For the sake of completeness, s 47 similarly provides that an 'egg donor' is not to be treated as the parent of a child unless parenthood is conferred under s 42, 43, or 46 or the donor has adopted the child. This reiterates the position made clear in s 33 that the genetic mother is to have no claim to 'legal *motherhood*', which exclusively vests in the gestational mother.

Reflections on the parenthood provisions in the HFEA 2008

At first sight, the HFEA 2008 is revolutionary. Having rejected the biological imperative that a child must have one legal father and one legal mother, the Act embraces a strong model of social parenthood unconstrained by genetics, gender, or heterosexuality. Thus an unmarried man or lesbian partner not tied to the child through blood or marriage (or civil partnership) can acquire legal parenthood by virtue of intention alone. A legally fatherless child with two female parents is therefore possible in English law. This 'radical' departure from the traditional heterosexual foundations of family life was inevitably strongly opposed. Critics have argued that this attempt to deny the reality that a child must have two biological parents of the opposite sex betrays the needs of the child.

T. Callus, 'First "Designer Babies", Now À La Carte Parents', (2008) 38 *Family Law* 143, 143, 145, 146–7

[Current legislation] appears to suggest that parental status itself may be dependent upon the mere intention of the would-be (wannabe?) parent. This is not wholly unprecedented. We have recognised the importance of intention in the process of adoption and more recently in the use of donated gametes in assisted conception techniques. However, giving effect to intention has been circumscribed within the heterosexual model, ideally of two parents to reflect the biological reality that a child is created by the fusion of male and female gametes. But the de-sexualisation of procreation through the use of assisted conception has resulted in a diversity of family forms and, in particular, the possibility of same-sex couples to 'parent' children. This has led to confusion between the parental role and parental status . . .

[The HFEA 2008] is remarkable because [it] grant[s] legal status to wider family forms based on the sole intention of the would-be parents who undergo treatment at a licensed clinic. Moreover, the proposals legally enshrine family models which deny the very basic fact that gametes of complementary sex are required to create the child. According to the Family Education Trust, they represent the 'lego-kit model of family construction' . . .

By recognising the status of two female parents, the child's identity is thrown into disarray because the recognition of two female parents conceals the necessary heterosexual element of human existence. Admittedly, even the present provisions on the use of donor gametes can lead to deception insofar as the parents may conceal their use of donated gametes, but the proposals double that deception.

[T]he [Act's] provisions are merely one example of a move towards recognising legal parental status on the basis of individual choice. Yet this choice may be transient and exercised in complete ignorance of the interest of the child.

---

128 See, e.g., *Re Q (Parental Order)* [1996] 1 FLR 369, decided under the HFEA 1990.

Unquestionably, for many commentators the HFEA 2008 constitutes a step too far from the 'natural' biological imperatives of parenthood. However, others have criticized the Act, not for exploding the heterosexual parenting paradigm, but for its inherent conservatism. It is argued that the HFEA 2008 remains firmly wedded to a gendered, heterosexual model of parenthood that is binary, structured around the central and exclusive role of the legal 'mother', and precludes a more radical re-visioning of parenthood capable of embracing gay fatherhood, the fragmentation of motherhood and fatherhood into multiple biological and social components, and parenting outside the sexual norm.[129]

J. McCandless and S. Sheldon, 'The Human Fertilisation and Embryology Act (2008) and the Tenacity of the Sexual Family Form', (2010) 73 *Modern Law Review* 175, 188, 190–2, 193, 197

[T]he sexual family ideal has retained a significant hold...This can be seen in the ongoing significance of the formally recognised adult couple; law's continued adherence to a two-parent model; what we describe as 'parental dimorphism' (which, within the two-parent model, allows only for one mother plus one father or female parent); and the notion that the couple must be (at least potentially) in a sexual relationship...

In the context of widespread political and cultural disagreement regarding on what grounds parents should be recognised, acceptance of the fact that we can have two—and only two—'real' parents has proved a unifying article of faith. The two parent model retains a grip on the law which appears to have outlived any inevitable relationship between legal parenthood and either biological fact or marital convention...[T]his reform process saw no discussion of the question of whether if two parents are better than one, three parents might be better than (or, at least, as good as) two...[L]ack of further attention to this issue signals just how ingrained in our collective imagination is the notion that a child has only two parents, even in the context of assisted reproduction where more than two people may contribute biologically to the reproductive process...

[T]he sexual family model continues to resonate in a steadfast resistance to the possibility that a child can have two 'mothers' (or indeed two 'fathers'). The two parent model thus appears to encompass an assumption of what might be loosely termed 'parental dimorphism', by which we mean that the two parents are seen as occupying complementary yet different legal roles. This was seen...in the fact that a lesbian co-mother is not to be legally recognised as a 'mother'...but as a 'female parent' (a status awarded on grounds which closely parallel those by which men obtain fatherhood)...

It seems not to have been considered that the status provisions might be further adapted to allow two men to be recognised as parents from the moment of birth...[T]o recognise two gay men as parents under the status provisions would be a significant step further again, and one which simply stretches the current legal imagination too far, as it would involve moving beyond the idea that the birth mother is a legal mother (or, alternatively, recognising three parents from the moment of birth)...

---

[129] See generally Diduck (2007); Lind and Hewitt (2009); McCandless and Sheldon (2010).

Alison Diduck captures the essence of these concerns, concluding:

A. Diduck, ' "If Only We Can Find the Appropriate Terms to Use the Issue Will Be Solved": Law, Identity and Parenthood', (2007) 19 *Child and Family Law Quarterly* 458, 466–7

It thus seems to me that the new legal status 'parent' does not overcome either the biological or 'proper' nuclear family privilege that attaches to the concept of legal parenthood which has underpinned the Human Fertilisation and Embryology Act 1990 since its inception. Like fatherhood under the Human Fertilisation and Embryology Act 1990, lesbian parenthood is acquired on a basis that mimics rather than overcomes traditional norms and biology. It applies a type of presumption of paternity to partnered lesbian women and instantiates rather than challenges hetero normativity and 'nature', It both biologises and heterosexes 'parent' by ascribing that status on the basis of a person forming an exclusive sexual link with the biological parent...[W]e are left with a situation in which legal parenthood remains limited in number and subtly gendered.

The latest development in this area is the ability to create embryos using genetic material from more than two people. The reason for considering this is to prevent mitochondrial disease, which is a form of genetic disorder caused by unhealthy mitochondria (which are part of human cells, required to make them function properly, but comprising only about 0.1 per cent of our total DNA).[130] There are many forms of mitochondrial disease, some entirely asymptomatic and others fatal. The mitochondria form part of the egg itself, but separate from the so-called 'maternal spindle' which contains the woman's main DNA material. Scientific advances mean that it is now possible to remove the chromosomes from one woman's egg and implant them in another woman's egg, such that the unhealthy mitochondria would be left behind. In 2014, the UK government consulted on whether to allow this process to take place, and in February 2015 the relevant amendments were passed.[131]

9.4.4 THE CHILD'S RIGHT TO KNOW HIS OR HER GENETIC PARENTAGE

Assisted reproduction, as regulated under the HFEA 1990, presents a direct challenge to the common law's preference for genetics. A policy choice had to be made and the HFEA favoured social over genetic parenthood. Whilst this may be welcomed as affording greater recognition to the importance of social parenthood, it leaves open the question of what, if any, role genetic parents play in the child's future. The preference for social parenthood in the legislation is arguably at variance with moves elsewhere in English law to recognize the right of children to know the truth about their genetic parentage.[132] In recent years, the government has therefore faced increasing pressure to protect this right of children conceived using donated gametes.

---

[130] DH (2014), 9.

[131] Human Fertilisation and Embryology (Mitochondrial Donation) Regulations 2015, SI 2015/572.

[132] E.g. *Re H (A Minor) (Blood Tests: Parental Rights)* [1997] Fam 89, discussed above at p 617–19.

Why is the right to know important?

The importance of knowing the truth about one's genetic background is described in moving terms by Joanna Rose, an AID child, as quoted by the court in *R (Rose)*.

R (Rose) v Secretary of State for Health [2002] EWHC 1593

SCOTT BAKER J:

7.... Ms Rose describes the importance of the information to her in the following terms:

'I feel that these genetic connections are very important to me, socially, emotionally, medically, and even spiritually. I believe it to be no exaggeration that non-identifying information [information about the genetic parents that cannot lead to their identity becoming known] will assist me in forming a fuller sense of self identity and answer questions that I have been asking for a long time. I am angry that it has been assumed that this would not be the case, and can see no responsible logic for this (given the usual pre-eminence accorded to the rights and welfare of the child), unless it is believed that if we are created artificially we will not have the natural need to know to whom we are related. I feel intense grief and loss, for the fact that I do not know my genetic father and his family...

I need to find out more about my medical, genealogical and social heritage. Other people who come from families, where they have known both of their natural parents are able to discover this through the process of time. This includes information about their background and religion, where certain of their talents and skills may come from (eg parents or relations with musical or artistic skills), why they look the way they do etc. I have a strong need to discover what most people take for granted. While I was conceived to heal the pain of others (ie my parents' inability to conceive children naturally), I do not feel that there are sufficient attempts to heal my pain.'

There is a growing body of research, largely conducted in the field of adoption, providing strong support for the argument that knowledge of one's genetic background is crucial to the development of a secure sense of identity and sense of self. As Michael Freeman explains, 'identity as what we know and what we feel is an organizing framework for holding together our past and our present and it provides some anticipated shape to future life'.[133] Denying children the truth about their genetic parentage can lead to a sense of 'genealogical bewilderment'.[134] O'Donovan highlights just some of the problems that can result.

K. O'Donovan, 'Interpretations of Children's Identity Rights', in D. Fottrell (ed), *Revisiting Children's Rights* (The Hague; Boston: Kluwer Law International, 2000), 75

Effects of identity confusion have been documented as long term. Low self-esteem, loss of trust in others, inability to form intimate relationships, depression, anxiety, lack of parenting skills, have all been noted. Security about identity is the basis for self-confidence.

---

[133] Freeman (1996), 290.
[134] Van Bueren (1998), 123 and Fortin (2009b), 469.

There is, however, an important distinction between the need for knowledge about one's genetic background and establishing a social relationship with the genetic parents. As Fortin observes, research in the field of adoption suggests that whilst adopted children may experience a strong need for the former, this is not necessarily accompanied by any desire for the latter.[135] Recognition of the right of children to know the truth about their genetic background does not therefore involve any necessary revision of the *legal status* or *social role* of the genetic parent.[136]

There is not, however, complete consensus surrounding the child's right to know. The analogy often drawn with adoption has been questioned, with commentators suggesting that the secrecy surrounding AID may not be as damaging as that surrounding adoption given the very different circumstances in which they operate. It is argued that the fact that the child is the result of a deliberate procreative act by the would-be parents, is desperately wanted, does not have to face the psychological difficulty of dealing with the fact of relinquishment and, in the majority of cases, has a genetic link with one of the parents, stands AID apart from adoption. In these circumstances, it is suggested that revealing the truth about genetic parentage may not be in the child's best interests, certainly as perceived by the parents.[137]

I. Turkmendag, R. Dingwall, and T. Murphy, 'The Removal of Donor Anonymity in the UK: The Silencing of Claims by Would-Be Parents', (2008) 22 *International Journal of Law, Policy and the Family* 283, 289

Adoption is a family-building activity that involves pre-existing individuals, whereas donor conception is directed towards creating a child in order to create a family. In other words, adoption is a *substitute* for procreation whereas donor conception is a *form* of procreation: the act has its own integrity and completeness – it is the would-be parent(s)' act and the child is unquestionably their child... In this act, social links are established between the procreator and the child, not with the donor.

Unlike an adopted child, a donor-conceived child usually has a biological connection with one of their social parents as a result of pregnancy and birth. In (traditional) adoption, both parents are biologically unrelated to the child. The donor conceived child usually has access to full genetic information about one of his/her biological parents. In addition, the donor's medical history is available for the resultant child on the HFEA registers. Adopted children are usually deprived of such information unless it is provided on their birth registers.

In gamete donation, it is easy for the parents to hide the method of their child's conception whereas 'adoption can only be the worst-kept "secret" around'... Despite the difference between adoption and donor conception, much of the evidence on the harm caused by secrecy and the importance for a child to know her/his origins is drawn from the literature on adoption. If the child knows that he/she was adopted, the feeling of relinquishment and the desire to seek reasons for being 'given up' may well cause emotional distress. By contrast, donor offspring were desired by their parents, parents have

---

135 Fortin (2009b), 467.

136 This is the same point made *Re H (A Minor) (Blood Tests: Parental Rights)* [1997] Fam 89). See discussion above at p 618.

137 Turkmendag, Dingwall, and Murphy (2008), 302.

often contributed gametes, and their birth stories do not involve relinquishment. It is then questionable whether donor offspring's interest in knowing their origins is identical to that of adopted children and whether the research findings on the latter can simply be read across.

There has also been some criticism of the importance these arguments place on the role of genetics in determining 'who we are' and 'what we become'. The nature versus nurture argument has long polarized scholars. Some argue that the current emphasis on genealogical background is simply crude genetic determinism. It is also suggested that the desperate need expressed by some to know the truth about their genetic background is socially constructed. In other words, it is the emphasis placed by society on the importance of genetics that creates the strongly held need to know the truth.[138] Changing social attitudes may therefore be a more effective solution than further entrenching these attitudes by enshrining the right to know in legislation. Melanie Roberts disagrees.

M. Roberts, 'Children by Donation: Do They Have a Claim to their Genetic Parentage?', in J. Bridgeman and D. Monk (eds), *Feminist Perspectives on Child Law* (London: Cavendish, 2000), 47, 63

As the importance which society places on the genetic tie is socially constructed, it could be argued that information about the donor's identity should not be provided, as this reinforces the importance of the genetic link. However, denying children information about genitors is not the way in which to diminish the importance placed on the genetic tie and to raise the importance of the social family. Concepts of anonymity and secrecy reinforce the importance of the blood tie. These concepts fuel the notion that the genetic family is the 'norm' and any other family formation is 'unnatural' and must be hidden. Recognition of, and respect for, the different ways in which families can be formed is needed, and the way to achieve this is to be honest and open about the formation and structure of families.

Furthermore, as O'Donovan points out, telling AID or adopted children that their perceived need for knowledge about their genetic origins is socially constructed does nothing to lessen the very real pain and profound sense of loss and bewilderment they are currently suffering.[139]

The right to know in the HFEA 1990

Background to the HFEA

Until recently, the HFEA guaranteed complete secrecy concerning the conception of a child using donated gametes. The complex reasons behind this approach have been strongly criticized by Roberts. She suggests that the medical underpinnings of assisted reproduction have led to the privileging of the prospective parents' interests (the patients being treated) at the expense of the child.

---

[138] Ibid, 291.
[139] Cited in Van Bueren (1998), 123.

M. Roberts, 'Children by Donation: Do They Have a Claim to their Genetic Parentage?', in J. Bridgeman and D. Monk (eds), *Feminist Perspectives on Child Law* **(London: Cavendish, 2000), 47, 49, 53–4**

Donation is surrounded with secrecy. When artificial insemination by donor was first introduced, it was assumed that secrecy was the best stance to take and was taken for granted. Secrecy stems from fear: fear that the child will reject the social parent in favour of the genitor; fear that the genitor will interfere; and fear of societal disapproval. As use of donor sperm far outweighs the use of donor ova, it is the infertile man in particular who is protected by a policy of secrecy. There is some evidence that there may be particular problems in relation to openness and male infertility. Western culture attaches much significance to the association between fertility and power. Male infertility is thus seen as a source of shame and weakness, with feelings of masculinity being damaged by the discovery of infertility. The myth that fertility and virility are related and the attitudes of others means that couples often wish to keep the problem of infertility and the means of conception secret. A quest for 'normality' can result in secrecy and dishonesty. For men, parenthood means genetic parenthood. Secrecy stems from patriarchal concern to protect male pride in hiding male infertility and what is considered a failure: the inability to pass on one's genetic heritage.

However, the secretive approach that marked the initial years of the HFEA was not inevitable given the somewhat mixed and inconsistent messages from the Warnock Committee. On the one hand, the Committee expressed great concern about the secrecy surrounding AID children.

DHSS, *Report of the Committee of Inquiry into Human Fertilisation and Embryology,* **Cm 9314 (London: HMSO, 1984)**

4.12 ... AID has tended, partly because of the legal situation, to be surrounded with secrecy. This secrecy amounts to more than a desire for confidentiality and privacy, for the couple may deceive their family and friends, and often the child as well. Indeed couples who achieve pregnancy may come to look on their AID child as a true child of the marriage. However the sense that a secret exists may undermine the whole network of family relationships. AID children may feel obscurely that they are being deceived by their parents, that they are in some way different from their peers, and that the men whom they regard as their fathers are not their real fathers. We have little evidence on which to judge this. But it would seem probable that the impact on children of learning by accident that they were born as a result of AID would be harmful—just as it would be if they learned by accident that they were adopted or illegitimate. However, while we agree that it is wrong to deceive children about their origins, we regard this as an argument against current attitudes, not against AID in itself.

However, although the Committee were concerned about 'family secrets' they unequivocally endorsed preserving the 'absolute anonymity of the donor'. The rationale was to 'give legal protection to the donor' and protect the integrity of the family unit by 'minimizing the invasion of the third party into the family'.[140]

---

[140] DHSS (1984), para 4.22.

The legal framework in the HFEA 1990[141]

Donor anonymity was one of the most controversial issues in the parliamentary debates on the HFEA 1990.[142] However, although donor anonymity was initially firmly entrenched in the legislation, that anonymity was removed in 2004 (although not retrospectively) and greater openness further extended by the HFEA 2008. The legal framework governing the collection, storage, and disclosure of information relating to the conception of a child is found in ss 31–5 of the legislation. Sections 31–31ZE are the core provisions on information to be provided to the child and donor. Under s 31(1)–(2), the HFEA is required to keep a register of any identifiable individual who has received treatment services using donated gametes, details of any individual whose gametes have been kept or used in the provision of treatment services, and details of any identifiable individual who was, or may have been, born as a result of treatment services using donated gametes. Under s 31ZA a donor-conceived child has the right, upon reaching the age of 16, to have access to non-identifying information about his or her genetic parentage and/or any genetically related siblings (specifically the number of such siblings, the sex of each, and the year of birth). Upon reaching the age of 18, the child has the right to access identifying information about the donor. Since the new right is not retrospective, children born by AID before 1 April 2005 are restricted to receiving non-identifying information. The exact information to be provided to the child is specified in regulations. Under s 31ZD a donor-conceived child may obtain identifying information about any donor-conceived genetic siblings who have also attained the age of 18 and who have agreed to identifying information being released to a genetically related sibling requesting such information. Finally, the child has the right, upon reaching the age of 16, to know (with the specified person's consent) whether they may be related to a specified person with whom they intend to: (i) enter into a marriage; (ii) enter into a civil partnership; or (iii) engage in an intimate physical relationship.[143] Before any of this information is disclosed, the donor-conceived child and any other affected person (genetic sibling and 'specified person') must have been given the opportunity to receive proper counselling about the implications of the disclosure.[144]

One innovation of the 2008 reforms was the introduction of the right of donors to access non-identifying information about any children (specifically the number of children, the children's sex, and the year of the children's birth) conceived through the use of their donated gametes.[145] The donor may also be notified when a donor-conceived child has made a request for information about the donor. The donor will not, however, be informed about the child's identity.[146] The HFEA is also authorized to establish a voluntary contact register which may assist children, donors, and genetic siblings to make contact with one another where all relevant parties consent but there is no right to identifying information under the legislation.[147]

Despite the child's right to know now being entrenched in the legislation, children conceived using donated gametes may still face several obstacles in acquiring information about their genetic background. The first and most difficult to overcome through legal

---

[141] As amended by the HFEA 2008.
[142] DH (2001a), para 1.15.
[143] HFEA 1990, s 31ZB.
[144] Ibid, ss 31ZA(3)(b), 31ZB(3)(c), 31ZE(3)(c).
[145] Ibid, s 31ZD.
[146] Ibid, s 31ZC.
[147] Ibid, s 31ZF.

change alone is that many parents who conceive using donated gametes may still prefer to conceal the facts about the child's conception.[148] Research carried out into donor insemination families in the UK, Italy, the Netherlands, and Spain, found that only 12 per cent of the mothers interviewed planned to inform the child that they were conceived using donated gametes.[149] Similar studies in the United States and Australia found that up to 90 per cent of parents had not disclosed the use of donated gametes to the child.[150] With no legal obligation on the parent (or the state) to tell children about their conception, most will remain ignorant about their genetic background. The Warnock Committee's suggestion that 'by donation' be added to the birth certificate after the non-genetic parent's name in order to alert the child to the truth of their conception (and thereby encourage parents to be open with the child) was considered again in the 2008 reform process but rejected.[151] The Joint Parliamentary Committee in their recommendations on the draft Human Tissue and Embryos Bill expressed deep concern at this omission, commenting that the authorities 'may be colluding in a deception'.[152] In response, whilst acknowledging the importance of donor-conceived children having access to information about their genetic background, the government argued that it is 'preferable that parents are educated about the benefits of telling children that they were donor-conceived rather than forcing the issue through the annotation of birth certificates'.[153] Although the government agreed to keep the issue under review,[154] its failure to act has disappointed some who point out that the government's approach perpetuates a deception and fundamentally undermines the child's right to know.

A. Bainham, 'What is the Point of Birth Registration?', (2008) 20 *Child and Family Law Quarterly* **449, 463–4**

Our concern here...is with the process of birth registration in cases where donation has taken place. Here the position stands in stark contrast to the position which we saw in relation to adoption. In the case of donor-conceived children there is only *one* birth certificate. This records as the legal parents the birth mother and her husband or, where the mother is unmarried, her partner who joins in the registration with her...At the point of registration, the registration officer will be completely unaware of the fact that donation has taken place...[T]he baby will be registered as the presumptive biological child of both parties (except in the case of same-sex partners where it will be clear that one cannot be), as is the case with the registration of births which do not involve donation. The birth certificate which is issued will record the legal, and apparently biological, parents of the child. The concern that legal parentage should correspond with biological parentage, which as we have seen is a central feature of birth registration, is absent here except to the extent that the Registration Service has no reason of course to believe or suspect that it is doing anything other than registering two biological parents.

In common with adopted children (who have no legal right to be told that they are adopted), donor conceived persons have no legal right to be told that they are donor

---

[148] Turkmendag, Dingwall, and Murphy (2008), 298.
[149] DH (2001a), para 1.25.
[150] HFEA (2002), para 20.
[151] DHSS (1984), para 4.25.
[152] DH (2007), 19, Recommendation 28.
[153] Ibid, para 69.
[154] Ibid, para 70.

conceived. But because of the way the registration system works, this is a far more serious matter for the latter than it is for the former. There is no attempt in the context of
donation to maintain a clear distinction between genetic and social parents even though
many of those registering the birth will be clear that this distinction in fact exists . . . While
it is true that from April 2005 donors have lost their right to anonymity and the child will
be able to access identifying information about them at 18, unless there is a revolution in
current practice, the great majority will never discover that they are donor-conceived and
hence will effectively be unable to exercise these rights to knowledge about biological
origins.

A second potential difficulty lies in the consistency of information provided by donors.
Since 1991, the HFEA has collected personal information about donors such as name at
time of donation, name at time of birth, place of birth, sex, and whether the donor has
children. It has also recorded donors' physical characteristics such as height, weight,
ethnic group, eye colour, hair colour, and skin colour. Information about donors'
religion, occupation, and interests is optional, as is the provision of a pen portrait.[155]
Clinics are advised to encourage donors to record as much non-identifying information about themselves as they are happy to provide but studies suggest the information
provided is sparse.[156] Many children born before the removal of anonymity will be disappointed by the information they receive. As regards children conceived after 2004,
regulations make the provision of information about the donor's religion, occupation,
interests, skills, and reasons for donating compulsory but provision of a pen portrait
remains optional.[157] The available information is therefore likely to remain limited
in scope.[158]

The downside of reform

One of the strongest arguments against removing anonymity was the perceived risk that
it would cause a drop in donors. Evidence from Sweden, where donor anonymity was
removed in 1985, suggested that such fears may be unfounded: whilst numbers declined
immediately following the change in the law, over time they recovered to their former
level.[159] Unfortunately, the emerging picture in the UK following the removal of anonymity is not encouraging. In 2014, the British Fertility Society warned of a major lack of
available sperm, with one in four samples of donated sperm being imported from abroad,
compared with one in ten in 2005.[160] Many couples are therefore having to wait months
for treatment or are even being denied treatment altogether. This has led some commentators to observe that the 'frustration, despair and anxiety' of those seeking treatment has been ignored in a misplaced, and ultimately vain, attempt to promote greater
openness.[161]

---

[155] HFEA (2002), para 9.
[156] Roberts (2000), 52.
[157] Human Fertilisation and Embryology Authority (Disclosure of Donor Information) Regulations
2004, SI 2004/1511, reg 2(2)(f)–(h).
[158] See Roberts (2000), 52–3.
[159] Ibid, 57; HFEA (2002), para 34.
[160] <http://www.bbc.co.uk/news/health-28061263>. See also Turkmendag, Dingwall, and Murphy
(2008), 284 and 296–7.
[161] Ibid, 304–5.

9.5 SURROGACY

9.5.1 EARLY ATTITUDES TO SURROGACY

Surrogacy is a controversial topic. The Warnock Committee found the issue particularly difficult and were divided over the correct approach. Having rehearsed the main arguments, the majority of the Committee was swayed by the arguments against surrogacy, particularly in a commercialized form, and strongly opposed introducing any measures that appeared to sanction or encourage the practice.

DHSS, *Report of the Committee of Inquiry into Human Fertilisation and Embryology*, Cm 9314 (London: HMSO, 1984)

8.10 The objections turn essentially on the view that to introduce a third party into the process of procreation which should be confined to the loving partnership between two people, is an attack on the value of the marital relationship...Further, the intrusion is worse than in the case of AID, since the contribution of the carrying mother is greater, more intimate and personal than the contribution of a semen donor. It is also argued that it is inconsistent with human dignity that a woman should use her uterus for financial profit and treat it as an incubator for someone else's child. The objection is not diminished, indeed it is strengthened, where the woman entered an agreement to conceive a child, with the sole purpose of handing the child over to the commissioning couple after birth.

8.11 Again, it is argued that the relationship between mother and child is itself distorted by surrogacy. For in such an arrangement a woman deliberately allows herself to become pregnant with the intention of giving up the child to which she will give birth and this is the wrong way to approach pregnancy. It is also potentially damaging to the child, whose bonds with the carrying mother, regardless of genetic connections, are held to be strong, and whose welfare must be considered to be of paramount importance. Further it is felt that a surrogacy agreement is degrading to the child who is to be the outcome of it, since for all practical purposes, the child will have been bought for money.

8.12 It is also argued that since there are some risks attached to pregnancy, no woman ought to be asked to undertake pregnancy for another, in order to earn money. Nor, it is argued should a woman be forced by legal sanctions to part with a child, to which she has recently given birth, against her will.

8.13 If infertility is a condition which should, where possible, be remedied, it is argued that surrogacy must not be ruled out, since it offers to some couples their only chance of having a child genetically related to one or both of them. In particular, it may well be the only way that the husband of an infertile woman can have a child. Moreover, the bearing of a child for another can be seen, not as an undertaking that trivialises or commercialises pregnancy, but, on the contrary, as a deliberate and thoughtful act of generosity on the part of one woman to another. If there are risks attached to pregnancy, then the generosity is all the greater.

8.14 There is no reason, it is argued, to suppose that carrying mothers will enter into agreements lightly, and they have a perfect right to enter into such agreement if they so wish, just as they have a right to use their own bodies in other ways, according to their own decision. Where agreements are genuinely voluntary, there can be no question of exploitation, nor does the fact that surrogates will be paid for their pregnancy of itself entail exploitation of either party to the agreement.

> 8.17 . . . In the first place we are all agreed that surrogacy for convenience alone, that is, where a woman is physically capable of bearing a child but does not wish to undergo pregnancy, is totally ethically unacceptable. Even in compelling medical circumstances the danger of exploitation of one human being by another appears to the majority of us far to outweigh the potential benefits in almost every case. That people should treat others as a means to their own ends, however desirable the consequences, must always be liable to moral objection. Such treatment of one person by another becomes positively exploitative when financial interests are involved. It is therefore with the commercial exploitation of surrogacy that we have been primarily, but by no means exclusively, concerned.

The majority thus recommended that any agency, profit- or non-profit-making, creating and supporting surrogacy agreements should be subject to criminal sanctions.[162] They also recommended that professionals knowingly assisting in establishing a surrogacy should be made criminally liable.[163] The Committee held back from recommending that the commissioning parents and the surrogate mother should be liable to criminal prosecution, concerned that children should not be 'born to mothers subject to the taint of criminality'.[164] They did, however, recommend that all surrogacy agreements be designated illegal contracts, unenforceable in the courts.

The minority was less hostile, accepting that there may be rare circumstances where surrogacy could be beneficial to couples as a very last resort.[165] They therefore felt that the door to surrogacy should 'be left slightly ajar'[166] and that medical practitioners should be able to recommend such a course to their patients without acting unlawfully. Whilst agreeing that surrogacy for mere convenience was totally unacceptable and that commercial agencies should be subject to criminal prohibitions, they argued in favour of bringing surrogacy within the remit of the regulatory authority and allowing the licensing of non-profit-making agencies to provide proper advice and support to those for whom surrogacy was deemed appropriate.[167] They also recommended that in order to regularize the legal relationship between the child and the commissioning parents some form of adoption procedure should be made available.[168] Given their view that surrogacy should not stand outside the law, they also disagreed with the majority's recommendation that all surrogacy arrangements should be unenforceable, arguing that each case should be dealt with on its own facts.[169]

9.5.2 THE STATUTORY FRAMEWORK FOR SURROGACY

Surrogacy is a difficult area on which to legislate. On one hand, the practice is now so well established (though it is difficult to say how many surrogacy arrangements are made or implemented each year[170]) that it is very difficult to prevent simply by pushing such arrangements

---

[162] DHSS (1984), para 8.18.
[163] Ibid.
[164] Ibid, para 8.19.
[165] Ibid, Expression of dissent, para 1.
[166] Ibid, para 9.
[167] Ibid, paras 3–5.
[168] Ibid, para 7.
[169] Ibid, para 8.
[170] The number of parental orders has risen in recent years, from 40 or 50 per year in the early and mid-2000s to 83 in 2010 and 149 in 2011 following the introduction of the Human Fertilisation and Embryology (Parental Orders) Regulations 2010: Crawshaw, Blyth, and van den Akker (2012).

beyond the law, particularly as surrogacy can be successfully carried out within the privacy of the home on a 'DIY' basis. There is, moreover, a danger that criminalizing the practice will drive it underground, compromising safety and increasing the dangers of exploitation for all those involved. On the other hand, to bring surrogacy within a regulatory regime would give it the stamp of legitimacy and risk encouraging a practice believed to be of dubious moral and ethical standing. Parliament has therefore taken the middle ground, neither fully endorsing a prohibitive approach, nor facilitating the practice. The current law on surrogacy is found in the Surrogacy Arrangements Act 1985 (SAA 1985) and the HFEA 2008, ss 54–5.

Surrogacy Arrangements Act 1985

The SAA 1985 targets the commercial aspects of surrogacy. Surrogacy agreements are made unenforceable but neither the commissioning parents nor the surrogate commit a criminal offence by entering into such an arrangement. However, those who engage in surrogacy for financial gain are liable to criminal prosecution. The scope of the legislation is broad, covering, for example, the distributor of a newspaper that the distributor knows contains an advertisement relating to the making of surrogacy agreements.

The key provisions of the SAA 1985 can be summarized as follows. First, it makes surrogacy arrangements unenforceable by or against any party to those agreements.[171] Secondly, the Act makes it a criminal offence to initiate or take part in (or even to offer to take part in) negotiations about a commercial surrogacy arrangement,[172] though because the aim is to prevent commercial enterprises from engaging in surrogacy arrangements, women who might be potential surrogates and individuals who might be commissioning parents are exempted from criminal sanction.[173] Non-profit organizations are also exempted, so long as any payments received by it are a reasonable reflection of its costs.[174] The SAA 1985 also criminalizes the advertising of surrogacy services in certain circumstances.[175]

The exclusion of non-profit organizations from the remit of the criminal sanctions has allowed such agencies to facilitate surrogacy arrangements and support and advise infertile couples seeking to enter into such arrangements. COTS (Childlessness Overcome Through Surrogacy) has established itself as the UK's leading surrogacy agency. Agencies, such as COTS, whilst operating within the law, are unregulated as they fall outside the regulatory framework of the HFEA. If, however, the parties to a surrogacy agreement seek treatment from a licensed clinic, the clinic is subject to the HFEA's Code of Practice which provides that clinics should only consider using assisted conception techniques to produce a surrogate pregnancy where, 'the commissioning mother is unable for physical or other medical reasons to carry a child or where her health may be impaired by doing so'.[176]

The lack of regulation of voluntary agencies assisting commissioning couples and surrogates has given rise to some concern. A review carried out for the government by Professors Brazier, Campbell, and Golombok in 1997, concluded that regulation was desirable but, as surrogacy was more akin to adoption, the HFEA was not the appropriate regulatory body.[177]

---

171 SAA 1985, s 1A.
172 Ibid, s 2(1).
173 Ibid, s 2(2).
174 Ibid, s 2A.
175 Ibid, s 3.
176 HFEA (2003), para 3.17.
177 Ibid, 52–3.

It thus recommended that all agencies should be registered with the Department of Health on pain of criminal prosecution.[178] It was further suggested that surrogacy agencies should be subject to a Code of Practice similar to the HFEA's Code of Practice for fertility clinics and a parental order (see discussion below) should only be made if the commissioning couple had complied with the Code. McFarlane J supported these calls for greater regulation in *Re G (Surrogacy: Foreign Domicile)*.[179] He strongly criticized COTS for its role in facilitating a surrogacy arrangement for a Turkish couple not domiciled in the UK and providing inaccurate legal advice as to the courts' jurisdiction to grant them a parental order under s 30 of the HFEA 1990 and their ability (with the surrogate's permission) to remove the child from the UK for adoption overseas.[180]

Determining parentage in a surrogacy arrangement: the HFEA 2008

The child's mother and father

The SAA 1985, apart from making surrogacy agreements unenforceable, does not deal with the legal consequences of such agreements, in particular as regards the parental status of the commissioning parents and their legal relationship with the child. These aspects of surrogacy are dealt with in the HFEA 2008, which seeks to strike a balance between protecting the surrogate whilst protecting the legal position of the commissioning parents and the child where all parties are happy to honour the original agreement.

The surrogate mother is given the strongest protection. Section 33 provides that having given birth to the child, the surrogate mother and no other woman, even if the commissioning mother is the genetic mother, will be regarded as the child's legal mother. The position of the commissioning father is more complicated. If the surrogate is unmarried and the commissioning father is the genetic father he will be able to rely on the common law principle that the genetic parent is accorded legal parenthood. If, however, the surrogate is married, the commissioning father will have to rebut the common law presumption that the surrogate's husband is the child's legal father. Similarly, if assisted reproduction techniques are used to bring about the pregnancy, even if the commissioning father's sperm is used in the treatment, the surrogate's husband will be deemed the legal father under s 35 unless it can be shown that he did not consent. Finally, if the surrogate is unmarried and donor sperm is used, the commissioning father may fall within the terms of s 36, provided he can satisfy the agreed fatherhood conditions under s 37. The weakest party is the commissioning mother who, under s 33, will be regarded as a complete legal stranger to the child.

Parental orders

Section 54 of the HFEA 2008 provides the only means by which the commissioning parents can secure their legal status with respect to the child without resorting to complicated and lengthy adoption proceedings. Under s 54, the court can make a 'parental order' in favour of the commissioning parents. A 'parental order' has the same legal effect as an adoption

---

[178] Ibid.
[179] [2007] EWHC 2814.
[180] Ibid, [23]–[29].

order, conferring legal parenthood on the commissioning parents and extinguishing the legal motherhood of the surrogate.[181] The making of a parental order is subject to a number of conditions:

Human Fertilisation and Embryology Act 2008, s 54

54 Parental orders

(1) On an application made by two people ("the applicants"), the court may make an order providing for a child to be treated in law as the child of the applicants if—

    (a) the child has been carried by a woman who is not one of the applicants, as a result of the placing in her of an embryo or sperm and eggs or her artificial insemination,

    (b) the gametes of at least one of the applicants were used to bring about the creation of the embryo, and

    (c) the conditions in subsections (2) to (8) are satisfied.

(2) The applicants must be—

    (a) husband and wife,[182]

    (b) civil partners of each other, or

    (c) two persons who are living as partners in an enduring family relationship and are not within prohibited degrees of relationship in relation to each other.

(3) Except in a case falling within subsection (11), the applicants must apply for the order during the period of 6 months beginning with the day on which the child is born.

(4) At the time of the application and the making of the order—

    (a) the child's home must be with the applicants, and

    (b) either or both of the applicants must be domiciled in the United Kingdom or in the Channel Islands or the Isle of Man.

(5) At the time of the making of the order both the applicants must have attained the age of 18.

(6) The court must be satisfied that both—

    (a) the woman who carried the child, and

    (b) any other person who is a parent of the child but is not one of the applicants (including any man who is the father by virtue of section 35 or 36 or any woman who is a parent by virtue of section 42 or 43),

have freely, and with full understanding of what is involved, agreed unconditionally to the making of the order.

(7) Subsection (6) does not require the agreement of a person who cannot be found or is incapable of giving agreement; and the agreement of the woman who carried the child is ineffective for the purpose of that subsection if given by her less than six weeks after the child's birth.

---

[181] HFEA 2008, s 55(1).

[182] Unlike other references to husband and wife in primary legislation, this provision was not amended by the Marriage (Same Sex Couples) Act 2013, though clearly a married same-sex couple would be eligible for a parental order.

(8) The court must be satisfied that no money or other benefit (other than for expenses reasonably incurred) has been given or received by either of the applicants for or in consideration of—

(a) the making of the order,

(b) any agreement required by subsection (6),

(c) the handing over of the child to the applicants, or

(d) the making of arrangements with a view to the making of the order, unless authorised by the court.

Assuming that these conditions are satisfied, the decision that the court must take is a welfare decision. Since 2010, this welfare determination has been informed by the same list of welfare considerations as exists in the adoption context.[183] By comparison with the pre-2010 position, Hedley J commented that 'welfare is no longer merely the court's first consideration but becomes its paramount consideration'.[184] Consequently, the balance to be struck between public policy and the child's welfare, as discussed in some of the pre-2010 cases,[185] is now weighted 'decisively in favour of welfare'.[186]

The s 54 conditions

The HFEA 2008 liberalized the eligibility criteria for applicants seeking parental orders. Under the 1990 Act, a parental order could only be made in favour of a married couple. The 2008 Act extended this to permit unmarried and same-sex couples who have entered into a surrogacy arrangement to apply to regularize their position in relation to the child. The crucial qualifying provisions for making an application are now that the applicants are either married, civil partners, or 'two persons who are living as partners in an enduring family relationship'. However, single applicants are barred from applying under s 54. It is difficult to see the justification for this restriction,[187] given that single applicants may adopt a child[188] and a single woman can be registered as the sole parent of a child conceived using donor sperm following treatment under the HFEA.[189]

The remaining conditions for making a parental order have been reproduced from the 1990 legislation. The requirement that the surrogate must have been impregnated by artificial means (s 54(1)(a)) is probably aimed at discouraging the 'adultery' involved in basic 'DIY' surrogacy. Section 54(1)(b) serves an important purpose. By insisting that the gametes of one of the commissioning parents were used in creating the embryo, applicants under s 54 are not 'mere' social parents: at least one must have a genetic tie to the child. This distinguishes such cases from pre-natal adoption, preventing surrogacy being used to circumvent the strict regulations concerning eligibility and suitability to adopt.

---

[183] The Human Fertilisation and Embryology (Parental Orders) Regulations 2010, SI 2010/985, import a modified version of s 1 of the ACA 2002 into s 54: the checklist in its adoption form is set out at 13.4.1.

[184] *Re L (Surrogacy: Parental Order)* [2010] EWHC 3146, [9].

[185] See, e.g., *Re X and Y (Foreign Surrogacy)* [2008] EWHC 3030, [24].

[186] *Re L (Surrogacy: Parental Order)* [2010] EWHC 3146, [10].

[187] In correspondence with the authors, the Department of Health suggested that the justification stemmed from the magnitude of the decision and the potentially volatile and traumatic situation involved. However, when set against the difficulties of the adoption process, this argument does not appear particularly compelling.

[188] ACA 2002, s 51.

[189] HFEA 2008, s 41.

Sections 54(4)(a) and 54(6) afford strong protection to the surrogate mother. The requirement that the child must be living with the commissioning parents at the time of the application means that the surrogate mother must have voluntarily surrendered the child after birth.[190] Section 54(4)(b) requires one or both of the applicants to be domiciled in the UK.[191] The surrogate is further protected by the requirement that she must freely consent to the order being made.[192] Any consent given within six weeks of the birth, when the surrogate is deemed physically and emotionally vulnerable, is invalid.[193] The commissioning parents cannot therefore use s 54 where the surrogate reneges on the agreement and wishes to keep the child. Unlike adoption, the court has no discretion to override the consent requirements: it is 'an absolute veto'.[194] The only alternative would be for the commissioning parents to pursue an adoption order under the ACA 2002 or, less satisfactorily from their perspective, apply for a child arrangements order by which the child is to live with them under s 8 of the CA 1989. There is a further potentially complicating factor in that the other 'parent' of the child, where it is not one of the applicants, must also consent to the order.[195] Where the surrogate is married this may mean her husband's consent is also required.

The other 'conditions' in subsections (2) to (8) have been given a wide interpretation in the case law, to the point where some of them appear to have been disregarded entirely by the courts. For example, despite the wording of subsection (4), in *A v P (Surrogacy: Parental Order: Death of Applicant)*, Theis J held that an order could be made where one of the applicants had died between the application being lodged and the order being made, on the basis that to say otherwise would be an undue interference with Article 8 rights under the ECHR.[196]

Perhaps more remarkably, the court has held that subsection (3)—that the application must be made within six months of the child's birth—does not impose a strict limitation. Earlier authority had suggested that there was no discretionary power to extend the time limit set: for example, in *JP v LP* Eleanor King J identified the policy aim of subsection (3) as being 'to provide for the speedy consensual regularisation of the legal parental status of a child's carers following a birth resulting from a surrogacy arrangement', which the judge said 'does not fit comfortably with extensions of time'.[197] However, in *Re X (Surrogacy: Time Limit)*,[198] Sir James Munby P took a different view. The President concluded, both as a matter of general principle and when considering the requirements of the ECHR, that the time limit was not strict and could be extended by the court in an appropriate case (which, in *Re X*, allowed an order to be made where the application was not made for 26 months after the child's birth). However, whatever may be the merits of such an approach, it is difficult to see how this interpretation can be reconciled with the plain wording of the Act.

The prohibition on financial reward set down in s 54(8) has been interpreted[199] following the approach taken in adoption cases,[200] that payments made to the surrogate in excess of

---

190 HFEA 2008, s 54(4)(a).
191 See *Re G (Surrogacy: Foreign Domicile)* [2007] EWHC 2814.
192 HFEA 2008, s 54(6).
193 Ibid, s 54(7).
194 *Re X and Y (Foreign Surrogacy)* [2008] EWHC 3030, [13].
195 HFEA 2008, s 54(6)(b).
196 [2011] EWHC 1738. This decision makes it all the more difficult to justify denying single applicants the ability to seek a parental order.
197 [2014] EWHC 595.
198 [2014] EWHC 3135. See Trimmings (2015).
199 *Re C; Application by Mr and Mrs X under s 30 of the Human Fertilisation and Embryology Act 1990* [2002] EWHC 157.
200 *Re Adoption Application (Payment for Adoption)* [1987] Fam 81.

reasonable expenses could be retrospectively authorized by the court. In *Re X and Y (Foreign Surrogacy)*, Hedley J considered the various factors that must be taken into consideration. The case concerned a surrogacy arrangement between a British couple and a Ukrainian woman. A payment had been made to her that covered not only her reasonable expenses but a deposit for a flat in the Ukraine. The tensions inherent in the court's task and Hedley J's disquiet at what the court is being asked to do in giving retrospective authorization to such payments are very clear.

Re X and Y (Foreign Surrogacy) [2008] EWHC 3030

HEDLEY J:

21. In relation to the public policy issues, the cases in effect suggest (and I agree) that the court pose itself three questions:

(i) was the sum paid disproportionate to reasonable expenses?

(ii) were the applicants acting in good faith and without 'moral taint' in their dealings with the surrogate mother?

(iii) were the applicants party to any attempt to defraud the authorities?

On the facts of this case I have no doubt that the applicants were acting in good faith and that no advantage was taken (or sought to be taken) of the surrogate mother who was herself a woman of mature discretion. Moreover there was never any suggestion of any attempt to defraud the authorities; quite the opposite: I am satisfied that these applicants sought at all times to comply with the requirements of English and Ukrainian law as they believed them to be.

23. In this case I am satisfied that the welfare of these children require that they be regarded as lifelong members of the applicants' family. Given my findings on the public policy considerations, I am able without great difficulty to conclude that I should in this particular case authorise the payments so made under Section 30(7) of the 1990 Act.

24. I feel bound to observe that I find this process of authorisation most uncomfortable. What the court is required to do is to balance two competing and potentially irreconcilably conflicting concepts. Parliament is clearly entitled to legislate against commercial surrogacy and is clearly entitled to expect that the courts should implement that policy consideration in its decisions. Yet it is also recognised that as the full rigour of that policy consideration will bear on one wholly unequipped to comprehend it let alone deal with its consequences (i.e. the child concerned) that rigour must be mitigated by the application of a consideration of that child's welfare. That approach is both humane and intellectually coherent. The difficulty is that it is almost impossible to imagine a set of circumstances in which by the time the case comes to court, the welfare of any child (particularly a foreign child) would not be gravely compromised (at the very least) by a refusal to make an order... If public policy is truly to be upheld, it would need to be enforced at a much earlier stage than the final hearing of a Section 30 [now s 54] application... It is, of course, not for the court to suggest how (or even whether) action should be taken, I merely feel constrained to point out the problem.

While this guidance remains helpful, the subsequent statutory importation of the welfare principle from s 1 of the ACA 2002 means that the considerations highlighted by Hedley J should be considered 'with the understanding that the court is only likely to refuse parental orders in the clearest case of the abuse of public policy where otherwise the child's welfare requires the order to be made'.[201]

Revoking parental orders

The HFEA itself provides no mechanism for revoking a parental order. However, in *G v G (Parental Order: Revocation)*,[202] the High Court considered that there was nonetheless a power to revoke a parental order. In *G v G*, the commissioning parents separated shortly after the parental order had been made and contact between the father and the child became the subject of litigation. The child had lived since birth with the commissioning mother. The father applied for the parental order to be revoked as a result of which the commissioning mother would be rendered a legal stranger to the child. However, the father, as the biological father, would retain parental responsibility. The father argued that the commissioning mother had deceived him, the surrogate mother, the parental reporter, and ultimately the court at the time the parental order was made in that she had already decided to leave him but concealed her intentions in order to secure the order. He therefore contended that the order had been made on a false premise, it being his position that had he known of his wife's true intentions he would not have proceeded and the order could not have been made. A number of other grave procedural flaws were identified in the making of the original order, including the order being made under the wrong legislation, the judge's failure to address the s 54 conditions (in particular the bar on making an order where the surrogate has been paid), and the judge's failure to consider the Cafcass report as to the child's welfare.

In his judgment, Hedley J noted that a parental order, like an adoption order, confers a lifelong legal status on both the child and the commissioning parents,[203] and thus the bar for challenging such an order once made 'is set very high'.[204] In making that assessment, the judge suggested that guidance can be taken from the authorities that relate to applications to revoke an adoption order.[205] Furthermore, Hedley J made clear that in determining the application the child's welfare is a relevant consideration. Taking into account the consequences of revocation for the legal relationship between the child and the commissioning mother (his primary carer) and the grave difficulty in finding a suitable alternative order to secure the mother's position should the parental order be set aside, Hedley J concluded, despite the serious procedural flaws, that the father's application should be refused.

Disputes when the surrogacy agreement breaks down

Evidence suggests that in only 4–5 per cent of cases do surrogates refuse to hand over the child.[206] However, where the surrogacy agreement does break down, there is rarely an easy answer as to whether the surrogate should be able to keep the child and, if so, the role if any that should be played by the commissioning parents. The courts have tended to take each case on its facts, applying the welfare principle as best they can. This has led to very different outcomes in individual cases depending on such factors as the circumstances surrounding

---

201 *J v G (Parental Order)* [2013] EWHC 1432, [21].
202 [2012] EWHC 1979.
203 Ibid, [33].
204 Ibid, [43].
205 See 13.2.
206 Brazier et al (1998), 26.

the surrogacy agreement, the reasons for the surrogate's refusal to proceed with the arrangement, and the court's general attitude towards surrogacy. The following two cases provide extreme examples of the difficult circumstances that can face the court and their reactions in trying to secure, as best they can, the child's interests.

In the early case of *A v C*,[207] the Court of Appeal made no secret of their intense disapproval of the commissioning couple and the circumstances surrounding the surrogacy agreement. The facts of *A v C* were somewhat colourful, and no doubt fuelled the court's hostility. The commissioning father was living with a slightly older woman who was no longer able to conceive. He desperately wanted a child of his own and so it was agreed that he would go down to Bow Street magistrates' court to select a suitable prostitute to act as surrogate. A 19-year-old surrogate was found and, in exchange for a substantial fee and the use of a flat during her pregnancy, she agreed to carry the child to be handed over to the commissioning parents after birth. She was artificially inseminated with the commissioning father's sperm. Unfortunately, she subsequently changed her mind and decided to keep the child. Immediately after the birth, the commissioning father applied to make the child a ward of court with care and control being vested in him. On advice, he withdrew this application but pursued an application for contact which both commissioning parents had enjoyed on a regular basis since the child's birth. The Court of Appeal dismissed the application, holding that 'to permit access to continue in the circumstances of this case is to perpetuate the most artificial situation that one can possibly imagine'.[208] In reaching this conclusion, whilst expressing sympathy for the surrogate, the court showed nothing but extreme distaste for the commissioning father and the 'sordid',[209] 'ugly',[210] 'bizarre and unnatural arrangement'[211] that he had orchestrated. The Court of Appeal made it clear that, in the circumstances, a mere genetic link between father and child was not sufficient to justify an ongoing social relationship.

More recently in *Re N (A Child)*[212] the court disapproved just as strongly of the behaviour of the surrogate mother and took the unusual and very surprising step of transferring the child's residence from the surrogate and her husband to the commissioning parents, even though the child had been living with the surrogate and her husband for the 18 months since her birth. The case was unusual given the surrogate mother's deliberate intention to obtain sperm for insemination by deceiving the commissioning parents into entering the surrogacy arrangement when she had no intention to relinquish the child. This deliberate deception led the court to conclude that the child's long-term interests would be better served with the commissioning parents, despite the high standards of care the surrogate and her husband had provided and the strong bond they had formed with the child. The Court of Appeal upheld this decision, paying little regard to whether the surrogate and her husband or the commissioning parents were to be regarded as the legal parents. However, whilst Thorpe LJ approached the case as one between two 'natural' parents—the surrogate mother and the commissioning father[213]—Lloyd LJ noted that under the HFEA 1990, the surrogate's husband would be the legal father.[214] Whilst this did not affect his assessment of

---

[207] [1985] FLR 445.
[208] Ibid, 457.
[209] Ibid (Cumming-Bruce LJ).
[210] Ibid, 461 (Stamp LJ).
[211] Ibid, 455 (Ormrod LJ).
[212] [2007] EWCA Civ 1053.
[213] Ibid, [13]–[14].
[214] Ibid, [19].

the child's welfare, it makes the decision all the more remarkable as the child was placed to live with two people who were legal strangers to him.

Whilst this pragmatic approach which seeks to protect each child's welfare has clear advantages, it also has the major disadvantage of uncertainty, particularly for the commissioning couple. The alternative approach of making surrogacy agreements enforceable like any other contractual arrangement would give much better protection to the commissioning parents and much greater certainty to all parties in the vast majority of surrogacy agreements that work. This intentional/contractual model has been adopted elsewhere, most notably California. Douglas, commenting on the decision of the Supreme Court of California in *Johnson v Calvert*,[215] provides an interesting analysis of the pros and cons of such an approach to determining legal parenthood both in surrogacy agreements and beyond.

G. Douglas, 'The Intention to Be a Parent and the Making of Mothers', (1994b) 57 *Modern Law Review* 636, 638–41

The California Court's reliance on intention...has potentially interesting consequences for our attitudes to parenthood and family formation in general. For instance, it has been argued that using intention in this way is a means of avoiding gender-based stereotypes and biologically-determined differences when determining issues of parenthood. While men and women cannot physically play the same role in the procreation of children, both can have the intention to become a parent. Giving weight to intention, rather than to biological roles, therefore provides a means to treat claims to parenthood equally, regardless of gender difference. On the other hand, it could be argued that focusing on intention is very much a *male* approach to parenthood because it fits far more closely to men's experience of procreation than to that of most women. Just as the commissioning mother was unable to carry and give birth to her own child, so too was her husband; for men, *all* women who carry children are surrogates. Relying upon their intention to produce and raise a child is a very convenient way for men to assert their parentage over children...

If the intention to have and rear a child were to be the main criterion for legal parenthood, anyone who had this intention could seek out gamete donors and a surrogate and claim the 'product' of these people's labours when the child was born. This would render irrelevant the assumption that to be the parents of a particular child presupposes a relationship (sexual or not) of not more than two persons of different sex. There would be no reason why more than two people could not be recognised as 'parents', nor why they should be of different sex.

But there may be practical difficulties in the emphasis on intent. First how does it relate to the welfare and interests of the child who is produced? The California majority relied upon the argument that 'the interests of children, particularly at the outset of their lives, are unlikely to run contrary to those of adults who choose to bring them into being.'...Secondly, how would proof of intention be established? The easiest way is by written agreement between the parties and there is certainly nothing new about this...Basing parenthood on intention implies a preparedness to recognise the free alienability of parental responsibility and hence the acceptability of surrogacy agreements. It comes closer to characterising children more openly as a form of property which can be transferred to others.

---

215 (1993) 5 Cal 4th 84.

Thirdly, the corollary of recognising intention as the determining factor of parenthood is to accept that *lack* of intention should be a means of avoiding parenthood. Hitherto, the law in the United Kingdom has generally refused to permit someone to avoid liability (if not responsibility) for a child on the ground that he or she had not *intended* the child's conception or birth...

Why, then, not take the more straightforward route of the California court and accept that the intention to act as parent should be the key indicator for parental status? The short answer is because of the disapproval of surrogacy as a form of assisted reproduction... But underlying these restrictions is a deeper assumption. We still require, or at least prefer, some sort of biological link to the child, be it genetic *or* gestational, because we view children as in some way the physical recreations of their parents. We still refuse to face up to the reality of our acceptance of the importance of social parenthood—to an idea of parenthood as departing from the traditional, pseudo-biological model of two people of the opposite sex creating and rearing their offspring. In *Johnson v Calvert*, probably unintentionally, the Supreme Court of California appears to have moved a little closer to such recognition.

9.6 ADOPTION

Adoption is the one method of acquiring legal parenthood in English law that does not require one or other of the parents to have a biological link (genetic or gestational) with the child. It permanently extinguishes the legal parenthood of the child's original parents (usually the genetic/biological parents) and replaces them with the adoptive parents (the social/intended parents) as if the child had been born their legitimate child.[216] Adoption thus provides unique recognition of the value of social parenthood. The absence of a genetic tie between parent and child means, however, that this method of acquiring legal parenthood is subject to the most detailed and rigorous scrutiny by the state. It is covered in detail in chapter 13.

9.7 CONCLUSION

This chapter has been primarily concerned with how one determines the identity of a child's legal parents under English law. As Douglas and Lowe point out, one can situate the various methods of acquiring legal parenthood on a sliding scale, with natural procreation at one end, adoption at the other, and the various methods of assisted reproduction located at different points in the middle.[217] As one progresses along the scale from natural to adoptive parenthood, one moves from a strong emphasis on genetic parenthood to greater acceptance of the value of social parents. However, as the genetic tie weakens, one also moves from no regulation of an individual's attempts to become a parent, to detailed and rigorous scrutiny of one's parenting credentials by the state. Such scrutiny reflects the law's long-standing preference for genetic parenthood and the ambivalence, and even suspicion, in which it holds 'mere' social parents.

---

[216] ACA 2002, ss 46 and 67.
[217] Douglas and Lowe (1992), 416–17.

Legal parenthood is clearly central to defining the child's core family relationships. However, as should be clear from the above discussion, it is not the only 'parent' or 'parent-like' relationship of importance to children. Advances in reproductive technology and the increasing fluidity and diversity in modern family life, have led to 'parenthood' becoming an increasingly fragmented concept. Three distinct concepts of 'parenthood' have thus emerged in English law: genetic parentage, legal parenthood, and social parenthood. This chapter has considered legal parenthood and, where legal parenthood is divorced from genetic parentage, the continuing role, if any, of the genetic parents. In the next chapter, we consider the child's social parents: those individuals who provide care and nurture for a child. Although in most cases the child's social parents will also be the child's legal (and probably genetic) parents, this is no longer necessarily the case: social parenting can be, and often is, located in someone other than the legal parents. The extent to which English law is able to accommodate this additional level of complexity forms the subject matter of the next chapter. It is to the concept of parental responsibility that we now turn.

ONLINE RESOURCE CENTRE

Questions, suggestions for further reading, and supplementary materials for this chapter (including updates on developments in this area of family law since this book was published) may be found on the Online Resource Centre at **www.oxfordtextbooks.co.uk/orc/familytcm3e/**.

10

PARENTAL RESPONSIBILITY

CENTRAL ISSUES

1. Understanding of the parent–child relationship has changed dramatically in recent years. From a concept dominated by rights, parenthood is now largely understood in terms of the parents' duties and responsibilities. Parental rights exist only insofar as they are necessary for parents to perform their parental duties.

2. Parenthood and parental responsibility are distinct legal concepts. Although largely undefined in the Children Act 1989 (CA 1989), parental responsibility gives an individual the power and authority to make decisions regarding the child's upbringing. Arguably, it is parental responsibility which confers the real legal status of parenthood.

3. Parental responsibility is conferred *automatically* on all mothers, married fathers, and civil partners accorded legal parenthood under s 42 of the Human Fertilisation and Embryology Act 2008 (HFEA 2008). Unmarried fathers (and second female parents accorded legal parenthood under s 43 of the HFEA 2008) must *acquire* parental responsibility in accordance with the legislative provisions. The difference in treatment between married and unmarried fathers is controversial but, in practice, of diminishing

significance. Indeed, some commentators are now suggesting that the balance has swung too far in conferring parental rights and responsibilities on disengaged fathers based on nothing more than the genetic tie.

4. A number of individuals can hold parental responsibility at any one time. In addition to the child's legal parents, parental responsibility may be held by social parents, such as step-parents and guardians, and 'corporate parents', such as the state. This raises the important question whether each individual holding parental responsibility can act unilaterally or whether the agreement of all members of the 'parenting team' must be obtained. Despite the clear statutory basis for unilateral action, the courts have suggested that there is a duty to consult and agree on a growing list of important issues.

5. The exercise of parental responsibility can be limited both by the child (upon reaching *Gillick* competence) and by the state. The state's intervention into the private decision-making realm of the parents is controversial, particularly when those holding parental responsibility are acting reasonably. The courts have been criticized for the limited weight given to parents' views once a dispute reaches court.

6. The parental responsibility of mothers, married fathers, and civil partners accorded legal parenthood under s 42 of the HFEA 2008 cannot be terminated, other than by way of a parental order under the HFEA 2008 or adoption. For these parents, 'parenthood is for life'. The parental responsibility of unmarried fathers, female second parents accorded legal parenthood under s 43 of the HFEA 2008, and 'mere' social parents can be terminated by the court. Arguably, in order to ensure the equal treatment of all parents, it should be possible to terminate the parental responsibility of any irresponsible and uninterested parent.

10.1 INTRODUCTION

Establishing the legal parenthood of a child under English law can be a complex and difficult process. However, establishing legal parenthood is only half the story. Although, as we have seen in chapter 9, a number of important rights and responsibilities attach to the mere fact of the parent–child relationship, in order to hold the full ambit of rights and responsibilities commonly associated with 'being a parent' and raising a child, an individual must also hold 'parental responsibility'. Indeed, it has been emphasized in the case law that it is parental responsibility that really confers the legal 'status of parenthood'.[1] Parental responsibility is thus a distinct legal concept. It is both narrower and wider than parenthood, in that, whilst some enduring rights and responsibilities attach exclusively to the parent–child relationship, other rights and responsibilities relating to the care and upbringing of the child attach exclusively to the concept of parental responsibility. For most parents, this disjunction between parenthood and parental responsibility poses no problems as the law both confers on them the status of legal parenthood and automatically regards them as holding parental responsibility. However, for some unmarried fathers the legal distinction is of enormous significance as they will not *automatically* hold parental responsibility for their children. Conversely, some social parents who have no genetic links with the child and do not hold the status of legal parenthood can acquire parental responsibility in accordance with the legislative provisions. Parental responsibility therefore plays an important role in the legal recognition of social parenthood, leading one commentator to remark that it is a 'potentially radical legal construct'.[2]

In understanding the parent–child relationship in English law, it is important to keep in mind this crucial distinction between the two legal concepts of parenthood and parental responsibility. Whilst chapter 9 dealt with the concept of parenthood, the focus of this chapter will be on parental responsibility. We begin by exploring the concept of parental responsibility and its legal significance in more detail, before considering the various legislative provisions dealing with who automatically holds parental responsibility, and how, and by whom, it may be acquired. We then examine the exercise of parental responsibility and the various restrictions that may be imposed on the decision-making authority of those who

---

[1] *Re S (A Minor) (Parental Responsibility)* [1995] 3 FCR 225, 234.
[2] Diduck (2007), 462.

hold it. The final section briefly considers the rights and responsibilities of those adults who care for a child but do not have parental responsibility.

10.2 WHAT IS PARENTAL RESPONSIBILITY?

10.2.1 FROM RIGHTS TO RESPONSIBILITY

The parent–child relationship

Section 3(1) of the CA 1989[3] defines parental responsibility in the following terms:

Children Act 1989, s 3

(1) In this Act 'parental responsibility' means all the rights, duties, powers, responsibilities and authority which by law a parent of a child has in relation to the child and his property.

'Parental responsibility' as a distinct legal concept was an innovation in the CA 1989. It was intended to mark a fundamental shift in understanding about the parent–child relationship from one dominated by rights to one dominated by duties and responsibilities. However, the same concept of parenthood can be seen to underpin *Gillick v West Norfolk and Wisbech AHA*.[4]

Gillick v West Norfolk and Wisbech Area Health Authority [1986] AC 112 (HL), 170, 183–5

LORD FRASER:

[P]arental rights to control a child do not exist for the benefit of the parent. They exist for the benefit of the child and they are justified only in so far as they enable the parent to perform his duties towards the child, and towards other children in the family.

LORD SCARMAN:

Parental rights clearly do exist, and they do not wholly disappear until the age of majority. Parental rights relate to both the person and the property of the child—custody, care, and control of the person and guardianship of the property of the child. But the common law has never treated such rights as sovereign or beyond review and control. Nor has our law ever treated the child as other than a person with capacities and rights recognised by law. The principle of the law, as I shall endeavour to show, is that parental rights are derived from parental duty and exist only so long as they are needed for the protection of the person and property of the child...

 The principle is that parental right or power of control of the person and property of his child exists primarily to enable the parent to discharge his duty of maintenance, protection, and

---

[3] Unless otherwise stated, all references to statutory provisions in this chapter are to the CA 1989.
[4] The facts of *Gillick* and further detailed extracts are found at 8.5.4.

education until he reaches such an age as to be able to look after himself and make his own decisions... [Blackstone] accepts that by statute and by case law varying ages of discretion have been fixed for various purposes. But it is clear that this was done to achieve certainty where it was considered necessary and in no way limits the principle that parental right endures only so long as it is needed for the protection of the child...

The *Gillick* approach to parenthood was heralded and later unequivocally endorsed by the Law Commission, before being enshrined in s 3.

Law Commission, *Family Law, Review of Child Law: Guardianship and Custody,* Law Com No 172 (London: HMSO, 1988c)

2.4 Scattered through the statute book at present are such terms as "parental rights and duties" or the "powers and duties", or the "rights and authority" of a parent. However, in our first Report on Illegitimacy we expressed the view that "to talk of parental 'rights' is not only inaccurate as a matter of juristic analysis but also a misleading use of ordinary language". The House of Lords in *Gillick v West Norfolk and Wisbech Area Health Authority*, has held that the powers which parents have to control or make decisions for their children are simply the necessary concomitant of their parental duties. To refer to the concept of "right" in the relationship between parent and child is therefore likely to produce confusion, as that case itself demonstrated. As against third parties, parents clearly have a prior claim to look after or have contact with their child but... that claim will always be displaced if the interests of the child indicate to the contrary. The parental claim can be recognised in the rules governing the allocation of parental responsibilities, but the content of their status would be more accurately reflected if a new concept of "parental responsibility" were to displace the ambiguous and confusing terms used at present. Such a change would make little difference in substance but it would reflect the everyday reality of being a parent and emphasise the responsibilities of all who are in that position.

The language of parental rights has not, however, been erased entirely from the statute books. Indeed, the 'rights' of parents are expressly included within the statutory definition of parental responsibility. It is, however, clear from the preparatory work of the Law Commission that such parental rights as are enshrined in the CA 1989 are meant in the *Gillick* sense. That is, they are instrumental: they exist only insofar as they are necessary for parents to perform their parental duties and responsibilities. It is therefore parental duties and responsibilities, not parental rights, which *should* be regarded as standing at the heart of parenthood. The Court of Appeal has reiterated the centrality of the responsibilities and burdens of parental responsibility in the practice of raising children.

Re W (Direct Contact) [2012] EWCA Civ 999

McFARLANE LJ:

74. ... I have stressed that, along with the rights, powers and authority of a parent, come duties and responsibilities which must be discharged in a manner which respects similarly-held rights, powers, duties and responsibilities of the other parent where parental responsibility is shared.

75. In all aspects of life, whilst some duties and responsibilities may be a pleasure to discharge, others may well be unwelcome and a burden. Whilst parenting in many respects brings joy, even in families where life is comparatively harmonious, the responsibility of being a parent can be tough. Where parents separate, the burden for each and every member of the family group can be, and probably will be, heavy. It is not easy, indeed it is tough, to be a single parent with the care of a child. Equally, it is tough to be the parent of a child for whom you no longer have the day-to-day care and with whom you no longer enjoy the ordinary stuff of everyday life because you only spend limited time with your child....

76. Where parental responsibility is shared by a child's parents, the statute is plain (CA 1989, s 3) that each of those parents, and both of them, share 'duties' and 'responsibilities' in relation to the child, as well as 'rights...powers...and authority'. Where all are agreed, as in the present case, that it is in the best interests of a child to have a meaningful relationship with both parents, the courts are entitled to look to each parent to use their best endeavours to deliver what their child needs, hard or burdensome or downright tough though that may be. The statute places the primary responsibility for delivering a good outcome for a child upon each of his or her parents, rather than upon the courts or some other agency...

However, while this judgment can be seen as reiterating the practical importance of parental responsibility, it is not easy to reconcile it with the courts' approach to making orders for parental responsibility which are expressly designed not to allow the parent concerned to play an active part in the child's upbringing.[5]

The parent–state relationship

The change in emphasis from focusing on parental rights to focusing on parental responsibilities also reflects a wider political agenda concerning the appropriate relationship between the child, the parent, and the state. As expressed by the government in its 1987 review of the public law on children, 'the prime responsibility for the upbringing of children rests with parents'.[6] In other words, in a policy which was typical of the privatizing trend of the Conservative Government of the time, caring for and supporting children was seen to be an individual, not a state, responsibility. The government's approach was encapsulated in Prime Minister Margaret Thatcher's remark that 'parenthood is for life'.[7] It served to emphasize the enduring nature of the individual responsibility of *both* parents for their children's upbringing, a responsibility that could not be transferred or surrendered to the state and would not be affected by the parents' changing relationship.[8]

Two distinct ideas therefore underpin the concept of 'parental responsibility' in the CA 1989: one focusing on the parent–child relationship; the other focusing on the parents' relationship with the state.[9] Eekelaar argues that, by the time the CA 1989 was enacted, there had been a decisive shift in emphasis from the Law Commission's initial concern with the duties and obligations owed by parents to their children, to the more politically

---

[5] See the court's approach to parental responsibility orders, discussed at 10.3.2.
[6] DHSS et al (1987), para 5.
[7] Quoted in Eekelaar (1991c), 43.
[8] See generally Lindley (1999) and Eekelaar (1991c), 42–3.
[9] Eekelaar (1991c), 38–9. See also Freeman (2000), 452.

contentious issue of the appropriate relationship between the parents and the state.[10] This was fuelled by the government's growing anxiety over the breakdown of the traditional family unit and the resulting growth in single motherhood. Traditionally, men were legally tied to their children through the institution of marriage. Changing social trends brought the effectiveness of this approach into question. It was widely perceived that the declining popularity of marriage, rising divorce rates, and the ever-increasing number of children born to unmarried mothers was resulting in a gradual transfer of parental responsibility from 'the husband' to the state. The growing 'irresponsibility' of men towards their children, and the wider social consequences of this phenomenon, was a matter of increasing concern.

J. Lewis, 'Family Policy in the Post-War Period', in S. Katz, J. Eekelaar, and M. Maclean (eds), *Cross Currents: Family Law and Policy in the United States and England* (Oxford: OUP, 2000), 81, 91–3

By the early 1990s, the political debate was dominated by those who stressed the irresponsibility and selfishness of men as well as of women. Michael Howard, then Home Secretary, said in a speech to the Conservative Political Centre in 1993: 'If the state will house and pay for their children the duty on [young men] to get involved may seem removed from their shoulders...And since the State is educating, housing and feeding their children the nature of parental responsibility may seem less immediate.'...

The prime concern of political commentators about men's obligation to maintain was often allied with a more generalised concern on the political Right, and the political Left, among politicians and the media, about an increase in male irresponsibility. All argued that the successful socialization of children required the active involvement of two parents. Dennis and Erdos sought to trace the rise of the 'obnoxious Englishman' to family breakdown. Their chief concern was the effect of lone motherhood on the behaviour patterns of young men. Lone parenthood was in their view responsible for at best irresponsible and at worst criminal behaviour in the next male generation.

The state was anxious to find a way of attaching children to their fathers other than through the traditional mechanism of marriage.[11] The most obvious legal status to which parental duties and responsibilities could be attached was parenthood.[12] However, the government has not always been consistent in its attitude towards the parenting role of unmarried fathers. As evidenced by the decision to withhold *automatic* parental responsibility from unmarried fathers,[13] there has persisted deeply entrenched suspicion about the 'value' of this particular group of men as parents. In the debates leading up to the CA 1989, a strong image of the unmarried father as a feckless, irresponsible individual emerged. Whilst successive governments have taken a clear and unequivocal position on the financial responsibilities of men towards their children,[14] they have shown considerably more ambivalence towards unmarried fathers and the *non-financial* responsibilities of parenthood. Indeed, it can be argued that a desire to move the *financial* burden

[10] Ibid, 40.
[11] Lewis (2000), 96.
[12] See Douglas (2000b), esp at 223–7.
[13] See detailed discussion below.
[14] As enshrined in the Child Support Act 1991, s 1.

of maintaining children from the state to *both* their parents has been at the heart of the rhetoric on 'parental responsibility'. However, whilst financial considerations clearly remain important, there was in the later years of the 1997–2010 Labour Government a discernible shift in attitude. Ambivalence about unmarried fathers gave way to a strong belief in the value of active engaged fathering to securing the best possible outcomes for children.[15] Suspicion was thus replaced by steadfast optimism, with the government keen to support and encourage fathers to embrace all aspects of their parenting responsibilities. The Labour Government's new found faith in the worth of the unmarried father was strongly reflected in its reforms to the birth registration system. No longer feckless and irresponsible, unmarried fathers were portrayed as crucial to children's welfare, and it was therefore seen as essential that they exercise parental responsibility in its broadest sense.

DCSF and DWP, *Joint Birth Registration: Recording Responsibility*, Cm 7293
(London: HMSO, 2008)

Ministerial foreword:

The role of both father and mother is important to a child's development. By jointly registering a birth an unmarried father gets parental responsibility and can have a say in such important matters as the child's name, medical decisions, schooling and religion. Currently, unmarried fathers do not automatically have these rights, which places unnecessary obstacles in the way of those fathers who want to take responsibility for their children.

Fathers' involvement in their child's life can lead to positive educational achievement, a good, open and trusting parent-child relationship during the teenage years and reduce the risk of mental health issues for children in separated families.

The Labour Government's concern with the parental responsibilities of unmarried fathers extended well beyond financial support.

R. Collier and S. Sheldon, *Fragmenting Fatherhood: A Socio-Legal Study*
(Oxford: Hart Publishing, 2008), 191–2

Given the broader policy context around the promotion of 'active fathering'...unmarried fathers' failure to obtain PR has been of growing concern to a government keen to foster men's commitment to their families in a more general sense. Granting automatic PR is thus seen as a way of entrenching paternal duty to provide for the child's emotional development, as well as their financial needs. Denying this 'stamp of approval' to unmarried fathers, it was suggested, risked alienating them and refusing the vital encouragement necessary for them to take on board family responsibilities, destabilising the family unit and further contributing to the creation of lone-parent families.

---

[15] The assumed value of fatherhood is a strong feature of the current debate over private law orders about children: see 11.7.1.

10.2.2 DEFINING PARENTAL RESPONSIBILITY

Parental responsibility has proved difficult to define with any specificity. The definition in s 3(1) raises more questions than it answers.[16] However, the Law Commission opposed attempts to articulate any kind of definitive list of parental rights and duties, citing impracticality, incompleteness, and a lack of flexibility as potential drawbacks of such an approach.[17]

'Parental responsibility' therefore remains largely undefined in the CA 1989. However, whilst acknowledging that the formulation of a comprehensive list would be difficult, Freeman argues that Parliament's refusal to provide some form of guidance as to what the law expects of those exercising parental rights and duties was to sacrifice 'principle to pragmatism'.[18] Gillian Douglas and Nigel Lowe attempt to identify the most important rights and duties enshrined within the concept.[19]

N. Lowe and G. Douglas, *Bromley's Family Law* (11th edn, Oxford: OUP, 2015), 337–8

- Bringing up the child.

- Having contact with the child.

- Protecting and maintaining the child.

- Disciplining the child.

- Determining and providing for the child's education.

- Determining the child's religion.

- Consenting to the child's medical treatment.

- Consenting to the child's marriage.

- Consenting to the child's adoption.

- Vetoing the issue of a child's passport.

- Taking the child outside the United Kingdom and consenting to the child's emigration.

- Administering the child's property.

- Naming the child.

- Representing the child in legal proceedings.

- Disposing of the child's corpse.

- Appointing a guardian for the child.

This list is frequently cited by other commentators. Despite the absence of a clear statutory definition of parental responsibility, there is fairly widespread consensus about what is core to the concept. In short, parental responsibility encapsulates all the decision-making power

---

[16] In *T v T* [2010] EWCA Civ 1366, [23], Black LJ said that the CA 1989 'gives a very clear exposition of the broad concept' of parental responsibility.

[17] Law Com (1985b), para 1.9.

[18] Freeman (2000), 455.

[19] This closely reflects the tentative list put forward by the Law Commission in 1985. Law Com (1985b), para 2.25. For detailed discussion of various of the matters listed, see Probert, Gilmore, and Herring (2009).

and authority that parents need to provide effective long-term care for a child. Black LJ has said that 'someone who has been granted parental responsibility has truly been recognised as a parent of the child'.[20] It is, however, notable that attempts to define parental responsibility tend to result in lists dominated by parents' rights and decision-making power. This probably accurately reflects the public's perception of parental responsibility and how it operates in practice. Despite the efforts of the Law Commission, the government, and the courts to shift the focus away from parental rights, Freeman may thus be justified in his opinion that the changes introduced in the CA 1989 can be exaggerated, and whilst 'the language and symbolism altered...there was not that much substance to the change'.[21]

10.3   HOW IS PARENTAL RESPONSIBILITY OBTAINED?

Unlike parenthood, where the law can only recognize a maximum of two legal parents, one of the distinguishing features of parental responsibility is that it can be held simultaneously by more than two people.

Children Act 1989, s 2

(5) More than one person may have parental responsibility for the same child at the same time.

(6) A person who has parental responsibility for a child at any time shall not cease to have that responsibility solely because some other person subsequently acquires parental responsibility for the child.

There are two routes by which individuals may come to hold parental responsibility: (i) they hold it automatically; or (ii) it has been acquired in accordance with the CA 1989.

10.3.1   MOTHERS

Regardless of marital status, the child's mother will *always* have *automatic* parental responsibility.

Children Act 1989, s 2

(1) Where a child's father and mother were married to each other at the time of his birth, they shall each have parental responsibility for the child.

(2) Where a child's father and mother were not married to each other at the time of his birth—

   (a) the mother shall have parental responsibility for the child...

---

[20] *T v T* [2010] EWCA Civ 1366, [23].
[21] Freeman (2000), 451.

10.3.2 FATHERS AND SECOND FEMALE PARENTS UNDER SS 42 AND 43 OF THE HFEA 2008

In legal terms, there is no material difference between the approach taken to fathers and to 'second female parents' under ss 42 and 43 of the HFEA 2008, so we deal with them together here. However, since the vast majority of cases involve a father rather than a second female parent, we refer primarily to 'fathers'.

Married fathers and second female parents who are married to, or are in a civil partnership with, the mother

Married fathers (and second female parents who are married to or in a civil partnership with the child's mother) *automatically* acquire parental responsibility for their children provided they were married to the child's mother 'at the time of [the child's] birth'.[22] This phrase is interpreted in accordance with s 1(4) of the Family Law Reform Act 1987 (FLRA 1987) to include any time between conception and birth. It also includes any child whose parents marry after the birth with the effect of 'legitimating' the child.[23] These provisions apply to void marriages, provided one or both of the parties reasonably believed that the marriage was valid.[24]

Unmarried fathers and second female parents

The position of an unmarried father (or second female parent) is considerably more complicated. If not married to the child's mother 'at the time of the child's birth', these parents do not automatically have parental responsibility. They must therefore acquire it in accordance with the legislative provisions.[25] Section 4 provides for three ways in which the child's *father* may acquire parental responsibility (with s 4ZA providing equivalent provisions for second female parents):

Children Act 1989, s 4

(1) Where a child's father and mother were not married to each other at the time of his birth, the father shall acquire parental responsibility for the child if—

   (a) he becomes registered as the child's father . . . ;

   (b) the father and the child's mother make an agreement (a "parental responsibility agreement") providing for him to have parental responsibility for the child; or

   (c) the court, on his application, orders that he shall have parental responsibility for the child.

---

[22] CA 1989, s 2(1).
[23] FLRA 1987, s 1(3)(b) and Legitimacy Act 1976, ss 2, 3, and 10.
[24] FLRA 1987, s 1(3)(a) and Legitimacy Act 1976, s 1(1). With respect to the status of a transsexual marriage and its affect on parenthood, see *J v C (Void Marriage: Status of Children)* [2006] EWCA Civ 551.
[25] CA 1989, s 2(2).

Registration

Section 4 of the CA 1989 was amended by the Adoption and Children Act 2002 (ACA 2002) to enable unmarried fathers who are entered as the child's father on the birth register[26] to acquire parental responsibility.[27] This is subject to the qualification that parental responsibility will not be acquired by means of registration if the father has previously made an unsuccessful application to the court for a parental responsibility order or, having previously held parental responsibility, the court had ordered that his parental responsibility should cease.[28] In 2012, only 5.7 per cent of children born in England and Wales were registered by the mother alone.[29] This means that all but a small minority of unmarried fathers now acquire parental responsibility by the simple act of registration. Indeed, the government identified this as one of the major benefits of the birth registration reforms.[30]

Parental responsibility agreements

A parental responsibility agreement is a formal agreement entered into by the child's parents that the father is to share parental responsibility with the mother. The agreement must be made on the prescribed form and registered at the Central Family Court in London.[31] In practice, they are rarely used.[32] It is generally recognized that the limited usage of parental responsibility agreements does not reflect a lack of interest in or commitment by unmarried fathers to their children. Rather it is a combination of the decreasing number of fathers who need such agreements following the reforms to the birth registration system, together with a lack of knowledge about the relevant provisions amongst some parents.

Parental responsibility orders (PRO)

For those small number of men unable to take advantage of the provisions on birth registration and who have not entered into a parental responsibility agreement, the only means by which they may acquire parental responsibility is by obtaining a court order under s 4 of the CA 1989. Many orders under s 4 come about from the father making a free-standing application for parental responsibility, but it is important to note that the court is *required* to make an order under this section if it is making a child arrangements order under which the child is to live with the father if he does not otherwise have parental responsibility.

---

[26] The registration must comply with the Births and Deaths Registration Act 1953, ss 10 and 10A in order to qualify for the purposes of the CA 1989, which means that a foreign birth certificate will not be sufficient (though the father may have obtained parental responsibility in the foreign country, in which case it will likely be recognized here): see *Re S (Relocation: Parental Responsibility)* [2013] EWHC 1295.

[27] ACA 2002, s 111. The new registration provisions came into effect on 1 December 2003 and have no retrospective effect. Fathers whose children were born before this date cannot therefore take advantage of them.

[28] S 4(1C).

[29] ONS (2013c). With just over half of all births being to parents who were married or in a civil partnership with each other, this means that around 88 per cent of children born to unmarried parents are registered with both parents' names on the birth certificate.

[30] DCSF and DWP (2008), para 9.

[31] S 4(2).

[32] In 2004, 5,831 agreements were registered, but the number fell after the 2002 reforms, with only 1,581 agreements registered in 2013. Thanks to DJ Hess for providing this information.

Children Act 1989, s 12

(1) Where—

(a) the court makes a child arrangements order with respect to a child,

(b) the father of the child, or a woman who is a parent of the child by virtue of section 43 of the Human Fertilisation and Embryology Act 2008, is named in the order as a person with whom the child is to live, and

(c) the father, or the woman, would not otherwise have parental responsibility for the child,

the court must also make an order under section 4 giving the father, or under section 4ZA giving the woman, that responsibility.

Conversely, if there is to be a child arrangements order under which the child is to spend time or otherwise have contact with the father, and the father does not otherwise have parental responsibility, then the court 'must decide whether it would be appropriate, in view of the provision made in the order with respect to the father or the woman, for him or her to have parental responsibility for the child and, if it decides that it would be appropriate for the father or the woman to have that responsibility, must also make an order under section 4 giving him, or under section 4ZA giving her, that responsibility'.[33] In other words, a PRO is *compulsory* if the child is to *live with* the father or second female parent, and must be *considered* if the child is to spend time or otherwise have contact.

In practical terms, an unmarried father's lack of parental responsibility often becomes a problem only when his relationship with the mother breaks down (if such a relationship ever existed) and a dispute develops over the child. Indeed, it is often at this point that the father learns for the first time that he lacks the necessary legal status to make key decisions with respect to his child's upbringing. Given the ease with which parents who were in agreement could either register the father's name on the birth certificate or enter into a parental responsibility agreement, it is unsurprising that most free-standing applications for a PRO are opposed.

The Court of Appeal has provided clear guidance on the factors which should be taken into account on an application for parental responsibility.[34] *Re H (Minors) (Local Authority: Parental Rights) (No 3)* concerned an application for a parental rights order under s 4(1) of the FLRA 1987 (the precursor to a parental responsibility order) but the criteria it set down have been approved and applied to applications under s 4 of the CA 1989.

Re H (Minors) (Local Authority: Parental Rights) (No 3) [1991] Fam 151 (CA), 158

BALCOMBE LJ:

In considering whether to make an order...the court will have to take into account a number of factors of which the following will undoubtedly be material (although there may well be

---

[33] S 12(1A).

[34] For a more detailed discussion of the case law on applications for parental responsibility orders, see Gilmore (2003).

others, as the list is not intended to be exhaustive): (1) the degree of commitment which the father has shown towards the child; (2) the degree of attachment which exists between the father and the child, and (3) the reasons of the father for applying for the order.

In subsequent case law, Balcombe LJ emphasized that these three factors provide only a *starting point* for the court.[35] Satisfying the *Re H (No 3)* criteria does not rise to a presumption in favour of making the order,[36] and on the other hand in some cases satisfying the criteria may not be necessary, depending on the circumstances.[37] All applications for parental responsibility remain subject to the overriding principle of the child's best interests.[38]

Re RH (A Minor) (Parental Responsibility) [1998] 2 FCR 89 (CA), 94

BUTLER-SLOSS LJ:

15. The three requirements set out by Balcombe LJ in *Re H* are, undoubtedly, the starting point for the making of an order but it is clear...that he did not intend them to be the only relevant factors in considering a parental responsibility order and that his list was not exhaustive. In any event, such an approach would be contrary to s 1 of the 1989 Act, which applies to parental responsibility orders and the welfare of the child is therefore paramount. The court has the duty in each case to take into account all the relevant circumstances and to decide whether the order proposed is in the best interests of the child. Of course, it is generally in a child's interests to know and have a relationship with his father but the appropriateness of the order has to be considered on the particular facts of each individual case. If, reviewing all the circumstances, the judge considers that there are factors adverse to the father sufficient to tip the balance against the order proposed, it would not be right to make the order, even though the three requirements can be shown by the father.

When determining the child's best interests in relation to an application for a parental responsibility order, several factors have proved particularly persuasive. The courts have generally taken the position that it is in the child's interests to have a father who is 'sufficiently concerned and interested' that he wishes to acquire the formal legal status of a parent. In support of this approach, the courts have placed great weight on the nature of a parental responsibility order, emphasizing that it confers a status on the unmarried father that a married father would enjoy as of right. Moreover, it is argued that granting parental responsibility and giving the father the court's 'stamp of approval' helps promote a positive image of him, a vital factor in developing the child's own secure sense of identity.[39] It is also stressed that parental responsibility is not about conferring rights on fathers, but imposing duties and responsibilities, something which invariably works to the child's advantage.[40]

---

[35] See *Re G (A Minor) (Parental Responsibility Order)* [1994] 1 FLR 504.

[36] Ward LJ came close to saying this in *Re P (Parental Responsibility)* [1997] 2 FLR 722, where he held that 'parental responsibility orders were essentially orders which conferred status on the unmarried father, and that the practice had developed where good reason had to be advanced why orders should not be granted in a committed father's favour'.

[37] *Re M (Parental Responsibility Order)* [2013] EWCA Civ 969.

[38] *Re W (Parental Responsibility Order: Inter-Relationship with Direct Contact)* [2013] EWCA Civ 335.

[39] *Re G (A Minor) (Parental Responsibility Order)* [1994] 1 FLR 504, 508 and *Re C and V (Contact and Parental Responsibility)* [1998] 1 FLR 392, 397.

[40] *Re C and V (Contact and Parental Responsibility)*, [1998] 1 FLR 392.

Re S (A Minor) (Parental Responsibility) [1995] 3 FCR 225 (CA), 234–6

WARD LJ:

It would...be helpful if the mother could think calmly about the limited circumstances when the exercise of true parental responsibility is likely to be of practical significance. It is wrong to place undue and therefore false emphasis on the rights and duties and the powers comprised in "parental responsibility" and not to concentrate on the fact that what is at issue is conferring upon a committed father the status of parenthood for which nature has already ordained that he must bear responsibility...

I have heard, up and down the land, psychiatrists tell me how important it is that children grow up with good self-esteem and how much they need to have a favourable positive image of the absent parent. It seems to me important, therefore, wherever possible, to ensure that the law confers upon a committed father that stamp of approval, lest the child grow up with some belief that he is in some way disqualified from fulfilling his role and that the reason for the disqualification is something inherent which will be inherited by the child, making her struggle to find her own identity all the more fraught.

BUTLER-SLOSS LJ:

It is important for parents...to remember the emphasis placed by Parliament on the order which is applied for. It is that of duties and responsibilities as well as rights and powers. Indeed, the order itself is entitled "parental responsibility". A father who has shown real commitment to the child concerned and to whom there is a positive attachment, as well as a genuine *bona fide* reason for the application, ought, in a case such as the present, to assume the weight of those duties and cement that commitment and attachment by sharing the responsibilities for the child with the mother. This father is asking to assume that burden as well as that pleasure of looking after his child, a burden not lightly to be undertaken.

In my judgment, this father should be allowed to share the burden of caring for his daughter which does not remove from the mother the day-to-day control of her daughter's welfare. But it gives to the father the status in which he can share in the responsibility for the child's upbringing and demonstrate that he will be as good a parent as he can make himself to this little girl.

Applying these principles, the Court of Appeal granted a parental responsibility order to the father of a seven-year-old girl, despite his recent conviction for the possession of obscene literature including paedophilic photographs of young girls.

The courts' emphasis on the *status* conferred by parental responsibility has been accompanied by a general tendency to downplay its *practical* significance. Although it is recognized parental responsibility confers important rights on the father,[41] the courts have made it clear that a parental responsibility order does not give the father a general licence to interfere in the day-to-day upbringing of the child. Fears concerning the father potentially misusing the order to interfere in the mother's day-to-day care have therefore been regarded as

---

[41] *Re RH (A Minor) (Parental Responsibility)* [1998] 2 FCR 89. These include the right to be heard in adoption proceedings and proceedings under the Hague Convention, as well as the right to be consulted on important matters regarding the child's upbringing, such as schooling.

insufficient to prevent the order being granted, particularly as such potential misuse can be controlled by the court under s 8.[42]

An alternative means by which the father's use of parental responsibility may be restricted is by subjecting the order to express conditions. This approach has sometimes been used when dealing with applications by known sperm donors, and we discuss it in detail below.[43] However, in restricting the father's exercise of parental responsibility, these decision are consistent with earlier authority holding that the fact that certain parental rights, duties, and responsibilities are currently incapable of being exercised or enforced by the father, whilst relevant, is no bar to the granting of a parental responsibility order.

Re C (Minors) [1992] 2 All ER 86 (CA), 88–9 and 93

MUSTILL LJ:

This appeal has required us to consider another possible factor, namely enforceability. The question can be posed in this way: is the court, when considering a PRO application, entitled or bound to take into account the fact that under the circumstances at the date of the application one or more or all of the parental rights may be valueless in practice because they are incapable of being exercised by force of circumstances or by order of the court?

Looking at that question as one of first impression without reference to authority, we would think that the answer must be Yes. The enforceability of the rights which he is being invited to confer is something that any judge would be entitled and bound to regard as relevant to the exercise of his discretion...

Given, therefore, that the prospective enforceability of parental rights is a relevant consideration for a judge deciding whether or not to grant them, there is, in our judgment, nothing in the 1987 Act to suggest that it should be an overriding consideration. It would be quite wrong, in our view, to assume that just because few or none of the parental rights happen to be enforceable under conditions prevailing at the date of the application it would necessarily follow as a matter of course that a PRO would be refused. That can be illustrated by looking—as the legislation clearly requires one to look—at the position of a lawful father in analogous circumstances. Conditions may arise (for example in cases of mental illness) where a married father has, regretfully to be ordered, in effect, to step out of his children's lives altogether. In such a case his legal status as a parent remains wholly unaffected, and he retains all his rights in law although none of them may be exercisable in practice. This does not mean that his parental status becomes a dead letter or a mere paper title. It will have real and tangible value, not only as something he can cherish for the sake of his own peace of mind, but also as a status carrying with it rights in waiting, which it may be possible to call into play when circumstances change with the passage of time. It is not difficult to imagine situations in which similar considerations would apply in the case of a natural father. Though existing circumstances may demand that his children see or hear nothing of him, and that he should have no influence upon the course of their lives for the time being, their welfare may require that if circumstances change he should be reintroduced as a presence, or at least as an influence, in their lives. In such a case a PRO, notwithstanding that only a few or even none of the rights under it may currently be exercisable, may be of

---

[42] See, e.g., *Re P (A Minor) (Parental Responsibility Order)* [1994] 1 FLR 578; *Re C And V (Contact and Parental Responsibility)* [1998] 1 FLR 392. See 11.8 on specific issue and prohibited steps orders.

[43] See 10.3.3.

value to him and also of potential value to the children. Although there may be other factors which weigh against the making of a PRO in such circumstances, it could never be right to refuse such an order out of hand, on the automatic ground that it would be vitiated by the inability to enforce it.

It is, however, important to note that the case law does not all point the same way and a parental responsibility order has been refused in a few cases where parental responsibility would be devoid of any practical meaning or effect. In *M v M (Parental Responsibility)* Wilson J reluctantly refused to make an order where the father had no *capacity* to exercise parental rights and responsibilities. *M v M* was a tragic case in which the child's father was seriously injured in a cycle accident resulting in significant mental impairment.

M v M (Parental Responsibility) [1999] 2 FLR 737 (Fam Div), 743–4

WILSON J:

[I]t is the third factor, namely the reasons of the father for applying for the order, which, when expanded to serve the demands of this particular inquiry, causes the most difficulty. Balcombe LJ's formulation presupposes that the father is capable of reason. Even more relevantly the statutory provisions themselves, namely ss 4(1) and 3(1) of the Children Act 1989, presuppose that the father is apt to be invested with responsibilities and is capable of exercising rights, of performing duties and of wielding powers in relation to the child. Parental responsibility, including as it does these rights, duties and powers, is not trivial. In *Re S (Parental Responsibility)* [1995] 2 FLR 648, Butler-Sloss LJ . . . spoke of the 'weight' of the relevant duties.

I ask whether it can be said with any degree of realism that this father's capacities are such that he should be invested with 'responsibility' for [the child]. It seems to me that he was only just across the borderline into being able to instruct lawyers to represent him in these proceedings. The general effect of the evidence is that, far from being able to exercise parental responsibility over another, for example to weigh up the merits of rival schools or to balance the potential benefits and risks of a surgical operation, this father requires something akin to parental responsibility to be exercised by others over himself . . .

I respect the weight of authority that misuse of a parental responsibility order can be controlled and that its spectre should not generally inhibit the making of an order. But those propositions presuppose the father's understanding of the concept of parental responsibility and of the likely repercussions of misuse . . .

I confess to having entertained a secret ambition that I would never be constrained to deny parental responsibility to a loving father. In the light of the tragedy which has broken the father's life, I feel a real sense of discomfort at a conclusion which does not at least give him that status. But my duty is to [the child] and, in my judgment, it dictates otherwise.

In *Re G (Parental Responsibility Order)*,[44] Hedley J similarly refused to uphold a 'suspended' parental responsibility order because it could not be exercised in any meaningful way. The child had been conceived following a 'one night stand' and was being raised by his mother and her new partner. The mother and step-father were strongly opposed to contact, leading

---

[44] [2006] EWCA Civ 745.

the judge at first instance to reduce direct contact from twice a month to just twice a year. However, in recognition of the father's commitment to his son and his determination to build a relationship with him, the judge made an order for parental responsibility. He then suspended that order on the mother's undertaking that she would provide certain information to the father about the child's health, education, and whereabouts. On appeal, Hedley J set aside the order holding that a parental responsibility order could not be suspended under s 4 of the CA 1989 and that it would be most unusual to make a parental responsibility order with one hand and then 'effectively draw all its teeth' with the other.[45] He suggested it would not be in the child's best interests to make an order for parental responsibility in circumstances where it had been determined that the father should not actually exercise that responsibility except in the most limited way.[46]

However, save for these few cases—which tend to be somewhat unusual on their facts—the courts have shown a strong propensity towards granting a parental responsibility order. Despite the initial view of the Law Commission that successful applications would be rare,[47] the vast majority of applications for a parental responsibility order are granted (though numbers are low). In 2011,[48] 5,586 parental responsibility orders were made in private law proceedings; in 45 cases the order was refused and in 40 'no order' was made, and 277 applications were withdrawn.[49] Indeed, the ease with which orders are granted makes the rationale for continuing court scrutiny unclear. That said, there are some grounds on which applications will be refused, albeit they tend to be somewhat exceptional. Amongst the reported cases abusive behaviour towards the child,[50] repeated imprisonment,[51] and 'demonstrably improper and wrong' motives for making the application,[52] have all been held to justify refusing the order.

10.3.3 'ALTERNATIVE FAMILIES'

In recent years there has been a steady flow of cases reaching the courts involving disputes between a lesbian co-parenting couple and a person usually termed a 'known sperm donor'. In most of these cases, the man has 'donated' the sperm to allow one of the women to conceive, but later wishes to develop or maintain a meaningful parental or quasi-parental role in the child's life. This involvement is often opposed by the co-parenting couple on the basis that it was never intended that the man would act as a father to the child, and that regular involvement could destabilize the child's primary care-giving unit.[53]

One of the first cases to address this situation in detail was *Re D (Contact and PR: Lesbian Mothers and Known Father) (No 2)*.[54] The sperm donor, Mr B, had understood that he was to

---

[45] Ibid, [23].

[46] Ibid.

[47] Law Com (1982b), para 7.27.

[48] 2011 was the final year for which this detailed breakdown was reported by the MOJ.

[49] MOJ (2012), table 2.4.

[50] *Re RH (A Minor) (Parental Responsibility)* [1998] 2 FCR 89.

[51] *Re P (Parental Responsibility)* [1997] 2 FLR 722.

[52] *Re P (Parental Responsibility)* [1998] 2 FLR 96. See also *W v Ealing London Borough Council* [1993] 2 FLR 788 (sole purpose of application to prevent adoption of the child) and *Re M (Contact: Parental Responsibility)* [2001] 2 FLR 342 (the father perceived the order as giving him the right to interfere in the child's upbringing which would destabilize and undermine the mother's care of the child—particularly important in this case because of the nature of the child's special needs and disabilities).

[53] For lesbian parents' views on these and other issues, see Smith (2006).

[54] [2006] EWHC 2.

have a continuing role in the child's upbringing, seeing her frequently and participating on an equal basis in important decisions. Conversely, the lesbian couple, Ms A and Ms C, had envisaged a more limited role: that he would be a 'real father' and enjoy regular contact, but he would not be a 'parent' involved in decisions regarding her upbringing. A and C feared that granting B parental responsibility would give him 'increased visibility' as 'a third parent', thereby compromising the security of their family unit and exacerbating the problems they faced in gaining social acceptance of their equal parenting roles. In trying to find a solution which recognized and affirmed the child's place within the primary care of A and C, yet also acknowledged the love and commitment of her biological father, Black J took what she described as a 'creative' approach to parental responsibility.

Re D (Contact and PR: Lesbian Mothers and Known Father) (No 2) [2006] EWHC 2

BLACK J:

33. Ms A and Ms C are anxious because they perceive same sex couples as having great difficulties in forming families which society recognises. Their experience is that most people focus on the biological mother as if she were a single mother of the type to which society has become used, treating the woman who is not the biological mother as redundant or in the background, rather than accepting the two women and their child as a family with two parents...The problem is compounded...by the shortcomings of language which does not yet have the terms to deal with the new ways of living that are evolving.

34. It is in this climate where, it seems to me, the law is advancing at a pace which is probably quicker than the pace of change in the views of society in general, where new ways of living have not yet wholly crystallised, and where language has not yet evolved to accommodate them, that I must adjudicate upon the issue of parental responsibility for Mr B, equipped only with concepts and language which were not designed with this in mind...

89. I confess that I have been anxious about whether making a parental responsibility order would be in D's interests for the sort of reasons that have influenced [the expert child and adolescent psychiatrist], notably the potential threat to the stability of D's immediate family from what I may loosely call "interference" from Mr B as well as the impact on society's perception of the family if he were, in fact, to use it to become more visible in D's life. On the other hand, I am very mindful of the authorities which stress the status aspect of parental responsibility and those which indicate that it is not appropriate to refuse to grant it because of a feared misuse which should more properly be controlled by s 8 orders. I am also mindful of the fact that such matters as those for which I have criticised Mr B in relation to his actions towards D's family fall far short of the sort of activity that has, in the past, been seen as sufficient to found a refusal of parental responsibility. Perhaps most importantly of all, I am considerably influenced by the reality that Mr B is D's father. Whatever new designs human beings have for the structure of their families, that aspect of nature cannot be overcome. It is to be hoped that as society accepts alternative arrangements more readily, as it seems likely will happen over the next few years, the impulse to hide or to marginalise a child's father so as not to call attention to an anomalous family will decline, although accommodating the emotional consequences of untraditional fatherhood and motherhood and of the sort of de facto, non-biological parenthood that is experienced by a step-parent or same sex partner will inevitably remain discomfiting.

90. The dilemma facing me has been greatly eased by Mr B's offer to be bound by conditions which would prevent him from being intrusive in the obvious situations which might be anticipated as problem areas, namely D's schooling and health care. It has rightly been

argued on behalf of Ms A and Ms C that it is not possible to anticipate all the situations that may arise and to guard against them but the course that Mr B proposes would cover the obvious ones. The court has power to regulate others, should they arise, through Children Act orders. Given that Mr B will know, following this judgment, the sort of context that the court anticipates there will be for his involvement in D's life, he will be able to forecast the likely consequences of attempts to become involved in areas of her life not covered by the proposed conditions and it is my judgment that that ought to be a brake upon his conduct.

91. Mr B's suggestion has allowed me to take a creative approach to parental responsibility in an attempt to make it serve the novel demands of a case such as this...I propose to grant him parental responsibility for D. The order will be considerably more detailed than normal and will recite that it is granted on the basis

    i) that Mr B will not visit or contact D's school for any purpose without the prior written consent of Ms A or Ms C

    ii) that Mr B will not contact any health professional involved in D's care without the prior written consent of Ms A or Ms C.

The grant of parental responsibility in this case thus had nothing to do with the actual 'doing' of parenthood; the imposition of conditions on the father's decision-making capacity stripped his parental responsibility of all meaningful practical effect. The order was made for purely symbolic and therapeutic reasons: to reflect the importance Black J attributed to the fact of B's biological fatherhood and to confer a sense of enhanced parental status on a committed and dedicated father unable to play the parenting role he desired.

However, other judges have refused to adopt the approach taken by Black J in *Re D*. For example, *TJ v CV* concerned a known 'sperm donor' (TJ) who had assisted his sister (S) and her civil partner (CV) to conceive a child and who wished to play a continuing parental role.[55] Hedley J considered it would be in the child's best interests to maintain a relationship with his father. However, he was equally clear that TJ should not have the status of a parent or play any kind of 'parental' role. In such circumstances, he held that the grant of a parental responsibility order would be inappropriate.[56]

In the later case of *MA v RS (Contact: Parenting Roles)*, Hedley J commented on the inadequacy of the available language to deal with these cases.

MA v RS *(Contact: Parenting Roles)* [2011] EWHC 2455

HEDLEY J:

9. The girls were conceived by IVF with the agreement and co-operation of all parties. This case provides a vivid illustration of just how wrong these arrangements can go. There are perhaps two particular issues that this cases raises. The first is the need for precise agreement

---

[55] [2007] EWHC 1952.

[56] See also *R v E and F (Female Parents: Known Father)* [2010] EWHC 417. Bennett J similarly refused a known 'sperm donor' parental responsibility, holding that where it was not intended that the donor would 'parent' the child (meaning not just caring emotionally and physically for the child but taking responsibility for all the day-to-day decisions) conferring the status of parental responsibility would not be appropriate. Bennett J was also strongly influenced by the expert evidence suggesting granting parental responsibility to the 'sperm donor' would be perceived as a direct threat to the autonomy of the nuclear family.

as to the roles that each is to play before any attempt is made to achieve a pregnancy; and secondly, this case, like others that I have been involved with, is bedevilled by a lack of a sufficient vocabulary to explain the true nature of the relationships. It is all too easy in these cases for biological fathers to see themselves in the same position as in separated parent cases in heterosexual arrangements, whereas this arrangement is, and was always intended to be, quite different....

16. As I have thought about this case, I have tried hard to see whether there are any other concepts than that of mother, father and primary carer, all conventional concepts in conventional family cases. The best that I have achieved, and I confess to having found it helpful in thinking about this case, is to contemplate the concept of principal and secondary parenting. The reason why this case is not equivalent to a separated parent is that there was a clear agreement that the respondents would do the principal parenting and that they would provide the two-parent care to these children. The second respondent clearly believes that her role in this regard has been brought into question, and it is certainly my view that her role in the concept of principal parenting, as one of the two principal parents, needs to be clearly affirmed and respected.

17. By the same token, I am satisfied that the applicants were acknowledged as having a parenting role, albeit in a secondary capacity. That parenting role was to fulfil at least three purposes. The first was indeed to give a clear sense of identity to the child or children in due course. The second was to provide the male component of parenting which all must be taken to have acknowledged. Thirdly, there was a more general role of benign involvement which would have, but would certainly not be confined to, an avuncular aspect.

However, in *A v B and C (Contact: Alternative Families)*, Thorpe LJ rejected Hedley J's suggestion of principal and secondary parenting.[57] In refusing to lay down specific guidance, the Court of Appeal noted how factually varied these cases could be, and reiterated that the only guiding principle for the courts is that the welfare of the child concerned is paramount.[58] Nonetheless, the court's approach is controversial. On the one hand, as Thorpe LJ said in *A v B and C*, from the child's point of view there may be advantages to having a legally recognized and protected relationship with more than two parents. The cases can also be seen as fitting with the law's general pro-father approach of recent years. On the other hand, some are critical of the courts precisely because they equate the sperm donor with a father. It can be said that the courts' decisions in these cases give insufficient respect to the nuclear family that the lesbian couple has formed, and place the stability and well-being of that family at risk in order to promote a relationship with a man that was never intended to be a 'father'. Although Hedley J's proposed labels have been rejected, it remains the case that the language available is inadequate and unhelpful in these cases—though it seems doubtful that finding better labels would help to resolve the underlying challenges.[59]

10.3.4 STEP-PARENTS

The CA 1989 was amended by the ACA 2002 and the Civil Partnership Act 2004 to allow 'step-parents' (which includes spouses and civil partners, but not cohabitants) to acquire parental responsibility for the children of their spouse or partner.

---

[57] [2012] EWCA Civ 285, [30].
[58] See also *Re SAB (A Child)* [2014] EWHC 384.
[59] See generally Diduck (2007).

Children Act 1989, s 4A

(1) Where a child's parent ("parent A") who has parental responsibility for the child is married to, or a civil partner of, a person who is not the child's parent ("the step-parent")—

    (a) parent A or, if the other parent of the child also has parental responsibility for the child, both parents may by agreement with the step-parent provide for the step-parent to have parental responsibility for the child; or

    (b) the court may, on the application of the step-parent, order that the step-parent shall have parental responsibility for the child.

This allows a step-parent to acquire parental responsibility through agreement with the child's parents or by order of the court. The agreement of the child's father or second female parent will only be required if he or she holds parental responsibility. If a parent holding parental responsibility withholds consent, an application to the court will be necessary.

Section 4A is an important provision. Before its introduction, step-parents wishing to formalize their legal relationship with their step-children had to resort to the sometimes artificial mechanism of obtaining a residence order or adopting the child. As there was usually no dispute over the child's residence, adoption was often the preferred option. However, step-parent adoption has a drastic effect on the legal position of the child: in addition to conferring parental responsibility on the step-parent, the adoption order terminated the parental responsibility and parental status of the non-adopting parent.[60] Indeed, once the adoption order has been made the child is to be treated for all purposes 'as if born as the child of the adopters or adopter'.[61] This effectively removes 'the very parenthood' of the non-adopting parent—usually the child's father—terminating any legal relationship between him and the child.

Growing awareness of the importance of genetic parentage and, wherever possible, preserving the child's familial links with *both* parents, regardless of whether the parents are divorced, separated, or have never lived together, has rendered step-parent adoption deeply problematic.[62] Section 4A thus provides an effective means of recognizing and supporting the social parenting role played by many step-parents, without undermining the importance of the child's relationship with both legal parents. It is thus a more measured response to the realities and complexities of the somewhat transient nature of modern family life. There remains, however, an apparent anomaly. As s 4A is specifically limited to a person who is married to, or a civil partner of, the child's parent, cohabitants cannot acquire parental responsibility for their partner's children via this route. This sits uneasily with the ACA 2002

---

[60] Under the Adoption Act 1976 the child's parent (parent A) had to make a joint application with his/her spouse (the step-parent), to adopt his/her own child. The ACA 2002 removes this wholly artificial requirement, providing that the partner of a child's parent can make a sole application to adopt the child and that the adoption will have no effect on parent A's own parental responsibility: ss 46(3)(b) and 51(2). However, the position of the child's other parent (the non-adopting parent) remains unchanged.

[61] ACA 2002, s 67(1).

[62] That said, it is clearly a matter of degree, and where the parent opposing the adoption has little or no involvement in the child's life, the balance of factors in the welfare assessment may still favour step-parent adoption: see *Re P (Step-Parent Adoption)* [2014] EWCA Civ 1174. Extracts from *Re P* can be found at 13.6.3.

which permits the 'partner' of a child's parent to apply for an adoption order.[63] It is perhaps regrettable that cohabitants may be forced into taking the more drastic step of adoption in order to consolidate their legal relationship with the child.

10.3.5 HOLDERS OF A CHILD ARRANGEMENTS ORDER

An alternative route by which step-parents, cohabitants, and others may acquire parental responsibility for their partner's children is by applying for a child arrangements order.[64] There are two mechanisms.

Orders that the child live with a person

If a child arrangements order is made *under which the child is to live with a person* then, if that person does not already have parental responsibility, he or she gets it automatically for the duration of the order.[65]

Children Act 1989, s 12

> (2) Where the court makes a child arrangements order and a person who is not a parent or guardian of the child concerned is named in the order as a person with whom the child is to live, that person shall have parental responsibility for the child while the order remains in force so far as providing for the child to live with that person.

In theory, anyone can acquire parental responsibility via this route, as s 10 of the CA 1989 provides that *any person* may apply for this kind of child arrangements order with respect to any child, although those falling outside certain defined categories will require leave.[66] It is important to remember, though, that the primary purpose of this form of child arrangements order is to determine the person or persons with whom a child is to live, and the conferral of parental responsibility is a necessary aside to enable the person with the order to provide for the child's care.

Orders that the child spend time or otherwise have contact with a person

Child arrangements orders under which the child is to live with a person provide one potential means by which that person can obtain formal recognition of their parenting role. When, however, there is no real dispute about the child's residence, it is questionable

---

63 ACA 2002, s 51(2). 'Partner' is defined in s 144 of the ACA 2002 as: 'a person is the partner of a child's parent if the person and the parent are a couple but the person is not the child's parent'. 'Couple' is defined as: '(a) a married couple, or (aa) two people who are civil partners of each other, or (b) two people (whether of different sexes or the same sex) living as partners in an enduring family relationship'.

64 Child arrangements orders are discussed in detail in chapter 11.

65 Note that if the applicant is the child's father or second female parent, a parental responsibility must be made order under s 4 of the CA 1989: CA 1989, s 12(1) (on which see pp 676–7). The reason is to ensure that the parental responsibility of the father or second female parent does not terminate if the child arrangements order ends, and to avoid the limitations discussed below.

66 See 11.3.2.

whether making that form of child arrangements order solely for the purpose of conferring parental responsibility on a person is appropriate. This issue caused a degree of difficulty for the courts until 2014, because the law provided no other means of conferring parental responsibility on people who were, in practice, performing a parenting role for a child but who were not covered by other provisions of the CA 1989. One such situation were cases of same-sex parents whose children were conceived outside the provisions of the HFEA 2008. Faced with these cases, some judges viewed the making of the order as being a pragmatic necessity and others saw it as an inappropriate use of a residence order (as it was then called).[67]

Much of this difficulty may now have been resolved by the introduction of a new s 12(2A) into the CA 1989 by the Children and Families Act 2014.

Children Act 1989, s 12

(2A) Where the court makes a child arrangements order and—

    (a) a person who is not the parent or guardian of the child concerned is named in the order as a person with whom the child is to spend time or otherwise have contact, but

    (b) the person is not named in the order as a person with whom the child is to live,

the court may provide in the order for the person to have parental responsibility for the child while paragraphs (a) and (b) continue to be met in the person's case.

This provision allows (but does not require) the court to make a free-standing parental responsibility order in favour of a person who is named in a child arrangements order but who is not a person with whom the child is to live. In other words, anyone who will be spending time or otherwise having contact with a child under a child arrangements order is now able to be given parental responsibility for that child for the duration of the order.

Limitations on parental responsibility arising from a child arrangements order

Parental responsibility acquired by a non-legal parent under either of these provisions is subject to important limitations. First, the non-legal parent's parental responsibility is contingent on the existence of the residence order. If the residence order terminates, so does parental responsibility.[68] This differs from the parental responsibility of a father or second female parent who acquires a parental responsibility order under s 4 or s 4ZA as an adjunct to the grant of a child arrangements order regulating the child's living arrangements under s 12(1) or s 12(1A). In this situation, the parental responsibility order has life independent from the child arrangements order. Secondly, there are two specific limits

---

[67] Compare, e.g., Thorpe J's early restrictive view in *Re WB (Residence Orders)* [1995] 2 FLR 1023 with his later expansive view in *Re G (Children)* [2005] EWCA Civ 462. The most recent authority on this issue is *Re G (Shared Residence: Biological Mother of Donor Egg Children)* [2014] EWCA Civ 336.

[68] S 12(2).

on the scope of a non-legal parent's powers if parental responsibility is acquired under s 12(2) or 12(2A).

Children Act 1989, s 12

(3) Where a person has parental responsibility for a child as a result of subsection (2) or (2A), he shall not have the right—

    (b) to agree, or refuse to agree, to the making of an adoption order, or an order under section 84 of the Adoption and Children Act 2002 with respect to the child; or

    (c) to appoint a guardian for the child.

Decisions relating to adoption and guardianship are amongst the most important with respect to a child's future and Parliament has therefore chosen to reserve such questions exclusively to legal parents.

10.3.6 SPECIAL GUARDIANS

Special guardianship orders (SGOs) confer parental responsibility on the applicants for the duration of the order.[69] A unique feature of SGOs is that whilst the parental responsibility of others is not terminated by the order, special guardians are entitled to exercise parental responsibility to the exclusion of any other person with parental responsibility.[70] Special guardianship is discussed in more detail in chapter 13.

10.3.7 GUARDIANS

A child's guardian has parental responsibility for the child for the duration of the appointment.[71] A guardian may be appointed by the court, a parent with parental responsibility, a previous guardian, or a special guardian.[72] Appointment by someone other than the court takes effect upon the death of the appointer, and may be revoked or disclaimed by the appointed person.[73] The appointment of an inter-testamentary guardian by a parent, guardian, or special guardian is the only mechanism available for conferring parental responsibility on an individual other than a parent or step-parent that does not require judicial scrutiny and approval.

10.3.8 ADOPTION

An adoption order confers parental responsibility on the adopter(s).[74] However, unlike other orders which confer parental responsibility on someone, an adoption order terminates the parental responsibility of any other person holding parental responsibility.[75] Parental

---

[69] S 14C(1)(a)
[70] S 14C(1)(b)
[71] S 5(6).
[72] S 5(3) and 5(4).
[73] S 6.
[74] ACA 2002, s 46(1).
[75] Ibid, s 46(2).

responsibility is thus transferred from the legal parents to the adoptive parent(s) who stand in relation to the child as if the child had been born their natural legitimate child.[76] In accordance with this approach, parental responsibility conferred by an adoption order is permanent and irrevocable save for a further adoption. The acquisition and exercise of parental responsibility by means of adoption is discussed in detail in chapter 13.

10.3.9 LOCAL AUTHORITIES

The state in the guise of the local authority automatically acquires parental responsibility for a child with respect to whom a care or emergency protection order is made.[77] However, to reinforce the lifelong responsibilities of the child's parents, the parents' parental responsibility is not terminated but is shared with the local authority. Whilst parental responsibility is shared, the local authority has the power to determine the extent to which the parents are actually able to exercise their legal responsibility for the child.[78] The acquisition and exercise of parental responsibility by a local authority is discussed in greater detail in chapter 12.

10.4 WHO SHOULD HAVE PARENTAL RESPONSIBILITY?

Since the CA 1989 was originally enacted, the provisions for conferring parental responsibility on people who do not have it automatically have expanded considerably. The position of unmarried fathers, in particular, has changed a lot, but unmarried fathers do not enjoy complete equality with the child's mother or a married father as regards their legal relationship with the child. There remains a small minority of unmarried fathers who, because they are not registered on the birth register or have not entered into a parental responsibility agreement with the mother, must still go to the expense and inconvenience of 'proving their worth' to the court before being accorded the full legal status of fatherhood. Furthermore, the parental responsibility of all unmarried fathers remains subject to termination by the court.[79] These anomalies are a continuing source of grievance for paternal rights activists who argue that all distinctions between the child's parents, whether based on sex or marital status, should be removed. On the other hand, whilst these technical distinctions remain, the reality following the birth registration reforms is that, save for a very small minority, all unmarried fathers will acquire parental responsibility. Any continuing 'discrimination' is thus more symbolic than real. Indeed, for some commentators, to confer parental responsibility on virtually all unmarried fathers as a consequence of the mere fact of birth registration is to go too far. It is argued that the assumed value of genetic fatherhood which underpins these reforms affords legal status to fathers who have no interest in playing any active part in the upbringing of their child, will do nothing to encourage men to take their parenting responsibilities more seriously, devalues the concept of parental responsibility as a practical parenting tool, and places vulnerable women and children at risk. The arguments

---

[76] Ibid, s 67(1).
[77] S 33(3).
[78] S 33(3)(b).
[79] See 10.6.

both for and against further reform are particularly revealing about prevailing attitudes towards the value of fatherhood in English law.

10.4.1 THE ARGUMENTS FOR FURTHER REFORM

The continuing distinction between married and unmarried fathers, even if largely symbolic, raises an important point of principle about the extent to which a diversity of family forms should be accorded equal respect under the law. There are strong public policy arguments in favour of recognizing and supporting a wide range of alternative family relationships, particularly where the rights and interests of children are involved. There is now widespread agreement amongst commentators that children should not be disadvantaged because of their parents' marital status. What is important to children is the quality of the parent–child relationship, not whether their parents are married.

The growing influence of human rights discourse in domestic law and policy provides further impetus for ensuring the children of unmarried parents are treated just the same way as children of married parents. From a children's rights perspective, the UN Convention on the Rights of the Child (UNCRC), appears to promote the importance of the child's relationship with *both* parents, regardless of marital status.[80] With particular reference to parental responsibility, Article 18 emphasizes the importance of *equality* between the child's parents.[81]

United Nations Convention on the Rights of the Child 1989, Article 18

> 1. States Parties shall use their best efforts to ensure recognition of the principle that both parents have common responsibilities for the upbringing and development of the child. Parents or, as the case may be, legal guardians have the primary responsibility for the upbringing and development of the child. The best interests of the child will be their basic concern.

A particularly strong argument in favour of affording equal legal status to married and unmarried fathers is the importance of eradicating any continuing legal distinction between 'legitimate' and 'illegitimate' children. This was acknowledged by the Law Commission during its review of illegitimacy in the 1980s.

Law Commission, *Family Law: Illegitimacy*, Law Com No 118
(London: HMSO, 1982b)

> 4.23...In the Working Paper we expressed the view that if the concept of illegitimacy were to be removed from family law it would be a *necessary* corollary that the distinction which the law now draws in relation to parental rights between, on the one hand, those children now "legitimate" and on the other, those now "illegitimate" would disappear along with all other distinctions based on legitimacy or illegitimacy. Thus our recommendation that

---

[80] See, e.g., Arts 7, 8, and 9.
[81] For commentary, see Lowe (1997a), 201–2.

fathers of illegitimate children should have parental rights was not intended to be an end in itself; it was merely a necessary incident of the abolition of all legal distinctions between children founded solely on their parents' marital status. We nevertheless thought it necessary to draw attention to the significance of parental rights in this context and to the consequences of such rights being automatically vested in all fathers. Our tentative conclusion was that any adverse consequences did not outweigh the benefits to be derived from abolition of the status of illegitimacy, but many commentators disagreed...

4.44...Some commentators expressed the view...that it would be perfectly possible to abolish the status of illegitimacy whilst preserving the existing rules whereby parental rights vest automatically only in married parents. We do not accept this view. The argument for "abolishing illegitimacy" (rather than merely removing such legal consequences of that status as are adverse to the child) is essentially that the abolition of any legal distinction based on the parents' marital status would itself have an influence on opinion. The marital status of the child's parents would cease to be *legally* relevant, and thus the need to refer to the child's distinctive legal status would (in this view) disappear. This consequence could not follow if a distinction—albeit relating only to entitlement to parental rights—were to be preserved between children which would be based solely on their parent's status. There would thus remain two classes of children: first, those whose parents were married and thereby enjoyed parental rights; secondly, those whose parents were unmarried and whose fathers did not enjoy such rights. In effect, therefore, the distinction between "legitimate" and "illegitimate" would be preserved.

4.45 We believe, therefore, that it is impossible to avoid the stark choice between abolition of the status of illegitimacy, and its retention (albeit coupled with a removal of the legal disadvantages of illegitimacy so far as they adversely affect the child).

Despite their initial view, the Law Commission finally recommended that fathers should not be accorded automatic parental rights. By retaining these differences between married and unmarried fathers, all legal distinctions between 'legitimate' and 'illegitimate' children have not therefore been removed from English law. The term 'illegitimate' may no longer be an acceptable part of legal discourse, but that should not disguise the fact that the legal relationship between children and unmarried parents is different from that enjoyed by children and their married parents. The Law Commission rationalized this continuing 'discrimination' on the basis that withholding automatic parental responsibility from unmarried fathers did not disadvantage the child, a conclusion with which not everyone would agree.

10.4.2 ARGUMENTS AGAINST CONFERRING EQUAL STATUS ON UNMARRIED FATHERS

The issue of whether unmarried fathers should be treated equally with mothers and married fathers highlights a basic tension in successive government policies on family life. Whilst wishing to ensure that responsibility for children, particularly those living outside the traditional married family unit, falls on the parents and not the state, successive governments have remained committed to promoting marriage as the preferred basis of family life.[82] Reform which may undermine the status of marriage is thus treated cautiously. It is clear from the various consultation papers on parental responsibility that there has been

---

[82] See, e.g., HO (1998) and the criticisms of that approach: HO (1999), ch 4.

deep-seated resistance to fully embracing a diversity of family forms, with suspicion about the value of unmarried fathers being particularly strong. Thus, whereas the commitment and worth of the married father has been simply assumed, the unmarried father, having failed to demonstrate his commitment to the mother and child through marriage, has been an uncertain figure, tainted by fears as to his reckless, irresponsible, and possibly even dangerous behaviour.[83] As the Law Commission's review of illegitimacy reveals, these concerns about the unmarried father were widely held. Although attitudes have undoubtedly moved on since the Law Commission was writing in the early 1980s, negative assumptions about the unmarried father remain a key part of the debate.

Law Commission, *Family Law: Illegitimacy*, Law Com No 118
(London: HMSO, 1982b)

4.24 In the Working Paper we summarised the case against automatically extending parental rights to the father of an illegitimate child in the following words—

"3.9 . . . It may be argued that [it is right that the father of a child born out of wedlock should have neither rights nor duties unless and until the court so orders] because of the very wide range of possible factual relationships between the father on the one hand and the mother and the child on the other. If the father wishes to participate in the child's upbringing and can make a substantial contribution to his welfare, the court can make appropriate orders even if the mother wishes to exclude him. If, on the other hand, he has nothing to offer it would, on this view, be wrong to give him rights (albeit rights of which the court would be able to divest him if the child's welfare so required). One can think of extreme and no doubt unrealistic examples. For instance, should a rapist, even in theory, be entitled to rights equal to those of the mother in relation to a child conceived as the result of the rape? If so, the rapist would in theory be entitled to ask whether he agreed to the child being adopted, and would have equal rights to the child's custody unless and until proceedings were taken formally to divest him of such rights. If such an issue were brought before a court it would of course be resolved by reference to the child's welfare, but, unless and until this was done, the rapist father would as a matter of law have the right to exercise full parental rights over the child and might in theory do so.

3.10 We have used the case of the rapist because it provides the most dramatic example of the consequences of abolishing discrimination not only against the child but also against his genetic father. There will, however, be other cases in which the father's relationship with the mother and her child is such that it might seem wrong to give him any, even *prima facie*, legal recognition, as where a child has been conceived as the result of a casual encounter.

3.11 It may be questioned whether this problem is of any real importance since in practice such a father would not seek to exercise rights. Even if he did, the court would be bound to override his rights if to do so would be in the child's interests. Looking at the position pragmatically, this may well be the right approach, but there are two reasons why it may be thought not to be an entirely satisfactory answer. First, the necessity to take legal proceedings to divest the father of his rights may in itself be distressing to the mother—so much so that it could, for example, affect her decision about placing the child for adoption if the result were that the father had to be made a party to the proceedings. Secondly, it would be necessary for the mother to take legal proceedings if she wanted to secure herself and the child against the risk of intervention by the father. Unless and until she did so, the father could (on the hypothesis that he had the same rights as the father of a legitimate child) properly exercise any of the parental rights over

[83] As to family law's construction of fathers, see Collier (2001) and (2003).

the child... Hence, to avoid this risk, mothers would no doubt often be advised to take steps to remove the father's rights, thus increasing not only the amount of litigation but also the mother's distress. These consequences must therefore be weighed in the balance in deciding whether or not the law should cease to discriminate against the genetic father."

Responses to the Law Commission's Working Paper identified a number of particular concerns with respect to conferring *automatic* parental responsibility on unmarried fathers.

4.26... (a) It was said that automatically to confer "parental rights" on fathers could well result in a significant growth in the number of mothers who would refuse to identify the father of their child. Mothers would be tempted to conceal the father's identity in order to ensure that in practice he could not exercise any parental rights. If this were to happen, it would detract from the desirable objective of establishing, recognising and fostering genuine familial links.

(b) It was said that to confer rights on the father might well be productive of particular distress and disturbance where the mother had subsequently married a third party, who had put himself *in loco parentis* to the child. The possibility—however unlikely in reality—of interference by the child's father could well engender a damaging sense of insecurity in the family: matters would be all the worse if the father did intervene. Some commentators argued that the result in such a case might be that the mother and her new partner would seek, for instance by an application for custody or adoption, to forestall any possible intervention by the natural father with the result that the child would be prematurely denied the possibility of establishing a genuine link with him.

(c) It was said that automatically to confer "rights" on the father of a child born outside marriage could put him in a position where he might be tempted to harass or possibly even to blackmail the mother at a time when she might well be exceptionally vulnerable to pressure. In this context a number of commentators made what seems to us to be the valid point that what is in issue is not so much how the law is perceived by the professional lawyer or the experienced social worker but how it might be perceived by a fearful and perhaps ill-informed mother. Sometimes what the law is thought to be may be almost as important as what it in fact is. Thus the parents of a child might well attach more significance to the fact that the law had given the father "rights" than would a lawyer who is accustomed to the forensic process and able dispassionately to consider the likelihood of a court in fact permitting a father to exercise those rights, given its overriding concern to promote the child's welfare.

As these responses to the Law Commission indicate, many commentators at the time were of the view that 'unmeritorious', unmarried fathers should be excluded from holding parental responsibility. Furthermore, as the Law Commission goes on to point out, the term 'unmeritorious fathers' was not necessarily restricted to a particularly deviant group of men, such as those convicted of a criminal offence.[84] Even men who had cohabited with the child's mother were still viewed as potentially problematic, as were men who had voluntarily acknowledged their paternity through, for example, registration on the birth register.[85] A similarly negative image of the unmarried father emerges from the writings of Deech, a particularly strong opponent of the focus on father's rights (rather than responsibilities) within these debates, at what she perceives to be the risk of marginalizing concern for the mother's autonomy and the welfare of the child.

[84] Law Com (1982b), para 4.30.
[85] Ibid, para 4.35.

R. Deech, 'The Unmarried Father and Human Rights', (1992) 4 *Journal of Child Law* 3

Applying a contractual approach, if the father wants all the rights appertaining to a married father, he should marry the mother. If he does not want to make that permanent connection, then he is asking for rights without the *quid pro quo* of responsibilities. If she does not want to marry him, she should not be forced into a quasi-marital situation by being subjected to fathers' rights, such as they are, save where imposed by court in the interests of the child. It is also taken as self-evident here that the law alone cannot make a father assume parental responsibilities that he does not want. It can make him pay support but it cannot make him visit or stay at home or care for his child....

Writers, mostly men, have argued for more fathers' rights, especially unmarried fathers', allegedly for the sake of the child's welfare. This connection can represent a confusion of thought. The basic rights of the child are not furthered by delivering more choice to the unmarried father. Legal rights which he may acquire are choices for him; that is, he may or may not choose to exercise them. Such choice is a limitation on the rights of the child. Moreover, the call for fathers' rights confuses abstract legal rights to have a say in long-term decisions about the child, with the existence of actual family contact with the child...If one sees parental rights as including protective rights, for example, the parent's right to consent to medical treatment, which gradually cedes with age to the child's choice, it is not clear that the absent unmarried father has any part to play. The proper exercise of a right such as consent to medical treatment of a minor depends fundamentally on intimate knowledge of the condition and maturity of the child and cannot sensibly be exercised otherwise...

Discrimination against [the unmarried father] is rooted in the perceived habits of fathers, married or not, who are absent from home, uncommunicative and unable to give guidance even when visiting...Criticism of absent fathers is to recognise, not to decry, the importance of a father's involvement...

The result of the intense consideration of fathers' rights internationally and in domestic policies has been seen in new legislation. Many of the rights claimed by men have been given to them. Has the movement gone too far? Has sufficient consideration been given to the need to plan for a child and the child's welfare?...The pressure for father's rights which has had so much effect is not directed towards making men take responsibility but only to allowing absent fathers to plant their name and the occasional visit on their children, as if they were pieces of property.

The question should not be, does the absent unmarried father have too few rights, but does he have too few responsibilities? Parenthood is defined in the Children Act 1989 as including duties, and 'rights' as a term has in general been replaced by 'responsibilities'. But does the average unmarried father know this new law? Does he now accept an equal responsibility to rear the child and provide a home for her, or if he is totally rejected by the mother, to do all in his power, materially and otherwise, to enable her to do so? Let us be clear about what is involved in parental responsibilities to make up for the law's deficiencies in defining them. They include feeding, washing and clothing the child, putting her to bed, housing her, educating and stimulating her, taking responsibility for arranging babysitting and day-care, keeping the child in touch with the wider family circle, checking her medical condition, arranging schooling and transport to school, holidays and recreation, encouraging social and possibly religious or moral development. Fatherhood that does not encompass a fair share of these tasks is an empty egotistical concept and has the consequence that the man does not know the child sufficiently well to be able sensibly to take decisions about education, religion, discipline, medical treatment, change of abode, adoption, marriage and property. Therefore the absent unmarried father as contrasted with the cohabiting father, should not automatically be entitled to these rights.

If it is the case that the mother is usually left with the sole day to day responsibility for the child born out of wedlock, and remembering that it is impossible to force a father to live with his child and her mother, the mother should not, in a one-sided way, be subjected to the absent father's rights and the legal disadvantages of marriage when she is not married and where the case for the improved welfare of the child stemming from the absent father's legal status has not been made out.

In stark contrast to the negative view of unmarried fathers, the unmarried mother is consistently portrayed as an inherently worthy parent, however the child was conceived. The perceived vulnerability of the unmarried mother is a further striking feature of the debates.

Law Commission, *Family Law: Illegitimacy*, Law Com No 118
(London: HMSO, 1982b)

4.39 It may, however, be argued that the father should be entitled to parental rights in cases where *both* parents of the child agree that he should. After all (it might be argued) the law already accords parental rights to all married parents without any prior scrutiny of what is in the child's best interests. Why should it not equally accord such rights to unmarried parents who are in agreement? We see force in this argument, but have nevertheless rejected it. The most powerful factor influencing our decision was the strong body of evidence from those best acquainted with the problems of the single parent family about the vulnerable position of the unmarried mother in many cases. Such mothers may well be exposed to pressure and even harassment, on the part of the natural father; and it would, in our view, give unscrupulous natural fathers undesirable bargaining power if they were to be placed in a position where they might more easily extort from the mother a joint "voluntary" acknowledgment, having the effect of vesting parental rights in the father, perhaps as the price of an agreement to provide for the mother or her child, or even as the price of a continuing relationship with the mother.

Concern for the mother has remained prominent in the debate over unmarried fathers and their 'right' to parental responsibility. All reforms to extend the rights of unmarried fathers have been qualified by the need to secure effective safeguards both for mother and child against the behaviour of 'irresponsible' fathers. This approach to the issue has found favour in the European Court of Human Rights, which considered whether it was discriminatory to withhold automatic parental rights from unmarried fathers in *McMichael v United Kingdom*.

McMichael v United Kingdom (A/308, ECHR) (1995)

94. ...In his submission, [the first applicant claimed] he had been discriminated against as a natural father contrary to Article 14 taken in conjunction with Article 6 para. 1 and/or Article 8...in that prior to his marriage to the second applicant he had no legal right to custody of [the child] or to participate in the care proceedings...

96. Under Scots law a child's father automatically acquires the parental rights of tutory, custody and access only if married to the child's mother...Further, only a "parent", that is a

person having parental rights, is entitled to attend at all stages of a children's hearing... The natural father of a child born out of wedlock may obtain parental rights by making an application to a court; such an application will be dealt with speedily if the mother consents...

Mr McMichael was therefore in a less advantageous position under the law than a married father...

97. According to the Court's well established case-law, a difference of treatment is discriminatory if it has no reasonable and objective justification, that is, if it does not pursue a legitimate aim or if there is not a reasonable relationship of proportionality between the means employed and the aim sought to be realized...

98. ...As the Commission remarked, "it is axiomatic that the nature of the relationships of natural fathers with their children will inevitably vary, from ignorance and indifference at one end of the spectrum to a close stable relationship indistinguishable from the conventional matrimonial-based family unit at the other"...As explained by the Government, the aim of the relevant legislation, which was enacted in 1986, is to provide a mechanism for identifying "meritorious" fathers who might be accorded parental rights, thereby protecting the interests of the child and the mother. In the Court's view, this aim is legitimate and the conditions imposed on natural fathers for obtaining recognition of their parental role respect the principle of proportionality. The Court therefore agrees with the Commission that there was an objective and reasonable justification for the difference of treatment complained of.

99. In conclusion, there has been no violation of Article 14 taken in conjunction with Article 6 para. 1 or Article 8... in respect of the first applicant.

The Court's reasoning in *McMichael* was applied to the specific issue of withholding automatic parental responsibility from unmarried fathers under the CA 1989 in *B v United Kingdom*.[86]

Despite attracting the support of the European Court, the purported justifications for withholding equal status from all unmarried fathers have been criticized on several grounds. It can be argued that unmarried fathers are being denied equal status on the basis of a negative stereotype that is unsupported by any kind of objective evidence.[87] To deny all unmarried fathers full legal responsibility for their children on the basis of unsubstantiated concerns about the behaviour of a small minority of men is arguably manifestly unjust. There are, after all, many irresponsible and uninterested married fathers, and indeed mothers, who are nevertheless 'given the benefit of the doubt' and encouraged to take an active role in their children's upbringing by the automatic grant of parental responsibility. Similarly, if the government is committed to encouraging active and meaningful relationships between children and fathers, there is a good case for saying that it should use parental responsibility positively to support that policy. As Pickford argues, denying unmarried fathers parental responsibility does not support the father–child relationship but rather undermines attempts to promote fathers' involvement with their children.[88]

These arguments feed into the wider debate about the cultural and social value of fatherhood in contemporary society. By making all men financially responsible for their children but denying them the full responsibilities of parenthood, the law not only constructs a negative image of the unmarried father but perpetuates outdated stereotypes of fathers as 'breadwinners' and 'providers', rather than 'nurturers' and 'carers', in contrast to mothers

---

[86] (App No 39067/97, ECHR) (1999). See also *Sporer v Austria* (App No 35637/03, ECHR).
[87] Bainham (1989), 227 and 230–1.
[88] Pickford (1999), 158.

who are depicted as the *automatic* natural carers for their children.[89] If one is committed to true equality in parenting, perpetuating these outdated, gendered stereotypes is deeply problematic. As Nigel Lowe has argued, the law needs to foster a 'culture of responsibility' whereby 'fathers have a duty to provide for their children's emotional and moral development as well as their financial needs'.[90]

In order to remove all legal distinctions between parents there are two further steps the government could take:

- place unmarried fathers in exactly the same position as mothers and married fathers: give them automatic parental responsibility which, like that of other parents, cannot be terminated or revoked;
- confer automatic parental responsibility on all unmarried fathers but retain the provisions on termination as an appropriate safeguard in extreme cases. This option could be pursued without compromising the principle of equality by rendering the parental responsibility of all parents subject to termination.[91]

Both of these options would address continuing concerns about the inequalities faced by unmarried fathers, whilst sending out a strong message to counter the problematic gendered stereotypes which arguably continue to pervade this area of law.

10.4.3 REVIEWING THE CURRENT POSITION

The 2002 reforms which enabled an unmarried father to acquire parental responsibility by registration clearly took much of the heat out of the debate. Prior to the birth registration reforms in 2009, registration on the birth register provided an effective mechanism for identifying those 'meritorious' fathers who had some form of continuing relationship with the child's mother, whilst requiring the minority of remaining fathers (who could be assumed to be more likely to fall into the category of 'irresponsible' or 'dangerous') either to apply to the court or enter into a parental responsibility agreement. However, the decision to make joint birth registration mandatory and thus, in effect, make the acquisition of parental responsibility automatic for virtually all genetic fathers has led to concern that the current focus on promoting (genetic) fatherhood is being unjustifiably pursued at the expense of other legitimate interests.

Far from dangerous and irresponsible, Sheldon and Collier suggest that the image of the unmarried father which has come to dominate family policy in recent years has changed dramatically.

R. Collier and S. Sheldon, *Fragmenting Fatherhood: A Socio-Legal Study*
(Oxford: Hart Publishing, 2008), 175–6

[T]he image of unmarried fathers as unworthy, irresponsible and uninterested in their children has been increasingly supplemented (in many contexts even supplanted) by a very different depiction: of men who are often deeply committed to their children, yet find themselves subject to discrimination, denied access to their children and unfairly dependent on the whims of selfish, sometimes hostile mothers.

---

[89] See, e.g., Collier (2001) and (2003) and McGlynn (2000) and (2001).
[90] Lowe (1997a), 207. See also Bainham (1989), 226–7.
[91] On terminating parental responsibility, see 10.6.

Against the background of this emerging image of the unmarried father as inherently worthy, it is argued that the tendency to use parental responsibility orders to confer mere parental status (or 'legitimation'[92]) on unmarried fathers is shifting parental responsibility further away from its original purpose of providing legal recognition and support to those carrying out the actual work of parenting and leaving parental responsibility devoid of any substantive meaning or purpose. Helen Reece is particularly critical of the decision in *Re D (Contact and PR: Lesbian Mothers and Known Father) (No 2)*, arguing that it represents the 'nadir' of a line of cases in which parental responsibility has become detached from parental decision-making. In her view, by awarding parental responsibility simply on the basis of biological fatherhood the distinction between parenthood and parental responsibility has become blurred.[93] These concerns are exacerbated by the effect of the birth registration reforms leaving parental responsibility 'meaning nothing whatsoever'.[94] As Reece points out, 'if almost all unmarried fathers are compelled to hold parental responsibility, their parental responsibility will no longer even imply official approval of them, as least as individual fathers'.[95] Harris and George echo these concerns.

P. Harris and R. George, 'Parental Responsibility and Shared Residence Orders: Parliamentary Intentions and Judicial Interpretations', (2010) 21 *Child and Family Law Quarterly* 151, 161, 163

From the high point of compliance with the scheme intended by Parliament there has been a consistent trend in the case law downplaying both the potency and primacy of parental responsibility, with the concept being constructed as a form of status recognition with limited or no practical effect . . . [T]he pattern that can be seen is that parental responsibility is increasingly granted to men who are going to play no real part in their children's upbringing, primarily as a means of placating them . . . [W]e would suggest that the courts have robbed parental responsibility of its substantive content. Granting parental responsibility to fathers who are to have little if any involvement in their children's lives, makes it almost impossible to argue that parental responsibility can be something of substantive significance.

In addition to these concerns over devaluing parental responsibility, it is doubtful that the government's objectives will be achieved: that conferring parental responsibility on all unmarried fathers will encourage them to undertake the responsibility and work of caring for their children. Insofar as the birth registration reforms are intended to effect a change in fathers' parenting behaviour, several commentators suggest they are naïvely optimistic and thus deeply flawed.[96]

---

92 Reece (2009), 85.
93 Ibid, 94, 101, and 102.
94 Ibid, 85.
95 Ibid, 97.
96 See also McCandless (2008) and Wallbank (2009); extracts from Wallbank (2009) can be found on the Online Resource Centre.

L. Smith, 'Clashing Symbols? Reconciling Support for Fathers and Fatherless Families after the Human Fertilisation and Embryology Act 2008', (2010) 22 *Child and Family Law Quarterly* 46, 55, 62–4, 69

[Joint birth registration] is motivated by the intention to develop a culture in which the welfare of children is paramount and people are clear that fatherhood as well as motherhood always comes with rights as well as responsibilities'. The White Paper sets out the optimistic view that the act of birth registration will, somehow, in and of itself, result in more fathers exercising their rights and responsibilities towards their children. This policy document too is supported by statements about the various unique advantages that children allegedly derive from the presence of an involved father, thus implicitly linking fathers with child welfare.

The position as a result of the reform is that the rights, duties, powers and responsibilities that comprise parental responsibility now follow upon the simple acknowledgement of genetic paternity. This creates an artificial link between biological and social fatherhood which assumes that the latter act follows the former fact...

These legislative and policy developments echo common law developments which have seen parental responsibility degraded from a mechanism for conferring rights and responsibilities to committed and attached fathers, to a simple recognition of status. Whereas, for the purpose of granting parental responsibility, the importance of unmarried fathers was once measured according to the role they actually played, it is now taken as a given. This once again shows a step backwards towards locating the importance of fatherhood in the genetic connection rather than the social relationship.

Smith concludes by suggesting that if the intention is to encourage more fathers to take an active interest in their children, the law would be better remaining faithful to the original purpose of parental responsibility and acknowledging and supporting the actual care a father provides rather than valorizing the genetic tie.

The irony of these developments is that the importance of genetic and social fatherhood has been fused using a tool which was designed to recognize that the two are not necessarily linked. The very existence of parental responsibility as a tool with which to graft practical aspects of parenting onto, or separate from, the duties and rights inherent in legal parenthood has always implied legal recognition that genetic and social parenthood may not always coincide. Moreover, when the concept of parental responsibility was introduced into English law, it encapsulated a view of parenthood as a care-giving role. More importantly...the *problem* with these developments is that merging the significance of genetic and social fatherhood makes it possible to assert that all fathers are valuable. By blurring the distinction between fathers who make an active and valuable contribution to their children's upbringing and those who do not, the trend makes it difficult to separate the former from the latter and thus to reject the importance of any father in terms of his potential contribution to his child's welfare...

[G]enuinely promoting the value of fatherhood actually depends on distinguishing genetic paternity from social parenting. Failing to distinguish between uninvolved genetic fathers and attentive social fathers devalues the care devoted by the latter. In that sense the confusion which suggests that it is simply a father, rather than the supportive parenting a father can provide, that is intrinsically valuable not only undermines fatherless families, but also undermines efforts to promote fatherhood itself. This means that the drive in family law and policy to promote the idea of responsible (ie involved) parenting to fathers has been undermined because the way in which the message has been presented has been counter-productive. By contrast, an approach to parenthood which emphasized the distinction between the fact of genetic parentage and the act of socially parenting could further the goal of promoting active fatherhood by encouraging more men to focus on the value of parenting their children, rather than just genetically fathering them.

According to this approach, legal parenthood should be left to deal with issues of parental status; parental responsibility should deal with those who actually undertake the job of parenting.[97]

10.5 EXERCISING PARENTAL RESPONSIBILITY

10.5.1 A DUTY TO CONSULT OR A RIGHT OF UNILATERAL ACTION?

The Children Act's approach to the acquisition of parental responsibility means that at any one time there may be several adults who hold parental responsibility for a particular child. While a child's 'parenting team' can cooperate over decisions relating to the child's upbringing, the fact that decision-making is shared poses no particular problems. However, difficulties develop where cooperation breaks down and different members of the 'parenting team' hold different views about what will best serve the child's interests. Disputes may arise over the child's school, medical treatment, surname, and in which religion, if any, the child should be raised.[98] The possibility of disagreement raises the important question of whether individuals holding parental responsibility can act unilaterally without consulting or seeking the agreement of the other members of the 'parenting team'. This is also an important issue where an individual holding parental responsibility has little or no contact with the child and that person's whereabouts may be unknown. Again, their estrangement from the child raises the question whether they must nevertheless be consulted and/or their agreement obtained with respect to important decisions concerning the child's upbringing.

These potential difficulties were anticipated by the Law Commission. Their proposed solution was to allow unilateral action by the individual holders of parental responsibility.

Law Commission, *Family Law, Review of Child Law: Guardianship and Custody*, Law Com No 172 (London: HMSO, 1988c)

(b) The power to act independently

2.10 . . . [W]e believe it important to preserve the equal status of parents and their power to act independently of one another unless and until a court orders otherwise. This should be seen as part of the general aim of encouraging both parents to feel concerned and responsible for the welfare of their children. A few respondents suggested that they should have a legal duty to consult one another on major matters in their children's lives, arguing that

---

[97] Lind and Hewitt (2009).
[98] For detailed discussion of these various aspects of parental responsibility, see Probert, Gilmore, and Herring (2009).

this would increase parental cooperation and involvement after separation or divorce. This is an objective which we all share. However, whether or not the parents are living together, a legal duty of consultation seems both unworkable and undesirable. The person looking after the child has to be able to take decisions in the child's best interests as and when they arise. Some may have to be taken very quickly. In reality, ...it is that person who will have to put those decisions into effect and that person who has the degree of practical control over the child to be able to do so. The child may well suffer if that parent is prevented by the other's disapproval and thus has to go to court to resolve the matter, still more if the parent is inhibited by the fear that the other may disapprove or by the difficulties of contacting him or of deciding whether what is proposed is or is not a major matter requiring consultation. In practice, where the parents disagree about a matter of upbringing the burden should be on the one seeking to prevent a step which the other is proposing, or to impose a course of action which only the other can put into effect, to take the matter to court. Otherwise the courts might be inundated with cases, disputes might escalate well beyond their true importance, and in the meantime the children would suffer. We recommend, therefore, that the equal and independent status of parents be preserved and, indeed, applied to others...who may share parental responsibility in future. This will not, of course, affect any statutory provision which requires the consent of each parent, for example, to the adoption of the child.

This recommendation was enshrined in s 2(7) of the CA 1989.[99]

Children Act 1989, s 2

(7) Where more than one person has parental responsibility for a child, each of them may act alone and without the other (or others) in meeting that responsibility; but nothing in this Part shall be taken to affect the operation of any enactment which requires the consent of more than one person in a matter affecting the child.

The only statutory restriction on this right of unilateral action is that a person exercising parental responsibility must not act incompatibly with a court order.[100]

Law Commission, *Family Law, Review of Child Law: Guardianship and Custody*, Law Com No 172 (London: HMSO, 1988c)

2.11 Allied to this is the principle that parents should not lose their parental responsibility even though its exercise may have to be modified or curtailed in certain respects, for example, if it is necessary to determine where a child will live after his parents separate. Obviously, a court order to that effect will put many matters outside the control of the parent who does not have the child with him. However, parents should not be regarded as losing their position, and their ability to take decisions about their children, simply because they are separated or in dispute with one another about a particular matter. Hence they should only be prevented from acting in ways which would be incompatible with an order made about the child's

---

[99] Specific provision is made for those holding parental responsibility under a special guardianship order. See s 14C(1)(b), (2) and (3).

[100] S 2(8).

upbringing. If, for example, the child has to live with one parent and go to a school near home, it would be incompatible with that order for the other parent to arrange for him to have his hair done in a way which will exclude him from the school. It would not, however, be incompatible for that parent to take him to a particular sporting occasion over the weekend, no matter how much the parent with whom the child lived might disapprove. These principles form part of our general aim of "lowering the stakes" in cases of parental separation and divorce, and emphasising the continued responsibility of both parents ...

Although a right of unilateral action avoids potential difficulties in trying to locate and obtain the agreement of an estranged parent, such an approach creates the possibility of members of the 'parenting team' taking contradictory decisions and undermining one another's care of the child. This is a particular concern for the resident parent who bears the burden of the day-to-day decision-making. As seen above, this issue has been raised in a number of s 4 applications where the mother has argued that parental responsibility may be misused by the father to exercise control over her and undermine her care of the child. In response to these concerns, the case law has stressed that such fears are based on a misunderstanding of the nature of a parental responsibility order: in particular, it does not provide a mandate to interfere in the day-to-day decision-making of the parent with whom the child is living.[101] However, the limited ability of a parent with whom the child is not living to participate in routine decisions about the child's day-to-day care does not exhaust the purpose and scope of parental responsibility. With respect to more important decisions concerning a child's upbringing, the position as regards consultation between the holders of parental responsibility is very different.

Despite the statutory basis for unilateral decision-making under s 2(7), the courts have imposed a duty to *consult* and, in effect, *agree* on certain important matters regarding the child's upbringing. The first case to suggest such a duty was *Re G (Parental Responsibility: Education)*. The case concerned a dispute between the child's parents over which school the child should attend. On the advice of the child's current headteacher, the child's father, with whom the child had lived since the parents' separation, wished the child to attend a local authority boarding school. The child's mother, who only became aware of the father's intentions at the eleventh hour, was strongly opposed to this course of action. She applied for a prohibited steps order[102] preventing the father from sending the child to the school until her own application for a residence order (as it was then called) could be determined. The application was dismissed, but, on appeal, the Court of Appeal made it clear that the mother should have been properly consulted over such an important decision.

Re G (Parental Responsibility: Education) [1995] 2 FCR 53 (CA), 56

GLIDEWELL LJ:

The great difficulty is, of course, on the one hand that the mother was not informed of the decision to send the boy to the boarding school and there is no doubt she should have been. Under s. 2 of the Children Act 1989 she has parental responsibility for both children, even though they are not living with her ...

---

[101] *Re P (A Minor) (Parental Responsibility Order)* [1994] 1 FLR 578.
[102] Prohibited steps orders are discussed at 11.8.

> So far no order has been made in respect of which the father is acting incompatibly, but equally there is no doubt, to my mind, that the mother, having parental responsibility, was entitled to and indeed ought to have been consulted about the important step of taking her child away from the day school that he had been attending and sending him to a boarding school. It is an important step in any child's life and she ought to have been consulted. Whether the local authority ought to have informed her I am not prepared to say, but that the father should have done I at once accept.

Support for imposing a duty to consult was taken a step further in *Re C (Minors) (Change of Surname)*, which concerned the mother's wish to change the children's surname from that of their father to that of her new husband. Following the parents' divorce it was agreed that the children would live with their mother and no residence order was therefore made. The children's contact with their father ceased just before the mother remarried. The fact that there was no residence order in force was significant because under s 13(1) of the CA 1989, had such an order been made, the mother would not have been able to change their surname without the written consent of everyone with parental responsibility or without first obtaining leave of the court.[103] However, following her remarriage, and on the advice of her solicitor, the mother attempted to change the children's surnames by deed poll without consulting her former husband or obtaining his agreement. Steps were then taken for the new surname to be used at official levels such as at school and on medical files. However, the headteacher and the local education authority requested confirmation that everyone with parental responsibility had consented to the change before being prepared to amend their records. Consequently, the mother applied for a specific issue order[104] requiring them to acknowledge and adopt the children's new surname. Holman J held that despite the various legislative provisions suggesting a unilateral right of action, on a matter as important as changing the child's surname, all those with parental responsibility should have been *consulted and their agreement obtained*.[105]

Re C (Minors) (Change of Surname) [1997] 3 FCR 310 (Fam Div), 312–19

HOLMAN J:

The argument for the mother

[Counsel's] argument was, in essence, as follows. Section 2(7) provides that where two or more people have parental responsibility each of them may act alone subject to any enactment which requires the consent of more than one person. In relation to a change of name the only relevant enactments are s. 13(1) and s. 33(7) [where the child is in the care of the local authority subject to a care order]. They do not apply to this case since there is no

---

[103] See 11.6.8

[104] Specific issue orders are discussed at 11.8.

[105] It has subsequently been suggested by the Court of Appeal that where one parent seeks to change the surname by which a child is known (usually the registered surname), the obligation to obtain the consent of all parents will apply regardless of whether a child arrangements order determining where the child should live is in force and regardless of which of the parents has parental responsibility. If the parent withholds consent, the leave of the court will be required. See *Dawson v Wearmouth* [1998] Fam 75.

residence or care order in force. Further, in private law cases, s. 13 provides an exhaustive statutory "code" of the circumstances in which the consents of all people having parental responsibility is required. Accordingly the mother had the right and power to change the surname...

In my judgment the conclusion and consequences of this argument are little short of bizarre. Where parents have not agreed about their child or not been able to trust each other so that a residence order has had to be made...the "rights" of both parents in relation to a change of name are carefully preserved; whereas where parents have been able to agree and have not caused or risked harm to their children, the "rights" of either parent can be unilaterally overborne by the other. Further, there would technically, and unless the mother obtained a court order, have been nothing to stop the father in the present case subsequently exercising *his* parental responsibility and executing another deed of name change, which would of course lead to chaos and be potentially very damaging to the children.

Moreover the argument, if correct, would run totally counter to the philosophy of the Children Act, for it would be likely to lead to an insistence on formal residence orders even when the parents were in complete agreement about the issue of with whom the child should live...In my judgment, Parliament neither intended nor enacted the result which the mother contends for...

Holman J went on to hold that the scope of parental responsibility as enshrined in the CA 1989 should be understood in light of any pre-existing limitations on parents' rights and responsibilities contained in the case law and/or legislation. He thus turned to examine the legal position on changing a child's surname as derived from the case law prior to the enactment of the CA 1989.

Analysis

The key is the meaning of "parental responsibility" in s. 3(1), namely "all the rights, duties, powers, responsibilities and authority which by law a parent of a child has in relation to the child and his property". In order to determine what rights, duties, powers, responsibilities and authority a parent actually has, it is necessary to look at the law. Where some provision of the Children Act or some other enactment is exhaustive, then of course that defines "the law". But vast areas of the law of parental responsibility are still derived from, and to be found in, the common law or a mixture of common law and statute...

In cases where there is no residence order, the old law derived from *Y. v Y.* still holds good. "By law" a parent of a child does not have a right, power or authority unilaterally to change its surname without the consent or agreement of the other parent if the child is legitimate. The very right or power itself only exists in law as a bilateral right or power, which is only capable of being exercised jointly with the other parent. So in relation to a change of surname, s. 3(1) has the effect that parental responsibility means a right or power jointly exercisable with all other persons having parental responsibility. The words "but nothing in this Part shall be taken to affect the operation of any enactment which requires the consent of more than one person in a matter affecting the child" in s. 2(7) do not preclude that the consent of more than one person may also be required by some other source of law than an enactment, notwithstanding the first limb of s. 2(7).

Eekelaar strongly criticized this decision, fearing it could be of much wider application.

J. Eekelaar, 'Do Parents Have a Duty to Consult?', (1998b) 114 *Law Quarterly Review* 337, 337–40

When two parents have parental responsibility, must one consult the other over important decisions regarding the child?...In 1988 the Law Commission thought it had resolved the question. "Whether or not the parents are living together, a legal duty of consultation seems both unworkable and undesirable" said the Law Commission, and recommended accordingly, but added that "this will not, of course, affect any statutory provision which requires the consent of each parent, for example, to the adoption of the child."...

[In *Re C*] Holman J held that [s 2(7)] did not "preclude that the consent of more than one person may also be required by some other source of law than an enactment, notwithstanding the first limb of s. 2(7)". He found such a source in the law as it existed prior to the implementation of section 2(7) which, in his view, prevented the parent of a legitimate child from changing its surname without the consent of the other parent.

...[I]t is certainly arguable that under a combination of statute and common law prior to the Children Act 1989 there was a legal duty to consult over "important" matters and that, if the second parent disagreed, the parent with the children could not act without permission of the court.

But this can hardly sustain the basis of Holman J.'s conclusion in [*Re C*]. For the Children Act 1975 was repealed by the Children Act 1989 and cannot form the source of rights thereafter and to hold that the common law position (whatever it was immediately before the implementation of the 1989 Act) overrides section 2(7) is to make the statute subject to the prior law it purported to replace and deprives it of all effect. An argument might be attempted that section 2(7) is consistent with the perpetuation of a duty to consult on the ground that all it does is to clarify that, should consultation fail to bring about agreement, either parent may take action "without the other" leaving the aggrieved party to seek eventual resolution of the dispute in court. Such an interpretation would depart from the intentions of the Law Commission...but there must now be some danger that it could be accepted...

It is suggested that the Law Commission was right in thinking that a general duty to consult would be unworkable. Apart from the problem of defining the range of issues upon which consultation would be required (what are "serious" issues? choice of school, probably; choice of curriculum, of extra-curricular activities? perhaps, perhaps not), what amounts to consultation or attempts at consultation? It cannot be sound policy to provide parties with increased opportunities for legal conflict and dispute...In most cases the best safeguard against surprise decisions lies in the hands of the outside parent. If he sees his children regularly, he will normally know about these "important issues", or will discover them quickly. It is striking that in [*Re C*] the attempt to change the children's name occurred only after direct contact between the father and the children had stopped for over a year. It is difficult to justify imposing a general duty to consult on the parent who is looking after the children when the other parent is not under a legally enforceable duty to involve himself with (or even visit) the children (and nor could such a duty be realistically imposed).

Holman J. commented that if the parents retained the right to independent action, there would have been nothing to stop the father from exercising *his* parental authority and executing another deed of name change, causing "chaos" and being potentially very damaging to the children. This argument against independent action could be made with respect to any exercise of parental responsibility, but is a red herring. Parental responsibility can best be understood as the legitimation of *practical actions* in exercising parenthood. A parent who is not actively involved in a child's life cannot effectively bring about a change in the name by which the child is known. Of course, should he attempt to do so and thus come into conflict with the other parent, the matter would need to be resolved by a court. But that would equally be the case if there was a requirement for his consent.

Indeed, Eekelaar's concern that, following *Re C*, a more general duty to consult and obtain agreement on a wide range of 'important' decisions might be imposed, has been borne out by the subsequent case law. Circumcision and immunization[106] have been added to the 'small group of important decisions'[107] on which consultation is necessary.

Re J (Child's Religious Upbringing and Circumcision) [2000] 1 FCR 307 (CA)

BUTLER-SLOSS P:

There is, in my view, a small group of important decisions made on behalf of a child which, in the absence of agreement of those with parental responsibility, ought not to be carried out or arranged by a one-parent carer although she has parental responsibility under s 2(7) of the Children Act 1989. Such a decision ought not to be made without the specific approval of the court. Sterilisation is one example. The change of a child's surname is another. Some of the examples, including the change of a child's surname, are based upon statute (see s 13(1) of the 1989 Act).

The issue of circumcision has not, to my knowledge, previously been considered by this court, but in my view it comes within that group. The decision to circumcise a child on grounds other than medical necessity is a very important one; the operation is irreversible, and should only be carried out where the parents together approve of it or, in the absence of parental agreement, where a court decides that the operation is in the best interests of the child.

The problem with this approach is the considerable uncertainty it causes. Whilst it is now clear that certain specific issues—schooling; change of surname; circumcision; sterilization; and immunization—fall within the class of case where consultation and agreement is necessary, other decisions potentially falling within this group will have to be determined on a case-by-case basis. The case law provides little guidance as to whether any particular decision will be regarded as sufficiently important as to require consultation. In *Re J*, Thorpe LJ suggested that such decisions should be regarded as exceptional and both Thorpe LJ and Butler-Sloss P pointed to the irreversible nature of a decision regarding circumcision (though, of course, that is true only if the decision is to proceed with circumcision: a decision not to circumcise can be revisited later). However, neither changing a child's surname nor decisions as to which school a child should attend can properly be regarded as irreversible. This alone cannot therefore be the distinguishing feature. The Court of Appeal recently suggested that 'in general terms, it must be the case that where two parents share parental responsibility, it will be the duty of one parent to ensure that the rights of the other parent are respected',[108] which suggests that the limitation on the exercise of parental responsibility may be very sizeable indeed. In turn, that issue raises questions about whether, in cases where a child has a primary carer, that person's autonomy is being undermined.

---

[106] *Re C (Welfare of Child: Immunisation)* [2003] EWHC 1376.
[107] Ibid, [16]–[17].
[108] *Re W (Direct Contact)* [2012] EWCA Civ 999, [47]. See also *Re C (Welfare of Child: Immunisation)* [2003] EWHC 1376, discussed by O'Donnell (2004).

The proper mechanism for resolving disputes between those holding parental responsibility is to apply for a specific issue or prohibited steps order under s 8 of the CA 1989 or, if the CA 1989 cannot provide an appropriate remedy, to invoke the inherent jurisdiction of the court.[109] In determining the dispute the child's welfare is the paramount consideration.

10.5.2 LIMITATIONS ON THE EXERCISE OF PARENTAL RESPONSIBILITY

The need for consultation and agreement between the holders of parental responsibility can serve as an important limitation on the decision-making authority of a parent. However, even where there is agreement their authority may still be subject to challenge by a third party. There are two major sources of external restraint on the decision-making authority of those holding parental responsibility: (i) the child and (ii) the state.

The *Gillick* competent child

Following the decision of the House of Lords in *Gillick v West Norfolk and Wisbech Health Authority*,[110] it is now well established that where children are of sufficient understanding to be deemed capable of making their own decisions, the child's parents lose their *exclusive* decision-making powers with respect to the care and upbringing of the child. As interpreted in the subsequent case law, *Gillick* competent children have the right, alongside their parents, to provide a valid consent on a range of important matters, such as contraception and medical treatment. As decision-making authority is effectively shared between them, neither the parent nor the child has a right of veto. Consequently, if, for example, the child and the parents are in dispute over the child's medical treatment, the doctors can proceed provided they have the consent of *either* the parents or the child.[111]

The state

A second and potentially more powerful constraint on the decision-making authority of those with parental responsibility is the state. Current policy generally dictates that parents should be left to raise their children as they see fit. Parental autonomy and protecting the privacy of the family unit against unnecessary intervention are seen as serving the child's interests (and thereby those of the state). With respect to the vast majority of decisions regarding the child's upbringing, the autonomy and authority of those holding parental responsibility is therefore respected.[112] However, the state retains the authority to override the unanimous wishes of those with parental responsibility where such intervention is necessary to protect the health and welfare of the child.[113]

It would generally be agreed that whatever rights a child's parents may have, they do not have the right to harm the child. There would probably also be general agreement that it is a legitimate function of the state to intervene into the private decision-making realm of

---

[109] *Re T (A Minor) (Child: Representation)* [1994] Fam 49. See also *Re R (A Minor) (Blood Transfusion)* [1993] 2 FLR 757.

[110] [1986] AC 112.

[111] For detailed discussion, see 8.5.4.

[112] See O'Donnell (2004), esp at 223.

[113] Ibid.

the family to protect a child who is vulnerable to such harm. It is important to remember, however, that not all cases in which the state seeks to intervene concern neglectful or abusive parents whose parenting would otherwise give rise to child protection concerns. Indeed, the parents embroiled in these disputes are most often devoted, committed parents who provide exemplary care. The problem occurs because the state disagrees with the parents' firmly held views as to the child's best interests and the nature of the harm being caused. The state, through the courts, justifies intervening into the private decision-making realm of the family on the basis of its historical obligation to protect the health and welfare of all minors falling within the protective jurisdiction of the Crown. The fundamental question, however, is whether, where the state and the parents disagree as to the child's welfare, the views of the parents or the state should prevail. To put the question another way: is the child's welfare for the individual family or the wider community to determine? For the courts, once their jurisdiction has been invoked, the answer is clear.

Re A (Children) (Conjoined Twins: Surgical Separation) [2001] Fam 147
(CA), 178–9

WARD LJ:

There is, however, this important safeguard to ensure that a child receives proper treatment. Because the parental rights and powers exist for the performance of their duties and responsibilities to the child and must be exercised in the best interests of the child, "...the common law has never treated such rights as sovereign or beyond review and control": per Lord Scarman in *Gillick* case...

Overriding control is vested in the court. This proposition is well established and has not been the subject of any challenge in this appeal. Because of the comment in the media questioning why the court should be involved, I add this short explanation. Long, long ago the sovereign's prerogative to protect infants passed to the Lord Chancellor and through him to the judges and it forms a part of the inherent jurisdiction of the High Court. The Children Act 1989 now contains a statutory scheme for the resolution of disputes affecting the upbringing of children. If a person having a recognisable interest brings such a dispute to the court, the court must decide it.

The protective jurisdiction of the court is most commonly invoked by a local authority or an NHS Trust seeking to override the unanimous views of those holding parental responsibility where a dispute has arisen over the child's medical treatment. There are two routes by which such a dispute may be brought before the courts: the third party may apply for a specific issue order under s 8 of the CA 1989 which authorizes them to administer or withhold certain treatment against the wishes of those with parental responsibility. Alternatively, the third party can invoke the High Court's inherent jurisdiction. Whichever procedural route is adopted, the welfare of the child is the court's paramount consideration.

The current approach: protecting the child's welfare and the paramountcy principle

The legal principles to be applied in disputes of this nature were set down in one of the most controversial cases to be decided in recent years: *Re T (a minor) (wardship: medical treatment)*. The court was asked to give permission for a liver transplant operation to be performed on a very young child against the wishes of the parents. The unanimous medical view was that without the operation the child would not live beyond two-and-a-half years. The Court of Appeal controversially refused the hospital's application.

Re T (A Minor) (Wardship: Medical Treatment) [1997] 1 WLR 242 (CA), 253–4

WAITE LJ:

The law's insistence that the welfare of a child shall be paramount is easily stated and universally applauded, but the present case illustrates, poignantly and dramatically, the difficulties that are encountered when trying to put it into practice...Loving and devoted parents have taken, after anxious consideration, a decision to withhold consent to operative transplant treatment. Although it is relatively novel treatment, still unavailable in many countries, doctors of the highest expertise have unanimously recommended it for this child on clinical grounds, taking the view that it involves a relatively minor level of risk which they regard as well worth taking in the child's long-term interests (which in this instance include an extension of life itself)...

What is the court to do in such a situation? It is not an occasion—even in an age preoccupied with "rights"—to talk of the rights of a child, or the rights of a parent, or the rights of the court. The cases cited by Butler-Sloss L.J. are uncompromising in their assertion that the sole yardstick must be the need to give effect to the demands of paramountcy for the welfare of the child. They establish that there are bound to be occasions when such paramountcy will compel the court, acting as a judicial parent, to substitute the judge's own views as to the claims of child welfare over those of natural parents—even in a case where the views of the latter are supported by qualities of devotion, commitment, love and reason. The judge, after anxious consideration, reached the conclusion that this case provides such an occasion. Was he right to do so?...

In this instance...I consider that the judge was betrayed into an error of law by his concern with the need to form a judgment about the reasonableness of the mother's approach.... [W]hen it comes to an assessment of the demands of the child patient's welfare, the starting point—and the finishing point too—must always be the judge's own independent assessment of the balance of advantage or disadvantage of the particular medical step under consideration. In striking that balance, the judge will of course take into account as a relevant, often highly relevant, factor the attitude taken by a natural parent, and that may require examination of his or her motives. But the result of such an inquiry must never be allowed to prove determinative. It is a mistake to view the issue as one in which the clinical advice of doctors is placed in one scale and the reasonableness of the parent's view in the other. Had the judge viewed the evidence more broadly from the standpoint of his own perception of the child's welfare when appraised in all its aspects, he would have been bound, in my view, to take significant account of other elements in the case...

All these cases depend on their own facts and render generalisations—tempting though they may be to the legal or social analyst—wholly out of place. It can only be said safely there is a scale, at one end of which lies the clear case where parental opposition to medical intervention is prompted by scruple or dogma of a kind which is patently irreconcilable with principles of child health and welfare widely accepted by the generality of mankind; and that at the other end lie highly problematic cases where there is genuine scope for a difference of view between parent and judge. In both situations it is the duty of the judge to allow the court's own opinion to prevail in the perceived paramount interests of the child concerned, but in cases at the latter end of the scale, there must be a likelihood (though never of course a certainty) that the greater the scope for genuine debate between one view and another the stronger will be the inclination of the court to be influenced by a reflection that in the last analysis the best interests of every child include an expectation that difficult decisions affecting the length and quality of its life will be taken for it by the parent to whom its care has been entrusted by nature.

Several important principles emerge from the Court of Appeal's judgments in *Re T*. All three members of the court made it clear that it is the paramountcy principle alone which applies. The courts are not therefore engaged in reviewing the parents' decision to determine whether it falls within a band of reasonable responses, with the court only being free to override the views of the parents if their decision is deemed unreasonable. The courts must undertake their own independent assessment of the child's welfare *de novo*. That is not to say that the views of the parents are irrelevant. Indeed, the Court of Appeal recognize that the parents' wishes may be crucial to the child's welfare if their opposition to the proposed course of action will directly impact upon the quality of care the child will receive or necessitate alternative care being sought. Furthermore, Waite LJ suggests that where the welfare arguments are finely balanced, the parents' reasonable views may carry considerable force. In such marginal cases, Waite LJ indicates that it would be appropriate to fall back on the principle that it is generally in the child's best interests for such difficult decisions to be taken by the people who care for and know the child best. In this case, the fact that the parents were well-informed health professionals, experienced in caring for sick children, seemed to add force to the Court of Appeal's view that, when all the relevant factors were taken into account, the parents' decision should be accorded significant weight within the welfare assessment.[114]

Whilst *Re T* was clearly exceptional, the legal principles set down by the Court of Appeal have been consistently applied in the case law. However, in *Re C (HIV Test)*, the court's attitude towards the parents' views was very different. In *Re C* the mother was HIV positive. The parents held unconventional views as to the diagnosis, cause, and appropriate treatment of HIV and therefore opposed the child, aged five months, being tested for the virus, maintaining that even if she tested positive they would not be prepared to consent to conventional treatment, preferring to rely on a healthy, holistic lifestyle. The mother was also determined to continue breastfeeding despite the increased risks of transmitting the disease to the child. Wilson J, whose decision was upheld by the Court of Appeal, granted the local authority's application for the child to be temporarily removed from her parents and tested. By the time the case was heard by the Court of Appeal, the parents had left the country, taking the child with them.

Re C (HIV Test) [1999] 2 FLR 1004 (Fam Div), 1006–17

WILSON J:

The parents contend that the application for an order is an affront to their parental autonomy... [W]elfare shall be the paramount consideration in my determination of this application.

[I]n some, if not all, circumstances [is] it possible, and, if so, helpful, to discern in the law a rebuttable presumption that the united appraisal of both parents will be correct in identifying

---

[114] Downie (2000), 198.

where the welfare of their child lies. Support for that proposition is arguably derived from s 1(5) of the 1989 Act, which prohibits the court from making any order under the Act unless it considers that to do so would be better for the child than not to do so. Not to do so is to leave the decision in the hands of those with parental responsibility for the child; and so any applicant for an order has, in effect, to persuade the court that there are positive grounds for taking the matter out of those hands. Furthermore, under Art 8...the parents and the baby all have a right to respect for their family life...

I collect from *Re T* the proposition that the views of these parents, looked at widely and generously, are an important factor in the decision, even, to some extent, irrespectively of the validity of the underlying grounds for their views.

But *Re T* also shows that the views of the parents may have another significance. The intervention proposed for the child may be, in effect, unworkable without their consent...A different, yet allied, situation may arise where to override the parents' wishes is to risk causing them such emotional distress as will disable them from caring properly for the child or, at any rate, as will indirectly affect the child's own emotional stability to a significant extent.

For all these reasons a court invited to override the wishes of parents must move extremely cautiously...

The concluding words of the father's eloquent final submissions were these: 'Whatever the outcome of this case, we would have lost if we had not stood up for our rights.' But this case is not at heart about the rights of the parents. And if...the father regards the rights of a tiny baby as subsumed within the rights of the parents, he is wrong. This baby has rights of her own.

[**Wilson J** then set down Articles 5, 6, and 24 of the UNCRC 1989 before confirming that under national law the case must be decided on the basis of the child's welfare. He went on to conclude that the arguments in favour of testing the baby were overwhelming.]

This conclusion was strongly endorsed by the Court of Appeal.

Re C (HIV Test) [1999] 2 FLR 1004 (CA), 1020–1

BUTLER-SLOSS LJ:

[Counsel] says that there has to be a space within which parents can reject the current orthodoxy, even though that may be based upon good medical evidence. There is an alternative view. They should be entitled to parental autonomy to make that choice, and that is something with which the courts should not intervene. He says that this is a continuing and developing area of medicine and that the parents ought to be free to make these decisions without the interference of the court...

The issue before this court is an issue of knowledge. What is the position of this child? In my view, the child is clearly at risk if there is ignorance of the child's medical condition. The degree of intrusion into the child of a medical test is slight. The degree of intrusion into the family of taking the child to the hospital for a medical test would for most people be comparatively slight. The parents have magnified this into a major issue because they do not accept any of the premises upon which the tests will be carried out. But the welfare of the child is paramount. The court has been asked to deal with the case. It cannot shirk its duty. The space sought by [counsel], which is a space in which parental decisions are final, undoubtedly exists, but it exists subject to s 1(1) of the Children Act. It does not matter whether the parents are responsible or irresponsible. It matters whether the welfare of the child demands that such a course should be taken…We are not talking about the rights of parents. We are talking about the rights of the child. Wilson J set out various Articles of the UN Convention on the Rights of the Child 1989. We do not in a sense need that. It is all encapsulated in s 1 of the Children Act, but it does give added strength to this most important of all points, that the parents' views, which are not the views of the majority, cannot stand against the right of the child to be properly cared for in every sense.

In accordance with *Re T*, the parents' views in *Re C (HIV Test)* were again mitigated through the welfare principle with the result that their somewhat unorthodox position was overruled by the court. Although there are undoubtedly some who would support the parents' approach, the weight of evidence before the judge provided no support for the parents' arguments. *Re C* perhaps therefore provides an example of the type of views described by Waite LJ in *Re T* as promoted by nothing more than 'scruple or dogma', totally and patently inconsistent with the child's welfare. Clearly, Waite LJ did not anticipate that such views should be accorded any great respect when carrying out the welfare assessment, and that is borne out by the decision in *Re C*.

Where there is room for genuine debate as to the child's interests and the parents adopt an entirely reasonable position within that debate, *Re T* suggested that their views would be treated with greater respect. This was put to the test in *Re A*, the case of the conjoined twins. The hospital treating the twins wished to undertake separation surgery to save the life of the stronger twin, Jodie, with the inevitable result that the weaker twin, Mary, would die. Without surgery, the prognosis for both twins was very poor, with the doctors predicting both would die within a few months. The parents, who were Roman Catholics with strong religious views on the matter, as well as practical concerns about raising a severely disabled child on the remote island where they lived, opposed the operation. This was a case with enormous scope for genuine disagreement amongst reasonable people as to what course of action would best serve the interests of the children. This was therefore one of those difficult, marginal cases in which deference to the parents' views might have been expected.

Re A (Children) (Conjoined Twins: Surgical Separation) [2001] Fam 147 (CA)

WARD LJ:

9. Giving due weight to the parents' wishes

9.1 The parents and the courts

…Since the parents have the right in the exercise of their parental responsibility to make the decision, it should not be a surprise that their wishes should command very great respect. Parental right is, however, subordinate to welfare. That was the view of the House of Lords in *In Re KD (A Minor) (Ward: Termination of Access)* [1998] AC 806, 824–825 where Lord Oliver of Aylmerton said:

" …Parenthood, in most civilised societies, is generally conceived of as conferring upon parents the exclusive privilege of ordering, within the family, the upbringing of children of tender age, with all that that entails. That is a privilege which, interfered with without authority, would be protected by the courts, but it is a privilege circumscribed by many limitations imposed both by the general law and, where circumstances demand, by the courts or by the authorities upon whom the legislature has imposed the duty of supervising the welfare of children and young persons. When the jurisdiction of the court is invoked for the protection of the child the parental privileges do not terminate. They do, however, become immediately subservient to the paramount consideration which the court has always in mind, that is to say, the welfare of the child . . . ".

In *J v C* [1970] AC 668, 715 Lord McDermott set out the rule which has served the test of time:

"While there is now no rule of law that the rights and wishes of unimpeachable parents must prevail over other considerations, such rights and wishes, recognised as they are by nature and society, can be capable of ministering to the total welfare of the child in a special way and must therefore preponderate in many cases. The parental rights, however, remain qualified and not absolute for the purposes of the investigation, the broad nature of which is still as described in the fourth of the principles enunciated by FitzGibbon LJ in *In Re O'Hara* [1990] 2 IR 232, 240."

That fourth principle . . . is stated thus:

"4. In exercising the jurisdiction to control or to ignore the parental right the court must act cautiously, not as if it were a private person acting with regard to his own child, and acting in opposition to the parent only when judicially satisfied that the welfare of the child requires that the parental right be suspended or superseded."

Finally, it is perhaps useful to repeat the passage in the judgment of Sir Thomas Bingham MR in *In Re Z (A Minor) (Identification: Restrictions on Publication)* [1997] Fam 1, 32–33 . . .

"I would for my part accept without reservation that the decision of a devoted and responsible parent should be treated with respect. It should certainly not be disregarded or lightly set aside. But the role of the court is to exercise an independent and objective judgment. If that judgment is in accord with that of the devoted and responsible parent, well and good. If it is not, then it is the duty of the court after giving due weight to the view of the devoted and responsible parent, to give effect to its own judgment. That is what it is there for. Its judgment may of course be wrong. So may that of the parent. But once the jurisdiction of the court is invoked its clear duty is to reach and give the best judgment that it can."

That is the law. That is what governs my decision. That is what I am desperately trying to do . . .

9.2 The role of the court: reviewer or decision-maker?

Is the court reviewing the parental decision as it reviews an administrative decision or does the court look at the matter afresh, in the round, with due weight given to the parental wish? If there was doubt about that, it has been resolved in favour of the latter approach by the decision of this court in *Re T (A Minor) (Wardship: Medical Treatment)* [1997] 1 WLR 242 . . .

9.3 The weight to be given to these parents' wishes

I would wish to say emphatically that this is not a case where opposition is "prompted by scruple or dogma." The views of the parents will strike a chord of agreement with many who reflect upon their dilemma. I cannot emphasise enough how much I sympathise with them in the cruelty of the agonising choice they had to make. I know because I agonise over the dilemma too. I fear, however, that the parents' wish does not convince me that it is in the children's best interest:

(i) From Jodie's point of view they have taken the worst possible scenario that she would be wheelchair bound, destined for a life of difficulty. They fail to recognise her capacity sufficiently to enjoy the benefits of life that would be available to her were she free and independent.

(ii) She may indeed need special care and attention and that may be very difficult fully to provide in their home country. This is a real and practical problem for the family, the burden of which in ordinary family life should not be underestimated. It may seem unduly harsh on these desperate *parents* to point out that it is the *child's* best interests which are paramount, not the *parents*'. Coping with a disabled child sadly inevitably casts a great burden on parents who have to struggle through these difficulties....

(iii) They are fully entitled to recoil at the idea, as they see it, of killing Mary. That is wholly understandable. This lies at the core of their objection. Yet they came to this country for treatment. They were aware of the possibility that Mary might be stillborn and they seemed reconciled to an operation which would separate Jodie from her. They seemed to have been prepared...[to] agree to the operation if Mary predeceased Jodie. The physical problems for Jodie would be the same, perhaps even worse in such an event. The parents appear to have been willing to cope in any event, and the burdens for parents and child cannot have changed. Mary is lost to them anyway.

(iv) In their natural repugnance at the idea of killing Mary they fail to recognise their conflicting duty to save Jodie and they seem to exculpate themselves from, or at least fail fully to face up to, the consequence of the failure to separate the twins, namely, death for Jodie. In my judgment, parents who are placed on the horns of such a terrible dilemma simply have to choose the lesser of their inevitable loss. If a family at the gates of a concentration camp were told they might free one of their children but if no choice were made both would die, compassionate parents with equal love for their twins would elect to save the stronger and see the weak one destined for death pass through the gates.

This is a terribly cruel decision to force upon the parents. It is a choice no loving parent would ever want to make. It gives me no satisfaction to have disagreed with their views of what is right for their family and to have expressed myself in terms they will feel are harshly and unfairly critical of them. I am sorry about that. It may be no great comfort to them to know that in fact my heart bleeds for them. But if, as the law says I must, it is I who must now make the decision, then whatever the parents' grief, I must strike a balance between the twins and do what is best for them.

[The Court of Appeal held that it would be in the twins' best interests for the operation to separate them to be performed.]

The parents' views were similarly rejected in *Re Wyatt*. *Re Wyatt* is significant because whereas *Re T, Re C*, and *Re A* all concerned intervention by the medical authorities with a view to prolonging life, *Re Wyatt* raised the opposite question: the proceedings were brought by the NHS Trust seeking to withhold potentially life-prolonging treatment against the parents' wishes. Cases such as this raise important questions about the appropriate distribution of NHS resources and whether the state is under a positive duty to preserve life at all costs, particularly as advances in technology mean that patients can be kept alive for much longer periods, even though suffering from the most severe disabilities and with little or no prospect of recovery. *Wyatt* was not, however, argued on this basis, the court simply focusing on the competing views of the doctors and the parents as to the child's best interests. Charlotte had been born at just 26 weeks gestation and was severely disabled. The issue was whether, should her breathing deteriorate, she should be given artificial ventilation to keep her alive, even though the chances of her surviving another 12 months, even with such intervention, were minimal. Whilst listening carefully to the parents' wishes and expressing great sympathy for their views, the court, in discharging its paramount obligation to protect the child's welfare, preferred the unanimous view of the medical professionals that artificial ventilation should not be pursued.

Re Wyatt (A Child) (Medical Treatment: Parents' Consent) [2004] EWHC 2247

HEDLEY J:

The law to be applied

21. This case evokes some of the fundamental principles that undergird our humanity. They are not to be found in Acts of Parliament or decisions of the courts but in the deep recesses of the common psyche of humanity whether they be attributed to humanity being created in the image of God or whether it be simply a self-defining ethic of a generally acknowledged humanism . . .

22. Charlotte, of course, is a baby. Whilst the sanctity of her life and her right to dignity are to be respected, she can exercise no choice of her own. In those circumstances someone must choose for her. That is usually her parents but here it is the court. That choice must be exercised on the basis of what is in her best interests. It is the understanding and application of that concept that presents the true difficulty in this kind of case . . . .

The views of the parents

32. Although this forms part of the consideration of best interests, it is a matter of sufficient importance to be dealt with in its own right. There is no doubt these parents have not relinquished hope and do not wish to accept Charlotte's death as inevitable. There is no doubt as to the genuineness of their view nor is there any doubt that they believe that they are in Charlotte's best interests. Moreover, there is no doubt that they have thought long and hard about the issues that confront them. Their views must be entitled to the greatest respect but what weight is to be attached to them?

33. There is no doubt that the law places final responsibility on the judge. This is not because parliament has expressly said so . . . but because the court is discharging its historic duty of overseeing the best interests of those who, for whatever reason, cannot make decisions for themselves. So although I have no doubt about the law, it leaves me a little uncomfortable . . . . I am being asked to override the views of these parents as to what is best for their daughter and undoubtedly I have the jurisdiction to do so.

34. I think the only way I can allay my discomfort is to remind myself in my consideration of Charlotte's best interests that Mr and Mrs Wyatt know her best. I should pay proper attention to their intuitive feelings whilst reminding myself that they may project those on to Charlotte. In approaching the case in this way, bearing in mind the breadth of the concept of best interests, I think I come closest to giving proper weight to their views whilst discharging the responsibility placed on the court.

Court's conclusions on best interests

38. I have given this case my most anxious and closest attention. I am only too aware of my own limitations in making so momentous a decision. Yet in the end I have come to a clear view. Subject to two observations that I wish to make at the end of this judgment, I do not believe that any further aggressive treatment, even if necessary to prolong life, is in her best interests. I know that that may mean that she may die earlier than otherwise she might have done but in my judgment the moment of her death will only be slightly advanced. I have asked myself: what can now be done to benefit Charlotte? I can only offer

three answers: first, that she can be given as much comfort and as little pain as possible; secondly, that she can be given as much time as possible to spend physically in the presence of and in contact with her parents; thirdly, that she can meet her end whenever that may be in what Mr Wyatt called the TLC of those who love her most. Although I believe and find that further invasive and aggressive treatment would be intolerable to Charlotte, I prefer to determine her best interests on the basis of finding what is the best that can be done for her.

39. In reaching that view I have of course been informed by the medical evidence as to the prospects and cost to her of aggressive treatment. I hope, however, that I have looked much wider than that and seen not just a physical being but a body, mind and spirit expressed in a human personality of unique worth who is profoundly precious to her parents. It is for that personality of unique worth that I have striven to discern her best interests. It is my one regret that my search has led to a different answer than that sought by these parents.

Hedley J made a declaration permitting the hospital to withhold artificial ventilation from Charlotte should her condition deteriorate.[115]

Although the courts clearly strive to reassure parents that considerable weight will be afforded to their views, the great deference which is shown to the medical authorities in these cases has led to concern that in reality it is the health-care professionals, and not the parents or the courts, who are determining the future of these children, even if the views of the children's parents are reasonable.[116] As Huxtable and Forbes suggest, when determining the child's welfare, the courts are prone to fall back on the objective, scientific evidence provided by the medical experts. This is a particular concern if the parents' views are, in contrast, treated with caution because of their inherent lack of objectivity, a factor which appears to have influenced Holman J in another difficult case regarding the withdrawal of treatment from a seriously sick child.

An NHS Trust v MB [2006] EWHC 507

HOLMAN J:

16. The views and opinions of both the doctors and the parents must be carefully considered. Where, as in this case, the parents spend a great deal of time with their child, their views may have particular value because they know the patient and how he reacts so well; although the court needs to be mindful that the views of any parents may, very understandably, be coloured by their own emotion or sentiment. It is important to stress that the reference is to the views and opinions of the parents. Their own wishes, however understandable in human terms, are wholly irrelevant to consideration of the objective best interests of the child save to the extent in any given case that they may illuminate the quality and value to the child of the child/parent relationship...

---

[115] This decision was subsequently reviewed and confirmed by Hedley J following receipt of further medical evidence in *Re Wyatt (No 3) (A Child) (Medical Treatment: Continuation of Order)* [2005] EWHC 693. Both decisions were subsequently upheld by the Court of Appeal in *Wyatt v Portsmouth Hospital NHS Trust* [2005] EWCA Civ 1181. See also *Re L (Medical Treatment: Benefit)* [2004] EWHC 2713.

[116] Huxtable and Forbes (2004), 352.

> 42. . . . I have to caution myself that [the mother] cannot, because of her relationship, be objective; but it is the fact that no one other person has spent so much time with M and been as intimate in their contact with him. I do consider that she is, in various respects, very understandably and humanly, deluding herself.

The father's religious beliefs were similarly dismissed as completely irrelevant to an objective assessment of the child's best interests.

> 49. The father is a practising Muslim. He said in his written statement: "One of my beliefs is that it is not right for people to choose whether another person should live or die." During the course of his oral evidence he said that he believes no one knows what time someone is born to die. No one knows exactly when the God who gives life takes it. We all have a certain time to die and should leave the decision to God.
>
> 50. This case concerns a child who must himself be incapable, by reason of his age, of any religious belief. An objective balancing of his own best interests cannot be affected by whether a parent happens to adhere to one particular belief, or another, or none. I have the utmost respect for the father's religious faith and belief, and for the faith of Islam which he practises and professes. But I regard it as irrelevant to the decision which I have to take and I do not take it into account at all.

This preference for the objectivity of science over faith was reiterated by Holman J in *The NHS Hospital Trust v A*, a case concerning Christian parents.

The NHS Hospital Trust v A [2007] EWHC 1696

> 68. I have already described (and [counsel] has accepted) the legal approach to faith. The presence or absence of religious faith and belief in either the parents or indeed myself are irrelevant. I must decide this case on the basis of medical knowledge and experience, the evidence, and reason. By definition, a miracle defies medical science and all known experience and reason. Whilst I respect the faith of the parents, I must leave entirely out of account any possibility of a miraculous cure.

Concerns about the way in which the views of parents are treated are clearly important. However, it should be remembered that the court's duty is to the child not the parents and, as the views of the parents carry no *independent* weight once the court has embarked upon its own assessment of the child's interests, the views of the parents, including their religious views, cannot be determinative. Whether this is the correct approach to these cases is a more difficult question.

10.5.3 WOULD A RIGHTS-BASED APPROACH BE PREFERABLE?

When faced with such difficult decisions, the courts have typically given only limited consideration to the human rights arguments. However, in all of the cases considered above, a rights-based analysis may well have brought an important and valuable new perspective to the issues. *Re T* may be seen as a substantial victory for the right to parental autonomy.

Indeed, the views of the parents were upheld to the extent that the Court of Appeal, in effect, sanctioned the inevitable death of a very young child. For this reason, the decision has been subjected to strong criticism, in particular for the way in which the interests of the child were subsumed within the interests of the child's mother.[117] Of clear importance in the Court of Appeal's decision was the central role to be played by the mother in the child's post-operative care. However, this welfare-orientated approach arguably led to the fundamental rights of the child, including most remarkably the child's right to life, being marginalized in the decision-making process. Waite LJ was unequivocal that a rights-based analysis was wholly misplaced. However, adopting a rights-based analysis may well have helped the court articulate and give more effective consideration to the different and potentially competing interests of the child.

Whilst a rights-based analysis in *Re T* may well have secured better protection of the child's independent interests, *Re C (HIV Test)* exemplifies the type of dispute in which a rights-based approach may have assisted the child's parents. It is in cases such as *Re C*, where the parents' views are inconsistent with mainstream orthodox thinking and thus are likely to be deemed contrary to the child's best interests, that a rights-based approach would ensure independent weight is accorded to their views. Recognition of the parents' right to decision-making autonomy gives the parents the space to reject orthodox opinion and raise their children in accordance with their own values and beliefs, free from the 'tyranny of the majority'. Such a right almost certainly falls within the scope of the parents' right to respect for their private and family life under Article 8 of the European Convention on Human Rights (ECHR), at least until the child becomes *Gillick* competent.[118] It is, of course, true that even adopting a rights-based analysis, the rights of the parents are vulnerable to being overridden by the competing rights of the child: it is unlikely that the court would prioritize the parents' right to autonomy over the child's right to life or a form of medical treatment which the evidence suggests is overwhelmingly in his or her best interests.[119] However, by starting from the position that the parents' decision-making authority should be respected, the rights-based approach does at least demand that the state justifies its intervention as being both necessary and proportionate to the legitimate aim of safeguarding the rights and interests of the child. In those cases which do not involve immediate 'life and death' decisions (which arguably would include *Re C*) or marginal cases where there is genuine debate as to the child's welfare, this burden should be much harder for the state to discharge.

The human rights arguments are clearly important where the interests of the parents and the child are potentially in conflict. However, as the *Wyatt* case demonstrates, a rights-based analysis may be of even greater importance in determining the outcome where the rights of the parents and the child are entirely consistent. In cases such as *Re C (HIV Test)* and *Re A (Conjoined Twins)*, the courts' view that the human rights arguments were of little assistance could be rationalized on the basis that the parents' right to decision-making autonomy would almost certainly be overridden by the competing rights of the child. However, in *Wyatt* the balancing exercise had the potential to take on a very different character. An important dimension of the *Wyatt* case was the possible conflict between the child's rights to life, health, and personal integrity, and the views of the medical authorities as to the child's best interests. Indeed, the rights of the child and the rights of the parents may well

---

[117] Downie (2000), 200.
[118] This would seem to be implicit in the decision of Silber J in *R (Axon) v Secretary of State for Health* [2006] EWHC 37, [123]–[132].
[119] Ibid, [44]. See also Downie (2000), 201.

have stood on the same side of the scales, underpinning and reinforcing, rather than counterbalancing one another. Given this alliance between the parents' and the child's rights, it would thus be much more difficult for the state to justify overriding the decision-making authority of the child's parents on the basis of the child's interests: an important consideration which the court overlooked by examining the issue through the exclusive prism of the welfare principle.

Although the domestic courts have made only limited reference to human rights arguments, the question has been considered by the European Court of Human Rights in *Glass v United Kingdom*. Glass concerned a dispute between the family of a severely disabled child and the hospital where he was being treated for respiratory failure. There was a history of problems between the hospital and the child's mother concerning the child's treatment, in particular as regards the administration of morphine. On this occasion, the doctors took the view that the child was dying and should be given diamorphine to relieve his pain and distress. They also placed a 'Do Not Resuscitate' order on the child's notes without consulting his mother. The mother believed her son was being covertly assisted to die by the use of diamorphine and wanted it stopped. Following a fight between the hospital staff and the child's family, the child was discharged into the care of his mother. Remarkably, given the hospital's view that he was dying, the child recovered. The European Court, applying a human rights framework, found against the UK government. However, the decision was firmly based not on the rights of the mother, but on the rights of the child.

Glass v United Kingdom (App No 61827/00, ECHR) (2004)

B. The court's assessment

1. As to the existence of an interference with Article 8

70. The court notes that the second applicant, as the mother of the first applicant—a severely handicapped child—acted as the latter's legal proxy. In that capacity, the second applicant had the authority to act on his behalf and to defend his interests, including in the area of medical treatment. The Government have observed that the second applicant had given doctors at St Mary's Hospital on the previous occasions on which he had been admitted authorisation to pursue particular courses of treatment...However, it is clear that, when confronted with the reality of the administration of diamorphine to the first applicant, the second applicant expressed her firm opposition to this form of treatment. These objections were overridden, including in the face of her continuing opposition. The Court considers that the decision to impose treatment on the first applicant in defiance of the second applicant's objections gave rise to an interference with the first applicant's right to respect for his private life, and in particular his right to physical integrity...It is to be noted that the Government have also laid emphasis on their view that the doctors were confronted with an emergency (which is disputed by the applicants) and had to act quickly in the best interests of the first applicant. However, that argument does not detract from the fact of interference. It is, rather, an argument which goes to the necessity of the interference and has to be addressed in that context...

72. [The court] would further observe that, although the applicants have alleged that the impugned treatment also gave rise to an interference with the second applicant's right to respect for her family life, it considers that it is only required to examine the issues raised from the standpoint of the first applicant's right to respect for his personal integrity, having regard, of course, to the second applicant's role as his mother and legal proxy.

The European Court went on to find against the UK on the narrow basis that the hospital's reasons for failing to refer the dispute to the High Court for resolution before the situation deteriorated and the treatment was imposed on the child against the mother's wishes were unconvincing. The state was therefore unable to justify the prima facie breach of the applicant's Article 8 rights. The Court did not address the wider issue of whether the state had struck an appropriate balance, in general terms, between the decision-making authority of the parents, the medical authorities, and the courts. Indeed, it appeared to give broad approval to the existing regulatory framework for resolving disputes over a child's medical treatment: the failure in this case had been a failure to properly invoke those procedures.

Given the limited grounds of the European Court's decision, it is important not to overstate the significance of this case. However, some commentators have suggested that *Glass* signals an important step towards the re-empowerment of parents. The decision imposes a clear obligation on the medical professionals to listen seriously to the concerns of parents and refer any dispute promptly to the High Court.[120] Of greater significance, however, is the underlying conceptual basis for the decision. The European Court adopts a very different approach from that adopted by the domestic courts. The Court starts from the position that the child has a right to self-determination and personal integrity exercised through proxy decision-makers. Any intervention by the medical professionals without the consent of those with parental responsibility therefore constitutes an interference with the child's rights and needs to be justified by the state in accordance with the requirements of Article 8(2). This principle would seem to apply whether or not the dispute is concerned with giving or withholding treatment. Such an approach reinforces the argument that the preferred locus for decision-making with respect to a child is the parents, not the hospital or the courts, and that the burden of justifying any departure from this position must therefore rest with the state.[121] The approach dictated by the European Court may make it increasingly difficult for the domestic courts to determine these disputes on the basis of the paramountcy principle alone.

10.6 TERMINATING PARENTAL RESPONSIBILITY

10.6.1 MOTHERS, MARRIED FATHERS, AND SECOND FEMALE PARENTS UNDER S 42 OF THE HFEA 2008

The restrictive circumstances under which the parental responsibility of mothers, married fathers, and second female parents under s 42 of the HFEA 2008 can be terminated, emphasizes that despite the occurrence of other events affecting the parties, such as, divorce, separation, or the removal of the children into care, parenthood is a lifelong commitment that cannot simply be surrendered to the state. Indeed, the only way in which the parental responsibility of a child's mother, married father, or second legal parent under s 42 of the HFEA 2008 can be terminated, however uninterested or unsuitable they are, is by making a parental order under s 54 of the HFEA 2008 (surrogacy agreements) or, more commonly, an adoption order. Under these orders the 'parenthood' of the child, including parental responsibility, is transferred to the adopters who, like natural parents, can only be divested of their parental responsibility by a second adoption order.

---

[120] Huxtable and Forbes (2004), 352.
[121] Ibid, 353.

An adoption order in favour of one legal parent can be used to divest the other legal parent of his or her parental responsibility. However, as noted above, adoption has far-reaching effects on the child's core family relationships beyond the termination of parental responsibility. This use of adoption to deprive an absent, irresponsible, or uninterested parent of parental responsibility is therefore an extreme measure. The issue was considered by the House of Lords in *Re B (A Minor) (Adoption: Natural Parent)*.[122] The child's father, who was worried about the security of his position as the child's residential carer, was seeking an adoption order with the sole purpose of permanently excluding the mother from the child's life.[123] Controversially, Lord Nicholls allowed the adoption order to stand, thereby making the child 'legally motherless', even though the father's position could have been consolidated using alternative, less drastic measures under the CA 1989.[124] The controversy surrounding this case highlights the important question of whether specific provision needs to be made for terminating the parental responsibility of mothers, married fathers, and second female parents under s 42 of the HFEA 2008, akin to the measures in place for terminating the parental responsibility of unmarried fathers, second female parents under s 43 of the HFEA 2008, and step-parents. This additional flexibility in the law, whilst inconsistent with the Children Act policy that 'parenthood is for life', would accommodate the somewhat transient nature of parenting in modern family life, recognizing the reality that there are absent, uninterested parents, who do not have a relationship with their children, and should not have to be consulted on important decisions regarding their upbringing. It would also have the additional benefit of formally acknowledging that the problem of the absent parent is not one restricted to the unmarried father: it is a problem of parenthood, not fatherhood.

10.6.2 UNMARRIED FATHERS, SECOND FEMALE PARENTS UNDER S 43 OF THE HFEA 2008, AND STEP-PARENTS

Unmarried fathers

The position of unmarried fathers regarding the acquisition of parental responsibility has improved considerably. However, unlike the parental responsibility of married fathers, the parental responsibility of unmarried fathers may still be terminated on application to the court by another holder of parental responsibility or, with leave, by the child.

Children Act 1989, s 4

(2A) A person who has acquired parental responsibility under subsection (1) [methods by which unmarried fathers may acquire parental responsibility] shall cease to have that responsibility only if the court so orders.

(3) The court may make an order under subsection (2A) on the application—

    (a) of any person who has parental responsibility for the child; or

    (b) with the leave of the court, of the child himself,

---

[122] [2001] UKHL 70.
[123] This decision is discussed in detail at 13.6.4.
[124] For commentary, see Harris-Short (2002).

> subject, in the case of parental responsibility acquired under subsection 1(c), to section 12(4).
>
> (4) The court may only grant leave under subsection (3)(b) if it is satisfied that the child has sufficient understanding to make the proposed application.

If the court has made a parental responsibility order in favour of an unmarried father or a second female parent made under s 4 or 4ZA because a child arrangements order was made under which the child was to live with that parent, the parental responsibility order cannot be terminated while the relevant child arrangements order remains in force.[125]

The principles to be applied in determining an application under ss 4(2A) and 4(3) are set down in *Re W (Parental Responsibility: Consequential Orders)*. The father had parental responsibility by virtue of having been named on the child's birth certificate. He was subsequently convicted for sexual offences against the mother's two daughters by a previous relationship and sentenced to 48 months' imprisonment. On his release from prison, the mother sought an order revoking the father's parental responsibility. The father sought a specific issue order requiring the mother to provide him with annual reports about the child's progress, but indicated that he did not intend to seek any other orders. At first instance, Baker J followed the approach set out by Singer J in *Re P (Terminating Parental Responsibility)*,[126] which was then the only reported decision setting out any principles for such applications.

Re W (Parental Responsibility: Consequential Orders) [2013] EWHC 854

BAKER J:

59. . . . I find there is force in the mother's concerns that the father is motivated by wishing to become more involved in [the child's] life, to the detriment of the family including [the child]. As in *Re P*, I find that, if the father did not have parental responsibility, it is inconceivable it would now be granted to him, and that this is a factor I should take into account when considering this application to terminate his parental responsibility. Furthermore, like Singer J in *Re P*, I find that in this case there is no element of the bundle of responsibilities that make parental responsibility which this father could in present or foreseeable circumstances exercise in a way which would be beneficial for [the child].

60. I therefore make an order under section 4(2A) terminating the father's parental responsibility for [the child].

The father appealed on the basis that the principles set out by *Re P* in 1994 needed to be revised following the Human Rights Act 1998 and the modifications that had been made to the CA 1989 with respect to parental responsibility.

---

[125] S 12(4).
[126] [1995] 1 FLR 1048.

Re W (Parental Responsibility: Consequential Orders) [2014] EWCA Civ 315

RYDER LJ:

12. When a court is considering an application relating to the cessation of parental responsibility, . . . the child's welfare will be the court's paramount consideration. By section 1(4), there is no requirement upon the court to consider the factors set out in section 1(3) (the 'welfare checklist') but the court is not prevented from doing so and may find it helpful to use an analytical framework not least because welfare has to be considered and reasoned. Given that the cessation of parental responsibility is an order of the court, the court must also consider whether making such an order is better for the child than making no order at all (the 'no order' principle in section 1(5)).

13. The paramountcy test is overarching and no one factor that the court might consider in a welfare analysis has any hypothetical priority. Accordingly, factors that may be said to have significance by analogy or on the facts of a particular case, for example, the factors that the court considers within the overarching question of welfare upon an application for a parental responsibility order (the degree of commitment which the father has shown to the child, the degree of attachment which exists between the father and the child and the reasons of the father for applying for the order) may be relevant on the facts of a particular case but are not to be taken to be a substitute test to be applied . . .

14. An unmarried father does not benefit from a 'presumption' as to the existence or continuance of parental responsibility. He obtains it in accordance with the statutory scheme and may lose it in the same way. In both circumstances it is the welfare of the child that creates the presumption, not the parenthood of the unmarried father. The concept of rival presumptions is not helpful . . . There is also ample case law describing the imperative in favour of a continuing relationship between both parents and a child so that ordinarily a child's upbringing should be provided by both of his parents and where that is not in the child's interests by one of them with the child having the benefit of a meaningful relationship with both. A judge would not be criticised for identifying that, as a very weighty, relevant factor, the significance of the parenthood of an unmarried father should not be under estimated.

Having rejected the father's claim on this issue, Ryder LJ went on to reject the father's other grounds of appeal, including that Baker J had not considered the proportionality of the order made. Permission to appeal to the Supreme Court was refused on the basis that there was 'no error of law in the approach of any of the courts below'.[127]

Although *Re P* and *Re W* emphasize that the courts will be reluctant to terminate the parental responsibility of an unmarried father without very good grounds, the fact that the parental responsibility of an unmarried father (but not that of a mother or of a married father) can be terminated at all is a potential source of grievance for paternal rights advocates. However, the argument that it constitutes discrimination against unmarried fathers has been dismissed by the European Court of Human Rights.[128]

Second female parents under s 43 of the HFEA 2008

The parental responsibility of a second female parent under s 43 of the HFEA 2008 can be terminated on exactly the same basis as that of an unmarried father.[129]

---

[127] UKSC 2014/0172, 12 November 2014.
[128] *B v United Kingdom* (App No 39067/97, ECHR) (1999).
[129] S 4ZA(4)–(5).

Step-parents

The parental responsibility of step-parents is also subject to termination on the same basis as that of unmarried fathers and second female parents under s 43 of the HFEA 2008.[130] However, the possibility that the parental responsibility of a step-parent may be terminated on application to the court is considerably less controversial. A step-parent's relationship with a child will usually be very different from that of an unmarried father or second female parent under s 43 of the HFEA 2008, the marriage between the step-parent and one of the child's parents constituting the principal link between them. It therefore seems sensible to provide for the termination of the step-parent's parental responsibility should the step-parent's relationship with the child change upon his or her separation or divorce from the child's parent.

10.6.3 GUARDIANS, SPECIAL GUARDIANS, AND OTHERS

Guardians, special guardians, and those holding parental responsibility through a child arrangements order do not have a separate parental responsibility order in their favour: the holding of parental responsibility is regarded as an integral part of the appointment or order made. There are therefore no specific provisions for the termination of parental responsibility where parental responsibility is acquired through one of these mechanisms: it terminates automatically when the relevant appointment or order comes to an end.[131] Similarly, the parental responsibility of a local authority is automatically extinguished when the care order terminates.

10.7 CARING FOR CHILDREN WITHOUT PARENTAL RESPONSIBILITY

There will be many occasions when a child will be cared for by someone who does not have parental responsibility, such as, an unmarried father, a step-parent, a grandparent, a teacher, a foster carer, or a family friend. Without parental responsibility, these carers have no legally recognized decision-making authority. As regards the mundane, day-to-day decisions respecting the child, the carer's lack of parental responsibility poses no particular difficulties. Again, however, there may be problems if more important questions arise. For example, if the child is injured whilst in the care of one of these individuals, decisions may have to be made regarding the child's medical treatment. The position of a carer without parental responsibility is governed exclusively by s 3(5) of the CA 1989.

Children Act 1989, s 3

(5) A person who—

(a) does not have parental responsibility for a particular child; but

(b) has care of the child,

may (subject to the provisions of this Act) do what is reasonable in all the circumstances of the case for the purpose of safeguarding or promoting the child's welfare.

---

[130] S 4A.
[131] S 12(2) and 14C(1)(a).

This confers sufficient authority on the carer to make any decisions necessary to safeguard or promote the child's welfare. As there is little case law providing authoritative guidance on the correct interpretation of this provision, its exact meaning is unclear. In practice, it most probably means that where the child is being cared for by individuals on a short-term basis, they will only be able to make urgent decisions regarding, for example, whether the child should receive emergency medical treatment. In *Re S (Abduction: Hague and European Conventions)*,[132] Butler-Sloss LJ said that s 3(5) 'does not clothe the carers with control over the child other than the minimum necessary to provide for the day-to-day welfare of the child'.

Where, however, the child is in the more permanent care of an individual without parental responsibility, s 3(5) may confer on the child's carer the necessary authority to make longer-term decisions regarding such things as the child's education or religious upbringing. It depends on the context of the case.[133]

10.8 CONCLUSION

Parenthood is a very complex issue with different rights and responsibilities attaching to the two core concepts of legal parenthood and parental responsibility. In many ways, the complexity of the law on this issue is a positive factor. It provides scope for the legal recognition of a range of 'parents'—genetic, intentional, and social—who play an important role in the life of the child. In a social context where family life, including parenting, is increasingly transient, this flexibility in the regulation of the parent–child relationship is a great strength. Whilst the child's immediate family environment may be subject to unsettling changes, English law is able to provide positive support for the child's core relationships.

There are, however, some issues of concern. In recent years, the position of unmarried fathers has generated most debate. However, recent reforms to the birth registration system and s 4 of the CA 1989 have considerably improved the overall picture, such that the argument that unmarried fathers face an unjust struggle to achieve recognition of their parenting role is no longer convincing. Indeed, with the vast majority of unmarried fathers now able to acquire parental responsibility by the mere act of registration (or failing that by a relatively straightforward application to the court), the concern is now the other way. There are clear signs that parental responsibility is losing its distinct identity as a legal mechanism for providing legal recognition and support to those actively involved in raising a child and becoming no more than a useful device to confer enhanced parental status on (for the most part) unmarried fathers in the hope that it will encourage them to assume their parenting responsibilities. By routinely conferring parental responsibility on unmarried fathers, some of whom will play only a limited role in the life of the child, genetic fatherhood is being valorized whilst social parenthood and the actual work of parenting is marginalized. This has particularly worrying implications for mothers who still shoulder the bulk of the actual

---

132 [1997] 1 FLR 958, 962, aff'd [1998] 1 FLR 122, 127.
133 See *Re K (Abduction: Rights of Custody)* [2014] UKSC 29, [59], where Lady Hale lists a number of factors which could establish 'rights of custody' for the purposes of the Hague Convention on the Civil Aspects of International Child Abduction where a person has no formal legal rights, one of which is that the person has legal powers equivalent to those under s 3(5).

work and responsibility of parenting. From a position in which the law was dominated by overwhelmingly positive images of mothers as natural committed carers alongside negative stereotypes of unmarried fathers as irresponsible and dangerous, we have moved to a position in which the law on parenthood and parental responsibility is now dominated by assumptions as to the value of genetic fatherhood alongside suspicions about obstructive mothers. As we will see in the next chapter, whilst these changing attitudes towards motherhood and fatherhood and the gendered assumptions which underpin them now permeate family law, they are deeply problematic.

 ONLINE RESOURCE CENTRE
Questions, suggestions for further reading, and supplementary materials for this chapter (including updates on developments in this area of family law since this book was published) may be found on the Online Resource Centre at **www.oxfordtextbooks.co.uk/orc/familytcm3e/**.

11

PRIVATE DISPUTES OVER CHILDREN

CENTRAL ISSUES

1. When determining any private law dispute over a child's upbringing, the child's welfare is the paramount consideration. However, the application of that principle has been informed to varying degrees by the use of 'assumptions' or 'de facto presumptions' when resolving disputes about children's upbringing.

2. Many more mothers become the main carers of their children than fathers. However, when resolving disputes about children's living arrangements, the courts deny that they are applying a presumption in favour of mothers.

3. Claims that the judiciary discriminate against fathers in their approach to disputes about children's living arrangements must be examined carefully. The existing division of labour within intact families and the difficulties of 'co-parenting' post-separation make such claims difficult to sustain.

4. The courts are making increased use of orders for shared living arrangements as a solution to the problems of post-separation parenting. However, there are strong reasons to doubt whether requiring children to split their time equally between the two parents will commonly prove workable or fair. The use of shared orders for symbolic or psychological reasons has also attracted strong academic criticism.

5. When resolving disputes about children's upbringing between parents and non-parents, the courts have more openly applied a 'de facto presumption' in favour of the natural parent. Views differ as to whether this privileging of 'genetic' over 'social' parenting can be justified.

6. When resolving disputes about children spending time or having contact with a parent, the courts again apply a strong 'assumption' or 'de facto presumption' in favour of making such orders. Some say that this presumption is sometimes being applied inappropriately, so that abusive men are being granted contact at the expense of the safety and welfare of women and children.

7. Enforcing these orders is fraught with difficulty. The courts have recently adopted a more 'hard-line' approach to 'intransigent' mothers. Whether imprisoning the mother for disobeying a contact order can ever be in the child's interests, is a fiercely disputed question.

8. Successive governments have introduced important reforms aimed at moving contact disputes out of the courts. Using both 'soft' and 'hard' tools of persuasion, the aim is to transform the 'culture' of contact such that it becomes 'socially unacceptable' to deny children a relationship with both parents following separation or divorce.

11.1 INTRODUCTION

Private law disputes are typically, although not exclusively, concerned with disagreements between parents over some aspect of their child's upbringing. Disputes of this kind following the parents' separation or divorce are extremely common.[1] They are often bitter, heart-wrenching, and protracted. Perfect solutions which safeguard the welfare of the child whilst satisfying the wishes of both parties are rarely possible. Children cannot be physically split between two parents, and avoiding a win–lose mentality is difficult. Anger, betrayal, bitterness, and suspicion are just some of the emotions which make these disputes so hard to resolve—this is family law at its most raw.

In the last few years, private law disputes over children, prompted by the activities of groups such as Fathers4Justice, have increasingly attracted the media spotlight. It has become popularly portrayed as the modern-day 'battle of the sexes'. The gender dimension of intra-parental disputes has certainly added a heat and ferocity to the debate which has not always been helpful. Fathers' rights groups have launched highly successful media campaigns against what they perceive to be the strong bias in favour of women in this area. Anecdotal 'tug-of-love' stories in which fathers and children are victimized by malevolent, spiteful, selfish mothers, determined to deprive their children of any meaningful relationship with their fathers, are used to maximum impact. Policy-makers, government ministers, even the judiciary have, to varying degrees, been receptive to these complaints. On the other hand, women's rights groups have responded with their own accusations of violent and abusive men who have no genuine interest in their children simply using family court disputes to exercise power and control over their former partners. Cutting through the highly charged, and increasingly politicized, rhetoric to get a more balanced perspective on the important gender dimensions of this debate is not easy.[2]

This chapter explores the current legal framework for resolving private law disputes over children. We begin by considering procedural issues germane to all private law disputes, including the extent to which children are able to participate in these proceedings. The three main private law orders available under the Children Act 1989 (CA 1989)—child arrangements orders, specific issue orders, and prohibited steps orders—will then be considered, as well as recent initiatives to try and improve the way in which these cases are handled.

---

[1] Nearly 100,000 children a year in England and Wales experience parental divorce (ONS 2014a), though since nearly half of all children are born to parents who are not married (ONS 2013c), the number of children who experience parental *separation* is considerably higher. Around 120,000 children a year are involved in private law proceedings (MOJ 2012, table 2.1), though it is important to note that some of those children are involved in ongoing proceedings which run across more than one year, and that the majority of children whose parents separate are never the subject of court proceedings at all.

[2] See Collier (2005).

11.2 PRIVATE LAW ORDERS UNDER THE CHILDREN ACT 1989

In 2014, substantial changes were made to the orders that are made in private law proceedings under s 8 of the CA 1989, which are referred to collectively as 's 8 orders'. Following amendment by the Children and Families Act 2014 (CFA 2014), s 8(1) states:

Children Act 1989, s 8

(1) In this Act—

"[a] child arrangements order" means an order regulating arrangements relating to any of the following—

(a) with whom a child is to live, spend time or otherwise have contact, and

(b) when a child is to live, spend time or otherwise have contact with any person;

"a prohibited steps order" means an order that no step which could be taken by a parent in meeting his parental responsibility for a child, and which is of a kind specified in the order, shall be taken by any person without the consent of the court; and

"a specific issue order" means an order giving directions for the purpose of determining a specific question which has arisen, or which may arise, in connection with any aspect of parental responsibility for a child.

Child arrangements orders are a new creation, and replace two different orders which existed before the CFA 2014. Those orders were:

- *residence orders*, which were orders settling the arrangements as to the person with whom a child was to live; and
- *contact orders*, which required the person with whom the child lived to allow the child to visit or stay with the person named in the order, or for the person and the child otherwise to have contact with each other.

In practical terms, there is little difference between the two limbs of a child arrangements order and the two previous orders, all of which regulate the child's living arrangements and relationships with other people (usually parents and other family members). The rationale for the change was to remove the sense that some parents (especially fathers) perceived, that residence orders were 'better' than contact orders, or that the parent with a residence order was the 'main' parent. By removing the labels 'resident parent' and 'contact parent', and making a single order which covers all the main arrangements and both parents, the government hopes that any sense of 'winners' and 'losers' will be removed. It is not yet clear whether this aim will be achieved in practice.

There are provisions within Part II of the CA 1989 governing particular issues—removal of a child from the UK and change of the child's surname, for example—which we discuss below.[3] There are also other orders available under Part II—special guardianship orders,[4]

---

[3] See 11.6.8 and 11.9.

[4] CA 1989, s 14A; see 13.8. Unless stated otherwise all statutory references in this chapter are to the CA 1989.

orders for financial relief,[5] and family assistance orders[6]—which are not discussed here in detail.

11.3 PROCEDURAL MATTERS GERMANE TO ALL S 8 ORDERS

11.3.1 WHEN MAY A S 8 ORDER BE MADE?

A s 8 order may be made in any 'family proceedings' in which a question arises with respect to the child's welfare.[7] The court may act upon its own motion or upon an application being made.[8]

11.3.2 WHO MAY APPLY FOR A S 8 ORDER?

Subsections 10(1) and 10(2) identify two categories of applicant who can apply for a s 8 order: 'entitled applicants', and those who have obtained the court's leave.

Entitled applicants

Entitled applicants are divided into three groups. First, under s 10(4), any parent, guardian, or 'person who is named, in a child arrangements order that is in force with respect to the child, as a person with whom the child is to live' is entitled to apply for *any s 8 order*.[9] In this context, 'parent' includes both natural parents (meaning the legal parents) regardless of whether they hold parental responsibility.[10]

The second group of entitled applicants, specified in s 10(5), are entitled to apply as of right *only for a child arrangements order.*

Children Act 1989, s 10

(5) The following persons are entitled to apply for a child arrangements order with respect to a child—

(a) any party to a marriage (whether or not subsisting) in relation to whom the child is a child of the family;

(aa) any civil partner in a civil partnership (whether or not subsisting) in relation to whom the child is a child of the family;

(b) any person with whom the child has lived for a period of at least three years;

(c) any person who—

---

[5] S 15 and Sch 1; see 6.5.
[6] S 16.
[7] Ss 8(3)–(4).
[8] S 10(1).
[9] S 10(4).
[10] *M v C and Calderdale Metropolitan Borough Council* [1994] Fam 1.

> (i) in any case where a child arrangements order in force with respect to the child regulates arrangements relating to [any person] with whom the child is to live or when the child is to live with any person, has the consent of each of the persons named in the order as a person with whom the child is to live;
>
> (ii) in any case where the child is in the care of a local authority, has the consent of that authority; or
>
> (iii) in any other case, has the consent of each of those (if any) who have parental responsibility for the child;
>
> (d) any person who has parental responsibility for a child by virtue of provision made under section 12(2A).

'Child of the family' is defined to include: (i) a child of the parties to a marriage or civil partnership; and (ii) any other child who has been treated by the parties to a marriage or civil partnership as a child of their family (except children placed with them as foster carers).[11]

The third category of entitled applicants can apply *only for the type of child arrangements order under which the child would live with them* (previously called a residence order).

Children Act 1989, s 10

> (5A) A local authority foster parent is entitled to apply for a child arrangements order to which subsection (5C) applies with respect to a child if the child has lived with him for a period of at least one year immediately preceding the application.
>
> (5B) A relative of a child is entitled to apply for a child arrangements order to which subsection (5C) applies with respect to the child if the child has lived with the relative for a period of at least one year immediately preceding the application.
>
> (5C) This subsection applies to a child arrangements order if the arrangements regulated by the order relate only to either or both of the following—
>
> (a) with whom the child concerned is to live, and
>
> (b) when the child is to live with any person.

A 'relative' is defined as 'a grandparent, brother, sister, uncle or aunt (whether of the full blood or half blood or by marriage or civil partnership) or a step-parent'.[12] If an applicant does not fall within one of the categories of entitled applicant, the leave of the court will be required.

Applicants requiring leave

Any person, including a child, who is not entitled under either s 10(4), (5), (5A) or (5B) may apply for *any s 8 order* if the court grants them leave to do so. This 'open door' policy is subject to specific restrictions imposed on local authority foster parents—they may not apply for leave unless they have the consent of the local authority, they are a relative of the child,

---

[11] S 105(1). See *Re A (Child of the Family)* [1998] 1 FLR 347.
[12] S 105(1).

or the child has been living with them for at least one year preceding the application.[13] The Court of Appeal has held that where foster parents are precluded from applying for a s 8 order by virtue of these restrictions, the court can nevertheless act of its own motion.[14]

Principles to be applied on an application for leave

Applicants under s 10(9)

The principles to be applied on an application for leave, other than by the child forming the subject matter of the order, are set down in s 10(9).

Children Act 1989, s 10

(9) Where the person applying for leave to make an application for a section 8 order is not the child concerned, the court shall, in deciding whether or not to grant leave, have particular regard to—

(a) the nature of the proposed application for the section 8 order;

(b) the applicant's connection with the child;

(c) any risk there might be of that proposed application disrupting the child's life to such an extent that he would be harmed by it; and

(d) where the child is being looked after by a local authority—

(i) the authority's plans for the child's future; and

(ii) the wishes and feelings of the child's parents.

The question of whether considerations beyond those specified in s 10(9) can be taken into account has caused some difficulty. Initially, the courts observed that an application for leave was not a question relating to the upbringing of a child, and therefore that the child's welfare was not the paramount consideration.[15] Then it was said that an applicant had to have 'a good arguable case' on the merits before leave would be granted;[16] however, the Court of Appeal later queried this 'gloss' on the statutory wording, particularly in the light of Articles 6 and 8 of the European Convention on Human Rights (ECHR).[17] The Court of Appeal gave further guidance in *Re B (A Child) (Care Proceedings: Joinder)*.[18] Black LJ made clear that s 10(9) does not contain a 'test' as such, but merely picks out some relevant considerations for judges to assess. There is no limitation on any *other* considerations that might be relevant. Although 'leave will not be given for an application that is not arguable', the fact that an application is arguable is not in itself enough to justify allowing the application because all factors need to be taken together.[19] The extent of any investigation required to make the

---

[13] S 9(3). Where a child is placed with prospective adopters by a local authority adoption agency, the prospective adopters will be regarded as falling within the restrictions imposed on local authority foster parents by s 9(3). See *Re C (Adoption: Notice)* [1999] 1 FLR 384.

[14] *Gloucestershire County Council v P* [2000] Fam 1.

[15] *Re A and W* [1992] 2 FLR 154.

[16] See, e.g., *Re A (A Minor) (Residence Order: Leave to Apply)* [1993] 1 FLR 425; *Re S (Contact: Application by Sibling)* [1999] 1 Fam 283.

[17] *Re J (Leave to Issue Application for Residence Order)* [2002] EWCA Civ 1364.

[18] [2012] EWCA Civ 737.

[19] Ibid, [48]–[49].

decision will vary depending on the case, with a focus on 'ensur[ing] in each case that there is a fair determination of the claims of the parties and the issues in the case'.[20]

Obtaining leave does not give rise to any presumptions in favour of the applicant at the substantive hearing.[21]

Where the applicant is 'the child concerned': s 10(8)

Children are able to bring and defend Children Act proceedings in their own name.[22] In order to apply for a s 8 order, the child requires the court's leave under s 10(8).[23] In determining the application, the court must be satisfied that the child is of sufficient understanding to make the application.[24] Again, the child's welfare is not the court's paramount consideration and proceedings which are 'doomed to failure' will not be allowed to commence.[25] The application must also be sufficiently serious to merit intervention by the court.[26]

In determining a child's application for leave, the courts have been reluctant to allow children to make their own applications in the course of proceedings between their parents. The judicial disquiet about such applications was clear in *Re H (Residence Order: Child's Application For Leave)*,[27] in which a 12-year-old boy sought leave to make an application for a residence order in favour of his father in the course of his parent's divorce proceedings. The court refused the application, holding that the child could add nothing by way of argument or cross-examination to that which would be presented to the court on the father's behalf.[28] Johnson J also referred with concern to the 'spectre of a mother being faced across a courtroom by solicitor or counsel acting on behalf of the child she bore'.[29] Changing attitudes towards the participation of children in private family law disputes, including securing separate legal representation for the child where appropriate, may now encourage a more liberal approach to applications of this nature.[30]

Prohibited applicants

Section 9(2) prohibits a local authority from applying for a child arrangements order. This restriction is based on the important principle that a local authority seeking to intervene in the private realm of family life should be required to use its public law powers under Part IV of the CA 1989, rather than invoking private law proceedings. This prevents the local authority from circumventing the strict requirement under Part IV of the Act that the child must be suffering or likely to suffer significant harm before the state can intervene by way of compulsory measures. The local authority is permitted, with leave, to apply

---

[20] Ibid, [51].

[21] *Re W (Contact: Application by Grandparent)* [1997] 1 FLR 793.

[22] Family Procedure Rules 2010 (FPR 2010), r 12.3(1).

[23] In order to fall within the terms of this provision, the child must be applying for an order where he or she is 'the child concerned', meaning he or she must be the intended subject matter of the order. See *Re S (Contact: Application by Sibling)* [1999] Fam 283. A child applying for a s 8 order with respect to another child will have his or her application for leave determined in accordance with s 10(9).

[24] *Re SC (A Minor) (Leave to Seek Residence Order)* [1994] 1 FLR 96.

[25] Ibid. See also *Re H (Residence Order: Child's Application for Leave)* [1994] 1 FLR 26.

[26] *Re C (A Minor) (Leave to Seek Section 8 Orders)* [1994] 1 FLR 26.

[27] [2000] 1 FLR 780.

[28] Ibid, 783.

[29] Ibid.

[30] See discussion at 11.3.3.

for a specific issue or prohibited steps order but the court cannot make a specific issue order or prohibited steps order with a view to achieving a result which could be achieved by making a child arrangements order.[31] This leaves very little room for a local authority to make use of s 8 orders, even if it believes such orders would be a more nuanced response to the problems of a particular family than invoking its more confrontational powers under Part IV.[32]

Restricted applicants under s 91(14)

An important tool in the armoury of the judiciary is s 91(14), which empowers the court to prohibit a particular individual from making any further applications to the court in relation to a particular child without first obtaining the court's leave. The purpose of making restrictions of this kind is to protect the child and the child's carers from endless or vexatious litigation by requiring an applicant to obtain the court's leave before an application can be brought. Judges have been cautious about the use of s 91(14) orders, and the Court of Appeal laid down guidelines about when they should be made in *Re P (A Child) (Residence Order: Child's Welfare)*.[33]

A s 91(14) order will most commonly be made where there has been protracted litigation between the parties and it is in the child's best interests to bring proceedings to an end. In such cases, the prohibited applicant will usually have made repeated unmerited applications or will have conducted the litigation in an unreasonable manner.[34] However, s 91(14) orders are not to be used simply to give the parties breathing space from litigation or to allow time for new child arrangements to settle.[35]

A s 91(14) order can be made in the absence of a history of vexatious litigation provided the potential risks to the child of further litigation are sufficiently serious to warrant pre-emptive action.[36] Restrictions can be made for specified periods or until further order, and can relate either to applications for all orders in relation to a child or to specified types of application.

It is sometimes said that s 91(14) orders are controversial because they deny a person access to the court, which is a fundamental right protected by Article 6 ECHR. However, the precise nature of the restriction needs to be remembered.

Re P (A Child) (Residence Order: Child's Welfare) [2000] Fam 15 (CA), 38

BUTLER-SLOSS LJ:

The applicant is not denied access to the court. It is a partial restriction in that it does not allow him the right to an immediate *inter partes* hearing. It thereby protects the other parties and the child from being drawn into the proposed proceedings unless or until a court

---

[31] S 9(5)(a).

[32] See further discussion at 12.5.2.

[33] [2000] Fam 15. These guidelines were reaffirmed in *Re M (A Child) (Parental Responsibility: Father's Application for Parental Responsibility)* [2013] EWCA Civ 969.

[34] *B v B (Residence Order: Restricting Applications)* [1997] 1 FLR 139.

[35] *Re G (A Child) (Order: Restriction on Applications)* [2008] EWCA Civ 1468, [13]–[14]; *Re A (A Child) (Order: Restriction on Applications)* [2009] EWCA Civ 1548, [16]–[17].

[36] *Re Y (Child Orders: Restricting Applications)* [1994] 2 FLR 699.

has ruled that the application should be allowed to proceed. On an application for leave, the applicant must persuade the judge that he has an arguable case with some chance of success. That is not a formidable hurdle to surmount. If the application is hopeless and refused the other parties and the child will have been protected from unnecessary involvement in the proposed proceedings and unwarranted investigations into the present circumstances of the child.

If an order has been made under s 91(14), the applicant requires leave before making any further applications to the court. The principles to be applied on an application for leave were considered by the Court of Appeal in *Re A (Application for Leave)*.[37] The court held that the application was not to be determined in accordance with the principles set down under s 10(9), but on the basis of the simple question: 'does the application demonstrate that there is any need for renewed judicial investigation?'[38] The Court of Appeal has also confirmed that it is impermissible to attach conditions to a s 91(14) order, such as requiring a report from a psychiatrist demonstrating that the applicant has satisfactorily addressed his damaging behaviour, as such conditions would fetter the judge's discretion when hearing any future application and may, in effect, constitute a bar to the applicant seeking leave.[39] However, the court can give guidance as to what is expected of the parent before a new application is likely to be allowed.[40]

11.3.3 THE PARTICIPATION OF CHILDREN IN PRIVATE LAW DISPUTES

The recognition accorded to the developing decision-making capacity of children, and the importance of respecting children's views on issues that affect their lives, now forms a core consideration in many areas of family law.[41] This changing attitude towards children is particularly important with respect to their participation in court proceedings concerning their future care and upbringing. As noted above, children deemed to be of sufficient maturity and understanding can bring and defend Children Act proceedings in their own name. In the majority of cases, however, children will be mere 'spectators', observing their parents' dispute. In such cases, there remain strong differences of opinion about the extent to which a child should be able to participate in the proceedings. On the one hand, a children's rights approach emphasizes the importance of listening to and respecting the autonomous, decision-making abilities of children in all matters affecting them. Article 12 of the United Nations Convention on the Rights of the Child provides an underpinning of support for this approach, albeit qualified by reference to the 'age and maturity' of the child.[42]

---

[37] [1998] 1 FLR 1.

[38] Ibid, 4.

[39] *Re S (Children) (Restrictions on Applications)* [2006] EWCA Civ 1190, [72]–[80].

[40] *Re M-D (A Child)* [2014] EWCA Civ 1363, [18].

[41] See, e.g., *Re Roddy (A Child) (Identification: Restriction on Publication)* [2003] EWHC 2927, in which a 16-year-old child who had sufficient maturity and understanding was held to have the same rights to personal autonomy under Arts 8 and 10 ECHR as an adult.

[42] Support for this rights-based approach is also found in the European Convention on the Exercise of Children's Rights which came into force in 2000. The UK has not yet ratified the Convention.

United Nations Convention on the Rights of the Child 1989, Article 12

1. States Parties shall assure to the child who is capable of forming his or her own views the right to express those views freely in all matters affecting the child, the views of the child being given due weight in accordance with the age and maturity of the child.

2. For this purpose, the child shall in particular be provided the opportunity to be heard in any judicial and administrative proceedings affecting the child, either directly, or through a representative or an appropriate body, in a manner consistent with the procedural rules of national law.

On the other hand, there remains deep-seated concern amongst some family practitioners about exposing children to the burdens and responsibilities of the adult world of decision-making in matters as difficult and sensitive as family court proceedings.[43] However, as Fortin notes, there is a crucial difference between allowing the views of children to determine the outcome of court proceedings—in effect 'delegating the decision-making process to them'—and consulting children on matters that affect them.[44] English law is clearly far from adopting the former, more radical approach. However, although consultation is a more ambivalent offering, the family judiciary are taking this requirement more seriously.

English law has traditionally taken a cautious approach to the participation of children in family law proceedings. The child's voice is usually heard only indirectly through the reports and evidence of others. In many cases, the child's voice is not heard at all. In private law proceedings, the main medium through which the child's views will be expressed is a welfare report prepared by a Children and Family Reporter (CFR). However, a welfare report will not be ordered in every case.[45] Furthermore, even if the court does make a direction for a welfare report to be prepared, there is no clear obligation on the CFR to ascertain the child's wishes and feelings.[46] There are growing concerns that this mechanism for hearing from the child is unsatisfactory. Research carried out by May and Smart revealed that, from their sample of 430 cases, only 47 per cent had a welfare report on file and in only half of those cases had the child been consulted—though, of course, many children in family court proceedings are very young.[47]

In addition to the welfare report, the judge has a wide discretion as to whether to hear directly from the child.[48] The English judiciary have traditionally exercised that discretion cautiously.[49] There are several reasons why judges may be reluctant to speak to children.

P. Parkinson, J. Cashmore, and J. Single, 'Parents' and Children's Views on Talking to Judges in Parenting Disputes in Australia', (2007) 21 *International Journal of Law, Policy and the Family* 84, 85

[T]he accepted view in most common law jurisdictions is that it is better to rely on the work of trained experts to interview children and to interpret their wishes and feelings to the court.

---

[43] May and Smart (2004), 315.
[44] Fortin (2009b), 291.
[45] S 7.
[46] FPR 2010, r 16.33.
[47] May and Smart (2004), 308.
[48] *B v B (Minors) (Residence and Care Disputes)* [1994] 2 FLR 489.
[49] Family Justice Council (2008), [4].

> Not only are such professionals regarded as better able to interview children, but they are also seen as better qualified to interpret their views in the light of all the circumstances . . . Writing in 1983, three Canadian judges explained why the practice of judicial interviewing should be regarded as undesirable:
>
> "The interview is conducted in an intimidating environment by a person unskilled in asking questions and interpreting the answers of children. In the relatively short time these interviews take, it is difficult to investigate with sufficient depth and subtlety those perceptions of a child which may explain, justify or represent the child's wishes. Moreover, the interview may be perceived as a violation of the judge's role as an impartial trier of fact who does not enter the adversarial arena. The impartiality may also be compromised by the judge assuming the role of inquisitor in questioning children".

However, attitudes are changing in light of recent research suggesting many children want a greater level of involvement in the court proceedings, including being given the opportunity to speak directly to the judge.[50] Research into the views of Australian children revealed that 85 per cent would have liked the opportunity to speak to the judge; almost all their parents supported this position.[51] The children's and the parents' reasons were broadly similar.

P. Parkinson, J. Cashmore, and J. Single, 'Parents' and Children's Views on Talking to Judges in Parenting Disputes in Australia', (2007) 21 *International Journal of Law, Policy and the Family* **84, 102**

> Both referred to children's right to be heard and the importance of them having a say in the decision-making process. While both parents and children referred to the need for acknowledgment, and the more therapeutic benefits for children in being heard directly, there was a clear focus in many of their responses on the value of this information in the decision-making process. A number of parents and children thought that if children had the opportunity to talk with the judge directly, it was more likely that the truth would come out and that judges could get the 'real picture' without the distortions arising from the parents' conflict. Like the separately represented children in a recent British study . . . some children in this study also were concerned that their views be conveyed accurately to the court and indicated that speaking directly to the judge would be the best way of ensuring this.

Parents who opposed the child seeing the judge (27 per cent) raised three main concerns: first, that it would be intimidating for the children; secondly, that judges do not have the time or experience to ensure they are accurately eliciting the children's views; and thirdly, that the children may be being manipulated by one parent.[52] Despite these concerns, the Family Justice Council of England and Wales is now encouraging a more open approach.

---

[50] Ibid. See Fortin, Ritchie, and Buchanan (2006) and Parkinson, Cashmore, and Single (2007), 88–9.
[51] Parkinson, Cashmore, and Single (2007), 95.
[52] Ibid, 99–100.

Family Justice Council, *Guidelines for Judges Meeting Children who are Subject to Family Proceedings* (2010a)

5. If a Judge decides to meet a child, it is a matter for the discretion of the Judge, having considered representations from the parties—

(i) the purpose and proposed content of the meeting;

(ii) at what stage during the proceedings, or after they have concluded, the meeting should take place;

(iii) where the meeting will take place;

(iv) who will bring the child to the meeting;

(v) who will prepare the child for this meeting (this should usually be the Cafcass officer);

(vi) who shall attend during the meeting—although a Judge should never see a child alone;

(vii) by whom a minute of the meeting shall be taken, how that minute is to be approved by the Judge, and how it is to be communicated to the other parties.

It cannot be stressed too often that the child's meeting with the judge is not for the purpose of gathering evidence. That is the responsibility of the Cafcass officer. The purpose is to enable the child to gain some understanding of what is going on, and to be reassured that the judge has understood him/her.

6. If the meeting takes place prior to the conclusion of the proceedings—

(i) The Judge should explain to the child at an early stage that a Judge cannot hold secrets. What is said by the child will, other than in exceptional circumstances, be communicated to his/her parents and other parties.

(ii) The Judge should also explain that decisions in the case are the responsibility of the Judge, who will have to weigh a number of factors, and that the outcome is never the responsibility of the child.

(iii) The Judge should discuss with the child how his or her decisions will be communicated to the child.

(iv) The parties or their representatives shall have the opportunity to respond to the content of the meeting, whether by way of oral evidence or submissions.

It is thus possible that it will become much more common for judges to speak directly to children. Although the views of senior family judges appear to remain divided,[53] it has been suggested that 'the pendulum is swinging' towards judges more often seeing children directly.[54] However, meetings between judges and children should be short (no more than 20 minutes) and judges must not use a meeting with the child as a way to gather evidence.[55]

---

[53] See *Re W (Leave to Remove)* [2008] EWCA Civ 538, [33] (Thorpe LJ); [57] (Wilson LJ); [59]–[61] (Charles J).

[54] *Re P-S (Care Proceedings: Right to Give Evidence)* [2013] EWCA Civ 223, [23]. New Zealand family court judges appeared to become less anxious about meeting children as they became more experienced in doing so: Caldwell (2011).

[55] In *Re KP (Abduction: Judge Meeting Child: Conduct of Interview)* [2014] EWCA Civ 554, Parker J had met with a 13-year-old child for over an hour during which time she 'sought to probe and tease out what, if

If, unusually, evidence is required from a child, then 'an appropriate process' should be used which can be adapted based on the child's age and other characteristics.[56]

Where the child's views are before the court, they are relevant,[57] but they will not be determinative.[58] The weight to be accorded to the child's wishes is highly dependent on the child's age. May and Smart found that whereas younger children were generally regarded as incapable of forming a view, children over seven years of age were routinely asked whether they would prefer to live with mum or dad and they appeared to have no difficulty weighing up the various factors and expressing a clearly articulated view.[59] However, although May and Smart felt that the child's views were taken seriously both by the CFR and the court,[60] young adults looking back at their experiences of parental separation expressed less satisfaction with the way in which their views were taken into account both in the welfare report and by the court.[61]

The courts' general reluctance to override the wishes of an older child stems in part from welfare considerations. It has thus been held that having ascertained the child's wishes it is inappropriate to ignore them.[62] However, the courts' reluctance also stems from the futility of ordering contact if it is known that the children will refuse to comply.[63] The courts have recognized that there must come a point, particularly with older children, when it is counterproductive for the court to continue to force the issue.[64]

In particularly complex or difficult cases, the child can be made a party to the proceedings; usually the child will be represented by a children's guardian,[65] though the court may allow a solicitor to act as guardian where an older child is able to give instructions directly.[66] Section 41 of the CA 1989 was amended by the Adoption and Children Act 2002 (ACA 2002) to say that rules of court could be introduced which would give children an automatic right to separate representation in s 8 proceedings unless the court was satisfied that his or her interests could be adequately protected without it.[67] However, no such rules of court have ever been introduced, and it remains unusual for children to be separately represented in s 8 proceedings under the current Practice Direction.[68]

---

any, reasons there were behind [the child's] stated views'; the judge then relied on her impression of the child to reject a Cafcass recommendation. The Court of Appeal allowed the appeal.

[56] *Re LC (Children) (Abduction: Habitual Residence: State of Mind of Child)* [2014] UKSC 1, [55]; *Re KP (Abduction: Judge Meeting Child: Conduct of Interview)* [2014] EWCA Civ 554, [54].

[57] S 1(3)(a).

[58] *Re M (Family Proceedings: Affidavits)* [1995] 2 FLR 100.

[59] May and Smart (2004), 314–15.

[60] Ibid.

[61] Fortin, Ritchie, and Buchanan (2006), 220–1. Fewer than a third of the young people felt that the court took proper account of their views and less than a third felt that they had been able to say everything they wanted to the CFR. There is clearly scope for improving the way in which CFRs approach their work with children.

[62] *Re F (Minors) (Denial of Contact)* [1993] 2 FLR 677.

[63] *Churchard v Churchard* [1984] FLR 635.

[64] For a powerful discussion of these issues, see *Re S (Contact: Children's Views)* [2002] EWHC 540, [114]–[121].

[65] FPR 2010, rr 16.2 and 16.4.

[66] *Re LC (Children) (Abduction: Habitual Residence: State of Mind of Child)* [2014] UKSC 1, [46].

[67] S 41 as amended by ACA 2002, s 122.

[68] For excellent commentary, see Fortin (2007), 256–64. For the approaches of other jurisdictions, see Woodhouse (2014) (Italy and the United States), Coenraad (2014) (the Netherlands), and Singer (2014) (Scandinavia).

Practice Direction 16A—*Representation of Children* (2014)

7.1 Making the child a party to the proceedings is a step that will be taken only in cases which involve an issue of significant difficulty and consequently will occur in only a minority of cases. Before taking the decision to make the child a party, consideration should be given to whether an alternative route might be preferable, such as asking [a CFR] to carry out further work or by making a referral to social services or, possibly, by obtaining expert evidence.

7.2 The decision to make the child a party will always be exclusively that of the court, made in the light of the facts and circumstances of the particular case. The following are offered, solely by way of guidance, as circumstances which may justify the making of such an order—

(a) where [a CFR] has notified the court that in the opinion of that officer the child should be made a party;

(b) where the child has a standpoint or interest which is inconsistent with or incapable of being represented by any of the adult parties;

(c) where there is an intractable dispute over residence or contact, including where all contact has ceased, or where there is irrational but implacable hostility to contact or where the child may be suffering harm associated with the contact dispute;

(d) where the views and wishes of the child cannot be adequately met by a report to the court;

(e) where an older child is opposing a proposed course of action;

(f) where there are complex medical or mental health issues to be determined or there are other unusually complex issues that necessitate separate representation of the child;

(g) where there are international complications outside child abduction, in particular where it may be necessary for there to be discussions with overseas authorities or a foreign court;

(h) where there are serious allegations of physical, sexual or other abuse in relation to the child or there are allegations of domestic violence not capable of being resolved with the help of [a CFR];

(i) where the proceedings concern more than one child and the welfare of the children is in conflict or one child is in a particularly disadvantaged position;

(j) where there is a contested issue about scientific testing.

Occasionally, where a children's guardian has been appointed to act on the child's behalf, conflict develops between the guardian's duty to act in the child's best interests and the child's own views. In such circumstances, the child can apply for the guardian to be removed and for the child to conduct his or her own case.[69] In determining such an application, the court must be satisfied that the child has sufficient understanding to participate as a party to the proceedings without the guardian's assistance.[70] Thorpe LJ held that when determining this

---

[69] FPR 2010, r 16.6.
[70] Ibid, r 16.6(6).

question the courts must avoid paternalistic judgments and pay much greater respect to the rights and autonomy of the child.

Mabon v Mabon [2005] EWCA Civ 634

THORPE LJ:

25. In our system we have traditionally adopted the tandem model for the representation of children who are parties to family proceedings, whether public or private. First the court appoints a guardian ad litem who will almost invariably have a social work qualification and very wide experience of family proceedings. He then instructs a specialist family solicitor who, in turn, usually instructs a specialist family barrister. This is a Rolls Royce model and is the envy of many other jurisdictions. However its overall approach is essentially paternalistic. The guardian's first priority is to advocate the welfare of the child he represents. His second priority is to put before the court the child's wishes and feelings. Those priorities can in some cases conflict. In extreme cases the conflict is unmanageable. That reality is recognised by the terms of rule 9.2A [which was the predecessor to the current PD 16A]. The direction set by rule 9.2A(6) is a mandatory grant of the application provided that the court considers "that the minor concerned has sufficient understanding to participate as a party in the proceedings concerned." Thus the focus is upon the sufficiency of the child's understanding in the context of the remaining proceedings.

26. In my judgment the Rule is sufficiently widely framed to meet our obligations to comply with both Article 12 of the United Nations Convention and Article 8 of the ECHR, providing that judges correctly focus on the sufficiency of the child's understanding and, in measuring that sufficiency, reflect the extent to which, in the 21st Century, there is a keener appreciation of the autonomy of the child and the child's consequential right to participate in decision making processes that fundamentally affect his family life...

28....Although the tandem model has many strengths and virtues, at its heart lies the conflict between advancing the welfare of the child and upholding the child's freedom of expression and participation. Unless we in this jurisdiction are to fall out of step with similar societies as they safeguard Article 12 rights, we must, in the case of articulate teenagers, accept that the right to freedom of expression and participation outweighs the paternalistic judgment of welfare.

29. In testing the sufficiency of a child's understanding I would not say that welfare has no place. If direct participation would pose an obvious risk of harm to the child arising out of the nature of the continuing proceedings and, if the child is incapable of comprehending that risk, then the judge is entitled to find that sufficient understanding has not been demonstrated. But judges have to be equally alive to the risk of emotional harm that might arise from denying the child knowledge of and participation in the continuing proceedings...

32. In conclusion this case provides a timely opportunity to recognise the growing acknowledgement of the autonomy and consequential rights of children, both nationally and internationally. The Rules are sufficiently robustly drawn to accommodate that shift. In individual cases trial judges must equally acknowledge the shift when they make in individual cases a proportionate judgment of the sufficiency of the child's understanding.

Subsequently, Lady Hale has cautioned that 'the intrusion, the expense and the delay' that may result from making a child a party to proceedings will mean that, 'in the general run of cases', separate representation will not be justified.[71] Lord Wilson picked up the same theme

[71] *Re M (Children) (Abduction: Rights of Custody)* [2007] UKHL 55, [57].

when he warned that '[t]he intrusion of the children into the forensic arena, which enables a number of them to adopt a directly confrontational stance towards the applicant parent, can prove very damaging to family relationships even in the long term and definitely affects their interests'.[72] The differing positions on this issue can therefore be seen, but it does not seem that there is likely to be any change in practice soon, especially given the financial constraints under which the family justice system is currently operating.

11.4 GENERAL PRINCIPLES APPLICABLE TO ALL S 8 ORDERS

In any determination in relation to the upbringing of a child—which includes the making of *any* s 8 order, whether contested or agreed between the parties—the court's paramount consideration must be the welfare of the child.[73] The CA 1989 also contains a 'general principle' that delay in determining cases about children's upbringing 'is likely to prejudice the welfare of the child',[74] and the court is instructed that it should not make any order in relation to children 'unless it considers that doing so would be better for the child that making no order at all'.[75] When a court is considering making a s 8 order and that order is opposed by any party, the court must also consider the *welfare checklist* in s 1(3) of the CA 1989.

Children Act 1989, s 1

(3) In the circumstances mentioned in subsection (4), a court shall have regard in particular to—

  (a) the ascertainable wishes and feelings of the child concerned (considered in the light of his age and understanding);

  (b) his physical, emotional and educational needs;

  (c) the likely effect on him of any change in his circumstances;

  (d) his age, sex, background and any characteristics of his which the court considers relevant;

  (e) any harm which he has suffered or is at risk of suffering;

  (f) how capable each of his parents, and any other person in relation to whom the court considers the question to be relevant, is of meeting his needs;

  (g) the range of powers available to the court under this Act in the proceedings in question.

We discuss the welfare principle and the welfare checklist in more detail in chapter 8. As in other contexts, the difficulty arising from the welfare principle is how it should

---

[72] *Re LC (Children) (Abduction: Habitual Residence: State of Mind of Child)* [2014] UKSC 1, [48]. But cf *Cambra v Jones and Jones* [2014] EWHC 913, [12]–[14].
[73] S 1(1).
[74] S 1(2).
[75] S 1(5).

be applied to the facts of each case.[76] The way in which the child's best interests have been interpreted by the courts in the context of s 8 orders has varied over the years, and has provoked a range of criticisms. One of those criticisms—which we consider further below—was that some fathers' groups argued that family courts were biased in favour of mothers. The Family Justice Review in 2011 had concluded that 'the core principle of the paramountcy of the welfare of the child is sufficient and to insert any additional statements brings with it unnecessary risk for little gain'.[77] However, although the government rejected the claim of bias against the courts, it took the view that 'there should be a legislative statement of the importance of children having an ongoing relationship with both their parents after family separation, where that is safe, and in the child's best interests'.[78] Consequently, the CFA 2014 added a new presumption of parental involvement after family separation to s 1 of the CA 1989, which was brought into force on 22 October 2014.

Children Act 1989, s 1

(2A) A court, in the circumstances mentioned in subsection (4)(a) or (7), is as respects each parent within subsection (6)(a) to presume, unless the contrary is shown, that involvement of that parent in the life of the child concerned will further the child's welfare.

(2B) In subsection (2A) "involvement" means involvement of some kind, either direct or indirect, but not any particular division of a child's time.

(6) In subsection (2A) "parent" means parent of the child concerned; and, for the purposes of that subsection, a parent of the child concerned—

(a) is within this paragraph if that parent can be involved in the child's life in a way that does not put the child at risk of suffering harm; and

(b) is to be treated as being within paragraph (a) unless there is some evidence before the court in the particular proceedings to suggest that involvement of that parent in the child's life would put the child at risk of suffering harm whatever the form of the involvement.

As we will see, this principle was already well established by the courts, but the inclusion of this section in the Act was nonetheless controversial. Some groups—particularly fathers' rights groups—argued that the provision did not go far enough and would have no real effect, while other groups—women's groups and domestic violence organizations, in particular—suggested that the new provision would place some women and children at greater risk. Given that s 1(2B) makes clear that 'involvement' may be either direct or indirect, and the Act does not—as some campaign groups had favoured—include any presumption about how much time a child should spend with either parent, it is difficult to tell whether this provision will cause any change to the previous practice, or simply codify what the courts had already established.

---

[76] Fehlberg and Smyth with Trinder (2014).
[77] Family Justice Review (2011), para 4.40.
[78] MOJ and DFE (2012), para 61.

11.5 CHILD ARRANGEMENTS ORDERS: INTRODUCTION

When the CA 1989 came into force, it created two new orders in relation to children's upbringing—residence orders and contact orders. Residence orders were about the person or persons with whom a child was to live, and contact orders regulated the child's relationships with people with whom he or she was not living. Although designed to be purely factual descriptions, these labels became increasingly problematic. The campaigns by fathers' groups from the early 2000s onwards put particular focus on the way in which residence and contact disputes were resolved. Groups such as New Fathers 4 Justice[79] and Families Need Fathers[80] argued that by granting sole residence to the mother and restricting fathers to 'mere' contact, as often happened, the judiciary were basing their decisions on, and reinforcing, outdated stereotypes of men and women and their respective parenting roles.

This issue was considered as part of the Family Justice Review.

D Norgrove (Chair), *Family Justice Review: Final Report* (London: MOJ, 2011)

4.59. Whether to remove the terms contact and residence is clearly a matter of judgement, and it would be difficult to point to clear evidence either way. The balance of the responses to consultation was though firmly in favour of removal and we agree with that. We were also struck by the Chief Justice of Australia's clear view that removal of the terms had been beneficial there.

4.60. ...In the light of the consultation responses we propose that a broader, new order should be developed that would encompass all arrangements for children's care in private law. This could be termed a 'child arrangements order', which would set out the arrangements for the upbringing of the child. It would focus all discussions on resolving issues related to their care, rather than on labels such as residence and contact. It would of course, be necessary either in a Parenting Agreement or a court order to provide clarity on where a child would normally live and with whom a child would spend time.

The government subsequently accepted this recommendation, and residence and contact orders were abolished in favour of child arrangements orders by the CFA 2014. Consequently, there are no longer separate orders made in relation to a child, but just one order, though it seems that most orders specify within them where (or with whom) the child will normally reside and other people with whom he or she will spend time. Because of this, we divide our discussion into two parts—first we look at the part of a child arrangements order which regulates the people with whom a child is to live, and then we look at the part dealing with orders dealing with the child spending time or otherwise having contact with people with whom he or she does not live.

[79] <www.newfathers4justice.info>.
[80] <www.fnf.org.uk>.

11.6 CHILD ARRANGEMENTS ORDERS: LIVING ARRANGEMENTS

Our focus in this section is on the part of a child arrangements order which deals with the person or persons with whom a child is to live or when a child is to live with any person. There is little authority available about how the courts are approaching orders about children's living arrangements following the CFA 2014. However, it seems likely that there will have been little change from the position reached in relation to residence orders in the years immediately preceding the introduction of child arrangements orders. Put shortly, the order can set out many possible arrangements, including having the child living:

- with only one person (formerly called a sole residence order);
- with two or more people who live in the same household (formerly called a joint residence order); or
- with two or more people who live in different households (formerly called a shared residence order).

These lattermost orders, for shared living arrangements, can be made in a wide variety of circumstances, as we will see, which may—but often do not—involve an equal or near-equal division of the child's time between two households.

In the following sections, we address various approaches and criticisms that have been adopted over the years to explain how the courts came to the position that we find now. It must be borne in mind that, as Thorpe LJ once said, '[w]hen the law enters the field of child welfare, statements of principle may not hold their value much beyond the times in which they were expressed'.[81] Consequently, it is important to note the dates of some of the cases to which we refer: many things said a comparatively short time ago would almost certainly not be said today.

11.6.1 A 'PRESUMPTION' IN FAVOUR OF THE MOTHER?

At one time, the courts were clear in their approach to children's main living arrangements, at least with regard to younger children. For example, in *Re S (An Infant)* in 1958, the High Court said that there was a 'prima facie rule (which is now quite clearly settled) is that, other things being equal, children of this tender age should be with their mother'.[82] This approach was prevalent at the time: the 1959 UN Declaration on the Rights of the Child similarly included, as Principle 6, at statement that: 'A child of tender years shall not, save in exceptional circumstances, be separated from his mother'. However, matters rapidly moved on. By the early 1990s, judges were keen to recognize the emergence of the so-called 'new father', stressing the equal capacity of men in today's society to assume the responsibility of primary carer.[83]

---

81 *Re L (A Child) (Contact: Domestic Violence)* [2001] Fam 260, 294.
82 [1958] 1 WLR 391, 397.
83 See also *Re K (Residence Order: Securing Contact)* [1999] 1 FLR 583, 591.

Re S (A Minor) (Custody) [1991] FCR 155 (CA), 160

LORD DONALDSON MR:

What is clear is that there is a change in the social order, in the organization of society, whereby it is much more common for fathers to look after young children than it used to be in bygone days. It must follow that more fathers are equipped to undertake these sorts of duties than was formerly the case. From that it must follow that courts could more readily conclude in an individual case that it was in the interests of a young child that it be with its father than they would have done previously. Now, as always, the duty of the court is to consider the welfare of the child, and that is usually the paramount consideration.

Nonetheless, in several cases, the courts' denial that they were applying a presumption in favour of mothers was immediately qualified by the suggestion that, despite the absence of any 'presumption in law', it was nevertheless 'natural' for children, particularly young children, to be with their mother. As it was put by Cumming-Bruce LJ, it is 'not a principle but a matter of human nature in the case of the upbringing of children of tender years, that given the normal commitment of a father to support the family, the mother, for practical reasons, is usually the right person to bring up her children.'[84]

This same appeal to the 'natural order of things' appeared in two key judgments of Butler-Sloss LJ.

Re S (A Minor) (Custody) [1991] FCR 155 (CA), 158

BUTLER-SLOSS LJ:

The welfare of the child is the first and paramount consideration . . . [T]here is no presumption that one parent should be preferred to another parent at a particular age. It used to be thought many years ago that young children should be with the mother, that girls approaching puberty should be with mother and that boys over a certain age should be with father. Such presumptions, if they ever were such, do not, in my view, exist today. There are *dicta* of this court to the effect that it is likely that a young child, particularly perhaps a little girl, would be expected to be with her mother, but that is subject to the overriding factor that the welfare of the child is the paramount consideration. When there is a dispute between parents as to which parent should take the responsibility of the care of the child on a day to day basis, it is for the justices or for the Judge to decide which of those parents would be the better parent for the child, who cannot have the best situation since they are not together caring for her. I would just add that it is natural for young children to be with mothers, but, where it is in dispute, it is a consideration but not a presumption.

In the second key judgment, Butler-Sloss LJ attempted to clarify what she meant by her comment in *Re S* that 'it is natural for young children to be with mothers'.

---

[84] *Re H (A Minor: Custody)* [1990] 1 FLR 51, 56.

Re A (A Minor) (Custody) [1991] FCR 569 (CA), 575–6

BUTLER-SLOSS LJ:

[The first argument for the mother] was that it was natural for a mother to have the care of a six year old girl. This was, in my judgment, a misunderstanding of the decision of this court in *Re S (A Minor) (Custody)*... where I said that: "it is natural for young children to be with mothers but, where it is in dispute, it is a consideration but not a presumption".

In cases where the child has remained throughout with the mother and is young, particularly when a baby or toddler, the unbroken relationship of the mother and child is one which it would be very difficult to displace, unless the mother was unsuitable to care for the child. But where the mother and child have been separated and the mother seeks the return of the child, other considerations apply and there is no starting-point that the mother should be preferred to the father and only displaced by a preponderance of evidence to the contrary.

In this case the mother and child had been separated at the time of the hearing for nearly 12 months and at the age of six, she is not within the category of very young children. There is no presumption which requires the mother as mother to be considered as the primary caretaker in preference to the father. The welfare of the child is paramount and each parent has to be looked at by the Judge in order to make as best he can the assessment of each and to choose one of them to be the custodial parent. In so far as the Judge appears to have started with the proposition that little girls naturally go to their mothers, the Judge was in error and applied the wrong test. The second point, the conflict of guidance over matters peculiar to her sex, is, in the context of a case like this, and probably generally, unimportant and ought not to be in itself placed in the balance unless there were recognizable difficulties which had already occurred or were likely to occur...

Butler-Sloss LJ thus placed two key qualifications on her general statement in *Re S* that it is 'natural for young children to be with their mothers'. The first related to the age of the child, with Butler-Sloss LJ suggesting that this 'fact of nature' will only be of particular importance in the case of very young children, particularly babies and toddlers. The second qualification related to the need for there to exist an unbroken relationship between mother and child. In the absence of such an unbroken bond, the courts are more willing to displace the 'presumption' that young children should be with their mothers in favour of the alternative carer.[85]

These comments reflect a deeply traditional and arguably outdated notion of family life in which the father's role is one of breadwinner and provider and the mother's role that of primary child-care provider. Clare McGlynn is critical of this approach, arguing that it reflects an 'ideology of motherhood' in which motherhood is portrayed as something instinctive and innate, and thus the natural and appropriate role for all women.[86] As McGlynn points out, this ideology has been underpinned in the law by a welfarist discourse, often termed the 'tender years doctrine', which emphasizes the strong emotional and physical dependence of a young child on the care of his or her mother.[87] The result has been a privileging of the mother–child relationship in law.

---

[85] See, e.g., *Re K (Residence Order: Securing Contact)* [1999] 1 FLR 583.
[86] McGlynn (2000), 31 and (2001), 325–30.
[87] Ibid. See also Neale and Smart (1999), 36.

R. van Krieken, ' "The Best Interests of the Child" and Parental Separation: On the "Civilizing of Parents" ', (2005) 68 *Modern Law Review* **25, 30**

Most commentators will speak of the emergence of a more or less judicially explicit 'maternal preference rule' as the 'dominant doctrine in most Western countries', in conjunction with a 'tender years doctrine', that the younger a child is the more preferable it is for the mother to retain care and control.

In the decades leading up to the 1970s, there were two lines of argument about post-separation childhood which dominated the way in which the best interests standard was interpreted. The first concerning the understanding of the mother-child relationship, and its placement at the centre of children's emotional development, such as in the work of John Bowlby. As Maidment puts it:

For more than the next twenty years psychologists explored the mother-child dyad to the exclusion of all other relationships, fathers were excluded from all aspects of their children's birth, a maternal preference prevailed in custody cases, mothers were discouraged from working and thus leaving their children, and policy-makers discouraged alternative care arrangements for children such as day nurseries.

Bowlby himself was happy to see the biological mother replaced by another carer, what mattered was the continuity of care, but for all practical purposes his position was understood as emphasising the importance of an undisturbed close relationship between mothers and their children: fathers (or secondary carers) were seen as important but not crucial. In a custody dispute between the two it was clear that the mother's claim was the stronger.

By the late 1990s, the courts were explicitly moving against this approach. In *Re A (A Minor: Residence Order)*, the Court of Appeal considered a case where the trial judge had relied in the 1959 UN Declaration to justify making a residence order in favour of the mother. The Court of Appeal upheld the father's appeal on the basis that the judge's use of this outdated, gendered principle was wholly erroneous.

Re A (A Minor) (Residence Order) [1998] 2 FCR 633 (CA), 638–9

THORPE LJ:

The relevance and value of the declaration is most doubtful. In terms of relevant social policy it could be said to be almost antiquated since it is now nearly 40 years old and in terms of social development and in terms of understanding of child development and welfare that is an exceedingly long time. Nor is that principle reflected in the United Nations Convention on the Rights of the Child...a convention ratified by this nation, as indeed by most other nations of the developed world. As [opposing counsel] points out, the corresponding article of the convention, art 9, is in strictly neutral terms. It states that the parties shall ensure that a child shall not be separated from his or her parent against their will except when competent authorities, subject to judicial review, determine, or where the parents are living separately and a decision must be made as to the child's place of residence. In modern terminology that is gender neutral...

In brief conclusion, it is, in my judgment, plainly demonstrated that in this case, most unfortunately, the trial judge fell into error in...applying what he erroneously accepted as a principle, that since J was of tender years his interests would best be served by him being cared for by his mother.

Despite these judicial moves against the presumption in favour of mothers, fathers' rights groups continued to say that deeply engrained within the collective psyche of the judiciary is a privileging of motherhood and a strong ambivalence towards fatherhood. According to this view, the law is guilty of constructing fathers as uninterested, irresponsible, and even dangerous figures—a construction without foundation. Unfortunately, official statistics on the making of s 8 orders under the CA 1989 are not broken down into gender. There is therefore no official record of how many sole residence orders (to use the old language) were granted to mothers in litigated cases and how many were granted to fathers. However, research carried out on the general population of post-divorce families, which includes those cases where children's living arrangements are agreed without going to court, strongly suggests that post-divorce parenting remains highly gendered. Studies done in the early 2000s suggested that over 80 per cent of children of separated parents lived primarily with their mother;[88] 12 per cent of parents operated a shared care arrangement.[89] More recent research based on a study of court files suggests that similar patterns continue.[90]

However, gender bias in the courts is not the only explanation for these outcomes. For example, one factor tending to advantage the mother is her greater availability, for practical reasons, to take on the role of primary carer post-separation. With many women in the UK choosing not to return to work after the birth of a child or, if returning to work, doing so on a part-time basis,[91] they can more easily assume the burden of child-care without having to rely as heavily on alternative carers, such as members of the extended family or childminders. Of course, as with the status quo argument, the employment and child-care responsibilities of the parties is often established pre-separation and carried through into the immediate post-separation period. If for whatever reason the mother has been the primary carer pre-separation, she is likely to be well placed to argue that she should continue in that role in any post-separation dispute.

11.6.2 A 'PRESUMPTION' IN FAVOUR OF THE STATUS QUO?

The status quo is an important factor in all disputes about where a child should live, but has again been a particular concern of fathers' rights groups.[92] There is no 'presumption' in favour of maintaining the status quo and the courts have certainly been prepared to move a child from a settled placement.[93] However, in accordance with the welfare checklist, where the child is settled and happy, the courts have generally required some good reason for disturbing that position.

---

[88] DCA and DFES (2004), 2.

[89] Peacey and Hunt (2008), 19.

[90] Harding and Newnham (2014).

[91] In a survey conducted for the Equality and Human Rights Commission in 2009, 63 per cent of women were in employment, of whom 43 per cent were full time and 57 per cent part time. That compares with 89 per cent of men in employment, of whom just 7 per cent were part time: Ellison, Barker, and Kulasuriya (2009), 33.

[92] Geldof (2003), 189.

[93] See, e.g., *Re N (A Child)* [2007] EWCA Civ 1053, a surrogacy case in which the child was removed from the care of the surrogate mother and her husband and placed with the commissioning couple after 18 months of 'high standards of care' living with the former.

Re F (A Child) [2009] EWCA Civ 313

WARD LJ:

9. The mother's case was strongly advanced on an argument that the status quo was with her and that, accordingly, the children should not be moved without good reason. There is obviously a case for an argument about preserving the status quo but I venture to suggest that since the Children Act of 1989 it would be better to address the checklist factors than rely on any presumption of fact which may arise from an argument of that kind. The status quo argument means no more than that, if the children are settled in one place, then the court is to have regard to section 1(3)(b) of the Act and consider the likely effect on them of any change in circumstances...

17. [I]f, as the judge found, the children will be well looked after and be safe and would thrive in either household, a finding he made, then the defect in the judgment is the inadequate explanation of the reasons which justified a change from a settled position, as settled it had become in the 12 months after the final separation of the parties.

Similar statements can be found in the Supreme Court's decision in *Re B (A Child)*, which reinstated magistrates' decision to leave a four-year-old boy—named Harry in the Supreme Court judgment—with his grandmother, rather than transferring his main home to his father with whom he had never lived.[94]

Re B (A Child) [2009] UKSC 5

LORD KERR:

42. ...What we heard...confirmed the view that considerable disruption to Harry's life would have been involved in a transfer to live with his father.... Transfer of his residence would involve a great deal more than a change of address. Many of the familiar aspects of his life which anchor his stability and sense of security would be changed. The justices were therefore right to give significant weight to the desirability of preserving the status quo. This is a factor which will not always command the importance that must be attached to it in the present case but we are satisfied that it was of considerable significance in the debate as to where this child's best interests lay.

In principle, the status quo argument can work in favour of either parent.[95] However, the usual pattern following relationship breakdown is for the children to remain in the family home with the mother and for the father to move out into alternative accommodation. This places the mother in much the stronger position in any subsequent dispute, enabling her to quickly establish her position as the sole primary carer. Because of long delays in the court process, the mother is able to entrench that position by the time of the final hearing. There may, of course, be a very good reason for this trend in parenting patterns in the immediate post-separation period: it may accurately reflect the division of parenting responsibilities pre-separation and therefore be a 'natural' extension of established parenting roles. Although some would argue that parenting roles and responsibilities should be renegotiated

---

[94] See further extracts from this case at 11.6.7.
[95] See, e.g., *Re A (A Minor) (Custody)* [1991] FCR 569.

upon separation to meet the demands of the new situation, it is reasonable to look to past patterns of care in evaluating what arrangements will best promote the child's future interests. However, fathers' rights groups see the opportunity afforded to the mother to entrench her position as primary carer as a serious cause of injustice.

11.6.3 VICTIMS OF GENDER DISCRIMINATION: MOTHERS, FATHERS, OR BOTH?

Despite the absence of any legal presumption in favour of mothers, the courts therefore give weight to several factors that tend to favour them as the more suitable primary carer. But does this constitute gender discrimination against fathers? Whilst many scholars within the feminist school would share the concerns of fathers about some of the outdated gender stereotypes underpinning these cases, the contention that the law is thereby discriminating against fathers is more problematic. Indeed, it is important to recognize that the 'maternal preference' rule and the *ideology* of motherhood which underpins it can work against the interests of women as well as men, particularly as competing discourses on 'gender equality' and the 'new father' gain in strength and popularity. Moreover, many feminists are concerned that the highly publicized allegations of bias against fathers are based on erroneous assumptions about the reality of child-care responsibilities in the UK and risk ignoring the huge investment and sacrifices made by women in developing their parenting role—in short, that the success of the fathers' rights movement has led to a worrying devaluation of motherhood.[96]

The ideology of motherhood and the tender years doctrine have had both positive and negative consequences for women. As Boyd points out, the maternal preference approach can be empowering for women. However, she shares McGlynn's concerns about the wider implications of the 'ideology of motherhood' for women's equality in the public sphere, particularly in the field of employment.

S. Boyd, 'From Gender Specificity to Gender Neutrality? Ideologies in Canadian Child Custody Law', in C. Smart and S. Sevenhuijsen (eds), *Child Custody and the Politics of Gender* (London: Routledge, 1989), 126, 133

The ideology attached to the tender years principle had conflicting implications for women. On the positive side, it arguably empowered women by allowing them to leave abusive husbands without forfeiting their children, and to play the role of head of a family unit. In addition, it may have increased women's bargaining power within marriage and during divorce or separation. While usually lacking the economic clout of their husbands, mothers could play upon the emotional incentive which men had to keep their marriage intact, lest they lose their children...On the negative side, the ideological aspects of the tender years doctrine which strengthened women's position in custody disputes rendered them ill-suited for public life. That is, the ideology underlying the tender years doctrine was one of inequality in that it enhanced the view of women as wives and mothers within the private sphere of the home...[W]omen were considered only as mothers rather than complete human beings. In turn, any deviation from the 'ideal' vision of motherhood such as leaving a child in the care

[96] Collier (2005).

of another person working outside the home, or engaging in an adulterous relationship could defeat the maternal preference...As long as women are allocated primary responsibility for child rearing and housework, even when employed...they tend to take employment which allows them to reconcile paid work with household and child rearing responsibilities. Such work is normally undervalued in terms of prestige and pay, is often part time, and tends to be 'dead-end' leading to few promotions...Pay and prestige differentials between male and female dominated jobs in turn lead to a tendency for mothers to withdraw from the labour force to care for young children, rather than fathers with better salaries and perhaps greater psychological investment in their employment...The 'traditional' sexual division of labour is thus maintained in spite of significant changes to women's pattern of involvement in the labour market.

As more women enter full-time employment and struggle to live up to the 'ideal' of the self-sacrificing, full-time mother, the 'ideology of motherhood' has become less empowering and increasingly problematic for women. Against the background of the 'new father' rhetoric, it has been observed that in other Commonwealth jurisdictions women's parenting has been subjected to intense scrutiny, with women who deviate from the ideal of a 'good mother', including women who work and those who 'abandon' their children upon separation, being viewed particularly harshly.[97] In contrast, the parenting qualities of men face minimal scrutiny.[98] The simple fact that a father applies for a child arrangements order is enough to make him a good father. As the father often cannot rely on his own positive history as shared or primary carer, this disproportionate and unfair scrutiny of the mother is encouraged by the father's tendency to focus on the mother's defects.[99]

Boyd argues that there is an important tension within the law. The prevailing appeal of the traditional ideology of motherhood has not been displaced but it has been complicated by competing 'gender neutral ideologies' that have devalued the mothering role of many women and 'render[ed] invisible to the legal eye social and economic differences between the sexes'.[100] Judgments are thus increasingly founded on an idealized but essentially illusionary principle of gender equality that leaves women vulnerable both to the decline of 'maternal preference' and the rise of the 'new father' rhetoric.

S. Boyd, 'From Gender Specificity to Gender Neutrality? Ideologies in Canadian Child Custody Law', in C. Smart and S. Sevenhuijsen (eds), *Child Custody and the Politics of Gender* (London: Routledge, 1989), 126, 138–42

Increasingly, the starting point for judges in custody cases is a supposedly gender neutral assumption that women and men are equally situated and thus equally able to assume domestic responsibilities such as child care. The difficulty for judges in the current conjuncture is in applying this gender neutral assumption to an area of social relations which is not yet gender neutral, and where ideologies of male and female behaviour still prevail. The fact that 43 per cent of women with children are not employed...and that women 'continue to bear

---

[97] Boyd (1989) (Canada) and Moloney (2001) (Australia).
[98] Moloney (2001), 373.
[99] Brophy (1989), 236.
[100] Boyd (1989), 136.

the primary burden of family and home care' even if employed...may not be appropriately acknowledged when judges apply gender neutral standards...

Recent Canadian cases involving employed mothers illustrate that the gender-neutral principle of equality and its closely related 'individual-based ideology' can be applied in such a way as to undervalue primary caregiving...[M]istaken assumptions of equality encourage judges to jump to the conclusion that mothers and fathers have shared parenting more or less equally if there is evidence that fathers have engaged in child care to any extent more than the standard model of paternal conduct. Especially where mothers have been employed outside the home, it is often erroneously assumed that domestic work and child care are shared equally between parents, an assumption which devalues the double burden of work carried by most employed mothers...Some judges are also too ready to assume that fathers who have engaged in at least minimal child care can easily adopt the role of primary caregiver of children, while minimizing the value of primary caregiving performed by mothers in the past.

These observations provide an important insight into our own case law and the way in which the parenting of the mother is evaluated in comparison to that of the alternative carer.[101]

11.6.4 OTHER IMPORTANT CONSIDERATIONS IN DISPUTES BETWEEN PARENTS

Gay and lesbian parents

Two distinct situations may arise regarding a parent's sexual orientation. First, there may be disputes between parents where one parent has left a heterosexual relationship to form a same-sex relationship. There was a flurry of reported cases addressing this issue in the early 1990s, though very little can be seen by way of more recent authority. The courts have consistently held that homosexuality does not bar a parent from becoming a child's main carer. However, in the early 1990s judges also made it clear that a parent's sexuality could be relevant to welfare. Indeed, although the case is now quite old, the court in *C v C (Custody of Child)* took a particularly conservative line in evaluating the 'merits' of parenting within a same-sex family when compared with other, more 'conventional', alternatives.

C v C (Custody of Child) [1991] FCR 254 (CA), 260, 262–3

GLIDEWELL LJ:

Despite the vast change over the past 30 years or so in the attitude of our society generally to the institution of marriage, to sexual morality, and to homosexual relationships, I regard it as axiomatic that the ideal environment for the upbringing of a child is the home of loving, caring and sensible parents, her father and her mother. When the marriage between father and mother is at an end, that ideal cannot be attained. When the court is called upon to decide which of two possible alternatives is then preferable for the child's welfare, its task is to choose the alternative which comes closest to that ideal.

---

[101] See, e.g., *Re A (A Minor) (Residence Order)* [1998] 2 FCR 633; *Re K (Residence Order: Securing Contact)* [1996] 1 FLR 583; *Re W (Residence)* [1999] 2 FLR 390.

Even taking account of the changes of attitude to which I have referred, a lesbian relationship between two adult women is an unusual background in which to bring up a child. I think that the mother herself recognizes this, because the Judge recorded her as saying that she was sensitive to the problems that could arise, and did not flaunt the sexual nature of her relationship...

I make it clear that I am not saying that the fact that a mother is living in a lesbian relationship is conclusive, or that it disqualifies her from ever having the care and control of her child. A court may well decide that a sensitive, loving lesbian relationship is a more satisfactory environment for a child than a less sensitive or loving alternative. But that the nature of the relationship is an important factor to be put into the balance seems to me to be clear.

For this reason I would allow the appeal and set aside the Judge's order.

Interestingly, although the Court of Appeal favoured the 'normal' family environment offered by the father, the first instance judge rehearing the case granted residence to the mother.[102]

While this authority has never formally been overruled, it is difficult to see that it can remain good law in the light of the many other changes that have occurred in the law's attitude to sexual orientation.[103] Perhaps most significantly, it has been held by the European Court of Human Rights that it is contrary to Articles 8 and 14 ECHR to discriminate between parents on the basis of sexual orientation when determining disputes about where a child should live. In *da Silva Mouta v Portugal*, the Portuguese Court of Appeal had denied residence to the child's father on the basis of his homosexuality.

---

da Silva Mouta v Portugal (App No 33290/96, ECHR) (1999)

1. Existence of a difference in treatment...

28. The Court does not deny that the Lisbon Court of Appeal had regard above all to the child's interests when it examined a number of points of fact and of law which could have tipped the scales in favour of one parent rather than the other. However, the Court observes that in reversing the decision of the Lisbon Family Affairs Court and, consequently, awarding parental responsibility to the mother rather than the father, the Court of Appeal introduced a new factor, namely that the applicant was a homosexual and was living with another man.

The Court is accordingly forced to conclude that there was a difference of treatment between the applicant and M.'s mother which was based on the applicant's sexual orientation, a concept which is undoubtedly covered by Article 14 of the Convention...

2. Justification for the difference in treatment

29. In accordance with the case-law of the Convention institutions, a difference of treatment is discriminatory within the meaning of Article 14 if it has no objective and reasonable justification, that is if it does not pursue a legitimate aim or if there is not a reasonable relationship of proportionality between the means employed and the aim sought to be realised...

---

102 *C v C (No 2)* [1992] FCR 206.
103 In *Re G (Residence: Same-Sex Parents)* [2006] EWCA Civ 372, [40], Thorpe LJ said, with reference to *C v C*, that 'judicial attitudes to homosexual parenting were very different in that earlier age'. (This case was reversed on other grounds in the House of Lords: [2006] UKHL 43.)

30. The decision of the Court of Appeal undeniably pursued a legitimate aim, namely the protection of the health and rights of the child; it must now be examined whether the second requirement was also satisfied.

31. In the applicant's submission, the wording of the judgment clearly showed that the decision to award parental responsibility to the mother was based mainly on the father's sexual orientation, which inevitably gave rise to discrimination against him in relation to the other parent.

32. The Government submitted that the decision in question had, on the contrary, merely touched on the applicant's homosexuality. The considerations of the Court of Appeal to which the applicant referred, when viewed in context, were merely sociological, or even statistical, observations. Even if certain passages of the judgment could arguably have been worded differently, clumsy or unfortunate expressions could not in themselves amount to a violation of the Convention.

33. The Court reiterates its earlier finding that the Lisbon Court of Appeal, in examining the appeal lodged by M.'s mother, introduced a new factor when making its decision as to the award of parental responsibility, namely the applicant's homosexuality... In determining whether the decision which was ultimately made constituted discriminatory treatment lacking any reasonable basis, it needs to be established whether, as the Government submitted, that new factor was merely an *obiter dictum* which had no direct effect on the outcome of the matter in issue or whether, on the contrary, it was decisive.

34....The Court of Appeal...weighed the facts differently from the lower court and awarded parental responsibility [equivalent to residence] to the mother. It considered, among other things, that "custody of young children should as a general rule be awarded to the mother unless there are overriding reasons militating against this...". The Court of Appeal further considered that there were insufficient reasons for taking away from the mother the parental responsibility awarded her by agreement between the parties.

However, after that observation the Court of Appeal added "Even if that were not the case...we think that custody of the child should be awarded to the mother"...The Court of Appeal then took account of the fact that the applicant was a homosexual and was living with another man in observing that "The child should live in...a traditional Portuguese family" and that "It is not our task here to determine whether homosexuality is or is not an illness or whether it is a sexual orientation towards persons of the same sex. In both cases it is an abnormality and children should not grow up in the shadow of abnormal situations"...

35. It is the Court's view that the above passages from the judgment in question, far from being merely clumsy or unfortunate as the Government maintained, or mere *obiter dicta*, suggest, quite to the contrary, that the applicant's homosexuality was a factor which was decisive in the final decision. That conclusion is supported by the fact that the Court of Appeal, when ruling on the applicant's right to contact, warned him not to adopt conduct which might make the child realise that her father was living with another man "in conditions resembling those of man and wife" (ibid.).

36. The Court is therefore forced to find, in the light of the foregoing, that the Court of Appeal made a distinction based on considerations regarding the applicant's sexual orientation, a distinction which is not acceptable under the Convention...

The Court cannot therefore find that a reasonable relationship of proportionality existed between the means employed and the aim pursued; there has accordingly been a violation of Article 8 taken in conjunction with Article 14.

The Court's decision therefore seems to prohibit treating sexual orientation, in and of itself, as a relevant consideration in a dispute about the child's place of residence, and clearly not as a decisive factor.

A second type of case is where same-sex parents (most commonly two women) have separated.[104] In principle, these cases are no different from any other post-separation parental disputes: 'the issues arising are just the same as those which may arise between heterosexual couples. The legal principles are also the same'.[105] However, as we discuss below,[106] there has been some debate about the potential relevance of the genetic and gestational tie which may exist between one of the parents and the child, but not the other. While that issue is by no means restricted to cases between former same-sex partners, some of the key authorities discussing it have arisen in this context. Moreover, there are more intricate factual patterns that can arise which are either rare or impossible in heterosexual relationships. For example, in *Re G (Shared Residence Order: Biological Mother of Donor Egg Children)*,[107] the applicant woman's eggs had been fertilized by anonymous donor sperm and then implanted in the respondent woman, who carried the twin children to birth. The question in that case was whether a shared residence order should be made for the principal purpose of conferring parental responsibility on the applicant,[108] the parties having already agreed the role that each would play in the child's upbringing following their separation.

Racial, religious, and cultural factors

Race, religion, and culture are often regarded as fundamentally important to a person's sense of identity and belonging. When separating parents are from different racial, cultural, or religious backgrounds, the battle over the person with whom the child should live can take on an even greater significance. It is more than just a battle over where the child should live: it is a dispute over the child's whole way of life. The courts have recognized the importance of these issues. However, whilst religion, race, and culture are relevant, they are not afforded any special significance in the welfare balance. The European Court of Human Rights has made it clear that a decision concerning residence must not be based 'solely or principally' on the applicant's religion: in and of itself it cannot be a determining factor.[109] The courts must also avoid making abstract judgements about the tenets, beliefs, or practices of particular religions or cultures. The European Court has, however, confirmed that it is legitimate for the domestic authorities to take into account the *effect* of the applicant's religious practices on the child's lifestyle and upbringing.[110] This is the approach adopted by the English courts.

The leading case on this issue did not involve a dispute about where the children should live (which was agreed between the parties), but rather about their schooling and educational upbringing, which would be dealt with under a specific issue order. Nonetheless, Munby LJ's discussion of the issues is of broader relevance. The parents in *Re G (Education: Religious Upbringing)* came from families which were part of the Chassidic (Hasidic) or Chareidi community of Ultra Orthodox Jews. In the Chareidi community, all aspects of life are governed by the Torah and, of particular relevance to the case, children attend single-sex

---

104 On disputes between same-sex couples and the 'other parent' about contact, see pp 793–4.

105 *Re G (Children) (Residence: Same-Sex Partner)* [2006] UKHL 43, [6].

106 Below, 11.6.7.

107 [2014] EWCA Civ 336.

108 Note that CA 1989, ss 12(1A) and 12(2A) were not in force when this case was decided, which would now offer an easier means of conferring parental responsibility on similar facts: see 10.3.2 and 10.3.5.

109 *Palau-Martinez v France* (App No 64927/01, ECHR) (2004).

110 *Ismailova v Russia* (App No 37614/02, ECHR) (2007), [55]–[63].

schools. Although the mother had grown up in this community, she no longer considered herself to be part of it, though she still considered herself to be an Orthodox Jew.[111]

Re G (Education: Religious Upbringing) [2012] EWCA Civ 1233

MUNBY LJ:

35. Religion—whatever the particular believer's faith—is not the business of government or of the secular courts, though the courts will, of course, pay every respect to the individual's or family's religious principles. Article 9 of the European Convention for the Protection of Human Rights and Fundamental Freedoms, after all, demands no less. The starting point of the common law is thus respect for an individual's religious principles, coupled with an essentially neutral view of religious beliefs and a benevolent tolerance of cultural and religious diversity.

36. It is not for a judge to weigh one religion against another. The court recognises no religious distinctions and generally speaking passes no judgment on religious beliefs or on the tenets, doctrines or rules of any particular section of society. All are entitled to equal respect, so long as they are "legally and socially acceptable" (Purchas LJ in *Re R (A Minor) (Residence: Religion)* [1993] 2 FLR 163, 171) and not "immoral or socially obnoxious" (Scarman LJ in *Re T (Minors) (Custody: Religious Upbringing)* (1981) 2 FLR 239, 244) or "pernicious" (Latey J in *Re B and G (Minors) (Custody)* [1985] FLR 134, 157, referring to scientology).

37. The Strasbourg jurisprudence is to the same effect....

38. The important point for present purposes is that the Convention forbids the State to determine the validity of religious beliefs and in that respect imposes on the State a duty of what the Strasbourg court has called neutrality and impartiality...

39. Within limits the law – our family law – will tolerate things which society as a whole may find undesirable. A child's best interests have to be assessed by reference to general community standards, making due allowance for the entitlement of people, within the limits of what is permissible in accordance with those standards, to entertain very divergent views about the religious, moral, social and secular objectives they wish to pursue for themselves and for their children....

40. Where precisely the limits are to be drawn is often a matter of controversy. There is no 'bright-line' test that the law can set. The infinite variety of the human condition precludes arbitrary definition.

41. Some things are nevertheless beyond the pale: forced marriages (always to be distinguished of course from arranged marriages to which the parties consent), female genital mutilation and so-called, if grotesquely misnamed, 'honour-based' domestic violence. Plainly, as I wish to emphasise, we are not here in that territory....

43. Some manifestations of religious practice may be regulated if contrary to a child's welfare. Although a parent's views and wishes as to the child's religious upbringing are of great importance, and will always be seriously regarded by the court, just as the court will always pay great attention to the wishes of a child old enough to be able to express sensible views on the subject of religion, even if not old enough to take a mature decision, they will be given effect to by the court only if and so far as and in such manner as is in accordance with the child's best interests. In matters of religion, as in all other aspects of a child's upbringing, the interests of the child are the paramount consideration.

---

[111] Further extracts from *Re G* can be found at 8.2.1.

Munby LJ then quoted from an earlier Court of Appeal decision which had related to the upbringing of a child as a Jehovah's Witness.

Re T (Minors) (Custody: Religious Upbringing) (1981) 2 FLR 239 (CA), 244–5

SCARMAN LJ:

We live in a tolerant society. There is no reason at all why the mother should not espouse the beliefs and practice of Jehovah's Witnesses. It is conceded that there is nothing immoral or socially obnoxious in the beliefs and practice of this sect. . . . It is as reasonable on the part of the mother that she should wish to teach her children the beliefs and practice of the Jehovah's Witnesses as it is reasonable on the part of the father that they should not be taught those practices and beliefs.

It is not for this court, in society as at present constituted, to pass any judgment on the beliefs of the mother or on the beliefs of the father. It is sufficient for this court that it should recognize that each is entitled to his or her own beliefs and way of life, and that the two opposing ways of life considered in this case are both socially acceptable and certainly consistent with a decent and respectable life. What follows from that? It follows, in my judgment, that there is a great risk, merely because we are dealing with an unpopular minority sect, in overplaying the dangers to the welfare of these children inherent in the possibility that they may follow their mother and become Jehovah's Witnesses. Of course, most of us like to play games on Saturdays, to go out to children's parties and to have a quiet Sunday—some of us will go to church, and some of us will not. This appears to be the normal and happy, even though somewhat materialistic, way of life, accepted by the majority of people in our society. It does not follow, however, that it is wrong, or contrary to the welfare of children, that life should be in a narrower sphere, subject to a stricter religious discipline, and without the parties on birthdays and Christmas that seem so important to the rest of us. These are factors that must be considered, but I think it is essential in a case of this sort to appreciate that the mother's teaching, once it is accepted as reasonable, is teaching that has got to be considered against the whole background of the case and not as in itself so full of danger for the children that it alone could justify making an order which otherwise the court would not make.

After quoting this passage, Munby LJ observed that, in determining a case where these considerations were relevant, the court should not automatically prefer the parent whose way of life was seen as being 'more acceptable', because it was not necessarily contrary to a child's welfare to be part of a minority group. Munby LJ drew a distinction between commenting upon the tenets, doctrines, or rules of a religion or other group, and looking at the impact of those tenets, doctrines, or rules on the child's welfare. The former is outside the court's role, but the latter is required when making a welfare determination under s 1 of the CA 1989. However, as Rachel Taylor has commented, it is difficult to draw this distinction: 'If adherence to a particular religion requires a certain behaviour, then to discriminate between parents on the basis of that behaviour is, in effect, to risk discriminating on the basis of religion itself'.[112]

In preference to allowing religious or cultural factors to become a dominant factor in residence disputes, the courts have tended to rely on making generous provision for contact

---

[112] Taylor (2013), 341.

to satisfy the child's need for knowledge of both sides of his or her religious and/or cultural heritage.[113] Indeed, in some cases equal time arrangements have been made as 'one way of trying to guard against the risk that the religious perspective of either parent will predominate'.[114]

11.6.5 SHARED LIVING ARRANGEMENTS

One of the biggest changes in how the courts have approached children's living arrangements following parental separation over the last two decades has been the rise of orders referred to, before the 2014 change in terminology, as *shared residence orders*—these orders will now be child arrangements orders specifying that the child should live with more than one person in different households.[115] Support for the greater use of shared residence orders is firmly rooted in the discourse on shared parenting. Shared parenting post-divorce is an integral part of the normative model of the 'civilized divorce'.[116] The hostility promoted by the 'win–lose' mentality of previous models of post-divorce parenting is regarded as particularly damaging to children, with shared parenting perceived as one means by which hostilities can be reduced.[117] The normative model of post-divorce parenting emerging from these debates is explained by Bren Neale and Carol Smart.

B. Neale and C. Smart, 'In Whose Best Interests? Theorising Family Life Following Parental Separation or Divorce', in S. Day Sclater and C. Piper (eds), *Undercurrents of Divorce* (Aldershot: Ashgate, 1999), 33, 37–9

Since the early 1980s the model of lone/reconstituted family has gradually been replaced by that of a co-parenting/biological family. The original family is no longer to be broken under the 'clean break' philosophy, nor is it to be replaced by a reconstituted family...The potential to care for a child without the other parent, even if this is bound up with a new marriage or partnership, has a diminished value under this new ideology and, barring exceptional circumstances, can no longer be legally sanctioned. If the family can't remain intact and under one roof (still, of course the preferred option) then, as Day Sclater and Piper argue...it must re-invent itself as a 'bi-nuclear' family spread across two households. Divorce has thus been recast as a 'stage' (albeit a painful one) in the newly extended life course of the indelible nuclear family...

This new model dovetails with a welfare discourse that has been radically reformulated. Children are no longer said to need one stable home, one primary carer and the restabilising influence of the stepfamily. What they are now said to need is two biological parents and the restabilising influence of the non-residential father. One notable feature of this reformulated welfare discourse is that the child's needs are now defined in terms of what they are lacking: the lack of proper fathering and the limitations of mothering, which has culminated in a link between the 'child of divorce' and the pervasive but largely undefined notion of harm...

---

[113] *Re T (A Child)* [2005] EWCA Civ 1397.
[114] *Re N (Religion: Jehovah's Witness)* [2011] EWHC 3737, [75].
[115] In relation to the pre-2014 cases, we continue to refer to 'shared residence' from time to time.
[116] Krieken (2005), 34–45.
[117] Brophy (1989), 222 and Krieken (2005), ibid.

> The assumption that children are 'damaged' by divorce is accompanied by another assumption—that this damage can be mitigated if particular forms of parenting and therapeutic interventions are put in place. Parents are to ameliorate the worst effects of their actions by prioritising their children's welfare, playing a joint part in their children's day to day care and developing a co-operative and unselfish sharing of parental authority.

As Neale and Smart point out, the shared parenting discourse is underpinned by a significant shift in the welfare discourse. Whereas the interests of children under the 'tender years doctrine' were clearly identified with those of the mother, the rise of the 'new father' rhetoric has seen the interests of children increasingly viewed as dependent on their relationship with their father.[118] As we have seen in other areas of the law, fathers' rights groups have thus been able to argue that the imperative for improving the legal position of fathers comes from within the welfare discourse itself.

> [T]he new model is underpinned by a fresh articulation of the rights of fathers who argue that, since they are just as capable as mothers of caring for their children they should be granted equal legal rights to them . . .
>
> It is important to recognise that what is transformed under the new model is how fatherhood is constituted within legal and policy discourse. It seems that where mothers, as the day to day carers, were once constructed as vital to their children, it is fathers, as the restabilisers and potential carers, who are now constructed as essential, at least following divorce. That fathers might want a more direct involvement in day to day care is a relatively new phenomenon, deserving of explanation. According to Beck, it is linked to wider social changes under which the traditional gendering of parental care and financial support is breaking down . . .
>
> The changed attitude can also be understood in terms of the value that is increasingly placed upon emotional fulfilment within family relationships. If marriage and, perhaps more to the point, remarriage can no longer be relied upon to provide this, then the parent-child relationship may increasingly become the focus of such fulfilment. This, in turn, is linked to the rise in a romanticised vision of children as priceless emotional assets which, in the interests of parental equality, are best divided equally than awarded to one parent alone. Where mothers were once seen to be the holders of onerous responsibilities, requiring sustained emotional commitment, hard physical work and a range of socio-economic sacrifices (and deserving, therefore, of custodial status and state support), they are now seen to be in possession of valuable commodities, and any unwillingness to share them seen as discriminatory against fathers.

Shared parenting does not necessarily mean 50:50 shared care as advocated by some fathers' rights groups. Although 50:50 care perhaps represents the most 'pure' form of shared parenting, the retention of parental responsibility by both parents (allied with generous contact to the non-resident parent) already ensures that they both have the necessary legal status to remain actively engaged in their children's lives post-separation.

Development of the courts' approach

The early case law, both before and after the CA 1989 entered force, was generally hostile to orders for shared care, the prevailing view being that children require one settled home.

---

[118] Brophy (1989).

A shared residence order was therefore regarded as 'wholly exceptional',[119] and it had to be shown that the proposed departure from the conventional orders conferred some 'positive benefit' on the child.[120] Opposition to shared residence was particularly strong where there was continuing hostility between the parents.

However, judicial attitudes towards such orders have undergone significant change.[121] A more liberal approach was clear from the Court of Appeal judgment in *D v D (Shared Residence Order)*. The case was one in which there was 'an exceptionally high level of animosity between the parents'. The children lived with their mother but had substantial levels of contact with their father. The judge found that the mother used the fact she had sole residence as a weapon in the parents' 'war'. He therefore made an order for shared residence in an attempt to reduce the level of conflict between them.

D v D (Shared Residence Order) [2000] EWCA Civ 3009

HALE LJ:

20. [Counsel] who appears for the mother, has argued that the authorities indicate that shared residence orders should only be made either in exceptional circumstances or, at the very least, where it can be demonstrated that they would show a positive benefit for the children. In this particular case there were no exceptional circumstances, no evidence of positive benefit and thus, no reason to change the legal arrangements which had been in place for some time. He also argues that access to information was irrelevant or given too much weight because the father already had parental responsibility and was entitled to that information. Thus that, by itself, could not be regarded as an exceptional circumstance or of positive benefit...

22. The background to the Children Act provision lies in the Law Commission's Working Paper No. 96, published in 1986, on Custody and the Law Commission's Report, Law Com. No. 172, published in 1988, on Guardianship and Custody. If I may summarise the basic principles proposed, the first was that each parent with parental responsibility should retain their equal and independent right, and their responsibility, to have information and make appropriate decisions about their children. If, of course, the parents were not living together it might be necessary for the court to make orders about their future, but those orders should deal with the practical arrangements for where and how the children should be living rather than assigning rights as between the parents...

24....[D]ealing with residence orders the Commission said this at paragraph 4.12 of the Law Com No. 172:

"Apart from the effect on the other parent, which has already been mentioned, the main difference between a residence order and a custody order is that the new order should be flexible enough to accommodate a much wider range of situations. In some cases, the child may live with both parents even though they do not share the same household. It was never our intention to suggest that children should share their time more or less equally between their parents. Such arrangements will rarely be practicable, let alone for the children's benefit. However, the evidence from the United States is that where they are practicable they can work well and we see no reason

---

[119] *J v J* [1991] 2 FLR 385; *Re H (A Minor) (Shared Residence)* [1994] 1 FLR 717.

[120] *A v A (Minors) (Shared Residence Order)* [1994] 1 FLR 669.

[121] Trinder (2014) describes the evolving attitude to shared care as going through five phases: rarity, expansion, politicization, internationalization, and finally symbolism.

why they should be actively discouraged. None of our respondents shared the view expressed in a recent case [Riley v Riley] that such an arrangement, which had been working well for some years, should never have been made. More commonly, however, the child will live with both parents but spend more time with one than the other. Examples might be where he spends term time with one and holidays with the other, or two out of three holidays from boarding school with one and the third with the other. It is a far more realistic description of the responsibilities involved in that sort of arrangement to make a residence order covering both parents rather than a residence order for one and a contact order for the other. Hence we recommend that where the child is to live with two (or more) people who do not live together, the order may specify the periods during which the child is to live in each household. The specification may be general rather than detailed and in some cases may not be necessary at all." . . .

31. It is quite clear that in [*A v A (Minors)* [1994] 1 FLR 669, Butler-Sloss LJ] was moving matters on from any suggestion, which is not in the legislation, that these orders require exceptional circumstances . . .

32. If . . . it is either planned or has turned out that the children are spending substantial amounts of their time with each of their parents then, as both the Law Commission and my Lady indicated in the passages that I have quoted it may be an entirely appropriate order to make. For my part, I would not add any gloss on the legislative provisions, which are always subject to the paramount consideration of what is best for the children concerned.

33. This case is one in which, as the judge said, the arrangements have been settled for some considerable time. The children are, in effect, living with both of their parents. They have homes with each of them . . .

34. In those circumstances it seems to me that there is indeed a positive benefit to these children in those facts being recognised in the order that the court makes. There is no detriment or disrespect to either parent in that order. It simply reflects the reality of these children's lives. It was entirely appropriate for the judge to make it in this case and neither party should feel that they have won or lost as a result. I would, therefore, dismiss the appeal.

This case marked an important change in approach towards shared residence orders. Hale LJ made clear that the courts should not feel constrained in making a shared residence order where such an order reflects the reality of the children's lives. It is, however, often very difficult to determine where the boundary lies between, on the one hand, a reality of shared care justifying a shared residence order and, on the other, a more conventional arrangement best reflected in orders for residence and contact. It is a question of degree. Absolute equality is not required.[122] Nor is geographical proximity between the parents[123] or a pattern of care whereby the child spends alternative weeks in the home of each parent.

It is clear from *D v D* that high levels of hostility between the parents will not prevent the court making a shared residence order where it is otherwise justified; a good relationship between the parties is not a prerequisite.[124] Indeed, it has been suggested that a shared residence order may actually help to ease the conflict between the parents by sending out the strong message that they have equal *status* in the eyes of the law.[125] That point developed in some judges' thinking to the point where there were clear authorities for the

---

[122] *Re K (A Child)* [2008] EWCA Civ 526, [6].

[123] *Re F (Children)* [2003] EWCA Civ 592; *Re H (Children)* [2009] EWCA Civ 245, [8].

[124] See also *Re R (Children)* [2005] EWCA Civ 542, [11]–[12].

[125] Cf Harris-Short (2010), who suggests that by getting a shared care order, the expectations of the non-primary carer for 'real equality' (i.e. an actual 50:50 sharing of time) will be raised and the dispute will then turn to focus on the minutiae of the division of time under the terms of the order.

proposition that a shared residence order could be justified for symbolic or psychological reasons (particularly to acknowledge the equal status of the parents) even in the absence of an underlying reality of shared care. This suggestion first emerged in a judgment of Sir Mark Potter P.[126]

Re A (A Child) (Joint Residence: Parental Responsibility) [2008] EWCA Civ 867

POTTER P:

66. The making of a shared residence order is no longer the unusual order which once it was. Following the implementation of the Act and in the light of s 11(4) of the Act which provides that the court may make residence orders in favour of more than one person, whether living in the same household or not, the making of such an order has become increasingly common. It is now recognised by the court that a shared residence order may be regarded as appropriate where it provides legal confirmation of the factual reality of a child's life or where, in a case where one party has the primary care of a child, it may be psychologically beneficial to the parents in emphasising the equality of their position and responsibilities.

Although *Re A* fell into the sub-category of cases where a shared residence order is necessary to confer parental responsibility on the non-resident parent,[127] the President's judgment was approved by Wilson LJ as summarizing the principles governing shared residence orders and applied to a routine intra-parental residence dispute.

Re W (Shared Residence Order) [2009] EWCA Civ 370

WILSON LJ:

13. With respect to [counsel], I see no subsisting foundation for his submission to us today that, unless the time to be spent by a child in the two households is close to being equal, unusual circumstances are required before a shared residence order should be made. Fifteen years ago his submission would have been valid...But at any rate for the last 8 years the better view has been that, while of course a need remains for the demonstration of circumstances which positively indicate that the child's welfare would thereby be served, there is no such gloss on the appropriateness of an order for shared residence as would be reflected by the words 'unusual' or indeed 'exceptional'...

17....[Counsel] began by presenting to us statistics which he had compiled and which, according to him...indicate that, under the arrangements made by consent between the parties, K [the child] is to spend with the father only 25% of her time...His submission reminded me of comments which, as a temporary member of this court, I made in *Re F (Shared Residence Order)*...to the effect that statistics of that character were usually only of limited value. [Counsel] ultimately described as the main plank of his appeal the fact that a shared residence order did not reflect the situation on the ground...But it was in that same

---

[126] Although see also *Re K (A Child)* [2008] EWCA Civ 528, [6], where Wilson LJ hinted at a similar approach.

[127] In this case the child had been raised for two years by his mother's partner who mistakenly believed that he was the legal (genetic) father. Note that s 12(2A) was not in force when this decision was made, and would have offered an alternative means of granting parental responsibility: see 10.3.5.

short judgment of mine...that I attempted to explode the *canard* that a shared residence order was appropriate only in circumstances in which the children would be spending their time evenly, or more or less evenly, in the two homes.

The shared residence order was thus upheld even though the 'reality' of the child's care was a long way from 50:50 shared care.[128]

Making a shared residence order, regardless of the 'reality' of the division of the child's time, in order to try to control the conflict between the separated parents seems reasonable and laudable. Any approach which may help 'lessen the stakes' and reduce the problems associated with the 'win–lose' mentality of litigation will ultimately further the child's welfare. However, despite the initial attractions of this approach, it can be questioned whether it is focused on the child's welfare as opposed to the adults' desires. The rise of shared residence arrangements which did not reflect shared care was criticized for its inconsistency with the original scheme intended by the Law Commission and Parliament, and for undermining the essential purpose of a residence order.

P. Harris and R. George, 'Parental Responsibility and Shared Residence Orders: Parliamentary Intentions and Judicial Interpretations', (2010) 22 *Child and Family Law Quarterly* **151, 155–6, 166–9**

The [Law] Commission...recommended that, where both parties had parental responsibility, the court be limited to dealing with concrete and practical issues about with whom the child should live, what contact she would have with others, and any disputed matters relating to the exercise of parental responsibility...[I]t is important to note that the Commission was clear that the orders should reflect the *realities*...In reflecting that overarching policy, while the Commission in their Review favoured shared residence orders where the child shared 'their time more or less equally between their parents', it thought such orders appropriate only in the rare cases where such an order was a 'more realistic description of that...sort of arrangement...than a residence order for one [parent] and a contact order for the other'. That approach was also echoed in Parliament when Lord Chancellor Mackay explained that 'contact' included 'staying with' the non-residential parent and that 'shared residence [would be] rare'. Thus both the Commission and Parliament appear to have emphasised that shared residence orders were to be contemplated only where they reflected *the reality* of the *concrete* arrangement...

Having reviewed the case law on shared residence orders and the trend to make such orders in order to affirm the equal status of the parents, Harris and George argue that this development was closely linked to the recent degradation of parental responsibility such that the latter is now a meaningless concept.

We suggest that this alternative approach [to shared residence] came about, in part, because of the courts' earlier dilution of the potency of parental responsibility. The problem from the courts' perspective was that, if a man convicted of possessing child pornography and who was to have no direct contact with his child was worthy of parental responsibility, surely a

---

[128] See also *Re O (A Child)* [2009] EWCA Civ 1266.

good father who already had parental responsibility and who was to continue to play some active involvement in his child's upbringing ought to have something more.

Using shared residence orders to resolve the difficulty created by the dilution of parental responsibility was not initially obvious, given the courts' historical resistance to such orders. However, we have now reached the point where academics can suggest that 'a[s] parental responsibility has been diluted, shared residence orders have arguably come to represent the new way of giving separated parents equal authority', and practitioners can ask 'whether the rise of the shared residence order is inextricably linked to the perceived ineffectual nature of parental responsibility'...

It is arguable that the courts are starting on the same road with shared residence as was seen with parental responsibility. Whereas parental responsibility was down-graded so as to be given to fathers who had no practical role to play in their children's lives at all, now shared residence is being down-graded to give it to fathers who are involved, but not in day-to-day care. Where parents live in reasonable proximity to one another, and their children spend considerable time living in both households, there is no reason not to call that shared residence. Where the parents live far apart, but their children live, say, with one for the school term and with the other for the holidays, there is equally no difficulty with calling that shared residence. But when the child merely visits one parent, even if those visits involve overnight stays, such arrangements should not be called residence, for they are not.[129]

Senior judges were also somewhat divided as to whether it was appropriate to use shared residence to deal with questions of parental status even where there was no underlying reality of shared care.[130]

Re H (Children) [2009] EWCA Civ 902

Ward LJ:

13. [A] shared residence order must reflect the reality of the children's lives. Where the children are spending a substantial amount of time with both parents, a shared residence order reflects the reality of their lives...[A] residence order is about where a child is to live and it is not about status. I want to emphasise that here the father's status is recognised by the parental responsibility agreement and order which has been made. That gives him equal say in how the children are to be brought up, so that when they are with him he will determine when they brush their teeth and when they go to bed and whether they have cornflakes or porridge for breakfast...So in terms of status he has it, and shared residence is not going to affect status. Shared residence is about the reality of where they live. And the best test I can think of...is to postulate the question, ask the children, where do you live? If the answer is "I live with my mummy but I go and stay with my daddy regularly", then you have the answer to your problem. That answer means a residence order with mummy and contact with daddy, but if the situation truly is such that the children say, "Oh we live with mummy for part of the time and with daddy for the other part of the time", then you have the justification for making a shared residence order.

The House of Lords addressed the issue of shared residence orders in *Holmes-Moorhouse v London Borough of Richmond upon Thames*.[131] The case raised the interesting question

---

[129] See also Newnham (2011).
[130] This was also the view taken by Hale LJ in *Re A (Children)* [2001] EWCA Civ 1795, [17].
[131] [2009] UKHL 7.

of the relationship between the court's power to make an order for shared residence and the local authority's obligations to provide public housing to a parent in whose favour such an order has been made and who is claiming to be in priority need as a 'person with whom dependent children reside or might reasonably be expected to reside.'[132] The court had made a shared residence order in favour of the applicant and his former partner by consent, with the children expected to live with each parent on alternate weeks. Despite the order, the local authority refused to accommodate the father even though he claimed to have priority need. The local authority argued that even though the court had made a shared residence order, the local authority had to reach an independent judgement under the Housing Act as to whether the applicant's expectation that a dependent child would live with him was reasonable. The House of Lords agreed, holding that the provision of public housing was a matter for the housing authority exercising its statutory duties and responsibilities and could not be controlled or pre-judged by the court through the making of a shared residence order, whether or not the order was made by consent or following a disputed hearing. As Lord Hoffmann points out, these are two different questions decided by different authorities on a different basis and 'must not be allowed to become entangled with one another'.[133] The fact that an applicant for public housing has a shared residence order in his or her favour (determined on the basis of the child's welfare but which for various reasons may not have been the subject of thorough forensic examination) is just one factor for the housing authority to take into account when determining whether the applicant has a priority need, alongside other material considerations such as the limited availability of suitable family housing in the area.[134] The shared residence order cannot determine the matter.[135]

The judgment of Baroness Hale is particularly interesting for the general guidance it provides.

Holmes-Moorhouse v London Borough of Richmond upon Thames [2009] UKHL 7

BARONESS HALE:

30. When any family court decides with whom the children of separated parents are to live, the welfare of those children must be its paramount consideration: Children Act 1989, s 1(1). This means that it must choose from the available options the future which will be best for the children, not the future which will be best for the adults. It also means that the court may be creative in devising options which the parents have not put forward. It does not mean that the court can create options where none exist...

37.... [I]n my view, this order should not have been made. A residence order is "an order settling the arrangements to be made as to the person with whom a child is to live"...Although, as I have said, the parents are free to depart from it by agreement if they wish, it is an order which can be enforced, by physical removal of the children if need be...It is one thing to make such an order when each parent has a home to offer the children, even if it is not exactly what they have been used to before their parents split up. It is another thing entirely to make such an order when one parent is living in the family home and the other parent has no accommodation at all to offer them and no money with which to feed and clothe them....

---

[132] Housing Act 1996, ss 193 and 189(1)(b).
[133] [2009] UKHL 7, [8], [9], [14], and [17].
[134] Ibid, [16].
[135] Ibid, [17].

38. Family court orders are meant to provide practical solutions to the practical problems faced by separating families. They are not meant to be aspirational statements of what would be for the best in some ideal world which has little prospect of realisation. Ideally there may be many cases where it would be best for the children to have a home with each of their parents. But this is not always or even usually practicable. Family courts have no power to conjure up resources where none exist. Nor can they order local authorities or other public agencies to provide particular services unless there is a specific power to do so...The courts cannot even do this in care proceedings, whose whole aim is to place long term parental responsibility upon the state, to look after and safeguard and promote the welfare of children who are suffering or likely to suffer harm in their own homes...A fortiori they cannot do this in private law proceedings between the parents. No doubt all family courts have from time to time tried to persuade local authorities to act in what we consider to be the best interests of the children whose welfare is for us the paramount consideration. But we have no power to order them to do so. Nor, in my view, should we make orders which will be unworkable unless they do. It is different, of course, if we have good reason to believe that the necessary resources will be forthcoming in the foreseeable future. The court can always ask the local authority for information about this...

39. But the family court should not use a residence order as a means of putting pressure upon a local housing authority to allocate their resources in a particular way despite all the other considerations which...they have to take into account. It is quite clear that this was what the family court was trying to do in this case...

Baroness Hale's approach, emphasizing the importance of s 8 orders being grounded in reality and offering practical solutions to the problems facing post-separation families, has clear echoes of her earlier judgments on shared residence orders. Although it is only possible to speculate, there is nothing in this judgment to suggest Baroness Hale would now depart from the clear principles she established in *D v D* to endorse the approach to shared residence orders that has been favoured in more recent years by some members of the Court of Appeal. Baroness Hale also emphasizes the particular importance of listening to the voice of the child in cases of shared residence, 'because it is the children who will have to divide their time between two homes and it is all too easy for the parents' wishes and feelings to predominate'.[136]

Questions about orders for shared living arrangements and the shared parenting ideal

Government policy

The question of whether legislation should contain a positive presumption in favour of shared living arrangements has been a focus of successive governments for some years. In 2004, the Labour Government rejected the idea of introducing a 50:50 presumption into the CA 1989. The government stressed its commitment to having both parents involved in their children's lives, and to the welfare principle in s 1 of the Children Act, but thought that a 50:50 presumption would not work.[137] A similar view was later taken by the Family Justice Review in its final report. The Family Justice Review took account of a range of international

---

[136] Ibid, [36].
[137] DCA, DFES, and DTI (2004).

experiences, as well as research evidence (though as we will see below, the picture from the research is not entirely clear).

D. Norgrove (Chair), *Family Justice Review: Final Report* (London: MOJ, 2011), 138–9

4.22 We made clear in our interim report and have again emphasised it earlier in this report our view that children benefit from a relationship with both parents post separation, where this is safe. The question is how best to achieve this without inadvertently encouraging arrangements which involve frequent changes of carer or home for a very young child, or exposing children to ongoing parental conflict. In particular the issue for us was to recommend what role the law and the courts should play.

4.23 Drawing on international and other evidence we opposed legislation to encourage 'shared parenting'. The evidence showed that people place different interpretations on this term, and that it is interpreted in practice by counting hours spent with each parent, disregarding the quality of the time. The thorough and detailed evidence from Australia showed the damaging consequences for many children. So we recommended that:

- no legislation should be introduced that creates or risks creating the perception that there is a parental right to substantially shared or equal time for both parents.

4.27 Having thoroughly reconsidered the evidence, we remain firm in our view that any legislation that might risk creating an impression of a parental 'right' to any particular amount of time with a child would undermine the central principle of the Children Act 1989 that the welfare of the child is paramount. We also believe that legislation is a poor instrument for social change in this area. ...

4.28 So we maintain our view that the focus should instead be on supporting and fostering a greater awareness of shared parental responsibility and on the duties and roles of both parents from birth onwards. Legislation is not the means through which to achieve this. As one legal adviser, responding to the online consultation put it: 'education, not legislation.'

However, in 2012 the Coalition Government indicated that it did not accept this conclusion of the Family Justice Review. A consultation paper was issued which indicated that the government intended to introduce legislation to promote shared parenting. The government observed that the principle that, ordinarily, both parents should be actively involved in their children's lives following parental separation was already factored into court decisions. However, it was suggested that the lack of a clear principle on the face of any legislation meant that some people had a misconception about the law. In particular, the government thought that, given that most separating parents make arrangements for their children's living arrangements without going to court, it was important to 'reinforce the expectation at societal level that both parents are jointly responsible for their children's upbringing'.

DFE and MOJ, *Co-operative Parenting Following Family Separation: Proposed Legislation on the Involvement of Both Parents in a Child's Life* (London: TSO, 2012)

4.3 The legislative change will send a clear signal to separated parents that courts will take account of the principle that both should continue to be actively involved in their children's lives. It will help to dispel the perception that there is an in-built legal bias towards fathers or mothers. The Government believes that this will encourage more separated parents to resolve their disputes out of court and agree care arrangements that fully involve both parents....

4.4 This legislative change is categorically not about equality in the time that a child spends with each parent after separation. There is no intention that equal time, or indeed any prescribed notion of an 'appropriate' division of time, should be the starting point of the court's considerations. The quality of time a child spends with each parent, the need for stability in a child's life, and the sustainability of arrangements are the most important factors. Every family and every child's circumstances are different, and the courts will continue to make decisions on this basis.

However, while there was initial uncertainty about how these aims would be implemented in legislation, the newly created s 1(2A) of the CA 1989 (which gives effect to this policy aim) in fact says nothing about shared parenting. Rather, it is a presumption that, where it is safe and in the child's best interests, children should have ongoing direct or indirect involvement with both parents following separation.[138]

Research evidence

The empirical work of Smart and Neale is instructive in understanding concerns about how the post-divorce parenting debate has developed. Based on a sample of 60 parents, the research reveals the reality of pre- and post-divorce parenting patterns and the differing attitudes of mothers and fathers towards their respective parenting roles. In particular, their findings unveil the 'myth' of the equal, hands-on 'new father' within intact families, one of the driving forces behind the calls for greater equality in post-divorce parenting.

C. Smart and B. Neale, *Family Fragments?* (Cambridge: Polity Press, 1999), 45–66

[I]t is clear that in Western cultures there are significant differences in both the responsibilities associated with mothering and with fathering, and with the meaning(s) associated with being a mother and being a father. Moreover, while motherhood may have imparted a fairly stable identity, the meaning of fatherhood has become highly contested and uncertain in Britain in the 1990s...

Almost all of our interviewees became parents while married or cohabiting and so entered into parenthood with the assumption that there would be two parents available to raise the children. Moreover the majority had settled into a form of parenting where responsibilities and duties had been allocated and become established. We found, not surprisingly, that the typical pattern was one where mothers gave up work or worked part-time in order to become primary carers. The fathers therefore tended to develop rather different relationships with their children because they spent less time with them and inevitably took less day-to-day responsibility for them. We found a pattern of relationships which was very similar to that described by Backett in her study of parenting in intact households. Basically fathers were one step removed from their children and their relationship with them was sustained via their relationship with the mother...Of considerable interest in Backett's research was her discovery that fathers did not have to do equal amounts of caring in order to be regarded as good fathers. Thus child-rearing was often described as being equally shared when in fact it was nothing of the sort...

---

[138] S 1(2A) is discussed above at 11.4.

Very few of our fathers were willing to allow their careers or job prospects to suffer in order to take more responsibility for their children while they had a relationship with the mother...[O]nly one father stayed at home in a 'role reversal' arrangement...[F]or most their ability to spend equal amounts of time with their children and to assume a shared responsibility at a day-to-day level was actually compromised by their paid employment.

The accounts of the mothers in our sample focused on two aspects of childcare, the physical work (e.g. feeding, bathing, toilet training) and the emotional care (e.g. monitoring the child's moods, anticipating needs). In some instances mothers were disappointed that fathers did relatively little of the former, or felt angry that after a 'promising start' they lapsed into a more traditional role. In other instances the mothers were not unduly concerned about the physical work, or acknowledged that the fathers had undertaken a reasonable amount of this burden, but they pointed to the fact that fathers rarely seemed to be 'in tune' with the children or that they did not notice or anticipate emotional states, illnesses or preferences. As with the mothers in Backett's study, these mothers tended to assume that they held the 'real' responsibility for the children while the fathers either helped or hindered...

The gendered nature of parenting within the intact family has important implications for the transition to post-separation family life.

The fact that mothers tended to see themselves as responsible and as more experienced in childcare made the transition to post-divorce parenting hard. During their marriage or cohabitation, being a good mother meant taking this responsibility and, to some extent, taking it for granted too. But on divorce they found that they were expected to relinquish this feeling of responsibility to someone who (usually) had not actually shared it during their relationship and who might be viewed as fairly inept at the physical care work, let alone the emotional caring.

This division of labour mitigated against sharing responsibility later, especially if children were very young...

How parents view themselves, and how much of their personal identity is bound up with their parenthood, has an important bearing on how parenthood operates in practice. People's biographies as parents assume importance because parental identities are not made instantly or ascribed but, much like other kin relationships, are negotiated and forged over considerable periods of time. From this perspective, parenthood can be seen as part of a nexus of life commitments. It is a matter of conscious choice, which must be weighed against competing life interests such as employment, leisure pursuits, geographical mobility and, following separation, the pursuit of new intimate partnerships. How this balancing is undertaken and to what extent parents make themselves available for their children in preference to other life chances will have a strong influence on how post divorce parenthood is negotiated and established.

Where the activities of parental care are gendered then the parental identities which arise from them are also likely to be gendered. Motherhood and fatherhood are not perceived as identical subject positions. Many of the mothers in our sample had made their parenthood a central part of their lives...

The strong identity as mothers which these parents express arises in part from dominant cultural constructions which idealize motherhood. It also arises, more concretely, from their experience as full-time parents who gave up their jobs when they had children...[E]ven where the mothers in our sample were working full time in the early years of parenthood (nine out of thirty-one cases) they continued to take the main responsibility for the children's day-to-day care, for 'being there' when needed and for organising substitute care. For these women, therefore, their maternal identity was (for a time at least) more significant than identities arising from their engagement in paid work.

The father's identity is less likely to be derived from such an intense focus on parenthood...But this does not mean that men do not have identities as fathers, but this is often linked to their work as financial providers. This work of financial provision is crucially important, yet it means deriving a sense of identity from outside the home and the family. Although some fathers are now more actively involved in their children's lives, they are more likely to spend time sharing leisure pursuits with the children, rather than engaging in the basics of childcare. There is, therefore, a sense in which fathers have more freedom to opt in or out of such interactions and to choose how and when to balance fatherhood with their other commitments or interests. It is now quite acceptable for men to assume either the identity of the 'good provider' father or the 'new man' father...

[S]ome fathers...gradually develop a new identity as fathers as a consequence of having their children living with them part of the time...But relatively few fathers in our sample were either able or willing to do this, and the majority remained 'good provider' fathers (in that they paid child support and saw their children occasionally) or simply fell back on the minimalist paternal identity as mere biological progenitors who had no other investment in fatherhood.

Parenthood therefore still appears to have very different meanings for mothers and fathers, both before and after separation, although the meanings of both are currently subject to change. But it is important to realize that it is how motherhood and fatherhood are perceived and experienced that will have a major impact on how parents negotiate over their children after separation...[139]

To ignore the reality of pre-separation parenting patterns in the debate on post-separation parenting is unhelpful. With women still investing so heavily in motherhood, they may find it extremely difficult to surrender that key part of their identity post-separation and to share the parenting role with someone they regard as having been essentially disengaged from hands-on parenting whilst living together.

One of the difficulties facing judges and policy-makers in this area is that the research evidence that is available about the effects of different care arrangements on children's welfare is unclear and highly contested. A lot of research has been conducted over the last few years, especially in Australia and the United States, but scholars disagree about what the findings of that research show.

One view is that shared care arrangements work well for a minority of separating families—usually a sub-group of those who are not involved in litigation—but can be problematic for other children.

B. Fehlberg, B. Smyth, M. Maclean, and C. Roberts, 'Legislating for Shared Time Parenting After Separation: A Research Review', (2011) 25 *International Journal of Law, Policy and the Family* 318, 321–3

Shared time parenting is likely to work well when arrangements are child-focused, flexible, and cooperative. These same characteristics also mean that parents are likely to move away from shared time to accommodate their children's evolving needs and wishes.

---

[139] As to the existence of the 'new father', see also Kaganas (2002).

The research suggests that families with such arrangements tend to involve parents with features not typical of the broader separating population. These features include being tertiary educated, being socio-economically well-resourced, having some flexibility in working hours, living near each other, fathers who have been involved in children's daily care prior to separation and children of primary school age (although the features present vary from case to case) . . . Studies also repeatedly find that parents in this group have agreed to shared time arrangements without recourse to lawyers or the courts . . .

The 'warning flags' for when shared time parenting is not workable (meaning that the stress and burden for children outweighs the benefits for them) are essentially the flipside of those that facilitate it: in particular, high ongoing parental conflict, family violence and abuse, and rigidity.

Fehlberg et al observe that the two groups of families that they identify—the highly cooperative and the high conflict—represent only the two ends of a spectrum. They consider that not enough is known about the effects of shared care arrangements on children in families who come between these two extremes. However, they suggest that the research evidence is strong enough to show that 'shared time arrangements present particular risks for children when mothers express ongoing "safety concerns", where there is high ongoing parental conflict and when children are very young—or some combination of these'.[140]

However, in a sign of how complex the debate about research in this area can be, other scholars take a different view of what the evidence shows about overnight contact or shared care arrangements.

R. Warshak, 'Social Science and Parenting Plans for Young Children: A Consensus Report', (2014) 20 Psychology, Public Policy, and Law 46, 59–60

Research on children's overnights with fathers favors allowing children under four to be cared for at night by each parent rather than spending every night in the same home. We find the theoretical and practical considerations favoring overnights for most young children to be more compelling than concerns that overnights might jeopardize children's development. Practical considerations are relevant to consider when tailoring a parenting plan for young children to the circumstances of the parents. Such considerations may not be evident in the laboratory, or measured by existing studies, but they are readily apparent to parents and consultants who must attend to the feasibility of parenting plan options. Overnights create potential benefits related to the logistics of sharing parenting time.

. . . Parenting schedules that offer the father and child 2-hr blocks of time together, two or three times per week, can unduly stress their contacts. Overnights help to reduce the tension associated with rushing to return the child, and thus potentially improve the quality and satisfaction of the contact both for the parent and child. Overnights allow the child to settle in to the father's home, which would be more familiar to the child who regularly spends the night in the home compared with one who has only 1-hr segments in the home (allowing for transportation and preparation for the return trip). . . . Spending the night allows the father to participate in a wider range of bonding activities, such as engaging in bedtime rituals and comforting the child in the event of nighttime awakenings. . . .

---

[140] Fehlberg et al (2011), 323. The principal research that underpins the claim in relation to young children (meaning those aged under four years) comes from a large Australian study by McIntosh et al (2010).

> Nonetheless, because of the relatively few studies currently available, the limitations of these studies, and the predominance of results that indicate no direct benefit or drawback for overnights per se outside the context of other factors, we stop short of concluding that the current state of evidence supports a blanket policy or legal presumption regarding overnights. Because of the well documented vulnerability of father-child relationships among never-married and divorced parents, and the studies that identify overnights as a protective factor associated with increased father commitment to child rearing and reduced incidence of father drop-out, and because no study demonstrates any net risk of overnights, decision makers should recognize that depriving young children of overnights with their fathers could compromise the quality of their developing relationship.

The controversy associated with these studies demonstrates the difficulty in drawing any clear conclusions from the available research evidence. However, there may be an increasing consensus around one issue, namely that while *some* amount of overnight time away from a main carer does not harm young children (meaning aged three and under), there is reason to be cautious about *high frequency* overnight time, especially if there is parental conflict or if the child's bond with one parent is not yet formed.[141]

11.6.6 AN ALTERNATIVE APPROACH: A 'PRIMARY CARER' PRESUMPTION?

One of the key problems emerging from these debates is how to encourage greater equality in post-divorce parenting without undermining women's greater investment in mothering. Boyd suggests an alternative approach. She suggests that living arrangements should be determined on the basis of a primary carer presumption.[142] This approach has the advantage that it is gender neutral but nevertheless has the capacity to recognize and take account of the actual burden of child-care carried by most women.[143] Equally, whilst valuing the reality of women's investment in motherhood, the work of men who make an equal or greater contribution to parenting is similarly recognized and valued.[144] A presumption in favour of the primary carer also sits well with an approach giving greater weight to the status quo, in which the quality and strength of the child's existing relationships are seen as central in determining the arrangements which will best promote the child's interests during this difficult period of transition. Indeed, as Julie Wallbank points out, it could be argued that rather than 'favouring mothers' and 'discriminating against fathers', this is what the courts are already doing in faithful adherence to the paramountcy of the child's welfare.

J. Wallbank, 'Getting Tough on Mothers: Regulating Contact and Residence',
(2007) 15 *Feminist Legal Studies* 189, 207–8

> The question therefore arises about how...the roles of mothers and fathers should be treated when the parents' relationship breaks down...It is necessary for the courts to consider the pattern of care that existed before the relationship breakdown. The inquiry

---

[141] Warshak (2014); Pruett, McIntosh, and Kelly (2014).
[142] Boyd (1989), 148–52.
[143] Ibid.
[144] Ibid.

into future residence should focus on the past relationship of each parent to the child and should do so in a "more precise and individualised way than...the best interests standard requires". By looking at the pattern of care that existed during the adults' relationship the traditional objectives of promoting continuity and stability for the child are more effectively accommodated...[T]he status quo of the pre-breakdown situation needs to be foregrounded in order to protect the children from undue disruption...[D]espite the formal legal position of gender neutrality in relation to residence and contact, it is overwhelmingly the case that women will continue to have primary responsibility for children on separation, with men seeking contact. Very often, courts will do nothing more than make orders to retain the *status quo*. In the vast majority of cases decisions about residence and contact are reached informally. In respect of court decisions, sole residence and contact orders are used to best match the circumstances and the maintenance of the *status quo* is a feature of the welfare checklist. Rather than presenting evidence of a legal bias against the men, the pattern of residence and contact is reflective of the factual situation where women carry out the bulk of childcare.

The major disadvantage of such an approach is that it is essentially reactive rather than proactive: it tends to preserve the status quo in terms of the current patterns of pre- and post-separation parenting with all the wider disadvantages for women that such divisions in child-care create. However, changes in post-separation parenting rely heavily on changes to parenting within intact families, which requires, in turn, a fundamental restructuring of both private and public life, including most importantly the field of employment. This is clearly something beyond the limited reach of the Children Act.[145]

11.6.7 A 'PRESUMPTION' IN FAVOUR OF A NATURAL PARENT?

The majority of disputes about children's living arrangements involve competing claims by the child's parents. However, it is not uncommon for these disputes to involve a non-parent, such as a grandparent or—in proceedings which straddle private and public law, which many do—a prospective adopter. Such disputes must be determined in accordance with the welfare principle. However, in interpreting the child's welfare in this context, the key question is whether a 'presumption' in favour of the 'natural' parent can be justified on the basis that it will usually be in the child's best interests to be raised by a natural parent.[146] The issue again raises the important question of the value to be placed on 'biological' as opposed to 'social' or 'psychological' parenthood.[147] Determining the weight to give to the 'blood tie' and to social parenthood remains a difficult and controversial issue, with conflicting arguments found in court judgments over time and in different contexts.

---

145 Brophy (1989), 228, 232, and 234.

146 The term 'natural' parent is generally used throughout the case law to indicate the 'genetic' parent. This essentially ignores the complexity which will arise in a small minority of cases from the fact that the legal parent may not be the genetic parent. However, for the purposes of this discussion we will use the term 'natural' parent in accordance with the case law, particularly as the significance of 'natural' parenthood in the welfare balance is clearly linked to the perceived importance of the genetic tie. The term 'non-parent' will be used to denote all non-genetic parents.

147 See also chapters 9 and 13.

Applying a 'presumption'?

The traditional starting point for determining a residence dispute involving a non-parent is Lord Templeman's judgment in *Re KD (A Minor) (Ward: Termination of Access)*.

Re KD (A Minor) (Ward: Termination of Access) [1988] AC 806 (HL), 812

LORD TEMPLEMAN:

The best person to bring up a child is the natural parent. It matters not whether the parent is wise or foolish, rich or poor, educated or illiterate, provided the child's moral and physical health are not endangered. Public authorities cannot improve on nature. Public authorities exercise a supervisory role and interfere to rescue a child when the parental tie is broken by abuse or separation. In terms of the English rule the court decides whether and to what extent the welfare of the child requires that the child shall be protected against harm caused by the parent, including harm which could be caused by the resumption of parental care after separation has broken the parental tie.

Whilst it is clear that the only relevant principle to be applied is the welfare principle, this dictum has generally been interpreted and applied in subsequent case law as amounting to a de facto 'presumption' in favour of the natural parents.[148]

Factors favouring the 'presumption'

Jane Fortin identifies several reasons behind the courts' preference for the biological blood tie in residence disputes.

J. Fortin, 'Re D (Care: Natural Parent Presumption) Is Blood Really Thicker Than Water?', (1999b) 11 *Child and Family Law Quarterly* 435, 437, 442

In the late 1980s and early 1990s, a series of decisions emerged which gave the biological link a far greater significance than before. An analysis of the decisions suggests that this change in approach was particularly influenced by three concerns. First, in 1988 Lord Templeman had provided a stirring reminder of the 'naturalness' of the child-parent relationship. Secondly, there appeared to be anxieties that comparisons between the homes of relatively well-off foster carers and of disadvantaged birth parents would inevitably favour the former, leading to decisions which might be criticised as amounting to 'social engineering'. Thirdly, ideas about children's rights had also started to have some impact on judicial thinking and the concept of children having a 'right' to be brought up by their birth parents conveniently encapsulated the new approach...

[U]nderpinning such a view is the societal assumption that it is 'natural' for a child to be brought up by at least one of his 'natural' parents. Furthermore, there is also the growing view that children gain a great deal from knowing about their genetic origins and that this knowledge should be enhanced, if possible, by their having a social relationship with their biological parents.

---

[148] See also *Re K (A Minor) (Ward: Care and Control)* [1990] 1 WLR 431; *Re D (Care: Natural Parent Presumption)* [1999] 1 FLR 134 and *Re R (A Child) (Residence Order)* [2009] EWCA Civ 358, [116] (Wall LJ).

All of these factors have been evident in the developing case law. For example, *Re K (A Minor) (Ward: Care and Control)* concerned a dispute between the father and the mother's half-sister and her husband ('Mr and Mrs E') with whom the child had lived since the mother's suicide. The Court of Appeal granted residence to the father, stressing that in the case of a residence dispute between a parent and non-parent, the judge was wrong to embark on a straightforward balancing exercise to decide which of the respective parties would be best able to promote the child's welfare. Relying on *Re KD*, the Court of Appeal held that the correct approach was to ask whether the welfare of the child positively demanded that the normal presumption in favour of the natural parent should be displaced. Moreover, any reasons put forward to displace the presumption must, in the words of Waite J, be 'compelling'. The Court of Appeal rationalized their approach on the basis that the natural parent had a 'right' to raise his own child, albeit they identified this parental 'right' with an identical right in the child.

The parent's *right* to residence is given further weight by Article 8 ECHR.[149] The approach of the European Court is clear from *Görgülü v Germany* where the child ('C') had been living with prospective adopters for two years and was therefore securely settled. The European Court found there had been a violation of the father's Article 8 right, the German courts having failed to do enough to rehabilitate the child with his father.

Görgülü v Germany (App No 74969/01, ECHR) (2004)

44. ...[T]he Court of Appeal considered that although the applicant was in a position, together with his wife who had already raised two children, to care for C, granting the applicant custody would not be in C's best interest, as a deep social and emotional bond had evolved between the child and his foster family and a separation from the latter would lead to severe and irreparable psychological damage on the part of the child...

45. The Court is aware that the fact that the applicant and C have at no time lived together may be of relevance when striking a balance between the conflicting rights and interests of the applicant and the rights of Mr and Ms B. and C. The Court recalls its case-law, which postulates that where the existence of a family tie with a child has been established, the State must act in a manner calculated to enable that tie to be developed... Article 8 of the Convention thus imposes on every State the obligation to aim at reuniting a natural parent with his or her child... [T]he Court also notes that effective respect for family life requires that future relations between parent and child not be determined by the mere passage of time...

46. The Court concedes that an instant separation from C's foster family might have had negative effects on his physical and mental condition. However, bearing in mind that the applicant is C's biological parent and undisputedly willing and able to care for him, the Court is not convinced that the Naumburg Court of Appeal examined all possible solutions to the problem. In particular, that court does not appear to have examined whether it would be viable to unify C and the applicant under circumstances that would minimise the strain put on C. Instead, the Court of Appeal apparently only focused on the imminent effects which a separation from his foster parents would have on the child, but failed to consider the long-term effects which a permanent separation from his natural father might have on C. The solution envisaged by the District Court, namely to increase and facilitate contacts between the applicant and C, who would at an initial stage continue to live with his foster family, was seemingly not taken into consideration...

---

149 For more detailed discussion, see Fortin (1999b), 444–5.

The natural parent 'presumption' has also been justified by the need to avoid the dangers of 'social engineering', particularly when the dispute is between a parent and a 'perfect' prospective adopter.[150] The Supreme Court has recently given judgment on the importance of children having a relationship with their natural parents if at all possible in the context of public law child protection proceedings.[151]

Re B (Care Proceedings: Appeal) [2013] UKSC 33

LORD NEUBERGER P:

77. It seems to me to be inherent in section 1(1) that a care order should be a last resort, because the interests of a child would self-evidently require her relationship with her natural parents to be maintained unless no other course was possible in her interests. That is reinforced by the requirement in section 1(3)(g) [of the CA 1989] that the court must consider all options, which carries with it the clear implication that the most extreme option should only be adopted if others would not be in her interests. As to article 8, the Strasbourg court decisions cited by Lady Hale in paras 195–198 make it clear that such an order can only be made in "exceptional circumstances", and that it could only be justified by "overriding requirements pertaining to the child's welfare", or, putting the same point in slightly different words, "by the overriding necessity of the interests of the child". I consider that this is the same as the domestic test...

78. The high threshold to be crossed before a court should make an adoption order against the natural parents' wishes is also clear from UNCRC. Thus, *Hodgkin and Newell, Implementation Handbook for the Convention on the Rights of the Child*, Unicef, 3rd ed (2007), p 296, state that "there is a presumption within the Convention that children's best interests are served by being with their parents wherever possible". This is reflected in UNCRC, which provides in article 7 that a child has "as far as possible, the right to know and be cared for by his or her parents", and in article 9, which requires states to ensure that

"a child shall not be separated from his or her parents against their will, except when competent authorities subject to judicial review determine, in accordance with applicable law and procedures, that such separation is necessary for the best interests of the child".

104. ....Although the child's interests in an adoption case are "paramount" (in the UK legislation and under article 21 of UNCRC), a court must never lose sight of the fact that those interests include being brought up by her natural family, ideally her natural parents, or at least one of them.

LADY HALE:

179. Since well before the Children Act came into force, the courts have recognised that there is a line to be drawn between parents whose personal characteristics mean that they may be less than perfect parents and parents who may cause harm to their children. Lord Templeman put the point this way in his well-known words in *In re KD (A Minor) (Ward: Termination of Access)* [1988] AC 806, 812:

"The best person to bring up a child is the natural parent. It matters not whether the parent is wise or foolish, rich or poor, educated or illiterate, provided the child's moral and physical health are not endangered. Public authorities cannot improve on nature."

---

[150] For early cases addressing this issue, see *Re K (Private Placement for Adoption)* [1991] FCR 142; *Re O (A Minor) (Custody or Adoption)* [1992] 1 FCR 378.

[151] See further extracts from *Re B* at 8.4.4, 12.5.3, and 13.4.3.

If, by that last sentence, Lord Templeman was making a factual statement, then some might disagree: if local authorities remove children from unsatisfactory parents at birth and swiftly place them with highly satisfactory adoptive parents they can undoubtedly improve on nature. But in my view Lord Templeman was making a normative statement: public authorities have no right to improve on nature.

198. ... [I]t is quite clear that the test for severing the relationship between parent and child is very strict: only in exceptional circumstances and where motivated by *overriding requirements* pertaining to the child's welfare, in short, where nothing else will do.

In the private law context, it is worth noting the comments of the Court of Appeal in *Re B (Transfer of Residence to Grandmother)*,[152] which concerned an appeal from the order of the first instance judge transferring residence of a child to the paternal grandmother because of the mother's opposition to contact. In allowing the mother's appeal, Thorpe LJ observed that he knew of no other case in which transfer of residence to a grandparent had been used against an obdurate parent in a dispute about time spent with the grandparent. Of particular interest are the Court of Appeal's observations regarding the general position of grandparents in such disputes, making it clear that '[m]anifestly grandparents are not on an equal footing with parents' and that '[i]nevitably there are disbenefits for a child to be brought up by an adult of a different generation to either of her parents'.[153]

Factors opposing a 'presumption'

Not everyone is convinced by these arguments privileging biological parenting. Fortin, for example, suggests that the argument that children have the right to be raised by their natural parents has, at times, been 'distorted' to further the rights and interests of the parents rather than those of the child.[154] The result is that equally important considerations for the child, such as the potential damage caused to the child's psychological health by disrupting the emotional bonds formed with alternative carers, have been accorded insufficient weight. Fortin questions whether it is right to talk of the child's 'right' to be cared for by his or her natural parents when the child has lived apart from them.[155] In those circumstances she questions whether the 'blood-tie' has any real value to the child and whether, indeed, it would make more sense to talk of the child's right to be cared for by his or her *psychological parents*.[156]

The weight to be accorded to the 'blood-tie' in purely private law disputes between parents was revisited by the House of Lords in *Re G (Children) (Residence: Same-Sex Partner)* and by the Supreme Court in *Re B (A Child)*. These decisions suggest that it is wrong to talk of any 'presumption' in favour of the natural parent. It remains somewhat unclear, however, what weight, if any, should be placed on the significance of the 'blood tie' when determining the best interests of the child.

Re G concerned a residence dispute between a same-sex couple, CG and CW. The children were born to CG as a result of donor insemination (prior to the enactment of the Human

---

152 [2012] EWCA Civ 858.
153 Ibid, [13].
154 Fortin (2009b), 520.
155 Ibid, 518.
156 Ibid, 518 and 524–5.

Fertilisation and Embryology Act 2008 (HFEA 2008)). CW had been fully involved in every aspect of the children's upbringing. In earlier proceedings a shared residence order had been made in favour of both parties to confer parental responsibility on CW; the dispute concerned the sharing of time under that order. The Court of Appeal had held that the children's primary home should be with CW because of CG's obstructive attitude towards contact. The House of Lords reversed that decision. Baroness Hale placed great emphasis on the importance of the biological tie, although she denied that this raised a *presumption* in favour of the 'natural mother'.[157]

Re G (Children) (Residence: Same-Sex Partner) [2006] UKHL 43

BARONESS HALE:

36. Of course, in the great majority of cases, the natural mother combines all three. She is the genetic, gestational and psychological parent. Her contribution to the welfare of the child is unique. The natural father combines genetic and psychological parenthood. His contribution is also unique. In these days when more parents share the tasks of child rearing and breadwinning, his contribution is often much closer to that of the mother than it used to be; but there are still families which divide their tasks on more traditional lines, in which case his contribution will be different and its importance will often increase with the age of the child.

37. But there are also parents who are neither genetic nor gestational, but who have become the psychological parents of the child and thus have an important contribution to make to their welfare. Adoptive parents are the most obvious example, but there are many others. This is the position of CW in this case...

38. ...While CW is their psychological parent, CG is...both their biological and their psychological parent. In the overall welfare judgment, that must count for something in the vast majority of cases. Its significance must be considered and assessed. Furthermore, the evidence shows that it clearly did count for something in this case. These children were happy and doing very well in their mother's home. That should not have been changed without a very good reason.

44. My Lords, I am driven to the conclusion that the courts below have allowed the unusual context of this case to distract them from principles which are of universal application. First, the fact that CG is the natural mother of these children in every sense of that term, while raising no presumption in her favour, is undoubtedly an important and significant factor in determining what will be best for them now and in the future. Yet nowhere is that factor explored in the judgment below...

Although denying the existence of a 'presumption' in favour of the natural parent, Baroness Hale's strong preference for biological over psychological parenting appeared to be clear. To repeat her words, being both the biological and psychological parent 'must count for something'. It is 'undoubtedly an important and significant factor' in determining the welfare of the child.[158] In his short judgment, Lord Nicholls appeared to agree.

---

[157] See further the extracts from *Re G* at 9.2.1
[158] Some commentators were critical of this focus on biology (e.g. Diduck 2007).

LORD NICHOLLS:

2. ... In reaching its decision the court should always have in mind that in the ordinary way the rearing of a child by his or her biological parent can be expected to be in the child's best interests, both in the short term and also, and importantly, in the longer term. I decry any tendency to diminish the significance of this factor. A child should not be removed from the primary care of his or her biological parents without compelling reason. Where such a reason exists the judge should spell this out explicitly.

This decision, whilst explicitly rejecting any notion of a presumption in favour of the natural parent, appeared essentially consistent with existing case law on the importance to be attributed to the genetic or biological tie. However, in the Supreme Court decision of *Re B*, Lord Kerr, giving the judgment of the court, seemed to retreat from a position in which the blood tie would be accorded particular weight in the welfare balance. As we saw earlier, *Re B* concerned a dispute between the maternal grandmother and the father over the residence of four-year-old Harry, who had lived with the grandmother all his life. The Supreme Court expressed concern at the apparent 'misunderstanding' of the true import of *Re G* and the principles to be derived from that judgment.[159] The court reasserted the importance of a 'pure' application of the welfare principle, untrammelled by assumptions about the significance of biological parenthood, observing that the argument that a child had a right to be raised by his or her biological parent could obscure or distort a proper analysis of the child's best interests.

Re B (A Child) [2009] UKSC 5

LORD KERR:

19. The theme that it was preferable for children to be raised by their biological parent or parents was developed by the judge ... He stated that it was the right of the child to be brought up in the home of his or her natural parent. (It is clear from the context that the judge was using the term 'natural parent' to mean 'biological parent'.) We consider that this statement betrays a failure on the part of the judge to concentrate on the factor of overwhelming – indeed, paramount – importance which is, of course, the welfare of the child. To talk in terms of a child's rights – as opposed to his or her best interests – diverts from the focus that the child's welfare should occupy in the minds of those called on to make decisions as to their residence.

20. The distraction that discussion of rights rather than welfare can occasion is well illustrated in the latter part of [the] judgment. [The judge] suggested that, provided the parenting that Harry's father could provide was "good enough", it was of no consequence that that which the grandmother could provide would be better. We consider that in decisions about residence such as are involved in this case; there is no place for the question whether the proposed placement would be "good enough". The court's quest is to determine what is in the best interests of the child, not what might constitute a second best but supposedly adequate

---

[159] For insight into the background to the judgments in *Re G*, see Hale (2014), 30–1. Note in particular Lady Hale's comments that she was 'anxious to produce an opinion with which all the other members of the appellate committee could agree', and that it would have been better to have 'referred to them both as mothers, rather than to one as the mother and the other as the other parent'.

alternative. As the Court of Appeal pointed out . . . the concept of 'good enough' parenting has always been advanced in the context of public law proceedings and of care within the wider family as opposed to care by strangers . . .

34. [In reliance on a passage from Lord Nicholls' judgment in *Re G*], the justices stated that a child should not be removed from the primary care of biological parents. A careful reading of what Lord Nicholls actually said reveals, of course, that he did not propound any general rule to that effect. For a proper understanding of the view that he expressed, it is important at the outset to recognise that Lord Nicholls' comment about the rearing of a child by a biological parent is set firmly in the context of the child's welfare. This he identified as "the court's paramount consideration". It must be the dominant and overriding factor that ultimately determines disputes about residence and contact and there can be no dilution of its importance by reference to extraneous matters.

35. When Lord Nicholls said that courts should keep in mind that the interests of a child will normally be best served by being reared by his or her biological parent, he was doing no more than reflecting common experience that, in general, children tend to thrive when brought up by parents to whom they have been born. He was careful to qualify his state-ment, however, by the words "*in the ordinary way* the rearing of a child by his or her bio-logical parent can be expected to be in the child's best interests" (emphasis added). In the ordinary way one can expect that children will do best with their biological parents. But many disputes about residence and contact do not follow the ordinary way. Therefore, although one should keep in mind the common experience to which Lord Nicholls was refer-ring, one must not be slow to recognise those cases where that common experience does not provide a reliable guide . . .

37. . . . All consideration of the importance of parenthood in private law disputes about resi-dence must be firmly rooted in an examination of what is in the child's best interests. This is the paramount consideration. It is only as a contributor to the child's welfare that parenthood assumes any significance. In common with all other factors bearing on what is in the best interests of the child, it must be examined for its potential to fulfil that aim.

The Supreme Court thus seems to have 'downgraded' biological parenthood from a factor of undoubted importance and significance (*Re G*), to just one more factor to be taken into account in the welfare balance, its weight to be determined on the individual facts of each case. How this decision fits with the renewed focus on a child's birth family in care proceed-ings is unclear.

11.6.8 EFFECT OF A CHILD ARRANGEMENTS ORDER WHICH DETERMINES LIVING ARRANGEMENTS

Conferring parental responsibility

A child arrangements order which determines a child's living arrangements has a number of important subsidiary legal effects, the most important of which is that it confers parental responsibility on the person holding the order. Unlike other cases where a person has or obtains parental responsibility, parental responsibility acquired in this way lasts only as long as the relevant part of the order is in force.[160]

---

[160] See 10.3.5.

Imposing certain restrictions

Whilst a child arrangements order which deals with a child's living arrangements is in force, certain restrictions are imposed on those holding parental responsibility.

Children Act 1989, s 13

(1) Where a child arrangements order to which subsection (4) applies is in force with respect to a child, no person may—

    (a) cause the child to be known by a new surname; or

    (b) remove him from the United Kingdom;

without either the written consent of every person who has parental responsibility for the child or the leave of the court.

(2) Subsection 1(b) does not prevent the removal of a child, for a period of less than one month, by a person named in the child arrangements order as a person with whom the child is to live.

(3) In making a child arrangements order to which subsection (4) applies the court may grant the leave required by subsection 1(b), either generally or for specified purposes.

(4) This subsection applies to a child arrangements order if the arrangements regulated by the order consist of, or include, arrangements which relate to either or both of the following—

    (a) with whom the child concerned is to live, and

    (b) when the child is to live with any person.

In many ways, s 13 is redundant as it is clear that a parent cannot remove a child from the jurisdiction[161] or change the child's surname[162] without the consent of everyone with parental responsibility, whether or not a relevant child arrangements order is in force. Where a relevant child arrangements order is in force, the applicant can either apply for leave under s 13(1) or apply for a specific issue order under s 8.[163] If no order is in force, the application must be brought under s 8. Either way, in determining the application, the child's welfare will be the paramount consideration. Technically, the welfare checklist applies only to s 8, not s 13,[164] but it has been made clear that this anomaly will have no substantive effect.[165]

Leave to remove from the jurisdiction

This issue is dealt with below.[166]

---

[161] Child Abduction Act 1984, s 1.

[162] *Dawson v Wearmouth* [1999] 2 AC 308.

[163] It has been suggested by George (2008b) that this view that there are two routes is based on a misunderstanding of the wording of the CA 1989; for detailed discussion of this jurisdictional issue, see Gilmore (2004c), 376–8.

[164] S 1(4).

[165] *Dawson v Wearmouth* [1998] Fam 75, 80–2, aff'd on other grounds [1999] 2 AC 308; *Payne v Payne* [2001] EWCA Civ 166, [33].

[166] See 11.9.

Changing the child's surname

The principles to be applied in determining a dispute over a child's surname were summarized by Butler-Sloss LJ in *Re W (A Child) (Illegitimate Child: Change of Surname)*.

Re W (A Child) (Illegitimate Child: Change of Surname) [2001] Fam 1 (CA)

BUTLER-SLOSS LJ:

9. The present position, in summary, would appear to be as follows.

(a) If parents are married they both have the power and the duty to register their child's names.

(b) If they are not married the mother has the sole duty and power to do so.

(c) After registration of the child's names, the grant of a residence order obliges any person wishing to change the surname to obtain the leave of the court or the written consent of all those who have parental responsibility.

(d) In the absence of a residence order, the person wishing to change the surname from the registered name ought to obtain the relevant written consent or the leave of the court by making an application for a specific issue order.

(e) On any application, the welfare of the child is paramount, and the judge must have regard to the s 1(3) criteria.

(f) Among the factors to which the court should have regard is the registered surname of the child and the reasons for the registration, for instance recognition of the biological link with the child's father. Registration is always a relevant and an important consideration but it is not in itself decisive. The weight to be given to it by the court will depend upon the other relevant factors or valid countervailing reasons which may tip the balance the other way.

(g) The relevant considerations should include factors which may arise in the future as well as the present situation.

(h) Reasons given for changing or seeking to change a child's name based on the fact that the child's name is or is not the same as the parent making the application do not generally carry much weight.

(i) The reasons for an earlier unilateral decision to change a child's name may be relevant.

(j) Any changes of circumstances of the child since the original registration may be relevant.

(k) In the case of a child whose parents were married to each other, the fact of the marriage is important and I would suggest that there would have to be strong reasons to change the name from the father's surname if the child was so registered.

(l) Where the child's parents were not married to each other, the mother has control over registration. Consequently on an application to change the surname of the child, the degree of commitment of the father to the child, the quality of contact, if it occurs, between father and child, the existence or absence of parental responsibility are all relevant factors to take into account.

The Court of Appeal has recently reiterated the value of these guidelines, while emphasizing that the factors identified by Butler-Sloss LJ should not be seen as a straitjacket because ultimately '[t]he test is welfare, pure and simple'.[167]

---

[167] *Re W (Children) (Change of Name)* [2013] EWCA Civ 1488, [13]. For an example of a change of surname case where the mother sought to protect the children from the effects of detrimental material

11.7 CHILD ARRANGEMENTS ORDERS: SPENDING TIME AND OTHERWISE HAVING CONTACT WITH PEOPLE

Child arrangements orders which are not about the people with whom a child is to live can take various forms, differing as to both quantity and quality. They can involve spending time directly with someone (face-to-face) and/or having indirect contact (e.g. having Skype or phone contact, or sending letters, emails, cards, or presents) and may take place according to a strictly regulated regime or on a more informal, ad hoc basis. Where there are particular concerns about the child's safety or general welfare, spending time or having contact may be 'supported' or more closely 'supervised' by a third party, often at designated contact centres.[168] The courts have wide powers under s 11(7) to attach conditions to the order or make detailed directions as to how it is to be carried out.[169] Disputes about these orders are often amongst the most bitter, protracted, and difficult in family law. Due in large part to the campaign of fathers' rights groups, there have been many important changes to the law and changes to the way in which such disputes are tackled. However, the polarized and overly simplistic way in which the issue has been portrayed in the media may well have led to many important factors in these disputes being marginalized or ignored.

11.7.1 A 'PRESUMPTION' IN FAVOUR OF ORDERS TO SPEND TIME OR HAVE CONTACT?

The courts' approach

As a matter pertaining to the 'upbringing' of the child, the paramountcy principle applies to an application for spending time or having contact. If the application is opposed, the welfare checklist must be considered.[170] However, whilst the statutory framework for resolving such disputes previously contained no *legal* presumption in favour of contact, the new s 1(2A) of the CA 1989 specifies that there is a presumption of parental *involvement* in the child's life, so long as the parent can be involved in the child's life without putting the child at risk of suffering harm. Whether this statutory change will make any practical difference is difficult to judge, because (as the government acknowledged before introducing the new presumption) the courts have applied a strong de facto presumption in favour of parents having an ongoing relationship for many years.[171]

The courts' approach has been articulated in various ways. Some early cases conceptualized it as a *right* of the child to contact with the non-resident parent, albeit that right may have to give way to welfare considerations.

which the father published about them and the mother online, see *Re F (Children: Contact, Name, Parental Responsibility)* [2014] EWFC 42.

168 For the difference between 'supported' and 'supervised' contact, see CASC (2001), 3.18–3.19.
169 *Re O (A Minor) (Contact: Indirect Contact)* [1996] 1 FCR 317.
170 S 1(3)–(4).
171 Bailey-Harris et al (1999b), 114–15; Gilmore (2008).

M v M (Child: Access) [1973] 2 All ER 81 (Fam Div), 85

WRANGHAM J:

[T]he companionship of a parent is in any ordinary circumstances of such immense value to the child that there is a basic right in him to such companionship. I for my part would prefer to call it a basic right in the child rather than a basic right in the parent. That only means this, that no court should deprive a child of access to either parent unless it is wholly satisfied that it is in the interests of that child that access should cease, and that is a conclusion at which a court should be extremely slow to arrive.

This rights-based approach is enshrined in the United Nations Convention on the Rights of the Child.

United Nations Convention on the Rights of the Child 1989, Article 9

(3) States Parties shall respect the right of the child who is separated from one or both parents to maintain personal relations and direct contact with both parents on a regular basis, except if it is contrary to the child's best interests.

The parent may also claim a corresponding right to contact, and this issue clearly falls within the scope of the right to respect for family life under Article 8 ECHR.[172] However, at least at the level of rhetoric, the English courts have been at pains to make clear that insofar as it makes sense to talk of rights in this context, the right is that of the child and not the parent. The Human Rights Act 1998 did not change this basic approach.[173]

In preference to the rights-based approach, more recently the courts have tended to conceptualize the 'presumption' in favour of contact as a straightforward application of the welfare principle albeit the courts take as their starting point that the benefits of contact with a non-residential parent can be *assumed*. The courts have emphasized that a long-term view should be taken of the child's best interests and that they should not be unduly concerned about any temporary or short-term distress to the child.[174]

The absence of any requirement to adduce positive evidence of the benefits of contact means that contact is one issue where, although conceptually very different,[175] *in practice* the rights-based and welfare-based approaches are unlikely to lead to a substantive difference in approach or outcome.[176] The courts' strong predisposition to order contact was made

---

[172] See, e.g., *Hokkanen v Finland* (App No 32346/96, ECHR) (1996) and *Glaser v United Kingdom* (App No 32346/96, ECHR) (2000). For an illustration of the difference between a rights-based approach and a welfare-based approach, see *Sahin v Germany; Sommerfeld v Germany* (App No 30943/96, ECHR) (2003), [79]–[95] where the European Court held that it constituted discrimination under Art 14 to apply a rights-based approach to married fathers but a welfare-based approach to unmarried fathers. See also Herring (1999a), 234–5.

[173] *Re H (Children) (Contact Order) (No 2)* [2001] 3 FCR 385.

[174] See, e.g., *Re M (Contact: Long-Term Best Interests)* [2005] EWCA Civ 1090.

[175] Herring (1999a), 230–2.

[176] *Re L (A Child) (Contact: Domestic Violence)* [2001] Fam 260, 294.

clear in *Re O (A Minor) (Contact: Indirect Contact)*, which is still regarded as the leading authority.[177]

Re O (A Minor) (Contact: Indirect Contact) [1996] 1 FCR 317 (CA), 323–7

BINGHAM MR:

It may perhaps be worth stating in a reasonably compendious way some very familiar but nonetheless fundamental principles. First of all, and overriding all else as provided in s. 1(1) of the 1989 Act, the welfare of the child is the paramount consideration of any court concerned to make an order relating to the upbringing of a child. It cannot be emphasized too strongly that the court is concerned with the interests of the mother and the father only in so far as they bear on the welfare of the child.

Second, where parents of a child are separated and the child is in the day-to-day care of one of them, it is almost always in the interests of the child that he or she should have contact with the other parent. The reason for this scarcely needs spelling out. It is, of course, that the separation of parents involves a loss to the child, and it is desirable that that loss should so far as possible be made good by contact with the non-custodial parent, that is the parent in whose day-to-day care the child is not...

Fourth, cases do, unhappily and infrequently but occasionally, arise in which a court is compelled to conclude that in existing circumstances an order for immediate direct contact should not be ordered, because so to order would injure the welfare of the child...The courts should not at all readily accept that the child's welfare will be injured by direct contact. Judging that question the court should take a medium-term and long-term view of the child's development and not accord excessive weight to what appear likely to be short-term or transient problems...

Fifth, in cases in which, for whatever reason, direct contact cannot for the time being be ordered, it is ordinarily highly desirable that there should be indirect contact so that the child grows up knowing of the love and interest of the absent parent with whom, in due course, direct contact should be established....

The caring parent also has reciprocal obligations. If the caring parent puts difficulties in the way of indirect contact by withholding presents of [sic] letters or failing to read letters to a child who cannot read, then such parent must understand that the court can compel compliance with its orders; it has sanctions available and no residence order is to be regarded as irrevocable. It is entirely reasonable that the parent with the care of the child should be obliged to report on the progress of the child to the absent parent for the obvious reason that an absent parent cannot correspond in a meaningful way if unaware of the child's concerns...

[T]he truth is that the mother is subject to an enforceable duty to promote contact where the court judges that contact will promote the welfare of the child.

The resident parent's *duty* to promote contact with the non-resident parent has become a central feature of the contact debate.

In *Re M (Minors) (Contact)*, Wilson J attempted to re-focus the courts' attention on the welfare test, and the s 1(3) criteria in particular, and rejected counsel's submission

---

[177] See, e.g., *Re W (Direct Contact)* [2012] EWCA Civ 999, [37], describing *Re O* as 'the definitive exposition of the relevant principles'.

that the circumstances must be 'wholly exceptional' to defeat the presumption in favour of contact.

Re M (Minors) (Contact) [1995] 1 FCR 753 (Fam Div), 758

WILSON J:

I personally find it helpful to cast the principles into the framework of the check-list of considerations set out in s. 1(3) of the Children Act 1989 and to ask whether the fundamental emotional need of every child to have an enduring relationship with both his parents (s. 1(3)(b)) is outweighed by the depth of harm which, in the light *inter alia* of his wishes and feelings (s. 1(3)(a)), this child would be at risk of suffering (s. 1(3)(e)) by virtue of a contact order.

Although cited with approval by the Court of Appeal in *Re L (A Child) (Contact: Domestic Violence)*,[178] Wilson J's attempt to return to a 'purer' application of the welfare test has not proved persuasive. The courts have continued to reiterate that 'it is almost always in the interests of the child to have contact with the parent with whom the child is not living, has been approached by judges, both before and since the decision in *Re O*, as requiring the presence of "cogent reasons" for departing from that general principle'.[179]

Although the presumption in favour of contact is undoubtedly strongest in the postdivorce context, it has been consistently applied to unmarried fathers. In line with the growing importance generally attached to the father–child relationship, the inherent value of maintaining a relationship between children and their fathers through contact has generally been accepted. At one time, there appeared to be some distinction drawn between cases in which the father has an established, meaningful relationship with the child, so the question is one of *maintaining* an existing relationship, and cases where the applicant is in effect seeking to *establish* a *new* relationship.[180] However, in practice, the distinction appears to have carried very little weight.

R. Bailey-Harris, J. Barron, and J. Pearce, 'From Utility to Rights? The Presumption of Contact in Practice', (1999b) 13 *International Journal of Law, Policy and the Family* 111, 117–19

[S]ome of the case law demonstrates the courts' willingness to *establish* a relationship which was tenuous in the first place or which has been interrupted for a considerable period... Many district judges apparently have an unquestioning belief that contact will always be in the best interests of the children; hence they tend automatically to try to re-establish contact, even after a long break or where the parent has had no opportunity to form any kind of relationship with a very young child, and when there is no certainty that the absent parent will be consistent in maintaining contact in future. This practice holds

---

[178] [2001] Fam 260, 274. In his judgment Thorpe LJ expressed a preference for an 'assumption' rather than a 'presumption' in favour of contact.

[179] *Re W (Direct Contact)* [2012] EWCA Civ 999, [39].

[180] See, e.g., Thorpe LJ in *Re L (A Child) (Contact: Domestic Violence)* [2001] Fam 260, 294–5.

despite the lack of evidence that this will be for the child's good and even when the child exhibits signs of considerable distress before, during or after contact. It can be interpreted as indicating the court's conception of its duty as one of establishing, rather than simply maintaining, contact.

Indeed, more recently it has been said that the effect of the judgments of the European Court of Human Rights,[181] as well as the growing domestic jurisprudence, is that courts must take positive action both to maintain and to restore contact.

Re C (Direct Contact: Suspension) [2011] EWCA Civ 521

MUNBY LJ:

47. ... There is a positive obligation on the State, and therefore on the judge, to take measures to maintain and to reconstitute the relationship between parent and child, in short, to maintain or restore contact. The judge has a positive duty to attempt to promote contact. The judge must grapple with all the available alternatives before abandoning hope of achieving some contact. He must be careful not to come to a premature decision, for contact is to be stopped only as a last resort and only once it has become clear that the child will not benefit from continuing the attempt. ...

Is the 'presumption' in favour of spending time and having contact well-founded?

Fathers

The consensus across various disciplines about the importance of spending time and having contact with both parents is remarkable. Research by Bailey-Harris et al suggests it is extremely rare for the benefits of contact with the child's *father* to be questioned by any of the professionals involved in a case.[182] Successive governments have been equally committed to the 'contact is good' mantra.

DFE and MOJ, *Co-operative Parenting Following Family Separation: Proposed Legislation on the Involvement of Both Parents in a Child's Life* (London: TSO, 2012)

3.2 The majority of parents who separate reach their own agreements about the care arrangements for their children, and many manage this in a co-operative way, taking account of the child's needs. When disputes about these arrangements arise, however, there is a risk that children's needs are overlooked. Whether courts are involved or not, in too many cases one parent is left in a position where it is very hard to retain a strong and influential relationship with his or her child. This can result in children losing contact completely with

---

[181] See, e.g., *Kosmopoulou v Greece* (App No 60457/00, ECHR) (2004); *Kopf v Austria* (App No 1598/06, ECHR) (2012).

[182] Bailey-Harris et al (1999b), 118.

one parent (usually the father), often with a lasting impact on their lives. The Government firmly believes that parents who are able and willing to play a positive role in their child's care should have the opportunity to do so. The aim of the legislative amendment is also to reinforce the expectation at societal level that both parents are jointly responsible for their children's upbringing.

The evidential base on which this unwavering faith in the value of contact is founded is, however, open to question. For example, Bailey-Harris et al suggest that the current consensus on contact is based on little more than 'self-reinforcing professional received wisdom'.

R. Bailey-Harris, J. Barron, and J. Pearce, 'From Utility to Rights? The Presumption of Contact in Practice', (1999b) 13 *International Journal of Law, Policy and the Family* 111, 117–19

[O]ur overall conclusion was that the various professionals involved supported each other in a somewhat circular and self-confirming fashion. Contact is presumed to be for the good of the child—but no evidence has been produced to demonstrate this. Solicitors nevertheless advise their clients to accede to contact because that is what the courts expect. The judges order contact because no one really opposes it—so if they do they are being 'unreasonable' and not listening to the advice of their solicitors. Court welfare officers (who, of all the professionals, are beginning to develop doubts about the 'automatic' pro-contact presumption) nonetheless know that they need to make their arguments all the stronger if they are to persuade the court against ordering contact in any particular case. One district judge told us that the reason for emphasis on 'contact at (almost) any cost' is the belief that the higher courts would overrule a refusal of contact. Thus the rights/rule approach to the determination of contact disputes has become entrenched through the cumulative effect of self-reinforcing professional received wisdom.

Thorpe LJ has recognized the importance of the courts only proceeding on the basis of the best available expert evidence.

Re L (A Child) (Contact: Domestic Violence) [2001] Fam 260 (CA), 295

THORPE LJ:

The assumption that contact benefits the child cannot be derived from legal precedent or principle. It must find its foundation in the theory and practice of the mental health professions. Perhaps the largest single ingredient of a child's welfare is health, giving that word a broad definition to encompass physical, emotional and psychological development and well-being. So both judicial general assumption and judicial assessment of welfare in the individual case are to be derived from the expertise of mental health professionals whose training and practice has centred on the development needs and vulnerability of children. So for me the proposition that children benefit from contact with the parent with whom they no longer live must be drawn from current opinion shared by the majority of mental health professionals.

Qualified support for the prevailing judicial approach was indeed provided in *Re L* in the form of an expert psychiatric report co-authored by Dr Claire Sturge and Dr Danya Glaser.[183] The report was widely disseminated and provides some general support for the courts' pro-contact stance. However, whilst the report points to a number of factors in favour of contact, it does not provide unqualified support for the current pro-contact culture. The report makes it clear that each case must be considered on its own particular merits with the welfare of the individual child as the core consideration. It therefore provides no support for the sweeping presumption in favour of contact that has been typical of the courts' approach. The report also identified a number of specific risks attaching to both direct and indirect contact.

Re L (A Child) (Contact: Domestic Violence) [2001] Fam 260 (CA), 269

BUTLER-SLOSS P:

The overall risk was that of failing to meet and actually undermining the child's developmental needs or even causing emotional abuse and damage directly through contact or as a consequence of the contact. Specifically that included: escalating the climate of conflict around the child which would undermine the child's general stability and sense of emotional well being. The result was a tug of loyalty and a sense of responsibility for the conflict in all children except young babies which affected the relationships of the child with both parents. There might be direct abusive experiences, including emotional abuse by denigration of the child or the child's resident carer. There might be continuation of unhealthy relationships such as dominant or bullying relationships, those created by fear, bribes or emotional blackmail, by undermining the child's sense of stability and continuity by deliberately or inadvertently setting different moral standards or standards of behaviour, by little interest in the child himself or by unstimulating or uninteresting contact. They indicated a series of situations where there were risks to contact: where there were unresolved situations, where the contact was unreliable and the child frequently let down, where the child was attending contact against his wishes so he felt undermined, where there was little prospect for change such as wholly implacable situations, where there was the stress on the child and resident carer of ongoing proceedings or frequently re-initiated proceedings.

The commitment of successive governments to contact has been driven by wider social and political concerns. For example, the Green Paper preceding the Children and Adoption Act 2006 (CAA 2006) focused on the social 'dangers' of lone, as opposed to shared, parenting, emphasizing the poor educational and social outcomes for children who experience loss of contact with the non-resident parent post-separation. Similarly, the assumption underpinning the consultation paper leading to the CFA 2014 continued this theme.[184] However, the evidence suggesting children of separated parents are socially and educationally disadvantaged is controversial. In particular, the assumption that loss of contact is the principal cause of these problems is highly questionable,[185] with

---

[183] Sturge and Glaster (2000).
[184] DFE and MOJ (2012).
[185] Rhoades (2002), 81.

the social and economic difficulties often associated with family breakdown undoubt-edly a major factor.[186]

Recent research with young people who, as children, went through parental separation, sheds light on how children themselves experience different contact arrangements.

J. Fortin, J. Hunt, and L. Scanlan, *Taking a Longer View of Contact: The Perspectives of Young Adults Who Experienced Parental Separation in their Youth: Summary* (University of Sussex/University of Oxford, 2012), 4–5

The importance of retaining a relationship with both parents

Our respondents saw contact between children and their non-resident parents as being vitally important in principle... This was considered to be the case even amongst those who had never had any contact themselves and those whose own experience of contact had not been particularly happy....

But despite this view that contact was immensely important, for many this was a principled answer to a theoretical question which had no reality in their own lives. Many chose to termi-nate unsatisfactory contact when they felt able to do so, Furthermore, there was overwhelm-ing agreement that there were circumstances, such as an abusive parent/child relationship, where contact should never take place. There was also a strong view that contact should not start or continue if it did not promote the child's best interests and that no contact was better than bad contact.

The ingredients for successful contact

Our findings showed that for contact to be successful it needs to be continuous. Respondents who had had unbroken contact throughout their childhood were most likely to rate their con-tact in positive terms. Responsibility for contact not happening at all or not being regularly maintained was very largely attributed to the non-resident parent, and typically explained in terms of that parent's lack of commitment to the child....

One of the most striking findings of the study was the importance of the pre-separation relation-ship between the child and the parent who subsequently became non-resident. Where relation-ships had been very close contact was most likely to be both continuous and a positive experience for the child. The foundations of successful contact, then, are laid down pre-separation.

Respondents were also more likely to rate their experience of contact with the non-resident parent as being positive if the following factors were present: the parents involved their children in the decision-making; there was little or no post-separation conflict between the parents; there was no domestic violence or serious concerns about the care the non-resident parent could provide; the resident parent encouraged the relationship between the child and the non-resident parent; the non-resident parent made time for the child; the child felt equally at home in both the resident and non-resident parent's homes; the non-resident parent either did not re-partner or the child got on well with their new partner.

Non-parents

The assumed value of contact between a parent and the child is not applied to relationships with other family members, no matter how significant. The courts have been fairly consistent

---

[186] Gilmore (2006); Mooney, Oliver, and Smith (2009).

in refusing to apply a 'presumption' in favour of contact with members of the extended family, such as siblings, step-parents, or grandparents. In these cases a 'pure' unfettered application of the welfare principle is followed,[187] though the courts more recently have appeared unconcerned about making contact orders which preserve existing relationships between children and non-parents. For example, in *Re R (Parental Responsibility)*,[188] Peter Jackson J refused to make a parental responsibility order but did order continuing contact every other weekend between a boy aged four and a man who had initially thought he was the father, but who was in fact not genetically related to the child at all.

Same-sex couples and the 'other parent'

A particularly difficult issue for the courts has been whether, and how, to recognize a relationship between a child and a person (usually a man) who has provided genetic material leading to that child's birth, but where the child was always intended to be raised by a same-sex couple (usually two women). While the courts sometimes refer to the person concerned as the 'father' of the child, this terminology is controversial for some, given its implications of a child-raising function in cases where, on one view, the man's intended role was often more akin to a sperm donor.[189] On the other hand, Black LJ has suggested that the term 'donor' might be inappropriate when the man's identity was known, since it 'is capable of conveying the impression that the father is giving his child away and that is misleading'.[190]

While the courts have been addressing these cases for some time, they are still seen as 'new territory', and the Court of Appeal has declined to issue any specific guidance on them.[191] In the leading case of *A v B and C (Contact: Alternative Families)*, Black LJ encouraged parties entering into such arrangement to make their intentions as clear as possible at the outset, but stressed that agreement neither could nor should be determinative: 'Biology, human nature and the hand of fate are liable to undermine it and to confound their expectations. Circumstances change and adjustments must be made. And above all, what must dictate is the welfare of the child and not the interests of the adults'.[192] However, given the inherent lack of certainty in the meaning of 'the welfare of the child',[193] it could be said that the Court of Appeal was simply begging the question with this approach. The very dispute is whether a child's welfare is better served by having a clear, stable 'nuclear family' with the couple who intended to be his or her parents and to the potential exclusion of the male biological progenitor, or by having a relationship with that man which is legally recognized and protected in the face of opposition from the primary carers.

Despite this controversy, it seems increasingly that the courts are willing to promote relationships between the child and the male progenitor in the face of opposition from the same-sex couple who had intended to be the child's only parents. Baker J's decision in *Re G (Sperm Donor: Contact Order); Re Z (Sperm Donor: Contact Order)* is one such case.[194] The case concerned a dispute between the lesbian co-parents of a child (civil partners 'D' and 'E') and the 'known sperm donor father' ('S'). S wanted to have a 'father-like' relationship

---

[187] See *Re S (Contact: Application by Sibling)* [1999] Fam 283 (siblings); *Re H (A Minor) (Contact)* [1994] 2 FCR 419 (step-father); *Re H (A Child)* [2014] EWCA Civ 271 (grandmother).

[188] [2011] EWHC 1535.

[189] See, e.g., Zanghellini (2012), 477.

[190] *A v B and C (Contact: Alternative Families)* [2012] EWCA Civ 285, [48].

[191] Ibid.

[192] Ibid, [44].

[193] See 8.2.2.

[194] [2013] EWHC 134.

with the child. D and E's position was that there were 'three cardinal points' of the arrangement they had entered into: S was to have no parental title, no parental responsibility, and no financial commitment—he was to be known to the child as no more than a friend of the parents.

In accordance with the terms of s 42(1) of the HFEA 2008, D and E were deemed the child's legal parents, entered as such on the birth certificate, and enjoyed shared parental responsibility. S thus had no legal status in relation to the child (as confirmed in s 45(1) of the HFEA 2008) and thus required the leave of the court under s 10(9) to make a s 8 application for contact. The court's judgment is notable not just for its clarification of the correct principles to be applied on an application for leave but also for its developing jurisprudence on alternative families, particularly in a context such as this where the known sperm donor has no legal status as 'father'. Significantly, the court held that the sperm donor's lack of legal status as 'father' was not to be determinative of whether or not he should be allowed to develop a social or psychological relationship with the child and leave to make the contact application should therefore be granted. It is important to note on the facts of this case that S had enjoyed fairly regular contact with the child from birth and, moreover, S and his partner, T, had enjoyed significant contact with the child's older sibling, of whom S was the legal father pursuant to a similar donor agreement with D and E which had been entered into prior to the HFEA reforms on legal parenthood. Nonetheless, the case is striking in that Baker J was willing to allow the case to proceed to a full hearing about the biological father's role in the child's life, despite the law's determination as to legal parenthood.[195]

11.7.2 DISPLACING THE 'PRESUMPTION'

Even where the courts apply a 'presumption' in favour of spending time or having contact, individual welfare considerations are not redundant. Whether one approaches the issue from a rights-based or welfare-based perspective, the burden is placed on the parent opposing contact to adduce positive evidence as to why it should not take place. As it was put by Butler-Sloss LJ in *Re R (A Minor) (Contact: Biological Father)*, 'there are cases where serious risk factors are identified which form cogent reasons why there should not be contact between the father or mother and the child and those cogent reasons are sufficient to displace the general proposition of continuing contact'.[196]

Several factors are identified in the case law as *potentially* constituting a 'cogent reason' for displacing the presumption in favour of contact. Thorpe LJ has provided a tentative list.

Re L (A Child) (Contact: Domestic Violence) [2001] Fam 260 (CA), 300

THORPE LJ:

[T]he factors that may offset the assumption in favour of contact are probably too legion to be either listed or categorised. Abuse must form the largest compartment: as well as physical abuse of the other parent and/or a child there is equally sexual and emotional abuse within the family. Then there is the self-abuse of either drugs or alcohol and the failure to maintain sexual boundaries appropriate to the development of the child. Additionally mental illness or

---

[195] For comment, see Zanghellini (2012), Smith (2013), Bremner (2014).
[196] [1993] 2 FLR 762.

personality disorder may be a dominant factor as may malign motives prompting the applicant to pursue a seemingly justifiable application for the covert purpose of threatening or
dominating the primary carer.

The more controversial of these factors are considered below.

Implacable hostility of the residential carer

The courts have engaged in a lot of 'hard talking' on the problem of the so-called 'implacably
hostile' or 'intransigent' mother.[197] It is clear that the hostility of the residential parent, usually the mother, is not, without more, justification for refusing contact.

Re A (Intractable Contact Dispute) [2013] EWCA Civ 1104

McFARLANE LJ:

39. Where, as in the present case, there is an intractable contact dispute, the authorities indicate that the court should be very reluctant to allow the implacable hostility of
one parent to deter it from making a contact order where the child's welfare otherwise
requires it (*Re J (A Minor) (Contact)* [1994] 1 FLR 729). In such a case contact should only
be refused where the court is satisfied that there is a serious risk of harm if contact were
to be ordered (*Re D (Contact: Reasons for Refusal)* [1997] 2 FLR 48). ...Further, in *Re J*,
where contact was refused in order to avoid placing the child in a situation of stress as a
result of the mother's implacable hostility to contact, Balcombe LJ rightly acknowledged
that affording paramount consideration to the child's welfare may, in some cases, produce an outcome which is seen as 'an injustice' from the perspective of the excluded
parent...

In other cases, the court has emphasized that, despite the mother's hostility, it should not be
assumed that she will not obey the court's orders.[198] However, in many cases, the mother's
intention to disobey is patently clear. In such circumstances, the courts have held that they
will not 'abdicate their responsibility' by capitulating to such 'threats'. The order, if in the
child's interests, will still be made,[199] and a 'robust' response is to be expected.[200] Mothers
who are regarded as 'implacably hostile' may be directed or ordered to attend classes or
counselling aimed at persuading them to cooperate.[201]

In some cases the mother's 'hostility' is more accurately described as 'fear' or 'anxiety'.
Indeed, this fear or anxiety, even if lacking a rational basis, may be so strong that ordering contact will cause such enormous distress that the mother's ability to care for the
child will be compromised. It is accepted that in such extreme cases, provided the mother's fears and anxiety are genuine, an order for contact may well be inimical to the child's

---

[197] 'Implacable hostility' is used to mean opposition to contact which has no reasonable basis, and
does not apply where a parent opposes contact for objectively good reasons: see *Re D (Contact: Reasons for
Refusal)* [1997] 2 FLR 48.

[198] *Re H (A Minor) (Contact)* [1994] 2 FCR 419.

[199] *Re W (A Minor) (Contact)* [1994] 2 FLR 441.

[200] *Re A (Children)* [2009] EWCA Civ 1141, [21]. On the courts' responses to such cases, see below.

[201] Ss 11A–11G.

interests.[202] Similarly, where the mother's opposition is such that the child, acutely aware of his mother's anxiety and distress, is being placed in an impossibly stressful position, contact should not be ordered. In *Re L (Contact: Genuine Fear)*, the father had a history of serious violence (including stabbing his former wife) which the mother claimed had persisted throughout their relationship. She vehemently opposed contact, having developed what the judge described as a 'phobic disorder' with respect to the father. Somewhat surprisingly given the facts, the judge found her fears were genuine but had no rational basis. He nevertheless dismissed the father's application for direct contact, making an order for indirect contact instead.

There will also, of course, be many cases where the mother's deeply held fears over contact are based on reasonable concerns about the father's behaviour. The courts have therefore recognized the importance of distinguishing between cases of 'intransigence' or 'implacable hostility' and cases where the hostility arises from legitimate concern.[203] Whether judges have sustained this distinction in practice is, however, fiercely disputed. Indeed, feminist scholars have criticized the courts for perpetuating the 'myth' of the 'selfish', 'irresponsible' mother by marginalizing genuine and reasonably held fears over contact. In the current climate, it is argued that, if *any* opposition to contact is simply dismissed as 'unreasonable' and mothers who resist contact classed as 'deviant', mothers and children who are vulnerable may be placed at heightened risk of abuse.[204]

Domestic violence

The stereotype of the 'selfish' intransigent mother has proved particularly contentious where there is a history of domestic violence between the parties. Rhoades argues that the 'image of the self-interested "no-contact mother" has helped to obscure the extent to which the child's right to contact provides abusive men with litigation-based tools for harassing the child's carer'.[205] In her view, such is the strength of the dominant welfare discourse that 'father absence' is widely regarded as a much greater social problem than domestic violence. Thus, she says, the usual dispute over spending time or having contact turns into a 'hostile mother/thwarted father problem and only exceptionally a protective mother/harmful father problem'.[206] Adrienne Barnett agrees, arguing that such is the dominance of the pro-contact culture that women are frightened to raise issues of domestic violence for fear of being labelled a hostile or intransigent mother.[207]

Until recently, judicial attitudes towards domestic violence have given more than sufficient grounds for concern. *Williams v Williams* provides a striking example of how the courts previously minimized the effects of domestic violence on both the mother and child and tended to regard a history of abuse as irrelevant to the issue of contact. It was found on the evidence that there had been violence during the marriage, some witnessed by the children.

---

[202] *B v A (Illegitimate Children: Access)* (1982) 3 FLR 27.
[203] *Re D (Contact: Reasons for Refusal)* [1997] 2 FLR 48; *Re P (Minors) (Contact: Discretion)* [1999] 1 FCR 566.
[204] Kaganas (2013).
[205] Rhoades (2002), 77.
[206] Ibid, 83.
[207] Barnett (2000), 142–3; see also Kaganas (2013).

Williams v Williams [1985] FLR 509 (CA), 512–13

DUNN LJ:

If these children are denied any contact with their father during their minority, and not only denied access but actively encouraged to be frightened of him, there is a real danger, such as has already begun to happen with the girl, that they may acquire what the psychologist called 'a generalized fear of men'...

I do not underestimate the traumatic effect upon the mother of the violence that she has suffered at the hands of this man, but it is plain from the evidence that in her dealings with the children she has not sought to forget it, or push the memory into the background, or to help them to come to terms with it; but rather she has fired and stimulated the memories and encouraged them in the minds of the children so that she has made such memories as they have worse and more vivid in the course of conduct that she has taken in the 2 years or so since she has been separated from their father. And in doing that she has placed a very heavy burden of responsibility upon herself...

If the mother stimulates, and continues to stimulate, the children's fears of their father and if the little girl continues to show the signs of emotional instability which, to a large extent at any rate, appears to have been caused by the mother's action, and if the mother refuses to co-operate..., then at some future time the court may have to consider whether this mother is fit to be entrusted with the care of these children and some other arrangement will have to be made in their interests. That is not a threat, it is simply a statement of the situation.

This expectation that, as a 'good mother', a victim of domestic violence should be able to prioritize her child's interests by putting aside her own 'selfish' fears in order to promote a good relationship between father and child was reiterated in subsequent cases.[208]

Research by Bailey-Harris et al suggests that, until recently, these attitudes were deeply entrenched at all levels of the court system. Their study of practice in the county courts revealed that the issue of domestic violence was routinely marginalized, with district judges adopting a 'no fault discourse' in which the accepted mantra was to 'look forward not back'. Past conduct, including domestic violence, was thus rendered irrelevant to the contact application.[209]

Since 2000, however, there has been a shift in judicial attitudes regarding the relevance of domestic violence to issues of contact. This has been driven by the growing body of evidence as to the harm caused to children who witness incidents of abuse.[210] The potential dangers of promoting contact between a child and a violent parent are dealt with at length in the Sturge and Glaser report,[211] which was used extensively by the Court of Appeal.

Re L (A Child) (Contact: Domestic Violence) [2001] Fam 260 (CA), 270

BUTLER-SLOSS P:

The [Sturge and Glaser] report then moved to the central issue of domestic violence. They agreed...that there needs to be greater awareness of the effect of domestic violence on

---

208 See, e.g., *Re P (A Minor) (Contact)* [1994] 2 FLR 374.
209 Bailey-Harris et al (1999b), 123.
210 Barnett (2000), 139.
211 See also Humphreys and Harrison (2003), 239–40. Humphreys and Harrison point to similar research suggesting that where children live with domestic violence, the risk that they themselves will be subjected to physical or sexual abuse is markedly increased.

children, both short-term and long-term, as witnesses as well as victims. The research was entirely consistent in showing the deleterious effects on children of exposure to domestic violence and that children were affected as much by exposure to violence as to being involved in it. All children were affected by significant and repeated inter-partner violence even if not directly involved. Research indicates that even when children did not continue in violent situations emotional trauma continued to be experienced. The context of the overall situation was highly relevant to decision making. The contribution of psychiatric disorder to situations of domestic violence and emotional abuse must be considered. In situations of contact there might be a continuing sense of fear of the violent parent by the child. The child might have post-traumatic anxieties or symptoms the proximity of the non-resident violent parent might re-arouse or perpetuate. There might be a continuing awareness of the fear the violent parent aroused in the child's main carer. The psychiatric report highlighted the possible effects of such situations on the child's own attitudes to violence, to forming parenting relationships and the role of fathers. Research shows that attitudes in boys were particularly affected.

These concerns are important given the evidence that family breakdown often acts as a catalyst for violence, with the risks of escalation and even homicide being particularly high in the first six months after separation.[212] Worryingly, it has been shown that victims of domestic violence are particularly vulnerable to further abuse when contact is taking place.[213] An analysis of 300 court files carried out by the Department for Constitutional Affairs (DCA) revealed that in 35 per cent of cases there were safety concerns relating to the child or the resident parent.[214]

In *Re L (A Child) (Contact: Domestic Violence)*, the courts' general approach to contact where there are allegations of past or present domestic violence was comprehensively reviewed. The Sturge and Glaser report had recommended that in cases of domestic violence there should be a presumption *against* direct contact, with the violent partner having to meet a number of requirements before contact could be deemed beneficial.

Re L (A Child) (Contact: Domestic Violence) [2001] Fam 260 (CA), 271

BUTLER-SLOSS P:

Dr Sturge and Dr Glaser considered the question in what circumstances should the court give consideration to a child having no direct contact with the non-resident parent. In their view there should be no automatic assumption that contact to a previously or currently violent parent was in the child's interests, if anything the assumption should be in the opposite direction and he should prove why he can offer something of benefit to the child and to the child's situation. They said

"Domestic violence involves a very serious and significant failure in parenting – failure to protect the child's carer and failure to protect the child emotionally (and in some cases physically – which meets any definition of child abuse.)

Without the following we would see the balance of advantage and disadvantage as tipping against contact:

(a) some (preferably full) acknowledgment of the violence;

---

[212] Ibid, 241. Barnett (2000), 143.
[213] Humphreys and Harrison (2003).
[214] DCA, DFES, and DTI (2004), 10. See also Hunt and Macleod (2008), 6 and Trinder et al (2005), iii.

(b) some acceptance (preferably full if appropriate i.e. the sole instigator of violence) of respon-sibility for that violence;

(c) full acceptance of the inappropriateness of the violence particularly in respect of the domestic and parenting context and of the likely ill effects on the child;

(d) a genuine interest in the child's welfare and full commitment to the child i.e. a wish for contact in which he is not making the conditions;

(e) a wish to make reparation to the child and work towards the child recognising the inappro-priateness of the violence and the attitude to and treatment of the mother and helping the child to develop appropriate values and attitudes;

(f) an expression of regret and the showing of some understanding of the impact of their behaviour on the ex-partner in the past and currently;

(g) indications that the parent seeking contact can reliably sustain contact in all senses."

They suggested that without (a)–(f) above they could not see how the non-resident parent could fully support the child and play a part in undoing the harm caused to the child and sup-port the child's current situation and need to move on and develop healthily. There would be a significant risk to the child's general well-being and his emotional development.

The Court of Appeal also had before them a report by the Advisory Board on Family Law, Children Act Sub-Committee (chaired by Wall J) on parental contact in cases of domestic violence ('the CASC report').[215] The CASC report did not support a presumption against contact in cases of domestic violence but set down a number of guidelines as to how allega-tions of domestic violence should be handled in such disputes.[216] Both the expert evidence of Drs Sturge and Glaser and the recommendations of the CASC report informed the court's approach.

Re L (A Child) (Contact: Domestic Violence) [2001] Fam 260 (CA), 272–5

BUTLER-SLOSS P:

The family judges and justices need to have a heightened awareness of the existence of and consequences (some long-term) on children of exposure to domestic violence between their parents or other partners. There has, perhaps, been a tendency in the past for courts not to tackle allegations of violence and to leave them in the background on the premise that they were matters affecting the adults and not relevant to issues regarding the children. The general principle that contact with the non-resident parent is in the interests of the child may sometimes have discouraged sufficient attention being paid to the adverse effects on chil-dren living in the household where violence has occurred. It may not necessarily be widely appreciated that violence to a partner involves a significant failure in parenting – failure to protect the child's carer and failure to protect the child emotionally.

In a contact or other application under section 8 of the Children Act 1989, where allegations of domestic violence are made which might have an effect on the outcome, those allegations must be adjudicated upon and found proved or not proved. It will be necessary to scrutinise such allegations which may not always be true or may be grossly exaggerated. If however there is a

---

215 CASC (2000).
216 Ibid, Sec 5.

firm basis for finding that violence has occurred, the psychiatric advice becomes very important. There is not, however, nor should there be, any presumption that, on proof of domestic violence, the offending parent has to surmount a prima facie barrier of no contact. As a matter of principle, domestic violence of itself cannot constitute a bar to contact. It is one factor in the difficult and delicate balancing exercise of discretion. The court deals with the facts of a specific case in which the degree of violence and the seriousness of the impact on the child and on the resident parent have to be taken into account. In cases of proved domestic violence, as in cases of other proved harm or risk of harm to the child, the court has the task of weighing in the balance the seriousness of the domestic violence, the risks involved and the impact on the child against the positive factors, if any, of contact between the parent found to have been violent and the child. In this context, the ability of the offending parent to recognise his past conduct, be aware of the need to change and make genuine efforts to do so, will be likely to be an important consideration...[217]

In expressing these views I recognise the danger of the pendulum swinging too far against contact where domestic violence has been proved. It is trite but true to say that no two child cases are exactly the same. The court always has the duty to apply section 1 of the Children Act 1989 that the welfare of the child is paramount and, in considering that welfare, to take into account all the relevant circumstances, including the advice of the medical experts as far as it is relevant and proportionate to the decision in that case...

In conclusion, on the general issues, a court hearing a contact application in which allegations of domestic violence are raised, should consider the conduct of both parties towards each other and towards the children, the effect on the children and on the residential parent and the motivation of the parent seeking contact. Is it a desire to promote the best interests of the child or a means to continue violence and/or intimidation or harassment of the other parent? In cases of serious domestic violence, the ability of the offending parent to recognise his or her past conduct, to be aware of the need for change and to make genuine efforts to do so, will be likely to be an important consideration.

The importance of taking allegations of domestic violence seriously is thus clearly established. However, the Court of Appeal firmly rejected any suggestion that past or present violence by the non-resident parent should constitute a bar to contact. More controversially, they also rejected the recommendation by Drs Sturge and Glaser that where there is a history of violence there should be a presumption against direct contact.[218]

The Court of Appeal's rejection of this more robust approach in favour of a 'pure' application of the welfare principle disappointed many.[219] However, the Court of Appeal set down a number of positive requirements, which were subsequently enshrined in Practice Directions, designed to ensure that an allegation of domestic violence is taken seriously and dealt with effectively by the courts.[220] However, recent cutbacks and changes to the procedures raise concerns about whether the progress that was made will now be undermined. For example, whereas previously the court was *required* to obtain an initial screening from Cafcass in all contact applications involving allegations of domestic violence, the current Practice Direction provides that, when considering applications for child arrangements

---

[217] Note that '[g]ood intentions are no guarantee, and provide scant evidence, that the victims of abuse will be safe if exposed again to the abuser': Kaganas (2010), 126.

[218] Sturge and Glaser (2000), 623.

[219] For a critique of the decision, see Kaganas (2000), and for an alternative way in which the case might have been decided, Kaganas (2010).

[220] It is compulsory to comply with the Practice Direction: see, e.g., *Re Z (Children)* [2009] EWCA Civ 430; *Re W (Children: Domestic Violence)* [2012] EWCA Civ 528.

orders which raise domestic violence concerns, the court should *consider* directing a report from Cafcass unless satisfied that it is not necessary to do so.[221] Similarly, whereas previously the court was *required* to hold a fact-finding hearing in every case where there were concerns over domestic violence, they are now conducted only when 'necessary'.[222]

Practice Direction 12J—*Child Arrangements and Contact Order: Domestic Violence and Harm* (2014)

36. In the light of any findings of fact the court should apply the individual matters in the welfare checklist with reference to those findings; in particular, where relevant findings of domestic violence or abuse have been made, the court should in every case consider any harm which the child and the parent with whom the child is living has suffered as a consequence of that violence or abuse, and any harm which the child and the parent with whom the child is living, is at risk of suffering if a child arrangements order is made. The court should only make an order for contact if it can be satisfied that the physical and emotional safety of the child and the parent with whom the child is living can, as far as possible, be secured before during and after contact, and that the parent with whom the child is living will not be subjected to further controlling or coercive behaviour by the other parent.

37. In every case where a finding of domestic violence or abuse is made, the court should consider the conduct of both parents towards each other and towards the child; in particular, the court should consider –

(a) the effect of the domestic violence or abuse on the child and on the arrangements for where the child is living;

(b) the effect of the domestic violence or abuse on the child and its effect on the child's relationship with the parents;

(c) whether the applicant parent is motivated by a desire to promote the best interests of the child or is using the process to continue a process of violence, abuse, intimidation or harassment or controlling or coercive behaviour against the other parent;

(d) the likely behaviour during contact of the parent against whom findings are made and its effect on the child; and

(e) the capacity of the parents to appreciate the effect of past violence or abuse and the potential for future violence or abuse.

Where the court has made a finding of domestic violence but nevertheless considers that direct contact is in the best interests of the child, the court must also consider whether the contact should be supervised or whether conditions need to be imposed requiring the violent party to seek advice and/or treatment for his behaviour.[223] The CA 1989 also includes provision for an abusive parent to be directed or ordered to attend 'programmes, classes and counselling or guidance sessions of a kind that may, by addressing a person's violent behaviour, enable or facilitate contact with a child'.[224] Where direct contact is considered inappropriate the court must consider whether to make an order for indirect contact.[225]

---

[221] Practice Direction 12J (2014), [21].
[222] Ibid, [16]–[17].
[223] Ibid, [38].
[224] S 11A(5).
[225] Practice Direction 12J (2014), [39].

Is there a problem over contact?

Several important considerations may displace the presumption in favour of contact. However, contrary to the impression which the media may have created, the strength of the presumption in favour of contact is such that it is very rare for contact to be refused. The statistics are striking: less than 1 per cent of applications are refused.[226] Moreover, the majority of applicants obtain both the type and amount of contact sought.[227] Which begs the question: why are so many fathers angry and disillusioned over contact? The answer: the problems surrounding enforcement. And it is to this problem we now turn.

11.7.3 ENFORCING ORDERS TO SPEND TIME OR HAVE CONTACT

According to fathers' rights groups, non-compliance with contact orders is a huge problem,[228] with large numbers of women routinely flouting orders out of pure malevolence and spite. The courts have borne the brunt of the criticism, coming under sustained attack for their apparent inability or unwillingness to tackle the problem effectively. In response, it is argued on behalf of mothers that they are simply acting to protect their children, their concerns about the child's welfare having been given inadequate weight when contact was ordered. The problem of non-compliance with these orders has generated bitter debate in which gender has again emerged as the dominant factor.

Modes of enforcement

Breach of an order to allow a person to spend time with or otherwise have contact with a child constitutes contempt of court punishable by fine or committal to prison for a maximum of two years. Committal proceedings can be initiated by another party to the proceedings or, in exceptional cases, by the court acting of its own motion.[229] Alternatively, under s 11J of the CA 1989, the court can make an enforcement order imposing 'an unpaid work requirement' on the party in breach.[230] Repeated refusals to allow contact with the non-residential parent can also be addressed by changing the child's place of residence.

Whether the courts should seek to secure compliance with an order by invoking one of these measures is exceptionally difficult. If the mother disregards the order and the court fails to act, the welfare of the child, as determined by the court, will be undermined. On the other hand, decisive action which sees the mother imprisoned or deprived of residence is unlikely to further the child's interests, particularly if the father cannot provide the child with an alternative home. Matters are further complicated where the child, having become alienated from the father, also opposes contact.[231] The welfare of the child is not, however, the only consideration: there is a wider public interest in ensuring compliance with the

---

[226] DCA, DFES, and DTI (2004), 13.

[227] Hunt and Macleod (2008), 4.

[228] It is difficult to assess the extent to which this is true. In 2011, 38,405 children were the subject of contact applications, and fewer than 1,500 applications for enforcement measures were brought: Trinder et al (2013). However, that says nothing about the number of cases in which there were difficulties which were not taken to court.

[229] *Re M (A Minor) (Contempt of Court: Committal of Court's Own Motion)* [1999] Fam 263.

[230] Inserted by s 4 of the CAA 2006.

[231] See, e.g., *Re N (A Minor) (Access: Penal Notice)* [1992] 1 FLR 134.

courts' terms. In determining the weight to be afforded to these various factors the courts have adopted strongly differing views.

Committal proceedings

The dilemma facing the courts where one party to a contact dispute seeks to enforce the order by committal has been graphically illustrated by Ward LJ.

Re M (A Minor) (Contempt of Court: Committal of Court's Own Motion) [1999] Fam 263 (CA), 281–2

WARD LJ:

The judge was, of course, uniquely well placed to assess what the welfare of the children demanded with regard to the maintenance of a link with their father through contact, but here the judge was assuming that coercive powers of the court would achieve that desired result. He did not, however, appear to consider what effect a committal application (carrying with it the possibility of a prison sentence) may have had on the children, especially in the light of his findings about the mother's proven capacity to influence the children against their father. It does not require much imagination to envisage the domestic scene where mother dramatically proclaims to the children that she is about to face a prison sentence because she is doing what they want - saving them from contact with their horrible father. There is an almost inevitable and serious risk that the committal proceedings might themselves exacerbate the poor relationship between children and father and so hinder not help contact. The committal proceedings do not carry such a certain outcome of good for the children as would justify the judge proceeding of his own motion on the basis of their benefit.

The courts have therefore been extremely reluctant to enforce contact orders by imprisoning the child's residential carer. Indeed, at one time it was held that concerns about the impact of committal proceedings on the child rendered such proceedings utterly 'futile',[232] and committal was understood to be a weapon of very last resort, if appropriate at all.[233] More recently, there has, however, been a clear hardening of attitudes. This more robust approach has been marked by a shift in the welfare discourse with a much greater focus on the importance of securing the long-term benefits of contact with the non-residential parent than the short-term distress caused by the imprisonment of the residential carer.[234] The courts' greater willingness to invoke committal proceedings has also been marked by a move away from an almost exclusive focus on the child's welfare to place much greater emphasis on the need to uphold the dignity and authority of the court. The leading authority on this more hard-line approach is *A v N (Committal: Refusal of Contact)* in which the mother of a four-and-a-half-year-old girl was adamant that she would rather go to prison than allow the girl to have contact with her father. The mother was committed to prison for 42 days for her persistent breach of the court's orders. The Court of Appeal refused her appeal.

---

232 See, e.g., *Churchard v Churchard* [1984] FLR 635.

233 See, e.g., *Re N (A Minor) (Access: Penal Notice)* [1992] 1 FLR 134 and *Re M (A Minor) (Contempt of Court: Committal of Court's Own Motion)* [1999] Fam 263.

234 See, e.g., *Re L (Minors) (Access Order: Enforcement)* [1989] 2 FLR 359 and *B v S* [2009] EWCA Civ 548. In the latter case the Court of Appeal upheld the mother's committal to prison even though she had a three-month-old baby and the father no longer wished to see her committed.

A v N (Committal: Refusal of Contact) [1997] 2 FCR 475 (CA), 482–4

WARD LJ:

[In an application for committal for breach] the upbringing of the child is not a paramount consideration. It is obviously a material consideration and every Judge who does any family work at all is always alive to the grievous effect the implementation of an order is likely to have on the life of the children whom the mother is unwisely seeking to protect in her own misguided way. . . . [The judge] was fully mindful of the distressing consequence of imprisonment on the child . . . but he balanced against that the long-term damage that she will suffer, especially if she grows up under a deliberate false impression as to whom her father really is. He did, therefore, take proper account of welfare factors and his balance is not one with which I would interfere.

The stark reality of this case is that this is a mother who has flagrantly set herself upon a course of collision with the court's order. She has been given endless opportunities to comply with sympathetic attempts made by the Judge to meet her flimsy objections to contact taking place. She has spurned all of those attempts. For it to be submitted that the hardship to the child is the result of the court imposing the committal order is wholly to misunderstand the position. This little child suffers because the mother chooses to make her suffer. This mother had it within her power to save T that suffering, but she did not avail of that opportunity . . .

[I]t is perhaps appropriate that the message goes out in loud and in clear terms that there does come a limit to the tolerance of the court to see its orders flouted by mothers even if they have to care for their young children. If she goes to prison it is her fault, not the fault of the Judge who did no more than his duty to the child which is imposed upon him by Parliament.

It may be noted that recent judgments have increasingly focused on the technical elements that have to be proved to show contempt, with judges conscious that contempt hearings must comply with the standards of criminal proceedings. It has been stressed that a contempt has to be proved beyond all reasonable doubt, and that only a deliberate failure to comply with a clear, unambiguous, and injunctive order will suffice.[235] A number of recent attempts to bring such proceedings have failed on these technical points,[236] which raises questions about whether contempt proceedings are an effective solution to the difficulties of enforcing private law orders in relation to children.

Enforcement measures under the CA 1989

The CAA 2006 introduced a number of new measures into the CA 1989 aimed at improving implementation and enforcement of contact. The CA 1989 provides that the court may ask an officer of Cafcass to monitor and, if necessary, report back to the court as to compliance.[237] The period of monitoring may not exceed 12 months.[238] The intention behind it is to ensure

---

[235] See, e.g., *Re A (Abduction: Contempt)* [2008] EWCA Civ 1138, [6]; *Re LW (Contact Order: Committal)* [2010] EWCA Civ 1253.

[236] See, e.g., *Re Jones (Alleged Contempt of Court)* [2013] EWHC 2579.

[237] S 11H(2).

[238] S 11H(6).

breaches are immediately brought to the judge's attention. Furthermore, additional advice, support, and assistance to help parents adjust to contact in difficult cases may now be more readily available under a family assistance order.[239] Family assistance orders appear to have been little used in private law disputes,[240] although their potential has been recognized in the academic literature.[241]

On the specific issue of enforcement, the CAA 2006 amended the CA 1989 to increase the range of measures available to the courts. As an alternative to imposing a fine or imprisonment, the courts may make an enforcement order imposing an 'unpaid work requirement' unless the person in breach can satisfy the court, on the balance of probabilities, that there was a reasonable excuse for non-compliance.[242] Before making the enforcement order the court must be satisfied that: (i) the order is necessary to secure compliance with the contact order; and (ii) the enforcement order is *proportionate* to the seriousness of the offence.[243] The court must also take into account the child's welfare, though not as the paramount consideration. Compliance with an unpaid work requirement is monitored by an officer of Cafcass.[244] Research by Tinder et al suggests that these orders are rarely made, but judges may raise the spectre of such enforcement by ordering an assessment or making a suspended order, which can be effective to secure compliance with the original contact order.[245]

Where breach of a contact order causes financial loss, such as the cost of a cancelled holiday, the court can order the person in breach to pay compensation.[246] To avoid the order, the person in breach must satisfy the court, on the balance of probabilities, that he or she had a reasonable excuse for failing to comply. In determining whether to make the order and, if so, for how much, the court must take into account the individual's financial circumstances and the welfare of the child concerned.

Transferring residence

A similar hardening of attitudes is discernible in the courts' use of their final weapon in intractable contact disputes: moving the child from the 'intransigent' parent to live primarily with the other parent.[247] The Court of Appeal has again made it clear that the transfer of the child's main home is a 'judicial weapon of last resort'—such a move should not be taken lightly.[248] Where the child has been denied contact, there will be obvious risks in transferring residence to a parent who may well be a relative stranger. However, despite the risks, the courts have made it clear that they are increasingly willing to employ this measure against 'unreasonable mothers' to protect the child's long-term interests. The key question for the court is whether there is a greater risk of harm to the child by reason

---

[239] S 16(4A).

[240] For recent examples in a cases involving complex private law disputes, see *Re N (A Child) (Religion: Jehovah's Witness)* [2011] EWHC 3737; *Re L and M (Children: Private Law)* [2014] EWHC 939.

[241] Seden (2001).

[242] S 11J(2)–(4).

[243] S 11L.

[244] S 11M.

[245] Trinder et al (2013).

[246] S 11O.

[247] For examples see *Re C (A Child)* [2007] EWCA Civ 866; *Re A (Suspended Residence Order)* [2010] 1 FLR 1679; *Re S (Transfer of Residence)* [2010] 1 FLR 1785.

[248] *Re A (Children)* [2009] EWCA Civ 1141, [18].

of the disruption and distress caused by a transfer of residence or by denying him or her a relationship with the other parent, which requires a careful balancing of the pros and cons of a move.

Re M (Children) (Contact) [2012] EWHC 1948

PETER JACKSON J:

65. In relation to the children's needs, there are factors that strongly speak against a change of residence:

- In all other respects, they have made very good progress in their mother's care....
- They are securely attached to their mother, and to [their half-brothers], and have a good relationship with their stepfather Mr A, who they admire. The relationship between the boys and their younger half-brothers is very important to them and a change of residence not only means that they would see much less of them, but that their upbringings would inevitably diverge.
- A change of residence disrupts the pattern of care within the home that the children have been used to all their lives, despite several changes of address while in their mother's care.
- They are doing well at school, despite several changes of school.
- The children have at the moment persuaded themselves that they do not want to see their father, let alone live with him.
- Without the mother's support, the children would be very difficult to move and they may not settle with their father.
- Arrangements for contact with their mother and siblings would be difficult, at least at the outset.

66. A move would therefore bring real losses for the children, and risks, which could easily amount to harm if the transition was unsuccessful.

68. Against these factors:

- A move is the only way of restoring the children's relationships with their father and wider family.
- There is no available therapeutic mechanism that can restore their relationship with their father, given the distances, the lack of funds and the mother's current attitude.
- The children's true feelings are, as I have found, being stifled.
- The father is, I find, capable of bringing up the children appropriately and meeting their needs. Although he is untested as a full-time carer, there is no reason to believe that he cannot take on that role successfully with the support network that he has, and the flexibility that his employment allows.
- I discount the suggestion that the children would come to harm in the father's care as a result of any acts or failures on his part.
- The father is likely to support the children's relationship with their mother to the extent that it is within his power to do so.

Jackson J then moved to look at how these factors would be balanced in the case before him, taking into account the short, medium, and long-term consequences of each option. The judge concluded that it was necessary to make an order transferring the children's residence from their mother to their father. However, he gave the mother 'one final opportunity' to comply with the contact order, by making a condition that his order for a transfer of the children's main residence was not to take effect if the mother and her new partner started to comply with the original order.[249]

Although controversial, this more hard-line approach to enforcement finds support in the ECHR. It was held in *Hokkanen v Finland* that the state has a positive obligation under Article 8 to 'facilitate' the parent–child relationship, including taking all reasonable steps to enforce private law orders for contact.[250] However, the European Court recognized that the state's obligation cannot be absolute and that any coercive measures against the parent in breach must be limited by the need to take into account the rights and interests of others, in particular those of the child. These principles were approved and applied in *Glaser v United Kingdom*.[251]

11.7.4 TAKING CONTACT OUT OF THE COURTS

As the courts struggle to find appropriate and effective solutions to the more difficult and intractable contact disputes, it has been questioned more broadly whether the courts are the most appropriate forum for dealing with disputes of this nature. Long-term, deep-rooted problems, which are incapable of resolution at a discrete point in time, often underpin such disputes. The blunt tool of ordering and enforcing contact will not address the underlying cause of the resident parent's hostility. Counselling or therapy may be the only way such problems can be effectively resolved.

Re L (A Child) (Contact: Domestic Violence) [2001] Fam 260 (CA), 296–8

THORPE LJ:

[T]here is in my opinion validity in questioning the future role of the family justice system in relation to contact. I have already expressed how limited is the capacity of the family justice system to produce good outcomes in disputed areas of personal relationship. Yet a great deal of the resources of the system are taken up with contested contact cases. The disputes are particularly prevalent and intractable. They consume a disproportionate quantity of private law judicial time. The disputes are often driven by personality disorders, unresolved adult conflicts or egocentricity. These originating or contributing factors would generally be better treated therapeutically, where at least there would be some prospect of beneficial change, rather than given vent in the family justice system . . .

I would question whether the investment of public funds in litigation as the conventional mode of resolving contact disputes is comparatively productive. In many cases the same investment in therapeutic services might produce greater benefit. Within the National Health Service, child and mental health services work with warring parents to try and help them separate their parenting role from the breakdown of the partnership. If one parent has a mental illness or personality disorder the service can help the family to manage perhaps by providing

---

[249] *Re M (Children) (Contact)* [2012] EWHC 1948, [76].

[250] *Hokkanen v Finland* (Case No 50/1993/445/524, ECHR) (1996).

[251] (App No 32346/96, ECHR) (2000). See also *Damnjonovic v Serbia* (App No 5222/07, ECHR) (2009), [75]–[78] and *Kaleta v Poland* (App No 11375/02, ECHR) (2009), [52].

sessions with the children to help them understand their situation. Within the voluntary sector there are exceptional facilities...that provide more than neutral space for contact, and perhaps some professional supervision or assessment. Such centres attempt to address the underlying dysfunction in family relationship that expresses itself in the absence or failure of contact. In some cases they may work with the family therapeutically for weeks before attempting any direct contact. It must at least be arguable that that expenditure of effort and cost is likely to achieve more than an equal expenditure on litigation with its tendency to increase alienation through its adversarial emphasis. Of course there will always be many cases that are only fit for referral to litigation. But in my opinion judges with responsibility for case management should be thoroughly informed as to available alternative services in the locality and astute in selecting the service best suited to promote the welfare of the child in each case.[252]

Numerous initiatives have been introduced over the last few years which attempt to promote non-court solutions to private law children disputes. One approach has been to introduce initiatives aimed at changing the attitudes and behaviour of separating parents through tools of *persuasion*. The hope was to achieve a change in *culture* regarding contact disputes, whereby 'it becomes socially unacceptable for one parent to impede a child's relationship with its other parent wherever it is safe and in the child's best interests'.[253] Parents were thus to be 'educated' to understand that the 'civilized divorce' and 'good parenting' requires them to put their children's interests before their own and that this means facilitating contact.

The first step towards this goal was to provide better access to information and advice through existing agencies such as NCH, Sure Start, and Relate. Information targeted at both parents and children[254] include parenting plans containing examples of various contact arrangements which have been shown to work well.[255] Several measures have been introduced which are aimed at promoting a more conciliatory approach to resolving disputes. A collaborative law programme is now operated by some law firms, whereby both parents' lawyers must be committed to achieving settlement; in the absence of agreement, different lawyers must be instructed.[256]

Most recently, where applications are made to the court (unless it is for an application for a consent order), the government has made it mandatory except in cases involving domestic violence for the parties to attend a Mediation Information and Assessment Meeting (MIAM) to see whether the case is suitable for mediation.[257] The parties can attend the MIAM separately or together. While it is not strictly compulsory to attend a MIAM, the court may adjourn proceedings pending attendance if it does not consider that the parties have a good reason for non-attendance.[258] At the same time, legal aid has been withdrawn from almost all private law proceedings (except in a limited class of cases involving domestic violence, plus a few other limited exceptions). This move is predicated on the Coalition

---

[252] See also *Re D (Intractable Contact Dispute: Publicity)* [2004] EWHC 727.

[253] DCA, DFES, and DTI (2005), 7.

[254] For comment on engaging children in this process of securing the 'civilized divorce', see Kaganas and Diduck (2004).

[255] DCA, DFES, and DTI (2005), 19–21.

[256] Ibid.

[257] Practice Direction 3A—*Family Mediation and Information Assessment Meetings (MIAMS)* (2014). See 1.2.7.

[258] Ibid, [37].

Government's view that most private law disputes should not be in court and therefore that the state should not fund legal representation for such cases.[259]

11.8 SPECIFIC ISSUE AND PROHIBITED STEPS ORDERS

In essence, specific issue and prohibited steps orders constitute two sides of the same coin. A specific issue order (SIO) is a positive order providing for a particular step to be taken with respect to the child's upbringing.[260] A prohibited steps order (PSO) is a negative order preventing a particular step being taken. As discussed in chapter 10, such orders are commonly used to resolve disputes between the holders of parental responsibility. However, subject to the requirement for leave, anyone may in theory apply to the court for a particular issue to be determined. SIOs and PSOs have been used to resolve a wide range of disputes concerning a child, the one requirement being that it must engage some aspect of parental responsibility.[261] Some of the more common include: changing a child's surname,[262] preventing the removal of a child from the jurisdiction,[263] medical treatment,[264] choice of school,[265] and the publication of information about the child.[266]

Whilst the potential use of SIOs and PSOs is extremely broad, there are some important restrictions on their use. An SIO or PSO cannot be made with a view to achieving a result which could be achieved by making a child arrangements order.[267] Nor may a SIO or PSO be made with a view to placing a child in local authority care.[268] Finally, a SIO or PSO cannot be used to 'oust' someone from the family home, the proper route for such an application being under Part IV of the Family Law Act 1996.[269]

An application for a SIO or PSO is determined on the basis of the child's welfare.

11.9 RELOCATION DISPUTES

Relocation disputes are cases which arise when one parent seeks to take the child to live in another geographic location, and the other parent opposes the proposal. According to recent research, the vast majority of applications (95 per cent) are brought by mothers, and the children involved are typically in middle childhood (ages four to nine).[270] In terms of litigated cases, two-thirds of proposed international moves and just over 70 per cent of contested domestic moves end with the relocation being permitted, though a great many

---

[259] MOJ (2010b); for a strong critique, see Eekelaar (2011) and George (2012a), ch 1.
[260] Gilmore (2004c).
[261] *Re J (Specific Issue Order: Leave to Apply)* [1995] 1 FLR 669.
[262] *Dawson v Wearmouth* [1999] 2 AC 308; *Re W (A Child) (Illegitimate Child: Change of Surname)* [2001] Fam 1.
[263] *Re K (Application to Remove from Jurisdiction)* [1998] 2 FLR 1006.
[264] *Re HG (Specific Issue Order: Sterilisation)* [1993] 1 FLR 587; *Re R (A Minor) (Blood Transfusion)* [1993] 2 FLR 757.
[265] *Re G (Education: Religious Upbringing)* [2012] EWCA Civ 1233.
[266] *Re Z (A Minor) (Freedom of Publication)* [1997] Fam 1.
[267] CA 1989, s 9(5)(a). See *Re H (Prohibited Steps Order)* [1995] 1 WLR 667.
[268] Ibid, ss 9(5)(b) and 100(2).
[269] *Pearson v Franklin* [1994] 1 WLR 370; *Re D (Prohibited Steps Order)* [1996] 2 FLR 273.
[270] George (2013a).

factors can be identified which influence outcomes in particular cases.[271] Unlike many other jurisdictions,[272] English law draws a distinction between proposed relocations to places outside the UK and proposed moves which are within the UK.

11.9.1 INTERNATIONAL RELOCATION CASES

It is not known how many international relocation cases there are each year, but a number in the low hundreds is probably about right.[273] However, although there are comparatively few of these cases, they have such significant consequences for the children involved that they have been one of the major areas of debate in English law over the last few years. As we saw earlier, s 13 of the CA 1989 imposes an automatic prohibition on a parent removing a child from the UK (except for a holiday) when a child arrangements order is in force which determines where the child should live.[274] However, in any case where both parents have parental responsibility and are spending any amount of time with the child, removal from the UK without the written consent of everyone with parental responsibility or the court's permission will be child abduction, which has important civil and criminal law consequences.[275]

The leading modern authority on the principles to be applied in determining a contested application for leave to remove a child from the UK is the Court of Appeal decision in *Payne v Payne*.

Payne v Payne [2001] EWCA Civ 166

THORPE LJ:

40. ...To guard against the risk of too perfunctory an investigation resulting from too ready an assumption that the mother's proposals are necessarily compatible with the child's welfare I would suggest the following discipline as a prelude to conclusion:

(a) Pose the question: is the mother's application genuine in the sense that it is not motivated by some selfish desire to exclude the father from the child's life? Then ask, is the mother's application realistic, by which I mean founded on practical proposals both well researched and investigated? If the application fails either of these tests, refusal will inevitably follow.

(b) If, however, the application passes these tests then there must be a careful appraisal of the father's opposition: is it motivated by genuine concern for the future of the child's welfare or is it driven by some ulterior motive? What would be the extent of the detriment to him and his future relationship with the child were the application granted? To what extent would that be offset by extension of the child's relationships with the maternal family and homeland?

---

[271] Ibid. The factors include child-care arrangements, proposed destination, applicant's and respondent's motivations, and process issues such as whether the parties had lawyers representing them or not.

[272] For comparison with New Zealand, see George (2014).

[273] George (2014).

[274] See 11.6.8.

[275] Child Abduction Act 1984; Child Abduction and Custody Act 1985. Over 90 countries are signatories to the Hague Convention on the Civil Aspects of International Child Abduction 1980, which aims to secure the prompt return of any child removed or retained internationally without lawful consent.

(c) What would be the impact on the mother, either as the single parent or as a new wife, of a refusal of her realistic proposal?

(d) The outcome of the second and third appraisals must then be brought into an overriding review of the child's welfare as the paramount consideration, directed by the statutory checklist in so far as appropriate.

41. In suggesting such a discipline I would not wish to be thought to have diminished the importance that this court has consistently attached to the emotional and psychological wellbeing of the primary carer. In any evaluation of the welfare of the child as the paramount consideration great weight must be given to this factor.

BUTLER-SLOSS P:

85. In summary I would suggest that the following considerations should be in the forefront of the mind of a judge trying one of these difficult cases...

(a) The welfare of the child is always paramount.

(b) There is no presumption created by s 13(1)(b) in favour of the applicant parent.

(c) The reasonable proposals of the parent with a residence order wishing to live abroad carry great weight.

(d) Consequently the proposals have to be scrutinised with care and the court needs to be satisfied that there is a genuine motivation for the move and not the intention to bring contact between the child and the other parent to an end.

(e) The effect upon the applicant parent and the new family of the child of a refusal of leave is very important.

(f) The effect upon the child of the denial of contact with the other parent and in some cases his family is very important.

(g) The opportunity for continuing contact between the child and the parent left behind may be very significant.

The decision in *Payne* has provoked considerable discussion. In the first ten years after *Payne* was decided, the bulk of that commentary was critical of the decision for various reasons.

M. Hayes, 'Relocation Cases: Is the Court of Appeal Applying the Correct Principles?', (2006) 18 *Child and Family Law Quarterly* 351, 362, 364

The 'discipline' in *Payne* imposes a gloss on the welfare principle. It tells a judge trying a relocation case to focus on particular matters. On its face the discipline appears relatively even-handed. But a closer analysis reveals that it expects a judge to approach his task in a manner which is weighted towards one party. The judge is expected to give more attention to the proposals of the primary carer, who, in practice, is almost always the mother, than he is to those of the other parent, in practice almost always the father...

The combined effect of paragraphs [40](c) and [41] [see *Payne* above] leads to the outcome that a judge evaluating the impact on a mother of denial of leave does not start his investigation with an open mind. Instead, he is told to approach his task with certain preconceptions in mind. He is instructed to treat the impact of his ruling on the mother as the most significant consideration. He is told that he must have in mind the importance that the court has consistently attached to the emotional and psychological well-being of the primary carer when weighing this matter within his overriding review of the child's welfare. He is told that he must carefully evaluate the impact of refusal of leave on the new family and on the stepfather or prospective stepfather.

By contrast, a judge is not instructed to have any preconceptions in his mind when he carries out his investigation of the detriment to the father under paragraph [40](b)...

The parent/child relationship is a fundamental bond that is central to the deepest emotions experienced by mothers and fathers. It is central to the deepest emotions experienced by children. The discipline values the bond between the child and the primary carer, but gives less value to the bond between the child and the non-residential parent. The weight that a trial judge is required by the discipline in *Payne* and subsequent case-law to give to considerations that favour the mother offends the fundamental principle that justice should be even-handed. The bias has developed because the discipline is built around the assumption that a child's relationship with his mother as the primary caring parent is of most importance to his or her welfare. But, of course, depending on the circumstances of each case, such an assumption may, or may not, be correct.

Hayes' answer to the biases within *Payne* is to insist that the judge undertake a full examination of the welfare principle in every case, with all relevant factors in the welfare checklist given due consideration.[276]

Herring and Taylor have been similarly critical of *Payne*, but for different reasons. They argue that it is not so much the outcomes in the relocation cases which give rise to concern but the process of reasoning that is employed.[277] They criticize the way in which the welfare principle has been used in these cases 'to tilt the scales heavily in favour of the relocating parent'.[278] However, rather than a return to a 'pure' application of the welfare principle, they advocate a rights-based approach which, in their view, would not lead to a greater number of decisions favouring the non-resident parent but would ensure the individual interests of each family member were properly identified and weighed in the decision-making process. Much greater transparency and accountability would thereby be secured. They begin by identifying the competing rights likely to be engaged within the context of a relocation dispute.

J. Herring and R. Taylor, 'Relocating Relocation', (2006) 18 *Child and Family Law Quarterly* 517, 530–2

The rights involved...will depend on the particular facts of the case, but even in simple cases the court is likely to be faced with a range of conflicting rights...[T]he rights of the adults involved will include, at a minimum, the resident parent's Article 8 right to freedom of movement and the non-resident parent's Article 8 right to maintain and develop a relationship with his child. The rights of the child are also complex: in many cases the child herself will have conflicting rights. On the one hand, the child will have a right under Article 8 to stability in her residential family life. On the other hand, it is clear that a child has a right to contact with both parents under Article 8. Even if the overall duration of contact between the father and the child is maintained, changes to the nature of that contact may affect the

---

276 Hayes (2006), 371–2.
277 Herring and Taylor (2006), 518.
278 Ibid, 518–19.

relationship between the father and child and engage Article 8. Further where the child is old enough to form and express her own views, she may have a right under Article 8 for those views to be considered.

The question of how the inevitable conflict between these competing rights can be resolved is then addressed.

Given the range of rights involved in the simplest case, it is important to consider how a court may assign weight to each right in the 'ultimate balancing exercise': if the rights are incommensurable, the rights-based approach will not be capable of producing a principled resolution to the clash of rights. It is our view that a principled balancing of rights can be achieved by focusing on the values that underlie each right....While the answer will vary between cases, it is possible to identify the values that are most commonly raised in relocation cases.

Strasbourg jurisprudence shows that notions of personal autonomy lie at the heart of Article 8 and its interpretation. At the heart of the right to autonomy is the right to develop one's vision of the good life free from improper interference from either the State or other people. This gives us some assistance in considering competing rights under Article 8: the right to autonomy. The closer the desired act is to the individual's vision of their life and their self, the stronger the claim is and the greater the justification required to interfere with it. ...So, just because two parties can claim competing Article 8 rights does not mean that their claims are equal. Not all interferences with autonomy are equal. Some are major setbacks in plans for life; others are minor interruptions....

[W]hen dealing with a clash between the rights of the mother and father in a relocation case, the court should consider which interference will constitute a greater blight on the vision of the good life that each had.

Payne was also criticized for being based on outdated gendered assumptions as to the usual pattern of post-separation parenting, in particular that it now incorrectly assumes a pattern of mother as primary carer. Mostyn J was particularly outspoken in his criticism and the perceived emphasis that *Payne* is sometimes thought to place on the impact of refusal on the child's primary carer.[279]

Subsequently, some of the heat has been taken out of the debate about the *Payne* approach to international relocation disputes by the Court of Appeal's decision in *K v K (International Relocation: Shared Care Arrangement)*.[280] Although focused on the question of how the *Payne* guidelines should be applied to an equal or near-equal shared care arrangement, the judgments of Moore-Bick and Black LJJ have wider significance to the relocation debate.

K v K (Relocation: Shared Care Arrangement) [2011] EWCA Civ 793

MOORE-BICK LJ:

86. ...Guidance of the kind provided in *Payne v Payne* is, of course, very valuable both in ensuring that judges identify what are likely to be the most important factors to be taken into account and the weight that should generally be attached to them. It also plays a valuable role

---

[279] *Re AR (A Child: Relocation)* [2010] EWHC 1346, [12]; note the criticism of Mostyn J's comments by George (2014), 148–9, who sees the judge's approach as 'adult-centred'.

[280] [2011] EWCA Civ 793.

in promoting consistency in decision-making. However, the circumstances in which these difficult decisions have to be made vary infinitely and the judge in each case must be free to weigh up the individual factors and make whatever decision he or she considers to be in the best interests of the child.

BLACK LJ:

141. The first point that is quite clear is that, as I have said already, the principle—the only authentic principle—that runs through the entire line of relocation authorities is that the welfare of the child is the court's paramount consideration. Everything that is considered by the court in reaching its determination is put into the balance with a view to measuring its impact on the child.

142. Whilst this is the only truly inescapable principle in the jurisprudence, that does not mean that everything else—the valuable guidance—can be ignored. It must be heeded for all the reasons that Moore-Bick LJ gives but as guidance not as rigid principle or so as to dictate a particular outcome in a sphere of law where the facts of individual cases are so infinitely variable.

143. Furthermore, the effect of the guidance must not be overstated. . . . [In her judgment in *Payne*,] Dame Elizabeth referred, of course, to the effect on the parent with residence (paragraphs 83 and 84) but she also stressed that the relationship with the other parent is highly relevant and that there are many other factors which may arise in an individual case (paragraph 84). I detect in her discussion of the factors and in her summary at paragraph 85 no weighting in favour of any particular factor. . . .

144. *Payne* therefore identifies a number of factors which will or may be relevant in a relocation case, explains their importance to the welfare of the child, and suggests helpful disciplines to ensure that the proper matters are considered in reaching a decision but it does not dictate the outcome of a case. . . .

It is clear that *K v K* does not overrule *Payne*, but rather highlights that the factors highlighted by *Payne* form part of a holistic analysis of the child's welfare. The effect is to say that the *Payne* guidance remains relevant to all international relocation cases, but that judges must assess the extent to which the facts of the case in front of them require them to modify or depart from that guidance.

This approach was subsequently reinforced by Munby LJ in *Re F (Relocation)*.[281] The facts of *Re F* were relatively unusual in that the application to remove was being made by the non-residential carer, the child's primary care having changed following the mother's return to Spain herself without the child a year earlier. It is particularly notable that Munby LJ considered that the judgments of Moore-Bick and Black LJJ encapsulate the correct approach to *all* relocation applications, and not just those involving shared care arrangements.

Re F (Relocation) [2012] EWCA Civ 1364

MUNBY LJ:

45. . . . The four-stage process set out in sub-paragraphs (a) to (d) [in para 40 of Thorpe LJ's "discipline" in *Payne*] is of course highly relevant where the applicant is a primary

---

281 [2012] EWCA Civ 1364.

carer. But as a consideration of the content of those sub-paragraphs demonstrates, the discipline is not relevant only to such cases. For the issues canvassed in sub-paragraphs (a) to (d) will arise in many relocation cases where the application is being made by someone other than a primary carer. So, ...applying the approach indicated in *K v K* by Moore-Bick LJ and Black LJ, the guidance which Thorpe LJ gave in *Payne v Payne* at paragraph [40] is not, in my judgment, confined to cases where the applicant is the primary carer. It is guidance that, in my judgment, may be utilised in other kinds of relocation case if the judge thinks it helpful and appropriate to do so. In saying this I am merely agreeing with the majority view in *K v K*.

By aligning himself with the judgments of Moore-Bick and Black LJJ, Munby LJ has thus attempted to bring the debate over the relevance of the *Payne* guidance to relocation cases to an end.[282] Nonetheless, there are practitioners and academics who continue to think that this area of the law needs to be reviewed.[283] Devereux and George consider the position of the law following *K v K* and its reinterpretation of *Payne*. They identify three risks that they say arise from the approach taken by *K v K*.

E. Devereux and R. George, 'When Will the Supreme Court Put Us Out of Our Payne?' (2014) *Family Law*, 44: 1586, 1587 and 1589–90

First, ...[m]ost judges hearing relocation cases are not specialists in international family law, and the issues arising in a relocation case are in many ways very different from the 'standard' private law children dispute. Having an approach which involves firmly stated guidance, coupled with a later amendment suggesting that it be read loosely, is a recipe for confusion in the trial courts.

Secondly, it is not clear what is now to happen in cases where there is a genuine dispute between the parents about which of them should provide the child's main residence. *Payne* itself says that those cases are different...However, both *K v K* (per Black LJ) and *Re F*, at paras [58]–[61] say that there is to be only one approach, with no 'classes' of relocation case. Again, ...the question remains – how is the conscientious trial judge to deal with such a case, and how are lawyers supposed to advise clients?

Thirdly, and most fundamentally, the guidance offered by *Payne v Payne* is not appropriate for all international relocation cases. As noted above, the guidance is premised on the applicant being the clear primary carer. There must, therefore, be serious doubt about whether that guidance can be modified, on a case by case basis by trial judges, to fit the very different facts which arise where there is no one clear primary carer of the child. While there are elements of the *Payne v Payne* guidance which will indeed be relevant to all international relocation cases (in particular, the questions of whether the proposal is made in good faith, and whether the plans for relocation are well researched and realistic), other elements are applicable only when the applicant is clearly the primary carer, and trial judges are being led into error by the Court of Appeal's instruction that they should apply the *Payne* guidance in a modified manner...

---

[282] The unsuccessful father in *Re F* sought permission from the Supreme Court to appeal the Court of Appeal's decision, but the application was refused. For commentary on *Re F*, see George (2012c).

[283] For discussion of how relocation law might be reformed, see George (2014), ch 6.

Despite these and other calls for reform, it seems that the pressure for change which once existed in international relocation cases has lessened in recent years.[284] It is consequently unclear when any review of the *Payne* approach is likely to take place.

11.9.2 RELOCATION WITHIN THE UK

Neither the restrictions in s 13(1) nor the guidance in *Payne* applies to cases of proposed relocation within the UK. So-called cases of 'internal relocation' usually arise as a result of a parent with whom the child is not living attempting to impose conditions as to the other parent's place of residence, either within the child arrangements order or using a prohibited steps order to prevent the other parent from relocating. The Court of Appeal has made it clear that it will be unusual for a parent's freedom of movement to be restricted in this way. In *Re E (Residence: Imposition of Conditions)*, the child's mother wished to relocate from London to Blackpool; the Court of Appeal removed the conditions from her residence order preventing her from doing so.

Re E (Residence: Imposition of Conditions) [1997] EWCA Civ 3084

BUTLER-SLOSS LJ:

18. . . . The wording of [s 11(7)] is wide enough to give the court the power to make an order restricting the right of residence to a specified place within the United Kingdom. But in my view a restriction upon the right of the carer of the child to chose where to live sits uneasily with the general understanding of what is meant by a residence order. . . .

20. A general imposition of conditions on residence orders was clearly not contemplated by Parliament and where the parent is entirely suitable and the court intends to make a residence order in favour of that parent, a condition of residence is in my view an unwarranted imposition upon the right of the parent to chose where he/she will live within the United Kingdom or with whom. There may be exceptional cases, for instance, where the court, in the private law context, has concerns about the ability of the parent to be granted a residence order to be a satisfactory carer but there is no better solution than to place the child with that parent. . .

21. The correct approach is to look at the issue of where the children will live as one of the relevant factors in the context of the cross-applications for residence and not as a separate issue divorced from the question of residence. If the case is finely balanced between the respective advantages and disadvantages of the parents, the proposals put forward by each parent will assume considerable importance.

The Court of Appeal later said that the imposition of a condition on a primary carer's right to choose where he or she lives was 'a truly exceptional order'.[285] However, more recent decisions suggest that, as in the context of international relocation cases, there has been some

---

[284] See, e.g., Mostyn J in *NJ v OV* [2014] EWHC 4130, [7], saying that he did not agree that there was need for a reconsideration of relocation law following *K v K* and *Re F* since the law was now 'clear and stable'. Given his earlier calls for reform, this position surprised many, particularly since Mostyn J's judgment in *Re TC v JC (Children: Relocation)* [2013] EWHC 292 (which also post-dated *K v K* and *Re F*) had reiterated his earlier criticisms of the law.

[285] *Re B* [2007] EWCA Civ 1055, [7].

movement towards seeing the earlier authorities as mere guidance, with the focus on the child's overall welfare.

The movement started with *Re L (Internal Relocation: Shared Residence Order)* in 2009, in which Wall LJ said that the 'correct approach' to internal relocation cases was 'to look at the underlying factual matrix in welfare terms'.[286] In other words, the judge's task is 'to examine the underlying factual matrix, and to decide in all the circumstances of the case whether or not it is in the child's interest to relocate with the parent who wishes to move'.[287]

The same theme was picked up by Wilson LJ the following year. The judge identified three features of the internal relocation case law which he found 'puzzling'. The first was the multitude of orders which it was possible to seek which would address internal relocation. The second was the difference between the law on internal relocation as compared with international relocation.

Re F (Internal Relocation) [2010] EWCA Civ 1428

WILSON LJ:

25. The third [puzzling] feature relates to the early insinuation into the principles governing internal relocation of a test of exceptionality. The development of the case-law in this regard offers an interesting insight into the way in which law is made, perhaps not always satisfactorily. No one could quarrel with a proposition that it would rarely be in the interests of a child for the residential parent to be prevented from moving home with the child within the UK. The way in which, in *Re E*, Butler-Sloss LJ chose to express that proposition was to turn it round and to say, at 642D, that 'there may be exceptional cases' which justified refusal. Thus were the seeds of a new test sown. In the first of the decisions in *Re S (Residence Order: Condition)* [2001] EWCA Civ 847, Thorpe LJ, at [24], described the cases in which refusal would be legitimate as 'highly exceptional' and Clarke LJ, at [35], described them as 'genuinely exceptional'. By the time of this court's second decision in relation to S, namely *Re S (A Child) (Residence Order: Condition) (No 2)* [2002] EWCA Civ 1795, exceptionality had become part of 'the principle'....

26. In two entirely different contexts I have previously had occasion to refer to the danger that a decision-maker's attempt to explain his decision in terms which include reference to exceptionality gives rise to the subsequent elevation of a concept of exceptionality as the governing criterion... It is too late for it to be permissible for this court to rule that, in internal relocation cases, the analysis of the child's welfare, informed by consideration of the matters specified in s 1(3) of the Act, should not be conducted through the prism of whether the circumstances are exceptional. ....But, for the reasons given, I believe that, had I not felt bound by authority, I might have wished to suggest that a test of exceptionality was an impermissible gloss on the inquiry mandated by s 1(1) and (3) of the Act.

Because of the generally relatively short distances involved, internal relocation cases tend to be seen as less complex than their international counterparts. However, the consequences in terms of the child's relationship with the non-moving parent can potentially be as serious. Moreover, if the relocation involves the child moving between the three jurisdictions of

---

286 [2009] EWCA Civ 20, [51].
287 Ibid, [36]. See also *Re S (Residence Order: Internal Relocation)* [2012] EWCA Civ 1031.

the UK (from England and Wales to Scotland or to Northern Ireland), there are potentially complex legal implications in terms of enforcing ongoing s 8 orders.[288] For these reasons amongst others, there are some who think that it would be better to have a single approach to relocation disputes, regardless of the proposed destination.[289]

11.10 TERMINATING S 8 ORDERS

Any s 8 order can be made for a specified period[290] or until further order. Most s 8 orders cannot be made beyond the child's 16th birthday unless the case is exceptional.[291] However, this restriction is specifically disapplied in relation to child arrangements orders when they are only about the person with whom the child is to live, and which can therefore readily continue until the child is 18 if that is in the child's best interests.[292]

A s 8 order can be discharged by the court, either on an application by a relevant person or, if proceedings are already underway, of its own motion;[293] an order discharging a s 8 order *is in itself* a s 8 order,[294] and so is a welfare decision to which s 1 applies. Under s 11(5), a child arrangements order which regulates the child's living arrangements terminates automatically if the child has two parents who both have parental responsibility, and the parents then live together continuously for a period of six months.

11.11 CONCLUSION

The law on private disputes over children gives rise to a wide range of issues, bringing into sharp relief many of the key themes discussed in the previous three chapters. The courts are routinely called upon to grapple with such fundamental questions as the appropriate parenting roles of mothers and fathers; whether biological or social parenting should be prioritized; whether the 'bi-nuclear' or 'reconstituted' family is the more secure basis for post-separation parenting; whether multiple parenting figures can be sustained; and the extent to which alternative family forms, such as gay and lesbian parenting, should be accepted as equal to conventional heterosexual arrangements. In searching for the answers to these questions, the courts are required to make the child's welfare their paramount consideration. However, nothing demonstrates the vagaries of the welfare principle more effectively than the shifts in the courts' approach to these disputes over the last 40 years. Whilst some evolution of judicial thinking is to be expected, and indeed applauded, in line with the best available evidence on the developmental needs and outcomes for children living in separated families, the case law and legislative reforms considered in this chapter highlight the extent to which these trends are often driven by social and political factors well beyond the control of the courts. Thus, whilst orthodox wisdom used to dictate the importance of

---

[288] Family Law Act 1986; for an example of the complexity, see *Re W-B (Family Jurisdiction: Appropriate Jurisdiction within UK)* [2012] EWCA Civ 592.
[289] George (2014), ch 6.
[290] S 11(7)(c).
[291] S 9(6).
[292] S 9(6A)–(6B).
[293] S 10(1).
[294] S 8(2).

mothering over fathering, social over biological parenting, and the reconstituted over the 'bi-nuclear' family, various social and political factors have converged to transform these trends so that what we now see, at least in the post-divorce or post-separation context, is a dramatic reversal in the fortunes of one figure: the genetic father. Although there may be some disquiet that the highly politicized debate surrounding fathers' rights has distorted many of the underlying issues, the greater value placed on genetic fathering is not necessarily a cause for concern. Indeed, it may be something to be welcomed. However, in such a highly charged political atmosphere as that generated by some fathers' rights groups, the courts must ensure they do not become distracted by this powerful and often superficially persuasive rhetoric. Decision-making in the courts must remain firmly focused on the needs and interests of the individual child.

ONLINE RESOURCE CENTRE

Questions, suggestions for further reading, and supplementary materials for this chapter (including updates on developments in this area of family law since this book was published) may be found on the Online Resource Centre at **www.oxfordtextbooks.co.uk/orc/familytcm3e/**.

12

CHILD PROTECTION

CENTRAL ISSUES

1. Child protection is a challenging topic. It requires the state to draw a difficult balance between respecting the integrity of the family whilst ensuring vulnerable family members are protected. Tragic cases attracting strong media interest serve as a constant reminder of the dangers of under and over-reacting to suspicions of abuse.

2. Part III of the Children Act 1989 (CA 1989) seeks to support families through the provision of voluntary services to 'children in need'. These aims will be seriously compromised if local authorities are under-resourced.

3. The state cannot remove children from their parents' care on the basis of a simple best interests test: a threshold involving 'significant harm' must first be established. The threshold for state intervention at various stages of the child protection process has been extremely controversial. It has been the subject of several recent House of Lords/Supreme Court decisions.

4. Concern regarding the impact of delay on children suffering significant harm has led to a strong drive towards securing speedier and more robust decision-making by professionals and an emphasis on securing permanency for looked after children within a more tightly defined timetable.

5. The Human Rights Act 1998 (HRA 1998) has reinforced the importance of children's and parents' rights throughout the child protection process, necessitating some changes to both substantive law and procedure.

12.1 INTRODUCTION

The death of a child at the hands of her parents always engenders strong feelings. When that child is known to be at risk and is supposedly under the care and protection of the state, the child's death attracts great public anger and concern. Kimberley Carlile, Victoria Climbié, Baby Peter, Khyra Ishaq, and Keanu Williams are just some of the children who have died in such tragic circumstances.[1] Finding answers to what went wrong and, more importantly, how such deaths can be prevented is exceptionally difficult. Deception and manipulation by the child's parents, the naïve optimism of social workers, the complacency of health professionals and teachers, overworked, inexperienced, and poorly trained staff, and a serious lack of local authority resources are all too familiar stories. However, even the best resourced, trained, and supported professionals would not be able to prevent the death of every child at risk of harm from abusive parents. Child protection is an inherently difficult process. Every case requires a delicate balancing exercise to be performed between respecting and supporting the integrity of the family whilst ensuring vulnerable family members are protected. A strong, robust, and highly interventionist approach by professionals can be just as harmful as the 'hands-off' complacency which marked the cases of Victoria Climbié and Baby Peter.[2] The unjustified removal of large numbers of children in Cleveland in 1987, Rochdale in 1990, and Orkney in 1991 because of misplaced suspicions of ritualized sexual abuse provides a chilling reminder of the dangers of misguided, 'crusading', albeit well-meaning, professionals.[3] Although state intervention into the family is not necessarily a bad thing—indeed, help offered to the family by the local authority on a consensual basis can be both positive and supportive—the wrongful removal of a child can be devastating.[4]

The legal framework provided by the CA 1989 has to ensure that child protection professionals can respond quickly and effectively to children at risk of harm, whilst guarding against unnecessary and potentially harmful intervention into the family.[5] It is a difficult balance, exacerbated by the increasingly difficult and challenging environment in which the child protection system operates. Against a backdrop of severe budgetary constraints on local authorities and the courts, there has been a dramatic increase in the number of local authority applications for care orders driven both by social work reaction to the public outcry following the death of Baby Peter and a perception amongst policy-makers that social workers wait far too long before initiating legal proceedings to secure the removal of a child from abusive and neglectful parents.[6] At the same time, it cannot be forgotten that families facing the removal of their children are often themselves intensely vulnerable, with mothers in particular suffering from a myriad of problems necessitating professional understanding, intervention, and support.[7] These ever increasing demands have brought the child protection system to crisis point, characterized by systemic delay (care proceedings in 2012 took an average of 55 weeks to complete)[8] and poor decision-making. In the words of David Norgrove, we have 'a system that is not a system, characterised by mutual distrust and lack of leadership, by incoherence and without solid evidence based knowledge about how it

---

[1] For short accounts of the circumstances surrounding the deaths of Maria Colwell, Jasmine Beckford, Kimberley Carlile, and Victoria Climbié see Cretney (2003a), ch 20. As to Baby Peter, see LSCB (2009); Khyra Ishaq, see Radford (2010); and Keanu Williams, see Lundberg (2013).

[2] Lord Laming (2003).

[3] Butler-Sloss (1988).

[4] For a striking example of such a miscarriage of justice see, *Re W (Children)* [2009] EWCA Civ 59.

[5] Unless otherwise stated, all references to statutory provisions in this chapter are to the CA 1989.

[6] The number of care applications jumped dramatically in 2009 from an average of 20,000 per year to what is now a relatively stable level of 30,000 per year. See MOJ (2014a), 14. As to concerns regarding the slow and cautious response of social workers to situations of neglect, see Norgrove (2011), 91 and House of Commons (2012/13).

[7] Masson, Pearce, and Bader (2008), 20.

[8] MOJ (2014a), 17.

really works. The consequence for children is unconscionable delay'.[9] The Family Justice Review ('Norgrove') made a number of recommendations to address these problems which were accepted by government and are now enshrined within the Children and Families Act 2014 (CFA 2014), the most notable of which are a statutory time limit for the disposal of care proceedings of 26 weeks, a more restricted approach to the use of expert evidence, and a reduced role for the judiciary in the scrutiny of care plans.[10]

Within the context of this challenging environment, this chapter considers the law governing state intervention into family life where a child is considered to be 'in need' or at risk of harm. We begin by outlining the competing approaches to state intervention and the principles underpinning the CA 1989. We then examine the legal framework governing voluntary state intervention for children in need under Part III of the CA 1989 before considering the law and procedure regulating compulsory intervention into family life by means of care proceedings under Part IV. We conclude by considering the various emergency and interim measures available to protect a child thought to be at risk of immediate harm.

12.2 PRINCIPLES OF STATE INTERVENTION INTO FAMILY LIFE

12.2.1 COMPETING APPROACHES AND THE CHILDREN ACT 1989

When determining the basis upon which state intervention into family life is justified, two key questions have to be addressed: (i) the principles which should govern the state's initial intervention; and (ii) the long-term goals which should guide decision-making once some form of intervention is deemed necessary. Lorraine Fox-Harding has identified four models of state intervention into family life which suggest differing answers to these two key questions:

L. Fox-Harding, 'The Children Act 1989 in Context: Four Perspectives in Child Care Law and Policy (1)', (1991a) 13 *Journal of Social Welfare and Family Law* 179, 181–2

(1) Laissez-faire and patriarchy

The term *laissez-faire* is used here to describe the perspective which sees the role of the state in child care as ideally one of minimal intervention, while the privacy and sanctity of the original family should in most circumstances be respected. However, in *extreme* cases of poor parental care, state intervention is not only acceptable but preferably of a strong and authoritative kind, transferring the child from the original parent(s) to a secure substitute placement with a new set of parent figures. The new family unit should then be accorded the same rights, and respect by the state, as the original one...

(2) State paternalism and child protection

The terms "state paternalism and child protection" are taken to indicate a school of thought which favours much more extensive state intervention to protect children from poor parental

---

[9] Norgrove (2011), 3.
[10] CFA 2014, ss 13–15.

care. Where parental care is deemed inadequate, then in this perspective finding the child a new permanent home where good quality care will be provided is usually the appropriate response. Therefore the rights and liberties of parents and the integrity of the original birth family are given a low priority in this perspective; while the welfare of the child, as this is construed, is paramount.

(3) The defence of the birth family and parents' rights

A third, pro-birth family perspective encapsulates the idea that birth or biological families are extremely important both for children and parents, and should be maintained wherever possible. Where families have to be separated through children entering substitute care, then parent-child links should usually be kept up. The role of the state is seen as, ideally, neither paternalist nor *lasseiz-faire*, but positively supportive of families, providing various services that they need to function well and remain together. At the same time, class, poverty and deprivation are seen as important elements in child care, explaining much of what appears to be inadequate parenting, while the (usually coercive) response of the state is disproportionately directed to lower class and deprived families.

(4) Children's rights and child liberation

The terms "children's rights and child liberation" are used here for a perspective which emphasises the importance of *the child's* own viewpoint and wishes, seeing the child as a separate entity with rights to autonomy and freedom, rather like an adult. The idea of the control of children, either through the state or by adults individually, is called into question by the emphasis on rights and liberation, as therefore are notions of custody and parental rights. The strength and competence of children, and their similarity to adults, are emphasised, rather than their vulnerability; children are not seen as in need of protection, but empowerment; but it is not clear how far children would be expected to carry the burdens and duties of adult status as well. A less extreme position would emphasise that children should at least have more say in what happens to them.

Fox-Harding contends that elements of all four approaches can be identified in the CA 1989, albeit she argues that paternalism and defence of the birth parents' rights predominate.[11] Indeed, these were strong themes in the government's Review of Child Care Law preceding the legislation. The importance placed on preserving the integrity of the birth family and supporting it wherever possible both before and after intervention is particularly clear.

DHSS, *Review of Child Care Law. Report to Ministers of an Interdepartmental Working Party* (London: HMSO, 1985)

2.8 A distinction is often drawn between the interests of children and the interests of their parents. In the great majority of families, including those who are for one reason or another in need of social services, this distinction does not exist. The interests of the children are best served by their remaining with their families and the interests of their parents are best served by allowing them to undertake their natural and legal responsibility to care for their own children. Hence the focus of effort should be to enable and assist parents to discharge

---

[11] Fox-Harding (1991b), 299.

those responsibilities. Even where a child has to spend some time away from home, every effort should be made to maintain and foster links between the child and his family to care for the child in partnership with rather than in opposition to his parents, and to work towards his return to them.

As Fox-Harding notes, the emphasis placed on providing extensive state *support* for the birth family is surprising.[12] Given the CA 1989 was sponsored by a Conservative Government whose political ideology traditionally favours protecting the autonomy of the family and affords only a minimal role to the state, a more laissez-faire approach might have been expected. This would also have been more consistent with what some commentators have identified as the 'privatizing' trend underpinning the CA 1989, which, as encapsulated by s 1(5) (the 'no order' principle), seeks to place the primary responsibility for the care and upbringing of children on the child's parents and is generally characterized by a marked withdrawal of the state from family life.[13] None of this is consistent with the imposition of wide-ranging duties on local authorities to provide a comprehensive range of services to help and support families in need. Yet, this is what Part III of the CA 1989 purports to do.

Unfortunately, no matter how much help and support is provided, there will always be some families for whom support will have to give way to more coercive forms of intervention. One of the hardest questions in child protection is determining when that point is reached. In recent years there has been a shift towards earlier and more decisive intervention with a view to securing permanency for the child.[14] Growing concern about the life-chances of children left to 'drift' in and out of care,[15] has led to a strong focus on ensuring effective planning for children known to social services and securing long-term alternative placements for those children in care.[16] Given the evidence regarding the woeful life-experiences and long-term prospects of 'looked after' children, this emphasis on the importance of permanency planning, even at the potential expense of long-term engagement with the birth family, is understandable.[17] However, as Norgrove recognizes, this drive towards permanency within much tighter timescales can be difficult to reconcile with perceptions as to birth parents' rights:

D. Norgrove (Chair), *Family Justice Review: Final Report* (London: MOJ, 2011), 13

The system struggles to cope with the weight of its responsibilities. Understandable sympathy for parents and an acute awareness of the enormity of the decisions encourages a wish to explore every avenue. The idea of a proportionate approach comes across as

---

[12] Ibid.

[13] Bainham and Gilmore (2013), 82.

[14] House of Commons (2012/13); House of Lords (2013), [56]–[87].

[15] DFES (2004).

[16] See, e.g., House of Lords (2013), [56]–[87] and DFE (2013a). See also Parkinson (2003), 147–8. For an important recent study examining decision-making and outcomes for young children under 12 months old deemed to be suffering or likely to suffer significant harm, see Ward, Brown, Westlake, and Munro (2010). The research findings support concerns as to the over-optimistic and almost deferential approach of social workers to parents, the damaging impact of delay on these very vulnerable young children, and the lack of understanding about these dangers amongst professionals.

[17] DFES (2004).

seeming to risk denial of the parent's right to a fair hearing. We were told and we agree that the right of the parents to a fair hearing has come too often to override the paramount welfare of the child.

12.2.2 THE HUMAN RIGHTS DIMENSION

The fundamental rights of the child and the parents must be safeguarded throughout the child protection process. From the child's perspective, two key rights under the European Convention on Human Rights (ECHR) are engaged: Article 3 and Article 8.[18] These provisions impose positive obligations on the state to protect a child from parental abuse. Clearly the state cannot provide absolute guarantees against the abuse of children. Given the secretive nature of child abuse, particularly sexual abuse, many incidences of abuse will go undetected without any degree of fault or responsibility resting with state officials. Even in those cases known to the local authority, the need to prioritize and allocate scare resources means that the protection afforded to individual children cannot ever be absolute. However, the European Court of Human Rights has held that under Articles 3 and 8 the state owes individual children a positive duty as regards the detection, investigation, and management of child abuse. That obligation includes the need to remove children from situations of known risk where appropriate.[19]

However, as the European Court also recognizes, where the local authority is or should be aware that a child is at risk, it is not a straightforward matter of simply removing the child.[20] In all of these cases children have important countervailing rights: whilst ensuring the child is adequately protected against abuse, the state must also respect the integrity of the child's family. In particular, when considering what child protection measures are necessary, Article 8 requires the state to take all necessary steps to ensure that any measures of intervention are proportionate to the harm suffered and that no child is unnecessarily removed from the care of his or her family. It is a difficult line for the local authority to tread. Both over-reacting (removing without good cause) and under-reacting (failing to remove) may give rise to liability under s 7 of the HRA 1998 or (at the suit of the child) in common law negligence.[21]

The child's parents enjoy similar rights under the ECHR.[22] The European Court has consistently stressed that under Article 8 the state has both negative and positive obligations

---

[18] See also Art 19 of the United Nations Convention on the Rights of the Child 1989 (UNCRC). For an excellent analysis of the impact of human rights law on child protection, see Kaganas (2010).

[19] *Z v United Kingdom* (App No 29392/95, ECHR) (2001).

[20] Ibid, [74].

[21] *TP and KM v United Kingdom* (App No 28945/95, ECHR) (2001). See also *D v East Berkshire Community Health NHS Trust* [2003] EWCA Civ 1151; *APB, BBB, CBB and DBB v Milton Keynes Council* [2011] EWHC 2745 (QB).

[22] *RK and AK v United Kingdom* (App No 38000/05, ECHR) (2008) and *MAK and RK v United Kingdom* (App Nos 45901/05 and 40146/06, ECHR) (2010). Note, however, that whilst the parents may bring a claim under the HRA 1998, domestic authorities have yet to find that the local authority owes them a duty of care under common law negligence, at least if they are the suspected perpetrators of the abuse: *D v East Berkshire Community Health NHS Trust* [2005] UKHL 23 and *Lawrence v Pembrokeshire County Council* [2007] EWCA Civ 446. A duty of care may be owed to parents in circumstances where, because the parent is not the suspected abuser, there is no potential conflict of interest between parent and child: *Merthyr Tydfil County Borough Council v C* [2010] EWHC 62. For a strong critique of the European Court of Human Rights' approach to parents' rights in this context, see Greasley (2010).

towards the child's parents. The various demands of Article 8 are summarized in the case
of *Haase v Germany*.

Haase v Germany (App No 11057/02, ECHR) (2005)

[90]...While the authorities enjoy a wide margin of appreciation in assessing the necessity
of taking a child into care, in particular where an emergency situation arises, the Court must still
be satisfied in the particular case that there existed circumstances justifying the removal of the
child, and it is for the respondent State to establish that a careful assessment of the impact of
the proposed care measure on the parents and the child, as well as of the possible alternatives
to taking the child into public care, was carried out prior to implementation of such a measure...

[92] Following any removal into care, a stricter scrutiny is called for in respect of any further
limitations by the authorities, for example on restrictions on parental rights and access, and
on any legal safeguards designed to secure the effective protection of the right of parents
and children to respect for their family life. Such further limitations entail the danger that the
family relations between the parents and a young child might be effectively curtailed...

[93] The taking into care of a child should normally be regarded as a temporary measure
to be discontinued as soon as circumstances permit, and any measures of implementation
of temporary care should be consistent with the ultimate aim of reuniting the natural parent
and child...In this regard a fair balance has to be struck between the interests of the child
remaining in care and those of the parent in being reunited with the child...In carrying out
this balancing exercise, the Court will attach particular importance to the best interests
of the child which, depending on their nature and seriousness, may override those of the
parent...In particular, a parent cannot be entitled under Article 8 to have such measures
taken as would harm the child's health and development...

[94] Whilst Article 8 contains no explicit procedural requirements, the decision-making process involved in measures of interference must be fair and such as to ensure due respect for
the interests safeguarded by Article 8. The Court must therefore determine whether, having
regard to the circumstances of the case and notably the importance of the decisions to be
taken, the applicants have been involved in the decision-making process, seen as a whole, to
a degree sufficient to provide them with the requisite protection of their interests...

The judiciary have broadly welcomed the reception of a rights-based discourse into the
public law on children.[23] The right to respect for family life reinforces the importance of
preserving the integrity of the family unit which has long formed a core principle of child
protection policy. The courts have thus issued strong warnings as to the need for fundamental changes in the prevailing 'culture' and 'mindset' of local authorities, demanding
far-reaching improvements in both the procedural and substantive aspects of local authority decision-making before, during, and after formal care proceedings.[24] With the Article 8
rights of the child and the parents engaged, ECHR arguments are now a routine feature of
public law cases and must form an *explicit* part of the judge's reasoning.[25] Indeed, arguments
over alleged breaches of Articles 6 and 8 ECHR are so commonly made that some judges

---

[23] For further discussion, see Harris-Short (2005), 340–50.

[24] *Re G (Care: Challenge to Local Authority's Decision)* [2003] EWHC 551; *Re L (Care: Assessment: Fair Trial)* [2002] EWHC 1379.

[25] *EH v Greenwich London Borough Council; Re A (Children) (Non-Accidental Injury)* [2010] EWCA Civ 344; *Re M and B (Children) (Care Proceedings: Family Life)* [2010] EWCA Civ 821; *Re V (A Child) (Care Proceedings: Human Rights Claims)* [2004] EWCA Civ 54.

have expressed concern that human rights arguments are hindering local authority applications and causing unnecessary expense and delay.[26]

12.2.3 THE PROBLEM OF RESOURCES

The strong protection given to the parents' rights under Article 8 makes the recent shift in favour of permanency planning at the potential expense of repeated attempts at rehabilitation with the birth family all the more surprising. However, it is arguable that given the severe fiscal restraints of recent years, the government's emphasis on permanency planning is driven more by pragmatic concerns than any major ideological shift in child protection policy. A model of state intervention based on providing a range of effective support services to families in need is resource-intensive, requiring large-scale investment in local authority services. Without such investment, an approach focusing on supporting the birth family is almost certain to fail. This is an issue where idealism meets head-on the harsh economic realities of life. The serious problem of poorly resourced local authorities[27] means there is a tendency to divert resources away from voluntary family support services to deal with the more serious and immediate problems of children requiring compulsory care.[28] A local authority culture of crisis intervention is thereby perpetuated.[29] Keenan argues that inadequate funding is a key factor behind the adoption of a more hard-line, authoritarian approach to child protection.[30]

12.3 STATE SUPPORT FOR CHILDREN AND FAMILIES UNDER PART III

Part III of the CA 1989 enshrines the then Conservative Government's commitment to promoting the upbringing of children within their birth families by the provision of help and support to families in need. In accordance with the principle that 'prevention is better than cure',[31] this section of the CA 1989 brings together a wide range of services aimed at ensuring that children's needs are met within their families before more coercive intervention becomes necessary. 'Partnership' is the 'buzz' word of these provisions.[32] Intervention under Part III should be non-coercive, based on mutual cooperation, and, most importantly, voluntarily accepted by the parents. The government was keen to remove any stigma attached to receiving help from the local authority, stressing that the provision of services under Part III should be viewed as a positive, supportive measure for the family, not a sign of 'parental shortcomings' or failure.[33] To emphasize the distinction between these services and any compulsory measures taken within the context of care proceedings under Part IV, all coercive measures that the state could formerly take when a

---

[26] *Re V (Care: Pre-Birth Actions)* [2004] EWCA Civ 1575; *Re J (A Child) (Care Proceedings: Fair Trial)* [2006] EWCA Civ 545.
[27] See, e.g., *R (G) v Barnet London Borough Council* [2003] UKHL 57, [10].
[28] Bainham and Gilmore (2013), 468.
[29] See generally, Smith (2002).
[30] Keenan (2006), 48.
[31] Bainham and Gilmore (2013), 27.
[32] Ibid, 85.
[33] DHSS et al (1987), paras 17, 21.

child was being voluntarily looked after by the local authority were removed.[34] In practice, this marked a significant erosion of state power and an important correlative strengthening of the parents' rights.[35]

Before the CA 1989, the provision of support and assistance to families in need was contained within a complicated patchwork of legislative provisions.[36] One of the major aims of the CA 1989 was to rationalize and consolidate the legal basis for the provision of services into one comprehensive, coherent piece of legislation.[37] As a result of this consolidation process, the scope of Part III is extremely broad. It covers a wide and disparate range of children's needs, from the provision of respite care for disabled children to the provision of more long-term accommodation for children in need as a result of parental neglect.

12.3.1 THE GENERAL DUTY TO CHILDREN IN NEED: S 17

Section 17(1) sets down the general duty owed by local authorities to children in need.

Children Act 1989, s 17

(1) It shall be the general duty of every local authority (in addition to the other duties imposed on them by this Part)—

(a) to safeguard and promote the welfare of children within their area who are in need; and

(b) so far as is consistent with that duty to promote the upbringing of such children by their families,

by providing a range and level of services appropriate to those children's needs.

In order to qualify for the provision of services under s 17 the child must be 'a child in need'. 'Child' is defined in s 105(1) as 'a person under the age of eighteen'. The meaning of a child 'in need' is set down in s 17(10).

Children Act 1989, s 17

(10) For the purposes of this Part a child shall be taken to be in need if—

(a) he is unlikely to achieve or maintain, or to have the opportunity of achieving or maintaining, a reasonable standard of health or development without the provision for him of services by a local authority under this Part;

(b) his health or development is likely to be significantly impaired, or further impaired without the provision for him of such services; or

(c) he is disabled . . .

---

[34] Bainham and Gilmore (2013), 465.
[35] For discussion of the previous powers of the state, see Bainham and Gilmore (2013), 29.
[36] Ibid, 27.
[37] DHSS et al (1987), paras 7–8.

'Development' is further defined as 'physical, intellectual, emotional, social or behavioural development'.[38] 'Health' is further defined as physical or mental health.[39] It was held by the Supreme Court in *R (A) v London Borough of Croydon*,[40] that a distinction needs to be drawn between the question of whether or not a young person is 'a child' for the purposes of the CA 1989 and the question of whether or not that child is 'in need' for the purposes of Part III.[41] The former is a straightforward objective question of fact (to which there is a right and wrong answer) and, in cases of dispute, is to be determined, on the evidence, by the court.[42] In contrast, the question of whether the child is 'in need' involves 'a number of different value judgments' and is thus to be made by the local authority, 'subject to the control of the courts on the ordinary principles of judicial review'.[43]

The House of Lords has held that the s 17 duty is a general or 'target' duty owed to all children in need within the local authority area.[44] This means there is no specific duty on the local authority to carry out an assessment of a child's needs which can be enforced at the suit of an individual child. The majority also dismissed the argument that the general duty under s 17 'crystallizes' into a specific enforceable duty once the child has been assessed and a particular need identified.[45] However, whilst there is therefore no duty on the local authority to provide an assessed service, the local authority's refusal can be challenged by way of judicial review.[46] Bearing in mind the policy underpinning the CA 1989, it was held by Munby LJ in *R (VC) v Newcastle City Council and Secretary of State for the Home Department*, that a local authority's refusal to provide services to a child in need would be subject to 'strict and, it may be, sceptical scrutiny, particularly if there is no available argument based on lack of resources'.[47]

To assist the local authority to carry out its s 17(1) duty, Sch 2, Part I sets down a range of more specific duties and powers.[48] These include identifying and assessing children in need within their area,[49] taking reasonable steps to prevent abuse and neglect,[50] taking reasonable steps to prevent the need for care proceedings under Part IV, providing accommodation to a member of the child's household to protect the child from ill-treatment,[51] and providing services for children living at home (including the provision of advice, guidance and counselling, occupational, social, cultural, or recreational activities, home help, and assistance with holidays).[52] Section 17(6) further provides that services may include the provision of accommodation (although a child provided with accommodation under s 17 is not a 'looked after' child), giving assistance in kind or, in exceptional circumstances, cash.[53] Services may

---

[38] S 17(11).

[39] Ibid.

[40] [2009] UKSC 8, [26].

[41] Ibid, [26], [32].

[42] Ibid, [27] (Lady Hale); [51], [53] (Lord Hope).

[43] Ibid, [26], [28] (Lady Hale). See also *Re J (Specific Issue Order: Leave to Apply)* [1995] 1 FLR 669.

[44] *R (On the Application of G) v Barnet London Borough Council* [2003] UKHL 57, [106].

[45] Lord Nicholls dissented.

[46] *R (VC) v Newcastle City Council and Secretary of State for the Home Department* [2011] EWHC 2673 (Admin).

[47] Ibid, [25]–[26]

[48] S 17(2).

[49] Sch 2, Part I, paras 1 and 3.

[50] Ibid, para 4.

[51] Ibid, para 5.

[52] Ibid, para 8.

[53] S 17(6) was amended by the Adoption and Children Act 2002, s 116 to make clear that accommodation could be provided under s 17 following contrary decisions in *R (A) v Lambeth London Borough Council* [2001] EWCA Civ 1624 and *R (J) v Enfield Borough Council* [2002] EWHC 432.

be provided to the child or a member of the child's family. Before determining what, if any, services to provide under this section the local authority must, so far as is reasonably practicable, ascertain and give due consideration to the child's wishes.[54]

12.3.2 PROVIDING ACCOMMODATION FOR A CHILD

The duty to accommodate: s 20(1)

In stark contrast to the wide discretion conferred on the local authority under s 17, s 20(1) confers a clear duty on the local authority to accommodate a child if certain conditions are met.

Children Act 1989, s 20

(1) Every local authority shall provide accommodation for any child in need within their area who appears to them to require accommodation as a result of—

    (a) there being no person who has parental responsibility for him;

    (b) his being lost or having been abandoned; or

    (c) the person who has been caring for him being prevented (whether or not permanently, and for whatever reason) from providing him with suitable accommodation or care.

In the case of children in need who are over 16 years of age, the duty to provide accommodation will only arise if the local authority considers it likely that the child's welfare will be 'seriously prejudiced' if it does not provide the child with accommodation.[55]

If the local authority is under a duty to accommodate a child pursuant to s 20 of the CA 1989, it cannot avoid the more extensive obligations owed to a 'looked after' child by purporting to accommodate the child under some other statutory provision. The issue has become of particular significance for young people approaching the age of 18 whose entitlement to local authority financial and other support services is dependent on whether or not the child is or has been a 'looked after' child under s 20 of the CA 1989. The question of the relationship between a local authority's general powers under s 17 and its more specific duty to accommodate a child under s 20 arose in the case *of R (H) v Wandsworth London Borough Council*.[56] Holman J held that in determining whether a duty arises under s 20 the local authority may need to exercise judgement over certain matters, such as the relevance of the child's wishes.[57] However, once it has been determined that the s 20 duty arises (or at least should be deemed to have arisen), there is no room for discretion: the local authority is bound to act pursuant to that duty and cannot avoid its more onerous responsibilities by purporting to accommodate the child under some other statutory provision, including its

---

[54] S 17(4A).

[55] S 20(3). See *Re T (Accommodation by Local Authority)* [1995] 1 FLR 159.

[56] [2007] EWHC 1082.

[57] Baroness Hale similarly suggested in *R (M) v London Borough of Hammersmith and Fulham* [2008] UKHL 14, [43] that not all homeless 16- and 17-year-olds would 'require accommodation' (as opposed, e.g., to requiring help to secure accommodation) under s 20 and that it would be very unlikely that a competent child would be accommodated as a 'looked after' child against his or her wishes. She reiterated this view in *R (G) v London Borough of Southwark* [2009] UKHL 26, [28](4) and (6).

various duties and powers under the Housing Act 1996.[58] Holman J's approach has subsequently been endorsed by the House of Lords in *R (G) v London Borough of Southwark*[59] and *R (M) v Hammersmith and Fulham London Borough Council.*[60]

ONLINE RESOURCE CENTRE

Extended extracts from these authorities can be found on the Online Resource Centre.

It is important to note that the duty imposed on the local authority under s 20(1) is a duty to provide accommodation for the *child*. It does not include providing accommodation for members of the child's family. This was made clear by the House of Lords in *R (G) v Barnet London Borough Council*. Two of the three conjoined cases concerned a child who had been assessed as in need of accommodation because the mother had been rendered homeless and was not entitled to assistance under the homelessness legislation. Whilst the local authorities were not prepared to accommodate both mother and child under s 17, they were, if necessary, prepared to accommodate the child pursuant to their duties under s 20(1). The appellants contended that this policy was unlawful, arguing that as the local authority was under a duty to promote the upbringing of children within their families, s 20(1) should be read as imposing a duty on the local authority to house both mother and child together. In support of this argument, the appellants relied on the duty imposed on the local authority under the CA 1989 to make arrangements to enable the child to live with, amongst others, a parent unless 'that would not be reasonably practicable or consistent with his welfare'. The majority of the House of Lords again rejected this argument:

R (On the Application of G) v Barnet London Borough Council [2003] UKHL 57

LORD HOPE:

99. There are...four hurdles that the appellants must cross if they are to succeed in their argument. First, they must show that their children are children in need within the meaning of section 17(10). It was not suggested that there would have been any serious room for doubt on this point. Their mothers were unable to provide them with accommodation, and in both cases the children were at serious risk of having no roof over their heads at all. Leaving them to sleep in doorways was not an option in their case. Children who are reduced to this level of destitution are plainly children in need. Their health or development is likely to be significantly impaired if they are not provided with services by the local social services authority: section 17(10)(b).

---

[58] [2007] EWHC 1082, [53], [55], and [58].

[59] [2009] UKHL 26, [9]. Applied in *R (TG) v Lambeth London Borough Council* [2011] EWCA Civ 526.

[60] [2008] UKHL 14. Note, however, that on the facts of *M* where the child had never been referred to the local authority's Children's Services Department and the local authority had thus never addressed its mind to the question of whether a duty may be owed under the CA 1989, the House of Lords held that the local authority could not be deemed to have accommodated the child pursuant to its Children Act responsibilities. For a good critique of this decision, see Driscoll and Hollingsworth (2008). The case was distinguished by the Court of Appeal in *R (TG) v Lambeth London Borough Council* [2011] EWCA Civ 526 where it was held that the fact that the young person had been assessed by a local authority social worker experienced in the provision of children's services was sufficient to impute a duty to accommodate to the Children's Services Department under the CA 1989.

100. The appellants must show, in the second place, that the respondents were under a duty to provide their children with accommodation. Local social services authorities are under a duty to provide accommodation for a child in need within their area who appears to them to require accommodation as a result, among other things, of the person who has been caring from [sic] him being prevented (whether or not permanently, and for whatever reason) from providing him with suitable accommodation or care: section 20(1)(c). This provision must be read in the light of the general duties set out in section 17(1). Among these duties there is the duty to safeguard and promote the welfare of the child. At first sight the concept of the carer being prevented from providing the child with suitable accommodation or care does not sit easily with the situation where the carer has chosen to refuse offers of accommodation or other forms of assistance by the relevant local authority. But the words "for whatever reason" indicate that the widest possible scope must be given to this provision. The guiding principle is the need to safeguard and promote the child's welfare. So it makes no difference whether the reason is one which the carer has brought about by her own act or is one which she was resisting to the best of her ability. On the facts, it is plain that the respondents were under a duty to provide accommodation for the appellants' children under section 20(1).

101. The appellants must then show, in the third place, that section 23(6) applies to their case [now replaced by s 22C(2)–(4)]. That subsection applies where a local social services authority "are looking after a child." This expression is defined in section 22(1), which provides that any reference in the Act to a child "who is looked after by a local authority" is a reference to a child who is either in their care or is provided with accommodation by the authority in the exercise of any functions referred to the social services committee, including the functions under the Act…[I]t is clear that if the stage had been reached where the respondents were fulfilling their duty to provide accommodation for them under section 20(1)(c), the children would have been children who were being looked after by the local authority within the meaning of section 22(1).

102. This brings me to the crucial point in this part of the case, which is whether a local authority looking after a child is under a duty to provide accommodation to any of the persons mentioned in section 23(6)(a) and (b) [now s 22C(3)], who include the child's parent, to enable the child to live with that person. The duty, as expressed in the subsection, is to "make arrangements to enable" the child to live with any one of the persons mentioned. It is qualified by the words "unless that would not be reasonably practicable and consistent with his welfare". The appellants' argument is that among the arrangements that may be made in the performance of this duty is the provision of accommodation to the person mentioned so that the child will be able to live with that person. They also submit…that neither the cost of doing this nor the availability of resources have any bearing on what is or is not reasonably practicable as to permit this would downgrade the duty into a discretionary power…

104. Section 23(6) [now s 22C(2)–(4)] appears to have been framed on the…assumption [that the person with whom the child is to be placed or the person with whom the child may be allowed to live already has accommodation which will enable the child to live with that person]. The context in which it appears suggests that this is so. But the wording of the subsection, and its content, reinforce the argument. The arrangements to which it refers are arrangements enabling the child to live with that person. Nothing is said about providing that person with accommodation. Moreover the duty to make the arrangements to which it refers is not restricted to enabling the child to live with his family. If it had been so restricted there might have been some force in the argument that the duty in this subsection was to be read together with the general duty in section 17(1) to promote the upbringing of the child by his family. But the person with whom the child may be enabled to live under this

subsection include relatives other than his parents...The width of this class of persons indicates that what Parliament had in mind when it was enacting this provision was that these were persons who already had accommodation of their own. The fact that the duty is qualified by reference to what is reasonably practicable and consistent with the child's welfare is entirely consistent with this approach. It permits the local authority to have regard to the nature of the accommodation which that person is able to provide before it takes its decision as to whether, and if so with whom, the child is to be accommodated under this subsection. It is not concerned with the resources of the local authority, because the duty does not extend to the provision of accommodation for that person at its own cost or from its own resources.

The power to accommodate: voluntary accommodation under s 20(4)

In addition to its duty to provide accommodation, the local authority has the *power* to provide accommodation to a child if it 'considers that to do so would safeguard or promote the child's welfare'.[61] This power to receive children into voluntary care was intended as a positive measure for struggling parents. The government hoped that its position within Part III of the legislation would encourage families to seek local authority support when needed.[62] To this end, s 20(7) explicitly provides that a local authority may not provide accommodation for a child if a person with parental responsibility objects and is willing and able to provide or arrange alternative accommodation. To reinforce this point, it is further provided that a person with parental responsibility can remove the child at any time and without notice from local authority care.[63]

The importance of 'partnership' between the local authority and the parents is evident throughout these provisions. However, the Children Act's strong commitment to protecting the voluntary nature of accommodation under Part III and the weakening of the local authority's position relative to that of the parents has been the subject of strong criticism. It is argued that children in this position can end up drifting in and out of care throughout their childhood, with the local authority being used by parents as nothing more than a convenient dumping ground.[64] In particular, commentators have expressed concern that inappropriate use of voluntary care may prevent proper long-term planning for children spending significant periods of time away from their families. The government has therefore recently consulted on proposals to impose new duties on local authorities to properly prepare for and support the return of a child from voluntary care.[65] The proposed new duties will include a requirement for local authorities to prepare a return 'plan' setting out the support and services to be offered to the child's family. Where the return home was unplanned, the local authority will be under a duty to visit and review the child at home within ten days of his or her removal from care.

Judith Masson has also expressed concern about the inappropriate use of voluntary care but on rather different grounds. She argues that parents are often pressured into agreeing to voluntary accommodation by the local authority to avoid the threat of care proceedings

---

[61] S 20(4).

[62] DHSS et al (1987), para 21.

[63] S 20(8) and (9). Relying on comments of Munby J in *R (G) v Nottingham City Council* [2008] EWHC 152, Bainham contends that s 3(5) of the CA 1989 provides sufficient authority for anyone with de facto care of the child to refuse to hand the child over to a parent with parental responsibility if the parent appears to pose an imminent risk to the child's health and safety. See Bainham (2008c), 261–2.

[64] Smith (1992), 350.

[65] DFE (2013a), ch 5.

or because the parents believe they have no choice.[66] In one particularly worrying case, Munby J was strongly critical of the actions of Nottingham County Council in unlawfully removing a newborn baby from its distressed mother in reliance on the fact that she did not 'raise objection'. As Munby J points out, 'helpless acquiescence' or 'submission in the face of asserted State authority' cannot be equated with consent and 'in this context, nothing short of consent will suffice'.[67]

The drive to divert cases away from costly and difficult court proceedings by reaching a voluntary agreement with the parents is now formally enshrined in the pre-proceedings Public Law Outline.[68] From the perspective of the local authority, the use of voluntary care secured through the pre-proceedings process has many advantages. It is more cost effective and avoids the difficulties of making a potentially complicated and expensive application to the court. However, coercing parents into agreeing to voluntary accommodation to avoid court proceedings is of concern if the local authority would not have been able to make out the grounds for compulsory intervention under Part IV.[69] As Kaganas points out, whilst proceeding in this way may have certain benefits for the parents, this informal mode of 'state regulation' also denies them the protection of procedural rights and guarantees, including adequate legal representation, which characterize a judicial process.[70]

F. Kaganas, 'Child Protection, Gender and Rights', in J. Wallbank, S. Choudhry, and J. Herring (eds), *Rights, Gender and Family Law* (Abingdon: Routledge, 2010), 43, 53–5

[W]hile there might be a drop in the number of applications to court, this does not necessarily mean that families are not going to be regulated. What it might mean is that families will be subject to forms of regulation that take even less account of their rights and give them less chance of making their side of the story heard or of resisting the assessments of the professionals. It is true that the safeguards offered by the HRA are triggered at all decision-making stages of the child protection process, but since they relate primarily to information consultation and presence at meetings, they do not necessarily provide a bulwark against pressure to reach agreement...

[T]he partnership between social workers and parents is generally weighted in favour of the professionals. The balance of power between parents and professionals is not equal and professionals are in a position to dictate what is expected of families...This presents risks for parents...The pressure exerted, coupled with parents' lack of understanding, means that they may agree to arrangements they cannot maintain. Failure to abide by the terms of the agreement can be used to demonstrate parents' unfitness or refusal to co-operate...

---

[66] Masson (1992). Discussed in Bainham and Gilmore (2013), 465.

[67] *R (G) v Nottingham City Council (No 2)* [2008] EWHC 400, [55] and [61]. See also the guidance given by Hedley J in *Coventry City Council v C* [2012] EWHC 2190, [46].

[68] MOJ (2008), Flowchart: Pre-proceedings Public Law Outline, superceded by President of the Family Division (2010), sec 10. See also Masson (2010). For an excellent discussion of the three key reviews informing the Public Law Outline, see Masson (2007).

[69] Bainham and Gilmore (2013), 465–6.

[70] As to the inadequacy of legal representation for parents at the pre-proceeding stage, see Holt et al (2013). More generally as to concerns regarding the compatibility with the ECHR of this pre-proceedings process and the shift to decision-making within an 'administrative' rather than judicial setting, see Holt and Kelly (2012).

Clearly then, partnership and co-operative working can involve monitoring and regulation of the family. And that regulation is unimpeded by the kind of scrutiny that court proceedings would entail. The arrangements are not open to challenge by, for example, lawyers or a children's guardian. And any challenge on the part of the parents carries the risk of court proceedings in which they could be branded as uncooperative and unreasonable.

Increased pressure to proceed by way of voluntary agreement under the pre-proceedings protocol also has worrying implications for the child who is denied the independent voice and protection of a children's guardian:

P. Welbourne, 'Safeguarding Children on the Edge of Care: Policy for Keeping Children Safe after the *Review of the Child Care Proceedings System, Care Matters and the Carter Review of Legal Aid*', (2008) 20 *Child and Family Law Quarterly* 335, 343–57

The contrast between the situation in the courts, with the children's guardian, lawyers and the welfare principle guiding decision making, and that for a child having arrangements made in a FGC [Family group conference] or other informal setting is very marked... There is no mechanism for assuring that the best interests of the child will be a primary consideration in local authority gateway meetings, despite the gravity of the decisions being taken, nor in any ADR [alternative dispute resolution] process used. In these settings the child's interests compete with other, very powerful, interests such as the wishes of family members and financial and audit considerations of the local authority... Alternative dispute resolution places the child in a disadvantaged position as the only non-legally advised 'party' to the process.

Three key aspects of a court hearing are absent: (a) independence of the person making or ratifying the decision about the child's best interests; (b) independent representation of the child and parents; and (c) enforceability of decisions made. Decisions may be reached in 'informal' processes that seriously affect parents' and children's family life, but they are decisions that may be lawfully disregarded by parents, leaving children at continuing risk of serious harm. Agreements need to be carefully monitored for compliance, but there is no right of access to the child following negotiated agreements and no statutory requirement that local authorities carry out regular reviews or systematically follow up the placement. There is no framework for reviewing the progress of children in informal arrangements. There may be reviews under child protection procedures if the child continues to be at risk... but these have a narrower focus on issues of safety and protection...

For the children and families involved in section 31 proceedings, the court's powers are 'draconian' and the parents' (and children's) circumstances 'dire'. For this reason, the right of children to adequate representation is hard to overvalue. Decisions have to be made about their future safety and welfare, and only in court can they be assured of legal representation, a children's guardian and the prioritisation of their interests over those of others.

The use of the pre-proceedings process can also simply be a further cause of delay.[71]

---

71 Masson et al (2013).

12.3.3 LOCAL AUTHORITY DUTIES WITH RESPECT TO LOOKED AFTER CHILDREN

Section 22 of the CA 1989 details the various duties and responsibilities of local authorities with respect to children in their care. Although these provisions are located in Part III of the legislation, the duties are owed to all children 'looked after' by the local authority: this includes not only children who are in voluntary care but children who are in local authority care pursuant to a care order, interim care order, or emergency protection order under Parts IV and V.[72] The core duty of the local authority set down in s 22(3) is to safeguard and promote the child's welfare.[73] This is not the same as making each individual child's welfare the paramount consideration. The justification for not imposing the paramountcy principle on local authorities is clear. Local authorities owe duties and responsibilities to large numbers of children in their care. In such circumstances it would obviously be inappropriate to prioritize the interests of just one child to the detriment of others. This is particularly so given the limited resources with which local authorities typically have to contend. In making decisions with respect to individual children, local authorities therefore have a wide discretion permitting them to take into account a broad range of factors other than the assessed needs and interests of the child in question.[74]

The way in which local authorities discharge their duties and responsibilities under s 22(3) is crucially important. However, the task is not easy. On 31 March 2013, there were 68,110 looked after children in care, a 2 per cent increase from the previous year and an increase of 12 per cent compared with March 2009.[75] Many of these children have come from abusive homes and have complex and challenging needs. The difficulty of ensuring that all looked after children enjoy the highest possible standards of accommodation and care, particularly where resources are limited, should not be underestimated. However, despite recent reforms and improvements, outcomes for many looked after children remain poor.[76]

Department for Education, *Statistical First Release, Outcomes for Children Looked After by Local Authorities in England, as at 31 March 2013*
(London: HMSO, 2013c), 1.

Looked after children have poorer educational outcomes than non-looked after children. A high proportion (67.8 per cent) have special educational needs and their emotional and behavioural health is often a cause for concern.... The attainment gaps between looked after and non-looked after children for the main key stage 1, 2 and 4 measures have decreased or remained the same from 2012 to 2013. However the gaps are still large, especially for key stage 4, where 15.3 per cent of looked after children achieved 5 or more A*-C GCSEs

---

[72] S 22(1).
[73] S 22(3)(a).
[74] See, e.g., *Re T (Judicial Review: Local Authority Decisions Concerning Child in Need)* [2003] EWHC 2515.
[75] DFE (2013b), 1.
[76] The CA 1989 was amended by the CA 2004 to place a particular duty on the local authority to promote the child's educational achievement (CA 1989, s 22(3A)). The Children and Young Persons Act 2008 introduced further amendments to place a duty on the local authority to ensure, so far as is reasonably practicable, that the child's placement does not disrupt the child's education and training (CA 1989, s 22C(8)(b)).

or equivalent including English and maths compared with 58 per cent of non-looked after children. Although this gap has narrowed in recent years to 42.7 percentage points, it is still higher than it was in 2009.

During the year ending 31 March 2013, 6.2 per cent of looked after children aged 10–17 had been convicted or subject to a final warning or reprimand and 3.5 per cent of all looked after children had a substance misuse problem. Looked after children are twice as likely to be permanently excluded from school and nearly three times more likely to have a fixed term exclusion than all children. Around half of all looked after children aged 5–16 were considered to be 'borderline' or 'cause for concern' in relation to their emotional and behavioural health.

Educational achievement, youth offending rates, and longer term health and employment prospects are all thus significantly poorer for looked after children.

In addition to the general duty to promote the welfare of looked after children, s 22 of the CA 1989 imposes a number of more specific duties on the local authority. Before making any decision with respect to a looked after child, the local authority is under a duty, so far as is reasonably practicable, to ascertain and give due respect to the wishes and feelings of the child and the child's parents.[77] This includes an unmarried father without parental responsibility. The local authority must also pay particular regard to the 'child's religious persuasion, racial origin and cultural and linguistic background'.[78]

When a child is in voluntary care, the duty to act in partnership with the parents is particularly strong. Indeed, it was held in *R v Tameside Metropolitan BC, ex parte J* that when a child is in care pursuant to Part III of the CA 1989, the local authority must not only consult the child's parents but obtain their consent to any significant changes regarding the child's care, including where the child is accommodated.[79] The position with respect to a child 'in care' pursuant to a care order is different because under s 33(3)(a) the local authority acquires parental responsibility for the child and thereby shares decision-making authority with the parents.[80]

In determining *where* a looked after child should be accommodated, the local authority has a number of options.[81] Although the child is being looked after by the local authority, the local authority remains under a duty to promote the child's upbringing within his or her family. Section 22C(2)–(4) thus provide that unless it is not practicable to do so or contrary to the child's welfare, the local authority should 'make arrangements' for the child to be accommodated with a parent, a person other than a parent who has parental responsibility or a person with whom the child was living under a child arrangements order prior to the care order being made. The local authority may provide financial support for the placement.[82] If the local authority is unable to make

---

[77] S 22(4) and (5). As to the importance of respecting the child's wishes and feelings, see *R (CD) v Isle of Anglesey County Council* [2004] EWHC 1635.

[78] S 22(5)(c).

[79] [2000] 1 FCR 173, 179–81. Note also that a voluntarily accommodated child may be made a ward of court without offending s 100 of the CA 1989 which prevents the court using wardship to require a child to be placed in local authority care: *Re E (Wardship Order: Child in Voluntary Accommodation)* [2012] EWCA Civ 1773.

[80] *Tameside MBC*, ibid. See discussion below at 12.5.6.

[81] S 22C(2)–(4) and (6). See also Arrangements for Placement of Children (General) Regulations 1991, SI 1991/890.

[82] S 22C(10)(a).

arrangements for the child in accordance with s 22C(2), then it is under a duty to place the child in the most appropriate placement, giving priority to a relative, friend, or connected person who is also a local authority foster parent.[83] If there is no relative or friend able to care for the child then the child can be placed with other local authority foster parents or in a secure unit, residential school, residential home, or hostel.[84] So far as is reasonably practicable the child should be placed within the local authority area, as near to his or her home as possible and, where relevant, with his or her siblings.[85] The majority of looked after children are placed with local authority foster parents previously unknown to the child.[86] In this regard, the CFA 2014 introduced a new duty on local authorities in order to encourage early placement with a view to adoption and minimize the disruption caused to children by potentially multiple short-term placements.[87] The priority afforded to kinship placements under s 22C(6)(a) remains, but where such a placement is not deemed most appropriate and the local authority are satisfied that the child ought to be placed for adoption but are not authorized to place the child under s 19 or 21 of the Adoption and Children Act 2002, they must consider placing the child with a prospective adopter who has also been approved as a local authority foster parent for these purposes.[88]

Whilst a child is being looked after by the local authority, great emphasis is placed upon maintaining the child's familial links. The local authority is thus under a duty, if reasonably practicable and consistent with the child's welfare, to promote contact between the child and, amongst others, the parents.[89] Where the child has infrequent contact with family members and is not regularly visited by anyone the local authority may appoint an independent visitor to 'visit, advise and befriend the child'.[90] The local authority is also under a duty to ensure that looked after children are visited by a representative of the authority who will provide them with advice, support, and assistance.[91]

The local authority must review the case of a looked after child within four weeks of the date on which the child first entered care. The second review must be carried out no more than three months after the first and thereafter a review must be carried out every six months.[92] An independent reviewing officer (IRO) is appointed for every child and is responsible for monitoring the local authority's performance, participating in any reviews of the child's case, ensuring the child's wishes and feelings are taken into consideration, and, if appropriate, referring the child's case to an officer of Cafcass (Children and Family Court Advisory Support Service) who will be able to initiate legal proceedings on the child's behalf.[93] Strong concern has, however, been expressed as to the ineffectiveness of the IRO

---

[83] S 22C(5)–(9). These provisions replaced s 23 of the CA 1989 under which there had been considerable difficulties of construction with respect to the status of children placed with kinship carers: see *R (SA) v Kent County Council* [2011] EWCA Civ 1303. It is no longer possible for the local authority to 'make arrangements' for a relative or friend to care for a child who is not a local authority approved foster parent under s 22C(6).

[84] S 22C(6). On 31 March 2013, 9 per cent of looked after children were accommodated in a secure unit, residential school, home, or hostel (a decrease from 10 per cent in 2009). DFE (2013b), 4.

[85] S 22C(8)–(9).

[86] On 31 March 2013, 75 per cent of looked after children were living with foster parents, the vast majority of which were unknown to the child. DFE (2013b), 4–5.

[87] S 22C (9A)–(9B).

[88] For further discussion, see pp 938–9.

[89] Part II, Sch II, para 15(1). The obligation extends to friends and any person connected with the child.

[90] S 23ZB; Part II, Sch II, para 17(1)–(2).

[91] S 23ZA.

[92] Review of Children's Cases Regulations 1991, SI 1991/895, reg 3.

[93] Ss 25A–C.

system in safeguarding the interests of children in care not least of which is their lack of independence from the local authority.[94]

12.3.4 PART III: A SUCCESS?

The aims behind Part III of the CA 1989 are certainly admirable. It is difficult to argue with the principle that 'prevention is better than cure' and that, wherever possible, children should be helped and supported within their families. However, as noted above, an approach based on prevention and support will only be successful if properly resourced. The absence of much needed investment in local authority services has resulted in local authorities being crisis-led and focusing most of their time and resources on 'managing child protection cases'.[95] Local authorities thus become trapped in a vicious circle. The less time, money, and effort invested in prevention and support, the more resources needed to deal with cases requiring immediate, coercive intervention. Conversely, if more resources were diverted to providing effective services under Part III, the need for intervention under Parts IV and V should decline. It is therefore disappointing that more than 20 years after implementation of the CA 1989, 'child protection' cases under Parts IV and V remain the main focus of concern.

12.4 THE CHILD PROTECTION SYSTEM: INVESTIGATING ALLEGATIONS OF CHILD ABUSE

12.4.1 SECTION 47 INVESTIGATION

There is no general duty on the public to report suspected cases of child abuse to the authorities. Concerns about the welfare of a child should, however, be referred to their local children's services department. Within one working day of a referral being received, the local authority must decide how to proceed. If further investigation is needed, the local authority must carry out an assessment in accordance with the guidelines set down in *Working Together to Safeguard Children*.[96] The local authority's assessment should be informed by the views of the child and his or her family and the relevant health and education professionals.[97] Whenever possible the child should be seen by the social worker without the parents being present.[98] Although *Working Together* no longer prescribes a strict timetable for carrying out an assessment, it does stipulate that the assessment should be completed within 45 days from initial referral unless there are good reasons justifying a longer timescale.[99] If the local authority has *reasonable cause to suspect* that the child is suffering or likely to suffer significant harm, the local authority must carry out a full investigation under s 47 of the CA 1989. If the parents

---

94 House of Lords (2013), [114]–[128].
95 Smith (2002), 254–5.
96 DFE (2013d), esp 18–22.
97 Ibid, para 38.
98 Ibid, para 38.
99 Ibid, para 57. *Working Together* was substantially revised (and edited down) following Professor Eileen Munro's review of child protection. Munro concluded that the child protection system was being undermined by the extent of prescription and regulation imposed on social workers to the detriment of the exercise of professional judgement in the interests of children. See Munro (2011).

refuse to cooperate with the investigation, the local authority must apply for an emergency protection order (EPO), child assessment order (CAO), or care or supervision order unless satisfied that the child's welfare is adequately protected without one.[100] The preferred route for obtaining access to the child is a CAO under s 43. The court can only make the order if certain conditions are met:

Children Act 1989, s 43

(1) On the application of a local authority or authorised person for an order to be made under this section with respect to a child, the court may make the order if, but only if, it is satisfied that—

(a) the applicant has reasonable cause to suspect that the child is suffering, or is likely to suffer, significant harm;

(b) an assessment of the state of the child's health or development, or of the way in which he has been treated, is required to enable the applicant to determine whether or not the child is suffering, or is likely to suffer, significant harm; and

(c) it is unlikely that such an assessment will be made, or be satisfactory, in the absence of an order under this section.

If the order is made, the assessment can be carried out without the parents' consent. The parents are placed under a duty to produce the child to any person named in the order and must comply with any specified directions for carrying out the assessment.[101] A child of sufficient understanding can, however, refuse to submit to a medical, psychiatric, or other assessment.[102] The order can last for a specified period of no more than seven days from the date on which the assessment is to begin.[103]

The purpose of the local authority assessment is to determine the nature and level of the child's needs, any risk factors, and what services are to be provided.[104] If the concerns leading to the initiation of a s 47 investigation are substantiated and the child is believed to be at continuing risk, the local authority should convene a child protection conference (CPC)—usually within 15 days of the s 47 inquiries being initiated.[105] The aim of the CPC is to bring together all relevant professionals and the family to plan how best to safeguard and promote the child's welfare.[106] The parents should normally attend and be provided with sufficient information to enable them to participate effectively in the proceedings.[107] If of sufficient age and understanding, the child may also attend.[108] If the child's attendance is not appropriate, the child's social worker or advocate should convey the child's wishes and

---

[100] S 47(6).

[101] S 43(6).

[102] S 43(8). Although it would seem that the court, exercising its inherent jurisdiction, can override the child's refusal. See *South Glamorgan County Council v W and B* [1993] 1 FLR 514, decided within the context of an interim care order.

[103] S 43(5).

[104] DFE (2013d), para 43.

[105] Ibid, 38–46.

[106] Ibid.

[107] *Re M (Care: Challenging Decisions by Local Authority)* [2001] 2 FLR 1300 and *Re G (Care: Challenge to Local Authority's Decision)* [2003] EWHC 551.

[108] DFE (2013d), 38.

feelings to the meeting. The child will be recorded as at risk of harm under an initial category of abuse: physical, emotional, sexual, neglect, or multiple. Neglect is the most common category (41 per cent of cases).[109] The CPC must decide whether the child should be subject to a formal child protection plan and establish a core group, headed by a lead professional, to be responsible for developing, implementing, and monitoring the plan.[110] The plan must include clear actions and timescales for change. A child protection review conference will be held within three months of the initial conference and thereafter every six months.[111] The plan may be terminated at any time if the review concludes the child is no longer at risk of significant harm.

Within the context of the child protection plan, the local authority remains responsible for determining whether an application should be made to the court for a care or supervision order.[112] Before doing so the local authority should comply with statutory guidance on the pre-proceedings process which requires a letter before proceedings to be sent to the parents setting out the local authority's concerns and inviting them to attend a pre-proceedings meeting at which they are entitled to be legally represented.[113] The local authority is under no legal duty to initiate care proceedings even if satisfied the child is suffering or is likely to suffer significant harm.[114] It has been argued this creates an unfortunate gap in the statutory framework. Although the local authority's decision not to initiate care proceedings can be challenged through the local authority internal complaints procedure or by way of judicial review,[115] as Eekelaar notes, it is 'surprising that the imposition of extensive and elaborate duties to inquire do not lead to a clear and unambiguous duty to take action on the basis of the results of the inquiries where the child is likely to be harmed if no such action is taken'.[116] Similarly, just as the court is unable to direct the local authority to take any specific steps to protect a child, it is equally unable to grant injunctive relief to restrain the local authority from investigating a child's circumstances under s 47, even if the court is already seized of a private law dispute between the parents.[117] If the local authority decides to initiate care proceedings, the local authority's actions should be challenged by way of defending the proceedings. Only in wholly exceptional circumstances will it be appropriate to bring an application for judicial review.[118]

The potentially indeterminate outcome of a local authority investigation under s 47 can be problematic. Essentially, where there are grounds for continuing concern the local authority may simply decide to keep monitoring the situation and respond as and when appropriate. This can leave parents accused of abuse or neglect in a difficult state of limbo. Whilst care proceedings constitute a high level of intervention into the family, they do at least provide the opportunity for parents to formally challenge the local authority's allegations and for those allegations to be properly scrutinized by the court. Without such proceedings, it is

[109] DFE (2013e), 7–8.
[110] DFE (2013d), 40.
[111] Ibid, 44.
[112] S 47(3)(a).
[113] DFE (2014a), ch 2. See also Masson (2010), 369.
[114] See *Nottinghamshire County Council v P* [1994] Fam 18.
[115] *R v East Sussex County Council, ex parte W* [1998] 2 FLR 1082.
[116] Eekelaar (1990), 486.
[117] *D v D (County Court Jurisdiction: Injunctions)* [1993] 2 FLR 802. The Court of Appeal solved this problem by making a prohibited steps order to restrain the father from exercising his parental responsibility to consent to such investigations. The local authority were investigating the mother's treatment of her children at the behest of the father, against the background of a residence dispute.
[118] *Re M (Care Proceedings: Judicial Review)* [2003] EWHC 850.

difficult for parents to 'clear their name' in the face of the local authority's continuing suspicion. This problem was considered in *R (S) v Swindon Borough Council*,[119] which concerned a consultant gynaecologist suspected of sexually assaulting the teenage daughter of his former partner. Following his acquittal in the criminal proceedings, he wished to set up home with his new partner, Mrs X, but was unable to do so whilst the local authority, believing he may pose a continuing risk, refused to provide the necessary assurance that it would not take steps to protect Mrs X's two daughters should he and Mrs X begin to cohabit. The claimant sought judicial review of the local authority's position, arguing that it needed to reach a final decision as to whether the allegations were substantiated and, on the basis of that decision, either initiate care proceedings to protect Mrs X's daughters or leave him alone to get on with his life. Scott Baker J dismissed the application, stressing that whilst the local authority must respect the claimant's private and family life, it had an overriding duty to monitor the situation in order to protect the two children. The judgment makes clear that at the early stages of an investigation into child abuse, the thresholds for state intervention are necessarily low and there is therefore no requirement for the local authority to substantiate allegations of abuse on the balance of probabilities. The judge concluded that 'the critical question is whether the authority *have reasonable cause to suspect* a child is likely to suffer significant harm',[120] and emphasized that the fact of an acquittal in a criminal trial would never be conclusive as to whether a local authority should start or continue a s 47 investigation.

If at any point throughout this process the local authority believes the child to be in need of urgent protection, the local authority should request that the police take the child into police protection or apply for an emergency protection order under Part V.[121]

12.4.2 SECTION 37 INVESTIGATION

An alternative route by which a family may find themselves subject to a local authority investigation is under s 37 of the CA 1989:

Children Act 1989, s 37

(1) Where, in any family proceedings in which a question arises with respect to the welfare of any child, it appears to the court that it may be appropriate for a care or supervision order to be made with respect to him, the court may direct the appropriate authority to undertake an investigation of the child's circumstances.

It was held in *Re H (A Minor) (Section 37 Direction)* that the 'child's circumstances' should be widely construed to include 'any situation which may have a bearing on the child being likely to suffer significant harm in the future'—even if the child is currently settled, well cared for, and happy.[122] The purpose of the investigation is for the local authority to decide whether or not they should apply for a care or supervision order. The local authority must

---

[119] [2001] EWHC 334.
[120] Ibid, [34].
[121] See 12.6.
[122] *Re H (A Minor) (Section 37 Direction)* [1993] 2 FLR 541, 549.

report back to the court within eight weeks.[123] If the local authority decides not to apply for a care or supervision order, the reasons for the decision must be explained and the court informed of any alternative action they propose to take.[124] However, regardless of the local authority's findings, the local authority again has no duty to begin proceedings and the court has no power to direct proceedings to be initiated.[125]

12.5 CARE AND SUPERVISION PROCEEDINGS UNDER PART IV

Part IV of the CA 1989 provides for two key orders permitting compulsory intervention into family life: care and supervision orders. A care order is defined under s 31(1)(a) as an order 'placing the child with respect to whom the application is made in the care of a designated local authority'. A supervision order is a less interventionist measure and is simply defined as an order putting the child 'under the supervision of a designated local authority'.[126]

12.5.1 WHO MAY APPLY FOR A CARE OR SUPERVISION ORDER?

Under s 31(1), only a 'local authority' or 'authorized person' may apply for a care or supervision order. 'Authorized person' is defined in s 31(9) as the NSPCC and any other person authorized by the Secretary of State to bring proceedings. To date no such other person has been authorized. The child, the mother, and the father if he has parental responsibility, are automatically joined as respondents.[127] The local authority must serve notice of the proceedings on a father without parental responsibility but he has no right to participate in the proceedings: he must apply for leave to be joined as a party.[128] Leave will, however, ordinarily be granted unless there is some clear reason for refusing the application.[129]

12.5.2 WHEN MAY A CARE OR SUPERVISION ORDER BE MADE?

An application for a care or supervision order may be made in any 'family proceedings' or in free-standing care proceedings.[130] As noted above, only a local authority or the NSPCC can make the application; the court cannot act of its own motion. Indeed, s 100(2) of the CA 1989 explicitly removes the power of the court to place a child into local authority care pursuant

---

[123] S 37(4).

[124] S 37(3).

[125] *Nottinghamshire County Council v P* [1994] Fam 18.

[126] S 31(1)(b).

[127] Family Procedure Rules 2010 (FPR 2010), r 12.3(1). A father with parental responsibility whose whereabouts are known can be discharged as a party to the proceedings and service dispensed with, but only in the most exceptional circumstances: *M v M (Children)* [2009] EWHC 3172.

[128] FPR 2010, r 12.8 and Practice Direction 12C. Only in exceptional circumstances will this requirement be waived: *Re AB (Care Proceedings: Service on Husband Ignorant of Child's Existence)* [2003] EWCA Civ 1842.

[129] *Re K (Care Proceedings: Joinder of Father)* [1999] 2 FLR 408; *Re P (Care Proceedings: Father's Application to be Joined as Party)* [2001] 1 FLR 781.

[130] For the meaning of 'family proceedings', see s 8(3)–(4).

to its inherent jurisdiction. Although this lack of jurisdiction has frustrated some, it ensures no child can be placed into local authority care on the basis of a simple best interests test (as was the case under the inherent jurisdiction): the threshold of harm justifying state intervention into the family as set down in s 31 must always be established. For similar reasons, the local authority is constrained from acting to protect a child by applying for private law orders under s 8. Section 9(2) thus prohibits a local authority from applying for a child arrangements order and whilst the local authority is permitted, with leave, to apply for a specific issue or prohibited steps order, the court cannot, in accordance with s 9(5)(a), make an order with a view to achieving a result that could be achieved under a child arrangements order. This leaves very little room for local authorities to make use of s 8 orders, even if they believe such orders would be a more nuanced response to the problems of a particular family than invoking their more drastic and confrontational powers under Part IV.

The limitations imposed on local authorities and the various problems such limitations can create for the courts are dramatically illustrated in *Nottinghamshire County Council v P*.[131] As regards local authorities and the courts working in partnership to protect children at risk of harm, this case represents a particular low point with Sir Stephen Brown P expressing clear frustration at the local authority. The case concerned two young girls whose older sister had made allegations of sexual abuse against the father. The parents denied the allegations. The court found that the father had sexually abused the eldest daughter and that the two younger girls were now at serious risk. The court also found that the mother had no capacity to protect the children against their father. However, rather than apply for a care order under Part IV, the local authority applied for a prohibited steps order requiring the father not to reside in the same household as his daughters and prohibiting contact. Owing to the restrictions contained in ss 9(2) and 9(5)(a), Ward J, at first instance, held that he was unable to make the order sought and, in the face of the local authority's refusal to apply for a care order, he instead made a child arrangements order in favour of the mother, subject to two conditions: (i) that the father was not to reside in the family home; and (ii) was not to be allowed contact with the children. All parties appealed:

Nottinghamshire County Council v P [1994] Fam 18 (CA), 38–43

SIR STEPHEN BROWN P:

In the view of this court the application for a prohibited steps order by this local authority was in reality being made with a view to achieving a result which could be achieved by making a [child arrangements order]...

The court is satisfied that the local authority was indeed seeking to enter by the "back door" as it were. It agrees with Ward J. that he had no power to make a prohibited steps order in this case...

A wider question arises as to policy. We consider that this court should make it clear that the route chosen by the local authority in this case was wholly inappropriate. In cases where children are found to be at risk of suffering significant harm within the meaning of section 31 of the Children Act 1989 a clear duty arises on the part of local authorities to take steps to protect them. In such circumstances a local authority is required to assume responsibility and to intervene in the family arrangements in order to protect the child. Part IV specifically provides them with wide powers and a wide discretion...A prohibited steps order would not

---

[131] For commentary, see Brasse (1993).

afford the local authority any authority as to how it might deal with the children. There may be situations, for example where a child is accommodated by a local authority, where it would be appropriate to seek a prohibited steps order for some particular purpose. However, it could not in any circumstances be regarded as providing a substitute for an order under Part IV of the Act of 1989. Furthermore, it is very doubtful indeed whether a prohibited steps order could in any circumstances be used to "oust" a father from a matrimonial home...

The Court of Appeal then went on to consider Ward J's decision to make a child arrangements order subject to conditions under s 11(7). The difficulty with this order was that it was being imposed on the mother against her wishes yet, unlike an order under Part IV, provided no power or responsibility to the local authority to monitor, regulate, or enforce it:

In our judgment these orders cannot stand. Even if the judge had a theoretical power to assume authority by reason of section 10 of the Act of 1989, the orders were plainly not appropriate even in the unhappy circumstances of this case. In the result the appeals against these orders must be allowed.

In the result there are now no orders in force which are capable of regulating and safeguarding the position of these children... Since the fact of the risk of significant harm to the children has been established and not contradicted there remains upon the local authority the clear duty to take steps to safeguard the welfare of these children. It should not shrink from taking steps under Part IV of the Act...

This court is deeply concerned at the absence of any power to direct this authority to take steps to protect the children. In the former wardship jurisdiction it might well have been able to do so. The operation of the Children Act 1989 is entirely dependent upon the full co-operation of all those involved. This includes the courts, local authorities, social workers, and all who have to deal with children. Unfortunately, as appears from this case, if a local authority doggedly resists taking the steps which are appropriate to the case of children at risk of suffering significant harm it appears that the court is powerless. The authority may perhaps lay itself open to an application for judicial review but in a case such as this the question arises, at whose instance? The position is one which it is to be hoped will not recur and that lessons will be learnt from this unhappy catalogue of errors.

Once the local authority has made an application under s 31 and the court is satisfied the threshold conditions are satisfied, the court has much greater freedom to shape its orders in accordance with the child's welfare.[132]

12.5.3 THE THRESHOLD CRITERIA

In *Humberside County Council v B*, Booth J established a two-stage approach to care proceedings.[133] First, before the court acquires the jurisdiction to make a care or supervision order, the threshold criteria set down in s 31(2) must be satisfied. The Supreme Court has explained that whether or not the threshold is crossed is not an exercise of discretion but a 'value judgement' which must be made on the basis of established facts. The child's welfare is irrelevant to this exercise.[134] Once the threshold criteria have been established, the court

---

132 See below at pp 871–3.
133 [1993] 1 FLR 257.
134 *Re B (Care Proceedings: Appeal)* [2013] UKSC 33, [44] (Lord Wilson).

can move on to the second stage of the inquiry: whether it is in the child's best interests to make the order. This is generally known as the welfare stage.

Section 31(2) performs a crucial 'gate-keeping' function. It ensures the state can take coercive action against a child's primary carers only once a certain threshold of harm has been established. It thus plays a crucial role in balancing the importance of respecting family integrity against the need to protect children from inadequate or abusive parenting.[135] The threshold criteria are set out in s 31(2) of the CA 1989:

Children Act 1989, s 31

(2) A court may only make a care order or supervision order if it is satisfied—

    (a) that the child concerned is suffering, or is likely to suffer, significant harm; and

    (b) that the harm, or likelihood of harm, is attributable to—

        (i) the care given to the child, or likely to be given to him if the order were not made, not being what it would be reasonable to expect a parent to give to him; or

        (ii) the child's being beyond parental control.

There are thus two basic limbs to the threshold criteria, both of which must be satisfied:

- the child must be suffering or be likely to suffer significant harm; and
- the harm must be attributable to the care given to the child not being what it would be reasonable to expect a parent to give or to the child being beyond parental control.

We will take these requirements in turn.

Is suffering or likely to suffer significant harm

'Harm'

Harm is very widely defined in s 31(9) as the 'ill-treatment or the impairment of health or development including, for example, impairment suffered from seeing or hearing the ill-treatment of another'.[136] 'Ill-treatment' includes 'sexual abuse and forms of ill-treatment which are not physical'. Importantly, as made clear by the Supreme Court in *Re B (Care Proceedings: Appeal)* this includes emotional harm caused by the parents' behaviour and/or particular personality traits.[137] 'Health' includes both physical and mental health. 'Development' means 'physical, intellectual, emotional, social or behavioural development'. In determining whether a child has been subjected to 'harm', the courts are prepared to tolerate diverse standards of parenting taking into account the social, cultural, and religious background of the family.

---

[135] *Re G (Care Proceedings: Threshold Conditions)* [2001] EWCA Civ 968.

[136] As amended by the Adoption and Children Act 2002, s 120.

[137] [2013] UKSC 33, [65]. The harm relied on by the local authority was the impact on the child of the mother's somatization disorder, factitious illness disorder, her lying and dishonesty, and her inability to engage constructively with professionals. On the facts of the case, the Supreme Court were satisfied, Baroness Hale dissenting, that the impact of this behaviour on the child's emotional development was sufficiently serious to conclude that the making of a care order was both necessary and proportionate.

Re L (Care: Threshold Criteria) [2007] 1 FLR 2050

HEDLEY J:

[50] What about the court's approach, in the light of all that, to the issue of significant harm? In order to understand this concept and the range of harm that it's intended to encompass, it is right to begin with issues of policy. Basically it is the tradition of the UK, recognised in law, that children are best brought up within natural families... It follows inexorably from that, that society must be willing to tolerate very diverse standards of parenting, including the eccentric, the barely adequate and the inconsistent. It follows too that children will inevitably have both very different experiences of parenting and very unequal consequences flowing from it. It means that some children will experience disadvantage and harm, while others flourish in atmospheres of loving security and emotional stability. These are the consequences of our fallible humanity and it is not the provenance of the state to spare children all the consequences of defective parenting. In any event, it simply could not be done.

The importance to be accorded to diversity in family life has been reiterated by the House of Lords.

Re B (Children) (Care Proceedings: Standard of Proof) [2008] UKHL 35

BARONESS HALE:

20. Taking a child away from her family is a momentous step, not only for her, but for her whole family, and for the local authority which does so. In a totalitarian society, uniformity and conformity are valued. Hence the totalitarian state tries to separate the child from her family and mould her to its own design. Families in all their subversive variety are the breeding ground of diversity and individuality. In a free and democratic society we value diversity and individuality. Hence the family is given special protection in all the modern human rights instruments including the European Convention on Human Rights (art 8), the International Covenant on Civil and Political Rights (art 23) and throughout the United Nations Convention on the Rights of the Child. As Justice McReynolds famously said in *Pierce v Society of Sisters* 268 US 510 (1925), at 535, "The child is not the mere creature of the State".

'Significant'

Section 31(10) provides that where the question of whether the harm suffered is significant turns on the child's health or development, then the child's health or development should be compared with that which could be reasonably expected of a similar child.[138] 'Significant' is not otherwise defined by the legislation. The meaning of significant harm was considered at length by the Supreme Court in *Re B (Care Proceedings: Appeal)* in 2013, with the majority being anxious not to complicate the relatively straightforward statutory wording with unnecessary judicial gloss and 'encrustation'.[139] However, Lady Hale cites as 'helpful' the

---

138 See *Re O (A Minor) (Care Order: Education: Procedure)* [1992] 2 FLR 7, 10.

139 [2013] UKSC 33, [26] (Lord Wilson); [56] (Lord Neuberger). Lady Hale dissented, considering that Art 8 had a bearing on the ultimate decision and that it should be borne in mind when considering the sufficiency of the harm. For commentary on the Supreme Court decision, see Doughty (2013).

ordinary dictionary definition of 'significant', which demands that the harm must be 'considerable', 'noteworthy', or 'important'.[140] As she goes on to point out, the threshold would be irrelevant if it could be crossed by trivial or unimportant harm.[141] Both Lady Hale and Lord Wilson also suggest that the 'significance' or seriousness of the harm must be considered in parallel with its likelihood, such that, whilst only a slight possibility of very grave harm may be sufficient to cross the threshold, a very strong possibility may be required of harm which is of much less significance.[142]

'Is suffering'

This is the most straightforward way of establishing the first limb of the threshold criteria. It raises a simple question of fact: is the child suffering significant harm? The usual civil standard of proof applies, so the burden is on the local authority to prove the alleged facts on the balance of probabilities.[143] Although relatively straightforward, questions have arisen regarding *when* the alleged state of affairs must be shown to exist. In *Re M (A Minor) (Care Orders: Threshold Conditions)*, the child, (G), when just four months old, witnessed his father brutally murder his mother, for which the father was serving life imprisonment. The local authority applied for a care order. After a short period in foster care, G went to live with Mrs W, his mother's cousin, who was also caring for his three older half-siblings. By the time the local authority's application for a care order was heard, the child was well settled and well cared for in Mrs W's home. Mrs W applied for a residence order. This was supported by the local authority who decided not to pursue its application. However, the guardian ad litem (now 'children's guardian', who represents the child's interests in the proceedings) and the father supported making a care order, hoping the child could be adopted outside the family. The question arose whether, in this commonplace scenario of a child being 'rescued' from a harmful situation by the local authority, the child had to be suffering significant harm at the time of the hearing, or whether it sufficed for the purposes of the threshold criteria that the child had been suffering significant harm at the point the local authority first intervened to protect the child. The House of Lords, emphasizing the need to 'avoid the tyranny of language', preferred the latter interpretation.

Re M (A Minor) (Care Orders: Threshold Conditions) [1994] 2 AC 424 (HL), 433–4

LORD MACKAY:

There is nothing in section 31(2) which in my opinion requires that the conditions to be satisfied are disassociated from the time of the making of the application by the local authority. I would conclude that the natural construction of the conditions in section 31(2) is that where, at the time the application is to be disposed of, there are in place arrangements for the protection of the child by the local authority on an interim basis which protection has been continuously

---

[140] *Re B*, ibid, [185]. This was the approach endorsed by Booth J in *Humberside CC v B* [1993] 1 FLR 257. Note that in *Re MA (Care Threshold)* [2009] EWCA Civ 853, the majority of the Court of Appeal appeared to accept that physical abuse that could be defended as 'reasonable chastisement' does not amount to significant harm. Similarly, the Court of Appeal upheld the finding of the trial judge that witnessing the parents' cruel physical abuse of another (non-biological) child would not cause the children significant emotional harm. See Masson (2010) and Keating (2011) for strong critiques.

[141] *Re B*, ibid.

[142] Ibid, [187]–[190] (Lady Hale) and [26] (Lord Wilson).

[143] Discussed in detail below at pp 864–6.

in place for some time, the relevant date with respect to which the court must be satisfied is the date at which the local authority initiated the procedure for protection under the Act from which these arrangements followed. If after a local authority had initiated protective arrangements the need for these had terminated, because the child's welfare had been satisfactorily provided for otherwise, in any subsequent proceedings, it would not be possible to found jurisdiction on the situation at the time of initiation of these arrangements. It is permissible only to look back from the date of disposal to the date of initiation of protection as a result of which local authority arrangements had been continuously in place thereafter to the date of disposal.

It has to be borne in mind that this in no way precludes the court from taking account at the date of the hearing of all relevant circumstances. The conditions in subsection (2) are in the nature of conditions conferring jurisdiction upon the court to consider whether or not a care order or supervision order should be made. Conditions of that kind would in my view normally have to be satisfied at the date on which the order was first applied for. It would in my opinion be odd if the jurisdiction of the court to make an order depended on how long the court took before it finally disposed of the case.

It was subsequently suggested in *Southwark London Borough Council v B* that the relevant date at which the 'local authority initiated the procedure for protection' may include voluntary arrangements entered into under Part III, provided protective arrangements have been continuously in place since that date.[144]

The issue of timing arose again in *Re G (Care Proceedings: Threshold Conditions)*.[145] The question this time was whether the local authority could rely on information acquired *after* they had first intervened to protect the child in order to help establish that the threshold conditions were satisfied at the point of intervention. The Court of Appeal drew a distinction between: (i) information and events which went towards proving the alleged state of affairs at the point of intervention; and (ii) completely unrelated information and events which, whilst in themselves capable of constituting evidence of significant harm, had no bearing on the initial reasons for the local authority intervening. It was held that whilst the former was clearly relevant and should be admitted, evidence falling into the latter category could not be relied upon by the local authority to 'retrospectively valid[ate] a concern which was not in fact justified at the time'.[146] Wall LJ has provided further clarification on this issue, holding in *Re L (Children) (Care Proceedings)*[147] that the local authority is free to advance grounds for establishing the threshold criteria at trial which are different from the grounds relied on when it first intervened provided the alternative grounds actually existed (whether or not known to the local authority) at the date of intervention.[148] This differs from the situation where a new unrelated event giving rise to grounds for concern occurs *after* the date of intervention, which, in accordance with Hale LJ's judgment in *Re G*, would remain excluded from consideration. In such circumstances the local authority would simply have to start proceedings again.

'Is likely to suffer'

The alternative basis on which the local authority can satisfy the first limb of the threshold criteria under s 31(2)(a) is the likelihood of future significant harm. It has been suggested

---

144 [1998] 2 FLR 1095, 1109.
145 [2001] EWCA Civ 968.
146 Ibid, [15].
147 [2006] EWCA Civ 1282.
148 Ibid, [42]–[45]

that when looking forward the local authority is not restricted to the immediate or even medium-term future, anticipated harm even years in advance will suffice.[149] Satisfying the prospective limb of s 31(2)(a) is, however, in many ways a difficult task, relying as it does on various hypotheses about the future. There are now a number of House of Lords/Supreme Court authorities on the point, notably *Re H (Minors) (Sexual Abuse: Standard of Proof)*,[150] *Re B (Children) (Care Proceedings: Standard of Proof)*,[151] *Re J (Care Proceedings: Possible Perpetrators)*,[152] and *Re B (Care Proceedings: Appeal)*.[153]

Re H concerned applications for care orders with respect to three children (D2, D3, and D4). A fourth child (D1, the eldest sister) alleged she had been sexually abused by the step-father (Mr R) over a number of years. He was charged with rape but acquitted at the criminal trial. The local authority continued with the care proceedings, the sole ground for the care orders being the likelihood of future significant harm given the alleged sexual abuse of the eldest daughter. It did not contend that any of the three children were currently suffering significant harm. This was therefore a case where the issue was whether or not the alleged abuse of another child had taken place—if proven, the identity of the perpetrator was not an issue.

The House of Lords were all agreed that 'likely' should be interpreted to mean there was a 'real possibility' of future significant harm: there was no need to show that the harm was 'probable' in the sense of 'more likely than not'. However, the House of Lords were divided as to the evidential base required in order to make a positive finding that the child was likely to suffer significant harm. The majority held that the court must be satisfied on the balance of probabilities that there was a real possibility the child would suffer significant harm, the burden of proof resting on the local authority. Lord Nicholls went on to hold that the court could only proceed on the basis of 'proper material', meaning the court would only be able to find a real possibility of future harm on the basis of established facts not mere doubts or suspicions—which in this case meant the local authority would need to prove on the balance of probabilities that the eldest daughter had been sexually abused. The minority disagreed, arguing that a number of 'unproven' facts, when taken together, could prove equally probative. The point is important, going as it does to the heart of child protection policy. Is the state justified in removing a child from his or her parents on the basis of mere suspicion of past neglect or abuse? The majority say 'no', setting a much higher threshold for state intervention than the minority.

Re H (Minors) (Sexual Abuse: Standard of Proof) [1996] AC 563 (HL), 588–92, 572–4

LORD NICHOLLS [with whom Lord Goff and Lord Mustill agreed]:

A conclusion based on facts

The starting point here is that courts act on evidence. They reach their decisions on the basis of the evidence before them. When considering whether an applicant for a care order has shown that the child is suffering harm or is likely to do so, a court will have regard to the undisputed evidence. The judge will attach to that evidence such weight or importance as he

---

[149] *Re H (A Minor) (Section 37 Direction)* [1993] 2 FLR 541, 548.
[150] [1996] AC 563.
[151] [2008] UKHL 35.
[152] [2013] UKSC 9.
[153] [2013] UKSC 33.

considers appropriate. Likewise with regard to disputed evidence which the judge accepts as reliable. None of that is controversial. But the rejection of a disputed allegation as not proved on the balance of probability leaves scope for the possibility that the non-proven allegation may be true after all. There remains room for the judge to have doubts and suspicions on this score. This is the area of controversy.

In my view these unresolved judicial doubts and suspicions can no more form the basis of a conclusion that the second threshold condition in section 31(2)(a) has been established than they can form the basis of a conclusion that the first has been established...

A decision by a court on the likelihood of a future happening must be founded on a basis of present facts and the inferences fairly to be drawn therefrom....

An alleged but non-proven fact is not a fact for this purpose... [T]here must be facts from which the court can properly conclude there is a real possibility that the child will suffer harm in the future... [I]f the facts are disputed, the court must resolve the dispute so far as necessary to reach a proper conclusion on the issue it has to decide...

The range of facts which may properly be taken into account is infinite... And facts, which are minor or even trivial if considered in isolation, when taken together may suffice to satisfy the court of the likelihood of future harm. The court will attach to all the relevant facts the appropriate weight when coming to an overall conclusion on the crucial issue.

I must emphasise a further point. I have indicated that unproved allegations of maltreatment cannot form the basis for a finding by the court that either limb of section 31(2)(a) is established. It is, of course, open to a court to conclude there is a real possibility that the child will suffer harm in the future although harm in the past has not been established. There will be cases where, although the alleged maltreatment itself is not proved, the evidence does establish a combination of profoundly worrying features affecting the care of the child within the family. In such cases it would be open to a court in appropriate circumstances to find that, although not satisfied the child is yet suffering significant harm, on the basis of such facts as are proved there is a likelihood that he will do so in the future.

That is not the present case. The three younger girls are not at risk unless D1 was abused by Mr. R in the past. If she was not abused, there is no reason for thinking the others may be. This is not a case where Mr. R has a history of abuse. Thus the one and only relevant fact is whether D1 was abused by Mr. R as she says. The other surrounding facts, such as the fact that D1 made a complaint and the fact that her mother responded unsatisfactorily, lead nowhere relevant in this case if they do not lead to the conclusion that D1 was abused. To decide that the others are at risk because there is a possibility that D1 was abused would be to base the decision, not on fact, but on suspicion: the suspicion that D1 may have been abused. That would be to lower the threshold prescribed by Parliament...

Conclusion

As I read the Act, Parliament decided that the threshold for a care order should be that the child is suffering significant harm, or there is a real possibility that he will do so. In the latter regard the threshold is comparatively low. Therein lies the protection for children. But, as I read the Act, Parliament also decided that proof of the relevant facts is needed if this threshold is to be surmounted. Before the section 1 welfare test and the welfare 'checklist' can be applied, the threshold has to be crossed. Therein lies the protection for parents. They are not to be at risk of having their child taken from them and removed into the care of the local authority on the basis only of suspicions, whether of the judge or of the local authority or anyone else. A conclusion that the child is suffering or is likely to suffer harm must be based on facts, not just suspicion.

Lord Lloyd and Lord Browne-Wilkinson dissented, concerned that the majority approach set the threshold for state intervention too high and left children in unacceptable situations of risk.[154]

LORD BROWNE-WILKINSON:

I agree that the judge can only act on evidence and on facts which, so far as relevant, have been proved. He has to be satisfied by the evidence before him that there is a real possibility of serious harm to the child.

Where I part company is in thinking that the facts relevant to an assessment of risk ('is likely to suffer...harm') are not the same as the facts relevant to a decision that harm is in fact being suffered. In order to be satisfied that an event has occurred or is occurring the evidence has to show on balance of probabilities that such event did occur or is occurring. But in order to be satisfied that there is a risk of such an occurrence, the ambit of the relevant facts is in my view wider. The combined effect of a number of factors which suggest that a state of affairs, though not proved to exist, may well exist is the normal basis for the assessment of future risk. To be satisfied of the existence of a risk does not require proof of the occurrence of past historical events but proof of facts which are relevant to the making of a prognosis.

Let me give an example, albeit a dated one. Say that in 1940 those responsible for giving air-raid warnings had received five unconfirmed sightings of approaching aircraft which might be enemy bombers. They could not, on balance of probabilities, have reached a conclusion that any one of those sightings was of an enemy aircraft: nor could they logically have put together five non-proven sightings so as to be satisfied that enemy aircraft were in fact approaching. But their task was not simply to decide whether enemy aircraft were approaching but whether there was a risk of an air raid. The facts relevant to the assessment of such risk were the reports that unconfirmed sightings had been made, not the truth of such reports. They could well, on the basis of those unconfirmed reports, have been satisfied that there was a real possibility of an air raid and given warning accordingly...

My Lords, I am anxious that the decision of the House in this case may establish the law in an unworkable form to the detriment of many children at risk. Child abuse, particularly sex abuse, is notoriously difficult to prove in a court of law. The relevant facts are extremely sensitive and emotive. They are often known only to the child and to the alleged abuser. If legal proof of actual abuse is a prerequisite to a finding that a child is at risk of abuse, the court will be powerless to intervene to protect children in relation to whom there are the gravest suspicions of actual abuse but the necessary evidence legally to prove such abuse is lacking.

The majority position was affirmed by the House of Lords in *Re B (Children) (Care Proceedings: Standard of Proof)*. Thus the court cannot be satisfied that child A is likely to suffer significant harm on the basis that there is a 'real possibility' or 'suspicion' that child B has suffered similar harm in the past at the hands of one or both parents.

Re B (Children) (Care Proceedings: Standard of Proof) [2008] UKHL 35

LORD HOFFMANN:

2. If a legal rule requires a fact to be proved (a "fact in issue"), a judge or jury must decide whether or not it happened. There is no room for a finding that it might have happened. The

---

[154] See also Keating (1996) and (2009). Cf Cobley and Lowe (2009), 468.

law operates a binary system in which the only values are 0 and 1. The fact either happened or it did not. If the tribunal is left in doubt, the doubt is resolved by a rule that one party or the other carries the burden of proof. If the party who bears the burden of proof fails to discharge it, a value of 0 is returned and the fact is treated as not having happened. If he does discharge it, a value of 1 is returned and the fact is treated as having happened.

3. The effect of the decision of the House in *Re H (Minors) (Sexual Abuse: Standard of Proof)* [1996] AC 563 is that section 31(2)(a) of the Children Act 1989 requires any facts used as the basis of a prediction that a child is "likely to suffer significant harm" to be proved to have happened. Every such fact is to be treated as a fact in issue. The majority of the House rejected the analogy with facts which merely form part of the material from which a fact in issue may be inferred, which need not each be proved to have happened. There is of course no conceptual reason for rejecting this analogy, which in the context of some predictions (such as Lord Browne-Wilkinson's example of air raid warnings) might be prudent and appropriate. But the House decided that it was inappropriate for the purposes of section 31(2)(a). It is this rule which the House reaffirms today.

BARONESS HALE:

22. This case is about the meaning of the words "is likely to suffer significant harm". How is the court to be satisfied of such a likelihood? This is a prediction from existing facts, often from a multitude of such facts, about what has happened in the past, about the characters and personalities of the people involved, about the things which they have said and done, and so on. But do those facts have to be proved in the usual way, on the balance of probabilities? Or is it sufficient that there is a "real possibility" that they took place, even if the judge is unable to say that it is more likely than not that they did? ...

32. In our legal system, if a judge finds it more likely than not that something did take place, then it is treated as having taken place. If he finds it more likely than not that it did not take place, then it is treated as not having taken place. He is not allowed to sit on the fence. He has to find for one side or the other. Sometimes the burden of proof will come to his rescue: the party with the burden of showing that something took place will not have satisfied him that it did. But generally speaking a judge is able to make up his mind where the truth lies without needing to rely upon the burden of proof.

54. The reasons given by Lord Nicholls for adopting the approach which he did in *Re H* remain thoroughly convincing. The threshold is there to protect both the children and their parents from unjustified intervention in their lives. It would provide no protection at all if it could be established on the basis of unsubstantiated suspicions: that is, where a judge cannot say that there is no real possibility that abuse took place, so concludes that there is a real possibility that it did. In other words, the alleged perpetrator would have to prove that it did not. [Counsel] accepts that it must be proved on the balance of probabilities that a child "is suffering" significant harm. But nevertheless he argues that those same allegations, which could not be proved for that purpose, could be the basis of a finding of likelihood of future harm. If that were so, there would have been no need for the first limb of section 31(2)(a) at all. Parliament must be presumed to have inserted it for a purpose. Furthermore, the Act draws a clear distinction between the threshold to be crossed before the court may make a final care or supervision order and the threshold for making preliminary and interim orders. If Parliament had intended that a mere suspicion that a child had suffered harm could form the basis for making a final order, it would have used the same terminology of "reasonable grounds to suspect" or "reasonable grounds to believe" as it uses elsewhere in the Act. Instead ... it speaks of what the child is suffering or is likely to suffer ...

59. To allow the courts to make decisions about the allocation of parental responsibility for children on the basis of unproven allegations and unsubstantiated suspicions would be to deny them their essential role in protecting both children and their families from the intervention of the state, however well intentioned that intervention may be. It is to confuse the role of the local authority, in assessing and managing risk, in planning for the child, and deciding what action to initiate, with the role of the court in deciding where the truth lies and what the legal consequences should be. I do not under-estimate the difficulty of deciding where the truth lies but that is what the courts are for.

Re H was concerned with the issue of whether or not past abuse to child A had been proven and could thus form the basis of the care order application with respect to child B. This needs to be distinguished from cases where the issue is not whether or not past abuse has occurred to child A but as to the *identity* of the alleged perpetrator of the abuse. So the factual matrix in this alternative scenario is an allegation by the local authority that child B is at risk of significant harm as a result of proven abuse suffered by child A but there is uncertainty as to the identity of the perpetrator of the abuse.[155] This particular problem was addressed by the Supreme Court in the case of *Re J (Care Proceedings: Possible Perpetrators)*.[156]

In *Re J* the care order application was being advanced, somewhat artificially, on the *sole* basis that the child was *likely to suffer significant harm* because he or she was being cared for by an individual who *may* have caused harm (that harm being proven) to *another* child. In other words, the basis of the application was that one of child B's carers was within the 'pool of possible perpetrators' for causing harm to child A. It is important to note that the decision does not apply to cases where a previous child (child A) has been harmed whilst in the care of the parents (although it is not possible to say which of the two parents was the perpetrator) but the family unit remains intact such that a subsequent child (child B) who now forms the basis of the care order application is being cared for within a family unit where it is known that one of the parents *must* have been the perpetrator of the previous abuse. The care order application in *Re J* related to three children in the care of 'the mother' and 'the father'. The mother was the biological mother of the youngest child only. The father was the biological father of the two oldest children only. The youngest child was the mother's third child by her previous partner. Her first child with her previous partner died aged three weeks. The baby was found to have suffered multiple non-accidental injuries and died as a result of asphyxia caused either deliberately or by the mother's former partner taking her to bed with him. In care proceedings relating to the mother's second child, the judge could not identify the perpetrator of the non-accidental injuries suffered by the first child but found in any event that both parents were culpable having colluded in hiding the truth in order to protect the person responsible. For the purposes of the current care proceedings, the local authority chose not to seek to rely on the finding that both the mother and her former partner had colluded to hide the truth and had failed to protect a child in their care. The local authority proceeded instead on the single basis that the mother fell within the pool of possible perpetrators for causing non-accidental injuries to the baby. The question for the Supreme Court was whether this was *sufficient* for the threshold criteria to be crossed in relation to

---

[155] Note also that this needs to be distinguished from cases where the basis for the local authority's application is proven abuse to the child who is the *subject* of the application but the identity of the perpetrator is unknown. This is the scenario dealt with by *Lancashire CC v B* [2000] 2 AC 147 (threshold) and *Re O and N* [2003] UKHL 18 (welfare), discussed at pp 859–62 and 869–71 below.

[156] [2013] UKSC 9.

the third child and her two older step-siblings in the new family unit. The unanimous decision of the Supreme Court was that this fact was not by itself *sufficient* for a finding that the three children currently living within the mother's household were likely to suffer significant harm, it never having been proved on the balance of probabilities that the mother had caused non-accidental injuries to another child. Lady Hale gave the lead judgment in which, having set out the issue, she started by referring to the earlier case of *Re S-B*, in which (in obiter comments) she had appeared to answer this question:

Re S-B (Non-Accidental Injury) [2009] UKSC 17

LADY HALE:

49. There is a further reason to remit the case. The judge found the threshold crossed in relation to William [the child who had suffered no actual harm] on the basis that there was a real possibility that the mother had injured Jason. That, as already explained, is not a permissible approach to a finding of likelihood of future harm. It was established in *Re H* and confirmed in *Re O*, that a prediction of future harm has to be based upon findings of actual fact made on the balance of probabilities. It is only once those facts have been found that the degree of likelihood of future events becomes the 'real possibility' test adopted in *Re H*. It might have been open to the judge to find the threshold crossed in relation to William on a different basis, but she did not do so.

Having quoted this passage as being an apparent source of 'consternation',[157] Lady Hale continued to review the so-called 'trilogy' of House of Lords decisions in this area, namely *Re H (Minors) (Sexual Abuse: Standard of Proof)*,[158] *Lancashire County Council v B*,[159] and *Re O (Non-Accidental Injury)*.[160] From her review, Lady Hale concluded that none of the earlier authorities was directly on point, but that the principles emerging from them were 'entirely consistent' with paragraph 49 of *Re S-B*, and consequently it could be said that that paragraph 'represents a correct statement of the law, and should be followed'.[161]

The policy rationale lying behind this conclusion is important. Lady Hale stresses the importance of s 31 in striking the correct balance between protecting children from the risk of harm whilst according due respect to family autonomy and protecting the family from unwarranted state intervention. The threshold criteria is crucial to striking that balance, with Lady Hale emphasizing that the various tests set out under s 31 must be looked at together in assessing whether that balance has been correctly struck:

Re J (Care Proceedings: Threshold Criteria) [2013] UKSC 9

LADY HALE:

44. Time and again, the cases have stressed that the threshold conditions are there to protect both the child and his family from unwarranted interference by the state. There must

---

157 [2013] UKSC 9, [20].
158 [1996] AC 563, as discussed above.
159 [2000] 2 AC 147, which we discuss below.
160 [2003] UKHL 18, which we discuss below.
161 *Re J (Care Proceedings: Threshold Criteria)* [2013] UKSC 9, [43].

be a clearly established objective basis for such interference. Without it, there would be no "pressing social need" for the state to interfere in the family life enjoyed by the child and his parents which is protected by article 8 of the ECHR. Reasonable suspicion is a sufficient basis for the authorities to investigate and even to take interim protective measures, but it cannot be a sufficient basis for the long term intervention, frequently involving permanent placement outside the family, which is entailed in a care order....

49. Having adopted a flexible test of likelihood, it became all the more important to hold that an objective factual basis was required from which to draw the inference that future harm was likely.

Lord Wilson gave a concurring judgment in which he strongly agreed with Lady Hale on the fundamental issue at stake and the rationale underpinning the Supreme Court's approach:

LORD WILSON:

71. Stockton [the local authority] does not dispute that a prediction of likelihood of significant harm must be founded on proven facts. There is, of course, no express statement of such a requirement in the Act itself. It arises as a result of judicial interpretation at the highest level... Stockton argues, instead, that a person's consignment to a pool of possible perpetrators of harm to a child is itself a finding of fact which can found a prediction that a second child is likely to suffer significant harm; or, even if not, that, when added to a finding (being on any view a finding of fact) that the first child did suffer harm, it provides the requisite foundation upon which it would be open to the court to predict the likelihood.

72. Is a bald statement that there is a real possibility that X caused the injuries a statement of fact? I personally do not find the answer easy. But there is no need for an answer. For the consignment of two (or more) persons to a pool of possible perpetrators goes further than that: it is a statement not only that there is a real possibility that X caused the injuries and alternatively that Y caused them but also that no one else caused them, i.e that one or other of them did cause them. I am clear that such a conclusion does amount to a finding of fact. But is it a fact relevant to the threshold? Where X and Y remain together as a unit and are putting themselves forward as carers for an unharmed child, it is certainly relevant and might well suffice in enabling the threshold to be crossed in relation to that child; for in those circumstances the fact is that somebody in the child's proposed home did perpetrate injuries to another child. But the difficulty arises in the case, reflective of the facts in this appeal, in which X and Y no longer remain together as a unit and in which only one of them, X, is put forward as a carer. The consignment of X to a pool is not a finding that X did cause the injuries. So the question arises whether in that situation such a finding of fact is relevant.

73. Here is the crux of this appeal. Stockton's case is deeply illogical. Stockton argues that the children are at risk of suffering significant harm because of the presence in their home of [the mother]. So the requisite foundational facts must relate to [the mother]. To point to no more than the fact that [the mother's first child] suffered grave non-accidental injuries is, on any view, insufficient. A second fact is needed such as relates to [the mother]. Stockton seeks to make the link with her by relying on her consignment to the pool of possible perpetrators of the injuries. But her consignment to the pool is not a relevant fact because it falls short of ascribing their perpetration to her. The result is that there is no relevant second fact. In both *In re H* and *In re B*, cited above, it was clear that, if in each case the girl had suffered harm, it had been at the hands of her step-father; in the event, however, the court's conclusion was no more than that there was a real possibility that she had suffered the harm. Stockton does not challenge the principle established by those cases that such a conclusion

was insufficient to found a likelihood that the step-father would cause significant harm to other children. The present appeal presents the precisely obverse situation; there was no doubt that [the mother's first child] had suffered harm and the only issue, which in the event was unable to be resolved save in terms of a real possibility, related to the identity of the perpetrator. There is in my view no basis for departing from that principle in this precisely obverse, yet analogous, situation. The harm and the person's responsibility for it are the two planks on which any conclusion about likelihood must rest and they must be equally sturdy.

75. If and insofar (so Stockton proceeds to submit) as the basis of the appeal is illogical, then so be it; for otherwise legalism would triumph over child protection. But - in my view - logic is the blood which runs through the veins of the law: allow it to escape and ultimately the edifice collapses. Nor is the rigid approach to the factual foundation properly categorised as legalism.

76. My view remains that the need for the local authority to prove the facts which give rise to a real possibility of significant harm in the future is a bulwark against too ready an interference with family life on the part of the state. And, subject to the caveat that the court received no argument on the impact of article 8 of the European Convention on Human Rights, I incline to the view that nothing less than a factual foundation would justify such grave interference with the rights of the child and the parents thereunder to respect for their family life ...

77. I therefore conclude that the mother's consignment to the pool of possible perpetrators of the injuries to T-L is irrelevant to whether the three subject children are likely to suffer significant harm.

Although agreeing on the central point, Lord Wilson (supported by Lord Sumption) did however depart from the majority on the important question of whether the consignment of the mother to a pool of possible perpetrators could be of *any relevance* at all to establishing the threshold. Lady Hale,[162] Lord Hope, and Lord Reed (with whom Lord Clarke and Lord Carnworth agreed) were of the view that such a finding, whilst not *by itself sufficient* to cross the threshold, could be *relevant* to establishing the threshold criteria, such that, when taken together with other established facts (e.g. other failings in parental capacity which contributed to the previous child's injuries) it could be found to be sufficient. This point is made most clearly in Lord Hope's judgment:

LORD HOPE:

86. To identify what is and is not a "finding of fact" for the purposes of the threshold, which looks to the future, is only the first step in the analysis. Views may differ as to what is truly a "fact" for this purpose, but I do not think that one need dwell on this question. Anything that is proved on a balance of probabilities may be taken into account to see what can be made of it. The crucial steps are to identify what is *relevant* and what is not, and then to determine whether what is found to be relevant is *sufficient* for a finding that the threshold has been crossed. If it is not, the question will be whether there are other facts and circumstances that can be brought into account to satisfy this requirement.

87. Let us assume that the question is whether the child would be at risk while in the care of X. A finding that X is in the pool of two or more possible perpetrators of harm that a child sustained in the past is a finding of fact. It means that, because X is in the pool, it is possible that X was the perpetrator. If the perpetrators are still together, it will be relevant, and may

---

162 See at [51]–[54] of her judgment.

on its own be sufficient, to show that the threshold has been crossed. If the parties have separated and X is the carer, I decline to say that a finding that X was in the pool will no longer be relevant. That is so for two reasons: first, because it is information which invites further inquiry as to whether the subsequent child is likely to suffer harm while in the care of X; and, second, because, in combination with other facts and circumstances that the inquiry reveals about X's attitude or behaviour, it may help to show that this threshold has been crossed. It may have a bearing on the weight of the evidence when looked at as a whole, including an assessment of the balance of probabilities.

88. ...So I do not, with respect, agree with Lord Wilson that the finding can never be relevant. But it will not on its own be sufficient. The crucial point is this: it cannot, and must not, be treated on its own as a finding of fact that it was X who caused or contributed to the injuries.

As Lord Hope indicated, Lord Wilson (supported by Lord Sumption) strongly disagreed with this view:

LORD WILSON:

80. ...I feel driven to the conclusion that their suggestion is illogical; and that if, for the purpose of the requisite foundation, X's consignment to a pool has a value of zero on its own, it can, for this purpose, have no greater value in company. I can only hope that their suggestion, highly authoritative though it will be, will not destabilise the requisite foundation; will not in practice lead to a prediction about a real possibility in the future being founded, in part, on no more than a real possibility about what happened in the past.

The position following the Supreme Court's decision in *Re J* can thus be summarized as follows:

- the consignment of a child's carer to a pool of possible perpetrators for causing non-accidental injuries to *another* child cannot by itself constitute a sufficient factual basis for a finding that the unharmed child who is the subject of the present care order application is likely to suffer future significant harm;

- however, whilst the consignment of the child's carer to a pool of possible perpetrators is not by itself sufficient for the threshold to be crossed, it is a relevant fact for the court to consider and when taken together with other relevant facts may constitute a sufficient factual basis for a finding that the unharmed child who is the subject of the present care order application is likely to suffer future significant harm.

The Supreme Court's approach to unknown perpetrators at the threshold stage in *Re J* has met with a mixed academic response. Bainham welcomed the decision as striking the correct balance between protecting the family from unwarranted intervention and protecting children from harm.[163] The majority's reasoning has, however, been subjected to strong criticism by Gilmore as being 'formalistic and unconvincing'.[164] Gilmore argues that Lady Hale was too focused on whether the majority's approach could be justified as a matter of 'legal logic' at the expense of grappling in any convincing way with the important underlying

---

[163] Bainham (2013), 269.
[164] Gilmore (2013), 236.

questions of legal policy. Insofar as Lady Hale does address those questions, Gilmore criticizes her for a misplaced emphasis on the role of the threshold criteria in acting as a bulwark for parents against unwarranted state intervention into family life as opposed to focusing on the overriding necessity of protecting children:

S. Gilmore, 'Re J (Care Proceedings: Past Possible Perpetrators in a New Family Unit) [2013] UKSC 9: Bulwarks and Logic – The Blood Which Runs Through the Veins of Law – But How Much Will Be Spilled in Future?' (2013) 25 *Child and Family Law Quarterly* 215, 230

Lord Nicholls was clear in the earlier uncertain perpetrator cases that the policy that outweighs all others is child protection and that children are not to be put at risk simply because a possible perpetrator of proven harm to a child cannot be identified. . . . Some sound reasons underlie that policy. As Professor Hayes has observed, the policy that should prevail in the debate concerning how the balance should be held between parents' and children's interests in child protection cases is informed by consideration of the relative risks involved. In a case such as *Re J*, this involves considering the nature of the harm to the child which might occur if the court were not to permit protection of the child on the basis of a person's possible perpetration of harm to another child, as against the harm which might occur if intervention were permitted and later found to have an erroneous basis because it is discovered that the person did not perpetrate any harm. Both are errors with serious consequences, but which of two outcomes is likely to be potentially worse for the child: a false finding of anticipated abuse or a false finding that there is no risk of future abuse? In a case like *Re J*, the potential consequences to a child of not permitting intervention (possible death or physical injury) may be regarded as more serious than the consequences of what may turn out to have been unwarranted state intervention. . . . *Re H* is not authority for a general principle that inferences about future harm must *always* be based upon facts proved on the balance of probabilities. By contrast, in *Re J* the basis for inferring a risk of future harm was not mere suspicion of past harm; it was qualitatively different. While it could only be said that the mother *might* be the source of risk to the children in *Re J*, the fact remained that there was a proven risk to the children in *Re J*, founded on the proven fact of harm to another child. The facts of *Re J* – given the proven past harm to another child – were in this regard crucially different from *Re H's* finding of no judicially determined risk at all.

'Is attributable to the care given to the child not being what it would be reasonable to expect a parent to give to him'

The second limb of the threshold test similarly raises the difficult question of whether the local authority must be able to prove on the balance of probabilities that the harm is attributable to one or other or both of the parents before the s 31(2) criteria are met. It is important to note at the outset that by this stage of the inquiry the court will be satisfied that the child is suffering or likely to suffer harm. The issue at this stage will thus typically arise in cases where it has been established on the balance of probabilities that the child who is the subject of the application has suffered harm but the identity of the perpetrator remains open to question. The issue again has important implications as to the overall threshold for state intervention into the family. It was confirmed by Lady Hale in *Re S-B (Non-Accidental Injury)* that the test to be applied when identifying the perpetrator is the balance of probabilities.[165] The problem arises when the local authority is unable to discharge that burden with respect to any one particular individual. The problem of the 'unknown perpetrator' was addressed by the House of Lords in *Lancashire CC v B*.[166] Lord Nicholls again gave judgment for the majority, arguably sanctioning state intervention in circumstances where, contrary to his judgment in *Re H* and the subsequent decision of the Supreme Court in *Re J*, there was only a *suspicion*, as opposed to established fact, that the child had suffered significant harm *at the hands of the parents*. The case concerned the now common scenario where the care of the child had been shared between the parents and a childminder, although the problem of the 'unknown perpetrator' also frequently arises where the parents have separated and the local authority is unable to establish whether one or other or both of the parents is responsible for the harm. There was no dispute that the child had suffered significant harm. The question was whether in order to satisfy the second limb of the threshold, it had to be established, on the balance of probabilities, which of the three possible perpetrators: the mother, the father, or the childminder, had been responsible for the harm.

Lancashire CC v B [2000] 2 AC 147 (HL), 164–7

LORD NICHOLLS:

In a case based on present harm ("is suffering...significant harm") the attributable condition requires the court to be satisfied that the harm is attributable to the care given to the child or, which is not this case, to the child's being beyond parental control. That nexus must be established on the basis of proved facts. But that prompts the question: care by whom? The contention of A's parents is that, having regard to the statutory context and the legislative policy behind Part IV of the Children Act 1989, "the care given to the child" in section 31(2)(b)(i) means the care given to the child by the parents or other primary carers. The contrary contention, advanced by the local authority and A's guardian, is that no such limiting words are to be read into the statute: the relevant phrase means the care given by anyone who plays a part in the care arrangements for the child.

Counsel [for the parents] submitted that a strictly literal interpretation of the phrase under consideration would lead to an absurdity. Parliament cannot have intended that a child should be at risk of being removed from his family, and the parents at risk of losing their child, because of an unforeseeable failure of care by a third party to whom the parents, wholly unexceptionably, had temporarily entrusted the child....

This is a forceful argument, up to a point. I accept that the interpretation of the attributable condition urged on behalf of the respondents [the Local Authority]...is too wide and loose. For this one needs to look no further than [counsel for the appellant's] example of the one-off temporary entrustment of the child to a person reasonably believed by the parents to be suitable. Injury inflicted by the temporary carer would satisfy the threshold conditions. But the appellants' argument goes too far in the other direction. The interpretation urged on behalf of the appellants is too rigid. As with the respondents' submission, so also with the appellants' submission: the conclusion to which it leads cannot be right. As the present case exemplifies, the appellants' argument, if accepted, produces the result that where a child has repeatedly sustained non-accidental injuries the court may nevertheless be unable to intervene to protect the child by making a care order or, even, a supervision order. In the

---

165 [2009] UKSC 17, [34].
166 [2000] 2 AC 147.

present case the child is proved to have sustained significant harm at the hands of one or both of her parents or at the hands of a daytime carer. But, according to this argument, if the court is unable to identify which of the child's carers was responsible for inflicting the injuries, the child remains outside the threshold prescribed by Parliament as the threshold which must be crossed before the court can proceed to consider whether it is in the best interests of the child to make a care order or supervision order. The child must, for the time being, remain unprotected, since section 31 of the Children Act 1989 and its associated emergency and interim provisions now provide the only court mechanism available to a local authority to protect a child from risk of further harm.

I cannot believe Parliament intended that the attributable condition in section 31(2)(b) should operate in this way. Such an interpretation would mean that the child's future health, or even her life, would have to be hazarded on the chance that, after all, the non-parental carer rather than one of the parents inflicted the injuries. Self-evidently, to proceed in such a way when a child is proved to have suffered serious injury on more than one occasion could be dangerously irresponsible.

There is a further factor which weighs with me. Sadly, the unhappy facts of the present case are far from being exceptional. As the Court of Appeal observed, the task of caring for children is often shared nowadays between parents and others. When questions of non-accidental injury or abuse arise, the court is frequently unable to discover precisely what happened. This is not surprising. And yet, on the appellants' construction of the attributable condition, in this common form situation of shared caring the court is powerless to make even a supervision order if the judge is unable to penetrate the fog of denials, evasions, lies and half-truths which all too often descends in court at fact finding hearings...

Against this background, I consider that a permissible and preferable interpretation of section 31(2)(b)(i), between the two extremes, is as follows. The phrase "care given to the child" refers primarily to the care given to the child by a parent or parents or other primary carers. That is the norm. The matter stands differently in a case such as the present one, where care is shared and the court is unable to distinguish in a crucial respect between the care given by the parents or primary carers and the care given by other carers. Different considerations from the norm apply in a case of shared caring where the care given by one or other of the carers is proved to have been deficient, with the child suffering harm in consequence, but the court is unable to identify which of the carers provided the deficient care. In such a case, the phrase "care given to the child" is apt to embrace not merely the care given by the parents or other primary carers; it is apt to embrace the care given by any of the carers. Some such meaning has to be given to the phrase if the unacceptable consequences already mentioned are to be avoided. This interpretation achieves that necessary result while, at the same time, encroaching to the minimum extent on the general principles underpinning section 31(2). Parliament seems not to have foreseen this particular problem. The courts must therefore apply the statutory language to the unforeseen situation in the manner which best gives effect to the purposes the legislation was enacted to achieve.

Lord Nicholls recognized the difficulties caused by this approach but held that the known risk of harm to the child outweighed any potential unfairness to the parents:

I recognise that the effect of this construction is that the attributable condition may be satisfied when there is no more than a possibility that the parents were responsible for inflicting the injuries which the child has undoubtedly suffered. That is a consequence which flows from giving the phrase, in the limited circumstances mentioned above, the wider meaning those circumstances require. I appreciate also that in such circumstances, when the court proceeds to the next stage and considers whether to exercise its discretionary power to make a care order or supervision order, the judge may be faced with a particularly difficult problem. The judge will not know which individual was responsible for inflicting the injuries. The child may suffer harm if left in a situation of risk with his parents. The child may also suffer harm if removed from parental care where, if the truth were known, the parents present no risk. Above all, I recognise that this interpretation of the attributable condition means that parents who may be wholly innocent, and whose care may not have fallen below that of a reasonable parent, will face the possibility of losing their child, with all the pain and distress this involves. That is a possibility, once the threshold conditions are satisfied, although by no means a certainty. It by no means follows that because the threshold conditions are satisfied the court will go on to make a care order. And it goes without saying that when considering how to exercise their discretionary powers in this type of case judges will keep firmly in mind that the parents have not been shown to be responsible for the child's injuries.

I recognise all these difficulties. This is indeed a most unfortunate situation for everyone involved: the child, the parents, the child-minder, the local authority and the court. But, so far as the threshold conditions are concerned, the factor which seems to me to outweigh all others is the prospect that an unidentified, and unidentifiable, carer may inflict further injury on a child he or she has already severely damaged.

Following *Lancashire CC v B*, it is clear that in order to satisfy the second limb of the threshold it is not necessary where it is known the subject child has suffered harm to identify the perpetrator of the harm. However, establishing the identity of the perpetrator where possible remains of considerable importance as the proceedings progress to the welfare stage and the court is required to determine the future arrangements for the child. Thus, whilst unnecessary to meet the threshold criteria, where the perpetrator can be identified on the balance of probabilities, the court has a duty to do so.[167] There is, however, a limit as to what the court can be expected to do.[168] The Court of Appeal has emphasized that where identification is simply not possible on the evidence, it is the 'duty of the judge to state that as his or her conclusion.'[169] The question then arises what more, if anything, the court should do where the perpetrator cannot be identified. The Supreme Court addressed this particular aspect of the problem in *Re S-B (Non-Accidental Injury)*, holding that it is still important for the court to identify the 'pool of possible perpetrators' because 'it will help to identify the real risks to the child and the steps needed to protect him. It will help the professionals working with the family. And it will be of value to the child in the long run.'[170]

The test for identifying the 'pool of possible perpetrators' was addressed in *North Yorkshire CC v SA*.[171] The Court of Appeal held that applying a test of 'no possibility' to *exclude* a possible perpetrator from the pool was 'patently too wide': it may leave in the pool 'anyone who had even a fleeting contact with the child in circumstances in which there was the opportunity to cause injuries'.[172] Butler-Sloss P suggested that the test for *inclusion* in the pool should be 'likelihood or real possibility'.[173] This approach was approved in *Re S-B*.

[167] *Re D (Children) (Non-Accidental Injury)* [2009] EWCA Civ 472, [12].
[168] Ibid.
[169] Ibid.
[170] [2009] UKSC 17, [40].
[171] [2003] EWCA Civ 839.
[172] Ibid, [25].
[173] Ibid, [26].

Re S-B (Non-Accidental Injury) [2009] UKSC 17

LADY HALE:

43. The cases are littered with references to a "finding of exculpation" or to "ruling out" a particular person as responsible for the harm suffered. This is...to set the bar far too high. It suggests that parents and other carers are expected to prove their innocence beyond reasonable doubt. If the evidence is not such as to establish responsibility on the balance of probabilities it should nevertheless be such as to establish whether there is a real possibility that a particular person was involved. When looking at how best to protect the child and provide for his future, the judge will have to consider the strength of that possibility as part of the overall circumstances of the case.

Two further points regarding the correct interpretation of the 'attributable to' limb of the threshold criteria should be noted. It was established in *Lancashire CC v B* that the phrase 'attributable to' connotes a causal connection between the harm and the care being given to the child, but the care in question need not be the 'sole or dominant or direct cause'; a contributory cause, such as a parent's failure to protect, is sufficient.[174] Lord Nicholls also addressed the standard of care to be expected of the caregiver, emphasizing that it was not a question of attributing blame or culpability but establishing that the care had fallen below an objectively acceptable level.[175] It is a wholly 'objective' test, thus the reasonable parent is not to be imbued with the particular characteristics of the parent in question when determining whether the care provided has fallen below the required standard.[176] Similarly, there is no subjective mental element: the parent does not have to *intend* to cause harm.[177] It is also important to distinguish between the parents' particular personality or characteristics and the impact of those characteristics on their ability to adequately parent the child. As made clear by the Supreme Court in *Re B (Care Proceedings: Appeal)*,[178] only the latter is relevant. The fact a parent may have learning difficulties or a long criminal history or is a compulsive liar are all irrelevant unless they impact in some way on the quality of the care afforded to the child.

In determining the objective standard of care to be expected of parents, it has been held by Munby J that social and cultural differences may be taken into consideration. *Re K*[179] concerned applications for various orders with respect to a 16-year-old Kurdish Iraqi girl whose family had moved to the UK following her father being granted asylum. In accordance with the family's cultural and religious practices, the girl had entered into an arranged (not forced) marriage at the age of 15 in a religious ceremony in the UK. She subsequently alleged that she had been raped and sexually abused by her 'husband' and physically abused by her father. The police and local authority intervened and she became estranged from her family. Although she maintained her allegations of rape, she later returned to the family home and refused to cooperate with social services. The local authority applied for a supervision order and orders under the court's inherent jurisdiction to prevent the parents removing her from the UK or consenting to a further marriage whilst she was under the age

---

[174] [2000] 2 AC 147, 162.
[175] Ibid.
[176] *Re D (A Child) (Care Order: Evidence)* [2010] EWCA Civ 1000, [35].
[177] [2013] UKSC 33, [31] (Lord Wilson).
[178] [2013] UKSC 33.
[179] [2005] EWHC 2956.

of 18. The applications were dismissed. In considering the question of whether the harm suffered by the girl as a result of the arranged marriage was attributable to the care given by the parents, Munby J held that whilst the care afforded by the parents was to be judged in accordance with an objective standard, the court must be sensitive to the social, cultural, and religious world-view of the family and evaluate the parents' behaviour accordingly.[180] Taking into account the parents' cultural and religious beliefs and the fact that the mother was herself married to the father at the age of 14, Munby J went on to observe that he would be very reluctant to find that parents who had only recently settled in the UK had fallen below an acceptable standard of parenting if when judged against the standards of their own community they would be regarded as having done nothing wrong.[181] Indeed, it was evident in this case that the parents were genuinely upset and bemused as to why an arranged marriage at the age of 15 should have been regarded as abusive and have caused such outrage amongst the relevant professionals. This judicial sensitivity to cultural difference has not, however, been welcomed by all who fear it sanctions a relativist approach to child protection. Keating, for example, has noted with caution that the judgment 'could lend weight to the idea that children from different ethnic backgrounds could legitimately receive different levels of protection from harm' and that 'any such inference would be deeply wrong'.[182]

Establishing the threshold criteria

The standard of proof

In order to satisfy both limbs of the threshold criteria, it is clear the local authority will need to establish a number of key facts. It was held by Lord Nicholls in *Re H*, that the usual civil standard of proof applies, placing the burden on the local authority to satisfy the court on the balance of probabilities as to any disputed factual issues. None of this is particularly contentious.[183] However, more controversially, Lord Nicholls went on to explain how, in his view, this standard of proof would be applied in the case of serious allegations of child abuse.

Re H (Sexual Abuse: Standard of Proof) [1996] AC 563, 586

LORD NICHOLLS:

Where the matters in issue are facts the standard of proof required in non-criminal proceedings is the preponderance of probability, usually referred to as the balance of probability. This is the established general principle. There are exceptions such as contempt of court applications, but I can see no reason for thinking that family proceedings are, or should be, an exception...

The balance of probability standard means that a court is satisfied an event occurred if the court considers that, on the evidence, the occurrence of the event was more likely than not.

---

[180] Ibid, [25]–[26].
[181] Ibid.
[182] Keating (2011), 126.
[183] See, e.g., a straightforward reminder that the burden is on the local authority to prove their case as to the parents causing non-accidental injuries to a child (and not on the parents to prove that the injuries were accidental or to provide a satisfactory explanation as to how they were caused in the absence of which a non-accidental cause will be assumed) in *Re M (Fact-Finding Hearing: Burden of Proof)* [2012] EWCA Civ 1580.

When assessing the probabilities the court will have in mind as a factor, to whatever extent is appropriate in the particular case, that the more serious the allegation the less likely it is that the event occurred and, hence, the stronger should be the evidence before the court concludes that the allegation is established on the balance of probability. Fraud is usually less likely than negligence. Deliberate physical injury is usually less likely than accidental physical injury. A stepfather is usually less likely to have repeatedly raped and had non-consensual oral sex with his under age stepdaughter than on some occasion to have lost his temper and slapped her. Built into the preponderance of probability standard is a generous degree of flexibility in respect of the seriousness of the allegation.

Although the result is much the same, this does not mean that where a serious allegation is in issue the standard of proof required is higher. It means only that the inherent probability or improbability of an event is itself a matter to be taken into account when weighing the probabilities and deciding whether, on balance, the event occurred. The more improbable the event, the stronger must be the evidence that it did occur before, on the balance of probability, its occurrence will be established.

Lord Nicholls' judgment was interpreted to mean that the more serious the allegation, the more cogent and convincing the evidence would need to be to tip the balance of probabilities in favour of the local authority.[184] Lord Lloyd gave a strong dissenting judgment in *Re H* itself, describing such an approach as 'bizarre'. It was also subjected to convincing academic criticism, both in terms of its untested assumptions and its potential implications for children.[185]

The House of Lords revisited the issue in *Re B (Children) (Care: Proceedings)*.[186] The suggestion that Lord Nicholls had intended to apply a 'heightened' civil standard of proof to care proceedings was firmly denied: in the words of Baroness Hale, 'it is time for us to loosen its grip and give it its quietus'.[187] The House of Lords unanimously held that the usual civil standard of proof was to be applied without further gloss or elaboration. That said, both Lord Hoffmann and Baroness Hale went on to state that the inherent improbability of an event occurring *may* be relevant, an alleged improbable 'fact' being harder to prove on the balance of probabilities than a probable one. However, whilst noting the potential relevance of inherent probabilities to discharging the burden of proof, both expressly disagreed with Lord Nicholls' basic assertion that the seriousness of the allegation bears any relationship to the inherent improbability of the event occurring.

Re B (Children) (Care Proceedings) [2008] UKHL 35

BARONESS HALE:

70. . . . I would go further and announce loud and clear that the standard of proof in finding the facts necessary to establish the threshold under section 31(2) or the welfare considerations in section 1 of the 1989 Act is the simple balance of probabilities, neither more nor less. Neither the seriousness of the allegation nor the seriousness of the consequences should

---

184 *Re U (A Child) (Serious Injury: Standard of Proof)* [2004] EWCA Civ 567, [13].
185 See, e.g., Keenan (2005), Keating (2006).
186 [2008] UKHL 35.
187 Ibid, [64].

make any difference to the standard of proof to be applied in determining the facts. The inherent probabilities are simply something to be taken into account, where relevant, in deciding where the truth lies...

72. As to the seriousness of the allegation, there is no logical or necessary connection between seriousness and probability. Some seriously harmful behaviour, such as murder, is sufficiently rare to be inherently improbable in most circumstances. Even then there are circumstances, such as a body with its throat cut and no weapon to hand, where it is not at all improbable. Other seriously harmful behaviour, such as alcohol or drug abuse, is regrettably all too common and not at all improbable. Nor are serious allegations made in a vacuum. Consider the famous example of the animal seen in Regent's Park. If it is seen outside the zoo on a stretch of greensward regularly used for walking dogs, then of course it is more likely to be a dog than a lion. If it is seen in the zoo next to the lions' enclosure when the door is open, then it may well be more likely to be a lion than a dog.

The House of Lords have thus silenced many of the critics of Lord Nicholls' judgment in *Re H*.[188]

12.5.4 THE WELFARE STAGE

Once the court is satisfied the threshold conditions are met, it acquires jurisdiction to make an order. It can thus move on to the second stage of the proceedings. Whether the court should make the order sought is a question relating to the child's upbringing and the child's welfare is thus the paramount consideration.[189] Section 1(4) directs the court to have particular regard to the welfare checklist in s 1(3), of which the following are of particular note.

'Ascertainable wishes and feelings of the child'

In certain specified public law cases,[190] including applications for care or supervision orders, the child is made a party to the proceedings. To this end, s 41 provides that the court shall appoint a children's guardian to safeguard the child's interests unless satisfied that it is not necessary to do so.[191] The core responsibilities of children's guardians include providing the court with their professional assessment as to the child's best interests and advising the court as to the child's wishes and feelings.[192] It is clear that there is no rebuttable presumption that the wishes and feelings of children should be followed, even in the case of mature minors.[193] The child's wishes must be considered within the context of the whole welfare balance. Children's guardians are also responsible for appointing and instructing a solicitor to represent the child unless the guardian is authorized to conduct litigation.[194] If the child and the guardian disagree over the handling of the case, the child may instruct the solicitor directly provided the solicitor, the children's guardian, or the court considers the child is of

---

[188] Keating (2009).

[189] *Humberside County Council v B* [1993] 1 FLR 257, 261.

[190] S 41(6).

[191] See also FPR 2010, r 16.3.

[192] FPR 2010, r 16.20.

[193] *Re P-S* [2013] EWCA Civ 223, [43].

[194] Criminal Justice and Court Services Act 2000, s 15.

sufficient understanding to do so.[195] In such circumstances, the guardian will continue to act, subject to the directions of the court, and may, with leave, appoint his or her own legal representation.[196]

Although the child may be a party to public law proceedings, the child is not entitled to attend court if represented by a children's guardian or solicitor.[197] Indeed, the courts have strongly discouraged guardians from allowing children to be present at hearings, requiring such presence to be justified to the judge.[198] Alternatively, the judge may choose to speak to the child directly.[199] In April 2010, the Family Justice Council issued guidance for judges meeting children.[200] The guidelines make clear that the purpose of the meeting is to benefit the child—it is not to gather evidence. Particular caution is therefore required where the proceedings have not yet concluded to ensure that the evidence is not 'contaminated' by the judge hearing directly from a child in circumstances where the usual procedural safeguards, such as the right to cross-examine, do not apply. The guidelines were considered by the Court of Appeal in *Re A (Fact-Finding: Judge Meeting Child)*.[201] It is clear from that decision that there remains considerable disquiet amongst the judiciary about the appropriateness and 'risks' of the judge meeting the child, particularly when the judge is engaged in a fact-finding exercise as opposed to making a forward-looking welfare decision.[202]

Whether the child should give evidence in the more conventional sense has also been the subject of Supreme Court authority and subsequent guidance by the Family Justice Council.[203] In *Re W (Children) (Abuse: Oral Evidence)* it was argued on behalf of the father who had been accused of serious sexual abuse by his partner's daughter that in order to protect the Convention rights of all parties, including the father's right to a fair trial, there should be no presumption against a child giving evidence in care proceedings. The Supreme Court, Lady Hale giving judgment, agreed that there could be no such 'starting point' or 'presumption' but ultimately concluded that when the balancing exercise is carried out, weighing the right to a fair trial against the potential harm to the child, the balance is very likely to continue to fall against a child giving evidence—children giving evidence will thus remain the exception rather than the rule. The Supreme Court's approach was quickly challenged in the Court of Appeal in the case of *Re P-S (Care Proceedings: Right to Give Evidence)*.[204] *Re P-S* was a very different case in that it was the child who wanted to give evidence so he could press upon the court the strength of his opposition to a care order being made. He argued that as a party to the proceedings, he had a right to give evidence. Ward LJ dismissed the argument. He confirmed in accordance with Article 12 of the UN Convention on the Rights of the Child that children do have the 'right to be heard in family proceedings'.[205] He went on, however, to explain that the child's right may be realized in a

---

[195] FPR 2010, r 16.21. For a more detailed explanation, see *Re M (Minors) (Care Proceedings: Child's Wishes)* [1994] 1 FLR 749.

[196] FPR 2010, r 16.21.

[197] FPR 2010, r 12.14(3).

[198] *Re C (A Minor) (Care: Child's Wishes)* [1993] 1 FLR 832, 840–1.

[199] *Re M (Minors) (Care Proceedings: Child's Wishes)* [1994] 1 FLR 749, 755.

[200] Family Justice Council (2010a). For further discussion and extracts from the guidance, see 11.3.3.

[201] [2012] EWCA Civ 185. See also the child abduction case of *Re KP (Abduction: Judge Meeting Child: Conduct of Interview)* [2014] EWCA Civ 554.

[202] See also *Re P-S (Care Proceedings: Right to Give Evidence)* [2013] EWCA Civ 223, [42].

[203] *Re W (Children) (Abuse: Oral Evidence)* [2010] UKSC 12. See also Family Justice Council (2010b).

[204] [2013] EWCA Civ 223.

[205] Ibid, [36].

variety of ways. There is thus no right to give evidence (as was argued in *Re P-S*)[206] nor is there a right to see the judge. It will all depend on the circumstances of the case. In many cases the child's right to be heard will be properly realized only through his or her guardian conveying the child's wishes and feelings to the court.

'Any harm which he has suffered or is at risk of suffering'

In order to get to this stage of the proceedings it must already have been established that the child is suffering or is likely to suffer significant harm. At this point the court may take into account not only the harm established at the threshold stage but any additional harm the child may suffer as a result of the court making or refusing to make the orders sought. Importantly, this includes any emotional harm the child may suffer as a result of separation from his or her primary carers, as well as the advantages and disadvantages of 'corporate parenting' through long-term foster or residential care.[207]

The Court of Appeal has held that when considering harm at the welfare stage, the same principles set down by Lord Nicholls in the House of Lords in *Re H* will apply. Only harm which is established on the balance of probabilities can therefore be considered; mere suspicion about existing or likely future harm must be excluded.

Re M and R (Minors) (Sexual Abuse: Expert Evidence) [1996] 4 All ER 239 (CA), 246–8

BUTLER-SLOSS LJ:

In the case before us [counsel] submitted that the House of Lords [in *Re H*] were concerned only with the threshold stage and that the majority view had no relevance to the welfare stage. So far as the latter stage was concerned, he submitted that since the judge in the present case was also clearly of the view that there was a real possibility that the children had been sexually abused, this was sufficient to establish that the children were at risk of suffering like harm in the future. Since a risk of harm is included in the welfare checklist set out in s 1(3) of the 1989 Act, the judge was wrong to exclude it from consideration. [Counsel] submitted that the justification for approaching s 1 in a way rejected by the House of Lords for s 31 was that under s 1 the welfare of the child was the paramount consideration, which justified and indeed required the court to act on possibilities rather than proof on the preponderance of probability...

In our judgment these submissions cannot be supported. They amount to the assertion that under s 1 the welfare of the child dictates that the court should act on suspicion or doubts, rather than facts. To our minds the welfare of the child dictates the exact opposite...

The court must reach a conclusion based on facts, not on suspicion or mere doubts. If, as in the present case, the court concludes that the evidence is insufficient to prove sexual abuse in the past, and if the fact of sexual abuse in the past is the only basis for asserting a risk of sexual abuse in the future, then it follows that there is nothing (except suspicion or mere doubts) to show a risk of future sexual abuse...

Section 1(3)(e)...does not deal with what *might* possibly have happened or what future risk there *may* possibly be. It speaks in terms of what *has* happened or what *is* at risk of

---

[206] Ibid, [39].
[207] *Humberside County Council v B* [1993] 1 FLR 257, 267, recently reiterated by the Court of Appeal in *Re G (Care Proceedings: Welfare Evaluation)* [2013] EWCA Civ 965, [46]–[47].

happening. Thus, what the court must do (when the matter is in issue) is to decide whether the evidence establishes harm or the risk of harm.

We cannot see any justification for the suggestion that the standard of proof in performing this task should be less than the preponderance of probabilities. Were such a suggestion to be adopted, it would mean in effect that instead of acting on what was established as probably the case, the court would have to act on what was only possibly the case, or even on the basis of what was probably not the case. This, as Lord Nicholls pointed out in *Re H*, is the same as saying that the court should act on the basis of suspicion rather than on the basis of fact.

Such a proposition has, to our minds, only to be stated to be rejected. The same applies to the suggestion that the paramountcy of the welfare of the child requires such a method of proceeding, for this equally entails the proposition that the future of the child should be decided on the basis of suspicion rather than fact. We can find nothing in the 1989 Act which begins to suggest that Parliament intended that all-important decisions as to the future of a child should be made on such a basis, which to our minds would be a recipe for making decisions which were not in the best interests of the child...

Finally, we find support for our analysis of the position from the odd results which would follow were [counsel's] submissions to be accepted.

Firstly, it would be extraordinary if Parliament intended that evidence which is insufficient to establish that a child is likely to suffer significant harm for the purposes of s 31, should nevertheless be treated as sufficient to establish that a child is at risk of suffering harm for the purposes of s 1...

Secondly, it is clear from the speech of Lord Nicholls in *Re H*...that s 31 provides, among other things, protection for parents...

That protection would be entirely removed in circumstances similar to those of the present case, if, on reaching the second stage for reasons which might well not justify permanently removing the children, the court could act on the basis of such suspicions to make an order for permanent removal which would not be justified on the matters that had been properly proved.

As at the threshold stage, a different approach is taken to the question of the *identity* of the perpetrator. In line with the House of Lords decision in *Lancashire CC v B*, it was held by Lord Nicholls in *Re O and N (Minors) (Care: Preliminary Hearing)* that when considering the risk of harm to the child at the welfare stage, a possible perpetrator should not be excluded simply because the local authority is unable to establish culpability on the balance of probabilities. Consequently, whilst the question of whether the child has suffered or is at risk of suffering harm must be determined on the basis of facts proved on the balance of probabilities,[208] there is no requirement to establish the identity of the perpetrator on the same basis.

Re O and N (Minors) (Care: Preliminary Hearing) [2003] UKHL 18

LORD NICHOLLS:

The welfare stage: 'uncertain perpetrator' cases

26. The first area concerns cases of the type involved in the present appeals, where the judge finds a child has suffered significant physical harm at the hands of his parents but is unable to say which. I stress one feature of this type of case. These are cases where it has

---

[208] *Re M and R (Minors) (Sexual Abuse: Expert Evidence)* [1996] 4 All ER 239.

been proved, to the requisite standard of proof, that the child is suffering significant harm or is likely to do so.

27. Here, as a matter of legal policy, the position seems to me straightforward. Quite simply, it would be grotesque if such a case had to proceed at the welfare stage on the footing that, because neither parent, considered individually, has been proved to be the perpetrator, therefore the child is not at risk from either of them. This would be grotesque because it would mean the court would proceed on the footing that neither parent represents a risk even though one or other of them was the perpetrator of the harm in question.

28. That would be a self-defeating interpretation of the legislation. It would mean that, in 'uncertain perpetrator' cases, the court decides that the threshold criteria are satisfied but then lacks the ability to proceed in a sensible way in the best interests of the child. The preferable interpretation of the legislation is that in such cases the court is able to proceed at the welfare stage on the footing that each of the possible perpetrators is, indeed, just that: a possible perpetrator...This approach accords with the basic principle that in considering the requirements of the child's welfare the court will have regard to all the circumstances of the case...

31. In 'uncertain perpetrator' cases the correct approach must be that the judge conducting the disposal hearing will have regard, to whatever extent is appropriate, to the facts found by the judge at the preliminary hearing...When the facts found at the preliminary hearing leave open the possibility that a parent or other carer was a perpetrator of proved harm, it would not be right for that conclusion to be excluded from consideration at the disposal hearing as one of the matters to be taken into account. The importance to be attached to that possibility, as to every feature of the case, necessarily depends on the circumstances. But to exclude that possibility altogether from the matters the judge may consider would risk distorting the court's assessment of where, having regard to all the circumstances, the best interests of the child lie...

34. I wholly understand that parents are apprehensive that, if each of them is labelled a possible perpetrator, social workers and others may all too readily rule out the prospect of rehabilitation with either of them because the child would be 'at risk' with either of them...

35. I understand this concern. Whether it is well founded, generally or in particular cases, is an altogether different matter. Whether well founded or not, the way ahead cannot be for cases to proceed on an artificial footing.

As Lord Nicholls clearly acknowledges, his approach means that a parent faces losing his or her child without the state ever proving on the balance of probabilities that the parent in question was responsible for the harm caused. In *Re B (Children)*, Baroness Hale dismissed the argument that this was inconsistent with the decisions of the House of Lords in *Re H* and the Court of Appeal in *Re M and R*, holding that 'the court cannot shut its eyes to the undoubted harm which has been suffered simply because it does not know who was responsible'.[209]

Whilst now well established that at the welfare stage the court can treat all possible but unproven perpetrators as posing a potential risk to the child, it remains somewhat unclear as to whether the court should attempt to assess the *degree of risk* posed by the individual in question. Lord Nicholls seemed to suggest in *Re O and N* that it was entirely appropriate for the court to attempt to assess the degree of likelihood that a particular individual was the perpetrator of the harm.[210] Lady Hale has been more cautious, suggesting it is unhelpful to

209 [2008] UKHL 35, [61].
210 [2003] UKHL 18.

try and assign percentage chances to each possible perpetrator. Whilst not precluding the possibility that the court could find that one individual is 'more likely' to be the perpetrator than others within the pool,[211] she has given strong support to Thorpe LJ's comment that the courts 'should be cautious about amplifying a judgment in which they have been unable to identify a perpetrator: "better to leave it thus"'.[212]

'The range of powers available to the court'

Once the threshold criteria have been established, the court has considerable freedom to shape its orders in accordance with the child's needs. It is open to the court on an application for a care order to make a supervision order and on an application for a supervision order to make a care order. As care proceedings constitute family proceedings, the court may also make a s 8 or a special guardianship order. This enables the court, even where the threshold conditions are satisfied, to make a private law order preventing the removal of the child into local authority care.[213] Despite the wide scope of the court's discretion, it is clear that there must be 'cogent and strong reasons to force upon the local authority a more draconian order than that for which they have asked'.[214] However, even where all the parties are agreed on the most appropriate order, the court is still under a duty to conduct an 'appropriate judicial investigation' and having considered all the circumstances of the case make the order it considers to be in the child's best interests.[215] As expressed by McFarlane LJ in *Re G (Care Proceedings: Welfare Evaluation)*, 'the judicial task is to undertake a global, holistic evaluation of each of the options available for the child's future upbringing', with both the positives and negatives of all the options properly assessed and weighed in the balance.[216] To this end, a 'linear' approach which starts with the least interventionist measure and works its way through the options to the most interventionist is to be avoided.[217] Such an approach risks the judge settling on the most extreme measure standing at the end of the line simply because all those that have come before it have been rejected as lacking in some way but without the judge at any time giving proper consideration to the potential problems and disadvantages of that most interventionist option.

When determining the appropriate order the court must consider the need for a proportionate response: that is, it should adopt the least interventionist measure possible to protect the child.[218] The importance of this principle has been reinforced by the implementation of the HRA 1998: in order to justify any prima facie interference with the rights of the parents under Article 8(1), any measures taken by the state must, under Article 8(2), be shown to have been no more than necessary to protect the competing rights and interests of the child. This was reiterated by Hale LJ in *Re C and B*, a case concerning the removal of two very young children from their parents on the basis of the intellectual and emotional impairment caused to two older siblings by their mother's deteriorating mental health. Hale LJ held that the removal of the two younger children without any evidence that either of them were currently suffering significant harm was a wholly disproportionate response.

---

[211] *Re T (Non-Accidental Injury)* [2009] EWCA Civ 1208, [60]–[65].
[212] *Re S-B (Non-Accidental Injury)* [2009] UKSC 17, [44].
[213] *Northamptonshire CC v S* [1993] 1 FLR 554.
[214] *Oxfordshire County Council v B* [1998] 3 FCR 521, 525.
[215] *Re T (A Child) (Care Order)* [2009] EWCA Civ 121, [44] and [49].
[216] [2013] EWCA Civ 965, [50]–[54].
[217] Ibid.
[218] [1998] 3 FCR 521, 526.

Re C and B (Children) (Care Order: Future Harm) [2000] 2 FCR 614 (CA)

HALE LJ:

30. I . . . accept that there are cases in which the local authority is not bound to wait until the inevitable happens: it can intervene to protect long before that. But there has to be a balance. The cases where it is appropriate to do that are likely to involve long-standing problems which interfere with the capacity to provide even 'good enough' parenting in a serious way, such as serious mental illness, or a serious personality disorder, or intractable substance abuse, or evidence of past chronic neglect, or abuse, or evidence of serious ill-treatment and physical harm. None of those was involved in this case. Nor can it follow that every case where there is any significant risk of harm to a young child should result in a care order in which the care plan is adoption. Again, one quite understands why this may be considered by the local authority to be the appropriate course of action because, if there is early intervention before problems have escalated, the chance of placing the child successfully for adoption are much increased. The prospects are much less favourable if the child remains and damage is in fact sustained.

31. Nevertheless one comes back to the principle of proportionality. The principle has to be that the local authority works to support, and eventually to reunite, the family, unless the risks are so high that the child's welfare requires alternative family care. I cannot accept [counsel's] submission that this was a case for a care order with a care plan of adoption or nothing. There could have been other options . . .

34. There is a long line of European Court of Human Rights jurisprudence . . . which emphasises that the intervention has to be proportionate to the legitimate aim. Intervention in the family may be appropriate, but the aim should be to reunite the family when the circumstances enable that, and the effort should be devoted towards that end. Cutting off all contact and the relationship between the child or children and their family is only justified by the overriding necessity of the interests of the child.

A number of recent cases have emphasized the importance of the court complying with its obligations under Article 8 ECHR when making a care order. In the case of *EH v Greenwich London Borough Council; Re A (Children) (Non-Accidental Injury)*,[219] Baron J, sitting in the Court of Appeal, suggested that in order to demonstrate that the judge has Article 8 fully in mind and that the care order is both necessary and proportionate, the judge should refer fully and explicitly to the terms of Article 8 in the course of the judgment.[220] The Court of Appeal also reiterated that in accordance with the demands of Article 8 the local authority's core obligation when intervening into family life is to work to support the family and ensure rehabilitation has 'a reasonable prospect of success'.[221] On the facts, the local authority were strongly criticized for not providing the mother with the rigorous support work she needed in order to give rehabilitation a realistic chance—the local authority having decided at an early stage on finding permanence for the children outside the birth family.[222] Wall LJ was particularly trenchant in his criticism of the local authority, stressing that, whatever the

---

[219] [2010] EWCA Civ 344.
[220] Ibid, [64]. Wilson LJ has expressed ambivalence about the necessity for this: see *Re M and B (Children) (Care Proceedings: Family Life)* [2010] EWCA Civ 821, [22].
[221] *EH v Greenwich London Borough Council; Re A (Children) (Non-Accidental Injury)* [2010] EWCA Civ 344, [14].
[222] Ibid, [55].

difficulties of the work, the social workers' aim whenever possible had to be to unite families rather than separate them.[223]

The responsibility on the court to ensure strict compliance with Article 8 is particularly important when the care plan is to place the children for adoption thereby severing all ties (legal and factual) between the parent and child.[224] As the Supreme Court made clear in *Re B (Care Proceedings: Appeal)*, Article 8 demands a 'high degree of justification' before a determination that a child should be placed in care with a view to adoption.[225] In the words of Lady Hale, the circumstances must be 'exceptional', giving rise to an 'overriding' welfare imperative. In short, the court must be satisfied 'nothing else will do'.[226]

12.5.5 THE CARE PLAN

An important consideration when it is proposed to a take a child into care is the local author-ity care plan.[227] Section 31A of the CA 1989 thus provides that where the local authority makes an application on which a care order may be made, it must prepare a care plan.[228] The content of the care plan is prescribed by regulations but should include: the child's identified needs, including needs arising from race, culture, religion, special education, or health needs; the aim of the plan; the proposed timescale for implementation; the proposed placement; arrangements for contact and reunification; a contingency plan if the placement breaks down; the parents' and the child's wishes and views; and plans for the parents ongo-ing participation in the decision-making process.[229] The courts expect the local authority to produce evidence supporting the plan focusing on its feasibility and the likelihood of success.[230]

In a move to encourage more robust decision-making, the CFA 2014 has dramatically curtailed the extent to which the court is *expected* to scrutinize the care plan before deter-mining whether or not a care order is in the best interests of the child. Section 31(3A) of the CA 1989 now provides that when deciding whether to make a care order the court is only *required* to consider the permanence provisions of the plan (i.e. whether the child is to live with a parent or kinship carer, is to be adopted, or will remain in long-term care) and the local authority's intentions as regards contact between the child and family members.[231] Although the legislation does not prevent the court going beyond the prescribed matters, it is now extremely doubtful that the care plan will be subjected to the kind of 'rigorous scrutiny' previously envisaged by the courts.[232] The thinking behind the imposition of these restrictions was the perception that the courts' 'exhaustive' preoccupation with the details of local authority care plans was causing further delay and was a waste of time and money. It was also suggested by the Family Justice Review that the courts had been inappropriately

---

223 Ibid, [110].

224 For the most recent analysis of the Convention principles as applied to domestic law by the European Court of Human Rights, see *YC v United Kingdom* (App No 4547/10, ECHR) (2012), discussed in more detail at 13.4.2.

225 [2013] UKSC 33, [34] (Lord Wilson).

226 Ibid, [195]–[198] (Lady Hale). See also [74]–[79] (Lord Neuberger); [130] (Lord Kerr).

227 Although always an important consideration, the care plan was only given statutory force in 2002.

228 S 31A(1).

229 Set down in *Re J (Minors) (Care: Care Plan)* [1994] 1 FLR 253, 258–9.

230 Ibid, 261–2.

231 CA 1989 as amended by CFA 2014, s 15.

232 See *Re J (Minors) (Care: Care Plan)* [1994] 1 FLR 253.

encroaching into areas with which they were ill-equipped to deal and in the process under-mined the confidence and decisiveness of local authority decision-makers for the children in their care.[233] The shift away from judicial scrutiny of local authority care plans does, however, require a certain faith in the local authority to plan appropriately and to effectively monitor and review the implementation of the care plan. It also places increased responsi-bility for safeguarding the rights and welfare of looked after children in the hands of IROs. As noted below, this might be problematic.[234]

Although the role of the court is likely to be much more limited in the future, the court must still be satisfied that the core elements of the care plan are in the child's best interests before making the care order. There thus remains the potential for disagreement between the court and the local authority as to the core elements of the plan, raising the question as to how such disagreements are to be resolved. In practice, the answer is that there is very little the court can do if it disagrees with what the local authority intends. As observed by Munby J, if the court seeks to alter the local authority's care plan it must 'achieve its objective by persuasion rather than by compulsion.'[235] Where persuasion fails and the local authority will not reconsider its position, the only option available to the court is to refuse to make the care order.[236] It would be a brave judge who refused to make a care order where the threshold conditions were satisfied and the child's welfare otherwise demanded it. In practice such cases are rare.[237]

The frustration caused by the limited range of options available to the court where it disagrees with the local authority care plan is exacerbated by the restrictions placed on the court once a care order has been made. Often the problem is not so much that the court disagrees with the plan, but that the plan is incomplete or uncertain. Before the CA 1989, the High Court had the power to monitor the implementation of care plans and, if neces-sary, give directions to the local authority regarding a child within its care or bring a case back before the court for further consideration and review. The CA 1989 removed these powers.[238] Under the current legislative scheme, once the care order has been made, respon-sibility for the child, save for on issues relating to contact, passes to the local authority.[239] Decisions regarding the implementation of the care plan, including making major changes such as abandoning attempts to rehabilitate the child to her family, are regarded as falling within the discretion of the local authority. Consequently, the only way in which the deci-sion of a local authority can be challenged is by bringing an application to discharge the care order under s 39 of the CA 1989, applying for judicial review, or, if there has been a violation of the child's or the parents' rights under Article 6 or 8 ECHR, by bringing an application under ss 7 and 8 of the HRA 1998.[240]

The courts' inability to monitor or review the implementation of the care plan has been a matter of considerable concern amongst the judiciary. This concern is based on more than simple indignation at the court's inability to control matters once a certain point has been reached. In recent years, worrying evidence has emerged as to the number of children said

---

[233] Norgrove (2011), 3.17.
[234] Discussed below at p 877.
[235] *Re K* [2007] EWHC 393, [15].
[236] *Re S and D (Child Case: Powers of Court)* [1995] 1 FCR 626 (CA).
[237] Ibid, [21].
[238] S 100(2). See *Re J (Minors) (Care: Care Plan)* [1994] 1 FLR 253, 258.
[239] See below at 12.5.7.
[240] *Re M (Care: Challenging Decisions by Local Authority)* [2001] 2 FLR 1300. For a recent example of a guardian challenging the local authority care plan by way of judicial review and under the HRA 1998, see *Re B (Transfer of Foster Placement)* [2013] 1 FLR 633. This was, however, a case in which the guardian remained involved because final care orders had yet to be made.

to be 'lost in care'.[241] These are children for whom no clear care plan has ever been in place or for whom the care plan has simply failed or been forgotten. As was acknowledged by Lord Nicholls, these children are grossly let down by the system.[242] Concern about the number of children 'lost in care' prompted calls across the legal profession for the introduction of better judicial safeguards for children in care. It was against this background that *Re S (Minors) (Care Order: Implementation of Care Plan)* came before the House of Lords.

It was contended in *Re S* that the current legislative scheme risked infringing the ECHR rights of both parents and children by the lack of judicial oversight of the implementation of the care plan once a care order had been made. As regards the rights of the parents, the House of Lords disagreed. As regards the rights of the child, it recognized the potential for breach but declined to provide a remedy. Lord Nicholls' judgment begins by making clear the sensible rationale behind the current division of responsibility between the local authority and the court:

Re S (Minors) (Care Order: Implementation of Care Plan) [2002] UKHL 10

LORD NICHOLLS:

25. ...The [Children] Act delineated the boundary of responsibility with complete clarity. Where a care order is made the responsibility for the child's care is with the authority rather than the court. The court retains no supervisory role, monitoring the authority's discharge of its responsibilities. That was the intention of Parliament...

27. ...The change brought about by the Children Act gave effect to a policy decision on the appropriate division of responsibilities between the courts and local authorities...The particular strength of the courts lies in the resolution of disputes...But a court cannot have day to day responsibility for a child. The court cannot deliver the services which may best serve a child's needs. Unlike a local authority, a court does not have close, personal and continuing knowledge of the child. The court cannot respond with immediacy and informality to practical problems and changed circumstances as they arise. Supervision by the court would encourage 'drift' in decision making, a perennial problem in children cases. Nor does a court have the task of managing the financial and human resources available to a local authority for dealing with all children in need in its area. The authority must manage these resources in the best interests of all the children for whom it is responsible.

28. ...The court operates as the gateway into care, and makes the necessary care order when the threshold conditions are satisfied and the court considers a care order would be in the best interests of the child. That is the responsibility of the court. Thereafter the court has no continuing role in relation to the care order. Then it is the responsibility of the local authority to decide how the child should be cared for.

Lord Nicholls went on to consider whether the current legislative scheme violated the ECHR, concluding that the CA 1989 per se was not incompatible with Article 8:

54. Clearly, if matters go seriously awry, the manner in which a local authority discharges its parental responsibilities to a child in its care may violate the rights of the child or his parents under this article. The local authority's intervention in the life of the child, justified at the

---

241 See, e.g., Waterhouse (2000) and *Re F; F v Lambeth London Borough Council* [2002] 1 FLR 217.
242 *Re S (Minors) (Care Order: Implementation of Care Plan)* [2002] UKHL 10, [29]–[30].

outset when the care order was made, may cease to be justifiable under article 8(2). Sedley LJ pointed out that a care order from which no good is coming cannot sensibly be said to be pursuing a legitimate aim. A care order which keeps a child away from his family for purposes which, as time goes by, are not being realised will sooner or later become a disproportionate interference with the child' s primary article 8 rights . . .

55. Further, the local authority's decision making process must be conducted fairly and so as to afford due respect to the interests protected by article 8. For instance, the parents should be involved to a degree which is sufficient to provide adequate protection for their interests . . .

56. However, the possibility that something may go wrong with the local authority's discharge of its parental responsibilities or its decision making processes, and that this would be a violation of article 8 so far as the child or parent is concerned, does not mean that the legislation itself is incompatible, or inconsistent, with article 8 . . .

57. If an authority duly carries out [its] statutory duties, in the ordinary course there should be no question of infringement by the local authority of the article 8 rights of the child or his parents. Questions of infringement are only likely to arise if a local authority fails properly to discharge its statutory responsibilities. Infringement which then occurs is not brought about, in any meaningful sense, by the Children Act. Quite the reverse. Far from the infringement being compelled, or even countenanced, by the provisions of the Children Act, the infringement flows from the local authority's failure to comply with its obligations under the Act. True, it is the Children Act which entrusts responsibility for the child's care to the local authority. But that is not inconsistent with article 8 . . .

58. Where, then, is the inconsistency which is alleged to exist? As I understand it, the principal contention is that the incompatibility lies in the absence from the Children Act of an adequate remedy if a local authority fails to discharge its parental responsibilities properly and, as a direct result, the rights of the child or his parents under article 8 are violated . . .

59. In my view this line of argument is misconceived. Failure by the state to provide an effective remedy for a violation of article 8 is not itself a violation of article 8. This is self-evident. So, even if the Children Act does fail to provide an adequate remedy, the Act is not for that reason incompatible with article 8. This is the short and conclusive answer to this point.

Lord Nicholls then considered the arguments under Article 6, concluding that as the parents could effectively challenge any decision made by the local authority regarding implementation of the care plan by judicial review or under ss 7 and 8 of the HRA 1998, any potential breach of their Article 6 rights would be more illusory than real.[243] The child's position was more difficult, Lord Nicholls holding that the *child's* inability to bring legal proceedings to challenge any potential breach of Article 8 gave rise to a *possible* incompatibility between the legislative scheme and the child's rights under Article 6:

82. I must note also a difficulty of another type. This concerns the position of young children who have no parent or guardian able and willing to become involved in questioning a care decision made by a local authority. This is an instance of a perennial problem affecting children. A parent may abuse a child. The law may provide a panoply of remedies. But this avails nothing if the problem remains hidden. Depending on the facts, situations of this type may give rise to difficulties with Convention rights. The Convention is intended to guarantee rights which are practical and effective. This is particularly so with the right of access to the courts, in view of the prominent place held in a democratic society by the right to a

---

243 Ibid, [75]–[81].

> fair trial... The guarantee provided by article 6(1) can hardly be said to be satisfied in the case of a young child who, in practice, has no way of initiating judicial review proceedings to challenge a local authority's decision affecting his civil rights. (In such a case, as already noted, the young child would also lack means of initiating section 7 proceedings to protect his article 8 rights.)
>
> 83. My conclusion is that in these respects circumstances might perhaps arise when English law would not satisfy the requirements of article 6(1) regarding some child care decisions made by local authorities. In one or other of the circumstances mentioned above the article 6 rights of a child... are capable of being infringed.

Having found, however, that the legislative scheme gave rise to a *potential* breach of Article 6, Lord Nicholls declined to decide whether this 'lacuna' did in fact render the legislation incompatible with the child's ECHR rights, concluding that it was unnecessary to do so on the particular facts of the case.

The House of Lords' judgment in *Re S* thus did little to improve the position of children badly let down by the local authority. That is not to say that the House of Lords did not recognize the need for change. Indeed, Lord Nicholls concluded his judgment by urging the legislature to take appropriate steps to address the problem. Parliament responded by introducing two important amendments.[244] First, the local authority was placed under a statutory duty to keep the child's care plan under review.[245] Secondly, the local authority must now appoint an IRO who will participate in the local authority's six-monthly review of every case, monitor the performance of the local authority, and refer the case to Cafcass if it is deemed appropriate to do so.[246] If the child's Article 8 rights are at risk of being infringed by changes to or non-implementation of the care plan, the potential breach should therefore be brought to the attention of a Cafcass officer who has the responsibility to bring an action in judicial review or under s 7 of the HRA 1998 on the child's behalf. The effectiveness of the IRO system is, however, questionable. Research conducted by Timms and Thoburn in 2006 for the NSPCC suggested that many young people within the care system have little faith in the IRO to challenge local authority decision-making effectively: lack of power and lack of independence being key concerns.[247] The researchers go on to comment that the fact that 'very few, if any, cases have been referred by IROs to children's guardians since this section was implemented in 2004 does not encourage confidence that the distress and dissatisfaction with contact and placement plans expressed by some... children... will be alleviated by this particular legislative change.'[248] These concerns are strongly borne out by *A and S (Children) v Lancashire County Council*,[249] where Jackson J details the systemic problems facing the IRO system.

Against the backdrop of these concerns, attempts to circumvent the courts' inability to monitor care plans by other means have also ultimately proved unsuccessful. It was held in *Kent County Council v C* that it was inappropriate to add a direction to a care order providing for the continued involvement of the guardian so that she could monitor the

---

[244] Amendments introduced by the Adoption and Children Act 2002.
[245] S 26(2)(f).
[246] Ss 26(2)(k) and 26(2A). Review of Children's Cases Regulations 1991, SI 1991/895, reg 2A.
[247] Timms and Thoburn (2006), 168.
[248] Ibid.
[249] [2012] EWHC 1689. See also House of Lords (2013), paras 114–124 and House of Commons (2012), paras 87–90.

local authority's progress.[250] Similarly, it has been held to be inappropriate for the court to adjourn questions of contact with a view to keeping an attempt at rehabilitation under review.[251] The same approach has been taken to the use of interim orders when employed as a means of monitoring or supervising the local authority. It was accepted in *Re J (Minors) (Care: Care Plan)* that a court could refuse to make a final care order if it was not satisfied about 'material aspects of the care plan'.[252] However, Wall J emphasized that interim orders should only be used with caution and should not be used 'as a means of exercising the now defunct supervisory role of the court'.[253] He went on to point out that the court should not be unduly concerned if there were continuing elements of doubt and uncertainty about the plan. This approach was confirmed in *Re S*:

Re S (Minors) (Care Order: Implementation of Care Plan) [2002] UKHL 10

LORD NICHOLLS:

90. From a reading of section 38 as a whole it is abundantly clear that the purpose of an interim care order...is to enable the court to safeguard the welfare of a child until such time as the court is in a position to decide whether or not it is in the best interests of the child to make a care order. When that time arrives depends on the circumstances of the case and is a matter for the judgment of the trial judge. That is the general, guiding principle. The corollary to this principle is that an interim care order is not intended to be used as a means by which the court may continue to exercise a supervisory role over the local authority in cases where it is in the best interests of a child that a care order should be made.

91. An interim care order, thus, is a temporary 'holding' measure...

92. When a local authority formulates a care plan in connection with an application for a care order, there are bound to be uncertainties. Even the basic shape of the future life of the child may be far from clear. Over the last ten years problems have arisen about how far courts should go in attempting to resolve these uncertainties before making a care order and passing responsibility to the local authority. Once a final care order is made, the resolution of the uncertainties will be a matter for the authority, not the court.

93. In terms of legal principle one type of uncertainty is straightforward. This is the case where the uncertainty needs to be resolved before the court can decide whether it is in the best interests of the child to make a care order at all...In such a case the court should finally dispose of the matter only when the material facts are as clearly known as can be hoped...

94. More difficult, as a matter of legal principle, are cases where it is obvious that a care order is in the best interests of the child but the immediate way ahead thereafter is unsatisfactorily obscure. These cases exemplify a problem, or a 'tension', inherent in the scheme of the Children Act. What should the judge do when a care order is clearly in the best interests of the child but the judge does not approve of the care plan?...

95. In this context there are sometimes uncertainties whose nature is such that they are suitable for immediate resolution, in whole or in part, by the court in the course of disposing

---

[250] [1993] Fam 57, 62.
[251] *Re S (A Minor) (Care: Contact Order)* [1994] 2 FLR 222.
[252] [1994] 1 FLR 253, approving *C v Solihull Metropolitan Council* [1993] 1 FLR 290.
[253] Ibid. See also *Re L (Sexual Abuse: Standard of Proof)* [1996] 1 FLR 116, 124–6.

of the care order application. The uncertainty may be of such a character that it can, and should, be resolved so far as possible before the court proceeds to make the care order. Then, a limited period of 'planned and purposeful' delay can readily be justified as the sensible and practical way to deal with an existing problem...

97. Frequently the case is on the other side of this somewhat imprecise line. Frequently the uncertainties involved in a care plan will have to be worked out after a care order has been made and while the plan is being implemented...

98. ...Quite apart from known uncertainties, an element of future uncertainty is necessarily inherent in the very nature of a care plan. The best laid plans 'gang aft a-gley'. These are matters for decision by the local authority, if and when they arise. A local authority must always respond appropriately to changes, of varying degrees of predictability, which from time to time are bound to occur after a care order has been made and while the care plan is being implemented. No care plan can ever be regarded as set in stone...

100. Cases vary so widely that it is impossible to be more precise about the test to be applied by a court when deciding whether to continue interim relief rather than proceed to make a care order. It would be foolish to attempt to be more precise. One further general point may be noted. When postponing a decision on whether to make a care order a court will need to have in mind the general statutory principle that any delay in determining issues relating to a child's upbringing is likely to prejudice the child's welfare: section 1(2) of the Children Act.

Subsequent case law has made clear that where there remains doubt over a fundamental question such as whether a child should be placed for adoption or remain in long-term foster care, a final care order should not be made.[254] This would appear to be the case even if there is no question of the child returning home and thus the making of a final care order is at some point inevitable. The practical advantages of the court refusing to make the care order final in these circumstances have been highlighted by the Court of Appeal:

Re G (Care Orders) [2010] EWCA Civ 1271

BLACK LJ:

53. I think it would be fair to say that it was an uphill task for counsel for the mother to produce arguments to justify the course that the recorder took in granting full care orders when he had pronounced himself in such fundamental disagreement with the local authority's care plan and was unwilling to grant the placement orders necessary to take it forward...

55. The guardian's counsel has set out very clearly a number of the disadvantages for the children in the course that the recorder took, not least potential delay and lack of continuing independent input into decisions about their future. The making of the care order and dismissal of the placement application brought the involvement of the guardian and the children's solicitor to an end; similarly [the mother's] legal representation would come to an end. The instruction of the new expert would be a matter for the local authority's

---

254 *Re G (Care Orders)* [2010] EWCA 1271.

internal processes. They would have to obtain funding for it. The guardian and her solicitor would no longer be available to contribute their expertise to the instruction. The court
would have no role in scrutinising the suitability of the chosen person, the questions
that were to be addressed by him or her and the timetable for the report. Any input the
parents had would be entirely a matter between them and the local authority. It would
be up to the local authority to decide when, if at all, to recommence proceedings for a
placement order...

58. ...[T]he recorder failed to take account of the practical difficulties that the dismissal of
the placement applications would pose for the local authority...They would...have to reis-
sue the placement applications and await directions hearings thereafter rather than a further
hearing of the existing adjourned placement application being scheduled...to tie in with the
care proceedings.

59. As counsel for the guardian puts it, this was a case in which the court should have
retained control over the proceedings, the evidence and the timetable for the children. The
consequence of the court not doing this is that the children have been left in limbo without a
clearly defined or timetabled path to permanence.

The approach endorsed by Black LJ in this case should be contrasted with her approach in
Re D O'H (Children).[255] The issue in dispute in *Re D O'H* was not the principle of adoption
but the type of adoption placement, in particular whether there should be provision for
post-adoption contact or not. The Court of Appeal held that where the principle of adoption
had been resolved and the only matter outstanding was post-adoption contact the judge had
been correct in proceeding to make a final care order.[256]

12.5.6 EFFECT OF A CARE ORDER

The legal effects of a care order are set down in s 33 of the CA 1989. The primary effect
of the order is to place a duty on the local authority to receive the child into care and to
keep the child in care whilst the order remains in force.[257] A child can be 'in care' but
remain living at home.[258] The care order gives the local authority the power to remove
the child from the parents without further recourse to the courts, although, except in
emergencies, the local authority must provide the parents with proper notice of the decision and involve them fully in the decision-making process.[259] Whilst the care order is in
force, the local authority holds parental responsibility. That responsibility is shared with
the parents but the local authority has the power to determine the extent to which the
parents may exercise it.[260] This means the local authority not only has the right to make
day-to-day decisions with respect to the child's upbringing and, where necessary, override the wishes of the parents, but to effectively exclude them from the decision-making
process.[261] Any restrictions imposed on the parental responsibility of the parents must
be necessary to safeguard and promote the child's welfare.[262] Whilst the child is in care,

---

[255] [2011] EWCA Civ 1434.
[256] Ibid, [39]–[40].
[257] S 33(1).
[258] Placement of Children with Parents etc Regulations 1991, SI 1991/893.
[259] Ibid, reg 11. See *G v N County Council* [2009] 1 FLR 774, [20], [29]–[30].
[260] S 33(3)(a).
[261] *Re P (Children Act 1989, ss 22 and 26: Local Authority Compliance)* [2000] 2 FLR 910.
[262] S 33(4).

the local authority must also comply with the substantive and procedural requirements of Article 8.

Re G (Care: Challenge to Local Authority's Decision) [2003] EWHC 551

MUNBY J:

43. The fact that a local authority has parental responsibility for children pursuant to section 33(3)(a) of the Children Act 1989 does not entitle it to take decisions about those children without reference to, or over the heads of, the children's parents. A local authority, even if clothed with the authority of a care order, is not entitled to make significant changes in the care plan, or to change the arrangements under which the children are living, let alone to remove the children from home if they are living with their parents, without properly involving the parents in the decision-making process and without giving the parents a proper opportunity to make their case before a decision is made. After all, the fact that the local authority also has parental responsibility does not deprive the parents of their parental responsibility.

44. A local authority can lawfully exercise parental responsibility for a child only in a manner consistent with the substantive *and procedural* requirements of article 8. There is nothing in section 33(3)(b) of the Act that entitles a local authority to act in breach of article 8. On the contrary, section 6(1) of the 1998 Act requires a local authority to exercise its powers under both section 33(3)(a) and section 33(3)(b) of the 1989 Act in a manner consistent with both the substantive and the procedural requirements of article 8.

The CA 1989 imposes further limits on the local authority's parental responsibility. The local authority cannot: (i) cause the child to be brought up in a different religion; (ii) refuse or consent to the child's adoption; or (iii) appoint a guardian.[263] More generally, whilst a care order is in force no one can cause the child to be known by a new surname or remove the child from the jurisdiction without either the written consent of everyone holding parental responsibility or the court's leave.[264]

A care order can be made for a specified period or until further order.

12.5.7 CONTACT WITH A CHILD IN CARE

If the local authority plan is to try and rehabilitate the child with the parents, it is obviously important that the child's familial relationships are sustained through generous provision of contact. Where, however, the local authority's plan is to place the child with a permanent alternative family, the benefits of maintaining contact are more questionable. It used to be the dominant professional view that contact in such circumstances was unhelpful, it being believed that the continued presence of the birth family may prevent the child bonding with the new family and destabilize the placement.[265] That view has changed as the importance of the child maintaining positive links with the birth family has been recognized, not just whilst the child is in care, but in the longer term if the child is adopted.

---

[263] S 33(6).
[264] S 33(7).
[265] This is discussed in greater detail in the context of adoption. See below at pp 940 and 968–79.

Re E (Children in Care: Contact) [1994] 1 FCR 584 (CA), 594

SIMON BROWN LJ:

[Even] when the s. 31 criteria are satisfied, contact may well be of singular importance to the long-term welfare of the child: firstly in giving the child the security of knowing that his parents love him and are interested in his welfare; secondly, by avoiding any damaging sense of loss to the child in seeing himself abandoned by his parents; thirdly, by enabling the child to commit himself to the substitute family with the seal of approval of the natural parents; and, fourthly, by giving the child the necessary sense of family and personal identity. Contact, if maintained, is capable of reinforcing and increasing the chances of success of a permanent placement, whether on a long-term fostering basis or by adoption.

This marked change in professional attitudes towards contact has been reinforced by the European Court of Human Rights. The Court has stated repeatedly that terminating contact between parent and child constitutes a grave interference with Article 8 as it effectively ends any meaningful relationship between them. Any 'radical' decision by the national courts to terminate contact will therefore be subjected to the most 'anxious scrutiny', only being justified in exceptional circumstances.[266] It should, however, be noted that in recent years the government has questioned this strong commitment to preserving contact between a looked after child and his or her parents, particularly if the child is to be placed permanently outside the family.[267]

Despite the government's concerns, the importance of contact between a child in care and members of the child's family remains firmly entrenched within the CA 1989. The local authority is under a general duty to promote contact between a looked after child and the child's parents.[268] This is reinforced by s 34(1) which provides that the local authority shall, subject to its duty to safeguard and promote the child's welfare, allow 'reasonable contact' between them.[269] Initially it will be for the local authority to determine what constitutes reasonable contact having regard to the child's welfare. However, one of the most important policy changes enshrined in the CA 1989 was to remove the local authority's almost unfettered authority over contact decisions.[270] Before making a care order the court must always consider the local authority's proposed arrangements for contact and may make an order of its own motion.[271] An application may also be made to the court for a defined contact order, in determining which the child's welfare is the paramount consideration.[272]

The most important change introduced by the CA 1989 was to remove the local authority's power to terminate contact. That power now rests with the court. The local authority can only prohibit contact between the child and a person specified in s 34(1) for a maximum

---

[266] *S and G v Italy* (App Nos 39221/98 and 41963/98, ECHR) (2000), [170].

[267] DFE (2012a).

[268] Sch 2, para 15.

[269] S 34 was amended by s 8 of the CFA 2014 to make clear that the duty to allow reasonable contact is subject to the child's welfare and may be restricted on the facts of a particular case. This amendment was a response to concerns that in some cases the amount of contact being promoted between a child in care (especially young babies) and his or her parent was 'being driven by a view that contact should take place, rather than on the basis of the individual needs, circumstances, views and wishes of the child.' See DFE (2012a).

[270] For a brief account of the approach to contact prior to the CA 1989, see *Re B (Minors) (Termination of Contact: Paramount Consideration)* [1993] Fam 301, 306–8.

[271] S 34(11) and 34(5).

[272] For the test to be applied on an application for leave, see *Re W (Care Proceedings: Leave to Apply)* [2004] EWHC 3342.

of seven days if it is an emergency and the local authority is satisfied that it is necessary to safeguard and promote the child's welfare.[273] In all other cases, the local authority must apply to the court under s 34(4) for permission to terminate contact. It is clear from the case law that the court must take this jurisdiction seriously and not simply abdicate its responsibility to the local authority. Thus, it is inappropriate for the court to give the local authority general authorization to terminate or suspend contact should it consider it necessary.[274] This principle applies even if the local authority is certain that at some point in the future contact will need to be terminated.[275]

The court's jurisdiction over contact constitutes an important exception to the principle that once the care order has been made, responsibility for the child passes to the local authority. It raises the possibility of conflict between the local authority's care plan and the court's view on contact, which may in turn reflect a more fundamental disagreement between them as to the child's long-term future. The issue arose in *Re B (Minors) (Termination of Contact: Paramount Consideration)*. The local authority applied to terminate contact between two children and their mother in order to place the children for adoption. The guardian opposed the application, concerned that the possibility of rehabilitation with the mother had not been properly assessed. The Court of Appeal upheld the guardian's appeal, making it clear that where the local authority and the court disagree, the court must do what it considers to be in the child's best interests, even if continuing contact is inconsistent with the local authority's care plan.

Re B (Minors) (Termination of Contact: Paramount Consideration) [1993] Fam 301 (CA), 310–12

BUTLER-SLOSS LJ:

A section 34 application is clearly a substantive application in which the court is determining a question with respect to the upbringing of the child....

At the moment that an application comes before the court, at whichever tier, the court has a duty to apply section 1, which states that when a court determines any question with respect to the upbringing of a child, the child's welfare shall be the court's paramount consideration...

Contact applications generally fall into two main categories: those which ask for contact as such, and those which are attempts to set aside the care order itself. In the first category there is no suggestion that the applicant wishes to take over the care of the child and the issue of contact often depends on whether contact would frustrate long-term plans for the child in a substitute home, such as adoption, where continuing contact may not be for the long-term welfare of the child. The presumption of contact, which has to be for the benefit of the child, has always to be balanced against the long-term welfare of the child and, particularly, where he will live in the future. Contact must not be allowed to destabilise or endanger the arrangements for the child and in many cases the plans for the child will be decisive of the contact application. There may also be cases where the parent is having satisfactory contact with the child and there are no long-term plans or those plans do not appear to the court to

---

[273] S 34(6).

[274] *Re L (Sexual Abuse: Standard of Proof)* [1996] 1 FLR 116; *Re S (Children) (Termination of Contact)* [2004] EWCA Civ 1397.

[275] *Re H (Children) (Termination of Contact)* [2005] EWCA Civ 318.

preclude some future contact. The proposals of the local authority, based on their apprecia-tion of the best interests of the child, must command the greatest respect and consideration from the court, but Parliament has given to the court, and not to the local authority, the duty to decide on contact between the child and those named in section 34(1). Consequently, the court may have the task of requiring the local authority to justify their long-term plans to the extent only that those plans exclude contact between parent and child. In the second category, contact applications may be made by parents by way of another attempt to obtain the return of the children. In such a case the court is obviously entitled to take into account the failure to apply to discharge the care order, and in the majority of cases the court will have little difficulty in coming to the conclusion that the applicant cannot demonstrate that contact with a view to rehabilitation with the parent is a viable proposition at that stage, particularly if it had already been rejected at the earlier hearing when the child was placed in care. The task for the parents will be too great and the court would be entitled to assume that the plans of the local authority to terminate contact are for the welfare of the child and are not to be frustrated by inappropriate contact with a view to the remote possibility, at some future date, of rehabilitation.

But in all cases the welfare section has to be considered, and the local authority have the task of justifying the cessation of contact. There may also be unusual cases where either the local authority have not made effective plans or there has been considerable delay in implementing them and a parent, who has previously been found by a court unable or unwill-ing to care for the child so that a care order has been made, comes back upon the scene as a possible future primary carer. If the local authority with a care order decide not to consider that parent on the new facts, [counsel for the parents] argued that it is for the court, with the enhanced jurisdiction of the Act of 1989, to consider whether even at this late stage there should be some investigation of the proposals of the parent, with the possibility of reconsid-ering the local authority plans. [Counsel for the local authority] argued that the court cannot go behind the long-term plans of the local authority unless they were acting capriciously or were otherwise open to scrutiny by way of judicial review.

I unhesitatingly reject the local authority argument. As I have already said, their plan has to be given the greatest possible consideration by the court and it is only in the unusual case that a parent will be able to convince the court, the onus being firmly on the parent, that there has been such a change of circumstances as to require further investigation and reconsidera-tion of the local authority plan. If, however, a court were unable to intervene, it would make a nonsense of the paramountcy of the welfare of the child which is the bedrock of the Act, and would subordinate it to the administrative decision of the local authority in a situation where the court is seized of the contact issue. That cannot be right.

But I would emphasise that this is not an open door to courts reviewing the plans of local authorities.

This decision thus makes some limited inroads into the local authority's otherwise unfet-tered control over the content and implementation of the care plan. It is clear that, although unusual, in the second category of case (where the dispute over contact is really a dispute over whether the child should be rehabilitated with the parents), the court has the jurisdic-tion to order contact with a view to rehabilitation even if the local authority is thereby forced to reconsider its long-term plan to place the child permanently outside the family. Similarly, in the first category of case (where the parent is not seeking to have the child returned to his or her care), although Butler-Sloss LJ recognizes that contact should not be allowed to destabilize or jeopardize the local authority's long-term plan—an outcome which will rarely be in the child's best interests—the judge may nevertheless test the local authority's position and can refuse to terminate contact where it is not satisfied that the care plan and contact are necessarily inconsistent.[276]

Section 34 ensures that any attempt by the local authority to terminate contact between parent and child is subjected to independent judicial scrutiny. The court is thus very much cast in the role of safeguarding and defending the parents' rights. Indeed, if necessary, the court can attach a penal notice to the order and enforce it against the local authority by way of committal.[277] Of course, it is not necessarily the case that it is the court that is supportive of contact in the face of the local authority's opposition, raising the question whether the court has jurisdiction to terminate contact against the local authority's wishes. Despite early indications to the contrary,[278] however, the Court of Appeal has held that, given the clear legislative objectives behind s 34, the court has no jurisdiction to make an order prohibiting contact.[279]

12.5.8 EFFECT OF A SUPERVISION ORDER

A supervision order provides for a much lower level of intervention into the family than a care order. The effect of the supervision order is to place the child, not the parent, under 'supervision'.

Children Act 1989, s 35

(1) While a supervision order is in force it shall be the duty of the supervisor—

  (a) to advise, assist and befriend the supervised child;

  (b) to take such steps as are reasonably necessary to give effect to the order; and

  (c) where—

    (i) the order is not wholly complied with; or

    (ii) the supervisor considers that the order may no longer be necessary,

  to consider whether or not to apply to the court for its variation or discharge.

Further provisions with respect to supervision orders are found in Sch 3, Parts I and II. Conditions cannot be attached to a supervision order.[280] The supervision order may, however, require the supervised child to comply with certain directions given by the supervisor. This may include directions that the child reside at a particular place for a particular period of time; keep the supervisor informed of any change in address; allow the supervisor to visit him or her; attend certain appointments; or participate in various activities.[281] The

---

[276] See also *Re E (Children in Care: Contact)* [1994] 1 FCR 584, *Berkshire County Council v B* [1997] 1 FLR 171, and *Re K* [2007] EWHC 393, [24], [26].

[277] *Local Authority v HP, MB and P-B (Children)* [2009] EWCA Civ 143, [45], [50].

[278] See *Kent County Council v C* [1993] 1 FLR 308, 311 and *Re D and H (Care: Termination of Contact)* [1997] 1 FLR 841.

[279] *Re W (A Child) (Parental Contact: Prohibition)* [2000] Fam 130, 136–7.

[280] *Re S (Care or Supervision Order)* [1996] 1 FLR 753 and *Re V (A Minor) (Care or Supervision Order)* [1996] 2 FCR 555, 564. Similarly, the court has no jurisdiction to accept undertakings on the making of a supervision order: *Re B (Supervision Order: Parental Undertaking)* [1996] 1 FLR 676.

[281] Sch 3, Part I, paras 2 and 8.

supervision order may also require the child to submit to medical or psychiatric examination or treatment.[282] If the child is of sufficient understanding, the child must consent to the inclusion of such a provision in the order.[283] The supervision order may also include a requirement that a 'responsible person' take all reasonable steps to ensure that the supervised child complies with these directions.[284] The 'responsible person' may also be directed to participate in certain activities, to keep the supervisor informed of the responsible person's and the child's address, and to allow the supervisor to have reasonable contact with the child.[285] A 'responsible person' is defined as 'any person who has parental responsibility for the child and any other person with whom the child is living'.[286] As with a child of sufficient understanding, the 'responsible person' must consent to the inclusion of these provisions.[287]

In contrast to the position under a care order, it has been held that the children's guardian may continue to act until the supervision order has ceased to have effect.[288] The guardian's role will differ depending on the circumstances of each case but may include monitoring the implementation of the order to ensure its goals are being met.[289] The hope is that the continued engagement of the guardian can give the supervision order 'added teeth'.

A supervision order can only be made initially for a period of up to 12 months.[290] The order can be extended for further specified periods not exceeding three years in total from the date on which it was first made.[291] The problems caused by the limited duration of supervision orders were raised in *T v Wakefield Metropolitan District Council*.[292] In order to avoid the statutory restrictions, the judge made the order for 12 months and then immediately extended it for a further two years to give the maximum protection of three years. Whilst acknowledging the pragmatism and common sense behind the judge's order, the Court of Appeal held that such an approach was impermissible as it was clearly artificial for the court to make the order and then immediately extend it, thereby circumventing the clear statutory language.[293] The Court of Appeal did, however, confirm that on an application for the original order to be extended, it could be extended for a full two-year period rather than being limited to the 12-month maximum period of the initial order.[294]

An application to extend a supervision order is determined on the basis of the child's welfare.[295] It is not necessary for the local authority to prove that the threshold conditions still apply.[296] If after the three-year period has expired the local authority is of the view that the supervision order needs to remain in place, it must make a fresh application under s 31 at which the threshold conditions will again need to be proved to the satisfaction of the court.[297]

---

[282] Ibid, paras 4–5.
[283] Ibid, paras 4(4) and 5(5).
[284] Ibid, para 3(1)(a) and (b).
[285] Ibid, paras 3(1)(c), 3(3) and Part II, para 8(2).
[286] Ibid, para 1.
[287] Ibid, para 3(1).
[288] *Re H (Care Proceedings: Children's Guardian)* [2002] 1 FCR 251.
[289] Ibid, [35].
[290] CA 1989, Sch 3, Part II, para 6(1).
[291] Ibid, para 6(3).
[292] [2008] EWCA Civ 199.
[293] Ibid, [18].
[294] Ibid, [19].
[295] *Re A (Supervision Order: Extension)* [1995] 1 WLR 482, 486.
[296] Ibid.
[297] Ibid, 485–6.

When is a supervision order appropriate?

From the point of view of the parents, a supervision order obviously has a number of advantages over a care order. The order is time-limited to an absolute maximum of three years, during which time the child remains living at home. The decision-making capacity of the local authority is severely limited because it does not acquire parental responsibility, and although various obligations can be imposed on the parents, their consent and cooperation is required.[298] The entirely voluntary nature of the parents' participation makes enforcement of a supervision order extremely difficult. The only sanction for non-compliance is for the supervisor to return to court to apply to vary or discharge the order or to issue a fresh application for a care order.[299]

Perhaps the most important limitation on the power of the local authority under a supervision order is that it does not have the authority to remove a child from home should the situation deteriorate and the immediate removal of the child be deemed necessary. In such circumstances, the local authority has to face the delay, expense, and inconvenience of returning to court to apply for a care order or emergency protection order. These restrictions can compromise the local authority's ability to protect the child, making a care order, from their perspective, considerably more advantageous.[300]

As the care order confers parental responsibility on the local authority, it not only enables the local authority to remove the child from the parents without the cost and delay of returning to court, it is able to control and monitor the child's welfare much more effectively. A care order can also protect the child over a longer period of time, remaining in force until the court orders otherwise, thereby vesting much greater control in the court as to when the protective measures in place for the child can be safely lifted.[301] A care order may therefore be felt to be more appropriate where it is believed the child will continue to be at risk for a number of years or where it is believed the risk of abuse will be particularly high as the child reaches a certain age.[302] It has also been suggested that a care order is advantageous because of the direct duties and responsibilities imposed on the local authority where the child is a looked after child, in particular to keep the child safe and to safeguard his or her welfare.[303]

The perceived inadequacies of a supervision order led to a number of cases in which the appeal court overturned a supervision order in favour of a care order.[304] However, some of these perceived inadequacies have been questioned by Hale J and the benefits of proceeding under a supervision order emphasized—not least of which is that, as a less interventionist

---

[298] *Leicestershire County Council v G* [1994] 2 FLR 329.

[299] *Re V (A Minor) (Care or Supervision Order)* [1996] 2 FCR 555, 565.

[300] *Re S (J) (A Minor) (Care or Supervision Order)* [1993] 2 FCR 193, 228–31 (Fam Div).

[301] *Re D (A Minor) (Care or Supervision Order)* [1993] 2 FLR 423, 429. Note, however, that it was held by the Court of Appeal in *Re T (A Child) (Care Order)* [2009] EWCA Civ 121, [63], that where the judge has decided rehabilitation with the parents is appropriate and there is no suggestion that the child will need to be urgently removed (thus making the case eminently suitable for a supervision order), it is not for the judge to decide how long the protective regime needs to be in place: that is something to be left to the discretion of the local authority when it comes to decide whether or not it should apply for the supervision order to be extended.

[302] *Re T (A Minor) (Care or Supervision Order)* [1994] 1 FLR 103.

[303] *Re S (J) (A Minor) (Care or Supervision Order)* [1993] 2 FCR 193 (Fam Div), 223–6. See above at 12.3.3.

[304] *Re T (A Minor) (Care or Supervision Order)* [1994] 1 FLR 103; *Re S (Care or Supervision Order)* [1996] 1 FLR 753; *Re V (A Minor) (Care or Supervision Order)* [1996] 2 FCR 555; and *Re S(J) (A Minor) (Care or Supervision Order)* [1993] 2 FCR 193.

measure, a supervision order will often constitute a more proportionate response to concerns about the child.[305]

12.5.9 LEAVING CARE

The discharge and variation of care and supervision orders is dealt with under s 39. A care or supervision order may be discharged on application by the local authority/supervisor, the child, or any person who has parental responsibility for the child.[306] An individual who is affected by a condition or requirement imposed by a supervision order may also apply for its variation or discharge.[307] In determining the application, the court applies a simple welfare test.[308] Where a care order is in force, the court can substitute a supervision order without first having to re-establish that the threshold conditions are met.[309] The making of a child arrangements order regarding where the child should live, special guardianship order, or adoption order will also have the automatic effect of discharging a care order.[310]

Sadly, for many children the route out of local authority care will not be by way of discharge of the care order because they are returning home or because they have successfully been adopted. For many children, the care order will simply cease to have effect because they have grown up and have left the care of the local authority. As we have seen, young adults leaving care are exceptionally vulnerable.[311] Most have a poor educational background, little prospect of employment, and poor coping skills. Few have a family on whom they can rely for help and support. Adjusting to a life of independence outside the care system is very difficult for these young people. In recognition of this, the CA 1989 was amended by the Children (Leaving Care) Act 2000 to increase substantially the duties and responsibilities on local authorities to provide assistance and support to looked after children or formerly looked after children who have been in local authority care for a specified period of time.[312] The support now provided, depending on the child's particular status, may include the appointment of a personal adviser, the preparation of a pathway plan, advice and assistance (including financial support) for young people undertaking education, training, and employment, and the provision of, or assistance with the cost of obtaining, suitable accommodation.[313]

ONLINE RESOURCE CENTRE

A more detailed discussion of the leaving care provisions can be found on the Online Resource Centre.

---

[305] *Re O (Minors) (Care or Supervision Order)* [1997] 2 FCR 17; *Oxfordshire County Council v B* [1998] 3 FCR 521; *Re O (A Child) (Supervision Order: Future Harm)* [2001] EWCA Civ 16.

[306] S 39(1)–(2). It was confirmed in *Re A (Care: Discharge Application by Child)* [1995] 1 FLR 599, that the child does not require leave to bring an application.

[307] S 39(3), (3A), and (3B).

[308] *Re S (Discharge of Care Order)* [1995] 2 FLR 639. The same test applies to an application by the local authority for permission to withdraw a care order application. See *WSCC v M, F and others* [2010] EWHC 1914.

[309] S 39(4) and (5).

[310] *Re SC (A Minor) (Leave to Seek Residence Order)* [1994] 1 FLR 96.

[311] See above at p 836–7.

[312] For the various qualifying conditions, see ss 23A, 23C, and Sch 2, para 19B.

[313] Ss 23B, 23C, 23CA, 23E, 24, 24A, 24B, and Sch 2, paras 19B and 19C. For more detailed discussion of all these provisions, see Bainham and Gilmore (2013), 499–502.

12.6 EMERGENCY PROTECTION UNDER PART V

Although there is now a statutory time limit of 26 weeks for care proceedings to be concluded (subject only to 'necessary' extensions), it will still typically take many months before a final care order can be made.[314] Pending final order, the court may need to take interim steps to protect the child. In serious cases of abuse it often becomes necessary for the local authority to intervene as a matter of urgency. Part V of the Children Act provides for two key mechanisms by which the state may intervene in an emergency to protect a child from harm: (i) police protection; and (ii) EPOs.

12.6.1 POLICE PROTECTION POWERS

Children Act 1989, s 46

Where a constable has reasonable cause to believe that a child would otherwise be likely to suffer significant harm, he may—

(a) remove the child to suitable accommodation and keep him there; or

(b) take such steps as are reasonable to ensure that the child's removal from any hospital, or other place, in which he is then being accommodated is prevented.

Thus, the threshold criteria for police intervention in an emergency is '*reasonable cause to believe*' that the child is 'likely to suffer significant harm'—much lower than the threshold for state intervention under s 31. The police exercising their protective powers do not acquire parental responsibility for the child, but must do what is reasonable to safeguard and promote the child's welfare.[315] The child must be placed in local authority accommodation and the parents allowed such contact as the police consider reasonable and in the child's best interests.[316] As soon as the child is taken into police protection a designated officer must begin an inquiry and release the child if no longer satisfied that there is reasonable cause to believe that the child is likely to suffer significant harm.[317] The child cannot be kept under police protection for more than 72 hours.[318] During this period, there is no mechanism by which the parents can challenge the actions of the police. In order to protect the child beyond this period, the police may apply on behalf of the local authority for an emergency protection order.[319]

Police protection powers should only be used as a last resort.[320] However, research suggests that police protection is widely used as the first step in child protection proceedings, often out of administrative convenience and particularly when the local authority wish to initiate protective measures outside normal working hours.

---

[314] CA 1989, s 32(1)(a) as amended by the CFA 2014, s 14.
[315] S 46(9).
[316] S 46(3)(f) and (10).
[317] S 46(3)(e).
[318] S 46(6).
[319] S 46(7).
[320] DFE (2013d), 52.

J. Masson, 'Fair Trials in Child Protection', (2006) 28 *Journal of Social Welfare and Family Law* 15, 22

Where the local authority was unable to obtain an EPO, the social worker contacted the police and requested that the child be taken into police protection. There were three situations where such requests were made. First, if the need to protect was immediate; for example where a parent was insisting that their child left hospital immediately. Secondly, where the magistrates' legal adviser took a restrictive approach to without notice hearings, requiring additional information before considering an application, concern about the time taken to persuade the court to agree would encourage the local authority lawyers to suggest that the social worker should approach the police. Magistrates' legal advisers were also said to suggest this course of action, in order to avoid the need to arrange an immediate hearing. Thirdly, if the need to protect the child arose out of normal working hours, social work emergency duty teams usually contacted the police rather than seeking a court order.

Masson's study of emergency protection carried out between 2001 and 2004 revealed that in 45 per cent of EPO applications, the child had already been taken into police protection.[321] In 74 per cent of those cases the police acted at the request of social services.[322]

The widespread use of police protection is concerning given there are some important disadvantages to invoking these powers rather than proceeding by way of an application for an EPO.

J. Masson, 'Emergency Intervention to Protect Children: Using and Avoiding Legal Controls', (2005) 17 *Child and Family Law Quarterly* 75, 79, 95

Police protection is a power, not a court order; the individual officer who exercises the power takes responsibility for it, subject only to a review of its continuation by the designated officer. In most forces, police protection is exercised by ordinary officers with very limited training and experience in child protection, not officers from specialist Family Protection Units. In contrast, EPOs are sought by social workers from specialist child protection teams who generally work closely with specialist lawyers. They can be granted only after a hearing before a magistrate; the court provides an external check that it is appropriate to make the order and give the local authority the power to remove or detain the child... Using police protection avoided the system in the Children Act 1989 for securing legal local authority accountability... Using police protection denied the parents any opportunity to challenge the initial decision to remove or detain the child.

Echoing these concerns, it has been held by the Court of Appeal that, save in exceptional cases, removing a child in an emergency should always be carried out under the auspices of an EPO rather than relying on police protection.[323]

---

[321] Masson (2005), 78–9.
[322] Ibid.
[323] Applied in *A v East Sussex County Council* [2010] EWCA Civ 743, in which Hedley J gives a useful exposition of the correct approach to emergency powers.

Langley v Liverpool City Council [2005] EWCA Civ 1173

DYSON LJ:

36. ...The statutory scheme shows that Parliament intended that, if practicable, the removal of a child from where he or she is living should be authorised by a court order and effected under section 44. Parliament could have provided simply that specified persons could remove children if the statutory criteria are satisfied without any court involvement at all. But the removal of children, usually from their families, is a very serious matter. It is, therefore, not at all surprising that Parliament decided that the court should play an important part in the process. This is a valuable safeguard. The court must be satisfied that the statutory criteria for removal exist.

37. There are a number of important differences between the section 44 and section 46 regimes. They include the following. First, the court can give directions with respect to contact, examinations and assessments. This is a valuable power not available to the police. Secondly, an EPO gives the applicant parental responsibility, whereas while a child is being kept in police protection under section 46 neither the constable nor the designated officer has parental responsibility. Thirdly, no child can be kept in police protection for more than 72 hours, whereas an EPO may have effect for a period not exceeding 8 days (section 45(1)), and this period may be extended by up to 7 days (section 45(5)).

38. In my judgment, the statutory scheme clearly accords primacy to section 44. Removal under section 44 is sanctioned by the court and it involves a more elaborate, sophisticated and complete process than removal under section 46...

39. It is also relevant to point out that children who require emergency protection and have to be removed are often already well known to the Social Services Department within whose area the children are ordinarily resident. It is obviously preferable for the removal of a child to be effected if possible by, or at least with the assistance of, social workers who are known to the child, rather than by uniformed police officers who will almost certainly be strangers to the child. Whether known to the child or not, a social worker has skills in dealing with the removal of children from their homes which the most sensitive police officer cannot be expected to match.

40. I would, therefore, hold that (i) removal of children should usually be effected pursuant to an EPO, and (ii) section 46 should be invoked only where it is not practicable to execute an EPO. In deciding whether it is practicable to execute an EPO, the police must always have regard to the paramount need to protect children from significant harm.

Although there are clear concerns about the widespread use of police protection, Masson notes that where police protection has been used as a prelude to an application for an EPO, the EPO proceedings are likely to be fairer.[324] The window of time created by the fact the child is safe in police protection makes it more likely the EPO application will be heard on full notice, giving the parents the opportunity to obtain representation and give instructions.[325] It also makes it more likely that the child will be represented by a children's guardian.[326]

---

[324] Masson (2006), 24.
[325] Ibid.
[326] Ibid.

12.6.2 EMERGENCY PROTECTION ORDERS

The alternative means by which immediate action can be taken to protect a child is by applying to the court for an EPO under s 44. There are two basic grounds on which an EPO can be made: (i) that the *court* is satisfied there is *reasonable cause to believe* the child is at immediate risk of suffering significant harm; and (ii) inquiries are being conducted by the local authority or the NSPCC, those inquiries are being frustrated by access to the child being unreasonably withheld, and the *local authority or the NSPCC have reasonable cause to believe* that access is required as a matter of urgency. Where necessary, an EPO can be obtained very quickly. The application can be made ex parte and heard by a judge sitting outside normal business hours.[327] In practice very few applications are contested and it is rare for a local authority application to be refused.[328]

The legal effects of an EPO are set down in s 44(4).

Children Act 1989, s 44

(4) While an order under this section ('an emergency protection order') is in force it—

    (a) operates as a direction to any person who is in a position to do so to comply with any request to produce the child to the applicant;

    (b) authorises—

        (i) the removal of the child at any time to accommodation provided by or on behalf of the applicant and his being kept there; or

        (ii) the prevention of the child's removal from any hospital, or other place, in which he was being accommodated immediately before the making of the order; and

    (c) gives the applicant parental responsibility for the child.

An EPO thus authorizes the local authority to remove the child where necessary to safeguard the child's welfare.[329] The local authority must return the child to the parents as soon as it considers it safe to do so although whilst the order remains in force the local authority has the power to remove the child again should it be deemed necessary.[330]

In order to protect the child without necessitating the child's removal from home, the court has the power to attach to the EPO a provision excluding a specified individual from residing within the same dwelling-house as the child.[331] In order to make the exclusion order the court must have reasonable cause to believe that by so doing the child will be protected from suffering significant harm or the NSPCC's or local authority's inquiries will cease to be frustrated.[332] The court must also be satisfied that there is another person residing within the dwelling-house who is willing and able to care for the child and who

---

[327] Ibid, 89–90.
[328] Ibid, 96 and Masson (2004), 475.
[329] S 44(5)(a).
[330] S 44(10) and (12).
[331] S 44(1) and (3).
[332] S 44A(2)(a).

consents to the exclusion order.[333] A power of arrest may also be attached.[334] The court may accept an undertaking in lieu of the exclusion order but it cannot attach a power of arrest.[335]

Whilst the EPO is in force the local authority obtains parental responsibility for the child, although it may only take such action as is reasonably required to safeguard or promote the child's welfare.[336] The local authority must allow the child reasonable contact with, amongst others, the parents.[337] The court may also make a direction for a medical or psychiatric examination or other assessment of the child, subject to the child's consent if of sufficient understanding.[338]

An EPO has effect initially for a maximum of eight days.[339] Upon application by the local authority it may be extended once for a further seven days (15 days in total) provided there is reasonable cause to believe that the child is likely to suffer significant harm if the extension is not granted.[340] An application to discharge the order may be brought by the child, the parents, any person with parental responsibility, and any person with whom the child was living immediately before the order was made, subject to the important restriction that an application cannot be brought by anyone who was given notice of the proceedings and was present at the hearing.[341] This restriction makes the growing practice of hearing applications on abridged notice to the parents particularly troublesome.

J. Masson, 'Fair Trials in Child Protection', (2006) 28 *Journal of Social Welfare and Family Law* 15, 24–7

Abridged notice appeared to be seen by both legal advisers and local authority solicitors as a compromise solution, securing a speedy decision for the local authority whilst giving the parents the opportunity to participate in the hearing...

Where notice of the application was abridged, parents were less likely to attend the hearing or to be represented. Only half of the parents who were given short notice of the EPO hearing were represented, compared with over 70% of those with full notice...

Parents who attended were doubly disadvantaged. They lost the right to challenge the EPO available in without notice cases...but had little real opportunity to participate in the proceedings...Children were also less likely to be represented. There were no arrangements between local authorities and CAFCASS to provide children's guardians with early notification of applications...

Overall, the compromise of holding EPO hearings on short notice appeared to undermine the rights of parents rather than to protect them. Although the proceedings might give the appearance of fairness, the more limited opportunity for representation and the loss of the right to challenge the order meant that the parents had less opportunity to be involved in

---

[333] S 44A(2)(b).
[334] S 44A(5).
[335] S 44B.
[336] S 44(5)(b).
[337] S 44(6)(a) and (13).
[338] S 44(6)(b) and (7). In appropriate cases, the child's refusal to consent can be overridden by the court exercising its inherent jurisdiction. See *South Glamorgan County Council v W and B* [1993] 1 FLR 574.
[339] S 45(1).
[340] S 45(4)–(6).
[341] S 45(8)–(11).

the process than if either the hearing had been on full notice or without any notice at all. The same could also be said for the child, whose own involvement was frequently thwarted because no representative was appointed until after the order had been made.

There is no right of appeal against the making of an EPO or against a decision to extend or discharge the order.[342]

An EPO is thus a drastic order, often made in the absence of the parents[343] and with little effective scrutiny by the courts.[344] These shortcomings are compounded by the severe restrictions placed on challenging the order, raising questions as to the compatibility of this statutory regime with Article 8. The principles to be applied are firmly established in the Strasbourg case law.[345]

Haase v Germany (App No 11057/02, ECHR) (2005)

95. The Court accepts that when action has to be taken to protect a child in an emergency, it may not always be possible, because of the urgency of the situation, to associate in the decision-making process those having custody of the child. Nor may it even be desirable, even if possible, to do so if those having custody of the child are seen as the source of an immediate threat to the child, since giving them prior warning would be liable to deprive the measure of its effectiveness. The Court must however be satisfied that the national authorities were entitled to consider that there existed circumstances justifying the abrupt removal of the child from the care of its parents without any prior contact or consultation. In particular, it is for the respondent State to establish that a careful assessment of the impact of the proposed care measure on the parents and the child, as well as of the possible alternatives to the removal of the child from its family, was carried out prior to the implementation of a care measure.

In a detailed obiter judgment, Munby J has identified various points of tension between the statutory regime governing EPOs and the demands of the ECHR, outlining what measures are necessary to avoid incompatibility:

X Council v B (Emergency Protection Orders) [2004] EWHC 2015

MUNBY J:

57. . . .

i) An EPO, summarily removing a child from his parents, is a "draconian" and "extremely harsh" measure, requiring "exceptional justification" and "extraordinarily compelling reasons". Such an order should not be made unless the FPC [Family Proceedings Court] is

---

[342] S 45(10). See *Essex County Council v F* [1993] 1 FLR 847 and *Re P (Emergency Protection Order)* [1996] 1 FLR 482.

[343] Masson (2004), 475. Masson points out that even if the proceedings are heard on notice, given the limited time available to them the parents are often unable to actively contest the order.

[344] Ibid, 461 and Masson (2005).

[345] See *K and T v Finland* (App No 25702/94, ECHR) (2001) and *P, C and S v United Kingdom* (App No 56547/00, ECHR) (2002).

satisfied that it is both necessary and proportionate and that no other less radical form of order will achieve the essential end of promoting the welfare of the child. Separation is only to be contemplated if immediate separation is essential to secure the child's safety; "imminent danger" must be "actually established".

ii) Both the local authority which seeks and the FPC which makes an EPO assume a heavy burden of responsibility. It is important that both the local authority and the FPC approach every application for an EPO with an anxious awareness of the extreme gravity of the relief being sought and a scrupulous regard for the Convention rights of both the child and the parents.

iii) Any order must provide for the least interventionist solution consistent with the preservation of the child's immediate safety.

iv) If the real purpose of the local authority's application is to enable it to have the child assessed then consideration should be given to whether that objective cannot equally effectively, and more proportionately, be achieved by an application for, or by the making of, a CAO under section 43 of the Act.

v) No EPO should be made for any longer than is absolutely necessary to protect the child. Where the EPO is made on an ex parte (without notice) application very careful consideration should be given to the need to ensure that the initial order is made for the shortest possible period commensurate with the preservation of the child's immediate safety.

vi) The evidence in support of the application for an EPO must be full, detailed, precise and compelling...

vii) Save in wholly exceptional cases, parents must be given adequate prior notice of the date, time and place of any application by a local authority for an EPO. They must also be given proper notice of the evidence the local authority is relying upon.

viii) Where the application for an EPO is made ex parte the local authority must make out a compelling case for applying without first giving the parents notice. An ex parte application will normally be appropriate only if the case is genuinely one of emergency or other great urgency – and even then it should normally be possible to give some kind of albeit informal notice to the parents – or if there are compelling reasons to believe that the child's welfare will be compromised if the parents are alerted in advance to what is going on.

ix) The evidential burden on the local authority is even heavier if the application is made ex parte...

xii) ...The local authority must apply its mind very carefully to whether removal is essential in order to secure the child's immediate safety. The mere fact that the local authority has obtained an EPO is not of itself enough. The FPC decides whether to make an EPO. But the local authority decides whether to remove. The local authority, even after it has obtained an EPO, is under an obligation to consider less drastic alternatives to emergency removal. Section 44(5) requires a process within the local authority whereby there is a further consideration of the action to be taken after the EPO has been obtained. Though no procedure is specified, it will obviously be prudent for local authorities to have in place procedures to ensure both that the required decision making actually takes place and that it is appropriately documented.

xiii) Consistently with the local authority's positive obligation under Article 8 to take appropriate action to reunite parent and child, sections 44(10)(a) and 44(11)(a) impose on the local authority a mandatory obligation to return a child who it has removed under section 44(4)(b)(i) to the parent from whom the child was removed if "it appears to [the local authority] that it is safe for the child to be returned." This imposes on the local authority a continuing duty to keep the case under review day by day so as to ensure that parent and child are separated for no longer than is necessary to secure the child's safety. In this, as in other respects, the local authority is under a duty to exercise exceptional diligence.

xiv) Section 44(13) requires the local authority, subject only to any direction given by the FPC under section 44(6), to allow a child who is subject to an EPO "reasonable contact" with his parents. Arrangements for contact must be driven by the needs of the family, not stunted by lack of resources.

These guidelines were strongly endorsed by McFarlane J in *Re X (Emergency Protection Orders)*.[346]

12.7 INTERIM CARE AND SUPERVISION ORDERS

If, following the making of the EPO, there are continuing grounds for concern, the next step is for the local authority to initiate care proceedings. Once proceedings have begun, the court has jurisdiction to adjourn the proceedings and make an interim order to protect the child until the parties are ready to proceed to the final hearing.[347] The court can also make an interim order whilst a s 37 investigation is carried out.[348] Interim orders are dealt with under s 38. The threshold for making an order at this interim stage is higher than that for an EPO but lower than that required for the making of a full care order.

Children Act 1989, s 38

(2) A court shall not make an interim care order or interim supervision order under this section unless it is satisfied that there are *reasonable grounds for believing* that the circumstances with respect to the child are as mentioned in s.31(2) [child is suffering or is likely to suffer significant harm]. (Emphasis added)

If the threshold is crossed then the child's welfare is again the court's paramount consideration in the same way as it is when making a final order.[349] In determining this second question,[350] the Court of Appeal has held that the child should only be removed from the parents pending the final hearing if the child's safety demands immediate separation.[351] As Black LJ makes clear in *Re L (Care Order: Prison Mother and Baby Unit)*, the court's focus at the interim stage must be on preserving the parent–child relationship pending final hearing

---

[346] [2006] EWHC 510.
[347] S 38(1).
[348] Ibid.
[349] *Re C (Interim Care Order)* [2011] EWCA Civ 918, [3].
[350] *Re B (Refusal to Grant Interim Care Order)* [2012] EWCA Civ 1275.
[351] *Re H* [2001] 1 FCR 350, [39]. It has been held that the suggestion made by Ryder J in *Re L* [2008] 1 FLR 575 that there must be 'imminent risk of really serious harm' before intervention can be justified does not establish any new principle of law. See *Re L-A (Children)* [2009] EWCA Civ 822, [7].

unless there is an immediate danger to the child's physical or emotional safety.[352] It is 'a very high standard'.[353] To describe the test in Convention-compliant language (an approach preferred by Sir Nicholas Wall P in *Re S (Care Proceedings: Human Rights)*), removal must be proportionate to the risk of harm to which the child will be exposed in his or her parents' care.[354] This is not a new or different test from that of 'safety demands': whether or not the child's safety (physical or emotional) demands immediate removal will be crucial to determining proportionality.[355] Proportionality will clearly be more difficult, albeit not impossible, to establish in the absence of an imminent risk of physical harm.[356]

An interim order has the same legal effects as a final order. Under an interim care order the local authority therefore acquires parental responsibility and ultimate decision-making authority.[357] The local authority has a clear duty to consult with the parents when an interim order is in force but the weight to be attached to the parents' views will differ from case to case and is a matter for the local authority.[358] Consultation must, however, be genuine and such as to safeguard the parents' rights to participate in the decision-making process; 'consultation' is not a means for simply conveying predetermined decisions.[359] Conditions cannot be attached to an interim care order although a suspected abuser may be excluded from the child's home.[360] Contact between the child and the parents is governed by s 34. However, pending the final hearing, terminating contact will only be considered appropriate in exceptional circumstances.[361]

An interim order can be made for such period as is determined by the court.[362] The main purpose of an interim care order is to maintain the status quo until the final hearing.[363] It was the original intention that the 'holding period' under an interim care order would be short: on average 12 weeks.[364] The reality is very different. Care proceedings have become riddled with delays, such that by 2010 cases were taking on average between 48 weeks and 61 weeks to complete depending on whether the case was being heard in a county court care centre or in the FPC (magistrates).[365] With a view to tackling these delays, a *Protocol for Judicial Case Management in Public Law Children Act Cases* was introduced in June 2003, followed in 2008 by the Public Law Outline, and in 2010 by a new Practice Direction. These all failed to have any impact on reducing the delays, resulting in the government's decision following the recommendation of the Family Justice Review to introduce a statutory time limit of 26 weeks.[366] The new time limit, which is extendable only if 'necessary' for the just disposal of the proceedings, has had a dramatic impact: the average time for

[352] [2013] EWCA Civ 489, [60].

[353] *Re L-A (Children)* [2009] EWCA Civ 822, [7].

[354] *Re B (Care Proceedings: Interim Care Orders)* [2009] EWCA Civ 1254. This test which focuses on ensuring removal would be consistent with the parties' Art 8 rights was preferred by the former President, Sir N Wall P, in *Re S (Care Proceedings: Human Rights)* [2010] EWCA Civ 1383.

[355] *Re L (Care Order: Prison Mother and Baby Unit)* [2013] EWCA Civ 489, [39]–[42].

[356] See *Re F (Children)* [2010] EWCA Civ 826; cf *Re C (Interim Care Order)* [2011] EWCA Civ 918.

[357] *Re L (Interim Care Order: Power of Court)* [1996] 2 FLR 742.

[358] *R (H) v Kingston Upon Hull City Council* [2013] EWHC 388 (Admin), [52].

[359] Ibid, [59]–[63].

[360] S 38A.

[361] *A v M and Walsall Metropolitan Borough Council* [1993] 2 FLR 244.

[362] CA 1989, s 38(4), as amended by the CFA 2014, s 14. The CFA removed the previous time limits on interim care orders: an initial period of eight weeks renewable for periods of four weeks.

[363] *Re G (Minors) (Interim Care Order)* [1993] 2 FCR 557 (CA), 562–3.

[364] DCA (2002), para 24.

[365] Norgrove (2011), 91.

[366] CA 1989, s 32(1)(a), as amended by CFA 2014, s 14(2).

disposal of a care or supervision application had dropped by the second quarter of 2014 to just under 30 weeks.[367]

Although ultimate responsibility for the child passes with the interim care order to the local authority, the court retains control of the care proceedings. This gives the court limited authority to direct the local authority to undertake certain assessments involving the child for the purposes of the final hearing.

Children Act 1989, s 38

(6) Where the court makes an interim care order, or interim supervision order, it may give such directions (if any) as it considers appropriate with regard to the medical or psychiatric examination or other assessment of the child; but if the child is of sufficient understanding to make an informed decision he may refuse to submit to the examination or other assessment.

The scope of the power conferred on the court by s 38 has given rise to considerable controversy and has now been considered by the House of Lords on two occasions. Dispute has centred, in particular, on whether the court can order the local authority to undertake a programme of 'treatment' or 'therapy' rather than 'assessment' and whether an assessment which is primarily aimed, not at the child, but at the parents falls within the scope of the section. The issue was first considered by the House of Lords in *Re C (A Minor) (Interim Care Order: Residential Assessment)* which appeared to widen the scope of permissible directions to include assessments other than those of a medical or psychiatric nature and to include assessments involving the parents as well as the child. The case concerned whether the court could order an expensive residential assessment of the family which was primarily aimed at evaluating the parents' parenting ability.

Re C (A Minor) (Interim Care Order: Residential Assessment) [1997] AC 489 (HL), 500–4

LORD BROWNE-WILKINSON:

[F]or the purpose of making its ultimate decision whether to grant a full care order, the court will need the help of social workers, doctors and others as to the child and his circumstances. Information and assessments from these sources are necessary not only to determine whether the section 31 threshold has been crossed (including the cause of the existing or anticipated harm to the child from its existing circumstances) but also in exercising its discretion whether or not to make a final care order... Section 38(6) deals with the interaction between the powers of the local authority entitled to make decisions as to the child's welfare in the interim and the needs of the court to have access to the relevant information and assessments so as to be able to make the ultimate decision. It must always be borne in mind that in exercising its jurisdiction under the Act, the court's function is investigative and non-adversarial...

Against that background, I turn to consider the construction of section 38(6)... There are two possible constructions of subsection (6)..., one narrow, the other purposive and broader. The

---

[367] MoJ (2014a), 2.

Court of Appeal in *Re M (Minors) (Interim Care Order: Directions)* [1996] 3 FCR 137 adopted the narrow view. They held that the words "other assessment of the child" had to be construed as ejusdem generis with the words "medical or psychiatric examination". They attached decisive importance to the fact that the subsection only refers to the examination or assessment "of the child" and makes no reference to the examination or assessment of any other person in relation to the child. They further held that for the court to order a residential assessment of the parents and child together at a specified place would involve the court in an unwarranted usurpation by the court of the local authority's power (as the authority having parental responsibility under the interim care order) to regulate where the child is to reside . . . [Counsel] for the local authority in the present appeal, submitted that Parliament cannot have intended the court to have power to require the local authority against its own judgment to expend scarce resources: he submitted that the local authority is the only body which can properly assess how such resources are to be allocated as between the social services and the other services it has to provide and as between the various calls on its social services budget.

My Lords, I cannot accept this narrow construction of the subsection. The Act should be construed purposively so as to give effect to the underlying intentions of Parliament. As I have sought to demonstrate, the dividing line between the functions of the court on the one hand and the local authority on the other is that a child in interim care is subject to control of the local authority, the court having no power to interfere with the local authority's decisions save in specified cases. The cases where, despite that overall control, the court is to have power to intervene are set out, inter alia, in subsection (6) . . . The purpose of subsection (6) is to enable the court to obtain the information necessary for its own decision, notwithstanding the control over the child which in all other respects rests with the local authority. I therefore approach the subsection on the basis that the court is to have such powers to override the views of the local authority as are necessary to enable the court to discharge properly its function of deciding whether or not to accede to the local authority's application to take the child away from its parents by obtaining a care order. To allow the local authority to decide what evidence is to go before the court at the final hearing would be in many cases, including the present, to allow the local authority by administrative decision to pre-empt the court's judicial decision . . .

Next, it is true that subsection (6) . . . only refer[s] to the assessment "of the child" and not, as is proposed in the present case, a joint assessment of the child and the parents, including the parents' attitude and behaviour towards the child. But it is impossible to assess a young child divorced from his environment. The interaction between the child and his parents or other persons looking after him is an essential element in making any assessment of the child . . .

Much the most powerful of [counsel's] submissions is that based on the expenditure of scarce resources by the local authority in the carrying out of an expensive assessment. In the overwhelming majority of care cases, the parties are in straitened circumstances and there is no one to pay for any examination or assessment under section 38(6) other than the local authority. In the present case, the proposed residential assessment is going to cost some £24,000 and the local authority, taking as it does a gloomy view of the result of the assessment, considers that expenditure on that scale is not a sensible allocation of its limited resources, a decision which it is far better qualified to take than the court. I accept the force of this submission but it proves too much. [Counsel] was not able to argue that if the court directed a medical examination of the child himself, which examination would be very expensive, the local authority could refuse to carry it out simply on the grounds of the expense involved and the unwise allocation of limited resources. In such a case, it will be for the court to take into account in deciding whether or not to make an order for the medical examination the expense that it involves. If that is so, the issue of resources cannot affect the proper construction of subsection (6). The consideration of the resource consequences of

making the order must be the same whether the court is making an order for medical examination of the child or an order for the other assessment of the child. Therefore it is impossible
to construe section 38(6) in the narrow sense simply because the court is less suitable than
the local authority to assess the financial considerations.

In my judgment, therefore, subsection (6)...of section 38 of the Act [is] to be broadly
construed. [It] confer[s] jurisdiction on the court to order or prohibit any assessment which
involves the participation of the child and is directed to providing the court with the material
which, in the view of the court, is required to enable it to reach a proper decision at the final
hearing of the application for a full care order. In exercising its discretion whether to order
any particular examination or assessment, the court will take into account the cost of the
proposed assessment and the fact that local authorities' resources are notoriously limited.

This judgment was subsequently seized upon as a potential means of directing the local
authority to provide expensive treatment and therapy for individuals other than the child.
This gave rise to considerable litigation in the face of local authorities' objections to being
forced to fund treatment with which they did not agree.[368] The second House of Lords'
decision responded to these concerns, attempting to rein back the potentially expansive
scope of s 38(6), and imposing firm restrictions on the nature of the directions that may be
imposed. The proposed assessment in this case involved intensive psychotherapy for the
child's mother to be provided over a period of months.

Re G (A Minor) (Interim Care Order: Residential Assessment) [2005] UKHL 68

BARONNESS HALE:

64. The purpose of [ss 38(6) and 38(7)] is...not only to enable the court to obtain the information it needs, but also to enable the court to control the information-gathering activities
of others. But the emphasis is always on obtaining information. This is clear from the use of
the words "examination" and "other assessment". If the framers of the Act had meant the
court to be in charge, not only of the examination and assessment of the child, but also of the
medical or psychiatric treatment to be provided for her, let alone for her parents, it would have
said so. Instead, it deliberately left that in the hands of the local authority.

65. A fortiori, the purpose of section 38(6) cannot be to ensure the provision of services
either for the child or his family. There is nothing in the 1989 Act which empowers the court
hearing care proceedings to order the provision of specific services for anyone. To imply such
a power into section 38(6) would be quite contrary to the division of responsibility which was
the "cardinal principle" of the 1989 Act...

66. I appreciate, of course, that it is not always possible to draw a hard and fast line
between information-gathering and service-providing. Some information can only be gathered through the provision of services. It may be necessary to observe the parents looking
after the child at close quarters for a short period in order to assess the quality of the child's
attachment to the parents, the degree to which the parents have bonded with the child, the
current parenting skills of the parents, and their capacity to learn and develop...

67. But the court only has power to insist where this is relevant to the questions which
the court has to answer. Where the threshold criteria are in issue, it must be recalled that

---

[368] See, e.g., *Re B (Psychiatric Therapy for Parents)* [1999] 1 FLR 701; *Re D (Jurisdiction: Programme of Assessment or Therapy)* [1999] 2 FLR 632; *Re B (Interim Care Order: Directions)* [2002] 1 FLR 545.

> these are phrased (in section 31(2)) in the present tense...Where the threshold is found or conceded but the proper order is in issue, the welfare checklist is likewise focussed on the present...The capacity to change, to learn and to develop may well be part of that. But it is still the present capacity with which the court is concerned. It cannot be a proper use of the court's powers under section 38(6) to seek to bring about change.
>
> 68. These conclusions are reinforced by the Act's emphasis on reaching decisions without delay. It cannot have been contemplated that the examination or assessment ordered under section 38(6) would take many months to complete. It would be surprising if it were to last more than two or three months at most. The important decision for the court is whether or not to make a care order, with all that that entails...The court may sometimes have to accept that it is not possible to know all that is to be known before a final choice is made, because that choice will depend upon how the family and the child respond and develop in the future.

Nonetheless, within the framework provided by the House of Lords, Munby J has emphasized the continuing wide scope of s 38(6).[369]

Recent case law has also seen a different argument raised in support of applications for an assessment under s 38(6). It has been suggested that if by refusing an up-to-date assessment under s 38 the parent would be left, in effect, unable to challenge the making of the care order because of the weight of previous negative assessments (which may well have led to the removal of older siblings), the proceedings would be unfair and violate the parents' rights under Articles 6 and 8. That argument has been dismissed by the Court of Appeal. The court made clear in *Re T (Residential Parenting Assessment)* that there is no absolute right in the parent to bring any possible evidence before the court.[370] In determining whether to order an assessment under s 38(6), the court must have a mind both to the child's welfare and the potential harm of delay and if further assessment would be futile and/or could not hope to establish a realistic prospect of reunification within a reasonable timescale for the child, it should not be ordered.[371]

12.8 CHALLENGING LOCAL AUTHORITY DECISIONS

The relationship between the local authority and a family struggling to keep their child is often going to be fraught with tension. There are a number of ways in which local authority decisions can be challenged depending on the nature of the complaint and where proceedings have reached. Every local authority is required to establish a complaints procedure covering Parts III, IV, and V of the CA 1989. The decisions of a local authority are also subject to judicial review on the usual grounds of illegality, irrationality, and procedural impropriety. Judicial review is most commonly used to challenge decisions under Part III as any decisions made under Part IV are more appropriately challenged within the ongoing care proceedings where the child's welfare can be more fully considered as opposed to the bare legality of the decision.[372] Where ECHR rights of the parties are engaged, the local authority's actions may

---

[369] *Re A (A Child)* [2009] EWHC 865.
[370] [2011] EWCA Civ 812.
[371] Ibid, [53], [61], [93], [95].
[372] *R(CD) v Isle of Anglesey County Council* [2004] EWHC 1635, [12]; *Re C (Adoption: Religious Observance)* [2002] 1 FLR 1119, 1134.

also be challenged under s 7 of the HRA. Again where possible such claims should be brought within the existing proceedings.[373]

12.9 CONCLUSION

Protecting children from abuse and neglect involves a difficult balancing exercise. Whilst children must not be left in situations of known risk, the decision to remove a child from the child's parents carries a heavy responsibility. It causes deep loss to both parents and child. Parents in this position are often deeply troubled and vulnerable, they have a right to expect help and support from the state. Better resourced support services may help keep more vulnerable families together. The inadequate funding of services under Part III is thus an issue of crucial importance. However, the sad reality is that even if the state had unlimited resources, for some parents it would never be enough. In serious cases of abuse and neglect or for parents battling against multiple long-term problems, there will come a point at which the child's right to a safe and secure childhood must come first. Deciding when that point has been reached is never easy, but children cannot be expected to wait forever. Whilst the rights of the parents must be taken seriously throughout the child protection process, parents do not have the right to cause irreparable harm to their children. That basic principle should not be forgotten.

When children are received into local authority care, they look to the state to give them the safe and secure childhood so many other children are able to take for granted. Munby J is right to observe that 'if the State is to justify removing children from their parents it can only be on the basis that the State is going to provide a better quality of care than that from which the child in care has been rescued.'[374] Sadly, for many children, the state fails them too.[375] As we have seen, the state's own parenting record is poor. However, the children for whom the state has assumed this heavy responsibility are often deeply scarred by their early experiences. They arrive in care deeply troubled and vulnerable. The state does not have a magic wand. It cannot make deep-rooted problems just disappear. However, it can try and repair some of the damage by giving these children the best possible care that it can. And where children cannot return home, successive governments have firmly believed that the best possible care is not that of the state, but the love and support of an alternative 'forever family'. And for many children that means adoption.

ONLINE RESOURCE CENTRE

Questions, suggestions for further reading, and supplementary materials for this chapter (including updates on developments in this area of family law since this book was published) may be found on the Online Resource Centre at **www.oxfordtextbooks.co.uk/orc/familytcm3e/**.

---

[373] *Re L (Care Proceedings: Human Rights Claims)* [2003] EWHC 665; *Re V (A Child) (Care Proceedings: Human Rights Claims)* [2004] EWCA Civ 54.
[374] *F v Lambeth London Borough Council* [2002] 1 FLR 217, 234.
[375] Ibid.

13

ADOPTION

CENTRAL ISSUES

1. Adoption is a controversial topic. Successive governments have been strongly committed to increasing the number of children adopted out of care and speeding up the entire adoption process. However, the drive to ensure more children are adopted more quickly has met with concern that the 'rush to adoption' has resulted in the need to ensure adoption is in the best interests of each individual child being lost.

2. An adoption order terminates the legal relationship between the birth parents and the child. It is permanent and irrevocable. The adoptive parents become the child's legal parents as if the child had been born their own legitimate child. As the social purpose of adoption has changed, this concept of adoption has found itself under increasing pressure. It is, however, a concept of adoption which remains important to prospective adoptive parents. This tension has been particularly evident in the recent reforms which have sought to reassert a more 'traditional' concept of adoption.

3. Whenever a decision is made in relation to the adoption of a child, the child's welfare is the paramount consideration. Parental consent to the adoption can be dispensed with if the child's welfare requires it. The exclusively child-centred approach of the Adoption and Children Act 2002 (ACA 2002) raises questions as to whether adequate consideration is given to the birth parents' rights and interests throughout the adoption process.

4. The weight to be placed on a child's ethnic, cultural, and religious background when a child is to be adopted is a particularly difficult issue. It was one of the most controversial questions arising from the reforms enshrined in the Children and Families Act 2014 (CFA 2014).

5. Recent years have seen a shift to a more open concept of adoption which ensures children are provided with information about their birth parents and, where appropriate, provides for indirect or even direct contact between the child and the birth family post-adoption. However, this again sits uneasily with the more traditional concept of adoption and can deter prospective adopters at a time when the government is trying to encourage more people to put themselves forward.

6. Special guardianship was introduced by the ACA 2002 as an alternative means of securing permanency for the child. It is used primarily by kinship carers.

13.1 INTRODUCTION

Adoption is an area of family law beset by tensions and contradictions. As one important route to 'becoming a parent', adoption is for many people a 'good news' story. For adoptive parents, it can fulfil a lifetime's dream to become a parent providing vital recognition of the value and importance of social parenthood. For children in care or voluntarily relinquished by their parents it can be a life-line, providing the opportunity to be part of a 'normal', loving, and devoted 'forever family', perhaps for the first time in their short and often troubled lives. For others, however, behind this 'good news' story lies sadness and despair. A price must be paid for the creation of this new adoptive family—and that price is paid by the birth family. For them, adoption represents the termination of their legal relationship with the child. Put simply, in legal terms, the child is lost to them forever. Often young, vulnerable, and marginalized, it is usually the birth mother who pays the greatest price, many facing a lifetime of unresolved grief. For children too, adoption can be a paradox. Whilst the gains for the child can be enormous, so too can the losses, with many adopted children being profoundly affected by the loss of their birth family relationships. That deep sense of loss can remain with children throughout their lives, often intensifying as they grow older. Adoption is thus a complex issue. It marks both the beginning and the end of what for many is the core, defining relationship of their lives—that of parent and child.

The tensions and contradictions inherent in adoption make this a particularly appropriate topic with which to end the book. Contemporary debates surrounding adoption encapsulate many of the key themes explored within the previous chapters. It brings into focus key questions such as the respective value to be placed on biological as opposed to social parenthood, the value to be placed on traditional as opposed to alternative family forms, the importance of a child's cultural and religious heritage, the importance of preserving original family ties as opposed to supporting and prioritizing new and reconstituted families, the responsibilities of the state when it compulsorily removes a child from its family of birth, and the advantages and disadvantages of law over other methods of social governance. Adoption thus retains great symbolic importance. What the law has to say about adoption tells us a great deal about prevailing social attitudes to marriage, non-marital relationships, biological parenting, social parenting, and the role of the state in family life. As Murray Ryburn puts it, 'the practice of adoption goes to the heart of many issues that are critical in determining the kind of society we live in or wish to live in'.[1]

This chapter explores the legal framework for adoption as enshrined in the ACA 2002. We begin by examining the legal concept of adoption before turning to consider whether this traditional western concept meets the particular needs of children adopted from care. We then move on to consider the statutory provisions in more detail, beginning with two core principles running throughout the legislation: the welfare principle and the requirement for the birth parents' consent. The statutory test for dispensing with parental consent will be considered, particularly its compatibility or otherwise with the European Convention on Human Rights (ECHR). The adoption process as enshrined in the ACA 2002 is then examined in detail, including the application of the welfare principle to three particularly contentious issues: (i) the

---

[1] Ryburn (1998a), 53–4.

importance of the birth family in an adoption dispute; (ii) trans-racial adoption; and (iii) step-parent adoptions and adoptions by a sole natural parent. We conclude our discussion of adoption by examining the increasingly important question of 'open adoption', focusing in particular on adopted children's right to information about their birth families and provision for post-adoption contact. Finally, we turn to consider special guardianship, the main alternative to adoption for securing permanence outside of local authority care.

13.2 WHAT IS ADOPTION?

The legal effects of an adoption order are enshrined in ss 46 and 67 of the ACA 2002.[2]

Adoption and Children Act 2002, s 46

(1) An adoption order is an order made by the court...giving parental responsibility for a child to the adopters or adopter.

(2) The making of an adoption order operates to extinguish—

(a) the parental responsibility which any person other than the adopters or adopter has for the adopted child immediately before the making of the order...

Adoption and Children Act 2002, s 67

(1) An adopted person is to be treated in law as if born as the child of the adopters or adopter...

(3) An adopted person—

(a) if adopted by one of a couple is to be treated in law as not being the child of any person other than the adopter and the other one of the couple, and

(b) in any other case, is to be treated in law...as not being the child of any person other than the adopters or adopter...

In the case of a 'stranger-adoption',[3] an adoption order completely terminates any legal relationship between the birth parents and the child. Save for the limited exceptions specified in s 74 of the ACA 2002,[4] it is as if the birth parents had never been: there is a total and absolute transplanting of the legal relationship of parent and child. The adoptive parents become the child's legal parents and are vested with parental responsibility. By an act of legal fiction, they stand in relation to the child as if the child had been born their natural legitimate child.

---

[2] Unless otherwise stated, all references to statutory provisions in this chapter are to the ACA 2002.

[3] This term refers to adoption by anyone other than a parent or step-parent, including members of the extended family.

[4] Marriage within the prohibited degrees; the offence of engaging in sexual intercourse with an adult relative; and acquisition of British nationality.

For the adoptive parents, adoption thus represents full and unequivocal recognition of their parental status.

A step-parent adoption has similar effects, although the legal status of the birth parent with whom the child is to live remains unchanged.[5] In contrast, the legal relationship between the non-resident birth parent and the child is completely extinguished just as in a stranger adoption. The child is to be treated as if born to the resident birth parent and his or her new partner.[6]

The courts have strongly endorsed this model of adoption, prioritizing the need to support the adoptive family by treating them in every way as if they were a 'normal' family unit. This has been evident in their approach to whether conditions should be imposed on the adoption order. The courts have firmly resisted this, arguing that to impose conditions on the adoptive family undermines the concept of adoption as a total legal transplant and treats the adoptive parents as something less than an ordinary, natural family: as 'second-class' parents. They have thus generally refused to attach any conditions to the order which interfere with the adoptive parents' decision-making authority. This approach was tested in *Re S (A Minor) (Adoption: Blood Transfusion)*. The prospective adopters were Jehovah's Witnesses who, under pressure from the judge, had undertaken that they would not withhold consent to the child receiving a blood transfusion without first applying to the court. The adoptive parents appealed, wishing to be released from the undertaking. The Court of Appeal allowed the appeal.

Re S (A Minor) (Adoption: Blood Transfusion) [1995] 2 FCR 177 (CA), 182

STAUGHTON LJ:

If one were to look over the whole field of imposing conditions on adoptive parents against their will, it might become very common indeed. To my mind this should be a very rare course...The best thing for the child in the ordinary way is that he or she should become as near as possible the lawful child of the adopting parents. That is what the child's welfare requires. I would not, in this case, regard it as in any way appropriate to impose a condition which derogated from that, and which made very little difference as to what would in fact happen, in circumstances which were in any event unlikely to arise.

As with natural parenthood, 'adoption is for life'. Subject only to the very limited circumstances in which an adoption order can be revoked on statutory grounds under the ACA 2002,[7] the legal parenthood of the adoptive parents can only be terminated by invoking the inherent jurisdiction of the High Court or by a further adoption order. The permanent, irrevocable nature of adoption sets it apart from any other form of social parenthood. This was dramatically illustrated in *Re B (Adoption: Jurisdiction to Set Aside)*, in which an adopted child sought to set aside the adoption order 36 years after it was made. The applicant's birth mother was Roman Catholic and the birth father was a Muslim Arab from Kuwait. The child was mistakenly placed with an Orthodox Jewish couple

---

[5] S 67(3). It is thus no longer necessary for the birth parent with whom the child is living to adopt his or her own child.

[6] S 67(2)(b).

[7] See ACA 2002, s 55 (child adopted by a sole natural parent who subsequently marries the other natural parent thereby legitimating the child).

who subsequently adopted him. The applicant sought to set the adoption order aside under the court's inherent jurisdiction arguing it had been made under a fundamental mistake of fact as to his racial and ethnic origins. As Simon Brown LJ commented, 'it is difficult to imagine a more ill-starred adoption placement'. The Court of Appeal nevertheless refused the application.

Re B (Adoption: Jurisdiction to Set Aside) [1995] Fam 239 (CA), 245–9

SWINTON THOMAS LJ:

In my judgment such an application faces insuperable hurdles...

There are certain specific statutory provisions for the revocation of an adoption order...There are cases where an adoption order has been set aside by reason of what is known as a procedural irregularity...Those cases concern a failure to effect proper service of the adoption proceedings on a natural parent or ignorance of the parent of the existence of the adoption proceedings. In each case the application to set aside the order was made reasonably expeditiously. It is fundamental to the making of an adoption order that the natural parent should be informed of the application so that she can give or withhold her consent. If she has no knowledge at all of the application then, obviously, a fundamental injustice is perpetrated. I would prefer myself to regard those cases not as cases where the order has been set aside by reason of a procedural irregularity, although that has certainly occurred, but as cases where natural justice has been denied because the natural parent who may wish to challenge the adoption has never been told that it is going to happen....

There is no case which has been brought to our attention in which it has been held that the court has an inherent power to set aside an adoption order by reason of a misapprehension or mistake. To allow considerations such as those put forward in this case to invalidate an otherwise properly made adoption order would, in my view, undermine the whole basis on which adoption orders are made, namely that they are final and for life as regards the adopters, the natural parents, and the child. In my judgment [counsel], who appeared as amicus curiae, is right when he submits that it would gravely damage the lifelong commitment of adopters to their adoptive children if there is a possibility of the child, or indeed the parents, subsequently challenging the validity of the order. I am satisfied that there is no inherent power in the courts in circumstances such as arise in this case to set aside an adoption order. Nobody could have other than the greatest sympathy with the applicant but, in my judgment, the circumstances of this case do not provide any ground for setting aside an adoption order which was regularly made.

As the Court of Appeal notes, an adoption order can only be challenged under the High Court's inherent jurisdiction in circumstances where there has been a fundamental breach of natural justice. An adoption order was set aside on these grounds in *Re K (Adoption: Foreign Child)*.[8] The case concerned the adoption of a Bosnian Muslim child wrongly assumed to have no surviving relatives. The order was set aside for a 'plethora of procedural irregularities' including the failure to appoint a guardian ad litem, the failure to ensure the guardian appointed by the Bosnian government could participate effectively in the proceedings, and the failure to have proper regard to an edict of the Bosnian government prohibiting the adoption of Bosnian children.[9] In the absence of such significant

---

[8] [1997] 2 FCR 389.
[9] Ibid, 395–7.

procedural errors giving rise to a fundamental breach of natural justice, the adoption order must stand.[10]

This restrictive approach similarly applies where an adoption has irretrievably broken down and it is the adoptive parents who are no longer willing or able to provide a home for the child. The court will not revoke the adoption order but, as it would with a natural non-adopted child, make a care order so the child can be received back into care.[11] The adoptive parents will only cease to be the child's legal parents if a subsequent adoption order is made.

An adoption order can be appealed in accordance with the usual principles. In an attempt to circumvent the strict approach to the revocation of an adoption order, some applicants have sought instead to appeal against an adoption order out of time. This was successful in the case of *Re M* in which a natural father was allowed to appeal against an adoption order out of time because his ignorance of certain material facts—that the natural mother was suffering from terminal cancer—was held to have vitiated his consent.[12] However, as was made clear by Parker J in *Re PW (Adoption)*, the same overriding policy considerations apply and in the absence of some fundamental challenge to the propriety of the original adoption order, the court is very unlikely to be persuaded to allow applicants to pursue this route, particularly if there has been a significant passage of time since the adoption order was made.[13]

13.3 THE CHANGING FACE OF ADOPTION

13.3.1 FROM CHILDLESS COUPLES AND TROUBLE-FREE BABIES...

The nature and social purpose of adoption has changed dramatically over the course of the twentieth century.

C. Bridge, 'Adoption Law: A Balance of Interests', in J. Herring (ed), *Family Law: Issues, Debates, Policy* (Cullompton: Willan, 2001), 198–9

Formal legal adoption is a relatively modern concept. Its roots lie in the changes evident in society after the first world war: numbers of orphaned children needed the permanency and stability that family life supposedly provided and cohabitation, which had become increasingly common, gave rise to the need for secure legal arrangements for both children and birth parents. The first Adoption Act was passed in 1926 with these social purposes in mind. In comparison with the current law that Act was limited. It did not provide for the child's full integration into the adoptive family, it set out only limited grounds for permitting adoption without parental consent, and did not fully address inheritance issues. Adoption was, as Cretney and Masson suggest, a 'private or amateur activity'. But as the nature of

---

[10] See also *W v Norfolk County Council* [2009] EWCA Civ 59.

[11] *Re W (Inherent Jurisdiction: Permission Application: Revocation and Adoption Order)* [2013] EWHC 1957.

[12] *Re M (Minors) (Adoption)* [1991] 1 FLR 458.

[13] [2013] 1 FLR 96.

social problems changed so the nature and purpose of adoption also changed. Adoption became a way of dealing with some of the uncomfortable social and human problems that emerged during the 1950s and 60s. Its upsurge during this period was due, primarily, to the increasing numbers of young single mothers unable to care for their illegitimate babies. Social, moral, financial and a variety of practical measures combined to present adoption as the way out for both mother and child. By having the baby adopted straight after birth the mother was perceived as enabled to resume her life untarnished by the product of past immoral conduct. For the baby, adoption was widely perceived as a lucky escape from the shame of illegitimacy. Illegitimacy still carried a social stigma yet the numbers of such births were high. Sexual liberation had arrived but the contraceptive pill had yet to become widely available and abortion was unlawful. As a result, large numbers of white babies were adopted by childless married couples—those whom Lowe and Douglas describe as seeking to avoid the 'oppressive taint of infertility'. In a secretive process designed to facilitate an irrevocable transfer of all legal rights and powers from birth parents to adoptive parents, such babies became the lawful offspring of their new family, born to them as 'a child of the marriage'. The image this conjured up is one of a traditional family more redolent of the 1950s than the twenty-first century, and although it smacks of legislation of earlier times, that is not so.

At its peak in 1968 there were 24,831 adoptions.[14] However, important social changes in the second half of the twentieth century saw a dramatic decline in the number of adoption orders made. Contraception, the ready availability of abortion, and the loss of stigma surrounding single motherhood and illegitimacy drastically reduced the number of babies available for adoption.[15] Increased understanding of the causes of infertility and the availability of new treatments similarly rendered adoption a less attractive option for childless couples. By 1999, the annual number of adoption orders had reached its lowest point at just 4,100.[16] In only a tiny proportion of these cases was the child voluntarily relinquished by the child's mother immediately after birth. Approximately half were adoptions of children out of care, the other half were made up of step-parent and inter-country adoptions.[17] Thus, by the end of the twentieth century the social role played by adoption had changed dramatically.[18] Adoption was no longer about providing childless couples with unwanted, 'trouble-free babies'. The majority of adoptions were either step-parent adoptions or adoptions of children out of care, the latter having stabilized at about 2,000 per year.[19] However, since 2000 successive governments have been strongly committed to promoting adoption as a central plank of child protection policy. With steadily increasing numbers of children entering the care system, central to this policy has been the principle that 'no child is un-adoptable' and that the number of adoptions from care need to be significantly increased.

---

[14] Cretney (2003a), 596.

[15] Bridge (1993), 83. In 1968 approximately half of the 25,000 adoptions were of babies under 12 months old. By 2012, only 2.2 per cent of adoptions were of babies under 12 months: DH (1993), 4 and ONS (2013e).

[16] Cabinet Office (2000), 10.

[17] Ibid.

[18] Ibid.

[19] Ibid. Out of the total number of children looked after by the local authority each year, this represents an adoption rate of about 4 per cent. Cabinet Office (2000), 11.

13.3.2 LOOKED AFTER CHILDREN: DOES ADOPTION OFFER THE BEST SOLUTION?

One of the major factors driving the ACA 2002 was the then Labour Government's desire to increase the use of adoption as a route to 'permanence' for looked after children unable to return home: put simply, there should be 'more adoptions more quickly'.[20] The new legislation, hailed as the 'most radical overhaul of adoption law in 25 years', was accompanied by National Adoption Standards and performance targets aimed at increasing by 40 per cent the number of children adopted from care by 2004–5.[21] From the outset, the 2002 reforms were marked by a strong 'saving children in care' rhetoric.[22] This theme was taken forward in equally strong terms during the more recent reforms spearheaded by the Conservative-led coalition.[23] In 2011, Martin Narey was appointed as government adviser on adoption shortly after publishing in *The Times* a 'blueprint' for reform:

M. Narey, 'The Narey Report: A Blueprint for the Nation's Lost Children',
The Times, 5 July 2011

How can it be, when there is such unanimity about the transformational impact of adoption, that numbers of adoption in England are historically modest and, rather than growing, beginning to fall in number...[I]n so many cases, we are talking about something entirely positive, rescuing children from abject neglect and giving them a family who will love and value them...I am absolutely clear in my conclusion, which is that we need to see many more adoptions and of much younger children in the UK. At the moment we are denying far too many children the loving and stable childhood that they need and deserve.

Continuing problems with children left to 'drift in care' and strong disillusionment with the perceived professional emphasis on keeping children within inadequate birth families further fuelled the calls for reform:

M. Narey, 'The Narey Report: A Blueprint for the Nation's Lost Children',
The Times, 5 July 2011

Adoption is the ultimate intervention in the life of a child and one that, we know, can and does transform lives, particularly when the adoption is made at an early age. But adoption generally becomes a possibility only when a child has been taken into care, that is, removed from his or her birth parents. And that process can often begin too late and then take far too long, endangering the chances of a successful adoption (if that is what is best for the child) or in

---

[20] Harris-Short (2001), 407.

[21] DH (2000), 5. These targets met with limited success. The number of adoption orders made in 2004 was 5,360, an increase of 16 per cent from a low of 4,617 in 1998. However, from a high point of 5,486 in 2002, the number of adoptions began to decline again, with the number of orders made in 2007 falling to 4,637 and by 2010 to 4,472: ONS (2013e), 2–3. The renewed reform efforts of the Conservative-led coalition led to a focus on adoption and numbers rising again with 5,206 orders made in 2012, an increase of 9.8 per cent since 2011. However, the most recent figures suggest another imminent drop with the number of placement orders made in 2014 declining quite significantly. MOJ (2014a), 22.

[22] Cabinet Office (2000), 3; Harris-Short (2001), 406.

[23] See DFE (2012b).

some cases preventing adoption. Central to this report is my belief that there is a very strong case for radically increasing the number of adoptions in England and the rest of the UK. But to do so will require us to intervene earlier in the lives of large numbers of deeply neglected children and to resolve their permanent future much more quickly. Delay in intervention and then delay in achieving permanency for children is deeply damaging...

[It is] sad reality that too often we wait too long before removing a child from parental neglect, sometimes because of an unjustified optimism about the capacity of parents to improve... Why do we allow children to be damaged in this way? Sometimes it is because sustained changes in parenting capacity can be and are achieved. But the current system is gripped by an unrealistic optimism about the capacity of deeply inadequate parents to change.[24]

There is a considerable body of evidence supporting the case for increased numbers of adoption. Although there have been recent efforts to improve the care system and it is important to recognize that for many children care can be a positive experience,[25] adoption consistently emerges as by far the better alternative. Research on outcomes for adopted children is generally very positive, particularly for children *voluntarily relinquished and placed as babies*.

J. Castle, C. Beckett, and C. Groothues, 'Infant Adoption in England: A Longitudinal Account of Social and Cognitive Progress', (2000) 24 *Adoption and Fostering* 26–7

Baby adoptions are viewed as a group for whom successful outcomes are usual. In general, studies of children placed as babies have shown favourable levels of psychosocial functioning, high parental satisfaction and low levels of adoption disruption. Data from the National Child Development Study (NCDS) indicated that adopted children outperformed birth comparisons on maths and reading tests at age seven, and on a measure of general ability at age eleven.

Although children adopted as babies fare extremely well, there have been conflicting findings regarding psychosocial outcome. In their report of adopted adolescents in residential treatment, Grotevant and McRoy mentioned studies from several countries showing increased referral rates for treatment of emotional disturbance in children adopted as infants by childless couples, compared with the normal population. However, where clinical referrals were concerned, it was possible that adoptive parents were more likely to make use of mental health services because of a lower threshold of concern so there are limitations in generalising from clinical cases to the general population of adopted children.

Castle, Beckett, and Groothues' study of 52 adopted children support these findings, with children placed under six months and reviewed at ages four and six, 'showing favourable cognitive and social progress... and high levels of satisfaction with adoption among parents'.[26] However, the outcomes for children *adopted out of care* are less convincing. Disruption rates for children adopted at around the pre-school age (the average age for children placed out of care in England and Wales) are about 5 per cent.[27] A longitudinal study carried out by

---

[24] Delays in taking children into care and the length of care proceedings were identified by Ofsted as key factors preventing the timely adoption of looked after children. Ofsted (2012), 12–15. See also DFE (2012b), 7–9 and 14–15.

[25] House of Commons Select Committee on Education (2012/13).

[26] Castle et al (2000), 32. See also IJzendoorn and Juffer (2005); Maugham, Collishaw, and Pickles (1998); and Brand and Brinich (1999).

[27] Triseliotis (2002), 25.

Dance and Rushton of 99 children placed from care aged between five and eleven years revealed that whilst six years after placement 49 per cent of adoptions were continuing and positive, 28 per cent were continuing but assessed as 'difficult', and 23 per cent had disrupted (child returned to local authority care).[28] Disruption rates for children placed in adolescence are significantly higher, between a third and a half disrupting within a three- to five-year period. Studies focusing more specifically on the psychosocial and behavioural adjustment of later placed children also reveal a more mixed picture. Howe, Shemmings, and Feast report that older placed children are 'at increased risk of poor mental health, behavioural problems and relationship difficulties'.[29]

Despite these somewhat mixed outcomes it is important not to lose sight of the fact that children adopted out of care still generally fare better than the most relevant comparator groups: similarly disadvantaged children who remain in institutional care or who are placed in long-term foster care.[30] Evidence suggests that when compared against these alternative forms of substitute care, adoption is a superior, generally effective form of intervention, with the potential to help children make significant strides towards overcoming their earlier damaging experiences. The greater permanence and security offered by adoption appears to be a particularly significant factor in achieving better outcomes.

J. Triseliotis, 'Long-Term Foster Care or Adoption? The Evidence Examined',
(2002) 7 *Child and Family Social Work* 23, 31

Two broad conclusions can be drawn...First, because of the type of child currently being adopted or fostered, differences in breakdown rates and in adjustment between these two forms of substitute parenting are diminishing and in some age groups evening out. Yet at least one recent study reported that foster care rarely offers permanence. Its placements are too liable to break down. Second, compared with long-term fostering, adoption still provides higher levels of emotional security, a stronger sense of belonging and a more enduring psychosocial base in life for those who cannot live with their birth families.

The main limitation of long-term fostering is its unpredictability and the uncertain and ambiguous position in which the children find themselves. Taken together these conditions appear to generate long-standing feelings of insecurity and anxiety in children. One other possible explanation for this is the different expectations placed on adopters and foster carers and the different commitment that is brought to the task by each of these two groups of 'substitute' parents.

Adoption also fares better when compared with outcomes for a child returning home. A recent study by Thoburn, Robinson, and Anderson revealed that whilst returning to live

---

[28] Dance and Rushton (2005), 269. In Farmer et al's study of 149 looked after children, at six months following the adoption placement 40 per cent were positive with no issues, 27 per cent identified problems, 18 per cent had significant challenges, 5 per cent were at risk of breaking down, and 5 per cent had already disrupted. Younger age and lack of behavioural problems were key indicators of success. See Farmer et al (2010), 7.

[29] Howe, Shemmings, and Feast (2001), 337. See also IJzendoorn and Juffer (2005), 327.

[30] Brand and Brinich (1999) and IJzendoorn and Juffer (2005). But see Biehal et al (2009) who found that when measuring emotional, behavioural, and educational outcomes children in stable long-term foster care were doing just as well as adopted children. For an excellent discussion of the differences between adoption and long-term foster care, see the judgment of Black LJ in *Re V* [2013] EWCA Civ 913.

with a parent is the most likely route out of care (about 40 per cent of looked after children return home), it is the least successful permanence option with only a 40–50 per cent chance of success in cases of serious maltreatment.[31] Within two years of return, many children will simply find themselves back in care.[32]

Studies suggesting more mixed outcomes for children adopted out of care do not therefore undermine the drive to make greater use of adoption as a route to permanence for looked after children. However, the research does suggest that caution is needed when considering adoption for older children with difficult, challenging backgrounds. Adoption will not provide a 'happy ending' for every child and children who are already vulnerable should not be unnecessarily exposed to the risk of failure. Clearly adoption is not a panacea and it should not be pursued at all costs. Adoption needs to be underpinned by a clear focus on the welfare of the particular child: not political ideology, government targets, rigid timescales, or budgetary constraints.[33]

13.3.3 ADOPTING CHILDREN OUT OF CARE: NEW CHALLENGES

As the use of adoption has changed, so too has the profile of adopted children. This explains the poorer outcomes for children adopted out of care. These are not the 'trouble-free babies' that once characterized adoption.[34] Children adopted out of care are typically older[35] and acutely vulnerable as a result of 'challenging backgrounds' marked by abuse and neglect. Not surprisingly, these children have a range of 'complex needs'.[36] Problems are compounded by the length of time looked after children typically spend in care before being adopted, many experiencing a number of unsettling moves before they are successfully placed.[37] These difficult pre-placement experiences increase the risk of an adoption disrupting.[38] The changed profile of adopted children raises important policy questions about how adoption practice needs to change to meet the demands of its new 'client group'.

---

[31] Thoburn, Robinson, and Anderson (2012), 2, 12.

[32] For statistics on the numbers of children returned to care, see ibid, 5.

[33] See generally Sagar and Hitchings (2007). The social workers interviewed as part of their study all expressed concern at the new target-driven approach to adoption, arguing that it was likely to lead to a greater number of unsuitable placements disrupting. Ibid, 207.

[34] Cabinet Office (2000), 14.

[35] In 2012 the percentage of children adopted from care aged 1–4 was 63 per cent; aged 5–9 was 24 per cent; aged 10–14 was 8.4 per cent; and aged 15–17 was 3.2 per cent. The percentage of children adopted under the age of 12 months was just 2.2 per cent. These figures when compared with those in 1999 do, however, show a trend towards the average age of children adopted out of care falling. ONS (2013e), 4–5.

[36] Cabinet Office (2000), 14.

[37] Figures from 1999 suggest that the average length of time a child spent in care before being adopted was two years and ten months, with 36 per cent waiting more than three years. Forty-seven per cent of children experienced two or more placements before being successfully placed for adoption. Ibid, 13–14. See Howe, Shemmings, and Feast (2001), 337. By 2011, the average time between a child entering care and being successfully placed for adoption had fallen to 21 months. For children entering care aged over 2½ years, the wait for adoption increased to almost 30 months (DFE 2012b). Ofsted's new inspection regime expects all children identified for adoption to be placed by the agency within 12 months of the formal agency decision unless there are exceptional circumstances. Ofsted (2012).

[38] Dance and Rushton (2005), 279; Selwyn, Frazer, and Quinton (2006).

Post-adoption support

Children adopted out of care often have a range of physical, social, and educational needs requiring skilled and sensitive parenting. Adoptive parents face a difficult task for which ongoing professional support may be essential. There is a strong argument that having removed these troubled children from their birth parents, the state cannot simply walk away—it has a continuing responsibility to support the child and the adoptive parents as they face the many challenges of adoption. This approach is clearly at odds with the traditional concept of adoption and, from the government's perspective, one of its major advantages: that once the adoption order has been made the adoptive family is legally and socially autonomous, neither expecting nor requiring any additional assistance or support. So strongly is this notion of the new autonomous family embedded within society's understanding of adoption, that many adoptive parents actively resist post-adoption services and support, believing such intervention makes them less than the ideal.[39] However, it has been argued persuasively by Nigel Lowe that if the adoption of children out of care is to work, this 'mindset' has to change.

N. Lowe, 'The Changing Face of Adoption—The Gift/Donation Model versus the Contract/Services Model', (1997b) 9 *Child and Family Law Quarterly* 371, 382–3

[R]eference [has been] made to the 'mind-set' which seems to stem from the practice of baby adoptions, that essentially adoption is a gift and is the final and irrevocable act in which the mother has given away her child...It is the thesis of this article that this 'mind set' is certainly inadequate for the adoption of older children and, even possibly, for all types of adoption, yet, notwithstanding the virtual ending of baby adoption, this type of thinking still permeates the law, and legal and social work practice...

The 'gift/donation' model sits uneasily with the adoption of older children...and it seems clear that a new model is needed. At the very least with regard to older children (if not all children) it needs to be accepted that adoption is not the end of the process but only a stage (albeit an important stage) in an ongoing and often complex process of family development. It is further suggested that adoption of older children out of care is best understood as some kind of informal 'contract' between the birth family, the child and the adoptive family—a 'contract' which brings with it a pattern of reciprocal obligations between the 'parties' and between the adoption agency...

Under this 'contract/services' model the State should expect to provide substantial support both before, during and after the adoption; the adopters should expect to be informed fully of all the circumstances of the child and to be warned properly of the risks of 'failure' both for the child and for themselves. They should also expect that adoption will not necessarily mean the end of contact with members of the birth family and, although this proposition is made much more tentatively, they may also have to expect that the price of ongoing support is that they may not be in complete control of the child's upbringing...

Consistent with the general thesis that adoption should not be regarded as the end of the process, the State cannot consider that its obligations towards such children as being *ipso facto* discharged by the making of the order.

---

[39] Rushton (2003), 46; Sagar and Hitchings (2007).

Fundamental to Lowe's 'contract/service model' of adoption is the state's responsibility to provide a comprehensive post-adoption support service, including, where appropriate, financial support in the form of an adoption allowance. Adoption should not be regarded as 'a cheap option for bringing up children currently languishing in care'.[40] However, the extent to which the state should be responsible for the provision of comprehensive post-adoption support services remains a contentious issue: an issue which the recent reform process failed to resolve.[41]

Open adoption

Children adopted out of care bring with them a very different relationship with their birth family than babies voluntarily relinquished at birth. As Bridge points out, these children know their families and no matter how inadequate or even abusive their parenting may have been, the children will retain 'history, memories and attachments which cannot be erased'.[42] Statutory provisions aimed at eradicating the birth parents from the child's life and 'drawing a veil of secrecy'[43] over the adoption are obviously pointless in the case of older children who have developed and retain close emotional ties to their birth family. Seeking to deny the importance of these ties may well be inimical to the child's interests. The adoption of children out of care has therefore brought with it a demand for greater openness in adoption.

Openness can take a variety of forms, from simply providing the child with information about the birth family, to facilitating regular indirect (letter-box contact) or direct contact with members of the birth family after the adoption. However, protecting, fostering, and encouraging the child's relationship with the birth parents can be difficult to reconcile with the traditional concept of adoption as a total legal transplant of the parent–child relationship.[44] The challenge posed to the adoptive parents by greater openness in adoption is also a particular concern in an environment in which the government is trying to increase the pool of prospective adopters. There is thus discernible in the recent reforms an attempt to reassert the more traditional transplant model of adoption which marginalizes any continuing role for the birth family. As Narey observes, 'that view of the adoptive child as having two families, the adoptive and the real family, even when adopted as a baby or tiny child, is not uncommon but must offend and hurt those who raise adoptive children unequivocally as their own, as well as sometimes confusing and distressing the child.'[45] It is a difficult question whether retreating into a more traditional concept of adoption serves the needs and interests of looked after children by potentially increasing the pool of prospective adopters or whether it simply promotes and prioritizes the interests of the adoptive parents at the expense of the child's welfare. To put it starkly, is a closed 'transplant' model of adoption which may be less than the ideal from the child's perspective better

[40] Lowe (1997b), 385–6. Changes introduced by the ACA 2002 to the provision of post-adoption support will be discussed below at 13.7.2.
[41] House of Lords (2013), 54.
[42] Bridge (1993), 87.
[43] Ibid, 82.
[44] We consider below at 13.7.1 whether the ACA 2002 makes adequate provision for greater openness in adoption.
[45] Narey (2011).

than no adoption at all? Or can we find a form of permanency that better serves the needs and interests of all parties?

A different model of adoption

The changing profile of adopted children has clearly placed the traditional concept of adoption under increasing pressure. Indeed, the needs of looked after children are so different from the children for whom adoption was originally conceived that government efforts would arguably be better focused on developing more appropriate forms of alternative care.[46] As Sagar and Hitchings suggest, not enough attention has been paid to the crucial question of whether adoption *should* be the preferred means of securing permanency for looked after children.[47] At the very least, commentators suggest that the legal concept of adoption needs to be fundamentally transformed if it is to successfully fulfil its changing social purpose.

P. Parkinson, 'Child Protection, Permanency Planning and Children's Right to Family Life', (2003) 17 *International Journal of Law, Policy and the Family* 147, 161, and 168

It is correct to say that other permanency options are not as final as adoption. They can be revoked. But there is nothing magic about the concept of adoption which makes it the only form of irreversible parenting order. It is possible to devise new forms of order which provide for such permanence without severing the legal relationship of a child's extended family. Indeed, adoption itself might become a more widely used option if it were reinvented to remove the legal fiction of rebirthing into a new family in a way which denies the importance of pre-adoption relationships in the family of origin. The Law Commission of New Zealand has recommended that adoption be recharacterized as having the effect of permanently transferring full parental responsibility from the birth parents to the adoptive parents, making the adoptive parents the legal parents of the child but in so doing the law should recognize that the birth family still exists and may have a role in the child's life. The failure to provide certainty and stability to long-term foster carers may be nothing more than a failure of legal imagination...

Despite these calls for finding more imaginative ways of providing permanence for looked after children, the traditional legal concept of adoption remains firmly entrenched within the ACA 2002. Furthermore, whilst there was some concern expressed at the government's overemphasis on adoption at the expense of other routes to permanence, it is striking that these fundamental questions about the legal concept of adoption did not figure at all in the recent debates surrounding reform.[48] With that in mind, policy-makers are perhaps reluctant to grapple with the difficult question of whether the current legal framework really meets the welfare needs of the children it serves.

---

[46] For arguments against adoption in this context, see Parkinson (2003), 156–61.
[47] Sagar and Hitchings (2007), 211–12.
[48] See, e.g., House of Lords (2013), 14–16; House of Commons Select Committee on Education (2012/13).

13.4 ACA 2002: THE CORE PRINCIPLES

13.4.1 THE WELFARE PRINCIPLE

The ACA 2002 provides that whenever 'a court or adoption agency' is 'coming to a decision' relating to the adoption of a child, the child's welfare must be the paramount consideration.[49] The principle is thus of wide application, binding all key decision-makers throughout the adoption process. In recognition of the life-long consequences of adoption, regard must be had to the welfare of the child 'throughout his life'. This allows the decision-maker to take into account a broad range of factors relating to the child's childhood and beyond.[50] To guide the decision-maker, the legislation provides a 'welfare checklist' similar to that within s 1(3) of the Children Act 1989 (CA 1989):

Adoption and Children Act 2002, s 1

(4) The court or adoption agency must have regard to the following matters (among others)—

    (a) the child's ascertainable wishes and feelings regarding the decision (considered in light of the child's age and understanding),

    (b) the child's particular needs,

    (c) the likely effect on the child (throughout his life) of having ceased to be a member of the original family and becoming an adopted person,

    (d) the child's age, sex, background and any of the child's characteristics which the court or agency considers relevant,

    (e) any harm (within the meaning of the Children Act 1989 (c. 41)) which the child has suffered or is at risk of suffering,

    (f) the relationship which the child has with relatives, and with any other person in relation to whom the court or agency considers the relationship to be relevant, including—

        (i) the likelihood of any such relationship continuing and the value to the child of its doing so,

        (ii) the ability and willingness of any of the child's relatives, or of any such person, to provide the child with a secure environment in which the child can develop, and otherwise to meet the child's needs,

        (iii) the wishes and feelings of any of the child's relatives, of any such person, regarding the child.

---

[49] S 1(1)–(2).

[50] See *ASB and KSB v MQS and Secretary of State for the Home Department* [2009] EWHC 2491, in which an adoption order was made with respect to a 17-year-old boy, Bennett J being satisfied that the applicants genuinely intended to exercise parental responsibility for him (the adoption was not a mere device to gain the child a right of abode in the UK), the child was happy and settled both at school and in the applicant's home, and there was a real and substantial risk to the child's welfare if he had to return to Pakistan. Bennett J was thus satisfied that the adoption order would 'confer real benefits on him' not just for the remainder of his childhood but throughout his life. Ibid, [35] and [42].

Many of these factors are familiar, having come directly from s 1(3) of the CA 1989. Of particular note, however, are the provisions relating specifically to the effect of the adoption on the child's legal status (s 1(4)(c)) and the child's existing and future relationship with the birth family (s 1(4)(f)). The term 'relative' expressly includes the child's parents regardless of whether they hold parental responsibility.[51]

The paramountcy principle entrenched in s 1 of the ACA 2002 ensures the law on adoption is in line with the CA 1989 and complies with Article 21 of the United Nations Convention on the Rights of the Child (UNCRC) which provides that any state recognizing or permitting the system of adoption must ensure that the best interests of the child are the paramount consideration.[52] However, the weight to be attributed to the child's welfare in adoption is controversial. Under the previous legislation the child's welfare was the *first* but not the paramount consideration enabling the decision-maker to take into account factors other than the child's interests, most importantly the rights and interests of the birth parents.[53] This is precluded by a strict application of the paramountcy principle, something which is arguably problematic. As adoption entails the irrevocable severance of the parent–child relationship it has profound effects on both the birth parents and the child. Thus, as Bainham notes, 'the total severance of the parent–child relationship ought not to occur without a thorough examination of the *parent's* claims and interests as well as those of the child'.[54] Given the importance of adoption for the birth family, it is questionable whether focusing exclusively on the child's interests is right in principle. It also raises serious questions about the compatibility of the ACA 2002 with the ECHR.

In considering the requirements of Article 8, it is instructive to go back to *Johansen v Norway*.[55] In *Johansen* the applicant mother argued that the decision of the Norwegian authorities to terminate her parental rights and responsibilities and place her daughter (S) for adoption shortly after birth breached her Article 8 right to respect for family life. The Court made clear that such a grave interference with the birth parent's rights could not be justified under Article 8(2) on the basis of a simple welfare test.

Johansen v Norway (App No 17383/90, ECHR) (1997)

78. The Court considers that taking a child into care should normally be regarded as a temporary measure to be discontinued as soon as circumstances permit and that any measures of implementation of temporary care should be consistent with the ultimate aim of reuniting the natural parent and the child. In this regard, a fair balance has to be struck between the interests of the child in remaining in public care and those of the parent in being reunited with the child. In carrying out this balancing exercise, the Court will attach particular importance to the best interests of the child, which, *depending on their nature and seriousness*, may override those of the parent. In particular, as suggested by the Government, the parent cannot be

---

[51] ACA 2002, s 1(8)(b).

[52] For an excellent analysis of the requirements of the UNCRC as regards adoption and the compatibility or otherwise of English law, see Sloan (2013).

[53] Adoption Act 1976 (AA 1976), s 6.

[54] Bainham (2005), 266–7. This is arguably what a complete reading of the UNCRC demands. See Sloan (2013), 45–6.

[55] See earlier discussion at 8.4.4. The issue of step-parent adoption is dealt with in *Re P (A Child)* [2014] EWCA Civ 1174. Discussed below at 13.6.3.

entitled under Article 8 of the Convention to have such measures taken as would harm the child's health and development.

In the present case the applicant had been deprived of her parental rights and access in the context of a permanent placement of her daughter in a foster home with a view to adoption by the foster parents. These measures were particularly far-reaching in that they totally deprived the applicant of her family life with the child and were inconsistent with the aim of reuniting them. Such measures should only be applied in exceptional circumstances and could only be justified if they were motivated by an overriding requirement pertaining to the child's best interests...

84....The Court does not consider that the decision...in so far as it deprived the applicant of her access and parental rights in respect of her daughter, was sufficiently justified for the purposes of Article 8(2), it not having been shown that the measure corresponded *to any overriding requirement* in the child's best interests.

Therefore the Court reaches the conclusion that the national authorities overstepped their margin of appreciation, thereby violating the applicant's rights under Article 8 of the Convention. [emphasis added]

It would appear clear from this decision that in a contested adoption the birth parents have *independent* rights which must be carefully weighed against the rights and interests of the child. Thus, whilst 'particular importance' may be attached to the child's welfare, the child's interests are not paramount in the sense of the *only* or *determinative* consideration. The birth parents' rights are on the scales.[56] Moreover, the court makes clear that the need to strike a *fair* balance between these potentially competing rights means the adoption must be *proportionate* to the child's needs. Where the interference with the birth parents' rights and interests is particularly far-reaching, only very weighty and substantial welfare considerations will therefore be sufficient to justify the interference—in marginal cases where the welfare of the child is finely balanced, the adoption will be neither necessary nor proportionate.[57]

It can be argued that the paramountcy principle does not permit this required balancing of interests to occur. In interpreting the welfare of the child, ss 1(4)(c) and 1(4)(f) direct the court or the adoption agency to take into account the wishes and feelings of the birth parents and their relationship with the child. However, as these factors must be mitigated through the framework of the welfare principle, this is not the same as giving *separate* consideration to the rights and interests of the birth parents which are strictly only relevant insofar as they bear upon the interests of the child.[58]

---

[56] The adoptive parents may also have a right to respect for family life under Art 8.

[57] Harris-Short (2001), 423 and Bonner et al (2003), 582–3. See also the comments of Baroness Hale in *Down Lisburn Health and Social Services Trust v H* [2006] UKHL 36, [33]–[34]. Although in more recent cases the European Court has begun to adopt the language of paramountcy when referring to the child's best interests, including in cases of adoption, the European Court's judgments remain ambiguous, with the terms 'primary' and 'paramount' being used interchangeably. Certainly when read within context, the European Court does not appear to understand the term 'paramount' in quite the same way as it is understood in English law. See, e.g., *Neulinger and Shuruk v Switzerland* (App No 41615/07, ECHR) (2010), discussed above at 8.4.4.

[58] Harris-Short (2001), 419–20.

13.4.2 PARENTAL CONSENT

Concerns about the marginalization of the rights and interests of the birth parents under the ACA 2002 are further exacerbated when considered alongside the issue of parental consent.[59] At key points along the pathway to adoption, the process can only move forward if the court is satisfied that 'each parent or guardian of the child' has consented or that the parent or guardian's consent should be dispensed with.[60] Whenever the legislation requires parental consent, the issue must be dealt with in accordance with s 52. 'Parent' for these purposes is defined as 'a parent having parental responsibility'.[61] The consent of an unmarried father without parental responsibility is therefore not required. Consent must be given 'unconditionally' and with 'full understanding of what is involved'.[62] Consent given by the mother of a child within six weeks of the child's birth is ineffective.[63] In the absence of parental consent, the court is able to dispense with this requirement if certain conditions are satisfied:

Adoption and Children Act 2002, s 52

(1) The court cannot dispense with the consent of any parent or guardian of a child to the child being placed for adoption or to the making of an adoption order in respect of the child unless the court is satisfied that—

(a) the parent or guardian cannot be found or is incapable of giving consent, or

(b) the welfare of the child *requires* the consent to be dispensed with. [emphasis added]

Except in the limited circumstances provided for in s 52(1)(a), this provision means parental consent can arguably be dispensed with on the basis of a simple welfare test. This again differs significantly from the previous law which provided for six grounds on which the court could dispense with parental consent.[64] The most widely used was that the parent or guardian was withholding his or her agreement unreasonably.[65] Although this was subject to differing interpretations, it was tolerably clear from the case law that in determining whether consent was being unreasonably withheld, the birth parent's rights and interests were highly relevant. In other words, it was accepted that a reasonable parent would have regard to his or her own wishes and feelings when deciding whether to consent to the child's adoption: the child's welfare was not the only or decisive consideration.[66] When the ACA 2002 was passed there was some uncertainty as to whether s 52(1)(b) would be interpreted to allow the courts

---

[59] We discuss the application of the welfare principle to particularly contentious issues at 13.6.

[60] The two key stages are placing the child for adoption and making the adoption order.

[61] S 52(6).

[62] S 52(5).

[63] S 52(3). In order to place a child under six weeks old for adoption the mother must enter into a written agreement with the adoption agency permitting placement. Once the child is six weeks old the mother should be asked to formally give a 's 19 consent' to placement. Failure to obtain the 's 19 consent' once the child is six weeks old will mean that the consent requirements for making an adoption order under s 47(4) will not have been met and the mother's consent will need to be dispensed with. See *A Local Authority v GC* [2008] EWHC 2555.

[64] AA 1976, s 16.

[65] AA 1976, s 16(2)(b).

[66] *Re W (An Infant)* [1971] AC 682; *Re H; Re W (Adoption: Parental Agreement)* (1983) FLR 614; and *Re C (A Minor) (Adoption: Parental Agreement: Contact)* [1993] 2 FLR 260.

the same opportunity to consider the birth parents' various rights and interests. Subsequent case law suggests this will not be the case, at least outside the s 1(4) welfare test.

The correct interpretation of s 52(1)(b) was first raised by Wall LJ in *Re S (A Child) (Adoption Order or Special Guardianship Order)*.[67] There had been speculation in the academic literature that the use of the term 'requires' in s 52(1)(b) may be interpreted by the courts to demand a higher threshold for dispensing with consent than a straightforward application of the welfare test.[68] Although reaching no final view on the matter, Wall LJ rejected this argument, suggesting a straightforward welfare test would be applied so that once adoption has been found to be in the child's best interests parental consent would automatically be dispensed with.[69]

Wall LJ was given the opportunity to revisit the issue in *Re P (A Child)*.[70] It was argued on behalf of the mother that the preliminary view expressed by Wall LJ in *Re S* was 'at odds' with both the ordinary meaning of the word 'requires' and the intention of Parliament when passing the 2002 Act.[71] Rather than a simple application of the welfare test, it was argued that the word 'requires' conveyed 'a sense of the imperative; something which was a necessity; and a demand which was the antithesis of something voluntary or optional'.[72] In other words, it demanded an 'enhanced' welfare test unlikely to be satisfied where an alternative long-term placement such as fostering was an equally viable if not preferable way forward.[73] In support of this position, counsel for the mother relied on parliamentary material suggesting a balance must be struck between the rights of the birth parents and the rights of the child as demanded by the Strasbourg case law. Counsel on behalf of the adoption agency took a different approach, arguing against an 'enhanced' welfare test which would require the court to revisit the question of welfare applying a higher or different test when dealing with parental consent. In her submission, the court should simply apply the welfare test as set down in s 1(4) which would mean, as suggested by Wall LJ in *Re S*, that once adoption had been found to be in the child's best interests, it would automatically follow that parental consent should be dispensed with.[74]

Having identified one of the key objectives of the 2002 Act as being 'to shift the emphasis to a concentration on the welfare of the child',[75] the Court of Appeal appeared to confirm this latter approach, firmly rejecting the need to apply an 'enhanced' welfare test to dispensing with consent. However, in the course of its reasoning, the court also appeared to agree, rather curiously, with the submissions made on behalf of the mother that the word 'requires' does indeed convey the essence of the Strasbourg jurisprudence that adoption must be 'imperative' or 'demanded' rather than 'merely optional or reasonable or desirable'. These apparently contradictory positions can be reconciled, according to the Court of Appeal, through the application of the extended welfare test enshrined in s 1(4) and in particular the requirement that the court is to have regard to the child's welfare *throughout his or her life*—to which the loss of the child's existing familial relationships will be particularly significant.

---

[67] [2007] EWCA Civ 54.
[68] See, e.g., Choudhry (2003), 122–4.
[69] [2007] EWCA Civ 54, [71]–[72].
[70] [2008] EWCA Civ 535.
[71] Ibid, [75].
[72] Ibid.
[73] Ibid, [83]–[84].
[74] [2008] EWCA Civ 535, [99]–[101].
[75] Ibid, [32].

Re P (Children) (Adoption: Parental Consent) [2008] EWCA Civ 535

WALL LJ:

116. . . . The guidance is, we think, simple enough. The judge must, of course, be aware of the importance to the child of the decision being taken. There is, perhaps, no more important or far-reaching decision for a child than to be adopted by strangers. However, the word "requires" in section 52(1)(b) is a perfectly ordinary English word. Judges approaching the question of dispensation under the section must, it seems to us, ask themselves the question to which section 52(1)(b) of the 2002 [Act] gives rise, and answer it by reference to section 1 of the same Act, and in particular by a careful consideration of all the matters identified in section 1(4).

117. In summary, therefore, the best guidance which in our judgment this court can give is to advise judges to apply the statutory language with care to the facts of the particular case. The message is, no doubt, prosaic, but the best guidance, we think, is as simple and as straightforward as that . . .

118. Without wishing to qualify in any way the clarity and simplicity of what we have just said, . . . we think we should add a few words about the Strasbourg jurisprudence . . .

119. Plainly Article 8 is engaged; and it is elementary that, if Article 8 is not to be breached, any intervention under Part IV or Part V of the 1989 Act, and any placement or adoption order made without parental consent in accordance with section 52(1)(b) of the 2002 Act, must be proportionate to the legitimate aim of protecting the welfare and interests of the child . . .

120. "Necessary" takes its colour from the context but in the Strasbourg jurisprudence has a meaning lying somewhere between "indispensable" on the one hand and "useful", "reasonable" or "desirable" on the other hand. It implies the existence of what the Strasbourg jurisprudence calls a "pressing social need" . . .

124. In assessing what is proportionate, the court has, of course, always to bear in mind that adoption without parental consent is an extreme – indeed the most extreme – interference with family life. Cogent justification must therefore exist if parental consent is to be dispensed with in accordance with section 52(1)(b). Hence the observations of the Strasbourg court in *Johansen v Norway* (1996) . . .

125. This is the context in which the critical word "requires" is used in section 52(1)(b). It is a word which was plainly chosen as best conveying, as in our judgment it does, the essence of the Strasbourg jurisprudence. And viewed from that perspective "requires" does indeed have the connotation of the imperative, what is demanded rather than what is merely optional or reasonable or desirable.

126. What is also important to appreciate is the statutory context in which the word "requires" is here being used, for, like all words, it will take its colour from the particular context. Section 52(1) is concerned with adoption – the making of either a placement order or an adoption order – and what therefore has to be shown is that the child's welfare "requires" *adoption* as opposed to something short of adoption. A child's circumstances may "require" statutory intervention, perhaps may even "require" the indefinite or long-term removal of the child from the family and his or her placement with strangers, but that is not to say that the same circumstances will necessarily "require" that the child be adopted. They may or they may not. The question, at the end of the day, is whether what is "required" is adoption.

127. In our judgment, however, this does not mean that there is some enhanced welfare test to be applied in cases of adoption, in contrast to what [counsel] called a simple welfare test. The difference, and it is an important, indeed vital, difference, is simply that between section 1 of the 1989 Act and section 1 of the 2002 Act.

128. In the first place, section 1(2) of the 2002 Act, in contrast to section 1(1) of the 1989 Act, requires a judge considering dispensing with parental consent in accordance with

section 52(1)(b) to focus on the child's welfare "throughout his life." This emphasises that adoption, unlike other forms of order made under the 1989 Act, is something with lifelong implications. In other words, a judge exercising his powers under section 52(1)(b) has to be satisfied that the child's welfare now, throughout the rest of his childhood, into adulthood and indeed throughout his life, requires that he or she be adopted. Secondly, and reinforcing this point, it is important to bear in mind the more extensive 'welfare checklist' to be found in section 1(4) of the 2002 Act as compared with the 'welfare checklist' in section 1(3) of the 1989 Act; in particular, the provisions of section 1(4)(c) – which specifically directs attention to the consequences for the child "throughout his life" – and section 1(4)(f). This all feeds into the ultimate question under section 52(1)(b): does the child's welfare *throughout his life* require adoption as opposed to something short of adoption?

The practical effect is that the welfare stage and the consent stage of an adoption/placement application have in practice become indistinguishable such that once adoption is deemed to be in the child's best interests, parental consent will be dispensed with without further thought or consideration of the birth parents' interests or the demands of the specific wording of s 52(1)(b). Moreover, in determining the child's welfare, the Court of Appeal's judgment strongly defends the position that the welfare test, as set down in s 1(4), is sufficient, without more, to comply with the requirements of the ECHR.[76]

Notably, Wall LJ finds strong support for his approach in *Re P* in the European Court decision of *YC v United Kingdom*.[77] In addressing the issue, the Court held that the extended range of factors to which the court must give consideration when applying the welfare checklist in s 1(4) is sufficient to meet the required balancing of interests under Article 8(2). The case concerned the making of a final care order and a placement order in circumstances in which the mother was asking for a further assessment of her capacity to parent following separation from the child's father.

YC v United Kingdom (App No 4547/10, ECHR) (2012)

134. The Court reiterates that in cases concerning the placing of a child for adoption, which entails the permanent severance of family ties, the best interests of the child are paramount (see *Johansen v Norway*, 7 August 1996, [78]...). In identifying the child's best interests in a particular case, two considerations must be borne in mind: first, it is in the child's best interests that his ties with his family be maintained except in cases where the family has proved particularly unfit; and second, it is in the child's best interests to ensure his development in a safe and secure environment (see *Neulinger and Shuruk*, [136]...). It is clear from the foregoing that family ties may only be severed in very exceptional circumstances and that everything must be done to preserve personal relations and, where appropriate, to "rebuild" the family (see *Neulinger and Shuruk*, [136]...). It is not enough to show that a child could be placed in a more beneficial environment for his upbringing...However, where the maintenance of family ties would harm the child's health and development, a parent is not entitled under Article 8 to insist that such ties be maintained (see *Neulinger and Shuruk*...[136]).

135. The identification of the child's best interests and the assessment of the overall proportionality of any given measure will require courts to weigh a number of factors in the balance. The

---

[76] For critique, see Sloan (2013), 55–6.
[77] (App No 4547/10, ECHR) (2012).

Court has not previously set out an exhaustive list of such factors, which may vary depending on the circumstances of the case in question. However, it observes that the considerations listed in section 1 of the 2002 Act broadly reflect the various elements inherent in assessing the necessity under Article 8 of a measure placing a child for adoption. In particular, it considers that in seeking to identify the best interests of a child and in assessing the necessity of any proposed measure in the context of placement proceedings, the domestic court must demonstrate that it has had regard to, inter alia, the age, maturity and ascertained wishes of the child, the likely effect on the child of ceasing to be a member of his original family and the relationship the child has with relatives.

13.4.3. RIGHTS, WELFARE, REFORM, AND THE FUNDAMENTAL PRINCIPLES OF ADOPTION

On any reading of *Re P*, the Court of Appeal was keen to make clear that the rights and interests of the birth family, even if not afforded independent weight and consideration, could not be ignored in the adoption process, the birth family being inextricably linked to any proper understanding of the child's welfare.[78] The debate over the child's welfare and the weight, if any, to be placed on the rights and interests of the birth parents has, however, developed against a backdrop of increasing government pressure on local authorities to increase the number and speed of children adopted out of care. The birth family and their opposition to adoption undoubtedly constitutes an important cause of delay in many cases. Tensions perhaps inevitably developed between the drive to increase the numbers of children adopted out of care and the need to ensure there was no 'rush to judgement', with children being inappropriately made subject to a care order and placed for adoption against their birth parents' consent in circumstances where the birth family had not been given fair opportunity to prove themselves. The need to ensure proper regard for the child's relationship with the birth family (and thus proportionality) in cases of non-consensual adoption was very firmly set out by the Supreme Court in *Re B (Care Proceedings: Appeal)*. The Supreme Court made clear that care and placement orders could only be justified as a very last resort. In the succinct words of Lady Hale, 'it is quite clear that the test for severing the relationship between parent and child is very strict: only in exceptional circumstances and where motivated by *overriding requirements* pertaining to the child's welfare, in short, where nothing else will do'.[79] The Supreme Court were unanimous in endorsing that very clear test:

Re B (Care Proceedings: Appeal) [2013] UKSC 33[80]

LORD NEUBERGER P:

74. A care order in a case such as this is a very extreme thing, a last resort, as it would be very likely to result in Amelia being adopted against the wishes of both her parents.

---

[78] Again Sloan argues that this understanding of the child's welfare is entrenched within the UNCRC. Sloan (2013), 47.

[79] The Supreme Court had previously made very clear the fundamental principles which were to be applied to a non-consensual adoption both as a matter of domestic law and policy but also to ensure compliance with the ECHR in the Scottish case of *ANS v ML* [2012] UKSC 30, [34]–[44] (Lord Reed).

[80] For further extracts see 8.4.4. and 11.6.7. The decision was applied in *Re P (Care Proceedings: Balancing Exercise)* [2013] EWCA Civ 963.

75. As already mentioned, it is clear that a judge cannot properly decide that a care order should be made in such circumstances, unless the order is proportionate bearing in mind the requirements of article 8.

76. It appears to me that, given that the Judge concluded that the section 31(2) threshold was crossed, he should only have made a care order if he had been satisfied that it was necessary to do so in order to protect the interests of the child. By "necessary", I mean, to use Lady Hale's phrase... "where nothing else will do". I consider that this conclusion is clear under the 1989 Act, interpreted in the absence of the Convention, but it is put beyond doubt by article 8. The conclusion is also consistent with UNCRC.

77. It seems to me to be inherent in section 1(1) that a care order should be a last resort, because the interests of a child would self-evidently require her relationship with her natural parents to be maintained unless no other course was possible in her interests. That is reinforced by the requirement in section 1(3)(g) that the court must consider all options, which carries with it the clear implication that the most extreme option should only be adopted if others would not be in her interests. As to article 8, the Strasbourg court decisions cited by Lady Hale... make it clear that such an order can only be made in "exceptional circumstances", and that it could only be justified by "overriding requirements pertaining to the child's welfare", or, putting the same point in slightly different words, "by the overriding necessity of the interests of the child". I consider that this is the same as the domestic test...

78. The high threshold to be crossed before a court should make an adoption order against the natural parents' wishes is also clear from UNCRC. Thus, *Hodgkin and Newell, Implementation Handbook for the Convention on the Rights of the Child*, Unicef, 3rd ed (2007), p 296, state that "there is a presumption within the Convention that children's best interests are served by being with their parents wherever possible".

82. What the Strasbourg jurisprudence requires (and, I would have thought, what the rule of law in a modern, democratic society would require) is that no child should be adopted, particularly when it is against her parents' wishes, without a judge deciding after a proper hearing, with the interests of the parents (where appropriate) and of the child being appropriately advanced, that it is necessary in the interests of the child that she is adopted...

104. ...All give added weight to the importance of emphasising the principle that adoption of a child against her parents' wishes should only be contemplated as a last resort – when all else fails. Although the child's interests in an adoption case are "paramount" (in the UK legislation and under article 21 of UNCRC), a court must never lose sight of the fact that those interests include being brought up by her natural family, ideally her natural parents, or at least one of them.

105. Hodgkin and Newell, *op cit*, suggest that, under UNCRC, an "adoption can only occur if parents are unwilling or are deemed by judicial process to be unable to discharge" their responsibilities towards the child. The assessment of that ability to discharge their responsibilities must, of course, take into account the assistance and support which the authorities would offer.... It means that, before making an adoption order in such a case, the court must be satisfied that there is no practical way of the authorities (or others) providing the requisite assistance and support.

The Supreme Court's approach was forcefully reiterated by the President of the Family Division in *Re B-S*, a case concerned with an application for leave to oppose an adoption application. Expressing clear concern that children were being placed for adoption without sufficient rigour being exercised in the decision-making process, Munby P restated in unequivocal terms the 'fundamental principles' governing adoption:

Re B-S (Children) (Adoption: Application of Threshold Criteria) [2013]
EWCA Civ 1146

SIR JAMES MUNBY P:

20. Section 52(1)(b) of the 2002 Act provides, as we have seen, that the consent of a parent with capacity can be dispensed with only if the welfare of the child "requires" this. "Require" here has the Strasbourg meaning of necessary, "the connotation of the imperative, what is demanded rather than what is merely optional or reasonable or desirable": [*Re P(Children) (Adoption: Parental Consent)*]. This is a stringent and demanding test.

21. Just how stringent and demanding has been spelt out very recently by the Supreme Court in *Re B (Care proceedings: Appeal)* . . . *Re B* is a forceful reminder of just what is required.

22. The language used in *Re B* is striking. Different words and phrases are used, but the message is clear. Orders contemplating non-consensual adoption – care orders with a plan for adoption, placement orders and adoption orders – are "a very extreme thing, a last resort", only to be made where "nothing else will do", where "no other course [is] possible in [the child's] interests", they are "the most extreme option", a "last resort – when all else fails", to be made "only in exceptional circumstances and where motivated by *overriding requirements* pertaining to the child's welfare, in short, where nothing else will do" . . .

23. Behind all this there lies the well-established principle, derived from s 1(5) of the 1989 Act, read in conjunction with s 1(3)(g), and now similarly embodied in s 1(6) of the 2002 Act, that the court should adopt the 'least interventionist' approach . . . .

25. Implicit in all this are three important points emphasised by Lord Neuberger in *Re B*.

26. First (*Re B* paras 77, 104), although the child's interests in an adoption case are paramount, the court must never lose sight of the fact that those interests include being brought up by the natural family, ideally by the natural parents, or at least one of them, unless the overriding requirements of the child's welfare make that not possible.

27. Second (*Re B* para 77), as required by section 1(3)(g) of the 1989 Act and section 1(6) of the 2002 Act, the court "must" consider all the options before coming to a decision. As Lady Hale said (para 198) it is "necessary to explore and attempt alternative solutions". What are these options? That will depend upon the circumstances of the particular cases. They range, in principle, from the making of no order at one end of the spectrum to the making of an adoption order at the other. . . . [T]he possible list of options is long. We return to the implications of this below.

28. Third (*Re B* para 105), the court's assessment of the parents' ability to discharge their responsibilities towards the child must take into account the assistance and support which the authorities would offer. So "before making an adoption order . . . the court must be satisfied that there is no practical way of the authorities (or others) providing the requisite assistance and support." . . .

29. It is the obligation of the local authority to make the order which the court has determined is proportionate work. The local authority cannot press for a more drastic form of order, least of all press for adoption, because it is unable or unwilling to support a less interventionist form of order. Judges must be alert to the point and must be rigorous in exploring and probing local authority thinking in cases where there is any reason to suspect that resource issues may be affecting the local authority's thinking . . .

33. Two things are essential – we use that word deliberately and advisedly – both when the court is being asked to approve a care plan for adoption and when it is being asked to make a non-consensual placement order or adoption order.

> **Adoption – essentials: (i) proper evidence**
>
> 34. First, there must be proper evidence both from the local authority and from the guardian. The evidence must address *all* the options which are realistically possible and must contain an analysis of the arguments *for* and *against* each option...
>
> 41. The second thing that is essential, and again we emphasise that word, is an adequately reasoned judgment by the judge...
>
> 44. We emphasise the words [from McFarlane LJ's judgment in *Re G (A child)* [2013] EWCA Civ 965] "global, holistic evaluation". This point is crucial. The judicial task is to evaluate *all* the options, undertaking a global, holistic and...multi-faceted evaluation of the child's welfare which takes into account *all* the negatives and the positives, *all* the pros and cons, of *each* option...

In the immediate aftermath of this decision the numbers of children being placed for adoption, which had risen significantly following the reforms initiated by the Conservative-led coalition, dramatically declined.[81] It is important to note, however, that as was pointed out in clear terms by Munby P in *Re R (A Child)*, the decision in *Re B-S* did not change the law in any way—it simply reiterated the existing principles.[82] The court must be satisfied that adoption is *required* in the child's best interests; in other words, that following a holistic evaluation of all the *realistic* options, nothing else will do.

13.5 THE ADOPTION PROCESS

13.5.1 MAKING ARRANGEMENTS FOR THE ADOPTION OF A CHILD

Every local authority must provide an adoption service either directly or through a registered adoption society (referred to as an 'adoption agency'). The adoption service must cover two primary functions: (i) making and participating in arrangements for the adoption of children; and (ii) making and participating in arrangements for the provision of adoption support services. If the child's parents wish to voluntarily relinquish the child for adoption they must approach an adoption agency to make the necessary arrangements. It is an offence for anyone other than an adoption agency to make arrangements for the adoption of a child unless: (i) acting pursuant to an order of the High Court; or (ii) the prospective adopters are parents, relatives, or guardians of the child; or (iii) the prospective adopter is the partner of a parent of the child.[83] The extensive statutory restrictions on arranging a 'private adoption' are intended to prevent a black market developing in unwanted babies. They are reinforced by ss 95 and 96 of the ACA 2002 which make it an offence to make or receive any payment for or in consideration of the adoption of a child, other than a payment to a registered adoption society made by a parent or guardian of the child or a prospective adopter in respect of reasonable expenses incurred by the society in connection with the adoption.[84]

---

[81] See National Adoption Leadership Board (2014).
[82] *Re R (A Child)* [2014] EWCA Civ 1625.
[83] ACA 2002, ss 92–93 and 123.
[84] Ss 95 and 96.

In the case of a looked after child, the local authority begins the adoption process once the local authority care plan identifies adoption as the preferred option for permanence. The plan for adoption will only be confirmed following approval by a senior local authority social worker known as the agency decision-maker. Once the decision to place the child for adoption has been properly made, the local authority is under a duty to take the necessary legal steps to obtain authorization to place the child.[85]

13.5.2 FINDING PROSPECTIVE ADOPTERS

English law currently does not recognize a right to adopt. This has also been the clear position under the ECHR although the Strasbourg jurisprudence may now be moving on the issue. In *EB v France*, the European Court reiterated that there is no right to adopt under the family life limb of Article 8. However, it left open whether such a right may now be found to fall within the right to respect for private life.

EB v France (App No 43546/02, ECHR) (2008)

41. The Court, noting that the applicant based her application on Article 14 of the Convention, taken in conjunction with Article 8, reiterates at the outset that the provisions of Article 8 do not guarantee either the right to found a family or the right to adopt... Neither party contests this. The right to respect for "family life" does not safeguard the mere desire to found a family; it presupposes the existence of a family..., or at the very least the potential relationship between, for example, a child born out of wedlock and his or her natural father..., or the relationship that arises from a genuine marriage, even if family life has not yet been fully established..., or the relationship that arises from a lawful and genuine adoption...

43. The Court has, however, previously held that the notion of "private life" within the meaning of Article 8 of the Convention is a broad concept which encompasses, inter alia, the right to establish and develop relationships with other human beings..., the right to "personal development"...or the right to self-determination as such...It encompasses elements such as names..., gender identification, sexual orientation and sexual life, which fall within the personal sphere protected by Article 8..., and the right to respect for both the decisions to have and not to have a child...

45. It should...be noted that the applicant claimed to have been discriminated against on the ground of her avowed homosexuality, resulting in a violation of the provisions of Article 14 of the Convention taken in conjunction with Article 8.

46. The court is not therefore called upon to rule whether the right to adopt, having regard to, inter alia, developments in legislation in Europe and the fact that the Convention is a living instrument which must be interpreted in the light of present day conditions...should or should not fall within the ambit of Art 8 of the Convention taken alone.

The European Court's failure to grapple directly with the question of whether the right to adopt is protected within the private life limb of Article 8 has been subjected to convincing criticism, particularly in light of the Court's recent jurisprudence on assisted reproduction.[86]

---

[85] S 22.
[86] See 9.4.2.

I. Curry-Sumner, 'E.B. v France: A Missed Opportunity', (2009) 21 *Child and Family Law Quarterly* 356, 362

[I]f one does not accept that the right to adopt should fall within the ambit of Article 8, an otherwise unjustifiable distinction will arise between couples wishing to adopt and those wishing to use artificial reproduction techniques. If the court now accepts that the decision to have or not to have a child falls within the scope of Article 8, which the court already acknowledged in *Evans v UK*, why does this not also apply to those who have chosen to follow the route of adoption…[T]he court expressly stated that 'the right to respect for both the decisions to become and not to become a parent' falls within the ambit of Article 8. Is this not also true of adoptions? Obviously, the 'decision to adopt' does not and nor should it lead to a 'right to adopt', in the same way that a 'decision to have a child using artificial insemination techniques does not guarantee a 'right to a child'. However, in recognising that adoption is a method through which individuals and couples are able to realise their wish to raise a child and thus provide a child in need with a familial home, is this decision equally deserving of the protection laid down by the Convention as the desire to raise one's own genetic child?

The selection of prospective adopters under English law is a matter for the adoption agency, although it must comply with any statutory restrictions as to who may apply for an adoption order.[87] All people wishing to adopt in England and Wales are subjected to rigorous vetting procedures. Applicants who are unhappy with the decision of an adoption agency as to their suitability to adopt, may apply for the decision to be reviewed by an independent review panel.[88]

The pool of prospective adopters was widened considerably by the ACA 2002. Section 49(1) provides that an application for an adoption order may be made by a 'couple' or one person. 'Couple' is defined in s 144(4) as a married couple, two people who are civil partners of each other, or two people (whether of different sexes or the same sex) living as partners in an enduring family relationship. Hedley J has held that in determining whether a couple are 'living as partners in an enduring family relationship' it is not necessary for them to be living together in the same property—'what is required is: first, an unambiguous intention to create and maintain family life, and secondly, a factual matrix consistent with that intention'.[89] The Labour Government's decision to allow same-sex and unmarried opposite-sex couples to adopt under the ACA 2002 was, at the time, controversial. Under the previous legislation an adoption order could not be made in favour of more than one person unless the couple were married.[90] This meant opposite-sex cohabiting couples and same-sex couples could not adopt 'as a couple', although one of them could apply as a single applicant and a residence order made to confer parental responsibility on the non-adopting partner.[91] This reflected the belief that family units headed by a married couple provided adopted children with much greater security and stability—a view which apparently still prevails amongst some members of the legislature and the senior judiciary.[92] With the need to widen the pool

---

[87] For a useful illustration of how the approval process works see *R (On the Application of Hofstetter and another) v Barnet Borough Council* [2009] EWHC 3282 (Admin).

[88] ACA 2002, s 12. Independent Review of Determinations (Adoption) Regulations 2005, SI 2005/3332, reg 3.

[89] *T and M v OCC and C* [2010] EWHC 964, [16]–[17].

[90] AA 1976, s 14.

[91] *Re AB (A Minor) (Adoption: Parental Consent)* [1996] 1 FCR 633.

[92] See, e.g., *Re P (Adoption: Unmarried Couple)* [2008] UKHL 38, [12]–[13] (Lord Hoffmann) and [108]–[112] (Baroness Hale).

of prospective adopters, the Labour Government decided late in the legislative process to lift the restriction.[93]

The government's decision pre-empted developments in the Strasbourg jurisprudence. Although the European Court has avoided giving any determinative answer to the question of whether Article 8 per se protects the right to adopt, it is clear that should the state choose to go beyond its ECHR obligations and allow individuals to apply, it cannot do so in a discriminatory manner.[94] It is not therefore permissible for states to exclude a prospective adopter from consideration on the grounds (whether direct or indirect) of his or her sexuality.

EB v France (App No 43546/02, ECHR) (2008)

48. The prohibition of discrimination enshrined in Article 14...extends beyond the enjoyment of the rights and freedoms which the Convention and the Protocols thereto require each State to guarantee. It applies also to those additional rights, falling within the general scope of any Convention Article, for which the State has voluntarily decided to provide. This principle is well entrenched in the Court's case-law...

49. The present case does not concern adoption by a couple or by the same-sex partner of a biological parent, but solely adoption by a single person. Whilst Article 8 of the Convention is silent as to this question, the Court notes that French legislation expressly grants single persons the right to apply for authorisation to adopt and establishes a procedure to that end. Accordingly, the Court considers that the facts of this case undoubtedly fall within the ambit of Article 8 of the Convention. Consequently, the State, which has gone beyond its obligations under Article 8 in creating such a right – a possibility open to it under Article 53 of the Convention – cannot, in the application of that right, take discriminatory measures within the meaning of Article 14...

50. The applicant alleged in the present case that, in the exercise of her right under the domestic law, she had been discriminated against on the ground of her sexual orientation. The latter is a concept covered by Article 14 of the Convention...The Court also points out that in *Fretté v. France*..., to which the parties expressly referred, the applicant complained that the rejection of his application for authorisation to adopt had implicitly been based on his sexual orientation alone. The Chamber found that Article 14 of the Convention, taken in conjunction with Article 8, was applicable...

51. Accordingly, Article 14 of the Convention, taken in conjunction with Article 8, is applicable in the present case...

The Court's assessment...

84. The Court...notes that the administrative courts went to some lengths to rule that although regard had been had to the applicant's sexual orientation, it had not been the basis for the decision in question and had not been considered from a hostile position of principle.

85. However, in the Court's opinion the fact that the applicant's homosexuality featured to such an extent in the reasoning of the domestic authorities is significant...[The Court] observes that the manner in which certain opinions were expressed was indeed revealing in that the applicant's homosexuality was a determining factor....

---

[93] Although the shortage of suitable approved adopters remains a cause of considerable delay: Ofsted (2012), 25. Recruitment of adopters who are able and willing to meet the needs of today's looked after children is a significant problem.

[94] *EB v France* (App No 43546/02, ECHR) (2008), [49].

87. Regarding the systematic reference to the lack of a "paternal referent", the Court disputes not the desirability of addressing the issue, but the importance attached to it by the domestic authorities in the context of adoption by a single person. The fact that it is legitimate for this factor to be taken into account should not lead the Court to overlook the excessive reference to it in the circumstances of the present case.

88. Thus, notwithstanding the precautions taken by the Nancy Administrative Court of Appeal, and subsequently by the *Conseil d'Etat*, to justify taking account of the applicant's "lifestyle", the inescapable conclusion is that her sexual orientation was consistently at the centre of deliberations in her regard and omnipresent at every stage of the administrative and judicial proceedings.

89. The Court considers that the reference to the applicant's homosexuality was, if not explicit, at least implicit. The influence of the applicant's avowed homosexuality on the assessment of her application has been established and, having regard to the foregoing, was a decisive factor leading to the decision to refuse her authorisation to adopt...

90. The applicant therefore suffered a difference in treatment. Regard must be had to the aim behind that difference in treatment and, if the aim was legitimate, to whether the different treatment was justified.

91. The Court reiterates that, for the purposes of Article 14, a difference in treatment is discriminatory if it has no objective and reasonable justification, which means that it does not pursue a "legitimate aim" or that there is no "reasonable proportionality between the means employed and the aim sought to be realised"...Where sexual orientation is in issue, there is a need for particularly convincing and weighty reasons to justify a difference in treatment regarding rights falling within Article 8...

92. In that connection the Court observes that the Convention is a living instrument, to be interpreted in the light of present-day conditions...

93. In the Court's opinion, if the reasons advanced for such a difference in treatment were based solely on considerations regarding the applicant's sexual orientation this would amount to discrimination under the Convention...

94. The Court points out that French law allows single persons to adopt a child..., thereby opening up the possibility of adoption by a single homosexual, which is not disputed. Against the background of the domestic legal provisions, it considers that the reasons put forward by the Government cannot be regarded as particularly convincing and weighty such as to justify refusing to grant the applicant authorisation...

96. Having regard to the foregoing, the Court cannot but observe that, in rejecting the applicant's application for authorisation to adopt, the domestic authorities made a distinction based on considerations regarding her sexual orientation, a distinction which is not acceptable under the Convention...

98. There has accordingly been a breach of Article 14 of the Convention taken in conjunction with Article 8.

Although the European Court does not explicitly state as such, the decision in *EB v France* effectively overrules the earlier decision of the Court in *Fretté v France* in which it held that the rejection of a single gay man as a prospective adopter on the basis of his sexual orientation was justified to protect the interests of children, particularly in light of the wide margin of appreciation afforded to states on such sensitive matters.[95]

[95] *Fretté v France* (App No 36515/97, ECHR) (2003). For an excellent critique of the decision in *EB v France*, see Curry-Sumner (2009).

Of crucial importance to the decision in *EB v France* is the fact that the French authorities permit adoption by single 'heterosexual' applicants and cannot therefore discriminate against single 'homosexual' applicants. The issue would be different if the domestic authorities imposed wider restrictions on adoption such as limiting it to married couples. The question then is whether the state is justified in precluding from consideration all unmarried cohabiting couples and single applicants, regardless of sexual orientation. In the case of *Gas and Dubois v France*, the European Court held that such a restriction would not constitute discrimination.[96] However, in dealing with such restrictions on adoption in Northern Ireland, the House of Lords took a different view, holding that such difference in treatment between married and unmarried couples is contrary to Articles 8 and 14 ECHR.[97] Whilst expressing some sympathy for the view that it is better for children to be raised by a couple who have given each other the commitment of marriage, the House of Lords held that a 'bright line' exclusion of all unmarried couples could not be justified on the basis of protecting the child's welfare. Indeed, to the contrary, the House of Lords took the view that it is in the interests of children for the 'door to adoption' to be opened as widely as possible.[98]

English law's now fairly long-standing acceptance that same-sex couples and opposite-sex cohabiting couples should be permitted to adopt provides important recognition of the diverse nature of family life in contemporary society. However, the way in which this change was secured in 2002, and the concerns which underpinned the change, have been the subject of criticism. In particular, Dey notes that the extension of adoption rights to same-sex couples was done as a matter of expedience, with the issue never being addressed as a matter of principle.[99] This failure to tackle the question of same-sex adoption as a matter of principle has potentially wider repercussions. It is clear under the Equality Act 2010 that an adoption agency cannot refuse to provide adoption services to same-sex couples wishing to adopt, even if such adoptions would contravene the agency's religious principles.[100] However, as Dey argues, less direct discriminatory practices in the selection of prospective adopters may well continue. Indeed, s 45(2) of the ACA 2002 provides that in determining the suitability of adopters, regulations may provide that 'proper regard is to be had to the need for stability and permanence in their relationship'.[101] This arguably provides a basis on which the greater 'stability and permanence' offered by traditional heterosexual marriage can continue to be privileged over other 'less enduring' family forms—a position given some support by the House of Lords in *Re P*.[102] Commentators have observed how 'adoption for the homosexual parent only seems to occur where the child has special needs or behavioural problems, and the homosexual parent concerned has exceptional caring qualities to offer, perhaps beyond what may be expected of the "normal parent".'[103] It thus seems that there are two pools of prospective adopters: the preferred traditional family unit deemed suitable to care for any

---

[96] *Gas and Dubois v France* (App No 25951/07, ECHR) (2011). For commentary, see Johnson (2012).

[97] Lord Walker dissented on a point of constitutional law.

[98] *Re P (Adoption: Unmarried Couple)* [2008] UKHL 38, [54] (Lord Hope). For an excellent commentary, see Kilkelly (2010).

[99] Dey (2005).

[100] See Equality Act 2010, ss 12 and 29, replacing the Equality Act (Sexual Orientation) Regulations 2007, SI 2007/1263. As a result of these provisions Catholic adoption agencies in England and Wales have either had to close or sever their ties with the church. See <www.telegraph.co.uk/news/newstopics/religion/7952526/Last-Catholic-adoption-agency-faces-closure-after-Charity-Commission-ruling.html>.

[101] It does not appear that this has been expressly included within the regulations. See Adoption Agencies Regulations 2005, SI 2005/389.

[102] [2008] UKHL 38, [12]–[13] (Lord Hoffmann) and [108]–[112] (Baroness Hale).

[103] Marshall (2003), 843–4.

child and a second group who provide a fall-back option for particularly difficult to place children or who can establish some particular reason on the basis of the child's welfare why placing the child in this less than optimal family setting is justified.[104] There is, in other words, no *general* acceptance of the *equal* parenting worth of single, same-sex, and possibly also opposite-sex cohabiting couples. Yet, as Tobin and McNair argue, there is nothing within the empirical research on gay and lesbian parenting to justify this continuing caution.[105]

13.5.3 PLACING THE CHILD FOR ADOPTION

Placing a child with prospective adopters is a vitally important step in the adoption process. An adoption agency can only place a child for adoption in accordance with ss 18–29 of the ACA 2002. Consent is a crucial issue at this stage of the proceedings because in many contested cases the parents will be unable to reopen consent at the final adoption hearing.

Placing the child with the birth parent's consent

If the birth parents consent to the adoption, the adoption agency can place the child without the courts' prior authorization.[106] The birth parents have the option of consenting only to a specific placement or of consenting generally to any placement chosen by the agency.[107] At the same time as consenting to the placement of the child, the birth parents may give their advance consent to the making of an adoption order.[108] Consent can again be general or limited to adoption by the specific individuals with whom the child is to be placed.[109] At the same time as giving consent, or any time thereafter, the parents can give notice to the adoption agency that they do not wish to be informed of any subsequent adoption application.[110] The birth parents can withdraw this notice and their advance consent to the adoption at any time up to the point the adoption order is made.[111]

If the child is voluntarily relinquished by the mother and the mother wishes to keep the fact of the birth and subsequent adoption secret, questions have arisen as to whether she is entitled to have her wish for confidentiality respected or whether the birth father should be notified and the possibility of a placement with him or the extended maternal or paternal family investigated. The courts have consistently taken the position that birth fathers should be informed about the adoption and their views considered before the child is placed for adoption.[112] This is always subject to the particular facts of the case including practical considerations such as whether it is feasible to identify and locate the father, as well as welfare considerations concerning the child.[113] In *Re L (Adoption: Contacting Natural Father)*,[114]

---

[104] For a worrying small-scale study of social work attitudes towards homosexual applicants post-2002 legislation, see Hitchings and Sagar (2007).

[105] Tobin and McNair (2009), 127.

[106] ACA 2002, s 19(1).

[107] Ibid.

[108] S 20(1).

[109] S 20(2).

[110] S 20(4)(a).

[111] S 20(3) and (4)(b).

[112] For an excellent article which makes the case for women to be able to preserve confidentiality and privacy in these circumstances, see Marshall (2012).

[113] *Re H and G (Adoption: Consultation of Unmarried Fathers)* [2001] 1 FLR 646.

[114] [2007] EWHC 1771.

Munby J held that 'where there exists family life within the meaning of Art 8 of the ECHR as between the mother and the father, one generally requires "strong countervailing factors"...to justify the exclusion from the adoption process of an unmarried father without parental responsibility'.[115] The issue arose again before the Court of Appeal in *C v X, Y, Z County Council*.[116] It was argued on the child's behalf that there was a statutory duty on the local authority to notify the child's father and extended family members even where, as on the facts of this case, the mother wished the child's birth to remain a secret. 'Compelling reasons' would thus be required to prevent disclosure taking place, particularly to the child's father.[117] Such a duty was suggested to serve two important purposes: first, it enabled inquiries to be made as to the possibility of a long-term placement for the child within the extended family; secondly, even if such a placement did not materialize, important information could be gathered about the birth families which would be important for the child as he or she grew older.

In a decision which arguably devalues the child's relationships (both actual and potential) with the birth family and pays little regard to the procedural and substantive rights of the child's father, the Court of Appeal disagreed:

C v X, Y, Z County Council [2007] EWCA Civ 1206

ARDEN LJ:

3. In my judgment...when a decision requires to be made about the long-term care of a child, whom a mother wishes to be adopted, there is no duty to make enquiries which it is not in the interests of the child to make, and enquiries are not in the interests of the child simply because they will provide more information about the child's background: they must genuinely further the prospect of finding a long-term carer for the child without delay. This interpretation does not violate the right to family life. The objective of finding long-term care must be the focus of making any further enquiries and that means the court has to evaluate evidence about those prospects. That did not happen in this case....

14. This is a question of statutory interpretation. It is necessary to go back to s 1 [of the ACA 2002]. In my judgment, the governing provision is subs (2), because it lays down a 'paramount' or overarching consideration, and not surprisingly that paramount consideration is the child's welfare. Parliament has added that the reference to welfare is to welfare throughout a child's life and not simply in the short term future or the child's childhood. All the other provisions of s 1 about decision-making take effect subject to this provision.

15. The result is that s 1 is child-centred. It is not "mother-centred". The emphasis is on the interests of the child and not those of the mother. As the European Court of Human Rights ("the Strasbourg court") expressed it in one case, adoption means "giving a family to a child and not the child to a family"... The interests of the child will include the child's interest in retaining its identity, and this is likely to be important to the child in adulthood. But identity is only one factor in the balance that has to be struck. S 1 does not privilege the birth family over adoptive parents simply because they are the birth family...

---

[115] Ibid, [25]. On the facts, Munby J was 'sceptical' as to whether the father would have any right under Art 8.
[116] [2007] EWCA Civ 1206.
[117] Ibid, [23].

16. S 1 then lists a number of matters that the court or adoption agency must have in mind when it makes any decision about adoption. Importantly, those matters include delay (subs (3))...

17. ...The legislation is not prescriptive...[Section] 1 does not establish any preference for any particular result or prescribe any particular conclusion. Importantly, as I have said, it does not express a preference for following the wishes of the birth family or placing a child with the child's birth family, though this will often be in the best interests of the child. The one exception is delay. Delay is always to be regarded as in some degree likely to prejudice the child's welfare: see subs (3). Parliament has here made a value judgement about the likely impact of delay and it is not open to the court or the adoption agency to quarrel with that basic value judgement.

18. In this particular case, subs (4) (c) and (f) are particularly important...

20. Subs (4) (f) requires the court to have regard to the wishes and feelings of a child's relatives and their ability and willingness to provide the child with long-term care. However, that assumes that information is reasonably available about these matters. If the information is not readily available, the court or adoption agency may want to obtain it. But in the light of subs (2) there [sic] are only required to do so, if that is required for the purposes of the child's welfare and if they consider it right to take those steps notwithstanding that any delay is likely to prejudice the child's welfare.

21. It can be seen from this analysis that when a decision requires to be made about the long-term care of the child, whom a mother wishes to be adopted, there is no duty to make enquiries of an absolute kind. There is only a duty to make enquiries, if it is in the interests of the child to make those enquiries. In the present case, the judge considered that in adult life the child would benefit from more information about the child's father. But in the context of the decision-making with which the judge was concerned, I do not consider that that fact could of itself animate indeed the exercise of discretion. The immediate question with which the guardian and local authority were concerned was who would look after the child on a long-term basis. The enquiries had to be focused on that result. That meant looking at the evidence about the prospective carers within the mother's family. It was not enough simply to say that it would be in the child's interests to be placed with her birth family...Finding out more about the child's background for E's information in the future was secondary to that objective, and it would inevitably lead to delay...

24. The logical consequence of my interpretation of s 1 is that exceptional situations can arise in which relatives, or even a father, of a child remain in ignorance about the child at the time of its adoption. But this result is consistent with other provisions of the 2002 Act.

The ECHR arguments are considered by Arden LJ but ultimately she holds that there is nothing within them that requires disclosure. As to the right to respect for family life, she holds in accordance with the Strasbourg jurisprudence that an unmarried father ('who is only a one-night stand') has no right to respect for family life that would be infringed by non-disclosure.[118] As regards the mother's extended family, whilst she recognizes that grandparents and other close relatives may have a right to respect for family life, she holds that any prima facie violation will be justified by the fact that the decision as to disclosure will have been based on the child's welfare.[119] No final conclusion is reached on the question of whether the child may have a right to respect for family life which requires inquiries to

---

[118] Ibid, [39].
[119] Ibid.

be made as to whether she can be raised by her natural father. As with the extended family, Arden LJ holds that any such right would be capable of being overridden by the competing welfare considerations under Article 8(2).[120] The child's right to information about her family, as protected under the private life limb of Article 8, is also considered. However, Arden LJ concludes that the current provisions of the ACA 2002 fall well within the state's margin of appreciation in determining appropriate measures to meet this particular requirement of Article 8.[121]

The Court of Appeal's judgment in *C v X, Y, Z Council* sent out a clear message as to the overriding priorities entrenched within the ACA 2002: the child's welfare is determinative; avoiding delay is of paramount importance; and the purported rights and interests of the birth family must not divert attention away from these two core objectives. In the words of Thorpe LJ, the ACA 2002 does not compel the adoption agency to 'inform and assess all and sundry'—including the child's father.[122] The opportunity to 'fast-track [the child] into adoption in accordance with her mother's wishes' must not be lost.[123]

However, the decision in *C v X, Y, Z Council* whilst perhaps consistent with the general tenor of the ongoing adoption reforms, appeared to depart from a number of earlier authorities which had clearly established the principle that the child's father should be told of the child's existence unless there were 'exceptional circumstances' or 'strong countervailing reasons' justifying non-disclosure. This departure was surprising given the apparent demands of Articles 6 and 8 ECHR. The Court of Appeal has, however, revisited the issue in *Re A*, upholding the previous line of authority. Lady Justice Black gave the fullest judgment. Dealing first with the judgments of the Court of Appeal in *C v X, Y, Z Council*, she held that there was 'no reason to suppose that the court was contemplating a radical departure from [previous] authorities'.[124] She continued:

Re A (Father: Knowledge of Child's Birth) [2011] EWCA Civ 273

BLACK LJ:

43. [Counsel] accept that "the starting point is that [F] should know of the existence of his son and should be able to participate in future care and adoption proceedings" and that "only in an exceptional case should that general rule be overridden". This realistic position accords with the authorities as I see them...

44. The appellant's complaint is that the judge did not just look for exceptional circumstances but proceeded on the basis that only a significant physical risk would do and this was to set the test too high.

45. I agree that the authorities do not impose a requirement of significant physical risk. Harm and risk come in many guises and...I would be anxious about attempting to define what may make a case exceptional enough to justify departing from normal principles. It may be a moot point whether [the judge] was actually setting himself a test involving significant physical harm or...simply emphasising the high hurdle that will have to be overcome before a father who is married to the child's mother and also living with her is kept in

---

120 Ibid, [35].
121 Ibid, [33].
122 Ibid, [78].
123 Ibid, [69]. For critique, see Sloan (2013), 52.
124 *Re A (Father: Knowledge of Child's Birth)* [2011] EWCA Civ 273, [38]–[42].

ignorance of the fact that he has a child and deprived of the chance to participate in the legal process relating to that child. Whatever the judge had in mind, however, the balance was inevitably going to come down against [the mother's] applications and his determination is not in any way undermined by this reference of his to a significant physical risk.

The test for non-disclosure thus remains a high one of exceptionality. This will be particularly hard to satisfy, as in *Re A*, where the parents are or have been in a significant relationship to which family life rights will attach.

Placing the child without consent: placement orders

Where the birth parents do not consent, or the local authority has applied for a care order, the adoption agency must apply to the court under s 21 for a placement order authorizing them to place the child for adoption.[125] A placement order confers general authorization on the adoption agency to place the child with any prospective adopters considered appropriate.[126] The welfare principle applies,[127] and the order can only be made if the parent(s) or guardian(s) consent or the court is satisfied consent should be dispensed with. The consent requirements must be dealt with in accordance with s 52. Further conditions on making the order are set down in s 21(2):

Adoption and Children Act 2002, s 21

(2) The court may not make a placement order in respect of a child unless—

  (a) the child is subject to a care order,

  (b) the court is satisfied that the conditions in section 31(2) of the 1989 Act (conditions for making a care order) are met, or

  (c) the child has no parent or guardian.

Before placing a child for adoption, the threshold conditions for state intervention into family life as set down in s 31 of the CA 1989 must therefore be met: the child must be suffering or likely to suffer significant harm attributable to the parents' care. This ensures that no child can be placed for adoption against the birth parents' wishes on the basis of a simple welfare test.

However, in order to eliminate delays in the adoption process, s 22 of the ACA 2002 places a duty on the local authority to apply for a placement order as soon as they are satisfied that a looked after child should be placed for adoption. This duty applies whether or not a care order is in force provided the local authority 'consider' that the threshold conditions are satisfied. This means that a child can be placed for adoption against the birth parents' wishes without a care order ever being made.

The important question of whether the practice of 'dual planning' could be reconciled with the duties of the local authority under s 22 was addressed by the Court of Appeal in *Re P (Children) (Adoption: Parental Consent)*.[128] The legal issue was whether the court could be said to be 'satisfied that the child ought to be placed for adoption' in circumstances where

---

[125] S 19(3).
[126] S 21(1).
[127] S 1(1) and (7).
[128] [2008] EWCA Civ 535, [134]–[140] and [156]–[159].

the local authority acknowledged that finding a suitable adoptive placement was likely to prove difficult and, in light of this uncertainty, had adopted a 'dual planning' approach. It was argued on behalf of the mother that if both long-term fostering and adoption were regarded as potentially suitable placements, it could not be said that a placement order 'ought' to be made or was required in the children's best interests.

The Court of Appeal rejected this argument in favour of a pragmatic approach, holding that whilst there were important legal, philosophical, and practical differences between adoption and fostering, provided the local authority were satisfied that adoption was in the child's best interests they could, and indeed ought, to apply for a placement order without precluding undertaking a simultaneous search for long-term foster parents. In the Court of Appeal's judgment, this dual approach was entirely sensible for 'compelling pragmatic reasons': the chances of finding a suitable adoptive home were considerably improved by having the placement order firmly in place whilst any further delay for the child would be avoided if an adoptive home could not be found.

The situation in *Re P (Children) (Adoption: Parental Consent)* needs to be distinguished from that which was considered by a differently constituted Court of Appeal in *Re T (Children: Placement Order)*.[129] *Re T* was concerned with a case where, because of the very serious nature of the children's problems, it was recommended that they be placed in a therapeutic foster home for at least six months before a final decision was made as to their long-term placement. Although the local authority agreed that adoption would theoretically be in the long-term interests of the children, that plan remained purely hypothetical given not only the uncertainty of finding a placement but, more importantly, the uncertainty as to whether the children would be deemed suitable for adoption—an uncertainty which would only be resolved after the therapeutic placement. Given it could not be said with certainty that adoption would be in the children's best interests, the Court of Appeal held that it was premature to make a placement order under s 22.[130] Thus, whilst a placement order can and should be made despite uncertainty over finding a suitable placement, a placement order cannot be made if it has not yet been determined that adoption is in the child's best interests.

Section 22 is clearly intended to minimize any delay in placing looked after children for adoption. The importance of moving children through the care system with greater speed has been reinforced by the imposition of tighter timescales for decision-making at every stage of the process.[131] Tackling the problem of 'drift in care' and eradicating any *unnecessary* delays between a child coming into care and being found a permanent alternative home are laudable objectives. The concern that delays in the adoption process can prejudice the chance of a successful outcome is borne out by research.[132] Closely associated with this problem of delay is the number of short-term placements a looked after child may experience before finally being placed with prospective adopters. As part of the most recent reforms the government therefore decided to tackle this particular issue by providing a statutory basis for the practice of 'fostering for adoption'.[133] Section 22C of the CA 1989 was amended to place a duty on local authorities when 'considering' adoption for a child or upon reaching the decision that the child 'ought' to be placed for adoption, to place the child with prospective adopters who are also approved for this purpose as local authority foster parents.[134]

---

[129] [2008] EWCA Civ 248.
[130] Ibid, [18].
[131] DH (2001b), Part A, para 2.
[132] Selwyn, Frazer, and Quinton (2006).
[133] DFE (2012b), 25–7.
[134] CA 1989, s 22C(9A)–(9C) as amended by CFA 2014, s 2.

Children can thus now be placed with prospective adopters before the local authority has determined that the child 'ought' to be adopted, before an application for a placement order has been made, or, perhaps most importantly, before the court has determined that adoption is in the child's best interests. The intention behind the change is to minimize the disruption of multiple placements for the child. The clear advantage from the child's perspective is that if rehabilitation with the birth family is ruled out and the decision is made that the child should be adopted the child will already be settled with the prospective adopters. There is, however, some disquiet that these provisions create a 'fast-track' to adoption which may deprive children of the opportunity of being successfully rehabilitated with their birth parents.[135] Concern was expressed to the House of Lords Select Committee on Adoption that once a child has been placed with prospective adopters bonds and attachments will begin to form and the birth family will face a virtually impossible uphill struggle to successfully contest a placement order—the court being faced, in effect, with a *fait accompli*. It is, of course, a difficult balance but the Select Committee concluded that provided pre-proceedings work with the birth family has been properly carried out, 'fostering for adoption' would not unfairly tip the balance against the birth parents:

House of Lords Select Committee on Adoption Legislation, 1st Report of Session 2012–13, *Adoption: Pre-Legislative Scrutiny. Report,* **HL Paper 94** (London: TSO, 2012)

56. We are not persuaded that the ability of birth parents to challenge the application for a placement order would be adversely affected by fostering for adoption, so long as all reasonable steps have been taken by the local authority to explore reunification of the child with the birth family at the earliest opportunity, and the parents have been able effectively to participate in the decision-making process. We do not believe that such concerns should be allowed to outweigh the potential benefit to the child of moving as early as possible into a permanent placement.

Consequences of the child being placed or being authorized to be placed for adoption

Whilst a child is placed or authorized to be placed for adoption, parental responsibility is given to the adoption agency.[136] If the child is placed with prospective adopters then the prospective adopters also acquire parental responsibility for the duration of the placement, the adoption agency having the power to determine to what extent the prospective adopters will be able to exercise their responsibility.[137] The birth parents do not lose parental responsibility by virtue of the fact the child is placed or authorized to be placed for adoption but again the adoption agency has the power to determine to what extent they can exercise that responsibility.[138] If a care order was made at the same time as the placement order or the child was subject to a care order when the placement order was made, the care order ceases

---

[135] Harris-Short (2001); Sagar and Hitchings (2007).
[136] S 25(1)–(2).
[137] S 25(3)–(4).
[138] Ibid.

to have effect whilst the placement order is in force.[139] The child is therefore no longer 'in care' although a child placed or authorized to be placed for adoption by a local authority is still regarded as a looked after child.[140]

Contact with a child who is placed or authorized to be placed for adoption

Contact is a crucially important issue at this stage of the proceedings as the pattern of contact established at this point can determine whether provision is made for post-adoption contact at the final hearing. For members of the birth family, ensuring contact is continued throughout the placement period can thus be of vital importance.

Although during placement the child has the status of a looked after child, local authorities are exempt from the duty under Sch 2, para 15 of the CA 1989 to endeavour to promote contact between looked after children and their parents.[141] Furthermore, any existing orders for contact made under s 8 or 34 of the CA 1989 cease to have effect.[142] The court can, however, order contact under s 26 of the ACA 2002.[143] The court is under a duty before making a placement order to consider the adoption agency's proposals for contact.[144]

A s 26 contact order remains in force whilst the child is placed or authorized to be placed for adoption.[145] The adoption agency retains the authority to terminate contact in an emergency for a maximum of seven days if satisfied that it is necessary to do so to safeguard and promote the child's welfare.[146]

Restrictions on removing a child who is placed for adoption

When a child is placed for adoption under s 19 (with parental consent) only the adoption agency can remove the child from the prospective adopters.[147] If the parents withdraw their consent to the placement the child must be returned to their care within 14 days unless an application has been made for a placement order or the prospective adopters have applied for an adoption order, special guardianship order, or child arrangements order, in which case the child can only be removed with the court's leave.[148] If an adoption agency is authorized to place a child under s 19 but the parents withdraw their consent before the child is placed, the child must be returned to the parents within seven days.

Where a placement order is in force, nobody, other than the local authority, can remove the child.[149] Where the adoption agency decides that a child should be removed from prospective adopters, the prospective adopters must return the child within seven days of receiving notice of return unless they have applied for an adoption order, special guardianship

---

[139] S 29(1).

[140] S 18(3).

[141] Adoption Agencies Regulations 2005, SI 2005/389, reg 45(2)(d).

[142] ACA 2002, s 26(1).

[143] Upon application by the child, the adoption agency, the birth parents, the child's relatives, a guardian, or any person in whose favour a child arrangements order was in force or who had care of the child under the High Court's inherent jurisdiction immediately before the placement order was made. Any other person may apply with leave. The court may also act of its own motion. S 26(2)–(4).

[144] S 27(4).

[145] S 27(1).

[146] S 27(2).

[147] S 30(1).

[148] Ss 32(2) and 32(5).

[149] S 34(1).

order, or child arrangements order, in which case the court's leave to remove the child is required.[150] It was held by Charles J in *DL, ML v London Borough of Newham* that the fact that the decision to remove a child is made by the adoption agency and not the court is not a breach of Article 6.[151] The prospective adopters are able to challenge the adoption agency's decision to give notice to return by way of judicial review or under the Human Rights Act 1998. The notice to return may be stayed pending review of the local authority's decision.[152] Where the child has lived with the prospective adopters for any period of time, Article 8 rights will be engaged giving both substantive and procedural protection to the prospective adopters.[153] Where the child needs to be removed urgently (before the seven days notice has expired) the local authority will have to apply for an emergency protection order or an interim care order authorizing removal.[154] Charles J thus concluded that the legislative scheme was Convention compliant.

Where it is the prospective adopters who wish to return the child to the adoption agency, the adoption agency must receive the child back into care within seven days.[155]

Revoking the placement order

Once a placement order has been made, the birth parents will face an uphill struggle to prevent the adoption proceeding. The placement order is of unlimited duration, remaining in force until revoked or an adoption order is made.[156] Moreover, opportunities to challenge the order are limited. A placement order can be revoked on the application of any person, but only the child or the adoption agency can apply as of right.[157] All other applicants require leave under s 24, and leave will only be granted if the child is not already placed and there has been a change in circumstances since the original order was made.[158]

The test to be applied on an application for leave to revoke a placement order was considered by the Court of Appeal in *Re M (Children) (Placement Order).*[159] It was argued on the mother's behalf that if she was able to establish a change in circumstances the court would be required to grant leave. The local authority disagreed, contending that establishing a change in circumstances was only 'the necessary precursor to the court's exercise of a discretion' and that in exercising its discretion the children's welfare would be a relevant consideration.[160] The Court of Appeal agreed with the local authority, holding that establishing a change in circumstances was not determinative of the application. Wilson LJ held that the decision whether to grant leave to revoke a placement order was not 'coming to a decision relating to the adoption of a child' within the meaning of s 1(7) of the Act.[161]

---

150 Ss 35(2) and 35(5).
151 [2011] EWHC 1127 (Admin).
152 Ibid, [110].
153 Ibid, [122].
154 Ibid, [112]–[115].
155 S 35(1).
156 S 21(4). For the problems this can cause, see *A and S v Lancashire County Council* [2012] EWHC 1689.
157 S 24(1)–(2).
158 S 24(2)–(3).
159 [2007] EWCA Civ 1084.
160 Ibid, [4].
161 S 1(7) provides: 'In this section, "coming to a decision relating to the adoption of a child", in relation to a court, includes – (a) coming to a decision in any proceedings where the orders that might be made by the court include an adoption order (or the revocation of such an order), a placement order (or the revocation of such an order) or an order under section 26 (or the revocation or variation of such an order); (b) coming to a decision about granting leave in respect of any action (other than the initiation of proceedings in any court)

The paramountcy principle under s 1(2) does not therefore apply. However, Wilson LJ went on to hold that this does not mean that the children's interests are irrelevant.[162] Indeed, in line with the approach taken to leave applications under s 10(9) of the CA 1989, he held that once a change in circumstances has been established,[163] the court has a discretion as to whether or not to grant leave, in the exercise of which the children's welfare and the applicant's prospects of success on the main application are relevant considerations.[164] He concludes that whilst in most cases the children's welfare will be subsumed within the broader inquiry into the applicant's prospects of success, they remain separate considerations.[165]

The Court of Appeal has also had to tackle a number of difficulties caused by related restrictions set down in s 24: (i) that an application to revoke a placement order cannot be made once the child has been placed for adoption; and (ii) a child cannot be placed for adoption without the court's leave when an application to revoke the placement order is pending. In *Re F (A Child) (Placement Order)*[166] the Court of Appeal confirmed, by a majority, that a child can lawfully be placed for adoption by the adoption agency even though the adoption agency knows that an application for leave to revoke the placement order has been made. The Court of Appeal held that in accordance with the strict wording of s 24(5), the prohibition on placement without the court's leave only applies once the substantive application for revocation has been made.[167] However, the Court of Appeal emphasized that good practice very clearly demanded that if, to the knowledge of the adoption agency, an application for leave has been issued, the child should not be placed (thereby defeating the application) without the permission of the court and, if necessary, an injunction can be sought to prevent them doing so until the application for leave has been determined.[168] The Court of Appeal also made clear that if the local authority decides to go ahead and place the child before the parent is able to issue the necessary legal proceedings, the actions of the local authority will be susceptible to judicial review.[169] In determining whether a child has 'been placed' for the purposes of s 24, it was held by the Court of Appeal in *Coventry City Council v O (Adoption)* that a child is not 'placed' until he begins to live with the proposed adopters or, if he is already living with them in their capacity as foster carers, when the adoption agency formally allows him to continue to live with them in their fresh capacity as prospective adopters.[170]

---

which may be taken by an adoption agency or individual under this Act, but does not include coming to a decision about granting leave in any other circumstances.' The Court of Appeal held that an application for leave to revoke a placement order was an application to *initiate proceedings* and therefore was specifically excluded from the scope of s 1(7). Cf an application for leave to defend adoption proceedings, discussed below at 946–51.

[162] [2007] EWCA Civ 1084, [24].

[163] Although the change in circumstances will usually relate to the parent and the parent's capacity to resume full-time care of the child, this will not always be the case. A change in circumstances which relates to the child and renders the plan for adoption no longer appropriate may constitute a sufficient change in circumstances for the purposes of s 24 and establish the applicant has a 'real prospect of success' in revoking the order—even if it remains impossible for the child to return home. See *NS-H v Kingston-Upon-Hull City Council* [2008] EWCA Civ 493.

[164] [2007] EWCA Civ 1084, [26]–[29].

[165] Ibid, [29].

[166] [2008] EWCA Civ 439.

[167] Ibid, [33], [69].

[168] Ibid, [99], [111].

[169] Ibid, [36], [94].

[170] [2011] EWCA Civ 729, [44].

13.5.4 THE ADOPTION APPLICATION

If the child is successfully placed with prospective adopters or, in the case of a non-agency adoption, is already living with the prospective adopter(s), the next stage is to issue the application for an adoption order.

Preliminaries to making the application

Residence conditions

Before prospective adopters can apply to adopt a child, the child must have lived with them for a specified period of time, the exact period depending on the circumstances of the adoption. If the child was placed for adoption by an adoption agency, pursuant to an order of the High Court, or the applicant is a parent of the child, the child must have lived with the prospective adopter(s) for ten weeks preceding the application.[171] If the applicant is the partner of a parent of the child (i.e. a step-parent adoption) the child must have lived with the applicant for six months.[172] If the applicants are local authority foster parents, the child must have lived with them for 12 months unless the court gives leave to apply.[173] In all other cases, the child must have lived with the prospective adopters for not less than three of the previous five years unless again the court gives leave to apply.[174] One of the main purposes of these provisions is to ensure that the local authority or adoption agency has had sufficient opportunity to observe the prospective adopters and the child together in their home environment.[175]

Where the prospective adopters require leave to apply for an adoption order, the Court of Appeal has held that the same principles apply as in an application for leave to revoke a placement order.[176] Thus, it was held in *TL v Coventry City Council* that the child's welfare is a relevant but not paramount consideration and the court should take into account whether the application has a real prospect of success.[177]

In addition to the restrictions on removing a child from the care of prospective adopters when the child has been placed for adoption by an adoption agency (see above), once an application to adopt has been made in non-agency cases (i.e. private arrangements, foster parent, and step-parent adoptions), the child cannot be removed from the care of the prospective adopters without the court's leave.[178] This prohibition also applies where an application for leave to apply has been made in non-agency cases.[179]

The requirement to give notice

Where the child was not placed with the prospective adopters by an adoption agency, the adoption order cannot be made unless the prospective adopters have given notice to the local authority of their intention to apply.[180] Notice must be given no more than two years or less

---

[171] S 42(2).
[172] S 42(3).
[173] S 42(4) and (6).
[174] S 42(5)–(6).
[175] S 42(7).
[176] *Re M (Children) (Placement Order)* [2007] EWCA Civ 1084.
[177] [2007] EWCA Civ 1383, [10].
[178] Ss 36–7.
[179] Ss 36 and 40.
[180] S 44(2).

than three months before the date on which the application is made.[181] Applicants requiring leave cannot give notice of their intention to adopt until leave has been granted.[182] On receiving notice, the local authority must investigate and prepare a report for the court.[183] Once notice of an intention to adopt has been given, nobody can remove the child from the prospective adopters' care without the court's leave, save in the following circumstances: (i) the local authority can remove the child in exercise of a statutory power including the authority to place the child with prospective adopters of the local authority's choice pursuant to a placement order;[184] (ii) if the child has been in the care of the foster parents for more than one year but less than five years and is being looked after by the local authority pursuant to a voluntary agreement under Part III of the CA 1989, a person with parental responsibility may remove the child;[185] or (iii) where a notice of an intention to adopt has been given by a step-parent but the child has lived with the step-parent for less than three years, a parent or guardian can remove the child.[186]

13.5.5 THE FINAL HEARING
Conditions on making the adoption order

Age restrictions

In the case of an application by a single person, the applicant must have attained the age of 21 years.[187] Where the prospective adopters are a couple, both must have attained the age of 21 years unless one of them is a parent of the child in which case the parent must be at least 18 years of age.[188] No maximum age limit is specified in the legislation.

Applications by one person

Applications by one person are subject to additional conditions. An order can be made in favour of one person where the applicant is a parent's partner. Otherwise, if the applicant is married or has a civil partner, the application will only be allowed if: the court is satisfied that the person's spouse/civil partner cannot be found, the spouses/civil partners have separated and are living apart and the separation is likely to be permanent, or the person's spouse/civil partner is incapable by reason of ill-health from making an application to adopt.[189] Interestingly there is no similar prohibition on someone living within an 'enduring family relationship' applying to adopt as a single person.[190]

Although it may on the face of it seem odd, a parent may apply to adopt his or her own child. Such adoptions are now rare, but they once served the important purpose of legitimating the child. The law on legitimacy having been comprehensively reformed, adoption by a sole natural parent is now contentious because it terminates any familial ties with one half of the child's family without giving the child the opportunity to build new

---

[181] S 44(3).
[182] S 44(4).
[183] S 44(5).
[184] *Coventry City Council v O (Adoption)* [2011] EWCA Civ 729, [23]–[24].
[185] Ss 38(5) and 40.
[186] Ss 39(3) and 40.
[187] S 51.
[188] S 50.
[189] S 51(3)–(3A).
[190] Bainham (2008d), 481.

relationships with an alternative family. Applications by a sole natural parent are subject to additional conditions:

Adoption and Children Act 2002, s 51

(4) An adoption order may not be made on an application under this section by the mother or the father of the person to be adopted unless the court is satisfied that—

   (a) the other natural parent is dead or cannot be found,

   (b) by virtue of the provisions in subsection (5) [s 28 of the Human Fertilisation and Embryology Act 1990 (HFEA 1990) and ss 34–47 of the HFEA 2008], there is no other parent, or

   (c) there is some other reason justifying the child's being adopted by the applicant alone,

and where the court makes an adoption order on such an application, the court must record that it is satisfied as to the fact mentioned in paragraph (a) or (b) or, in the case of paragraph (c), record the reason.

Section 51(4) reproduces, albeit with a slight change in wording, the same conditions on adoption by a sole natural parent as were contained within s 15(3) of the AA 1976. Section 15(3) was the subject of House of Lords authority in which Lord Nicholls rejected a restrictive interpretation of the requirement that there must be 'some other reason' justifying the adoption. Adopting Lord Nicholls' approach, provided it can be shown that adoption by the natural parent is in the child's best interests these additional conditions will present no real obstacle to the adoption proceeding.

Re B (A Minor) (Adoption: Natural Parent) [2001] UKHL 70

LORD NICHOLLS:

11. ... The Adoption Act permits adoption in the circumstances of child A, but only if there is reason to exclude the mother. The intervention by the court is to protect the interests of the child ... [T]he interference must meet a pressing social need and be proportionate to that need. Hale LJ [in the Court of Appeal] said ... :

'... it is difficult indeed to argue that there is a pressing social need to deprive A of all legal relationship with one half of her family of birth.... she already has a full and secure legal and factual relationship with her father. If there is any need to give her more, it can be provided for in a package of orders along the lines discussed. In my view, it would be a disproportionate response to her current needs to turn her from the child of two legal parents, with two legal families, into the child of only one parent, with only one legal family. Section 15(3) has to be given effect in such a way as to avoid that result.' ...

22. On its face this permanent exclusion of the child's mother from the life of the child is a drastic and detrimental consequence of adoption so far as the child is concerned. How serious this loss is likely to be depends on the circumstances of the case. In deciding whether to make an order having this consequence the court must always be satisfied that this course is in the best interests of the child. There must be some reason justifying the exclusion of the other natural parent. The reason must be sufficient to outweigh the adverse consequences

such an order may have by reason of the exclusion of one parent from the child's life. Consent of the excluded parent is not of itself a sufficient reason, but it is a factor to be taken into account. Its weight will depend on the circumstances.

23. In so far as the Court of Appeal construed section 15(3)(b) more restrictively than this, I am unable to agree. Section 15(3) imposes a prerequisite to the making of an adoption order on the application of the mother or father alone. One or other of the exceptions set out in paragraphs (a) and (b) must be satisfied. The three exceptions listed in paragraph (a) are instances where the other natural parent cannot have, or is unlikely to have, any further part in the child's upbringing and life. But these three exceptions are not an exhaustive list of the circumstances in which a natural parent is unlikely in practice to have a further role in a child's life. Further, there may be other situations when the welfare of the child justifies the exclusion of a natural parent. Abandonment, or persistent neglect or ill-treatment of the child, could be instances.

24. It is not surprising, therefore, that the exception stated in paragraph (b) ['some other reason'] is altogether open-ended. No doubt this was a deliberate choice of language. I can see no ground for importing into this exception an unexpressed limitation whereby 'some other reason' must be comparable with the death or disappearance of the other natural parent. What is required by paragraph (b), and all that is required, is that the reason, whatever it be, must be sufficient to justify the exclusion of the other parent. Whether any particular reason satisfies this test depends on the circumstances. This is a matter left to the decision of the court. On this question of interpretation I respectfully consider the Court of Appeal was unduly restrictive in its approach.

Lord Nicholls held that it would be in the child's best interests to make the adoption order thereby permanently excluding the child's mother from playing any further role in the child's life and giving the father the additional security he desired.[191]

Consent and leave to defend the adoption proceedings

In most cases, the issue of consent is unlikely to arise as the question will have been determined at the placement stage. The rather complicated provisions bearing on consent are contained in s 47.

Adoption and Children Act 2002, s 47

(1) An adoption order may not be made if the child has a parent or guardian unless one of the following conditions is met, but this section is subject to section 52.

(2) The first condition is that, in the case of each parent or guardian of the child, the court is satisfied—

(a) that the parent or guardian consents to the making of the adoption order,

(b) that the parent or guardian has consented under section 20 (and has not withdrawn the consent) and does not oppose the making of the adoption order, or

(c) that the parent's or guardian's consent should be dispensed with.

(3) A parent or guardian may not oppose the making of an adoption order under subsection 2(b) without the court's leave.

(4) The second condition is that—

---

[191] For further discussion, see below at pp 964–6.

(a) the child has been placed for adoption by an adoption agency with the prospective adopters in whose favour the order is proposed to be made,

(b) either—

(i) the child was placed for adoption with the consent of each parent or guardian and the consent of the mother was given when the child was at least six weeks old, or

(ii) the child was placed for adoption under a placement order, and

(c) no parent or guardian oppose the making of the adoption order.

(5) A parent or guardian may not oppose the making of an adoption order under the second condition without the court's leave.

(6) The third condition is that the child is free for adoption...[under the AA 1976].

(7) The court cannot give leave under subsection (3) or (5) unless satisfied that there has been a change in circumstances since the consent of the parent or guardian was given or, as the case may be, the placement order was made.

Section 47(4) deals with the position where the child was placed by an adoption agency. In such cases, the child will either have been placed with parental consent or pursuant to a placement order. Although s 47(4)(c) states that the order cannot be made if the adoption is opposed, s 47(5) provides that birth parents falling within this category of case will not be able to oppose the adoption without the court's leave.[192] Section 47(7) then goes on to provide that the court can only grant leave if satisfied there has been a change in circumstances since the consent was given or the placement order made.[193]

The relevance of the child's welfare to an application for leave under s 47(7) arose in *Re P (A Child) (Adoption Order: Leave to Oppose Making of Adoption Order)*.[194] The first question addressed by the Court of Appeal was whether the decision to grant leave was 'coming to a decision relating to the adoption of a child' thereby making the child's welfare the paramount consideration. In accordance with s 1(7) which provides that 'coming to a decision about granting leave in respect of any action (other than the initiation of proceedings)' is a decision relating to the adoption of a child, the Court of Appeal held that as an application for leave to defend the adoption order was *not* an application for leave to *initiate proceedings*, s 1(7) required the paramountcy principle to be applied:[195]

Re P (A Child) (Adoption Order: Leave to Oppose Making of Adoption Order)
[2007] EWCA Civ 616

WALL LJ:

26. In our judgment, analysis of the statutory language in sections 1 and 47 of the 2002 Act leads to the conclusion that an application for leave to defend adoption proceedings

---

[192] The parents will be notified of the proceedings and made respondents thereto. Family Procedure Rules 2010, r 14.3(1).

[193] The same restrictions on defending the adoption application apply under s 47(2)(b) where the birth parents gave advance consent to the adoption under s 20. If the parents wish to defend the proceedings, leave will be required in accordance with ss 47(3) and 47(7), the application to be determined in accordance with the principles set down in *Re P* and *Re B-S* below.

[194] [2007] EWCA Civ 616.

[195] Ibid, [19]–[21]. Cf where leave is sought to revoke a placement order discussed above at pp 941–2.

under section 47(5) of the 2002 Act involves a two stage process. First of all, the court has to be satisfied, on the facts of the case, that there has been a change in circumstances within section 47(7). If there has been no change in circumstances, that is the end of the matter, and the application fails. If, however, there has been a change in circumstances within section 47(7) then the door to the exercise of a judicial discretion to permit the parents to defend the adoption proceedings is opened, and the decision whether or not to grant leave is governed by section 1 of the 2002 Act. In other words, "the paramount consideration of the court must be the child's welfare throughout his life".

The Court of Appeal then expanded on what was meant by a 'change in circumstances':

30. . . . We do not think it permissible to put any gloss on the statute, or to read into it words which are not there. The change in circumstances since the placement order was made must, self-evidently and as a matter of statutory construction, relate to the grant of leave. It must equally be of a nature and degree sufficient, on the facts of the particular case, to open the door to the exercise of the judicial discretion to permit the parents to defend the adoption proceedings. In our judgment, however, the phrase "a change in circumstances" is not ambiguous . . .

31. . . . Furthermore, in our judgment, the importation of the word "significant" puts the test too high . . . The only limiting factor is that it must be a change in circumstances "since the placement order was made". Against this background, we do not think that any further definition of the change in circumstances involved is either possible or sensible.

32. We do, however, take the view that the test should not be set too high, because, as this case demonstrates, parents in the position of S's parents should not be discouraged either from bettering themselves or from seeking to prevent the adoption of their child by the imposition of a test which is unachievable. We therefore take the view that whether or not there has been a relevant change in circumstances must be a matter of fact to be decided by the good sense and sound judgment of the tribunal hearing the application.

Particularly in light of these words of caution regarding potential unfairness to the birth parents, making the child's welfare the paramount consideration on an application for leave to defend the proceedings may seem a little odd—this is, after all, a procedural hurdle and not the substantive hearing at which the child's welfare will clearly be determinative. Moreover, the Court of Appeal make clear that in determining the application for leave, there is no need for the court to conduct a full welfare inquiry with oral evidence and cross-examination.[196] Lord Justice Thorpe elaborated on this welfare stage of the inquiry in *Re W (A Child) (Adoption: Leave to Oppose)*, holding that at this discretionary stage the judge must have 'great regard to the impact of the grant of permission on the child within the context of the adoptive family' and such a step should not be taken unless the applicant 'demonstrates prospects of success that are not just fanciful'.[197] Lord Justice Thorpe suggested that it would only be in 'exceptionally rare circumstances' that the adoption could be halted in these circumstances.[198]

---

[196] Ibid, [53].
[197] *Re W (A Child) (Adoption: Leave to Oppose)* [2010] EWCA Civ 1535, [20].
[198] Ibid, [17].

Against the backdrop of growing concern amongst the senior family judiciary about the approach being adopted to non-consensual adoptions, the Court of Appeal revisited the correct test on applications for leave to defend in *Re B-S*. The President, giving the judgment of the court, retreated from any suggestion that leave would only be granted in 'exceptional' cases or that the test was a particularly 'stringent' one:

Re B-S (Children) (Adoption: Application of Threshold Criteria) [2013] EWCA Civ 1146

SIR JAMES MUNBY P:
Section 47(5) of the 2002 Act – fundamentals

68. We share...misgivings about Thorpe LJ's use of the phrase "exceptionally rare circumstances", as also about his use, followed by the President in *Re C*, of the word "stringent" to define or describe the test to be applied on an application under section 47(5). Both phrases are apt to mislead, with potentially serious adverse consequences. In the light of *Re B* [see above at pp 924–5] they convey quite the wrong message. Neither, in our judgment, any longer has any place in this context. Their use in relation to section 47(5) should cease.

70. Section 47(5) is intended to afford a parent in an appropriate case a meaningful remedy – and a remedy, we stress, that may enure for the benefit not merely of the parent but also of the child. Whilst we can understand what lay behind what Thorpe LJ said, we think that his use of the phrase "exceptionally rare circumstances" carries with it far too great a potential for misunderstanding, misapplication and indeed injustice for safety. The same, if in lesser measure, applies also to the word "stringent". Stringent, as we have said, is a word that appropriately describes the test that has to be surmounted before a non-consensual adoption can be sanctioned. It is not a word that comfortably describes the test that a parent has to meet in seeking to resist such an adoption.

71. Parliament intended section 47(5) to provide a real remedy. Unthinking reliance upon the concept of the "exceptionally rare" runs the risk – a very real and wholly unacceptable risk – of rendering section 47(5) nugatory and its protections illusory. Except in the fairly unusual case where section 47(4)(b)(i) applies, a parent applying under section 47(5) will always, by definition, be faced with the twin realities that the court has made both a care order and a placement order and that the child is now living with the prospective adopter. But, unless section 47(5) is to be robbed of all practical efficacy, none of those facts, even in combination, can of themselves justify the refusal of leave.

Section 47(5) of the 2002 Act – the proper approach

72. Subject only to one point which does not affect the substance, the law, in our judgment, was correctly set out by Wall LJ in *Re P*, though we fear it may on occasions have been applied too narrowly and indeed too harshly. The only qualification is that the exercise at the second stage is more appropriately described as one of judicial *evaluation* rather than as one involving mere *discretion*.

73. There is a two stage process. The court has to ask itself two questions: Has there been a change in circumstances? If so, should leave to oppose be given? In relation to the first question we think it unnecessary and undesirable to add anything to what Wall LJ said.

74. In relation to the second question – If there has been a change in circumstances, should leave to oppose be given? – the court will, of course, need to consider all the circumstances. The court will in particular have to consider two inter-related questions: one, the parent's

ultimate prospect of success if given leave to oppose; the other, the impact on the child if the parent is, or is not, given leave to oppose, always remembering, of course, that at this stage the child's welfare is paramount. In relation to the evaluation, the weighing and balancing, of these factors we make the following points:

i) Prospect of success here relates to the prospect of resisting the making of an adoption order, *not*, we emphasise, the prospect of ultimately having the child restored to the parent's care.

ii) For purposes of exposition and analysis we treat as two separate issues the questions of whether there has been a change in circumstances and whether the parent has solid grounds for seeking leave. Almost invariably, however, they will be intertwined; in many cases the one may very well follow from the other.

iii) Once he or she has got to the point of concluding that there has been a change of circumstances and that the parent has solid grounds for seeking leave, the judge must consider very carefully indeed whether the child's welfare really does necessitate the refusal of leave. The judge must keep at the forefront of his mind the teaching of *Re B*, in particular that adoption is the "last resort" and only permissible if "nothing else will do" and that, as Lord Neuberger emphasised, the child's interests include being brought up by the parents or wider family unless the overriding requirements of the child's welfare make that not possible. That said, the child's welfare is paramount.

iv) At this, as at all other stages in the adoption process, the judicial evaluation of the child's welfare must take into account *all* the negatives and the positives, *all* the pros and cons, of *each* of the two options, that is, either giving or refusing the parent leave to oppose. Here again, as elsewhere, the use of Thorpe LJ's 'balance sheet' is to be encouraged...

vi) As a general proposition, the greater the change in circumstances (assuming, of course, that the change is positive) and the more solid the parent's grounds for seeking leave to oppose, the more cogent and compelling the arguments based on the child's welfare must be if leave to oppose is to be refused.

vii) The mere fact that the child has been placed with prospective adopters cannot be determinative, nor can the mere passage of time. On the other hand, the older the child and the longer the child has been placed the greater the adverse impacts of disturbing the arrangements are likely to be.

viii) The judge must always bear in mind that what is paramount in every adoption case is the welfare of the child "throughout his life". Given modern expectation of life, this means that, with a young child, one is looking far ahead into a very distant future – upwards of eighty or even ninety years. Against this perspective, judges must be careful not to attach undue weight to the short term consequences for the child if leave to oppose is given...

ix) Almost invariably the judge will be pressed with the argument that leave to oppose should be refused, amongst other reasons, because of the adverse impact on the prospective adopters, and thus on the child, of their having to pursue a contested adoption application. We do not seek to trivialise an argument which may in some cases have considerable force, particularly perhaps in a case where the child is old enough to have some awareness of what is going on. But judges must be careful not to attach undue weight to the argument. After all, what from the perspective of the proposed adopters was the smoothness of the process which they no doubt anticipated when issuing their application with the assurance of a placement order, will already have been disturbed by the unwelcome making of the application for leave to oppose....

> x) We urge judges always to bear in mind the wise and humane words of Wall LJ in *Re P*,
> para 32. We have already quoted them but they bear repetition: "the test should not be
> set too high, because . . . parents . . . should not be discouraged either from bettering them-
> selves or from seeking to prevent the adoption of their child by the imposition of a test
> which is unachievable."

If the parents' application for leave is refused, the adoption application will be unopposed, thus satisfying the necessary conditions for making an adoption order. If the parents' application is successful, both the child's welfare and the issue of parental consent will fall to be fully re-litigated.[199]

In all other cases (i.e. step-parent adoptions and private placements), consent will not have been dealt with at an earlier stage of the proceedings and will thus fall to be determined at the final hearing. Section 47 thus provides that the court will only be able to make the adoption order if satisfied that the birth parents consent to the adoption or that their consent should be dispensed with in accordance with the terms of s 52.[200]

Welfare

Making an adoption order is clearly a 'decision relating to the adoption of a child'. The welfare principle in s 1(2) therefore applies and the child's welfare must be the court's paramount consideration. That said, as most applications will now be unopposed it is difficult to envisage many cases in which the adoption order will be refused. Under the previous legislation, almost 97 per cent of contested adoption applications were successful.[201] As Ryburn notes, although adoption is the final decision in a 'cumulative process where there were many other decisions along the way', it is difficult to imagine any other area of the law where the odds are so highly stacked against one party to the dispute.[202]

13.6 IN THE BEST INTERESTS OF THE CHILD? CONTROVERSIAL ISSUES

Although the birth parents face several obstacles in resisting an adoption, the court must still be satisfied both at the placement stage and at the final hearing that the adoption is in the child's best interests. In determining whether a child should be adopted a number of particularly controversial questions have dominated the case law.

13.6.1 BIRTH FAMILY V THE 'PERFECT' ADOPTIVE COUPLE

At the heart of many contested adoptions is the question of whether a child should be raised within the birth family, preferably by the parents, or be given the opportunity to start a new

---

[199] *Re B-S (Children) (Adoption: Application of Threshold Criteria)* [2013] EWCA Civ 1146.
[200] See 13.4.2 above.
[201] Ryburn (1998a), 56.
[202] Ibid.

life with the adoptive parents. A contested adoption thus raises in stark form the value to be placed on 'genetic' as opposed to 'social' or 'psychological' parenting. We have seen within the context of disputes over where a child should live how the law has tended to favour biological over social parenting.[203] The key factors justifying the 'natural parent presumption' in such disputes are particularly important in disputes concerning adoption. For example, the need to protect the child's developing sense of identity takes on particular significance when the order being sought will extinguish all legal ties with the birth family. Concerns over the dangers of 'social engineering' also take on a particular resonance when the birth parents, with all their problems and inadequacies, are facing competing claims from an adoptive couple who will have successfully come through a difficult and far-reaching vetting procedure.

The child's right to be brought up by his or her birth family has, in the past, formed the starting point for determining a contested adoption. This was made clear by Butler-Sloss LJ in *Re K (Private Placement for Adoption)*.[204] The case concerned a private arrangement between the birth parents and the prospective adopters which was entered into shortly after the child's birth and at a time when the birth mother was under enormous stress. The birth parents changed their mind and sought to have the child returned to their care. At the time of the hearing the child had been in the prospective adopters' care for seven-and-a-half months. The Court of Appeal returned the child to her parents.

Re K (Private Placement for Adoption) [1991] FCR 142 (CA), 147–8

BUTLER-SLOSS LJ:

The mother must be shown to be entirely unsuitable before another family can be considered, otherwise we are in grave danger of slipping into social engineering. The question is not: would the child be better off with the plaintiffs? But: is the natural family so unsuitable that... "the welfare of the child positively demanded the displacement of the parental right?" I agree...that it is the right of the child rather than the parent and, borrowing from the philosophy of the Children Act 1989, I would rephrase it as the displacement of the parental responsibility. Once the Judge found that this mother genuinely wanted her child back and was a mother who cared properly for the other two children, not to give her at least an opportunity to try to rehabilitate the family was to deprive the child of any chance of her own family.

The courts' preference for the birth parents has also extended to the wider kinship network.[205] It was held in *Re L (A Minor) (Care Proceedings: Wardship)* that the local authority should look first to the extended family for alternative care before considering stranger adoption. In determining whether members of the birth family are suitable, the court emphasized that adoption should not be regarded as a 'panacea' and that sometimes the known risks of the birth family would be preferable to the unknown risks of adoption.

---

[203] See 11.6.7.

[204] See also *Re O (A Minor) (Custody or Adoption)* [1992] 1 FCR 378.

[205] Ryburn contends that this is contrary to prevailing social work practice where the 'zero-cost' of stranger adoption is preferred. See Ryburn (1998b), 37.

Re L (A Minor) (Care Proceedings: Wardship) (No 2) [1991] 1 FLR 29
(Crown Court), 36–8

JUDGE WILLIS:

The whole crux of this case depends on how much weight should be given to the various 'pros' and 'cons' for the two alternative courses for this child, namely, going to the grand-parents or being adopted. We received the impression from the guardian, as we did from the local authority witnesses also, that they are far too keen on adoption and consider it the panacea for all problems. They all expressed a number of concerns or problems which might arise in the maternal grandparents' extended family if K [the child] is there. None of them envisaged any real problem in adoption in a child of this age. The impression they tried to give was that, as in every good fairy story, after placement, 'everyone lives happily ever after'...

The local authority's case is that there are far too many problems if K goes back to the family, i.e. to grandparents, and that a fresh start with adoption is a less risky course. K will be 'grafted' into a new family with the absence of access problems. This argument, however, fails to address the considerable problems which are more likely to arise in adoption, namely the psychological worry of who and what her family are, why she is not with them and why she was adopted...The great advantage in staying with the wider family is that the child maintains her roots. We consider this a very important aspect which has been totally ignored by the local authority and also by the guardian ad litem...[A]doption should only be the last resort when no one in the wider family is available and suitable to look after a child. Parentage is not always perfect, but parentage in the family is preferable to the unknown risks of adoption...We consider that every child has a right, whenever it is possible, to be brought up in its own genetic family. That right should not be taken away from it except in the last resort when there are strong, cogent and positive reasons for so doing. All the local authority's arguments are based on concerns which may or may not happen. Even if they did, the risk to K, we feel, would be less than the risks inherent in adoption.

The decision of the Court of Appeal in *C v X, Y, Z Council* questioned whether this 'privileging' of the birth family could be reconciled with a straightforward application of the welfare principle.[206] However, the importance of the birth family was reiterated by *Re B* and *Re B-S* (discussed in detail above), both of which firmly and unequivocally returned the law to the clear principle that the birth family must only be displaced by an order for adoption when adoption is 'required' or 'demanded' by the child's welfare—when nothing else will do.

Even given this entrenched respect for the right of the child to be raised whenever possible within the family of birth, there will, however, be very few cases in which the birth parents are successful in opposing the adoption.[207] The explanation for this lies in the strength of the countervailing considerations in a typical contested adoption where there will usually be a long history of serious and persistent failings in parenting. Even where there are no such failings, such as where the birth father was unaware of the child, the court is often faced with the problem of what amounts, in effect, to a *fait accompli*: by the time of the adoption hearing the child has been living with the adoptive parents for a substantial period of time and strong emotional bonds have developed between them. Where the child is strongly attached to the adoptive parents the courts are extremely reluctant to disrupt this position. In *Re O*

---

[206] [2007] EWCA Civ 1206.
[207] Ryburn (1998a), 56.

(Adoption: Withholding Agreement) the strong attachment which had developed between the child and the prospective adopters was held to constitute a compelling factor capable of displacing the preference for the birth family, even though the father, who had not been told of the child's existence, was perfectly capable of offering the child a secure and stable home.[208] Empirical research suggests that this reluctance to break the child's bond with the alternative carers is well founded. Dyer, for example, argues that breaking the bond between the child and the child's primary attachment figures, whether those attachments are to the birth or psychological parents, can have serious adverse consequences. He points to various empirical studies which link 'disturbed or disrupted attachment to personality disorders; poor functioning in the parental role as an adult; alcoholism; criminality; and sexual offending'.[209] However, against this, the court has to balance equally compelling evidence regarding the problems often suffered by adopted adolescents in developing a secure and positive sense of identity.[210] These are difficult cases to which there are no easy answers.

13.6.2 TRANS-RACIAL ADOPTION

Concerns over the child's developing sense of identity are particularly strong when there are ethnic, cultural, or religious factors involved. Indeed, no issue causes greater division within adoption.[211] Advocates on both sides of the debate can be particularly dogmatic in their approach.

Opponents of trans-racial adoption have focused on two key problems: (i) the difficulties ethnic minority children face in developing a strong, positive ethnic identity when placed in a white household; and (ii) the inability of the child's carers to help the child cope with the racism still endemic within British society. Goldstein's interview with John Small, a key opponent of trans-racial adoption and a leading figure in the development of social work policy on this issue during the 1980s, reveals the thinking behind current opposition to trans-racial placements:

B. Goldstein, 'Ethnicity and Placement. Beginning the Debate', (2000) 24
Adoption and Fostering 9, 9–10

The thing which is important to my mind is the psychological damage that is likely to occur when the identities of children are not recognised. For example, if you have a child from a West Indian, African [or] Indian background and they claim that their colour is another [ie white], that must be some deep psychological scar. They look into the mirror and what they see they don't like, and the reason why they don't like that is a direct result of what's happening to them in the social world that they are in. It is the question of what society is doing to children whose personalities are in the process of being formed and are actually influenced by what they see, bearing in mind that they develop their ideas and attitudes and they are shaped by the people with whom they interact.

---

[208] [1999] 2 FCR 262. For a more recent example, see *Re Q (Adoption)* [2012] EWCA Civ 1610, albeit there were additional welfare concerns in that case regarding the child moving to live with the father and his wife.

[209] Dyer (2004), 11.

[210] See detailed discussion at 9.4.4.

[211] We are typically talking here about placing black or Asian children in white households: a problem which is exacerbated by the low number of prospective adopters from black or Asian communities. DH (2000), para 6.4.

The psychological research has shown us about self and what constitutes self and how our self-image is derivative of the messages we obtain from significant others. So if society has this negative view of particular ethnic groups and transmits this through the media, through television, through the radio, through the print media, through the attitudes in society, through the attitudes of other children in the playground, those kinds of images come through. Identity is something you internalise from a range of things as you go through life, not something you search for later. This is why the messages parents and society give are important. You have to be very conscious of this with a black child in a racist society. Some white parents, they don't think that is important. They think love is enough—perhaps in a non-racist society but we certainly haven't reached that stage yet...

I realise that some well-meaning, white middle-class people tend to ignore the effects of racism because they can't understand the implications of racism for the black population generally. That leads them to deny that racism exists and, once they deny that, it is unlikely that they will be able to explain these things to their children or to the child that they have adopted.

As Hayes explains, opponents of trans-racial adoption have tried to shift the debate away from arguments that can be attacked as ideologically or politically driven because of their association with 'black identity politics', focusing instead on the individualized interests of the child. Opponents of trans-racial adoption have emphasized that it is the particular vulnerability of ethnic minority children in a racist society and the 'experience-based skills' of black and other ethnic minority parents in dealing with such issues—not their 'biological essences'—that make them the preferred carers for these children.[212]

It is, however, difficult to escape ideologically based arguments when issues of race and ethnicity are in question. Underlying disagreements about trans-racial adoption are fundamentally different 'world-views' on issues such as: the importance of racial identity in a liberal western society, whether ethnic identity is an innate or chosen characteristic, and whether or not it is accurate to describe contemporary British society as inherently racist. Hayes is a strong advocate of trans-racial adoption based on a clear philosophical commitment to a 'colour-blind' vision of life.[213]

P. Hayes, 'Giving Due Consideration to Ethnicity in Adoption Placements—A Principled Approach', (2003) 15 *Child and Family Law Quarterly* 255, 260–2

[A]ttempts at ethnic matching demonstrate a naïve understanding of ethnicity and culture that is every bit as flawed as the idea that all people who are not white can be simply lumped together as 'black'.

Three mistaken assumptions underlie precise ethnic matching: first, it is assumed that ethnic culture is a natural inheritance rather than a conventional construct; secondly, a minority child's culture is invariably assumed to be exclusive and particular to one ethnic group rather than being universally accessible; and thirdly, ethnic cultures are conceived of in essential, rather than nominal, terms.

---

[212] Goldstein (2000), 14 and Flynn (2000).
[213] See also Patel (2007), esp at 33. Patel argues against an 'essentialist view' of racial identity, contending that racial identity is 'flexible' and 'fluid' and that the individual is able 'to construct for themselves multiple racial identities'.

Nature and convention

Advocates of ethnic matching assume that the cultural elements of a child's ethnicity are passed down rather like genes so that they form a hereditary and predetermined element of the child's make-up. Religions, for example, are not defined as universally accessible communities that people might either enter and leave through choice or become acculturated to as they grow up. Instead, it is assumed that it is somehow natural for a child to inherit the religion of the birth parents or grandparents, whether or not the child has been raised in that religion. This is referred to, misleadingly, as the 'right' and 'need' of the child to belong to a particular religion. In fact, it is nothing to do with the child's individual rights, but is rather a collectivist argument that religiously defined communities can lay claim to a child as one of their own...

Particularism and universalism

Advocates of ethnic matching ignore cultural attributes that are universally accessible in favour of ones that are particular to a single ethnic culture. Culture is always viewed by such advocates as something that divides people, never as something that brings them together. But often culture unites people of different ethnic origins, for example, the character sketches of children advertised for adoption mention commonplace interests and pursuits such as football or pop music. These universally accessible pastimes are, in fact, part of these children's culture, although, as they are not associated with any one particular ethnic group, they are not conceived of as culture by those who favour ethnic matching.

Essentialism and nominalism

Ethnic cultures are not fixed concepts with discrete boundaries. Making essentialist distinctions between ethnic cultures ignores the way in which cultures can blend and change; ignores cultural synthesis, and fails to see that the components of culture are multifaceted so that people who nominally share the same ethnic culture may engage in diverse patterns of living. Culture is not tied to race. People of different races may share the same culture, while people who are racially similar may adopt different cultures. This cultural nominalism is not recognised by advocates of ethnic matching. The failings of the essentialist understanding of ethnic culture are particularly apparent in its inchoate response to the placement of mixed-race children. The culture of mixed-race children—like all minority children—is never seen as transcending their racial heritage, but is rather reduced to it. For mixed-race children this means breaking down their supposed culture into a set of discrete components derived from their various ancestors. Mixed-race children are then told to take pride in the ethnic mix within themselves, while at the same time any further mixing into a transracial placement is said to be potentially damaging to them.

Ethnic identity versus 'colour-blind' human beings

One difference between trans-racially adopted children and inracially adopted children has been singled out for particular criticism by advocates of ethnic matching. Transracially adopted children have often been found to be somewhat more likely to describe themselves as human beings first and foremost, or as taking a 'colour-blind' approach in their social relationships. This is a reasonable and viable way of defining yourself and others. It is, for example, a perspective by no means uncommon among minority adults who appear to be perfectly well-adjusted...

To be colour-blind is to assess each individual on his or her own merits. People who are colour-blind believe that generalisations about an ethnic group a person belongs to may well tell you little or nothing about what he or she is like as an individual. They also believe that a person's colour is not an intrinsic bar to achievement, and that neither should there be any bar to relationships between people of different colours, including the deepest marital and family relationships.

The idea of being colour-blind is closely associated with the philosophy of individualism. Those who adopt the colour-blind approach to life have neither reason nor tendency to assume that everyone else in society, or indeed their own children, necessarily thinks the same way that they do about ethnicity. Such an assumption of uniform thinking is quite at odds with the individualist insistence that people are able to make up their own minds about such issues. It is, therefore, incorrect to suggest that to be colour-blind is to assume that no one is racist, or that everyone takes the view that colour is irrelevant. However, advocates of ethnic matching appear to think that because they are fixated with issues of ethnicity, then so is everyone else, and it may be that they attribute to colour-blind parents their own faulty logic.

Advocates of trans-racial adoption have further stressed the absence of any empirical evidence to support the perceived problems caused by trans-racial placements.[214] The empirical evidence is, however, limited and the conclusions drawn somewhat tentative. On the basis of a review carried out of studies in the UK and the United States, Rushton and Minnis conclude that adoption breakdown rates are determined by age at placement rather than the type of placement and that 'developmental outcomes of transracially placed children appear to be good for the majority in terms of educational attainment, peer relations and behaviour'.[215] They also point out, however, that methodological flaws with the various studies preclude definitive conclusions.[216] The conclusions drawn by Moffat and Thoburn from a review of the existing literature and their own study of 254 ethnic minority children are similarly qualified, although again they find no significant evidence of harm resulting from trans-racial placements.

P. Moffatt and J. Thoburn, 'Outcomes of Permanent Family Placement for Children of Minority Ethnic Origin', (2001) 6 *Child and Family Social Work* 13, 14, 18, and 20

The majority of placements of children of minority ethnic origin were successful, at least in the sense that the young people remained in placement. This applied irrespective of gender, of whether they were of mixed race parentage or had two parents of the same ethnic background, and of whether they were placed in ethnically matched families or transracially. However, a worrying minority of the children experienced placement breakdown. The explanations for the success or otherwise of the placements appear broadly similar to those for white children. For the sample as a whole, no difference was found in breakdown rates between those placed in 'matched' and in 'transracial' placements...

Our qualitative data indicate that not all placements which last are successful when other outcome measures such as well-being, satisfaction or ethnic pride are the outcome measures

---

[214] Hayes (2003), 256–7 and 268; Simon and Altstein (1996).
[215] Rushton and Minnis (2000), 53.
[216] Ibid.

used. From a combination of the qualitative and the quantitative data we concluded that some white families can successfully parent children of a different ethnic origin, including helping them to combat the adverse effects of racism and feel pride in their appearance, culture and heritage. However, compared with the parents of minority ethnic origin, they have additional tasks to negotiate, and the job they have to do in parenting a child who has already suffered adversity and at least one separation and rejection is difficult enough without making it more difficult. We thus concur with the preference expressed in the UN Convention on the Rights of the Child, the Hague Convention on Inter-country Adoption and the England and Wales Children Act 1989 for children to be placed whenever possible with families from their own local or wider communities. But our data emphasize that placements in 'matched' families are also vulnerable to disruption and that long-term support must be available if the chances of success are to improve.

On the basis of the current available evidence, the majority of researchers thus remain cautious about trans-racial placements, concluding that, despite the absence of any positive evidence that trans-racial adoption is harmful, 'matched' placements provide better safeguards against feelings of ostracism and identity confusion and should therefore be the preferred option where available.[217]

The ACA 2002 as originally implemented sought to strike this balance between giving preference to 'matched' placements whilst not denying a black or ethnic minority (BME) child the benefits of adoption where matching was not possible:

Adoption and Children Act 2002, s 1

(5) In placing the child for adoption, the adoption agency must give due consideration to the child's religious persuasion, racial origin and cultural and linguistic background.

However, problems arose with the practical implementation of this policy. The preference for matched placements sat uneasily with the drive to eradicate delay. In practice, due to the small number of approved ethnic minority adopters, it was very difficult for the local authority to find suitable 'matched' placements within the prescribed timescales for decision-making and placement.[218] The Narey Report identified ethnic matching as a particularly pernicious cause of delay in the adoption of BME children:

M. Narey, 'The Narey Report: A Blueprint for the Nation's Lost Children', *The Times*, 5 July 2011

We live in an increasingly multicultural society and one where quite properly, the stereotyping of people because of their race is discouraged... The UK has moved on. But not in the case of adoption where there is, in my view, a continuing, unjustified obsession with ethnicity....

The now long established determination to find the right ethnic match for a child is, I would argue, based on a dubious emphasis on the significance of culture and heritage – particularly

---

[217] See also Kirton, Feast, and Howe (2000).

[218] As to the reasons why there are currently so few prospective adopters from ethnic minority communities, see Frazer and Selwyn (2005) and Sunmonu (2000).

when we are talking about a baby – and is certainly and demonstrably damaging to black and mixed-race children, where delay is persistent and unacceptable....

However well-intentioned the actions of practitioners in seeking a close or perfect ethnic match for a child...the consequences for BME children are incontrovertible....[T]hey face an adoption apartheid. White children in care are three times more likely to be adopted than black children.

Black as opposed to BME children fare particularly badly....[T]he option that we know offers the best prospects for a child's future, adoption, is extended to only about 10 per cent of black children leaving care and only about 15 per cent of Asian children, while 35 per cent of white children leaving care become adopted...

The reality is that the overarching warning against the damaging consequences of delay – based on a wealth of research – has for some years now been ignored in favour of a rigid interpretation of the ethnicity and cultural provisions in the Act, the effect of which is to leave black and Asian children languishing in care....

In light of the perceived delays caused by this apparent 'obsession' with ethnic matching the government decided (but only extending to England) to revoke s 1(5) of the ACA 2002.[219] This legislative amendment did not meet with widespread support. It was first argued that the 'problem' had been wrongly identified. The evidence on which Narey and the government relied in support of its case for reform was challenged as much more nuanced than suggested. Indeed, the Joint Committee on Human Rights concluded that the evidence relied on by the government (which showed Asian children taking on average less time to be adopted than white children), 'not only fails to support but positively undermines its justification for repealing the statutory requirement'.[220] Whilst acknowledging that recent research had identified ethnicity as a cause of delay in the adoption of BME children, particularly black children, the House of Lords Select Committee on Adoption pointed out that it was the *age* of the children which was found to be a more significant factor than ethnicity and inflexible social work practice:

House of Lords Select Committee on Adoption Legislation, 1st Report of Session 2012–13, *Adoption: Pre-Legislative Scrutiny. Report*, HL Paper 94 (London: TSO, 2012)

65. Overall, recent research has suggested a number of potential reasons for the delay in placing some BME children. Age remains the most important predictive factor. The search for an 'ideal' matched placement may be a factor in some cases. There is, however, also evidence from the recent research of flexibility in adoption agencies' approach to matching. A key finding in Professor Farmer's study[221] was that "29% of BME children were placed with families whose characteristics did not match their ethnicity, often in order to secure a placement for children with complex needs where the need to place was considered more important that finding an 'ideal' match".

66. Evidence from those working in adoption did not reveal wide-spread concern about current practice...

---

[219] CFA 2014, s 3. See DFE (2012b), 21–2.
[220] Joint Committee on Human Rights (2013), paras 24–8.
[221] Famer et al (2010).

Whilst questioning whether a rigid approach to ethnicity was the real cause of the problem,[222] the Select Committee also voiced strong concern about the 'solution':

> 72. Section 1 (4)(d) of the Act requires the court or adoption agency to have regard "to the child's age, sex, background and any of the child's characteristics which the court or agency considers relevant" (often referred to as the 'welfare checklist'). The Government have made clear their belief that this provision will allow considerations of race, religion, culture and language to be taken into account, once section 1(5) no longer applies.
>
> 73. This belief is not shared by all those who work in the sector. There is concern about the message this legislative change could send out to social workers on the ground. BAAF [British Association for Adoption and Fostering] pointed to Article 20 of the United Nations Convention on the Rights of the Child, which states that: "Children who cannot be looked after by their own family have a right to special care and must be looked after properly, by people who respect their ethnic group, religion, culture and language." They argued that a child's identity was an important part of their development, and that the four factors identified in Article 20 were an important part of that identity. BAAF considered that Article 20 and section 1(5) embodied this 'widely acknowledged' principle. In their view the proposal for section 1(5) to not apply in England brought with it a risk that these important considerations of identity would be neglected when making decisions for adoption matching....
>
> 77. We accept that it is important to ensure that appropriate weight is given to religion, race, language and culture when making adoption matches. However, we believe that the Government need to give further consideration to the practical effect of the proposed change to section 1(5) of the Adoption and Children Act 2002 on social work culture and practice...
>
> 79. We appreciate that the Government believe that section 1(5) has given a perception of prominence to considerations of ethnicity and that this has resulted in more weight being attached to ethnicity than some of the other factors identified at 1(4). The Government are concerned with ensuring that the appropriate weight is given to ethnicity, and to avoid any suggestion that legislation places consideration of religion, race, culture or language above the factors in s 1(2) to 1(4).
>
> 80. In order to attach the appropriate weight to considerations of religion, race, culture and language, we believe that these factors should be considered alongside those identified at 1(4)....
>
> 81. Placing the factors embodied in section 1(5) alongside the other elements of the welfare checklist at 1(4) will rule out any suggestion of prominence or pre-eminence for any one attribute, and will therefore meet the Government's stated aim. To remove mention of religion, race, culture and language altogether will run the risk of these important factors of identity being neglected in matching decisions.[223]

The government rejected this recommendation and pressed ahead with revoking s 1(5). Only time will tell what impact, if any, it will have on the adoption of BME children.

---

[222] See also Selwyn et al (2008) which concluded that whilst an overly narrow approach to matching may have contributed to problems in successfully placing BME children, age was the most important predictive factor as to whether a child was adopted or not. Notably black children were much older when they first became looked after than white, Asian, or mixed ethnicity children. Shortage of ethnic minority adopters remains a key problem.

[223] Joint Committee on Human Rights (2013), paras 29–33.

13.6.3 STEP-PARENT ADOPTION

Step-parent adoptions now account for just 5 per cent of the total number of annual adoptions.[224] The declining popularity of step-parent adoption is not surprising. During the 1970s, step-parent adoptions were seen by many as a natural means of consolidating and supporting a new family unit following divorce or separation. Reinforced by the 'clean break philosophy' underpinning divorce and a more ambivalent attitude towards the role of the father in the post-divorce context, it was thought by some that the child's interests would be better protected within the security and stability of the new nuclear family. The interests of the new family unit were thus prioritized, with the maintenance of links with the non-resident parent, invariably the father, viewed as potentially destabilizing, adding to the pressures on the new family and preventing it from firmly establishing itself as a 'normal', autonomous unit. However, even at this time, there were some strong concerns about the widespread use of step-parent adoption to exclude the non-resident parent from the child's life.[225]

Concerns about step-parent adoption strengthened as the important changes in family policy underpinning the CA 1989 became entrenched. The clean break model of divorce became supplanted by an ideal of cooperative joint parenting post-separation, supported by the enduring nature of parental responsibility and a strong presumption in favour of continuing contact with the non-resident parent. As Neale and Smart explain, the model of the reconstituted nuclear family was replaced by that of the bi-nuclear family spread across two households.[226] These key policy changes were reinforced by a fundamental reorientation of the welfare discourse such that the child's best interests were no longer viewed as resting primarily with the new family unit but in preserving strong healthy relationships with both sides of the birth family. These policy changes are fundamentally inconsistent with using adoption to sever irrevocably the child's relationship with the non-resident parent.

Cases in which step-parent adoption will be sanctioned are thus likely to be unusual. Section 8 orders can confer the desired security on the new family unit and regulate any problematic behaviour by the non-resident parent. The fact that the CA 1989 now allows a step-parent to acquire free-standing parental responsibility further reduces the need to resort to adoption—although, surprisingly, unlike applications for adoption under the ACA 2002, only married or civil partners of a birth parent can take advantage of these provisions.[227]

That is not to say, however, that a step-parent adoption will never be found to be in the child's best interests. It will depend on the particular circumstances of the case. McFarlane LJ has recently provided clear guidance on the approach to be taken to step-parent adoptions under domestic law.[228] Most notably, he distinguishes step-parent adoptions from non-consensual adoptions outside the family and holds that the high threshold which applies in the latter case ('nothing else will do') is not to be applied to the former. As his judgment makes clear, in his view step-parent adoptions are very often a much less drastic interference with family life than non-consensual adoptions outside the family and do not

---

[224] MOJ (2014a), 23.
[225] *Re B (A Minor) (Adoption by Parent)* [1975] Fam 127, esp 143 and 146.
[226] Neale and Smart (1999), 37.
[227] CA 1989, s 4A. See 10.3.4.
[228] The Strasbourg jurisprudence is contained in *Söderbäck v Sweden* (App No 113/1997/897/1109, ECHR) (1998). The European Court of Human Rights held that a step-parent adoption does not necessarily violate the rights of the non-adopting parent.

therefore require the same high degree of justification. Whether that is correct will clearly depend on the individual circumstances of each case. On the facts of *Re P*, the mother's partner was seeking to adopt her two children aged 14 and 12. The father of one of the boys had abandoned them shortly after birth; the other had not seen his son since the parents divorced and the mother relocated from Poland several years before:

Re P (A Child) (Adoption: Step-Parent) [2014] EWCA Civ 1174

McFARLANE LJ:

22. In a single applicant step-parent adoption case under the ACA 2002 regime, such as the present case, the result of these various provisions is that if a step-parent adoption order is made:

a) The child is treated as if born as a child of the step-parent [ACA 2002, s 67(1)];

b) Is to be treated in law as not being the child of any person other than the step-parent adopter and the natural parent who is that step-parent's partner [s 67(3)(a)];

c) The natural parent who is not the step-parent's partner (i.e. A's [the child's] natural father in the present case) has any parental responsibility for the child extinguished [s 46(2)(a)]; and

d) The adopter gains parental responsibility for the child [s 46(1)].

46. In an adoption application the key to the approach both to evaluating the needs of a child's welfare throughout his or her life and to dispensing with parental consent is proportionality. The strong statements made by the Justices of the Supreme Court in *Re B*...to the effect that adoption will be justified only where 'nothing else will do' are made in the context of an adoption being imposed upon a family against the wishes of the child's parents and where the adoption will totally remove the child from any future contact with, or legal relationship with, any of his natural relatives. Although the statutory provisions applicable to such an adoption (in particular ACA 2002, s 1 regarding welfare and s 52 regarding consent) apply in precisely the same terms to a step-parent adoption, the manner in which those provisions fall to be applied may differ and will depend upon the facts of each case and the judicial assessment of proportionality.

47. By way of example, in a child protection case where it is clear that rehabilitation to the parents is not compatible with their child's welfare, the court may be faced with a choice between adoption by total strangers selected by the local authority acting as an adoption agency or adoption by other family members. There is a qualitative difference between these two options in terms of the degree to which the outcome will interfere with the ECHR, Art 8 rights to family life of the child and his parents; adoption by strangers being at the extreme end of the spectrum of interference and adoption by a family member being at a less extreme point on the scale. The former option is only justified when 'nothing else will do', whereas the latter option, which involves a lower degree of interference, may be more readily justified.

48. Where an adoption application is made by a step-parent, the approach of the ECtHR in *Söderbäck v Sweden* should be applied according to the facts of each case. In doing so the following central points from the judgment in *Söderbäck* are likely to be important:

a) There is a distinction to be drawn between adoption in the context of compulsory, permanent placement outside the family against the wishes of parents (for example as in *Johansen v Norway*) and a step-parent adoption where, by definition, the child is remaining in the care of one or other of his parents;

b) Factors which are likely to reduce the degree of interference with the Art 8 rights of the child and the non-consenting parent ['Parent B'], and thereby make it more likely that adoption is a proportionate measure are:

i) Where Parent B has not had the care of the child or otherwise asserted his or her responsibility for the child;

ii) Where Parent B has had only infrequent or no contact with the child;

iii) Where there is a particularly well established family unit in the home of the parent and step-parent in which 'de facto' family ties have existed for a significant period.

49. In so far as the earlier domestic cases to which I have made reference establish that, in the event of Parent B being actively opposed to a step-parent adoption, practical arrangements should be dealt with by private law orders, that approach is entirely at one with the modern private law relating to children which seeks to determine aspects of the delivery of child-care and the discharge of parental responsibility either by parental agreement or by a child arrangements order under CA 1989, s 8.

50. The making of an adoption order is primarily, if not entirely, concerned with the legal status of the relationships between the child, his natural parent(s) and the adopter(s), rather than practical arrangements . . .

52. . . . [I]n the present application the detriment, in ECHR Art 8 terms, to each of these two children and their fathers of extinguishing their respective legal relationships is modest. The interference with Art 8 family life rights here is of an altogether lower level of intervention to that which is typically involved where the proposed adoption is by non-family members with all familial relationships being extinguished against the will of parents with whom the children have a real and active relationship . . .

54. . . . Caution is therefore required in reading [*Re P (Children) (Adoption: Parental Consent)*— discussed above at p 922–3] in the context of a step-parent adoption, albeit that the statutory test in s 52 is precisely the same for both categories of adoption. The reason for caution is that, whilst the statutory wording is the same, the degree of interference with family life and evaluation of proportionality under Article 8 are likely to be different . . .

61. . . . [T]he context of the particular case will be of particular significance: where on the spectrum of intervention by adoption does this case sit? In broad terms the spectrum will run from a fully opposed, public law 'stranger' adoption at one extreme, to an adoption within the child's existing 'de facto' family unit, which is made with the consent of both parents. In between there will be step-parent adoptions which are actively opposed by 'Parent B', who is himself fully involved in the life of his child, or step-parent adoptions, like the present, where Parent B, whilst not consenting, has played no active parental role for some years.

62. The reason why context is important is that, in each case, it is necessary to evaluate the proportionality of the intervention in family life that is being proposed. For the child, and for the child's welfare throughout his life, there will be a qualitative difference between adoption by strangers, with no continuing contact or legal relationship with any member of the birth family, on the one hand, and an adoption order which simply reflects in legal terms the reality in which the child's family life and relationships have been conducted for some significant time. In ECHR terms, no adoption order will be justified in terms of its interference with family life rights unless it is 'necessary' and 'proportionate', but in assessing those factors the degree to which there is an interference will be relevant. In short, in the present case, the loss to A, and the loss to her father, of his legal status as her father who holds parental responsibility for her, interferes with their respective family life rights to a relatively modest degree. In contrast, if the social services were to intervene and seek to remove her from the care of her mother and Mr TMI [the step-parent] by compulsory order to place her for adoption with strangers, the degree of interference would be extreme.

63. The judge in the present case was correct to approach the interpretation of 'requires' in s 52(1)(b) by reference to the 'connotation of imperative' that it has... But what is 'required'' varies from case to case and is firmly grounded, by the very words of s 52(1)(b), upon an evaluation of the child's welfare throughout his life. The use of the phrase 'connotation of imperative' in *Re P* does not mean (see *Re P* paragraph 127) that there is some enhanced welfare test to be applied in cases of adoption...

67. It follows that I do not agree that the judge was constrained by the words of the statute, as he considered that he was, to refuse to dispense with consent. I also consider that his decision on ordinary welfare terms was wrong. The finding that, as a matter of day to day existence, A's family life would continue in much the same way and that there were other routes by which Mr TMI might gain parental responsibility, failed to engage with the benefit that adoption would bring by marrying up the legal relationships with the 'de facto' relationships as they had become established within this small family unit. In almost every way Mr TMI had become A's and D's father. The making of an adoption order would confirm that status as a matter of law.

13.6.4 ADOPTION BY A SOLE NATURAL PARENT

Many of the concerns regarding step-parent adoption apply with added force in the case of an adoption by a sole natural parent. The only real remaining advantage of adopting one's own child, from the perspective of the adopting parent, is that it confers additional security on the resident parent by permanently terminating the parental responsibility of the non-adopting parent. It is thus an effective means of ensuring the non-resident parent can play no future role in the child's upbringing. The advantages of such an order from the child's perspective are more difficult to discern. Again, however, there will be some cases in which such an order is deemed to be in the child's best interests. In *Re B (A Minor) (Adoption: Natural Parent)*, the House of Lords controversially allowed an adoption order in favour of the child's natural father to stand. The facts of the case were relatively unusual in that the mother, having voluntarily relinquished the child at birth, wanted nothing more to do with her. The father discovered the child's existence by chance and immediately assumed responsibility for her care. The mother did not oppose his application to adopt.

Re B (A Minor) (Adoption: Natural Parent) [2001] UKHL 70

LORD NICHOLLS:

5. The father is seeking an adoption order primarily because he is anxious to secure A's future in his sole care. He feels insecure, and believes he will feel more secure knowing that the mother's parental responsibility for A has been removed. This can only be achieved by an adoption order. The mother has said repeatedly she does not wish to play any part in A's life. But the father is concerned that, without an adoption order, it will remain possible in future years for the mother to pose a threat to A's continued placement with him. He is concerned that the mother may marry and, with her new husband, ask to have A to live with her. The court might look favourably upon such an application. His vulnerability to an attempt by the mother to reclaim A is something which has caused him great anxiety. He is adamant in his

wish for an adoption order, although whatever order is made will not affect the strength of his commitment to A. He does not, in principle, exclude the possibility of future contact by the mother with A, provided the placement with him is secure . . .

6. In his report to the court the Official Solicitor, acting as A's guardian, opposed the application. The sole consequence of an adoption order would be to end the mother's relationship with A. This was not an order which could be said to safeguard and promote A's welfare. There was nothing in the history of the case to suggest that the mother would be likely to seek to disrupt the security of A's placement with her father. But any attempt by her to do so would not necessarily be to A's disadvantage . . .

25. An adoption order in favour of a single natural parent alone will . . . have the effect of permanently extinguishing any parental responsibility of the other natural parent . . . This will afford the adoptive parent a measure of additional security. But it is important here to keep in mind the wide range of powers the court now has under the Children Act 1989 to restrict the possibility of inappropriate intervention in the child's life by the other natural parent. Adoption is not intended to be used simply as the means by which to protect the child's life with one natural parent against inappropriate intervention by the other natural parent.

26. Another consequence adoption has in this type of case is that after adoption the child will be treated in law as if she had been born to her adoptive parent in wedlock . . . The significance of this benefit today should not be overstated. The social and legal status of children born outside marriage has changed greatly in recent years. The social stigma and legal disabilities attendant upon 'illegitimacy' have now largely gone. Two children in every five born in this country are born outside marriage. Unless a contrary intention appears, statutes enacted after 1987 are to be interpreted without regard to whether a person's parents were married at any time . . .

27. Having regard to all these matters, the circumstances in which it will be in the best interests of a child to make an adoption order in favour of one natural parent alone, thereby, in Hale LJ's words, taking away one half of the child's legal family, are likely to be exceptional. Bracewell J [at first instance] regarded the circumstances of the present case as exceptional. She said so. The father's case was that the mother's continuing status as a parent with parental responsibility for A would perpetuate insecurity for him and that this would potentially affect A's stability. The judge accepted this . . . Given the mother's attitude to A from the moment of A's birth, and her consent, adoption by the father was in A's best interests. Adoption was in A's best interests even though this would have the consequence of excluding the mother.

28. In my view, on the evidence before her this conclusion was open to Bracewell J . . . That an adoption order as sought by A's father will safeguard and promote A's welfare is a wholly tenable view. A residence order, together with an appropriate prohibited steps order, may not suffice to allay the father's genuine anxieties.

The decision met with strong criticism. It is certainly questionable whether rendering the child 'legally motherless', given the strong negative message of rejection this sends out, was in the child's interests, particularly when alternative orders were available under the CA 1989 to address the father's insecurity.[229] On a more general level, the case raises interesting questions as to whether parents (both mothers and fathers) should be able to reject parenthood by irrevocably terminating their 'very parenthood' through adoption or whether there should be a less drastic mechanism for removing parental responsibility from absent

---

[229] Harris-Short (2002).

or uninterested parents which does not have the same distorting effect on the child's core familial relationships.[230]

13.7 POST-ADOPTION ISSUES

13.7.1 OPEN ADOPTION

In order to protect the new relationship between the adoptive parents and the child, adoption was traditionally shrouded in secrecy with very careful restrictions in place to prevent children discovering the truth about their adopted status or birth parents discovering the whereabouts of the new adoptive family. In order to preserve the confidentiality of the placement approximately 80 per cent of people applying for an adoption order still ask for a serial number (rather than using their names) to be assigned to their case.[231] However, the fact that many adopted children are now older with strong emotional ties to their birth families, alongside emerging evidence as to the strong need felt by adopted adults to seek information about their biological parents, has severely challenged the closed nature of adoption. In the past few years, a more open concept of adoption has become entrenched within social work practice. However, the law has been more reluctant to embrace this change—a change which fundamentally challenges the orthodox 'legal transplant' model of adoption remaining entrenched within the legislation.

Openness can take many forms. At one end of the scale it can simply involve providing children with more detailed information about their birth parents and the circumstances surrounding their adoption. At the other end of the scale, it can involve regular direct contact between the child and members of the birth family. Between these extremes, openness can involve infrequent visits, indirect contact such as telephone calls and letters, and fairly frequent exchange of information between the adoptive parents and the birth family in the form of photographs, reports on the child's progress, and news about the birth family. Contact between the child and the birth mother, maternal grandparents, and siblings is common, but rarely involves the father and the wider paternal family.[232]

The right to information

Although much of the debate on open adoption now focuses on post-adoption contact, an important aspect of openness is the provision of information about the child's genealogical background and the circumstances surrounding the adoption. In some cases this will be sufficient to meet concerns about the child's identity and help assuage any feelings of confusion or loss. Under the ACA 2002, an adopted person has the right, upon reaching the age of 18, to apply through an adoption agency for information which will allow him or her to obtain a certified copy of the birth record.[233] For people adopted before the ACA 2002 came into force, this information can be obtained directly from the Registrar General. Disclosure of this information can only be withheld in exceptional circumstances by order of the

---

[230] See further discussion at 10.6.1. See also Harris-Short (2002).
[231] DCA (2006a), 19.
[232] Neil (2000), 314.
[233] S 60(2).

High Court.[234] An adopted person upon reaching the age of 18 also has the right to a copy of the adoption order and any prescribed information which had to be disclosed to the adopters.[235] The Registrar General must also maintain an adoption contact register. Part 1 of the register enables adopted persons over the age of 18 to record whether they would like to make contact with any of their birth relatives. Part II of the register contains information entered by birth relatives as to whether they wish to make contact with the adopted child. Where there is a 'match' between the two parts of the register, the Registrar General will notify the adopted person.[236]

The statutory requirements dealing with the recording, keeping, and disclosure of wider information about a child's adoption are contained within ss 56–65 of the ACA 2002. The information which an adoption agency must keep in relation to an adoption is prescribed by regulations and referred to as 'section 56 information'. It includes:

- the child's case record (includes the child's permanence report, a written record of the adoption panel proceedings, a record of the agency's decision on placement, any consents);

- any information that has been supplied by a natural parent or relative or other significant person in the adopted person's life, with the intention that the adopted person may, should he wish to, be given that information;

- any information supplied by the adoptive parents or other persons which is relevant to matters arising after the making of the adoption order;

- any information the adopted person has requested should be kept;

- any information given to the adoption agency in respect of an adopted person by the Registrar General (information that would enable an adopted person to obtain a certified copy of the record of his birth);

- any information disclosed to the adoption agency about an entry relating to the adopted person on the Adoption Contact Register.[237]

The adoption agency has discretion not to keep information supplied by a member of the birth family or the adoptive parents if satisfied that it would be prejudicial to the adopted person's welfare or it would not be reasonably practicable.[238] Any s 56 information which is 'identifying information', this is information which directly identifies a person or, whether taken alone or in conjunction with other information, could lead to an individual being identified, is referred to as 'protected information'.[239] Where an agreement is in place permitting disclosure, protected information may be disclosed.[240] Otherwise, an application must be made to the adoption agency which has a wide discretion as to whether disclosure should take place. There are no restrictions as to who can apply but the adoption agency does not have to proceed with an application if it does not consider

---

[234] S 60(3). This gives statutory recognition to the principle established in *R v Registrar General, ex parte Smith* [1991] 2 QB 393.

[235] S 60(2)(b) and (4).

[236] Adopted Children and Adoption Contact Registers Regulations 2005, SI 2005/924, reg 8.

[237] Disclosure of Adoption Information (Post-Commencement Adoptions) Regulations 2005, SI 2005/888, reg 4.

[238] Ibid, reg 4(4).

[239] ACA 2002, s 57.

[240] S 57(5). See also Disclosure of Adoption Information (Post-Commencement Adoptions) Regulations 2005, SI 2005/888, reg 11.

it appropriate to do so.[241] If it does consider it appropriate to proceed, it must take all reasonable steps to obtain the views of any affected person.[242] Where the protected information is about a person who is at the time of the application a child, the agency must take all reasonable steps to ascertain the views of the child's parent or guardian and, having regard to the child's age and understanding, the views of the child.[243] It is then within the discretion of the agency whether or not it considers it appropriate to disclose. In exercising this discretion, the adoption agency is directed to consider the welfare of the adopted person and the views of any person the information is about.[244] Where the information is about an adopted child who has not yet attained the age of 18, the child's welfare must be the agency's paramount consideration.[245] If the information is about any other child, the agency 'must have particular regard to the child's welfare'.[246] In the case of information which is not protected information, the adoption agency simply has a broad discretion whether or not to disclose.[247] In exercising its discretion under these provisions the adoption agency is entitled to adopt a general policy on disclosure but must consider each individual case on its merits.[248]

The child's right to know?

Whilst the adoption agency has a broad discretion to make disclosure of both identifying and non-identifying information to an adopted person, the legislation does not provide a *right* in the *child* to receive any information about the birth parents or the circumstances surrounding the adoption. It is therefore misleading to talk about the child's *right* to information in this context. This contrasts sharply with other areas of the law where the courts have moved towards accepting the child's *right* to know the truth about parentage.[249] Despite Parliament's reticence to enshrine such a right in the legislation, the National Minimum Standards on Adoption are clearly premised on the assumption that the adoptive parents will be open about the adoption and will be willing and able to share information with the child about the birth family and the circumstances surrounding the adoption when the child reaches an appropriate age.[250] Detailed guidance is provided on the importance of life story work.

Post-adoption contact

The most effective way of informing children about their birth family is through direct or indirect contact.

---

[241] ACA 2002, ss 61(2) and 62(2).
[242] Ss 61(3) and 62(4).
[243] S 62(3).
[244] Ss 61(5) and 62(7).
[245] S 62(6)(a).
[246] S 62(6)(b).
[247] S 58.
[248] See *Gunn-Russo v Nugent Care Society and Secretary of State for Health* [2001] EWHC 566 (decided under the AA 1976).
[249] See *Re H (A Minor) (Blood Tests: Parental Rights)* [1997] Fam 89, 107 and discussion at p 618.
[250] DFE (2014b), Standard 2, Promoting a Positive Identity, Potential and Valuing Diversity.

The empirical evidence on post-adoption contact

Based on the work of the child psychiatrist John Bowlby, many child-care professionals working in the 1970s considered that to consolidate the child within the new adoptive family existing attachments to the birth family must be severed.

B. Lindley, 'Open Adoption—Is the Door Ajar?', (1997) 9 *Child and Family Law Quarterly* 115, 117–18

Attachment theory was cited by some clinicians and social work practitioners as justification for the notion of closed, secretive adoption. Bowlby's work on attachment and the vital importance of the early relationship with one care-giver, normally the mother, was used to affirm the view that as far as adoption was concerned the child needed an exclusive environment free from interference from the birth family. Although he modified his theory later in his life, conceding that the child could have multiple attachment figures, albeit in some form of hierarchy, Bowlby's original thesis still remains very influential. This is partly due to the work of Goldstein, Freud and Solnit who asserted that, from their *clinical* experience in the UK and the USA, when children were apart from a parent, there should be a cessation of contact with that parent, otherwise the child would fail to bond with the new parent/carer and would also experience confusion and divided loyalties. They applied this theory both to children placed with new carers/families and to children whose parents were separated or divorced...Although their 'clean break' view was based on clinical rather than research evidence, it had a very strong influence on child care professionals at the time when the 'permanence' movement was developing during the 1970s and 1980s. Indeed, in spite of the recent practice development of greater openness, particularly for older children adopted from the care system, this view remains very influential today.

A child's ability to form multiple attachments strongly undermines the view that birth families must be totally excluded from the child's life if the child is to bond successfully with the adoptive family. Indeed, research suggests that continuing contact with the birth family has no affect on the child's sense of belonging with the adoptive parents and can even positively promote the child's integration into the new family. Lindley continues:

Subsequent studies of children moving to new families suggest that, rather than preventing children from settling, openness can *help* the child settle in the new family, providing the adults are not hostile to each other, or the idea. Fratter's study found that contact helped to provide continuity, a positive identity and an understanding for the child of the circumstances of the adoption. It enabled the child to feel free to attach to the new family whilst retaining a link with their birth family. Indeed, she concludes when commenting on the impact of contact, that 'contact was not thought to have adversely affected the attachment of any of the children placed under seven years of age, and had not given rise to divided loyalties, even where there had been fortnightly face-to-face contact'. However, she adds a qualification to this, namely that the attitude of the parents and parent figures to one another is crucial in freeing children from guilt and divided loyalties.

Other studies have found that the stability of the placements of older children was not threatened by maintaining links with their families of origin. They also show that older children may not be willing to move to a new family if contact with their original families is to be severed, although they do not always feel able to voice their opinion...

> Moreover, Hill et al found that when earlier attachments are disregarded, the feelings do not go away but are simply driven underground. Triseliotis et al also report some evidence which suggests that older children who are pressurised to abandon meaningful relationships with members of the birth family may find it difficult to attach themselves to the new family...

Direct knowledge of the birth parents can also help the child develop a secure and positive identity, avoiding what has been termed in the literature 'genealogical bewilderment'.[251] Ryburn identifies a number of further important benefits from post-adoption contact, perhaps most obviously these include benefits for both the birth parents and the child.

M. Ryburn, 'In Whose Best Interests?—Post-Adoption Contact with the Birth Family', (1998) 10 *Child and Family Law Quarterly* 53, 59–61

Advantages of contact for birth parents

Contact for birth parents with their children can make a significant difference. The studies indicate in particular that contact helps parents to resolve the grief of their loss, and to move on in their lives, and there is a well-established principle here. It is extremely difficult to manage grief when it has no clear focus... This, in reality, is the living death of a child...

The studies also indicate that one of the overwhelming needs of birth parents without contact is for reassurance that their child is well and happy, and contact is able, in general, to offer this reassurance. In some instances just the open exchange of information may be sufficient... Perhaps one of the most striking things to emerge from the studies is how concerned birth parents are that contact should not be a source of distress or disruption in the life of their child.

Advantages of contact for children

The research studies suggest that with indirect contact children's information needs begin to be met, but that with direct contact their questions are more likely to be met at a level that is satisfying. One of the key advantages of any contact is that facts can more readily replace speculation and fantasy. Children are also helped through contact to come to terms with difficult aspects of their past lives—aspects that might otherwise be a source of difficulty for them...

Children also appear to gain a sense of reassurance as a consequence of contact, particularly direct contact, with their birth relatives. In particular, it gives them a clear message that the placement is supported by their original family since otherwise they would not be visiting, and it is a visible symbol that their adoptive parents feel positively about their original family or contact would not be permitted. The largest study of adoption and permanent foster care placements ever undertaken in the UK... also found that birth family contact was the single factor which could be identified as enhancing the stability of placements. Finally, contact, in particular direct contact, appears to strengthen children's sense of attachment to their adoptive parents...

---

[251] Smith (2004), 330. See further discussion at 9.4.4.

Perhaps more surprisingly, Ryburn also identifies a number of advantages for the adoptive parents:

Effects of secrecy on adopters

Traditionally, adopters have been seen as those with the least to gain through post-adoption contact and certainly it was agencies claiming to represent the voice of adopters who were instrumental in introducing much greater secrecy...Without adequate information at the time of placement, and a way of accessing additional and up-to-date information as it is needed, adopters may feel hampered in the task of parenting a child born to someone else...

Advantages of contact for adopters

The studies indicate that adopters may gain significantly through contact. Adopters with continuing contact following adoption are generally comfortable with it. It would appear that contact can enhance children's attachments to their adopters, it provides a ready source of information and it appears to lead to more positive feelings towards birth relatives. This, in turn, is likely to aid children in the acquisition of positive identity.

The greatest gain to be attributed to contact—in this case direct contact—is a sense of security and permanence in the parenting role.

Although some researchers are more cautious than Ryburn in their reading of the empirical evidence,[252] most generally agree that the impact of post-adoption contact on adoption outcomes is fairly negligible: post-adoption contact with the birth family is not generally harmful to the child but neither is its absence.[253] There is little evidence that post-adoption contact leads to significantly better outcomes.[254]

Post-adoption contact in the courts

Practice within the social work profession has in many ways moved ahead of the empirical evidence. The importance of being open about adoption and the birth family, including promoting contact where appropriate, is emphasized at every stage of the process. There are consequently very few adoptions where there is no provision for some form of direct or indirect contact between the adopters and the birth family with 'letter-box' contact the most usual.[255] Indeed, unless prospective adopters are willing to facilitate openness their suitability to adopt is likely to be questioned. This positive attitude contrasts sharply with the attitude of the courts which have, in the past, been extremely reluctant to make any kind of formal provision for post-adoption contact—this reluctance stemming it would seem from their difficulty in reconciling a move towards greater openness with the traditional legal understanding of adoption.[256] The guiding principles to be applied on an application for post-adoption contact prior to the implementation of the ACA 2002 were established by

[252] See, e.g., Quinton and Selwyn (1998) and (2006).

[253] Neil (2009). For the most recent review of the research evidence see Neil et al (2012). See also Quinton and Selwyn (2006), 473. For an excellent summary of the current position, see Smith (2005), 315–17 and Logan and Smith (2005), 6–11.

[254] Neil (2009).

[255] Masson (2000) and Neil et al (2012), 4.

[256] See, e.g., *Re C (A Minor) (Adoption Order: Condition)* [1986] 1 FLR 315 (Sir John Donaldson) and *Re V (A Minor) (Adoption: Consent)* [1987] Fam 57 (CA), 68.

the House of Lords in *Re C (A Minor) (Adoption Order: Conditions)*. The House of Lords held that it would only be in exceptional cases that a contact order would be imposed on the adoptive parents.

Re C (A Minor) (Adoption Order: Conditions) [1989] 1 AC 1 (HL), 17–18

LORD ACKNER:

The cases rightly stress that in normal circumstances it is desirable that there should be a complete break, but that each case has to be considered on its own particular facts. No doubt the court will not, except in the most exceptional case, impose terms or conditions as to access to members of the child's natural family to which the adopting parents do not agree. To do so would be to create a potentially frictional situation which would be hardly likely to safeguard or promote the welfare of the child. Where no agreement is forthcoming the court will, with very rare exceptions, have to choose between making an adoption order without terms or conditions as to access, or to refuse to make such an order and seek to safeguard access through some other machinery, such as wardship. To do otherwise would be merely inviting future and almost immediate litigation.

Following *Re C*, the courts consistently refused to make provision for contact where the adoptive parents did not agree. Even where they did agree, the courts were extremely reluctant to formalize that agreement in an order, holding that such matters were best left to the 'good sense' of the adopters.[257]

The ACA 2002 was arguably intended to mark a shift away from this very cautious approach towards post-adoption contact. The duty on the court to consider contact at the placement stage suggested more birth parents were likely to retain contact throughout this crucial period which, in turn, would strengthen their case for post-adoption contact.[258] Moreover, regardless of whether or not the parent has made an application to the court, the court is under a mandatory duty to consider the proposals as to post-adoption contact when deciding whether or not to make the adoption order.[259] The court should be further prompted towards making some provision for contact by the welfare checklist which directs the court's attention to the child's existing relationships with members of the birth family, the value of those relationships continuing, and the wishes and feelings of the child's relatives.[260] The statutory regime governing post-adoption contact was, however, amended by the CFA 2014 to introduce a new statutory provision: s 51A. As originally implemented, the court retained the right under the ACA 2002 to make a s 8 order dealing with post-adoption contact alongside an adoption order.[261] This created the somewhat odd situation whereby the adoption order was governed by s 1(4) of the ACA 2002 whilst post-adoption contact was governed by s 1(3) of the CA 1989.[262] The introduction of s 51A means that the statutory regime is rationalized and post-adoption contact will now be governed exclusively under the ACA 2002 (the use of s 8 orders being specifically precluded).[263] However, in a significant

[257] *Re T (A Minor) (Contact After Adoption)* [1995] 2 FCR 537 (CA), 542–4.
[258] S 26.
[259] S 46(6).
[260] S 1(4)(f) and (6).
[261] S 46(5).
[262] ACA 2002, s 26(5). See *Oxfordshire County Council v X* [2010] EWCA Civ 581, [5].
[263] S 51A(8). S 26(5) is repealed.

change, whilst it had been held under the previous law that birth parents would be entitled to apply as of right for a contact order to be heard together with the adoption application at the final hearing,[264] s 51A imposes a leave requirement on the birth family applying for a contact order even before the final adoption order has been made. The criteria to be applied in determining leave are drawn from s 10(9) but include any representations made by the adoptive parents.[265] Section 51A also makes it possible for the court to make orders for 'no contact' to deal with the growing problem of birth families making unauthorized contact with adopted children (and sometimes vice versa) via social media.[266] Adoptive parents can apply for such an order as of right. Consequently, whilst the legislature back in 2002 may have intended a more positive approach to post-adoption contact, the recent amendments have a distinctly more negative and restrictive tone.[267] It will clearly now be much harder for the birth parents to be heard on the issue of post-adoption contact, particularly if the very restrictive approach to granting leave to birth parents post-adoption which prevailed under the previous law is adopted at the final hearing stage.[268]

It is thus clear that whatever may have been the original intentions, the statutory regime for post-adoption contact is very unlikely to bring about any fundamental change in the courts' approach. The view of the higher family judiciary has vacillated somewhat following implementation of the ACA 2002, but there is no evidence that there has been any shift in the general practice of the courts. Comments made by Wall LJ immediately prior to the implementation of the ACA 2002 appeared to make clear that the courts' approach to post-adoption contact would remain unchanged:

Re R (Adoption: Contact) [2005] EWCA Civ 1128

WALL LJ:

48. We were shown section 1 of the new Act, which is due in force later this year, which demonstrates the clear change of thinking there has been since 1976, when the Act was initially enacted, and which demonstrates that the court now will need to take into account and consider the relationship the child had with members of the natural family, and the likelihood of that relationship continuing and the value of the relationship to the child.

49. So contact is more common, but nonetheless the jurisprudence I think is clear. The imposition on prospective adopters of orders for contact with which they are not in agreement is extremely, and remains extremely, unusual.

However, just two years later in the case of *Re P (Children) (Adoption: Parental Consent)*, Wall LJ appeared to signal a cautious but important potential change in approach, holding that the courts now have a much more central role to play in securing post-adoption contact where appropriate.[269]

---

[264] ACA 2002, s 46. See *X and Y v A Local Authority (Adoption: Procedure)* [2009] EWHC 47, [18]–[19].
[265] S 51A(5).
[266] 51A(2)(b).
[267] It is notable that these reforms were opposed by some of the most experienced researchers in the field. See Neil et al (2012), 12–13.
[268] See *Re S (Contact: Application by Sibling)* [1999] Fam 283; *X and Y v A Local Authority* [2009] EWHC 47.
[269] See also the more positive comments of Baroness Hale regarding post-adoption contact in *Down Lisburn Health and Social Services Trust v H* [2006] UKHL 36, [6]–[8].

Re P (Children) (Adoption: Parental Consent) [2008] EWCA Civ 535

WALL LJ:

141. We approach this part of our judgment with caution, as we are conscious that these are early days, and the manner in which adoption agencies apply the terms of the 2002 Act will need to be worked out in practice over time...

142. Historically, post adoption contact between children and their birth parents has been perceived as highly exceptional...

147. All this, in our judgment, now falls to be revisited under section 26 and 27 of the 2002 Act, given in particular the terms of sections 1(4)(f), 1(6) and (7) and 46(6). In our judgment, the judge in the instant case was plainly right to make a contact order under section 26 of the 2002 Act, and in our judgment the question of contact between [the children], and between the children and their parents, should henceforth be a matter for the court, not for the local authority, or the local authority in agreement with prospective adopters...

148. . . . The making of the placement orders means, of course, that contact under the 1989 Act is no longer possible, but orders under sections 26 and 27 are not only possible but, in our judgment, necessary.

149. Furthermore, when the time comes for [the children] to be finally placed, it will be the court which will have to make the necessary orders – either for adoption, or for revocation of the placement orders if the children are not to be adopted. At that point, in our judgment, as the facts of this case currently stand, it will be for the court, before making an adoption order, to decide, in accordance with section 46(6) of the 2002 Act, what ongoing contact [the children] should have with each other – not for their prospective adopters to do so. The same principle will apply if the children are to be placed in long-term foster care.

150. The effect of the placement order is substantially to disempower [the children's] parents – see section 25(4) of the 2002 Act. In our judgment, as matters currently stand, the existence of the placement orders should not be an inhibition on the ability of [the mother] in particular to apply to the court to determine questions of contact – and in particular the question of contact between D and S. Indeed, it seems to us highly likely that the placement of the children with adopters or foster carers who are unwilling, in particular, to facilitate contact between [the children] would provide a proper basis for leave to be granted to [the mother] under section 24(2) of the 2002 Act (leave to make an application to apply for an order to revoke the placement order) or for leave to apply to oppose the making of an adoption order under section 47(5) of the 2002 Act.

151. On the facts of this case, there is a universal recognition that the relationship between [the children] needs to be preserved. It is on this basis that the local authority / adoption agency is seeking the placement of the children. In our judgment, this means that the question of contact between the two children is not a matter for agreement between the local authority/adoption agency and the adopters: it is a matter which, ultimately, is for the court. It is the court which will have to make adoption orders or orders revoking the placement orders, and in our judgment it is the court which has the responsibility to make orders for contact if they are required in the interests of the two children...

153. . . . [I]t is not, in our judgment, a proper exercise of the judicial powers given to the court under the 2002 Act to leave contact between the children themselves, or between the children and their natural parents to the discretion of the local authority and/or the prospective carers of [the children], be they adoptive parents or foster carers. It is the court which must make the necessary decisions if contact between the siblings is in dispute, or if it is argued that it should cease for any reason.

154. We do not know if our views on contact on the facts of this particular case presage a more general sea change in post adoption contact overall. It seems to us, however, that the stakes in the present case are sufficiently high to make it appropriate for the court to retain control over the question of the children's welfare throughout their respective lives under sections 1, 26, 27 and 46(6) of the 2002 Act; and, if necessary, to make orders for contact post adoption in accordance with section 26 of the 2002 Act, under section 8 of the 1989 Act. This is what Parliament has enacted. In section 46(6) of the 2002 Act Parliament has specifically directed the court to consider post adoption contact, and in section 26(5) Parliament has specifically envisaged an application for contact being heard at the same time as an adoption order is applied for. All this leads us to the view that the 2002 Act envisages the court exercising its powers to make contact orders post adoption, where such orders are in the interests of the child concerned.

A 'sea change' in approach did not materialize as a result of these comments. Indeed, in *Oxfordshire County Council v X*, Lord Neuberger MR held that it remains 'extremely unusual' to make a contact order against the wishes of the adoptive parents. He went on to distinguish *Re P*, holding that Lord Justice Wall's comments were inapplicable to a case where the application for contact is made after an adoption order has already been made—the correct approach to such cases remains that expressed in *Re R*.[270] The issue in *Oxfordshire* was whether the adoptive parents should be ordered to provide the birth parents with an annual photo of the child. Lord Neuberger's judgment is expressed in forceful terms:

Oxfordshire County Council v X [2010] EWCA Civ 581

LORD NEUBERGER MR:

36. It is a strong thing to impose on adoptive parents, it is "extremely unusual" to impose on adoptive parents, some obligation which they are unwilling voluntarily to assume, certainly where, as here, the adoption order has already been made. Was there a proper basis for taking that extremely unusual step? In our judgment there was not. The judge found that the adoptive parents were genuine when they expressed their concerns, so what was the justification for imposing on them something they conscientiously and reasonably objected to, particularly when, as we have seen, they say that they have not ruled out the possibility of letting the natural parents have photographs in the future? As we have said, they are not to be saddled with an order merely because a judge takes a different view. The adoptive parents are J's parents; the natural parents are not. The adoptive parents are the only people with parental responsibility for J. Why, unless the circumstances are unusual, indeed extremely unusual – and here, in our judgment, they are neither – should that responsibility be usurped by the court? We can see no good reason either on the facts or in law. On the contrary, there is much force in the point they make, that they wish their status as J's parents to be respected and seen to be inviolable – not for themselves but in order, as they see it, to give J the very best chance for the adoption to be successful.

Lord Neuberger's judgment was endorsed shortly thereafter by Lord Justice Wilson in *Re T (A Child) (Adoption: Contact)* as 'still reflecting the general approach'.[271] However, the

---

[270] *Oxfordshire County Council v X* [2010] EWCA Civ 581, [14] and [9]. For an excellent critique of this decision, see Hughes and Sloan (2011).
[271] [2010] EWCA Civ 1527.

debate still rumbles on, albeit quietly, with a somewhat different approach being taken by Ryder LJ in *Re P-M (A Child)*, in which, having made a 'limited' contact order in favour of the maternal grandmother, he observed that a more proactive approach by the courts to post-adoption contact, particularly between siblings, may be necessary in order to safeguard the children's interests:

Re P-M (A Child) [2013] EWHC 1838

RYDER LJ:

33. I have considered long and hard the divergent views about whether a contact order should be made and if so, on what basis. On the one hand an order could expose P-M [the child] to instability and split loyalties arising out of the reasonable anxieties that Ms D [the adoptive parent] would harbour with the risk that she would not be able to cope with what she says she can commit herself to voluntarily. A contact order could tend to be antagonistic to the rationale for the adoption order that I intend to make and everyone agrees that nothing must be allowed to put at risk the placement that P-M has with Ms D. On the other hand, Ms D must understand that it is my firm view that provided circumstances do not change for the worse, the contact that I have set out is in P-M's best interests and I expect him to be afforded the benefit of it. In particular, the contact between P-M and his sister is necessary for his welfare to be safeguarded throughout his life i.e. in the long term.

34. As the parties know only too well, I have changed my mind more than once. For what I believe to be good legal and evaluative reasons I intend to hold to the view with which I concluded the proceedings in January. I have decided to make a limited contact order alongside an adoption order. For me, they are inextricably linked on the facts of this case: both orders are necessary and the success of the adoption order is in part dependent upon a minimum level of contact with P-M's birth family particularly his sister and maternal grandmother. The balance of contact though desirable should not form part of an order as in my judgment that would go too far and be potentially antagonistic to the exercise of Ms D's parental responsibility.

35. Although this is not a part of the reasoning of the court, it has to be remarked that all too often adoption orders are made with all the best intentions for continuing sibling contact which are then thwarted for no particularly good reason. Too often the lack of post adoption support or any pro-active communication causes parties to drift so quickly that the absence of contact over time becomes a barrier with the very understandable fear on the part of adopters that its recommencement will be so unsettling that it may damage a placement: a fear that may well be justified. Perhaps more often than hitherto, courts faced with agreed contact post adoption might consider whether an order can give reassurance to the child by keeping an enduring relationship that is important and for some children critical to their welfare throughout their lives.

Should there be stronger intervention by the courts?

The much more positive comments in *Re P* and *Re P-M* as to the courts' role in securing post-adoption contact will be welcomed by advocates of open adoption. Commentators have argued that many of the courts' objections towards the making of formal orders have been somewhat overstated, particularly where the parties are in agreement. It is recognized that flexibility is crucial in dealing with post-adoption contact and that many adoptive parents are resistant to court orders—as opposed to proceeding by way of voluntary agreement—because of their rigidity and the fact that they take control out of the hands of the adoptive parents.[272] However, Lowe and Murch argue that the inflexibility of such orders can be exaggerated, with the court able to specify with no greater particularity that there should be 'reasonable contact', thereby leaving it to the adoptive parents to determine exactly what constitutes 'reasonable contact' in the particular circumstances of the case.[273] Moreover, it is pointed out that there are certain advantages to any voluntary agreement between the adoptive parents and the birth family being underpinned by the security of a contact order.[274] Without a court order the adopters can simply walk away from any earlier agreement, a significant possibility if their agreement was only given reluctantly in exchange for the birth parents' consent to the adoption.[275]

Other leading commentators have, however, questioned whether stronger legal intervention is the answer. Indeed, commentators have suggested that the courts are ill-equipped to deal effectively with disputes over post-adoption contact and a more robust legal response is therefore likely to be wholly ineffective, even counterproductive. Smith argues that whilst the law can provide an overarching framework for the resolution of such disputes, the actual job of facilitating post-adoption contact is best left to social welfare professionals working to promote greater trust and cooperation between the parties.[276]

C. Smith, 'Trust v Law: Promoting and Safeguarding Post-Adoption Contact',
(2005) 27 *Journal of Social Welfare and Family Law* 315, 326, 329

Law can require, regulate and enforce post-adoption contact. However, it cannot influence the qualitative experience of relationships and social interaction that enable adults to co-operate in the best interests of children. Additionally, while law can intervene in contact disputes at particular points in time, it lacks the capacity to continuously negotiate and respond to developing needs as these unfold. Law acts to reduce uncertainty but in so doing it constrains flexibility and the necessary use of discretion. Even while law may limit itself to ordering 'reasonable' contact, it reduces scope for the exercise of personal responsibility and moral competence on which mutually beneficial contact relies. As with post-divorce and post-separation contact disputes, law's intervention is unlikely to resolve conflicts unless underlying issues of trust are addressed. Law may enforce contact, but it cannot ensure beneficial experiences for those involved—particularly for children . . .

However, there are ways of enhancing the willingness and ability of adopters to support contact without recourse to legal regulation. Preparation of prospective adopters is crucial to helping them to understand the value of contact for children. The use of research which reports on adoptive parents' experience of beneficial contact can ameliorate fears and increase understanding, as can the inclusion of adopters and birth relatives preparation sessions. An important part of this work is to encourage adopters' confidence about making decisions in their child's best interests. Agencies should avoid negative evaluations of prospective adopters who want the sense of control and ownership over their children

---

272 Harris-Short (2001), 417–18.
273 Discussed, ibid.
274 Ibid.
275 Ibid.
276 See also Masson (2000).

that adoption conveys. There is evidence that this legal construction of (adoptive) parent-hood provides a secure base, which enables adoptive parents to be generous about contact arrangements...

The argument that formal intervention of the courts is unnecessary and unhelpful where the parties are in agreement as to the principle of contact and are able to cooperate in making and, where necessary, changing the arrangements in the interests of the child, is persuasive. However, in the absence of consensus the law's withdrawal is more problematic. Adoptive parents are not always reasonable and cannot always be trusted to act in the child's best interests. Where mediatory techniques fail to achieve cooperation, unless the adoptive parents are to be the final arbiter of the child's welfare, legal intervention may well be necessary to uphold and enforce certain normative standards.

Re-conceptualizing adoption

The courts have clearly struggled with the idea that retaining substantial links with the birth family can be consistent with adoption as traditionally understood. Commentators have thus argued that it may be easier to facilitate greater openness in the post-adoption context if adoption were to be 're-conceptualized'.[277] Adoption is a legal and social construct. There is therefore no inherent inconsistency between adoption and the preservation of ongoing relationships with the birth family—a permanent irrevocable transfer of parental respon-sibility can be achieved whilst maintaining the child's essential genealogical ties. In other words, the legal fiction that the child is to be treated as if born to the adoptive parents can be removed without compromising the powerful messages of permanence and stability tra-ditionally offered by adoption and which are still so highly valued by both children and adopters. However, not all commentators agree that transforming the legal concept of adop-tion will help encourage greater openness. Smith and Logan suggest that re-conceptualizing adoption may, from the perspective of the adoptive parents, fundamentally undermine the advantages of adoption over other permanent forms of alternative care which help them facilitate and support ongoing contact with the birth family. In particular, it is the 'total legal transplant' achieved through adoption that confers on the adoptive parents the 'entitlement' to parent, thereby giving them the sense of confidence, authority, and legitimacy to engage constructively with the birth family.

C. Smith and J. Logan, 'Adoptive Parenthood as a "Legal Fiction"—Its Consequences for Direct Post-Adoption Contact', (2002) 14 *Child and Family Law Quarterly* 281, 292, 293–4, 295, and 300

[W]e want to suggest an alternative understanding of the relationship between adoption and contact, which indicates that emphatic calls for change in policy and law may be misplaced and points to the significance of adoption's legal and social effects in facilitating contact...

We asked each of the 59 adoptive mothers and 49 adoptive fathers whom we interviewed why they wanted to adopt, rather than to care for children through some other arrange-ment... Unsurprisingly, the vast majority of adopters wanted the legal security and permanence

---

[277] See, e.g., Bridge (1993), 101–2 and Parkinson (2003), 161.

afforded by adoption…However, it was clear from our interviews that adoption achieves far more than legal security—it constructs parenthood. It was the experience and meaning of parenthood—legally, socially and emotionally—that was of enormous significance to the adopters in our sample. For many adoptive parents the phenomenology of parenthood is intrinsically characterised by a sense of ownership and control—those very features of adoption that some advocates of contact wish to dismantle. In answer to an open-ended question about what features of adoption were important to them, at least one adoptive parent in 49 (83%) families spontaneously identified factors associated with 'ownership' of their children…

Adoption is remarkably powerful, not only in its legal effects, but in the way it operates to construct new phenomenological identities and relationships. For our adopters, the experience of ownership and control expresses a complex 'package' of attributes that characterise parenthood, and which can only be achieved through adoption. The perceived relationship between parenthood and 'family belonging' was also apparent, with at least one adopter in 27 (46%) families emphasising the creation of a family as an important consequence of adoption. What is particularly noteworthy, in the context of this discussion, is the way in which ownership and control serve to facilitate the maintenance of direct contact…

It seems to us that what our adopters are trying to convey is a sense of parenthood that is phenomenologically distinct from its legal definition in adoption. They can willingly accommodate direct contact because they are the child's legal, social and emotional parents. Birth parents and other birth family members become something 'other'—the phenomenological equivalent of the legal concept of a 'former' parent. While critics of this 'legal fiction' fear that it distorts the nature of relationships and may hinder, rather than promote, post-adoption contact, we found no indication that this is the case. Rather, the 'legal fiction' and its phenomenological counterpart can act to facilitate contact and to make it a beneficial experience for the children concerned…[W]e are suggesting, on the basis of empirical research, that the way in which adopters experience the 'legal fiction' can confirm their sense of parenthood and, at the same time, accommodate the ongoing significance of birth family members through continuing contact…

[We] disagree with any assertion that the most effective way to promote contact must be through policy change, more intrusive judicial intervention or a social and legal assault on the phenomenology of adoption and adoptive parenthood. On the contrary, our research, which is supported by other studies, suggests that contact will be facilitated by enhancing adopters' confidence and confirming the phenomenology that they describe.

13.7.2 POST-ADOPTION SUPPORT

The ACA 2002 provides that adoption support services must be designed to meet the needs of 'adopted persons, their parents, natural parents and former guardians'.[278] It is clear that the duty to provide adoption support services to 'adopted children' includes post-adoption support. The Adoption Support Services Regulations 2005 explicitly provide that in addition to 'counselling, advice and information',[279] adoption support services must

---

[278] S 3(1). The duty to provide certain adoption services (i.e. financial support and therapeutic services) is restricted under the regulations to 'agency adoptions'. Other services (i.e. those concerned with facilitating post-adoption contact) must be available to members of the child's wider family including siblings and other birth relatives: Adoption Support Services Regulations 2005, SI 2005/691, reg 4. The local authority has a discretion but not a duty to extend the provision of services to individuals falling outside these prescribed categories: ACA 2002, s 3(3).

[279] ACA 2002, s 2(6).

include: the payment of adoption allowances; providing assistance in relation to arrangements for contact between an adopted child and the birth family; assisting the adoptive family where the placement is at risk of disrupting; and meeting the 'therapeutic needs' of an adoptive child.[280] Individuals assessed for the provision of adoption support services may now be awarded a 'personal budget' which enables them to control the acquisition of such services as they determine best.[281] Every local authority must appoint an adoption support services adviser who is responsible for advising those affected by an adoption as to how to access appropriate services.[282] The CFA 2014 also introduced a new duty on local authorities to provide adoptive parents, including prospective adopters, with a range of information about available post-adoption services including their right to request an assessment for such services under s 4.[283] An 'adoption passport' has been introduced at a national level which sets down the minimum level of support that adoptive families are entitled to receive.[284]

The need for effective post-adoption support services formed a central plank of the 2002 legislation. It was recognized that if greater use was to be made of adoption for 'looked after' children, better support would be needed to prevent these often challenging placements from breaking down. Under the previous legislation the provision of post-adoption support services was woefully inadequate.[285] The duties imposed on local authorities under the ACA 2002 were intended to lead to a substantial improvement in services. There are, however, weaknesses in the legislative scheme. Under s 4(1) the local authority must on request carry out an assessment of a person's need for adoption support services.[286] However, the local authority is under no duty to meet those needs. The local authority must simply decide whether to provide the person with appropriate support, although if it decides to provide the person with services other than advice and information on more than one occasion it must prepare a plan and keep the plan under review.[287] The approach taken to the provision of financial support is even more restricted with regulations imposing additional conditions on the payment of adoption allowances. Financial support will only be payable if:

- necessary to ensure that the adoptive parent can look after the child;
- the child needs special care which requires greater expenditure of resources by reason of illness, disability, emotional or behavioural difficulties, or the continuing consequences of past abuse or neglect;
- necessary for the local authority to make any special arrangements to facilitate the placement or the adoption by reason of the age or ethnic origin of the child or the desirability of placing the child with a sibling;
- necessary to meet the recurring costs in respect of travel for the purpose of visits between the child and a related person;

[280] Adoption Support Services Regulations 2005, SI 2005/691, reg 3.
[281] ACA 2002, s 4A, as amended by CFA 2014, s 5.
[282] Ibid, reg 6.
[283] ACA 2002 s 4B, as amended by CFA 2014, s 6.
[284] DFE (2012b), 33.
[285] Lowe et al (1999), 430; Rushton (2003), 46; and Selwyn and Quinton (2004), 12.
[286] The local authority is only under a duty to assess a person's need for particular adoption support services if the local authority is under a duty to extend the provision of the service in question to that particular category of person: Adoption Support Services Regulations 2005, SI 2005/691, reg 13.
[287] ACA 2002, s 4(4)–(5). Adoption Support Services Regulations 2005, SI 2005/691, reg 16.

- the local authority considers it appropriate to make a contribution to meet expenditure necessary for the purpose of accommodating and maintaining the child including, for example, alterations to and adaptations of the home.[288]

Financial support may include an element of remuneration where the adoptive parents were previously local authority foster parents for the child. Such payments are, however, restricted to a time limit of two years unless the circumstances are exceptional.[289]

The absence of a clear duty on the local authority to meet an individual's assessed need for post-adoption support services was not resolved in the most recent reforms. Although the government introduced a number of measures aimed at 'signposting' adoptive families to the various support services to which they are entitled, the House of Lords Select Committee on Adoption was clear in its view that the government should be looking to do more:

House of Lords Select Committee on Adoption Legislation, 2nd Report of Session 2012–13, *Adoption: Post-Legislative Scrutiny. Report,* HL Paper 127 (London: TSO, 2013)

215. Children adopted from care have a range of needs due to their early life experiences which are not resolved simply by being adopted. As a result adoptive parents face challenges that many other families do not. Adoptive parents perform a vital social function in caring for very vulnerable and often damaged children, and thereby save the state money.

216. The failure of adoptive placements can be extremely expensive for local authorities in the short and long term, as well as causing significant harm to the children concerned. Well-targeted support services have the potential to ensure placement stability and to avoid these costs.

217. We believe that adoptive parents should receive greater and more consistent and continuing support. Calculations of cost need to take into account the contribution which support services make to preventing adoption breakdown and the associated costs. To support this, we recommend the Government commission an independent cost-benefit analysis setting out the cost of breakdown against the cost of providing support....

233. We welcome the Government's proposals for post-adoption support, but we regret that they fall short of a statutory duty to provide the support needs as assessed. There should be a statutory duty on local authorities and other service commissioning bodies to cooperate to ensure the provision of post-adoption support; this should include appropriate access to health, education, and Children and Adolescent Mental Health Services, and other services as necessary. These entitlements should form part of the Adoption Passport.

The government's failure to use the opportunity provided by the CFA 2014 to introduce such a duty clearly lies not in any lack of goodwill on the government's part to provide every possible support to adoptive families but in the resource implications of imposing such a duty on the local authority.[290] If post-adoption support were available as of right, significant investment would be needed into local authority adoption services.[291] However, it is by no means clear that this would be the most appropriate use of scarce public resources. Indeed, concern has been

---

[288] Adoption Support Services Regulations 2005, SI 2005/691, reg 8.
[289] Ibid.
[290] DFE (2012b).
[291] Harris-Short (2001), 412.

expressed at the impact post-adoption support has on other local authority services to fami-lies in need.[292] The duties owed by local authorities to adoptive families are more extensive than those owed to 'children in need' under s 17 of the CA 1989.[293] Providing greater support to adoptive families than other struggling families is not easy to rationalize, particularly if it detracts from the local authority's ability to provide effective support services under Part III of the CA 1989.[294] These concerns are heightened by the fact adoptive parents tend to have high levels of 'family functioning', scoring highly on such things as 'problem-solving, communica-tion skills, cohesiveness and future orientation'.[295] Where resources are limited, it is certainly questionable whether adoptive families, many of whom have the capacity to obtain the neces-sary professional help from the private sector, should be prioritized over other, perhaps more vulnerable, families.

Differences regarding the priority which should be afforded to post-adoption support reflect continuing ambivalence about the nature of adoptive parenthood.

B. Luckock and A. Hart, 'Adoptive Family Life and Adoption Support: Policy Ambivalence and the Development of Effective Services', (2005) 10 *Child and Family Social Work* 125, 126, and 133–4

Are adoptive parents more like foster carers, high on any priority list for extra support, or more like any other parents in the community who have to take their turn, according to their assessed needs and agency eligibility criteria?...

[G]overnment tries to have it both ways. It has reinforced the traditional expectations of the autonomy of the adoptive family and explicitly distinguished adoption from 'corporate parent-ing' and its instability. But it has also emphasized the importance to the success of adoption of additional support. This leads to mixed messages being received on the ground and some confusion about which way to move services forward. Analysis of the new legislation and guidance reveals an inherent ambivalence in policy. This is both in relation to the appropriate focus of adoption support services and about the nature of eligibility for those services of the different people affected by the adoption. This ambivalence...can be traced primarily to the ambiguous expectations of the adoptive family and to a persisting uncertainty about how best to understand adoptive family life and kinship itself.

Luckock and Hart argue that we need to recognize adoption gives rise to a wholly distinctive form of family life that should not be gauged against either biological or 'corporate' parent-ing. By continuing to measure adoptive parenting against these benchmarks, it is argued that we obscure the real reason adoptive families should be prioritized and attract high levels of support from the state:

[W]e propose that the invigoration of a responsive culture of adoption support requires a fresh approach to be taken to understanding adoptive family life and kinship and its distinc-tive claims for support. Instead of attempts to press these claims by emphasizing the special social expectations of adoptive parenting or to limit them by pointing to the autonomy (and

---

292 Masson (2003), 646–7.
293 See 12.3.1.
294 Masson (2003), 646–7.
295 Rushton (2003), 44; O'Brien and Zamostny (2003), 690.

consumer power) of adoptive families, eligibility for adoption support needs to be argued in an alternative way. Adoption is a different way of 'doing' family life, and the nature of that difference must be understood if services are to be effective. So what is it that makes the difference distinctive in adoption? And what implications does this have for the nature of local service collaboration?

We think it is time to move on from discussions of difference in adoption that use either normative procreational families or 'corporate parenting' models as their benchmark or template. The limitations of current government policy, where both points of reference are drawn on simultaneously, show how difficult it is trying to have it both ways.

When the benchmark for adoptive family life is the procreational family and its life-cycle, difference is defined in terms of the additional 'adoption-related' tasks faced by children and parents in 'adjusting' or 'adapting' to the autonomous family norm...When the template is 'corporate parenting', difference is understood in terms of the capacity of adoptive parents to implement care plans designed to enhance child development and achievement.

Both aspects of adoptive family are recognizable...Nonetheless, although recognizable, they do not convey the real difference that makes adoption distinctive and its service claims exceptional. This difference derives, we think, from the *way* adoptive family life and kinship is established rather than simply from the nature of any social tasks that family is expected to perform...

What makes adoptive family life and kinship distinctive, however, is the fact that its origins lie in an enforced transition and an obligatory collaboration with professionals...

It is this quality of being an autonomous family life, yet formed from the outset through the support and surveillance of the state, that makes adoption distinctive within a community of family differences. It is on this basis that its exceptional claims for support should now be based.

13.8 ALTERNATIVES TO ADOPTION: SPECIAL GUARDIANSHIP

Although the Labour Government was strongly committed to adoption as the preferred option for children in care, it recognized that there would remain some children for whom adoption was not appropriate. The ACA 2002 therefore amended the CA 1989 to make available a new alternative order for securing permanence outside the care system termed special guardianship. The rationale behind this new order is explained in the 2000 White Paper:

Department of Health, *Adoption: A New Approach*, Cm 5017
(London: HMSO, 2000)

5.8 Adoption is not always appropriate for children who cannot return to their birth parents. Some older children do not wish to be legally separated from their birth families. Adoption may not be best for some children being cared for on a permanent basis by members of their wider birth family. Some minority ethnic communities have religious and cultural difficulties with adoption as it is set out in law. Unaccompanied asylum-seeking children may also need secure, permanent homes, but have strong attachments to their families abroad. All these children deserve the same chance as any other to enjoy the benefits of a legally secure, stable permanent placement that promotes a supportive, lifelong relationship with their carers, where the court decides that it is in their best interests...

5.10 The Government will legislate to create [a] new option, which could be called 'special guardianship'. It will be used only to provide permanence for those children for whom adoption is not appropriate and where the court decides it is in the best interests of the child or young person. It will:

- give the carer clear responsibility for all aspects of caring for the child or young person, and for taking the decisions to do with their upbringing. The child or young person will no longer be looked after by the council;

- provide a firm foundation on which to build a lifelong permanent relationship between the carer and the child or young person;

- be legally secure;

- preserve the basic link between the child or young person and their birth family;

- be accompanied by proper access to a full range of support services including, where appropriate, financial support.

These proposals are now enshrined in ss 14A–F of the CA 1989. An application for a special guardianship order may be made by: (i) the child's guardian; (ii) any person in whose favour a child assessment order (CAO) providing for a child to live with him/her is in force with respect to the child; (iii) any person with whom the child has lived for at least three years; (iv) any person who has the consent of any person in whose favour a CAO is in force; (v) the local authority if the child is in care; (vi) any person who has the consent of all persons with parental responsibility for the child; and (vii) a local authority foster parent with whom the child has lived for a period of at least one year immediately preceding the application. Anyone else may apply with leave.[296] The court may also make a special guardianship order of its own motion in any family proceedings.[297]

The main effect of the order is to confer parental responsibility on the special guardian.[298] Special guardianship is, however, intended as a stronger, more permanent measure than a CAO. The special guardian is thus entitled to exercise parental responsibility to the exclusion of any other person.[299] Whilst the order is in force the child's surname cannot be changed and the child cannot be removed from the jurisdiction other than by the special guardian for a period of no more than three months without leave of the court.[300] Unlike an adoption order, a special guardianship order does not automatically discharge a s 8 order. A child arrangements order providing for contact in favour of the child's parents may therefore continue in force, although the court must consider whether the order should be varied or discharged.[301] Where no child arrangements order is in force the court must consider whether it should make provision for contact before granting the special guardianship order.[302]

---

[296] CA 1989, s 14A(3) and (5).
[297] Ibid, s 14A(6).
[298] CA 1989, s 14C(1)(a). See also *A Local Authority v Y, Z and others* [2006] 2 FLR 41.
[299] S 14C(1)(b).
[300] S 14C(3) and (4).
[301] S 14B(1)(a).
[302] S 14B(1)(b).

A key feature of special guardianship is that it is intended to confer a much greater sense of security and permanence on the child's carers than that conferred by a child arrangements order, without having the irrevocable consequences of adoption. Section 14D provides that the order may be varied or discharged on application by: (i) the special guardian; (ii) the child if of sufficient understanding; (iii) any parent or guardian of the child; (iv) any person in whose favour a child arrangements order is in force with respect to the child; (v) any other person who immediately before the making of the special guardianship order had parental responsibility for the child; or (vi) the local authority.[303] The court may also vary or discharge the order of its own motion. In order to protect the special guardians from potentially destabilizing and distressing challenges to their parenting role, applicants other than the local authority require leave to apply for a variation or discharge of the order.[304] Leave will not be granted, other than on application by the child, unless the court is satisfied that there has been a 'significant change' in circumstances since the order was made.[305] Wilson LJ has somewhat tentatively held that despite the specific requirement in s 14D(5) that the change in circumstances must be 'significant' (a qualification which does not appear in s 24(3) of the ACA 2002), that difference in statutory language should be disregarded and an identical approach taken to an application for leave to discharge a special guardianship order as that set down in *Re M (Children) (Placement Order)*[306] for an application for leave to revoke a placement order.[307] This decision will not help assuage the concerns of commentators such as Parkinson who has argued that the provisions purporting to confer security on the special guardians are weak and the hurdles for challenging the order set too low.[308] In this regard, it has been noted with concern that parents do not require leave to apply for a child arrangements order with respect to contact when a special guardianship order is in force, thus leaving the special guardians vulnerable to repeated unsettling applications by the birth family.[309]

The Court of Appeal has provided helpful guidance on special guardianship in three important cases.[310] The three cases were all concerned with one central issue: whether it was more appropriate for the child to be adopted or made the subject of a special guardianship order. The three appeals were heard by differently constituted courts but Wall LJ, giving judgment in *Re S (A Child) (Adoption Order or Special Guardianship Order)*,[311] provided a general 'commentary' on the new legislative provisions which was adopted in all three appeals.

Wall LJ begins his judgment in *Re S* with some general comments as to when a special guardianship order may be deemed more appropriate than adoption, making it clear that there is no presumption that a special guardianship order is preferable to adoption in any particular category of case.

---

[303] S 14D(1).
[304] S 14D(3).
[305] S 14D(5).
[306] [2007] EWCA Civ 1084. Discussed above at pp 941–2.
[307] *Re G (A Child) (Special Guardianship Order: Leave to Discharge)* [2010] EWCA Civ 300, [11]–[14].
[308] Parkinson (2003), 161.
[309] *Re S (A Child) (Adoption Order or Special Guardianship Order)* [2007] EWCA Civ 54, [62]–[68].
[310] Ibid; *Re M-J (A Child) (Adoption Order or Special Guardianship Order)* [2007] EWCA Civ 56; *Re AJ (A Child)* [2007] EWCA Civ 55.
[311] [2007] EWCA Civ 54.

Re S (A Child) (Adoption Order or Special Guardianship Order) [2007]
EWCA Civ 54

WALL LJ:

46. ... [I]n addition to the fundamental difference in status between adopted children and those subject to special guardianship orders, there are equally fundamental differences between the status and powers of adopters and special guardians. These, we think, need to be borne in mind when the court is applying the welfare checklist under both section 1(3) of the 1989 Act and section 1 of the 2002 Act.

47. Certain other points arise from the statutory scheme:–

(i) The carefully constructed statutory regime (notice to the local authority, leave requirements in certain cases, the role of the court, and the report from the local authority—even where the order is made by the court of its own motion) demonstrates the care which is required before making a special guardianship order, and that it is only appropriate if, in the particular circumstances of the particular case, it is best fitted to meet the needs of the child or children concerned.

(ii) There is nothing in the statutory provisions themselves which limits the making of a special guardianship order or an adoption order to any given set of circumstances. The statute itself is silent on the circumstances in which a special guardianship order is likely to be appropriate, and there is no presumption contained within the statute that a special guardianship order is preferable to an adoption order in any particular category of case. Each case must be decided on its particular facts; and each case will involve the careful application of a judicial discretion to those facts.

(iii) The key question which the court will be obliged to ask itself in every case in which the question of adoption as opposed to special guardianship arises will be: which order will better serve the welfare of this particular child? ...

49. We would add ... that, although the no order principle as such is unlikely to be relevant, it is a material feature of the special guardianship regime that it is "less intrusive" than adoption. In other words, it involves a less fundamental interference with existing legal relationships. The court will need to bear Article 8 of ECHR in mind, and to be satisfied that its order is a proportionate response to the problem, having regard to the interference with family life which is involved. In choosing between adoption and special guardianship, in most cases Article 8 is unlikely to add anything to the considerations contained in the respective welfare checklists. Under both statutes the welfare of the child is the court's paramount consideration, and the balancing exercise required by the statutes will be no different to that required by Article 8. However, in some cases, the fact that the welfare objective can be achieved with less disruption of existing family relationships can properly be regarded as helping to tip the balance.[312]

Wall LJ then went on to deal with the particular issue of whether special guardianship is more appropriate than adoption when the child is to live with a member of the extended family:

50. It is clear from the White Paper that special guardianship was introduced at least in part to deal with the potential problems arising from the use of adoption in the case of placements within the wider family ...

---

[312] It is reiterated in *Re M-J* [2007] EWCA Civ 56, [17]–[19] that although special guardianship may constitute a more proportionate response to the parents' inability to care for the child this does not give rise to a presumption in favour of special guardianship as the least interventionist measure.

51. A particular concern is that an adoption order has, as a matter of law, the effect of making the adopted child the child of the adopters for all purposes. Accordingly, where a child is adopted by a member of his wider family, the familial relationships are inevitably changed. This is frequently referred to as the "skewing" or "distorting" effect of adoption, and is a factor which the court must take into account when considering whether or not to make an adoption order in such a case. This is not least because the checklist under section 1 of the 2002 Act requires it to do so: – see section 1(4)(f) ("the relationship which the child has with relatives."). However, the weight to be given to this factor will inevitably depend on the facts of the particular case, and it will be only one factor in the overall welfare equation.

52. As will be seen, the three appeals before this court illustrate the different weight to be placed on this factor in different circumstances, and that in some it may be of only marginal importance. In particular, as the case of Re AJ demonstrates, both children and adults are capable of penetrating legal forms and retaining hold of the reality....

In *Re AJ*, Wall LJ added that the distorting effect of adoption on the child's core familial relationships should not be overplayed.[313]

Finally, Wall LJ confirmed that, as the statute explicitly contemplates the court making a special guardianship order of its own motion, the court has the power to impose a special guardianship order on an unwilling party against his or her wishes.[314] In determining whether it should do so, Wall LJ held that the court should apply the welfare checklist taking into account the reasons for the opposition and how that impacts on the child's welfare. However, he emphasized that if the court reaches the view that special guardianship will best serve the child's interests, then that is the order it should make.[315]

Commentators were generally sceptical about whether special guardianship orders would successfully bridge the gap between child arrangements orders and adoption.[316] There would appear, however, to be growing enthusiasm for special guardianship. In 2006 there were just 70 special guardianship orders granted but by 2012 that number had risen quite significantly to 2,130.[317] Special guardianship has proved particularly popular with foster carers (in whose favour the majority of orders are now made) and kinship carers for whom adoption would not have been considered appropriate.[318] It has thus quickly positioned itself as a much more effective alternative to a child arrangements order where children who would otherwise have entered or remained in care are to be cared for within the extended family or by former carers and where the greater security and permanence of adoption is unnecessary.[319] Like adoption, special guardianship thus constitutes an increasingly important part of the state's child protection policy. In keeping with this 'public service function', special guardianship is highly regulated and can attract similar support services as fostering and adoption, including financial support—it should not be regarded as a cheap alternative to the child remaining in local authority care.[320] The reality, however, is that many special guardians are exceptionally vulnerable:

---

[313] [2007] EWCA Civ 55, [44] and [51]. See also *N v B (Adoption by Grandmother)* [2013] EWHC 820, where the skewing of family relationships resulting from an adoption order is recognized as an important but not determinative consideration when deciding between special guardianship and adoption.

[314] [2007] EWCA Civ 54, [73].

[315] Ibid, [73]–[77].

[316] Parkinson (2003), 147.

[317] ONS (2013e), 3.

[318] Ibid.

[319] Hall (2008), 373. See Wade et al (2009).

[320] On the issue of financial support, see *B v London Borough of Lewisham* [2008] EWHC 738; *R (Barrett) v Kirklees Metropolitan Council* [2010] EWHC 467; and *R (TT) v London Borough of Merton* [2012] EWHC 2055.

House of Lords Select Committee on Adoption Legislation 2nd Report of Session 2012-13, *Adoption: Post-Legislative Scrutiny. Report,* **HL Paper 127** (London: TSO, 2013)

235. Special guardians and kinship carers receive little of the training and preparation that is given to prospective adopters; they also receive few of the benefits and financial support arrangements that foster carers receive. Several of our witnesses expressed concern that such carers were struggling to meet the needs of the children in their care....The profile of kinship carers and special guardians is older...and poorer than the average adopter. In addition, they often have to manage complex contact arrangements, where the birth parent seeking contact may be their own child...A survey by the Kinship Care Alliance found that 68% of respondents who sought help from their local authority did not receive the services they required...

237. Children in special guardianship and kinship placements deserve the same support which we recommend for adopted children.[321]

13.9 CONCLUSION

Adoption is a very different way of 'becoming a parent', bringing great rewards, but also many challenges. The law has supported and protected these sometimes fragile family units by treating them in every way as if they were an 'ordinary' natural family. Any legal measures which may mark them out as different, as second-class parents, have been consistently resisted. In many ways, this approach is to be welcomed, recognizing as it does the equal value and importance of social parenting. Adoption can therefore be a liberating force within the law. Freed from biological constraints, it allows a multitude of ways of 'being a family'. Yet adoption is a paradox. Whilst the ACA 2002 recognizes a diverse range of prospective parents, it continues to construct the family unit in accordance with the married (legitimate), heterosexual norm. The courts can perpetuate this myth by assimilating adoptive parenting to the biological 'ideal' and minimizing the extent to which adoptive family life is different: most importantly, that adoptive parenting cannot always be exclusive of the birth family. This reluctance to embrace the difference of adoption betrays the law's true ambivalence towards alternative ways of 'doing family'. The married, heterosexual, autonomous family unit remains the norm and whilst adoption provides a snapshot of the rich complexity of contemporary family life, English law's response to that complexity remains in many ways problematic.

---

[321] See also Wade et al (2009).

BIBLIOGRAPHY

This bibliography contains citations available as hard copy, hard copy and electronic, and solely electronic. Those available as hard copy and electronic are listed in full, with an Online Resource Centre symbol in the margin, to indicate that a link is available on the Online Resource Centre for this book (www.oxfordtextbooks.co.uk/orc/familytcm3e/). Those available only via the internet have URLs listed against them. These links are up to date as of 1 December 2014. If a link becomes broken, please navigate to the Online Resource Centre, as we will regularly monitor links and provide the most up-to-date iterations there.

ACPO (2008). *Guidance on Investigating Domestic Abuse*. <www.acpo.police.uk/documents/crime/2008/2008-cba-inv-dom-abuse.pdf>.

ADAM, S. AND BREWER, M. (2010). *Couple Penalties and Premiums in the UK Tax and Benefit System*. IFS Briefing Note BN 102. <www.ifs.org.uk/bns/bn102.pdf>.

ALGHRANI, A. AND HARRIS, J. (2006). 'Reproductive Liberty: Should the Foundation of Families be Regulated?'. *Child and Family Law Quarterly*, 18: 10.

ALLEN, A. AND GOLDSTEIN, A. (2012). *Survey of Child Maintenance Options Outcomes 2009/10*. CMEC Research Report No 4.

ALLEN, D.W. AND GALLAGHER, M. (2007). 'Does Divorce Law Affect the Divorce Rate? A Review of Empirical Research, 1995–2006'. iMAPP Research Brief, 1(1). <www.marriagedebate.com/pdf/imapp.nofault.divrate.pdf>.

ALTMAN, S. (2003). 'A Theory of Child Support'. *International Journal of Law, Policy and the Family*, 17: 173.

ANCILLARY RELIEF ADVISORY GROUP (1998). *Report to the Lord Chancellor of the Ancillary Relief Advisory Group*. London.

ANDREWS, G. (2007). 'The Presumption of Advancement: Equity, Equality and Human Rights'. *Conveyancer and Property Lawyer*, 340.

ANDREWS, S., ARMSTRONG, D., MCLERNON, L., MEGAW, S., AND SKINNER C. (2011). *Promotion of Child Maintenance: Research on Instigating Behaviourial Change*. CMEC Research Report. <http://webarchive.nationalarchives.gov.uk/20120716161734/http://www.childmaintenance.org/en/pdf/research/Main-Report-Vol-I.pdf>.

ANTOKOLSKAIA, M. (2014). 'Dissolution of Marriage in Westernised Countries', in J. Eekelaar and R. George (eds), *Routledge Handbook of Family Law and Policy*. Abingdon: Routledge.

ARCHBISHOP OF CANTERBURY'S GROUP (1984). *No Just Cause: The Law of Affinity in England and Wales: Some Suggestions for Change*. London: CIO Press.

ARTHUR, S., LEWIS, J., MACLEAN, M., FINCH, S., AND FITZGERALD, R. (2002). *Settling Up: Making Financial Arrangements after Divorce or Separation*. London: National Centre for Social Research.

ATKINSON, A. AND MCKAY, S. (2005). *Child Support Reform: The Views and Experiences of CSA Staff and New Clients*. DWP RR 232. <http://webarchive. nationalarchives.gov.uk/20130314010347/http://research.dwp.gov.uk/asd/asd5/ rports2005-2006/rrep232.pdf>.

AUCHMUTY, R. (2007). 'Unfair Shares for Women: The Rhetoric of Equality and the Reality of Inequality', in H. Lim and A. Bottomley (eds), *Feminist Perspectives on Land Law*. Abingdon: Routledge-Cavendish.

AUCHMUTY, R. (2008). 'What's so Special About Marriage? The Impact of *Wilkinson v Kitzinger*'. *Child and Family Law Quarterly*, 20: 475.

AUCHMUTY, R. (2009). 'Beyond Couples'. *Feminist Legal Studies*, 17: 205.

BAILEY-HARRIS, R. (1992). 'Child Support: Is the Right the Wrong One?'. *International Journal of Law and the Family*, 6: 169.

BAILEY-HARRIS, R. (1996). 'Law and the Unmarried Couple—Oppression or Liberation?'. *Child and Family Law Quarterly*, 8: 137.

BAILEY-HARRIS, R. (2005). 'The Paradoxes of Principle and Pragmatism: Ancillary Relief in England and Wales'. *International Journal of Law, Policy and the Family*, 19: 229.

BAILEY-HARRIS, R., BARRON, J., AND PEARCE, J. (1999a). 'Settlement Culture and the Use of the "No Order" Principle under the Children Act 1989'. *Child and Family Law Quarterly*, 11: 53.

BAILEY-HARRIS, R., BARRON, J., AND PEARCE, J. (1999b). 'From Utility to Rights? The Presumption of Contact in Practice'. *International Journal of Law, Policy and the Family*, 13: 111.

BAINHAM, A. (1989). 'When is a Parent Not a Parent? Reflections on the Unmarried Father and His Child in English Law'. *International Journal of Law and the Family*, 3: 208.

BAINHAM, A. (1990). 'The Privatisation of the Public Interest in Children'. *Modern Law Review*, 53: 206.

BAINHAM, A. (1998). 'Changing Families and Changing Concepts—Reforming the Language of Family Law'. *Child and Family Law Quarterly*, 10: 1.

BAINHAM, A. (1999). 'Parentage, Parenthood and Parental Responsibility', in A. Bainham, S. Day Sclater, and M. Richards (eds), *What is a Parent? A Socio-Legal Analysis*. Oxford: Hart Publishing.

BAINHAM, A. (2007a). '"Truth Will Out": Paternity in Europe'. *Cambridge Law Journal*, 66: 278.

BAINHAM, A. (2007b). 'Who or What is a Parent?'. *Cambridge Law Journal*, 66: 30.

BAINHAM, A. (2008a). 'Arguments About Parentage'. *Cambridge Law Journal*, 67: 322.

BAINHAM, A. (2008b). 'What is the Point of Birth Registration?'. *Child and Family Law Quarterly*, 20: 449.

BAINHAM, A. (2008c). 'Removing Babies at Birth: A More Than Questionable Practice'. *Cambridge Law Journal*, 67: 260.

BAINHAM, A. (2008d). 'Homosexual Adoption'. *Cambridge Law Journal*, 67: 479.

BAINHAM, A. (2013). 'Suspicious Minds: Protecting Children in the Face of Uncertainty'. *Cambridge Law Journal*, 72: 266.

BAINHAM, A. AND GILMORE, S. (2013). *Children: The Modern Law*, 4th edn. Bristol: Jordan Publishing.

BAMFORTH, N. (2001). 'Same-Sex Partnerships and Arguments of Justice', in R. Wintemute and M. Andenæs (eds), *Legal Recognition of Same-Sex Partnerships*. Oxford: Hart Publishing.

BAMFORTH, N. (2007a). '"The Benefits of Marriage in All But Name?" Same-Sex Couples and the Civil Partnership Act 2004'. *Child and Family Law Quarterly*, 19: 133.

BAMFORTH, N. (2007b). 'Same-Sex Partnerships: Some Comparative Constitutional Lessons'. *European Human Rights Law Review*, 12: 47.

BAMFORTH, N. (2011). 'Families By Not (Yet) Marriages? Same-Sex Partners and the Developing European Convention "Margin of Appreciation"'. *Child and Family Law Quarterly*, 23: 128.

BARKER, N. (2012). 'Civil Partnership: An Alternative to Marriage? *Ferguson and others v UK*'. *Family Law*, 42: 548.

BARLOW, A. (2004). 'Regulation of Cohabitation, Changing Family Policies and Social Attitudes: A Discussion of Britain within Europe'. *Law and Policy*, 26: 57.

BARLOW, A. AND DUNCAN, S. (2000). 'New Labour's Communitarianism, Supporting Families and the "Rationality Mistake": Part II'. *Journal of Social Welfare and Family Law*, 22: 129.

BARLOW, A. AND JAMES, G. (2004). 'Regulating Marriage and Cohabitation in 21st Century Britain'. *Modern Law Review*, 67: 143.

BARLOW, A. AND LIND, C. (1999). 'A Matter of Trust: The Allocation of Rights in the Family Home'. *Legal Studies*, 19: 468.

BARLOW, A. AND SMITHSON, J. (2010). 'Legal Assumptions, Cohabitants' Talk and the Rocky Road to Reform'. *Child and Family Law Quarterly*, 22: 328.

BARLOW, A. AND SMITHSON, J. (2012). 'Is Modern Marriage a Bargain? Exploring Perceptions of Pre-Nuptial Agreements in England and Wales'. *Child and Family Law Quarterly*, 24: 304.

BARLOW, A., BURGOYNE, C., AND SMITHSON, J. (2007). *The Living Together Campaign: An Investigation of its Impact on Legally Aware Cohabitants*. Ministry of Justice Research Series 5/07. <http://lawcommission.justice.gov.uk/docs/living-together-research-report.pdf>.

BARLOW, A., BURGOYNE, C., CLERY, E., AND SMITHSON, J. (2008). 'Cohabitation and the Law: Myths, Money and the Media', in A. Park et al (eds), *British Social Attitudes: The 24th Report*. London: Sage.

BARLOW, A., DUNCAN, S., JAMES, G., AND PARK, A. (2001). 'Just a Piece of Paper? Marriage and Cohabitation in Britain', in A. Park, J. Curtice, K. Thomson, L. Jarvis, and C. Bromley (eds), *British Social Attitudes: The 18th Report—Public Policy, Social Ties*. London: Sage.

BARLOW, A., DUNCAN, S., JAMES, G., AND PARK, A. (2005). *Cohabitation, Marriage and the Law*. Oxford: Hart Publishing.

🌐 BARNARD, C. (2008). 'The "Opt-Out" for the UK and Poland from the Charter of Fundamental Rights: Triumph of Rhetoric over Reality?', in S. Griller and J. Ziller (eds), *The Lisbon Treaty: EU Constitutionalism without a Constitutional Treaty*. New York: Springer. <www.law.cam.ac.uk/faculty-resources/summary/barnard-uk-opt-out-and-the-charter-of-fundamental-rights/7309/pdf>.

BARNES, H., DAY, P., AND CRONIN, N. (1998). *Trial and Error: A Review of UK Child Support Policy*, Occasional Paper 24. London: Family Policy Studies Centre.

🌐 BARNES, L. (2007). '*Stack v Dowden*: The Principles in Practice'. <www.familylaw-week.co.uk/site.aspx?i=ed642>.

BARNETT, A. (2000). 'Contact and Domestic Violence: The Ideological Divide', in J. Bridgeman and D. Monk (eds), *Feminist Perspectives on Child Law*. London: Cavendish.

BARNETT, H. (1998). *Introduction to Feminist Jurisprudence*. London: Cavendish Publishing.

BARRON, J. (2002). *Five Years On: A Review of Legal Protection from Domestic Violence*. Bristol: Women's Aid Federation of England.

BARTON, C. (1998). 'Third Time Lucky for Child Support?—The 1998 Green Paper'. *Family Law*, 28: 668.

BARTON, C. (1999). 'Child Support—Tony's Turn'. *Family Law*, 29: 704.

BARTON, C. (2002). 'White Paper Weddings—The Beginnings, Muddles and Ends of Wedlock'. *Family Law*, 32: 431.

BARTON, C. AND BISSETT-JOHNSON, A. (2000). 'The Declining Number of Ancillary Relief Financial Orders'. *Family Law*, 30: 94.

BARTON, C. AND DOUGLAS, G. (1995). *Law and Parenthood*. London: Butterworths.

BEAUJOUAN, É. AND NÍ BHROLCHÁIN, M. (2011). 'Cohabitation and Marriage in Britain Since the 1970s'. *Population Trends*, 145: 1.

BENDALL, C. (2014). 'Some are More "Equal" than Others: Heteronormativity in the Post-*White* Era of Financial Remedies'. *Journal of Social Welfare and Family Law*, 36: 3.

BEVERIDGE REPORT (1942). *Social Insurance and Allied Services: A Report by Sir William Beveridge*, Cmd 6404. London: HMSO.

🌐 BIEHAL, N., ELLISON, S., BAKER, C., AND SINCLAIR, I. (2009). Characteristics, Outcomes and Meanings of Three Types of Permanent Placement – Adoption by Strangers, Adoption by Carers and Long-Term Foster Care. DCSF-RBX-09-11. <www.york.ac.uk/inst/spru/research/pdf/3types.pdf>.

BIRD, R. AND BURROWS, D. (2009). *Child Maintenance: The New Law*. Bristol: Jordan Publishing.

BLACK, J., BRIDGE, J., BOND, T., GRIBBIN, L., AND REARDON, M. (2012). *A Practical Approach to Family Law*, 9th edn. Oxford: OUP.

BLACKSTONE, W. (1765). *Commentaries on the Laws of England, Volume I: Of the Rights of Persons*. Facsimile edition (1979) S. Katz (ed). Chicago: University of Chicago Press.

BLACKWELL, A. AND DAWE, F. (2003). *Non-Resident Parental Contact—Final Report*. London: Office for National Statistics.

BODEN, R. AND CHILDS, M. (1996). 'Paying for Procreation: Child Support Arrangements in the UK'. *Feminist Legal Studies*, 4: 131.

BOELE-WOELKI, K., DETHLOFF, N., AND GEPHART, W. (eds) (2014). *Family Law and Culture in Europe*. Cambridge: Intersentia.

BOELE-WOELKI, K., FERRAND, F., GONZÁLEZ BEILFUSS, C., JÄNTERÄ-JAREBORG, M., LOWE, N., MARTINY, D., AND PINTENS, W. (2004). *Principles of European Family Law Regarding Divorce and Maintenance Between Former Spouses*. Antwerp; Oxford: Intersentia.

BONNER, D., FENWICK, H., AND HARRIS-SHORT, S. (2003). 'Judicial Approaches to the HRA'. *International and Comparative Law Quarterly*, 52: 549.

BOOTH COMMITTEE (1985). *Report of the Matrimonial Causes Procedure Committee*. London: HMSO.

BOTTOMLEY, A. (1984). 'Resolving Family Disputes: A Critical View', in M. Freeman (ed), *State, Law and the Family*. London: Tavistock.

BOTTOMLEY, A. (1993). 'Self and Subjectivities: Languages of Claim in Property Law'. *Journal of Law and Society*, 20: 56.

BOTTOMLEY, A. (1998). 'Women and Trust(s): Portraying the Family in the Gallery of Law', in S. Bright and J. Dewar (eds), *Land Law: Themes and Perspectives*. Oxford: OUP.

BOTTOMLEY, A. AND WONG, S. (2006). 'Shared Households: A New Paradigm for Thinking About the Reform of Domestic Property Relations', in A. Diduck and K. O'Donovan (eds), *Feminist Perspectives on Family Law*. Abingdon: Routledge.

BOWCOTT, O. (2014). 'Couple Launch Legal Challenge Against Ban on Heterosexual Civil Partnerships'. *Guardian*, 2 December 2014. <www.theguardian.com/lifeandstyle/2014/dec/02/couple-challenge-ban-heterosexual-civil-partnerships/print>.

BOYD, S. (1989). 'From Gender Specificity to Gender Neutrality? Ideologies in Canadian Child Custody Law', in C. Smart and S. Sevenhuijsen (eds), *Child Custody and the Politics of Gender*. London: Routledge.

BRADNEY, A. (1984). 'Arranged Marriages and Duress'. *Journal of Social Welfare and Family Law*, 6: 278.

BRADNEY, A. (1994). 'Duress, Family Law and the Coherent Legal System'. *Modern Law Review*, 57: 963.

BRADSHAW, J. AND MILLAR, J. (1991). *Lone Parent Families in the UK*, Department of Social Security Research Report No 6. London: HMSO.

BRADSHAW, J., STIMSON, C., SKINNER, C., AND WILLIAMS, J. (1999). *Absent Fathers?* London: Routledge.

BRAND, A. AND BRINICH, P. (1999). 'Behavior Problems and Mental Health Contacts in Adopted, Foster, and Nonadopted Children'. *Journal of Child Psychology and Psychiatry*, 40: 1221.

BRASSE, G. (1993). 'The Section 31 Monopoly—*Nottinghamshire CC v P* Considered'. *Family Law*, 23: 691.

BRASSE, G. (2006). 'It's Payback Time! *Miller, McFarlane* and the Compensation Culture'. *Family Law*, 36: 647.

BRAZIER, M., CAMPBELL, A., AND GOLOMBOK, S. (1997). *Surrogacy—Review for the UK Health Ministers of Current Arrangements for Payments and Regulation. Consultation Document and Questionnaire*. London: DH.

BRAZIER, M., CAMPBELL, A., AND GOLOMBOK, S. (1998). *Surrogacy—Review for Health Ministers of Current Arrangements for Payments and Regulation. Report of the Review Team*, Cm 4068. London: HMSO.

BREMNER, P. (2014). 'Lesbian Parents and Biological Fathers – Leave to Apply for Contact'. *Journal of Social Welfare and Family Law*, 36: 79.

BRIDGE, C. (1993). 'Changing the Nature of Adoption: Law Reform in England and New Zealand'. *Legal Studies*, 13: 81.

BRIDGE, C. (2001). 'Adoption Law: A Balance of Interests', in J. Herring (ed), *Family Law: Issues, Debates, Policy*. Cullompton: Willan.

BRIDGE, S. (1998). 'Transferring Tenancies of the Family Home'. *Family Law*, 28: 26.

BRIDGE, S. (2001). 'Marriage and Divorce: The Regulation of Intimacy', in J. Herring (ed), *Family Law: Issues, Debates, Policy*. Cullompton: Willan.

BRITISH ACADEMY WORKING GROUP (2009). *Social Science and Family Policies*. London: British Academy.

BROPHY J. (1989). 'Custody Law, Child Care, and Inequality in Britain', in C. Smart and S. Sevenhuijsen (eds), *Child Custody and the Politics of Gender*. London: Routledge.

BROWN, J. AND DAY SCLATER, S. (1999). 'Divorce: A Psychodynamic Perspective', in S. Day Sclater and C. Piper (eds), *Undercurrents of Divorce*. Dartmouth: Ashgate.

BRYAN, M. AND SANZ, A. (2008). *Does Housework Lower Wages and Why? Evidence for Britain*. ISER Working Paper 2008-3. <www.iser.essex.ac.uk/publications/working-papers/iser/2008-03.pdf>.

BRYSON, C., ELLMAN, I., McKAY, S., AND MILES, J. (2015). *Child Maintenance: How Would the British Public Calculate What the State Should Require Parents to Pay?* London: Nuffield Foundation. <www.nuffieldfoundation.org/public-views-child-support>.

BRYSON, C., SKIPP, A., ALLBESON, J., POOLE, E., IRELAND, E., AND MARSH, V. (2013). *Kids Aren't Free: The Child Maintenance Arrangements of Single Parents on Benefit 2013*. London: Nuffield Foundation. <www.nuffieldfoundation.org/sites/default/files/files/Kids%20aren%27t%20free%20-%20full%20report_04_07_13.pdf>.

BURGOYNE, C. AND SONNENBERG, S. (2009). 'Financial Practices in Cohabiting Heterosexual Couples: A Perspective from Economic Psychology', in J. Miles and R. Probert (eds) (2009), below.

BURROWS, D. (2009a). 'Do Child Support Committal Applications Breach Human Rights?'. *New Law Journal*, 159: 653.

BURROWS, D. (2009b). 'Enforcement of Child Maintenance: *Kehoe*'. *Family Law*, 39: 1086.

BURROWS, D. (2010). 'Delay and Enforcement of Child Support Arrears'. *Family Law*, 40: 269.

BURTON, M. (2003a). 'Third Party Applications for Protection Orders in England and Wales: Service Provider's Views on Implementing Section 60 of the Family Law Act 1996'. *Journal of Social Welfare and Family Law*, 25: 137.

BURTON, M. (2003b). 'Criminalising Breaches of Civil Orders for Protection from Domestic Violence'. *Criminal Law Review*, 301.

BURTON, M. (2004a). '*Lomas v Parle*—Coherent and Effective Remedies for Victims of Domestic Violence: Time for an Integrated Domestic Violence Court?'. *Child and Family Law Quarterly*, 16: 17.

BURTON, M. (2004b). 'Domestic Violence—From Consultation to Bill: Closer Integration of the Civil and Criminal Justice Systems'. *Family Law*, 34: 128.

BURTON, M. (2006). 'Judicial Monitoring of Compliance: Introducing "Problem Solving" Approaches to Domestic Violence Courts in England and Wales'. *International Journal of Law, Policy and the Family*, 20: 366.

BURTON, M. (2008a). *Legal Responses to Domestic Violence*. Abingdon: Routledge-Cavendish.

BURTON, M. (2008b). *Domestic Abuse Literature Review*. <www.reading.gov.uk/documents%5Ccommunity-living%5Ccommunity-safety/13535/DomesticAbuseLiteratureReview.pdf>.

BURTON, M. (2009a). 'Failing to Protect: Victims' Rights and Police Liability'. *Modern Law Review*, 72: 283.

BURTON, M. (2009b). 'Civil Law Remedies for Domestic Violence: Why are Applications for Non-Molestation Orders Declining?'. *Journal of Social Welfare and Family Law*, 31: 109.

BURTON, M. (2010). 'The Human Rights of Victims of Domestic Violence: *Opuz v Turkey*'. *Child and Family Law Quarterly*, 22: 131.

BURTON, M., McCRORY, A., AND BUCK, T. (2002). *The Civil Remedies for Domestic Violence under the Family Law Act 1996: Is Section 60 the Way Forward?* Unpublished report submitted to the LCD, October.

BUTLER-SLOSS, E. (1988). *Report of the Inquiry into Child Abuse in Cleveland 1987*, Cm 412. London: HMSO.

ⓦ CABINET OFFICE PERFORMANCE AND INNOVATION UNIT (2000). *Prime Minister's Review of Adoption*. <http://webarchive.nationalarchives.gov.uk/+/http://www. cabinetoffice.gov.uk/strategy/downloads/su/adoption/adoption.pdf>.

CALDERWOOD, L. (2008). 'Family Demographics', in K. Hansen and H. Joshi (eds), *Millennium Cohort Survey: Third Survey—A User's Guide to Initial Findings*. London: Centre for Longitudinal Studies.

CALDWELL, J. (2011). 'Common Law Judges and Judicial Interviewing'. *Child and Family Law Quarterly*, 23: 41.

CALLUS, T. (2008). 'First "Designer Babies", Now À La Carte Parents'. *Family Law*, 38: 143.

CAMERON, E. (2001). 'Foreword' to R. Wintemute and M. Andenæs (eds), *Legal Recognition of Same-Sex Partnerships*. Oxford: Hart Publishing.

CAMPBELL, T. (1992). 'The Rights of Minor: As Person, as Child, as Juvenile, as Future Adult'. *International Journal of Law and the Family*, 6: 1.

CARACCIOLO DI TORELLA, E. AND REID, E. (2002). 'The Changing Shape of the "European Family" and Fundamental Rights'. *European Law Review*, 27: 80.

CARBONE, J. (1996). 'Feminism, Gender and the Consequences of Divorce', in M. Freeman (ed), *Divorce: Where Next?* Dartmouth: Ashgate.

ⓦ CASC (2000). *Report on the Question of Parental Contact in Cases Where There is Domestic Violence*. <http://webarchive.nationalarchives.gov.uk/+/http://www.dca.gov. uk/family/abfla/dvconreport.pdf>.

ⓦ CASC (2001). *Making Contact Work. The Facilitation of Arrangements for Contact between Children and their Non-Residential Parents; and the Enforcement of Court Orders for Contact*. <http://webarchive.nationalarchives.gov.uk/+/http://www.dca.gov.uk/ family/abfla/mcwrep.pdf>.

CASHMORE, J. AND PARKINSON, P. (2011). 'Parenting Arrangements for Young Children: Messages from Research'. *Australian Journal of Family Law*, 25: 236.

CASTLE, J., BECKETT, C., AND GROOTHUES, C. (2000). 'Infant Adoption in England. A Longitudinal Account of Social and Cognitive Progress'. *Adoption and Fostering*, 24: 26.

CAVE, E. AND WALLBANK, J. (2012). 'Minors' Capacity to Refuse Treatment: A Reply to Gilmore and Herring'. *Medical Law Review*, 20: 423.

ⓦ CENTRE FOR SOCIAL JUSTICE (2009). *Every Family Matters: An In-Depth Review of Family Law in Britain*. London: Centre for Social Justice. <www.centreforsocialjustice. org.uk/UserStorage/pdf/Pdf%20reports/CSJEveryFamilyMattersWEB.pdf>.

ⓦ CENTRE FOR SOCIAL JUSTICE (2012). *Beyond Violence: Breaking Cycles of Domestic Abuse*. <www.centreforsocialjustice.org.uk/publications/beyond-violence-breaking-cycles-of-domestic-abuse>.

CHAU, P.-L. AND HERRING, J. (2004). 'Men, Women, People: The Definition of Sex', in B. Brooks-Gordon, L. Gelsthorpe, M. Johnson, and A. Bainham (eds), *Sexuality Repositioned: Diversity and the Law*. Oxford: Hart Publishing.

CHOUDHRY, S. (2003). 'The Adoption and Children Act 2002, the Welfare Principle and the Human Rights Act 1998—A Missed Opportunity'. *Child and Family Law Quarterly*, 15: 119.

CHOUDHRY, S. AND FENWICK, H. (2005). 'Taking the Rights of Parents and Children Seriously: Confronting the Welfare Principle under the Human Rights Act'. *Oxford Journal of Legal Studies*, 25: 453.

CHOUDHRY, S. AND HERRING, J. (2006a). 'Righting Domestic Violence'. *International Journal of Law, Policy and the Family*, 20: 95.

CHOUDHRY, S. AND HERRING, J. (2006b). 'Domestic Violence and the Human Rights Act 1998: A New Means of Legal Intervention?'. *Public Law*, 752.

CHOUDHRY, S. AND HERRING, J. (2010). *European Human Rights and Family Law*. Oxford: Hart Publishing.

CHURCH OF ENGLAND (2003). *Response to Civil Partnership Consultation*. <www.churchofengland.org/media/45595/civil.pdf>.

CHURCH OF ENGLAND (2013). *Response to Equal Marriage Consultation*. <www.churchofengland.org/media/1475149/s-s%20marriage.pdf>.

CLARKE, L. AND BERRINGTON, A. (1999). 'Socio-Demographic Predictors of Divorce', in *One Plus One Marriage and Partnership Research, High Divorce Rates: The State of the Evidence on Reasons and Remedies*. Lord Chancellor's Department Research Report Series 2/99, 1(1). Summary at <http://webarchive.nationalarchives.gov.uk/+/http://www.dca.gov.uk/research/1999/299-1esfr.htm>.

CLIVE, E. (1980). 'Marriage: An Unnecessary Legal Concept?', in J. Eekelaar and S. Katz (eds), *Marriage and Cohabitation in Contemporary Societies*. London: Butterworths.

CMEC (2012). *The Child Support Maintenance Calculations Regulations 2012: A Technical Consultation on the Draft Regulations*. <www.gov.uk/government/consultations/child-support-maintenance-calculation-regulations-2012-technical-consultation>.

COAST, E. (2009). 'Currently Cohabiting: Relationships, Attitudes, Expectations and Outcomes'. LSE Research Online. <http://eprints.lse.ac.uk/23986/1/Currently_cohabiting_(LSERO).pdf>.

COBLEY, C. AND LOWE, N. (2009). 'Interpreting the Threshold Criteria under Section 31(2) of the Children Act 1989—The House of Lords Decision in *Re B*'. *Modern Law Review*, 72: 463.

COENRAAD, L. (2014). 'Voices of Minor Children Heard and Unheard in Judicial Divorce Proceedings in the Netherlands'. *Journal of Social Welfare and Family Law*, 36: 370.

COLEMAN, K. AND OSBORNE, S. (2010). 'Homicide', in K. Smith et al (eds), *Homicides, Firearm Offences and Intimate Violence 2008/09: Supplementary Volume 2 to Crime in*

England and Wales 2008/09. Home Office Statistical Bulletin 01/10. <http://webarchive. nationalarchives.gov.uk/20110218135832/http:/rds.homeoffice.gov.uk/rds/pdfs10/ hosb0110.pdf>.

COLEMAN, L. AND GLENN F. (2010). *When Couples Part: Understanding the Consequences for Adults and Children.* London: One Plus One.

COLEMAN, N., SEEDS, K., AND NORDEN, O. (2007). *Child Maintenance Redesign Survey: Indications of Future Behaviours and Choice.* DWP Research Report No 444. <http://webarchive.nationalarchives.gov.uk/20130314010347/http://research.dwp.gov. uk/asd/asd5/rports2007-2008/rrep444.pdf>.

COLLIER, R. (1994). 'The Campaign Against the Child Support Act: "Errant Fathers" and "Family Men"'. *Family Law,* 24: 384.

COLLIER, R. (1995). *Masculinity, Law and the Family.* London: Routledge.

COLLIER, R. (1999). 'The Dashing of a "Liberal Dream"?—The Information Meeting, the "New Family" and the Limits of Law'. *Child and Family Law Quarterly,* 11: 257.

COLLIER, R. (2001). 'A Hard Time to be a Father?: Reassessing the Relationship Between Law, Policy, and Family (Practices)'. *Journal of Law and Society,* 28: 520.

COLLIER, R. (2003). 'In Search of the 'Good Father': Law, Family Practices and the Normative Reconstruction of Parenthood', in J. Dewar and S. Parker (eds), *Family Law Processes, Practices and Pressures—Proceedings of the Tenth World Conference of the International Society of Family Law, July 2000, Brisbane, Australia.* Oregon: Hart Publishing.

COLLIER, R. (2005). 'Fathers 4 Justice, Law and the New Politics of Fatherhood'. *Child and Family Law Quarterly,* 17: 511.

COLLIER, R. (2014). 'Men, Gender and Fathers' Rights "After Legal Equality": New Formations of Rights and Responsibilities in Family Justice', in R. Leckey (ed), *After Legal Equality: Family, Sex, Kinship.* Abingdon: Routledge.

COLLIER, R. AND SHELDON, S. (2008). *Fragmenting Fatherhood. A Socio-Legal Study.* Oxford: Hart Publishing.

COLLINS, L. (ed) (2014). *Dicey, Morris and Collins on the Conflict of Laws,* 15th edn. London: Sweet & Maxwell.

CONWAY, H. (2002). 'Money and Domestic Violence—Escaping the *Nwogbe* Trap'. *Family Law,* 32: 61.

COOK, D., BURTON, M., ROBINSON, A., AND VALLELY, C. (2004). *Evaluation of Specialist Domestic Violence Courts/Fast Track Systems.* London: Crown Prosecution Service/ Department of Constitutional Affairs.

COOKE, E. (2007). '*Miller/McFarlane*: Law in Search of Discrimination'. *Child and Family Law Quarterly,* 19: 98.

COOKE, E. (2009). 'The Future of Ancillary Relief', in G. Douglas and N. Lowe, *The Continuing Evolution of Family Law.* Bristol: Family Law.

COOKE, E. (2011a). 'In the Wake of *Stack v Dowden*: The Tale of TR1'. *Family Law,* 41: 1142.

COOKE, E. (2011b). 'White v White: A Late Instalment in a Long Story', in S. Gilmore, J. Herring, and R. Probert (eds), Landmark Cases in Family Law. Oxford: Hart Publishing.

COOKE, E., BARLOW, A., AND CALLUS, T. (2006). Community of Property: A Regime for England and Wales? London: Policy Press.

COUNCIL OF EUROPE (2011). Convention on Preventing and Combating Violence Against Women and Domestic Violence. CETS 210. <www.conventions.coe.int/Treaty/Commun/QueVoulezVous.asp?CL=ENG&NT=210>.

CPAG (2006). CPAG Response to Government Consultation on Henshaw Review of Child Support. London: CPAG.

CPAG (2014). Welfare Benefits and Tax Credits Handbook 2014/2015. London: CPAG.

CPAG (2014). Child Support Handbook 2014/2015. London: CPAG.

CPS (2006). Domestic Violence Monitoring Snapshot. <www.cps.gov.uk/publications/prosecution/domestic/snapshot_2005_12.html#06>.

CPS (2008). Guidance on Section 1, Domestic Violence, Crime and Victims Act 2004. <www.cps.gov.uk/legal/d_to_g/guidance_on_section_1_domestic_violence_crime_and_victims_act_2004/>.

CPS (2009). CPS Policy for Prosecuting Cases of Domestic Violence. <www.cps.gov.uk/publications/prosecution/domestic/domv.html>.

CPS (2014a). 'DPP Announces Highest Ever Conviction Rate for Domestic Violence at Women's Aid Conference'. <www.cps.gov.uk/news/latest_news/vawg_report_2014/>.

CPS (2014b). Violence against Women and Girls Crime Report 2013–14. <www.cps.gov.uk/publications/docs/cps_vawg_report_2014.pdf>.

CPS (2014c). The Prosecution of Domestic Violence Cases. <www.cps.gov.uk/consultations/dv_2014_consultation.html>.

CRAWFORD, C., GOODMAN, A., GREAVES, E., AND JOYCE, R. (2012). 'Cohabitation, Marriage and Child Outcomes: An Empirical Analysis of the Relationship Between Marital Status and Child Outcomes in the UK using the Millennium Cohort Study'. Child and Family Law Quarterly, 24: 176.

CRAWSHAW, M., BLYTH, E., AND VAN DEN AKKER, O. (2012). 'The Changing Profile of Surrogacy in the UK: Implications for National and International Policy and Practice'. Journal of Social Welfare and Family Law, 34: 265.

CRETNEY, A. AND DAVIS, G. (1997). 'The Significance of Compellability in the Prosecution of Domestic Assault'. British Journal of Criminology, 37: 75.

CRETNEY, S. (1992). 'Divorce—A Smooth Transition?'. Family Law, 22: 472.

CRETNEY, S. (1996a). 'Divorce Reform: Humbug and Hypocrisy or Smooth Transition?', in M. Freeman (ed), Divorce: Where Next? Aldershot: Dartmouth.

CRETNEY, S. (1996b). 'From Status to Contract?', in F. Rose (ed), Consensus ad Idem: Essays in the Law of Contract in Honour of Guenter Treitel. London: Sweet & Maxwell.

CRETNEY, S. (1998). *Law, Law Reform and the Family*. Oxford: OUP.

CRETNEY, S. (1999). 'Contract Not Apt in Divorce Deal'. *Law Quarterly Review*, 115: 356.

CRETNEY, S. (2003a). *Family Law in the Twentieth Century: A History*. Oxford: OUP.

CRETNEY, S. (2003b). 'Community of Property Imposed by Judicial Decision'. *Law Quarterly Review*, 119: 349.

CRETNEY, S. (2006a). *Same Sex Relationships*. Oxford: OUP.

CRETNEY, S. (2006b). 'Marriage, Mothers-in-Law and Human Rights'. *Law Quarterly Review*, 122: 8.

CRETNEY, S. AND MASSON, J. (1990). *Principles of Family Law*, 5th edn. London: Sweet & Maxwell.

CRETNEY, S., MASSON J., AND BAILEY-HARRIS, R. (2002). *Principles of Family Law*, 7th edn. London: Sweet & Maxwell.

CROMPTON, L. (2004). 'Civil Partnerships Bill 2004: The Illusion of Equality'. *Family Law*, 34: 888.

CROMPTON, L. (2013). 'DVP Notices and Orders: Vulnerable to Human Rights Challenge?'. *Family Law*, 43: 1588.

CROMPTON, L. (2014). DVP Notices and Orders: Protecting Victims or the Public Purse?'. *Family Law*, 44: 62.

CURRY-SUMNER, I. (2006). *All's Well that Ends Registered*. Antwerp; Oxford: Intersentia.

CURRY-SUMNER, I. (2009). '*E.B. v France*: A Missed Opportunity'. *Child and Family Law Quarterly*, 21: 356.

DANCE, C. AND RUSHTON, A. (2005). 'Predictors of Outcome for Unrelated Adoptive Placements Made During Middle Childhood'. *Child and Family Social Work*, 10: 269.

DAVIES, C. (1993). 'Divorce Reform in England and Wales: A Visitor's View'. *Family Law*, 23: 331.

DAVIS, G. (1988). *Partisans and Mediators*. Oxford: OUP.

DAVIS, G. (2000). *Monitoring Publicly Funded Family Mediation—Summary Report to the Legal Services Commission*. London: Legal Services Commission.

DAVIS, G. AND MURCH, M. (1988). *Grounds for Divorce*. Oxford: Clarendon Press.

DAVIS, G. AND ROBERTS, M. (1989). 'Mediation and the Battle of the Sexes'. *Family Law*, 19: 305.

DAVIS, G. AND WIKELEY, N. (2002). 'National Survey of Child Support Agency Clients—The Relationship Dimension'. *Family Law*, 32: 522.

DAVIS, G., CRETNEY, S., AND COLLINS, J. (1994). *Simple Quarrels: Negotiating Money and Property Disputes on Divorce*. Oxford: OUP.

DAVIS, G., PEARCE, J., BIRD, R., WOODWARD, H., AND WALLACE, C. (2000). 'Research: Ancillary Relief Outcomes'. *Child and Family Law Quarterly*, 12: 43.

DAVIS, G., WIKELEY, N., AND YOUNG, R., WITH BARRON, J. AND BEDWARD, J. (1998). *Child Support in Action*. Oxford: Hart Publishing.

DAY SCLATER, S. (1999). 'Experiences of Divorce', in S. Day Sclater and C. Piper (eds), *Undercurrents of Divorce*. Dartmouth: Ashgate.

DAY SCLATER, S., BAINHAM, A., AND RICHARDS, M. (1999). 'Introduction', in A. Bainham, S. Day Sclater, and M. Richards (eds), *What is a Parent? A Socio-Legal Analysis*. Oxford: Hart Publishing.

DCA (2002). *Scoping Study on Delay in Children Act Cases Findings and Action Taken*. <www.dca.gov.uk/family/scopestud.htm>.

DCA (2006a). *Judicial Statistics (Revised) England and Wales for the Year 2005*, Cm 6903. London: TSO. <www.official-documents.gov.uk/document/cm69/6903/6903.pdf>.

DCA (2006b). *Separate Representation of Children*. London: HMSO.

DCA (date unknown). 'Government Policy concerning Transsexual People'. <www.dca.gov.uk/constitution/transsex/policy.htm>.

DCA AND DFES (2004). *The Government's Response to the Children Act Sub-Committee (CASC) Report: 'Making Contact Work'*. <http://webarchive.nationalarchives.gov.uk/+/http://www.dca.gov.uk/family/abfla/cascresponse.pdf>.

DCA, DFES, AND DTI (2004). *Parental Separation: Children's Needs and Parents' Responsibilities*, Cm 6273. London: HMSO.

DCA, DFES, AND DTI (2005). *Parental Separation: Children's Needs and Parents' Responsibilities—Next Steps*, Cm 6452. London: HMSO.

DCLG (2009). *Housing in England 2007–8*. London: DCLG.

DCLG (2014). *English Housing Survey: Headline Report 2012–13*. <www.gov.uk/government/uploads/system/uploads/attachment_data/file/284648/English_Housing_Survey_Headline_Report_2012-13.pdf>.

DCMS (2014a). *Civil Partnership Review (England and Wales): A Consultation*. <www.gov.uk/government/consultations/consultation-on-the-future-of-civil-partnership-in-england-and-wales>.

DCMS (2014b). *Civil Partnership Review (England and Wales): Report and Conclusions*. <www.gov.uk/government/consultations/consultation-on-the-future-of-civil-partnership-in-england-and-wales>.

DCSF (2009). *Statistical First Release – Children Looked After in England (Including Adoption and Care Leavers) Year Ending 31 March 2009*, SFR 25/2009. London: DCSF.

DCSF and DWP (2008). *Joint Birth Registration: Recording Responsibility*, Cm 7293 (London: HMSO). <www.gov.uk/government/uploads/system/uploads/attachment_data/file/243115/7293.pdf>.

DE WAAL, A. (2008). *Second Thoughts on the Family*. London: Civitas.

DEECH, R. (1977). 'The Principles of Maintenance'. *Family Law*, 7: 229.

DEECH, R. (1980a). 'Williams and Glyn's and Family Law'. New Law Journal, 130: 896.

DEECH, R. (1980b). 'The Case Against the Legal Recognition of Cohabitation'. International and Comparative Law Quarterly, 29: 480.

DEECH, R. (1982). 'Financial Relief: The Retreat from Precedent and Principle'. Law Quarterly Review, 98: 621.

DEECH, R. (1984). 'Matrimonial Property and Divorce: A Century of Progress?', in M. Freeman (ed), State, Law, and the Family. London: Tavistock Publications.

DEECH, R. (1990). 'Divorce Law and Empirical Studies'. Law Quarterly Review, 106: 229.

DEECH, R. (1992). 'The Unmarried Father and Human Rights'. Journal of Child Law, 4: 3.

DEECH, R. (1996). 'Property and Money Matters', in M. Freeman (ed), Divorce: Where Next? Aldershot: Dartmouth.

DEECH, R. (2009a). Divorce Law—A Disaster? Gresham Lectures 2009–10, <www.gresham.ac.uk/event.asp?PageId=45&EventId=946> and Family Law, 39: 1048.

DEECH, R. (2009b). Cohabitation and the Law. Gresham Lectures 2009–10, <www.gresham.ac.uk/lectures-and-events/cohabitation-and-the-law> and Family Law, 40: 39.

DEECH, R. (2009c). What's a Woman Worth? The Maintenance Law. Gresham Lectures 2009–10, <www.gresham.ac.uk/lectures-and-events/what%E2%80%99s-a-woman-worth-the-maintenance-law> and Family Law, 39: 1140.

DEPARTMENT OF JUSTICE (2008). Spousal Support Advisory Guidelines. <www.justice.gc.ca/eng/fl-df/spousal-epoux/ssag-ldfpae.html>.

DEVEREUX, E. AND GEORGE, R. (2014). 'When Will the Supreme Court Put Us Out of Our Payne?'. Family Law, 44: 1586.

DEWAR, J. (1997). 'Reducing Discretion in Family Law'. Australian Journal of Family Law, 11: 309.

DEWAR, J. (1998a). 'The Normal Chaos of Family Law'. Modern Law Review, 61: 467.

DEWAR, J. (1998b). 'Land, Law and the Family Home', in S. Bright and J. Dewar (eds), Land Law: Themes and Perspectives. Oxford: OUP.

DEWAR, J. (2003). 'Families', in P. Cane and M. Tushnet (eds), The Oxford Handbook of Legal Studies. Oxford: OUP.

DEY, I. (2005). 'Adapting Adoption: A Case of Closet Politics?'. International Journal of Law, Policy and the Family, 19: 289.

DFE (2012a). Contact Arrangements for Children: A Call for Views. <http://dera.ioe.ac.uk/15557/1/contact%20arrangements%20for%20children%20a%20call%20for%20views.pdf>.

DFE (2012b). An Action Plan for Adoption: Tackling Delay. <www.gov.uk/government/uploads/system/uploads/attachment_data/file/180250/action_plan_for_adoption.pdf>.

DFE (2013a). Improving Permanence for Looked After Children. <www.gov.uk/government/uploads/system/uploads/attachment_data/file/245513/consultation_document.pdf>.

DFE (2013b). *Statistical First Release. Children Looked After in England (Including Adoption and Care Leavers) Year Ending 31 March 2013*, SFR 36/2013. <www.gov.uk/government/uploads/system/uploads/attachment_data/file/244872/SFR36_2013.pdf>.

DFE (2013c). *Statistical First Release, Outcomes for Children Looked After by Local Authorities in England, as at 31 March 2013*, SFR 50/2013. <www.gov.uk/government/uploads/system/uploads/attachment_data/file/264385/SFR50_2013_Text.pdf>.

DFE (2013d). *Working Together to Safeguard Children*. <www.gov.uk/government/uploads/system/uploads/attachment_data/file/281368/Working_together_to_safeguard_children.pdf>.

DFE (2013e). *Statistical First Release, Characteristics of Children in Need in England, 2012–13*, SFR45/2013. <www.gov.uk/government/uploads/system/uploads/attachment_data/file/254084/SFR45-2013_Text.pdf>.

DFE (2014a). *Statutory Guidance on Court Orders and Pre-Proceedings for Local Authorities*. <www.gov.uk/government/uploads/system/uploads/attachment_data/file/339926/Statutory_Guidance_on_court_orders_and_pre-proceedings_18_2.pdf>.

DFE (2014b). *Adoption: National Minimum Standards*. <www.gov.uk/government/uploads/system/uploads/attachment_data/file/336069/Adoption_NMS_July_2014_for_publication.pdf>.

DFE (2014c). *Childcare and Early Years Survey of Parents 2012–2013*. <www.gov.uk/government/uploads/system/uploads/attachment_data/file/275992/SFR06-2014_Childcare_and_Early_Years_Survey_of_Parents_2012-13_final.pdf>.

DFE AND MOJ (2012). *Co-operative Parenting Following Family Separation: Proposed Legislation on the Involvement of Both Parents in a Child's Life*. London: TSO.

DFES (2004). *Statistics of Education: Outcome Indicators for Looked After Children—Twelve Months to 30 September 2003, England*. London: TSO.

DH (1993). *Adoption: the future*, Cm 2288. London: HMSO.

DH (2000). *Adoption—A New Approach. A White Paper*, Cm 5017. London: HMSO.

DH (2001a). *Donor Information Consultation—Providing Information about Gamete or Embryo Donors*. London: HMSO.

DH (2001b). *National Adoption Standards for England*. LAC (2001)22. London: HMSO.

DH (2006). *Review of the Human Fertilisation and Embryology Act. Proposals for Revised Legislation (Including Establishment of the Regulatory Authority for Tissue and Embryos)*, Cm 6989. London: HMSO. <www.hfea.gov.uk/docs/Review_HFEA_Act_White_Paper_DH.pdf>.

DH (2007). *Government Response to the Report from the Joint Committee on the Human Tissue and Embryos (Draft) Bill*, Cm 7209. London: HMSO. <www.gov.uk/government/uploads/system/uploads/attachment_data/file/243182/7209.pdf>.

DH (2014). *Mitochondrial Donation: A Consultation on Draft Regulations to Permit the Use of New Treatment Techniques to Prevent the Transmission of a Serious Mitochondrial Disease from Mother to Child*. <www.gov.uk/government/uploads/

system/uploads/attachment_data/file/285251/mitochondrial_donation_consultation_document_24_02_14_Accessible_V0.4.pdf>.

DHSS (1974). *Report of the Committee on One-Parent Families, Vol 1*, Cm 5629. London: HMSO.

DHSS (1984). *Report of the Committee of Inquiry into Human Fertilisation and Embryology*, Cm 9314. London: HMSO.

DHSS (1985). *Review of Child Care Law. Report to Ministers of an Interdepartmental Working Party*. London: HMSO.

DHSS, HO, LCD, DES, WO, AND SO (1987). *The Law on Child Care and Family Services*. London: HMSO.

DIBDIN, K., SEALEY, A., AND AKTAR, S. (eds) (2001). *Judicial Statistics Annual Report*. London: The Court Service.

DIDUCK, A. (1995). 'The Unmodified Family: The Child Support Act and the Construction of Legal Subjects'. *Journal of Law and Society*, 22: 527.

DIDUCK, A. (1999). 'Dividing the Family Assets', in S. Day Sclater and C. Piper (eds), *Undercurrents of Divorce*. Dartmouth: Ashgate.

DIDUCK, A. (2001). 'A Family by Any Other Name . . . or Starbucks Comes to England'. *Journal of Law and Society*, 28: 290.

DIDUCK, A. (2003). *Law's Families*. London: Butterworths.

DIDUCK, A. (2005). 'Shifting Familiarity'. *Current Legal Problems*, 58: 235.

DIDUCK, A. (2007). ' "If Only We Can Find the Appropriate Terms to Use the Issue Will Be Solved": Law, Identity and Parenthood'. *Child and Family Law Quarterly*, 19: 458.

DIDUCK, A. (2010). '*In re G (Children) (Residence: Same-Sex Partner)*—Judgment', in R. Hunter, C. McGynn, and E. Rackley (eds), *Feminist Judgments: From Theory to Practice*. Oxford: Hart Publishing.

DIDUCK, A. (2011a). 'Ancillary Relief: Complicating the Search for Principle'. *Journal of Law and Society*, 38: 272.

DIDUCK, A. (2011b). 'What is Family Law For?'. *Current Legal Problems*, 64: 287.

DIDUCK, A. AND KAGANAS, F. (2006). *Family Law, Gender and the State*. Oxford: Hart Publishing.

DIDUCK, A. AND ORTON, H. (1994). 'Equality and Support for Spouses'. *Modern Law Review*, 57: 681.

DINGWALL, R. (1988). 'Empowerment or Enforcement? Some Questions About Power and Control in Divorce Mediation', in R. Dingwall and J. Eekelaar (eds), *Divorce Mediation and the Legal Process*. Oxford: OUP.

DINGWALL, R. AND GREATBATCH, D. (1993). 'Who is in Charge? Rhetoric and Evidence in the Study of Mediation'. *Journal of Social Welfare and Family Law*, 14: 367.

DIXON, M. (2007a). 'Anything to Declare? Express Declaration of Trust on Land Registry Form TR1: The Doubts Raised in *Stack v Dowden*'. *Conveyancer and Property Lawyer*, 71: 364.

DIXON, M. (2007b). 'The Never-Ending Story: Co-ownership after *Stack v Dowden*'. *Conveyancer and Property Lawyer*, 71: 456.

DIXON, M (2012). 'The Still Not Ended, Never-Ending Story'. *Conveyancer and Property Lawyer*, 76: 83.

DNES, A. (1998). 'The Division of Marital Assets Following Divorce'. *Journal of Law and Society*, 25: 336.

DOBASH, R. AND DOBASH, R. (1992). *Women, Violence and Social Change*. London: Routledge.

DOBASH, R. AND DOBASH, R. (2004). 'Women's Violence to Men in Intimate Relationships'. *British Journal of Criminology*, 44: 324.

DOGGETT, M. (1992). *Marriage, Wife-Beating and the Law in Victorian England*. London: Weidenfield & Nicolson.

DONOVAN, C., HESTER, M., HOLMES, J., AND McCARRY, M. (2006). *Comparing Domestic Abuse in Same Sex and Heterosexual Relationships*. <www.equation.org. uk/wp-content/uploads/2012/12/Comparing-Domestic-Abuse-in-Same-Sex-and-Heterosexual-relationships.pdf>.

DOUGHTY, J. (2013). '*Re B (A Child) (Care Order)* (2013) UKSC 33'. *Journal of Social Welfare and Family Law*, 35: 491.

DOUGLAS, G. (1991). *Law, Fertility and Reproduction*. London: Sweet & Maxwell.

DOUGLAS, G. (1993). 'Assisted Reproduction and the Welfare of the Child'. *Current Legal Problems*, 46: 53.

DOUGLAS, G. (1994a). 'Marriage—Nullity'. *Family Law*, 24: 17.

DOUGLAS, G. (1994b). 'The Intention to be a Parent and the Making of Mothers'. *Modern Law Review*, 57: 636.

DOUGLAS, G. (2000a). 'The Family, Gender and Social Security', in N. Harris (ed), *Social Security Law in Context*. Oxford: OUP.

DOUGLAS, G. (2000b). 'Marriage, Cohabitation and Parenthood—From Contract to Status?', in S. Katz, J. Eekelaar, and M. Maclean (eds), *Cross Currents: Family Law and Policy in the US and England*. Oxford: OUP.

DOUGLAS, G. (2003). '*Re J (Leave to Issue Application for Residence Order)*'. *Child and Family Law Quarterly*, 15: 103.

DOUGLAS, G. (2004a). *An Introduction to Family Law*, 2nd edn. Oxford: OUP.

DOUGLAS, G. (2004b). 'Case Report: Child Support—Human Rights'. *Family Law*, 34: 399.

DOUGLAS, G. (2009). Case Comment on *Kehoe v UK*. *Family Law*, 39: 107.

DOUGLAS, G. (2012). 'Simple Quarrels? Autonomy vs. Vulnerability', in R. Probert and C. Barton (eds), *Fifty Years in Family Law: Essays for Stephen Cretney*. Cambridge: Intersentia.

DOUGLAS, G. AND LOWE, N. (1992). 'Becoming a Parent in English Law'. *Law Quarterly Review*, 108: 414.

DOUGLAS, G. AND PERRY, A. (2001). 'How Parents Cope Financially on Separation and Divorce—Implications for the Future of Ancillary Relief'. *Child and Family Law Quarterly*, 13: 67.

DOUGLAS, G., PEARCE, J., AND WOODWARD, H. (2007a). 'Dealing with Property Issues on Cohabitation Breakdown'. *Family Law*, 37: 36.

⊚ DOUGLAS, G., PEARCE, J., AND WOODWARD, H. (2007b). *A Failure of Trust: Resolving Property Disputes on Cohabitation Breakdown*. <www.law.cf.ac.uk/researchpapers/papers/1.pdf>.

DOUGLAS, G., PEARCE, J., AND WOODWARD, H. (2008). 'The Law Commission's Cohabitation Proposals: Applying Them in Practice'. *Family Law*, 38: 351.

DOUGLAS, G., PEARCE, J., AND WOODWARD, H. (2009). 'Money, Property, Cohabitation and Separation: Patterns and Intentions', in J. Miles and R. Probert (eds) (2009), below.

DOUGLAS, G., MURCH, M., SCANLAN, L., AND PERRY, A. (2000). 'Safeguarding Children's Welfare in Non-Contentious Divorce: Towards a New Conception of the Legal Process?'. *Modern Law Review*, 63: 177.

DOUGLAS, G., DOE, N., GILLIAT-RAY, S., SANDBERG, R., AND KHAN, A. (2012). 'The Role of Religious Tribunals in Regulating Marriage and Divorce'. *Child and Family Law Quarterly*, 24: 139.

DOUGLAS, G. AND MEMBERS OF THE NETWORK ON FAMILY, REGULATION AND SOCIETY (2011). 'Contact is Not a Commodity to be Bartered for Money'. *Family Law*, 41: 491.

DOWNIE, A. (2000). '*Re C (HIV Test)* The Limits of Parental Autonomy'. *Child and Family Law Quarterly*, 12: 197.

DRISCOLL J. AND HOLLINGSWORTH, K. (2008). 'Accommodating Children in Need: *R (M) v Hammersmith and Fulham London Borough Council*'. *Child and Family Law Quarterly*, 20: 522.

DSS (1990). *Children Come First*, Cm 1264. London: HMSO.

DSS (1995). *Improving Child Support*, Cm 2745. London: HMSO.

DSS (1999). *A New Contract for Welfare: Children's Rights and Parents' Responsibilities*, Cm 4349. London: DSS.

⊚ DTI (2004). *Final Regulatory Impact Assessment: Civil Partnership Act 2004*. URN 04/1336. <http://webarchive.nationalarchives.gov.uk/+/http://www.berr.gov.uk/files/file23829.pdf>.

⊚ DUNCAN, S. ET AL (2013). *Living Apart Together: Uncoupling Intimacy and Co-Residence*. London: NatCen. <www.natcen.ac.uk/our-research/research/living-apart-together/>.

DUNCAN, S. AND PHILLIPS, M. (2008). 'New Families? Tradition and Change in Modern Relationships', in A. Park et al (eds), *British Social Attitudes: The 24th Report*. London: Sage.

DUNCAN, S., CARTER, J. , PHILLIPS, M., ROSENEIL, S., AND STOILOVA, M. (2012). 'Legal Rights for People Who "Live Apart Together"?'. *Journal of Social Welfare and Family Law*, 34: 443.

DUNNE, P. (2014). 'Marriage Dissolution as a Pre-Requisite for Legal Gender Recognition'. *Cambridge Law Journal*, 73: 506.

DWP (2006a). *A Fresh Start: Child Support Redesign—the Government's Response to Sir David Henshaw*, Cm 6895. London: TSO.

DWP (2006b). *A New System of Child Maintenance*, Cm 6979. London: TSO. <https://www.gov.uk/government/uploads/system/uploads/attachment_data/file/272384/6979.pdf>.

DWP (2007). *Report on the Child Maintenance White Paper: Reply by the Government*, Cm 7062. <www.gov.uk/government/uploads/system/uploads/attachment_data/file/243430/7062.pdf>.

DWP (2010). *Fraud and Error in the Benefit System, October 2008 to September 2009*. London: DWP. <www.gov.uk/government/uploads/system/uploads/attachment_data/file/214334/tackling-fraud-and-error.pdf>.

DWP (2011). *Strengthening Families, Promoting Parental Responsibility: The Future of Child Maintenance*, Cm 7990. <www.gov.uk/government/uploads/system/uploads/attachment_data/file/220421/strengthening-families.pdf>.

DWP (2012). *Impact Assessment for the Child Support Maintenance Calculation Regulations 2012*. IA No DWP 0013. <www.gov.uk/government/uploads/system/uploads/attachment_data/file/184682/cmec-annual-profile-costs-benefits-ia.pdf>.

DWP (2013). *Child Maintenance Reforms: CSA Case Closure, Introducing CMS Fees, Supporting Family-Based Arrangements*. IA No DWP0031. <www.gov.uk/government/uploads/system/uploads/attachment_data/file/259694/cm-case-closure-and-charges-regs-ia-final.pdf>.

DWP (2014a). *Households Below Average Income: An Analysis of the Income Distribution 1994/95–2012/13*. <www.gov.uk/government/statistics/households-below-average-income-hbai-199495-to-201213>.

DWP (2014b). *Family Resources Survey, UK, 2012–13*. <www.gov.uk/government/statistics/family-resources-survey-2012-to-2013>.

DWP (2014c). *Decision Makers' Guide*. <http://./dwp.gov.uk/publications/specialist-guides/decision-makers-guide/>.

DYER, F. (2004). 'Termination of Parental Rights in Light of Attachment Theory'. *Psychology, Public Policy and Law*, 10: 5.

EDWARDS, S. (1989). *Policing 'Domestic' Violence: Women, the Law and the State*. London: Sage.

EDWARDS, S. (2001). 'Domestic Violence and Harassment: An Assessment of the Civil Remedies', in J. Taylor-Browne (ed), *What Works in Reducing Domestic Violence? A Comprehensive Guide for Professionals*. London: Whiting and Birch.

EDWARDS, S. AND HALPERN, A. (1991). 'Protection for the Victim of Domestic Violence: Time for Radical Revision?'. *Journal of Social Welfare and Family Law*, 13: 94.

EEKELAAR, J. (1986). 'The Emergence of Children's Rights'. *Oxford Journal of Legal Studies*, 6: 161.

EEKELAAR, J. (1987). 'A Woman's Place—A Conflict Between Law and Social Values'. *Conveyancer and Property Lawyer*, 51: 93.

EEKELAAR, J. (1990). 'Investigation under the Children Act 1989'. *Family Law*, 20: 486.

EEKELAAR, J. (1991a). 'Are Parents Morally Obliged to Care for Their Children?'. *Oxford Journal of Legal Studies*, 11: 340.

EEKELAAR, J. (1991b). *Regulating Divorce*. Oxford: Clarendon Press.

EEKELAAR, J. (1991c). 'Parental Responsibility: State of Nature or Nature of the State?'. *Journal of Social Welfare and Family Law*, 13: 37.

EEKELAAR, J. (1994). 'A Jurisdiction in Search of a Mission: Family Proceedings in England and Wales'. *Modern Law Review*, 57: 839.

EEKELAAR, J. (1995). 'Family Justice: Ideal or Illusion? Family Law and Communitarian Values'. *Current Legal Problems Part II*, 48: 191.

EEKELAAR, J. (1998a). 'Should Section 25 be Reformed?'. *Family Law*, 28: 469.

EEKELAAR, J. (1998b). 'Do Parents have a Duty to Consult?'. *Law Quarterly Review*, 114: 337.

EEKELAAR, J. (1999). 'Family Law: Keeping Us "On Message"'. *Child and Family Law Quarterly*, 11: 387.

EEKELAAR, J. (2000). 'Uncovering Social Obligations: Family Law and the Responsible Citizen', in M. Maclean (ed), *Making Law for Families*. Oxford: Hart Publishing.

EEKELAAR, J. (2002). 'Beyond the Welfare Principle'. *Child and Family Law Quarterly*, 14: 237.

EEKELAAR, J. (2004). 'Children Between Cultures'. *International Journal of Law, Policy and the Family*, 18: 178.

EEKELAAR, J. (2006a). 'Property and Financial Settlements on Divorce: Sharing and Compensating'. *Family Law*, 36: 754.

EEKELAAR, J. (2006b). *Family Law and Personal Life*. Oxford: OUP.

EEKELAAR, J. (2010). 'Financial and Property Settlement: A Standard Deal?'. *Family Law*, 40: 359.

EEKELAAR, J. (2011). '"Not of the Highest Importance": Family Justice under Threat'. *Journal of Social Welfare and Family Law*, 33: 311.

EEKELAAR, J. (2014). '"Perceptions of Equality: The Road to Same-Sex Marriage in England and Wales". *International Journal of Law, Policy and the Family*, 28: 1.

EEKELAAR, J. AND MACLEAN, M. (1986). *Maintenance after Divorce*. Oxford: OUP.

EEKELAAR, J. AND MACLEAN, M. (1997). 'Property and Financial Adjustment after Divorce in the 1990s—Unfinished Business', in K. Hawkins (ed), *The Human Face of Law*. Oxford: Clarendon Press.

EEKELAAR, J., MACLEAN, M., AND BEINART, S. (2000). *Family Lawyers: The Divorce Work of Solicitors*. Oxford: Hart Publishing.

EHRC (2009). *Working Better: Fathers, Family and Work—Contemporary Perspectives*. Research Summary 41. <www.equalityhumanrights.com/uploaded_files/research/41_ wb_fathers_family_and_work.pdf>.

ELLISON, L. (2003). 'Responding to Victim Withdrawal in Domestic Violence Prosecutions'. *Criminal Law Review*, 760.

ELLMAN, I. (1997). 'The Misguided Movement to Revive Fault Divorce, and Why Reformers Should Look Instead to the American Law Institute'. *International Journal of Law, Policy and the Family*, 11: 216.

ELLMAN, I. (2000). 'Divorce', in S. Katz, J. Eekelaar, and M. Maclean (eds), *Cross Currents: Family Law and Policy in the US and England*. Oxford: OUP.

ELLMAN, I. (2005). 'Do Americans Play Football?'. *International Journal of Law, Policy and the Family*, 19: 257.

ELLMAN, I. (2007). 'Financial Settlements on Divorce: Two Steps Forward, Two to Go'. *Law Quarterly Review*, 123: 2.

ELLMAN, I. AND BRAVER, S. (2011). 'Lay Intuitions about Child Support and Marital Status'. *Child and Family Law Quarterly*, 23: 465.

ELLMAN, I., MCKAY, S., MILES, J., AND BRYSON, C (2014). 'Child Support Judgments: Comparing Public Policy to the Public's Policy'. *International Journal of Law, Policy and the Family*, 28: 274.

EMMERSON, D. AND PLATT, J. (2014). 'Legal Aid, Sentencing and Punishment of Offenders Act 2012: LASPO Reviewed'. *Family Law*, 44: 515.

ESKRIDGE, W. (2001). 'The Ideological Structure of the Same-Sex Marriage Debate (And Some Postmodern Arguments for Same-Sex Marriage)', in R. Wintemute and M. Andenæs (eds), *Legal Recognition of Same-Sex Partnerships*. Oxford: Hart Publishing.

ETHERTON, T. (2009). 'Constructive Trusts and Proprietory Estoppel: The Search for Clarity and Principle'. *Conveyancer and Property Lawyer*, 73: 104.

FAHEY, T. (2014). 'Divorce Trends and Patterns: An Overview', in J. Eekelaar and R. George (eds), *Routledge Handbook of Family Law and Policy*. Abingdon: Routledge.

FAMILIES NEED FATHERS (2007). Written Memorandum to Public Bill Committee, on Child Maintenance and Other Payments Bill 2007. <www.publications.parliament. uk/pa/cm200607/cmpublic/childmain/memos/memocm2.htm>.

FAMILY AND PARENTING INSTITUTE (2009). *Ending Child Poverty: Making it Happen—A Response from the Family and Parenting Institute*. <www.endchildpoverty. org.uk/files/c1109_ending_child_poverty.doc>.

FAMILY JUSTICE COUNCIL (2008). *Enhancing the Participation of Children and Young People in Family Proceedings: Starting the Debate.* <www.judiciary.gov.uk/wp-content/uploads/JCO/Documents/FJC/voc/Participation_of_young_people.pdf>.

FAMILY JUSTICE COUNCIL (2010a). *Guidelines for Judges Meeting Children who are Subject to Family Proceedings.* <www.judiciary.gov.uk/wp-content/uploads/JCO/Documents/FJC/voc/Guidelines_+Judges_seeing_+Children.pdf>.

FAMILY JUSTICE COUNCIL (2010b). *Guidelines in Relation to Children Giving Evidence in Family Proceedings.* <www.judiciary.gov.uk/wp-content/uploads/JCO/Documents/FJC/Publications/Children+Giving+Evidence+Guidelines+-+Final+Version.pdf>.

FAMILY LAW WEEK (2007). 'Child Support Reform "A Disaster", says Commons Public Accounts Committee'. <www.familylawweek.co.uk/site.aspx?i=ed724>.

FARMER, E. AND DANCE, C., WITH BEECHAM, J., BONIN, E., AND OUWEJAN, D. (2010). *An Investigation of Family Finding and Matching in Adoption – Briefing Paper.* DFE-RBX-10-05. <www.adoptionresearchinitiative.org.uk/briefs/DFE-RBX-10-05.pdf>.

FEHLBERG, B. (1997). *Sexually Transmitted Debt: Surety Experience and English Law.* Oxford: Clarendon Press.

FEHLBERG, B. AND MACLEAN, M. (2009). 'Child Support Policy in Australia and the United Kingdom: Changing Priorities but a Similar Tough Deal for Children?'. *International Journal of Law, Policy and the Family*, 23: 1.

FEHLBERG, B. AND SMYTH. B. (2002). 'Binding Pre-Nuptial Agreements in Australia: The First Year'. *International Journal of Law, Policy and the Family*, 16: 127.

FEHLBERG, B. AND SMYTH, B., WITH TRINDER, L. (2014). 'Parenting Issues After Separation: Developments in Common Law Countries', in J. Eekelaar and R. George (eds), *Routledge Handbook of Family Law and Policy*. Abingdon: Routledge.

FEHLBERG, B., SMYTH, B., MACLEAN, M., AND ROBERTS, C. (2011). 'Legislating for Shared Time Parenting After Separation: A Research Review'. *International Journal of Law, Policy and the Family*, 25: 318.

FELDBLUM, R. (2001). 'The Limitations of Liberal Neutrality Arguments in Favour of Same-Sex Marriage', in R. Wintemute and M. Andenæs (eds), *Legal Recognition of Same-Sex Partnerships*. Oxford: Hart Publishing.

FERGUSON, L. (2008). 'Family, Social Inequalities, and the Persuasive Force of Interpersonal Obligation'. *International Journal of Law, Policy and the Family*, 22: 61.

FERGUSON, L. (2013a). 'Arbitration in Financial Dispute Resolution: The Final Step to Reconstructing the Default(s) and Exception(s)?'. *Journal of Social Welfare and Family Law*, 35: 115.

FERGUSON, L. (2013b). 'Not Merely Rights for Children but Children's Rights: The Theory Gap and the Assumption of the Importance of Children's Rights'. *International Journal of Children's Rights*, 21: 177.

FERGUSON, L. (2015). 'Arbitral Awards: A Magnetic Factor of Determinative Importance – Yet Not to be Rubber-Stamped?'. *Journal of Social Welfare and Family Law*, 37: forthcoming.

ⓦ FERGUSON, S. ET AL (2011). *Application of Ferguson et al v United Kingdom, File number 8254-11*, 2 February. <www.petertatchell.net/campaigns/Equal%20Love/Equal_Love_ECHR_Application_2_Feb.pdf>.

FINEMAN, M. (2004). *The Autonomy Myth: A Theory of Dependency*. New York: The New Press.

ⓦ FINNEY, A. (2006). *Domestic Violence, Sexual Assault and Stalking: Findings from the 2004/05 British Crime Survey*. Home Office Online Report 12/06. <http://webarchive.nationalarchives.gov.uk/20110218135832/http:/rds.homeoffice.gov.uk/rds/pdfs06/rdsolr1206.pdf>.

FINNIS, J. (1993). 'Law, Morality and "Sexual Orientation"'. *Notre Dame Law Review*, 69: 1049.

FISHER, H. AND LOW, H. (2009). 'Who Wins, Who Loses and Who Recovers from Divorce?', in J. Miles and R. Probert (eds) (2009), below.

FLAHERTY, J., VEIT-WILSON, J., AND DORNAN, P. (2004). *Poverty: The Facts*, 5th edn. London: CPAG.

ⓦ FLUDGER, D. AND DOUGHERTY, S. (2014). 'Household Satellite Accounts – Valuing Household Clothing and Laundry Services in the UK'. <www.ons.gov.uk/ons/dcp171776_384852.pdf>.

FLYNN, L. AND LAWSON, A. (1995). 'Gender, Sexuality and the Doctrine of Detrimental Reliance'. *Feminist Legal Studies*, 3: 105.

FLYNN, R. (2000). 'Black Carers for White Children. Shifting the "Same-Race" Placement Debate'. *Adoption and Fostering*, 24: 47.

FORTIN, J. (1994). '*Re F:* "The Gooseberry Bush Approach"'. *Modern Law Review*, 57: 296.

FORTIN, J. (1999a). 'The HRA's Impact on Litigation Involving Children and Their Families'. *Child and Family Law Quarterly*, 11: 217.

FORTIN, J. (1999b). '*Re D (Care: Natural Parent Presumption)* Is Blood Really Thicker Than Water?'. *Child and Family Law Quarterly*, 11: 435.

FORTIN, J. (2004). 'Children's Rights: Are the Courts Now Taking Them More Seriously?'. *Kings College Law Journal*, 15: 253.

FORTIN, J. (2006). 'Accommodating Children's Rights in a Post Human Rights Act Era'. *Modern Law Review*, 69: 299.

FORTIN, J. (2007). 'Children's Representation Through the Looking Glass'. *Family Law*, 37: 500.

FORTIN, J. (2009a). 'Children's Right to Know Their Origins—Too Far, Too Fast?'. *Child and Family Law Quarterly*, 21: 336.

FORTIN J. (2009b). *Children's Rights and the Developing Law*, 3rd edn. Cambridge: CUP.

FORTIN, J. (2014). 'Children's Rights: Flattering to Deceive?'. *Child and Family Law Quarterly*, 26: 51.

FORTIN, J., HUNT, J., AND SCANLAN, L. (2012). *Taking a Longer View of Contact: The Perspectives of Young Adults Who Experienced Parental Separation in their Youth: Summary*. University of Sussex/University of Oxford. <www.sussex.ac.uk/law/documents/nuffield-foundation-research-summary-16nov2012.pdf>.

FORTIN, J., RITCHIE, C., AND BUCHANAN, A. (2006). 'Young Adults' Perceptions of Court-Ordered Contact.' *Child and Family Law Quarterly*, 18: 211.

FOX, L. (2001). 'Co-ownership of Matrimonial Property: Radical Proposals for Reform'. *Northern Ireland Legal Quarterly*, 52: 20.

FOX, L. (2003). 'Reforming Family Property—Comparisons, Compromises and Common Dimensions'. *Child and Family Law Quarterly*, 15: 1.

FOX, L. (2005). 'Creditors and the Concept of "Family Home": A Functional Analysis'. *Legal Studies*, 25: 201.

FOX HARDING, L. (1991a). 'The Children Act 1989 in Context: Four Perspectives in Child Care Law and Policy (I)'. *Journal of Social Welfare and Family Law*, 13: 179.

FOX HARDING, L. (1991b). 'The Children Act 1989 in Context: Four Perspectives in Child Care Law and Policy (II). *Journal of Social Welfare and Family Law*, 13: 285.

FRAZER, L. AND SELWYN, J. (2005). 'Why Are We Waiting? The Demography of Adoption for Children of Black, Asian and Black Mixed Parentage in England'. *Child and Family Social Work*, 10: 135.

FREEMAN, M. (1984). 'Legal Ideologies, Patriarchal Precedents, and Domestic Violence', in M. Freeman (ed), *State, Law, and the Family: Critical Perspectives*. London: Tavistock.

FREEMAN, M. (1989). 'The Abuse of the Elderly—Legal Responses in England', in J. Eekelaar and D. Pearl (eds), *An Aging World: Dilemmas and Challenges for Law and Social Policy*. Oxford: OUP.

FREEMAN, M. (1992). 'Taking Children's Rights More Seriously'. *International Journal of Law and the Family*, 6: 52.

FREEMAN, M. (1996). 'The New Birth Right? Identity and the Child of the Reproductive Revolution'. *International Journal of Children's Rights*, 4: 273.

FREEMAN, M. (2000). 'Disputing Children', in S. Katz, J. Eekelaar, and M. Maclean (eds), *Cross Currents: Family Law and Policy in the US and England*. Oxford: OUP.

GAFFNEY-RHYS, R. (2005). 'The Law Relating to Affinity after *B and L v UK*'. *Family Law*, 35: 955.

GAFFNEY-RHYS, R. (2006). '*Sheffield City Council v E and Another*—Capacity to Marry and the Rights and Responsibilities of Married Couples'. *Child and Family Law Quarterly*, 18: 139.

GAFFNEY-RHYS, R. (2009). 'The Law Relating to Marriageable Age from a National and International Perspective'. *International Family Law*, 228.

GAFFNEY-RHYS, R. (2013). 'Am I Married? Three Recent Case Studies of the Effect of Non-Compliant Marriage Ceremonies'. *International Family Law*, 53.

GARDNER, S. (1993). 'Rethinking Family Property'. *Law Quarterly Review*, 109: 263.

GARDNER, S. (2008). 'Family Property Today'. *Law Quarterly Review*, 124: 422.

GARDNER, S. (2013). 'Problems in Family Property'. *Cambridge Law Journal*, 72: 301.

GARDNER, S. (2014). 'Material Relief Between Ex-Cohabitants 2: Otherwise than via Beneficial Entitlement'. *Conveyancer and Property Lawyer*, 78: 202.

GARDNER, S. AND DAVIDSON, K. (2011). 'The Future of *Stack v Dowden*'. *Law Quarterly Review*, 127: 13.

GARDNER, S. AND DAVIDSON, K. (2012). 'The Supreme Court on Family Homes'. *Law Quarterly Review*, 128: 178.

GARRISON, M. (2014). 'The Changing Face of Marriage', in J. Eekelaar and R. George (eds), *Routledge Handbook of Family Law and Policy*. Abingdon: Routledge.

GELDOF, B. (2003). 'The Real Love that Dare Not Speak its Name', in A. Bainham, B. Lindley, M. Richards, and L. Trinder (eds), *Children and their Families*. Oxford: Hart Publishing.

GENERAL REGISTER OFFICE (2003). *Civil Registration: Delivering Vital Change*. London: HMSO. <http://webarchive.nationalarchives.gov.uk/+/http:/www.statistics.gov.uk/downloads/registration/01Chapters1-11.pdf>.

GENN, H. (2010). 'Civil Mediation: A Measured Approach?'. *Journal of Social Welfare and Family Law*, 32: 195.

GEORGE, R. (2008a). '*Stack v Dowden*—Do As We Say, Not As We Do?'. *Journal of Social Welfare and Family Law*, 30: 49.

GEORGE, R. (2008b). 'Changing Names, Changing Places: Reconsidering Section 13 of the Children Act 1989'. *Family Law*, 38: 1121.

GEORGE, R. (2011). 'Cutting Legal Aid Will Undermine Whole Family Law System'. *The Telegraph*, 25 February. <www.telegraph.co.uk/news/newstopics/lawreports/8346866/Cutting-legal-aid-will-undermine-whole-family-law-system.html>.

GEORGE, R. (2012a). *Ideas and Debates in Family Law*. Oxford: Hart Publishing.

GEORGE, R. (2012b). 'The International Relocation Debate'. *Journal of Social Welfare and Family Law*, 34: 141.

GEORGE, R. (2012c). 'International Relocation, Care Arrangements and Case Taxonomy'. *Family Law*, 42: 1478.

GEORGE, R. (2013a). *Relocation Disputes in England and Wales: First Findings from the 2012 Study*. Oxford Legal Research Paper 91/2013. <http://ssrn.com/abstract=2306097>.

GEORGE, R. (2013b). 'Family Finances and the Corporate Veil: *Prest v Petrodel*'. *Family Law*, 43: 991.

GEORGE, R. (2014). *Relocation Disputes: Law and Practice in England and New Zealand*. Oxford: Hart Publishing.

GEORGE, R. (2015). 'The Child's Welfare in European Perspective', in J. Scherpe (ed), *European Family Law, Vol III: Family Law in European Perspective*. London: Elgar.

GEORGE, R., HARRIS, P., AND HERRING, J. (2009). 'Pre-Nuptial Agreements: For Better or For Worse?'. *Family Law*, 39: 934.

GIBB, F. (2008). 'Family Justice System is At Risk, Warns New Chief Judge'. *The Times*, 24 March.

GIBSON, C. (1994). *Dissolving Wedlock*. London: Routledge.

GILLESPIE, G. (2002). 'Child Support—When the Bough Breaks'. *Family Law*, 32: 528.

GILLIES, V. (2009). Understandings and Experiences of Involved Fathering in the United Kingdom: Exploring Classed Dimensions. *Annals, AAPSS*: 624.

GILMORE, S. (2003). 'Parental Responsibility and the Unmarried Father—A New Dimension to the Debate'. *Child and Family Law Quarterly*, 15: 21.

GILMORE, S. (2004a). 'Duration of Marriage *and* Seamless Preceding Cohabitation?'. *Family Law*, 34: 205.

GILMORE, S. (2004b). '*Re P (Child) (Financial Provision)*—Shoeboxes and Comical Shopping Trips—Child Support from the Affluent to Fabulously Rich'. *Child and Family Law Quarterly*, 16: 103.

GILMORE, S. (2004c). 'The Nature, Scope and Use of the Specific Issue Order'. *Child and Family Law Quarterly*, 16: 367.

GILMORE, S. (2006). 'Contact/Shared Residence and Child Well-Being: Research Evidence and its Implications for Legal Decision-Making'. *International Journal of Law, Policy and the Family*, 20: 344.

GILMORE, S. (2007). '*Re B (Contact: Child Support)*—Horses and Carts: Contact and Child Support'. *Child and Family Law Quarterly*, 19: 357.

GILMORE, S. (2008). 'Disputing Contact: Challenging Some Assumptions'. *Child and Family Law Quarterly*, 20: 285.

GILMORE, S. (2011). '*Corbett v Corbett*: Once a Man, Always a Man?', in S. Gilmore, J. Herring, and R. Probert (eds), *Landmark Cases in Family Law*. Oxford: Hart Publishing.

GILMORE, S. (2013). '*Re J (Care Proceedings: Past Possible Perpetrators in a New Family Unit)* [2013] UKSC 9: Bulwarks and Logic – The Blood Which Runs Through the Veins of Law – But How Much Will Be Spilled in Future?'. *Child and Family Law Quarterly*, 25: 215.

GILMORE, S. AND HERRING, J. (2011). '"No" is the Hardest Word: Consent and Children's Autonomy'. *Child and Family Law Quarterly*, 23: 3.

GINGERBREAD (2011). '*Strengthening Families, Promoting Parental Responsibility*' – *Government Plans for Child Maintenance*. Gingerbread Briefing February. <www.gingerbread.org.uk/file_download.aspx?id=7360>.

GINGERBREAD (2012a). *The Only Way is Up? The Employment Aspirations of Single Parents*. <www.gingerbread.org.uk/content/667/Policy-work---employment>.

GINGERBREAD (2012b). *The Draft Child Support Maintenance Calculation Regulations 2012: Response from Gingerbread to the Technical Consultation*. <www.gingerbread.org.uk/file_download.aspx?id=7718>.

GLENDINNING, C., CLARKE, K., AND CRAIG, G. (1994). 'The Impact of the Child Support Act on Lone Mothers and their Children'. *Journal of Child Law*, 7: 18.

GLENDON, M. (1974). 'Is There a Future for Separate Property?'. *Family Law Quarterly*, 8: 315.

GLENNON, L. (2005). 'Displacing the 'Conjugal Family' in Legal Policy—A Progressive Move?'. *Child and Family Law Quarterly*, 17: 141.

GLENNON, L. (2008). 'Obligations Between Adult Partners: Moving from Form to Function?'. *International Journal of Law, Policy and the Family*, 22: 22.

GLENNON, L. (2010). 'The Limitations of Equality Discourses on the Contours of Intimate Obligations', in J. Wallbank, S. Choudhry, and J. Herring (eds), *Rights, Gender and Family Law*, Abingdon: Routledge.

GLISTER, J. (2010). 'Section 199 of the Equality Act 2010: How Not to Abolish the Presumption of Advancement'. *Modern Law Review*, 73: 807.

GOLDSTEIN, B. (2000). 'Ethnicity and Placement. Beginning the Debate'. *Adoption and Fostering*, 24: 9.

GONZÁLEZ, L. AND VIITANEN, T. (2006). *The Effect of Divorce Laws on Divorce Rates in Europe*. IZA Discussion Paper No 2023. <http://ssrn.com/abstract=892354>.

GOODMAN, A. AND GREAVES, E. (2010). *Cohabitation, Marriage and Child Outcomes*. London: Institute for Fiscal Studies. <www.ifs.org.uk/comms/comm114.pdf>.

GOVERNMENT ACTUARY'S DEPARTMENT (2005). *Marriages Abroad*. London: GAD.

GOVERNMENT EQUALITIES OFFICE (2012). *Equal Civil Marriage: A Consultation*. <www.gov.uk/government/uploads/system/uploads/attachment_data/file/133258/consultation-document_1_.pdf>.

GRACE, S. (1995). *Policing Domestic Violence in the 1990s*. Home Office Research Study 139. London: HMSO.

GRAY, K. (1977). *Reallocation of Property on Divorce*. Abingdon: Professional Books.

GRAY, K. AND GRAY, S. (2009). *Elements of Land Law*, 5th edn. Oxford: OUP.

GRAY, K. AND GRAY, S. (2011). *Land Law*, 7th edn. Oxford: OUP.

GRAYCAR, R. AND MORGAN, J. (2002). *The Hidden Gender of Law*, 2nd edn. Leichhardt, New South Wales: The Federation Press.

GREASLEY, K. (2010). 'A Negligent Blow to Children at Risk: *MAK and RK v United Kingdom* (European Court of Human Rights)'. *Modern Law Review*, 73: 1026.

GREATBATCH, D. AND DINGWALL, R. (1999). 'The Marginalization of Domestic Violence in Divorce Mediation'. *International Journal of Law, Policy and the Family*, 13: 174.

GREEN, L. (2011). 'Sex-Neutral Marriage'. *Current Legal Problems*, 64: 1.

HAFEN, B. AND HAFEN, J. (1995–96). 'Abandoning Children to their Autonomy: The United Nations Convention on the Rights of the Child'. *Harvard International Law Journal*, 37: 449.

HALE, B. (2004). 'Unmarried Couples in Family Law'. *Family Law*, 34: 419.

HALE, B. (2009). 'The Future of Marriage', in G. Douglas and N. Lowe (eds), *The Continuing Evolution of Family Law*. Bristol: Jordan Publishing.

HALE, B. (2014). 'New Families and the Welfare of Children'. *Journal of Social Welfare and Family Law*, 36: 26.

HALE, M. (1736). *The History of the Pleas of the Crown*. (1971) P. Glazebrook (ed). London: Professional Books.

HALL, A. (2008). 'Special Guardianship and Permanency Planning: Unforeseen Consequences and Missed Opportunities'. *Child and Family Law Quarterly*, 20: 359.

HALL, S. (2000). 'What Price the Logic of Evidence?'. *Family Law*, 30: 423.

HALLEY, J. (2001). 'Recognition, Rights, Regulation, Normalisation: Rhetorics of Justification in the Same-Sex Marriage Debate', in R. Wintemute and M. Andenæs (eds), *Legal Recognition of Same-Sex Partnerships*. Oxford: Hart Publishing.

HARDING, M. (2009). 'Defending *Stack v Dowden*'. *Conveyancer and Property Lawyer*, 309.

HARDING, M. AND NEWNHAM, A. (2014). 'Initial Research Findings: The Typical Levels of Parental Involvement Where Post-Separation Parenting is resolved by Court Order'. *Family Law*, 44: 672.

HARDING, R. (2007). 'Sir Mark Potter and the Protection of the Traditional Family: Why Same-Sex Marriage is (Still!) a Feminist Issue'. *Feminist Legal Studies*, 15: 223.

HARDING, R. (2014). '(Re)inscribing the Heteronormative Family: Same-Sex Relationships and Parenting "After Equality"', in R. Leckey (ed), *After Legal Equality: Family, Sex, Kinship*. Abingdon: Routledge.

HARDING, R. (2015). 'Playing House of Lords Bingo: A Critical Discourse Analysis of Hansard Debates on Civil Partnership and Same Sex Marriage, in J. Miles, P. Mody, and R. Probert (eds), *Marriage Rites and Rights*. Oxford: Hart Publishing.

HARPER, M., DOWNS, M., LANDELLS, K., AND WILSON, G. (2005). *Civil Partnership: The New Law*. Bristol: Jordan Publishing.

HARRIS, D.J., O'BOYLE, M., AND WARBRICK, C. (1995). *Law of the European Convention on Human Rights*. London: Butterworths.

HARRIS, J. (1995). 'The Right to Found a Family', in R.E. Ladd (ed), *Children's Rights Re-Visioned: Philosophical Readings*. Belmont, California: Wadsworth Publishing.

HARRIS, J. (2000). *An Evaluation of the Use and Effectiveness of the Protection from Harassment Act 1997*. Home Office Research Study 203. London: Home Office. <http://webarchive.nationalarchives.gov.uk/20110218135832/rds.homeoffice.gov.uk/rds/pdfs/hors203.pdf>.

HARRIS, N. (1996). 'Unmarried Cohabiting Couples and Social Security in Great Britain'. *Journal of Social Welfare and Family Law*, 18: 123.

HARRIS, P. (2008). 'The Miller Paradoxes'. *Family Law*, 38: 1096.

HARRIS, P. AND GEORGE, R. (2010). 'Parental Responsibility and Shared Residence Orders: Parliamentary Intentions and Judicial Interpretations.' *Child and Family Law Quarterly*, 22: 151.

HARRIS-SHORT, S. (2001). 'The Adoption and Children Bill—A Fast Track to Failure?'. *Child and Family Law Quarterly*, 13: 405.

HARRIS-SHORT, S. (2002). '*Re B (Adoption: Natural Parent)* Putting the Child at the Heart of Adoption?'. *Child and Family Law Quarterly*, 14: 325.

HARRIS-SHORT, S. (2003). 'An "Identity Crisis" in the International Law of Human Rights? The Challenge of Reproductive Cloning'. *International Journal of Children's Rights*, 11: 333.

HARRIS-SHORT, S. (2005). 'Family Law and the Human Rights Act 1998—Restraint or Revolution?'. *Child and Family Law Quarterly*, 17: 329.

HARRIS-SHORT, S. (2010). 'Resisting the March Towards 50/50 Shared Residence. Rights, Welfare and Equality in Post-Separation Families'. *Journal of Social Welfare and Family Law*, 32: 257.

HASKEY, J. (2001a). 'Cohabitation in Great Britain: Past, Present and Future Trends—And Attitudes'. *Population Trends*, 103: 4.

HASKEY, J. (2001b). 'Cohabiting Couples in Great Britain: Accommodation Sharing, Tenure and Property Ownership'. *Population Trends*, 103: 26.

HASKEY, J. AND LEWIS, J. (2006). 'Living-Apart-Together in Britain: Context and Meaning'. *International Journal of Law and Context*, 2: 37.

HASSON, E. (2006). 'Wedded to "Fault": The Legal Regulation of Divorce and Relationship Breakdown'. *Legal Studies*, 26: 267.

HASTINGS, G. (2010). '*Re A (Children) (Conjoined Twins: Surgical Separation)*—Judgment', in R. Hunter, C. McGynn, and E. Rackley (eds), *Feminist Judgments: From Theory to Practice*. Oxford: Hart Publishing.

HAYES, M. (1990). 'The Law Commission and the Family Home'. *Modern Law Review*, 53: 222.

HAYES, M. (2006). 'Relocation Cases: Is the Court of Appeal Applying the Correct Principles?'. *Child and Family Law Quarterly*, 18: 351.

HAYES, M. AND WILLIAMS, C. (1999). *Family Law: Principles, Policy and Practice*. London: Butterworths.

HAYES, P. (2003). 'Giving Due Consideration to Ethnicity in Adoption Placements—A Principled Approach'. *Child and Family Law Quarterly*, 15: 225.

HAYWARD, A. (2012). ' "Family Property" and the Process of "Familialisation" of Property Law'. *Child and Family Law Quarterly*, 24: 284.

HEAPHY, B., SMART, C., AND EINARSDOTTIR, A. (2013). *Same-Sex Marriages: New Generations, New Relationships*. Basingstoke: Palgrave Macmillan.

HENRICSON, C. AND BAINHAM, A. (2005). *The Child and Family Policy Divide: Tension, Convergence and Rights*. York: Joseph Rowntree Foundation.

HENSHAW, D. (2006). *Recovering Child Support: Routes to Responsibility*, Cm 6894. London: TSO. <www.gov.uk/government/uploads/system/uploads/attachment_data/file/272335/6894.pdf>.

HERRING, J. (1999a). 'The Human Rights Act and the Welfare Principle in Family Law—Conflicting or Complementary?'. *Child and Family Law Quarterly*, 11: 223.

HERRING, J. (1999b). 'The Welfare Principle and the Rights of Parents', in A. Bainham, S. Day Sclater, and M. Richards (eds), *What is a Parent? A Socio-Legal Analysis*. Oxford: Hart Publishing.

HERRING, J. (2005a). 'Why Financial Orders on Divorce should be Unfair'. *International Journal of Law, Policy and the Family*, 19: 218.

HERRING, J. (2005b). 'Farewell Welfare?'. *Journal of Social Welfare and Family Law*, 27: 159.

HERRING, J. (2010). Family/Divorce Comment. *New Law Journal*, 160: 1551.

HERRING, J. (2011). 'Elder Abuse and Stressing Carers', in J. Bridgman, H. Keating, and C. Lind (eds), *Regulating Family Responsibilities*. Farnham: Ashgate.

HERRING, J. (2012). 'Divorce, Internet Hubs and Stephen Cretney', in R. Probert and C. Barton (eds), *Fifty Years in Family Law*. Cambridge: Intersentia.

HERRING, J. (2013). 'Capacity to Cohabit: Hoping "Everything Turns Out Well in the End"'. *Child and Family Law Quarterly*, 25: 471.

HERRING, J. (2014). 'Making Family Law Less Sexy . . . and More Careful', in R. Leckey (ed), *After Legal Equality: Family, Sex, Kinship*. Abingdon: Routledge.

HERRING, J. AND TAYLOR, R. (2006). 'Relocating Relocation'. *Child and Family Law Quarterly*, 18: 517.

HERRING, J., BARKER, N., AND FOX, M. (2010). '*Sheffield County Council v E*', in R. Hunter et al (eds), *Feminist Judgments: From Theory to Practice*. Oxford: Hart Publishing.

HERRING, J., PROBERT, R., AND GILMORE, S. (2012). *Great Debates: Family Law*. Basingstoke: Palgrave Macmillan.

HERRING, J., HARRIS, P., AND GEORGE, R. (2011). 'Ante-Nuptial Agreements: Fairness, Equality and Presumptions'. *Law Quarterly Review*, 127: 335.

HESTER, M. (2005). 'Making it Through the Criminal Justice System: Attrition and Domestic Violence'. *Social Policy and Society*, 5: 79.

HESTER, M. (2009). *Who Does What to Whom? Gender and Domestic Violence Perpetrators*. Bristol: University of Bristol in association with the Northern Rock Foundation. <http://www.nr-foundation.org.uk/downloads/Who-Does-What-to-Whom.pdf>.

HESTER, M., PEARCE, J., AND WESTMARLAND, N. (2008). *Early Evaluation of the Integrated Domestic Violence Court, Croydon*. MOJ Research Series 18/08. <www.bristol. ac.uk/media-library/sites/sps/migrated/documents/rk6668reportpart2.pdf>.

HESTER, M., WESTMARLAND, J., PEARCE, J., AND WILLIAMSON, E. (2008). *Early evaluation of the Domestic Violence, Crime and Victims Act 2004*. MOJ Research Series 14/08. <http://dro.dur.ac.uk/5093/1/5093.pdf>.

HFEA (2002). *Response to the Department of Health's Consultation on 'Donor Information: Providing Information about Sperm, Egg and Embryo Donors'*. <www.hfea. gov.uk/cps/rde/xbcr/SID-3F57D79B-F8EA46AD/hfea/Donor_Info_response.pdf>.

HFEA (2003). *Code of Practice*, 6th edn. <www.hfea.gov.uk/cps/rde/xbcr/SID-3F57D79B-EA722370/hfea/Code_of_Practice_Sixth_Edition_-_final.pdf>.

HFEA (2005). *Tomorrow's Children. Report of the Policy Review of Welfare of the Child Assessments in Licensed Assisted Conception Clinics*. <www.hfea.gov.uk/docs/ TomorrowsChildren_report.pdf>.

HFEA (2012). *Fertility Treatment in 2012: Trends and Figures*. <www.hfea.gov.uk/ docs/FertilityTreatment2012TrendsFigures.PDF>.

HIBBS, M. (2001). 'Surrogacy—Who Will Be Left Holding The Baby?'. *Family Law*, 31: 736.

HIBBS, M., BARTON, C., AND BESWICK, J. (2001). 'Why Marry? Perceptions of the Affianced'. *Family Law*, 31: 197.

HITCHINGS, E. (2009a). 'Chaos or Consistency? Ancillary Relief in the "Everyday" Case', in J. Miles and R. Probert (eds) (2009), below.

HITCHINGS, E. (2009b). 'From Pre-Nups to Post-Nups: Dealing with Marital Property Agreements'. *Family Law*, 39: 1056.

HITCHINGS, E. (2010). 'The Impact of Recent Ancillary Relief Jurisprudence in the "Everyday" Ancillary Relief Case'. *Child and Family Law Quarterly*, 22: 93.

HITCHINGS, E. (2011). *A Study of the Views and Approaches of Family Practitioners Concerning Marital Property Agreements*. <www.bristol.ac.uk/law/research/ researchpublications/2013/maritalpropertyagreements.pdf>.

HITCHINGS, E. AND SAGAR, S. (2007). 'The Adoption and Children Act 2002: A Level Playing Field for Same-Sex Adopters?'. *Child and Family Law Quarterly*, 19: 60.

HITCHINGS, E., MILES, J., AND WOODWARD, H. (2013). *Assembling the Jigsaw Puzzle: Understanding Financial Settlement on Divorce*. <www.bristol.ac.uk/media-library/ sites/law/migrated/documents/assemblingthejigsawpuzzle.pdf>.

HM CPS INSPECTORATE AND HM INSPECTORATE OF CONSTABULARY (2004). *Violence at Home: A Joint Thematic Inspection of the Investigation and Prosecution of Cases Involving Domestic Violence*. <http://www.hmcpsi.gov.uk/documents/reports/ CJJI_THM/BOTJ/DomVio0104Rep.pdf>.

HMCS, HO, AND CPS (2008). *Justice with Safety: Specialist Domestic Violence Courts Review 2007–08*. <www.cps.gov.uk/publications/equality/sdvc_review.html>.

HM GOVERNMENT (2009). *Together We Can End Violence Against Women and Girls: A Strategy.* <http://webarchive.nationalarchives.gov.uk/20100419081706/http://homeoffice.gov.uk/documents/vawg-strategy-2009/end-violence-against-women2835.pdf?view=Binary>.

HM GOVERNMENT (2010). *Call to End Violence against Women and Girls.* <www.gov.uk/government/uploads/system/uploads/attachment_data/file/118150/vawg-paper.pdf>.

HM GOVERNMENT (2012). *Equal Marriage: The Government's Response.* <www.gov.uk/government/uploads/system/uploads/attachment_data/file/133262/consultation-response_1_.pdf>.

HM GOVERNMENT (2014). *Consultation on the Child Poverty Strategy 2014–17.* <www.gov.uk/government/consultations/child-poverty-a-draft-strategy>.

HM INSPECTORATE OF CONSTABULARY (2014). *Everyone's Business: Improving the Police Response to Domestic Abuse.* <www.justiceinspectorates.gov.uk/hmic/wp-content/uploads/2014/04/improving-the-police-response-to-domestic-abuse.pdf>.

HM TREASURY (2003). *Every Child Matters*, Cm 5860. London: HMSO.

HM TREASURY AND INLAND REVENUE (2002). *The Child and Working Tax Credits: The Modernisation of Britain's Tax and Benefits System.* London: HM Treasury.

HO (1998). *Supporting Families: A Consultation Document.* London: HMSO.

HO (1999). *Supporting Families: Summary of Responses to the Consultation Document.* London: TSO. <http://webarchive.nationalarchives.gov.uk//http://www.homeoffice.gov.uk/documents/sfamr.pdf?view=Binary>.

HO (2000). *Domestic Violence: Revised Circular to Police.* Home Office Circular No 19/2000.

HO (2003). *Safety and Justice: The Government's Proposals on Domestic Violence,* Cm 5847. <www.archive2.official-documents.co.uk/document/cm58/5847/5847.pdf>.

HO (2005). *Domestic Violence: A National Report.* <http://www.brokenrainbow.org.uk/sites/default/files/Government%20Report%20on%20DV%202005.pdf>.

HO (2006). *National Domestic Violence Delivery Plan: Progress Report 2005/06.*

HO (2008). *Government Response to the Sixth Report from the Home Affairs Committee 2007–8 HC263: Domestic violence, Forced Marriage and "Honour"-Based Violence,* Cm 7450. London: TSO. <www.official-documents.gov.uk/document/cm74/7450/7450.pdf>.

HO (2009). *National Domestic Violence Delivery Plan: Annual Progress Report 2008/9.* <http://webarchive.nationalarchives.gov.uk/20100418065544/http://www.homeoffice.gov.uk/documents/dom-violence-delivery-plan-08-092835.pdf?view=Binary>.

HO (2011). *Domestic Violence Protection Notices and Domestic Violence Protection Orders: Interim Guidance Document for Police Regional Pilot Schemes.* <www.gov.uk/government/uploads/system/uploads/attachment_data/file/97864/DV-protection-orders.pdf>.

HO (2012). *Cross-Government Definition of Domestic Violence – A Consultation. Summary of Responses.* <www.gov.uk/government/uploads/system/uploads/attachment_data/file/157800/domestic-violence-definition.pdf>.

HO (2014a). *Strengthening the Law on Domestic Abuse – A Consultation.* <www.gov.uk/government/uploads/system/uploads/attachment_data/file/389002/StrengtheningLawDomesticAbuseResponses.pdf>.

HO (2014b). *Strengthening the Law on Domestic Abuse Consultation – Summary of Responses.* London: HO. <www.gov.uk/government/uploads/system/uploads/attachment_data/file/389002/StrengtheningLawDomesticAbuseResponses.pdf>.

HOBSON, B. AND FAHLÉN, S. (2011). 'Parent's Work-Life Balance: Beyond Responsibilities and Obligations to Agency and Capabilities', in J. Bridgeman, H. Keating, and C. Lind (eds), *Regulating Family Responsibilities.* Farnham: Ashgate.

HOFF, L. (1990). *Battered Women as Survivors.* London: Routledge.

HOGGETT, B. (1980). 'Ends and Means: The Utility of Marriage as a Legal Institution', in J. Eekelaar and S. Katz (eds), *Marriage and Cohabitation in Contemporary Societies.* Toronto: Butterworths.

HOGGETT, B. (1989). 'The Children Bill: The Aim'. *Family Law*, 19: 217.

HOLCOMBE, L. (1983). *Wives and Property.* Toronto: University of Toronto Press.

HOLT, K. AND KELLY, N. (2012). 'Rhetoric and Reality Surrounding Care Proceedings: Family Justice Under Strain'. *Journal of Social Welfare and Family Law*, 34: 155.

HOLT, K., BROADHURST, K., DOHERTY, P., AND KELLY, N. (2013). 'Access to Justice for Families? Legal Advocacy for Parents Where Children are on the "Edge of Care": An English Case Study'. *Journal of Social Welfare and Family Law*, 35: 163.

HOME AFFAIRS SELECT COMMITTEE (2008). *Domestic Violence, Forced Marriage and "Honour"-Based Violence*, HC 263. London: TSO. <www.publications.parliament.uk/pa/cm200708/cmselect/cmhaff/263/263i.pdf>.

HOPKINS, N. (2009). 'Regulating Trusts of the Home: Private Law and Social Policy'. *Law Quarterly Review*, 125: 310.

HORTON, M. (1995). 'Improving Child Support—A Missed Opportunity'. *Child and Family Law Quarterly*, 7: 26.

HOUSE OF COMMONS JUSTICE COMMITTEE (2012). *Pre-Legislative Scrutiny of the Children and Families Bill, Fourth Report of Session 2012–13*, HC 739. <www.publications.parliament.uk/pa/cm201213/cmselect/cmjust/739/739.pdf>.

HOUSE OF COMMONS SELECT COMMITTEE ON EDUCATION (2012/13). *Children First: The Child Protection System in England.* <www.publications.parliament.uk/pa/cm201213/cmselect/cmeduc/137/137.pdf>.

HOUSE OF LORDS SELECT COMMITTEE ON ADOPTION LEGISLATION (2012). 1st Report of Session 2012–13, *Adoption: Pre-Legislative Scrutiny. Report*, HL Paper 94. <www.publications.parliament.uk/pa/ld201213/ldselect/ldadopt/94/94.pdf>.

(ⓦ) HOUSE OF LORDS SELECT COMMITTEE ON ADOPTION LEGISLATION (2013). 2nd Report of Session 2012–13, *Adoption: Post-Legislative Scrutiny. Report*, HL Paper 127. <www.publications.parliament.uk/pa/ld201213/ldselect/ldadopt/127/127.pdf>.

HOWE, D., SHEMMINGS, D., AND FEAST, J. (2001). 'Age at Placement and Adult Adopted People's Experience of Being Adopted'. *Child and Family Social Work*, 6: 337.

HOYLE, C. (1998). *Negotiating Domestic Violence*. Oxford: Clarendon Press.

HOYLE, C. AND SANDERS, A. (2000). 'Police Response to Domestic Violence: From Victim Choice to Victim Empowerment'. *British Journal of Criminology*, 40: 14.

HUGHES, K. AND SLOAN, B. (2011). 'Post-Adoption Photographs: Welfare, Rights and Judicial Reasoning'. *Child and Family Law Quarterly*, 23: 393.

HUMPHREYS, C. AND HARRISON, C. (2003). 'Focusing on Safety—Domestic Violence and the Role of Child Contact centres'. *Child and Family Law Quarterly*, 15: 237.

HUMPHREYS, C. AND KAYE, M. (1997). 'Third-Party Applications for Protection Orders: Opportunities, Ambiguities and Traps'. *Journal of Social Welfare and Family Law*, 19: 403.

HUMPHREYS, C. AND THIARA, R. (2003). 'Neither Justice nor Protection: Women's Experiences of Post-Separation Violence'. *Journal of Social Welfare and Family Law*, 25: 195.

(ⓦ) HUNT, J. AND MACLEOD, A. (2008). *Outcomes of Applications to Court for Contact Orders After Parental Separation or Divorce. Briefing Note*. London: Ministry of Justice. <http://dera.ioe.ac.uk/9145/1/outcomes-applications-contact-orders.pdf>.

HUNT, J., MASSON, J., AND TRINDER, L. (2009). 'Shared Parenting: The Law, the Evidence and Guidance from Families Need Fathers'. *Family Law*, 39: 831.

(ⓦ) HUTTON, J. (2006). *Ministerial Statement: Child Support Redesign*. <http://webarchive.nationalarchives.gov.uk/+/http://www.dwp.gov.uk/aboutus/2006/24-07-06.asp>.

HUXTABLE, R. AND FORBES, K. (2004). '*Glass v United Kingdom*: Maternal Instinct v Medical Opinion'. *Child and Family Law Quarterly*, 16: 339.

IJZENDOORN, M.H. VAN AND JUFFER, F. (2005). 'Adoption is a Successful Natural Intervention Enhancing Adopted Children's IQ and School Performance'. *Current Directions in Psychological Science*, 14: 326.

INGLEBY, R. (1989). 'Rhetoric and Reality: Regulation of Out-of-Court Activity in Matrimonial Proceedings'. *Oxford Journal of Legal Studies*, 9: 230.

(ⓦ) INLAND REVENUE (2004). 'Tax and Civil Partners', Rev BN 28. <http://webarchive.nationalarchives.gov.uk/20091222074811/http://www.hmrc.gov.uk/budget2005/revbn28.pdf>.

(ⓦ) INSTITUTE FOR FISCAL STUDIES (2010). 'Conservatives to Recognise One Third of Marriages in Tax System'. <www.ifs.org.uk/pr/marriage_pr.pdf>.

JACKSON, E. (2002). 'Conception and the Irrelevance of the Welfare Principle'. *Modern Law Review*, 65: 176.

JACKSON, E. (2006). 'What is a Parent?', in A. Diduck and K. O'Donovan (eds), *Feminist Perspectives on Family Law*. Abingdon: Routledge-Cavendish.

JACKSON, E. AND WASOFF, F., WITH MACLEAN, M. AND DOBASH, R. (1993). 'Financial Support on Divorce: The Right Mixture of Rules and Discretion?'. *International Journal of Law and the Family*, 7: 230.

(ω) JAMES, B. (2007). 'Domestic Violence and Ex Parte Applications: Getting the Affidavits Right'. *Family Law Week*, December. <www.familylawweek.co.uk/site.aspx?i=ed901>.

JAMES, G. (2009). 'Mothers and Fathers as Parents and Workers: Family-Friendly Employment Policies in an Era of Shifting Identities'. *Journal of Social Welfare and Family Law*, 31: 271.

JOHNSON, M. (1999). 'A Biomedical Perspective on Parenthood', in A. Bainham, S. Day Sclater, and M. Richards (eds), *What is a Parent? A Socio-Legal Analysis*. Oxford: Hart Publishing.

JOHNSON, P. (2012). 'Adoption, Homosexuality and the European Convention on Human Rights: *Gas and Dubois v France*'. *Modern Law Review*, 76: 1123.

JOINT COMMITTEE ON HUMAN RIGHTS (2003). *Third Report, Scrutiny of Bills: Progress Report*, HL 23/HC252 2003/04. London: HMSO.

(ω) JOINT COMMITTEE ON HUMAN RIGHTS (2004). *Fifteenth Report of Session 2003–04: Civil Partnership Bill*, HL Paper 136, HC 885. London: HMSO. <www.publications.parliament.uk/pa/jt200304/jtselect/jtrights/136/13602.htm>.

(ω) JOINT COMMITTEE ON HUMAN RIGHTS (2007). *Legislative Scrutiny: Child Maintenance and Other Payments Bill: Third Report of Session 2007–08*, HL Paper 28, HC 198. <www.publications.parliament.uk/pa/jt200708/jtselect/jtrights/28/28.pdf>.

(ω) JOINT COMMITTEE ON HUMAN RIGHTS (2009). *Legislative Scrutiny: Welfare Reform Bill, Fourteenth Report of Session 2008–09*. HL Paper 78, HC 414. <www.publications.parliament.uk/pa/jt200809/jtselect/jtrights/78/78.pdf>.

(ω) JOINT COMMITTEE ON HUMAN RIGHTS (2013–14). *Legislative Scrutiny: Children and Families Bill*. <www.publications.parliament.uk/pa/jt201314/jtselect/jtrights/29/2902.htm>.

JONES, S. (2007). 'Civil Partnerships and Social Security'. *Journal of Social Security Law*, 14: 9.

KAGANAS, F. (1999a). '*B v B (Occupation Order)* and *Chalmers v Johns*: Occupation Orders under the Family Law Act 1996'. *Child and Family Law Quarterly*, 11: 193.

KAGANAS, F. (1999b). 'Contact, Conflict and Risk', in S. Day Sclater and C. Piper (eds), *Undercurrents of Divorce*. Aldershot: Ashgate.

KAGANAS, F. (2000). '*Re L (Contact: Domestic Violence)* … Contact and Domestic Violence'. *Child and Family Law Quarterly*, 12: 311.

KAGANAS, F. (2002). 'Shared Parenting—A 70% Solution'. *Child and Family Law Quarterly*, 14: 365.

KAGANAS, F. (2007). 'Domestic Violence, Men's Groups and the Equivalence Argument', in A. Diduck and K. O'Donovan (eds), *Feminist Perspectives on Family Law*. Abingdon: Routledge-Cavendish.

KAGANAS, F. (2010). 'Child Protection, Gender and Rights', in J. Wallbank, S. Choudhry, and J. Herring (eds), *Rights, Gender and Family Law*. Abingdon: Routledge.

KAGANAS, F. (2011). '*In re L (Contact: Domestic Violence)*—Judgment', in R. Hunter, C. McGynn, and E. Rackley (eds), *Feminist Judgments: From Theory to Practice*. Oxford: Hart Publishing.

KAGANAS, F. (2013). 'A Presumption that "Involvement" of Both Parents is Best: Deciphering Law's Messages'. *Child and Family Law Quarterly*, 25: 270.

KAGANAS, F. AND DIDUCK, A. (2004). 'Incomplete Citizens: Changing Images of Post-Separation Children'. *Modern Law Review*, 67: 959.

KAHN-FREUND, O. (1952). 'Inconsistencies and Injustices in the Law of Husband and Wife'. *Modern Law Review*, 15: 133.

KAHN-FREUND, O. (1955). 'Matrimonial Property Law in England', in W. Friedmann (ed), *Matrimonial Property Law*. London: Stevens.

KAHN-FREUND, O. (1959). 'Matrimonial Property—Some Recent Developments'. *Modern Law Review*, 22: 241.

KAHN-FREUND, O. (1967). 'The Law Commission: Reform of the Grounds of Divorce. The Field of Choice'. *Modern Law Review*, 30: 180.

KAHN-FREUND, O. (1971). 'Matrimonial Property and Equality Before the Law: Some Sceptical Reflections'. *Human Rights Journal*, 4: 493.

KAY, R. (2004). 'Whose Divorce is it Anyway—The Human Rights Aspect'. *Family Law*, 34: 892.

KEATING, H. (1996). 'Shifting Standards in the House of Lords—*Re H and others (Minors) (Sexual Abuse: Standard of Proof)*'. *Child and Family Law Quarterly*, 8: 157.

KEATING, H. (2009). 'Suspicions, Sitting on the Fence and Standards of Proof'. *Child and Family Law Quarterly*, 21: 230.

KEATING, H. (2011). 'Case Commentary: *Re MA*: The Significance of Harm'. *Child and Family Law Quarterly*, 23: 115.

KEENAN, C. (2005). 'The Impact of *Cannings* on Civil Child Protection Cases'. *Journal of Social Welfare and Family Law*, 27: 173.

KEENAN, C. (2006). 'Lessons from America? Learning from Child Protection Policy in the USA'. *Child and Family Law Quarterly*, 18: 43.

KELLY, L. (1999). *Domestic Violence Matters: An Evaluation of a Development Project*. Home Office Research Study 193. London: Home Office. <http://webarchive.nationalarchives.gov.uk/20110218135832/rds.homeoffice.gov.uk/rds/pdfs/hors193.pdf>.

KELLY, L., ADLER, R., HORVATH, M., LOVETT, J., COULSON, M., KERNOHAN, D. AND GRAY, M. (2013). *Evaluation of the Pilot of Domestic Violence Protection Orders*. Home

Office Research Report 76. <www.gov.uk/government/publications/evaluation-of-the-pilot- of-domestic-violence-protection-orders>.

Kewley, A. (1996). 'Pragmatism before Principle: The Limitations of Civil Law Remedies for the Victims of Domestic Violence'. *Journal of Social Welfare and Family Law*, 18: 1.

Kiernan, K. and Mueller, G. (1998). *The Divorced and Who Divorces?*, Centre for Analysis of Social Exclusion, CASE Paper 7. <http://eprints.lse.ac.uk/6529/1/The_Divorced_and_Who_Divorces.pdf>.

Kilkelly, U. (2010). 'In *Re P*: Adoption, Discrimination and the Best Interests of the Child'. *Child and Family Law Quarterly*, 22: 115.

Kingdom, E. (2000). 'Cohabitation Contracts and the Democratization of Personal Relationships'. *Feminist Legal Studies*, 8: 5.

Kirton, D., Feast, J., and Howe, D., (2000). 'Searching, Reunion and Transracial Adoption'. *Adoption and Fostering*, 24: 6.

Krieken, R. van (2005). 'The "Best Interests" of the Child and Parental Separation: On the "Civilising of Parents" '. *Modern Law Review*, 68: 25.

Laming, (2003). *The Victoria Climbié Inquiry*. London: HMSO.

Langdridge, D. and Blyth, E. (2001). 'Regulation of Assisted Conception Services in Europe: Implications of the New Reproductive Technologies for "the Family"'. *Journal of Social Welfare and Family Law*, 23: 45.

Law Commission (1966). *Reform of the Grounds of Divorce: The Field of Choice*, Law Com No 6. London: HMSO.

Law Commission (1969). *Report on Financial Provision in Matrimonial Proceedings*, Law Com No 25. London: HMSO.

Law Commission (1970). *Report on Nullity of Marriage*, Law Com No 33. London: HMSO.

Law Commission (1971). *Family Property Law*, Published Working Paper 42. London: HMSO.

Law Commission (1973a). *Report on Solemnisation of Marriage in England and Wales*, Law Com No 53. London: HMSO.

Law Commission (1973b). *First Report on Family Property: A New Approach*, Law Com No 52. London: HMSO.

Law Commission (1978). *Family Property: The Matrimonial Home (Co-ownership and Occupation Rights) and Household Goods*, Law Com No 86. London: HMSO.

Law Commission (1980). *The Financial Consequences of Divorce: The Basic Policy. A Discussion Paper*, Law Com No 103. London: HMSO.

Law Commission (1981). *The Financial Consequences of Divorce*, Law Com No 112. London: HMSO.

Law Commission (1982a). *The Implications of Williams & Glyn's Bank Ltd v Boland*, Law Com No 115. London: HMSO.

Law Commission (1982b). *Family Law: Illegitimacy*, Law Com No 118. London: HMSO.

Law Commission (1985a). *Polygamous Marriages: Capacity to Contract a Polygamous Marriage and Related Issues*, Law Com No 146. London: HMSO.

Law Commission (1985b). *Family Law, Review of Child Law: Guardianship*, Law Com Working Paper 91. London: HMSO.

Law Commission (1988a). *Facing the Future: A Discussion Paper on the Ground for Divorce*, Law Com No 170. London: HMSO.

Law Commission (1988b). *Family Property: Matrimonial Property*, Law Com No 175. London: HMSO.

Law Commission (1988c). *Family Law, Review of Child Law: Guardianship and Custody*, Law Com No 172. London: HMSO.

Law Commission (1990). *The Ground for Divorce*, Law Com No 192. London: HMSO.

Law Commission (1992). *Family Law: Domestic Violence and Occupation of the Family Home*, Law Com No 207. London: HMSO.

Law Commission (2002). *Sharing Homes: A Discussion Paper*, Law Com No 278. London: HMSO.

Law Commission (2006). *Cohabitation: The Financial Consequences of Relationship Breakdown*, Law Com CP 179. London: TSO. <www.lawcommission.justice.gov.uk/docs/cp179_Cohabitation_Consultation.pdf>.

Law Commission (2007). *Cohabitation: The Financial Consequences of Relationship Breakdown*, Law Com No 307. London: TSO. <www.lawcommission.justice.gov.uk/docs/lc307_Cohabitation.pdf>.

Law Commission (2008). *Tenth Programme of Law Reform*, Law Com No 311. London: TSO. <www.justice.gov.uk/lawcommission/docs/lc311_10th_Programme.pdf>.

Law Commission (2009). *Conspiracy and Attempts*, Law Com No 318. London: TSO. <www.justice.gov.uk/lawcommission/areas/conspiracy-and-attempts.htm>.

Law Commission (2011). *Marital Property Agreements*, Law Com CP 198. London: TSO. <http://lawcommission.justice.gov.uk/docs/cp198_Marital_Property_Agreements_Consultation.pdf>.

Law Commission (2012). *Marital Property, Needs and Agreements – A Supplementary Consultation Paper*, Law Com CP 208. London: TSO. <lawcommission.justice.gov.uk/docs/cp208_matrimonial_property.pdf>.

Law Commission (2014). *Matrimonial Property, Needs and Agreements*, Law Com No 343. London: TSO. <http://lawcommission.justice.gov.uk/docs/lc343_matrimonial_property.pdf>.

Law Commission (2015). *Enforcement of Family Financial Orders*, Law Com CP 219. London: TSO. <http://lawcommission.justice.gov.uk/docs/cp219_enforcement_family_financial_orders.pdf>.

Law Reform Advisory Committee for Northern Ireland (2000). *Matrimonial Property*, Report No 10. Belfast: TSO.

LAW SOCIETY (2003). *Financial Provision on Divorce: Clarity and Fairness*. London: The Law Society.

LAW SOCIETY (2010). *Family Law Protocol*, 3rd edn. London: The Law Society.

LAWSON, A. (1996). 'The Things We Do for Love: Detrimental Reliance in the Family Home'. *Legal Studies*, 26: 218.

LCD (1990). *Judicial Statistics Annual Report for 1989*, Cm 1154. London: HMSO.

LCD (1992). *Judicial Statistics Annual Report for 1991*, Cm 1990. London: HMSO.

LCD (1993). *Looking to the Future—Mediation and the Ground for Divorce*, Cm 2424. London: HMSO.

LCD (1995). *Looking to the Future, Mediation and the Ground for Divorce*, Cm 2799. London: HMSO.

LCD (1999). 'Implementation of Family Law Act Part II Delayed Pilots Show Disappointing Response to Information Meetings'. Press Release No 159/99, 17 June.

LCD (2001). 'Divorce Law Reform—Government Proposes to Repeal Part II of the Family Law Act 1996'. Press Release No 20/01.

LCD (2002). *Moving Forward Together: A Proposed Strategy for Marriage and Relationship Support for 2002 and Beyond*.

LE GRICE, V. (2013). 'A Critique of Non-Marriage'. *Family Law*, 43: 1278.

LECKEY, R. (2013). 'Marriage and the Data on Same-Sex Couples'. *Journal of Social Welfare and Family Law*, 35: 179.

LEE, N. (2014). *Revenue Law: Principles and Practice*, 32nd edn. London: Bloomsbury Professional.

LEE, R. (2008). '*Stack v Dowden*—A Sequel'. *Law Quarterly Review*, 124: 209.

LEES, K. (2012). '*Geary v Rankine*: Money Isn't Everything'. *Conveyancer and Property Lawyer*, 76: 412.

LEGAL SERVICES COMMISSION, *Funding Code Decision-Making Guidance*. <www.legalservices.gov.uk/civil/guidance/funding_code.asp>.

LEGAL SERVICES COMMISSION, *Funding Code: Part 1—Criteria*. <www.legalservices.gov.uk/docs/civil_contracting/Funding_code_criteria_Jul07.pdf>.

LEWIS, J. (1998). 'The Problem of Lone-Mother Families in Twentieth-Century Britain'. *Journal of Social Welfare and Family Law*, 20: 251.

LEWIS, J. (2000). 'Family Policy in the Post-War Period', in S. Katz, J. Eekelaar, and M. Maclean (eds), *Cross Currents: Family Law and Policy in the US and England*. Oxford: OUP.

LEWIS, J. (2001a). 'Debates and Issues Regarding Marriage and Cohabitation in the British and American Literature'. *International Journal of Law, Policy and the Family*, 15: 159.

LEWIS, J. (2001b). *The End of Marriage? Individualism and Intimate Relations*. Cheltenham: Edward Elgar.

LEWIS, J. (2004). 'Adoption: The Nature of Policy Shifts in England and Wales 1972–2002'. *International Journal of Law, Policy and the Family*, 18: 235.

LEWIS, J. (2009). 'Balancing "Time to Work" and "Time to Care": Policy Issues and Implications for Mothers, Fathers and Children'. *Child and Family Law Quarterly*, 21: 443.

LEWIS, J., WITH DATTA, J. AND SARRE, S. (1999). *Individualism and Commitment in Marriage and Cohabitation*. LCD Research Series No 8/99. London: Lord Chancellor's Department.

LEWIS, R. (2004). 'Making Justice Work: Effective Legal Interventions for Domestic Violence'. *British Journal of Criminology*, 44: 204.

LIM, H. (1996). 'Messages from a Rarely Visited Island: Duress and Lack of Consent in Marriage'. *Feminist Legal Studies*, 4: 195.

LIND, C. (2004). 'Sexuality and Same-Sex Relationships in Law', in B. Brooks-Gordon, L. Gelsthorpe, M. Johnson, and A. Bainham (eds), *Sexuality Repositioned*. Oxford: Hart Publishing.

LIND, C. AND HEWITT, T. (2009). 'Law and the Complexities of Parenting: Parental Status and Parental Function'. *Journal of Social Welfare and Family Law*, 31: 391.

LINDLEY, B. (1997). 'Open Adoption—Is the Door Ajar?'. *Child and Family Law Quarterly*, 9: 115.

LINDLEY, B. (1999). 'State Intervention and Parental Autonomy in Children's Cases: Have We Got the Balance Right?', in A. Bainham, S. Day Sclater, and M. Richards (eds), *What is a Parent? A Socio-Legal Analysis*. Oxford: Hart Publishing.

Ⓦ LOCAL SAFEGUARDING CHILDREN BOARD, HARINGEY ('LSCB') (2009). *Serious Case Review: Baby Peter*. <www.haringeylscb.org/executive_summary_peter_final.pdf>.

LOGAN, J. AND SMITH, C. (2005). 'Face-to-Face Contact Post-Adoption: Views from the Triangles'. *British Journal of Social Work*, 35: 3.

Ⓦ LORD LESTER's Civil Partnership Bill 2002. <www.odysseustrust.org/civil_partnershipsindex.html>.

LOWE, N. (1997a). 'The Meaning and Allocation of Parental Responsibility—A Common Lawyer's Perspective'. *International Journal of Law, Policy and the Family*, 11: 192.

LOWE, N. (1997b). 'The Changing Face of Adoption—The Gift/Donation Model versus the Contract/Services Model'. *Child and Family Law Quarterly*, 9: 371.

LOWE, N. (2011). '*J v C*: Placing the Child's Welfare Centre Stage', in S. Gilmore, J. Herring, and R. Probert (eds), *Landmark Cases in Family Law*. Oxford: Hart Publishing.

LOWE, N. AND DOUGLAS, G. (2007). '*Bromley's Family Law*, 10th edn. Oxford: OUP.

LOWE, N. AND DOUGLAS, G. (2015). *Bromley's Family Law*, 11th edn. Oxford: OUP.

LOWE, N., MURCH, M., BORKOWSKI, M., WEAVER, A., BECKFORD, V., WITH THOMAS, C. (1999). *Supporting Adoption—Reframing the approach*. London: BAAF.

LUCKOCK, B. AND HART, A. (2005). 'Adoptive Family Life and Adoption Support: Policy Ambivalence and the Development of Effective Services'. *Child and Family Social Work*, 10: 125.

LUNDBERG, B. (2013). *Serious Case Review in Respect of the Death of Keanu Williams: Born 11th December 2008, Died 9th January 2011*. Birmingham: Birmingham Safeguarding Children Board. <www.lscbbirmingham.org.uk/images/stories/downloads/executive-summaries/Case_25__Final_Overview_Report_02.10.13.pdf>.

LUNDBERG, S., POLLAK, R., AND WALES, T. (1997). 'Do Husbands and Wives Pool Their Resources? Evidence from the United Kingdom Child Benefit'. *Journal of Human Resources*, 32: 463.

MACLEAN, M. AND EEKELAAR, J. (1993). 'Child Support: The British Solution'. *International Journal of Law and the Family*, 7: 205.

MACLEAN, M. AND EEKELAAR, J. (1997). *The Parental Obligation: A Study of Parenthood across Households*. Oxford: Hart Publishing.

MACLEAN, M. AND EEKELAAR, J. (2009). *Family Law Advocacy: How Barristers Help the Victims of Family Failure*. Oxford: Hart Publishing.

MACLEAN, M. WITH KURCZEWSKI, J. (2011). *Making Family Law: A Socio Legal Account of the Legislative Process in England and Wales, 1985 to 2010*. Oxford: Hart Publishing.

MADDEN DEMPSEY, M. (2006). 'What Counts as Domestic Violence? A Conceptual Analysis'. *William and Mary Journal of Women and the Law*, 12: 301.

MAPLETHORPE, N., CHANFREAU, J., PHILO, D., AND TAIT, C. (2010). *Families with Children in Britain: Findings from the 2008 Families and Children Study (FACS)*. DWP RR 656. <www.gov.uk/government/uploads/system/uploads/attachment_data/file/214426/rrep656.pdf>.

MARSH, A. AND VEGERIS, S. (2004). *The British Lone Parent Cohort and their Children 1991–2001*. DWP Research Report No 209. Leeds: Corporate Document Service. <http://webarchive.nationalarchives.gov.uk/20130314010347/http://research.dwp.gov.uk/asd/asd5/rports2003-2004/rrep209.pdf>.

MARSHALL, A. (2003). 'Comedy of Adoption—When is a Parent Not a Parent?'. *Family Law*, 33: 840.

MARSHALL, J. (2012). 'Concealed Births, Adoption and Human Rights Law: Being Wary of Seeking to Open Windows into People's Souls'. *Cambridge Law Journal*, 71: 325.

MASSON, J. (1992). 'Managing Risk under the Children Act 1989: Diversion in Child Care'. *Child Abuse Review*, 1: 103.

MASSON, J. (2000). 'Thinking about Contact—A Social or Legal Problem?'. *Child and Family Law Quarterly*, 12: 15.

MASSON, J. (2003). 'The Impact of the Adoption and Children Act 2002—Part 2—The Provision of Services for Children and Families'. *Family Law*, 33: 644.

MASSON, J. (2004). 'Human Rights in Child Protection: Emergency Action and its Impact', in P. Lødrup and E. Modvar (eds), *Family Life and Human Rights*. Oslo: Gyldendal Norsk Forlag AS.

Masson, J. (2005). 'Emergency Intervention to Protect Children: Using and Avoiding Legal Controls'. *Child and Family Law Quarterly*, 17: 75.

Masson, J. (2006). 'Fair Trials in Child Protection'. *Journal of Social Welfare and Family Law*, 28: 15.

Masson, J. (2007). 'Reforming Care Proceedings—Time for a Review'. *Child and Family Law Quarterly*, 19: 411.

Masson J. (2008). 'Controlling Costs and Maintaining Services—The Reform of Legal Aid Fees for Care Proceedings.' *Child and Family Law Quarterly*, 20: 425.

Masson, J. (2010a). 'A New Approach to Care Proceedings'. *Child and Family Social Work*, 15: 369.

Masson, J. (2010b). '(Mis)understandings of Significant Harm'. *Child Abuse Review*, 19: 291.

Masson, J., Bailey-Harris, R., and Probert, R. (2008). *Cretney: Principles of Family Law*, 8th edn. London: Sweet & Maxwell.

Masson, J., Pearce, J., and Bader, K. (2008). *Care Profiling Study*. Ministry of Justice Research Series 4/08. Ministry of Justice. <http://research-information.bristol. ac.uk/files/9073958/care_profiling_study_Rpt.pdf>.

Masson, J., Bader, K., Dickens, J., and Young, J. (2013). 'The Pre-Proceedings Process for Families on the Edge of Care Proceedings'. University of Bristol and University of East Anglia. <http://research-information.bristol.ac.uk/files/9073836/ Partnership_by_law.pdf>.

Maughan, B., Collishaw, S., and Pickles, A. (1998). 'School Achievement and Adult Qualifications among Adoptees: A Longitudinal Study'. *Journal of Child Psychology and Psychiatry*, 39: 669.

May, V. and Smart, C. (2004). 'Silence in Court?—hearing children in residence and contact disputes'. *Child and Family Law Quarterly*, 16: 305.

McCafferty, C. (2002). 'Gays, Transsexuals and the Right to Marry'. *Family Law*, 32: 362.

McCandless, J. (2008). 'Status and Anomaly: *Re D (Contact and Parental Responsibility: Lesbian Mothers and Known Father)* [2006] EWHC 2 (Fam), [2006] 1 FCR 556'. *Journal of Social Welfare and Family Law*, 30: 63.

McCandless, J. and Sheldon, S. (2010). 'The Human Fertilisation and Embryology Act (2008) and the Tenacity of the Sexual Family Form'. *Modern Law Review*, 73: 175.

McCann, K. (1985). 'Battered Women and the Law: The Limits of the Legislation', in J. Brophy and C. Smart (eds), *Women in Law: Explorations in Law, Family and Sexuality*. London: Routledge.

McClean, D. and Hayes, M. (2011). 'But I Didn't Really Want to Get Married', in S. Gilmore et al (eds), *Landmark Cases in Family Law*. Oxford: Hart.

McFall, S. (ed) (2012). *Understanding Society: Findings 2012*. Colchester: Institute for Social and Economic Research, University of Essex. <www.understandingsociety. ac.uk/research/publications/findings/2012>.

McGlynn, C. (2000). 'Ideologies of Motherhood in European Community Sex Equality Law'. *European Law Journal*, 6: 29.

McGlynn, C. (2001). 'European Union Family Values: Ideologies of "Family" and "Motherhood" in European Union Law'. *Social Politics*, 8: 325.

McIntosh, J., Smyth, B., Kelaher, M., Wells, Y., and Long, C. (2010). *Post-Separation Parenting Arrangements and Developmental Outcomes for Infants and Children*. North Carlton, Australia: Family Transitions.

McLellan, D. (1996). 'Contract Marriage—The Way Forward or Dead End?'. *Journal of Law and Society*, 23: 234.

Mee, J. (1999). *The Property Rights of Cohabitees*. Oxford: Hart Publishing.

Mee, J. (2004). 'Property Rights and Personal Relationships: Reflections on Reform'. *Legal Studies*, 24: 414.

Mee, J. (2009). 'The Limits of Proprietary Estoppel: *Thorner v Majors*'. *Child and Family Law Quarterly*, 21: 367.

Mee, J. (2011). '*Burns v Burns*: The Villain of the Piece?' in S. Gilmore et al (eds), *Landmark Cases in Family Law*. Oxford: Hart Publishing.

Mee, J. (2012). '*Jones v Kernott*: Inferring and Imputing in Essex'. *Conveyancer and Property Lawyer*, 76: 167.

Mee, J. (2013). 'Proprietary Estoppel and Inheritance: Enough is Enough?' *Conveyancer and Property Lawyer*, 77: 280.

Middleton, S., Ashworth, K., and Braithwaite, I. (1997). *Small Fortunes: Spending on Children, Childhood Poverty and Parental Sacrifice*. York: Joseph Rowntree Foundation.

Miles, J. (2001). 'Domestic Violence', in J. Herring (ed), *Family Law: Issues, Debates, Policy*. Cullompton: Willan Publishing.

Miles, J. (2003). 'Property Law v Family Law: Resolving the Problems of Family Property'. *Legal Studies*, 23: 624.

Miles, J. (2005). 'Principle or Pragmatism in Ancillary Relief: The Virtues of Flirting with Academic Theories and Other Jurisdictions'. *International Journal of Law, Policy and the Family*, 19: 242.

Miles, J. (2008). '*Charman v Charman (No 4)*: Making Sense of Need, Compensation and Equal Sharing after *Miller/McFarlane*'. *Child and Family Law Quarterly*, 20: 378.

Miles, J. (2009). '*Radmacher v Granatino*: Upping the Ante-Nuptial Agreement'. *Child and Family Law Quarterly*, 21: 513.

Miles, J. (2011a). 'Responsibility in Family Finance and Property Law', in J. Bridgeman, H. Keating, and C. Lind (eds), *Regulating Family Responsibilities*. Aldershot: Ashgate.

Miles, J. (2011b). 'Family Abuse, Privacy and State Intervention'. *Cambridge Law Journal*, 70: 32.

Miles, J. (2011c). 'Marriage and Divorce in the Supreme Court and the Law Commission: For Love or Money?'. *Modern Law Review*, 74: 430.

MILES, J. (2011d). 'Legal Aid, Article 6 and "Exceptional Funding" under the Legal Aid (etc.) Bill 2011'. *Family Law*, 41: 1003.

MILES, J. (2011e). 'Legal Aid and Exceptional Funding: A Postscript'. *Family Law*, 41: 1268

MILES, J. (2012). 'Marital Agreements: "The More Radical Solution"', in R. Probert and C. Barton (eds), *Fifty Years in Family Law: Essays for Stephen Cretney*. Cambridge: Intersentia.

MILES, J. AND PROBERT, R. (eds) (2009). *Sharing Lives, Dividing Assets: An Inter-Disciplinary Study*. Oxford: Hart Publishing.

MILL, J.S. (1869). *Three Essays: On Liberty, Representative Government and the Subjection of Women* (1975) R. Wollheim (ed). Oxford: OUP.

MILLAR, J. (1996). 'Family Obligations and Social Policy: The Case of Child Support'. *Policy Studies*, 17: 181.

MILLER, G. (2003). 'Pre-Nuptial Agreements and Financial Provision', in G. Miller (ed), *Frontiers of Family Law*. Dartmouth: Ashgate.

MILLWARD, E. (2008). 'The Domestic Violence, Crime and Victims Act 2004: Is it Working?'. *Family Law*, 38: 493.

MIRRLEES-BLACK, C. (1999). *Domestic Violence: Findings from a New British Crime Survey Self-Completion Questionnaire*. Home Office Research Study 191. London: HMSO. <http://webarchive.nationalarchives.gov.uk/20110218135832/rds.homeoffice.gov.uk/rds/pdfs/hors191.pdf>.

MITCHELL, M., DICKENS, S., AND O'CONNOR, W. (2009). *Same-Sex Couples and the Impact of Legislative Changes*. London: NatCen. <www.natcen.ac.uk/our-research/research/same-sex-couples/>.

MNOOKIN, R. (1975). 'Child-Custody Adjudication: Judicial Functions in the Face of Indeterminacy'. *Law and Contemporary Problems*, 39: 225.

MNOOKIN, R. AND KORNHAUSER, L. (1979). 'Bargaining in the Shadow of the Law: The Case of Divorce'. *Yale Law Journal*, 88: 950.

MODY, P. (2015). 'Forced Marriage: Rites and Rights', in J. Miles, P. Mody, and R. Probert (eds), *Marriage Rites and Rights*. Oxford: Hart Publishing.

MOFFATT, P. AND THOBURN, J. (2001). 'Outcomes of Permanent Family Placement for Children of Minority Ethnic Origin'. *Child and Family Social Work*, 6: 13.

MOJ (2008). *The Public Law Outline. Guide to Case Management in Public Law Proceedings*. London: HMSO. <www.bournemouth-poole-lscb.org.uk/inter-agency_safeguarding_procedures/part_one/pictures/content34/public_law_outline.pdf>.

MOJ (2010a). *Judicial and Court Statistics 2009*. <www.justice.gov.uk/downloads/statistics/mojstats/jcs-stats-2009-211010.pdf>.

MOJ (2010b). *Proposals for the Reform of Legal Aid in England and Wales*, Cm 7967. London: TSO. <www.gov.uk/government/uploads/system/uploads/attachment_data/file/228970/7967.pdf>.

MOJ (2012). *Judicial and Court Statistics 2011*. <www.gov.uk/government/statistics/judicial-and-court-statistics-annual>.

MOJ (2013). *Code of Practice for Victims of Crime*. London: TSO. <www.gov.uk/government/uploads/system/uploads/attachment_data/file/254459/code-of-practice-victims-of-crime.pdf>.

MOJ (2014a). *Court Statistics Quarterly, April to June 2014*. <www.gov.uk/government/uploads/system/uploads/attachment_data/file/358230/court-statistics-quarterly-april-to-june-2014.pdf>.

MOJ (2014b). *Legal Aid Statistics in England and Wales, 2013–2014*. London: HMSO. <www.gov.uk/government/uploads/system/uploads/attachment_data/file/358100/legal-aid-statistics-2013-14.pdf>.

MOJ (2014c). *Marriages by Non-Religious Belief Organisations*. London: MOJ. <www.gov.uk/government/consultations/marriages-by-non-religious-belief-organisations>.

MOJ (2014d). *Report of the Family Mediation Task Force*. <www.justice.gov.uk/downloads/family-mediation-task-force-report.pdf>.

MOJ (2014e). *Marriages by Non-Religious Belief Organisations: Summary of Written Responses to the Consultation and Government Response*. London: MOJ. <www.gov.uk/government/consultations/marriages-by-non-religious-belief-organisations>.

MOJ/DFE (2012). *The Government Response to the Family Justice Review: A System with Children and Families at its Heart*, Cm 8273. <www.gov.uk/government/uploads/system/uploads/attachment_data/file/177097/CM-8273.pdf>.

MOJ/LEGAL AID AGENCY (2014). *Ad Hoc Managements Information: Legal Aid Exceptional Case Funding Application and Determination: 1 April 2014 to 30 June 2014*. <www.gov.uk/government/uploads/system/uploads/attachment_data/file/358092/legal-aid-statistics-apr-jun-2014.pdf>.

MOLONEY, L. (2001). 'Do Fathers "Win" or Do Mothers "Lose"? A Preliminary Analysis of Closely Contested Parenting Judgments in the Family Court of Australia'. *International Journal of Law, Policy and the Family*, 15: 363.

MONAGHAN, K. AND HARDING R. (2010). '*Wilkinson v Kitzinger*', in R. Hunter, C. McGlynn, and E. Rackley (eds), *Feminist Judgments: From Theory to Practice*. Oxford: Hart Publishing.

MOONEY, A., OLIVER, C., AND SMITH, M. (2009). *Impact of Family Breakdown on Children's Well-Being. Evidence Review*. Research Report DCSF-RR113. London: DfCSF and Thomas Coram Research Unit. <www.education.gov.uk/research/data/uploadfiles/DCSF-RR113.pdf>.

MOOR, P. AND LE GRICE, V. (2006). 'Periodical Payments Orders following *Miller* and *McFarlane*—A Series of Unfortunate Events'. *Family Law*, 36: 655.

MORGAN, P. (2000). *Marriage-Lite: The Rise of Cohabitation and its Consequences*. London: Institute for the Study of Civil Society.

MORLEY, R. AND MULLENDER, A. (1994). *Preventing Domestic Violence to Women*. Crime Prevention Unit Series Paper No 48. London: Home Office.

MORRIS, A. (2000). 'Couples and Benefits Claims: A Comment on *Relying on the State, Relying on Each Other'. Journal of Social Security Law*, 7: 228.

MORRIS, A. AND GELSTHORPE, L. (2000). 'Re-Visioning Men's Violence Against Female Partners'. *The Howard Journal*, 39: 412.

MORRIS, A. AND NOTT, S. (2005). 'Marriage Rites and Wrongs: Challenges to Orthodoxy'. *Journal of Social Welfare and Family Law*, 27: 43.

MORRIS, C. (2005). 'Divorce in a Multi-Faith Society'. *Family Law*, 35: 727.

MORTIMER COMMISSION (1966). *Putting Asunder: A Divorce Law for Contemporary Society.* London: SPCK.

MOSTYN, N. (1999). 'The Green Paper on Child Support—Children First: A New Approach to Child Support'. *Family Law*, 29: 95.

MULLENDER, A. AND MORLEY, R. (1994). 'Context and Content of a New Agenda', in A. Mullender and R. Morley (eds), *Children Living with Domestic Violence.* London: Whiting and Birch.

MÜLLER-FREIENFELS, W. (2003). 'The Emergence of *Droit de Famille* and *Familienrecht* in Continental Europe and the Introduction of Family Law in England'. *Journal of Family History*, 28: 31.

MUMFORD, A. (2007). 'Working Towards Credit for Parenting: A Consideration of Tax Credits as a Feminist Enterprise', in A. Diduck and K. O'Donovan (eds), *Feminist Perspectives on Family Law.* Abingdon: Routledge-Cavendish.

MUNBY, J. (2014a). 'The Family Justice Reforms: Remarks by Sir James Munby. 29 April 2014'. <www.judiciary.gov.uk/announcements/the-family-justice-reforms-remarks-by-sir-james-munby/>.

MUNBY, J. (2014b). Press Conference, 29 April. <www.judiciary.gov.uk/wp-content/uploads/2014/05/munby-press-conference-290420141.pdf>.

MUNRO, E. (2011). *The Munro Review of Child Protection: Final Report. A Child-Centred System*, Cm 8062. <www.gov.uk/government/uploads/system/uploads/attachment_data/file/175391/Munro-Review.pdf>.

MURPHY, J. (2000). 'Rationality and Cultural Pluralism in the Non-Recognition of Foreign Marriages'. *International and Comparative Law Quarterly*, 49: 643.

MURPHY, J. (2003). 'Children in Need: The Limits of Local Authority Accountability'. *Legal Studies*, 23: 103.

NAPO (2012). *Probation: Domestic Abuse Programmes and Budgets.* <www.napo.org.uk/sites/default/files/BRF07-12%20Probation%20Domestic%20Abuse%20Programmes%20and%20Budgets.pdf>.

NAREY, M. (2011). 'The Narey Report: A Blueprint for the Nation's Lost Children'. *The Times*, 5 July.

NATIONAL ADOPTION LEADERSHIP BOARD (2014). *Impact of Court Judgments on Adoption. What the Judgments Do and Do Not Say.* <www.cypnow.co.uk/digital_assets/635/ALB---Impact-of-Court-Judgments-on-Adoption---November-2014-(1)-(1).pdf>.

Neale, B. and Smart, C. (1999). 'In Whose Best Interests? Theorising Family Life Following Parental Separation or Divorce', in S. Day Sclater and C. Piper (eds), *Undercurrents of Divorce*. Dartmouth: Ashgate.

Neil, E. (2000). 'The Reasons Why Young Children are Placed for Adoption: Findings from a Recently Placed Sample and a Discussion of Implications for Subsequent Identity Development'. *Child and Family Social Work*, 5: 303.

Neil, E. (2009). 'Post-Adoption Contact and Openness in Adoptive Parents' Minds: Consequences for Children's Development'. *British Journal of Social Work*, 39: 5.

Neil, E., Beek, M., Thoburn, J. et al (2012). *Contact Arrangements for Adopted Children: What can be Learned from Research?* UEA: Centre for Research on the Child and Family.

Neuberger, D. (2008). 'The Conspirators, the Tax Man, the Bill of Rights, and a Bit about Lovers'. Chancery Bar Association Annual Lecture, 10 March. <www.chba.org.uk/for-members/library/annual-lectures/the-conspiratorsthe-taxman-the-bill-of-rights.pdf>.

Neuberger, D. (2009). 'The Stuffing of Minerva's Owl? Taxonomy and Taxidermy in Equity'. *Cambridge Law Journal*, 68: 537.

Newcastle Centre for Family Studies (2001a). *Information Meetings and Associated Provisions within the Family Law Act 1996: Key Findings from Research*. London: LCD. <http://webarchive.nationalarchives.gov.uk/+/http:/www.dca.gov.uk/family/fla/flapt2.htm>.

Newcastle Centre for Family Studies (2001b). *Information Meetings and Associated Provisions within the Family Law Act 1996: Summary of the Final Evaluation Report*. London: LCD. <http://webarchive.nationalarchives.gov.uk/+/http:/www.dca.gov.uk/family/fla/flapt2.htm>.

Newcastle Centre for Family Studies (2004). *Picking Up the Pieces: Marriage and Divorce Two Years After Information Provision*. <http://webarchive.nationalarchives.gov.uk/+/http://www.dca.gov.uk/pubs/reports/family2004-webpageintro.htm>.

Newnham, A. (2011). 'Law's Gendered Understandings of Parents' Responsibilities in Relation to Shared Residence', in J. Bridgeman, H. Keating, and C. Lind (eds), *Regulating Family Responsibilities*. Farnham: Ashgate.

Newnham, A. (2013). 'Common Intention Constructive Trusts: A Way Forward'. *Family Law*, 43: 718.

NHS (2014) *Gender Dysphoria*. <www.nhs.uk/Conditions/Gender-dysphoria/Pages/Introduction.aspx>.

Noon, R. (2008). 'Compensation for Domestic Abuse after *Singh v Bhakar*'. *Family Law Week*, September. <www.familylawweek.co.uk/site.aspx?i=ed25932>.

Norgrove, D. (2011). *Family Justice Review: Final Report*. London: MOJ. <www.gov.uk/government/uploads/system/uploads/attachment_data/file/217343/family-justice-review-final-report.pdf>.

Norrie, A. (2010). 'The Coroners and Justice Act 2009—Partial Defences to Murder (1) Loss of Control'. *Criminal Law Review*, 275.

NORRIE, K. (2000). 'Marriage is for Heterosexuals—May the Rest of Us Be Saved From It'. *Child and Family Law Quarterly*, 12: 363.

O'BRIEN, K. AND ZAMOSTNY, K. (2003). 'Understanding Adoptive Families: An Integrative Review of Empirical Research and Future Directions for Counseling Psychology'. *The Counseling Psychologist*, 31: 679.

O'DONNELL, K. (2004). '*Re C (Welfare of Child: Immunisation)*—Room to Refuse? Immunisation, Welfare and the Role of Parental Decision-Making'. *Child and Family Law Quarterly*, 16: 213.

O'DONOVAN, K. (1982). 'Should All Maintenance of Spouses be Abolished?'. *Modern Law Review*, 45: 424.

O'DONOVAN, K. (1985). *Sexual Divisions in Law*. London: Weidenfield & Nicolson.

O'DONOVAN, K. (1993). *Family Law Matters*. London: Pluto Press.

O'DONOVAN, K. (2000). 'Interpretations of Children's Identity Rights', in D. Fottrell (ed), *Revisiting Children's Rights*. The Hague; Boston: Kluwer Law International.

O'KEEFFE, M. ET AL (2007). *UK Study of Abuse and Neglect of Older People: Prevalence Survey Report*. London: NatCen.

O'NEILL, O. (1992). 'Children's Rights and Children's Lives'. *International Journal of Law and the Family*, 6: 24.

O'NEILL, R. (2005). *Fiscal Policy and the Family*. London: Civitas <www.civitas.org.uk/pdf/OneillFiscalPolicy.pdf>.

OECD (2014). *Family Database: Marriage and Divorce Rates*. <www.oecd.org/els/family/SF3_1_Marriage_and_divorce_rate_Jan2014.pdf>.

OFSTED (2012). *Right on Time. Exploring Delays in Adoption*. London: HMSO. <www.ofsted.gov.uk/sites/default/files/documents/surveys-and-good-practice/r/Right%20on%20time%20exploring%20delays%20in%20adoption.pdf>.

OLDHAM, M. (2001). 'Financial Obligations Within the Family—Aspects of Intergenerational Maintenance and Succession in England and France'. *Cambridge Law Journal*, 60: 128.

ONS (2003). *Census 2001 National Report for England and Wales*. London: TSO.

ONS (2005b). *Focus on Ethnicity and Identity*. London: HMSO.

ONS (2007). *Focus on Families*. London: Palgrave Macmillan. <www.ons.gov.uk/ons/rel/family-demography/focus-on-families/2007/focus-on-families-summary-report.pdf>.

ONS (2008). 'Report: divorces in England and Wales during 2007'. *Population Trends*, 133: 71.

ONS (2009). *Marriage, Divorce and Adoption Statistics*. Series FM2 no 34. <www.ons.gov.uk/ons/rel/vsob1/marriage--divorce-and-adoption-statistics--england-and-wales--series-fm2-/no--34--2006/marriage--divorce-and-adoption-statistics--england-and-wales--series-fm2-.pdf>.

ONS (2010a). *Marriage, Divorce and Adoption Statistics*. Series FM2 no 36, 2007. <www.ons.gov.uk/ons/publications/re-reference-tables.html?edition=tcm%3A77-39669>.

ⓦ ONS (2010b). *2008-Based Marital Status Population Projections*. <www.ons.gov.uk/ons/taxonomy/index.html?nscl=Population+Projections+by+Marital+Status>.

ⓦ ONS (2010c). *Marriage Statistics 2008, Provisional*. <www.ons.gov.uk/ons/rel/vsob1/marriages-in-england-and-wales--provisional-/2008/marriages-in-england-and-wales--provisional----marriage-statistics.xls>.

ⓦ ONS (2010d). *Social Trends*, 40. London: TSO. <www.ons.gov.uk/ons/rel/social-trends-rd/social-trends/social-trends-40/index.html>.

ⓦ ONS (2012a). *Marriages in England and Wales, 2010*. <www.ons.gov.uk/ons/dcp171778_258307.pdf>.

ⓦ ONS (2012b). *Ethnicity and National Identity in England and Wales 2011*. <www.ons.gov.uk/ons/dcp171776_290558.pdf>.

ⓦ ONS (2012c). *Religion in England and Wales 2011*. <www.ons.gov.uk/ons/dcp171776_290510.pdf>.

ⓦ ONS (2013a). *Families and Households in England and Wales, 2011*. <www.ons.gov.uk/ons/dcp171776_296986.pdf>.

ⓦ ONS (2013b). *Civil Partnerships in the UK, 2012*. <www.ons.gov.uk/ons/dcp171778_329457.pdf>.

ⓦ ONS (2013c). *Statistical Bulletin: Live Births in England and Wales by Characteristics of Mother 1, 2012*. <www.ons.gov.uk/ons/dcp171778_330664.pdf>.

ⓦ ONS (2013d). *Families and Households, 2013*. <www.ons.gov.uk/ons/rel/family-demography/families-and-households/2013/index.html>.

ⓦ ONS (2013e). *Adoptions in England and Wales 2012*. <www.ons.gov.uk/ons/dcp171778_322848.pdf>.

ⓦ ONS (2013f). *Women in the Labour Market*. <www.ons.gov.uk/ons/dcp171776_328352.pdf>.

ⓦ ONS (2014a). *Divorces in England and Wales, 2012*. <www.ons.gov.uk/ons/dcp171778_351693.pdf>.

ⓦ ONS (2014b). *2011 Census Analysis: How Do Living Arrangements, Family Type and Family Size Vary in England and Wales?* <www.ons.gov.uk/ons/dcp171776_366963.pdf>.

ⓦ ONS (2014c). *Births in England and Wales 2013*. <www.ons.gov.uk/ons/dcp171778_371129.pdf>.

ⓦ ONS (2014d). *Crime Statistics: Focus on Violent Crime and Sexual Offences, 2012/13*. <www.ons.gov.uk/ons/rel/crime-stats/crime-statistics/focus-on-violent-crime-and-sexual-offences--2012-13/index.html>.

ⓦ ONS (2014e). *Marriages in England and Wales (Provisional), 2012*. <www.ons.gov.uk/ons/dcp171778_366530.pdf>.

ⓦ ONS (2014f). *How Many Marriages of Same Sex Couples Have Been Formed in England and Wales So Far?* <www.ons.gov.uk/ons/rel/vsob1/marriages-in-england-and-wales--provisional-/for-same-sex-couples-q1-and-q2-2014/sty-same-sex-marriages.html>.

ⓦ ONS (2014g). *How Have Living Arrangements and Marital Status in England and Wales Changed Since 2001?* <www.ons.gov.uk/ons/dcp171776_356002.pdf>.

ⓦ ONS (2014h). *UK Labour Market, November 2014*. <www.ons.gov.uk/ons/rel/lms/labour-market-statistics/november-2014/statistical-bulletin.html>.

ORMEROD, D. (2011). *Smith and Hogan's Criminal Law*, 13th edn. Oxford: OUP.

PAHL, J. (1985). *Private Violence and Public Policy: The Needs of Battered Women and the Response of Public Services*. London: Routledge and Kegan Paul.

PAHL, J. (2005). 'Individualisation in Couple Finances: Who Pays for the Children?'. *Social Policy and Society*, 4: 381.

ⓦ PARADINE, K. AND WILKINSON, J. (2004). *Protection and Accountability: The Reporting, Investigation and Prosecution of Domestic Violence Cases*. London: HMIC. <www.justiceinspectorates.gov.uk/cjji/wp-content/uploads/sites/2/2014/04/DomVio0104LitRev.pdf>.

PARKER, S. (1991). 'Child Support in Australia: Children's Rights or Public Interest?'. *International Journal of Law and the Family*, 5: 24.

PARKER, S. (1992). 'Rights and Utility in Anglo-Australian Family Law'. *Modern Law Review*, 55: 311.

PARKINSON, P. (1999). 'The Diminishing Significance of Initial Contributions to Property'. *Australian Journal of Family Law*, 13: 52.

PARKINSON, P. (2003). 'Child Protection, Permanency Planning and Children's Right to Family Life'. *International Journal of Law, Policy and the Family*, 17: 147.

PARKINSON, P. (2007). 'Reengineering the Child Support Scheme: An Australian Perspective on the British Government's Proposals'. *Modern Law Review*, 70: 812.

PARKINSON, P. (2011). *Family Law and the Indissolubility of Parenthood*. Cambridge: CUP.

PARKINSON, P., CASHMORE, J., AND SINGLE, J. (2007). 'Parents' and Children's Views on Talking to Judges in Parenting Disputes in Australia'. *International Journal of Law, Policy and the Family*, 21: 84.

PATEL, T. (2007). 'Theorising the Racial Identity Development of Transracial Adoptees. A Symbolic Interactionist Perspective'. *Adoption and Fostering*, 31: 32.

PEACEY, V. AND HUNT, J. (2008). *Problematic Contact After Separation and Divorce? A National Survey of Parents*. London: One Parent Families/Gingerbread.

PEARCE, N. (2013). '*AI v MT* [2013] EWHC 100 (Fam)'. *Journal of Social Welfare and Family Law*, 35: 259.

PEEL, E. (2015). 'Civil Partnership Ceremonies: (Hetero)normativity, Ritual and Gender', in J. Miles, P. Mody, and R. Probert (eds), *Marriage Rites and Rights*. Oxford: Hart Publishing.

PERRY, A. (2000). '*Lancashire County Council v B*. Section 31—Threshold or Barrier?'. *Child and Family Law Quarterly*, 12: 301.

PERRY, A., DOUGLAS, G., MURCH, M., BADER, K., AND BORKOWSKI, M. (2000). *How Parents Cope Financially on Marriage Breakdown*. London: Family Policy Studies Centre/Joseph Rowntree.

PHILLIPS, R. (1991). *Untying the Knot: A Short History of Divorce*. Cambridge: CUP.

PICKFORD, R. (1999). 'What is a Parent? A Socio-Legal Analysis', in A. Bainham, S. Day Sclater, and M. Richards (eds), *What is a Parent? A Socio-Legal Analysis*. Oxford: Hart Publishing.

PINTENS, W. (2011). 'Matrimonial Property Law in Europe', in K. Boele-Woelki, J. Miles, and J. Scherpe (eds), *The Future of Family Property in Europe*. Cambridge: Intersentia.

PIPER, C. (1996). 'Norms and Negotiation in Mediation and Divorce', in M. Freeman (ed), *Divorce: Where Next?* Aldershot: Dartmouth.

PIPER, C. AND KAGANAS, F. (1997). 'Family Law Act 1996, Section 1(d)—How will "They" Know There is a Risk of Violence?'. *Child and Family Law Quarterly*, 9: 269.

PIRRIE, J. (2006). 'Child Support in Danger'. *Solicitors Journal*, 150: 1089.

PIRRIE, J. (2007). 'The Legal Dig'. *New Law Journal*, 16 March: 382.

PISKA, N. (2008). 'Intention, Fairness and the Presumption of Resulting Trust after *Stack v Dowden*'. *Modern Law Review*, 71: 120.

PISKA, N. (2009). 'Constructing Trusts and Constructing Intention', in M. Dixon (ed), *Modern Studies in Property Law, volume 5*. Oxford: Hart Publishing.

PIZZEY, E. (1974). *Scream Quietly or the Neighbours will Hear*. London: IF Books.

PLATT, J. (2008). 'The Domestic Violence, Crime and Victims Act 2004 Part 1: Is it Working?'. *Family Law*, 38: 642.

PLATT, J., ASOKAN, M., FINDLAY, L., AND TRUMAN, D. (2009). *Injunctions and Orders against Anti-Social or Violent Individuals*. Bristol: Jordan Publishing.

PLAYDON, Z. (2004). 'Intersecting Oppressions: Ending Discrimination Against Lesbians, Gay Men and Trans People in the UK', in B. Brooks-Gordon, L. Gelsthorpe, M. Johnson, and A. Bainham (eds), *Sexuality Repositioned*. Oxford: Hart Publishing.

POLIKOFF, N. (2008). *Beyond (Straight and Gay) Marriage: Valuing All Families Under the Law*. Boston, MA: Beacon Press.

POOLE, E., SPEIGHT, S., O'BRIEN, M., CONNOLLY, S., AND ALDRICH, M. (2013). *What Do We Know About Non-Resident Fathers?* <www.modernfatherhood.org/wp-content/uploads/2013/11/Briefing-paper-tables-Non-resident-fathers-embargoed-20.11.13.pdf>.

POULTER, S. (1998). *Ethnicity, Law and Human Rights*. Oxford: OUP.

PRACTICE DIRECTION (2010). *Public Law Proceedings Guide to Case Management*. <www.judiciary.gov.uk/NR/rdonlyres/3FEA2F29-47D5-4BEB-8DB2-19B9EDD1ABC5/0/public_law_outline_PD_April_2010.pdf>.

PRACTICE DIRECTION 3A (2014). *Family Mediation and Information Assessment Meetings (MIAMS)*. <www.justice.gov.uk/courts/procedure-rules/family/practice_directions/pd_part_03a>.

(w) PRACTICE DIRECTION 12J (2014). *Child Arrangements and Contact Order: Domestic Violence and Harm*. <www.justice.gov.uk/courts/procedure-rules/family/practice_directions/pd_part_12j>.

(w) PRACTICE DIRECTION 16A (2014). *Representation of Children*. <www.justice.gov.uk/courts/procedure-rules/family/practice_directions/pd_part_16a>.

(w) PRACTICE GUIDANCE (2014). Issued by the President of the Family Division, 13 October. <www.familylawweek.co.uk/site.aspx?i=ed134189>.

PRICE, D. (2009). 'Pension Accumulation and Gendered Household Structures: What are the Implications of Changes in Family Formation for Future Financial Inequality?', in J. Miles and R. Probert (eds) (2009), above.

PROBERT, R. (1999). 'The Controversy of Equality and the Matrimonial Causes Act 1923'. *Child and Family Law Quarterly*, 11: 33.

PROBERT, R. (2001). 'Trusts and the Modern Woman—Establishing an Interest in the Family Home'. *Child and Family Law Quarterly*, 13: 275.

PROBERT, R. (2002a). 'When Are We Married? Void, Non-Existent and Presumed Marriages'. *Legal Studies*, 22: 398.

PROBERT, R. (2002b). 'Sharing Homes—A Long-Awaited Paper'. *Family Law*, 32: 834.

PROBERT, R. (2004a). 'Family Law—A Modern Concept?'. *Family Law*, 34: 901.

PROBERT, R. (2004b). 'Lord Hardwicke's Marriage Act—Vital Change 250 Years On?'. *Family Law*, 34: 585.

PROBERT, R. (2004c). 'Cohabitation in Twentieth Century England and Wales: Law and Policy'. *Law and Policy*, 26: 13.

PROBERT, R. (2004d). '*Sutton v Mischon de Reya and Gawor & Co*—Cohabitation Contracts and Swedish Sex Slaves'. *Child and Family Law Quarterly*, 16: 453.

PROBERT, R. (2005a). 'How Would *Corbett v Corbett* be Decided Today?'. *Family Law*, 35: 382.

PROBERT, R. (2005b). 'The Wedding of the Prince of Wales: Royal Privileges and Human Rights'. *Child and Family Law Quarterly*, 17: 363.

PROBERT, R. (2007a). '*Hyde v Hyde*: Defining or Defending Marriage?'. *Child and Family Law Quarterly*, 19: 322.

PROBERT, R. (2007b). 'A Review of Cohabitation: The Financial Consequences of Relationship Breakdown'. *Family Law Quarterly*, 41: 521.

PROBERT, R. (2008a). 'Hanging on the Telephone: *City of Westminster v IC*'. *Child and Family Law Quarterly*, 20: 395.

PROBERT, R. (2008b). 'Equality in the Family Home?'. *Feminist Legal Studies*, 15: 341.

PROBERT, R. (2009a). 'Parental Responsibility and Children's Partnership Choices', in R. Probert, S. Gilmore, and J. Herring (eds), *Responsible Parents and Parental Responsibility*. Oxford: Hart Publishing.

PROBERT, R. (2009b). *Marriage Law and Practice in the Long Eighteenth Century: A Reassessment*. Cambridge: CUP.

PROBERT, R. (2009c). 'Cohabitation: Current Legal Solutions'. *Current Legal Problems*, 62: 316.

PROBERT, R. (2009d). 'The Cohabitation Bill'. *Family Law*, 39: 150.

PROBERT, R. (2011a). 'The *Roos* Case and Modern Family Law', in S. Gilmore, J. Herring, and R. Probert (eds), *Landmark Cases in Family Law*. Oxford: Hart Publishing.

PROBERT, R. (2011b). 'The Evolution of the Common Law Marriage Myth'. *Family Law*, 41: 283.

PROBERT, R. (2011c). 'For Richer, for Poorer – But How Does One Find Out Which?'. *Law Quarterly Review*, 127: 28.

PROBERT, R. (2012a). 'Marriage at the Crossroads in England and Wales', in M. Garrison and E. Scott (eds), *Marriage at the Crossroads: Law, Policy and the Brave New World of Twenty-First-Century Families*. Cambridge: CUP.

PROBERT, R. (2012b). *The Changing Legal Regulation of Cohabitation: From Fornicators to Family, 1600–2010*. Cambridge: CUP.

PROBERT, R. (2013a). 'The Evolving Concept of Non-Marriage'. *Child and Family Law Quarterly*, 25: 314.

PROBERT, R. (2013b). 'For Better or for Worse? Encouraging Marriage through the Tax System'. *Family Law*, 43: 285.

PROBERT, R. AND BARLOW, A. (2000). 'Displacing Marriage—Diversification and Harmonisation within Europe'. *Child and Family Law Quarterly*, 12: 153.

PROBERT, R., GILMORE, S., AND HERRING, J. (eds) (2009). *Responsible Parents and Parental Responsibility*. Oxford: Hart Publishing.

PRUETT, M., MCINTOSH, J., AND KELLY, J. (2014). 'Parental Separation and Overnight Care of Young Children, Part I: Consensus Through Theoretical and Empirical Integration'. *Family Court Review*, 52: 240.

QUINTON, D. AND SELWYN, J. (1998). 'Contact with Birth Parents in Adoption—A Response to Ryburn'. *Child and Family Law Quarterly*, 10: 349.

QUINTON, D. AND SELWYN, J. (2006). 'Adoption: Research, Policy and Practice'. *Child and Family Law Quarterly*, 18: 459.

RADFORD, J. (2010). Serious Case Review under Chapter V111 "Working Together to Safeguard Children": In Respect of the Death of a Child: Case Number 14'. Birmingham: Birmingham Safeguarding Children Board. <www.nscb.norfolk.gov.uk/documents/birmingham_case14.pdf>.

RAITT, F. (1996). 'Domestic Violence and Divorce Mediation'. *Journal of Social Welfare and Family Law*, 18: 11.

RAKE, K. (2000). *Women's Incomes over the Lifetime*. London: TSO.

REECE, H. (1996). 'The Paramountcy Principle: Consensus or Construct?'. *Current Legal Problems*, 49: 267.

REECE, H. (2003). *Divorcing Responsibly*. Oxford: Hart Publishing.

REECE, H. (2006). 'The End of Domestic Violence'. *Modern Law Review*, 69: 770.

REECE, H. (2009). 'The Degradation of Parental Responsibility', in R. Probert, S. Gilmore, and J. Herring (eds), *Responsible Parents and Parental Responsibility*. Oxford: Hart Publishing.

REECE, H. (2014). 'Leaping without Looking', in R. Leckey (ed), *After Legal Equality: Family, Sex, Kinship*. Abingdon: Routledge.

RESOLUTION (2000). *Fairness for families: Proposals for Reform of the Law on Cohabitation*. London: SFLA.

RESOLUTION (2009). *Precedents for Consent Orders*, 8th edn. London: Resolution.

RESOLUTION (2010). *Family Agreements: Seeking Certainty to Reduce Disputes*. London: Resolution.

RESOLUTION (2012). *Guides to Good Practice*. <www.resolution.org.uk/site_content_files/files/guides_to_good_practice_2012_lo_res_merged.pdf>.

RHEINSTEIN, M. (1972). *Marriage Stability, Divorce and the Law*. London: University of Chicago Press.

RHOADES, H. (2002). 'The "No Contact Mother": Reconstructions of Motherhood in the Era of the "New Father" '. *International Journal of Law, Policy and the Family*, 16: 71.

RICHARDS, M. (1995). 'But What About the Children? Some Reflections on the Divorce White Paper'. *Child and Family Law Quarterly*, 7: 223.

RICHARDS, M. (1996). 'Divorce Numbers and Divorce Legislation'. *Family Law*, 26: 151.

ROBERTS, M. (1992). 'Who is in Charge? Reflections on Recent Research and the Role of the Mediator'. *Journal of Social Welfare and Family Law*, 13: 372.

ROBERTS, M. (1996). 'Family Mediation and the Interests of Women—Facts and Fears'. *Family Law*, 26: 239.

ROBERTS, M. (2000). 'Children by Donation: Do They Have a Claim to Their Genetic Parentage?', in J. Bridgeman and D. Monk (eds), *Feminist Perspectives on Child Law*. London: Cavendish.

ROBINSON, A. AND COOK, D. (2006). 'Understanding Victim Retraction in Cases of Domestic Violence: Specialist Domestic Violence Courts, Government Policy, and Victim-Centred Justice'. *Contemporary Justice Review*, 9: 189.

ROE, S. (2010). 'Intimate Violence: 2008/09 BCS', in K. Smith et al (eds), *Homicides, Firearm Offences and Intimate Violence 2008/09: Supplementary Volume 2 to Crime in England and Wales 2008/09*. Home Office Statistical Bulletin 01/10. <http://rds.homeoffice.gov.uk/rds/pdfs10/hosb0110.pdf>.

ROGERSON, C. (2002). *Developing Spousal Support Guidelines in Canada: Beginning the Discussion—Background Paper*. <www.justice.gc.ca/eng/rp-pr/fl-lf/spousal-epoux/ss-pae/>.

ROGERSON, C. (2014). 'Child Support, Spousal Support and the Turn to Guidelines', in J. Eekelaar and R. George (eds), *Routledge Handbook of Family Law and Policy*. London: Routledge.

ROSS, A. AND SACKER, A. (2010). 'Understanding the Dynamics of Attitude Change', in A. Park et al (eds), *British Social Attitudes: The 26th Report*. London: Sage.

ROSS, H., GASK, K., AND BERRINGTON, A. (2011). 'Civil Partnership Five Years On'. *Population Trends* 145 (Autumn): 1.

ROTHERHAM, C. (2004). 'The Property Rights of Unmarried Cohabitees: The Case for Reform'. *Conveyancer and Property Lawyer*, 68: 268.

ROWTHORN, R. (1999). 'Marriage and Trust: Some Lessons from Economics'. *Cambridge Journal of Economics*, 23: 661.

ROYAL COMMISSION ON MARRIAGE AND DIVORCE (1956). Cm 9678. London: HMSO.

RUMNEY, P. (1999). 'When Rape isn't Rape: Court of Appeal Sentencing Practice in Cases of Marital and Relationship Rape'. *Oxford Journal of Legal Studies*, 19: 243.

RUSHTON, A. (2003). 'Support for Adoptive Families. A Review of Current Evidence on Problems, Needs and Effectiveness'. *Adoption and Fostering*, 27: 41.

RUSHTON, A. AND MINNIS, H. (2000). 'Research Review: Transracial Placements'. *Adoption and Fostering*, 24: 53.

RYBURN, M. (1998a). 'In Whose Best Interests?—Post-Adoption Contact with the Birth Family'. *Child and Family Law Quarterly*, 10: 53.

RYBURN, M. (1998b). 'A New Model of Welfare: Re-asserting the Value of Kinship for Children in State Care'. *Social Policy and Administration*, 32: 28.

SAGAR, T. AND HITCHINGS, E. (2007). '"More Adoptions, More Quickly": A Study of Social Workers' Responses to the Adoption and Children Act 2002'. *Journal of Social Welfare and Family Law*, 29: 199.

SALTER, D. (2007). 'Couples, Children and Taxation—The Need for Consistency and Coherence' in R. Probert (ed), *Family Life and the Law: Under One Roof*. Dartmouth: Ashgate.

SANDLAND, R. (2000). 'Not "Social Justice": The Housing Association, the Judges, the Tenant and His Lover'. *Feminist Legal Studies*, 8: 227.

SCHERPE, J. (2007a). 'A Comparative View of Pre-Nuptial Agreements'. *International Journal of Family Law*, 18.

SCHERPE, J. (2007b). 'Family and Private Life, Ambits and Pieces'. *Child and Family Law Quarterly*, 19: 390.

SCHERPE, J (ed) (2011a). *Marital Agreements and Private Autonomy in Comparative Perspective*. Oxford: Hart Publishing.

SCHERPE, J. (2011b). 'Fairness, Freedom and Foreign Elements – Marital Agreements in England and Wales after *Radmacher v Granatino*'. *Child and Family Law Quarterly*, 23: 513.

SCHERPE, J. (2012). 'Towards a Matrimonial Property Regime for England and Wales', in R. Probert and C. Barton (eds), *Fifty Years in Family Law: Essays for Stephen Cretney*. Cambridge: Intersentia.

SCHNEIDER, C. (1992). 'Discretion and Rules: A Lawyer's View', in K. Hawkins (ed), *The Uses of Discretion*. Oxford: OUP.

SCHNEIDER, E. (1994). 'The Violence of Privacy', in M. Fineman and R. Mykitiuk (eds), *The Public Nature of Private Violence*. New York: Routledge.

SCHOFIELD, G. (2010). *Bankruptcy and Divorce: A Practical Guide for the Family Lawyer*. Bristol: Family Law.

SCHUZ, R. (1993). 'Divorce Reform'. *Family Law*, 23: 630.

SCHUZ, R. (1996). 'Divorce and Ethnic Minorities', in M. Freeman (ed), *Divorce: Where Next?* Aldershot: Dartmouth.

SCOTT, E. (2002). 'Marital Commitment and the Legal Regulation of Divorce', in A. Dnes and R. Rowthorn (eds), *The Law and Economics of Marriage and Divorce*. Cambridge: CUP.

SCOTT, J. AND DEX. S. (2009). 'Paid and Unpaid Work: Can Policy Improve Gender Inequalities?', in J. Miles and R. Probert (eds) (2009), above.

SCOTTISH LAW COMMISSION (1981). *Report on Aliment and Financial Provision*, Scot Law Com No 67. Edinburgh: HMSO.

SCOTTISH LAW COMMISSION (1984). *Report on Matrimonial Property*, Scot Law Com No 86. Edinburgh: HMSO.

SCOTTISH LAW COMMISSION (1992). *Report on Family Law*, Scot Law Com No 135. Edinburgh: HMSO.

SCULLY, A. (2003). 'Case Commentary: *Parra v Parra*—Big Money Cases, Judicial Discretion and Equality of Division'. *Child and Family Law Quarterly*, 15: 205.

SEDEN, J. (2001). 'Family Assistance Orders and the Children Act 1989: Ambivalence about Intervention or a Means of Safeguarding and Promoting Children's Welfare?'. *International Journal of Law, Policy and the Family*, 15: 226.

SELECT COMMITTEE (1975). *Report from the Select Committee in Violence in Marriage*. London: HMSO.

SELWYN, J. AND QUINTON, D. (2004). 'Stability, Permanence, Outcomes and Support'. *Adoption and Fostering*, 28: 6.

SELWYN, J., FRAZER, L., AND QUINTON, D. (2006). 'Paved with Good Intentions: The Pathway to Adoption and the Costs of Delay'. *British Journal of Social Work*, 36: 561.

SELWYN, J., HARRIS, P., QUINTON, D. ET AL (2008). *Pathways to Permanence for Black, Asian and Mixed Ethnicity Children: Dilemmas, Decision-Making and Outcomes*. DCSF-RBX-18-08. <www.bristol.ac.uk/media-library/sites/sps/migrated/documents/rk6417finalreport.pdf>.

🔊 Sentencing Guidelines Council (2006a). *Overarching Principles: Domestic Violence*. <www.sentencingcouncil.org.uk/wp-content/uploads/web_domestic_violence.pdf>.

🔊 Sentencing Guidelines Council (2006b). *Breach of a Protective Order*. <www.sentencingcouncil.org.uk/wp-content/uploads/web_breach_of_protective_order.pdf>.

Shah, P. (2003). 'Attitudes to Polygamy in English Law'. *International and Comparative Law Quarterly*, 52: 369.

Sheldon, S. (2009). 'From "Absent Objects of Blame" to "Fathers Who Want to Take Responsibility": Reforming Birth Registration Law'. *Journal of Social Welfare and Family Law*, 31: 373.

Shepherd, N. (2009). 'Ending the Blame Game: Getting No Fault Divorce Back on the Agenda'. *Family Law*, 39: 122.

Shultz, M. (1982). 'Contractual Ordering of Marriage: A New Model for State Policy'. *California Law Review*, 70: 204.

Simmonds, C. (2012). 'Paramountcy and the ECHR: A Conflict Resolved?' *Cambridge Law Journal*, 71: 498.

Simon, J. (1964). *With All My Worldly Goods . . .* Holdsworth Club Presidential Address, University of Birmingham.

Simon, R. and Altstein, H. (1996). 'The Case for Transracial Adoption'. *Children and Youth Services Review*, 18: 5.

Singer, A. (2014). 'Voices Heard and Unheard: A Scandinavian Perspective'. *Journal of Social Welfare and Family Law*, 36: 381.

Sloan, B. (2013). 'Conflicting Rights: English Adoption Law and the Implementation of the UN Convention on the Rights of the Child'. *Child and Family Law Quarterly*, 25: 40.

Sloan, B. (2015). 'Keeping Up With the *Jones* Case: Establishing Constructive Trusts in "Sole Legal Owner" Scenarios'. *Legal Studies:* forthcoming but already available via Wiley Online Library.

Smart, C. (1984). *The Ties that Bind: Law, Marriage and the Reproduction of Patriarchal Relations*. London: Routledge.

Smart, C. (1989). *Feminism and the Power of Law*. London: Routledge.

Smart, C. (2000). 'Divorce in England 1950–2000: A Moral Tale?', in S. Katz, J. Eekelaar, and M. Maclean (eds), *Cross Currents: Family Law and Policy in the US and England*. Oxford: OUP.

Smart, C. and Neale, B. (1999). *Family Fragments?* Cambridge: Polity Press.

Smart, C. and Stevens, P. (2000). *Cohabitation Breakdown*. London: Family Policy Studies Centre.

Smith, C. (1997). 'Children's Rights: Judicial Ambivalence and Social Resistance'. *International Journal of Law, Policy and the Family*, 11: 103.

SMITH, C. (2004). 'Autopoietic Law and the "Epistemic Trap": A Case Study of Adoption and Contact'. *Journal of Law and Society*, 31: 318.

SMITH, C. (2005). 'Trust v Law: Promoting and Safeguarding Post-Adoption Contact'. *Journal of Social Welfare and Family Law*, 27: 315.

SMITH, C. AND LOGAN, J. (2002). 'Adoptive Parenthood as a "Legal Fiction"—Its Consequences for Direct Post-Adoption Contact'. *Child and Family Law Quarterly*, 14: 281.

SMITH, L. (1989). *Domestic Violence: An Overview of the Literature*. Home Office Research Study No 107. London: HMSO.

SMITH, L. (2006). 'Is Three a Crowd? Lesbian Mothers' Perspectives on Parental Status in Law'. *Child and Family Law Quarterly*, 18: 231.

SMITH, L. (2010). 'Clashing Symbols? Reconciling Support for Fathers and Fatherless Families after the Human Fertilisation and Embryology Act 2008'. *Child and Family Law Quarterly*, 22: 46.

SMITH, L. (2013). 'Tangling the Web of Legal Parenthood: Legal Responses to the Use of Known Donors in Lesbian Parenting Arrangements'. *Legal Studies*, 33: 355.

SMITH, R. (2002). 'The Wrong End of the Telescope: Child Protection or Child Safety?'. *Journal of Social Welfare and Family Law*, 24: 247.

SMITH, V. (1992). 'Children Act 1989: The Accommodation Trap'. *Family Law*, 22: 349.

SMYTH, B. (2005). 'Parent–Child Contact in Australia: Exploring Five Different Post-Separation Patterns of Parenting'. *International Journal of Law, Policy and the Family*, 19: 1.

SNAPE, D. AND MOLLOY, D. (1999). *Relying on the State, Relying on Each Other*. Research Report No 103. London: Department of Social Security.

SOLICITORS JOURNAL (2006). 'Family Lawyers Fear Inclusion of Conduct in Divorces'. *Solicitors Journal*, 150: 485.

SONI, B. (2007). 'Domestic Violence and Family Law: A New Era'. *Family Law Week*, July. <www.familylawweek.co.uk/site.aspx?i=ed725>.

SPAHT, E. (2002). 'Louisiana's Covenant Marriage Law: Recapturing the Meaning of Marriage for the Sake of the Children', in A. Dnes and R. Rowthorn (eds), *The Law and Economics of Marriage and Divorce*. Cambridge: CUP.

STAFFORD, B. AND ROBERTS, S. (2009). *The Impact of Financial Incentives in Welfare Systems on Family Structure*. DWP Research Report No 569. London: DWP.

STONE, L. (1990). *Road to Divorce: England 1530–1987*. Oxford: OUP.

STRASSER, M. (2014). 'Family, Same-Sex Unions and the Law', in J. Eekelaar and R. George (eds), *Routledge Handbook of Family Law and Policy*. Abingdon: Routledge.

STURGE, C. AND GLASER, D. (2000). 'Contact and Domestic Violence—The Experts' Court Report'. *Family Law*, 30: 615.

STYCHIN, C. (2006). 'Family Friendly? Rights, Responsibilities and Relationship Recognition', in A. Diduck and K. O'Donovan (eds), *Feminist Perspectives on Family Law*. Abingdon: Routledge-Cavendish.

STYLIANOU, C. (1998). 'The Tensions between Family Mediation Principles and the Formal Legal System'. *Family Law*, 28: 211.

SUGARMAN, S. (1990). 'Dividing Financial Interests on Divorce', in S. Sugarman and H. Kay (eds), *Divorce Reform at the Crossroads*. New Haven: Yale University Press.

SUNMONU, Y. (2000). 'Why Black Carers are Deterred from Adoption'. *Adoption and Fostering*, 24: 59.

SWADLING, W. (2007). 'The Common Intention Constructive Trust in the House of Lords: An Opportunity Missed'. *Law Quarterly Review*, 123: 511.

SYMES, P. (1985). 'Indissolubility and the Clean Break'. *Modern Law Review*, 48: 44.

TADROS, V. (2005). 'The Distinctiveness of Domestic Abuse: A Freedom-Based Account', in R. Duff and S. Green (eds), *Defining Crimes*. Oxford: OUP.

TALWAR, D. (2010). 'Many Muslims not Legally Wed'. BBC website, 2 February. <http://news.bbc.co.uk/1/hi/uk/8493660.stm>.

TAUB, N. AND SCHNEIDER, E. (1998). 'Women's Subordination and the Role of Law' in D. Kairys (ed), *The Politics of Law: A Progressive Critique*, 3rd edn. New York: Basic Books.

TAYLOR, R. (2013). 'Secular Rights and Sacred Values: *Re G (Education: Religious Upbringing)*'. *Child and Family Law Quarterly*, 25: 336.

THOBURN, J., ROBINSON, J., AND ANDERSON, B. (2012). 'Returning Children Home from Public Care', Research briefing, Social Care Institute for Excellence.

THORPE, M. (2008). 'Statutory Arbitration and Ancillary Relief'. *Family Law*, 30: 26.

TIMMS, J. E. AND THOBURN, J. (2006). 'Your Shout! Looked After Children's Perspectives on the Children Act 1989'. *Journal of Social Welfare and Family Law*, 28: 153.

TOBIN, J. AND McNAIR, R. (2009). 'Public International Law and the Regulation of Private Spaces: Does the Convention on the Rights of the Child Impose an Obligation on States to Allow Gay and Lesbian Couples to Adopt?'. *International Journal of Law, Policy and the Family*, 23: 110.

TRIMMINGS, K. (2015). 'Six Month Deadline for Applications for Parental Orders Relaxed by the High Court'. *Journal of Social Welfare and Family Law*, 37: forthcoming.

TRINDER, L. (2014). 'Climate Change? The Multiple Trajectories of Shared Care Law, Policy and Social Practice'. *Child and Family Law Quarterly*, 26: 30.

TRINDER, L., FIRTH, A., AND JENKS, C. (2010). '"So Presumably Things Have Moved on Since Then?" The Management of Risk Allegations in Child Contact Dispute Resolution'. *International Journal of Law, Policy and the Family*, 24: 29.

TRINDER, L., CONNOLLY, J., KELLETT, J., AND NOTLEY, C. (2005). *A Profile of Applicants and Respondents in Contact Cases in Essex*. DCA Research Series 1/05.

<www.familieslink.co.uk/download/july07/A%20Profile%20of%20Applicants%20 and%20Respondents%20in%20Essex.pdf>.

TRINDER, L., HUNT, J., MACLEOD, A., PEARCE, J., AND WORWOOD, H. (2013). *Enforcing Contact Orders: Problem-Solving or Punishment?*. Exeter: University of Exeter.

TRINDER, L., HUNTER, R., HITCHINGS, E., MILES, J., MOORHEAD, R., SMITH, L., SEFTON, M., HINCHLY, V., BADER, K., AND PEARCE, J. (2014). *Litigants in Person in Private Family Law Cases*. <www.gov.uk/government/uploads/system/uploads/ attachment_data/file/380479/litigants-in-person-in-private-family-law-cases.pdf>.

TRISELIOTIS, J. (2002). 'Long-Term Foster Care or Adoption? The Evidence Examined'. *Child and Family Social Work*, 7: 23.

TURKMENDAG, I., DINGWALL, R., AND MURPHY, T. (2008). 'The Removal of Donor Anonymity in the UK: The Silencing of Would-Be Parents'. *International Journal of Law, Policy and the Family*, 22: 283.

UNICEF (2006). *Behind Closed Doors: The Impact of Domestic Violence on Children*. <www.unicef.org/protection/files/BehindClosedDoors.pdf>.

VAN BUEREN, G. (1998). *International Law on the Rights of the Child*. The Hague: Kluwer Law International.

VALLELY, C., ROBINSON, A., BURTON, M., AND TREGIDGA, J. (2005). *Evaluation of Domestic Violence Pilot Sites at Caerphilly (Gwent) and Croydon 2004/05: Final Report*. <www.cps.gov.uk/publications/docs/eval_dv_pilots_04-05.pdf>.

VARDAG, A. AND MILES, J. (2015). 'The Rite that Defines the Rights? The Contemporary Role and Practice of Pre-Nuptial Agreement', in J. Miles, P. Mody, and R. Probert (eds), *Marriage Rites and Rights*. Oxford: Hart Publishing.

VERKAIK, R. (2006). 'Divorce Laws "Are Destroying Marriage"'. *The Independent*, 26 August, 1.

VINEY, J. AND BRUNSDON-TULLY, M. (2014). 'Compensation in Financial Remedy Cases: Parthian Shots and the Emperor's New Clothes'. *Family Law Week*. <www. familylawweek.co.uk/site.aspx?i=ed131966>.

VOGLER, C. (2005). 'Cohabiting Couples: Rethinking Money in the Household at the Beginning of the Twenty First Century'. *Sociological Review*, 53: 1.

VOGLER, C. (2009). 'Managing Money in Intimate Relationships: Similarities and Differences Between Cohabiting and Married Couples', in J. Miles and R. Probert (eds) (2009), above.

VOGLER, C., LYONETTE, C., AND WIGGINS, R. (2008). 'Money, Power and Spending Decisions in Intimate Relationships'. *The Sociological Review*, 56: 117.

WAALDIJK, K. (2003). 'Taking Same-Sex Partnerships Seriously: European Experiences as British Perspective?'. *International Family Law*: 84.

WADE J., DIXON, J., AND RICHARDS, A. (2009). *Implementing Special Guardianship*. DCSF-RBX-09-17. <www.york.ac.uk/inst/spru/research/pdf/SpecialG.pdf>.

WALBY, S. (2009). *The Cost of Domestic Violence: Up-date 2009*. Lancaster University.

WALBY, S. AND ALLEN, J. (2004). *Domestic Violence, Sexual Assault and Stalking: Findings from the British Crime Survey.* Home Office Research Study 276. London: HMSO. <http://webarchive.nationalarchives.gov.uk/20110218135832/rds.homeoffice.gov.uk/rds/pdfs04/hors276.pdf>.

WALBY, S. AND MYHILL, A. (2001). 'Assessing and Managing Risk', in J. Taylor-Browne (ed), *What Works in Reducing Domestic Violence? A Comprehensive Guide for Professionals.* London: Whiting Birch. <http://webarchive.nationalarchives.gov.uk/20110218135832/rds.homeoffice.gov.uk/rds/prgpdfs/assess.pdf>.

WALKER, J. (1991). 'Divorce—Whose Fault?'. *Family Law,* 21: 234.

WALKER, J. (1996). 'Is there a Future for Lawyers in Divorce?'. *International Journal of Law, Policy and the Family,* 10: 52.

WALKER, J. (2000). 'The Development of Family Mediation', in Newcastle Centre for Family Studies, *Information Meetings and Associated Provisions within the Family Law Act 1996: Final Evaluation of Research Studies Undertaken.* <http://webarchive.nationalarchives.gov.uk/+/http://www.dca.gov.uk/family/fla/chap18.pdf>.

WALKER, J. AND MCCARTHY, P. (2004). 'Picking Up the Pieces'. *Family Law,* 34: 580.

WALLBANK, J. (1997). 'The Campaign for Change of the Child Support Act 1991: Reconstituting the "Absent" Father'. *Social and Legal Studies,* 6: 191.

WALLBANK, J. (2007). 'Getting Tough on Mothers: Regulating Contact and Residence'. *Feminist Legal Studies,* 15: 189.

WALLBANK, J. (2009). ' "Bodies in the Shadows": Joint Birth Registration, Parental Responsibility and Social Class'. *Child and Family Law Quarterly,* 21: 267.

WALSH, E. (2004). 'The Future of Family Mediation', in J. Westcott (ed), *Family Mediation: Past, Present and Future.* Bristol: Jordan Publishing.

WARD, J., BROWN, R., WESTLAKE, D., AND MUNRO, E. (2010). 'Infants Suffering, or Likely to Suffer, Significant Harm: A Prospective Longitudinal Study'. Research Brief, DFE-RB053. <www.lboro.ac.uk/media/wwwlboroacuk/content/ccfr/publications/dfe-rb053.pdf>.

WARSHAK, R. (2014). 'Social Science and Parenting Plans for Young Children: A Consensus Report'. *Psychology, Public Policy, and Law,* 20: 46.

WASOFF, F., MILES, J., AND MORDAUNT, E. (2010). *Legal Practitioners' Perspectives on the Cohabitation Provisions of the Family Law (Scotland) Act 2006,* and Briefing Paper No 51. <www.crfr.ac.uk/cohabitation/>.

WATERHOUSE, R. (2000). *Lost in Care—Report of the Tribunal of Inquiry into the Abuse of Children in Care in the Former County Council Areas of Gwynedd and Clwyd.* London: HMSO.

WELBOURNE, P. (2008). 'Safeguarding Children on the Edge of Care: Policy for Keeping Children Safe after the *Review of the Child Care Proceedings System, Care Matters and the Carter Review of Legal Aid*'. *Child and Family Law Quarterly,* 20: 335.

WELSH ASSEMBLY GOVERNMENT (2009). *Living in Wales, 2008.* <http://wales.gov.uk/docs/statistics/2009/091130livingwales2008en.pdf>.

WESTWOOD, S. (2013). ' "My Friends are my Family": An Argument about the Limitations of Contemporary Law's Recognition of Relationships in Later Life'. *Journal of Social Welfare and Family Law*, 35: 347.

WIKELEY, N. (2000). 'Child Support—The New Formula, Part I'. *Family Law*, 30: 820.

WIKELEY, N. (2006a). *Child Support: Law and Policy.* Oxford: Hart Publishing.

WIKELEY, N. (2006b). 'A Duty But Not a Right: Child Support after *R (Kehoe) v Secretary of State for Work and Pensions'. Child and Family Law Quarterly*, 18: 287.

ⓦ WIKELEY, N. (2007a). *Written Memorandum to Public Bill Committee, on Child Maintenance and Other Payments Bill 2007.* <www.publications.parliament.uk/pa/cm200607/cmpublic/childmain/memos/memocm1.htm>.

WIKELEY, N. (2007b). 'Child Support Reform—Throwing the Baby Out With the Bathwater?'. *Child and Family Law Quarterly*, 19: 434.

WIKELEY, N. (2007c). 'Family Law and Social Security', in R. Probert (ed), *Family Life and the Law: Under One Roof.* Dartmouth: Ashgate.

WIKELEY, N. (2008). 'The Strange Demise of the Liable Relative Rule'. *Family Law*, 38: 52.

ⓦ WIKELEY, N., BARNETT, S., BROWN, J., DAVIS, G., DIAMOND, I., DRAPER, T., AND SMITH, P. (2008). *Relationship Separation and Child Support Study.* DWP RR 503. <http://webarchive.nationalarchives.gov.uk/20130314010347/http://research.dwp.gov.uk/asd/asd5/rports2007-2008/rrep503.pdf>.

ⓦ WIKELEY, N., ET AL (2001). *National Survey of Child Support Agency Clients.* DWP Research Report No 152. Leeds: Corporate Document Service. <http://webarchive.nationalarchives.gov.uk/20130314010347/http://research.dwp.gov.uk/asd/asd5/rrep152.pdf>.

WILLIAMS, G. (1947). 'Legal Unity of Husband and Wife'. *Modern Law Review*, 10: 16.

ⓦ WILLIAMS, Z. (2011). 'So We Can't Afford Legal Aid? Look at the Costs Without It'. *The Guardian*, 23 June 2011. <www.theguardian.com/commentisfree/2011/jun/22/legal-aid-cuts-will-not-save>.

WILSON, B. AND SMALLWOOD, S. (2007). 'Understanding Recent Trends in Marriage'. *Population Trends* 128: 24.

WILSON, B. AND STUCHBURY, R. (2010). 'Do Partnerships Last? Comparing Marriage and Cohabitation Using Longitudinal Census Data'. *Population Trends*, 139: 37.

WILSON, G. (2006). 'The Non-Resident Parental Role for Separated Fathers: A Review'. *International Journal of Law, Policy and the Family*, 20: 286.

WILSON, G. (2007). 'Financial Provision in Civil Partnerships'. *Family Law*, 37: 31.

WILSON, N. (1999). 'Response of the Judges of the Family Division to Government Proposals (Made by Way of Submission to the Lord Chancellor's Ancillary Relief Advisory Group)'. *Family Law*, 29: 159.

Ⓦ WOMEN AND EQUALITY UNIT (2003a). *Civil Partnership: A Framework for the Legal Recognition of Same-Sex Couples.* London: HMSO. <http://webarchive. nationalarchives.gov.uk/+/www.womenandequalityunit.gov.uk/research/civ_par_con.pdf>.

Ⓦ WOMEN AND EQUALITY UNIT (2003b). *Responses to Civil Partnership: A Framework for Legal Recognition of Same-Sex Couples.* London: DTI. <http://webarchive. nationalarchives.gov.uk/+/www.womenandequalityunit.gov.uk/publications/CP_responses.pdf>.

Ⓦ WOMEN'S AID (2005). *Women's Aid Briefing on Domestic Violence: A National Report.* <www.womensaid.org.uk/default.asp>.

WONG, S. (2009). 'Caring and Sharing: Interdependency as a Basic for Property Redistribution?', in A. Bottomley and S. Wong (eds), *Changing Contours of Domestic Life, Family and Law.* Oxford: Hart Publishing.

Ⓦ WOODHEAD, L. (2014). *An Error in the House of Bishops Guidance on Same Sex Marriage.* <www.thinkinganglicans.org.uk/archives/006460.html>.

WOODHOUSE, B. (2014). 'Listening to Children: Participation Rights of Minors in Italy and the United States'. *Journal of Social Welfare and Family Law,* 36: 358.

WOODWARD, H. AND SEFTON, M. (2014). 'Pensions on Divorce: A Study on How and When They Are Taken into Account'. *Family Law,* 44: 509.

Ⓦ WOODWARD, H. WITH SEFTON, M. (2014). *Pensions on Divorce: An Empirical Study.* Cardiff: Cardiff University. <orca.cf.ac.uk/56700/1/14%2002%2011%20Pensions%20on%20divorce%20final%20report.pdf>.

Ⓦ WORK AND PENSIONS SELECT COMMITTEE (2007), *Fourth Report: Child Support Reform,* HC 219-I, 219-II. <www.publications.parliament.uk/pa/cm/cmworpen.htm>.

YOUNG, C. (2009). 'Taking Spousal Status into Account for Tax Purposes: The Pitfalls and Penalties', in A. Bottomley and S. Wong (eds), *Changing Contours of Domestic Life, Family and Law.* Oxford: Hart Publishing.

ZANGHELLINI, A. (2012). '*A v B and C* [2012] EWCA Civ 285 – Heteronormativity, Poly-Parenting and the Homo-Nuclear Family'. *Child and Family Law Quarterly,* 24: 475.

ZUCKERMAN, A. (1978). 'Ownership of the Matrimonial Home—Common Sense and Reformist Nonsense'. *Law Quarterly Review,* 94: 26.

INDEX